THE LAW OF MARINE COLLISION

The *Stockholm* in dry dock after her collision with the *Andrea Doria,* July 25, 1956.

THE LAW OF MARINE COLLISION

by Nicholas J. Healy
Adjunct Professor of Law, New York University

and

Joseph C. Sweeney
John D. Calamari Distinguished Professor of Law,
Fordham University

CORNELL MARITIME PRESS
Centreville, Maryland

Library of Congress Cataloging-in-Publication Data

Healy, Nicholas J.
The law of marine collision / Nicholas J. Healy and Joseph C. Sweeney. — 1st ed.
p. cm.
Includes bibliographical references and index.
ISBN 0-87033-505-7 (hardcover)
1. Collisions at sea—United States. 2. Liability for marine accidents—United States. I. Sweeney, Joseph C. (Joseph Conrad), 1933– . II. Title.
KF1107.H43 1997
346.7303′22—dc21 97-45202
CIP

Manufactured in the United States of America
First edition

TO MARGARET HEALY AND ALICE SWEENEY

CONTENTS

FOREWORD

Despite the advances in marine technology and new electronic and other navigational aids, as well as new training methods for those on board vessels, maritime accidents generally—and marine collisions specifically—continue to feature prominently in annual maritime casualty statistics. Although collisions rarely represent a major sector of such statistics, when they do occur they always involve significant losses. This is, of course, not surprising. When two large steel structures come into contact, especially at speed, severe damage to the vessels involved, and consequent other losses, including death and personal injury, marine pollution, fire, explosion, cargo damage, and delays, are often the result.

Over its long history, admiralty law has developed a very complex and highly specialized sector related especially to marine collision. The very complexity of the subject has assured its very sparse literature, with marine collision treatises and texts appearing at considerable intervals in the United Kingdom and even more infrequently in the United States. As a result, the appearance of this book is a significant event for maritime literature generally and for U.S. admiralty law especially. This is particularly so for a book written by one author who can easily be called the dean of U.S. admiralty law and practice and by another who is one of the leading U.S. academic specialists in the field. In fact, a work such as this could not have been compiled by anyone better qualified than Nicholas Healy and Joseph Sweeney.

Professor Healy, the most senior active member of the Maritime Law Association of the United States, has had an outstanding career as an admiralty law practitioner and academic, spanning some six decades. During this period he has been president of the Maritime Law Association of the United States, vice president of the Comité Maritime International, coauthor of the principal U.S. admiralty law casebook, editor of the *Journal of Maritime Law and Commerce,* and representative of various U.S. maritime law interests at many important national, regional, and international gatherings. Professor Sweeney, long-time professor of maritime law at Fordham University in New York City, has also been in the forefront of U.S. admiralty law as a practitioner and academic for many years. He has represented his country in the area of marine law and policy at three diplomatic conferences and at a number of meetings of the United Nations. Both authors have had some sea experience, and acquired substantial experience in handling collision cases while serving with the U.S. Navy and in private practice, giving them practical illustrations of the problems they describe in this book.

This is a massive work involving an extensive examination of collision law, probably matched only by Marsden's *Collisions at Sea,* now part of the *British Shipping Laws* series. The depth of the book's research base reflects the fact that it is the culmination of many years of intensive research work and very thorough legal scholarship. In the very early stages of the book's development, one of the authors was to have been the late Alex J. Parks, of Portland, Oregon, another well-known U.S. admiralty law practitioner and author. Following his untimely death, Nicholas Healy and Joseph Sweeney carried on alone.

It is neither necessary nor appropriate to say anything specific about the actual content of a work that speaks for itself. Suffice it to say that it is one of the best and most important maritime law books to appear anywhere in many years. It treats an extremely complex area of the law clearly, yet provides the necessary background and detail required by all involved and interested in the field, whether practitioner, academic, policy maker, student, or mariner. While the book provides an important insight into the intricacies of U.S. admiralty collision law, it will also be of interest to many outside the United States.

As a maritime law professor, admiralty lawyer, and former ship's captain (who has faced "the agony of collision"), I found this to be an immensely practical work that neither disguises the complexity of the subject nor suffers from the unnecessary verbiage of many legal treatises. Nicholas Healy and Joseph Sweeney have, once again, provided an important service for maritime law by producing a work that will undoubtedly be well received, but which will also be with us for many years to come. It is a singular honor to have been asked to write a foreword for this important book that very much fills a significant void in the U.S. and international maritime law literature.

—Edgar Gold, Q.C., Ph.D., FNI*

* Member, Order of Canada; Past President, Canadian Maritime Law Association; Titulary Member, Comité Maritime International; Adjunct Professor of Maritime Law and Resource and Environmental Law, Dalhousie University, Halifax, Nova Scotia, Canada; Visiting Professor of Maritime Law and Canadian Member of the Board of Governors, World Maritime University, Malmö, Sweden; Member, Governing Board, IMO-International Maritime Law Institute, Malta; Sr. Partner, Huestis Holm, Barristers & Solicitors, Halifax, Nova Scotia, Canada

PREFACE

Twenty-five hundred years ago the beleaguered but ultimately victorious Athenian admiral, Themistocles, expressed the thought that a collision at sea could spoil your entire day. His warships, as well as those of the enemy, were propelled by oars, and the principal mode of attack was the deliberate ramming of the enemy vessel. Nevertheless, even at the slow speeds of which ships were then capable, accidental collisions occurred. Propulsion by sail did not decrease their frequency, especially in crowded harbors where maneuvering was difficult.

Nor did the technological innovations that appeared in quick succession during the nineteenth century and the earlier part of the twentieth: steam propulsion, the propeller, the diesel engine, the fathometer, electric lighting, sound signals, wireless telegraphy, and radio. More recent innovations such as radar, ARPA, LORAN, sonar, and electronic charts have helped to some degree, although before ships' officers were properly trained in the use of radar what some courts called "radar assisted collisions" were not unknown.

Science seems incapable of preventing marine collisions; they continue to occur as ships make greater speeds and the shipping industry finds it increasingly difficult to hire ships' officers and crews skilled in the proper use of the latest technology.

When we were introduced to the fundamentals of navigation and seamanship, thanks to the U.S. Navy, a prudent master would not willingly close another ship on the high seas in anything less than a five-mile radius. Today, greater speeds and sometimes crew fatigue call for still wider separation, but it is not always provided. On the other hand, a positive factor is the work of the International Maritime Organization (I.M.O.). Its valiant efforts to create uniform standards have done much to make the seas safer, but they are still very dangerous.

This book necessarily reaches into many areas beyond the International Collision Regulations (COLREGS) and the American Inland Rules: protection of the marine environment from pollution, distribution of cargo losses resulting from collisions, limitation of shipowners' liability, salvage, general average, and marine insurance.

We are conscious of the manifold emanations that a single collision can produce. The most tragic example is the collision of the outbound Norwegian grain carrier *Imo* and the inbound French munitions ship *Mont Blanc* in the Narrows of Halifax Harbor during World War I. The ensuing explosion and fire destroyed many other vessels and devastated a square mile of homes, schools, churches, and factories, as well as the entire waterfront area. It took the lives of almost 2,000 people afloat and ashore, injured 9,000 others, and left 25,000 homeless. (The disaster is the central theme of Hugh MacLennan's novel, *Barometer Rising,* and is the introduction to the series of animated training films on the Rules of the Road at Sea prepared by the Walt Disney Studios for use during World War II.)

This book reviews the many developments in substantive law and practice in collision litigation generally since World War II, and more particularly since COLREGS entered into force in 1977 and the Inland Rules became effective in inland waters generally in 1981 and on the Great Lakes in 1983. This is not to say that we have ignored the leading older cases, in our discussion of which we have benefited from the work of our distinguished predecessors, John W. Griffin and his editor, Arnold W. Knauth, in the United States, and Reginald C. Marsden and his editor, Kenneth C. McGuffie, in the United Kingdom. Other authorities we have found helpful are listed in the Bibliography (appendix 12).

COLREGS and the Inland Rules are discussed in the order in which they appear in the relevant convention and statutes. Other subjects are treated generally as they are now grouped in the *Digests of American Maritime Cases.*

ACKNOWLEDGMENTS

This book has only two authors, but many other persons have contributed to its formation. We are most grateful to all of them.

As professors of Admiralty law for many years, we hope that we have transmitted our love of the subject to our students, but we must also acknowledge the great extent to which their questions and research have stimulated our thinking. Similarly we must recognize the contributions of partners, associates, trainees, and other friends to the development of this volume.

David Owen read the initial drafts of several chapters with a critical eye, and made a number of extremely valuable suggestions—even the title of the book. Edgar Gold was kind enough to study the book while it was still in manuscript form and then to write his gracious foreword. Graydon Staring also studied the manuscript in order to prepare his thorough book review for the *M.L.A. Report,* and in the process made several very helpful suggestions. John Sims and Antonio Rodriguez generously exchanged material and ideas with us. Frank Wiswall read portions of the manuscript and made helpful comments concerning them.

Marianna Rubino and Helle Thorsen lent very efficient editorial and research assistance. Valuable research assistance was also provided by Brian O'Keefe, Andrea Rinaldi, and John Taylor.

Dolores Fleck's secretarial expertise; her skill with the word processor, the scanner, and other technological marvels; and her infinite patience and devotion to her work did much to make this book possible.

Fordham University and the dean and faculty of its law school have provided generous assistance in the form of faculty fellowships in 1986 and 1992, summer research and writing grants for the years 1987 to 1997, and secretarial support.

With the usual caveat about the possibility of inadvertently omitting a name, we list, in alphabetical order, others who have helped us, in one way or other in the production of this book: Richard H. Brown, Robert Conway, Patrick Griggs, Margaret Healy, Stuart Hetherington, Kap-You Kim, John Koster, Howard McCormack, Gordon Paulsen, Pedro Pablo Perez-Segnini, Catherine Sieman, Alice Sweeney, Joachim Wölters, and Genrong Yu.

TABLE OF CASES

B

C

D

E

H

I

N

O

P

Q

R

S

T

U

X

Y

Z

THE LAW OF MARINE COLLISION

CHAPTER ONE

BASIC PRINCIPLES OF COLLISION LAW

Section A. Introduction

1. *Definition*

"Collision" (Latin *collisio*) is defined as a violent encounter of one moving body with another.[1] In the maritime sphere, therefore, this means the coming together of moving vessels, although the term is commonly used as well when a moving vessel comes into contact with one that is motionless. The term "allision" is more etymologically accurate in describing a contact between a moving vessel and a stationary one, or a bridge, pier, wharf, or other fixed object,[2] but such a contact is often described as a "collision," and it will generally be so referred to in this text.

2. *Historical Background*

The definitive history of the subject is David R. Owen's *The Origins and Development of Marine Collision Law*,[3] a scholarly and exhaustive article to which the authors are greatly indebted for much of the brief historical summary that follows.

---

1. The revised fourth edition of *Black's Law Dictionary* defined the term "collision," as used in maritime law, as "The act of ships or vessels striking together," citing, *inter alia, Wright v. Brown*, 4 Ind. 95, 97 (1853), for the statement that "In its strict sense, collision means the impact of two vessels both moving, and is distinguished from *allision*, which designates the striking of a moving vessel against one that is stationary. But collision is used, in a broad sense, to include allision, and perhaps other species of encounters between vessels, and between a vessel and other floating, though non-navigable, objects." See, e.g., *In re Exxon Shipping Co.*, 869 F.2d 843, 1989 AMC 1422 (5th Cir. 1989), where the court applied the term "collision" to a contact between a moving vessel and a wreck.

2. Defined in *Black's Law Dictionary* (6th ed.) as "The running of one vessel into or against another, as distinguished from a collision, i.e., the running of two vessels against each other. But this distinction is not very carefully observed."

Some courts use the term "allision" in a broader sense, to include the contacts of moving vessels not only with stationary vessels or other floating structures, but also with piers, wharves, bridges, and other shoreside installations. See, e.g., *Georgia Ports Authority v. The Atlantic Towing Co.*, 1985 AMC 332 (SD Ga. 1983).

3. 51 Tul. L. Rev. 759 (1977) (hereinafter "Owen"). The article is an enlargement of a paper presented at the Tulane Admiralty Law Institute's Symposium on the American Law of Collision, held at New Orleans in March 1977, while Mr. Owen was president of the Maritime Law Association of the United States.

The origins of collision law are obscure. While the Justinian Digest (533 A.D.) mentions general average and ascribes the doctrine to the ancient Rhodians,[4] it makes no such attribution with respect to the law of collision. The first known written Roman law on that subject was the *Lex Aquilia*, which may have been drafted by L. Aquilio Gallo, who was Tribune of the Plebes in 467 B.C.[5] The Justinian Digest mentions a few cases of collision, but treats them under the general heading of fault liability.[6] Thus, as in other tort cases, contributory fault was a bar to recovery for negligent marine collision.[7]

There was a statement of collision law in the maritime code of the Eastern Roman Empire, compiled in the seventh or eighth century A.D., and called the Rhodian Sea Law in recognition of Rhodes as the earliest known source of maritime law.[8] Collision was treated in three of the medieval Mediterranean sea codes: the Constitutum Usus of Pisa (ca. 1160),[9] the Statutes of Ancona (ca. 1350),[10] and the Consolat de Mar, originally compiled at Barcelona in the thirteenth century.[11] Beyond the Mediterranean, collision was dealt with in the famous Rolls of Oleron (ca. 1150)[12] and the Laws of Wisby (Visby),[13] headquarters of the Hanseatic League until 1361.

Collision was one of the subjects included in the Ordonnance de la Marine of Louis XIV of France (1681),[14] the most significant of a number of national maritime codes adopted in Europe during the seventeenth century. *Inter alia*, the Ordonnance provided for the equal division of damages in cases of collision between two ships underway, regardless of fault.[15]

While the English Admiralty Court is generally considered to have originated in 1360, when the Lord High Admiral was granted jurisdiction in civil maritime cases,[16] continuous records of the court date only from 1530, and for the following 259 years very few collision cases were reported. Owen ascribes this to the low incidence of collisions and the limitations imposed

4. Bk. 14, tit. 2, frag. 1: "It is provided by the Rhodian Law that if merchandise is thrown overboard to lighten the ship, the loss occasioned for the benefit of all must be made good by the contribution of all." 2 Digest of Justinian 385 (W. Buckland translation, 1909).

5. E. Vincenzini, *L'Urto Di Navi Nel Diritto Marittimo Romano (Collisions at Sea in Roman Maritime Law)*, 1977 Il Diritto Marittimo 690.

6. Owen, supra note 3, at 760.

7. Id.

8. Id.

9. Id. at 761.

10. Id.

11. Id. at 761–62.

12. Id. at 762; Runyan, *Rolls of Oleron and the Admiralty Court in Fourteenth Century England*, 19 Am. J. Legal History 95 (1975).

13. Owen, supra note 3, at 763.

14. Id. at 764.

15. Id.

16. See R. Marsden, *Select Pleas in the Court of Admiralty*, Introduction, lxxxiii, 6 Selden Society Publications (London, 1894).

upon the court's jurisdiction by statute and by the writs of prohibition issued by the courts of common law under Lord Coke and his successors.[17]

The most frequently cited English collision decision of the period 1798–1838 was a sole fault case, *The Woodrop-Sims,*[18] decided by Sir William Scott (later Lord Stowell). In dicta he stated four basic principles of collision law: (1) each vessel bears her own loss in cases of inevitable accident; (2) damages are divided equally when both vessels are to blame; (3) there is no right of recovery when the damaged vessel is alone to blame, and (4) the damaged vessel is entitled to a full recovery when the other is solely at fault.[19] The first, third, and fourth principles are universally true today; the second was abolished in England in 1911, when Parliament adopted in its place the comparative fault rule of the 1910 Brussels Collision Convention,[20] and in the United States in 1975, when the Supreme Court adopted the same rule by its decision in *United States v. Reliable Transfer Co.*[21]

Modern Anglo-American collision law was developed very largely by Stephen Lushington, judge of the English High Court of Admiralty from 1838 to 1867.[22] During this period collision cases became much more frequent—a phenomenon ascribed by Owen to the coincidence of a number of events, including, *inter alia,* the advent of steam, the promulgation of a set of collision regulations by Trinity House, and the enactment by the British Parliament of legislation greatly expanding the jurisdiction of the Admiralty Court, enabling it to hear and decide cases of collision in tidal waters.[23]

Surprisingly, very few reported collision cases were decided by the vice admiralty courts of the American colonies, although they exercised a wider jurisdiction than the English High Court of Admiralty exercised in the seventeenth and eighteenth centuries. As Owen states, the foundations of American collision law rest largely on the decisions of some of the leading federal district court judges of the nineteenth century, including Samuel Betts, Addison Brown, Henry Brown, Peleg Sprague, and Ashur Ware. These judges were not innovators; their philosophy was to follow the general maritime law

17. Owen, supra note 3, at 765–66.

18. 2 Dods. 83, 165 Eng. Rep. 1422 (Adm. 1815).

19. The equal division rule in both-to-blame cases laid down in *The Woodrop-Sims* was approved by the House of Lords in *Hay v. Le Neve,* II Shaw's Rep. 395 (H. L. 1824). See Owen, supra note 3, at 767, n.45.

20. International Convention for the Unification of Certain Rules of Law with Respect to Collisions between Vessels, Sept. 23, 1910 (hereinafter "the 1910 Collision Convention"). The French text, which is the only official one, is reprinted in 212 Consol. Treaty Series, at 178. The Convention was implemented in the United Kingdom by the Maritime Conventions Act of 1911, 1 & 2 Geo. 5, ch. 57. See J. Griffin, *The American Law of Collision* 852 (1949) (hereinafter "Griffin"). The American translation into English is reproduced in appendix 4. See Bowman & Harris, *Multilateral Treaties, Index and Current Status*) (1984 and Tenth Cumulative Supp. 1993) (hereinafter "Bowman & Harris") for a list of the 84 State parties to the convention.

21. 421 U.S. 397, 1975 AMC 541 (1975).

22. Owen, supra note 3, at 769.

23. Id. at 768.

as enunciated in the English and Continental courts.[24] The Supreme Court decided no collision cases until 1840.[25] Between that year and 1880 the volume gradually increased, and some of the Court's decisions were of considerable importance. In the 1880s the volume decreased steadily, and by the turn of the century the Court's concern with the subject had become minimal. As of 1997 the Court has decided twenty-six collision cases, including *Reliable Transfer*,[26] which actually involved a stranding, but which had a profound effect on the American (and Liberian)[27] law of collision, since it replaced the old equal division of damages rule in both-to-blame cases with the comparative negligence rule.

Before 1840 there were no statutory rules or regulations governing navigation, although certain customs, not all of which were consistent, were generally followed by mariners,[28] and in England the Royal Navy had, for many years, a set of standing sailing orders. The increase in both the number and the seriousness of marine collisions resulting from the introduction of steam as a means of propulsion prompted the promulgation of the Trinity House navigational rules in 1840.[29]

The British Parliament enacted the first statute embodying a navigational rule—one requiring approaching steam vessels to keep to starboard—in 1846.[30] The same statute authorized the Lords Commissioners of the Admiralty to prescribe the lights to be displayed by steamers, which they did in 1848.[31] Additional statutory rules were adopted in 1851,[32] 1854,[33] and 1858.[34] These statutes applied only to British vessels, but an 1862 statute[35] authorized the issuance of rules to which other States would be encouraged to conform. Accordingly, the Board of Trade promulgated a relatively complete set of regulations in 1863.[36] France agreed by a treaty with the United Kingdom to follow the regulations,[37] and by 1868, thirty-three other countries had noti-

24. Id. at 772–73.

25. Id. at 777.

26. Supra note 21.

27. Since § 30 of the Liberian Maritime Law adopts the general maritime law of the United States as the general maritime law of Liberia, the effect of *Reliable Transfer* was to make the proportional fault rule part of the general maritime law of that country.

28. See R. Marsden, *Collisions at Sea* 424–25 (11th ed., K. McGuffie, editor, 1961, 4 British Shipping Laws, hereinafter "Marsden"); Owen, supra note 3, at 769–70.

29. Trinity House Regulations, reprinted in 166 Eng. Rep. 654–56 (1924). See Owen, supra note 3, at 783 and n.133. The issuance of the 1840 Regulations appears to have been prompted by the decision of Sir John Nichol in *The Perth* (1838) 3 Hag. Adm. 414. See F. Wiswall, Jr., *Uniformity in Maritime Law,* 57 Tul. L. Rev. 1208, 1215–16 (1983).

30. 9 & 10 Vict., ch. 100, §§ 9, 13, 36 (1846). See Owen, supra note 3, at 784.

31. Id. and n.139.

32. 14 & 15 Vict., ch. 79, §§ 27, 48 (1851).

33. 17 & 18 Vict., ch. 104, §§ 4, 296–97 (1854).

34. Admiralty Notice Respecting Lights and Fog Signals, reprinted at 166 Eng. Rep. 1252 (1924), Swab. App. vi (1860). See Owen, supra note 3, at 784.

35. Id.

36. The Merchant Shipping Act of 1862, 25 & 26 Vict. ch. 63, Table C (1862).

37. Owen, supra note 3, at 784.

fied the United Kingdom that their vessels would be bound by them, even when outside British waters.[38] The United States adopted them for inland waters as well as the high seas.[39]

By an order in council[40] new regulations were issued, prescribing "optional" whistle signals to indicate a vessel's movements—a system that had been observed by British masters to be working well in American waters. Most maritime countries then adhered to the system.

Meanwhile, the U.S. Congress enacted legislation relating to navigational lights in 1838 and 1849[41] and, in 1851,[42] the U.S. Navy, by regulation, required all U.S. steam vessels to display a white masthead light and red and green sidelights. The following year Congress authorized a newly created body, the Supervising Inspectors, to issue "Pilot Rules" governing navigation of vessels in inland waters.[43] A decisive move toward international uniformity was made in 1864, when Congress enacted a set of high seas rules almost identical to the British Regulations of 1863. The British rules were revised in 1884 and Congress adopted the same revised rules the following year.[44]

The first diplomatic conference on navigational rules was called by the President of the United States and was held in Washington in 1889.[45] This resulted in a set of rules that became effective throughout the world in 1897.[46] Relatively minor changes in the rules resulted from conferences held in Brussels in 1910[47] and in London in 1948[48] and 1960.[49]

The navigational rules currently in force in international waters were adopted in 1972 at a diplomatic conference held in London, called by the Intergovernmental Maritime Consultative Organization (IMCO), a specialized agency of the United Nations (now called the International Maritime Organization [I.M.O.]).[50] The 1972 Rules, which became effective July 15, 1977,[51] are commonly called "COLREGS," and will hereinafter be referred to by the latter designation. They constitute a thorough revision of the earlier version. COLREGS amendments were effected as of June 1, 1983, November

38. Id.
39. Id. at 784–85.
40. Regulations for Preventing Collisions at Sea, 4 P.Div. 241 (1879), modified, 9 P.Div. 247 (1884). See Owen, supra note 3, at 785.
41. Act of July 7, 1838, ch. 191, § 10, 5 Stat. 306; Act of Mar. 3, 1849, ch. 105, § 5, 9 Stat. 382. See Owen, supra note 3, at 785.
42. Id., n.154, citing *Jones v. The Hanover,* 13 F. Cas. 971, 973 n.1 (No. 7,466) (SDNY 1851).
43. Act of Aug. 30, 1852, ch. 191, § 18, 10 Stat. 70. See Owen, supra note 3, at 785.
44. Act of Apr. 29, 1864, ch. 69, arts. 1–20, 13 Stat. 58. See Owen, supra note 3, at 785–86.
45. Id. at 786.
46. Id.
47. Id.
48. Id.
49. Id.
50. Id.
51. The rules are embodied in the Convention on the International Regulations for Preventing Collisions at Sea, 1972, 28 U.S.T. 3459. The Convention became effective by a proclama-

19, 1989, and April 19, 1991,[52] but these were mainly technical in nature. COLREGS were the first rules adopted in the form of an international convention.[53]

Most countries have enacted statutes making COLREGS applicable in local waters, although in some instances special rules have been added to govern particular local conditions.[54] In the United States, however, prior to December 24, 1981, there were three sets of statutory rules for inland waters: the "Inland Rules,"[55] the "Western Rivers Rules,"[56] and the "Great Lakes Rules,"[57] and each set was supplemented by a corresponding set of "Pilot Rules," issued by the commandant of the U.S. Coast Guard pursuant to statutory authority.[58]

All three sets of statutory rules and the corresponding sets of pilot rules have now been replaced by the Inland Navigation Rules (Inland Rules),[59] which became effective on the Western Rivers and other inland waters, ex-

---

tion of President Gerald Ford issued Jan. 19, 1977, 42 F.R. 17112, reprinted in 33 U.S.C.A. following § 1602, which authorized the president to proclaim the regulations.

For an account of the difficulties encountered in connection with adoption of the regulations by the United States, and the part played by the Maritime Law Association of the United States in securing adoption, see Owen, supra note 3, at 788–89.

52. See the proclamation of President Ronald Reagan dated June 16, 1983, 48 F.R. 28634, reprinted following 33 U.S.C.A. § 1602, which also authorized the president to proclaim any amendment to the regulations adopted in accordance with Article VI of COLREGS and to which the United States did not object. See also, proclamations of President George Bush dated June 29, 1989, 54 F.R. 3885, and Mar. 19, 1991, 57 F.R. 292, reprinted following 33 U.S.C. §1602.

53. Owen, supra note 3, at 788.

54. 2 T. Schoenbaum, *Admiralty and Maritime Law* 256 (2d ed.) (hereinafter "Schoenbaum"); Owen, supra note 3, at 790.

55. Navigation Rules for Harbors, Rivers and Inland Waters Generally, 33 U.S.C. §§ 151–232. Sections 154–232 were repealed as of Dec. 24, 1981, the effective date of the new Uniform Inland Rules, 33 U.S.C. §§ 2001–38, with respect to the Western Rivers and inland waters generally. See note following 33 U.S.C.A. § 2001. The 1948 rules were, however, adopted at a diplomatic conference together with the 1948 Safety of Life at Sea (SOLAS) Convention, and the 1960 rules were adopted at the same conference that adopted the 1960 SOLAS Convention, 16 U.S.T. 185, T.I.A.S. No. 5780, 536 U.N.T.S. 27. Thus, the text of the 1960 SOLAS Convention was Annex "A" to the final act of the 1960 Conference and the collision regulations constituted Annex "B."

56. Navigation Rules for the Great Lakes and their Connecting and Tributary Waters, 33 U.S.C. §§ 241–95, repealed as of Mar. 1, 1983, the effective date of the new Inland Rules with respect to the Great Lakes.

57. Navigation Rules for the Red River of the North and Rivers Emptying into the Gulf of Mexico, 33 U.S.C. §§ 301–56, repealed as of Dec. 24, 1981, the effective date of the new Inland Rules with respect to the Western Rivers and inland waters generally. See note following 33 U.S.C.A. § 2001.

58. Inland Pilot Rules, 33 C.F.R. former §§ 80.01–80.36; Great Lakes Pilot Rules, 33 C.F.R. former §§ 90.01–90.30, and Western Rivers Pilot Rules, 33 C.F.R. former §§ 95.01–95.80. These Pilot Rules ceased to apply when the new Inland Rules became effective.

59. Supra note 55.

cept the Great Lakes, on December 24, 1981,[60] and came into force on the Lakes on March 1, 1983.[61] The Inland Rules include a few provisions concerning special navigational problems encountered in navigating the Western Rivers[62] and the Great Lakes,[63] but otherwise the same rules apply on all U.S. waters not governed by COLREGS.[64] Moreover, the Inland Rules are in most instances identical to the corresponding COLREGS; even the numbering system of COLREGS has been followed.[65] As will be discussed in chapters 5 and 8, the principal remaining difference is in the meaning of the sound signals to be exchanged by vessels approaching each other on head-on, crossing, or overtaking courses.[66] The dividing lines between waters governed by the Inland Rules and those where the International Rules apply have been established by Congress.

3. The Incidence of Marine Collisions

The widespread use of radar, ARPA (automatic radar plotting aid), and other sophisticated navigational aids, the schooling of ships' officers in their proper use, and the adoption of traffic separation schemes in congested waterways have reduced the number of marine collisions, but they continue to occur with discouraging frequency. In 1988, the latest year for which statistics were available as of 1997, a total of 1,593 collisions involving U.S. flag commercial vessels of all sizes were reported to the Coast Guard. Of these, 47 resulted in total losses and 1,546 in damage.[67] During the year, 36 deaths and 175 injuries were caused by collision.[68]

---

60. Pub. L. No. 96-591, § 7, provided that the new rules were to become effective twelve months after the date of enactment of the law (Dec. 24, 1980), except that the effective date with respect to the Great Lakes was to be established by the Secretary of Transportation.

61. See 47 F.R. 15135, Apr. 8, 1982.

62. See Rule 14(d), 33 U.S.C. § 2014(d), providing that a power-driven vessel operating on the Western Rivers and other rivers designated by the Secretary of Transportation, and on the Great Lakes, and proceeding downbound with a following current, has the right of way over an upbound vessel. See also Rule 24(i), relating to special lights for power-driven vessels when pushing ahead or towing alongside on the Western Rivers and other waters designated by the secretary.

63. See Rule 23(d), 33 U.S.C. § 2023(d), relating to an all-around white light which a power-driven vessel operating on the Great Lakes may carry in lieu of the second masthead light and sternlight required elsewhere. See also Rule 14(d), supra note 62, which applies to the Great Lakes as well as to the Western Rivers.

64. Rule 1, 33 U.S.C. § 2001.

The Inland Rules also apply to U.S. vessels on the Canadian waters of the Great Lakes to the extent that there is no conflict with Canadian law. Id.

65. See the comparative table in the U.S. Coast Guard publication, *Navigation Rules, International-Inland (1990)*. See also 12 J. Mar. L. & Com. 543 (1981), setting out those Inland Rules which differ from the corresponding International Rules.

66. Compare Rules 9 and 34 of COLREGS with Rules 9 and 34 of the Inland Rules.

67. See U.S. Coast Guard, *Statistics of Casualties—1988,* 48 Proceedings of the Merchant Marine Safety Council, No. 1, 25 (1991).

68. Id. at 28–29.

Section B. Jurisdiction in Collision Cases

1. Subject Matter Jurisdiction in Civil Cases

The U.S. Constitution extends the federal judicial power to "all cases of admiralty and maritime jurisdiction."[69] This constitutional grant was implemented by the Judiciary Act of 1789,[70] which established the lower federal courts and defined their powers. Section 9 provided, *inter alia,* that the "district courts shall have, exclusively of the courts of the several States, . . . exclusive original cognizance of all civil cases of admiralty and maritime jurisdiction, . . . saving to suitors, in all cases, the right of a common law remedy, where the common law is competent to give it . . . ."[71] This provision, in more modern English, was reenacted as part of Title 28 of the United States Code in 1948 and now reads:

> § 1333. The district courts shall have original jurisdiction, exclusive of the courts of the States, of: (1) Any civil case of admiralty or maritime jurisdiction, saving to suitors in all cases all other remedies to which they are otherwise entitled.

While federal admiralty jurisdiction in contract cases depends upon the maritime nature of the contract, in tort cases, with minor exceptions, it rests upon two elements: (a) that the tort be consummated on waters within the admiralty jurisdiction of the United States, and (b) "that the wrong bears a significant relationship to traditional maritime activity."[72] Waters navigable by commercial vessels of any size or type are within the admiralty jurisdiction of the United States if they form part of a navigable highway of commerce between two or more states of the United States, or between two or more countries.[73] Thus, not only are the high seas included, but so are rivers and canals, even those located in foreign countries, if they are navigable to the sea, or to other navigable waterways which connect them to the sea.[74] Navigable lakes of the United States are likewise within the admiralty jurisdiction if they lie between two or more American states,[75] even if they have no navigable outlet to the sea. In theory, a navigable lake connecting two or more foreign countries but having no navigable outlet to the sea would appear to be included, although as far as is known the question has never been decided. The locality test is therefore met in the case of a collision occurring on any navigable wa-

69. U.S. Const., art. III, § 2.

70. Ch. 20, § 9, 1 Stat. 73.

71. The language preserving the right of a common law remedy is commonly referred to as the "saving to suitors" clause.

72. *Executive Jet Aviation, Inc. v. City of Cleveland,* 409 U.S. 249, 268, 1973 AMC 1, 15–16 (1972).

73. *The Genesee Chief v. Fitzhugh,* 53 U.S. 443 (1852); *Fretz v. Bull,* 53 U.S. 466 (1851).

74. *Ex Parte Boyer,* 109 U.S. 629 (1884).

75. *Davis v. United States,* 185 F.2d 938, 1951 AMC 93 (9th Cir. 1950).

terway, except one confined to a single state of the United States, or to a single foreign country, and having no navigable outlet to the sea, or to another state or country.

When the vessels involved in a collision are commercial vessels, the second test for subject matter jurisdiction is plainly met, since there is "a significant relationship to traditional maritime activity." In recent years, however, a question has arisen as to whether a collision between two pleasure craft occurring on waters within the admiralty jurisdiction meets this second test. The question was decided in the affirmative in *Foremost Ins. Co. v. Richardson*,[76] but by a Court divided five to four. In that case, two pleasure boats, one 16 feet and the other 18 feet in length, collided on the Amite River in Louisiana, resulting in the death of an occupant of one of the vessels. Justice Marshall, for the majority, wrote that because the wrong involved the negligent operation of a vessel on navigable waters, it had "a sufficient nexus to traditional maritime activity to sustain admiralty jurisdiction in the District Court."[77]

In a strongly worded dissent, in which Chief Justice Burger and Justices Rehnquist and O'Connor joined, Justice Powell wrote that "In centuries past—long before modern means of transportation by land and air existed—rivers and oceans were the basic means of commerce, and the vessels that used the waterways were limited primarily to commercial and naval purposes.... Thus, the 'traditional' connection emphasized in *Executive Jet* is absent where pleasure boats are concerned."[78]

It is submitted that the majority opinion in *Foremost* is sound. If the minority view had prevailed, a number of questions would have remained unsettled. For example, would there have been admiralty jurisdiction if one of the vessels involved in *Foremost* had been a small commercial fishing vessel? Or if the collision had been between two large steam- or diesel-powered yachts crossing the Atlantic? Or between such a yacht and a cargo vessel? The majority opinion in *Foremost* makes it plain that *a fortiori* admiralty would have jurisdiction in any of these cases.[79]

In the great majority of collision actions brought in the United States the admiralty jurisdiction of one of the federal district courts is invoked by the

76. 457 U.S. 668, 1982 AMC 2253 (1982).

77. 457 U.S. at 674, 1982 AMC at 2258.

78. 457 U.S. at 681–82, 1982 AMC at 2263–64.

79. See N. Healy, *Admiralty and Shipping*, 1982 Annual Survey of American Law 1.

The *Foremost* analysis of admiralty tort jurisdiction continues to enjoy the support of a majority of the Supreme Court. In *Sisson v. Ruby*, 497 U.S. 358, 1990 AMC 1801 (1990), not a collision case, there was a challenge to admiralty jurisdiction over a fire on a noncommercial vessel at a marina on a navigable waterway because "navigation" was not involved. The Supreme Court rejected the argument because "... the need for uniform rules of maritime conduct and liability is not limited to navigation but extends at least to any other activities traditionally undertaken by vessels, commercial or non-commercial." 497 U.S. at 368, 1990 AMC at 1808.

In *Jerome B. Grubart, Inc. v. Great Lakes Dredge & Dock Co.*, 513 U.S. 527, 1995 AMC 913 (1995), also not a vessel collision case, there was a challenge to admiralty jurisdiction in the

plaintiff and, if this is done, the defendant has no right to have the case remanded to a state court, even if there is no diversity of citizenship.[80] Conversely, in the now extremely rare instance of a plaintiff electing to sue for collision damages in a state court, as he or she may under the "saving to suitors" clause,[81] the defendant has no right of removal to the federal district court as a court of admiralty jurisdiction.[82] If there is diversity of citizenship, the plaintiff may, however, have the case removed to the federal district court as a "diversity" court.[83] In that case the action will proceed as an ordinary civil case, and there will be a right of trial by jury.

When the plaintiff properly invokes the district court's admiralty jurisdiction, there will be no right of jury trial (if the case is not one arising on the Great Lakes),[84] and the procedure will be governed by the special provisions of the Federal Rules of Civil Procedure applicable when the admiralty jurisdiction is invoked,[85] and by the Supplemental Rules for Certain Admiralty and Maritime Claims, annexed to the Federal Rules.[86]

2. *Jurisdiction* In Personam *and* In Rem

Although the federal district courts, as courts of admiralty, have subject matter jurisdiction of all collisions occurring on waters within the admiralty jurisdiction of the United States, they are of course unable to exercise that jurisdiction unless they also have jurisdiction of the defendant, or the *res* against which the action is brought. Jurisdiction *in personam* is ordinarily obtained by a voluntary appearance (as where the plaintiff's attorney obtains an agreement to appear in the action from an attorney who he knows regularly represents the defendant), or by service of a writ of summons. In the latter case, service is made in the same manner as in any other district court civil action.[87] This may include service by mail on a defendant abroad, pursuant to a state "long arm" statute.[88] But where it is impossible to serve a summons on

---

flooding of a Chicago railroad tunnel because of pile-driving in the Chicago River above the tunnel. The Supreme Court rejected the challenge and approved the jurisdictional characterization, "repair or maintenance work on a navigable waterway performed from a vessel."

80. 1 Schoenbaum 62.

81. 28 U.S.C. § 1333.

82. See Note, *Removal of Maritime Actions,* in N. Healy & D. Sharpe, *Cases and Materials on Admiralty* 94–95 (2d ed. 1986).

83. Id.

84. Rule 38(e). Fed. R. Civ. P. With respect to jury trials in Great Lakes cases, see 28 U.S.C. § 1873. See also Note, *Jury Trials under the Great Lakes Act,* in N. Healy & B. Currie, *Cases and Materials on Admiralty* 28 (1965).

85. See Rules 1, 9(h), and 14(c), Fed. R. Civ. P.

86. The Supplemental Rules are lettered A to F. Rule A defines the scope of the rules. Rule B is concerned with maritime attachment and garnishment, Rule C with actions *in rem,* and Rule D with possessory, petitory, and partition actions. Rule E contains general provisions relating to actions under Rules B, C, and D. Rule F concerns limitation of liability proceedings.

87. Rule 4(c), Fed. R. Civ. P.

88. *Elefteriou v. The Archontissa,* 443 F.2d 185 (4th Cir. 1971).

the defendant personally because he cannot be "found" within the federal district wherein the action is brought, jurisdiction *in personam* may be obtained by "maritime attachment" or "garnishment" of any goods, chattels, credits, or effects of the defendant within the district. Thus, if after a reasonable effort it has not been possible to "find" the defendant within the district for the purpose of serving him with process, a vessel or other property belonging to him that may be found within the district may be attached or garnished, up to the amount sued for.[89] If he or she fails to appear in the action, a default judgment may then be taken against the defendant, for not more than the value of the property attached or garnished. On the other hand, if the defendant wishes to defend the action, and fails to defeat the claim on the merits, the court is empowered to enter judgment against him or her *in personam* for the full amount of the provable damages, even if they exceed the value of the property attached or garnished.[90] It may then be possible to recover, in some other jurisdiction where the defendant has assets, whatever part of the judgment cannot be recovered out of the property attached or garnished.

An appearance in an action may be expressly restricted to the defense of a maritime claim with respect to which the defendant's property has been attached or garnished. Such an appearance does not constitute an appearance for the purposes of any other claim with respect to which process of maritime attachment and garnishment is not available, or has not been served.[91] Suppose, for example, that a plaintiff were to bring an admiralty action *in personam* for collision damages in the U.S. District Court for the Southern District of New York, and were to join with the collision claim a nonmaritime claim against the defendant; that the defendant could not be "found" within the district, and that the plaintiff caused the defendant's New York bank account to be garnished with respect to the collision claim. In such a case the defendant could enter an appearance specifically restricted to the defense of the collision claim, without submitting to the jurisdiction of the court with respect to the nonmaritime claim.

---

89. Supplemental Rule B, Fed. R. Civ. P. See *Teyseer Cement Co. v. Halla Maritime Corp.*, 794 F.2d 472, 1986 AMC 2705 (9th Cir. 1986); *Belcher Co. v. The Maratha Mariner,* 724 F.2d 1161, 1163–65, 1984 AMC 1679, 1681 (5th Cir. 1984).

90. See, e.g., *United States v. An Article of Drug,* 725 F.2d 976, 982 (5th Cir. 1984); *Belcher Co. v. The Maratha Mariner,* supra note 89.

A defendant whose liquid assets have been attached and who wishes to defend the action may, however, apply to the court under Supplemental Rule E(6), Fed. R. Civ. P., for the release of any excessive amount of assets attached. Likewise, if he has furnished a surety bond or other approved security for the release of the attachment, he may apply under the same rule for a reduction in the amount of the security alleged to be excessive.

91. See Supplemental Rule E(8), Fed. R. Civ. P., which provides: "Restricted Appearance. An appearance to defend against an admiralty and maritime claim with respect to which there has issued process *in rem,* or process of attachment and garnishment whether pursuant to these Supplemental Rules or to Rule 4(e), may be expressly restricted to the defense of such claim, and in that event shall not constitute an appearance for the purposes of any other claim with respect to which such process is not available or has not been served."

An interesting by-product of the unification of the old General Admiralty Rules of the Supreme Court with the Federal Rules of Civil Procedure in 1966 was the addition, to the plaintiff's remedies in an *in personam* action, of any attachment remedies that may be available under the law of the state wherein the federal district court is located.[92] Thus, even though in a particular case there may be no right of maritime attachment (e.g., because the plaintiff can be "found" within the federal district wherein the action has been brought), there may nevertheless be a right of attachment under the local state law because the defendant has been removing assets from the jurisdiction in fraud of creditors.[93]

Another result of the unification of the General Admiralty Rules and the Federal Rules of Civil Procedure is that the marshal of one federal district is now authorized to serve a summons in a collision or other admiralty action anywhere within the state wherein the federal district is located. Thus, the Marshal of the Southern District of New York, which includes the Borough of Manhattan, may serve a summons on a defendant in the City of Buffalo, which is within the Western District of New York. But even though it may be possible to find and serve the defendant in Buffalo, the defendant's property located in Manhattan or elsewhere in the Southern District of New York may be attached or garnished if he or she cannot be "found" within the Southern District for the purpose of service of a summons there.[94]

While the avowed purpose of a maritime attachment is to "compel" the appearance of a defendant who cannot validly be served with a summons within the district, a defendant whose property has been properly attached or garnished cannot have the attachment or garnishment vacated if he or she subsequently appears in the action.[95] The attachment or garnishment thus has the incidental, but sometimes highly valuable result of affording security for the plaintiff's claim.

3. Maritime Liens and Arrests In Rem

Under American law, a negligently caused collision immediately impresses the offending vessel with an inchoate maritime lien, which may be perfected by the successful prosecution of an action *in rem* against her. Under English law, the prevailing view appears to be that a maritime lien is simply a security

92. Supplemental Rule B(1), Fed. R. Civ. P.

93. See, e.g., New York Civil Practice Law and Rules (CPLR) § 6201.

94. See R. Jarvis, *An Introduction to Maritime Attachment Practice under Rule B,* 20 J. Mar. L. & Com. 521, 527 (1989), citing *Det Bergenske Damps. v. Sabre Shipping Corp.,* 341 F.2d 50, 1965 AMC 234 (2d Cir. 1965).

95. *Construction Exporting Enterprises v. Nikki Maritime, Ltd.,* 558 F. Supp. 1372, 1984 AMC 344 (SDNY 1983), appeal dismissed, 742 F.2d 1432, 1984 AMC 342 (2d Cir. 1983); Jarvis, supra note 94, at 534.

device; an action *in rem* will lie only when the shipowner is liable *in personam.*[96] In the United States, on the other hand, the ship is personified, and for certain purposes is treated almost as a corporate entity.[97] Thus, the ship may be held liable for the torts of those lawfully in charge of her, even under circumstances where her owner is under no liability. Two classic examples of this feature of American maritime law are compulsory pilotage and operation by a bareboat charterer. The shipowner is not liable *in personam* for the faults of a compulsory pilot, i.e., one whom the law requires, since the owner has no choice in the selection of the pilot, and the latter is therefore not the owner's agent or servant.[98] Similarly, the shipowner is not liable *in personam* for the faults of the master or crew of a bareboat-chartered vessel, since they are, respectively, the agent and servants of the bareboat charterer, to whom possession and control of the vessel has been surrendered for the term of the charter.[99]

But in both compulsory pilotage and bareboat charter cases, the vessel herself is liable *in rem,* and may be sued *in rem* in much the same way as an individual or corporate defendant may be sued in an *in personam* action. Any action against the vessel *in rem,* however, must be brought in a federal district court, and the court's admiralty jurisdiction must be invoked. This is so because an action *in rem* by a private party against a vessel (or other maritime property, i.e., cargo or freights) is a remedy wholly unknown to the common law, and was therefore not saved to suitors by the Judiciary Act of 1789, or its modern counterpart.[100]

In a collision case, where no compulsory pilotage is involved, the plaintiff will usually endeavor to sue the vessel *in rem* and the shipowner (or bareboat charterer, if the vessel is operating under a bareboat charter) *in personam,* in the same action. There are decided advantages in doing so, in many instances. Thus, a maritime lien is the best possible security; under American law the lienor has a proprietary interest in the vessel to the extent of the lien,[101] which means that the lienor has priority over all creditors of the owner (or bareboat charterer) who do not have maritime liens, or have maritime liens of inferior rank. On the other hand, an action *in personam* may be desirable when there is a possibility that the provable damages may exceed

---

96. See *The China,* 74 U.S. 53 (1868). See also the discussion in Marsden 60–81. But see § 638 of the Canada Shipping Act, providing for application of the proportionate fault rule "[w]here, by *the fault of two or more vessels,* damage is caused to one or more of those vessels, to their cargoes or freight . . ." (emphasis added).

97. *The Young Mechanic,* 30 F. Cas. 873, 876 (No. 18,180) (CCD Me. 1855); *The China,* supra note 96; *Salazar v. The Atlantic Sun,* 881 F.2d 73, 1989 AMC 2594 (3d Cir. 1989).

For a thorough discussion of the personification doctrine see Hon. A. Howard, *Personification of the Vessel: Fact or Fiction?* 21 J. Mar. L. & Com. 319 (1990).

98. *Homer Ramsdell Transp. Co. v. Compagnie Generale Transatlantique,* 182 U.S. 406 (1901).

99. See *The Barnstable,* 181 U.S. 464 (1901). But a vessel is not liable *in rem* for the faults of persons unlawfully in possession. *United States v. The Malek Adhel,* 43 U.S. 210 (1844).

100. *The Moses Taylor,* 71 U.S. 411 (1867); *The Hine v. Trevor,* 71 U.S. 555 (1867).

101. *The John G. Stevens,* 170 U.S. 113 (1898).

the value of the *res*, and of course it will be the only available remedy when the offending vessel has been lost, or does not come to waters within the jurisdiction of a court in which an *in personam* action may be brought. Any judgment *in rem* could never be effective for more than the value of the vessel, less the amount of any other judgments *in rem* against her in favor of lienors whose liens outrank the plaintiff's collision lien.

Supplemental Rule E(8), Fed. R. Civ. P.,[102] cited above in relation to maritime attachment and garnishment, also applies to *in rem* proceedings. If, for example, an action for collision damage in the amount of $3 million is brought *in rem* only, the vessel's owner may file a "claim of owner"[103] and defend the action without submitting to the jurisdiction of the court for any other purpose. If the plaintiff obtains a judgment *in rem* for $3 million and the vessel brings only $1 million at a judicial sale (over and above marshal's fees and other expenses) the plaintiff's recovery will be limited to $1 million.[104]

4. Forum Non Conveniens

While a district court may have subject matter jurisdiction of a collision, and jurisdiction of the owner or operator, or the vessel, or both, under the *forum non conveniens* (F.N.C.) doctrine it may in certain circumstances have discretion to decline to exercise its jurisdiction, or to exercise it upon conditions.

Until recently it was generally thought that the doctrine could properly be applied only when all of the interested parties were foreign, except where an American plaintiff sued as assignee or subrogee of a foreign party.[105] However, the tendency appears to be for the courts to apply the doctrine with increasing frequency, even in cases where the plaintiffs are Americans.

---

102. Supra note 91.

103. Under Supplemental Rule C(6), Fed. R. Civ. P. the owner or other person claiming a vessel or other maritime property proceeded against *in rem* must file a "claim of owner" within 10 days after execution of the process *in rem,* unless further time is allowed by the court. Such a claim in an *in rem* proceeding is analogous to a notice of appearance in an action *in personam.* As of 1997, a committee of the Maritime Law Association of the United States was considering a recommendation to change the terms "claim" and "claimant," as used in proceedings *in rem,* because the terms have a very different meaning when used in limitation of liability proceedings.

104. Where a plaintiff is unable to obtain jurisdiction of the party who owned the vessel at the time of the collision (e.g., because he cannot be served with process within the district and has no property there subject to maritime attachment, the vessel having been sold) it would seem that the plaintiff should be entitled to bring an action against the former owner in another district where he can be served, or has property subject to attachment, to recover the amount by which the provable damages exceed the recovery in the proceeding *in rem.* But see the discussions of somewhat similar problems in *The Monte A.*, 12 F. 331 (SDNY 1882), and in Comment, *Application of the Doctrine of Res Judicata to Successive In Personam and In Rem Actions in Admiralty,* 27 Chicago L. Rev. 381 (1990).

105. *The Tricolor,* 1 F. Supp. 934, 1932 AMC 1256 (SDNY 1932), aff'd, 65 F.2d 392, 1933 AMC 919 (2d Cir. 1933).

Thus, it was applied in *The Nordic Regent*,[106] where a Liberian vessel struck a pier in Trinidad owned by an American corporation, causing extensive damage. The pier owner brought an action in the U.S. District Court for the Southern District of New York, where the Liberian shipowner had an office. The United States Court of Appeals for the Second Circuit held, in a nine-to-two *en banc* decision, that the trial court's dismissal of the action on F.N.C. grounds was a proper exercise of its discretion.[107] The decision had an important effect: under Trinidadian law, in the absence of a showing of "actual fault or privity" of the shipowner the limit of liability would have been £8 per ton of the ship's gross tonnage, or about $570,000 in the case of the *Nordic Regent*,[108] whereas under American law the limit would have been the damaged value of the vessel, plus any voyage earnings, or about $8 million, assuming that it was found that the collision was not caused with the "privity or knowledge" of the shipowner.[109]

5. *Civil Jurisdiction in Other Countries*

The English concept of subject matter jurisdiction in collision cases appears to be substantially the same as the American: the English Admiralty Court, now part of the Queen's Bench Division of the High Court of Justice, has jurisdiction of collisions occurring on navigable waters anywhere in the world, at least if they are tidal, regardless of the flags of the vessels involved, provided the defendant can be served with a writ of summons or his vessel can be arrested in English waters.[110] The law of Canada, Australia, and other Commonwealth countries is similar.[111]

---

106. 654 F.2d 147 (2d Cir. 1980). The citation is to the revised opinion. The earlier opinion, which was withdrawn, is reported at 1980 AMC 309. For a critical discussion of *The Nordic Regent*, see E. Dennard, *Forum Non Conveniens in International Maritime Collision Litigation in the Federal Courts: A Suggested Approach*, 16 Cornell Int'l L.J. 121 (1983).

107. 654 F.2d at 159–60.

108. Id. at 159.

109. Id.

110. The inherent jurisdiction of the old High Court of Admiralty in collision cases is preserved by the Administration of Justice Act 1956. In addition, the jurisdiction of the modern Admiralty Court in such cases is specifically recognized by § 20(1)(b),(3)(b) of the Supreme Court Act 1981.

While in the United States the test is navigability (*The Genesee Chief v. Fitzhugh*, 53 U.S. 443 [1852]), the traditional test in England has been what Lord Donaldson, M. R., called "tidality" in his dissenting opinion in *The Goring*, [1987] 1 Q.B. 689 (C.A.), aff'd, [1988] 2 W.L.R. 460 (H.L.), a salvage case, i.e., the admiralty jurisdiction in the geographical sense extends as far as the tide ebbs and flows. See W. Hastings, *Non-tidal Salvage in the United Kingdom:* Goring, Goring, *Gone*, 19 J. Mar. L. & Com. 473 (1988), wherein the author states that "It is unfortunate that navigability got translated into tidality, but this is potentially explicable because most [English] rivers were only navigable by ocean-going vessels up to the tidal limit. . . ." Id. at 479. In referring to *The Genesee Chief*, supra note 73, Hastings remarks that in that case "Taney C. J. astutely explained the English test of tidality as nothing more than a test of navigability." Id. at 19, n.73.

111. See F. Berlingieri, *Jurisdiction and Choice of Law in Collision Cases and an Overview of the Concept of Fault and Its Apportionment*, 51 Tul. L. Rev. 866 (1977) (hereinafter "Berlingieri"), an article based on a paper presented by Professor Berlingieri, then president, and later president of

The concept is quite different under the laws of the continental European countries, where it is necessary to show certain contacts with the forum State.[112] Thus, the defendant's domicile in that State is considered relevant in France, Germany, Greece, Sweden, and the former U.S.S.R.[113] The fact that the place of the tort is the forum State is sufficient to support subject matter jurisdiction in Denmark, Germany, France, Greece, Italy, Portugal, Spain, Sweden, and the former U.S.S.R.[114] The call of a vessel at a port within the forum State is a relevant consideration in France, Italy, Portugal, and the former U.S.S.R.[115]

6. *The Civil Jurisdiction Convention of 1952*

At its twenty-second Plenary Session, held at Naples in 1951, the Comité Maritime International (C.M.I.)[116] drafted a convention, adopted at a diplomatic conference held at Brussels the following year, called the International Convention on Certain Rules Concerning Civil Jurisdiction in Matters of Collision (the Civil Jurisdiction Convention),[117] which entered into force in 1955. However, it has not been adopted by a number of important maritime States, including the United States, Brazil, Japan, the Netherlands, the former U.S.S.R., and the Scandinavian countries.[118]

The convention applies not only to collisions, but to damages caused by improper maneuvers, failures to maneuver, or noncompliance with regulations, even when there has been no actual collision.[119] It does not affect domestic laws relating to collisions involving warships or vessels owned by or in the service of a government,[120] claims arising from contracts of carriage or other contracts,[121] or cases covered by the revised Rhine Navigational Convention of October 17, 1868.[122] It applies to all interested parties when all the vessels concerned belong to contracting States, but a contracting State may apply it to interested parties belonging to a noncontracting State conditional

---

honor of the Comité Maritime International, at the Tulane Admiralty Law Institute's Symposium on the American Law of Collision, held at New Orleans in March 1977.

112. Id. at 867.

113. Id., and n.10.

114. Id., and n.11.

115. Id., and n.12.

116. As of 1997 the C.M.I., founded in 1897 for the purpose of promoting international uniformity in maritime law, was composed of the national maritime law associations of 53 countries, including the United States. See *Comité Maritime International Yearbook (1996)* 29–69.

117. 439 U.N.T.S. 217 (hereinafter "Civil Jurisdiction Convention"). The convention is reprinted in full in appendix 4.

118. There were 63 ratifications and adherences as of 1997.

119. Civil Jurisdiction Convention, art. 4.

120. Id., art. 5.

121. Id., art. 6.

122. Id., art. 7.

upon reciprocity. When all interested parties belong to the forum State, national law, and not the convention, applies.[123]

Under the convention, an action will lie for damages caused by collision between seagoing vessels or between a seagoing vessel and an inland navigational craft (a) where the defendant has his or her habitual residence or a place of business, (b) where the defendant ship or a sister ship has been lawfully arrested or security has been furnished in lieu of arrest, or (c) in the case of a collision within the limits of a port or in inland waters where the collision occurs.[124] The choice among these jurisdictions is that of the plaintiff,[125] but a plaintiff may not bring a further action against the same defendant on the same facts in another jurisdiction without discontinuing an action already instituted.[126] These provisions are without prejudice to the right of the parties to bring a collision action before a court chosen by agreement, or to arbitrate the claims.[127]

Counterclaims arising out of the same collision may be brought before the court having jurisdiction of the principal action,[128] and if there are several claimants, any claimant may bring an action before the court previously seized of an action against the same party arising out of the same collision.[129] The convention does not prevent any court seized of an action under its provisions from exercising jurisdiction under its national laws in further actions arising out of the same incident.[130]

The contracting States undertake to arbitrate disputes arising out of the convention, without prejudice to the obligations of contracting States that have agreed to submit disputes to the International Court of Justice.[131]

As will be seen, the Civil Jurisdiction Convention represents a compromise between common law and civil law concepts of jurisdiction: it follows the civil law principle that there must be a connecting factor, but adds to the list of acceptable factors the possibility of arresting the vessel or the obtaining of security to avoid an arrest.[132] The proceeding *in rem*—a concept familiar to maritime lawyers and judges in the common-law States, but not to those in States following the civil law—is thus recognized.

Professor Berlingieri suggests that one reason for the failure of the 1952 Convention to achieve wide acceptance is the absence of rules for the avoidance of duplication of actions.[133] Under the convention there is no provision

123. Id., art. 8.
124. Id., art. 1(1).
125. Id., art. 1(2).
126. Id., art. 1(3).
127. Id., art. 2.
128. Id., art. 3(1).
129. Id., art. 3(2).
130. Id., art. 3(3).
131. Id., art. 9.
132. Id., art. 1(1).
133. Berlingieri, supra note 111, at 868.

for "compulsory" counterclaims; the defendant may forego filing a counterclaim in the original action, and may instead institute a separate action in another forum. Professor Berlingieri expresses doubt that duplication of actions can always be avoided, stating, "In any event, two conditions appear indispensable to achievement of this result: (1) the defendant must be given the choice of an alternative forum; and (2) limiting the defendant's choice must be contingent upon providing satisfactory security by the claimant."[134]

Other reasons have been suggested for the lack of wide support for the Civil Jurisdiction Convention, including its exclusion of all government vessels (even those used for commercial purposes), the absence of choice of law provisions, and the absence of provisions concerning recognition and enforcement of judgments.[135]

7. *The C.M.I. Draft Convention of 1977*

In the hope of meeting these objections, the C.M.I., at its thirty-first Plenary Session, held in Rio de Janeiro in 1977, formulated a new Draft Convention on Civil Jurisdiction, Choice of Law, and Recognition and Enforcement of Judgments in Matters of Collision (the Draft Convention).[136] This was submitted to IMCO (now I.M.O.), following the Rio de Janeiro Conference, but as of 1997 it had not been taken up by that organization's legal committee. However, the committee plans to consider it after completing current work on matters of higher priority, such as marine pollution.

Although not in force, a brief summary of the provisions of the Draft Convention concerning jurisdiction is set out below, because the draft represents a consensus of the concepts of many of the leading maritime States concerning the subjects which it treats, and a convention based upon it may eventually be adopted.

The Draft Convention consists of a preliminary article and eight others, grouped under four titles: (I) Jurisdiction, (II) Choice of Law, (III) Recognition and Enforcement of Judgments, and (IV) General Provisions. These subjects will be discussed on pages 21–22 and 38–39.

Paragraph (1) of the Preliminary Article (Article 1) would make the convention applicable to "collision" actions, including recourse (indemnity) actions, for damages resulting from loss of or damage to a vessel or to property on board. "Collision" is defined as "contact between two or more vessels, one of which at least is seagoing, and any other accident involving such vessels, arising from a manoeuvre, or a failure to manoeuvre, or from a failure to

134. Id.

135. See Report of the C.M.I. International Subcommittee on Collision, 3 1977 C.M.I. Documentation 138, at 154 (hereinafter "Collision Report"). A preliminary draft prepared by the Subcommittee was the basis of the discussions at the Rio de Janeiro Plenary Session, which resulted in formulation of the Draft Convention.

136. 2 1977 C.M.I. Documentation 104.

comply with any applicable rules of navigation, statutory or otherwise, even if no actual contact has occurred."

This broad definition corresponds to that in Article 4 of the 1952 Civil Jurisdiction Convention, and is designed to include "crowding" cases, i.e., cases where faulty navigation by one vessel forces a second vessel into collision with a third. The "collision" definition would also include "wash damage" to another vessel or its cargo, resulting from navigating in a crowded waterway at an excessive rate of speed.

Recourse (indemnity) actions are not specifically covered by the 1952 Convention. Their express inclusion in the Draft Convention would make it clear that in a "crowding" case, if the owners of Ship A were to sue Ship B's owners for collision damage, and B's owners were to allege that faulty maneuvering by Ship C contributed to the collision, a recourse action by B's owners against C's owners would fall under the Draft Convention.

The 1952 Civil Jurisdiction Convention does not apply when none of the vessels involved is seagoing; the Draft Convention contains a similar provision.[137] It was suggested that drilling rigs should be specifically included, or that there be added a definition of "vessel" sufficiently broad to include such structures. However, it was decided to omit such a definition, and to leave it to the courts to rule on what structures are "vessels," as was done in the 1910 Collision Convention and the 1952 Civil Jurisdiction Convention.

Unlike the 1952 Civil Jurisdiction Convention, the Draft Convention would not apply to personal injury and wrongful death claims. However, while the penultimate paragraph of Article 9 would abrogate the 1952 Convention for most purposes as between States accepting the Draft Convention, the 1952 Convention would continue to apply to personal injury and death claims, as between States subscribing to that convention.[138]

Article 1(2) of the Draft Convention would exclude warships and public vessels, but government-owned commercial vessels and ferries would be included.

Article 2(1) would provide that unless the parties otherwise agreed, collision actions could be brought only in the courts of five possible places, at the plaintiff's option:

1. The place of the defendant's "habitual residence or domicile, or principal place of business";[139]
2. The State in whose internal waters or territorial sea the collision occurred;[140]

---

137. Civil Jurisdiction Convention, art. 1(1); Draft Convention, art. 1(1).
138. See Civil Jurisdiction Convention, art. 4; Draft Convention, art. 9.
139. Draft Convention, art. 2(1)(a).
140. Id., art. 2(1)(b).

3. A State where the colliding vessel, or a sister ship lawfully subject to arrest, had been arrested, or security had been provided to avoid arrest;[141]
4. A State where the defendant had property which was subject to attachment under the domestic law, and such property had been attached or security had been provided to avoid attachment;[142]
5. A place where a limitation fund had been properly constituted by the defendant.[143]

The first sentence of Article 2(2), corresponding to Article 1(3) of the 1952 Convention, concerns *lis pendens.* However, while the 1952 Convention would require the discontinuance of the first action before a plaintiff would be permitted to bring a further action against the same defendant in another jurisdiction, the Draft Convention would permit a second action if prosecution of the first action was simply stayed in accordance with local law.[144]

The second sentence of Article 2(2) concerns *res judicata.* It provides that once judgment on the merits has been rendered in an action in one State, one party will not be entitled to bring a further action against other parties on the same facts unless the judgment cannot be fully satisfied in the State where rendered, in accordance with the law of that State.[145] There is no corresponding provision in the 1952 Convention.

As will be seen in the discussion of Title III of the Draft Convention on pages 38–39, in the case of States which had agreed to the application of that title as between themselves, an action in a second State for an unpaid balance of a judgment would be unnecessary. However, the provision would serve a purpose as between States that did not agree to the application of Title III as between themselves.

Article 3 of the Draft Convention would permit an action, by way of counterclaim or otherwise, to be brought against any party on any claim arising out of the casualty, before the court seized of the original action. A cargo owner, for example, would be entitled to bring an action against both a plaintiff shipowner and a defendant shipowner in the court in which the litigation between the shipowners was pending.

8. *Penal Jurisdiction*

In the United States, with a few exceptions, such as cases of treason and terrorism, the courts do not have jurisdiction to try persons accused of crimes unless the crimes charged were alleged to have been committed within

141. Id., art. 2(1)(c).
142. Id., art. 2(1)(d).
143. Id., art. 2(1)(e).
144. Id., art. 2(2), first sentence.
145. Id., art. 2(2), second sentence.

American territory or on board American vessels.[146] Thus, in high seas collision cases, a charge of willful misconduct on the part of the master or a member of the crew of an American flag vessel involved would be within the criminal jurisdiction of a federal district court. Such cases are, however, not brought very frequently. More often, there is no criminal proceeding; instead, the person charged with recklessness is subjected to disciplinary proceedings instituted by the U.S. Coast Guard, and if the charges are upheld he or she can be subjected to a civil penalty, or his or her license can be revoked or suspended.[147]

The United States is not a party to the 1952 Brussels Convention on Penal Jurisdiction in Matters of Collision or Other Incidents of Navigation (the Penal Jurisdiction Convention).[148] This convention, which was also drafted by the C.M.I., was adopted as a result of the decision of the International Court of Justice in the famous case of *The Lotus*.[149] It provides that in the event of a collision or any other incident of navigation involving the penal or disciplinary responsibility of the master or any other person in the service of a seagoing vessel, criminal or disciplinary proceedings may be instituted only before the judicial or administrative authorities of the flag State,[150] and no arrest or detention of the vessel may be ordered, even as a measure of investigation, by any court other than one of the flag State.[151] Any State may, however, permit its own authorities to take any action in respect of certificates of competence or licenses issued by that State, or to prosecute its own nationals for offenses committed while on board a vessel of another State.[152]

The Penal Jurisdiction Convention is inapplicable to collisions or other incidents of navigation occurring within the limits of a port or in inland waters, and contracting States may, at the time of signature, ratification, or accession to the convention, reserve to themselves the right to take proceedings in respect of offenses committed within their own territorial waters.[153]

The contracting States undertake to arbitrate disputes between themselves arising out of the interpretation or application of the Penal Jurisdiction Convention, without prejudice to the obligations of contracting States that have agreed to submit disputes to the International Court of Justice.[154]

The provisions of the Penal Jurisdiction Convention have been taken over, in part, by Article 11(1) of the Geneva High Seas Convention of 1958,

146. See *United States v. Flores,* 289 U.S. 137, 1933 AMC 649 (1933).

147. 46 U.S.C. §§ 2103–09; 7701–03.

148. The pertinent provisions of the Penal Jurisdiction Convention, 439 U.N.T.S. 233, are contained in appendix 4.

149. *France v. Turkey (The Lotus),* P.C.I.J., Ser. A, No. 10 (1927), 1928 AMC 1 (Permanent Court of International Justice [the "World Court"] 1927).

150. Penal Jurisdiction Convention, Art. 1.

151. Id., art. 2.

152. Id., art. 3.

153. Id., art. 4.

154. Id., art. 5.

which provides that no penal proceedings may be instituted against the navigating officers of a vessel except before the authorities of the flag State or the State of which the officers are nationals.[155] As of 1997 the High Seas Convention had been ratified or adhered to by fifty-nine States.[156] The U.N. Convention on the Law of the Seas ("UNCLOS") entered into force on Nov. 16, 1994; art. 97(1) is virtually the same as art. 11(1) of the High Seas Convention. As of 1997, 112 States had ratified or adhered to UNCLOS.[157]

Section C. Choice of Law

1. *Substantive and Remedial Questions*

Once a court having jurisdiction of the subject matter of a collision acquires jurisdiction of the defendant, or the vessel, or both, the next question to be considered is what substantive and remedial law should be applied. The determination of this question must necessarily be made in accordance with the conflict of laws principles of the forum State.[158]

2. *Jurisdiction, Practice, and Procedure*

There appears to be universal agreement that remedial questions, including questions relating to subject matter jurisdiction and jurisdiction of the defendant, are governed by the law of the forum State.[159] However, as will be seen, not all States agree on which questions are remedial and which are substantive.[160]

3. *Maritime Liens*

Under U.S. law a maritime lien is a property interest in a vessel and not merely a security device. It follows that in the United States, the question as to whether a negligently caused collision gives rise to a maritime lien which can be enforced by a proceeding *in rem* against the offending vessel should be treated as a question of substantive law, to be decided in accordance with the same principles as those governing other substantive questions.[161]

---

155. 13 U.S.T. 2312, T.I.A.S. No. 5200, 450 U.N.T.S. 82.

156. 6B *Benedict,* Doc. 10-1 at 10-13. See Bowman & Harris for a list of the State parties to the convention.

157. 1982 United Nations Convention on the Law of the Sea, U.N.A./CONF. 62/122, 21 I.L.M. 1261 (1982), U.N. Pub. E.83.V.5 (1983), which entered into force on Nov. 16, 1994.

158. *Restatement (Second) of Conflict of Laws* § 6.

159. *Restatement (Second) of Conflict of Laws* §§ 122–38; 3 Beale, *Conflict of Laws* 1601 (1935); *Bournias v. Atlantic Maritime Co.,* 220 F.2d 152, 154, 1955 AMC 523, 525 (2d Cir. 1955).

160. See subsection 6, infra (damages), and subsection 7, infra (effect of mutual fault).

161. See Griffin, *Collision* 50–51.

In discussing the question as to when a maritime lien, with its accompanying right of an action *in rem*, arises out of a collision occurring in foreign territorial waters, Mr. Griffin, in *The American Law of Collision*, summarized the principles to be applied as follows:

> (a) *Proceedings in rem presuppose a maritime lien.* . . .[162]
> (b) *A maritime lien is a property right in the res.* . . .[163]
> (c) *Whether a maritime lien arises from the collision or other tort depends on the lex loci.* That is the law governing occurrences at the place in question and, in accordance with the principles already discussed, that is the law which of necessity must determine whether the property right known as a maritime lien has been created.
> (I) If, therefore, the *lex loci* allows a lien, a proceeding *in rem* may be maintained. . . .[164]
> (II) If the *lex loci* denies a lien, the courts elsewhere cannot create or enforce one. . . .[165]
> (III) If the case is one in which the general maritime law, as administered in the United States, gives a lien, as in cases of collision . . . and if there is no proof that the *lex loci* denies a lien, it has been held in several cases that the lien given by the general maritime law will be recognized and enforced.[166]

Under modern choice of law principles the basic rules thus summarized may be subject to an exception in a case where the place of the collision is merely fortuitous, and there are no other "contacts" calling for application of the *lex loci*. An example is a case where at the time of the collision the vessels were merely passing through the territorial waters of a country to which neither was bound. In such a case, if the law relating to maritime liens for collision damage is the same in both flag States, the court might apply that law, rather than the *lex loci*, just as it might apply the law common to both flag States relating to the effect of mutual fault.[167] If, however, the law relating to maritime liens for collision damage is not common to both flag States, e.g., where under the law of one State there is a lien, and under the law of the other there is none, or where there is no showing of what the law is in either

---

162. At 50, citing *The Maggie Hammond,* 76 U.S. 435 (1870); *The Bold Buccleugh,* 7 Moore P.C. 267, 13 Eng. Repr. 884 (1851); *The Lamington,* 87 F. 752 (EDNY 1898); *The Rock Island Bridge,* 73 U.S. 213 (1867); *The Cuzco,* 225 F. 169 (WD Wash. 1915).

163. Id., citing *The John G. Stevens,* supra note 101, at 116; *The Lottawanna,* 88 U.S. 558, 579 (1875); *The J. E. Rumbell,* 148 U.S. 1, 11 (1893); *The Lamington,* supra note 162; *The Bold Buccleugh,* supra note 162.

164. At 51, citing *The J. E. Rumbell,* supra note 163; *The Maud Carter,* 29 F. 156 (D Mass. 1886); *The Cuzco,* supra note 162; *The Scotland,* 105 U.S. 24, 29 (1882).

165. Id., citing *The Lamington,* supra note 162; *The Egyptian Monarch,* 36 F. 773 (D N.J. 1888); *The Cuzco,* supra note 162.

166. Id., citing *The Avon,* 2 F. Cas. 255 (No. 680) (Cir. Ct., ND Ohio 1873); *The Kaiser Wilhelm der Grosse,* 175 F. 215 (SDNY 1909); *The West Cherow,* 276 F. 585 (ED Va. 1921).

167. See *In re Seiriki Kisen Kaisha (The Seiryu—The Stena Freighter),* 629 F. Supp. 1374, 1392, 1986 AMC 913, 939 (SDNY 1985), infra, subsection 7.

State, a U.S. court will presumably apply U.S. law as the *lex fori*, and hold that a lien was created. The same principles will apply in the case of a high-seas collision.[168]

In sum, if a particular collision is governed by the substantive law of a country whose law does not create a maritime lien (or a privilege or other charge similar to a maritime lien) for collision damage, any action brought in the United States for damages resulting from the collision may properly be brought *in personam* only, but if the foreign law creates a lien, it will be enforced in an action *in rem* brought in a U.S. district court having jurisdiction of the *res*.

4. *Equipment and Manning*

In *The State of Alabama*[169] the law of the forum (and of the flag of one of the vessels involved in a high-seas collision) required exhibition of a certain type of light, while the law of the flag of the other vessel did not. It was held that the other vessel was not at fault for not carrying the light. It should be noted that this and other decisions involving differences between the *lex fori* and the flag law with respect to equipment of vessels were decided before the formulation of international rules governing equipment of vessels employed on the high seas, which have since been adopted by virtually all maritime coun-

168. See *The Scotland*, supra note 164, quoted in subsection 7, infra.

The "contacts" approach has recently been taken with increasing frequency in the case of contract liens. See, e.g., *Gulf Trading & Transp. Co. v. The Hoegh Shield*, 658 F.2d 363, 1982 AMC 1138 (5th Cir. 1981); *Cardinal Shipping Corp. v. The Seisho Maru*, 744 F.2d 461, 1985 AMC 2630 (5th Cir. 1984); *Gulf Trading & Transp. Co. v. The Tento*, 694 F.2d 1191, 1983 AMC 872 (9th Cir. 1982). See also 1 Schoenbaum 515–17. But in the case of necessaries, the most significant "contact" remains the place where they were furnished to the vessel. See *The Hoegh Shield*, supra; *Ocean Ship Supply Ltd. v. The Leah*, 729 F.2d 971, 1984 AMC 2089 (4th Cir. 1984).

The Canadian and South African law appears to be the same as that of the United States with respect to recognition of liens created under foreign law: the *lex loci delicti* or the *lex loci contractūs* will generally be applied in preference to the *lex fori*. See *The Strandhill v. W. Hodder & Co.*, [1926] S.C.R. 680, 1927 AMC 244 (S. Ct. of Canada 1926); *Todd Shipyard Corp. v. Altema Cia. Maritima (The Ioannis Daskalelis)*, [1974] S.C.R. 1248, 1973 AMC 176 (S. Ct. of Canada 1972); *Marlex Petroleum, Inc. v. The Har Rai*, [1984] 2 F.C. 345, 1984 AMC 1649 (Canadian Federal Ct. of Appeal, Ottawa 1984); *Southern Steamship Agency v. The Khalij Sky*, 1985 AMC 2794 (Supreme Ct. of South Africa, Admiralty Div., Cape of Good Hope 1984).

In the last two cases cited the courts refused to follow the decision of the Privy Council in *Bankers Trust Int'l Ltd. v. Todd Shipyards (The Halcyon Isle)*, 1980 AMC 1221, [1980] 2 Lloyd's Rep. 325 (P.C.), where the majority, over a strong dissent, refused to apply U.S. law, under which a lien arose for repairs effected in the United States, because the *lex fori* (Singapore, whose law in this respect was found to be the same as English law) did not recognize a lien for repairs.

On the reasoning of the majority in *The Halcyon Isle*, it would appear that if under English law no lien would have arisen under the particular circumstances had the collision occurred in English waters, the English courts would not recognize a lien, even though one was created under the *lex loci delicti*.

169. 17 F. 847 (SDNY 1883). See Griffin 46.

tries having seagoing merchant or public vessels.[170] The possibility of such differences occurring today is therefore rather remote.

However, as of this writing, substantial differences in manning requirements still remain.[171] If a colliding vessel was properly manned in accordance with the law of the vessel's flag, it is submitted that she would not be held improperly manned by the American courts, even though she was not manned in accordance with U.S. manning requirements.[172]

The 1978 Convention on Standards of Training, Certification, and Watchkeeping for Seafarers[173] was finally ratified by the United States in 1991. The convention had previously been adopted by some eighty States, representing more than 75 percent of the world's merchant tonnage. This convention establishes precise navigational, watchkeeping, and look-out requirements, violations of which could bear materially upon the outcome of collision litigation involving vessels of States subscribing to it.[174]

5. Navigation

There appears to be complete agreement that the navigation of a vessel is, for obvious reasons, governed by the navigational rules applicable to the waters where a vessel is operating. The only conceivable exception to this principle lies where one of two approaching vessels is navigating in waters governed by one set of rules and the other in waters where different rules are in force. Thus, in *The Arkansan—The Knoxville City*,[175] when two approaching vessels commenced navigating with respect to each other, one was in waters governed by the old Inland Rules and the other in waters governed by the then current International Rules. The court held that since it was apparent that they would both be in "inland" waters when they would presumably pass each other, they should have exchanged the sound signals required by the Inland Rules.

---

170. See, e.g., the International Convention for the Safety of Life at Sea (SOLAS), 1974, 32 U.S.T. 47, T.I.A.S. 9700, 6B Benedict, Doc. 14–8, 14–37 (1990).

171. See, e.g., 46 U.S.C. §§ 8101–9308, governing the manning of U.S. vessels, and Canada Shipping Act, S.C. 1934, ch. 49, as amended, part II, §§ 101–276, governing the manning of Canadian vessels. Reflagging Kuwaiti oil tankers under U.S. flag during the Iran-Iraq War produced a strained interpretation of the U.S. wage and hours statutes in *Cruz v. Chesapeake Shipping Co.*, 932 F.2d 218, 1991 AMC 2017 (3d Cir. 1991), to the effect that Filipino crew members of U.S. flag vessels were not protected by those statutes because the vessels never traded to the United States.

172. See *In re Hellenic Lines, Ltd. (The Hellenic Carrier—The Lash Atlantico)*, 1984 AMC 57, 71 (ED Va. 1982), modified on other grounds, 730 F.2d 139, 1984 AMC 2713 (4th Cir. 1984).

173. 3 Schoenbaum 252.

174. See also the IMCO Recommendation on Operational Guidance for Officers in Charge of a Navigational Watch, which is an annex to the Convention on Standards of Training, Certification and Watchkeeping for Seafarers (STCW), 6C Benedict Doc. 14–6.

175. 112 F.2d 223, 1940 AMC 889 (9th Cir. 1940).

6. Damages

Except with respect to the effect of mutual fault and limitation of liability, both of which are discussed infra, there is very little American authority on the question of choice of law applicable to the computation of damages in collision cases. The reason may be that there is substantial uniformity in the law of the principal maritime countries concerning questions such as what items are recoverable as collision damages.

Section 171 of the *Restatement (Second) of Conflict of Laws* provides that the law selected by application of the rule of § 145 determines the measure of damages. That section provides that rights and liabilities with respect to an issue in tort are determined by the local law of the State which, with respect to that issue, has the most significant relationship to the parties under the principles of § 6, and that the contacts to be taken into account in applying those principles include (a) the place of the injury, (b) the place where the conduct causing the injury occurred, (c) the parties' domicile, residence, nationality, place of incorporation, and place of business, and (d) the place where any relationship between the parties is centered.

Section 6, in turn, provides that, subject to constitutional restrictions, a court will follow a statutory directive of its own State on choice of law, and that in the absence of such a directive, the factors relevant to the choice include (a) the needs of the interstate and international systems, (b) the relevant policies of the forum, (c) the relevant policies of other interested States and their relevant interests in determining the issue, (d) the protection of justified expectations, (e) the basic policies underlying the particular field of law, (f) certainty, predictability, and uniformity of result, and (g) ease in the determination and application of the law to be applied.

Since under modern U.S. concepts issues of damages are treated as substantive, it would seem that, except in cases where foreign law is applicable, damages in a collision action brought in the United States should be governed by the general maritime law prevailing uniformly throughout the United States, and not by the law of the forum, whether the forum is a court of one of the American states, or a federal district court sitting as a "diversity" court, or one sitting as a court of admiralty jurisdiction.

Consideration of principles such as those enunciated in the *Restatement* should therefore be necessary only when the choice required to be made is one between American law and foreign law, e.g., where a collision occurs in a foreign port, but the litigation takes place in the United States. In such a case, it would seem that in the event of a conflict between the U.S. law and the law of the place of the collision on an issue of damages, an American court trying the case should apply the law of the place of collision, in the absence of strong countervailing factors.

It appears that in England the law relating to damages is partly procedural and partly substantive. In *Chaplin v. Boys*[176] Lord Guest stated:

> There would appear to be a distinction between questions affecting heads of damages which are for the *lex loci delicti* and quantification of damages which is for the *lex fori*. This is well illustrated in Dicey and Morris, *Conflict of Laws*, 8th ed. (1967), at p. 944, where the kind of damage is a matter of substantive law and the method of compensating the plaintiff for his loss which is for the *lex fori (ibid.*, at p. 1092). *Cheshire on Private International Law,* 7th ed., at p. 602, is to the same effect.

In 1987 the Comité Maritime International formulated the "Lisbon Rules"[177] in an effort to unify the rules followed in maritime countries relating to collision damages. Like the York-Antwerp Rules 1994, the Lisbon Rules are not intended to be incorporated in an international convention or in domestic legislation in the States constituting the C.M.I. Instead, shipowners, hull insurers, protection and indemnity associations, and cargo insurers may agree, following a collision, that the rules shall apply to any damage issues that may arise. In most respects the Lisbon Rules appear to be in harmony with existing U.S. law.

7. *Effect of Mutual Fault*

One of the principal areas where choice of law problems may arise with respect to collisions is the effect of mutual fault, (a) on the rights and obligations of the colliding vessels vis-à-vis each other, and (b) on the rights of "innocent" cargo against one or both of them. There appears to be a divergence of views as to whether the effect of mutual fault should be treated as remedial, and therefore governed by the *lex fori*, or whether it should be treated as a substantive question to which the rules governing choice of substantive law should be applied.

In the United States and, it appears, in most other countries, the effect of mutual fault is considered a substantive matter.[178] Under English law, on the other hand, it is treated as a remedial matter, and the English courts will therefore apply the *lex fori*, regardless of the place of the collision, the flags of the colliding vessels, or any other factors.[179]

---

176. [1971] A.C. 356, [1969] 2 Lloyd's Rep. 487, 496 (H.L. 1969).

177. The rules are contained in appendix 5, and are also printed in 18 J. Mar. L. & Com. at 577 (1987), where they are followed by a comment prepared by Jean Warot, chairman of the C.M.I. international subcommittee that drafted the rules. The American member of the subcommittee was James F. Moseley, Jr., president of the Maritime Law Association of the United States as of 1997. The British member was Patrick Griggs of London, president of the C.M.I. as of 1997.

178. *The Belgenland,* 114 U.S. 355, 370 (1885); Griffin 565, citing *The Kookaburra—The Ellen Bushey (Louis-Dreyfus Co. v. Seaboard Great Lakes Corp.),* 69 F.2d 71, 1934 AMC 215 (2d Cir. 1934).

179. See Marsden 269.

In the case of high-seas collisions between vessels of the same flag, American courts will apply the flag law to substantive questions, including the effect of mutual fault.[180] Likewise, when the colliding vessels are of different flags, but the substantive law on the points at issue is common to both, that law will be applied. Thus, if the point at issue is the effect of mutual fault, and the colliding vessels are both British, the court will apply the 1910 Collision Convention, to which the United Kingdom is a party. If one vessel is Japanese and the other is a Cayman Islands vessel, it will apply the convention as the law common to both countries, since both have adopted the convention.[181]

But if the vessels are of different flags, and the flag States do not have a common law on the point in issue, an American court will apply the *lex fori*, i.e., American law, since it would be unfair to give preference to the law of one flag State over that of the other.

In *The Scotland*, the U.S. Supreme Court stated the rule as follows:

> [I]f a collision occurs on the high seas, where the law of no particular state has exclusive force, but all are equal, any forum called upon to settle the rights of the parties would *prima facie* determine them according to its own law, as presumptively expressing the rules of justice; but if the contesting vessels belonged to the same foreign nation, the court would assume that they were subject to the law of their nation carried under their common flag, and would determine the controversy accordingly. If they belonged to different nations having different laws, since it would be unjust to apply the law of either to the exclusion of the other, the law of the forum, that is the maritime law as received and practiced therein, would properly furnish the rule of decision.[182]

Where there is no cargo loss or damage it is no longer of importance in most cases whether the law applicable to the effect of mutual fault is U.S. law or the law common to both colliding vessels. This is so because most of the important maritime countries, other than the United States and Liberia, are parties to the 1910 Collision Convention, and the most significant feature of that convention—the proportional fault rule—is now, as a result of *Reliable Transfer*,[183] part of the general maritime law of those two countries, insofar as concerns the effect of mutual fault in collisions not resulting in any cargo loss or damage.

However, *Reliable Transfer* did not affect the "innocent cargo" rule: under American law, in a both-to-blame case cargo on one vessel may still recover from the other vessel, as a joint tort-feasor, the full amount of its loss

180. *The Eagle Point,* 142 F. 453 (3d Cir. 1906).

181. See *In re Seiriki Kisen Kaisha (The Seiryu—The Stena Freighter),* supra note 167, where one vessel was Japanese and the other was a Cayman Islands vessel. Japan and the Cayman Islands both subscribe to the 1910 Collision Convention.

182. 105 U.S. 24, 29 (1882).

183. Supra note 21.

(subject to possible limitation of liability). Furthermore, the other vessel may still recover indemnity from the carrier with respect to a portion of the non-carrier's liability to cargo, in an amount corresponding to the carrier's proportion of blame, even though the carrier may be shielded from direct liability to its cargo by reason of the "errors in navigation" exception of an applicable convention, statute, charter party, or other contract of affreightment.[184] The question of choice of law therefore arises with greater frequency in high-seas collision cases where there is cargo loss or damage than in those where there is vessel damage only. But in either type of case the same choice of law rules apply: if the vessels are of different flags and the flag States do not have a common law governing the effect of mutual fault, the general maritime law as interpreted in the forum State will govern, whereas if the vessels are of the same flag, or are of States having a common law on the effect of contributory fault, the matter will be governed by the flag law, or the law common to both States, as the case may be.

The basic rule traditionally applied by American courts to collisions in inland and territorial waters is that the *lex loci delicti* governs substantive questions, including the effect of mutual fault. The leading case is *The Mandu*,[185] where the U.S. Court of Appeals for the Second Circuit applied the 1910 Collision Convention to a both-to-blame collision between a German vessel and a Brazilian vessel in the harbor of Santos, Brazil. In accordance with the convention, the court allowed cargo interests a recovery against the noncarrying vessel only to the extent of the degree of blame chargeable to that vessel, whereas if U.S. law had been applicable, the noncarrier, as a joint tort-feasor, would have been liable for 100 percent of the cargo damage. The court stated the principles as follows:

> Both Germany and Brazil are parties to the Convention. The United States has not adopted it, and under our maritime law it is still the rule that where both vessels are at fault in a collision, innocent cargo may recover full damages against either. *The Atlas*, 93 U.S. 302, 23 L.Ed. 863 (1876).
>
> Liability for tort caused by collision in the territorial waters of a foreign country is governed by the laws of that country. *Smith v. Condry*, 42 U.S. 28, 11 L.Ed. 35 (1843); Restatement of Conflict of Laws § 409. That law not only determines the existence of the liability but also generally determines the measure of it. *Northern Pacific R. Co. v. Babcock*, 154 U.S. 190, 14 S.Ct. 978, 39 L.Ed. 958 (1894). . . . "The injustice of imposing a greater liability than that created by the law governing the conduct of the parties at the time of the act or omission complained of is obvious." *Western Union Tel. Co. v. Brown*, 234 U.S. 542, 547, 34 S.Ct. 955, 58 L.Ed.

184. *Allied Chemical Corp. v. Hess Tankship Co.*, 661 F.2d 1044, 1982 AMC 1271 (5th Cir. 1981).

185. *The Mandu—The Denderah (Petition of Cia. de Nav. Lloyd Brasiliero)*, 102 F.2d 459, 1939 AMC 287 (2d Cir. 1939).

> 1457 (1914). . . . [T]he liability of the *Mandu* is determined by Brazilian law; the extent of the liability will in no event exceed what is proper under the Brussels Convention, the rules embodied in that Convention being part of the law of Brazil, and the particular article here involved, Art. 4, clearly relating to right rather than remedy. See *The Eagle Point,* 142 F. 453 (3d Cir. 1906), cert. denied, 201 U.S. 644, 26 S.Ct. 760, 50 L.Ed. 902. . . .
>
> It may be noted that the Great American has no fair grievance against the rules of the Brussels Convention. After all, its rights are only those of cargo owners who were content to ship their goods on a German vessel, and Germany as well as Brazil abides by the Convention. Even if the collision had occurred on the high seas, the law common to both vessels, the Convention, would control their liabilities to one another, and to cargo. *The Belgenland,* 114 U.S. 355, 5 S.Ct. 860, 29 L.Ed. 152 (1885). The petitioner therefore had the right to interpose the Brussels Convention when beset by claims of cargo on the *Denderah,* and the court below did not err in overruling the claimant's exceptions.[186]

Although the court mentioned the fact that both vessels were of States subscribing to the convention, it is evident from the opinion that the result would have been the same even if the collision had involved vessels flying the flags of States that were not parties to it, the controlling factor being the occurrence of the collision in the territorial waters of a State that had adopted the convention.

While in *The Mandu* the vessels were within a Brazilian port when they collided, under American conflict of laws principles prevailing in 1939, when the case was decided, the result would presumably have been the same if they had simply been passing through the Brazilian territorial sea, en route between non-Brazilian ports. Under more modern conflicts principles, however, it is doubtful that the *lex loci delicti* would be applied in such a case.

In *Matter of Seiriki Kisen Kaisha (The Seiryu—The Stena Freighter),*[187] Judge Sand of the U.S. District Court for the Southern District of New York expressed doubt as to whether the place of collision should be the sole criterion in choosing the substantive law to be applied. There, a both-to-blame collision occurred about 8 miles off the western tip of Cuba, between a Japanese vessel and a Cayman Islands vessel. Japan and the Cayman Islands are both parties to the 1910 Collision Convention; Cuba is not a party. It appeared that under Cuban law (as under American law) the noncarrying vessel in a both-to-blame case is liable for the full amount of the cargo loss.

---

186. 102 F.2d at 463; 1939 AMC at 293–94. It will be noted that *The Atlas,* cited in the first paragraph of the extract, was decided before enactment of the Harter Act, 46 U.S. Code §§ 190–97, and the Carriage of Goods by Sea Act, 46 U.S. Code §§ 1300–16. Where either of these statutes is applicable, the carrying vessel is shielded from direct liability to its cargo for damage resulting from errors in navigation.

187. Supra note 167.

The two vessel owners contended that although Cuba claimed a 12-mile territorial sea, as of the date of the collision (1981) the American courts refused to recognize claims to territorial seas in excess of 3 miles,[188] that the collision therefore occurred on the high seas, and that since both vessels were of States subscribing to the 1910 Collision Convention, that convention was applicable. The cargo interests, on the other hand, pointed to a proclamation made by President Reagan in 1983 to the effect that the United States would recognize the claims of other countries to territorial seas of up to 12 miles in width, provided they respected American rights.[189] They argued that the proclamation should be applied retroactively, so as to make the place of collision one recognized by the United States as within Cuban territorial waters.

The *Seiryu*'s owners further contended that even if the court should hold that the President's announcement had retroactive effect, Cuban law should not be applied, because under modern concepts of conflict of laws, the mere fact that a collision occurred within the territorial waters of a country should not be enough to warrant application of the substantive law of that country; additional "contacts" should be necessary, such as using a harbor of the country, as the vessels involved in *The Mandu* were doing at the time they collided.

Judge Sand noted that no steps had been taken to implement the proclamation, and said that even if such steps were not necessary to bring it into force, it should not be applied retroactively. He therefore concluded that because under American law at the time of the collision the waters where it occurred were part of the high seas, and because both vessels were of 1910 Collision Convention States, the collision was governed by that convention. However, Judge Sand continued:

> This conclusion renders it unnecessary for us to determine whether, as the *Seiryu* argues, modern choice-of-law principles would compel application of the Brussels Convention even if the collision had occurred within Cuban territorial waters. We need only note that, while we do not decide the case on that basis, we find that the arguments in support of that position have considerable weight. See *Lauritzen v. Larsen*, 345 U.S. 571, 1953 AMC 1210 (1953); *Cruz v. Maritime Company of Philippines*, 549 F. supp. 285, 288, 1983 AMC 1617, 1620 (S.D.N.Y. 1982), aff'd, 702 F.2d 47, 1983 AMC 1615 (2d Cir. 1983).

---

188. *Esso Transport Co. v. Terminales Maracaibo*, 356 F. Supp. 1367, 1973 AMC 840 (SDNY 1973); *MISR Ins. Co. v. The Har Sinai*, 480 F. Supp. 398, 1979 AMC 2367 (SDNY 1979), aff'd, 628 F.2d 1345, 1980 AMC 2399 (2d Cir. 1980).

189. Proclamation No. 5030 and "White House Fact Sheet," 19 Weekly Compilation of Presidential Documents 383–85, 397.

Five years later President Reagan issued a proclamation extending the width of the U.S. territorial sea to 12 miles. See Proclamation No. 5928, 54 Fed. Reg. 777 (Jan. 9, 1989). For a discussion of the effect of the proclamation, see B. Alexander, *The Territorial Sea of the United States: Is It Twelve Miles or Not?* 20 J. Mar. L. & Com. 449 (1989), and note, *U.S. Territorial Sea Extension: Jurisdiction and International Environmental Protection,* 16 Ford. Int'l. L.J. 1208 (1993). As of early 1997, Congress had not yet conformed U.S. statutes to the 1989 proclamation.

> We recognize, of course, that the traditional view is that set forth in *The Mandu:*
>
> "Liability for tort caused by collision in the territorial waters of a foreign country is governed by the laws of that country." 102 F.2d at 463, 1939 AMC at 293.
>
> Whether that remains as absolute a principle as it was when *The Mandu* was decided is far from clear. Insofar as the equitable considerations are concerned, here the grounds for application of American law, other than the stipulation of the parties that this court would have jurisdiction of the matter, are slim. Further, as the court in *The Mandu* noted, the consequence of its determination was to relegate the cargo owners to the law which governed the ship on which they were content to ship their goods. It would appear that no more than that occurs here. There certainly has been no reliance on Cuban law.[190]

The choice of law provisions of the C.M.I. Draft Convention on Civil Jurisdiction, Choice of Law, and Recognition and Enforcement of Judgments in Matters of Collision[191] are similar to American concepts. Article 4 of the Draft Convention lays down two basic choice of law rules: (1) the *lex loci delicti* applies to collisions in internal waters or the territorial sea of a country, and (2) the *lex fori* applies to high-seas collisions. Only three exceptions to these basic rules would be recognized: (1) if the vessels were documented (or, in the case of undocumented vessels, owned) in the same country, the flag law would apply; (2) if they were documented (or, if not documented, owned) in different countries, all of which were parties to a convention, the court seized of the case would be required to apply the convention; and (3) the principles of a convention would apply to the extent that the vessels involved were of countries subscribing to a common principle of a convention, e.g., the proportional fault principle of the 1910 Collision Convention.

The primary purpose of the second exception is to require a court to apply the 1910 Collision Convention if the colliding vessels are documented in countries adhering to the convention. This exception was made because the convention is by its terms mandatorily applicable as between contracting States, regardless of the place of the collision.[192]

The third exception is designed to apply, e.g., to a both-to-blame collision between a Liberian vessel and an American vessel, because both the United States and Liberia have adopted the rule as part of their domestic law.

Article 5 of the Draft Convention provides as follows:

> The law applicable as provided in Article 4 shall be the law governing:

---

190. 629 F. Supp. at 1395, 1986 AMC at 944–45.
191. Supra note 136.
192. See *Collision Report,* supra note 135.

(1) the basis of liability;
(2) the grounds for exemption from liability and any division of liability;
(3) the kinds of damage for which compensation may be due;
(4) the quantum of damages;
(5) the persons who may claim damages in their own right;
(6) the liability of a principal for the acts or omissions of his agent, or of an employer for the acts or omissions of his employee, or of a vessel or her owner or operator for the acts or omissions of a pilot;
(7) the question whether a right to damages may be assigned or inherited;
(8) the burden of proof and presumptions;
(9) the rules concerning prescription.

The application of a law declared applicable under this title may be refused only when such application would be incompatible with public policy.

8. *Limitation of Liability*

In the United States and, it appears, in most other maritime countries, limitation of liability is considered remedial in nature, so that not only is the procedure for invoking a statutory right to limit liability governed by the law of the forum, but so too is the constitution of the limitation fund.[193]

However, in some countries the constitution of the fund is a matter of substantive law, and therefore governed by the *lex loci delicti,* or whatever other law may govern substantive questions arising out of the particular collision. This problem is treated in chapter 14, section A(1).

9. *Recognition and Enforcement of Judgments*

The recognition or enforcement of a judgment is necessarily governed by the law of the place where recognition or enforcement is sought.

The courts of each state of the United States are required, under the U.S. Constitution, to give "full faith and credit" to the judgment of a court of another state having jurisdiction of the subject matter of the action, and of the parties.[194] Therefore, in the rare instance of a collision action in a state court, a judgment in favor of the plaintiff would be recognized by, and could be enforced in the courts of any state of the United States where the defendant could be served with process or subjected to the court's jurisdiction in some

---

193. *Ocean Steam Nav. Co. v. Mellor (The Titanic),* 233 U.S. 718 (1914); *In re Cia. Gijonesa De Nav., S. A. (The Cimadevilla),* 590 F. Supp. 241, 1985 AMC 1469 (SDNY 1984). Cf. *Black Diamond S.S. Corp. v. Robert Stewart & Sons,* 336 U.S. 386, 1949 AMC 393 (1949).
194. U.S. Const., art. IV.

other way, such as by attachment of his property. It would of course be unnecessary to prove the facts upon which the judgment was based.[195] The only defenses possible in such an action would be that under the law of the state where it was rendered the court rendering it lacked jurisdiction to hear and determine collision cases, or that it did not have jurisdiction of the defendant, or that the judgment was procured by a fraud upon the court.[196]

When, as more often happens, the plaintiff in a collision case invokes the admiralty jurisdiction of a federal district court, enforcement of a judgment in another district does not necessitate an action upon it in the other district. Once the judgment becomes final by appeal or by expiration of time to appeal, it may be registered in any other district. The judgment then has the same effect as one obtained in that district.[197] This of course may be of importance in the case of a judgment *in personam.* Since a judgment *in rem* can be obtained only when there is a *res* before the court, i.e., a vessel or other maritime property, or when security has been provided to take the place of the *res,* and since a judgment *in rem* cannot be enforced for more than the value of the *res,* or the amount of security given in its place, the judgment can usually be satisfied to the maximum extent possible in the district wherein it is awarded, so that there will be no need to register it in any other district. An exception would lie in a case where the security took the form of an undertaking given by a person who failed to honor it, and had assets in another district.

In the case of a civil action for collision damages in a state court, the judgment can be *in personam* only, since only in a federal district court action wherein the court's admiralty jurisdiction is invoked can an action *in rem* be maintained.[198]

A foreign judgment *in personam* for collision damage, like any foreign judgment, will be recognized and enforced by an American court on principles of international comity, provided that the court rendering it had jurisdiction of the subject matter of the collision and jurisdiction of the defendant, that the judgment was not obtained by a fraud on the court, and that it was not contrary to American concepts of natural justice.[199] This last requirement does not mean that recognition will not be given to a foreign judgment simply because it is based upon laws or legal principles different from those of the United States; it means simply that recognition will be denied if it is based upon principles which shock the American court's notions of fair play, so that enforcement would be contrary to U.S. public policy.[200]

---

195. *Huntington v. Attrill,* 146 U.S. 657 (1892).

196. See *Feinberg v. Feinberg,* 40 N.Y.2d 124, 351 N.E.2d 725 (1976), aff'd, 70 A.D.2d 612, 415 N.Y.S.2d 1018 (1979).

197. 28 U.S.C. § 1963.

198. *The Moses Taylor,* supra note 100; *The Hine v. Trevor,* supra note 100.

199. See *Gull v. Constam,* 105 F. Supp. 107 (D Colo. 1952).

200. *Tahan v. Hodgson,* 662 F.2d 862, n.17 (D.C. Cir. 1981). See also *Restatement (Second), Conflict of Laws,* § 117, comment c.

The enforcement of a foreign judgment in the United States requires the plaintiff to bring an action upon it in an American court, just as enforcement of a state court judgment in a U.S. state other than the one in which it is rendered requires an action to be brought upon the judgment in that state.[201]

A foreign judgment against a vessel *in rem* can be enforced only by the court which rendered it, just as a judgment *in rem* rendered by a U.S. district court can be enforced only by that court, because a judgment can be obtained only against the *res* before the court or the security posted as a substitute for the *res*. Again, an exception might lie in the case of a judgment against a person who defaulted on an undertaking to pay a judgment *in rem*.

American courts, however, are occasionally confronted with questions concerning *recognition* of foreign judgments *in rem*, as when a vessel has been sold by an officer of a foreign court to enforce a judgment *in rem* rendered by the court. In such a case the rules are similar to those relating to recognition of foreign judgments *in personam:* recognition will be given to a foreign judgment which is truly *in rem* if it was rendered by a court having jurisdiction of the subject matter of the action and of the *res*, i.e., the vessel or other maritime property proceeded against, if it was not obtained by a fraud on the court, and if its rendition was not contrary to the American court's concepts of natural justice.[202]

A leading case on recognition of foreign judgments *in rem* is *The Trenton*.[203] While it did not involve a collision, the principles outlined in that case more than a century ago are completely valid today in any maritime case involving foreign judgments *in rem*. The libelants (plaintiffs) furnished supplies to the American Schooner *Trenton* at Cleveland, Ohio. Claiming a lien, they caused the vessel to be seized at Toronto, Ontario, under a warrant issued by the maritime court. One party intervened in the action, claiming wages as a watchman and ship-keeper, and another intervened with a claim for wages as mate. The libelants' claims were dismissed on the ground that the maritime court at Toronto had no jurisdiction to enforce a claim for necessaries furnished to an American vessel at a U.S. port. A decree (judgment) was rendered in favor of the intervenors, and the vessel was sold to satisfy the decree. The purchaser then had her registered in Toronto, presumably under Canadian flag.

The libelants subsequently brought an action *in rem* against the *Trenton* in the U.S. District Court for the Eastern District of Michigan for the supplies

---

201. See, e.g., New York CPLR § 5301-09, which is based on the Uniform Foreign Money Judgments Recognition Act.

202. *The Trenton*, 4 F. 657, 658 (ED Mich. 1880).

On the subject of judicial sales in actions *in rem* see W. Spicer, *Court-Ordered Sale of Vessels*, 11 J. Mar. L. & Com. 239 (1980). See also D. Owen, *Some Legal Troubles with Treasure: Jurisdiction and Salvage*, 16 J. Mar. L. & Com. 139, 164–65 (1985).

203. Supra note 202, 4 F. at 657.

for which they had sued unsuccessfully in Toronto. The purchaser at the judicial sale in the Canadian litigation filed a claim to the vessel, and pleaded that the sale gave him title, free and clear of all liens. Judge Henry B. Brown, one of the ablest nineteenth-century American admiralty judges, agreed. In dismissing the action he stated:

> In considering the effect of this sale, I assume that the Dominion parliament had the requisite authority to establish this court, and that it possesses the powers and jurisdiction which the act purports to vest in it....
>
> That the sale of a vessel, made pursuant to the decree of a foreign court of admiralty, will be held valid in every other country, and will vest a clear and indefeasible title in the purchaser, is entirely settled, both in England and America. . . .
>
> ... To say that the judicial sale of a vessel frees her only from such liens as the court making the sale had jurisdiction to enforce by original process, is a practical denial of the principle that such a sale vests a clear title in the purchaser. This would make the validity of the sale depend, not upon the power of the court to condemn and sell, but upon its authority to assume jurisdiction of all claims which, by the law of another country, might be liens upon her. There are probably no two countries in which the jurisdiction of the admiralty courts is identically the same. . . .
>
> Now, if the theory of the libelant [plaintiff] be correct, a judicial sale of a vessel in one country would free her from none of the liens which the courts of that country were unable to enforce. A sale under such circumstances would be utterly destructive of the interests of owners and a complete sacrifice of the vessel. No one could possibly know the value of his purchase, for no one could foresee the amount of claims that might be made against the vessel in other countries. It would also compel us to inquire in each case whether such foreign court could have taken cognizance of the claim, either by original proceeding or by petition against the proceeds of sale, and, as the foreign law in each case must be proved as a question of fact, the errors and confusion into which we should fall will be readily appreciated.[204]

As we have seen, the 1952 Civil Jurisdiction Convention[205] does not treat the subject of recognition and enforcement of judgments in collision cases. In fact, as of 1997 there was no convention on recognition and enforcement of judgments relating specifically to collisions, although in 1971 the countries that are members of The Hague Conference on Private International Law concluded a Convention on the Recognition and Enforcement of For-

204. Id. at 659–63.

In the federal courts of the United States, it is no longer necessary to plead and prove foreign law as fact; the courts may now take judicial notice of foreign law. See rule 44.1, Fed. R. Civ. P.

205. Supra note 117.

eign Judgments in Civil and Commercial Matters.[206] There are also in force a number of treaties and conventions relating to the recognition and enforcement of the judgments of particular countries, such as the European Economic Community Convention of 1968.[207]

As stated previously, the C.M.I. Draft Convention on Jurisdiction, Choice of Law, and Recognition and Enforcement of Judgments in Collision Cases[208] has not been adopted as of this writing. Nevertheless, its provisions relating to judgments, like those relating to jurisdiction and choice of law, are outlined here because its recognition and enforcement provisions reflect the general principles followed in most of the maritime countries. It will be seen that these principles are quite similar to those followed by the U.S. courts.

Title III of the Draft Convention—the title relating to judgments—would in effect be optional; its application would be limited to instances where the countries concerned had entered into a supplemental agreement making the title applicable as between themselves. Thus, if a judgment rendered in State A was not satisfied in that State, State B would be obligated to recognize and enforce it, provided such a supplemental agreement had been made.[209]

Title III would apply only to judgments that were "final" in the sense that the successful parties would be entitled to execution on them under the law of the country where rendered; the fact that some form of review might still be possible would not preclude its application.[210]

Under Article 8(1) the party seeking recognition or enforcement would be required to furnish authenticated copies of the judgment and the documents establishing its "finality" within the meaning of Article 7, with translations if required by the court of the country wherein recognition or enforcement was being sought.

Under Article 8(2), which is to some extent similar to Article 5 of The Hague Convention on Recognition and Enforcement of Foreign Judgments,[211] if a supplementary agreement was in force between the countries involved, recognition or enforcement could be refused only (a) if the court rendering the judgment did not have jurisdiction under the Draft Convention; or (b) if the judgment was obtained by fraud; or (c) if recognition or enforcement would be incompatible with the public policy of the country wherein recognition or enforcement was sought; or (d) if the judgment debtor had not been given reasonable notice of the proceedings and a fair

206. 1144 U.N.T.S. No. 249, The Hague, Feb. 1, 1971, 6A Benedict, Doc. 8-10, at 8-124.2.

207. European Economic Community Convention on Jurisdiction and the Enforcement of Civil and Commercial Judgments (Sept. 27, 1968), 1262 U.N.T.S. 153, tit. II, art. 6, reprinted in Bulletin of European Community, Supp. II, 1969. See Berlingieri, *Jurisdiction and Choice of Law,* supra note 111, at 869.

208. Supra note 136.

209. Id., art. 7(2), (3), and (4).

210. Id., art. 7(1).

211. Supra note 206.

opportunity to present its case. Enforcement could of course be refused to the extent that the judgment had been satisfied.

Section D. The Basis of Liability for Collision Damages

1. *Fault as the Basis of Liability*

It is universally accepted that liability for collision damages is based upon fault.[212] Indeed, there would seem to be no fair alternative to this concept. Thus, if strict liability were the rule, a small fishing vessel whose navigation was completely blameless could be held fully responsible for the loss of a valuable tanker whose gross fault brought about a collision resulting in an explosion and the total loss of the tanker. Similarly, if the law required an equal division of damages between two colliding vessels, regardless of fault, the owner of the innocent fishing vessel would, in the end, be responsible for half of the tanker owner's damages, less half of its own damages.[213]

Finally, if a no-fault concept were the rule, and the collision resulted in the total loss of the innocent fishing vessel, the latter's owner would be left without recourse for a loss for which neither it nor its employees were in any way responsible.[214]

2. *The Former "Major-Minor Fault" Rule*

The rule of equal division of damages prevailing in the United States before the *Reliable Transfer*[215] decision of 1975 frequently had very harsh results, as where the faults of one colliding vessel vastly outweighed those of the other. In an attempt to ameliorate the effects of the rule in such cases the courts devised the so-called major-minor fault rule. Under this rule, when the faults of one vessel were serious and alone sufficient to account for the collision, the court was not required to hold the other vessel liable to pay half the total damages under the divided damages rule unless her fault was clear and convincing. Instead, the court could assess full blame against the vessel guilty of the serious fault. However, one of the effects of the *Reliable Transfer* decision was the abolition of the "major-minor fault" rule as unnecessary, since in a case where there is a wide disparity between the faults of one vessel and those

---

212. See, e.g., the 1910 Collision Convention, art. 2; *The Clara,* 102 U.S. 200 (1880). See also R. Brown, *General Principles of Liability,* 51 Tul. L. Rev. 820 (1977) (hereinafter "Brown"), an article based upon a paper delivered at the Tulane Admiralty Law Institute's Symposium on the American Law of Collision, held at New Orleans in March 1977.

213. See N. Healy, *The Apportionment of Risk Between Shipowner and Third Parties—Shipowner and Shipowner Collisions,* in Report of C.M.I. Seminar on Apportionment of Risk in Maritime Law, held at Aix-en-Provence in September 1976.

214. Id.

215. Supra note 21.

of the other the court may now take the disparity into account by apportioning blame on other than an equal basis.[216] Thus, since *Reliable Transfer* the courts have had no hesitancy in apportioning fault on bases such as 85 percent–15 percent,[217] or even 90 percent–10 percent.[218]

3. *Error* In Extremis

On occasion one vessel is guilty of serious fault, such as the violation of a basic navigational rule, and her conduct compels an approaching vessel to make a quick decision in an effort to avoid collision. If the effort does not succeed, it may appear, on calm reflection following the collision, that the avoiding action taken by the second vessel was not the preferable maneuver. Under the error *in extremis* doctrine the selection of such avoiding action will not be held actionable fault, but will be excused as action taken under the emergency conditions created by the first vessel's fault.[219]

Unlike the "major-minor fault" rule, the error *in extremis* doctrine was not developed for the purpose of mitigating the harsh effects of the old divided damages rule, but is simply intended to require the court to judge by a more liberal standard of care the conduct of a vessel whose navigators are compelled to make a quick decision when suddenly faced with a dangerous situation created by the fault of an approaching vessel.[220] Thus, the doctrine concerns the question of whether any percentage of blame at all is properly chargeable to the second vessel, and not the proportion of fault attributable to each colliding vessel in a case where both of them are guilty of actionable fault; the *in extremis* doctrine has therefore not been affected by *Reliable Transfer.*[221]

4. *Last Clear Chance*

The applicability of the last clear chance doctrine to collision cases has been questioned, and in any event the doctrine has seldom been invoked in such

216. See *Neptune Maritime Co. v. The Essi Camilla,* 1984 AMC 2983, noted at 714 F.2d 132 (4th Cir. 1983).

217. *Rich Ocean Carriers, S.A. v. The Sanko Diamond,* 1989 AMC 220 (MD Fla. 1988).

218. See, e.g., *Amoco Transport Co. v. The Mason Lykes,* 550 F. Supp. 1264, 1983 AMC 1087 (SD Tex. 1982), rev'd on other grounds, 768 F.2d 659, 1986 AMC 563. For a statistical analysis of apportionments in English and Scandinavian cases decided before 1976, see G. Paulsen, *Apportionment of Fault in Both to Blame Collision Cases,* Mar. L. Ass'n Doc. No. 602 (Oct. 30, 1976). The apportionments made by the American courts since *Reliable Transfer* are tabulated in the AMC Five-year Digests, under "Collision," ¶ 2434.

219. *The Genessee Chief v. Fitzhugh,* supra note 73; *The Bywell Castle,* 4 P.D. 219 (C.A. 1879); *V/O Exportkhleb and Ins. Co. of U.S.S.R. v. The William A. Reiss,* 1983 AMC 728 (ND Ohio 1982).

220. See Brown, supra note 212, at 837.

221. Id.

cases.[222] It was apparently first applied in a collision case by Judge Learned Hand to ameliorate the effects of the former divided damages rule.[223] Even before *Reliable Transfer* the doctrine had fallen into desuetude, but since that decision there has been no reason at all for its continued existence. In the words of Circuit Judge Altimari in *Prudential Lines, Inc. v. McAllister Brothers, Inc.,*[224] "The disease of divided damages having been destroyed, the balm of last clear chance has become superfluous. The last clear chance doctrine will not be permitted to continue out of sheer inertia."[225]

5. *Inevitable Accident*

On relatively rare occasions it is found that a collision was caused by pure accident, and that no navigational error, and no failure to use due diligence with respect to seaworthiness of either vessel caused or contributed to the collision. Thus, a sudden squall might cause two small vessels meeting in restricted waters to collide. Another example would be the sudden failure of a vessel's steering gear, caused by an inherent defect in the casting of a metal part, which could not have been discovered by the vessel's owners by means of any test or inspection that might reasonably have been required. In cases of this kind, the collision is said to have been caused by "inevitable accident."[226]

There was a time when in a case of inevitable accident the damages sustained by the two vessels were divided equally between their respective owners, but this rule was abrogated many years ago and it is now clear that in a case of "inevitable accident" the owner or operator of neither vessel is liable to the other; each bears its own damages.[227]

6. *Inscrutable Fault*

On still rarer occasions, a collision has been held caused by "inscrutable fault." The circumstances may have been such that the court concludes that the collision would never have occurred unless someone erred, but it is impossible to determine where the error lay. Thus, if two vessels were to collide on a clear night in fair weather, and the collision were to result in the deaths of all those on watch on each vessel, the court might conclude from the weather conditions that the loss was caused by the fault of one or both of the vessels, but that it could not determine where the fault lay; it was inscrutable.

---

222. Id. at 836–37.

223. *Chemical Transporter, Inc. v. M. Turecamo, Inc.,* 290 F.2d 496, 1961 AMC 1520 (2d Cir. 1961).

224. 801 F.2d 616, 1987 AMC 231 (2d Cir. 1986).

225. Id. at 621.

226. *The Jumna,* 149 F.171 (2d Cir. 1906). See the discussion of inevitable accident in Griffin, at 537–50.

227. See *The Jumna,* supra note 226.

In such a case, as in the case of inevitable accident, the owner of neither vessel is entitled to recover from the other; the losses lie where they fall.[228] Thus, the result of a finding of "inscrutable fault" is the same as that of a finding of "inevitable accident."[229]

---

228. *The Grace Girdler,* 74 U.S. 196 (1869); *Lucas v. The Thomas Swann,* 15 F.Cas. 1065 (No. 8588) (D Ohio 1854).

229. The cases are thoroughly reviewed in S. Chameides, *Inscrutable Fault in Collision Litigation,* 9 J. Mar. L. & Com. 363 (1978).

CHAPTER TWO

ESTABLISHING A CAUSE OF ACTION

Section A. Burden of Proof, Presumptions, and Permissible Inferences

1. Collisions between Moving Vessels

In collision actions, as in other tort cases, the burden of proof rests upon the party asserting a cause of action against another to establish its existence, and this burden never shifts.[1] In the usual collision case, the owner or operator of each vessel alleges fault on the part of the other; where both vessels have suffered damage, and the owner of one institutes an action against the other, it is rare that the other's owner does not file a counterclaim against the first vessel, or her owner, or both. In such a case, each owner has the burden of proving a cause of action against the other.

In the case of a collision between two moving vessels, neither of which is shown to have committed a statutory fault, the burden of proof is normally met by evidence alone. However, as will be seen, in some collision cases presumptions and permissible inferences may be important factors in meeting the burden, e.g., when one vessel is stationary, or when one or both of the vessels are shown to have committed statutory faults.

2. Collisions of Moving Vessels with Anchored, Moored, and Grounded Vessels, and with Fixed Structures

When a moving vessel collides with one that is properly moored and anchored, or aground, and complying with the applicable rules, e.g., those relating to the display of lights or shapes and the sounding of signals, there is a presumption of fault on the part of the moving vessel.[2] Similarly, there is a

1. See the dissenting opinion of Holmes, C.J., in *The Victor,* 53 F.2d 200, 1946 AMC 431 (5th Cir. 1946).

2. *The Oregon,* 158 U.S. 186 (1895). See also *The Louisiana,* 70 U.S. 164 (1870), for a presumption of fault on the part of a vessel *drifting* from her moorings and striking another vessel aground out of the navigation channel. A recent case applying the *Louisiana* Rule is *Hood v. Knappton Corp.,* 986 F.2d 329, 1993 AMC 928 (9th Cir. 1992).

presumption of fault on the part of a moving vessel which collides with a fixed structure, such as a pier, a wharf, a bridge, or a buoy.[3]

Some courts have held that the owners of the stationary vessel or fixed object must first prove compliance with any pertinent statutes or regulations before obtaining the benefit of the presumption,[4] while others have held that it is for the owners of the moving vessel to establish noncompliance as a defense.[5] It is submitted that the cases requiring the plaintiff to first establish compliance were correctly decided. It would not seem right, for example, to apply the presumption in favor of a vessel anchored in a fairway at night without displaying anchor lights. In most cases, the question is not of major practical importance: the plaintiff will usually plead facts indicating compliance with the law, and will offer evidence in support of his allegations without waiting for the moving vessel's owner to attempt to prove violations on the part of the plaintiff.

3. The Pennsylvania *Rule*

The most frequently invoked presumption in collision cases is the *Pennsylvania* Rule—a rule named after the 1874 U.S. Supreme Court decision involving a vessel of that name.[6] The case arose out of a collision in dense fog between the British Bark *Mary Troop* and the British Steamer *Pennsylvania,* off Sandy Hook, New Jersey. The bark sank, her master and five crew members were drowned, and her cargo was totally lost. In litigation instituted by the cargo owners in England, the Privy Council held that the collision resulted solely from the excessive speed at which the steamer was proceeding in the fog. While noting that the bark had been sounding a bell instead of the foghorn then required by the rules for sailing vessels underway, and recognizing that the bark was at fault for so doing, the Privy Council found that the fault was not a contributing cause of the collision.[7]

Subsequent litigation in the United States between the two vessel owners, however, culminated in a Supreme Court decision holding both vessels to blame. In holding that the bark's statutory violation, as well as the steamer's excessive speed, contributed to the collision, the Court enunciated the now famous *Pennsylvania* Rule:

3. See, e.g., *City of Boston v. The Texaco Texas,* 773 F.2d 1396, 1986 AMC 676 (1st Cir. 1985), holding that Fed. R. Evid. Rule 307 does not affect the presumption.

4. See *Rogers v. Saeger,* 247 F.2d 758, 1958 AMC 71 (10th Cir. 1957); *Willis v. The Tugs Tramp and Mars,* 216 F. Supp. 901, 1965 AMC 411 (ED Va. 1962).

5. See, e.g., *Georgia Ports Authority v. Atlantic Towing Co.,* 1985 AMC 332 (SD Ga. 1983).

6. 86 U.S. 125 (1874).

7. *The Pennsylvania,* 28 L.T.R.N.S. 55 (1870).

> The liability for damages is upon the ship or ships whose fault caused the injury. But when, as in this case, a ship at the time of a collision is in actual violation of a statutory rule intended to prevent collisions, it is no more than a reasonable presumption that the fault, if not the sole cause, was at least a contributory cause of the disaster. In such a case the burden rests upon the ship of showing not merely that her fault might not have been one of the causes, or that it probably was not, but that it could not have been.[8]

It should be noted at the outset that the *Pennsylvania* Rule does not create a presumption of fault, but one of causation. The rule, as stated by the U.S. Supreme Court, presupposes that fault has first been proved: It applies when the vessel "is in actual violation of a statutory rule intended to prevent collision." The violation, which the Court refers to as "the fault," then imposes upon the violator the burden of proving that the fault *could not have been* one of the causes of the collision.

What persuaded the Court to impose this extraordinarily heavy burden remains unclear. Apparently counsel for the steamship did not argue that the Court should do so.[9] No precedent was cited in support of the unique provision of the rule imposing liability for a statutory violation in the absence of proof that *it could not have been* causative. The Privy Council's decision in *The Fenham,*[10] which the Court cited, simply held that "if it is proved that a vessel has not shown lights, the burden lies on her to show that her noncompliance with the regulations was not the cause of the collision."

If the *Pennsylvania* Rule were to be abrogated by the Supreme Court, or by an act of Congress, the American law would certainly be in complete accord with the rule stated by the Privy Council: the violation of a navigational rule would impose upon the violator the burden of proving that the violation was not causative. However, that burden could then be met in the ordinary way, i.e., by proving the absence of causation by a preponderance of the evidence. It would no longer be necessary to prove that the violation *could not have been* a cause of the collision.

The British statute[11] cited by the Supreme Court dealt with a very different presumption than the one created by the Court in *The Pennsylvania.* The statute concerned a presumption of fault, not one of causation. It applied only when a departure from a navigational rule was first shown to have been a cause of a collision. The burden was then upon the vessel departing from the

---

8. 86 U.S. at 136.

9. See the summary of the argument of attorneys for the owners of the *Pennsylvania,* 22 L.Ed. 148, at 149–50.

10. [1870] L.R. 3 P.C. 212, 23 Law Times 329. The only other decision mentioned in the opinion, *The Emperor,* Holt's Rules of the Road 38, was cited simply for the point that the regulations required a close adherence to what they prescribed.

11. The Merchant Shipping Amendment Act, 25 and 26 Vic. ch. 63 § 29 (1862).

rule to prove that the departure was made necessary by the circumstances of the case. In the absence of such proof, the departure from the rule would be presumed to have been a fault.

Whatever special meaning *fault* may have under the 1910 Collision,[12] or under the Supreme Court's 1975 decision in *Reliable Transfer*,[13] there is nothing in *The Pennsylvania* opinion to suggest that the Court meant anything by *fault* but a negligent or willful violation of a navigational rule.

In many cases the presumption against a vessel violating a statute designed to prevent collisions is impossible to overcome, but there are instances where the offender is able to prove absence of causation. Thus, if two vessels are on crossing courses, those on the port-hand vessel will be unable to see the starboard-hand vessel's green sidelight, because the screening of that light will prevent it from showing across the vessel's bow so as to be visible from a vessel on her port side. Therefore, if the green light has burned out and has not been replaced, the starboard-hand vessel will be able to prove that the absence of the green light—a statutory violation—could not have contributed to a collision caused by the port-hand vessel's failure to keep out of the way, as required by the starboard-hand rule.[14]

The *Pennsylvania* Rule is applicable to violations of regulations issued pursuant to statutory authority,[15] as well as to statutory violations. It has been applied not only to collisions but to other casualties, such as strandings resulting in cargo damage.[16]

Application of the rule to structures other than vessels was at one time a debatable question, but it is now plain that the rule applies to violations of statutes and regulations relating to the construction or operation of bridges and other fixed structures with which vessels may collide.[17]

Commencing in 1929 with the Second Circuit's two-to-one decision in *The Mabel*,[18] the courts have tended to interpret the *Pennsylvania* Rule realistically.

---

12. International Convention for the Unification of Certain Rules of Law with Respect to Collisions between Vessels, Brussels, Sept. 23, 1910 ("the 1910 Collision Convention"). The French text, the only official one, is reprinted in 212 Consol. Treaty Series, at 178. The English text appearing in Griffin, at 852–56 and in appendix 4, infra, is a translation included in the 1911 Report of the American Delegation to the Secretary of State on the 1910 Diplomatic Conference at which the Convention was adopted. The official British Translation, Parliamentary Paper, Miscellaneous, No. 5 (1911), is reprinted in R. Marsden, *Collisions at Sea* 891–94 (11th ed., K. McGuffie, editor, 1961) (hereinafter Marsden). The American translation differs slightly in wording from the British. Id., at 891, note 2.

13. 421 U.S. 397, 1975 AMC 541 (1975).

14. Rule 15, COLREGS and Inland Rules.

15. See *Afran Transport Co. v. United States*, 435 F.2d 213, 1971 AMC 335 (2d Cir. 1972).

16. See, e.g., *The Denali*, 112 F.2d 952, 1940 AMC 877 (9th Cir. 1940).

The Second Circuit, however, has limited application of the *Pennsylvania* Rule in other than collision cases. See, e.g., *In Re Marine Sulphur Queen*, 460 F.2d 89, 1972 AMC 1122 (2d Cir. 1972).

17. *Dorrington v. City of Detroit*, 223 F.232 (6th Cir. 1915).

18. 35 F.2d 731, 1929 AMC 1688 (2d Cir. 1929).

In *The Mabel* a tug ran through an anchorage and collided with an anchored barge whose lights the tug contended she did not see because instead of the 15 feet required by the applicable statute, there was a difference of only 3 feet between the heights of the forward and after anchor lights. The tug further alleged that the statutory violation prevented the barge from being seen against lights on the shore. In exonerating the barge, the court said, "All things are indeed possible, but even in applying the [*Pennsylvania* Rule] we are limited to the reasonable probabilities."[19]

In *The Aakre,*[20] the same court went even further, stating: "Indeed, however the *Pennsylvania* rule was originally stated, the history of its application shows that it has done no more than shift the burden of proof with regard to causality."[21] Citing *The Mabel,* the First Circuit stated, in *Seaboard Tug and Barge, Inc. v. Rederi AB/DISA:*[22]

> We cannot believe that the Supreme Court in *The Pennsylvania* intended to establish as a hard and fast rule that every vessel guilty of a statutory fault has the burden of establishing that its fault could not by any stretch of the imagination have had any causal relation to the collision no matter how speculative, improbable or remote. Indeed, our interpretation seems to be supported by the decision in *The Umbria,* 166 U.S. 404 (1897), and we do not see anything in *Lie v. San Francisco & Portland S.S. Co.,* 243 U.S. 291 (1917), that militates against it. Notwithstanding the dictum in *The Martello,* 153 U.S. 64, 75 (1894), that the offending ship has the burden of showing that its statutory fault "could not by any possibility have contributed" to the collision, we nevertheless feel that in applying the rule of *The Pennsylvania* "we are limited to the reasonable probabilities."

The Fifth Circuit gave the rule a similar interpretation in *China Union Lines, Ltd. v. A.O. Anderson & Co.:*

> Appellants would have us give birth to a rule, that every vessel guilty of a statutory fault has the burden of establishing that its fault could not, by any stretch of the imagination, have had a causal relation to the collision, no matter how speculative, improbable or remote. *The Pennsylvania* does not go that far and this Court so stated in *Compania De Maderas v. The Queenston Heights,* 220 F.2d 120, 1966 AMC 1653 (5th Cir. 1955), *cert. denied,* 350 U.S. 824 (1955).[23]

---

19. 35 F.2d at 732; 1929 AMC at 1690.
20. 122 F.2d 469, 1941 AMC 1263 (2d Cir. 1941).
21. 122 F.2d at 474, 1941 AMC at 1270. See also *Lind v. United States (The Abner Doubleday—The Mary),* 156 F.2d 231, 1946 AMC 971 (2d Cir. 1946).
22. 213 F.2d 772, 775, 1954 AMC 1498, 1502 (1st Cir. 1954).
23. 364 F.2d at 782, 1966 AMC at 1669.

Griffin advocates restricting application of the *Pennsylvania* Rule to navigational faults.[24] That eminent authority expresses doubt as to whether the rule was correctly interpreted in cases such as *The Denali,*[25] where a divided court held it applicable to a violation of the "watch and watch" statute,[26] requiring three licensed mates. However, as brought out in R. Zapf, *The Growth of the Pennsylvania Rule: A Study of Causation in Maritime Law,*[27] the rule has been applied in cases concerning violations of statutes and regulations such as the Load Line Act,[28] the Wreck Statute,[29] and a Coast Guard regulation requiring the owners of oil barges to notify the Coast Guard of leaks in cargo tanks.[30]

When *Reliable Transfer* sounded the death knell of the old divided damages rule and replaced it with proportional fault, there was speculation that the *Pennsylvania* Rule would also be held defunct, along with the major-minor fault rule. While there are such suggestions in several early cases, it is now clear that the *Pennsylvania* Rule, although occasionally subjected to criticism, is still very much alive.[31]

One of the principal reasons given for the refusal of the United States to ratify the 1910 Collision Convention was the inclusion of the provision in Article 6 abolishing "legal presumptions," which the U.S. authorities interpreted as meaning presumptions such as the presumption of causation under the *Pennsylvania* Rule.[32] This interpretation has been questioned. Thus, Benedict translates the term *présomptions légales,* used in the official French text, as "statutory presumptions."[33] If this were the correct translation, the Convention would not affect the *Pennsylvania* Rule, which is the creature of the judicial, rather than the legislative branch. Benedict's view, however, was rejected by the Ninth Circuit Court of Appeals in *Ishizaki Kisen Co. v. United States,*[34] which appears to be the only reported decision directly passing on the point. Judge Sneed's analysis of the *Pennsylvania* Rule is so clear that the authors are quoting it extensively below.

---

24. See J. Griffin, *The American Law of Collision* 579 (hereinafter Griffin).

25. Supra note 11.

26. Now 46 U.S.C. § 8104(d).

27. 7 J. Mar. L. & Com. 521 (1976).

28. Now 46 U.S.C. §§ 5101–16. See *The Long,* 439 F.2d 109, 1971 AMC 1147 (2d Cir. 1971). But see *India Supply Mission v. The Maru,* 459 F.2d 1370, 1972 AMC 1238 (2d Cir. 1972).

29. 33 U.S.C. §§ 409, 411, 412, 414, and 415. See *Peoples Coal Co. v. Second Pool Coal Co.,* 181 F. 609 (WD Pa. 1910), aff'd, 188 F.2d 892 (3d Cir. 1911).

30. 46 CFR § 35.15-1. See *Commercial Transport Co. v. Martin Oil Service,* 374 F.2d 813, 1967 AMC 2185 (7th Cir. 1967).

31. The cases so holding are reviewed in W. Peck, *The* Pennsylvania *Rule Since* Reliable Transfer, 15 J. Mar. L. & Com. 95 (1984).

32. Senate Executive Report No. 4, 76th Cong., 1st Sess. (1938).

33. See 9 Benedict, *Admiralty* (6th ed., Arnold Knauth, editor), at 263–69.

34. 510 F.2d 875, 1975 AMC 287 (9th Cir. 1975).

In *Ishizaki* a Japanese hydrofoil and a small U.S. Army vessel collided in Kure Harbor, Japan. The owners of the hydrofoil sued in the U.S. District Court for the Northern District of California, and the United States filed a counterclaim. If navigation of the two vessels was governed by the International Rules, the hydrofoil was required to give way as the port-hand vessel in a crossing situation. The Japanese Port Regulations, however, provided that "Miscellaneous Vessels must give way to other than Miscellaneous Vessels in harbors." The hydrofoil owners argued that the army vessel failed to fly her international call sign, which the Japanese Port Regulations Law required to be flown by all vessels transiting Kure Harbor which were *not* "miscellaneous" vessels. They further argued that this failure contributed to a mistaken belief on the part of the captain of the hydrofoil that the other vessel was a "miscellaneous" vessel and therefore was required to give way.[35] The trial court, placing on the hydrofoil owners the burden of proving that the violation contributed to the collision, found that there was no evidence that the failure affected the judgment of the hydrofoil captain in any way.

On appeal, the hydrofoil owners contended that the district court should have applied the *Pennsylvania* Rule.[36] In rejecting this contention, the Ninth Circuit Court of Appeals held that since the collision occurred in the territorial waters of Japan, it was governed by Japanese law. The court continued:

> [T]here is no showing that Japanese law ever contained a rule similar to the *Pennsylvania* Rule and, in any event, it is our view that any such rule would not have survived the Japanese adherence to the International Convention with Respect to Collisions, 1910. . . .
>
> Nor should the *Pennsylvania* Rule here be considered a part of the procedural law of the forum. Were the Rule designed merely to shift to the violator of the statutory rule the burden of going forward with the evidence, its characterization as "procedural" would be proper. § 134 *Restatement, Conflict of Laws 2d* (1971). The Rule, however, does much more. Its effect has been described as follows:
>
> "The shift in burden resulting from application of the *Pennsylvania* Rule is twofold. Not only must the violator meet the burden of producing evidence to counter the presumption of causation, but he must also persuade the trier of fact that his explanation should be adopted. In order to carry this burden of persuasion under the Rule as it was created, it appears that a statutory violator would have to demonstrate beyond all doubt that his violation did not cause the loss." (Citing *The* Pennsylvania *Rule: Charting a New Course for An Ancient Mariner,* 54 Boston U. L. Rev. 78, 80 [1974]).

35. 510 F.2d at 878, 1975 AMC at 289–90.
36. 510 F.2d at 879, 1975 AMC at 290.

This is in accord with our own decisions which hold that the vessel guilty of a statutory violation has the burden "to establish that the violation could not reasonably be held to have been a proximate cause of the collision." *Pacific Tow Boat Co. v. States Marine Corp.*, 1960 AMC 696, 700, 276 F.2d 745, 749 (9 Cir., 1960). . . .

Under the currently prevailing view with respect to the distinction between substance and procedure in the conflict of laws setting, rules designed to affect the decision of a particular issue are classified as substantive. *Restatement, Conflict of Laws 2d* (1971). . . .

We conclude, therefore, that the *Pennsylvania* Rule is more akin to substantive law than to rules of procedure concerned primarily with judicial administration. The consequence is that it should not be applied to this case merely because it constitutes a part of the law of the forum. . . .

We believe that Article 6 [of the 1910 Collision Convention] is addressed to presumptions such as the *Pennsylvania* Rule without regard to whether they rest on judicial or legislative authority. Consistency in the interpretation of Article 6 requires this result because such presumptions in some nations may be contained in statutes while in others in the opinions and judgments of courts. The *Pennsylvania* Rule, for example, is a judge-made rule in the United States while in the United Kingdom its equivalent was contained in the Merchant Shipping Act of 1894, which was repealed shortly after the United Kingdom signed the International Convention. To interpret the Convention to require the repeal of a statutory presumption, but not one[37] different in substance, derived from case law, irrationally enhances the source of the presumption at the expense of uniformity in the undertaking and application of the Convention.

It does not follow from this that Article 6 is intended to make inoperative all presumptions. Some, such as those which place upon a vessel the duty of going forward with the evidence, are not presumptions "in regard to liability for collision." They do not affect liability in the strong and direct way that the *Pennsylvania* Rule does. Once more, it is important to recognize that the *Pennsylvania* Rule more resembles a rule of substantive law than it does a mere procedural rule designed to expedite judicial proceedings. The latter rules survive Article 6. The *Pennsylvania* Rule, on the other hand, establishes an almost insurmountable burden of proof that virtually insures that some liability will be imposed upon the ship that is charged with such a burden. It strains reason to insist that it is not a legal presumption of fault "in regard to liability for collision."[38]

---

37. [*Sic.*] "Not one" should probably read "not one no" or the equivalent.

38. 510 F.2d at 880–83, 1975 AMC at 292–96; footnotes by the court omitted.

In using the phrase "legal presumption of fault" the court followed the American translation of the French text of the 1910 Convention into English. The statutory violation is itself a

Since there appears to be no reasonable possibility that the 1910 Collision Convention will ever be adopted by the United States, the question of what effect, if any, adoption would have on the *Pennsylvania* Rule is of academic interest only. The second sentence of Article 6 of the convention provides: "There shall be no legal presumptions of fault in regard to liability for collision." If *fault,* as used in the convention and in *Reliable Transfer,*[39] had the same meaning as *fault* as used in *The Pennsylvania,* it would appear that adoption of the convention would have no effect on the rule, since, as we have seen, it creates a presumption of causation when fault has first been shown. But *fault* in the convention has been interpreted by some authorities as a term of art meaning *causative fault.* Thus, the English courts, in apportioning damages in both-to-blame cases, take into account the degrees of causation, as well as the degrees of *fault* in the ordinary sense of the word. The English rule is explained by Mr. Justice Brandon (later Lord Brandon of Oakbrook) as follows:

> [O]nly causative faults are relevant in apportioning liability under the Act. The seriousness or weight of such faults can be looked at from two angles. First, a fault can be looked at from the angle of its blameworthiness or culpability, irrespective of the extent to which it contributed to the damage or loss concerned. Second, a fault can be looked at from the angle of the extent to which it contributed to the damage or loss concerned, irrespective of its blameworthiness or culpability. These two aspects of any relevant fault can conveniently be labelled culpability and causative potency, respectively.
>
> There are passages in certain judgments in collision cases decided under the Act, mainly earlier cases, that suggest that, in apportioning liability under it, the causative potency of the relevant faults should alone be taken into consideration. These passages do not, however, represent the true principle of law applicable, as it has been established by later and authoritative decisions of appellate courts, that in apportioning liability under the Act, both the culpability and the causative potency of all relevant faults must be taken into account and weighed in the balance. This proposition, which is of fundamental importance, can be made good by a brief citation from three comparatively recent cases in appellate courts, one of which observed that "[t]he investigation is concerned with 'fault' which includes blameworthiness as well as causation. And no true apportionment can be reached unless both factors are borne in mind.[40]

"fault." With respect, therefore, the meaning the drafters of the convention intended to convey might have been more accurately expressed by the use of a term such as "legal presumption of causation," or "legal presumption of causative fault."

39. Supra note 13.

40. See Brandon, *Apportionment of Liability in British Courts Under the Maritime Convention Act of 1911,* 51 Tulane Law Rev. 1025 (1977) (citing *inter alia, The Statue of Liberty,* [1971] 2 Lloyd's

A minority of federal courts have likewise taken both degrees of culpability and degrees of causation into account.[41] Presumably these courts would interpret the word *fault,* as used by the Supreme Court in *Reliable Transfer,* in the same way as the English courts do in interpreting the convention because the Court's statement of the proportional fault rule in that case is a very close paraphrase of the language of the convention. On this interpretation, adoption of the convention by the United States would presumably result in abrogation of the *Pennsylvania* Rule. On the other hand, it would have no effect on the Rule if *fault* as used in the convention and in *Reliable Transfer* were interpreted in its ordinary sense, as it was in *The Pennsylvania.*

Summarizing, the following conclusions may be drawn from the authorities cited:

(a) The *Pennsylvania* Rule is not a procedural device, but a rule of substantive law; its application *vel non* should therefore generally depend on the law governing the other substantive aspects of the collision.

(b) The *Pennsylvania* Rule is a legal presumption of "fault," as that term is used in the 1910 Collision Convention, which abolishes such presumptions.

(c) Therefore, even where the rule is part of the law of the forum State, in the absence of extraordinary supervening circumstances it should not be applied by the forum in the case of a collision governed by the substantive law of a State subscribing to the convention, e.g., because the collision occurred in a harbor of that State, or because it occurred on the high seas and the vessels involved were of convention countries.

It is submitted that the critics of the *Pennsylvania* Rule are correct, and that it should be abrogated, either by the Supreme Court or by an act of Congress. It has received varying interpretations among the circuits, and is therefore a hindrance to the cause of national uniformity in the maritime law. It is contrary to the 1910 Brussels Convention, so that its abolition would narrow the differences between U.S. collision law and that of the other major maritime countries remaining after adoption of the proportional rule by the United States in 1975. Since *Reliable Transfer,*[42] it has no place in a regime of law which permits the courts to apportion damages in accordance with the degree of causative fault chargeable to each of the colliding vessels.

Rep. 277, 282 (H.L.); *The Miraflores and The Abadesa,* [1967] A.C. 826, 845; *The British Aviator,* [1965] 1 Lloyd's Rep. 271, 277 [C.A.]). The Act (1 & 2 Geo. 5, c. 57) implements the 1910 Convention.

The article is based on a paper delivered by Mr. Justice Brandon at the Tulane Admiralty Law Institute's Symposium on the American Law of Collision in March 1977.

41. See the discussion in chapter 12, section B(1).

42. Supra note 13.

4. *The* Pennsylvania *Rule and Improper Manning or Equipment*

Proof that a collision was caused by improper manning or equipment will of course subject a vessel to liability for collision damage.[43] What has not always been as clear, however, is whether proof of causation is required when a statute or regulation relating to manning or equipment has been violated. Although, as stated, Griffin expresses the view that the *Pennsylvania* Rule should be applied only to violations of statutes and regulations relating to navigation,[44] most of the recent cases have interpreted the rule more broadly.

The leading case on the application of the *Pennsylvania* Rule to violations of statutes and regulations relating to vessel equipment is *The Chickasaw.*[45] In that case a vessel ran aground on Santa Rosa Island, off the coast of Southern California, and her navigational equipment, including her radio direction finder and fathometer, were found to have been in deplorable condition. The district court, in denying both exoneration and limitation of liability, rested its decision on negligence of the master in failing to check the fathometer after being notified that it was defective, and privity of the owner, who had delegated the entire responsibility for vessel repairs in the Far East to the master.

The decision was affirmed on appeal, but on the ground that the vessel was in violation of a statute requiring an efficient radio direction finder, properly adjusted and in operating condition. After citing its decision in *The Denali,*[46] where the *Pennsylvania* Rule was applied to a vessel that was improperly manned, the Ninth Circuit continued:

> Although the *Pennsylvania* rule has been applied mainly in "rules of the road" and "manning" cases, it is also applicable to failure to provide equipment required by statute. . . .
>
> "[T]he navigation of a ship defectively equipped by a crew aware of her condition does not relieve the owner of his responsibility or transfer unseaworthiness into bad seamanship." *Maria,* 91 F.(2d) 819, 824, 1937 AMC 934, 943 (4th Cir. 1937).
>
> We hold that the court's finding that the stranding was not caused by the ship's failure to have an efficient radio direction finder is, in the light of the *Pennsylvania* Rule, clearly erroneous.[47]

---

43. See *Chamberlain v. Ward,* 62 U.S. 548 (1859); *The J. Rich Steers,* 228 F.319 (2d Cir. 1915); Griffin 547–50.

44. Griffin 579.

45. *Waterman Steamship Co. v. Gay Cottons (The Chickasaw),* 414 F.2d 724, 1969 AMC 1682 (9th Cir. 1969).

46. Supra note 11.

47. 414 F.2d at 737, 1969 AMC at 1699–1700.

Like the Ninth Circuit, the Second[48] and Fourth[49] Circuits have held the *Pennsylvania* Rule applicable where there has been a violation of a statutory manning requirement.

5. *Failure to Call Material Witnesses*

If the owner or operator of a colliding vessel fails to call a material witness within his or her control, without a satisfactory explanation, the court may draw an inference that if he or she had been called, the witness's testimony would have been adverse.[50] Thus, in most deep-sea collision cases, the practice is to call the master, whether or not he was on the bridge at the material times, the watch officer, the helmsman, the lookout, and the engineering officer on duty in the engine room, if they are still in the owner's employ. The oiler on watch usually testifies if there is an issue relating to the receipt or execution of orders from the bridge to the engine room, as recorded in the engine bell book. In the case of a fully automated vessel the number of witnesses to be called will of course be fewer; if the engine is controlled from the bridge, and the vessel is on automatic pilot, the watch officer and the helmsman-lookout may be the only material witnesses in addition to the master.

No adverse inference will be drawn against a party for failing to call a witness who is no longer in its employ. Thus, in *The Merry Queen—The Tug Minerva and Tow,*[51] the Third Circuit held that a showing that the lookout was no longer employed by the party rebutted the inference that if called his testimony would have been adverse. Similarly, the court held that no unfavorable inference should be drawn for failing to call the helmsman, who was shown to be in an institution, suffering from a nervous breakdown.

6. *Failure to Produce Logbooks and Other Records*

An unexplained failure to comply with a request for the production of a logbook, bell book, or other material record, like an unexplained failure to call a material witness within the party's control, will give rise to an unfavorable inference.[52]

There is surprisingly little case law, however, on the effect of the destruction of preliminary writings, such as rough notes made before the events

48. *The New York Marine No. 10,* 109 F.2d 564, 1940 AMC 347 (2d Cir. 1940). In the context of tort law a similar problem frequently occurs when a criminal statute admitting no defenses is applied in a civil litigation to establish the standard of care. In these cases courts may conclude that violation of the statute was reasonable, if made to avoid more serious injury or damage. See *Tedla v. Ellman,* 280 N.Y. 124, 19 N.E. 2d 987 (1939).

49. *The City of Baltimore,* 282 F. 490 (4th Cir. 1922).

50. *The New York,* 175 U.S. 187 (1899).

51. 202 F.2d 575, 1953 AMC 482 (3d Cir. 1953).

52. *Cary-Davis Co. v. United States,* 8 F.2d 324, 1925 AMC 1630 (1925); Griffin 636–37.

leading up to a collision are entered in the vessel's log. It is submitted that the practice should be frowned upon, but it was excused in the one case found which deals with the precise problem.[53]

7. *Alterations and Erasures in Logbooks and Other Records*

In a leading case on this subject, *The Chicago—The Silverpalm,*[54] the Ninth Circuit stated the rule as follows: "The alteration of log books by erasure and substitution . . . has long been condemned in courts of admiralty. It not only casts suspicion on the whole case of the vessel, but creates a strong presumption that the erased matter was adverse to her contention."[55] If an error has been made in a logbook or other record, it should be corrected by drawing a line through the erroneous words in such a manner as to leave the original language legible.[56]

8. *Failure to Stand By*

Title 46 U.S.C. § 2303 requires the master or individual in charge of a vessel involved in a marine casualty to render necessary assistance to save persons from danger caused by the casualty, so far as he can do so without serious danger to his own vessel or those on board. He is also required to give his name and address and the identification of his vessel to the master or person in charge of any other vessel involved in the casualty, and to injured persons and the owners of any damaged property. A violation of this provision carries a fine of not more than $1,000 or imprisonment for not more than two years, and renders the vessel liable *in rem* to the government for the fine.

Section 2303 is based upon the Stand-by Act of 1890,[57] which, however, related only to collisions. The act was repealed in 1983, when portions of Title 46 were recodified.[58] After setting forth the obligations of the masters of the colliding vessels to render assistance and exchange information it provided: "If he fails so to do, and no reasonable cause for such failure is shown, the collision shall, in the absence of proof to the contrary, be deemed to have been caused by his wrongful act, neglect, or default."

---

53. *Staley Mfg. Co. v. Porto Rico Lighterage Co.,* 438 F.2d 1, 1970 AMC 2152 (5th Cir. 1971). In that case there was testimony that it was customary on tugs to destroy rough notes after entering their contents in the log. But see *The Eureka,* 84 F.2d 496, 1936 AMC 1179 (9th Cir. 1936).

54. 94 F.2d 754, 1937 AMC 1427 (9th Cir. 1937).

55. 94 F.2d at 762, 1937 AMC at 1441–42.

56. *The Eureka,* supra note 53.

57. 26 Stat. 425, Sept. 4, 1890, 33 U.S.C. former §§ 367–68. The text is contained in Griffin, at 858.

58. Pub.L. No. 98-89, 97 Stat. 599, Aug. 26, 1983.

No similar provision is contained in § 2303, and the rebuttable presumption created by the Stand-by Act has thus been abolished.[59] The result is that in this respect U.S. law is now in accord with that of the 1910 Collision Convention countries. As stated previously, Article 6 of that Convention provides that there shall be no legal presumptions of [causative] fault in regard to liability for collision. Article 8 is very similar to § 2303, except that it applies only to collisions; it requires the master of each colliding vessel to assist the other vessel, her passengers, and crew, as far as he can do so without serious danger to his own vessel, her passengers, and crew, and also requires an exchange of identification. Article 8 then provides: "A breach of the above provisions shall not of itself impose any liability on the owner of a vessel." The British Maritime Conventions Act of 1911, implementing the convention, contains a similar provision.[60]

Section B. Admissions in Pleadings

Fault may of course be established by admissions in pleadings. On occasion, the owner of one colliding vessel may confess fault but litigate an issue of contributory fault on the part of the other vessel, or the damage issues, or the owner may admit facts which the court finds constitute fault.

Rule 36(a), Fed. R. Civ. P., entitles a party to serve upon any other party a written request to admit the truth of any matters within the scope of Rule 36(d), relating to statements or opinions of fact, or the application of law to fact, including the genuineness of any documents described in the request. Rule 36(b) provides that any matter admitted under the rule "is conclusively established unless the court on motion permits withdrawal or amendment of the admission."

Under Rule 8(d), Fed. R. Civ. P., averments in a pleading to which a responsive pleading is required, other than averments as to the amount of damage, are admitted when not denied in the responsive pleading. Averments in a pleading to which no responsive pleading is required or permitted are taken as denied or avoided.

Admissions and agreements made at pre-trial conferences and incorporated in pre-trial orders in accordance with Rule 16, Fed. R. Civ. P., can of course be used to establish fault on the part of one or both of the vessels involved in a collision.

---

59. See *Answers of the Maritime Law Association of the United States to the Comité Maritime International's Questionnaire on Implementation of International Conventions,* 18 J. Mar. L. & Com. 589 (1987).

60. See § 4(2) of the act, 1 & 2 Geo. 5, c. 57; Marsden 422–44.

Section C. Judicial Notice

Rule 201 of the Federal Rules of Evidence governs judicial notice in all proceedings in the federal courts, including admiralty proceedings, with a few immaterial exceptions. Paragraph (b) of the rule defines a judicially noticed fact as "one not subject to reasonable dispute in that it is either (1) generally known within the territorial jurisdiction of the trial court or (2) capable of accurate and ready determination by resort to sources whose accuracy cannot reasonably be questioned."

A case illustrating the first type is *Mid-America Trans. Co. v. National Marine Service, Inc.,*[61] where the court took judicial notice of the fact that the stretch of the Mississippi River between St. Paul, Minnesota, and St. Louis, Missouri, "is navigated daily in complete safety by many vessels."

An example of the second type is *United States v. The Monsoon,*[62] an oil pollution case, where Chief Judge Bailey Aldrich of the Court of Appeals for the First Circuit said that an admiralty court must take judicial notice of "a seaman's ready knowledge of tides and currents."[63]

Section D. Evidence Admissible in Collision Litigation

1. *Introduction*

At the outset it is necessary to take note of the historical support for the idea that admiralty courts were not "imprisoned by procedural niceties"[64] and were free to adapt themselves to whatever evidentiary rules and procedures would adduce the facts necessary for decision.[65] This proposition can be explained by the facts that during the period from 1789 to 1845 U.S. courts sitting in admiralty fashioned their own rules, and that in the period from 1845 to 1966 the Supreme Court fashioned minimal rules applicable solely on the

61. 497 F.2d 776, 780, 1974 AMC 1943, 1948 (8th Cir. 1974).

62. 433 F.2d 95, 1971 AMC 269 (1st Cir. 1970).

63. 433 F.2d at 98, 1971 AMC at 271.

64. See *Levinson v. Deupree,* 345 U.S. 648 (1953). The quoted language of Frankfurter, J., at 651, is useful to convey the relaxation of land law rules and procedures which have been tolerated by the Supreme Court. At issue in *Levinson* was the applicability of a state statute of limitations to a state-created wrongful death claim (pre-*Moragne v. States Marine Lines, Inc.,* 398 U.S. 375, 1970 AMC 967 [1970]). Not only is the rule in *Erie R.R. v. Tompkins,* 304 U.S. 64 (1938), *not* applicable to federal courts sitting in admiralty, but the analogy to the time bar could be rejected under the laches doctrine.

65. A limitation on that tolerant and relaxed attitude was struck in *Miner v. Atlass,* 363 U.S. 641, 1960 AMC 1267 (1960), invalidating local admiralty rules for discovery-type depositions, since only depositions *de bene esse* were permissible to preserve testimony. In 1961 the Supreme Court enacted a new Rule 30A(a) for examinations before trial in admiralty for purposes of discovery.

admiralty side of the federal courts.[66] Thus, Judge Benedict could say: Courts of admiralty are not bound by all the rules of evidence which are applied in the courts of common law, and they may, where justice requires it, take notice of matters not strictly proved.[67]

It should be noted, however, that except in certain Great Lakes cases, trials in admiralty were always by judge alone (pre-*Romero*)[68] and appeals were regarded as trials *de novo,* at which new evidence could be taken (pre-*McAllister).*[69] It was undoubtedly because of the absence of a jury that the courts found it unnecessary to adopt common law rules of evidence in admiralty cases.

Two dramatic changes have affected the tolerant and relaxed attitude of the past, so that procedural cases before 1966 and evidentiary cases before 1975 must be used with caution as precedents. The changes are the unification of the Supreme Court Admiralty Rules and the Federal Rules of Civil Procedure in 1966,[70] causing the disappearance of the separate admiralty "side" of the federal district courts (with its own docket and its own terminology), and the adoption of the Federal Rules of Evidence in 1975.[71] Even after twenty-two years it does not appear that evidentiary hearings have become more technical under the Federal Rules of Evidence than under the tolerant and relaxed attitudes of the district courts when sitting in admiralty before their adoption. The statement made in Griffin in 1949 still holds true:

> In admiralty cases, where there is no jury, doubtful evidence should be received subject to objection "unless, indeed, it be so utterly irrelevant or immaterial that there could not possibly be any doubt about it" . . . in order that the appellate court may have the evidence before it, if it should consider it admissible.[72]

---

66. The Supreme Court Admiralty Rules, 44 U.S. IX (1845). The Court acted under the rule-making power granted by the Congress in 1842 (Act of Aug. 23, 1842, ch. 188 § 6; 5 Stat. 518 (R.S. §§ 862, 917)).

67. *The J. F. Spencer,* 13 F. Cas. 614 (EDNY 1869) (No. 7315), quoted by successor judges of that court in *The Boskenna Bay,* 22 F. 662, 667 (SDNY 1884) (Brown, J.), and *The Rosalia,* 264 F. 285, 289 (2d Cir. 1920) (Hough, J.).

68. *Romero v. International Terminal Operating Co.,* 358 U.S. 354, 1959 AMC 832 (1959).

69. *McAllister v. Magnolia Petroleum Co.,* 357 U.S. 221, 1958 AMC 1754 (1958).

70. The Supreme Court Admiralty Rules were rescinded, effective July 1, 1966. The Supplemental Rules for Certain Admiralty and Maritime Claims were added to the Federal Rules of Civil Procedure on Feb. 28, 1966, and became effective July 1, 1966.

71. See generally, H.R. Rep. No. 93–650, 93d Cong. 1st Sess. (1974).

72. Griffin 623, citing *Minnesota S.S. Co. v. Lehigh Valley Transp. Co.,* 129 F. 22, 30 (6th Cir. 1904). The last phrase of the quotation reflects the former practice, when admiralty appeals were trials *de novo.*

2. *Depositions* "De Bene Esse"

Despite the common-law preference for oral testimony before the fact-finder at the trial and the relatively few exceptions to the hearsay rule dealing with recorded testimony, the Admiralty Court in England inherited the "civil law" traditions of the courts with which it was associated in Doctors' Commons, favoring written testimony and evidentiary hearings at intervals over a prolonged period, since juries were not used. The Admiralty Court also recognized the perils of the sea and the likelihood that oral testimony by mariners at the time of trial would be impossible, since the mariners might be absent on long voyages or might have perished in disasters at sea, which were then all too frequent. Accordingly, depositions of seagoing witnesses were commonly taken in the English Admiralty as part of the custom and usage of the sea. Depositions of mariners "to preserve testimony" have traditionally been referred to as *"de bene esse"* (literally *"as being good"*) for the time, or *"provisionally,"* meaning that the testimony has been preserved lest the witnesses later be unavailable to testify. Since the purpose of depositions *de bene esse* was preservation of testimony, the deposition could be taken, on notice to the opponents, by the party who might wish to use it. Traditionally, it was not considered as part of discovery of the opponent's case.[73]

The first Congress of the United States, possibly influenced by the admiralty proctors in their midst, enacted the *de bene esse* deposition statute in 1789 as part of the first Judiciary Act, providing that the testimony of witnesses living at a distance from the place of trial greater than 100 miles, or bound on a voyage to sea, or about to leave the United States, or about to be at a distance greater than 100 miles from the place of trial, could be taken by deposition under oath before various federal and state authorities, on notice to the opposing party, unless urgent necessity would justify a judge's ordering the deposition without notice.[74] The 1789 legislation also provided for the admissibility of the deposition at trial (it having been taken down in writing and subscribed by the deponent) if the court was satisfied that the witness was then dead, outside the United States, more than 100 miles from the place of trial, or unable to attend the trial by reason of age, sickness, bodily infirmity, or imprisonment.[75]

---

73. See *Miner v. Atlass,* supra note 65.

74. Act of Sept. 24, 1789, ch. 20 § 30, 1 Stat. 88, subsequently amended by Act of Mar. 1, 1817, ch.30, 3 Stat. 350; Act of Feb. 26, 1853, ch. 80 § 3, 10 Stat. 168; Act of July 29, 1854, ch. 159 § 2, 10 Stat. 315; and Act of May 9, 1872, ch. 146, 17 Stat. 89.

75. Act of Sept. 24, 1789, ch. 20 § 30, 1 Stat. 88.

The 1789 statute passed into the Revised Statutes[76] was subsequently codified in Title 28[77] and was included in the Supreme Court Admiralty Rules.[78] It was finally included in the Federal Rules of Civil Procedure,[79]

---

76. R.S. §§ 863–65, subsequently renumbered as §§ 1472–74; also amended by Act of Mar. 9, 1892, 31 Stat. 182. The 1874 revision preserved *de bene esse* depositions at law only, although under earlier versions they could be used at law and in equity as well as in admiralty. By a subsequent revision, R.S. §§ 863–65, as amended, became applicable only in admiralty proceedings.

R.S. § 863, not subsequently repealed, although superseded, is reproduced here from the notes preceding Chapter 117 (§§ 1781–84) of Title 28 U.S.C.A.—"Evidence; Depositions":

> Sec. 863. The testimony of any witness may be taken in any civil cause depending in a district court by deposition de bene esse, when the witness lives at a greater distance from the place of trial than one hundred miles, or is bound on a voyage to sea, or is about to go out of the United States, or out of the district in which the case is to be tried, and to a greater distance than one hundred miles from the place of trial, before the time of trial, or when he is ancient and infirm. The deposition may be taken before any judge of any court of the United States, or any clerk of a district court, or any chancellor, justice, or judge of a supreme or superior court, mayor or chief magistrate of a city, judge of a county court or court of common pleas of any of the United States, or any notary public, not being of counsel or attorney to either of the parties, nor interested in the event of the cause. Reasonable notice must first be given in writing by the party or his attorney proposing to take such deposition, to the opposite party or his attorney of record, as either may be nearest, which notice shall state the name of the witness and the time and place of the taking of his deposition; and in all cases in rem, the person having the agency or possession of the property at the time of seizure shall be deemed the adverse party, until a claim shall have been put in; and whenever, by reason of the absence from the district and want of an attorney of record or other reason, the giving of the notice herein required shall be impracticable, it shall be lawful to take such depositions as there shall be urgent necessity for taking, upon such notice as any judge authorized to hold courts in such district shall think reasonable and direct. Any person may be compelled to appear and depose as provided by this section, in the same manner as witnesses may be compelled to appear and testify in court.

By the unification of the Supreme Court Admiralty Rules and the Federal Rules of Civil Procedure, R.S. §§ 862–65 have been superseded. Rules 26 and 32, Fed. R. Civ. P., now apply to all civil actions. See *Republic of France v. Belships Co.,* 91 F. Supp. 912, 1950 AMC 1625 (SDNY 1950). See also *Application of A. Pellegrino & Son,* 11 F.R.D. 209 (SDNY 1950).

77. 28 U.S.C. §§ 639–41 (1948). See *Standard S.S. Co. v. United States,* 126 F. Supp. 583, 1955 AMC 104 (D Del. 1954). See also former § 1781 of Title 28 U.S.C. (1948).

78. Former Supreme Court Admiralty Rule 32C. In *Miner v. Atlass,* supra note 65, 363 U.S. at 644–45, 1960 AMC at 1270–71, the Supreme Court accepted the view that admiralty depositions under this rule were not available for discovery purposes, extending the prohibition to local admiralty rules which purported to authorize depositions for discovery purposes. 363 U.S. at 651–52. The Supreme Court Admiralty Rules were amended in 1961, before those rules were rescinded in 1966.

79. Rule 30 Fed. R. Civ. P. is applicable to depositions upon oral examination.

See C. Wright, A. Miller & R. Marcus, 8A *Federal Practice and Procedure* § 2105 (1994), at 52–54, describing this special notice in lieu of leave of court as the resolution of a long and troublesome dispute between the admiralty bar and those whose experience is with general civil litigation. The authors describe the *de bene esse* deposition as a common practice in admiralty but note that this proved to be one of the most difficult points in the 1966 unification of admiralty and civil procedure. Thus, Rule 30 was amended in 1970 to replace the *de bene esse* statutes and authorize counsel to notice a deposition without leave of court when facts showing an urgent need for an immediate deposition have been certified. A further amendment in 1993 revised the entire rule and now requires, by Rule 30(a)(2)(C), that the notice itself must contain facts to

where it remains as Rule 30.[80] It is not, however, part of the specific deposition exceptions to the hearsay rule in Rule 803(4) of the Federal Rules of Evidence. Accordingly, depositions of mariners which have been taken, on notice, either for the purpose of preservation of testimony or for discovery may be admitted in evidence at trial.[81]

3. Documentary Evidence: Logbooks and Other Records of Regularly Conducted Activities aboard Vessels (Fed. R. Evid. 803[6])

(a) Relevance and Materiality. Fed. R. Evid. Rule 401 sets up a broad rule that evidence "having any tendency to make the existence of any fact that is of consequence to the determination of the action more probable or less probable than it would be without [it]" is relevant.[82] Further, by Rule 402, all relevant evidence is admissible unless otherwise provided.[83]

(b) Prior Evidentiary Problems. Griffin's 1949 text reflects the then prevailing narrow, common-law view that logbooks were admissible *against* the vessel keeping them, but as they were considered "self-serving" documents they could not be offered *for* the vessel, although witnesses' recollections could be refreshed with them.[84]

Griffin also gives a very narrow reading to the 1936 Statute on Admissibility of Logbooks,[85] noting that a collision narrative would not be admissible,

---

support the certification that the person to be examined is expected to leave the United States and be unavailable for examination in the United States unless deposed before the time specified in Rule 26(d), dealing with the requirement of a conference of the parties under Rule 26(f). The 1993 amendments of Rule 30 omit reference to Rule 11 sanctions, but amendments of Rule 26(g)(3) mention appropriate sanctions for certifications in violation of the duty of the signing attorney under Rule 26(g)(1).

Use of depositions in court proceedings is governed by Rule 32, also amended in 1993. Rule 32(a)(3) provides that the deposition may be used if the witness is dead; at a greater distance than 100 miles from the place of trial or is out of the United States, unless the absence was procured by the party offering the deposition; unable to attend because of age, illness, infirmity, or imprisonment; the party offering the deposition is unable to compel appearance by subpoena; or exceptional circumstances exist requiring it in the interest of justice.

80. Rule 804(a)(5), Fed. R. Evid., requires the party seeking the admission of deposition testimony to show *inability* to procure attendance through process or other reasonable means.

In *Carey v. Bahama Cruise Lines,* 864 F.2d 201, 1989 AMC 852 (1st Cir. 1988), the Court of Appeals held that the trial court had not abused its discretion in admitting deposition testimony of crew members who were at sea at the time of trial, even though they remained employees of the defendant. The court concluded that the testimony was admissible under Rule 32, Fed. R. Civ. P., and distinguished "procuring absence" from "doing nothing to facilitate presence." There was no showing that the employees had been concealed or deliberately removed. See also *In re E.M. Queeny,* 752 F.2d 874, 1986 AMC 74 (3d Cir. 1986).

81. Rule 26, Fed. R. Civ. P., for discovery and Rule 32 for preservation of testimony.

82. Fed. R. Evid. Rule 401.

83. Fed. R. Evid. Rule 402.

84. Griffin 635–36.

85. 49 Stat. 1561, 28 U.S.C. § 695 (1982). See also 28 U.S.C. § 1732 (1982).

whereas "entries customarily made with respect to navigation, engine orders, etc." would be admissible.[86]

(c) Modern Rules on Admissibility. The Federal Rules of Evidence now provide a number of justifications, under the exceptions to the hearsay rule, for the admissibility of logbooks, in addition to the principal exception for business records under Fed. R. Evid. 803(6). These other exceptions are:

present sense impressions;[87]
regularly conducted activity;[88]
absence of entry in records of regularly conducted activity;[89]
public records and reports;[90]
absence of public record or entry.[91]

The older rules for admissions against interest[92] and *res gestae* or spontaneous utterances[93] may also be available to justify the admission of logbooks.

(d) Logbooks Customarily Carried on Merchant Vessels. These include:

- *The official log (smooth copy).* This mandated official record is *not* usually written concurrently with the events described but is prepared from materials contained in other, unofficial logs. Failure to preserve the contemporaneous records in unofficial logs and notebooks may give rise to adverse inferences.[94]
- *Other logbooks and similar records customarily carried on merchant vessels*: rough deck log; maneuvering order book; bridge bell book; navigator's log book; engine room bell book; radio log; bridge to bridge radiotelephone log (required by 47 CFR 83.368).

All of these are admissible as business records or under the broad list of exceptions to the hearsay rule.[95] These records may not be maintained on

---

86. Griffin 636. Griffin, however, notes that the admissibility of logbooks did not appear to have been settled by the courts as of the time the book was written (1949). But see *International Produce v. The Frances Salman, Inc.*, 1975 AMC 1521 (SDNY 1975), and *Texas Eastern Transmission Corp. v. Garber Bros., Inc.*, 494 F. Supp. 832, summarized at 1982 AMC 302 (ED La. 1980), aff'd in part, 677 F.2d 114 (5th Cir. 1982).
87. Fed. R. Evid. Rule 803(1).
88. Fed. R. Evid. Rule 803(6).
89. Fed. R. Evid. Rule 803(7).
90. Fed. R. Evid. Rule 803(8).
91. Fed. R. Evid. Rule 803(10).
92. Fed. R. Evid. Rule 804(b)(3) and (5).
93. Fed. R. Evid. Rule 803(2).
94. See § A(6), supra.
The official log of a U.S. flag merchant vessel is deposited with the U.S. Coast Guard at the destination port where the shipping articles are closed out.
95. See Federal Rules of Evidence cited supra in notes 87–91.

board a vessel indefinitely, and owners' requirements will vary as to their preservation. After two or three years it can be expected that these records will have been sent to the owners or destroyed in due course.

(e) Logbooks Customarily Carried by U.S. Navy and U.S. Coast Guard Vessels. Included in this category are: rough deck log; smooth deck log; junior officer of the deck log—maneuvering orders; bridge engine order book; navigator's log book; first lieutenant's logbook; captain's night order book; combat information center (CIC) log; engine room bell book; and message log.

(f) Automatic Record-keeping Devices. The previous discussion makes two assumptions: (1) that the bridge does not control the engine room directly; (2) that there is no automatic gyrocompass recorder or other automatic record of courses, speeds, and times (the equivalent of aviation's "black box"). It should be noted, however, that while such automatic recording devices are not now mandated, they will become increasingly common and the recording devices and their products will be admissible in court.[96]

(g) Notebooks in Frequent Use as Business Records. These include chief officers' notebook (or formal logbook), containing principally cargo-loading plans and other stability information; navigator's notebooks; bos'n's notebook; quartermaster's notebook (on U.S. Navy and U.S. Coast Guard vessels); electrician's notebook; electronic navigation notebook; deck notebook (first lieutenant's notebook).

(h) Other Documents. Among other records of vessel activity are navigational charts; dead reckoning computations (Loran and Decca); maneuvering solutions (plots); radar, sonar, and fathometer notebooks, plots and traces; cargo loading plans; classification society certificates; and items

---

96. Cf. *The Statue of Liberty,* [1968] 1 Lloyd's Rep. 429 (Adm. Div. 1968), where defendant argued that a mechanically recorded film of radar pips or echoes was inadmissible because they were produced without human intervention and therefore did not come within an exception to the hearsay rule. The film was admitted on the analogy of a tape recorder or any camera. See also *Burgess v. The Tamano,* 382 F. Supp. 351, 1975 AMC 2174 (D Me. 1975), where the court noted that course recorder tapes need not be given more weight than other evidence, since they are not capable of highly precise interpretation. It should be noted that photographs with date and time affixed are often made of radar screens in vessel traffic control centers around the world. Cf. *Akron Shipping Co. v. The Militos,* 1975 AMC 1717, 1722–3:

> Since there was no proof that failure to use the course recorder contributed to the collision, nor was there any proof that defendant was required under applicable regulations to use the device, defendant's failure to use the course recorder was of no consequence.

Use of electronic charts will present a challenge to the parties and the courts unless some method of retrieving the screen presentation just prior to collision can be built in and required. See chapter 4, infra.

concerning personal injuries resulting from collisions: medical officer's log (if any); medical treatment records.

(i) The Master's Protest. Laws or customs in many countries require the master (or senior surviving officer) of a vessel in a collision to prepare a document giving the general details of the collision, including the vessels' names, and the location, time, and date of the collision, within a very short time after its occurrence. This document may trigger the running of the statutory limitation period in some legal systems and may have great weight in subsequent official investigations. It also serves to notify hull and P&I (protection and indemnity) insurers of the possibility of claims under the vessel's insurance. This document has no special legal position in the United States, but it would be admissible, at least as a business record, and possibly as a public record or an admission against interest, although it has been characterized as unreliable because of its self-serving nature.[97]

(j) Business Records Generally. The broad scope of this exception to the hearsay rule is still being developed by the courts and as of this writing (1997) it is not yet possible to conclude whether the effect of the Federal Rules of Evidence will be to imprison admiralty within procedural niceties.[98] But even if the record itself is held inadmissible it may be used to refresh the recollection of witnesses.

---

97. Id., 1975 AMC 1724. See generally, *Newark S.B. Co. v. The Tug Cumeo,* 1941 AMC 1492 (EDNY 1941).

98. Cases decided under Fed. R. Evid. Rule 803(6) which seem to broaden the admissibility rules are the following:

Fernandez v. Chios Shipping Co., 542 F.2d 145, 1976 AMC 1780 (2d Cir. 1976) (surveyors' reports as to cargo's condition and stowage); *Raphaely International Inc. v. Waterman Steamship Corp.,* 972 F.2d 498, 1994 AMC 1441 (2d Cir. 1992) (government cargo inspectors' certificates); *Morrison Grain Co., Inc. v. Utica Mutual Ins. Co.,* 632 F.2d 424, 1982 AMC 658 (5th Cir. 1980) (ocean bill of lading); Cf. *Hershey Foods Corp. v. Waterman Steamship Corp.,* 1994 AMC 2970 (SDNY 1994) (clean bill of lading concerns exterior of bags, not interior); *Liner v. J.B. Talley & Co.,* 618 F.2d 327, 1982 AMC 2693 (5th Cir. 1980) (admission of records from a witness unfamiliar with record-keeping held harmless error); *Capital Marine Supply, Inc. v. The Roland Thomas,* 719 F.2d 104, 1984 AMC 905 (5th Cir. 1983) (preferred ship mortgage); *Saks International Inc. v. The Export Champion,* 817 F.2d 1011, 1987 AMC 1899 (2d Cir. 1987) (loading tallies); *Bergen v. The St. Patrick,* 816 F.2d 1345, 1987 AMC 2024 (9th Cir. 1987), modified on other grounds, 866 F.2d 318 (9th Cir. 1989) (fishing vessel's earning records); *United States v. Farrell Lines,* 1982 AMC 1904 (D Md. 1982) (survey reports made by Lloyd's agent); *Black Sea & Baltic General Ins. Co. v. The Hellenic Destiny,* 575 F. Supp. 685, 1984 AMC 1055 (SDNY 1983) (Fed. R. Evid. Rule 803[6] permits and commercial invoices); *Kansas Packing Co. v. The Lash Italia,* 1984 AMC 277 (SDNY 1984) (bill of lading).

Admissibility of business records was narrowed in *Barnett v. Howaldt,* 757 F.2d 23, 1985 AMC 2048 (2d Cir. 1985) (port captain's accident report).

See generally the "harmless error" rule, Fed. R. Evid. Rule 103.

4. Public Records (Fed. R. Evid. 803[8])

The Federal Rules of Evidence contain a general exception to the hearsay rule for public records and public documents, in Rule 803(8). The limitation on this exception is the requirement for authenticity by way of official certification under Fed. R. Evid. 902(3).[99]

5. Records of Official Investigations (Fed. R. Evid. 803[8][c])

Two separate issues are involved here: accessibility and admissibility. Generally speaking, official investigations are conducted for a public safety purpose, so that use of these records in private litigation is, at best, a by-product. Nevertheless, since witnesses can be compelled to attend and testify (always saving the fifth amendment privilege against self-incrimination) and documentary production can be compelled, the official investigation may offer a preview of subsequent litigation and the testimony itself may be admissible therein.

---

99. Fed. R. Evid. Rule 902(3):

> Extrinsic evidence of authenticity as a condition precedent to admissibility is not referenced with respect to the following:
>
> (3) Foreign public documents. A document purporting to be executed or attested in his official capacity by a person authorized by the laws of a foreign country to make the execution or attestation, and accompanied by a final certification as to the genuineness of the signature and official position (A) of the executing or attesting person, or (B) of any foreign official whose certificate of genuineness of signature and official position relates to the execution or attestation or is in a chain of certificates of genuineness of signature and official position relating to the execution or attestation. A final certification may be made by a secretary of embassy or legation, consul general, consul, vice consul, or consular agent of the United States, or a diplomatic or consular official of the foreign country assigned or accredited to the United States. If reasonable opportunity has been given to all parties to investigate the authenticity and accuracy of official documents, the court may, for good cause shown, order that they be treated as presumptively authentic without final certification or permit them to be evidenced by an attested summary with or without final certification.

See also *United States v. Central Gulf Lines, Inc.*, 974 F.2d 621, 1993 AMC 2622 (5th Cir. 1993), and *United States v. Central Gulf Lines, Inc.*, 747 F.2d 315, 1985 AMC 1982 (5th Cir. 1984) (survey reports and shortlanding certificates); *Midwest Nut and Seed Co. v. The Great Republic*, 1979 AMC 379 (SDNY 1978) (government cargo inspection certificates); *Black Sea & Baltic General Ins. Co. v. The Hellenic Destiny*, supra note 98 (customs certificates); *Ins. Co. of North America v. The Italica*, 567 F. Supp. 59, 1984 AMC 136 (SDNY 1983) (weather records at the loading port); *Raphaely International Inc. v. Waterman Steamship Corp.*, supra note 98 (cargo-inspection certificates).

Records of shareholders' and directors' meetings of foreign corporations have been held admissible for a limited purpose as public records. See *Morgan Guaranty Trust Co. v. Hellenic Lines Ltd.*, 621 F. Supp. 198, 1986 AMC 626 (SDNY 1985):

> Minutes of corporation's directors meetings are admissible as business records under Fed. R. Evid. Rule 803(6) when supported by the testimony of a director present at those meetings, even though he was not the custodian of the records. Since Greek law requires the filing of all minutes of shareholders meetings of Greek corporations, the minutes are admissible under Fed. R. Evid. Rule 803(8) to prove that they were made and properly recorded, although not as evidence of the truth of their contents.

(a) Accessibility. Records of official investigations under the control of U.S. government agencies such as the National Transportation Safety Board (NTSB), the U.S. Coast Guard, the U.S. Navy, and other agencies operating vessels, are governed by the Federal Freedom of Information Act,[100] the Federal Right to Privacy Act,[101] and relevant departmental regulations.[102] The statutory restrictions on the disclosure of these reports are to protect trade secrets[103] and disclosure of documents which have been formally classified for national security purposes.[104] Coast Guard Regulations add additional restrictions.[105]

(b) Admissibility of Entire Reports (Fed. R. Evid. 803[8][c]). The reports of U.S. government investigations, whether informal or formal, or of the proceedings of courts of inquiry, have the same format:

(i) Findings of fact, supported by specific testimony or documents;
(ii) Opinions (or conclusions) based on specific findings of fact;
(iii) Recommendations to prevent recurrences and improve safety.

Such investigations, conducted in the interests of safety, may have come upon factors of causation and allocations of responsibility which the experience of the investigators, as experts in the field, would cause to be regarded as highly probative, if not determinative, in civil litigation. At the very least, there is substantial discovery of facts and witness behavior, since testimony is taken under the penalty of perjury, although cross-examination may have been minimal.

Before 1988 there were a number of decisions differentiating between *fact* and *opinion,* wherein the factual findings of official U.S. government investigation reports were held admissible, while opinions contained therein were held inadmissible. However, the Supreme Court's decision in *Beech Aircraft Co. v. Rainey*[106] upheld the admissibility of opinions expressed in official investigative reports if otherwise trustworthy and based on fact. In that case, the Supreme Court resolved the interpretation of Rule 803(8)(c) of the Federal Rules of Evidence to permit the use of opinions of official investigators in official reports. While the decision involved a Navy Report of Investigation, it is apparent that it would have been applied to reports of Coast Guard

---

100. 5 U.S.C. § 552 (1982).

101. 5 U.S.C. § 552a (b) (1982).

102. See, e.g., Department of Transportation Regulations, 49 CFR, pt. 7, 46 CFR § 4.13-1; 5 MSM 72-5-30 and 72-6-45.

103. 18 U.S.C. § 905. See also 49 CFR § 7.67 (1987).

104. 18 U.S.C. § 798.

105. Certain Boating Accident Reports, 46 U.S.C. § 6102: Boating Accident Reports submitted to state authorities under 33 CFR § 173 app. A(a). (It should be noted that such reports submitted directly to the U.S. Coast Guard under 33 CFR § 173 app. A(b) *are* accessible.)

106. *Beech Aircraft Co. v. Rainey,* 488 U.S. 153, 1989 AMC 441 (1988). The decision is analyzed in G. Paulsen & L. Lambert, *Admissibility of Government Agency Reports in Maritime Cases,* 21 J. Mar. L. & Com. 111 (1990).

investigations prior to enactment of a 1996 statute[107] prohibiting the use of Coast Guard investigation reports in civil litigation.

In *Beech Aircraft* a product liability claim was brought by the survivors of two U.S. Navy pilots killed in an aircraft accident, against the manufacturer and service contractor of a Navy aircraft, alleging defects in the fuel control system causing loss of power, known as a "rollback." Banking sharply to avoid another aircraft, the plane lost altitude and crashed, killing the flight instructor and her student during a training exercise at Middleton Field, Alabama. (The training exercise involved "touch and go" landings.) The Navy Investigative Report, which had been admitted in evidence, had concluded that the most probable cause of the fatal accident was pilot error. At trial, the issue was pilot error or equipment malfunction. The Court of Appeals for the Eleventh Circuit reversed judgment for the manufacturer after a jury verdict, on the ground that the opinions of the Navy investigators had been improperly admitted into evidence.

Traditionally, Navy Courts of Inquiry and later forms of investigations held in accordance with the *Manual of the Judge Advocate General (JAGMAN)* made sharp distinctions between "findings of facts," "opinion" based on the facts, and "recommendations." In 1974, the drafters of the Federal Rules of Evidence, in a general prohibition of hearsay contained in Rule 803, listed an exception to the hearsay rule of "factual findings" made in public records and reports which resulted from investigations made pursuant to authority granted by law, unless the sources of information or other circumstances indicated lack of trustworthiness (Rule 803[8][c]).

The issue before the Supreme Court in *Beech Aircraft* was whether the use of the phrase "factual findings" by Congress was meant to keep out opinions and conclusions drawn from the facts, even though a sharp line between "fact" and "opinion" was very difficult to draw and was often arbitrary.

Justice Brennan, speaking for an undivided Court on this issue, noted that the authors of the draft rule did not intend to make a sharp distinction between fact and opinion and that the legislative history of the rule was ambiguous, opposite conclusions having been drawn in House and Senate Judiciary Committee Reports. Further, the dictionary definition of a finding of fact included a conclusion by way of reasonable inference from the evidence. Accordingly, the "factual findings" exception does *not* exclude conclusions or opinions based on a factual investigation which satisfies the requirement of trustworthiness.

As of this writing the consequences of *Beech Aircraft Co. v. Rainey* are hard to predict. The decision dealt with the positive admissibility of a report under Fed. R. Evid. 803(8)(c) and was not concerned with statutory prohibitions on admissibility, such as will be found in 49 U.S.C. § 1154(b),

107. 46 U.S.C. § 6308. See chapter 17, § A(7).

involving the National Transportation Safety Board (NTSB).[108] Judicial interpretations of the former 49 U.S.C. § 1441(e) have changed over the years, and it may be that courts will now apply the Supreme Court's 1988 view that the fact-opinion distinction is inevitably arbitrary, so that all parts of the report will be admissible under Fed. R. Evid. 803(8)(c), so long as otherwise trustworthy and based on facts. *Beech Aircraft Co. v. Rainey* was a trendsetter on total admissibility of NTSB reports until the Congress enacted 46 U.S.C. § 6308 to prevent the admission in civil litigation of Coast Guard reports and reenacted former 49 U.S.C. § 1441(e) as 49 U.S.C. § 1154(b).

(c) National Transportation Safety Board Reports. Respecting the National Transportation Safety Board, Congress has continued the policy, originating with aircraft accidents,[109] whereby: "No part of any report of the . . . Board, relating to any accident or the investigation thereof, shall be admitted as evidence or used in any suit or action for damages growing out of any matter mentioned in such report or reports."

Beyond NTSB reports, however, congressional authority respecting safety investigations has been viewed as authority for the regulatory rule that such investigations ". . . are for the purpose of taking appropriate measures for promoting safety of life and property at sea and are not intended to fix civil or criminal responsibility."[110] The policy of the statutory prohibition has

108. Section 701(a) of the Federal Aviation Act of 1958 contained the original prohibition which was found in the Department of Transportation Act of 1966, 49 U.S.C. § 1441(e) (1988). In 1994 the provision was renumbered as 49 U.S.C. § 1154(b). The duty of the NTSB to investigate aircraft accidents includes the duty to investigate the *probable cause* of the accident, 49 CFR 801.35, with the purpose of promoting safety and preventing similar accidents in the future (49 CFR 831.4). Thus the Fifth Circuit interpreted 49 U.S.C. § 1441(e) to mean that opinions in a report are admissible unless they are conclusions as to probable cause or concern agency opinion as to negligence. *American Airlines, Inc. v. United States,* 418 F.2d 180 (5th Cir. 1969).

Interpreting both § 1441(e) and Fed. R. Evid. Rule 803(8)(c), it has been held that no part of an NTSB Report may be admitted as evidence in a subsequent action for damages *(Travelers Ins. Co. v. Riggs,* 671 F.2d 810 [4th Cir. 1982]) despite opinions chipping away at the absolute prohibition. See *American Airlines, Inc. v. United States,* supra; *Universal Airline, Inc. v. Eastern Air Lines, Inc.,* 188 F.2d 993 (D.C. Cir. 1951); *Fidelity and Casualty Co. v. Frank,* 227 F. Supp. 948 (D Conn. 1964); *Kline v. Martin,* 345 F. Supp. 31 (ED Va. 1972); *Mullan v. Quickie Aircraft Corp.,* 797 F.2d 845 (10th Cir. 1986).

For post-*Rainey* decisions, see *In re Air Crash Disaster at Stapleton International Airport, Denver, Colorado,* 720 F. Supp. 1943 (D Colo. 1989) (NTSB Report admitted); cf. *In re Air Crash Disaster at Sioux City, Iowa,* 734 F. Supp. 1425 (ND Ill. 1991).

109. 49 U.S.C. § 1441(e) (1982). See also 45 U.S.C. § 33 (1982) concerning railroad accidents. NTSB investigators may testify only as to the factual content within the report and not as to opinion. (See 49 CFR 835.)

110. 46 CFR 4.07-1(b) (1986). See *Huber v. United States,* 838 F.2d 398, 1988 AMC 1796 (9th Cir. 1988); *Smith v. Ithaca Corp.,* 612 F.2d 215, 1981 AMC 1029 (5th Cir. 1980); *In re American Export Lines, Inc.,* 73 F.R.D. 454, 1977 AMC 2632 (SDNY 1977) (NTSB and Coast Guard opinions excluded in a collision case); and *In re Cleveland Tankers,* 821 F. Supp. 463, 1993 AMC 865 (ED Mich. 1992) (NTSB report containing an opinion inadmissible by statute; Coast Guard report containing an opinion inadmissible by regulation); *Reliable Transfer Co. v. United States,* 53 F.R.D. 24, 1971 AMC 647 (EDNY 1971).

even been held to shelter the report from admissibility where the government is a party defendant and the report is being sought as an admission against interest.[111]

The public record exception to the hearsay rule permits use of the testimony taken at an official investigation as former testimony if the declarant is unavailable as a witness and the party *against* whom the testimony is now offered, or a predecessor in interest, had an opportunity and similar motive to develop the testimony by direct, cross- or redirect examination.[112]

Another justification for use of the testimony is found in the broad exception for "factual findings resulting from an investigation made pursuant to authority granted by law."[113] Under this provision, however, the source of information or other circumstances may not indicate a lack of trustworthiness.[114] There is no requirement that the witness be unavailable.

---

111. Fed. R. Evid. Rule 801(d)(2). See *Huber v. United States,* 838 F.2d 398, 403 (9th Cir. 1988), vacating and remanding the decision of the district court, where a Coast Guard accident report was held inadmissible by analogy to the congressional restriction on NTSB reports.

112. Fed. R. Evid. Rule 804(b)(1). See *Lloyd v. American Export Lines, Inc.,* 580 F.2d 1179 (3d Cir. 1978), where testimony at a Coast Guard license suspension and revocation proceeding was held admissible because the Coast Guard was a predecessor in interest to a party.

See Note, *Evaluation Reports and Predecessor in Interest Construed to Admit Coast Guard Hearing Report and Testimony Under Federal Rules of Evidence,* 4 Mar. Law. 155 (1979). But see the 1996 statute concerning Coast Guard reports, supra note 107.

113. Fed. R. Evid. Rule 803 (8)(C).

114. Id. See, e.g., *In re American Export Lines, Inc.,* supra note 110, where testimony during a Coast Guard investigation was considered eligible for admissibility but decision was reserved on the issue of the unavailability of the witness.

CHAPTER THREE

INTERNATIONAL AND INLAND RULES: PART A—GENERAL PROVISIONS

Section A. Rule 1: Application of the Rules

The historical background of COLREGS and the Uniform Inland Rules is briefly outlined in chapter 1, section A. As there stated, COLREGS were adopted as the Convention on the International Regulations for Preventing Collisions,[1] signed in London on October 20, 1972. The convention entered into force on July 15, 1977, and implementing U.S. legislation—the International Navigational Rules Act of 1977[2]—was signed by the President on July 27.

Article VI of the convention provides machinery for amending COLREGS,[3] and section 3(c) of the International Navigational Rules Act[4] authorizes the president to proclaim any amendment to COLREGS adopted in accordance with Article VI of the convention, and to which the United States does not object. Section 3(d)[5] requires the president, upon receiving a proposed amendment, to notify Congress promptly, and Congress then has the right to disapprove the amendment. As stated in chapter 1, COLREGS were amended in 1983 and 1989, but the amendments were relatively minor in nature. Both sets of amendments have been incorporated into COLREGS and require no discussion independent of the discussion of the COLREGS rules and annexes to which they relate.

COLREGS Rule 1(a) is worded broadly enough to include not only the high seas but harbors, roadsteads, rivers, lakes, and inland waterways connected with them, if they are navigable by seagoing vessels. This provision is, however, qualified by Rule 1(b), which permits appropriate governmental authorities to make special rules for such local waters, conforming as closely as possible to COLREGS.

---

1. 28 U.S.T. 3459, T.I.A.S. 8587, as amended T.I.A.S. 10672, 6 *Benedict on Admiralty* 3–35 (7th ed. rev., F. Wiswall, Jr., editor-in-chief, volumes on *International Maritime Law Documents and Commentary*, hereinafter "Benedict").

2. Pub. L. No. 95-75, 91 Stat. 308; 33 U.S. Code §§ 1601–08.

3. Under art. VI any State party may propose an amendment to the International Maritime Organization (I.MO.). If I.M.O. approves the proposal, the Secretary General must submit it to the State Parties. The proposed amendment then enters into force on a date set by the I.M.O. Assembly, unless more than a third of the States notify the assembly that they object to the proposal.

4. Supra note 2, 33 U.S. Code § 1602(c).

5. Supra note 2, 33 U.S. Code § 1602(d).

In the United States the local rules currently in force are the Inland Navigation Rules ("Inland Rules"),[6] which replaced the old Inland, Great Lakes, and Western Rivers Rules. They were enacted December 24, 1980, and became effective one year later, except on the Great Lakes, where their effective date was March 1, 1983.[7] Inland Rule 1(b)(i) provides that the rules constitute special rules made by an appropriate authority (the U.S. Congress) within the meaning of COLREGS Rule 1(b).

COLREGS consist of thirty-eight rules, grouped in five parts: A, General; B, Steering and Sailing Rules; C, Lights and Shapes; D, Sound and Light Signals; and E, Exemptions.[8] Part B is divided into three subparts or sections: I, Conduct of Vessels in Any Condition of Visibility; II, Conduct of Vessels in Sight of One Another; and III, Conduct of Vessels in Restricted Visibility. The Inland Rules are grouped in the same manner.

There are four annexes to COLREGS: I, Positioning and Technical Details of Lights and Shapes; II, Additional Signals for Fishing Vessels Fishing in Close Proximity; III, Technical Details of Sound Signal Appliances; and IV, Distress Signals. There are five annexes to the Inland Rules. The first four concern the same subjects as the four COLREGS annexes. Annex V of the Inland Rules consists of several Pilot Rules. These include rules requiring the carriage of copies of the Inland Rules on board vessels of 12 tons or more,[9] permitting the lowering of lights and shapes in passing under bridges,[10] permitting the display of flashing blue lights by law-enforcement vessels,[11] and regulating the display of lights by barges in certain positions[12] and by dredge pipelines.[13]

In this text, the rules and annexes are generally discussed in order, but in a few instances related provisions are treated together, e.g., the safe speed requirement of Rule 19 (Conduct of Vessels in Restricted Visibility) is included in the discussion of Rule 6 (Safe Speed), paragraph (a)(i) of which provides that the state of visibility must be taken into account in determining the safe speed the rule requires of all vessels.

The Inland Rules are in most respects identical to the corresponding provisions of COLREGS; even the arrangement and numbering of the rules are the same, except that there is no Rule 28 in the Inland Rules. There are a few differences in the numbering and lettering of paragraphs and subpara-

---

6. Pub. L. No. 96-591, 94 Stat. 3415, § 7, 33 U.S. Code §§ 2001–38.

7. Fed. Reg. 15, 135, 15135, Apr. 8, 1982. See 33 U.S.C.A., historical note following § 2001.

8. COLREGS are set out in full in appendix 1, as are those Inland Rules which differ from COLREGS.

9. 33 C.F.R. § 88.05.

10. 33 C.F.R. § 88.09.

11. 33 C.F.R. § 88.11.

12. 33 C.F.R. § 88.13.

13. 33 C.F.R. § 88.15.

graphs of certain rules. The most important remaining differences between COLREGS and the Inland Rules lie with respect to the sound signals given in head-on, crossing, and overtaking situations. These and other differences are discussed in chapter 5 and chapter 8.

Rule 1(a) of the Inland Rules makes those rules applicable to all vessels upon the inland waters of the United States, and to U.S. vessels on the Canadian waters of the Great Lakes to the extent they do not conflict with Canadian law. Actually, there is no conflict; the U.S. Inland Rules, including the special provisions of Rules 14(d) and 15(b) applicable to vessels on the Great Lakes, are substantially identical in all pertinent respects to the Canadian Inland/Great Lakes Rules.[14]

The lines of demarcation between waters subject to the Inland Rules and waters where COLREGS apply have been established by the U.S. Coast Guard, and are set out in the Code of Federal Regulations.[15]

While the Inland Rules contain a number of special provisions with respect to lights, shapes, and other equipment, this presents no problem for either U.S. or foreign seagoing vessels using U.S. domestic waters, since Rule 1(b)(ii) provides that all vessels complying with the construction and equipment requirements of COLREGS are considered to be in compliance with the Inland Rules.

COLREGS Rule 1(c) recognizes the special requirements of ships of war, ships sailing in convoy, and fishing vessels fishing as a fleet. It therefore permits governments to adopt special rules with respect to lights, shapes and whistle signals for such vessels, but provides that so far as possible they must be such that they cannot be mistaken for any lights, shapes or signals authorized elsewhere under COLREGS.

Inland Rule 1(c) is substantially identical, except that it designates the Secretary of the Navy as the authority to provide for any special lights, shapes, and whistle signals for ships of war and vessels in convoy, and the secretary of the department in which the Coast Guard is operating (the Transportation Department in peacetime and the Navy Department in time of war) as the authority with respect to fishing vessels fishing in a fleet. Notice of such special rules must be published in the Federal Register, and once they come into force they have the same effect as the Inland Rules themselves.

COLREGS Annex II specifies additional signals for fishing vessels fishing in close proximity. Inland Rules Annex II is virtually identical. These signals are briefly discussed in chapter 8.

Pursuant to the authority granted in COLREGS Rule 1(d), the International Maritime Organization (I.M.O.) has adopted a number of traffic

14. See Canadian Modifications to the International Regulations for the Prevention of Collisions at Sea 1972, issued under the Canada Shipping Act. Section 9 contains the Canadian Inland/Great Lakes Rules, which are also published in Canadian Government Publication No. TP/10/39.

15. 33 CFR §§ 80.01–80.1705.

separation schemes for the purposes of the rules. Inland Rule 1(d) authorizes establishment of traffic separation schemes and warns that vessel traffic service regulations may be in effect in certain areas. Traffic separation schemes and service regulations are discussed in chapter 4, section G.

Section B. Rule 2: Responsibility

1. Good Seamanship

Rule 2(a) of COLREGS and the Inland Rules is commonly called the rule of good seamanship. A good seamanship rule was included as Article 24 in the U.S. Revised Rules enacted in 1885,[16] which applied to all U.S. vessels on the high seas and in coastal waters, except "such as [were] otherwise provided for." A similar rule was included as Article 29 in the International Rules adopted at the 1889 International Marine Conference,[17] and became effective in 1897.

Article 29 of the former Inland Rules,[18] Rule 28 of the 1895 Great Lakes Rules,[19] Rule 26 of the 1864 Western Rivers Rules,[20] and Rule 26 of the 1949 Western Rivers Rules[21] were all identical to Article 29 of the 1897 International Rules.

There was no substantial change in any of these rules until COLREGS became effective in 1977 and the Inland Navigation Rules replaced the former Inland and Western Rivers Rules in 1981 and the Great Lakes Rules in 1983. The language in former Article 29, "any neglect to carry lights or signals or of any neglect to keep a proper look-out," was replaced in COLREGS and Inland Rule 2(a) by the words "any neglect to comply with these Rules."

Under COLREGS the requirement of a proper look-out was made the subject of the positive mandate of a separate Rule (No. 5), for greater emphasis. There was therefore no need to mention the requirement in Rule 2(a). Rule 5 is treated in section B of chapter 4. Similarly, there was no need to mention failure to carry lights or signals, as these are specifically required by the rules of Part C (Lights and Shapes), which are discussed in chapter 7.

While Article 29 of the former International, Inland, Western Rivers, and Great Lakes Rules made no specific mention of excessive speed, and while former Rule 16, the only rule specifically requiring moderate speed, was applicable only in or near restricted visibility areas, vessels were held li-

---

16. 23 Stat. 438. The 1885 Rules are reprinted in J. Griffin, *The American Law of Collision,* at 811–21 (hereinafter "Griffin").

17. 26 Stat. 320, 33 U.S. Code §§ 61–147. The 1889 International Rules and the 1889 Inland Rules as amended to May 20, 1948 are set out in parallel columns in Griffin at 645–80.

18. 30 Stat. 96; 33 U.S. Code §§ 151–232.

19. Griffin 727–41.

20. Id. at 761–71.

21. Id. at 770–87.

able under Article 29 for damage caused by their excessive speed in crowded harbors.[22] Under COLREGS and the Inland Navigation Rules, such vessels are liable under Rule 6, which requires vessels to proceed at a safe speed at all times. A high rate of speed in crowded waters would be a clear violation of Rule 6, and there would therefore be no reason to invoke Rule 2(a).

While Rule 2(a) and its predecessors are worded negatively, they have from the beginning been interpreted as not only mandating compliance with the statutory rules, but as affirmatively requiring the exercise of good seamanship in other respects as well, i.e., "that degree of the skill and care which are ordinarily to be found in a competent seaman."[23] The rule of good seamanship is therefore in essence the basic rule applicable in negligence cases: one is liable in damages for the foreseeable consequences of a failure to use the care expected of those of one's calling, whatever that calling may be.

Since the rule is thus a restatement of the rule of the common law and the general maritime law, its necessity has been questioned. In referring to Article 29 of the former rules (the good seamanship rule), Marsden states: "It seems difficult to attribute to it any legal effect. It was inserted in the regulations, probably *ex abundante cautela,* and as a declaration, not to be overlooked by seamen, of the legal consequences of negligence."[24] Thus, an able-bodied seaman is expected to be able to steer as a competent able-bodied seaman should. But he is not expected to be able to plot a course, or perform any of the other functions of a licensed deck officer. A master mariner, on the other hand, is expected to be able to function with the skill of a competent master mariner.

The line between an error in judgment and a negligent act is a fine one, and is sometimes difficult to draw. An error in judgment such as might be made even by a competent seaman will generally be held excusable. Thus in *Hutton Co. v. Arrow Builders Supply Corp.,*[25] the Second Circuit Court of Appeals held that a barge captain's mistaken belief concerning the direction of the tide was an error in judgment for which the barge owner was not liable. On the other hand, it has been held that a vessel is liable for the consequences of a navigator's error in judgment, which a careful and prudent navigator would not have made.[26]

In referring to former Rule 29, Professors Gilmore and Black succinctly state:

---

22. See, e.g., *The George H. Jones,* 27 F.2d 665, 1928 AMC 1504 (2d Cir. 1928). Older cases are collected in Griffin at 581.

23. *The Llanover,* 78 Ll. L. Rep. 198 (H.L. 1945).

24. R. Marsden, *Collisions at Sea* 603 (11th ed., K. McGuffie, editor) (hereinafter "Marsden"), citing *The Queen Mary,* 82 Ll. L. Rep. 303, 341 (H.L. 1949), where Lord MacDermott stated: "In my opinion, it [Article 29 of the former International Rules] is not aimed at authorizing departure from the regulations, and I doubt if it is more than a solemn warning that compliance therewith does not terminate the ever present duty of using reasonable skill and care. "

25. 371 F.2d 944, 1967 AMC 934 (2d Cir. 1967). See also *Petition of Reading,* 121 F. Supp. 808, 1954 AMC 1848 (SDNY 1954).

26. *The Old Reliable,* 269 F. 725 (3d Cir. 1921).

"Negligence" at sea does not differ, in principle, from "negligence" ashore. It is an elastic and open-textured concept, defined as the correlative of the equally vague standard of "due care"; "good" or "prudent" seamanship sometimes appears as a synonym. Thus, when vessels pass in close quarters it seems that the suction generated sometimes causes the smaller vessel to move toward the larger, and collision is thus brought about; the standards of prudent navigation therefore require that speed be slackened, when necessary, to avoid this result, though the Rules say nothing about it.[27] (Citing *The Fontana,*[28] *The Potomac,*[29] and *Gulf Oil Corp. v. United States.*[30])

What is good seamanship is a question of fact to be decided upon consideration of all the relevant circumstances.[31] It is no more possible to visualize every act or omission of a master or crew member that could conceivably be held poor seamanship than it is to visualize every act or omission of a shoreside factory manager or his subordinates that might be found to constitute negligence. The following examples are by no means intended as an exhaustive list; they are simply given to illustrate some of the acts or omissions of a vessel which, under the prevailing conditions, have been found to constitute actionable negligence, i.e., a failure to exercise good seamanship:

Selecting an improper anchorage;[32]
In anchoring, failing to keep clear of vessels previously anchored;[33]
Failing to take into account the effect of shallow water on a vessel's ability to steer;[34]
Failing to take proper precautions while at anchor to avoid endangering other vessels anchored in the area, e.g., by letting out more chain, or dropping a second anchor if the conditions require it;[35]
In entering a slip, failing to diminish speed if there is doubt concerning the maneuvers of another vessel that is leaving the slip;[36]

---

27. Gilmore & Black, *The Law of Admiralty* 509–10 (2d ed.). This was written before COLREGS and the current Inland Rules entered into force. Rule 6 of each set of rules specifically requires vessels to proceed at safe speeds at all times.

28. 119 F.853 (6th Cir. 1903).

29. 105 F.2d 94, 1939 AMC 1296. (App. D.C. 1939).

30. 98 F. Supp. 988, 1951 AMC 2084 (SDNY 1951).

31. Marsden 603, citing *The Heranger* [1939] A.C. 94, 101; *The Queen Mary,* supra note 24, 82 Ll. L. Rep. at 334, and *The F.J. Wolfe,* [1945] P. 91, 97.

32. *The Persian,* 181 F. 439 (2d Cir. 1910); *The Hilton,* 213 F. 997 (ED Va. 1914).

33. *The Juniata,* 124 F. 861 (ED Va. 1903). The English decisions prior to 1961 are discussed in Marsden at 611–14.

34. *The Excelsior,* (1867) L.R. 2A. & E. 268; *The Christiana,* (1850) 7 Moo. P.C. 160; Marsden 614.

35. *The Fort George,* 183 F. 731 (2d Cir. 1910); *The Columbus,* 2 Mar. L. Cas. (O.S.) Dig. 730; *The Olympic—The Hawke,* [1913] P. 214.

36. *City of New York v. Morania No. 12, Inc.,* 357 F. Supp. 234, summarized, 1974 AMC 2155 (SDNY 1973).

Failure of a descending vessel to hold back at a bend when conditions indicate the necessity of holding back;[37]
Failing to observe due care in backing across a channel.[38]

2. *Special Circumstances*

The special circumstances rule is designed to apply in two general categories of navigational situations: (1) those not covered by the steering and sailing rules, and (2) those where the conditions are such that a departure from one or more of the other rules is not only permissible but mandatory.

In the first category fall special maneuvers, such as maneuvering in and out of slips, approaching and leaving piers, picking up and discharging pilots, and entering, maneuvering in, and leaving anchorages. Also included are situations where three or more vessels are involved, e.g., where Vessel A and Vessel B are meeting head and head and Vessel C is heading so as to cross A's bow from port to starboard and B's bow from starboard to port. In the first category also fall wartime conditions, when certain rules, e.g., those relating to navigational lights and sound signals, may have been suspended by the authorities.

The steering and sailing rules were obviously not designed for application to vessels maneuvering into and out of berths, coming to anchor or leaving an anchorage, or taking on or dropping pilots. Such situations plainly involve special circumstances, and Rule 2(b) is therefore applicable: vessels engaged in such maneuvers must navigate with "due regard . . . to all dangers of navigation and collision and to any special circumstances, including the limitations of the vessels involved . . . ."

Similarly, there is nothing in the rules regulating the conduct of three vessels that may find themselves in a situation where Vessel A is head to head with Vessel B but is the starboard-hand vessel in a crossing situation with Vessel C. The steering and sailing rules simply will not work in such a situation: if the rules applied, as between A and B, A would be obliged to alter course to starboard in order to pass B port to port, but as to C, A would be required to hold course and speed as the starboard-hand vessel. As between A and C, C, as the port-hand vessel, would be obliged to give way if the rules applied, but as between B and C, C, as the starboard hand vessel, would be obliged to keep course and speed. Only B would be permitted to maneuver in substantially the same way with respect to both of the other vessels. As to A, B should alter course to starboard to pass A port to port, and as to C she should keep out of C's way, which would normally be done by altering course to starboard and coming up under C's stern. It is plain that this would be a situation of special

---

37. *The Talabot* (1890) 15 P.D. 194; *Farwell's Rules of the Nautical Road* 221–22 (7th ed., R. Smith, ed.) (hereinafter "Farwell").

38. *The Sicilian Prince,* 128 F. 133 (SDNY 1904), aff'd, 144 F.951 (2d Cir. 1905).

circumstances in which the three vessels involved would have to work out a solution apart from the steering and sailing rules.[39]

If in wartime the authorities were to direct vessels in convoy to sail blacked out, and to refrain from employing the sound signals normally required by COLREGS when vessels are altering course, or backing, this would create a situation of special circumstances. The COLREGS provisions governing lights and sound signals would not apply, and each vessel in the convoy would be bound to do whatever she could to avoid collision under the difficult conditions thus created.[40]

Still another situation for which the steering and sailing rules do not provide is one involving a disabled vessel. Thus, in *Tiger Shipping Co. v. The Carville,*[41] a collier collided with an empty barge in tow of a tug which was attempting to seek shelter from adverse winds and heavy seas by entering Hampton Roads. The weather conditions made it impossible for the tug to shorten her 1,200 foot hawser by more than 150 or 200 feet, although Pilot Rule 84.10, then in force, required shortening to 450 feet or less. The hawser became fouled and the tug and tow thereupon became unmaneuverable until the crew could clear the foul. While the tug was held partially at fault for the subsequent collision on other grounds, her inability to comply with Pilot Rule 84.10 was excused. After quoting the special circumstances rule (then Rule 27 of the Inland Rules), the court said:

> The weather, which made the shortening of the hawser before entering Hampton Roads impossible, may properly be construed as such a special circumstance permitting noncompliance with the rule providing for the shortening of hawsers, particularly since the *Carville* attempted to comply as soon as the situation made it possible.[42]

A departure from the steering and sailing rules necessitated by special circumstances is not only perfectly proper, but a failure to make the departure is in fact a violation of the special circumstances rule, and therefore an actionable wrong.[43] However, the special circumstances rule has been narrowly construed. If a vessel departs from the steering and sailing rules the burden is on her to prove that special circumstances made the departure necessary.[44] The special circumstances rule will not excuse a departure from one or more of the other rules merely because the navigator considers it better to maneuver in some way other than in accordance with their

---

39. *The C.R. Hoyt,* 136 F.671 (D N.J. 1905); *The B.S. Ford,* 1937 AMC 603 (ED Va. 1937). See Farwell 231–32.

40. *Thurlow v. United States,* 295 F.905 (D Mass. 1924).

41. 381 F. Supp. 1340, 1974 AMC 1957 (ED Va. 1974).

42. 381 F. Supp. at 1344, 1974 AMC at 1963.

43. See *The Mauch Chunk,* 154 F. 182 (2d Cir. 1907).

44. *Zim Israel Nav. Co. v. The American Press,* 222 F. Supp. 947, 1964 AMC 1008 (SDNY 1963), aff'd, 336 F.2d 150, 1964 AMC 2537 (2d Cir. 1964).

provisions.[45] The Supreme Court explained the special circumstances rule in *Belden v. Chase*:[46]

> [W]hile under Rule twenty-four [the predecessor of COLREGS Rule 2(b) then in force], in construing and obeying the rules, due regard must be had to all dangers of navigation and to any special circumstances which may exist in any particular case, rendering a departure from them necessary in order to avoid immediate danger, the burden of proof lies on the party alleging that he was justified in such departure. *The Agra,* L.R. 1 P.C. 501; *The General Lee,* Irish L.R. 3 Eq. 155. Indeed, in *The Agra,* it was ruled that not only must it be shown that the departure at the time it took place was necessary in order to avoid immediate danger, but also that the course adopted was reasonably calculated to avoid that danger.

The two principal situations falling into the second category of cases where the special circumstances rule applies are *in extremis* cases and cases where one vessel proposes a maneuver which is contrary to the steering and sailing rules and the other consents.

An example of an *in extremis* situation mandating application of the special circumstances rule is one where Vessel A and Vessel B are meeting head on, and instead of turning to starboard as required by COLREGS Rule 14, Vessel A turns to port. If Vessel B were then to follow Rule 14 and turn to starboard, a collision would be likely to occur. The situation is therefore one of special circumstances requiring a departure by B from the Rule 14 requirement to turn to starboard. B must instead take whatever action appears best suited to avoid collision. Depending on the particular circumstances, this may be maintaining course and speed, or backing, or turning to port.[47]

An example of a special circumstances situation created by an agreement to a maneuver which is contrary to the steering and sailing rules is one where the port-hand vessel in a crossing situation proposes, without any valid reason, that she cross ahead of the starboard-hand vessel, and the latter consents.[48] Such a departure from the starboard-hand rule creates a special circumstance requiring each vessel to take whatever steps may be necessary to avoid a collision. It should be mentioned that if a collision nevertheless occurs it will be virtually impossible for either vessel to meet her *Pennsylvania* Rule burden of proving that the violation could not have caused or contributed to the collision.[49]

---

45. *Board of Commissioners v. The Farmsum,* 1975 AMC 2100 (ED La. 1975).
46. 150 U.S. 674, 699 (1893).
47. See *The Bywell Castle,* L.R. 4 Prob. Div. 219 (C.A. 1879).
48. *The Newburgh,* 273 F. 436 (2d Cir. 1921). However, there are instances where a valid reason exists for a starboard-hand vessel to give way, e.g., to a tug on the port hand with a tandem tow and a strong tide under foot.
49. *The Newburgh,* supra note 48.

Section C. Rule 3: General Definitions

Twelve definitions are contained in COLREGS Rule 3, while Inland Rule 3 contains seventeen. There is no definition in the Inland Rules corresponding to the definition of "vessel constrained by her draft" contained in paragraph (h) of COLREGS Rule 3. There was no need to include the definition in the Inland Rules, because those rules contain no provision similar to that found in paragraph (d)(i) of COLREGS Rule 18. That paragraph, which is discussed in chapter 5, provides that a vessel other than one not under command or restricted in her ability to maneuver must, if the circumstances admit, avoid impeding the safe passage of a vessel "constrained by her draft," exhibiting the signals prescribed in Rule 28 (three all-round red lights in a vertical line by night or a cylinder by day).

The definitions contained in paragraphs (a) to (g) of both sets of rules are identical, except for an immaterial difference in phraseology between paragraph (g) of COLREGS Rule 3 and paragraph (g) of Inland Rule 3. Because the Inland Rules omit the definition of a vessel constrained by her draft found in paragraph (h) of COLREGS Rule 3, the paragraphs of Inland Rule 3 corresponding to paragraphs (i), (j), (k), and (l) of COLREGS are lettered, respectively, (h), (i), (j), and (k) in the Inland Rules. The contents of these paragraphs in each set of rules are identical.

The definition of "vessel" in paragraph (a) is similar to the definition contained in Rule 1(c)(i) of the 1960 International Rules, and to the statutory definition contained in 1 U.S.C. section 3,[50] except that after "water craft," it adds "including nondisplacement craft and seaplanes." The inclusion of "nondisplacement craft" was of course intended to make it clear that hydrofoils and hovercraft are to be treated under the rules in the same manner as more conventional vessels.

Paragraph (e) defines "seaplane" as including any aircraft designed to maneuver on the water.

Paragraphs (b), (c), (d), (f), (g), and (h) of COLREGS and paragraphs (b), (c), (d), (e), (f), and (g) of the Inland Rules all define either types of vessels, the activities in which they are engaged, or their condition at the relevant times. Thus, a "power-driven" vessel is one propelled by machinery (paragraph [b]), and a "sailing vessel" is one under sail and whose propelling machinery, if any, is not being used (paragraph [a]).

A "vessel engaged in fishing" is one fishing with nets, lines, trawls, or other apparatus restricting maneuverability; excluded from the definition are vessels fishing with trolling lines or any other apparatus that does not restrict maneuverability (paragraph [d]).

---

50. "The word 'vessel' includes every description of watercraft or other artificial contrivance used, or capable of being used, as a means of transportation on water."

A vessel "not under command" is one which through exceptional circumstances is unable to maneuver as required by the rules and therefore is unable to keep out of the way of other vessels (paragraph [d]). Likewise, paragraph (g) defines a "vessel restricted in her ability to maneuver" as one which from the nature of her work is restricted in her ability to maneuver as required by the rules and is therefore unable to keep out of the way of other vessels. The paragraph then lists six examples of activities restricting a vessel's ability to maneuver, stating that the list is not exclusive: (i) laying, servicing, or picking up a navigation mark, submarine cable, or pipeline; (ii) dredging, surveying, or engaging in underwater operations; (iii) replenishing or transferring persons, provisions, or cargo while underway; (iv) engaging in the launching or recovery of aircraft; (v) performing mine clearing operations, and (vi) performing towing operations that severely restrict the ability of the tug and tow to deviate from their course.

Paragraph (h) of COLREGS Rule 3 defines a "vessel constrained by her draft" as a power-driven vessel severely restricted in her ability to deviate from her course because of her draft relative to the available depth and width of navigable water.

Paragraphs (i), (k), and (l) of COLREGS Rule 3 and paragraphs (h), (j), and (k) of Inland Rule 3 are similar to the corresponding provisions of the former rules, except that paragraph (i) of COLREGS Rule 3 and paragraph (k) of Inland Rule 3 specifically include "sandstorms" among the conditions which may cause visibility to be restricted, the others being "fog, mist, falling snow, heavy rainstorms," and "any other similar causes."

COLREGS Rule 3(i) and Inland Rule 3(h) define "underway" as meaning that a vessel is not at anchor, or made fast to the shore, or aground. COLREGS Rule 3(j) and Inland Rule 3(l) define a vessel's "length" and "breadth" as meaning her length overall and her greatest breadth. COLREGS Rule 3(k) and Inland Rule 3(j) provide that vessels shall be deemed in sight of one another only when one can be observed visually from the other.

Paragraphs (l) to (q) of Inland Rule 3 have no counterpart in COLREGS, as they relate to domestic waters subject to the Inland Rules. Paragraph (l) defines "Western Rivers" as including (1) the Mississippi and its tributaries; (2) South Pass and Southwest Pass to the demarcation lines dividing the high seas from harbors, rivers, and other U.S. inland waters; (3) the Port Allen–Morgan City Alternate Route; and (4) that part of the Atchafalaya River above its junction with the Port Allen–Morgan City Alternate Route, including the Old River and the Red River.

Under paragraph (n), "Great Lakes" means (1) the lakes and their connecting and tributary waters, including specified portions of the Calumet and Chicago Rivers; and (2) the St. Lawrence River as far east as the lower exit of the St. Lambert Lock.

Paragraph (n) specifies that references in the Inland Rules to "Secretary" are to the secretary of the department in which the Coast Guard is operating, i.e., the Transportation Department in peacetime, and the Navy Department in time of war.

"Inland Waters" are defined in paragraph (o) as meaning (1) the navigable waters of the United States shoreward of the navigational demarcation lines; and (2) Great Lakes waters on the U.S. side of the International Boundary.

Under paragraph (p) references to "Inland Rules" or "Rules" are to the Inland Navigational Rules and their annexes, governing the conduct of vessels and the lights, shapes, and sound signals that apply on inland waters.

Finally, paragraph (q) provides that references to "International Regulations" in the Inland Rules are to the International Regulations for Preventing Collisions at Sea, 1972 [i.e., COLREGS], including the annexes currently in force in the United States.

CHAPTER FOUR

INTERNATIONAL AND INLAND RULES: PART B(I)—CONDUCT OF VESSELS IN ANY CONDITION OF VISIBILITY

Section A. Introduction

1. The Scope of the Chapter

This chapter concerns Rules 4–10, which constitute Section/Subpart I of Part B (the Steering and Sailing Rules), governing vessels in any condition of visibility. Rules 11–18, constituting Section/Subpart II, applicable to vessels in sight of one another, are treated in chapter 5, and Rule 19, the only rule in Section/Subpart III (relating to vessels in restricted visibility), is discussed in chapter 6, except that the safe speed mandate of Rule 19(b) is discussed in section C of this chapter in conjunction with the safe speed requirements of Rule 6.

Rule 4 (Application) paraphrases the title of Section/Subpart I; it simply reiterates that the rules in the section/subpart apply in any condition of visibility. Rule 5 (Look-out) is discussed in section B below; Rule 6 (Safe Speed) in section C; Rule 7 (Risk of Collision) in section D; Rule 8 (Action to Avoid Collision) in section E; Rule 9 (Narrow Channels) in section F; and Rule 10 (Traffic Separation Schemes) in section G.

Rules 4, 5, 6, and 7 of COLREGS and the correspondingly numbered Inland Rules are identical. The differences between COLREGS Rules 8, 9, and 10 and Inland Rules 8, 9, and 10 will be treated in their respective sections.

2. Electronic Aids to Navigation

Because electronic aids to navigation play such a significant role in the application of the rules discussed in this and certain of the following chapters, the authors consider it best to start with a brief examination of three of the more important developments of the past fifty years in this area. These are radar, ARPA (automatic radar plotting aid), and electronic charts.

a. Radar. A detailed explanation of the way in which radar functions is beyond the scope of this text and the technical competence of the authors. For the brief outline that follows they are indebted to a number of authorities.[1]

1. These include Medina, Ct. J., in *The Burgan—The Bergechief,* 274 F.2d 469, 473–74, 1960 AMC 1380 (2d Cir. 1960); U.S. Maritime Administration, *Radar Instruction Manual* (1978);

"Radar" is an acronym for "radio detecting and ranging." Marine radar equipment consists of a revolving antenna, erected high above a vessel's hull, wired to a radar console on the bridge. The core of the console is a cathode ray tube, the top of which forms a screen much like a television screen. The inner side of the screen is coated with phosphorus, so that it glows when struck by a cathode "gun" in the base of the tube.

When the radar is operated, a narrow beam of ultrahigh-frequency radio waves is transmitted by the antenna as it revolves. If the waves strike another vessel or some other solid object, an echo is returned to the transmitting vessel, where it appears as a small spot of light, or "pip," on the radar screen. The screen is calibrated in degrees, so that the relative bearing of an object that the waves strike can be readily observed. The screen also contains a number of concentric rings, the space between each representing a certain distance from the transmitting vessel which, except in the case of "true motion" radar, is always represented by the center of the screen.

By means of controls on the panel of the console, the range can be quickly changed. Thus, in the open sea the range may be set at 20 miles or more, but may be reduced to 10 miles after an observed vessel comes within that range, to 5 miles when she comes within a 5-mile range, and so on.

The pip appearing on the screen when the waves strike another object does not disappear immediately as the antenna revolves, but leaves an afterglow, or "contrail," which outlasts several revolutions, so that the pip remains on the screen and its position changes if either or both the observing vessel and the observed object (assuming it is a vessel) are underway, with way on.

While the principles of radar were discovered well before the Second World War, it was during that conflict that it was developed to the extent that it could be used effectively to detect the presence of enemy vessels in the area. It was kept highly secret, and only when the war ended did it become available for merchant vessels. Until then there was no feasible way for such vessels to detect the presence of other vessels hidden from view by fog or similar conditions until their fog signals could be heard. Radar made it possible to detect the presence of other vessels well before hearing their fog signals.

The Third Conference on Safety of Life at Sea, held in London in 1948, was the first to consider the effect of radar on marine navigation. While the delegates considered proposals to make changes in the rules so as to allow

---

R. Slack & P. Whittle, *Marine Radar Accidents;* F. Wylie, *The Use of Radar at Sea* (5th rev. ed. 1978); A. Martinez, *Marine Radar: A Proposal for Mandatory Usage,* 11 J. Mar. L. & Com. 109 (1970); F. Flyntz, *Radar Plotting : A Developing Requirement of Good Seamanship,* 14 J. Mar. L. & Com. 581 (1983); J. Meadows, *The Radar Annex and Rule 16 of the Regulations for Preventing Collisions at Sea, 1960, as They Affect Navigation in Restricted Visibility,* 5 Willamette L. J. 399 (1969); F. Coughlin, *Radar and the Rules of the Road,* 7 Proceedings of the Merchant Marine Council, U.S. Coast Guard, 102 (1975); T. Murphy, *The Legal Implications of Marine Radar,* 7 J. Mar. L. & Com. 573 (1976); D. Jacobsen, *Technology and Liability,* 51 Tulane L. Rev. 1075 (1977); R. Deschauer, Jr., *Radar and the 1972 Collision Regulations,* unpublished student note, New York University School of Law, 1978.

for radar, the proposals were discarded, and the only mention of the new navigational aid was in a resolution which formed no part of the rules:

> The Conference, while recognizing that the recent advances in radar and electronic navigational aids are of great service to shipping, is of the opinion that the possession of any such device in no way relieves the master of a ship from his obligation strictly to observe the requirements laid down in the international regulations for preventing collisions at sea, and in particular, the obligations contained in articles 15 and 16 of those regulations.[2]

Radar was again considered at the 1960 Safety of Life at Sea (SOLAS) Conference, and this time changes in the rules were adopted which took radar into account, although only with respect to navigation in restricted visibility.[3] A definition (ix) was included in Rule 1 (c) making it clear that vessels were to be considered in sight of one another only when one could be observed visually from the other. Thus, the "fog rules" (15 and 16 of the 1960 Rules) were to apply even if other vessels were observable by radar.

The same concept was followed in a preliminary note to the Steering and Sailing Rules (17–27 of the 1960 Rules), which provided that the rules governing end-on, crossing, and overtaking situations (17–24) were to apply only to vessels in sight of one another.

The 1960 Rules contained a "preliminary" note to the fog rules, reading:

> 1. The possession of information obtained from radar does not relieve any vessel of the obligation of conforming strictly with the Rules and, in particular, the obligations contained in Rules 15 and 16.
> 2. The Annex to the Rules contains recommendations intended to assist in the use of radar as an aid to avoiding collision in restricted visibility.

The Radar Annex referred to in the preliminary note was largely advisory in nature. It consisted of eight "Recommendations on the use of radar information as an aid to avoiding collisions at sea." Among other things, it warned that assumptions should not be made on scanty information; that it was essential to make sure that action to avoid a close-quarters situation was having the desired effect; that an alteration of course might be the most effective action to avoid close-quarters; that alterations of course to starboard were generally preferable, particularly when vessels were apparently

---

2. Recommendation No. 19 of the 1948 International Convention for the Safety of Life at Sea (SOLAS), U.S. Dept. of State Pub. No. 3282, 1953 AMC at 83.

3. The changes relating to radar adopted at the 1960 SOLAS Conference are outlined in N. Healy, *Radar and the New Collision Regulations,* 37 Tulane L. Rev. 621, 625–26 (1963). For a summary of all the changes effected by the rules adopted at the conference see Magennis, *International Regulations for Preventing Collisions at Sea as Revised at the 1960 SOLAS Conference,* 14 The JAG Journal 25 (1960).

approaching on opposite or nearly opposite courses; that alterations of course should be substantial, and that if a close-quarters situation was imminent, the most prudent action might be to take all way off the vessel.

The third and fourth "recommendations" contained in the annex read:

> (3) When navigating in restricted visibility the radar range and bearing alone do not constitute ascertainment of the position of the other vessel under Rule 16(b) sufficiently to relieve a vessel of the duty to stop her engines and navigate with caution when a fog signal is heard forward of the beam.
>
> (4) When action has been taken under Rule 16(c) to avoid a close quarters situation, it is essential to make sure that such action is having the desired effect. Alterations of course or speed or both are matters as to which the mariner must be guided by the circumstances of the case.

The former Inland, Western Rivers, and Great Lakes Rules made no mention of radar. The current Inland Rules relating to radar—5 (Lookout), 6 (Safe Speed), 7 (Risk of Collision), and 19 (Conduct of Vessels in Restricted Visibility)—either specifically or inferentially are identical to the correspondingly numbered COLREGS Rules.

b. ARPA. "ARPA" is the acronym for "automatic radar plotting aid." Its use was foreseen in COLREGS Rule 7(b) in the words, ". . . radar plotting or equivalent systematic observation of detected objects." ARPA uses a computer that has been integrated with the radar to process and store information for presentation of the data on the screen in order to track targets, to determine the course and speed of the targets, and, most important, to determine the closest point of approach (CPA) of a target and the observer's vessel and the time it will take to reach the CPA. ARPA makes unnecessary the use of a maneuvering board or a grease-pencil plot on the face of the radar screen. But ARPA, an integrated part of the radar system, cannot eliminate the risk of collision at sea. In high-density traffic, however, such as the English Channel, under conditions of restricted visibility, ARPA becomes an essential tool in the effort to avoid collision.

One expert has graphically described ARPA as follows:

> Boiled down to its essentials, an ARPA consists of a basic radar coupled to a computer. It may combine the two units in a single package or may be purchased as an "add-on" to an existing radar installation. By analyzing data obtained from the source radar, it is able to display the course and speed of other vessels, assess risk of collision, alert the watch officer to the presence of on-coming traffic, calculate precisely any deviation from course due to wind or tide, display graphically what heading to steer in order to avoid other vessels by a specific safety margin and can provide

> graphic features called tracklines defining traffic separation zones or areas of danger. It even provides a crystal ball in the form of a Trial Maneuver function. In this mode, the watch officer may ask the computer to predict the outcome of an intended maneuver in terms of passing distance from other vessels or navigational hazards. Obviously, an ARPA adds a level of technical sophistication to the art of problem solving which is far beyond that of mere basic radar.[4]

In re Waterstand Marine Ltd. (The Seapride II)[5] contains a good explanation of the practical use of ARPA as a navigational aid. A vessel struck and demolished an electrical tower while proceeding in dense fog at an excessive rate of speed. Among the faults for which the vessel's owners were held liable was the master's failure to use any of the computerized plotting features of the vessel's ARPA. Among the sixty-five findings of fact were the following:

> 42. At all material times, the ARPA was being used as a radar. None of the ARPA's computerized functions had been implemented or employed.
> 43. The ARPA's features, had they been used, would have permitted the *Seapride*'s navigators to determine the following:
> (a) Own vessel's course and speed instantaneously.
> (b) Instantaneous determination of own vessel's position in 1, 2, 3 or more minutes in reference to own ship's vector or projected line of travel.
> (c) Set forth the location and future activity of all acquired targets for continuous observation.
> (d) Identified any or all stationary targets for continuous reference.
> 44. The ship's heading, had it been supplemented with a vector as provided by the ARPA, would have indicated the vessel's location in 1, 2, 3 minutes or any other selected period of time at a glance.

4. S. M. Van Wyck's paper, entitled *"ARPA: Radar's Replacement. (If You Believe the Ads),"* is contained in the Transcript of the Maritime Law Association's Fall 1989 Seminar. See also R. Chernyaev, *Impact of ARPA Limitations on Collision Avoidance,* Seaways, Feb. 1989, at p. 13; and O'Sullivan, *Know Your ARPA,* Safety at Sea, Feb. 1989, p. 17; and National Research Council, *Charting a Course into the Digital Era, Guidance for NOAA's Nautical Charting Mission* (1994).

5. 1991 AMC 1785 (ED Pa. 1988). Additional cases dealing with ARPA are: *Cliffs-Neddrill Turnkey International Oranjestad v. The Rich Duke,* 947 F.2d 83, 1992 AMC 1 (3d Cir. 1991); *Dahlia Maritime Co., Ltd. v. The Nordic Challenger,* 1994 AMC 2208 (ED La. 1993); *Seacarriers Maritime Co. v. The Stolt Jade,* 823 F. Supp. 1311, 1994 AMC 191 (ED La. 1993); *Elenson v. The Forteleza,* 1992 AMC 1447 (SDNY 1991); *Deutsche Shell Tanker GmBH v. Placid Refining Co.,* 767 F. Supp. 762, 1992 AMC 196 (ED La. 1991) aff'd, 993 F.2d 466, 1993 AMC 2141 (5th Cir. 1993); *In re G&G Shipping Co. Ltd. of Anguilla,* 767 F. Supp. 398, 1994 AMC 170 (D P.R. 1991); and *In re Ocean Foods Boat Co.,* 692 F. Supp. 1253, 1989 AMC 579 (D Or. 1988).

> 45. Any fixed or moving targets acquired by the ARPA would have had their relative vectors instantaneously displayed so that a moving vessel, such as the *Seapride,* would have a continued visual presentation of where its projected path would carry it both as to direction and time and whether any risk of collision was involved.
> 46. The true vector displayed from a moving target would have given an immediate indication as to just where the target and own vessel would be at designated time intervals so that danger of collision or contact would be immediately apparent.
> 47. In other words, the computerized data information base would have provided the *Seapride*'s navigators with sufficient knowledge at all times to ascertain the best course and speed solution to avoid both the approaching target and the tower.
> 48. Within a minute after the target was acquired, the ARPA would have begun providing the *Seapride*'s navigators with usable information as to the target's course and speed. Such information would have been updated constantly so that the *Seapride*'s navigators could take appropriate avoiding action.
> 49. If the *Seapride*'s navigators had been making use of the ARPA, they would have known they were proceeding at a speed in excess of that estimated as they entered a low visibility situation and approached a turn in the river which required that they remain within the confines of the ship channel. . . .
> 52. The *Seapride*'s master and the pilot had not been trained in the proper use of Racal/Decca ARPA with which the *Seapride* was equipped. . . .
> 59. The owners and managers failed completely to provide necessary and effective guidance or instructions to the *Seapride*'s master and crew in the use of the ARPA. Further, the vessel's owners/managers did not require that the vessel's master be qualified on ARPA before employment.[6]

The court concluded that the collision was caused by failure to use the full capabilities of the vessel's ARPA, as well as by failure to maintain a proper lookout, proceeding at excessive speed, and failure to sound fog signals. Further, the court denied limitation of liability because of the failure of the vessel's management to train the master sufficiently in the use of ARPA.[7]

---

6. 1991 AMC at 1789–91.

7. 1991 AMC at 1800–01. See also *The Tug Ocean Prince v. United States,* 584 F.2d 1151, 1978 AMC 1786 (2d Cir. 1978).

While *Waterstand Marine* is concerned with collision fault, the consequence of improper use of ARPA in a cargo damage action should be considered. Equipping the vessel with ARPA does not satisfy the nondelegable duty to render the vessel seaworthy; furnishing personnel trained in ARPA before and at the beginning of the voyage would be required. For analogous

The International Maritime Organization (I.M.O.)[8] made the use of ARPA mandatory on new-building vessels of 10,000 gross tons if the keel was laid after September 1, 1984, but retrofitting of ARPA was required on existing tankers in a descending schedule in accordance with size. Thus, tankers of 40,000 gross tons or more were to be fitted with ARPA by January 1, 1985, while existing tankers were to be so fitted by January 1, 1986. Existing merchant ships other than tankers were not required to be retrofitted until large tankers had been dealt with. Thus, existing ships of 40,000 or more gross tons were to be fitted with ARPA by September 1, 1986; ships of 20,000 or more gross tons by September 1, 1987, and ships of 15,000 or more gross tons by September 1, 1988. Vessels fitted with noncomplying ARPA systems could be "grandfathered" until January 1, 1991, when conformity with I.M.O. ARPA standards was required.

c. The Electronic Chart. The electronic chart is *not* simply the electronic display of the contents of the paper chart. Rather, it is an entirely new system for navigation, in that it combines satellite technology, data processing, and information technology with the traditional paper chart so that mariners can plan and monitor their vessel's route in a real-time navigational system.

The basic requirements of paper charts, prepared before development of electronic charting systems, were set forth in the 1974 SOLAS Convention,[9] mandating that adequate and up-to-date charts necessary for the intended voyage be carried by all ships. From the late 1970s, the various components of electronic charting were developed and integrated into several competing systems, but the I.M.O., working with the International Hydrographic Office, prepared standards for a single form of electronic chart, the ECDIS (Electronic Chart Display and Information System), over a ten-year period.[10]

---

case law on the necessity for properly trained and qualified personnel to meet the standards of due diligence, see *The Maria,* 91 F.2d 819, 1937 AMC 934 (4th Cir. 1937); *Horn v. Cia. de Navegacion Fruco,* 404 F.2d 422, 1968 AMC 2548 (5th Cir. 1968); *Matter of Ta Chi Navigation (Panama), S.A.,* 513 F. Supp. 148, 1981 AMC 2350 (ED La. 1981), aff'd, 728 F.2d 699, 1984 AMC 2408 (5th Cir. 1984); *Sunkist Growers v. Adelaide Shipping Lines, Ltd.,* 603 F.2d 1327, 1979 AMC 2787 (9th Cir. 1979); *In re Delphinus Maritime, S.A.,* 523 F. Supp. 583, 1981 AMC 2362 (SDNY 1981); *In re Texaco, Inc.,* 570 F. Supp. 1272, 1985 AMC 1650 (ED La. 1983); and *In re Armatur, S.A.,* 710 F. Supp. 390, 1990 AMC 557 (D P.R. 1988).

8. I.M.O. Resolution A 422 (XI).

9. 1974 Safety of Life at Sea Convention, 32 U.S.T. 47, T.I.A.S. 9700, Chapter V, Regulation 20: "All ships shall carry adequate and up-to-date charts, sailing directions, lists of lights, notices to mariners, tide tables and all other nautical publications for the intended voyage." As of 1997 no reported case had considered whether ECDIS is the equivalent of the paper charts described in Regulation 20.

10. I.M.O. Maritime Safety Committee's Performance Standards for Electronic Chart Display and Information Systems (ECDIS), were adopted by the I.M.O. Assembly in the fall of 1995 (I.M.O. Resolution A.817 [XIX]). See generally, L. Alexander & F. Ganjon, *ECDIS: Current Status/Future Expectations,* Sea Technology, March 1995.

The ECDIS system provides a color display component with computer processing of its digital database and navigational sensor inputs from both outside the ship (such as from the U.S. Department of Defense GPS [Global Positioning Satellites] and the U.S. Coast Guard's Differential Global Positioning Services [DGPS] and Loran C) and also from shipboard sources such as the ship's gyrocompass, radar or ARPA, and depth finder. Other information can be added, such as currents, tides, visibility, locations of other vessels, and the presence of ice and other obstructions. The system provides a standard display and permits changes of scale. The ship's own position can be symbolized or shown in true scale and can operate in true motion display (the ship's symbol moving across the chart), or in relative motion display (the ship's symbol stationary and the charted elements moving).

The equivalent of the "black box" or in-flight data recorder of the aviation industry is achieved through the voyage recording capabilities of ECDIS that presumably cannot be tampered with or manipulated after the fact. Human ingenuity is such, however, that this aspect of ECDIS must be constantly challenged and analyzed. At one-minute intervals ECDIS records the ship's own track, position, heading, speed, and time, along with a record of the source, edition, date, and updating of the electronic navigational chart that was used. In addition to the 12-hour reconstruction, ECDIS records the complete track for the entire voyage, marked off by 4-hour periods.

Respecting potential tort liability[11] for inputs to ECDIS it must be noted that a 1994 statute[12] immunizes the U.S. National Imagery and Mapping Agency (NIMA—formerly the Defense Mapping Agency) from liability for any map, chart, or publication prepared or disseminated by it. This immunity cannot conceal the fact that the basic paper chart to which electronic inputs are made may be the cause of casualties, especially groundings where ECDIS is used, because of the great age of the surveys upon which the nauti-

---

11. Cartographers and their publishers have been held liable to users for damages caused by justifiable reliance on negligent chart-making. See *De Bardeleben Marine Corp. v. United States,* 463 F.2d 208 (10th Cir. 1972) (aeronautical chart); *EmpireTransport, Inc. v. United States,* 524 F.2d 1, 1975 AMC 1926 (2d Cir. 1975) (Defense Mapping Agency); *Southern Natural Gas Co. v. United States,* 711 F.2d 1251 (5th Cir. 1983) (National Oceanic and Atmospheric Administration). Cf. the Canadian decision in *Warwick Shipping Ltd. v. The Queen,* [1982] 2 F.C. 147, aff'd, 48 N.M.R. 378 (1983) (no proof of reliance on misleading chart and no duty of care to individual mariners). See Mukherjee, *The Charting and Safekeeping of Oceans and Waterways: Legal Implications,* 6 Dalhouise L.J. 578 (1981). See also *Inter-Cities Navigation Corp. v. United States,* 608 F.2d 1079, 1980 AMC 2831 (5th Cir. 1979); Troop, *The Legal Liability of the Chartmaker,* 62 International Hydrographic Review, 1 (1985).

12. 10 U.S.C. § 456 (Pub. L. No. 103 - 337, Div. A, Title X, § 1074(b), "Civil Actions Barred," enacted Oct. 5, 1994, and codified as 10 U.S.C. § 2798, renumbered and amended in 1996, provides:

> (a) Claims barred.—No civil action may be brought against the United States on the basis of the content of a navigational aid prepared or disseminated by the National Imagery and Mapping Agency.
>
> (b) Navigational Aids Covered.—Subsection (a) applies with respect to a navigational aid in the form of a map, a chart, or a publication and any other form or me-

cal chart may have been based.[13] (For example, some admiralty charts of South American waters still use the surveys conducted by the voyage of HMS *Beagle* on which Charles Darwin sailed from 1831 to 1836.) While certain U.S. government departments, notably the National Oceanic and Atmospheric Administration (NOAA) and the Coast Guard, are not covered by the 1994 statute, it is possible that the discretionary function exception of the Federal Tort Claims Act may be extended to protect government departments other than NIMA.[14] The 1994 statute does *not* presently immunize the *private* manufacturer of paper charts and components for negligently furnished errors in ECDIS.[15]

It can be assumed that the electronic chart will eventually be required on merchant vessels; as of 1996 the U.S. Navy was installing ECDIS in major combat ships and it is likely to be required soon on very large tankers. While the

---

dium of project or information in which the National Imagery and Mapping Agency prepares or disseminates navigational aids.

Section 1074(d) of Pub. L. No. 103-337 provides:

Effective Date.—§ 2798 of title 10, United States Code, as added by subsection (b), shall take effect on the date of the enactment of this Act and shall apply with respect to (1) civil actions brought before such date that are pending adjudication on such date, and (2) civil actions brought on or after such date.

In *Hyundai Merchant Marine Co. v. United States,* 888 F. Supp. 543, 1995 AMC 2391 (SDNY 1995), aff'd on opinion below, 75 F.3d 134, 1996 AMC 683 (2d Cir. 1996), a shipowner sued the United States in 1989 under the Suits in Admiralty Act, 46 U.S.C. app. §§ 741–52, for negligent failure to update an inaccurate nautical chart produced by the Defense Mapping Agency (DMA). DMA Chart 24271 of the coast of Brazil (13th ed., April 1983) did not accurately indicate the position of a shoal on which the *M/V Hyundai New World* went aground at Baia de Sao Marcos in November 1987 and became a total loss. Although DMA had received notices from the Brazilian and British governments indicating water depths lower than those charted, no U.S. Notice to Mariners was published prior to the grounding. Plaintiffs argued that the statutory language did not immunize DMA for failure to issue corrective notices, but merely for the content of its navigational aids. The argument was rejected as semantic, on the ground that Congress intended to immunize DMA from suits because of reliance on DMA products. Plaintiffs further argued that application of the statute retroactively to an action commenced more than five years before its enactment was unconstitutional, but this argument was also rejected.

13. See, e.g., National Transportation Safety Board, Marine Accident Report, Grounding of the U.K. Passenger Vessel RMS *Queen Elizabeth II* near Cuttyhunk Island, Vineyard Sound, Massachusetts, Aug. 7, 1992 (1993). Surveys made in 1939 were the most recent surveys on which charts in use 54 years later were based.

14. *In re Glacier Bay,* 71 F.3d. 1447, 1996 AMC 379 (9th Cir. 1995). The discretionary exception of the Federal Tort Claims Act, 28 U.S.C. § 2671(a), has been interpreted as applicable to the Suits in Admiralty Act, 46 U.S.C. app. § 741–52. See *Williams v. United States,* 747 F.2d 700 (11th Cir. 1984).

15. The leading cases deal with aeronautical charts. See *Saloomy v. Jeppesen,* 707 F.2d 671 (2d Cir. 1983) (negligence); *Brockelsby v. Jeppesen,* 753 F.2d 794 (9th Cir. 1985) (strict product liability). See also McCowan, *IFR—The Liability of the Chart Maker,* 44 J. Air L. & Comm. 375 (1979).

The question of the First Amendment on the chilling effect of strict product liability has not yet been tested. See, however, *Jones v. J.B. Lippincott Co.,* 694 F.Supp. 1216 (D Md.

system is costly (in 1996, cost exceeded $200,000) it is likely that owners and insurers will determine that the enhanced safety features outweigh any negative factors, so that "retrofitting" of ECDIS on merchant vessels may become a condition of vessel seaworthiness in the new century. As is the case with radar and ARPA, it can be expected that watchstanding officers will be required to be adequately trained in the operation of ECDIS to evidence due diligence to make the vessel seaworthy and properly manned.

Section B. Rule 5: Look-out

1. *Preliminary Note*

Rule 5 of COLREGS and the Inland Rules requires *every* vessel *at all times* to "maintain a proper look-out by sight and hearing as well as by all means appropriate in the prevailing circumstances and conditions so as to make a full appraisal of the situation and of the risk of collision."

The word "look-out" is not defined in that rule or elsewhere in the rules. However, Rule 3(k) of COLREGS and Rule 3(j) of the Inland Rules provide that "Vessels shall be deemed to be in sight of one another only when one can be observed visually from the other," which makes it abundantly clear that the phrase "by sight" used in Rule 5 refers to visual observations and not to observations by radar or other electronic means.

It will be noted that "look-out" is hyphenated in Rule 5. *The Oxford Universal Dictionary* gives two spellings of the word—one with and one without the hyphen. *Webster's New Universal Unabridged Dictionary*, on the other hand, spells it only without the hyphen. "Lookout," or "look-out," has several dictionary definitions, the two pertinent to a discussion of Rule 5 being (1) "a careful looking or watching for any person or thing," and (2) "a person detailed to watch."[16] It is plain that in the context in which it appears in Rule 5 "look-out" refers to the act of looking or watching, and not to the person who performs the act. Following the spelling of the word in Rule 5, in this text the word will be hyphenated when used to denote the act. To differentiate between the act and the person who performs the act, the word will be spelled without the hyphen when it is used to designate the person, except that in quotations the original spelling will be followed.

1988), where the publisher of a medical textbook was held not strictly liable to a nursing student who was injured by following instructions in the book which were incorrect, since liability based on mere publication would be inconsistent with fundamental free speech principles, citing *Gertz v. Robert Welch, Inc.*, 418 U.S. 323 (1974), which concerned defamation and invasion of privacy.

16. These are the *Webster's New Universal Unabridged Dictionary* definitions. Similar definitions are contained in the *Oxford Universal Dictionary*. Cf. *The Santander*, [1966] 2 Lloyd's Rep. 77, where Wilmer, J., described a look-out as "appreciation of what is taking place."

2. *Historical Overview*

The requirement of maintaining a proper look-out was statutorily recognized in the United States at least as far back as 1885, when Congress enacted the Revised International Rules and Regulations for Preventing Collisions at Sea, applicable to U.S. vessels on the high seas and on inland waters, "except such as [were] otherwise provided for."[17] Article 24 of those rules (the "Good Seamanship" Rule) provided, *inter alia,* that "Nothing in these rules shall exonerate any ship, or the owner, or master, or crew thereof, from the consequences of . . . any neglect to keep a proper lookout." Similar provisions were contained in Article 29 of the International Rules[18] and the U.S. Inland Rules effective in 1897.[19] These provisions remained substantially unchanged until COLREGS went into effect in 1977 and the Inland Navigation Rules became effective on inland waters other than the Great Lakes in 1981, and on the Lakes in 1983.

Rule 5 is the first statutory rule affirmatively mandating the maintenance of a proper look-out; the earlier rules simply recognized that duty as part of the general maritime law obligation of good seamanship, although the importance of the obligation had long been recognized by the courts. Thus, in *Delaware, L. & W. R. Co. v. Central R. Co. of New Jersey,*[20] Judge Ward said: "The fundamental rule of the admiralty is that a vigilant lookout must be kept on all vessels, so that collision may be prevented even with those which are violating the rules." Because cases decided prior to the respective effective dates of the current rules were based on the general maritime law and not on a positive statutory rule, they present certain problems that may no longer be relevant, and caution should therefore be used in citing some of the older cases as precedents.

3. *Rule 5 and Related Provisions*

When radar was first used on merchant vessels following World War II, there was some speculation that radar observations might under some circumstances be accepted as a substitute for the maintenance of a visual look-out. However, the courts in Canada, the United States, and the United Kingdom soon made it clear that no such substitution would be tolerated.[21] Rule 5

17. 23 Stat. 438, reprinted in J. Griffin, *The American Law of Collision* 811–21 (hereinafter "Griffin").

18. 26 Stat. 320.

19. 30 Stat. 96. The Inland Rules and the International Rules effective in 1897 are reprinted in parallel columns in Griffin at 645–77.

20. 238 F. 657, 660 (2d Cir. 1916). See also *Hosei Kaiun Shoji Co. v. The Seaspan Monarch,* 1981 AMC 2162 2179 (D Or. 1980), where Judge Burns stated that "The duty to maintain a proper lookout is perhaps the first rule of safe navigation . . . ."

21. *The Triton—The Baranof* [1963] Can. Exch. 74; *The Bucentaur—The Wilson Victory,* 125 F. Supp. 42, 1955 AMC 142 (SDNY 1954); *The Anna Salen,* [1954] 1 Lloyd's Rep. 475 (Adm.), 566 F. Supp. 962, 1983 AMC 2409 (MD Fla. 1983), aff'd, 761 F.2d 1558 (11th Cir. 1985).

continues the same thought, in specifically requiring the maintenance of a look-out "by sight and hearing," as well as "by all available means appropriate in the prevailing circumstances and conditions. . . ." That the drafters of Rule 5 had radar primarily in mind in using the term "by all available means" is clear from the parallel use of the term in paragraph (a) of Rule 7 (Risk of Collision) and the addition of the specific language of paragraph (b) of that rule requiring the proper use of radar equipment, if fitted and operational, to obtain early warning of risk of collision.

Rule 5 thus mandates the maintenance of a proper look-out in two ways: (1) "by sight and hearing," and (2) "by all available means in the prevailing circumstances and conditions," e.g., radar.

The discussion in this section will be limited to the main thrust of Rule 5, i.e., the required maintenance of a look-out "by sight and hearing." So much of the rule as relates to the use of other "available means," will be treated in the discussion of Rule 7 in section D of this chapter.

Closely related to Rule 5 are the 1978 International Convention on Standards of Training, Certification and Watchstanding for Seafarers,[22] which was drafted by the International Maritime Organization (I.M.O.), and the I.M.O.'s 1995 STCW Code, annexed to the Convention. Tables A-II/IV of the STCW Code govern the maintenance of a proper look-out. Certain of its provisions will be discussed *infra.*

4. *Applicability of Rule 5*

Griffin notes cases decided while Article 29 of the former rules was in force, requiring sailing vessels, tugs, hawser tows, ferryboats, and small vessels as well as large to maintain look-outs.[23] Rule 5 leaves no doubt about the vessels to which the rule's requirement of the maintenance of a proper look-out applies: it is applicable to *every* vessel.

Under Article 29 the maintenance of a look-out adequate for the prevailing conditions was required even in daylight in clear weather, while at night, or in restricted visibility areas, or in congested waters, special vigilance was required.[24] Again, Rule 5 leaves no doubt about when a proper look-out is man-

---

22. 6C Benedict, Doc. 14-6. As of 1996 the convention (hereinafter called "Convention on Standards of Training, Certification, and Watchkeeping") had been adopted by 110 States, including the United States, which ratified it on July 1, 1991. The pertinent portions of the convention and the recommendations are reprinted in appendix 4.

23. Griffin 264–65.

24. Id. 265–66, citing, *inter alia, The Oregon,* 158 U.S. 186, 193 (1895) (darkness); *The Sagamore,* 247 F. 243, 255 (1st Cir. 1917) (fog); *The Transfer No. 17,* 254 F. 673 (2d Cir. 1918) (congested waters).

datory: the rule specifically provides that one must be maintained *at all times.*[25]

However, that *every* vessel must *at all times* maintain a proper look-out by sight and hearing is not to say that on every vessel, regardless of type or size, and regardless of the prevailing circumstances, a look-out must be kept by a member of the crew specially designated as a lookout for the watch, and having no other duties. Thus, the I.M.O. Recommendations annexed to the Convention on Standards of Training, Certification, and Watchkeeping[26] would permit the assignment of other duties as long as they did not interfere with the keeping of a proper look-out. They would also permit the helmsman to serve as lookout in a small ship, if there was an unobstructed all-round view at the steering position and there was no impairment of night vision or other impediment. Finally, the recommendations would permit the officer of the watch to act as sole lookout in daylight, provided it was safe to do so, full account had been taken of all relevant factors, and assistance was immediately available if any change in the situation required it.

5. *Legal Effect of a Failure to Maintain a Proper Look-out*

As discussed in chapter 2, despite frequent criticism, the *Pennsylvania* Rule[27] is still applied by U.S. courts.[28] Since former Article 29 brought a failure to maintain a proper look-out within the looser concepts of "neglect," "lack of ordinary prudence of seamen," and "special circumstances," rather than a positive statutory mandate that a proper look-out must be maintained by every vessel at all times, this gave rise to the question as to whether or not the failure to maintain a proper look-out should be treated as a statutory violation subject to the *Pennsylvania* Rule.

---

25. In *Cliffs-Neddrill Turnkey International Oranjestad v. The Rich Duke,* 947 F.2d 83, 89, 1992 AMC 1, 11 (3d Cir. 1991), the court held that "The unambiguous dictates of Rule 5" required the maintenance of a proper look-out on anchored vessels, as well as on vessels under way. Griffin notes that most of the cases decided under the former rules held that a lookout was required on an anchored vessel, but that a failure to maintain one was frequently found to be a noncontributing fault, since nothing a lookout could have done would have averted the collision. Griffin 267.

In *Granholm v. The TFL Express,* 576 F. Supp. 435, 1984 AMC 943 (SDNY 1984), Judge Haight held that a single-handed sailing yacht was 50 percent to blame under Rule 5 for a high-seas collision with a containership because her operator had gone below to take his rest at night, rather than during daylight hours, when the yacht would have been more visible to other vessels.

26. See appendix 4.

27. *The Pennsylvania,* 86 U.S. 125 (1874).

28. See the remarks of the Second Circuit in *The Tug Ocean Prince, Inc. v. United States,* 584 F.2d 1151, 1978 AMC 1786 (2d Cir. 1978), to the effect that the vitality of the *Pennsylvania* Rule was not affected by the Supreme Court's *Reliable Transfer* decision, 421 U.S. 397, 1975 AMC 541 (1975). It reversed the district court, which had concluded that the failure of a tug to post a lookout was not the cause of a stranding. The Second Circuit held the tug owner at fault, since it had not demonstrated that the failure to maintain a proper look-out could not have contributed to the casualty. See also *California v. The Ilice,* 534 F.2d 836, 1976 AMC 2290 (9th Cir. 1976); *Atlantic Mut. Ins. Co. v. ABC Ins. Co.,* 645 F.2d 528, 1982 AMC 2405 (5th Cir. 1981); W. Peck, *The Pennsylvania Rule Since Reliable Transfer,* 15 J. Mar. L. & Com. 95 (1984).

The Second Circuit stated the burden of exoneration where a proper look-out was not kept to be an affirmative showing that if there had been a lookout, and he had done his duty in seeing and reporting other vessels, and the navigation had been in conformity with the information thus obtained, the collision would have happened nevertheless.[29] In another Second-Circuit case, Judge Learned Hand explained that the requirement of maintaining a proper look-out was so stringent that the consequences of a failure were the same as if it were a positive statutory obligation.[30] Other decisions in the Second and other circuits stated the principle rigidly, although the decisions were invariably based on facts considered to be inexcusable.[31]

The Fourth Circuit was the clearest voice in holding that under the former rules a failure to maintain a proper look-out was not a statutory fault to be visited with "the extreme consequences" of the *Pennsylvania* Rule.[32] Opinions in other circuits, where excusable facts may have been present, also derogated from the rule's heavy burden.[33] However, some courts which rejected the *Pennsylvania* Rule's consequences[34] did so on the basis of the major-minor fault rule.[35] As discussed in chapter 1, that rule originated as a reaction to the even harsher consequences of the equal division of damages

---

29. *The Anna W.,* 201 F. 58 (2d Cir. 1912). The burden was described as heavy in *The George W. Roby,* 111 F. 601 (6th Cir. 1902). But see *Otto Marmet Coal Co. v. Fieger Co.,* 259 F. 435 (6th Cir. 1919).

30. *The Madison,* 250 F. 850 (2d Cir. 1918). See also his statement in *Ulster v. Matton No. 20,* 210 F.2d 106, 1954 AMC 426 (2d Cir. 1953), affirming 109 F. Supp. 581, 1953 AMC 451 (EDNY 1953).

31. *The Russell Poling No. 29–The Corporal,* 252 F.2d 167, 1958 AMC 1093 (2d Cir. 1958), affirming 151 F. Supp. 11, 1957 AMC 1275; *The Burgan—The Bergechief,* 274 F.2d 469, 1960 AMC 1380 (2d Cir. 1960), affirming 170 F. Supp. 893, 1960 AMC 98 (SDNY 1959); *United States v. The J.A. Cobb,* 283 F.2d 754, 1960 AMC 2318 (2d Cir. 1960), affirming 182 F. Supp. 234, 1959 AMC 2277 (SDNY 1959). See also *First National Bank v. Material Services Corp.,* 544 F.2d 911, 1978 AMC 193 (7th Cir. 1976); *In re Ta Chi Nav. (Panama) Corp.,* 513 F. Supp. 148, 1981 AMC 271 (ED La. 1980), aff'd, 728 F.2d 699, 1984 AMC 2408 (mem.) (5th Cir. 1984); *Allied Chemical Co. v. Hess Tankship Corp.,* 661 F.2d 1044, 1982 AMC 1271 (5th Cir. 1981); *The Weyerhaeuser Steamship Co. v. United States (The Pacific),* 174 F. Supp. 663, 1959 AMC 1869 (ND Cal. 1959).

32. *Anthony v. International Paper Co.,* 289 F.2d 574, 1961 AMC 1890 (4th Cir. 1961); *Tiger Shipping Co. v. The Tug Carville,* 381 F. Supp. 1340, 1974 AMC 1957 (ED Va. 1974).

33. See *The Martha Anne—The Ceara,* 328 F.2d 66, 1964 AMC 2331 (5th Cir. 1964), where the Fifth Circuit said the *Pennsylvania* Rule must not be interpreted too narrowly. (One vessel sheered into another at a distance of 300 feet.) See also *The Sea Wolf—The Miss Judy,* 444 F.2d 514, 1971 AMC 1968 (9th Cir. 1971), where the Ninth Circuit said that the duty to maintain a look-out was not a duty under any and all circumstances. The court held that a fishing vessel, dead in the water on the high seas, fully lighted in a flat calm, on a clear night with good visibility, was not at fault for failing to maintain a look-out.

34. *The Star of Honduras—The Queenston Heights,* 220 F.2d 120, 1955 AMC 797 (5th Cir. 1955), modifying 121 F. Supp. 280, 1954 AMC 1395 (ED La. 1954). See also *Koch-Ellis v. Chemical Barge Lines, Inc.,* 224 F.2d 115, 1955 AMC 1536 (5th Cir. 1955), reversing 128 F. Supp. 89, 1955 AMC 356 (ED La. 1954), where a decree of divided damages was reversed because the failure to have a lookout on the lead barge was described as "technical," in the face of gross faults of the other vessel (a tug) passing in a canal.

35. *The City of New York,* 147 U.S. 72, 85 (1893).

rule and has been rendered obsolete by the Supreme Court's decision in *Reliable Transfer,* adopting the proportional fault rule.[36]

In any event, the requirement of a proper look-out is now a positive statutory mandate, and as long as the *Pennsylvania* Rule retains validity, it will be applied to a violation of Rule 5: to obtain exoneration from liability for collision damage a vessel in violation of the rule has the burden of proving that the violation could not have contributed to the collision.[37]

6. *Noncontributory Failure to Maintain a Proper Look-out*

The same court that decided *The Pennsylvania*[38] interpreted it in the next term in *The Sea Gull,*[39] in which the court found that the absence of a lookout could not have contributed, and therefore it was not a causative fault; it appeared that "the other vessel was seen by the officer of the deck in season to adopt every needful precaution, and that the want of a lookout or his failure to perform his duty as such [lookout] did not and could not have contributed to the disaster."

The argument made in these noncontributory cases is that either the bridge (i.e., the navigating officer or other officer with the conn) already possessed all of the information that a proper lookout could have given, or that the vessel was not required to take action (because it was a "privileged" [holding-on] vessel), or that the navigational errors of the other vessel were so egregious that a lookout would not have helped.

a. Where There Is Adequate Knowledge on the Bridge. A classic demonstration of the noncontributory failure to maintain a proper look-out can be found, to the embarrassment of the U.S. Navy, in the *Darby—Soya* collision.[40] In that case an untrained "lookout" failed to warn of the presence of another vessel, but the captain, who was standing on the crowded bridge of his vessel, coming out of Norfolk for a Naval Reserve training cruise, observed the risk of collision with binoculars and by the naked eye before it was too late to take proper action to avoid the collision. This and similar cases have involved either direct testimony that the situation constituting risk of collision had at least been *observed* on the bridge, if not appreciated as giving rise to a risk of collision, for some minutes before the collision occurred.[41] A lookout is not

36. Supra note 28.

37. *Trinidad Corp. v. The Keiyoh Maru,* 845 F.2d 818, 1989 AMC 627 (9th Cir. 1988); *Elenson v. The Fortaleza,* 1992 AMC 1447 (SDNY 1991); *In re Delphinus Maritima, S.A. (The Mari Boeing),* 523 F. Supp. 583, 1981 AMC 2362 (SDNY 1981).

38. Supra note 27.

39. 90 U.S. 165, 176 (1874).

40. *The Darby—The Soya,* 330 F.2d 732, 1964 AMC 898 (4th Cir. 1964), affirming 213 F. Supp. 7, 1963 AMC 1 (D Md. 1963).

41. *The Dexter,* 90 U.S. 69 (1875); *The Victory,* 168 U.S. 410 (1897); *Moran T. & T. Co. v. Connors-Standard Marine Corp.,* 285 F.2d 368, 1961 AMC 383 (2d Cir. 1961), affirming 189 F. Supp.

required to *interpret* the sights and sounds that he reports,[42] and a failure to report what has also been seen by the navigator is therefore noncausative.

b. Where No Action Is Required. In these cases the vessel which is not maintaining a proper look-out was one considered "privileged" because of status (e.g., a sailing vessel)[43] or position (e.g., the starboard-hand vessel in a crossing situation).[44] In a number of early cases cited in Griffin[45] the holding-on vessel's failure to maintain a proper look-out was excused as noncontributory, on the theory that no action on her part was required. However, in more recent decisions, including *The Devonian*[46] and *The J.W. Wonson—The Osceola,*[47] the holding-on vessel was held at fault.

Judge Lowell observed in *The Devonian:*

> . . .[T]he privileged vessel has no right to keep her course with her eyes shut. The rule requiring a lookout is imposed alike upon the burdened and privileged vessel. The duty of the privileged vessel is to hold her course; the duty of the burdened vessel is to keep off that course. But the privileged vessel is to hold her course, constantly observing the burdened vessel, in order to notice if the latter fails in her duty.

Under Rule 17 of COLREGS and the current Inland Rules, discussed in chapter 5, if it becomes apparent that the port-hand vessel is failing in her duty of giving way, the starboard-hand vessel may take action to avoid collision; if she finds herself so close that collision cannot be avoided by action of the give-way vessel alone, she *must* take such action. Furthermore, Rule 34(d) requires a danger signal of five or more short, rapid blasts when in doubt

---

955, 1960 AMC 1855 (SDNY 1960); *The Barge Dykes—The Dredge Essayons,* 302 F.2d 264, 1962 AMC 1208 (2d Cir. 1962), affirming 1961 AMC 1606 (SDNY 1961); *The Urubamba—The Tug Coot,* 171 F. Supp. 735, 1959 AMC 2505 (SDNY 1959); *The Pentelikon—The Verdi,* 312 F. Supp. 489, 1970 AMC 1134 (SDNY 1970), reversed on other grounds, 438 F.2d 854, 1971 AMC 584 (2d Cir. 1971); *The Red Star v. The Catherine,* 305 F. Supp. 639, 1971 AMC 1770 (SDNY 1969), aff'd, 431 F.2d 641, 1971 AMC 1778 (2d Cir. 1970); *The Atlas Maru—The Elene,* 301 F.2d 59, 1962 AMC 1043 (4th Cir. 1962), modifying 190 F. Supp. 201, 1961 AMC 242 (D Md. 1961); *The Michalakis—The Shadwell,* 178 F. Supp. 33, 1959 AMC 1254 (ED Va. 1959); *The Steel Designer—The Virginia,* 310 F. Supp. 775, 1970 AMC 761 (D Md. 1970), aff'd, 438 F.2d 535, 1971 AMC 1326 (mem.) (4th Cir. 1971); *The Union Reliance—The Berean,* 364 F.2d 769, 1966 AMC 1653 (5th Cir. 1966), affirming 222 F. Supp. 874, 1965 AMC 901 (SD Tex. 1963); *The Marine Leopard—The Howard Olson,* 152 F. Supp. 197, 1957 AMC 2477 (ND Cal. 1957), aff'd, 279 F.2d 662, 1960 AMC 1230 (9th Cir. 1960).

42. See *The Madison,* supra note 30.

43. See Rule 20 of the former rules, Rule 18 of COLREGS and the current Inland Rules.

44. See Rule 21 of the former rules, Rule 17 of COLREGS and the current Inland Rules.

45. *The Bermuda,* 17 F. 397 (SDNY 1883); *The Clarion,* 27 F. 128 (ED Mich. 1886); *The Havana,* 54 F. 411 (D Conn. 1893); *The Gadsby,* 120 F. 851 (EDNY 1902); *The Fannie Hayden,* 137 F. 280 (D Maine 1905); *The Pocomoke,* 150 F. 193 (ED Va. 1906); *The Anna W,* 181 F. 604 (EDNY 1910); *The Haida,* 191 F. 623 (SDNY 1911), aff'd, 196 F. 1005 (2d Cir. 1912); *The Norfolk,* 297 F. 251 (D Md. 1924); *The Eelbeck,* 1925 AMC 1631 (SDNY 1925).

46. 110 F. 588 (D Mass.1901).

47. 239 F. 857 (2d Cir. 1917).

whether sufficient action is being taken by an approaching vessel. It is plain that these rules cannot be complied with if a holding-on vessel is not maintaining a proper look-out.

Contrast the holding-on situation with the situation presented in *The Lynn—The Ventura,*[48] a true case where no action was required, involving a fishing vessel trawling on the high seas off Boston when she was struck and sunk by an overtaking tanker. The court found that even if there had been a lookout on the trawler who might have heard and reported the overtaking signal, the trawler should not have been navigated any differently than she was in fact navigated.

c. Egregious Navigational Errors of the Other Vessel. It is possible that under Rule 5 courts may continue to find the absence of a lookout to be non-contributory in cases where the navigational errors of the other vessel can be categorized as gross negligence.[49] Doubt about the continued validity of such a finding comes from the relation of this exception to the discarding of the major-minor fault rule, whereby courts would close their eyes to a minor statutory fault of one vessel in the face of gross faults on the part of the other vessel. In view of *Reliable Transfer*[50] a court may instead assess a small proportion of the blame to the vessel failing to maintain a proper look-out.

7. Maintenance of a Proper Look-out

The case law on this subject under former Article 29 and the few cases decided under Rule 5 as of the time of writing will be examined in accordance with the following principles: (a) the lookout must be competent; (b) the lookout must be vigilant; (c) the lookout must ordinarily have no other duties; (d) the lookout must be properly positioned; (e) the lookout must report sights and sounds to the bridge.

a. Competence.

- *Training.* Lookouts are required to be trained mariners of sufficient age and experience[51] who have been carefully instructed in their duties.[52] This requirement can be illustrated by a U.S. Navy case in which the court stated that an untrained

---

48. 225 F.2d 280, 1955 AMC 1968 (1st Cir. 1955), affirming 130 F. Supp. 176, 1955 AMC 320 (D Mass. 1954).

49. *The Schmidt Barge,* 475 F.2d 428, 1973 AMC 1053 (7th Cir. 1973).

50. Supra note 28.

51. *The Volund,* 181 F. 643 (2d Cir. 1910); *Commonwealth and Dominion Line v. United States,* 1925 AMC 1575 (EDNY 1925); *The Chagres,* 63 F. Supp. 948, 1945 AMC 1435 (SDNY 1944).

52. *The Hawaiian,* 38 F. Supp. 574, 1941 AMC 710 (D Md. 1941), aff'd, 124 F.2d 45, 1942 AMC 84 (4th Cir. 1942).

and inexperienced new recruit was unqualified to act as a lookout,[53] although the importance of the case is reduced by the conclusion that the failure was noncontributory. This does not mean that all noncommercial U.S. flag vessels must use as lookouts only personnel certificated by the Coast Guard: a mature person, knowledgeable about small craft and carefully instructed as to what to look for, is a proper lookout on a pleasure boat.[54] Respecting commercial vessels, where there are statutory manning levels of licensed and certificated seamen, no decision has yet permitted the performance of look-out duties by other than trained and experienced watchstanders.

- *Eyesight.* While perfect 20-20 eyesight may be required for naval officers of the line, what eyesight is required for lookouts on commercial vessels and pleasure craft is not defined, except that it must be "good."[55] One court has held that colorblindness does not disqualify a seafarer from serving as lookout,[56] stating that it is a defect that does not in any way impair one's ability to see objects or lights. Even with perfect eyesight, however, a watchstander at night who has not adapted his eyes to the darkened conditions is not a proper lookout.[57]
- *Hearing.* Traditionally, the hearing ability of mariners has not been checked as carefully (by audiologists using audiometrical equipment) as eyesight, and it is not yet possible to predict

Convention on Standards of Training, Certification, and Watchkeeping, amended annex, Ch. II, Reg. II/4 prescribes the minimum requirements for "ratings," i.e., unlicensed seafarers, forming part of a navigational watch. The regulation provides that on seagoing ships of 500 or more gross tons they must be not less than 16 years of age, of satisfactory medical fitness, particularly regarding eyesight and hearing, have completed not less than six months approved sea experience and not less than two months special training, and according to STCW Code, Ch. II, Sec. A-II/4, must be able "to keep a proper look-out by sight and hearing and report the approximate bearing of a sound signal, light or other object in degrees or points."

53. *United States v. The Malden (The Malden—The Gearing),* 224 F. Supp. 705, 1964 AMC 1108 (ED Va. 1964) aff'd, 341 F.2d 292 (4th Cir. 1965). See also *The Esso Balboa—The Mobilgas,* 155 F. Supp. 699, 1957 AMC 1898 (SDNY 1957), aff'd, 253 F.2d 758, 1958 AMC 830 (2d Cir. 1958), where members of a Navy gun crew, trained in gunnery but not in seamanship, were held unqualified to act as lookouts on a merchant ship.

54. See *Granholm v. The TFL Express,* supra note 25.

55. *The Avon,* 22 F. 905 (ND Ill. 1885). As stated, Regulation II/4 annexed to the Convention on Standards of Training, Certification, and Watchkeeping for Seafarers (see supra note 52) simply provides, *inter alia,* that a seafarer forming part of a navigational watch must have "satisfactory medical fitness, particularly regarding eyesight and hearing," and must be able to keep a proper look-out "by sight and hearing."

56. *Reading Co., Inc. v. Pope & Talbot, Inc. (The Waltham Victory—The Carfloat No. 23),* 192 F. Supp. 663, 1961 AMC 681 (ED Pa. 1961), aff'd, 295 F.2d 40 (3d Cir. 1961).

57. *The Whitehurst—The Hoyanger,* 265 F. Supp. 730, 1967 AMC 1047 (WD Wash. 1967).

how the general standard of aural acuity may be regulated in the future.[58]

b. Vigilance. Constant observation by the lookout through the senses of sight and hearing is required.[59] Momentary inattention to sights and sounds will result in collision liability unless the vessel can meet the heavy burden of showing noncontribution.[60] Needless to say, the absence of the lookout while washing his hands,[61] running an errand,[62] getting a cup of coffee,[63] or coiling a rope[64] will not excuse the failure to maintain a vigilant look-out. When a lookout leaves his position for any length of time he must be replaced;[65] even fear of imminent death will not excuse a failure to report.[66] Distraction caused by a spectacular sight, such as flaming gas on an oil production platform is, of course, no excuse for inattention.[67]

c. Performance of Other Duties. Chief Justice Taney described a proper lookout as one "... exclusively employed in watching the movements of vessels...,"[68] with "... no other duties to perform...."[69] Accordingly, prior to the adoption of the Convention on Standards of Training, Certification and Watchkeeping[70] it was held that on commercial vessels, neither the

---

58. See *Granholm v. The TFL Express,* supra note 25.

In *The Johs. Stove—The Kerkedyk,* 286 F. Supp. 69, 1968 AMC 2012 (SDNY 1968), the court held that a lookout's inability to hear fog signals over the noise of jet aircraft taking off and landing did not disqualify him as a proper lookout.

59. *The Sagamore,* supra note 24, describing the lookout as "the eyes and ears of the ship"; *Jett v. Texas Co.,* 73 F. Supp. 699, 1948 AMC 973 (D Del. 1947). In *The Australia Star—The Hindoo,* 172 F.2d 472, 1949 AMC 423 (2d Cir. 1949), the lookout spotted a mysterious green light which the bridge could not understand. The court held that he was not a proper lookout, since he failed to see and report the range lights.

60. *First National Bank v. Material Services,* 544 F.2d 911, 1978 AMC 193 (7th Cir. 1976); *Moran v. City of New York,* 620 F.2d 356, 1980 AMC 1414 (2d Cir. 1980).

61. *The Norwich Victory v. The Dump Scows 116, 120, 122,* 175 F.2d 556, 1949 AMC 2040 (3d Cir. 1949), affirming 77 F. Supp. 264, 1948 AMC 879 (ED Va. 1948).

62. *First National Bank v. Material Services Corp.,* supra note 31.

63. *The Norwich Victory v. The Dump Scows 116, 120, 122,* supra note 61.

64. *The Celtic—The Patriotic,* 85 F. Supp. 813, 1949 AMC 559 (SDNY 1949).

65. *The Glenville—The Drilling Platform B,* 210 F. Supp. 865, 1962 AMC 2311 (SD Tex. 1962); *The Stifinder,* 275 F. 271 (2d Cir. 1921).

66. *The Charles Kurz—The Rodas,* 80 F. Supp. 587, 1948 AMC 2042 (SDNY 1948). The bow lookout on a tanker spotted a vessel 500 yards ahead, crossing so as to involve risk of collision and, fearing an explosion, ran from his post to awaken the crew, without reporting the sighting to the bridge. Because the navigators on the bridge saw the other vessel at the same time and ordered full astern, the failure of the lookout to report was held noncontributory.

67. *The Willowpool—The Platform 199-2,* 214 F. Supp. 449, 1963 AMC 635 (ED Tex. 1963).

68. *The Gennessee Chief,* 53 U.S. 443, 462 (1852).

69. *Chamberlain v. Ward,* 62 U.S. 548, 571 (1859). See also *United States v. The Holland,* 151 F. Supp. 772, 1957 AMC 1322 (D Md. 1957); *Sun Oil Co. v. The Georgel,* 245 F. Supp. 537, 1966 AMC 662 (SDNY 1965), aff'd, 369 F.2d 406, 1967 AMC 1689 (mem.) (2d Cir. 1966).

70. See appendix 4 H.

helmsman[71] nor the navigating officer of the watch[72] nor the pilot[73] could be considered as a lookout, and that no seaman expected to perform ordinary tasks could properly be assigned additional service as lookout at the same time.[74] Pleasure craft or small boats customarily navigated by one person are not expected to have a lookout with no other duties.[75] As we have seen, the I.M.O. Recommendations annexed to the convention would permit the watch officer to act as lookout during daylight hours, in clear weather, and would also permit the helmsman on a small ship to act as lookout under certain specified conditions.

d. Proper Position of a Lookout. A lookout's position at the bow ("the eyes of the ship"), as far forward as possible and as near the surface of the water as practical, is the best location for sight and sound observation and reporting to the bridge.[76] Interpreting the look-out requirement under the ordinary practices of seamen in Article 29 of the former rules, the First Circuit said that while the broad general rule does not spell out under what circumstances a look-out must be kept, nevertheless a look-out must be maintained in every direction from which danger may reasonably be expected to arise.[77]

Given the construction of most merchant ships, with the navigational "island" amidships or aft, a lookout stationed on the bridge (either in the pilothouse itself or on one of the "wings") is generally deemed improperly

71. *The Pilot Boy,* 115 F. 873 (4th Cir. 1902); *The Atlantic Trader—The Steel Designer,* 1970 AMC 1371 (CD Cal. 1970); *The Orion,* 26 F.2d 603, 1928 AMC 1044 (1st Cir. 1928).

72. *The Atlantic Trader—The Steel Designer,* supra note 71; *The J.G. Gilchrist,* 183 F. 105 (2d Cir. 1910).

73. *The Atlas Maru—The Elene,* supra note 41; *United States v. The Holland,* supra note 69.

74. *The Otco—The Bayway,* 194 F. Supp. 920, 1961 AMC 420 (SDNY 1960), aff'd, 297 F.2d 367, 1962 AMC 389 (2d Cir. 1962). Nevertheless, the faulty look-out was found to be noncontributory. See generally *The Colorado,* 91 U.S. 692, 699 (1876); *The Arkansan,* 112 F.2d 223, 1940 AMC 889 (9th Cir. 1940); *The Supply No. 4,* 109 F.2d 101, 1940 AMC 188 (2d Cir. 1940).

75. *The Pocomoke,* 150 F. 193 (ED Va. 1906); *The Nacoochee,* 137 U.S. 330 (1890); *The Pallanza,* 189 F. 43 (2d Cir. 1911), and see *Granholm v. The TFL Express,* supra note 25.

76. *The Manchioneal,* 243 F. 80 (2d Cir. 1917), where Hough, J. said, "By the overwhelming weight of authority it is settled that the proper place for a lookout is, under ordinary circumstances, on the bow." See also, *The Burgan—The Bergechief,* supra note 31; *United States v. The Holland,* supra note 69; *Alaska Packers Ass'n., Inc. v. The East Point,* 421 F. Supp. 48, 1976 AMC 2228 (WD Wash. 1976).

77. Under ordinary conditions a lookout is not required to be posted at the stern, but one must be posted in special circumstances, e.g., in backing into a channel, or when a vessel is drifting or maneuvering in such a way that there may be danger astern. See Griffin 275–76 and cases cited. See also *Stevens v. United States Lines Co.,* 187 F.2d 670, 1951 AMC 617 (1st Cir. 1951), an overtaking case where both vessels were held to blame, the overtaken vessel for failing to keep "some sort of lookout around," and having seen the overtaking vessel, failing to keep her under "some sort of observation."

positioned.[78] Two recent decisions[79] have excused the posting of bow lookouts on small fishing vessels, although there is authority to the contrary. When a tug and tow are integrated, the proper position for a lookout is at the head of the tow.[80]

Again, where a bow lookout is required it is the burden of a vessel without one to establish that the failure did not and could not have contributed to the collision.[81] Bad weather has not been accepted as an excuse for not stationing the lookout at the bow,[82] but it has been held that on a clear night the absence of a bow lookout was justified.[83]

e. Reports to the Bridge. Lights and sounds essential to a vessel's navigation must be reported to the bridge for the navigator to determine their significance.[84] A trained and experienced lookout will be able to discern the reporting required in high seas navigation at night, where any single light may become significant, as well as in a crowded port with a confusion of sights and sounds. Failure to instruct the lookout on proper reporting to the bridge is as much faulty look-out[85] as the actual failure of the lookout to report what he

---

78. *The San Juan—The Seaboard 77,* 1961 AMC 2577 (SDNY 1961), reversed, 300 F.2d 496, 1962 AMC 2305 (2d Cir. 1962); *The Willowpool—The Platform 199-2,* supra note 67 (bridge lookout held inadequate where distance from bow to bridge was 150 feet); *United States v. The J.A. Cobb,* supra note 31 (bridge look-out held inadequate where the distance from bow to bridge was 175 feet); *The Bucentaur—The Wilson Victory,* supra note 21 (bridge look-out held inadequate where there were 300 feet from bow to bridge); *The Cartagena—The Syra,* 290 F. Supp. 260, 1968 AMC 2235 (D Md. 1968). See also *The Kearsage—The Oriana,* 231 F. Supp. 469, 1964 AMC 2163 (SD Cal. 1964).

But see *In re Seiriki Kisen Kaisha,* 629 F. Supp. 1374, 1986 AMC 913 (SDNY 1986) *(The Seiryu—The Stena Freighter),* a both-to-blame case decided before the United States became a party to the Convention on Standards of Training, Certification, and Watchkeeping, appendix, infra. The *Stena Freighter,* a fully automated vessel, was proceeding in the open sea on a clear night, on automatic pilot, with only the watch officer and one seaman above deck. After citing Rule 5, the court accepted expert testimony that "under today's manning standards, there is discretion as to whether to post a lookout on a ship in the open ocean." It found, however, that the watch officer of the *Stena Freighter* was at fault in permitting the seaman to leave the bridge in order to call the next watch when *The Seiryu* was close by, and then busying himself in plotting a fix. The expert opinion referred to by the court is contrary to the I.M.O. Recommendations annexed to the convention, insofar as the opinion would apply to vessels of more than 200 gross tons, when under way at night, such as the *Stena Freighter.*

79. *Capt'n Mark v. The Sea Fever,* 692 F.2d 163, 1983 AMC 2651 (1st Cir. 1982); *In re Hellenic Lines, Ltd. (The Hellenic Carrier),* 1984 AMC 57 (ED Va. 1982). But see *Empire Seafoods v. Anderson,* 398 F.2d 204, 1968 AMC 2664 (5th Cir. 1968).

80. *The Birney R—The Katherine II,* 198 F. Supp. 515, 1962 AMC 916 (ED La. 1962).

81. *The Weyerhaeuser Steamship Co. v. United States (The Pacific),* supra note 31.

82. *The Manchioneal,* supra note 76. But see *The Kaiserin Maria Theresa,* 149 F. 97 (2d Cir. 1906), and *The Jean Jadot,* 2 F. Supp. 942, 1933 AMC 247 (EDNY 1933).

83. *American Metal Co. v. Belleville,* 284 F. Supp. 1002, 1970 AMC 633 (SDNY 1965); *Chotin Transp. Co. v. The Hugh C. Blaske,* 356 F. Supp. 388, 1973 AMC 2690 (ED La. 1972), aff'd, 475 F.2d 1370 (5th Cir. 1973).

84. *The Cabins—The Rio Maracana,* 182 F. Supp. 811, 1960 AMC 1944 (ED Va. 1960), aff'd, 285 F.2d 592, 1961 AMC 239 (4th Cir. 1961); *The Francisville—The Matthew Luckenbach,* 215 F. Supp. 667, 1963 AMC 2280 (SDNY 1963), aff'd, 324 F.2d 563, 1964 AMC 1 (2d Cir. 1963).

85. *The Kearsage—The Oriana,* supra note 78.

has seen and heard.[86] Maintenance of good communication, by occasional checking, is also important in keeping a good look-out.[87]

Section C. Rule 6: Safe Speed

1. Introduction

Rule 6 of COLREGS and the Inland Rules requires every vessel to proceed at all times "at a safe speed so that she can take proper and effective action to avoid collision and be stopped within a distance appropriate to the prevailing circumstances and conditions." The rule then lists, in paragraph (a), six factors among those to be taken into account by *all* vessels in determining a safe speed and, in paragraph (b), six additional factors among those to be taken into account by vessels with operational radar.

The first factor listed in Rule 6(a) to be considered by all vessels is "the state of visibility." Paragraph (b) of Rule 19 (Conduct of Vessels in Restricted Visibility) requires every vessel to "proceed at a safe speed adapted to the prevailing circumstances and conditions of restricted visibility," and adds: "A power driven vessel shall have her engines ready for immediate maneuver," a precaution which would surely be required under the "good seamanship" rule even if it were not part of Rule 19(b).

Since paragraph (b) of Rule 19 relates to speed under restricted visibility conditions it will be considered together with Rule 6 insofar as that rule relates to speed under such conditions.[88] And because radar frequently plays such an important part in the conduct of vessels in restricted visibility, the six additional factors among those to be taken into account by radar-equipped vessels will be discussed together with speed under restricted visibility conditions.

The remaining five factors among those to be taken into account by all vessels in determining a safe speed are simply factors which common sense would dictate should be observed by any prudent navigator. These may be summarized as follows: (1) traffic density; (2) the vessel's maneuverability; (3) the presence of background light; (4) wind, sea, and current conditions and proximity of navigational hazards; and (5) the vessel's draft in relation to

86. *The Norwich Victory—The Dump Scows 116, 120, 122,* supra note 61; *The American Producer—The Dant,* 1972 AMC 642 (ND Cal. 1971); *United States v. The Tug Colette Malloy,* 507 F.2d 1019, 1975 AMC 938 (5th Cir. 1975).

87. *The Canon Forest v. The Beishu Maru,* 1979 AMC 1205 (D Or. 1979).

88. See *The Glucometer II—The St. Michael,* [1989] 2 Lloyd's Rep. 54 (Adm.), a fog case where, in referring to Rules 6 and 19(b), Mr. Justice Sheen stated: "The only material difference between those two rules is that under r. 19, a vessel is required to have her engines ready for immediate manoeuvre." The remaining provisions of Rule 19 are discussed in chapter 6 and chapter 8.

the available depth of water. With reference to these factors Cockcroft and Lameijer state:

> Information concerning stopping distances and turning circles is now supplied to many vessels and navigating officers are expected to be familiar with the manoeuvering characteristics of their own ship. The distance that a vessel will cover in a crash stop before being brought to rest from full speed is likely to be between 5 and 15 ship lengths, depending upon speed, displacement, type of machinery, etc. . . .
>
> The manoeuverability is to be taken into account with reference to the prevailing conditions. A vessel which is restricted in her ability to manoeuvre because of the nature of her work may not be justified in going at a high speed in regions of high traffic density and when approaching a relatively slow vessel so as to involve risk of collision.
>
> The reference to draught is intended to cover the possible restriction of manoeuvering space due to shallow water in the vicinity, or the hydrodynamic effects, such as bow cushion, bank suction and interaction between ships, which can generally be eliminated or reduced by a reduction of speed.[89]

With the exception of the presence of background light, the factors to be taken into account by all vessels in determining safe speed are relevant under restricted visibility conditions as well as in clear weather, as illustrated by some of the decisions cited in the discussion of safe speed in restricted visibility which follows. Insofar as they relate to clear weather conditions, they will also be discussed in subsection 9 (Safe Speed in Clear Weather).

2. *"Moderate" Speed under the Former Rules*

Except for the rule that the stand-on vessel in a crossing or overtaking situation was required to hold her course and speed, the only statutory rule specifically relating to speed in force in the United States before the adoption of the current rules was Article 16 of the former International, Inland, Great Lakes, and Western Rivers Rules. Article 16 required vessels to proceed at "moderate" speed in fog, mist, falling snow, or heavy rainstorms.[90] The 1960 International Rule added, "or any other condition of restricted visibility"; the former Great Lakes Rule added, "or other causes"; and the former Western Rivers Rule added "or any other condition similarly restricting visibility, whether by day or night."

---

89. A. Cockcroft & J. Lameijer, *A Guide to the Collision Avoidance Regulations* 46-47 (4th ed.) (hereinafter "Cockcroft & Lameijer").

90. Rule 16(a) of the 1960 International Rules, Pub. L. No. 88-131; first paragraph of Rule 16 of the former Inland Rules; Rule 26 of the former Western Rivers Rules, and Rule 15 of the former Great Lakes Rules. The former Inland, Great Lakes, and Western Rivers Rules are reprinted in Griffin at 645–787.

The first U.S. Supreme Court decision concerning the meaning of "moderate speed" under the former rules was *The Pennsylvania,*[91] now much better known for the famous presumption it announced. In that case the Court recognized that what is a moderate speed "may not be precisely definable," and continued: "It must depend upon the circumstances of each case. That may be moderate and reasonable in some circumstances which would be quite immoderate in others."[92]

In *The Martello,*[93] the Supreme Court stated that while a speed of 6 knots, even in dense fog, might not be excessive in the open ocean, a different rule applied to a vessel leaving a busy harbor, with the visibility a quarter of a mile. Such a vessel, the Court said, should "reduce her speed to the lowest point consistent with a good steerageway, which the Court finds in this case to be three miles an hour."[94]

Four years later, in *The Umbria,*[95] the Court articulated the rule which, although stated in varying ways, was generally followed thereafter by the American courts in determining whether or not a vessel's speed in or near a restricted visibility area was "moderate":

> The general consensus of opinion in this country is to the effect that a steamer is bound to use only such precautions as will enable her to stop in time to avoid a collision, after the approaching vessel comes in sight, provided such approaching vessel is herself going at the moderate speed required by law. In a dense fog this might require both vessels to come to a standstill, until the course of each was definitely ascertained. In a lighter fog it might authorize them to keep their engines in sufficient motion to preserve their steerageway.[96]

This rule has frequently been described as the "half-distance rule," the notion being that if each of two vessels, even when approaching the other head on, is proceeding at a speed sufficiently slow to enable her to stop within half the distance between them when they are first able to see each other, and at that moment each vessel acts promptly to take her way off, collision will be

---

91. 86 U.S. 125 (1873).
92. Id. at 133.
93. 153 U.S. 64 (1893).
94. Id. at 71.
95. 166 U.S. 404 (1897).
96. Id. at 417. While *The Umbria* is generally considered the leading U.S. Supreme Court case on the half-distance rule, the rule's origins may be traced to earlier decisions of the court. See *The Colorado,* 137 U.S. 692, 703 (1875); *The Nacooche,* 137 U.S. 330, 339 (1890).

The earlier lower court cases, including some in which the rule was misstated, are discussed in Griffin at 293–313. Note 4 (pp. 301–4) contains exhaustive lists of cases where speeds of specified numbers of knots were held moderate or immoderate under specified conditions. In comparing these cases with more recent decisions, their age must of course be considered. Apart from the fact that all of them arose before the advent of radar, changes in the size and design of vessels and their means of propulsion have been such that speeds condemned as excessive under particular circumstances 50 or 100 years ago might under the same circumstances be held safe speeds today.

avoided, whether or not either changes heading. The rule is stated in Griffin as follows:

> A vessel in thick weather must go at such speed only as will enable her (1) to keep clear of vessels which she is bound to avoid (e.g., sailing vessels, and vessels at anchor) and (2) to stop her headway within her share of her distance from an approaching vessel seen or heard ahead, -always assuming that the other vessel is herself complying with the law as to speed and signals. As applied to vessels sighting each other head and head, this means that each must be able to stop within half of the visible distance. As applied to a vessel approaching another at anchor, it means that she must be able to stop before reaching the anchored vessel. As applied to crossing vessels, the rule cannot be stated in general terms applicable to all angles of approach; but the vessel furthest from the point of intersection ought always to be able to stop before she reaches that point.[97]

With respect, the authors have some question about the portions of the quoted statement concerning "moderate" speed in relation to sailing vessels, anchored vessels, and vessels on crossing courses. Under restricted visibility conditions a vessel without operational radar ordinarily remains unaware of the presence of other vessels before their fog signals are heard. Until then she does not know whether the first vessel that will come within the limit of visibility will be a sailing vessel, a power-driven vessel, or, if navigating in inland waters, an anchored vessel. To be "moderate," as that word was interpreted under the former rules, her speed should therefore be such that she should be able to avoid collision with any vessel in the area that is herself obeying the law, whether that vessel is a sailing vessel or a power-driven one, or whether she is anchored or underway, and if underway with way on, whether she is on a head-on course, or a crossing course, or is being overtaken, or is on a course not involving risk of collision. Thus, if, under the former rules, a vessel's speed was required to be sufficiently slow to enable her to stop within half the distance between her and a similar power-driven vessel obeying the half-distance rule and approaching head on, it is submitted that she should be limited to that speed. The fact that she might be able to proceed at a faster rate and still stop in time to avoid collision with an anchored vessel, or a sailing vessel, or a vessel on a crossing course, should make no difference; she should be prepared to stop in time to avoid colliding with any vessel obeying the rules, including a power-driven vessel approaching head on.

It has been held under the half-distance rule that if the visibility conditions are such that a vessel moored or anchored in a safe place would not be able to maintain steerageway at a speed slow enough to allow her to stop

97. See Griffin 292.

within half the limit of visibility, she should not get underway.[98] Similarly, it has been held under the rule that if a vessel underway encounters fog so dense that she cannot stop within half the visibility limit, she should moor or anchor if it is possible for her to do so.[99] In applying the half-distance rule in determining moderate speed there could of course be a wide diversity in terms of knots, since, obviously, compliance with the rule would depend on a number of factors, including tidal and current conditions, the depth of water, and the ability of the particular vessel to take her way off in a relatively short distance.

In discussing the English law on moderate speed under the former rules, Marsden states:[100]

> "Moderate" speed is a relative term. It cannot be defined so as to apply to all cases; what it should be depends on the circumstances of each particular case; and the terms of rule 16 recognise this fact.
>
> It has been stated as a general rule that speed such that another vessel cannot be seen in time to avoid her is unlawful,[101] but in *Morris v. Luton*

98. *Holland America Line v. The Johs. Stove (The Johs. Stove—The Kerkedyk),* 1968 AMC 2012 (SDNY 1968); *Oil Transfer Co. v. Diesel Tanker F.A. Verdon, Inc. (The Otto New York—The F.A. Verdon),* 192 F. Supp. 245, 1960 AMC 2392 (SDNY 1960); *Hogge v. The Yorkmar,* 434 F. Supp. 715, 1977 AMC 805 (D Md. 1977). Cf. *Avondale Marine Ways, Inc. v. The Crescent City,* 184 F. Supp. 773, 776, 1960 AMC 1451 (ED La. 1960), aff'd, 287 F.2d 889, 1961 AMC 1040 (5th Cir. 1961), where a vessel was held entitled to proceed in dense fog to her destination when that was the closest safe port.

An exception is recognized in favor of passenger ferries where they are necessary for the movement of people. *The Orange,* 46 F. 408 (SDNY 1891); Griffin 308, 311–12. But the exception has been held inapplicable to ferries other than passenger ferries. Thus, in *Chesapeake & Ohio Ry. Co. v. Cleveland Tankers, Inc. (The Meteor—The Mead—The Pere Marquette No. 12),* 121 F. Supp. 830, 1954 AMC 1921 (ED Mich. 1954), the exception was held inapplicable to a freight car ferry on the Detroit River.

In England there is no rule of law requiring ferries to cease operating in dense fog. Marsden, *Collisions at Sea* 534 (11th ed. by K. McGuffie) (hereinafter "Marsden"), citing *The Tranmere,* [1920] P. 454, 15 Asp. Mar. Cas. (N.S.) 290 (Adm.). However, in that case, and in *The Lancashire,* (1873) L.R. 4 A.&E. 198, 2 Asp. Mar. Cas. (N.S.) 202 (Adm.), also cited in Marsden, ferries were held at fault for operating in dense fog under the particular circumstances.

99. *La Bourgogne,* 86 F. 475 (2d Cir. 1898); Griffin 308; See also *The Otto New York—The F.A. Verdon,* supra note 98. Cf. *Moran Towing & Transportation Co. v. United States (The Julia C. Moran—The Comet),* 1967 AMC 1348 (SDNY 1967), where the court found that although the visibility was only 75 feet, the master of a cargo vessel entering New York Harbor acted reasonably under the existing circumstances in deciding not to anchor, but to continue on, relying on radar and other navigational aids. The vessel was, however, held solely at fault on other grounds, including excessive speed (more than 8 knots, reduced to 7 by the time of the collision).

100. Marsden 526.

101. Citing, among other English cases, *The City of Brooklyn,* (1876) 1 P.D. 276, 3 Asp. Mar. Cas. (N.S.) 230 (C.A.), where on a dark night a steamer ran into and sank a barque sailing in the same direction. The barque was not displaying a stern light, but none was required at the time. In holding the steamer solely at fault Lush, J. stated: "I think the rule of law, with regard to travelling at sea, is identical with travelling on the high road. No one on a dark night has a right to go at such a rate of speed as not to be able to escape an accident if he happens to follow immediately in the wake of another, whether it be by sea or by land. . . ."

> *Corporation*[102] the Court of Appeal held unanimously that there is no rule of law that a person riding or driving in the dark must be held to be negligent if he is driving at such a speed that he is not able to pull up within the limit of his vision; the question is one of fact, dependent on the circumstances of each case. Any dicta in previous cases of collision, whether at sea or on land, which appear to state that the point is solely governed by a rule of law, cannot therefore be relied upon.

Assuming that the half-distance rule as applied in the United States under the former rules could properly be described as a rule of law, the rule did not require a vessel to be able to stop within her share of the visibility, regardless of the circumstances. Rather, it required that under ordinary circumstances she should be able to do so. Any difference between U.S. law and English law on moderate speed in restricted visibility under the former rules may therefore be more apparent than real.

Application of the half-distance rule was effectively restricted by a six-to-three decision of the U.S. Supreme Court in *Union Oil Co. v. The San Jacinto.*[103] In that case an upbound tanker was proceeding in fog on her own starboard side of the Columbia River, at a speed of seven knots, when a downbound tug suddenly turned to port across the tanker's bow, and collision followed. The U.S. Court of Appeals for the Ninth Circuit held both vessels to blame—the tanker for navigating at too great a speed to enable her to stop within half the limit of visibility. Accordingly, it divided the damages equally, as the old divided damages rule was then still in force in the United States. When the Supreme Court granted certiorari it was generally thought that it had done so for the primary purpose of deciding whether or not that rule should be discarded. However, the Court reversed on the merits, holding the tug solely at fault. It thus became unnecessary to pass upon the divided damages rule, which was to meet its demise three years later in *United States v. Reliable Transfer Co.*[104] In reversing the Court of Appeals, Justice Rehnquist said in *The San Jacinto:*

> . . . If two vessels, upon sighting each other, are proceeding at rates of speed such that each can stop before it reaches the point at which the courses of the two intersect, collision is impossible.
>
> There can be no quarrel with the salutary purpose of this "rule of thumb." It is premised on the notion that when a ship is traveling under foggy weather conditions in waters in which other ships might be proceeding on intersecting courses, the speed of each ship must be such as to enable her to stop within half the distance separating the ships when they first sight each other. Implicit in the rule, however, is the assumption

102. [1946] K.B. 114 (C.A.). This was not a maritime case, but one involving a bicycle which struck an unlighted air-raid shelter at night.

103. 409 U.S. 140, 1972 AMC 2675 (1972).

104. 421 U.S. 397, 1975 AMC 541 (1975).

> that vessels can reasonably be expected to be traveling on intersecting courses. If, on the facts of the case, it is totally unrealistic to anticipate the possibility that a vessel will travel on a particular heading that would intersect the course of another ship, the reason for the rule is rather clearly not present.[105]

In a vigorous dissent in which he was joined by Justices Brennan and Douglas, Justice Stewart stated:

> I would reaffirm the continued vitality of the "half-distance" rule and approve its application in this case. I cannot concur in the Court's decision, which while apparently approving the "salutary purpose" of the rule, guts its certainty by making its application turn on elusive concepts such as the reasonable possibility of collision, or the particular bearing that a vessel might be expected to take on emerging from a fog bank. In short, the Court today allows a vessel to proceed at an immoderate speed, provided that its crew does not expect a collision. I cannot agree.
>
> The half-distance rule is a rational interpretation of the command of Art. 16 of the Inland Rules that vessels shall proceed at a "moderate speed" in fog with a "careful regard to the existing circumstances and conditions." 33 U.S. Code, sec. 192. The rule does not simply require a vessel to be able to stop in one-half the distance of her forward visibility, but rather "to maintain only such a rate of speed as would enable her to come to a standstill, by reversing her engines at full speed, before she should collide with a vessel which she should see through the fog." *Nacoochee,* 137 U.S. 330, 339 (footnote omitted). As one scholar phrased the rule: "the vessels must be able to stop, not within the distance of visibility, but before they collide." J. Griffin, *The American Law of Collision,* 295 (1949). . . .
>
> Concepts such as "reasonable expectancy," "anticipated possibility," and "reasonable possibility," do little service to the half-distance rule. "[T]he genius of the Rules for Prevention of Collision is their certainty." *Hess Shipping Corp. vs. S.S. Charles Lykes,* 1969 A.M.C. 1787, 1793, 417 F.2d 346, 351 (Brown, J., dissenting). The half-distance rule is effective precisely because it is a measurable rule of thumb, a nautical speed limit. Speed limits would serve no useful purpose if they only applied when there was a foreseeable probability that an accident might occur.[106]

3. "Safe" Speed under COLREGS and the Inland Rules

As stated, the term "moderate" was used under the former rules only to describe the maximum speed at which a vessel was permitted to proceed when

---

105. 409 U.S. at 144–45, 1972 AMC at 2679.
106. 409 U.S. at 148–50, 1972 AMC at 2681-83.

visibility was restricted. On the other hand, under Rule 6 of COLREGS and the Inland Rules the term "safe" is used to describe the speed at which a vessel underway is required to proceed under the particular existing circumstances, whether or not those circumstances include restricted visibility, and the term "safe" is again used in Rule 19(b), relating to speed in or near restricted visibility areas. As of this writing (1997) there does not appear to have been any reported decision, at least in the English-speaking countries, specifically equating the terms "moderate speed," as used in the former rules, and "safe speed," as used in COLREGS and the U.S. Inland Navigation Rules. However, in *The Maritime Harmony*,[107] in referring to Article 24 of the Belgian Shipping Regulations for the Lower Scheldt, which provided that in restricted visibility vessels must proceed at a "moderate speed," Mr. Justice Sheen stated: "That regulation does not conflict with r. 6 of the 1972 Collision Regulations . . . ."

In any case, insofar as they relate to maximum permissible speeds in restricted visibility, the reported decisions have drawn no distinction between the terms "moderate" and "safe," or the terms "immoderate" and "unsafe." Presumably the adjective "safe," rather than "moderate," was employed in Rule 6 because under the earlier rules the use of "moderate" had been limited to a description of the maximum speed permitted for vessels proceeding in or near areas of restricted visibility. "Safe" is a broader term. Thus, under some circumstances, a speed so slow that there would be danger of losing steerageway could not be considered "safe."[108] On the other hand it could hardly be described as "immoderate." Since the term "safe" was used in Rule 6, and that rule applies to restricted visibility as well as to clear weather conditions, it was appropriate to use the same term in Rule 19(b) in describing the speed required when visibility is restricted.

4. *Applicability of Radar and ARPA to Safe Speed*

Long before radar became mandatory for most seagoing vessels the courts in a number of States, including the United States, the United Kingdom, and Canada, held it a fault for a radar-equipped vessel navigating in or near a fog bank or other restricted visibility area to fail to use her radar. The earliest of these decisions appears to have been *The Thomas Barry—The Medford*,[109]

---

107. [1982] 2 Lloyd's Rep. 400 (Adm.).

108. See *The Ring*, [1964] 2 Lloyd's Rep. 177 (Adm.) (decided under the former rules).

109. 65 F. Supp. 622, 1946 AMC 795 (EDNY 1946). See also *The Esso Plymouth*, [1955] 1 Lloyd's Rep. 429 (Adm.); *Continental Oil Co. v. The Glenville*, 210 F. Supp. 865, 1962 AMC 2311 (SD Tex. 1962); *The Lucille Bloomfield—The Ronda*, 298 F. Supp. 1239, 1969 AMC 2205 (SDNY 1969), aff'd, 422 F.2d 728, 1970 AMC 521 (2d Cir. 1970); *The Wuerttemberg—The Swerve*, 219 F. Supp. 211, 1963 AMC 1554 (ED S.C. 1963), modified, 330 F.2d 498, 1964 AMC 1098 (4th Cir. 1964); *Standard Dredging Corp. v. The Syra*, 290 F. Supp. 260, 1968 AMC 2235 (D Md. 1968); *Pacific Bulk Carriers, Inc. v. The Sadoharu Maru*, 639 F.2d 72, 1980 AMC 2530 (2d Cir. 1980); *The Duke of York—The Haiti Victory*, 131 F. Supp. 712, 1955 AMC 1160 (ED Va. 1955), aff'd on this point, 230 F.2d 139, 1956 AMC 275 (4th Cir. 1956), aff'd, 354 U.S. 129, 1957 AMC 1151 (1957); *Moran Scow*

decided in 1946 by the U.S. District Court for the Eastern District of New York. The U.S. Court of Appeals for the Second Circuit went a step further in *The Burgan—The Bergechief,*[110] holding that the failure of a vessel to use her radar when conditions warrant its use imposes upon her the burden of proving that her failure did not contribute to a collision.

Decisions such as those cited are applications of the maxim that one must make use of all means at hand to avoid a collision.[111] Or, as Lord Justice Willmer put it more colorfully in *The Nora,*[112] in referring to a radar-equipped vessel that collided with one not so equipped: "I think there is scope here for applying the Biblical maxim which says: 'For unto whomsoever much is given, of him shall be much required.'"

Another question that arose soon after radar came to be used extensively on merchant ships was whether or not an oceangoing vessel should be held unseaworthy if she was not radar-equipped. In *The Burgan—The Bergechief*[113] both vessels had radar on board, and it was therefore unnecessary to answer this question. However, Judge Medina prophesied that "a rule requiring radar, subject to some limitations and qualifications, [would] sooner or later be formulated." As events proved, the question whether the U.S. courts should formulate a rule requiring radar became moot when the Ports and Waterways Safety Act[114] was enacted not long after Judge Medina's prophecy. The act authorized the Coast Guard to "require vessels to install and use . . . any electronic or other device . . . which is necessary in the interests of vessel safety."[115] The Coast Guard promptly implemented the act by promulgating regulations requiring vessels subject to it to be equipped with radar.[116]

5. *Regulations Relating to Radar and ARPA*

The current Coast Guard Regulations concerning radar[117] provide that every self-propelled vessel of 1,600 or more gross tons (except vessels that are not destined for or departing from a port or place subject to U.S. jurisdiction and

---

Corp. v. The Boston, 342 F. Supp. 216, 1972 AMC 2027 (SDNY 1972); *The Johs. Stove—The Kerkedyk,* supra note 98.

In *The Australian Star—The Hindoo,* 74 F. Supp. 145, 1947 AMC 1630 (SDNY 1947), aff'd on this point, 172 F.2d 472, 1949 AMC 423 (2d Cir. 1949), a decision in a wartime case holding that a radar-equipped vessel, aware that a blacked-out vessel was on her port bow, was at fault for failing to continue radar observations, which would have revealed that the radar-equipped vessel was on a collision course.

110. Supra note 31.

111. See, e.g., *The Australian Star—The Hindoo,* supra note 109, 74 F. Supp. at 148–49, 1947 AMC at 1634–36.

112. [1956] 1 Lloyd's Rep. 617, 625–26 (Adm.).

113. Supra note 31, 274 F.2d at 474, 1960 AMC at 1386.

114. 33 U.S.C. §§ 1221–36.

115. 33 U.S.C. §§ 1223(a)(3).

116. The 1996 Coast Guard Navigation Safety Equipment Regulations are contained in 33 CFR ch. I §§ 164.35–164.38.

117. See note 116, supra.

are in innocent passage through the U.S. territorial sea or in transit through U.S. waters forming part of an international strait) must be equipped with a "marine radar system for surface navigation"; that every vessel of 10,000 or more gross tons must have a second marine radar system that operates independently of the first, and that on every tanker of 10,000 gross tons or more subject to Section 5 of the Port and Tanker Safety Act of 1978[118] the dual radar system must have both short-range and long-range capabilities, and must have "true north features consisting of a display that is stabilized in azimuth."

The regulations also provide that except when operating on the Great Lakes and their connecting and tributary waters, vessels of 10,000 gross tons or more, constructed on or after September 1, 1984, must be equipped with an ARPA (automatic radar plotting aid). Tankers of 10,000 gross tons or more—even those built before September 1, 1984—must be so equipped if they carry oil or hazardous materials in bulk as cargo or in residue on U.S. navigable waters, or if they transfer such materials in any port or place subject to the jurisdiction of the United States.[119]

6. *Factors to Be Taken into Account by Radar-Equipped Vessels*

The six additional factors which Rule 6(b) lists among those to be taken into account by vessels with operational radar are:

(i) the characteristics, efficiency, and limitations of the radar equipment;
(ii) any constraints imposed by the radar range scale in use;
(iii) the effect on radar detection of the sea state, weather, and other sources of interference;
(iv) the possibility that small vessels, ice, and other floating objects may not be detected by radar at an adequate range;
(v) the number, location, and movement of vessels detected by radar;
(vi) the more exact assessment of the visibility that may be possible when radar is used to determine the range of vessels or other objects in the vicinity.

This is the first mention of radar by name in the current rules, although radar was intended to be included among "all available means in the prevailing circumstances and conditions" by which Rule 5 requires a look-out to be kept.[120]

With respect to the first factor—it is self-evident that the highly sophisticated radar equipment of a modern ship of the line, operated by a thoroughly trained naval officer, will enable her to proceed safely at a greater speed than a small fishing vessel equipped with only a rudimentary type of radar.[121]

118. 46 U.S.C. § 391(a).
119. 33 CFR ch. I § 164.38 (1995).
120. *The Pulkovo—The Oden,* [1989] 1 Lloyd's Rep. 280, 287 (Adm.).
121. See Cockcroft & Lameijer 47–48.

Regarding the second factor—any constraints imposed by the radar range scale in use—Messrs. Cockcroft and Lameijer state in *A Guide to the Collision Avoidance Regulations:*

> Constraints may be imposed by every range scale that can be used. When using the longer range scales definition and discrimination are reduced and small targets are less likely to be detected, whereas shorter range scales do not permit early detection of targets and do not enable the observer to obtain an overall assessment when several vessels are in the vicinity. The range scale which is most suitable for the locality should be selected but the scale should be changed at regular intervals. The scale should not be changed when there is a dangerous target at close range.
>
> When two radar displays are available and in use it may be advantageous to select a different range scale on each display to avoid the necessity of switching scales.[122]

An example of a range scale problem is found in *Wakefield v. The Veendam,*[123] a case involving a both-to-blame fog collision between the *Veendam* and the *Tualatin.* The latter was equipped with two radars, but the only one in operation at the material times had only two scales, one a half-mile and the other a 6-mile scale. When operated on the half-mile scale the scope displayed an area with a radius of approximately three-quarters of a mile. While the court did not cite Rule 6, it recognized the constraints imposed by the range scale in use, stating, "With the radar set at the half mile scale, . . . the scope would not display both sides of Johnstone Strait during the entire transit thereof."[124] Another example is *The Nassau—The Brott,*[125] an English decision handed down under the former International Rules, where Mr. Justice Hewson stated:

> . . . If the master of the *Nassau* was relying upon radar to justify his speed in reduced visibility it was not good seamanship to have kept his radar permanently on the short range.
>
> It is a matter which I have thought about and discussed with the Elder Brethren, and we are agreed upon what I am about to say. They should have extended the range periodically at intervals appropriate to the circumstances to inform themselves of the general situation and, in particular, of the probable effect of the approach of otherwise invisible vessels upon the action of the vessel known to be, and seen to be, ahead of them, the *Brott.*

---

122. Id. 49.
123. 1980 AMC 2906 (WD Wash. 1980).
124. Id. 2912.
125. [1964] 2 Lloyd's Rep. 509, 515 (Adm.).

The third factor—the effect on radar detection of the sea state, weather, and other sources of interference—points up a shortcoming in the efficacy of radar as a means of detecting the presence of other vessels and objects. Messrs. Cockcroft and Lameijer point out that while proper use of the controls on a radar console should normally enable the "echoes" of other vessels to be distinguished from the "clutter" of waves and precipitation, when such interference is severe echoes from small craft are likely to remain undetected, and even large targets may be obscured.[126]

Regarding the fourth factor—the possibility that small vessels, ice, and other floating objects may not be detected by radar at an adequate range—the same authors explain:

> Minor targets such as small coastal vessels and trawlers should normally be detected at distances greater than 6 miles, provided the [radar] set is properly adjusted, but yachts, open boats and other small craft, especially boats of fibreglass construction, usually give poor echoes and may not be detected in time to take effective avoiding actions. The fitting of an efficient radar reflector is likely to considerably increase the probability of being detected and may double the range of detection for a small vessel.[127]

It is plain that the fifth factor—the number, location, and movement of vessels—is one that should be taken into account in the determination of safe speed by a radar-equipped vessel. As noted previously, Rule 6(a)(ii) requires *all* vessels to take traffic density into account in determining safe speed. Paragraph (b)(v) in effect repeats this requirement insofar as it requires radar-equipped vessels to take into account the number of vessels detected by radar.[128] The same paragraph adds that the location and movement of such vessels must also be taken into account. Obviously, a slower rate of speed should be followed when another vessel is observed by radar approaching on a reciprocal course so as to involve risk of collision than would be indicated if the other vessel were observed on the starboard bow on a course taking her away from that of the observing vessel.

The sixth factor is a practical use of radar observations. With no landmarks or other vessels in sight a vessel without operational radar may have difficulty in estimating the extent of the visibility. But if any vessels or other objects are in the area, the extent of the visibility can of course be measured quite accurately by observing their positions on the radarscope at the moment they can first be visually observed.

---

126. Cockcroft & Lameijer 49–50.

127. Id. 50.

128. See *Maritrans Operating Partners L.P. v. The Faith I,* 800 F. Supp. 133, 1993 AMC 385 (D N.J. 1992); *The Shansin Victory,* [1980] 2 Lloyd's Rep. 359 (Adm.).

7. *The Proper Use of Radar Information*

Soon after the courts began holding radar-equipped vessels at fault for failing to use the equipment under restricted visibility conditions, they went a step further and held that it must be used properly. As early as 1951 the Supreme Court of Canada stated in *The Chinook v. The Dagmar Salen:*[129] "If radar is to furnish a new sight through fog, then the report which it brings must be interpreted by active and constant intelligence on the part of the operator." And in *The Nora*[130] Justice Willmer held:

> . . . The possession of this radar equipment gives the *Westerdam* a great advantage over other vessels which are not similarly equipped; but it brings with it, in my judgment, a concurrent duty to see that intelligent and reasonable use is made of the equipment provided. If she makes a mistake, being so much better equipped than the *Nora,* so much the less does she have an excuse for doing so.

A substantial number of what have sometimes been called "radar-assisted collisions"[131] have occurred because the navigators of one or both of the colliding vessels failed to plot a series of radar observations of the other vessel either on a maneuvering board or with a grease pencil on the face of the radarscope, at timed intervals. The strongest early condemnation of a failure to plot was Judge Medina's dictum in *The Burgan—The Bergechief:*[132]

> It is likely that there was time for plotting, and this would have revealed the exact speed and course of the *Burgan.* We cannot be sure of this. Although her speed was diminishing, the estimate of five knots could not have been much out of the way; and it would seem to be a good general rule that if a radar pip shows another vessel nearby and forward on your starboard bow, you should stop and *make* the time for a plot.

While the Radar Annex to the 1960 Rules did not mention plotting, the first recommendation was that "Assumptions made on scanty information may be dangerous and should be avoided." The inference is that "scanty information" is the kind of information that can be obtained by casually observing the "pip" of another vessel on the radar screen, instead of either making and plotting a series of observations at timed intervals or employing an "equiva-

---

129. [1961] 4 D.L.R. 1, 1951 AMC 1253.

130. Supra note 112, [1956] 1 Lloyd's Rep. at 626.

131. *Ove Skou Rederi A/S v. Nippon Yusen Kaisha (The Marie Skou—The Chitouse Maru),* 1971 AMC 470 (Supreme Court of Canada 1970): "This was in truth a radar-assisted collision . . . ." See also *Avondale Marine Ways, Inc. v. The Crescent City,* supra note 98; *The Burgan—The Bergechief,* supra note 31; *Polarus S.S. Co. v. The Sandefjord,* 236 F.2d 270, 1956 AMC 1779 (2d Cir. 1956); *The Anna Salen,* [1954] 1 Lloyd's Rep. 475 (Adm.).

132. Supra note 31, 274 F.2d at 475, 1960 AMC at 1387–88. See *The Lucille Bloomfield—The Ronda,* supra note 109, where the *Lucille Bloomfield* was held at fault on several grounds, including the master's failure to use the vessel's radar, relying instead on visual observations to determine relative bearings of the *Ronda* and distances between the two vessels.

lent systematic observation of detected objects," as now specifically required by Rule 7 of COLREGS and the Inland Rules (Risk of Collision). Even experienced mariners can become confused by the relative motion presentation on the scope. This requirement of systematic observation has been implemented by the I.M.O. and the U.S. Coast Guard Regulations, which, as stated, now require sizeable vessels to be equipped with automatic radar plotting aids (ARPAs).

8. *The Half-Distance Rule under COLREGS and the Inland Rules*

Do COLREGS affect the applicability of the half-distance rule in any way? It is a fact of life that vessels commonly proceed at close to maximum speed in open waters, even during periods of dense fog.[133] This practice is certainly reprehensible in the case of vessels without operational radar, or if so equipped, without officers properly trained in its use. But in the case of a vessel with radar in good working order, carefully monitored by fully qualified officers, the practice would appear to be permissible under Rule 6(b) and Rule 19(b). It would make little sense to require a vessel entering an area in the mid-Atlantic where the visibility was 1 mile to slow to a speed enabling her to stop within a half-mile, if it was clear from long-range radar observations that there was no other vessel within 20 miles.

Once the "pip" of another vessel appears on the radar screen of a vessel proceeding in open waters in restricted visibility, she should, in accordance with Rule 19(d), "determine if a close-quarters situation is developing and/or risk of collision exists," and if so, she should "take avoiding action in ample time. . . ." But where fog or other restricted visibility conditions are encountered by a vessel navigating in confined waters, or waters where there is heavy vessel traffic, it is submitted that the half-distance rule still has validity: to be considered "safe," the vessel's speed should generally be sufficiently slow to enable her to stop within half the limit of visibility. For the reasons so clearly stated by Justice Stewart in his dissenting opinion in *The San Jacinto,*[134] the rule is a good one, and should be generally applied in determining what speed in fog is "safe" under such circumstances, just as before the current rules became effective, it was generally applied in determining what speed was "moderate." This is not to say that if a vessel can be stopped within half the limit of visibility her speed is necessarily "safe." For example, the traffic density, or the state of wind, sea, and current, or the proximity of navigational hazards, may be such that an even lower speed may be indicated. Or her speed may be so slow that proper steerageway cannot be maintained, and it is therefore not a "safe" speed.[135]

---

133. See *The Tenes,* [1989] 2 Lloyd's Rep. 367, 370 (Adm.).
134. Supra note 103, 409 U.S. at 148-150, 1972 AMC at 2681–83.
135. *The Ring,* supra note 108.

As of 1997 there did not appear to have been any reported American, English, or Commonwealth cases decided under COLREGS expressly applying the half-distance rule in determining whether or not a vessel's speed in restricted visibility was in violation of Rules 6 and (19)(b).[136] Instead, the courts have weighed the factors set out in Rule 6. In most instances, however, where vessels have been held in violation of Rule 6, their speeds were such that quite obviously they could not have stopped within half the limit of visibility.[137]

---

136. As of 1997 the most recent reported American decision expressly invoking the half-distance rule appears to have been *In re Hercules Carriers, Inc.*, 566 F. Supp. 962, 1983 AMC 2409 (MD Fla. 1983), aff'd, 720 F.2d 1201, 1984 AMC 2962 (11th Cir. 1985), holding that a speed of 13 knots in visibility of less than 500 feet was not a "moderate" speed under A. 16 of the former Inland Rules. Since there is no difference between "moderate" speed and "safe" speed in restricted visibility, the court would presumably have invoked the half-distance rule even if the collision (with the Sunshine Skyway Bridge at Tampa) had occurred after the current Inland Rules entered into force. The half-distance rule was involved by implication in *Burma Navigation Corp v. The Reliant Seahorse*, 99 F.3d 652, 1997 AMC 2184 (5th Cir. 1996).

See also *Getty Oil Company (Eastern Operations), Inc. v. The Ponce de Leon*, 409 F. Supp. 909, 1977 AMC 71 (SDNY 1976), aff'd, 555 F.2d 328, 1977 AMC 711 (2d Cir. 1976), where after citing the half-distance rule the court held 12 knots in dense fog was in excess of the "moderate" speed required by former Rule 16. And see Judge John R. Brown's vigorous dissent in *Hess Shipping Corp. v. The Charles Lykes*, 417 F.2d 346, 1969 AMC 1787 (5th Cir. 1969).

In *In re Waterstand Marine Inc.*, supra note 5, decided under the current Inland Rules, one of the court's findings of fact was, "At the time of the collision, visibility was reduced to less than 100 meters, or 300 feet—a distance significantly less than the vessel's overall length. At her speed before the collision, the *Seapride* could not stop in one-half the distance of visibility." In holding the vessel at fault for excessive speed, as well as other statutory violations, the court cited Rule 6. There was no further discussion of the half-distance rule, presumably because the vessel's speed was so excessive under the extremely limited visibility conditions prevailing that no such discussion was necessary; the speed was plainly unsafe and therefore a violation of Rule 6. However, from the fact that the court made a specific finding that the vessel could not stop in one-half the distance of visibility, it is apparent that it considered the half-distance rule valid under the current Inland Rules. Furthermore, as Rule 6 of COLREGS is the same as Rule 6 of the Inland Rules, it is likewise apparent that the court would consider the half-distance rule also valid under COLREGS.

137. COLREGS and Inland Rules decisions on safe speed in restricted visibility: In most of the decisions listed below, one or both of the vessels were found guilty of other faults as well as proceeding at excessive speed under restricted visibility conditions. A reading of the entire opinion may therefore be necessary in order to evaluate the full significance of the finding of unsafe speed in a particular case.

(a) American decisions: *Wakefield v. The Veendam*, supra note 123 (18 knots in patchy fog held unsafe); *In re Hellenic Lines, Ltd. (The Hellenic Carrier—The Lash Atlantico)*, 1984 AMC 57 (ED Va. 1982), remanded on other grounds, 730 F.2d 159, 1984 AMC 2713 (4th Cir. 1984) (speeds of 18 knots and 14 knots in intermittent fog held unsafe); *Elenson v. The Fortaleza (The Paige 2—The Fortaleza)*, 1992 AMC 1447 (SDNY 1991) (18 knots under near-zero visibility conditions held unsafe); *Amoco Transport Co. v. The Mason Lykes*, 550 F. Supp. 1264, 1983 AMC 1087 (SD Tex. 1982), reversed on other grounds, 768 F.2d 659, 1986 AMC 563 (5th Cir. 1985) (14 knots in visibility of a half mile held unsafe). See also *In re Waterstand Marine, Inc.*, supra note 5.

(b) English decisions: *The Filiatra Legacy*, [1986] 2 Lloyd's Rep. 257 (Adm.) (11 knots through the water, nearly 14 knots over the ground, held unsafe in dense fog); *The E.R. Wallonia*, [1987] 2 Lloyd's Rep. 485 (Adm.) (18 knots and 14 knots held unsafe under heavy tropical rain conditions); *The Pulkovo—The Oden*, [1989] 1 Lloyd's Rep. 280 (Adm.) (13 knots and "slightly more than 13 knots" held unsafe in visibility of about two cables, the Trinity Masters having advised the court that the vessels should have been proceeding at half speed, which they estimated

9. *Safe Speed in Clear Weather under Rule 6: Swell Damage*

While the former rules were expressly concerned with "moderate" speed only under restricted visibility conditions, vessels were frequently held at fault under the good seamanship rule, or on general principles of negligence, for casualties resulting from proceeding in clear weather at speeds considered excessive under particular circumstances. Rule 6 of COLREGS and the current Inland Rules, expressly requiring every vessel to proceed at a safe speed at all times, has therefore created no new law insofar as speed in clear weather is concerned: it has simply codified the existing decisional law. However, other rules, particularly Rule 7 (Risk of Collision) and Rule 8 (Action to Avoid Collision) may in certain circumstances have a bearing on the determination of what speed is the safe speed Rule 6 requires.

A majority of clear-weather speed cases fall into one or the other of two main categories: (a) damage by swells created by the excessive speed of a passing vessel, or (b) collisions in overtaking situations caused by hydrodynamic interaction between the vessels involved, commonly called "suction" in the United States. A major cause of such interaction is frequently the excessive speed of the overtaking vessel. This problem is treated in section C of chapter 5. At this point the discussion will be limited to swell damage and miscellaneous casualties resulting from proceeding at unsafe speeds in clear weather.

---

would not have exceeded 8 knots); *The Eglantine—The Credo—The Inez,* [1989] 1 Lloyd's Rep. 593 (Adm.), modified on other grounds, [1990] 2 Lloyd's Rep. 390 (C.A.) (13½ knots, 16 knots "and possibly more," and 9 knots held unsafe in dense fog); *The Sanshin Victory,* [1980] 2 Lloyd's Rep. 359 (Adm.) (16½ knots and 13½ knots held unsafe in dense fog, with visibility less than 300 yards and concentrations of fishing vessels likely to be in the area, the Trinity Masters having advised the court that assuming each vessel's radar was operating satisfactorily, that each vessel had maneuvering capabilities commensurate with her type and tonnage, that each vessel's master was using a reflection plotter, that lookouts were posted on the fo'c'sle and on the bridge wing, and that a quartermaster was at the wheel, a safe speed for each would have been 7.5 knots); *The Ouro Fino,* [1986] 2 Lloyd's Rep. 466 (Adm.) (12 knots, increasing to 15 knots, held unsafe in visibility of 1 to 2 miles, for a vessel failing to maintain a proper radar watch); *The Tenes,* [1989] 2 Lloyd's Rep. 367 (Adm.) (15 knots and 10 knots held unsafe in dense fog, the Trinity Masters having advised the court that the speeds should not have exceeded 10 knots and 8 knots, respectively); *The Roselina—The Eleni D.,* [1981] 2 Lloyd's Rep. 410 (Adm.) (speeds of 13 and 14 knots in dense fog held unsafe). See also *The Maritime Harmony,* [1982] 2 Lloyd's Rep. 400 (Adm.), where a speed of 8½ knots in visibility of about 3 to 4 cables was held not a "moderate" speed, as required by the Shipping Regulations for the Lower Scheldt, for a vessel which was not maintaining a proper radar watch; 7 knots would have been permissible if such a watch had been kept.

Cf. *The Glucometer II—The St. Michael,* [1989] 1 Lloyd's Rep. 54 (Adm.), where a speed of about 8 knots was held safe for a cargo vessel proceeding in dense fog with visibility of 75 meters or less, where the vessel's radar was in good working order, there were no constraints from the radar range scale in use, the weather and sea states were such as would not interfere with radar detection, any small vessel with a radar reflector could be detected at an adequate range, and other vessels had been detected without any problem. The collision, with a catamaran racing yacht engaged in the City of Plymouth Round Britain Race, was found to have been caused solely by faults of the yacht in failing to hoist a radar reflector, and in leaving an anchorage and proceeding into a shipping lane.

A vessel's speed in clear weather should be relative to her situation.[138] Full speed in mid-ocean, in a calm sea, with no other vessels in sight or observable by radar, is plainly permissible. On the other hand, the same speed in a narrow channel, or a crowded harbor, or when navigating through a group of drilling rigs or fishing vessels, is manifestly negligent. It was therefore a violation of the good seamanship rule even before COLREGS and the current Inland Rules became effective,[139] and it imposes similar liability under the safe speed mandate of Rule 6 of those rules.[140]

The reports are replete with decisions holding vessels liable for damage to property, including other vessels and their cargoes, caused by swells produced by vessels proceeding at excessive speeds. There are also cases where damages were awarded for wrongful deaths and personal injuries resulting from swells. The basic law on swell damage was succinctly summarized in *Alamia v. Chevron Transportation Corp.*[141] Swells produced when a tanker proceeded in a ship channel at speeds ranging from 8 to more than 11 knots caused damage to a shrimp boat and its catch of fish. In holding the tanker solely at fault under Rule 6(a)(ii) and (b)(v)[142] the court stated:

---

138. *The George H. Jones,* 27 F.2d 665, 1928 AMC 1504 (2d Cir. 1928). Examples of cases where speeds in clear weather have been held not excessive under particular circumstances are *Hood v. Knappton Corp.,* 1993 AMC 928 (9th Cir. 1993) (speeds of approximately 40–45 miles per hour held not excessive for two motorized fishing vessels engaged in an early morning bass fishing tournament, but vessels held 25 percent to blame for collisions with a drifting log raft, caused partly by improper mooring of the raft and partly by the vessels' failure to maintain proper look-outs); *Japan Line, Ltd. v. United States,* 1976 AMC 355 (ED Pa. 1973) (a large loaded tanker held not at fault for ascending Delaware River on flood tide at speeds of 5 to 8 knots, since any lesser speeds would have created a risk of losing steerageway); *Monsanto Co. v. Edwards Towing Corp.,* 318 F. Supp. 13, 1970 AMC 105 (ED Mo. 1969); *Breiwick v. United States,* 1972 AMC 2609 (WD Wash. 1972) (U.S. Coast Guard rescue vessel held not responsible for causing damage to fishing boats by proceeding at high speed in an effort to save a life).

139. See, e.g., *Peterson v. United States,* 367 F. Supp. 1072, 1974 AMC 378 (D D.C. 1973); *Chevron Oil Company v. The New Yorker,* 297 F. Supp. 412, 1970 AMC 514 (ED La. 1969).

140. See, e.g., *Alamia v. Chevron Transportation Corp.,* 660 F. Supp. 1123, 1988 AMC 1856 (SD Miss. 1987), discussed infra; *Pelican Marine Carriers, Inc. v. City of Tampa,* 791 F. Supp. 845, 1993 AMC 567 (MD Fla. 1992), aff'd without opinion, 4 F.3d 999 (11th Cir. 1993), quoted in note 144, infra; *The Toluca,* [1984] 1 Lloyd's Rep. 131 (C.A.), holding a vessel at fault under Rule 6 for proceeding at half speed (10.5 knots through the water) in a tortuous narrow channel; *The Coral 1,* [1982] 1 Lloyd's Rep. 441 (Adm.), holding a large vessel liable for proceeding at full maneuvering speed in the Suez Bay waiting area, resulting in a collision with a vessel anchored in the area. The court said that taking into account the facts that many vessels were anchored in the area, that there was no apparent straight passage between them, and that it was dark and there was background light from the anchored ships, a safe speed would have been half speed.

On the necessity of taking background light into account in determining safe speed under Rule 6(a)(iv), see also *The Golden Mistral,* [1986] 2 Lloyd's Rep. 407 (Adm.), where Mr. Justice Sheen said that if background light from the shore was making it difficult for a vessel proceeding in a fairway at about 6.5 knots through the water to observe ships ahead, she should have reduced her speed, which he found she in fact had done.

141. Supra note 140.

142. Rule 6(a)(ii) requires that in determining safe speed all vessels must take into account "the traffic density including concentrations of fishing vessels or any other vessels," and Rule 6(b)(v) requires vessels equipped with operational radar to take into account the number, location, and movement of vessels detected by radar.

2. This is a wake damage case. In such cases the rule of law is as follows:

> A vessel causing injury to others by her swell must be held responsible for any failure to appreciate the reasonable effect of her own speed and motion through the water at the particular place and under the particular circumstances where the injury occurred, and her officers are required to take into consideration others who may reasonably be expected to be affected, and to take all reasonable precautions to avoid their injury even though former experience has shown that in the ordinary and usual course of the events they are likely to escape injury or that the larger vessel was proceeding on ordinary course and at her customary speed. Smaller craft have the right to assume larger craft aware of their presence will observe reasonable precautions and are under no duty to warn the larger vessel of the danger. [Citing *Moran v. The Georgie May.*][143]

3. In cases where a large vessel must travel a narrow channel, the fact that the vessel needs to travel at a speed sufficient to avoid running aground or losing steerage does not relieve the vessel from liability for any damage incurred as a result of the certain wake to be produced by the displacement of water. In this situation, it has been observed that "there may well be a duty upon a moving vessel to proceed under the vessel's own power below steerage-way speed, relying upon tugs to provide all steering . . ." [Citing *Creole Shipping Ltd. v. Diamandis Pateras, Ltd.*][144]

4. The general admiralty rule and the Fifth Circuit rule, regarding wakes is that the fact of injury from swells established *prima facie* liability of the vessel creating the swell. *West India Fruit and S.S. Co. v. Raymond,* 190 F.2d 673, 674, 1951 AMC 1648, 1649 (5th Cir. 1951). The offending vessel must "exonerate herself from blame by showing that

---

143. 164 F. Supp. 881, 884–85, 1958 AMC 1152, 1156-57 (SD Fla. 1958).

144. 410 F. Supp. 313, 316, 1977 AMC 189, 192 (SD Ala. 1976), aff'd, 544 F.2d 1348, 1977 AMC 1648 (5th Cir. 1977). See also *Pelican Marine Carriers, Inc. v. City of Tampa,* supra note 140, where a heavily laden tanker sustained substantial damage when it collided with a large concrete cap located on the top of a sewer line constructed immediately outside a navigational channel. In holding the tanker partially to blame, the magistrate judge found:

> The *Louisiana* was traveling at a speed of 3 knots or more on its approach to the Freeport Sulphur dock from the Ybor City Turning Basin. Due to the torque caused by the bottoming effects and the excessive speed, directional control over the vessel was lost. This speed was excessive under the circumstances, especially due to the *Louisiana*'s close proximity to the *Pennsylvania Trader* [another tanker close by] and the berth.
>
> The Coast Guard investigation report concluded that the *Louisiana* was proceeding at an excessive rate of speed: "The apparent cause of the grounding was loss

> it was not in her power to prevent the injury by adopting any practical precautions." *Id. See also, Ladd v. United States,* 97 F. Supp. 80, 83, 1951 AMC 1186, 1189 (E.D. Va. 1951).[145]

To be entitled to the presumption that the moving vessel was at fault, the damaged vessel must prove that she was properly moored so as to resist the ordinary swells and suction that should be anticipated under the circumstances.[146] And the damaged vessel must meet its burden of proving that the damage was in fact caused by the swells before the presumption of fault on the part of the moving vessel arises.[147]

> of control of the vessel during its approach to dock. The primary contributing factor was excessive speed of the vessel (in excess of 2 knots) in the narrow channel."

145. 660 F. Supp. at 1127, 1988 AMC at 1857.

Cf. *California Transport Corp. v. The Tug Accentor,* 183 F. Supp. 817, 1961 AMC 926 (ED La. 1960), aff'd, 289 F.2d 822, 1961 AMC 1436 (5th Cir. 1961), where a large tanker upbound in the Mississippi at New Orleans collided with the lead barge while overtaking a tug and her tow. In holding the tanker solely at fault the court said:

> Sole fault for this collision must be attributed to the *Gage Lund.* Her initial fault was charging into a crowded area of the Mississippi River in the harbor of New Orleans at the entrance to the Industrial Canal where cumbersome tows could be expected to be, and were, encountered leaving and entering the Canal. Then, instead of proceeding ahead slowly in the face of this unwieldy traffic moving in all directions in the river, this super tanker continued to make good seven knots in the face of a two-knot current. Because of the traffic, she was forced into close quarters with the tow of the *Accentor,* causing the head of that tow to be pulled by suction down on her starboard quarter.
>
> It may be unfortunate that large oceangoing super tankers like the *Gage Lund* are required to share the nation's waterways with lowly tugs pushing tows. But tugs and tows have as much right in the Mississippi River as proud ocean liners, and these ocean liners are charged with the knowledge that tugs and tows are unwieldy and difficult to navigate and that due allowance must be made for these debilities. Here the *Gage Lund,* contemptuous of the low-lying craft, provoked simultaneously an overtaking situation with one tow and a passing situation with another. Under the circumstances, she assumed the risk of collision. As the overtaking vessel she was bound to stay clear of the *Accentor.* This she failed to do, and for this she must be held solely at fault.

See also *Nicholas Eustathiou & Co. v. United States,* 178 F. Supp. 33, 1959 AMC 1254 (ED Va. 1957), holding an LSD (landing ship dock) solely to blame for a collision with a cargo vessel. Among the faults of which the LSD was found guilty was approaching a busy intersection off Cape Henry at flank speed "when it was known, or should have been known, that both inbound and outbound vessels would be encountered from many directions, and that these vessels would be maneuvering to pick up, or discharge their pilots."

146. *Petroleum Fuel and Terminal Co. v. The Overseas Alaska,* 1991 AMC 2729 (MD La. 1991); *New Orleans Steamboat Co. v. The Hellespont Glory,* 562 F. Supp. 391 (ED La. 1983); *O'Donnell Transp. Co. v. The Maryland Trader,* 228 F. Supp. 903, 1964 AMC 453 (SDNY 1963).

147. See *Cities Service Tankers Corp. v. The Weser Agent,* 1977 AMC 1219 (D Mass. 1977), where a moored tanker pulled a section of the pier and a bollard to which a spring line was attached into the water after defendant's vessel passed 250 to 300 feet abeam at a speed of not over 6 knots. There was evidence that the strain on the line might have been caused when the moored vessel's engines were being warmed up. See also *Scalici v. Moran Towing and Transportation Co.,* 1986 AMC 2645 (EDNY 1986); *State Site, Inc. v. The Heragas,* 628 F. Supp. 1569, 1987 AMC 819 (ED Tex. 1986).

The presumption of fault does not extend to personal injuries on board a vessel that does not herself sustain damage from the wake of a passing vessel. In *Maxwell v. Hapag-Lloyd,*[148] plaintiff was in the hold of a fishing boat tied to a private mooring dock on the Columbia River. Alerted by a noise, he came out of the hold, fell between the boat and the dock, and broke his leg. He claimed that his fall was caused by an unusually large wake from a passing cargo vessel proceeding upriver at an excessive speed. The trial judge denied the plaintiff's request to charge that when the wake of a "passing ship . . . produces unusual motion [of a properly moored vessel] which causes injury to someone on board the vessel, there is a presumption of fault. . . ." In affirming a judgment on a defendant's verdict, the Ninth Circuit stated:

> A presumption of fault does not extend to personal injuries occurring as a result of a fall on properly moored vessels that do not themselves suffer damage. See Annotation, *Res Ipsa Loquitur With Respect to Personal Injuries or Death On or About Ship,* 1 ALR 3d 642, 657-660 (1965). In negligence actions generally, fault should not be presumed in the case of an injury resulting from a fall. Unlike damage to a properly moored vessel, an accidental fall does not justify a presumption that negligence caused it. See Keeton, *Prosser and Keeton on Torts* sec. 39 at 246 (1984).
>
> Maxwell misreads his authority for extending the presumption to personal injuries. In *Couch v. Bowman,* 263 F. Supp. 714 (ED Tenn. 1966), the district court found as a fact that Bowman negligently piloted his vessel and created a large wave which caused Couch to be thrown from his boat deck into the lake. A passage included in the decision referred to an opinion stating that the burden of proof was shifted to the defendant once the plaintiff proved that swells caused damage to a properly moored vessel. See *O'Donnell Transportation Co. v. M/V Maryland Trader,* 1964 AMC 453, 462, 228 F. Supp. 903, 909 (SDNY 1963). This passage was not necessary to the holding in *Couch.* See 263 F. Supp. at 716–17. Decisions involving personal injuries occurring while aboard a moving vessel that result from the wash of another moving vessel have imposed a duty of reasonable care but not a presumption of fault. See *Anthony v. International Paper Co.* 1961 AMC 1890, 1897–1900, 289 F.2d 574, 579–81 (4 Cir. 1961) (lookout duty); *Moran v. M/V Georgie May,* 1958 AMC 1152, 1156–57, 164 F. Supp. 881, 884–85 (SD Fla. 1958); see also *Byrd v. Belcher,* 203 F. Supp. 645, 648 (ED Tenn. 1962). But cf. *Sweeney v. Car/Puter International Corp.,* 1982 AMC 622, 627, 634–36, 521 F. Supp. 276, 280, 285–86 (D.S.C. 1981) (imposing a duty of reasonable care and discussing, but not relying upon, *res ipsa loquitur.*)[149]

148. 862 F.2d 767, 1989 AMC 330 (9th Cir. 1988).
149. 862 F.2d at 769, 1989 AMC at 332–33.

In most instances swells are from a vessel's wake. However, in *Bernert Towboat Co. v. The U.S.S. Chandler*[150] the United States was held liable for damage to a downbound barge and its cargo caused by a "soliton" (a kind of wave) produced ahead of a 563-foot guided missile destroyer proceeding up the Columbia River. After finding that the *Chandler* was traveling at a speed of more than 21 knots, and that under the circumstances her speed was, as a matter of law, a violation of Rule 6, Judge Belloni stated:

> Captain Easley [of the *Tug Mary B*, which was pushing the damaged barge and another at the time of the casualty] testified that he rode over an unusually large swell that was pushed ahead of the *Chandler* . . . The government initially contended that his explanation is physically impossible because a ship's wake is left behind the ship, not pushed ahead. However at trial the government's expert conceded that Captain Easley's explanation is plausible.
>
> Plaintiff's expert, Dr. Bruce Adee, is a Professor at the University of Washington. He is also a naval architect and a hydrodynamicist. He testified that in unrestricted waters a ship creates a transverse wave that makes an angle of about 20° with the ship's centerline. These waves are left behind the ship. However, a ship traveling at high speed in a restricted channel will create a much different wave pattern. The pattern created is a function of the ship's speed and the water depth. Professor Adee stated that based on the river depth and the ship's speed, the *Chandler* produced a swell that made an angle between 54° and 65° from the ship's centerline. This unusual wave, which is called a soliton, is relatively steep and creates a shelf of water. He estimated the soliton's height at four to six feet.
>
> William G. Day testified for the government on this point. He agreed with Professor Adee on the underlying scientific principles of soliton creation. He said that a soliton wave can be 90° to the ship's centerline and can even be pushed ahead of the ship. He opined that if the *Chandler* traveled faster than 19 knots it could produce a soliton.
>
> I find Captain Easley's and Professor Adee's testimony credible concerning the existence of the soliton. I find that the *Chandler* produced a soliton wave which was higher than five feet. I find that the soliton posed a danger to seaworthy vessels capable of meeting the ordinary risks of navigation on the Columbia River.[151]

---

150. 666 F. Supp. 1454, 1987 AMC 2919 (D Or. 1987).
151. 666 F. Supp. at 1458–59, 1987 AMC at 2924–25.

Section D. Rule 7: Risk of Collision

1. *Introduction*

Rule 7 of COLREGS and Rule 7 of the Inland Rules are identical. The basic mandate of the rule is found in paragraph (a); the remaining paragraphs concern some of the ways in which the mandate is to be carried out. Paragraph (a) requires every vessel "to use all available means appropriate to the prevailing circumstances and conditions to determine if risk of collision exists," and provides: "If there is any doubt such risk shall be deemed to exist." No such positive requirements were included in the former rules. However, they did contain a note to the Steering and Sailing Rules[152] entitled "Preliminary—Risk of Collision," advising that "Risk of collision can, when circumstances permit, be ascertained by carefully watching the compass bearing of an approaching vessel. If the bearing does not appreciably change, such risk should be deemed to exist." While Rule 7 is devoted entirely to risk of collision, and while that term is used in Rules 5, 8 (of COLREGS only),[153] 12, 14, 15, 18, and 19, it is not defined in Rule 3 (General Definitions), or in any other of the rules. Indeed, it is a term that defies precise definition.[154]

In *The Milwaukee*,[155] the *Lac la Belle* was held at fault for violating Article 16 of the rules then in force, which required every steamship, when approaching another ship "so as to involve risk of collision" to slacken speed, or if necessary, stop and reverse.[156] In discussing the rule the court stated:

> . . . The moment the *Milwaukee* starboarded [i.e., turned to port] there was danger of collision. It then, if not before, certainly became the duty of the *Lac la Belle* to slacken speed. I think, however, it is open to discussion under article 16 whether the obligation of a steamship approaching another vessel to slacken speed does not attach the moment risk of collision is involved, and whether, under that article, it is allowable for such ship to wait to see if there is absolutely danger of collision before doing so. Danger of collision is, of course, included in risk of collision, but it is not all there is of it. There is never danger of collision other than by inevitable or inscrutable accident, where all fully and completely obey the law. Danger of collision begins only when one vessel or the other begins to depart from the rules established by law. Risk of collision begins the very moment when the two vessels have approached so

152. Former International Rules and Inland Rules, Articles 17–27.

153. Para. (f) of COLREGS Rule 8 was added in 1989. An identical provision was added to Inland Rule 8 in 1991. See § E, infra (Action to Avoid Collision).

154. See, e.g., Marsden 462, citing Dr. Lushington in *The Mangerton,* (1857) Sw. 120.

155. 17 F. Cas. 427 (ED Mich. 1871) (No. 9626).

156. Act of Apr. 29, 1864, 13 Stat. 61.

> near each other and upon such courses, that by a departure from the rules of navigation, whether from want of good seamanship, accident, mistake, misapprehension of signals or otherwise, a collision might be brought about.[157]

On the other hand, in *The Aurania*[158] Judge Addison Brown equated the term "risk of collision" with "danger of collision": "'Risk of collision' means, not merely certainty of collision if no efforts be made to avert it, but danger of collision, and there is danger or risk of collision whenever it is not clearly safe to go on. . . ."[159] At the 1972 Diplomatic Conference at which COLREGS were adopted it was proposed that "risk of collision" be defined in the rules. In referring to the proposal, Messrs. Cockcroft and Lameijer state:

> The 1972 Conference rejected a proposed definition that "risk of collision" exists between vessels when their projected courses and speeds place them at or near the same location simultaneously. Had this definition been accepted a vessel detecting another at long range, slowly approaching from the port side with little change of bearing, would have been obliged to keep her course and speed for a long period, possibly several hours.
>
> In the Courts of the United Kingdom and other countries risk of collision has not been held to apply at long distances when there is a low speed of approach. As the above definition was not accepted the previous Court interpretation should also apply to the 1972 Rules.[160]

It is essential that a distinction be drawn between (1) the phrase "risk of collision," as used in rules relating to the actual existence of the risk, or to the determination of its existence or nonexistence, and (2) the phrase "*so as to*

157. Supra note 155, 17 F. Cas. at 433. The case was decided at a time when steering wheels were rigged like the tillers that preceded them, i.e., to turn the rudder (and the ship's heading) to the right, the wheel was turned to the left, and vice versa, just as even today on a small vessel without a steering wheel, to turn the rudder (and the vessel's heading) to the left the tiller is put to the right, and vice versa.

The old system for vessels equipped with steering wheels was abolished in the United Kingdom in 1932 by Act of 22 and 23 Geo. V, and in the United States by 49 Stat. 668 (1935), repealed in 1951, 65 Stat. 407, presumably because the practice of direct orders had long since become so universal that the statute had become unnecessary. The 1948 International Rules also contained a Rule (32) requiring direct orders, but the rule was deleted from the 1960 Rules, presumably for the same reason.

158. 29 F. 98 (SDNY 1886).

159. Id. at 123. Cf. *The Philadelphia,* 199 F. 299 (ED Pa. 1912), where the court said that "Risk of collision is different from 'immediate danger,' and means 'chance,' 'peril,' 'hazard,' or 'danger of collision.' There is 'risk of collision' when it is not clearly safe to go on." See also *Socony Vacuum Transp. Co. v. Gypsum Packet Co.,* 153 F.2d 773, 1946 AMC 309, 313 (2d Cir. 1946) ("'Risk of collision' does not mean certainty of collision, but only that prudence demands that the navigators shall watch each other's navigation, and be prepared to do whatever safety may demand.")

160. Cockcroft & Lameijer 54.

involve[161] risk of collision," as used in rules describing the manner in which a vessel must be approaching another before a particular rule will apply. Thus in Rule 5 (Look-out) the words are used in outlining the purpose of maintaining a proper look-out: "so as to make a full appraisal of the situation and of the *risk of collision.*" In Rule 18 (Responsibilities Between Vessels) they are used to describe the circumstances whereunder a seaplane on the water must comply with the Steering and Sailing Rules: "where *risk of collision exists.*" In Rule 19 the words are used in outlining the obligations of a vessel detecting the presence of another by radar alone: she must "determine if a close quarters situation is developing or *risk of collision exists,*" and if it does, she must take avoiding action.

On the other hand, the mandates of COLREGS Rule 8 and Rules 12, 14, and 15 of both COLREGS and the Inland Rules apply not to the *existence* of a risk of collision, or to a determination of whether or not it exists, but to the conduct of vessels approaching each other "*so as to involve* risk of collision." Thus Rule 8(f)(ii) of COLREGS (Action to Avoid Collision) provides that a vessel required not to impede the passage or safe passage of another is not relieved of this obligation if approaching the other "*so as to involve* risk of collision." Rule 12 (Sailing Vessels) applies to such vessels when they are approaching one another "*so as to involve* risk of collision." Rule 14 (Head-on Situation) applies to vessels meeting on reciprocal or nearly reciprocal courses "*so as to involve* risk of collision," and Rule 15 (Crossing Situation) applies when vessels are crossing "*so as to involve* risk of collision." Rule 13 (Overtaking) contains no such provision. The significance of its absence is discussed in chapter 5, section C.

The distinction between the actual existence of a risk of collision, or a determination of its existence or nonexistence, and a maneuver involving a risk of collision is clearly made in Griffin and Marsden. In referring to the phrase "so as to involve risk of collision," as used in the Steering and Sailing Rules, Griffin states:

> It will be noted that the phrase is not "so that there *is* risk of collision," but "so as to *involve* risk of collision." The words evidently refer to a time when there is not yet actual danger, but when the relation between the vessels is such that danger may shortly arise, if the rules are not obeyed. Thus Brett, M.R., in the *Beryl,* 9 Prob. Div. 137, 5 Asp. 321 [1884], said that the rules are intended "not merely for the purpose of preventing a collision, but for the purpose of preventing even a risk of collision." And Atkin, L.J., in the *Gulf of Suez,* [1921] Prob. Div. 318, 332, said that the phrase "to involve risk of collision . . . indicates a period before the risk has, so to speak, actually matured; it means a period at which there is a probability that there will be a risk of collision if precautions are not

161. Italics in this and the following paragraph have been supplied.

> taken." To same effect, the *Kirnwood,* 201 Fed. 428 [1912]; the *City of Rome,* C.C.A. 2, 38 F.2d 782, 1930 A.M.C. 524, 528. See too the *Banshee,* 6 Asp. 221 [1887], ...[162]

Marsden's observations are similar. In referring to *The Beryl*[163] Marsden states:

> The Master of the Rolls and the other members of the Court of Appeal (Bowen and Fry L.JJ.) held that the regulations were intended not only to prevent collision but to prevent risk of collision; and that it is a rule of interpretation of the regulations that "they are all applicable at a time when the risk of collision can be avoided, not that they are applicable when the risk of collision is already fixed and determined." The court laid stress upon the words "so as to involve risk of collision," which occur in several of the articles,[164] and held that they do not refer to an existing risk of collision, but point to a time before risk of collision has arisen, and where it is, or ought to be, apparent that there will be risk if nothing is done to prevent it.[165] "Another rule of interpretation of these regulations is (the object of them being to avoid risk of collision) that they are all applicable at a time when the risk of collision can be avoided—not that they are applicable when the risk of collision is already fixed and determined. We have always said that the right moment of time to be considered is that which exists at the moment before the risk of collision is constituted."[166] So, in *The Stanmore,*[167] Brett M.R. held the regulations to apply where there is "a probability of risk." In *The Gulf of Suez,*[168] it was said that the phrase "to involve risk of collision" indicates a period before the risk has, so to speak, actually matured; it means a period at which there is a probability that there will be a risk of collision if precautions are not taken. . . .[169]

The effect of the use of the term "so as to involve risk of collision" in COLREGS Rule 8 is discussed in section E of this chapter—Action to Avoid Collision. The effect of its use in Rules 12, 14, and 15 of COLREGS and the Inland Rules is discussed in chapter 5.

---

162. Griffin 23.

163. (1884) 9 P.D. 137, 5 Asp. Mar. Cas. (N.S.) 321. Marsden also refers to *The Dordogne,* (1885) 10 P.D. 6; *The Ebor,* (1886) 11 P.D. 24, 29; and *The Memnon,* (1889) 6 Asp. Mar. Cas. (N.S.) 317.

164. Citing former Rules 17–32 (the Steering and Sailing Rules).

165. In *The Bellanoch* [1907] P. 170, 192, it was stated that this was the rule laid down in *The Beryl,* supra note 163. By applying the rule stated in this form it is easy in most cases to determine the time when the regulations begin to govern the situation. (Marsden's note.)

166. Citing Brett, M.R., in *The Beryl,* supra note 163, 9 P.D. at 140.

167. (1885) 10 P.D. 134.

168. Citing Atkin, L.J., in *The Gulf of Suez,* [1921] P. 318 at 332.

169. Marsden 461.

2. *What Constitutes "All Available Means"*

The phrase "all available means appropriate to the prevailing circumstances," as used in paragraph (a) of Rule 7, certainly includes radar when the circumstances indicate that its use would assist in determining whether risk of collision exists, and paragraph (b) of the rule specifically so provides. But as Messrs. Cockcroft and Lameijer point out, other means may be necessary and even preferable under particular circumstances. For example, the taking of compass bearings may be important in determining whether or not there is a risk of collision with a vessel that has already been sighted visually. The use of VHF radiotelephone may also assist two approaching vessels in clarifying each other's intentions. And when a traffic separation scheme is being followed, information received by VHF concerning the movements of other vessels proceeding against the prescribed direction of the traffic flow may be helpful.[170] Messrs. Cockcroft and Lameijer observe that while the radiotelephone has proved valuable in some areas, including the Great Lakes, in other international waters difficulty in ascertaining from which of several vessels in the area a radiotelephone message is coming, as well as language barriers, place severe limitations on its use.[171]

3. *Radar and the Determination of Risk of Collision*

Rule 7(b) requires the proper use of radar equipment if fitted and operational, "including long range scanning to obtain early warning of risk of collision and radar plotting or equivalent systematic observation of detected objects." This requirement applies in clear weather as well as in restricted visibility.[172]

Rule 7(c), like the Radar Annex to the 1960 International Rules, prohibits the making of assumptions "on the basis of scanty information, especially scanty radar information." Paragraphs (b) and (c) are treated together in some of the decisions concerning Rule 7 and will be considered together here.

---

170. Cockcroft & Lameijer 55–56.

171. Id. Cf. *The Tenes,* [1989] 2 Lloyd's Rep. 367 (Adm.), involving a both-to-blame collision between a German vessel and an Algerian vessel, where Mr. Justice Sheen stated:

> It appears from the evidence that when *Tenes* was approaching *Darion,* the mate of *Darion* went to the V.H.F. set and endeavoured to speak to the *Tenes.* The Court strongly deplores this use of V.H.F. The nationality of the other ship cannot be known. Even if the master of the other ship speaks the same language, the use of V.H.F. may cause confusion.

172. *In re Ocean Foods Boat Company (The Tosca—The McKinley),* 692 F. Supp. 1253, 1989 AMC 579 (D Or. 1988); *Maritrans Operating Partners L.P. v. The Faith I,* 800 F. Supp. 133, 1993 AMC 385 (D N.J. 1993); *In re G&G Shipping Co.,* 767 F. Supp. 398, 1994 AMC 170 (D P.R. 1991) (burden of proving that a failure to use radar properly did not contribute to a collision is on the party failing to use it.) See also *Arabian American Oil Co. v. Hellenic Lines, Ltd.,* 633 F. Supp. 659 (SDNY 1986). But see *Granholm v. The TLF Express,* 576 F. Supp. 435, 1984 AMC 943 (SDNY 1983): (Rule 7[b] does not require use of radar in uncongested waters, in clear visibility).

Perhaps the earliest reported American decision holding a vessel at fault for a violation of Rule 7 is *Wakefield v. The Veendam.*[173] In that case a fishing vessel was held 65 percent to blame for a fog collision with a passenger liner in Canadian waters, where COLREGS applied. After pointing to deficiencies in the crew, Judge Beeks continued:

> As a consequence of the deficient and incompetent manning, she could not comply with the applicable rules of the road (Collision Regulations). She could not post a proper lookout (Rule 5), or determine if a risk of collision existed (Rule 7(a)). With her radar set on the half mile scale (Rule 7(b)), she had no idea there was another vessel in the vicinity until immediately prior to impact. Without knowledge that a risk of collision existed, she could not take action to avoid it (Rule 8), alter course to starboard (Rule 14(a)), or sound proper signals (Rules 34 and 35(a)).[174]

It is plain that in the case of a vessel equipped with ARPA its proper use is "systematic observation of detected objects" equivalent to radar plotting, within the meaning of Rule 7(b).[175] But as of 1997 no other system had been approved by the courts.

In *Matter of Hellenic Lines, Ltd. (The Hellenic Carrier—The Lash Atlantico),*[176] a fog case, the *Lash Atlantico* observed the *Hellenic Carrier* ahead by radar, 12 miles distant. No plot was made, but the *Lash Atlantico*'s watch officer systematically observed the echo of the *Hellenic Carrier* as it moved in relation to the cursor and a parallel grid on the radarscope—a method referred to as parallel indexing. In finding the *Lash Atlantico* 80 percent and the *Hellenic Carrier* 20 percent at fault for the ensuing collision, the district court held that while the *Hellenic Carrier* was at fault for excessive speed, "parallel indexing" was the equivalent of plotting, and she was therefore not in violation of Rule 7.

On appeal, however, the Fourth Circuit disagreed and remanded the case to the district court for reconsideration of the apportionment of fault, stating:[177]

---

173. 1980 AMC 2906 (WD Wash. 1980).

174. Id. at 2912.

175. See *In re Hellenic Lines, Ltd. (The Hellenic Carrier—The Lash Atlantico),* 730 F.2d 159, 1984 AMC 2713 (4th Cir. 1984); *Elenson v. The Fortaleza,* 1992 AMC 1447 (SDNY 1991). Cf. *In re Ocean Foods Boat Company (The Tosca—The McKinley),* supra note 172, where in holding the *Tosca* 35 percent to blame for a collision with a fishing vessel the court said:

> Dirland [the *Tosca's* watch officer] went to the ARPA, an automatic radar plotting aid that is computer assisted. The ARPA processes the radar data and generates predictive vectors and other ship movement information which is then used in collision avoidance. It can be set on either automatic or manual. That evening it was set on manual. Dirland could see nothing on the ARPA. Consequently, he could not use the ARPA to help avoid the collision. The testimony at trial established that the ARPA works as a "slave" to the radar. If the radar is misadjusted, then the ARPA may not work.

176. Supra note 175, remanding 1984 AMC 57 (ED Va. 1982).

177. 730 F.2d at 163, 1984 AMC at 2718.

We hold that "parallel indexing" is not "equivalent systematic observation" to radar plotting, because it is not *equivalent* or reasonably equal to radar plotting. *Hellenic*'s own expert, Captain Slack, testified that "parallel indexing" was not equivalent to radar plotting because "parallel indexing" does not give the relative motion, course and speed of the other vessel. It provides only the closest point of approach. A system that does not provide information as to the course, speed and relative motion of an approaching vessel cannot be the *equivalent* of a system that does.

No court has yet addressed the question of what constitutes "equivalent systematic observation." However, A. Cockcroft & J. Lameijer, who assisted in drafting the 72 Colregs, state:

"Even continuous observation by a competent person is unlikely to be accepted as proper use of radar to obtain early warning of risk of collision if the bearings and distances of approaching vessels are not taken at regular intervals and carefully evaluated by *plotting* or by some *equivalent method* (emphasis added)."[178]

Knight's Modern Seamanship, which has been the standby of mariners for generations, in its 16th edition (1977) states at page 566:

"The radar plot required by the International Rules includes a radar deflection plotter fitted over the scope, as well as plotting directly on the scope. 'Systematic observation' includes the plotting teams used on most naval vessels as well as computerized collision avoidance systems which process radar bearings and range data and display information on a cathode ray tube."

Several decisions have held vessels to blame for failing to carry out long-range scanning, as required by Rule 7(b). In *The Pulkovo and Oden*[179] both vessels were held equally to blame for excessive speed in fog. The *Oden* was also held at fault for breaching the long-range scanning requirement of Rule 7(b), and for making assumptions as to the *Pulkovo's* course and speed on the basis of scanty radar information, contrary to Rule 7(c).[180]

4. *The Duty to Watch Compass Bearings*

As stated, the preliminary note to the former Steering and Sailing Rules was worded, not as a positive mandate, but rather as an advisory note. Nevertheless, vessels were held at fault under the former rules for failing to observe the compass bearings of an approaching vessel, or to note that the bearings

---

178. Citing Cockcroft & Lameijer, *A Guide to the Collision Avoidance Rules* 56 (2d ed. 1976). The quotation appears at pp. 58–59 of the 4th edition of Cockcroft & Lameijer.

179. [1989] 1 Lloyd's Rep. 280 (Adm.).

180. See also *Elenson v. The Fortaleza,* supra note 175.

were remaining constant, and that there was therefore a risk of collision.[181] Rule 7(d)(i) of COLREGS and the Inland Rules, on the other hand, is worded positively; it provides that among the considerations that *"shall"* be taken into account in determining whether risk of collision exists is that "if the compass bearing of an approaching vessel does not appreciably change," the risk *"shall"* be deemed to exist.[182]

Under COLREGS and the Inland Rules vessels have been held at fault in a number of American and English decisions for failing to follow the requirements of Rule 7(d)(i). Thus, in *The Pulkovo and Oden,*[183] Mr. Justice Sheen put the following question to the Trinity masters:

> Assuming that *Pulkovo* had observed in her radar an echo fine on the port bow at a range of seven miles and that thereafter the bearing of that echo did not change appreciably, what action should have been taken and when?

Their answer, which Mr. Justice Sheen accepted, was:

> If the bearing does not change appreciably then a close quarters situation is developing. When this is confirmed avoiding action should be taken in ample time, preferably at a distance of not less than five miles. With the echo approaching from fine on the bow the situation should be deemed to be end on or nearly end on. *Pulkovo* should have made a bold alteration to starboard of not less than 35 deg. and preferably about 60 deg. so that the alteration may readily be seen on the other vessel's radar. Thereafter the effectiveness of the action should be carefully checked and the course resumed when the possibility of a close quarters situation no longer exists. We would add that when ships are approaching each other nearly end on a reduction of speed by itself does not avoid a close quarters situation. . . .[184]

In *Maritrans Operating Partners L.P. v. The Faith I,*[185] both vessels were held at fault for failing to take compass bearings or plot radar observations of each other in order to determine speed and speed changes.

181. See, e.g., *In re Pacific Far East Line (The Esso Seattle—The Guam Bear),* 314 F. Supp. 1339, 1970 AMC 1592 (ND Cal. 1970) (Beeks, D.J.), aff'd, 472 F.2d 1382, (9th Cir. 1973); *United States v. The Wuerttemberg,* 219 F. Supp. 211, 1963 AMC 1554 (D S.C. 1963), aff'd in part, rev'd in part on other grounds, 330 F.2d 498, 1964 AMC 1098 (4th Cir. 1964); *In re Ocean Steamship Co. (The City of Rome—The U.S.S. S-51),* 38 F.2d 782, 784, 1930 AMC 524, 526 (2d Cir. 1930) (L. Hand, Ct. J.); *The Philadelphia,* supra note 159.

182. Emphasis supplied.

183. Supra note 179.

184. Id., [1989] 1 Lloyd's Rep. at 287.

185. Supra note 128.

In *In re Ocean Foods Boat Company (The Tosca—The McKinley)*,[186] the owner of the *McKinley* was denied limitation of liability for loss of life and property damage because the collision was caused in part by the incompetence of the crew. As the distance between the vessels closed, the bearing of the *Tosca* did not change, but the only man on watch at the material times did not know that "this was a sure sign of an imminent collision with the *Tosca*."

While constant bearings of an approaching vessel are a sure indication that the vessels are on a collision course, the converse is not true: changes in bearings do not always mean that there is no risk of collision. This fact was recognized by the courts long before the adoption of COLREGS and the Inland Rules. In referring to the preliminary note to the Steering and Sailing Rules then in force, the Court of Appeals for the Ninth Circuit said, in *Wilders S.S. Co. v. Low*:[187]

> This section is not a rule of navigation, but merely a suggestion of one circumstance which denotes that there is danger of collision, and a steamer is not justified in assuming that there is no risk because there is an appreciable change in the compass bearing of the lights of a sailing vessel seen at night, which would manifestly be an unwarranted assumption under some circumstances.

The principle is specifically recognized in the final paragraph of Rule 7. Paragraph (d)(ii), unlike paragraph (d)(i), is not a positive mandate, but simply a caveat: it warns that risk of collision "may sometimes exist even when an appreciable bearing change is evident, particularly when approaching a very large vessel or a tow or when approaching a vessel at close range." Farwell gives a good example of the caveat:

> Thus, in the crossing situation, the bearings of a vessel on the starboard bow may be constant, indicating that the two vessels will reach the point of intersection at the same time; they may be drawing ahead, indicating the stand-on vessel will reach the point of intersection first; or they may be drawing aft, indicating the give-way vessel will reach that point first. The rapidity of change in bearing depends on the distance apart and the relative speeds of the two vessels. It would be a mistake to assume that only in the first case is there risk of collision. It is true that if the bearings of the stand-on vessel draw ahead with a certain degree of rapidity, there is a presumption that she will have clearance across the bow of the burdened vessel; but this does not relieve the latter of her obligation to watch the stand-on vessel closely, and to slow down or stop or reverse, if necessary, before coming into dangerous proximity. Conversely, if the

186. Supra note 175.
187. 112 F.161 (9th Cir. 1901).

bearings of the stand-on vessel draw aft with sufficient rapidity, there is a presumption that the burdened vessel might cross with safety; but wide indeed must be the margin in that case before she is legally justified in making the attempt. As a matter of law, it must be wide enough so that no risk of collision is involved; as a matter of practice and of common prudence, it should be wide enough so that no collision can occur no matter what the other vessel does.[188]

Section E. Rule 8: Action to Avoid Collision

1. Introduction

Rule 8 is new as a rule, but its substance is quite similar to the Recommendations on the Use of Radar as an Aid to Avoiding Collisions at Sea, annexed to the 1960 International Rules. As stated, paragraph (f) was added to COLREGS Rule 8 in 1989, and an identical paragraph was added to Inland Rule 8 in 1991.

Paragraph (a) of the rule lays down three basic requirements with respect to any action taken to avoid collision: "If the circumstances of the case admit," the action must be (1) positive, (2) taken in ample time, and (3) in accordance with good seamanship. While grammatically the limiting words "if the circumstances of the case admit" apply to all three requirements, the drafters of Rule 8 could never have intended it to apply to the third, which is simply an echo of Rule 2(a), the rule of good seamanship. As discussed in chapter 3, section A, that rule is essentially a requirement of the exercise of due care at all times, although the standard of care may be different when a vessel is in the jaws of collision as a result of the fault of another vessel than it is when there is ample time to decide on a proper maneuver. The true thrust of paragraph (a) is therefore that generally whatever action is taken to avoid collision must be positive and timely.

Paragraph (b) is a corollary of the paragraph (a) requirement of positive action: when the action taken consists of an alteration of course and/or speed, it must, again "if the circumstances of the case admit," be sufficiently large to be readily apparent to another vessel observing by sight or by radar. Avoidance of a series of minor course and/or speed alterations is specifically mandated.

Paragraphs (a) and (b) of Rule 8 are closely related to Rules 16 and 19(d). Rule 16, discussed in chapter 5, requires every vessel directed to keep

---

188. Farwell's *Rules of the Nautical Road* 134–35 (7th ed. by R. Smith) (hereinafter "Farwell").

189. The amendment to COLREGS Rule 8 is contained in the 1997 Pocket Supplement to 33 U.S.C.A., at pp.41–42, following § 1602. The amendment to Inland Rule 8 is contained at p. 78, under § 2008.

out of the way of another (e.g., the port-hand vessel in a crossing situation, or a vessel overtaking another) to "take early and substantial action to keep well clear." Rule 19(d), discussed in chapter 6, requires a vessel detecting the presence of another vessel by radar alone to determine if a close-quarters situation is developing or if risk of collision exists. In either case, she must "take avoiding action in ample time." If the action is a course alteration she must, so far as possible, avoid a port turn for a vessel forward of the beam (other than a vessel being overtaken), and an alteration of course toward a vessel abeam or abaft the beam.

Paragraph (c) suggests that where there is sufficient sea room, the most effective action to avoid a close-quarters situation *may* be an alteration of course alone, provided (1) that it is made in good time, (2) that it is substantial, and (3) that it does not result in another close-quarters situation. This suggestion is based on the fact that alterations of speed take longer to put into effect than alterations of course, and are therefore less likely to be readily observed by those on board an approaching vessel.[190] The first two provisos are simply a specific application of the mandate of paragraph (a) that *any* action taken to avoid collision must be positive and timely; the mandate remains applicable when the action taken is a change of course alone. The third proviso is obviously one of common sense: there would be no point in making a course alteration to avoid a close-quarters situation with Vessel A if that action would result in a close-quarters situation with Vessel B.

Paragraph (d) requires that whatever action is taken to avoid collision must be one that will result in passing the other vessel at a safe distance. It further requires that the effectiveness of the action taken must be carefully checked until the other vessel is past and clear. The rules do not quantify the term "safe distance." It is quite obvious that in terms of miles, or fractions of a mile, a safe distance for passing will vary with the circumstances, including the state of the visibility, the wind and sea conditions, the relative speeds of the two vessels, the power, turning ability, and other characteristics of the vessel taking the action, and the traffic conditions, e.g., whether the action is taken in the open sea or in a crowded harbor.

Nor do the rules define "close quarters," a term that is the antithesis of "safe distance"—i.e., if a passing is not made at a "safe distance," it means that a close-quarters situation has been created. In discussing close quarters, Messrs. Cockcroft and Lameijer suggest that "In the open sea distances of the order of 2 to 3 miles are usually considered to be the outer limits in restricted visibility but smaller distances, probably of the order of 1 mile, would probably be accepted for vessels in sight of each other . . . ."[191] The same authors further state:

190. See Cockcroft & Lameijer 65.
191. Id. 67.

> In restricted visibility, in the open sea, a close quarters situation is generally considered to begin to apply at a distance of at least 2 miles in any direction forward of the beam as this is the typical range of audibility for the whistle of a large vessel in still conditions (see Annex III(1)(c)). A minimum distance of 3 miles is sometimes suggested when determining whether a close quarters situation is developing as allowance should be made for the effects of errors in radar observations, especially at long range. However, distances of less than 2 miles may be considered sufficient when proceeding at reduced speed in congested waters, when in an overtaking situation, or, when a vessel is expected to pass astern.[192]

In *Hellenic Lines, Ltd. v. Prudential Lines, Inc.,*[193] the Fourth Circuit set aside a finding of the district court that the colliding vessels were set up to pass at a distance of 2 miles when the *Hellenic Carrier* made the first of two port turns, stating:

> Initially we consider the district court's determination that a close quarters situation was not developing. What constitutes close quarters is not defined in Rule 19 [Conduct of vessels in restricted visibility] and must be determined in each case primarily upon the location of the vessels and the space in which they have to maneuver. See A. Cockcroft & J. Lameijer, *A Guide to the Collision Avoidance Rules* p. 129 (2d ed. 1976).[194] Although the district court made no specific finding on what distance constituted close quarters in this case, it is clear from the fact that a collision occurred and the testimony of Captain Slack that any passing distance under two miles is close quarters in a fog.[195]

Paragraph (e) provides that where necessary to avoid a collision, or to allow more time to assess the situation, a vessel must slacken her speed or take all way off by stopping or reversing her engines. This is another commonsense requirement: obviously, as long as a vessel maintains whatever steerageway may be required for maneuvering in relation to another vessel, the slower the speed, the more time there will be to reach a proper decision as to

---

192. Id. 146. On passing at a safe distance, see id. 67; 116.

193. 730 F.2d 159, 1984 AMC 2713 (4th Cir. 1984).

194. See the fourth edition of Cockcroft & Lameijer 146.

195. 730 F.2d at 164, 1984 AMC at 2719–20. Cf. *In re G&G Shipping Co. Ltd. (The Wishing Star—The Nedlloyd Van Noort),* 767 F. Supp. 398, 410, 1994 AMC 170, 176 (D P.R. 1991):

> What constitutes a close-quarters situation is not defined in the 72 Colregs and must be determined on a case by case basis depending on the location of the vessels and the maneuverability space. The slim passage envisioned by Nieuwkoop [the *Nedlloyd Van Noort*'s mate on watch], less than twice the length of the *Van Noort,* attempted at night without any indication that the approaching *Wishing Star* had sighted the *Van Noort,* is particularly brazen. In light of Captain Van Loo's standing orders considering one mile to be safe passage, and the sufficient sea room to the *Van Noort's* starboard side, a c.p.a. [closest point of approach] of 1,000 feet is not substantial within the meaning of Rule 8(b) and 8(c).

the action best suited to avoid a collision with another vessel, and the less likelihood there will be of a collision occurring.

As stated, paragraph (f) was added to COLREGS in 1989 and to Inland Rule 8 in 1991. It consists of three subparagraphs. Subparagraph (i) provides that a vessel which is required by any of the rules not to impede the passage[196] or safe passage[197] of another vessel must, when the circumstances require, take early action for the other vessel's safe passage. Subparagraph (ii) provides that the vessel required not to impede is not relieved of this obligation if approaching the other vessel so as to involve risk of collision and must, when taking action, have full regard to the action which may be required by the Steering and Sailing Rules (Rules 4–19). Under subparagraph (iii) the vessel whose passage is not to be impeded remains fully obliged to comply with the Steering and Sailing Rules when the two vessels are approaching one another so as to involve risk of collision.

2. *Decisions Applying Rule 8*

Even before adoption of the Radar Annex to the 1960 International Rules[198] the courts recognized the desirability of positive action to avoid collision, rather than successions of small alterations of course or speed, or both.[199] Nevertheless, some ship's officers continue to follow the practice of making minor changes, despite the explicit requirements of Rule 8(a) and (b) and the repeated condemnation of vessels that violate the mandate of these paragraphs. The following are examples of American and English decisions holding vessels at fault for making minor course alterations instead of taking positive action, or for other violations of Rule 8.

In re Potomac Transport, Inc. (The Potomac—The Banglar Baani):[200] The *Baani* was the hold-on vessel and the *Potomac* the give-way vessel in a crossing situation. The *Potomac*'s mate on watch made three successive changes of course to starboard, one of 30 degrees, one of 10 degrees, and one of 20 degrees. The *Baani*'s watch officer testified that he did not detect the first course change, and assumed the *Potomac* was maintaining a steady course. He therefore began altering course to port, intending to pass astern of the

196. See COLREGS Rule 9(d), which prohibits a vessel from crossing a narrow channel or fairway if such crossing impedes the passage of a vessel that can only navigate within the channel or fairway. See also COLREGS Rule 10(j), which prohibits a vessel engaged in fishing from impeding the passage of a vessel following a traffic lane.

197. See COLREGS Rule 10(j), which prohibits a vessel of less than 20 meters in length from impeding the *safe* passage of a power-driven vessel following a traffic lane. (Emphasis added).

198. Recommendation 7 of the Radar Annex provided: "An alteration of speed, either alone or in conjunction with an alteration of course, should be substantial. A number of small alterations of speed should be avoided."

199. See, e.g., *Oliver J. Olson & Co. v. The Marine Leopard,* 152 F. Supp. 197, 205, 1957 AMC 2477, 2488 (ND Cal. 1957), aff'd, 279 F.2d 662 (9th Cir. 1960).

200. *In re Potomac Transport Inc. (The Potomac—The Banglar Baani),* 741 F. Supp. 395, 1990 AMC 798 (SDNY 1989), modified on other grounds, 909 F.2d 42, 1991 AMC 190 (2d Cir. 1990).

Potomac. As the *Baani* continued to swing to port the *Potomac* went hard right and full astern, and her bow then struck the *Baani's* starboard quarter.

The district court held the *Baani* 75 percent and the *Potomac* 25 percent to blame.[201] In affirming the apportionment, Judge Oakes of the Second Circuit said:

> Kampmann [the *Potomac*'s mate on watch] admitted in his testimony that he should have altered his course 88 degrees, rather than simply 30 degrees, to achieve his objective of passing astern of *Baani*. Instead, Kampmann embarked upon a course change which would have required incremental shifts in the angle of navigation, contrary to Rule 8(b) of the Rules of the Road, which cautions against a succession of course changes and states that a course change should "be large enough to be readily apparent to another vessel observing visually or by radar." 33 U.S.C. foll. §1602. By hastily selecting a course change which actually made collision with *Baani* more imminent, and by failing to make a sufficiently dramatic and detectable shift in course, *Potomac*'s officers were not free from fault for the collision.[202]

The Pulkovo and Oden:[203] While proceeding in dense fog the *Pulkovo* observed on her radar the echo of what proved to be the *Oden* fine on her port bow, distant 7 miles, and the bearing remained steady. In answer to a question put to them by Mr. Justice Sheen, the Trinity Masters advised that since this meant that a close quarters situation was developing, the *Pulkovo* should have taken avoiding action, preferably at a distance of at least 5 miles; she should have turned a minimum of 35 degrees to starboard, and preferably about 60 degrees, so that the change could be easily seen on the other vessel's radar.

Mr. Justice Sheen accepted this advice. In holding the two vessels equally at fault, he said:

> *Pulkovo* was at fault in the following respects. First, in proceeding at an excessive speed in conditions of restricted visibility contrary to rr. 6 and 19(b). Second, in not taking action to avoid a close quarters situation as required by r. 8. Third, when action was taken it was the wrong action in two respects, namely that it was a succession of small alterations of course contrary to r. 8(b) and it consisted of altering course to port contrary to r. 19(d)(i). Fourth, the radar observation was inadequate in that the substantial alteration of course made by *Oden* a few minutes before the collision was not observed. If it had been observed *Pulkovo* probably would

201. 741 F. Supp. at 409, 1990 AMC at 819.
202. 909 F.2d at 46, 1991 AMC at 195.
203. Supra note 179.

> not have altered course 10 deg. to port between two and three minutes before the collision.[204]

The *Sanshin Victory:*[205] The *Sanshin Victory* was proceeding in dense fog at a speed of 13.5 knots on a course of 285 degrees when she picked up on her radar the echo of the *C.K. Apollo,* which was proceeding at full speed on a course of 092 degrees. The *Sanshin Victory* took no action to avoid collision until three minutes before it occurred, when she altered course 3 degrees to starboard, i.e., to 288 degrees. Except for minor reductions in speed, both vessels continued on their respective courses of 092 degrees and 288 degrees until they were less than a half mile apart. The *C.K. Apollo* turned left to 066 degrees during the last minute before collision, while at about the same time the *Sanshin Victory* turned hard right, and her stem struck the *C.K. Apollo*'s starboard side aft at an angle of about 52 degrees. Both vessels were held at fault.

The *Sanshin Victory* was charged with excessive speed in violation of Rules 6 and 19, and with a violation of Rule 8. In discussing the latter violation Mr. Justice Sheen stated:

> An alteration of course by 3 deg. is certainly not large enough to be readily apparent to another vessel observing by radar. Furthermore, if before that alteration each vessel was on a steady bearing from the other then an alteration of 3 deg. to starboard would not be such as to result in passing at a safe distance even if the speed of *Sanshin Victory* had been maintained. As an order to reduce speed was given at the same time as this alteration of course was made, the effect of one order would nullify the effect of the other. The presence of fishing vessels not less than 30 deg. on the starboard bow of *Sanshin Victory* and not less than one mile away did not prevent *Sanshin Victory* from altering course 25 deg. or even 180 deg. The alteration of course of 3 deg. was a breach of r. 8.[206]

The *Eglantine, Credo and Inez:*[207] The *Eglantine* and the *Credo* collided in dense fog in the Dover Straits. Both were held at fault for excessive speed, but the most serious faults were those of the *Inez,* which had embarrassed the navigation of the colliding vessels by proceeding in the wrong direction in a traffic separation lane, without any valid reason. In a decision varying the apportionment of fault made by Mr. Justice Sheen in the Admiralty Court, Lord Justice Parker, writing for the Court of Appeal, quoted with approval from a portion of Mr. Justice Sheen's opinion concerning the *Inez:*

> Her initial fault was compounded by the fact that when action was taken by altering course to starboard her alteration of course consisted of two

204. Id. at 287.
205. [1980] 2 Lloyd's Rep. 359 (Adm.).
206. Id. at 364.
207. [1990] 2 Lloyd's Rep. 390 (C.A.).

> very small alterations of 5 deg. each and a further alteration of 20 deg. That action was a clear breach of r. 8(b). . . . At the moment when the master of *Inez* saw on his radar that a ship or ships were approaching rapidly from ahead (as he must have done) he should have made a bold alteration of course to starboard. By that I mean that he should have altered not less than 35 deg. and preferably as much as 60 deg. to starboard.[208]

Enelson v. The Fortaleza:[209] The *Paige 2,* a 42-foot diesel yacht, sank as a result of a collision with the *Fortaleza,* a 700-foot roll-on/roll-off vessel, 4 miles south of Ambrose Light at the entrance to New York Bay, in near-zero visibility. Both vessels were held to blame on various counts, including violations of Rule 8. The *Fortaleza* failed to take action until just before the collision, when the mate on watch altered course 10 degrees to starboard. The *Paige 2* was held in violation of paragraphs (a) and (d) of Rule 8 for taking no action until she observed the echo of the *Fortaleza,* distant a half mile, when the yacht was taken off automatic pilot and the speed was reduced to idling. As the *Fortaleza* came closer, the *Paige 2*'s navigator put the engines in neutral and came hard left. The *Fortaleza* then struck the yacht on her starboard side.

Zim Israel Navigation, Ltd. v. Special Carriers, Ltd. (The En Gedi—The Acadia Forest):[210] *The Acadia Forest,* the give-way vessel in a crossing situation, was held solely at fault for a collision with the *En Gedi,* the hold-on vessel, caused in part by her failure to take "early and substantial action to keep well clear" of the *En Gedi,* as required by Rules 8, 15, and 16. Concerning this violation the court stated:

> The *Acadia Forest* also violated Rule 8 by failing to take effective and early action to avoid the collision. Captain Barth's testimony shows that he was aware, from the time he first sighted the *En Gedi,* that the two ships were in a crossing situation so as to involve a risk of collision. Furthermore, under Rule 7, the collision continued to be evident to the *Acadia Forest* because there was a constant relative bearing with the approaching *En Gedi.*
>
> The *Acadia Forest* had both the time and the sea room to avoid this collision by altering her course to starboard, permitting a safe port-to-port passage with the *En Gedi.* A full six minutes prior to collision, nothing obstructed the *Acadia Forest* from making a radical turn to the right or even from making a full circle to the right. However, the *Acadia Forest* navigated as if she were the privileged vessel and maintained her course and speed from the time the *En Gedi* was first sighted until just two minutes prior to collision. Even then she merely reduced engine speed to dead slow ahead rather than turning to starboard or stopping her engines en-

---

208. Id. at 392.

209. 1992 AMC 1447 (SDNY 1991).

210. 611 F. Supp. 581, 1986 AMC 2016 (ED La. 1985), modified, 800 F.2d 1392, 1988 AMC 2110 (5th Cir. 1986).

tirely. Had she done so, even at this late stage, it is probable that the collision could have been avoided. In any event, Captain Barth's order to port one minute later was precisely the wrong move as it negated the effect of the *En Gedi*'s proper starboard turn, and caused the two vessels to collide.[211]

The Tenes:[212] The *Tenes* and the *Darion* were found guilty of excessive speed in dense fog. The vessels were proceeding in opposite directions, head-on. As the distance between them closed, the *Darion* made two minor alterations of course to starboard. After quoting paragraphs (a), (b), and (c) of Rule 8, Mr. Justice Sheen stated:

> This tragic collision would not have occurred if both ships had complied with this rule. It is important to avoid a close quarters situation in which the master of a ship may have to make a hasty, and therefore possibly a wrong, decision. In this case both ships were proceeding at an excessive speed after the presence of the other was known and, in this respect, *Tenes* was more at fault than *Darion*. But the real mischief which created the very close quarters situation was the fact that *Darion* made two alterations of course to starboard which would not have been readily apparent to *Tenes*.[213]

3. *Rule 8 in Relation to Other Rules*

That Rule 8 does not override the other rules, but rather must be read in conjunction with them, was made clear by the First Circuit in *Lo Vuolo v. Gunning*.[214] The decision involved a collision between two power-driven pleasure boats in Boston harbor. Lo Vuolo's boat was the hold-on vessel and Gunning's the give-way vessel in a crossing situation. Gunning first observed Lo Vuolo's boat bearing about 30 degrees on his starboard bow. He cut the engines and put the drive gears in neutral, but the boat continued its forward motion. Meanwhile, Lo Vuolo, upon sighting Gunning's boat, turned hard right, and the collision then occurred, the bow of Gunning's boat striking the port quarter of Lo Vuolo's.

The district court held both vessels to blame and divided the damages equally, holding that "Rule 8 [of the Inland Rules] states the overriding obligation of persons operating motor boats, notwithstanding the more specific provisions of Rules 15, 16 and 17 [the Starboard Hand Rule and its Corollaries]." On appeal, the First Circuit agreed that both vessels were at fault for

211. Id., 611 F. Supp. at 586, 1986 AMC at 2021–22.

212. [1989] 2 Lloyd's Rep. 367 (Adm.).

213. Id. at 371. Other decisions involving violations of Rule 8 include *Maritrans Operating Partners L.P. v. The Faith I,* 800 F. Supp. 133, 1993 AMC 385 (D N.J. 1992); *In re Ocean Foods Boat Company (The McKinley—The Tosca),* 692 F. Supp. 1253, 1989 AMC 579 (D Or. 1988), and *In re G&G Shipping Co., Ltd.,* supra note 195.

214. 925 F.2d 22, 1991 AMC 1651 (1st Cir. 1991).

failing to maintain a proper look-out, but held that the district court had erred in deciding that Rule 8 was the overriding obligation. It therefore vacated the decision and remanded the case to the district court for proper application of the Inland Rules and reallocation of fault and damages, stating:

> By allowing Rule 8 to override all other rules, the district court failed to weigh the full implications of the three crossing rules. Rule 15, the starboard [hand] rule, states the obligations of the give-way vessel, here the defendants' boat:
>
> "(a) When two power-driven vessels are crossing so as to involve risk of collision, the vessel which has the other on her starboard side shall keep out of the way and shall, if the circumstances of the case admit, avoid crossing ahead of the other vessel."[215]

The court then quoted Rule 16, requiring the give-way vessel, "so far as possible [to] take early and substantial action to keep well clear." It also quoted Rule 17, requiring the hold-on vessel ordinarily to keep her course and speed, but permitting her to take avoiding action when it becomes apparent that the give-way vessel is not taking appropriate action, and requiring avoiding action when collision cannot be avoided by the action of the give-way vessel alone. The court continued:

> Gunning, having sighted LoVuolo's vessel 30 degrees off his starboard bow, was clearly the give-way vessel. Rule 15. According to his own testimony, he saw LoVuolo's vessel "in the vicinity of approximately 200 feet." The crossing rules, largely ignored by the district court, dictate "early and substantial action to keep well clear." Rule 16. Gunning did not take such decisive action. . . .
>
> Plaintiff Lo Vuolo's responsibilities are similarly spelled out by the crossing rules. As the privileged vessel, he was to keep his course and speed unless, as here, "the vessel required to keep out of the way [Gunning's] is not taking appropriate action." Rule 17(a)(i), (ii). Culpable in failing to maintain adequate lookout, Lo Vuolo belatedly perceived Gunning's imminent failure to avert collision. Rule 17(b) requires that he then take "such action as will best aid to avoid collision." See *Pinto v. Fernwood,* 1976 AMC 744, 749, 507 F.2d 1327, 1330–31 (1 Cir. 1974) (maintaining that privileged vessel not required to keep to course in extenuating circumstances). Rule 17(c) then mandates a turn only to his starboard side, which LoVuolo attempted. The district court viewed this maneuver as too little, too late, and consequently held that neither party took appropriate action to avoid the collision under Rule 8. We do not

215. Id., 925 F.2d at 26–27, 1991 AMC at 1658.

challenge the district court's finding of the facts, only its failure to consider fully and evenhandedly all applicable navigational rules. . . .[216]

Section F. Rule 9: Narrow Channels

1. *Introduction*

As Griffin states, the narrow channel rule is a particular application of the general principle recognized in Rule 18 of the former International and Inland Rules (now Rule 14 of COLREGS and the current Inland Rules), requiring power-driven vessels meeting end-on, or nearly end-on, so as to involve risk of collision to alter course to starboard and pass port to port.[217] That rule was recognized by the U.S. Supreme Court as early as 1860,[218] and was included as Rule 18 of the 1864 Rules applicable to U.S. naval and merchant vessels.[219] There is, however, an essential difference between the end-on rule and the narrow channel rule, in that the former applies only when two vessels are meeting in sight of one another, whereas the narrow channel rule governs even when no other vessels are in sight.

The 1864 Rules did not contain a narrow channel rule. The first statutory narrow channel rule was introduced in the United States in 1885 as Article 21 of the rules enacted in that year,[220] governing American vessels on the high seas and in U.S. coastal waters. Article 21 simply provided that in narrow channels, when it was "safe and practicable," a steam vessel must keep to that side of the fairway or midchannel which lay on her starboard side. In the United States, the rule appears to have developed from a practice prevailing at least on the Hudson River.[221]

A rule in substantially the same language was included as Article 25 in the International and Inland Rules that became effective in 1897,[222] and no change was effected by the 1948 amendments to the Inland Rules.[223] Rule

216. Id., 925 F.2d at 27, 1991 AMC at 1659.

217. Griffin 88.

218. *New York & Baltimore Transportation Co. v. Philadelphia & Savannah Steam Nav. Co.*, 63 U.S. 461 (1860), involving a collision between a tug with a barge in tow and a steamship in the Delaware River: "Beyond question, the law is well settled that steamers approaching each other from opposite directions are respectively bound to port their helms [i.e., turn to the right] and pass each other on the larboard [i.e.. port] side." 63 U.S. at 472.

219. 13 Stat. 58, Rev. Stat. § 4233.

220. Act of Mar. 3, 1885, "Revised International Regulations for Preventing Collisions at Sea," ch. 354, 48th Cong., 2d Sess., 23 Stat. 438. The 1885 Rules are reproduced in Griffin at 811–21.

221. See *The Vanderbilt*, 73 U.S. 225 (1867).

222. Act of Aug. 19, 1890, effective Jan. 1, 1897, 26 Stat. 320 (International Rules); Act of June 7, 1897, effective Oct. 7, 1897, 30 Stat. 96 (Inland Rules). The two sets of rules are reproduced, in parallel columns in Griffin at 645–80.

223. Act of May 21, 1948, effective Jan. 1, 1949, Pub. L. No. 544, 80th Cong. ch. 328, 2d Sess., reproduced in Griffin at 681–84.

25(a) of the 1960 International Rules[224] was the same as Article 25 of the 1897 Rules, but two paragraphs were added. Paragraph(b) required a power-driven vessel nearing a bend in a channel where a vessel approaching from the other direction could not be seen, to sound a prolonged blast, to be answered by a similar signal by any power-driven vessel approaching from around the bend and hearing the first vessel's signal. Paragraph (c) prohibited a vessel of less than 65 feet in length from hampering the safe passage of a vessel which could navigate only inside the narrow channel.

Rule 9 (COLREGS and the current Inland Rules) is much more elaborate.[225] Paragraph (a) of COLREGS and paragraph (a)(i) of the Inland Rules are virtually the same as the corresponding provisions of the earlier rules, except that they apply not only to power-driven vessels, but to all vessels. Paragraph (a)(ii) of the current Inland Rules provides for an exception applicable to narrow channels or fairways on the Great Lakes, Western Rivers, or waters specified by the secretary (of the department in which the U.S. Coast Guard is operating): in those waters a power-driven vessel proceeding downbound with a following current has the right-of-way over an upbound vessel, and must propose the manner and place of passage; the upbound vessel must hold as necessary to permit safe passing. Paragraphs (b), (c), (f), and (g) of COLREGS Rule 9 and of Inland Rule 9 are identical.

There is a material difference between paragraph (e)(i) of COLREGS Rule 9 and paragraph (e)(i) of Inland Rule 9. COLREGS Rule 9(e)(i) is in line with the American concept of sound signals as signals of intention, rather than as rudder, or turning signals. It requires an exchange of signals before overtaking in a narrow channel, when the overtaking can take place only if the vessel to be overtaken has to take action in order to permit safe passing. Paragraph (e)(i) of Inland Rule 9, on the other hand, provides that any vessel intending to overtake another in a narrow channel or fairway must sound the signals prescribed by Rule 34(c) (one short blast if the intention is to pass on the starboard side of the vessel ahead, and two short blasts if the intention is to pass on the port side). If the vessel ahead agrees, she must answer with a like signal; if she disagrees she must sound a danger signal. In this respect the Inland Rule regarding overtaking in narrow channels does not differ from the rules governing overtaking situations in inland waters generally. Under COLREGS, on the other hand, when the overtaking is not in a narrow channel, or when it is in a narrow channel but no action by the vessel ahead is required to permit safe passing, no signals are sounded unless a change in heading is made.

Paragraph (e)(ii) of Rule 9 of COLREGS and the corresponding subparagraph of the Inland Rules are identical; they provide that "This Rule," which presumably refers to paragraph (e)(i), does not relieve the overtaking

224. 33 U.S.C. §§ 1051–94.

225. For ready reference, COLREGS Rule 9 is set out in appendix 1.

vessel of her obligation under Rule 13, i.e., the obligation to keep out of the way of the vessel being overtaken.

Paragraph (b) of both sets of rules prohibits sailing vessels and vessels of less than 20 meters in length from impeding the passage of vessels which can safely navigate only within a narrow channel or fairway. Paragraph (c) contains a similar prohibition with respect to vessels engaged in fishing, except that it applies to all other vessels navigating within a narrow channel or fairway, and not only to vessels which can navigate safely in such waters.

Paragraph (d) of Rule 9 of both sets of rules prohibits crossing a narrow channel or fairway if the crossing impedes the passage of a vessel which can safely navigate only in those waters. Paragraph (d) of COLREGS Rule 9 permits the latter vessel to sound a danger signal if in doubt as to the crossing vessel's intention. Paragraph (d) of Inland Rule 9 requires such a signal. Paragraph (f) of COLREGS Rule 9 and Inland Rule 9 provides for a bend signal. This signal is discussed in chapter 8, infra. Paragraph (g) of both sets of rules prohibits anchoring in a narrow channel "if the circumstances of the case admit."

2. *Purpose of the Rule*

The essence of the narrow channel rule, now applicable to all vessels and in all conditions of visibility,[226] is to require vessels to proceed on their own starboard side of a narrow channel or fairway so that there will be a port to port passing,[227] and in a crossing situation, the starboard-hand rule will be superseded by the narrow channel rule.[228] Since problems often occur where the narrow channel is in the vicinity of a busy harbor, it is almost inevitable that vessels will seek the middle of the channel rather than the outer limit of their own starboard side of the channel because of the fear of other vessels suddenly backing out of pier areas, with or without sound signals.

The narrow channel rule is a pragmatic attempt to resolve problems that can make navigation difficult: currents, tides, traffic congestion, restricted maneuvering areas, restricted channel widths, shallow waters, and the proximity of the banks of the channel or the shoreline. When the vessel's speed and draft are added to the preexisting conditions there can be unpredictable consequences, such as interaction, causing a rapid and uncontrollable sheer and forcing a vessel away from a nearby river bank, shelf, or

226. *Scindia Steam Nav. Co. v. Standard Oil Co. (N.J.) (The Marine Leader—The Jalaketu),* 121 F. Supp. 816, 1954 AMC 1327 (SDNY 1959), aff'd, 218 F.2d 604, 1955 AMC 419 (2d Cir. 1955). The Second Circuit expressed no opinion on the application of the narrow channel rule in fog. But see *The Strandella—The Andrew,* 108 F.2d 619, 1940 AMC 286 (5th Cir. 1939). It is clear that Rule 9 of COLREGS and the current Inland Rules applies in fog, since it is included in Part B, §/Subpart I (Conduct of Vessels in Any Condition of Visibility).

227. *Union Steamship Co. v. New York and Virginia Steamship Co.,* 65 U.S. 307, 314 (1860).

228. *The Victory—The Plymothian,* 168 U.S. 410 (1897).

seashore.[229] Because vessel direction is largely dictated by the contours of the narrow channel, compliance with the obligations of the rule are chiefly met by engine orders of slow, stop, or reverse.[230] Even though the rule has the built-in proviso of "safe and practicable," a proven violation of the rule obliges the violator to meet the proof burden of the *Pennsylvania* Rule.[231]

3. *Statutory Requirements of the Basic Rule (9[a])*

There are three essentials in Rule 9(a): The first is that there be a *"narrow channel or fairway,"* as opposed to a wide body of water such as the open sea or a harbor; the second is that the vessel must proceed on her own *starboard side* of the channel or fairway; the third is that she must proceed as near to the outer limit of that side as is *"safe and practicable."*

a. Defining a Narrow Channel. Neither the term "narrow channel" nor the term "fairway" is defined in Rule 3 (Definitions). Accordingly, these terms involve questions of law and fact together.[232] Official designations of waterways as "narrow channels" are not made by the U.S. Coast Guard, despite its placement of channel buoy markers.[233] The geographical index in each *Annual Index to American Maritime Cases* and in each AMC *Five Year Digest* can be useful in identifying waterways which have previously been held to be or not to be narrow channels but because, as stated, the status of a waterway as a narrow channel is a mixed question of law and fact, previous cases are not always suitable precedents.[234] Resolution of this mixed question may be influenced by

---

229. *United States v. The Pleiades,* 5 F.2d 834, 1926 AMC 201 (2d Cir. 1925); cf. *Pocahontas Steamship Co. v. New York, Philadelphia & Norfolk R.R. (The Isaac T. Mann),* 14 F.2d 1018, 1926 AMC 1044 (4th Cir. 1926); *The Detroiter,* 82 F.2d 234, 1936 AMC 382 (2d Cir. 1936).

230. *The New York,* 175 U.S. 187 (1899). See also *Jackson v. British and South American Steam Nav. Co. (The Monaires—The Hortensius),* 1 F.2d 13, 1924 AMC 922 (2d Cir. 1924). See also *Chesapeake & Delaware Steamboat Co. v. The Tug Pennsylvania (The Lillian Anne—The Pennsylvania),* 1934 AMC 569 (2d Cir. 1934).

231. *In re Tug Management Corporation,* 330 F. Supp. 486, 498, 1971 AMC 2511 (ED Pa. 1971); *Southern Pacific Co. v. United States (El Sol—The Sac City),* 72 F.2d 212, 1934 AMC 1185 (2d Cir. 1934). For a discussion of the *Pennsylvania* Rule, see chapter 2, supra.

232. *Marine Transport Lines, Inc. v. M/V Tako Invader,* 37 F.3d 1138, 1995 AMC 622 (5th Cir. 1994). See also *Commonwealth & Dominion Line, Ltd. v. Seaboard Transp. Co.,* 258 Fed. 707 (D Mass. 1919) (each vessel held at fault). For the meaning of "fairway," see *Merriam v. The Hawaiian,* 38 F. Supp. 574, 1941 AMC 710 (D Md. 1941), aff'd, 124 F.2d 45, 1942 AMC 84 (4th Cir. 1942). See also *The Koenigin Juliana,* [1973] 2 Lloyd's Rep. 308 (Adm.), [1974] 2 Lloyd's Rep. 353 (C.A.); [1975] 2 Lloyd's Rep. 111 (H. L.).

233. Lighted or unlighted bell or whistle can buoys and spar buoys (odd numbers), colored black, are used on the port side of channels entering from seaward, while lighted or unlighted bell or whistle can buoys and nun or spar buoys (even numbers), colored red, are used on the starboard side of channels entering from seaward. 33 CFR 62.23.

234. *Maritrans Operating Partners, L.P. v. The Faith I,* supra note 128. See also *Tempest v. United States (The Tempest II),* 277 F. Supp. 59, 1968 AMC 926 (ED Va. 1967), aff'd, 404 F.2d 870, 1968 AMC 2538 (4th Cir. 1968).

the size and character of the waterway, but also by the amount and character of the traffic.

"Narrow channel" does not require that the waters be confined within banks as in rivers or canals, so long as vessels customarily navigate in opposite directions in the waterway, whatever its name or description.[235] The fact that a waterway is a river does not, of itself, make it a narrow channel.[236] Further, a channel dredged for major shipping may still be a narrow channel, although surrounded on both sides by water of a depth navigable by shallow-draft vessels. Narrow channels may be of any length and may or may not follow the sinuosities of the riverbanks or shorelines; the obligations of the rule remain as long as it is "safe and practicable."[237]

b. Outer Limit of Starboard Side. In *Moran Towing & Transp. Co. v. Bouchard Transport Co.,*[238] the Moran tugs *Judy* and *Maureen* were towing the barge *Nepco 140* eastbound through the Kill van Kull, a tortuous narrow channel between New Jersey and Staten Island, New York, with the *Judy* secured to the barge's starboard quarter and the *Maureen* to its port quarter. The Bouchard tug *Rhea* was towing the empty barge *B115,* with the tug secured to the stern notch of the barge. The tug *Ellen* was secured to the barge's starboard quarter, but was not assisting in the towage. The *Judy*'s captain sighted the Bouchard flotilla as it entered the channel, and sounded one blast for a port to port passing. He then contacted the *Rhea*'s captain by radio and the two agreed to pass port to port. During the conversation the *Rhea*'s captain agreed to "get over some" to starboard. However, gusting northeast winds on the starboard side of the Bouchard flotilla prevented it from moving over sufficiently from the center of the channel. The *Rhea* sounded a danger signal, but the *Nepco 140* glanced along the side of the *B115,* which then collided with the *Maureen.* The *Rhea* was held in sole fault for failing to keep the

---

235. *The Florence,* 186 Fed. 57 (3d Cir. 1911); *The No. 4,* 161 Fed. 847 (2d Cir. 1908) ([Narrow] channels . . . are bodies of water navigated up and down in opposite directions); *The Bee,* 138 Fed. 304 (2d Cir. 1905) ([Narrow] Channel Rule applies to a channel in the Upper Bay of New York Harbor). See also *La Bretagne,* 179 Fed. 286 (2d Cir. 1910), also describing New York Harbor and noting five designated channels therein. But see *Skibs A/S Siljestad v. Luckenbach Steamship Corp (The Francisville—The Matthew Luckenbach),* 215 F. Supp. 667, 1963 AMC 2280 (SDNY 1963), aff'd, 324 F.2d 563, 1964 AMC 1 (2d Cir. 1963); *Pfeiffer Oil Co. v. The Ira S. Bushey,* 129 F.2d 606, 1942 AMC 1041 (2d Cir. 1942).

236. See *American Dredging Co. v. Calmar Steamship Co.,* 121 F. Supp. 255, 263, 1954 AMC 1211, 1233 (ED Pa. 1954), aff'd, 218 F.2d 823, 1955 AMC 541 (3d Cir. 1955): "There is no rule of law which limits the navigation of a vessel to a ship channel, as a land vehicle such as an automobile would be limited to operation on a highway. The vessel may navigate at any part of a river containing navigable water."

237. See notes 240–43, infra; *The Towboat No. 1,* 74 F. 906 (lst Cir. 1896); *The Merida,* 210 F. 440 (2d Cir. 1913).

238. 1989 AMC 365 (SDNY 1988). See also *Standard Navigation Co. v. The K.Z. Michalos,* 1981 AMC 748 (SD Tex. 1981). See also *Southern Transp. Co. v. The Dauntless II,* 140 F.2d 215, 1944 AMC 161 (2d Cir. 1944) (a vessel out of position in a narrow channel, having received a one-blast proposal from a vessel proceeding in the opposite direction, has a duty to respond with

flotilla on its starboard side of the centerline of the channel, as well as for improper lookout. The court found that the *Rhea*'s captain was negligent in failing to position the assisting tug *Ellen* in such a way as to counteract the effect of the gusting northeast wind, and thus keep the flotilla on the proper side of the channel.

It was held early on that a vessel is not necessarily entitled to take up a full one-half of a narrow channel. Thus, in *The Howard Reeder,*[239] it was held that a vessel which has to pass a long tow does not have the right to assume that her own starboard side of a narrow channel will remain completely clear for her use.

c. "Safe and Practicable." The "outer limit" requirement is subject to the "safe and practicable" condition, so that in complying with Rule 9, vessels are not expected to encounter such risks as shoal waters or rocks. As we have seen, the "safe and practicable" language has been included in the narrow channel rule since 1885.[240] An illustrative case is *National Iranian Tanker Co. N.V. v. The Tug Dalzell No. 2,*[241] where, in the channel north of Hellgate (the entrance to Long Island Sound from New York Harbor), a southbound tug with two carfloats had crossed the center of the channel and failed to sound the danger signal. The northbound tanker, keeping to her own side of the channel, had to turn sharply to starboard to round Hallets Point, and then gently to port to follow the channel so that in navigating its sinuous course the tanker might encroach slightly on the port side of the channel. The tanker sounded a port-to-port passing signal, but this was not answered by the tug, which moved into the tanker's side of the channel. A finding of sole fault of the tug was affirmed because the tug had no basis for believing that the tanker would not return to her own starboard side. The tanker was held to have followed a "safe and practicable" course in a sinuous channel. The court said each party was entitled to presume that the narrow channel rule would be observed.

"Safe and practicable," does not exclude a starboard-to-starboard passing, but such a proposal places a heavy burden on the proposer to establish

---

a one-blast signal and turn to starboard, rather than try to force a starboard-to-starboard passing). See also *Burma Navigation Corp. v. The Reliant Seahorse,* supra note 136.

239. 207 F. 929 (4th Cir. 1913). See Griffin 97.

240. For an explanation of the need for the "safe and practicable" language in the rule, see *The Three Brothers,* 170 F. 48, 50 (2d Cir. 1909): "Its purpose is to prevent collisions, not produce them. It is not an inflexible rule to be followed in all cases and, where it is manifest that a blind adherence will produce disaster, it is not only the right but the duty of the navigator to disregard it."

241. 411 F.2d 759, 1969 AMC 1187 (2d Cir. 1969). See also *Smoot Sand & Gravel Co. v. Baltimore Steamship Packet Co. (The District of Columbia—The Virginia),* 250 F.2d 422, 1958 AMC 44 (D.C. Cir. 1958), reversing 148 F. Supp. 269, 1959 AMC 701 (D D.C. 1957); *The Michael Tracy (The Cape Cod),* 43 F.2d 965, 1930 AMC 1855 (2d Cir. 1930); cf. *The Margaret,* 30 F.2d 923, 1929 AMC 1307 (2d Cir. 1929).

its necessity.[242] When something does go wrong in a starboard-to-starboard passage, both the proposer and the acceptor may be held in fault.[243] "Safe and practicable," rather than simple convenience, may justify a local custom to depart from some requirement of the rule.[244] Obviously, when fog is so thick that the channel cannot even be made out, then navigation in the channel is not "safe and practicable."[245]

d. The Requirement "Not to Impede." Paragraphs (b), (c), and (d) of COLREGS and Inland Rule 9 impose an obligation on specified types of vessels "not to impede" the navigation of other vessels.[246] The same phrase is used in paragraph (f) of COLREGS Rule 8. The obligation not to impede may be imposed on small vessels such as sailing vessels, fishing vessels, harbor craft, and even ferries, in situations where the narrow channel lies in constricted waters adjoining port facilities,[247] or where the channel is very narrow and deep, so that maneuvering is difficult for large vessels.[248] The normal

---

242. In *The Standard Oiler v. Hamburg-America Line,* 396 F.2d 115, 1968 AMC 920 (9th Cir. 1968), a 500-foot-long vessel approaching a narrow channel 300 feet in width, in Suisun Bay, San Francisco, visually observed a 200-foot vessel coming in the opposite direction but not yet in the channel; the 500-foot vessel gave a starboard-to-starboard passing signal and continued at full speed through the channel into collision with the 200-foot vessel. The trial court's finding of sole fault of the 200-foot vessel was reversed and mutual fault of both vessels was found. In *Taylor v. Tiburon,* 1975 AMC 1229 (ED La. 1975), a collision occurred between a houseboat and a tug with a tow while the vessels were navigating under a drawbridge. Instructions of the drawbridge tender to pursue a zigzag course through the narrow channel were held not to justify a violation of the flotilla's obligation to keep to starboard. See also *Marshall Field & Co. v. United States (The Antigone—The Gaelic Prince),* 48 F.2d 763, 1930 AMC 1736 (2d Cir. 1931). The court described the rule as "enforced rigidly," 48 F.2d at 765. See also *The Michael Tracy—The Cape Cod,* 43 F.2d 965, 1930 AMC 1855 (2d Cir. 1930), (where the rule was enforced despite a local custom at Hell Gate, New York Harbor).

243. Mutual fault cases include *The Varanger,* 50 F.2d 724, 1931 AMC 1186 (4th Cir. 1931); *The Edward W. Parkhill,* 53 F.2d 87, 88, 1931 AMC 1944 (EDNY 1931) ("... [T]he violation of the Narrow Channel Rule does raise a presumption of fault, at least to the extent of requiring explanation [of vessel owners] as to why they sought to pass starboard to starboard"); *National Motorship Co. v. Pennsylvania R.R. Co. (The Chester),* 160 F.2d 510, 1947 AMC 448 (2d Cir. 1947), reversing 65 F. Supp. 803, 1946 AMC 1055 (EDNY 1946); *Esso Standard Oil Co. v. The Tug Maluco I,* 332 F.2d 211, 1964 AMC 911 (4th Cir. 1964).

244. *Huntley v. The Tug J.C. Reichert,* 39 F.2d 970, 1930 AMC 571 (EDNY 1930); aff'd, 48 F.2d 1076, 1931 AMC 1424 (2d Cir. 1931); *Arctic Shipping Corp. v. Gulfcoast Transit Co. (The Arctic Reefer—The Martha Mac),* 333 F.2d 605, 1964 AMC 2158 (5th Cir. 1964).

245. Cf. *The Yarmouth,* 100 Fed. 667 (D Mass. 1900).

246. The words "avoid impeding" do not have the same unequivocal meaning as do the words "give way." See Farwell 170–71. After discussing the perils of the starboard-hand rule in narrow channels, Farwell notes, at 172: "It is important for the crossing vessel, who is well able to navigate outside the channel, to understand the concern on the bridge of the vessel confined to the channel. Early exchange of signals and/or unambiguous alterations of course and speed are essential in order to avoid forcing risky give-way action on the part of the vessel in the channel."

247. *Southern Pacific Co. v. Haglund (The Thoroughfare),* 277 U.S. 304, 1928 AMC 965 (1928) (sole fault of ferryboat).

248. *Deep Sea Tankers, Ltd. v. The Tug Long Branch (The Rincon Hills—The Long Branch),* 258 F.2d 757, 1950 AMC 28 (2d Cir. 1958) (loaded tanker grounded because of actions of tugs in crowding and interfering with tanker's navigation in narrow channel designed for deep-draft vessels in the East River, New York; tugs held solely at fault).

rules for vessels meeting head on[249] or overtaking[250] (requiring mutual agreement under Rule 9[e][i]) apply in the respective situations. Paragraph (d) of Rule 9 does not eliminate the normal crossing rules.[251] It was included in COLREGS and the current Inland Rules to discourage crossing a narrow channel at a time when the passage of vessels "which can safely navigate only within such channel" would be impeded. Thus the obligation of Rule 8(e) to slacken speed or take all way off must first be met before a vessel on the starboard hand of a vessel proceeding on her own starboard side of a narrow channel may hold her course across the channel.

e. Right-of-Way under the Inland Rules. As stated, in narrow channels or fairways on the Great Lakes, the Western Rivers, or other waters designated by the Secretary (of the department in which the Coast Guard is operating), paragraph (a)(ii) of Inland Rule 9 gives a "right-of-way" to downbound vessels with a following current,[252] while vessels upbound against the current have an obligation to "hold" as necessary to permit safe passing.[253]

f. Danger Signals. Paragraph (d) of Inland Rule 9, as we have seen, requires a danger signal to be sounded when the intention of a vessel crossing a narrow channel is in doubt. Paragraph (d) of COLREGS Rule 9, on the other hand, permits such a signal, but does not require one. Under Inland Rule 9(d), the failure to sound a danger signal has been held a statutory fault on the part of the vessel in doubt, imposing upon her the burden of proving that the fault was not contributive.[254]

g. Defenses to Departures from the Narrow Channel Rule. The simple language of the rule does not include any specific defenses to departures from

---

249. Meeting head-on: *The Summitville,* 74 F.2d 705, 1935 AMC 283 (2d Cir. 1935).

250. Overtaking: *Charles Warner Co. v. Independent Pier Co. (The Gulftrade);* 278 U.S. 85, 1928 AMC 1815 (1928); *The Admiral Nulton—The Orient,* 66 F.2d 326, 1933 AMC 1335 (9th Cir. 1933).

251. Crossing: *The Eastern Glade—El Isleo,* 101 F.2d 4, 1939 AMC 71 (2d Cir. 1939) rev'd on other grounds, 308 U.S. 378, 1940 AMC 1 (1940) on remand sub nom.; *Postal S.S. Corp. v. Southern Pacific Co.,* 112 F.2d 297, 1940 AMC 866 (2d Cir. 1940); *The Panther,* 79 F.2d 625, 1935 AMC 1510 (2d Cir. 1935) (false appearance of a crossing situation because of a curve in the channel).

252. Downbound: *Linehan v. United States Lines,* 559 F.2d 1208, 1979 AMC 1557 (3d Cir. 1977) (vessel downbound in the Delaware River held not at fault for turning to port after observing a sailing yacht on the downbound vessel's starboard side of the channel); *The New York Co. v. The Robin Doncaster,* 233 F.2d 889, 1956 AMC 1061 (3d Cir. 1956); *Moore McCormack Lines, Inc. v. Calmar S.S. Corp. (The Mormacguide—The Portmar),* 249 F. Supp. 464, 1966 AMC 1582 (SDNY 1966).

253. Upbound: *Flowers Transport Co. v. American River Transportation Co.,* 485 F. Supp. 731, 1982 AMC 2689 (ND Miss. 1980).

254. *Charles Warner Co. v. Independent Pier Co. (The Gulftrade),* supra note 33; *Reiss Steamship Co. v. Cia. Fletera Cajotami (The Elpis—The Charles C. West),* 374 F.2d 117, 1967 AMC 1201 (6th Cir. 1967).

its terms. Nevertheless, courts have traditionally used their power of statutory interpretation to find defenses which can be inferred from the nature of a rule, despite legislative silence.[255] Thus, an element of Rule 9(a) that proceeding along the course of a narrow channel must be "safe and practicable" will open up the rule to defenses such as "reasonably" safe and "reasonably" practicable.[256]

h. Reasonable Conduct. An illustration of a defense of reasonable conduct can be found in *Zeller Marine Equipment. Inc. v. The Chemical Transporter,*[257] where a northbound tug and tow, confronted with a wider open west draw of the Central R.R. of New Jersey Bridge in Newark Bay than the constricted east draw of the bridge, chose to cross from the flotilla's starboard side of the channel to its port side, so as to use the wider passage, which brought them into collision with a southbound tanker. Findings of absence of lookout, inattention, and improper signals resulted in a mutual fault holding, but the court refused to find the use of the west draw by the northbound tug and tow to be a fault.

4. *Local Customs*

There has been a consistent line of cases holding that local custom may vary the normal expectations of vessel conduct under the narrow channel rule.[258] The general rule, however, is that custom alone will not justify a departure

---

255. A classic example is found in *Tedla v. Ellman,* 280 N.Y. 124, 131–32, 19 N.E. 2d 987 (1939), where the New York Court of Appeals found that a defense of reasonable conduct applied to the statutory violation by pedestrians walking along the highway on the same side as the moving traffic instead of facing the oncoming traffic. See also, Restatement of Torts Second, § 288 A (2):

> Unless the enactment or regulation is construed not to permit such excuse, its violation is excused when
>
> (a) the violation is reasonable because of the actor's incapacity;
> (b) he neither knows nor should know of the occasion for compliance;
> (c) he is unable after reasonable diligence or care to comply;
> (d) he is confronted by an emergency not due to his own misconduct;
> (e) compliance would involve a greater risk of harm to the actor or to others.
>
> This list is not intended to be exclusive.

However, the Supreme Court has not allowed reasonable conduct defenses to violations of the Federal Safety Appliance Act. See *O'Donnell v. Elgin J. & E. R. Co.,* 338 U.S. 384 (1949). See generally, Morris, *Custom and Negligence,* 42 Colum. L. Rev. 1147 (1942).

256. *American Hawaiian Steamship Corp. v. Western Transportation Co. (The Barry K—The Pennsylvanian),* 139 F.2d 478, 1943 AMC 1330 (9th Cir. 1943). See note 255, supra.

257. 307 F. Supp. 138, 1970 AMC 1582 (SDNY 1969). Cf. *The Priscilla,* 55 F.2d 32, 1932 AMC 334 (lst Cir. 1932). The difference, however, is that in the latter case the tug crossed over to the port side of the waterway under the drawbridge for the sake of convenience, in accordance with local custom, but the defense was rejected by the First Circuit, which held the tug in sole fault.

258. *The Michael Tracy—The Cape Cod,* 43 F.2d 965, 1930 AMC 1855 (2d Cir. 1930); *Algonquin Deep Sea Research Corp. v. Perini Corp.,* 457 F.2d 755, 1972 AMC 562 (1st Cir. 1972) (mutual fault).

from the rule.[259] The meaning of these apparently conflicting statements is that vessels may conform to a local operating custom in some parts of a narrow channel where "safety and practicability" require it, but may not disregard the entire rule. Mississippi River navigation abounds in local customs, beginning with the rather general practice whereby upbound vessels run the points and downbound vessels run the bends.[260] Such local customs may be used to defend actions taken by the observant vessel and condemn the nonobservant. The point-bend custom is discussed in chapter 5.

5. *Correct Charts*

Channels marked by governmental authority for the purposes of safe navigation would seem to require that vessels proceeding in marked channels have the correct charts for areas where they expect to navigate. There are two distinct problems with the absence of the correct charts. As between colliding vessels, the absence of charts at least indicates fault,[261] and since the 1974 SOLAS Convention, it may mean statutory fault, with a *Pennsylvania* Rule burden of proof.[262] As between a carrying vessel and her cargo, the consequences of the absence of the correct charts means that the owner has failed to exercise due diligence to make the vessel seaworthy before and at the beginning of the voyage.[263]

A substantial review of the vessel owner's obligations with respect to charts was made by the House of Lords in the leading case of *The Marion*,[264] where the vessel collided with an oil pipeline, causing $25 million in dam-

259. See, e.g., *The Athens*, 18 F.2d 743, 1927 AMC 786 (2d Cir. 1927), where a northbound tug navigated on the west side of the East River for its own convenience, so as to avoid a strong flood tide.

260. *Graham v. United States (The Rosebud—The R. & Y. and Tow)*, 112 F. Supp. 43, 1953 AMC 824 (ED La. 1953) (College Point on the Mississippi); *Koch-Ellis, Inc. v. The Capetan Dimitris*, 176 F. Supp. 645, 1959 AMC 2288 (ED La. 1959) (Twelve Mile Point below New Orleans); *Schwabe v. The Birney R.*, 198 F. Supp. 515, 1962 AMC 916 (ED La. 1961) (Mississippi River at Algiers Point opposite New Orleans); *Valley Towing Service Inc. v. The American Wheat Freighters, Inc.*, 618 F.2d 341, 1981 AMC 436 (5th Cir. 1980) (Nine Mile Point below New Orleans). In *Marine Transport Lines, Inc. v. The Tako Invader*, supra note 232, the court remanded the case to the district court for explicit findings on the question as to whether a 1,200-foot-wide Luling Bridge section of the Mississippi is a "narrow channel" within the meaning of Inland Rule 9.

261. *Placid Oil Co. v. The Willowpool*, 214 F. Supp. 449, 1963 AMC 635 (ED La. 1963); *Continental Oil Co. v. The Glenville*, 210 F. Supp. 865, 1962 AMC 2311 (ED La. 1962); See generally *Davidson Steamship Co. v. United States*, 205 U.S. 187 (1907).

262. Safety of Life at Sea Convention, 1974 (SOLAS), ch. V, Regulation 20: "All ships shall carry adequate and up-to-date charts, sailing directions, lists of lights, notices to mariners, tide tables and all other nautical publications necessary for the intended voyage."

263. Vessels held unseaworthy because of the absence of the correct charts: *Weyerhaeuser Timber Co. v. The W.W. Bruce*, 94 F.2d 834, 1938 AMC 232 (2d Cir. 1938) (Harter Act case); *Matter of Thebes Shipping Co. (The Argo Merchant)*, 486 F. Supp. 436, 1980 AMC 1686 (SDNY 1980). But this absence must be causal under COGSA. See *The Iristo*, 137 F.2d 619, 1943 AMC 1043 (2d Cir. 1943).

264. *The Marion*, [1984] 1 A.C. 563 (H. L.).

ages. The vessel pleaded the defenses of negligent navigation and management as to the cargo damage claim and sought limitation of liability. The *Marion* had an area chart on board, but the chart was obsolete and did not show the pipeline. The negligence in management pleaded was the master's failure to keep the chart updated, and the owners introduced a letter to their masters, directing them to keep their charts up to date. In the view of the House of Lords, affirming the Court of Appeal, the shipowners' letter instruction was an inadequate measure to ensure that up-to-date charts were being used. Accordingly, the vessel was held unseaworthy with the actual fault of the owners, so that limitation of liability was denied.

Section G. Rule 10: Traffic Separation Schemes

1. *Introduction*

Rule 10 of COLREGS and the Inland Rules, headed "Traffic Separation Schemes," is entirely new.[265]

"Vessel traffic services" (VTS) is the external direction of ship movements by higher authority within specified areas set apart because of congestion and the historic frequency of accidents in the areas. The term at the least involves traffic separation by course direction ("traffic separation schemes" [TSS]). It may also include monitoring the position of vessels within an area ("vessel traffic reporting systems" [VTRS]). It may also involve positive control of the course and speed of vessels ("vessel traffic management system" [VTMS]). VTS have been established by I.M.O. in many areas of "converging routes of high traffic density."[266]

The concept of eastbound North Atlantic traffic following certain designated tracks, with westbound North Atlantic traffic following other separate designated tracks, was adopted voluntarily for collision avoidance by shipowners in 1898, long before the existence of IMCO (now I.M.O.).[267] It has been persuasively argued that one of the main catalysts for VTS was pollution avoidance.[268]

265. For ready reference, COLREGS Rule 10, as amended in 1987 and again in 1989, can be found in appendix 1.

266. *Ships' Routeing* (4th ed. 1978), published by I.M.O. (formerly IMCO).

267. D. O'Connell, *The International Law of the Sea* 833 (1984).

268. E. Gold, *Vessel Traffic Regulation: The Interface of Maritime Safety and Operational Freedom,* 14 J. Mar. L. & Com. 1, 2 (1983). Dr. Gold adds: "The basic purpose of all new regulatory approaches in the industry is to establish greater navigational safety, and thus reduce ship-generated pollution to the lowest possible incidence." The article traces the history of traffic separation and routing from the time they were first proposed in 1847 until COLREGS entered into force in 1977.

There are substantial analogies between VTS and similar situations in air law, despite governmental minimizing of similarities in order to avoid governmental liability.[269] The case law involving governmental liability is extensive in air law and may provide useful analogies. (In fact, the "automated advances surveillance" type of VTS uses the transponder in a radar system, aided by computers, which was developed for U.S. airports and air traffic controllers.) The analogy is, of course, imperfect, because the maritime sphere is horizontal only, whereas the air problem is both horizontal and vertical.

Probably the most familiar traffic separation scheme for highly congested high seas waters is that for the English Channel (La Manche in France) and the Dover Strait established by IMCO in 1967, where the English side is for westbound traffic and the French side is for eastbound traffic. For inland congested waters the St. Lawrence Seaway Marine Traffic Control System of 1959 established by the United States and Canada is a familiar example.

VTS are now determined by I.M.O.'s Subcommittee on Navigation, which has exclusive jurisdiction to establish schemes on the high seas and those coastal State waters where there is an established traffic pattern involving both high seas and coastal waters.[270] I.M.O.'s Subcommittee considers proposals from governments with industry input, and makes recommendations to the I.M.O. Maritime Safety Committee, which may forward a proposal to the I.M.O. Assembly or direct it to the proposing governments for adoption. A substantial revision of the 1985 VTS Regulations by I.M.O., in the direction of mandatory applicability, will come into force on Jan. 1, 1999.

Coastal States may establish VTS schemes in territorial waters, and the U.S. Coast Guard has established them in high-density port areas: initially in Puget Sound and Berwick Bay, Louisiana, and subsequently in San Francisco, New Orleans, and New York. OPA 90[271] mandated VTS in Prince William Sound (Alaska), New York, and New Orleans. VTS have been established since the 1950s for other great ports such as London, Rotterdam, Hamburg, and Bremerhaven, and for the entire east coast of Canada. The I.M.O. Subcommittee on Navigation is constantly reviewing the operation of VTS schemes and proposals for changes or additional schemes. This factor makes the provision of up-to-date charts and sailing directions essential.

---

269. See e.g. *Stanley v. United States,* 239 F. Supp. 973, 979 (ND Ohio, 1965): "The essence of the matter is that in visual flight rule weather the function of the control tower operator is advisory and the primary responsibility for avoiding mid-air collisions is upon the pilots."

270. 2 D. O'Connell, supra note 267, at 835 (1984). See also, *Ships' Routeing,* supra note 265, at 3–4. Knowledge of the existence of a vessel traffic separation scheme (TSS) prepared by the Japan Captains' Association for High Seas Areas off the Japanese Coast, but not approved by I.M.O., could not create an enforceable duty to observe it. *Complaint of Pacific Bulk Carriers,* 639 F.2d 72, 1980 AMC 2530 (2d Cir. 1980). See also *Zim Israel Navigation Co. Ltd. v. Special Carriers, Inc.,* 611 F. Supp. 581, 1986 AMC 2016 (ED La. 1985), modified in other respects, 800 F.2d 1392, 1988 AMC 2110 (5th Cir. 1986), concerning a voluntary safety fairway south of Southwest Pass sea buoy.

271. The Oil Pollution Act of 1990, 33 U.S.C. §§ 2701–61.

2. *Enforcement Issues under Public International Law*

Violations of VTS schemes on the high seas are still governed by the law of the flag,[272] whereas violations of VTS schemes in territorial waters are based upon the penal law of the coastal State.[273]

a. The 1958 Convention on the Territorial Sea and Contiguous Zone: Innocent Passage. The 1958 Convention begins with a positive endorsement of the right of innocent passage: ". . . [S]hips of all States, whether coastal or not, shall enjoy the right of innocent passage through the territorial seas." The convention further provides that "Passage is innocent so long as it is not prejudicial to the peace, good order or security of the coastal State. . .,"[274] and the coastal State "must not hamper innocent passage."[275]

b. The 1982 Law of the Sea Convention: Passage, Transit Passage, and Archipelagic Passage. The 1982 United Nations Convention on the Law of the Sea rephrases the provisions of the 1958 Convention and empowers further coastal State control of vessels in territorial waters. Thus, although the basic right is restated,[276] the convention defines passage as "navigation"[277] that must be "continuous and expeditious,"[278] and stopping and anchoring are authorized *only* insofar as they are incidental to ordinary navigation, or rendered necessary by force majeure or distress, or to render assistance to persons, ships, or aircraft in danger or distress.[279] The significant provision of the convention concerning innocent passage in the territorial sea is the long list of activities that are *not* considered to be innocent passage.[280]

Furthermore, the convention introduces new concepts of passage under conditions slightly at variance with traditional innocent passage through the

---

272. Convention on the High Seas, April 29, 1958, 13 U.S.T. 2312, 450 U.N.T.S. 82, T.I.A.S. No. 5200 Art. 2. UNCLOS III Art. 89.

273. See *Cunard S.S. Co. v. Mellon,* 262 U.S. 100 (1923), concerning the application of the Prohibition Amendment and laws enacted thereunder to British flag vessels in U.S. harbors, despite contrary treaty provisions. See generally *Wildenhus's Case,* 120 U.S. 1 (1887); see also *Trinidad Corp. v. The Keiyoh Maru,* 845 F.2d 818, 1989 AMC 627 (9th Cir. 1988).

274. Convention on the Territorial Sea and Contiguous Zone, April 29, 1958, 15 U.S.T. 1606, T.I.A.S. No. 5639, 516 U.N.T.S. 205, Art. 14(1) and Art. 14(4).

275. Id. Art. 15 (1).

276. United Nations Convention on the Law of the Sea, Dec. 10, 1982, U.N. Doc. A/CONF. 62/122, 21 Int'l. Leg. Mat. 1261 (1982), Art. 17.

277. Id. Art. 18 (1).

278. Id. Art. 18 (2).

279. Id.

280. Id. Art. 19 (2).

> Passage of a foreign ship shall be considered to be prejudicial to the peace, good order or security of the coastal State if in the territorial sea it engages in any of the following activities:
>
> (a) any threat or use of force against the sovereignty, territorial integrity or political independence of the coastal State, or in any other manner in violation of the principles of international law embodied in the Charter of the United Nations;

territorial sea: "transit passage" and "archipelagic passage." "Transit passage" is the continuous and expeditious transit of a strait between one part of the high seas (or an exclusive economic zone [EEZ]) and another part of the high seas (or an EEZ).[281] Again, there are lists of noninnocent activities.[282] "Archipelagic passage" is a right of passage through sea lanes designated by the archipelagic State,[283] further defined as ". . . all normal passage routes used as routes for international navigation . . ." and "all normal navigational channels."[284] Ships are forbidden to deviate more than 25 miles of either side of continuous axis lines from entry to exit points to be designated by the archipelagic State.[285]

c. The 1982 Convention and Vessel Traffic Services. Ten years after COLREGS were formulated, the 1982 Convention, the major recodification and legislation on law of the sea, touched on the subject of vessel traffic services, but did not expand the powers of the coastal State or restrict the powers of the flag State. The following provisions of the 1982 Convention apply to innocent passage in territorial waters:

Article 22

Sea lanes and traffic separation schemes in the territorial sea

> 1. The coastal State may, where necessary having regard to the safety of navigation, require foreign ships exercising the right of innocent passage through its territorial sea to use such sea lanes and traffic separation schemes as it may designate or prescribe for the regulation of the passage of ships.

(b) any exercise or practice with weapons of any kind;
(c) any act aimed at collecting information to the prejudice of the defense or security of the coastal State;
(d) any act of propaganda aimed at affecting the defense or security of the coastal State;
(e) the launching, landing or taking on board of any aircraft;
(f) the launching, landing or taking on board of any military device;
(g) the loading or unloading of any commodity, currency or person contrary to the customs, fiscal, immigration or sanitary laws and regulations of the coastal State;
(h) any act of wilful and serious pollution contrary to this Convention;
(i) any fishing activities;
(j) the carrying out of research or survey activities;
(k) any act aimed at interfering with any systems of communication or any other facilities or installations of the coastal State;
(l) any other activity not having a direct bearing on passage.

281. Id. Art. 38.
282. Id. Arts. 39(1)(2) And 40.
283. Id. Art. 53(1).
284. Id. Art. 53(4).
285. Id. Art. 53(5).

2. In particular, tankers, nuclear-powered ships and ships carrying nuclear or other inherently dangerous or noxious substances or materials may be required to confine their passage to such sea lanes.
3. In the designation of sea lanes and the prescription of traffic separation schemes under this article, the coastal State shall take into account:

(a) the recommendations of the competent international organization;
(b) any channels customarily used for international navigation;
(c) the special characteristics of particular ships and channels; and
(d) the density of traffic.

4. The coastal State shall clearly indicate such sea lanes and traffic separation schemes on charts to which due publicity shall be given.

The following provisions apply to transit passage in international straits:

Article 41

Sea lanes and traffic separation schemes in straits used for international navigation

1. In conformity with this Part, States bordering straits may designate sea lanes and prescribe traffic separation schemes for navigation in straits where necessary to promote the safe passage of ships.
2. Such States may, when circumstances require, and after giving due publicity thereto, substitute other sea lanes or traffic separation schemes for any sea lanes or traffic separation schemes previously designated or prescribed by them.
3. Such sea lanes and traffic separation schemes shall conform to generally accepted international regulations.
4. Before designating or substituting sea lanes or prescribing or substituting traffic separation schemes, States bordering straits shall refer proposals to the competent international organization with a view to their adoption. The organization may adopt only such sea lanes and traffic separation schemes as may be agreed with the States bordering the straits, after which the States may designate, prescribe or substitute them.
5. In respect of a strait where sea lanes or traffic separation schemes through the waters of two or more States bordering the strait are being proposed, the States concerned shall co-operate in formulating proposals in consultation with the competent international organization.

6. States bordering straits shall clearly indicate all sea lanes and traffic separation schemes designated or prescribed by them on charts to which due publicity shall be given.
7. Ships in transit passage shall respect applicable sea lanes and traffic separation schemes established in accordance with this article.

Provisions applicable to archipelagic passage are the following:

Article 53

Right of archipelagic sea lanes passage

1. An archipelagic State may designate sea lanes and air routes thereabove, suitable for the continuous and expeditious passage of foreign ships and aircraft through or over its archipelagic waters and the adjacent territorial sea.
2. All ships and aircraft enjoy the right of archipelagic sea lanes passage in such sea lanes and air routes.
3. Archipelagic sea lanes passage means the exercise in accordance with this Convention of the rights of navigation and overflight in the normal mode solely for the purpose of continuous, expeditious and unobstructed transit between one part of the high seas or an exclusive economic zone and another part of the high seas or an exclusive economic zone.
4. Such sea lanes and air routes shall traverse the archipelagic waters and the adjacent territorial sea and shall include all normal passage routes used as routes for international navigation or overflight through or over archipelagic waters and, within such routes, so far as ships are concerned, all normal navigational channels, provided that duplication of routes of similar convenience between the same entry and exit points shall not be necessary.
5. Such sea lanes and air routes shall be defined by a series of continuous axis lines from the entry points of passage routes to the exit points. Ships and aircraft in archipelagic sea lanes passage shall not deviate more than 25 nautical miles to either side of such axis lines during passage, provided that such ships and aircraft shall not navigate closer to the coasts than 10 per cent of the distance between the nearest points on islands bordering the sea lane.
6. An archipelagic State which designates sea lanes under this article may also prescribe traffic separation schemes for the safe passage of ships through narrow channels in such sea lanes.
7. An archipelagic State may, when circumstances require, after giving due publicity thereto, substitute other sea lanes or traffic separation schemes for any sea lanes or traffic separation schemes previously designated or prescribed by it.

> 8. Such sea lanes and traffic separation schemes shall conform to generally accepted international regulations.
> 9. In designating or substituting sea lanes or prescribing or substituting traffic separation schemes, an archipelagic State shall refer proposals to the competent international organization with a view to their adoption. The organization may adopt only such sea lanes and traffic separation schemes as may be agreed with the archipelagic State, after which the archipelagic State may designate, prescribe or substitute them.
> 10. The archipelagic State shall clearly indicate the axis of the sea lanes and the traffic separation schemes designated or prescribed by it on charts to which due publicity shall be given.
> 11. Ships in archipelagic sea lanes passage shall respect applicable sea lanes and traffic separation schemes established in accordance with this article.
> 12. If an archipelagic State does not designate sea lanes or air routes, the right of archipelagic sea lanes passage may be exercised through the routes normally used for international navigation.

Because penal enforcement of VTS is limited to the flag State or the territorial waters State, it is likely that a further enhancement of enforcement powers will occur along the lines of the enhancement of pollution prevention powers through the port State jurisdiction of the 1982 treaty.[286] I.M.O. was pushed in this direction by a series of oil spills in 1992–93 which energized the European Community[287] in the same way that a series of oil spills in 1989–90 pushed the U.S. Congress into enacting the 1990 Oil Pollution Act.[288] It is likely that a new treaty will be necessary to permit States other than the flag State and the territorial waters State to enforce VTS. A first step in that direction will be an amendment to chapter V of SOLAS to require vessels to report at a minimum the name of the vessel and her position, and possibly also her destination and the nature of her cargo.

3. Rules of the Road in the VTS

(a) Relationship between Rule 10 and Other Rules. Until COLREGS Rule 10(a) was amended in 1987 it was uncertain what effect violations of the other rules of the road at sea would have on the status of vessels operating under VTS. Thus it was argued that the context in which Rule 10 was placed—following the narrow channel rule and preceding the Steering and Sailing Rules for vessels in sight of one another—implied that all the rules of

---

286. Id. art. 218.
287. E.g., the spills at La Coruña, Spain, and the Shetland Islands.
288. See note 40, ch. 11, infra.

the road were to apply. The 1987 amendment to Rule 10(a)—"and does not relieve any vessel of her obligation under any other rule"—makes it clear that noncompliance with other rules is not excused by compliance with VTS. There is no indication that the vessel violating Rule 10 will be found in a greater degree of fault than the vessel violating other maneuvering requirements of COLREGS.[289]

(b) Violations of COLREGS Rule 10. Rule 10[290] itself deals with vessels using a VTS scheme and those not using it for some specific reason. Thus, vessels using a traffic separation scheme must proceed in the appropriate traffic lane[291] in the general direction of traffic flow; so far as practicable, keep clear of a traffic separation line[292] or zone; normally join or leave a traffic lane at its termination; when joining or leaving from the side they must do so at as small an angle to the general direction of traffic flow as practicable.

---

289. In *The Genimar,* [1977] 2 Lloyd's Rep. 17, 25 (Adm.), Mr. Justice Brandon (later Lord Brandon of Oakbrook) found a vessel violating a VTS scheme to be liable to a lesser degree than the vessel complying with it. The *Larry L,* a large Greek flag bulk carrier, bound from Antwerp to Canada, was proceeding in Dover Strait under the southwest heading for traffic near the English coast, while the *Genimar,* a much smaller Liberian flag vessel, was proceeding on a northeast course to Rotterdam, outside the VTS. When the *Genimar* appeared to be crossing the *Larry L,* neither vessel took appropriate action. The court applied the starboard-hand rule, with the result that the *Larry L* was held two-thirds at fault for first failing to give way and then turning to port, while the *Genimar* was held one-third at fault for failing to comply with the VTS and to hold course and speed. These *Genimar* faults were found to be less culpable and less causative than those of the *Larry L.* In summing up the navigation of both vessels, Mr. Justice Brandon commented on the faults of the *Larry L:*

> I have no doubt that the master of the *Larry L* navigated in the way he did in relation to the *Genimar* because of the existence of the traffic separation scheme. His attitude appears to have been that, since the *Genimar* was proceeding in the wrong direction in his lane, it was for her to keep out of the way of the *Larry L,* rather than for the *Larry L* to keep out of her way. This attitude is exemplified by his two peremptory signals of five short blasts and his failure to take any action under r. 19.
>
> In adopting this attitude the master of the *Larry L* was plainly wrong. He should have known that the Collision Regulations applied despite the existence of the traffic separation scheme . . . . [1977] 2 Lloyd's Rep. 25.

See also *The Estrella* [1977] 1 Lloyd's Rep. 525.

In *In re Texaco Inc.,* 570 F. Supp. 1272, 1985 AMC 1650 (ED La. 1983), *The Genimar* served as a useful authority to establish fault for a collision between a tanker and an oil rig in the Gulf of Mexico. The owner was not only held at fault but was denied limitation of liability because of its failure to require use of the safety fairway.

290. I.M.O. Resolution A/284 (VIII) defines and interprets the terms used in Rule 10. Thus, "traffic separation scheme" is defined as "A scheme which separates traffic proceeding in opposite or nearly opposite directions, by the use of a separation zone or line, traffic lanes, or by other means." Excellent illustrations of the application of COLREGS Rule 10 are found in Cockcroft & Lameijer, at 85–100.

291. "Traffic lane" is defined in the resolution as "An area within definite limits inside which one-way traffic is established."

292. The resolution defines "separation zone or line" as "a zone or line separating traffic proceeding in one direction from traffic proceeding in another direction. A separation zone may also be used to separate a traffic lane from the adjacent inshore traffic zone."

Rule 10 prohibits a vessel other than a crossing vessel or one joining or leaving a lane from entering a separation zone or crossing a separation lane except in cases of emergency, to avoid immediate danger or to engage in fishing within a separation zone.

Nonusers are directed to avoid the VTS, "by as wide a margin as is practicable,"[293] and all vessels are directed, so far as practicable, to avoid anchoring in a traffic separation scheme or in areas near its termination,[294] where all vessels are directed to navigate "with particular caution."[295]

Local traffic convenience is preserved by the provision for inshore traffic zones,[296] which may always be used by vessels of less than 20 meters in length and sailing vessels.[297] Such zones must not normally be used by through traffic which can safely use the appropriate traffic lane within the adjacent traffic separation scheme.[298]

Fishing in VTS traffic lanes and separation zones is not prohibited, although fishing vessels must not impede the passage of vessels in a VTS traffic lane and must proceed in the general direction of the traffic flow.[299] Thus far, the maintenance of navigational aids, the servicing of submarine cables, and fishing are the only activities specifically permitted in a VTS, other than navigation itself. Thus, activities such as salvage operations and pollution cleanup will have to be dealt with on a case-by-case basis.[300]

(c) VTS in the United States. As originally enacted, Inland Rule 10 (Vessel Traffic Services) simply provided that each vessel required by regulation to participate in a vessel traffic service must comply with the applicable regulations. In 1992 the Inland Rule was amended, and is now substantially identical to COLREGS Rule 10.[301] Authority to establish VTS plans in U.S. territorial waters was vested in the Coast Guard by the 1972 Ports and Waterways Safety Act.[302] Prior to enactment of that act the Coast Guard's authority to direct vessel movements was limited to situations involving national security and

---

293. Rule 10(h).

294. Rule 10(g).

295. Rule 10(f).

296. I.M.O. Resolution A/284 (VIII) defines "inshore traffic zone" as "A designated area between the landward boundary of a traffic separation scheme and the adjacent coast intended for coastal traffic."

297. Rule l0(d).

298. Id.

299. Rule l0(d)(i) and I.M.O. Resolution A/284(VIII).

300. See, e.g., *Martha's Vineyard Scuba Headquarters, Inc. v. Unidentified Wrecked and Abandoned Steam Vessel,* 833 F.2d 1059, 1988 AMC 1109 (1st Cir. 1987), upholding salvage of an abandoned vessel which had sunk in an area within a traffic separation scheme beyond territorial waters.

301. Pub. L. No. 102-587, § 5206 (2).

302. Pub. L. No. 92-340, 86 Stat. 424, 33 U.S.C. §§ 1221–36. See Legislative History of the 1972 Act in 1972 U.S. Code Cong. & Adm. News 2766. The Magnuson Act, 50 U.S.C. § 191 (1976), and even earlier legislation from the First World War emergency had empowered the President to control vessel movements as a matter of national security. See Legislative History of Port and Tanker Safety Act of 1978, 1978 U.S. Code Cong. & Adm. News 3270–71.

dangerous cargoes. Further legislation in 1978—the Ports and Tanker Safety Act[303]—expanded the powers of the Coast Guard. It was also sensitive to the problem of foreign flag vessels navigating in VTS safety zones, both inside and outside U.S. territorial waters.[304] Furthermore, Congress chose to append duties (and liabilities) to the master's traditional responsibility for the safe navigation of his vessel, without clarifying the liability of the government when positive control contributes to a disaster.[305] Failure to comply with the applicable Coast Guard Regulations is of course a fault,[306] and since the regulations were clearly designed to avoid collisions, a violation is sure to impose upon the violator the *Pennsylvania* Rule burden of proving that the violation could not have been a contributing cause of the casualty.

An essential part of any VTS scheme is the requirement of the transmission of the following information, in English: time of arrival/departure; name and type of vessel; position; estimated time of entering VTS; destination in VTS area; speed of vessel; length of vessel; nature of cargo.[307]

4. *Navigational Errors in the VTS*

(a) Errors on Board the Vessels. In the absence of case law applicable to Rule 10, it is necessary to use analogies from the law of pilotage on the crucial issue of the plenary power of a master to override the orders of a pilot.[308] In a larger view, it could be argued that coastal State pilotage laws and regulations were (and are) a primitive form of VTS, by utilizing the services of a local navigator to conn the vessel on entry into and departure from port. Thus, the pilot "has the conn," so that the helmsman and other bridge personnel are required to respond to his orders respecting courses and speeds and the use of anchors, unless the master, who knows the characteristics of his own vessel better than the pilot, intervenes and cancels the pilot's orders.[309] Of course the most obvious dissimilarity between pilotage and VTS navigation is that

---

303. Pub. L. No. 95–474, 92 Stat. 1471, 33 U.S.C. §§ 1221–32. See Legislative History of the 1978 Act, 1978 U.S. Code Cong. & Adm. News 3270. Where a VTS was established on a voluntary basis, failure to comply with it cannot be held a fault. *P.F. Pugh & Assoc. v. Arco Marine, Inc.,* 1986 AMC 2519 (ND Cal. 1984).

304. See 33 U.S.C. § 1223(d)(i), respecting the right of innocent passage through territorial waters and contiguous zones, and 33 U.S.C. § 1223(d)(2), respecting the right of transit passage through international straits.

305. 33 U.S.C. § 1223(a) (1982).

306. 33 CFR §§ 160–61 (1986).

307. 33 CFR 161.124; 161.28.

308. See chapter 9 infra. See generally, A. Parks and E. Cattell, *The Law of Tug, Tow, and Pilotage* (3d ed. 1994); Boland, *Vessel Traffic Services and Liability for Oil Spills and Other Marine Accidents,* 18 Colum. J. Trans. Law 482 (1979).

309. *Ralli v. Troop,* 157 U.S. 386, 402 (1889): "To the pilot, therefore, temporarily belongs the whole conduct of the navigation of the ship, including the duty of determining her courses and speed and the time, place and manner of anchoring her."

the pilot is exposed to danger on the bridge of the vessel being navigated, while the VTS "advice" is given from the safety of an on-shore operations center. For the purpose of this discussion on vessel liability it is not necessary to differentiate between "compulsory" and "voluntary" pilotage.[310]

(b) Government Liability for Navigational Errors under VTS. Tort liability requires a duty to the injured party who has relied on the careful and accurate performances of the function undertaken by the defendant government. *Indian Towing Co. v. United States*[311] provides the best maritime analogy for the recovery of damages for a collision or stranding caused by negligent advice from the VTS. In that case, plaintiff's barge grounded on an island where the U.S. Coast Guard had established an unmanned lighthouse which malfunctioned. No warning of the absence of the light had been given. The case (decided by a court divided 5 to 4) distinguishes government planning (which is discretionary and for the absence of which there is no liability) from operational activities for which there may be liability if negligently performed. Once the discretion to establish a lighthouse is exercised, the government is required to exercise due care to maintain and repair it, or warn of its absence. The same principle has resulted in government liability with respect to the failure of a naval escort vessel equipped with radar to warn convoy vessels not so equipped about a risk of collision,[312] or the negligent attempt to rescue a fishing vessel, relying on incompetent government personnel deficiently equipped—a reliance which cost the lives of five fishermen.[313]

Under the *Indian Towing* principle, the governmental duty (and consequent liability for failing to carry out the duty carefully) will depend upon the reliance induced by certain words and their context, including the intensity and volume of the statement. Presumably, VTS personnel will not usually order a vessel's watch officer to take a specific action. Most of the communications from VTS will be information about the navigational problem and special weather, current, or tidal conditions. Recommendations may also be forthcoming with or without a request from the vessel; at an early stage there may be a suggestion for action, such as speed reduction to prevent a close-

---

310. The distinction goes back to *The China,* 74 U.S. 53 (1986). The outbound *China,* under the conn of a "compulsory" pilot, collided with the inbound *Kentucky,* due solely to the negligence of the *China's* pilot. The Court held the *China* liable *in rem* for the fault of her acting servant, even though the owner could not be held liable *in personam* because there was no choice in the selection of the pilot (see chapter 9).

311. 350 U.S. 61 (1955).

312. *United States v. The Australia Star,* 172 F.2d 472, 1949 AMC 423 (2d Cir. 1949).

313. *United States v. Sandra & Dennis Fishing Corp.,* 372 F.2d 189 (1st Cir. 1967). Chief Judge Aldrich's response to the government's plea of no duty to rescue was his refusal to add to the honored motto "Semper Paratus" [always ready] the words "Interdum Prudens" [sometimes careful]. 372 F.2d, at 197. Nonliability of the United States for the negligence of the National Weather Service because of the discretionary function was stated in *Brown v. United States,* 790 F.2d 199, 1986 AMC 2100 (1st Cir. 1986).

quarters or *in extremis* situation from developing; at a later stage the recommendation may become more peremptory and be indistinguishable from a "direction" in a time of imminent peril. Nevertheless, under the present rules the master of the vessel is expected to have sufficient experience, good judgment, and skill to save himself (or herself), the crew, and the vessel from disaster. Videotapes of the radar plot and tape recordings of the communications between the vessel traffic center and the ship are made and should be discoverable.

The air traffic controller (ATC) presents an analogy for the potential liability of the United States for negligent operational activity of vessel traffic center personnel. The analogy is not perfect, for the mariner is usually not confronted with the extreme perils of a metropolitan airport, where aircraft may be landing at intervals of a minute or less, while other aircraft are taking off. It should also be noted that very precise wordings for communication between ATC and pilots have been prescribed in air traffic controller manuals. The position of the U.S. government is that the air traffic controllers give advice or suggestions which aircraft commanders may follow, while remaining at all times in command of the aircraft. Following are examples of cases in which the government was held liable for ATC negligence.

In *Eastern Air Lines v. Union Trust Co.*[314] the ATC ordered two planes to land on the same runway at the same time at National Airport, Washington, D.C. *United Air Lines, Inc. v. Wiener*[315] involved approval of an incorrect IFR (instrument flight rules) flight plan. *Ingham v. United States*[316] dealt with a landing clearance when the visibility was already below the minimum for landing. *Furumizo v. United States*[317] involved improper warning of turbulence at take-off, as did *Hartz v. United States,*[318] dealing with wingtip vortices creating dangerous take-off turbulence; while in *Stork v. United States*[319] the controller who cleared an aircraft for take-off failed to warn of zero visibility. *Yates v. United States*[320] involved turbulence affecting a Cessna aircraft landing just behind a commercial jet at the direction of the controller. *Rudelson v. United States*[321] involved the ATC duty to trainee pilots. *Beattie v. United States*[322] concerned ATC negligence in the Antarctic. In *Daley v. United States*[323] the negligence was in attempting to locate the missing aircraft for

314. 221 F.2d 62 (D.C. Cir. 1955), aff'd sub nom. *United States v. Union Trust Co.*, 350 U.S. 907 (1955).
315. 335 F.2d 379 (9th Cir. 1964).
316. 373 F.2d 227 (2d Cir. 1967).
317. 381 F.2d 965 (9th Cir. 1967).
318. 387 F.2d 870 (5th Cir. 1968).
319. 430 F.2d 1104 (9th Cir. 1970).
320. 497 F.2d 878 (10th Cir. 1974).
321. 602 F.2d 1326 (9th Cir. 1979).
322. 756 F.2d 91 (D.C. Cir. 1984); on remand, 690 F. Supp. 1068 (D.C. Cir. 1988).
323. 792 F.2d 1081 (11th Cir. 1986).

rescuers. *Rodriguez v. United States*[324] involved the ATC insufficiently warning a small-plane pilot of the risk of a midair collision. *Transco Leasing Corp. v. United States*[325] concerned mistaken communications as the controller confused "Armstrong" with "Arlington." *Nakajima v. United States*[326] involved the midair collision of a helicopter and a small plane due to negligent landing instructions. *In re Air Crash Disaster Near Cerritos, California*[327] again dealt with a midair collision due in part to ATC negligence.

There are, however, an even greater number of cases where air traffic controllers have been exonerated and the blame for the crash attributed to the pilot. Samples of the many decisions favoring the government's position are listed in the footnotes.[328]

---

324. 823 F.2d 735 (3d Cir. 1987).

325. 896 F.2d 1435 (5th Cir. 1990), judgment amended in part on rehearing, 905 F.2d 61 (5th Cir. 1990), vacated in part and remanded on issue of interest against the United States, 992 F.2d 552 (5th Cir. 1993).

326. 965 F.2d 987 (11th Cir. 1992).

327. 973 F.2d 1490 (9th Cir. 1992).

328. *United States v. Schulteus*, 277 F.2d 322 (5th Cir. 1960); *United States v. Miller*, 303 F.2d 703 (9th Cir. 1962); *Tilley v. United States*, 375 F.2d 678 (4th Cir. 1967); *Somlo v. United States*, 416 F.2d 640 (7th Cir. 1969); *Gill v. United States*, 429 F.2d 1072 (5th Cir. 1970); *Lightenburger v. United States*, 460 F.2d 391 (9th Cir. 1973); *In re Air Crash Disaster at New Orleans*, 544 F.2d 270 (5th Cir. 1976); *Zabala Clemente v. United States*, 567 F.2d 1140 (1st Cir. 1977); *Redhead v. United States*, 686 F.2d 178 (3d Cir. 1982); *Sellfors v. United States*, 697 F.2d 1362 (11th Cir. 1983); *Armstrong v. United States*, 756 F.2d 1407 (9th Cir. 1985); *Rawl v. United States*, 778 F.2d 1009 (4th Cir. 1985); *Murff v. United States*, 785 F.2d 552 (5th Cir. 1986); *Barbosa v. United States*, 811 F.2d 1444 (11th Cir. 1987); *Davis v. United States*, 824 F.2d 549 (7th Cir. 1987); *Apostol v. United States*, 838 F.2d 595 (1st Cir. 1988); *Biles v. United States*, 848 F.2d 661 (5th Cir. 1988); *Schuler v. United States*, 868 F.2d 195 (6th Cir. 1989); and *In re Air Crash at Dallas/Fort Worth Airport*, 919 F.2d 1079 (5th Cir. 1991).

CHAPTER FIVE

INTERNATIONAL AND INLAND RULES: PART B(II)—CONDUCT OF VESSELS IN SIGHT OF ONE ANOTHER

Section A. Introduction

While Section/Subpart I of Part B of COLREGS and the Inland Rules (the Steering and Sailing Rules) regulates the conduct of vessels in any condition of visibility, Section/Subpart II, comprising Rules 11 to 18, applies only to vessels in sight of one another.

Rule 11 (Application) simply paraphrases the title of the section/subpart, stating that the rules it embraces "apply to vessels in sight of one another." It will be remembered that COLREGS Rule 3(k) and Inland Rule 3(j) provide that "Vessels shall be deemed in sight of one another only when one can be observed visually from the other." When vessels are not in sight of one another—even if their position and movements may be known by radar, radio, or other means—their conduct is governed by Rule 19, the only rule contained in Section/Subpart III of Part B (Conduct of Vessels in Restricted Visibility). So much of that section/subpart as relates to speed in restricted visibility is discussed in chapter 4; section C, fog signals, is treated in chapter 8, and the balance of the section/subpart is covered in chapter 6.

Rule 12 regulates the conduct of sailing vessels approaching one another so as to involve risk of collision. Rules 13–17 regulate the conduct of power-driven vessels in the three basic navigational situations: overtaking, meeting head-on, and crossing. Rule 18 concerns responsibilities, i.e., priorities, among vessels of various categories, under various circumstances.

Section B. Rule 12: Sailing Vessels

Article 17 of the International Rules effective in 1897, the forerunner of COLREGS Rule 12, was designed primarily for square-rigged sailing vessels, a vast number of which were in active service at the time. The rule required a sailing vessel running free to keep out of the way of one close-hauled, and one close-hauled on the port tack to keep out of the way of one close-hauled on the starboard tack. It further provided that when both vessels were running free, with the wind on different sides, the vessel with the wind on the port side was obliged to keep out of the other's way, and that when both were running free with the wind on the same side, the vessel to windward was obliged to keep out of the way of the vessel to leeward. Finally, the rule required a vessel with the wind aft to keep out of the way of the other vessel.[1]

Article 17 of the Inland Rules effective in 1897[2] was identical to Article 17 of the former International Rules, as was Rule 17 of the 1948 Western Rivers Rules.[3] Rule 16 of the Great Lakes Rules was identical to Article 17 of the former International Rules, except that the Great Lakes Rule omitted the provision requiring a sailing vessel with the wind aft to keep out of the way of the other vessel.

Rule 17 of the International Rules remained unchanged until the 1960 Rules[4] became effective in 1967. It was then amended so as to provide, in paragraph (a)(i), that when two sailing vessels are approaching one another so as to involve risk of collision, and each has the wind on a different side, the vessel with the wind on the port side must keep out of the other's way; and (ii) that when both have the wind on the same side, the vessel to windward must keep out of the way of the vessel to leeward. Paragraph (b) then provided that for the purposes of Rule 17, the windward side should be deemed the side opposite the one on which the mainsail was carried, or, in the case of a square-rigged vessel, the side opposite to that on which the largest fore- and aft sail was carried.

The changes effected by the 1960 Rules with respect to sailing vessels were made in recognition of the fact that by the time the rules were drafted, square-riggers had all but disappeared from the seas, and most sailing vessels then in use were pleasure craft or small fishing and other commercial vessels, with schooner-type sails.[5]

Rule 12 of COLREGS and Rule 12 of the current Inland Rules are identical. They are worded precisely the same as Rule 17 of the 1960 International Rules, except that they add to paragraph (a) a new subparagraph (iii), which provides that "if a vessel with the wind on the port side sees a vessel to windward and cannot determine with certainty whether the other vessel has the wind on the port or on the starboard side, she shall keep out of the way of the other." This addition was sponsored by the International Yacht Racing Union, with a view to harmonizing COLREGS and the Union's yacht racing rules.[6]

1. 26 Stat. 320, reprinted in J. Griffin, *The American Law of Collision,* at 645–80 (hereinafter "Griffin").

2. 30 Stat. 96, reprinted in Griffin, at 645–80.

3. Act of May 21, 1948, Pub. L. No. 544, 80th Cong., reprinted in Griffin, at 772–87.

4. Former §§ 1151–53, 33 U.S. Code.

5. See 1980 U.S. Code Cong. & Adm. News, p. 7068, relating to Inland Rule 12, identical to COLREGS Rule 12.

6. Cockcroft & Lameijer, *Collision Avoidance Rules* 103 (4th ed.) (hereinafter "Cockcroft & Lameijer"). As to the applicability of COLREGS in a sailing regatta, see *Juno SRL v. The Endeavour,* 58 F.3d 1, 1995 AMC 2678 (1st Cir. 1995), noted, 26 J. Mar. L. & Com. 609 (1995), where the

Section C. Rule 13: Overtaking

1. Introduction

Rule 13 of COLREGS and Rule 13 of the Inland Rules are identical, except for one immaterial difference in verbiage.[7] A similar rule (Article 24) was contained in the International Rules effective in 1897, and was left unchanged when those rules were amended in 1960. The former Inland Rule was identical to the former International Rule, and Rule 22 of the 1948 Western Rivers Rules was similar. Rule 22 of the former Great Lakes Rules was similar to COLREGS and present Inland Rule 13(a), but contained no provisions such as those contained in paragraphs (b), (c), and (d) of that rule.[8]

The core of the overtaking rule is paragraph (a), which requires any vessel overtaking any other to keep out of the way of the vessel being overtaken. Paragraph (b) defines the term "overtaking." Paragraph (c) concerns cases where there is doubt as to whether a vessel is overtaking another. Paragraph (d) relates to the effect of changes in bearing after an overtaking situation has been created. These provisions of Rule 13 will be discussed in this section, as will the other rules that relate to overtaking.[9]

2. *Application of the Overtaking Rule*

Paragraph (a) specifically provides that the rule applies to *any* vessel overtaking another, notwithstanding anything contained in Rules 4 through 18.[10] Thus, the order of priority set out in Rule 18 does not apply as between an overtaking vessel and a vessel being overtaken: *any* vessel, including a sailing vessel, or a vessel restricted in her ability to maneuver, or a small power-driven vessel, or one engaged in fishing, must keep out of the way of a vessel she attempts to overtake, even if the vessel to be overtaken is a large power-driven vessel under command.[11] So, too, the priorities between sailing vessels set out in Rule 12 do not apply when one sailing vessel is overtaking another;

---

court held that race participants who agree to abide by the International Yacht Racing Rules, or other similar rules, waive conflicting provisions of COLREGS. See also *DeSole v. United States,* 947 F.2d 1169, 1992 AMC 242 (4th Cir. 1991), in which the issue of the tort defense of assumption of risk was raised but not decided.

7. The opening phrase of Inland Rule 13(a) is "Notwithstanding anything contained in Rules 4 through 18. . . ," whereas the corresponding phrase of COLREGS Rule 13 is "Notwithstanding anything contained in Part B, Sections I and II. . . ," i.e., the sections comprising Rules 4 through 18. These sections contain all of the Steering and Sailing Rules except Rule 19 (Conduct of Vessels in Restricted Visibility), which is the only rule in Section III of Part B.

8. For citations to the former International, Inland, Western Rivers, and Great Lakes Rules, see supra notes 1–4.

9. I.e., ¶ (e) of Rule 9 (Narrow Channels), Rule 16 (Action by Give-way Vessel), Rule 17 (Action by Stand-on Vessel), and Rule 34 (Maneuvering and Warning Signals).

10. I.e., Part B (Steering and Sailing Rules), Section/Subpart I (Conduct of Vessels in Any Condition of Visibility), and Section/Subpart II (Conduct of Vessels in Sight of One Another).

11. See Cockcroft & Lameijer 106.

the overtaking vessel must keep out of the way of the other, regardless of the wind direction.[12]

If the conditions are such that it would be safe for Vessel A to overtake Vessel B on her port side, in a narrow channel she would be obliged under Rule 13 to keep out of B's way, even though in doing so it would not be possible for her to keep to her own starboard side of the channel, as Rule 9(a) (the Narrow Channel Rule) would normally require.[13]

Under Rule 13(b) a vessel is to be deemed overtaking when "coming up" on another vessel from a direction more than 22.5 degrees (two points) abaft her beam, so that at night she would be able to see only her sternlight,[14] but not her range lights or either of her sidelights.[15] It follows, conversely, that if one vessel is approaching another from a direction abeam of the other vessel, or forward of her beam, or not more than 22.5 degrees abaft her beam, from such a direction that at night she would be able to see the range lights and either the red or the green sidelight of the other vessel, but not her sternlight, it is a crossing situation, and not an overtaking one. Thus, if she is approaching the other vessel's port side from such a direction that at night she would be able to see the other vessel's red sidelight (but not her green sidelight), she is the port-hand vessel in a crossing situation and must keep out of the way. If she is approaching the other vessel's starboard side from such a direction that at night she would be able to see her green sidelight (but not her red sidelight), she is the starboard-hand vessel in a crossing situation and has the primary obligation of holding course and speed.

Rule 13(c) provides that if in doubt as to whether the situation is an overtaking or a crossing one, a vessel coming up on another must assume that she is overtaking the other, and must act accordingly.[16] If she is coming up on the other's port side, she is a give-way vessel and is obliged to keep out of the way, whether it is a crossing or an overtaking situation, and in either case the

12. Id.

13. See *National Iranian Tanker Co. (Nederland), N.V. v. The Dalzell 2 (The Reza Shah The Great)*, 411 F.2d, 759, 1969 AMC 1187 (2d Cir. 1969). This was an end-on meeting case, but the same rule should be applied in overtaking cases. The case is discussed in chapter 4, section G, note 29.

14. Rule 21(c) defines a sternlight as a white light showing over an arc of the horizon of 135 degrees, fixed so as to show 67.5 degrees from right aft on each side of the vessel.

15. Rule 23 requires a power-driven vessel underway to exhibit (1) a range of masthead lights, one forward, and a second abaft of and higher than the forward one, (2) sidelights, and (3) a sternlight. The rule contains special provisions for certain small vessels.

Rule 21(a) defines "masthead light" as a white light placed over the vessel's centerline, showing over an arc of the horizon of 225 degrees, and fixed so as to show from right ahead to 22.5 degrees abaft the beam on either side.

Rule 21(b) defines "sidelights" as a green light on the starboard side and a red light on the port side, each showing over an arc of the horizon of 112.5 degrees, and fixed so as to show from right ahead to 22.5 degrees abaft the beam on either side of the vessel.

For the definition of "sternlight" see note 14, supra. For a more detailed discussion of lights, see chapter 7.

16. See *Jones v. Texaco Panama, Inc. (The Texaco Ohio)*, 428 F.Supp. 1333, 1977 AMC 1249 (ED La. 1977).

other vessel has the primary obligation of holding her course and speed.[17] But even if the first vessel is coming up on the other's starboard side and is in doubt, she must treat the situation as an overtaking one, and keep out of the way of the other vessel.

Under Rule 13(d) no subsequent change in bearing between the two vessels will make an overtaking vessel a crossing one or relieve her of her duty of keeping out of the way of the vessel ahead until she is finally past and clear of her. Thus, if she is overtaking the vessel ahead on that vessel's starboard side, she remains a give-way vessel even after she reaches a point where, at night, she would be able to see the other vessel's green sidelight and range lights on her own port side, and would no longer be able to see the other vessel's sternlight. This principle is sometimes stated as a maxim: "Once an overtaking ship, always an overtaking ship."[18]

3. Overtaking under COLREGS and under the Inland Rules

With respect to overtakings at sea or in U.S. inland waters other than narrow channels, the only difference between COLREGS and the Inland Rules lies in the area of sound signals. As discussed in chapter 8, under COLREGS the signals of one short blast and two short blasts are rudder signals: one short blast indicates that the rudder is being put to the right, so that the vessel is turning to starboard, and two short blasts indicate that the rudder is being put to the left, so that the vessel is turning to port.[19]

Under the Inland Rules, on the other hand, the function of the signals is to effect an agreement as to the method in which two vessels approaching each other on overtaking, head-on, or crossing courses will navigate with respect to each other. Thus, wherever the Inland Rules apply, whether the vessels are in a narrow channel or in open waters, if Vessel A proposes overtaking Vessel B on B's starboard side, she must sound one short blast, and if B accepts A's proposal she must reply with one short blast; if A proposes overtaking B on B's port side, A must sound two short blasts, and if B accepts the proposal, she must reply with two short blasts.[20] In either case, if B is in doubt about A's proposal, she must reply with a danger signal of five or more short, rapid blasts.[21]

Under COLREGS, with the exception noted in the following paragraph, an overtaking vessel sounds no signal unless it is necessary for her to alter course to effect a safe passing. In that case, if she alters to starboard she must sound one short blast; if to port she must sound two short blasts. The vessel

17. See Rule 17.
18. See R. Marsden, *Collisions at Sea* 553 (11th ed. 1961) (hereinafter "Marsden").
19. COLREGS Rule 34(a).
20. Inland Rule 34(c)(i) and (ii).
21. Inland Rule 34(c)(ii) and (d).

ahead likewise sounds no signal if she simply holds her course. If she is obliged to alter course, e.g., because she finds that the overtaking vessel requires more room to pass safely, she must sound one or two short blasts, depending upon whether she is altering course to starboard or to port.

The only provision in COLREGS calling for a passing agreement by sound signals is found in Rule 9(e)(i) (Narrow Channels). That paragraph stipulates that in a narrow channel or fairway, when overtaking can take place only if the vessel ahead takes action to permit a safe passing, the overtaking vessel must sound the appropriate signal prescribed in COLREGS Rule 34(d) i.e., two prolonged blasts, followed by one short blast, meaning "I intend to overtake you on your starboard side," or two prolonged blasts, followed by two short blasts, meaning "I intend to overtake you on your port side." Rule 9(e)(ii) provides that if the vessel to be overtaken agrees, she must take steps to permit a safe passing and sound the appropriate signal prescribed in Rule 34(e)(ii) i.e., one prolonged, one short, one prolonged, and one short blast, in that order, whether the proposal was to overtake her on the starboard side or on the port side. COLREGS Rule 9(e)(i) provides that if in doubt the vessel to be overtaken *may* sound the signal prescribed in Rule 34(d) i.e., five or more short, rapid blasts.

COLREGS Rule 9(e) appears to recognize an exception to the mandate of Rule 17, that "Where one of two vessels is to keep out of the way, the other shall keep her course and speed." As Rule 13(a) requires any vessel overtaking another to keep out of the way of the vessel being overtaken, the latter is normally required to hold her course and speed in accordance with Rule 17. But COLREGS Rule 9(e) never applies unless the proposed overtaking can take place only if the vessel to be overtaken has to take action to permit a safe passing. Therefore, implicit in a proposal to overtake in waters where Rule 9(e) applies, is a request to the vessel ahead *not* to keep her course and speed in accordance with Rule 17, but to take such action as is required under Rule 9(e) to permit a safe passing. Correspondingly, an assent by the vessel ahead implies an agreement to take the required action.

4. *Overtaking and Risk of Collision*

While Rule 14, governing the conduct of power-driven vessels meeting on reciprocal or nearly reciprocal courses, and Rule 15, governing the conduct of power-driven vessels crossing, specifically apply only when meeting or crossing "so as to involve risk of collision," no such limitation is expressed in Rule 13. Whether, despite the absence of such an express limitation, the rule applies only when one vessel is overtaking another "so as to involve risk of collision" is a question on which the courts have disagreed.

The question as to whether the overtaking rule may apply even before risk of collision becomes "involved," despite the absence of any mention of risk of collision in the rule itself, came before the English courts in two fairly recent cases, *The Nowy Sacz*[22] and *The Auriga.*[23] In *The Nowy Sacz,* the vessel of that name and the *Olympian* were proceeding northeasterly in the Atlantic on a clear night, on nearly parallel courses. At about 0245 the *Olympian*'s masthead lights were sighted, bearing about 25 degrees to 30 degrees abaft the starboard beam of the *Nowy Sacz.* At about 0300 the *Olympian*'s red sidelight was observed, as well as her masthead lights, then bearing less than 22.5 degrees abaft the beam. By about 0330 the *Nowy Sacz* was abeam to port of the *Olympian,* and appeared to be on a course crossing that of the *Olympian* from port to starboard at an angle of 25 degrees to 30 degrees. Each vessel took avoiding action, but without success, and the *Nowy Sacz*'s stern collided with the *Olympian*'s port quarter. The *Olympian* contended that it was a crossing situation, and that the *Nowy Sacz,* as the port-hand vessel, was obliged to keep out of the way. The *Nowy Sacz,* on the other hand, argued that it was an overtaking situation, and that it was therefore the *Olympian,* as an overtaking vessel, that was obliged to keep clear.

In the Admiralty Court, Mr. Justice Brandon (later Lord Brandon of Oakbrook), citing *The Banshee,*[24] held that the overtaking rule applies only when vessels are in sight of each other and there is risk of collision. He found that the vessels were in sight of one another at 0300, and that the *Olympian* was then probably bearing more than 22.5 degrees abaft the *Nowy Sacz*'s starboard beam. Nevertheless, he held that the overtaking rule was inapplicable because at that point there was no risk of collision. In his view, the risk did not arise until about 0330, when the *Nowy Sacz* was bearing on the *Olympian*'s port beam, about one mile distant. He therefore held that it was a crossing situation; that the *Nowy Sacz,* as the port-hand vessel, was 75 percent to blame for failing to keep out of the way, and the *Olympian,* the starboard-hand vessel, was 25 percent to blame for failing to take timely action when it became apparent that the *Nowy Sacz* could not avoid collision by her own actions alone. The *Nowy Sacz* decision was appealed, but before the appeal was heard *The Auriga* came before Mr. Justice Brandon who again held that the overtaking rule was inapplicable until there was risk of collision, at which time the vessels were on crossing courses.

On the *Nowy Sacz* appeal the Court of Appeal took a different view. Citing *The Beryl,*[25] Sir David Cairns stated, "A good reason for holding that r. 24 [the overtaking rule under the 1960 International Rules then in force] applies before there is a risk of collision is that it is the object of the regulations not only to avoid collisions but to avoid the risk of collisions."[26] In essence the court

22. [1977] 2 Lloyd's Rep. 91 (C.A.), modifying [1976] 2 Lloyd's Rep. 682 (Adm.).

23. [1977] 1 Lloyd's Rep. 384 (Adm.). *The Nowy Sacz* and *The Auriga* are thoroughly discussed in P. Mukherjee, *Overtaking or Crossing: Judicial Interpretation and the Mariner's Dilemma,* 23 J. Mar. L. & Com. 247 (1992).

24. (1887) 6 Asp. Mar. Law (N.S.) 221 (C.A.).

25. (1884) 9 P.D. 137 (C.A.).

26. [1977] 2 Lloyd's Rep., at 98.

held that the overtaking rule applies when one vessel is approaching another from a direction more than 22.5 degrees abaft the other vessel's beam, even when their respective courses are such that if neither changes course no collision will occur.[27] Mr. Justice Brandon's decision was modified by reversing the proportions of blame: the Court of Appeal held the *Olympian* 75 percent and the *Nowy Sacz* 25 percent at fault.

In *The Auriga* the vessels were on diverging courses, with the *Auriga* bearing 10 degrees on the starboard quarter of the *Manuel Campos.* When the *Auriga* reached a position less than 22.5 degrees abaft the beam of the *Manuel Campos,* and about 2½ miles distant, she altered course to 181 degrees, which put the vessels on converging courses, and soon thereafter they collided. *The Auriga* argued that the overtaking rule was inapplicable because danger of collision did not exist until she altered course to 181 degrees, thus creating a crossing situation, and that the *Manuel Campos,* as the port-hand vessel, was then obliged to keep out of the way. Mr. Justice Brandon agreed, but nevertheless held the *Auriga* 60 percent to blame for creating a dangerous situation by altering course, and for failing to take sufficient action under Rule 17 when it became apparent that the *Manuel Campos* was not giving way. Professor Mukherjee, in his article,[28] quotes with approval the argument made by counsel for the *Manuel Campos* in *The Auriga:* "[R]eading into the overtaking rule words that were deliberately omitted from it would lead to confusion among mariners who might reasonably take different views on the question whether risk of collision existed in a particular case or not." The *Auriga* decision is also criticized in S. Harley, *Overtaking or Crossing,*[29] wherein the author states:

> An officer-of-the-watch is generally more concerned with looking-out ahead rather than astern; now it appears that he is required to carefully watch a vessel coming up astern in order to ascertain whether or not risk of collision exists, so that if the overtaking vessel is on his starboard side he will be ready to keep out of her way should risk of collision not be present until the overtaking vessel's bearing has decreased to less than two points abaft the beam of the overtaken vessel! Surely the draftsman of the overtaking rule did not intend such an (impractical) interpretation.
>
> If the overtaking rule were intended to be so constrained then it is probable that words such as "so as to involve risk of collision" would have been expressly written into the rule, and the mariner would have been afforded guidance as to the ascertainment of risk of collision in an overtaking situation.

If, as the court held, the overtaking rule never became applicable because there was no risk of collision before the *Auriga* altered course when the

27. [1977] 2 Lloyd's Rep., at 97.
28. Supra note 23, 23 J. Mar. L. & Com. at 261, quoting [1977] 1 Lloyd's Rep., at 393.
29. Safety at Sea International, June 1977.

vessels were about 2½ miles apart, it would seem to follow that the *Auriga* was not at fault for changing course. And if, as the court also held, a crossing situation was created by the change, the *Auriga,* as the starboard-hand vessel, would have been obliged to hold course and speed under Rule 21 of the then current 1960 International Rules, until such time as it became apparent that the *Manuel Campos* could not avoid collision by her own actions alone.

5. *When Rule 13 Begins to Apply*

If one vessel is coming up on another from a direction more than 22.5 degrees abaft the other's beam, with the intention of overtaking her, at what point do the mandates of Rule 13 begin to apply? In *New York & Liverpool Co. v. Rumball,*[30] the Supreme Court said: "Rules of navigation . . . are obligatory upon vessels approaching each other, from the time the necessity for precaution begins. . . ." But this and similar judicial statements leave open the question, "When does the necessity for precaution begin?" Cf. *Hosei Kaiun v. Seaspan Monarch,*[31] where the court said that the logical time when the overtaking rule becomes applicable is when one vessel is (or should be) maneuvering vis-à-vis the other. But the court left open the question of when one vessel (presumably the court was referring to the overtaking vessel) should be maneuvering with respect to the other (i.e., the vessel to be overtaken).

In considering this question a distinction should be drawn between (a) overtakings in waters where the applicable regulations require an exchange of signals before one power-driven vessel may overtake another, and (b) overtakings where no such signals are required. The first category includes (i) all waters governed by the U.S. Inland Rules, (ii) inland waters of other countries where national or local rules require an exchange of signals,[32] and (iii) narrow channels governed by COLREGS, when action by the vessel ahead is necessary to effect a safe passing.[33] The second category embraces (i) all other waters subject to COLREGS, and (ii) inland waters of countries where no national or local rule requires an exchange of signals.

In considering overtakings where signals are required, it should be noted at the outset that whereas Inland Rule 34(a) requires power-driven vessels to sound maneuvering signals when meeting or crossing so as to pass each other within a half mile or less, Inland Rule 34(c), relating to overtaking, contains no provision concerning the distance between the overtaking vessel and the vessel to be overtaken at which the signals are to be sounded. As we have seen, it simply stipulates that "a power-driven vessel intending to overtake another power-driven vessel shall indicate her intention" by the

30. 62 U.S. 372 (1859).

31. 1981 AMC 2162 (D Or. 1980). (The case is discussed in chapter 7, sect. A[3].)

32. See, e.g., Rule 19 of the Rules of the Clyde Pilotage Authority, Marsden 705, at 710; Rule 17 of the Humber and Lower Trent Navigation Bye-laws, 1956, Marsden 733, at 739.

33. See COLREGS Rules 9(e)(i) and 34(c).

appropriate signal of one short blast (to pass on the starboard side of the vessel ahead) or two short blasts (to pass on the port side); that if the vessel ahead agrees, she must reply with a like signal, and that if she is in doubt, she must sound a danger signal.

The U.S. Inland Rules contain no provision for the sounding of an overtaking signal by an overtaking vessel, whether power-driven or under sail, when the vessel to be overtaken is one under sail. Nor is there any provision for the sounding of any signal by an overtaken vessel under sail, other than the danger signal which Rule 34(d) requires any vessel, whether power-driven or under sail, to sound when approaching in sight of another vessel if she fails to understand the other's intentions or actions, or is in doubt as to whether she is taking sufficient action to avoid collision.

COLREGS Rule 34(c), on the other hand, is not limited to power-driven vessels. Therefore, under the circumstances described in COLREGS Rule 9(e)(i), that is, in a narrow channel or fairway when overtaking can take place only if the vessel to be overtaken has to take action to permit safe passing, the sound signals required by COLREGS Rule 34(c) must be sounded, whether the overtaking vessel, or the overtaken vessel, or both, are under sail.[34]

Where an exchange of signals is required, the first signal must be sounded by the vessel seeking to overtake.[35] At what point must the overtaking vessel initiate the exchange of signals? There is no answer that will fit all cases; it will vary depending upon a number of factors, including the assumed audibility range of the vessel ahead, the relative speeds of the two vessels, the width and depth of the waterway where the proposed overtaking is to take place, and the maneuverability of the overtaking vessel.

Obviously, no purpose would be served if an overtaking vessel were to sound a signal before coming within the range of audibility of the vessel ahead. Annex III to the Inland Rules sets forth the technical requirements for sound signal appliances of vessels of various lengths. The annex then indicates the approximate range at which a whistle may usually be heard "on its forward axis in conditions of still air on board a vessel having average background noise level at the listening posts. . . ." These ranges are 0.5 mile for a vessel of 12 to less than 20 meters in length, 1 mile for one of 20 to less than 75 meters, 1.5 miles for one of 75 to less than 200 meters, and 2 miles for one of 200 meters or more. The audibility ranges indicated in Annex III of COLREGS are similar, although not identical.

While in a head-on situation the rate of approach is the sum of the speeds of the two vessels, in an overtaking situation, if one vessel is directly astern of the other, the rate is the difference between the two speeds. If a vessel making 15 knots is coming up directly astern of one making 5 knots, the

34. See Cockcroft & Lameijer 188.
35. See *Schomburg v. The Industry*, 29 F.2d 29, 1928 AMC 1894 (2d Cir. 1928).

rate of approach is 10 knots; if the respective speeds are, instead, 10 knots and 8 knots, the rate of approach is only 2 knots.[36]

Under the U.S. Inland Rules, or in narrow channels governed by COLREGS under circumstances where COLREGS Rule 9(e) applies, it would seem that in the first case, i.e., one where the rate of approach is, say, 10 knots, the vessel astern should signal her intention of overtaking promptly after coming within the probable range of audibility. This would leave ample time to receive a signal from the vessel ahead, and then make the appropriate maneuver, depending upon whether the signal is an acceptance or a rejection of the overtaking proposal. If the speeds of the vessel astern and the vessel ahead were, respectively, 10 knots and 8 knots, and if the vessel ahead was of 200 meters or more in length, it would take about 30 minutes for the vessel astern to reach the vessel ahead after coming within a 2-mile range of audibility. It would seem that in such a case she should not be obliged to sound an overtaking signal until she was fairly close to the vessel ahead, although under ordinary conditions there would seem to be no reason why she could not sound a signal promptly after coming within the assumed range of audibility. If no reply was heard, it might be because the audibility range was less than that assumed by the vessel astern, and the signal should be repeated once or more often.[37]

Under Inland Rule 34(h) a vessel that reaches agreement with another in an overtaking situation (as well as in a meeting or crossing situation) by using the radiotelephone as prescribed by the Bridge-to-Bridge Radiotelephone Act,[38] is not obliged to sound the whistle signals prescribed by Rule 34, but may do so. Paragraph (h) further provides that "If agreement is not reached, then whistle signals shall be exchanged in a timely manner and shall prevail." There are no comparable provisions in COLREGS.

In exchanging overtaking signals in U.S. inland waters the vessel astern recognizes that at least from that point on she is governed by Rule 13, and is obliged to keep out of the way of the vessel ahead until she is past and clear of her.[39] Once an overtaking signal is heard, the vessel ahead becomes bound by Rule 34(c)(ii) and (d) and must reply with a like signal if she accepts the proposal, or with a danger signal if she is in doubt about it. If she accepts, she becomes bound by Inland Rule 13, and must hold her course and speed in accordance with Rule 17(a)(i), unless and until it becomes apparent that the overtaking vessel is not taking appropriate action to keep out of the way. She may then take action to avoid collision in accordance with Rule 17(a)(ii). If

---

36. See Cockcroft & Lameijer 110, where, in referring to the overtaking situation, the authors state: "The distance at which the Rules apply will depend largely on the speed of approach; it may be less than a mile in the case of two slow vessels proceeding on similar courses with little difference in speed."

37. On the repetition of overtaking signals see *Erwin v. Neversink Steamboat Co.*, 88 N.Y. 184 (1882); *Farwell's Rules of the Nautical Road* 107 (7th ed., R. Smith, ed.) (hereinafter "Farwell").

38. 33 U.S.C. §§ 1201–8. The Act is reprinted in appendix 3.

39. See *The Aurania and The Republic*, 29 F.98, 108 (SDNY 1886); Griffin 163.

the overtaken vessel finds herself so close that collision cannot be avoided by the action of the overtaking vessel alone, she must, in accordance with Rule 17(b), take such action as will best aid in avoiding collision.

The question as to when COLREGS Rule 13 begins to apply in waters where no exchange of signals is required is more difficult to answer than when the rule becomes applicable in waters where an exchange is necessary. In waters where signals are not required, the overtaking vessel usually has unlimited space in which to maneuver. In such a case, it would seem that a vessel coming up on another from a direction more than two points abaft her beam, should, if she is not already on a diverging course, alter course to one diverging somewhat from that of the vessel ahead, so that when the two vessels are abeam of each other they will be so far apart that no collision can occur. Under COLREGS, the overtaking vessel would be required to sound one short blast if altering course to starboard, or two short blasts if altering to port and assuming she was within the audibility range of the vessel ahead, the signal would alert that vessel to the overtaking vessel's presence, if she was not already aware of it, e.g., by radar or radiotelephone. From that point on, it would seem that the vessel ahead should hold her course and speed until the overtaking vessel was past and clear, or until it appeared that she was not taking proper steps to keep out of the way.

6. *Conduct of the Overtaking Vessel*

As has been shown, the overriding obligation of the overtaking vessel is to keep out of the overtaken vessel's way. In carrying out this obligation, she must fulfill two principal subsidiary obligations: (a) she must select a safe place in which to overtake, and (b) she must pass the overtaken vessel at a safe speed and at a safe distance.

(a) The Selection of a Safe Place. Because the decision to overtake is that of the overtaking vessel alone, it is for her to select the place of overtaking. In a high-seas case the place is seldom significant, as there is usually unlimited sea room for the maneuver, and the water is usually of ample depth. In some cases, however, the sea room may be restricted by the presence of other vessels, or by underwater obstructions, and overtakings in such areas should of course be avoided. Similarly, overtakings should not be attempted in shallow water, because of the increased danger of "suction"—a subject discussed below.

The selection of an unsuitable place for the overtaking is more commonly a cause of collision when the overtaking is attempted in a narrow channel or other confined waterway. The overtaking vessel has the option of passing on the starboard side or on the port side of the vessel ahead, provided the side selected is a safe one. In a narrow channel this usually means that the overtaking will be on the port side, because if the vessel ahead is obeying Rule 9 (the narrow channel rule) she will be as near as possible to the outer limit of her own starboard side of the channel, and there will be insufficient room for another vessel to pass safely on her starboard side.[40] The overtaking vessel will be held at fault if she selects a place that is unsafe. Thus, in *In re Ocean Queen Inc.*,[41] the overtaking vessel was found at fault for proposing to overtake another vessel at Hell Gate, a particularly dangerous area of New York harbor, and the overtaken vessel was held to blame for accepting the proposal.

(b) Avoidance of Hydraulic Interaction (Suction). The inherent danger of an overtaking vessel attempting to pass the vessel ahead at an excessive rate of speed and without allowing an ample distance between the two vessels is obvious. Aside from the danger of "suction," there is always the possibility of contact between the two vessels; for example, if the vessel ahead should be proceeding at a very slow speed, and should momentarily lose steerageway and sheer toward the track of the overtaking vessel. But the principal danger is that of "suction." It has long been recognized that vessels passing in close proximity, particularly in overtaking situations in narrow channels, have a tendency to veer toward each other when one or both are proceeding at high speeds. This phenomenon is most frequently encountered in shallow waters. Courts in the United States usually call it "suction," which is really a misnomer. The English courts more properly refer to it as "hydraulic interaction."[42] Despite a number of scientific studies, some including experiments with small-scale ship models, knowledge of the precise way in which interaction affects vessels remains incomplete as of 1997.

A typical case of collision caused by "suction" is *International Bulktank Corp. v. The Shinto Maru.*[43] The *Overseas Alaska,* a 34,449-gross-ton tanker 731 feet in length, was proceeding outbound on the Columbia River, astern of the *Shinto Maru,* a 452-foot dry cargo vessel of 9,039 gross tons. When the vessels were about a quarter of a mile apart, the *Overseas Alaska* informed the *Shinto Maru* by radiotelephone that she wished to overtake, and the two vessels agreed to an overtaking at a certain reach of the river. The *Shinto Maru* thereafter reduced her speed to 8 to 9 knots over the ground, while the *Overseas Alaska* increased hers to about 15 knots. When the maneuver began, the lateral distance between the vessels was at most 200 feet. As the bow of the *Overseas Alaska* began to lap the *Shinto Maru*'s stern to pass on her port side, the *Overseas Alaska* asked the *Shinto Maru* to put her engine full ahead for better rudder control, which the *Shinto Maru* had already done on her own initiative. The pressure of the water ahead of the two vessels decreased the

40. Farwell 164–65.
41. 398 F. Supp. 1062, 1976 AMC 1404 (SDNY 1974).
42. See Professor A.M. Robb's *Note on Interaction between Vessels,* reprinted in Marsden at 920–22, cited with approval in *The Irish Coast,* [1956] 1 Lloyd's Rep. 165 (Adm.).
43. 422 F. Supp. 982, 1977 AMC 37 (D Or. 1976).

Overseas Alaska's speed to about 13 knots as she pulled alongside the *Shinto Maru.* To hasten the maneuver, the *Overseas Alaska* asked the *Shinto Maru* to reduce her speed, which was then slowed to 7 to 8 knots over the ground. As the *Overseas Alaska* drew up stem to stem with the *Shinto Maru,* the latter sheered 3 to 5 degrees to starboard. The sheer was corrected by putting the rudder 20 degrees to port for several seconds, and the *Shinto Maru*'s bow began to swing to port toward the *Overseas Alaska.* The *Shinto Maru*'s rudder was then put hard right and her engine full ahead. However, these efforts to counteract the sheer were unavailing; it continued until the *Shinto Maru*'s bow struck the *Overseas Alaska*'s starboard quarter.

In holding the *Overseas Alaska* solely at fault, Judge Beeks stated:

> . . . I have no doubt but that the collision was attributable to the hydrodynamic force commonly and traditionally called "suction."
>
> Suction is a well-known and long recognized hydrodynamic phenomenon that poses a significant potential hazard to vessels engaged in overtaking maneuvers. Several facts have been identified which independently (and cumulatively) increase its potency and the attendant risk of collision. Aggravating factors include: close proximity of vessels, a disparity in the size of the vessels—especially when the larger vessel is overtaking, high speed on the part of the overtaking vessel, high relative speed as between vessels, and navigation through shallow or confined waters. When, due to the presence of one or more of the above factors, a substantial suction force is set up, it is ordinarily the overtaken vessel which is overcome. Also, when a disparity in size exists, it is typically the smaller vessel which yields to the force. The collision at bar conformed to this normal pattern.
>
> It is now firmly established that an overtaking vessel assumes those risks inherent in the maneuver, and, should collision occur, such overtaking vessel shall accordingly bear the responsibility therefor absent proof of fault on the part of the overtaken vessel.
>
> . . . I find suction to have been an inherent and foreseeable risk associated with the overtaking at the time and under the circumstances in question. The likelihood of a significant hydrodynamic interaction should have been apparent to *Overseas Alaska* prior to commencement of the passing upon due consideration of known or observable vessel characteristics, the high speed of *Overseas Alaska,* the substantially slower speed of *Shinto Maru,* the character of the channel and the contemplated passing clearance.[44]

---

44. Other decisions imposing liability on overtaking vessels for collisions and groundings caused by "suction" include *Algoma Central Corp. v. The Prestigious,* 1994 AMC 1900 (Fed. Ct. of Canada, Trial Div. 1994); *Harbor Towing Corp. v. The Calmar,* 364 F.Supp. 804, 1974 AMC 1760 (D Md. 1973), aff'd, 507 F.2d 720 (4th Cir. 1974); *Union Oil Co. v. The Mary Mallow,* 414 F.2d 669, 1969 AMC 2254 (5th Cir. 1969); *The Mesaba,* 111 F. 215 (SDNY 1901); *The Potomac,* 105 F.2d 94,

While, as stated by Judge Beeks, the danger of "suction" is greater in shallow water, the phenomenon can also occur in deep water. In *The Queen Mary—The Curacoa*[45] the famous liner, making 28½ knots, was en route from New York to the Clyde in October 1942, with over 10,000 American troops on board, and was escorted by the British cruiser *Curacoa.* At the material times she was on the starboard leg of a zigzag maneuver, and was steering 131 degrees (T). The *Curacoa* was making 25 knots, on a course of 108 degrees (T). When the two vessels were a mile apart, the *Curacoa* was bearing about 45 degrees on the *Queen Mary*'s starboard bow. As the converging courses of the two vessels brought them very close to one another, each took avoiding action, but without success. The *Queen Mary*'s bow struck the port quarter of the *Curacoa,* which sank almost immediately, with the loss of 329 lives. There was some evidence that the collision was caused in part by "suction," although the depth of water in the area where the collision occurred was about 120 meters. On the question of suction, Lord Porter stated:

> No doubt the effect of the forces of interaction are very imperfectly known, and one cannot impute to the captains of the two ships any expert or exact knowledge of them, but I should have expected some allowance to have been made for their coming into play, in the sense that the ships should not have been allowed to approach so near to one another as to run a risk of their coming into action.

7. *Conduct of the Overtaken Vessel*

Since the overtaking vessel is obliged to keep out of the way, the overtaken vessel has the corresponding obligation, under Rule 17(a)(i), to keep her course and speed, unless and until avoiding action becomes allowable in accordance with Rule 17(a)(ii) or necessary in accordance with Rule 17(b).[46] But this provision is interpreted liberally: the overtaken vessel may make predictable changes in heading, e.g., in following the curvature of a river or channel.[47] Similarly, she may make such changes in engine speed as may be

---

95, 1939 AMC 1296 (D.C. Cir. 1939); *Pan American Petroleum & Transport Co. v. The Steelore,* 220 F.2d 688, 1955 AMC 765 (4th Cir. 1955); *A/S J. Ludwig Mowinckels Rederi v. The Sea Level II,* 1984 AMC 1110 (ED La. 1983).

45. 82 Ll. L. Rep. 303 (H.L. 1948), dismissing an appeal and a cross-appeal from the decision of the Court of Appeal, 80 Ll. L. Rep. 609 (C.A. 1947), holding the *Curacoa* two-thirds and the *Queen Mary* one-third to blame. The trial court had held the *Curacoa* solely at fault. 80 Ll. L. Rep. 178 (Adm. 1946). The case is discussed and diagramed in H. Holdert & C. Buzek, *Collision Cases—Judgments and Diagrams* 90–93 (2d ed.) and discussed in Cockcroft & Lameijer, 111–12, and Farwell 112–13.

46. On the obligation of the overtaken vessel to take avoiding action when necessary, see *The Menominee,* 197 F. 736 (3d Cir. 1912).

47. *The Roanoke,* [1908] P 231, 11 Asp. (N.S.) 253 (C.A.); *Sea-Land Service, Inc. v. The Nelly Maersk,* 1983 AMC 472 (SD Tex. 1982); *Schomburg v. The Industry,* 29 F.2d 29, 1928 AMC 1894 (2d Cir. 1928).

necessary to maintain steerageway.[48] The obligation to hold course and speed does not arise in U.S. inland waters until the overtaking vessel sounds the appropriate overtaking signal.[49] But when she does hear such a signal, the overtaken vessel is obliged to reply, with a like signal if she accepts the proposal, or with a danger signal if she does not.[50] A signal of one or two short blasts sounded by an overtaking vessel in U.S. inland waters is not only a proposal to overtake; it is also a request for information as to conditions ahead that are known to the overtaken vessel, but may not be known to the overtaking vessel.[51] If the overtaken vessel knows of a dangerous situation of which the overtaking vessel may have no knowledge, she is obliged to reject the proposal by sounding a danger signal.[52] But if the situation is one of which both vessels have knowledge, the overtaken vessel will not be held to blame for assenting to the proposal.[53]

The overtaken vessel must make the decision whether or not to consent to the proposal. In *Union Oil Co. v. The Issaquena,*[54] the overtaken vessel did not believe the overtaking vessel could effect a safe passing at the place where it was proposed that the overtaking would be made. Nevertheless, she left the decision to the overtaking vessel. A collision occurred, and both vessels were held to blame, the overtaken vessel for not rejecting the proposal.

Acceptance of an overtaking proposal is not a guaranty of its safety. The rule was stated by the Supreme Court in *The Gulftrade:*[55]

> We cannot conclude that the *Taurus* was in fault. She was prudently navigated in plain view of the *Gulftrade* who knew the relevant facts; and by assenting that the latter might pass she certainly did not assume responsibility for the maneuver. At most the *Taurus* obligated herself to hold her course and speed so far as practicable, to do nothing to thwart the overtaking vessel, and that she knew of no circumstances not open to the observation of the *Gulftrade* which would prevent the latter from going safely by, if prudently navigated. Of course no ship must ever lead another into a trap. There was ample room for the *Gulftrade* to pass. But if

48. *Sea-Land Service, Inc. v. The Nelly Maersk,* supra note 47; *Pinto v. The Fernwood,* 507 F.2d 1327, 1976 AMC 744 (5th Cir. 1974).

49. *In re B.F.T. No. Two Corp. (The Harbor Star),* 433 F. Supp. 854, 1977 AMC 1168 (ED Pa. 1977); *Linear v. The Mr. Lucky,* 275 F.Supp. 230 (ED La. 1967); *The M.J. Rudolph,* 292 F. 740, 1923 AMC 1108 (Sy.) (2d Cir. 1923); *Bockenheim Red. Schiff., MBH v. The Voyager,* 495 F.Supp. 521, 1983 AMC 448 (ED La. 1980); *Schomburg v. The Industry,* supra note 47.

50. *The Mesaba Ocean Steamship Co. v. United States,* 39 F.2d 553 (2d Cir. 1930).

51. *M.P. Howlett, Inc. v. Charles Warner Co.,* 58 F.2d 923, 1932 AMC 986 (3d Cir. 1932); Farwell 108.

52. Farwell 108.

53. See *The Ohio River Co. v. Continental Grain Co.,* 352 F. Supp. 505, 1973 AMC 711 (ND Ill. 1972).

54. 339 F. Supp. 1011, 1972 AMC 2175 (ND Miss. 1971), aff'd, 470 F.2d 875, 1973 AMC 493 (5th Cir. 1973).

55. 278 U.S. 85, 1928 AMC 1815 (1928). See also Griffin 174–75; Farwell 166–67.

> not, she should have slowed down and kept at a safe distance. Her fault was the direct and sole cause of the collision.

In a sizable number of cases the overtaking vessel has sought to hold the overtaken vessel at least contributorily at fault for failing to maintain a stern lookout. As long ago as 1896 the Supreme Court said, in *The Delaware,*[56] "[A]s a general rule, an overtaken vessel is under no duty to keep a look-out aft, but has the right to act on the presumption that the overtaking vessel will keep clear." But a vessel has no right to change course without looking around to make certain that no other vessel is close astern.[57]

Section D. Rule 14: The Head-on Situation

1. *Introduction*

As originally worded, Inland Rule 14 was identical to Rule 14 of COLREGS except for the very minor difference in verbiage in paragraph (b) mentioned below. However, in 1984 a fourth paragraph, (d), was added to Inland Rule 14, and paragraph (a) of the Inland Rule was amended to bring it into conformity with the new paragraph.[58]

Paragraph (b) of COLREGS Rule 14 defines a head-on situation as existing when "a vessel sees the other ahead or nearly ahead and by night she could see the masthead lights of the other in a line or nearly in a line or both sidelights and by day she observes the corresponding aspect of the other vessel." The only difference between paragraph (b) of COLREGS Rule 14 and paragraph (b) of the Inland Rule is that the latter reads "and/or both sidelights," while the COLREGS paragraph reads "or both sidelights." Paragraph (c) of both COLREGS and Inland Rule 14 provides that when a vessel is in any doubt as to whether a head-on situation exists, she must assume that it does and act accordingly.

The core of COLREGS Rule 14 is contained in paragraph (a), which requires each of two power-driven vessels meeting on reciprocal or nearly reciprocal courses so as to involve risk of collision to alter course to starboard and pass on the port side of the other. In this respect Rule 14 is related to paragraph 2 of Rule 9, the narrow channel rule, requiring a vessel to keep as near to her own starboard side of a narrow channel as is safe and practicable.

---

56. 161 U.S. 459 (1896). See also *Ellis Towing and Transp. Co. v. Socony Mobil Oil Co.,* 292 F.2d 91, 1961 AMC 1406 (5th Cir. 1961) (J.R. Brown, Ct. J.); *The M.J. Rudolph,* 292 F. 740 (2d Cir. 1923).

57. *The Philadelphian,* 61 F. 862 (1st Cir. 1894); *The Illinois,* 103 U.S. 298 (1880). See also *In re B.F.T. No. Two Corp. (The Harbor Star),* 1977 AMC 1168 (ED Pa. 1977), where a tug was held at fault for drifting into a major thoroughfare without a stern look-out, while shortening her towline.

58. Pub. L. No. 98-557, § 16(c)(1) and (2).

The 1984 amendment to paragraph (a) of Inland Rule 14 added the words "Unless otherwise agreed" at the beginning of the paragraph. This was done to avoid any inconsistency between paragraph (a) and the exception to it recognized in paragraph (d), which was added at the same time. Paragraph (d) codified the custom long followed on the Mississippi and other Western Rivers, the Great Lakes, and certain other inland waters, which gives a downbound power-driven vessel with a following current the right-of-way over an upbound vessel.[59] The paragraph requires the downbound vessel to propose the manner of passage, and to initiate the exchange of the appropriate maneuvering signals prescribed by Rule 34(a)(i).[60]

Paragraph (d) of the Inland Rule thus recognizes an exception to the port to port requirement of paragraph (a) of the rule: where it applies, a downbound vessel with a following current may propose a starboard to starboard passing. Paragraph (d) has no counterpart in COLREGS, which require that when risk of collision is involved in a head-on situation, any change of course must be to starboard, so that the vessels will pass port to port, and no exception is made for downbound vessels with a following current.

It is important to note that Rule 14, like Rule 15 (Crossing Situation), and unlike Rule 13 (Overtaking), applies only when risk of collision is involved.[61] Thus, if two vessels are approaching one another on reciprocal courses in such a way that they are clear to pass port to port without any alteration of course on the part of either, no risk of collision is involved, and Rule 14 is inapplicable. The rule is similarly inapplicable when they are approaching in such a way that they are clear to pass starboard to starboard without either vessel changing course. Again, Rule 14 is inapplicable, because risk of collision is not involved.

Once again, the most important difference between COLREGS and the Inland Rules lies in the meaning of the sound signals of one short blast and two short blasts. In the situations described in the two preceding paragraphs, under COLREGS neither vessel would sound any signal, because the COLREGS signals are rudder, or turning signals, and neither vessel would be making a turn. On the other hand, under the Inland Rules, the signals are signals of intention, and must be exchanged whenever power-driven vessels in sight of each other are meeting head-on or crossing so as to pass within a half mile of each other.[62] Thus, if the vessels are meeting port to port so as to pass within a half mile of each other without any alteration of course, one must sound a signal of one short blast, meaning "I intend to leave you on my

---

59. *Marine Transport Lines, Inc. v. The Tako Invader,* 37 F.3d 1138, 1995 AMC 622 (5th Cir. 1994).

60. I.e., one short blast if she intends to pass the upbound vessel on her port side, and two short blasts if she intends to pass on her starboard side.

61. See section C, supra, and section E, infra.

62. Rule 34(a).

port side," and the other must reply with one short blast if she agrees, or with a danger signal of five or more short and rapid blasts if she does not.[63] Similarly, if the vessels are so far to the starboard of each other that they are clear to pass starboard to starboard within a half mile of each other, without either altering course, one must sound a signal of two short blasts, meaning "I intend to leave you on my starboard side." The other vessel must then reply with two short blasts if she agrees, or with a danger signal if she does not.[64]

It must be stressed that except where paragraph (d) applies, in the head-on situation, if any change of course is required to effect a safe passing it must be to starboard, so that the vessels will pass port to port. Even if the courses are somewhat to the starboard of each other, but a safe starboard to starboard passing cannot be made without any alteration of course by either vessel, each must turn to starboard. This is so, even though it may mean that one vessel must cross the other's bow in order to pass port to port.[65]

2. *Head-on and Crossing Distinguished*

Under Rule 14(b) a head-on situation is deemed to exist when one vessel sees another ahead, or nearly ahead, and by night could see the other's masthead lights in a line, or nearly in a line, and/or both of her sidelights, and by day could observe the corresponding aspect of the other vessel. Thus, under ordinary circumstances, when risk of collision is involved, if at night both the red and the green lights of a vessel are visible ahead, it is a head-on situation, whereas if only the green (starboard) sidelight can be seen on the port bow, or only the red (port) sidelight can be seen on the starboard bow, it is a crossing situation.

Since under paragraph (c) of Rule 14, when there is any doubt as to whether a head-on situation exists a vessel must assume that it does and act accordingly, it follows that if a vessel is not certain whether she is a starboard-hand vessel required to hold course in a crossing situation, or whether she should turn to starboard to effect a safe port to port passing as both vessels are required to do in a head-on situation, she should turn to starboard. If two vessels were literally meeting head-on, their headings would of course be 180 degrees apart. Several decisions have attempted to distinguish between head-on and crossing situations in terms of the difference in degrees between the reciprocal courses of the two vessels. These decisions have not been entirely consistent, but the weight of authority appears to be that if both sidelights of each vessel are visible more than half a point, or about 6 degrees,

63. Id.
64. Id.
65. See Cockcroft & Lameijer 114.

on the other's bow, it is a crossing, and not a head-on situation. After citing *The Gulf Stream*[66] and *The Kaituna*[67] Griffin states:

> While there is singularly little direct authority on the subject, the foregoing cases would seem to indicate that, if one has the other half a point on her starboard bow and is herself half a point on the other's port bow, the divergence is not sufficient to take the case out of Article 18 [of the former International Rules corresponding to COLREGS Rule 14] (but cf. the *Koning Willem II,* (1908) Prob. Div. 125, 131), but that, if either has the other more than half a point on the bow, the case is one of crossing vessels. This view would seem consistent with the rule for night, which depends on the sidelights (the *Grand Republic,* 16 Fed. 424, 426 (1883)). A properly screened sidelight should not show more than half a point across the bow (the *Edwin Slick,* 286 Fed. 43, 47 (1923); The *Thingvalla,* 48 Fed. 764, 769 (1891)), and half a point is, therefore, the limit at which both sidelights would be displayed to the other vessel. If one vessel has the other more than half a point on the starboard bow, and therefore is showing her green light only to the other's red or red and green, it is a crossing situation. The same result should follow by day in similar situations.[68]

If one vessel is proceeding up, and another down a narrow channel at night, and each is keeping to starboard in accordance with Rule 9 (the narrow channel rule), in straight stretches each should of course see the other's red light, and not her green. But on a winding stretch it is possible that when one vessel first sights the other she will see the other's green light and not her red, because the curvature of the waterway results in the vessels' headings being temporarily at right angles to each other. This does not mean that Rule 15 (the starboard-hand rule) will apply. Each vessel is keeping to the starboard side of the fairway, no risk of collision is involved, and only when risk of collision is involved is the rule applicable. The principle was explained in *The Pekin:*[69]

> The cases of the *Velocity,* the *Ranger,* and the *Oceano* have explained and illustrated the distinction which exists in the effect of [the crossing] rule as regards vessels navigating the open sea and those passing along the winding channels of rivers. The crossing referred to in art. 16 [of the 1884 Rules] is "Crossing so as to involve risk of collision" and it is obvious that while two vessels in certain positions and at certain distances in regard to each other in the open sea may be crossing so as to involve risk of collision it would be completely mistaken to take the same view of two

66. 43 F. 895 (SDNY 1890).
67. [1933] Prob. Div. 234.
68. Griffin 66–67.
69. [1897] App. Cas. 532, 537, 8 Asp. (N.S.) 367, 368 (P.C.).

> vessels in the same positions and distances in the reaches of a winding river. The reason, of course, is that the vessels must follow and must be known to intend to follow the curves of the river bank. But vessels may, no doubt, be crossing vessels within art. 16, in a river; it depends on their presumable courses. If, at any time, two vessels, not end on, are seen, keeping the courses to be expected with regard to them respectively, to be likely to arrive at the same point at or nearly at the same moment, they are vessels crossing so as to involve risk of collision; but they are not so crossing if the course which is reasonably to be attributed to either vessel would keep her clear of the other. The question, therefore, always turns on the reasonable inference to be drawn as to a vessel's future course from her position at a particular moment, and this greatly depends on the nature of the locality where she is at that moment.

3. The Point-Bend Custom on the Mississippi, and Other Customs

Attention has already been called to Inland Rule 14(d), which was based on the long-standing custom prevailing on the Mississippi and certain other U.S. inland waters, giving a *downbound* vessel with a following current the right of way over an *upbound* vessel. Several other customs have been developed which involve departures from the basic port to port passing requirement of Rule 14. While these have not been codified in the way the right of way custom has been codified in Rule 14(d), some of them have been given effect by the courts. Such exceptions to Rule 14 can be considered as applications of Rule 2(b), the special circumstances rule. A good example of such a custom is the one prevailing at Hell Gate, a danger spot in New York harbor, where the East River meets Long Island Sound. Under this custom, vessels pass starboard to starboard on a flood tide. The custom has been recognized by the U.S. Court of Appeals for the Second Circuit as "a reasonable custom of navigation arising from the peculiarities of this locality."[70]

Another custom recognized by the courts, although not by statute, is the point-bend custom prevailing on the Mississippi River, whereby the *descending* vessel follows the main current around bends in the river, and the *ascending* vessel avoids the current to the extent possible by "running the points."[71]

70. *The Transfer No. 21,* 248 F. 459 (1917). Other decisions are cited in Griffin, at 71–72. On custom generally, see Griffin 572–76. Cf. Marsden 473–74; Farwell 37.

71. See *Canal Barge v. China Ocean Shipping Co.,* 579 F. Supp. 243, 1985 AMC 731 (ED La. 1984), aff'd, 770 F.2d 1357, 1986 AMC 2042 (5th Cir. 1985); *The John D. Rockefeller,* 272 F. 67 (4th Cir. 1921); Griffin 574–75. For a thorough discussion of the custom, see R. Lemon, *The Mississippi River "Point-Bend Custom,"* 19 J. Mar. L. & Com. 373 (1988).

In *Canal Barge,* supra, the late Judge Rubin wrote, "Analysis of our prior opinions dealing with the point-bend custom reveals that it may have the 'force of law,' but only after the litigants have established its applicability under the facts of that case. The district court was correct, therefore, in its observation that '[t]he "point-bend" custom is not a rule of law,' insofar as recognizing it as such a rule would make it invariably applicable." 770 F.2d at 1361, 1986 AMC at 2048. (Footnote by the court omitted.)

A "point" in this context is the land projecting into the water at a curve of the river; a "bend" is the side of the river opposite a "point." Thus, if the curve is such that a vessel descending the river will have to round the curve in clockwise fashion, the point will be on her starboard side and the bend on her port side. If the curve is such that a descending vessel will have to proceed counterclockwise, the point will be on her port side and the bend will be on her starboard side.

The codification of the custom giving a downbound vessel with a following current the right of way over an upbound vessel has not eliminated the point-bend custom. In *Marine Transport Lines, Inc. v. The Tako Invader,*[72] the court said that Rule 14(d) modifies Rule 14(a) in the same way that Rule 9(a)(ii) modifies Rule 9(a)(i): vessels descending the Mississippi are ordinarily required to keep to their own starboard side of the river, but may force a departure from this requirement, provided that in accordance with Rules 9(a)(ii) and 14(d) they propose the manner of passage by initiating the appropriate signals prescribed by Rule 34(a)(i). The court added that if Rule 14 required vessels always to keep to their own starboard side of the river, Rule 9(a)(ii) would be redundant. The court added, in a footnote, that it would also be inconsistent with the point-bend custom "which requires frequent departures from the port-to-port passing default [*sic*] rule."

In the usual case, the downbound vessel will presumably follow the bend in the river, and the upbound vessel will follow the point, in accordance with the custom. If the bend is on the right descending side of the river and the point is on the left ascending side, the downbound vessel should exercise its option under Rule 14(d) by sounding one short blast for a port to port passing. If no dangerous situation exists, the upbound vessel should accept the proposal by sounding a like signal. Similarly, if the bend is on the left descending side and the point is on the right, the descending vessel should sound a two-blast signal for a starboard to starboard passing, and in the absence of a dangerous situation the upbound vessel should accept the proposal by replying with two short blasts.

It appears that under the Fifth Circuit's decision in *The Tako Invader,* the position may be summarized as follows:

1. On straight stretches of the Mississippi where the narrow channel rule applies, each vessel should ordinarily keep to her own starboard side of the river.
2. But in straight stretches of the river, the downbound vessel may exercise its option under Rule 14(d) and propose a starboard to starboard passing by sounding a two-blast signal; in the absence of danger, the upbound vessel should reply with a like signal, and the vessels should pass starboard to starboard.

---

72. Supra note 59.

3. At bends in the river, where the point-bend custom is applicable, the downbound vessel should follow the custom and exercise its Rule 14(d) option by proposing a port-to-port passing if the bend is on her starboard side, or a starboard-to-starboard passing if it is on her port side. Again, in the absence of danger, the upbound vessel should reply with a like signal, and the vessels should pass in the manner proposed.

Section E. Rule 15: The Starboard-Hand Rule

1. Origins of the Starboard-Hand Rule

Of the three basic navigational situations—head-on, overtaking, and crossing—the crossing situation is perhaps the most trying one a navigator may have to face.[73] The basic starboard-hand rule, requiring a power-driven vessel on the port side in a crossing situation with another power-driven vessel to keep out of the other's way, originated soon after steam propulsion became common. It was introduced in the 1863 United Kingdom Regulations, drawn up by the British Board of Trade in consultation with the French Government, and adopted by more than thirty maritime countries, including the United States and Germany, by the end of 1864.[74] In the United States, the 1864 and 1885 Regulations required the starboard-hand vessel to hold her course, but did not provide that she must maintain her speed, nor did they stipulate that the port-hand vessel must avoid crossing ahead. Both vessels had the duty to slow, stop, and reverse, if necessary.[75]

Rule 19 of the 1897 International Regulations required the port-hand vessel in a crossing situation involving risk of collision to keep out of the way; Rule 22 required her to avoid crossing ahead of the starboard-hand vessel if the circumstances admitted, and Rule 21 required the latter to hold her speed as well as her course.[76] These rules were essentially left unchanged under the Regulations of 1910 and 1960, and their substance is now contained in Rules 15, 16, 17(a)(i), and 17(b) of COLREGS.

The starboard-hand vessel was traditionally called the "privileged" vessel and the port-hand vessel the "burdened" vessel, and some lawyers and judges so describe them even today.[77] The term "privileged," however, is actually a misnomer: both vessels are in fact "burdened," since the starboard-hand ves-

73. See Farwell 115–16.

74. See Cockcroft & Lameijer 14.

75. Rules 19, 21, and 23 of the 1864 Rules, as reenacted in 1874, Griffin 809; Articles 16, 18, and 22 of the 1885 Rules, id. 819–20.

76. The 1897 Rules are reprinted in full in Griffin, at 645–80.

77. See, e.g., *Trinidad Corp. v. The Keiyoh Maru,* 845 F.2d 818, 1989 AMC 627 (9th Cir. 1988); *American Employers Ins. Co. v. The Meneleus,* 1982 AMC 654 (ED La. 1980); *Zim Israel Nav. Co. v. Special Carriers Inc.,* 611 F. Supp. 581, 1986 AMC 2016 (ED La. 1985).

sel's primary obligation to hold course and speed is just as truly a "burden" as is the port-hand vessel's primary obligation to keep out of the other vessel's way. The COLREGS and U.S. Inland Rules designations, "stand-on" and "give-way," are much more appropriate than "privileged" and "burdened."

2. *Applicability of the Starboard-Hand Rule*

For the rule to apply, several conditions must exist:

1. The vessels must be in visual sight of one another; as in head-on and overtaking situations, the Steering and Sailing Rules do not apply in a crossing situation when the vessels can "see" each other only on their respective radar screens.[78] However, once they do become actually visible to each other, e.g., when a snowstorm is over, or the vessels emerge from a fog bank, the starboard-hand rule will apply, if the distance then separating the vessels is sufficient to permit navigation in accordance with the rule.[79] If the distance is not sufficient, the case is one of special circumstances and Rule 2(b) will apply.
2. Risk of collision must be involved. Thus, if the vessels are so far apart when they become visible to each other that risk of collision is not involved, each is free to maneuver in such a way as to avoid a close-quarters situation.[80]
3. The vessels must be under way, and at least one of them must have way on. The starboard-hand rule has been applied in several cases where the port-hand vessel was drifting and the starboard-hand vessel had way on.[81] It has likewise been applied where the starboard-hand vessel was drifting and the port-hand vessel had way on.[82]
4. If the starboard-hand vessel has way on she must be on a steady course and be maintaining a steady speed, so that the port-hand vessel is able to ascertain her movements. However, this does not rule out changes in the starboard-hand vessel's heading, or even in her engine speed. Thus, she may be on a "curved" course, in order to follow the curvature of a river or channel,[83] or the helmsman may have to make minor

---

78. COLREGS Rule 11 provides that "Rules in this Section [Rules 11–18] apply to vessels in sight of one another." Inland Rule 11 is identical, except that "Subpart" is used in place of "Section." COLREGS Rule 3(k) and Inland Rule 3(j) provide that "Vessels shall be deemed to be in sight of one another only when one can be observed visually from the other." See *Borcich v. Ancich,* 191 F.2d 392, 1951 AMC 1701 (9th Cir. 1951); *The California—The Curlew,* 105 F. Supp. 428, 1952 AMC 508 (D. Mass. 1952).

79. *The E.R. Wallonia,* [1987] 2 Lloyd's Rep. 485 (Q.B., Adm. Ct. 1987).

80. *The Plumleaf,* 7 Ll. L. Rep. 207 (C.A. 1921).

81. *The Umbria,* 153 F. 851 (2d Cir. 1907); *The City of Camden,* 44 F.2d 711, 1930 AMC 1822 (3d Cir. 1930); *The Broomfield,* 10 Asp. Mar. Cas. (N.S.)194 (Prob. 1905). See Griffin 113–14.

82. *The Cyclops,* 45 F. 122 (SDNY 1891); *The N.Y.C. No. 18,* 230 F. 299 (EDNY 1916).

83. *Commonwealth & Dominion Line v. United States,* 20 F.2d 729, 731, 1927 AMC 1690, 1692–93 (2d Cir. 1927), rev'd on other grounds, 278 U.S. 427, 1929 AMC 238 (1929); cf. *The Alcoa Rambler,* 82 Ll. L. Rep. 359 (P.C. 1948).

changes in heading to compensate for yawing in a rough sea. Likewise, where it is clear that the stand-on vessel is engaged in a maneuver which requires alterations in engine speed, it is not a violation of her obligation to maintain her speed if she continues to make such alterations. Thus, a ferryboat on the starboard hand in a crossing situation may follow her usual practice of slowing when entering her slip.[84]

As stated by Lord Alverstone in *The Roanoke:*[85]

> . . . In my judgment, "course and speed" in art. 21 [now Rule 17] mean course and speed in following the nautical manoeuvre in which, to the knowledge of the other vessel, the vessel is at the time engaged. It is not difficult to give many instances which support this view. The "course" certainly does not mean the actual compass direction of the heading of the vessel at the time the other is sighted. . . . A vessel bound to keep her course and speed may be obliged to reduce her speed to avoid some danger of navigation, and the question must be in each case "Is the manoeuvre in which the vessel is engaged an ordinary and proper manoeuvre in the course of navigation which will require an alteration of course and speed; ought the other vessel to be aware of the manoeuvre which is being attempted to be carried out?"

A fairly recent example of a case where the starboard-hand rule was found inapplicable is *Trinidad Corp. v. The Keiyoh Maru.*[86] The *Fort Worth* was proceeding in the southbound coastal shipping lane, heading into Los Angeles harbor, while the *Keiyoh Maru* was leaving the neighboring port of Long Beach. As the *Keiyoh Maru* passed through the Long Beach breakwater entrance, the harbor pilot conning the ship radioed the pilot boat to come alongside to pick him up. This was done, and the *Keiyoh Maru* then sailed through a restricted anchorage and attempted to cut across the bow of the *Fort Worth,* from port to starboard. Under the applicable U.S. Coast Guard rules, the *Fort Worth,* unlike the *Keiyoh Maru,* was entitled to be in the restricted area, since she was intending to enter Los Angeles harbor. The *Fort Worth* ordered full astern and sounded a five-blast warning signal. No evasive action was taken by the *Keiyoh Maru,* whose port bow tore into the bow of the *Fort Worth.* The *Keiyoh Maru* contended that she was the stand-on vessel in a crossing situation, and that the *Fort Worth,* as the give-way vessel, was obliged

---

84. *The Bronx,* 250 F. 843 (2d Cir. 1918). See also Griffin 145, quoting Judge Learned Hand's statement in *The Napoli,* 1928 AMC 97 (SDNY 1920), that if the starboard-hand vessel has been proceeding at a varied speed she should "keep varying that speed as before. . . . So I think that 'keeping her speed' means keeping the apparent variation of speed, not changing it to a constant velocity."

85. [1908] P. 231, 239 (C.A.) See also *Commonwealth & Dominion Line,* supra note 83; *United States v. The Soya Atlantic,* 330 F.2d 732, 737, 1964 AMC 898, 906 (4th Cir. 1964).

86. 845 F.2d 818, 1989 AMC 627 (9th Cir. 1988).

to keep out of her way. The district court ruled, however, that the starboard-hand rule was inapplicable, and the court of appeals affirmed, stating:

> In order to be considered a privileged vessel in a crossing situation, it must be on a steady course. "A ship is on a steady course, not only when her heading does not change, but whenever her future positions are certainly ascertainable from her present position and movements." *Commonwealth & Dominion Line v. United States,* 20 F.2d 729, 731, 1927 AMC 1690, 1692 (2d Cir. 1927), rev'd on other grounds, 278 U.S. 427, 429, 1929 AMC 238, 239 (1929); see also *United States v. S.S. Soya Atlantic,* 330 F.2d 732, 737, 1964 AMC 898, 906 (4th Cir. 1964). The district court found that the *Keiyoh Maru*'s navigation did not satisfy this test. The district court said: "Due to the constantly changing engine orders and constantly changing headings of the *Keiyoh Maru,* the *Keiyoh Maru* never established itself on a constant course and speed in a crossing situation with the *Fort Worth.*" Moreover, the *Keiyoh Maru*'s course could not possibly be characterized as "certainly ascertainable" because of her movement through the restricted anchorage area. The *Fort Worth* was entitled to assume that another vessel would not transgress a restricted area and embarrass its passage. The district court was correct in finding that no crossing situation existed. The *Fort Worth* had, therefore, no duty to stay clear of the *Keiyoh Maru.*

It is not always easy to distinguish between a crossing situation and an overtaking situation, or between a crossing situation and a head-on meeting situation. These problems are discussed in sections C and D, supra.

3. Obligations of the Port-Hand Vessel

The port-hand vessel's obligations are set out in Rules 15 and 16 of COLREGS. Rule 16 of the Inland Rules is identical to COLREGS Rule 16, and Rule 15(a) of the Inland Rules is identical to COLREGS Rule 15. However, Rule 15 of the Inland Rules includes a paragraph (b), which provides that notwithstanding paragraph (a), on the Great Lakes, Western Rivers, or other waters specified by the Secretary of Transportation, a vessel crossing a river must keep out of the way of an ascending or descending vessel.

Rule 15 of COLREGS and Rule 15(a) of the Inland Rules prohibit the port-hand vessel from crossing ahead under ordinary circumstances, but do not otherwise prescribe how she is to fulfill her obligation of keeping out of the starboard-hand vessel's way. Guidelines are, however, to be found in Rule 8, which sets forth generally the actions to be taken to avoid collision: if the circumstances admit, the actions should be positive, timely, and in accordance with good seamanship; alterations of course and speed should be large enough to be apparent to another vessel observing her visually or by radar; the action should be such as to result in passing at a safe distance, and should be carefully checked until the other vessel is past and clear. If necessary, the vessel should slacken speed, or stop and reverse.

Rule 16 provides that the port-hand vessel (or any vessel, such as an overtaking vessel that is required to keep out of the way) must, so far as possible, take early and substantial action to keep well clear.

Finally, Rule 17, prescribing the duties of the starboard-hand vessel, concludes with a paragraph (d), which makes it clear that the rule does not relieve the give-way vessel of her obligation to keep out of the way.

4. *Obligations of the Starboard-Hand Vessel*

Rule 17 specifies the stand-on vessel's obligations in a crossing situation. Another rule that frequently becomes applicable is 34(d), which requires a danger signal of at least five short and rapid blasts when one approaching vessel fails to understand the intentions or actions of the other, or is in doubt as to whether the other is taking sufficient action to avoid collision. The sound signal may be supplemented by a light signal of at least five short, rapid flashes.

In carrying out her primary obligation to hold her course and speed, the starboard-hand vessel has the right to assume at the outset that the give-way vessel will fulfill her statutory obligation of keeping out of the way. As stated by the U.S. Court of Appeals for the Second Circuit in *The Exmouth—The Hellenic Beach:*[87]

> Under ordinary circumstances *Hellenic,* as the privileged vessel, was entitled to maintain her course and speed. If *Hellenic* had to speculate that *Exmouth* would not obey the rules and engage in avoiding action on that assumption, the rules might as well be discarded. Navigation would be reduced to a game of bluff.

The most significant change in the crossing rules effected by COLREGS was the addition of paragraph (a)(ii) to Rule 17. Under the former rules, the stand-on vessel in a crossing situation was frequently placed in a very difficult position when the give-way vessel failed to take prompt steps to keep out of the way. If the stand-on vessel took avoiding action before reaching a point where collision could not be avoided by action on the part of the give-way vessel alone, she could be held in violation of the first part of old Rule 21, requiring her to keep her course and speed.[88] On the other hand, if she held course and speed beyond the point where the give-way vessel could not avoid colli-

---

87. 253 F.2d 473, 1958 AMC 1018, 1022 (2d Cir. 1958), citing *Wilson v. Pacific Mail S.S. Co.,* 276 U.S. 454, 1928 AMC 740 (1928); *The Delaware,* 161 U.S. 459 (1896); *National Bulk Carriers v. United States,* 183 F.2d 405, 1950 AMC 1293 (2d Cir. 1950); *Pacific-Atlantic S.S. Co. v. United States,* 175 F.2d 632, 1949 AMC 1120 (4th Cir. 1949); *The Nereus,* 23 F. 448 (SDNY 1885).

88. See *The Britannia,* 153 U.S. 130 (1894); *Pacific-Atlantic S.S. Co. v. United States (The Oregon—The New Mexico),* 81 F. Supp. 777, 1948 AMC 1727 (ED Va. 1948), aff'd, 175 F.2d 632, 1949 AMC 1120 (4th Cir. 1949). The courts were, however, generally unwilling to judge too severely the conduct of a stand-on vessel confronted with the failure of a give-way vessel to fulfill her obli-

sion by her own actions alone, the stand-on vessel could be held in violation of the second sentence of old Rule 21, requiring her to take action at that point.[89] When the old rules were in force, this meant that where U.S. or Liberian law was applicable, the stand-on vessel could be held liable for 50 percent of the total damages, no matter how grievous the faults of the give-way vessel may have been.[90]

The old rule was unworkable: it presupposed that the stand-on vessel was familiar with the maneuvering ability of the give-way vessel.[91] An estimate of the give-way vessel's capabilities was of course difficult by day, but virtually impossible at night, when only the give-way vessel's lights could be seen, and not the vessel herself. In theory, the stand-on vessel might have inquired by radio about the give-way vessel's maneuverability, but of course in the brief period of time that might have been available, a radio message urging the give-way vessel to obey old Rule 19 and keep out of the way would have been far more practicable than one asking her to describe her characteristics.

This mandatory provision has been carried over into COLREGS by Rule 17(b). This may have been the result of a compromise between the views of those delegates to the COLREGS diplomatic conference who wanted to keep the obligations of the stand-on vessel as they were before COLREGS, and the views of those who wanted to replace the second part of old Rule 19 with mandatory language similar to the permissive language eventually included as Rule 17(a)(ii) of COLREGS, with respect to action the stand-on vessel may take upon seeing that the give-way vessel is not complying with the rules.

In any case, as finally formulated, COLREGS contain two theoretically distinct provisions regarding the rights and obligations of a stand-on vessel in a crossing situation when confronted with the failure of a give-way vessel to take prompt steps to keep out of her way: (1) under paragraph (a)(ii) of Rule 17 she *may* take action to avoid collision by her maneuver alone, as soon as it becomes apparent to her that the give-way vessel is not taking appropriate action; (2) under paragraph (b) of Rule 17 she *shall* take such action as will best aid in avoiding collision when she finds herself so close to the give-way vessel that collision cannot be avoided by the action of that vessel alone.

The new rules thus give a stand-on vessel a decided benefit, in permitting her to take action before waiting for the moment to arrive when a give-way vessel that is failing to give way can no longer avoid collision by her own action alone. On the other hand, COLREGS, at least as interpreted by the U.S. and British courts, impose a correspondingly greater obligation on the

---

gation of keeping out of the way. See, e.g., the court of appeals decision in *The Oregon—The New Mexico,* supra.

89. *Yangtse Ins. Ass'n v. Furness,* 215 F. 859 (2d Cir. 1914).

90. *The Catharine v. Dickinson,* 58 U.S. 170 (1855), overruled in *United States v. Reliable Transfer Co.,* 421 U.S. 397, 1975 AMC 541 (1975).

91. See Cockcroft & Lameijer 123–24.

stand-on vessel to take appropriate action to avoid collision with a give-way vessel that is failing to fulfill her obligation to give way.

Paragraph (c) of Rule 17 of COLREGS and the Inland Rules provides that a starboard-hand vessel which takes action under paragraph (a)(ii) to avoid collision with the port-hand vessel "shall, if the circumstances of the case admit, not alter course to port for a vessel on her own port side." No corresponding provision was contained in the former rules, although good seamanship would dictate avoidance of an alteration of course toward the port-hand vessel, except in extraordinary circumstances. Other than this, and the general guideline contained in Rule 8 concerning actions to be taken to avoid collision, the rules do not prescribe the type of action which should be taken by the starboard-hand vessel in accordance with paragraph (a)(ii) of Rule 17.

By its terms, paragraph (c) of Rule 17 applies only to the action which may be taken under paragraph (a)(ii) when it appears that the port-hand vessel is not taking appropriate action. No similar provision is made with respect to the action the stand-on vessel must take under paragraph (b), presumably because that paragraph applies only when the vessels are so close that an unorthodox maneuver—conceivably even an alteration to port toward a give-way vessel on the port side—may be necessary to avoid collision.

The first reported U.S. decision under the new crossing rules appears to be *American Employers Ins. Co. v. The Menelaus,*[92] a case involving factual issues almost exclusively, where, in holding the give-way vessel solely at fault, the court simply stated:

> The only possible negligence which could be attributed to the *Menelaus* would be the failure to take evasive action sooner, considering that her attempts to contact the *Ann Bonney* by radio and by whistle and light signal went unanswered. We conclude that, considering her duty as a privileged vessel to maintain course and speed, the *Menelaus* was not negligent in failing to alter either course or speed until the collision seemed imminent. (Citing Gilmore & Black 504.)

In *Matter of Shaun Fisheries, Inc.,*[93] the Fishing Vessel *Shaun* collided with the Barge *Bandon,* in tow of the Tug *Mary Catherine.* The court found that the tug's ability to maneuver was not restricted within the meaning of COLREGS Rule 18,[94] and that as the port-hand vessel in a crossing situation, she should have given way to the *Shaun,* and was at fault for failing to do so. In holding the *Shaun* equally to blame, the court stated:

---

92. 1982 AMC 654 (D La. 1980).
93. 1984 AMC 2650 (D Or. 1983).
94. Rule 18 provides, in part, that except as otherwise required by Rules 9, 10, and 13, a power-driven vessel under way, a sailing vessel underway, and a vessel engaged in fishing, when underway, shall keep out of the way of a vessel restricted in her ability to maneuver.

> Even though *Shaun* did have the right of way, she had the duty to avoid collision when it became apparent that *Mary Catherine* was not obeying the rules of the road. *Shaun* had ample warning of that fact in *Mary Catherine*'s steady course and speed throughout the time the vessels were in sight of each other. As collision became more and more probable, *Shaun* could have radioed *Mary Catherine* and asked her intentions, or, as the vessels came still closer, have sounded a warning signal to alert the other ship. Even after *Shaun* passed abeam of the tug, she could have turned to port and avoided the collision. COLREG Rule 17 did not require her to hold course until collision became practically inevitable.
>
> I find that both ships were at fault in failure to give way. *Mary Catherine* was obliged to give way under the rules of the road. *Shaun* was obliged to avoid collision when *Mary Catherine* failed to give way.

It will be noted that the court did not rest its decision holding the stand-on vessel to blame on a violation of the mandatory provisions of paragraph (b) of Rule 17, but rather on her failure to act when it became apparent that the tug was not obeying the rules of the road. It is implicit in the court's language that under the circumstances it considered a failure to act under paragraph 17 (a) (ii) a fault, despite the permissive wording of that paragraph.

In *Matter of Sieriki Kisen Kaisha,*[95] the *Seiryu,* the give-way vessel in a crossing situation, failed to take any steps to keep out of the way of the *Stena Freighter,* the stand-on vessel, until very shortly before the collision, when she turned to port across the *Stena*'s bow, which struck the *Seiryu*'s starboard side at a right angle and almost cut her in two. The *Stena*'s watch officer testified that he had concluded from plotting successive positions of the *Seiryu* on the *Stena*'s radar reflection plotter that the *Seiryu* would pass astern of his vessel. He then busied himself with taking a fix and plotting it on the chart. About three minutes before the collision he permitted the helmsman-lookout—the only other person on the bridge—to go below to call the next watch. (The vessel's automatic pilot was in operation.) After plotting the fix he saw the *Seiryu* dead ahead, and the vessels collided as he ran to the controls and put the *Stena*'s variable pitch propeller levers on "STOP."

The *Seiryu* confessed fault, but argued that the *Stena* was also to blame, because of her failure to maintain a proper look-out, to sound a danger signal, and to take the avoiding action permitted under paragraph (a)(ii) of Rule 17 and required under paragraph 17(b). Pointing to the *Stena*'s maneuverability, the *Seiryu* argued that her watch officer could have stopped his vessel dead in the water in two or three minutes if he had sounded a danger signal and received no response, and that in the last minutes before collision would otherwise have occurred, he could have turned the *Stena* to starboard and passed astern of the *Seiryu.* In determining that the *Stena* was 40 percent

95. 629 F. Supp. 1374, 1986 AMC 913 (SDNY 1986).

to blame for the collision, the court placed "primary emphasis on its failure to give a whistle warning signal rather than its failure to make any specific maneuver." The court concluded that the *Stena*'s fault in having both the helmsman-lookout and the watch officer engage in other activities, although admittedly aware of the *Seiryu*'s close proximity, was a violation of COLREGS, and that the *Stena*'s failure to give a warning signal was a contributing cause of the collision.

The court did not attempt to differentiate between the *right* to take avoiding action under Rule 17(a)(ii) and the *obligation* to take such action under Rule 17(b). But again, it seems implicit from the court's discussion of the *Stena*'s faults that had the *Stena* been maintaining a proper look-out she should, at the very least, have sounded a danger signal as soon as it became apparent that the *Seiryu,* as the port-hand vessel, was not complying with her obligation under COLREGS to keep out of the *Stena*'s way.

The *Achilleus*[96] involved a nighttime collision between a vessel of that name and the *Cinderella,* in the approaches to Kieler Forde, while the *Achilleus* was en route from Finland to Calais and the *Cinderella* was on a voyage from Piraeus to Stockholm. At the material times the vessels were on crossing courses, the *Cinderella* being the starboard-hand vessel and the *Achilleus* the port-hand vessel. The *Achilleus* was held 70 percent to blame, for crossing a traffic separation zone and for failing to keep out of the way. Both faults were found to have resulted from her failure to maintain a proper look-out. The *Cinderella* had sounded a warning signal, but it was not heard on the *Achilleus.* The *Cinderella* was held 30 percent to blame, for failing to take avoiding action, because, if she had been maintaining a proper look-out, it should have been apparent to those on board that the *Achilleus* was not turning to starboard, but was going to cross ahead of the starboard-hand vessel.

Mr. Justice Sheen quoted paragraphs (a)(i), (a)(ii), and (b) of Rule 17. While in charging the *Cinderella* with fault he did not specify which paragraphs of Rule 17 he considered the *Cinderella* had violated, he stated:

> . . . No one on the bridge of *Cinderella* appears to have appreciated that *Achilleus* had headway and was apparently going to cross ahead of *Cinderella.*
>
> Whether Mr. Ohlsson [the *Cinderella*'s mate on watch] was looking at the radar or keeping a visual lookout, he ought to have observed what *Achilleus* was doing. His failure to observe *Achilleus* shows a complete lack of a sense of responsibility. When the propeller of *Cinderella* was put to full astern mode *Achilleus* cannot have been more than half a cable distant. Long before that moment it should have been apparent that *Achilleus* was not taking appropriate action to comply with r. 15.

96. [1985] 2 Lloyd's Rep. 338 (Q.B. [Adm. Ct.] 1985).

Again, it will be observed that Mr. Justice Sheen did not charge the *Cinderella* with fault on the basis of a failure to take avoiding action when the vessels were so close that action by the *Achilleus* alone could not have prevented the collision. Rather, he noted the advice of the experts that long before the *Cinderella*'s propeller was put to full astern mode it should have been apparent that the *Achilleus* was not complying with her Rule 15 obligation to keep out of the way, and that the *Cinderella* should *then* have taken off her headway. It is therefore clear that he considered the *Cinderella* at fault for failure to take avoiding action in accordance with paragraph (a)(ii) of Rule 17, even though that paragraph is worded as permitting such action, rather than as requiring it.

Still another decision treating a stand-on vessel's failure to take the avoiding action permitted under Rule 17(a)(ii) as a fault is *In re Ocean Foods Boat Co.*[97] The Fishing Vessel *McKinley*, the give-way vessel in a crossing situation, collided with the M/V *Tosca*. Both vessels were held at fault, the *McKinley* for failing to give way and for attempting to cross the *Tosca*'s bow, and the *Tosca* for failing to take avoiding action. In charging the *Tosca* with 35 percent of the blame, the court quoted both paragraph (a)(ii) and paragraph (b) of Rule 17, and continued: "Rule 17 allowed the *Tosca* to take unilateral action to avoid the collision once it became apparent that the *McKinley* was not following the rules and that the *Tosca*'s maneuver was necessary to avoid collision. The *Tosca* failed to take such action. She must accept some responsibility for the collision."

To summarize, from the U.S. and British decisions concerning the rights and obligations of the stand-on vessel in a crossing situation handed down since COLREGS entered into force in 1977, three principles may be deduced:

1. As soon as it becomes apparent that the port-hand vessel is not taking prompt steps to keep out of the way, the starboard-hand vessel *must* sound the warning signal of five or more short, rapid blasts, which Rule 34 (d) requires a vessel approaching another to sound if from any cause she fails to understand the intentions or actions of the other, or is in doubt as to whether sufficient action is being taken by the other to avoid collision.
2. While paragraph (a)(ii) of Rule 17 is worded permissively, a stand-on vessel will be chargeable with some degree of blame if she stubbornly persists in holding course and speed after it has become apparent to her that the give-way vessel is not taking appropriate action, even if it

97. 692 F. Supp. 1253, 1989 AMC 579 (D Or. 1988). See also *Rich Ocean Car Carriers v. The Sanko Diamond*, 1989 AMC 220 (MD Fla. 1988), where the court found the stand-on vessel 15 percent to blame for failing to sound the danger signal required by Rule 34(d) when it appeared that sufficient action was not being taken by the give-way vessel to avoid collision, and for failing to take avoiding action "in ample time," as required by Rule 8.

is possible to demonstrate that the vessels were not then so close that action by the give-way vessel alone could not avoid collision, and that the mandatory provisions of paragraph (b) of Rule 17 were therefore not yet applicable.

3. The stand-on vessel will of course be held at least partially to blame for a collision contributed to by her violation of paragraph (b) of Rule 17, in failing to take appropriate avoiding action when the vessels are so close that the give-way vessel cannot avoid collision by her own action alone.

Cockcroft & Lameijer's analysis of the four stages in a collision situation is particularly appropriate as an outline of the respective rights and obligations of the vessels involved in a crossing situation:

> When two vessels in sight of each other are approaching with no change of compass bearing, so that when there is risk of collision one of them is required to keep out of the way by a Rule from Section II, there may be four stages relating to the permitted or required action for each vessel:
>
> 1. At long range, before risk of collision exists, both vessels are free to take any action.
> 2. When risk of collision first begins to apply the give-way vessel is required to take early and substantial action to achieve a safe passing distance and the other vessel must keep her course and speed.
> 3. When it becomes apparent that the give-way vessel is not taking appropriate action in compliance with the Rules the stand-on vessel is required to give the whistle signal prescribed in Rule 34(d) and is permitted to take action to avoid collision by her manoeuvre alone, but a power-driven vessel must not alter course to port to avoid another power-driven vessel crossing from her own port side. The give-way vessel is not relieved of her obligation to keep out of the way.
> 4. When collision cannot be avoided by the give-way vessel alone the stand-on vessel is required to take such action as will best aid to avoid collision.
>
> The distances at which the various stages begin to apply will vary considerably. They will be much greater for high speed vessels involved in an overtaking situation. For a crossing situation involving two power-driven vessels in the open sea it is suggested that the outer limit of the second stage might be of the order of 5 to 8 miles and that the outer limit for the third stage would be about 2 to 3 miles.[98]

98. Cockcroft & Lameijer 129–30.

Section F. Rule 18: Responsibilities between Vessels

Rule 18 establishes an order of priority among vessels of various types and in various modes. COLREGS Rule 18 and Inland Rule 18 are identical, except that COLREGS Rule 18 provides, in paragraph (d)(i), that any vessel other than one not under command, or one restricted in her ability to maneuver, shall, if the circumstances admit, avoid impeding the safe passage of a vessel constrained by her draft and exhibiting the signals required by Rule 28 (three all around red lights in a vertical line, or a cylinder). Paragraph (d)(ii) of the COLREGS rule adds that a vessel constrained by her draft "shall navigate with particular caution having full regard to her special condition." Inland Rule 18 contains no similar provisions.

Apart from the special provisions of COLREGS Rule 18(d), the essence of COLREGS and Inland Rule 18 is that power-driven vessels under way must keep out of the way of sailing vessels, and that both power-driven and sailing vessels underway must keep out of the way of vessels that are not under command, or are restricted in their ability to maneuver, or are engaged in fishing. Paragraph (c) of each rule requires that vessels engaged in fishing when underway must, as far as possible, keep out of the way of vessels not under command or restricted in their ability to maneuver.

Paragraph (e) of COLREGS Rule 18 and paragraph (d) of Inland Rule 18 provide that a seaplane on the water shall, in general, keep well clear of all vessels and avoid impeding their navigation, but that where there is risk of collision it shall comply with the Steering and Sailing Rules (Rules 4–18). The provisions of Rule 18 apply "[e]xcept where Rules 9, 10 and 13 otherwise require." As we have seen, Rule 9 (the narrow channel rule) contains special provisions applicable in such waters. Thus, it prohibits sailing vessels and vessels of less than 20 meters in length from impeding the passage of vessels that can safely navigate only within a narrow channel or fairway, and prohibits vessels engaged in fishing from impeding the passage of any other vessel navigating within such a waterway. In narrow channels, therefore, a power-driven vessel underway may have priority over a sailing vessel, and a sailing vessel may have priority over a vessel engaged in fishing, thus reversing the order of priority ordinarily governing under Rule 18. (See generally, chapter 4, section F.)

Similarly, COLREGS and Inland Rule 10 (Traffic Separation Schemes) provides in paragraph (j) that vessels of less than 20 meters in length and sailing vessels shall not impede the safe passage of power-driven vessels following traffic lanes. Here again, Rule 18 does not apply, and a power-driven vessel underway has priority over sailing vessels and small powered vessels, even if they are engaged in fishing or restricted in their ability to maneuver. (See generally, chapter 4, section G.)

CHAPTER SIX

INTERNATIONAL AND INLAND RULES: PART B(III)—CONDUCT OF VESSELS IN RESTRICTED VISIBILITY

Section A. Introduction

Rule 19 is the only rule in Part B of COLREGS and the Inland Rules (the Steering and Sailing Rules) relating exclusively to the conduct of vessels under restricted visibility conditions. However, Rule 6, also in Part B, provides in paragraph (a)(i) that in determining the safe speed the rule requires of *all* vessels, account must be taken of the state of the visibility, and in paragraph (b)(vi) provides that vessels equipped with operational radar must take into account the more exact assessment of the visibility that may be possible when radar is used to determine the range of another vessel or object in the vicinity.

Paragraph (k) of Rule 3 (General Definitions), which is included in Part A of COLREGS, provides that vessels shall be deemed in sight of one another only when one can be observed visually from the other. Thus, another vessel whose presence is observed by radar alone is not "in sight" within the meaning of the rules. Paragraph *(l)* of the same rule defines "restricted visibility," and Rule 35, in Part D (Sound and Light Signals), prescribes the "fog signals" to be sounded by vessels of various types in various situations when the visibility is restricted.[1]

Section I of Part B (Steering and Sailing Rules) governs the conduct of vessels in *any* condition of visibility. Thus, Rule 5 (Look-out), 6 (Safe Speed), 7 (Risk of Collision), 8 (Action to Avoid Collision), 9 (Narrow Channels), and 10 (Traffic Separation Schemes) are applicable in restricted visibility conditions as well as in clear weather.

Rule 2 (Responsibility), which includes the "good seamanship rule" as paragraph (a) and the "special circumstances rule" as paragraph (b), sometimes becomes pertinent when the visibility is restricted. Rule 2 is included in Part A of COLREGS and the Inland Rules.

1. Paragraph (j) of Inland Rule 3 is identical to paragraph (k) of COLREGS Rule 3, and paragraph (k) of Inland Rule 3 is identical to paragraph (1) of COLREGS Rule 3.

Section B. Application of the "Fog Rules"

Paragraph (a) of Rule 19 limits the application of the rule to vessels that are not in sight of one another and are navigating in or near a restricted-visibility area. The definition of "restricted visibility" in Rule 3*(l)* of COLREGS (3[k] of the Inland Rules) is "any condition in which visibility is restricted by fog, mist, falling snow, heavy rainstorms, sandstorms, or any other similar causes." Smoke is not specifically mentioned, but the "fog rules" have been applied when visibility was restricted by smoke[2] or haze.[3]

The language of Rule 3(1) of COLREGS (3[k] of the Inland Rules) is in a sense redundant. "Restricted visibility" is defined as a condition "in which visibility is restricted" by fog and other specified causes, but the word "restricted" is not defined. Obviously, it could not have been intended to mean any condition of less than perfect visibility; otherwise the fog rules would apply most of the time. On the other hand, it could not have been intended to describe only dense fog or similar visibility conditions.

The absence of a definition of "restricted" is of no consequence insofar as the requirement to proceed at a "safe" speed under Rule 6 and Rule 19(b) is concerned. Under Rule 6, every vessel must proceed at a "safe" speed, and what is "safe" will vary with the extent of the visibility as well as other factors. Thus, if the visibility is such that it is not "safe" to proceed at full speed, the visibility is "restricted" and an appropriate reduction is mandated by the rules.

Likewise, the absence of a definition of "restricted" does not appear to be material with respect to a vessel's obligations under Rule 19(e); unless it has been determined that no risk of collision exists, a vessel hearing a fog signal apparently forward of her beam must reduce her speed to bare steerageway and, if necessary, take all her way off and in any event navigate with extreme caution until danger of collision is over. If a vessel hears another's fog signal, it is obvious that she is navigating either in a restricted-visibility area or near one, and in either case the mandates of paragraph (e) will apply.

However, the absence of a definition of "restricted" may present a question with respect to the third obligation of a vessel navigating in or near a "restricted visibility" area: the obligation to sound the fog signals required under Rule 35. That rule provides *inter alia* that in or near an area of restricted visibility, whether by day or night, a power-driven vessel making way through the water must sound a signal of one prolonged blast (defined in

---

2. *The Yosemite,* 28 F.2d 939, 1929 AMC 128 (6th Cir. 1928); *The Edward E. Loomis,* 86 F.2d 705, 1937 AMC 54 (2d Cir. 1936); *The Archie Grossman and The Gracie,* 106 F. 984 (SDNY 1900), aff'd, 106 F. 984 (2d Cir. 1901); *The Esso Plymouth,* [1955] 1 Lloyd's Rep. 429 (Adm.).

3. *The Papoose,* 85 F.2d 54, 1936 AMC 1126 (2d Cir. 1936). But mere darkness does not constitute "restricted visibility." *The Maui (Matson Nav. Co. v. Pope & Talbot, Inc.),* 149 F.2d 295, 1945 AMC 767 (9th Cir. 1945); J. Griffin, *The American Law of Collision* 290 (1949) (hereinafter "Griffin").

Rule 32[c] as one of from four to six seconds' duration) at intervals of not more than two minutes. Fog signals are discussed more fully in chapter 8, section D.

Before COLREGS and the current Inland Rules came into force, the rules made no mention of vessels *approaching* areas of restricted visibility. Nevertheless, the U.S. and British courts held that it was a fault if a vessel failed to follow the fog rules when *nearing* a fog bank or other area of limited visibility.[4] COLREGS and the Inland Rules codify this requirement; it will be noted that paragraph (a) of Rule 19 provides that the rule applies to vessels which are not in sight of one another, not only when navigating *in* an area of restricted visibility, but when navigating *near* such an area.

Rule 11, the first rule of Section/Subpart II of Part B of COLREGS and the Inland Rules, provides that the rules of the section/subpart apply to vessels in sight of one another. These include Rule 12, governing the conduct of sailing vessels; Rule 13, applying to the overtaking of one vessel by another; Rule 14, relating to vessels meeting on reciprocal or nearly reciprocal courses; Rules 15 and 17, governing vessels on crossing courses; Rule 16, relating to vessels required to keep out of the way; and Rule 18, defining responsibilities between vessels. Rule 11 does not explicitly provide that Rules 12–18 do not apply to vessels that are *not* in sight of one another. It was, however, presumably intended by the drafters that Rules 12–18 as such should *not* apply; otherwise, they would in some instances be at variance with Rule 19.

Thus, under Rule 14(a), power-driven vessels meeting on reciprocal or nearly reciprocal courses so as to involve risk of collision must, unless otherwise agreed, each alter course to starboard and pass port to port. Rule 14(b) provides that such a situation shall be deemed to exist when a vessel "*sees* the other ahead or nearly ahead,"[5] which would be impossible in restricted visibility.

Under Rule 16, a vessel required to keep out of the way of another must, so far as possible, take early and substantial action to keep well clear. If the rule were applied in restricted visibility, it would in almost every case result in a violation of the safe-speed requirement of Rules 6 and 19(b).

Rule 17 requires a stand-on vessel to keep her course and speed, which in restricted visibility would result in a violation of Rule 19(e) once a fog signal was heard apparently forward of the beam.

Rule 12, governing the navigation of sailing vessels, and Rule 18, relating to responsibilities between vessels, both require information which can be obtained only by a visual sighting of another vessel. It is plain that these rules cannot apply when the visibility is restricted.

---

4. *Valley Towing Service, Inc. v. The American Wheat,* 618 F.2d 341, 1981 AMC 436 (5th Cir. 1980); *Silver Line, Ltd. v. United States (The Chicago—The Silver Palm),* 94 F.2d 754, 1937 AMC 1427 (9th Cir. 1937); *The Milanese,* (1881) 4 Asp. Mar. Cas. 318 (H.L.).

5. Emphasis added.

Rule 34 provides for maneuvering and warning signals to be given when vessels are in sight of one another; vessels in or near an area of restricted visibility are required, instead, to sound the fog signals specified in Rule 35.

The only rule in Section/Subpart II of Part B that might be said to have any pertinence in areas of restricted visibility is Rule 13(a), which provides that notwithstanding anything contained in Rules 4 through 18, any vessel overtaking any other shall keep out of the other's way. If a vessel overtaking another in clear weather is obliged to keep out of the other's way, *a fortiori* a vessel overtaking another in fog should keep out of the way of the vessel being overtaken. It is submitted that a failure to observe this obvious precaution would impose liability on the overtaking vessel under Rule 2(a), the rule of good seamanship, even if Rule 13(a) as such were interpreted as applicable only to vessels in sight of each other.[6]

Once vessels come in sight of one another, as when heavy rain or snow stops, or the vessels emerge from a fog bank, the rules in Section/Subpart II of Part B will apply, provided the vessels are then sufficiently far apart to make navigation in accordance with the particular rule feasible.[7] If they are then too close for navigation in accordance with those rules, Rule 2(b), the special circumstances rule, will apply, and each vessel will be obliged to take whatever action appears best suited to avoid collision.[8]

Section C. Obligations of Vessels Navigating in or near Restricted Visibility Areas

1. *Safe Speed*

The mandate of the first sentence of Rule 19(b), requiring a vessel to proceed at a safe speed adapted to the prevailing circumstances and conditions of restricted visibility, is essentially a duplicate of the mandate of part of Rule 6. So, too, is the mandate of Rule 19(c), requiring vessels to have due regard to the prevailing circumstances and conditions of restricted visibility when complying with the Steering and Sailing Rules. Rule 6 requires every vessel to proceed at all times at a safe speed, so that she can take proper and effective action to avoid collision and can be stopped within a distance appropriate to the prevailing circumstances and conditions.

---

6. See the discussion in Griffin, at 327–29, concerning the applicability *vel non* of the meeting, overtaking, and crossing rules, and of former Rule 20, requiring a steam vessel to keep out of the way of a sailing vessel under restricted visibility conditions. See also Marsden, *Collisions at Sea* 540 (11th ed. 1961, K. McGuffie, ed.).

7. *The New Hampshire,* 136 F. 769 (2d Cir. 1905); *United States v. The Walter A. Luckenbach (The Eelbeck),* 1925 AMC 1631 (SDNY 1925); Griffin 329.

8. See, e.g., *Afran Transport Co. v. The Transcolorado,* 458 F.2d 164 (5th Cir. 1972); and *The Queen Elizabeth,* 122 F. 406 (2d Cir. 1903), both decided under the former special circumstances rule, which was substantially the same as Rule 2(f) of COLREGS and the Inland Rules.

The provision in Rule 19(b) requiring a power-driven vessel to have her engines ready for immediate maneuver when navigating under restricted visibility conditions is new. There was no such provision in the former fog rules, but a vessel navigating in fog without having her engines ready would have been in violation of Rule 2(a), the good seamanship rule, and therefore at fault for a resulting collision. The safe-speed provisions of Rule 19 have been fully discussed in section C of chapter 4, together with Rule 6, and need not be reexamined here.

2. *Avoidance of Close-Quarters Situations*

Former International Rule 16(c) *permitted* a power-driven vessel detecting the presence of another vessel, apparently forward of her beam, before hearing her fog signal or sighting her visually, to take "early and substantial action to avoid a close-quarters situation." Rule 19(d) of COLREGS and the Inland Rules, on the other hand, is not worded permissively. Instead, it first requires a vessel detecting the presence of another "by radar alone" to "determine if a close-quarters situation is developing and/or[9] risk of collision exists." The requirement is not restricted to instances where the other vessel is forward of the beam. If it is determined that a close-quarters situation is developing and/or that risk of collision exists, the vessel is then required to "take avoiding action in ample time." Neither the former rule nor the current one defines a "close-quarters situation," and there do not appear to be any reported U.S. or British decisions defining the term.[10]

Two limitations on the type of avoiding action required to be taken are specified: (1) so far as possible, the vessel must not alter course to port for another vessel forward of the beam, other than a vessel being overtaken, and (2) so far as possible, the vessel must not alter course toward another vessel abeam or abaft the beam.

3. *Action Required upon Detecting the Presence of Another Vessel Forward of the Beam*

Perhaps the most significant changes effected by COLREGS and the current Inland Rules in the obligations of a vessel navigating in or near an area of restricted visibility are those relating to a vessel's conduct upon hearing another vessel's fog signal apparently forward of her beam. Under Rule 16(b)

9. Inland Rule 19(d) reads "or" in place of "and/or." Otherwise, Rule 19 of the Inland Rules is identical to Rule 19 of COLREGS.

10. See Cockcroft & Lameijer, *A Guide to the Collision Avoidance Rules* 67 (4th ed.), where the authors state: "The distance at which a close quarters situation first applies will depend upon a number of factors, including the visibility. In the open sea distances of the order of 2 to 3 miles are usually considered as the outer limits in restricted visibility but smaller distances, probably of the order of 1 mile, would probably be accepted for vessels in sight of one another."

of the 1960 International Rules and the second paragraph of Rule 16 of the former Inland Rules, if the position of the other vessel was not ascertained, the vessel hearing the signal was required, "so far as the circumstances of the case admit[ted]," to stop her engines, and then navigate with caution until danger of collision was over. Rule 19(e) of COLREGS and the current Inland Rules, on the other hand, provides that except where it has been determined that a risk of collision does not exist, a vessel hearing another's fog signal apparently forward of her beam, or which cannot avoid a close-quarters situation with another vessel forward of her beam, must (1) reduce speed to bare steerageway; (2) if necessary, take all her way off; and (3) in any event, navigate with extreme caution until danger of collision is over.

It will be seen, first of all, that the exception to the applicability of Rule 19(e) is narrower than the corresponding exception to the applicability of former International Rule 16(b) and the second paragraph of former Inland Rule 16. Those provisions did not apply in a case where the position of the other vessel had been ascertained. Thus, if the position had been ascertained by the proper use of operational radar, the paragraph was inapplicable even when risk of collision still existed. Rule 19(e) of COLREGS and the current Inland Rules, on the other hand, provides that even if the position of the other vessel has been ascertained, e.g., by effective use of radar, the rule will continue to apply until it has been determined that no risk of collision exists.

Secondly, whereas the former rule applied only when a fog signal was heard apparently forward of the beam, Rule 19(e) is applicable not only in such a case, but whenever a close-quarters situation with another vessel forward of the beam cannot be avoided. It therefore applies, e.g., where another vessel is detected ahead by radar, too close to avoid a close-quarters situation, even if no fog signal is heard from her.

It will be observed that Rule 19(e) provides that a vessel required to reduce speed to bare steerageway or to take all of her way off, must, after doing so, then "navigate with extreme caution until danger of collision is over." In this respect Rule 19(e) is the same as former International Rule 16(b) and the second paragraph of former Inland Rule 16, except for the addition of the adjective "extreme" before "caution."

CHAPTER SEVEN

INTERNATIONAL AND INLAND RULES: PART C—LIGHTS AND SHAPES

Section A. Introduction

1. Historical Background of the Light Rules

Long sea voyages requiring night operations did not become common until after the sixteenth-century age of discovery, when the custom developed of carrying a large lantern between dusk and dawn to indicate the vessel's position to mariners on other vessels. Custom became legal obligation in the United States in the age of steam, with an 1838 federal statute requiring steam vessels to indicate their positions with one or more lights,[1] a necessary concomitant of the greater speed and maneuverability of these vessels. Lights indicating vessel characteristics were introduced in an 1849 statute applicable to the Great Lakes and other northern and western lakes.[2] Thereafter, the Supervising Inspectors (predecessors of the U.S. Coast Guard) developed additional rules to prevent collisions, including rules requiring whistle signals and the combination of port (red), starboard (green), and masthead (white) lights for night operations.[3] Further improvements were introduced in statutes enacted in 1864, 1885, 1897, and 1929.[4] Thus, before the introduction of radar, a system of lights had been devised that informed observing mariners at night of a vessel's function,[5] position,[6] and general

1. Act of July 7, 1838, ch. 191, § 10, 5 Stat. 304: ". . . Every steamboat, running between sunset and sunrise to carry one or more signal lights, that may be seen by other boats navigating in the same waters. . . ."

2. Act of Mar. 3, 1849, ch. 105, § 5, 9 Stat. 382: ". . . [D]uring the night, vessels on the starboard tack shall show a red light, vessels on the larboard [port] tack a green light, and vessels going off large, or before the wind, or at anchor, a white light. . . ."

3. Steamboat Inspection Act, Aug. 30, 1852, ch. 106, 10 Stat. 61, setting up the Board of Supervisory Inspectors in the Treasury Department. These inspectors prepared the 1858 Pilot Rules, under the authority of § 29 of ch. 106 (the statutory passing rules).

4. Act of Apr. 29, 1864, ch. 69, arts. 1–20, 13 Stat. 58. Cases under the 1929 Rules and earlier versions are collected in J. Griffin, *The American Law of Collision,* at 230–61 (hereinafter "Griffin").

5. E.g., whether it was a sailing vessel, a fishing vessel, a vessel towing astern or pushing, a mine-sweeping vessel, a pilot vessel, or a seaplane.

6. E.g., the masthead lights or the sternlight would indicate the vessel's relative bearing from the observing vessel.

direction.[7] Further requirements were introduced in the post-radar 1948 and 1960 International Rules. In 1972 the technical specifications for installation of the lights were removed from the International Rules themselves and placed in Annex I to COLREGS, while the rules were reorganized and somewhat simplified in Part C—Lights and Shapes (Rules 20 to 31). Similarly, the technical specifications for lights governed by the Inland Rules are contained in Annex I to those rules.

2. *Applicability of the Light Rules*

While the arrangement of the language is slightly different, paragraphs (a) and (b) of Rule 20 of COLREGS and the U.S. Inland Rules are substantially the same as Rule 1(b) of the 1960 International Rules. Decisions interpreting the earlier rule will therefore presumably govern the interpretation of COLREGS and Inland Rule 20(a) and (b). Rule 20(a) provides that the Sound and Light Rules apply in all weather, and Rule 20 (b) requires the light rules to be complied with from sunset to sunrise. It will be noted that current Rule 20 requires the display of the prescribed lights during periods of restricted visibility encountered between sunrise and sunset, as well as at night.[8] This was a salutary change; the former international rule merely permitted the display of the lights when the visibility was restricted during daylight hours. The only discretionary provision remaining is that the lights *may* also be exhibited "in all other circumstances when it is deemed necessary." COLREGS and Inland Rule 20(a) explicitly forbids the display of any lights from sunset to sunrise that are unauthorized by the rules and might confuse observing mariners.[9]

It is to be noted that the display of the lights required by the rules is in no way diminished by modern reliance on radar and other electronic aids to navigation.

3. *The* Pennsylvania *Rule and the Light Rules*

Because the mandatory running lights and anchor lights have precise meanings, there can be no substitutes for them, and it is not possible to escape liability if it cannot be shown that incorrect lighting could not have caused or contributed to a collision.[10] Improper lights, however, do not excuse fault on

---

7. E.g., while the running lights do not indicate a vessel's course as does ARPA or plotting a radar contact, they do show the general direction in which the observed vessel is proceeding.

8. Rule 20(c) provides that the lights prescribed by the rules ". . . shall . . . also be exhibited from sunrise to sunset in restricted visibility. . . ."

9. Rule 20(b): "[D]uring such times no other lights shall be exhibited, except such lights as cannot be mistaken for the lights specified in these Rules. . . ."

10. "If maritime collisions are to be avoided, knowledge of the character and course of oncoming vessels is indispensable. The light rules embody an elaborate code designed to convey

the part of another vessel.[11] Thus, failure of a vessel to be equipped with or to display the required lights does not relieve another vessel from observing the rules and acting with caution when the first vessel's failure causes uncertainty.[12]

Lights that are lost or destroyed due to accident or weather must be replaced promptly. If a vessel navigates at night a backup system in working order must be provided. Thus, in *The Chester O. Swain*,[13] a vessel was held not excused from the requirement of precise lighting, even at anchor, by a fire on the previous day that had damaged the running lights, since they could have been repaired before the collision.

The *Pennsylvania* Rule has long been applied to failures to be *equipped* with proper anchor lights, if anchored, or running lights, if underway with or without way on, and to failures to display the required lights, if equipped with them. The day shapes indicating vessels not under command, even if underway, and vessels engaged in restrictive functions such as cable laying, towing submerged objects, dredging (whether by stationary dredges or by self-propelled suction dredges underway), conducting diving operations, mine sweeping, and stationing alongside wrecks or over submarine construction, must be displayed during daylight operations, including periods of twilight, and not merely from sunrise to sunset. Vessels engaged in these

---

that information. The extreme blackness of water at night makes any departure from light rules, 'one of the most recklessly unlawful faults a vessel can commit.'" *First National Bank v. Material Service Corp.*, 597 F.2d 1110, 1118, 1980 AMC 817, 826 (7th Cir. 1979), quoting *Bradshaw v. The Virginia*, 176 F.2d 526, 530, 1949 AMC 1580, 1585 (4th Cir. 1949). In this nighttime collision of a motor boat with a barge displaying an improper flashing amber light, the Seventh Circuit held it was error *not* to apply the *Pennsylvania* Rule. See also *Matter of Interstate and Ocean Transp. Co.*, 717 F.2d 752, 1983 AMC 2971 (2d Cir. 1983), where the Second Circuit affirmed a finding of 80 percent fault for a failure to show the white bow light on an unmanned barge and for the tug's failure to shorten the towing hawser to 450 feet; and *Cap't Mark Co. v. The Sea Fever*, 692 F.2d 163, 1983 AMC 2651 (1st Cir. 1982).

11. In *The Samuel H. Crawford*, 6 F.906 (EDNY 1881), the Steamship *Niagara* was proceeding southerly out of New York Harbor, while the Schooner *Samuel H. Crawford* was proceeding inbound. There was a forward house on the schooner and the sidelights were placed on its corners, so that the headsails possibly obstructed the view of the steamer. The court found the sidelights to be improperly located (they were required to be in the rigging) but that this was not causative, while the schooner's failure to exhibit a lighted torch to an approaching vessel, as then required, was causative, and thus the schooner was to blame. The steamer was also found at fault for improper lookout, but this was also not causative because of the presence of the helmsman and one other in the wheelhouse of the steamer who might have noticed the torch if it had been displayed. Both vessels being at fault, the damages were apportioned equally.

12. See *Cleary Bros. v. The Dauntless*, 178 F.2d 72, 1950 AMC 44 (2d Cir. 1949), where an assisting tugboat was also held at fault for displaying "deceptive running lights while at anchor."

13. 76 F.2d 890, 1935 AMC 613 (2d Cir. 1935). Temporary lights were rigged on the vessel, which was anchored in a fairway: one oil lantern at the bow jack-staff and the other on the aft awning spreader, plus four clusters of working lights. Judge Augustus Hand described the anchored vessel's burden: "She had the burden of showing that her makeshift lights could not have been replaced by proper ones, were not confusing to the *Swain* and did not contribute to the collision, and that the accident would have still occurred if her lighting had conformed to law." 76 F.2d at 892, 1935 AMC at 617.

EXAMPLES OF LIGHTS AND SHAPES DESCRIBED IN CHAPTER 7

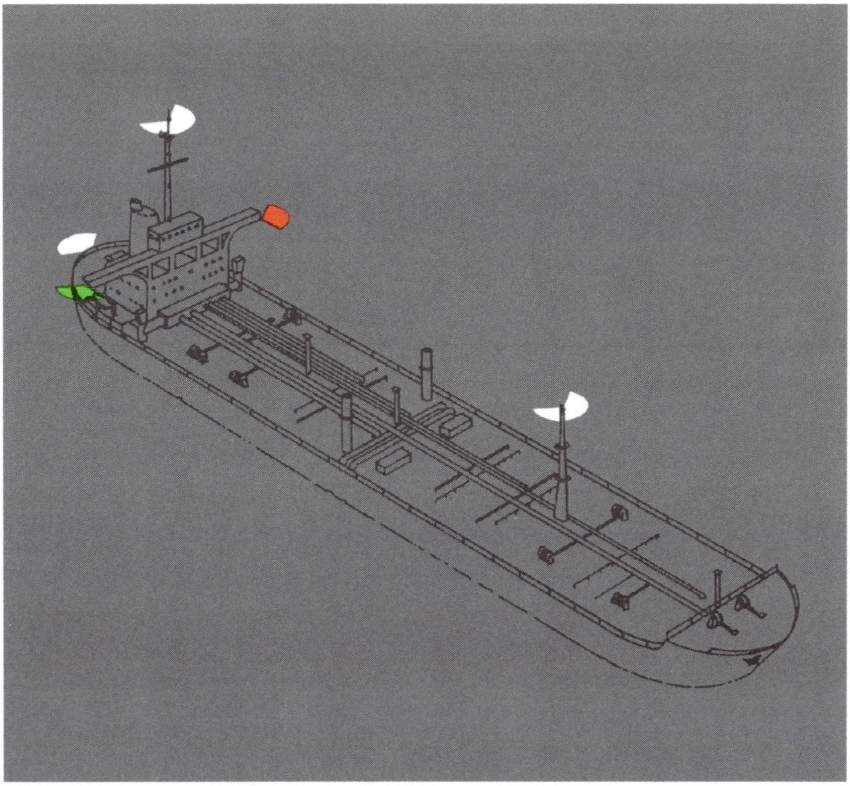

1. Arrangement of lights on a power-driven vessel 50 meters or longer underway (Rule 23(a)(i))

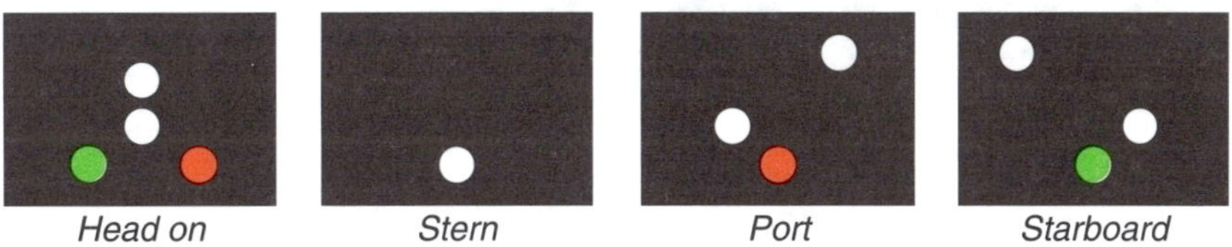

2. Power-driven vessel 50 meters or longer underway (Rule 23(a)(i)

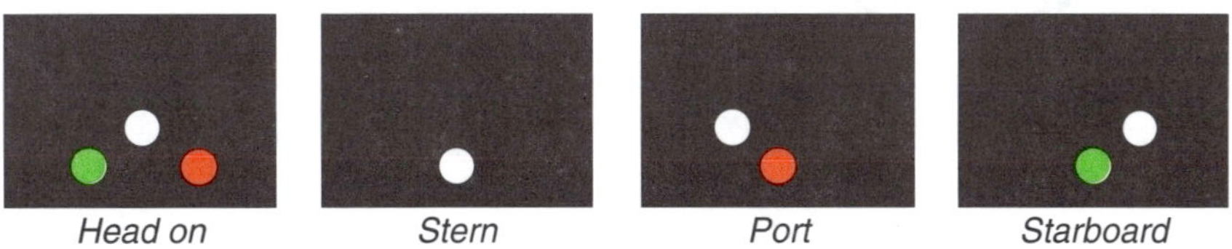

3. Power-driven vessel less than 50 meters long underway (Rule 23(a)(ii))

Head on *Stern* *Port* *Starboard*

4. Power-driven vessel less than 12 meters long underway—under International Rules may be combined in a lantern (Rule 23(c))

Head on *Stern* *Port*

5. Sailing vessel with optional mast lights (Rule 25(a) and (c))

Head on *Stern* *Port* *Day shape Under sail being propelled by machinery*

6. Sailing vessel less than 20 meters long (Rule 25(b))

Head on *Stern* *Port* *Day shape*

7. Vessel at anchor (Rule 30(a))

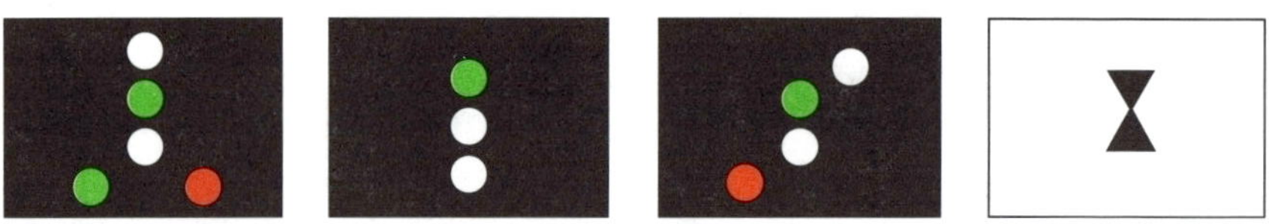

Head on *Stern* *Port* *Day shape*

8. Vessel 50 meters or more in length—trawling—underway—making way (Rule 26(b))

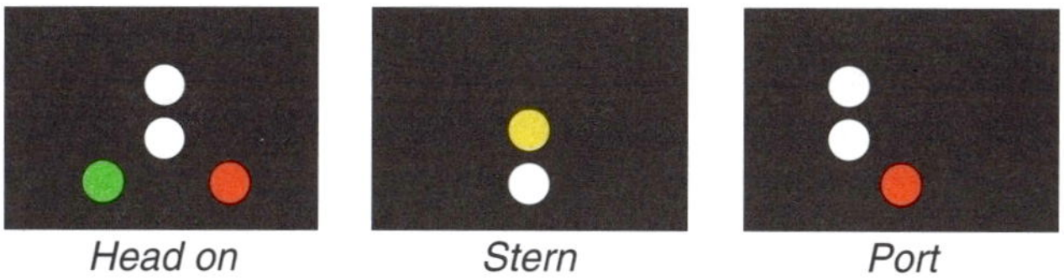

9. Vessel less than 50 meters long towing astern with tow 200 meters or less in length (Rule 24(a))

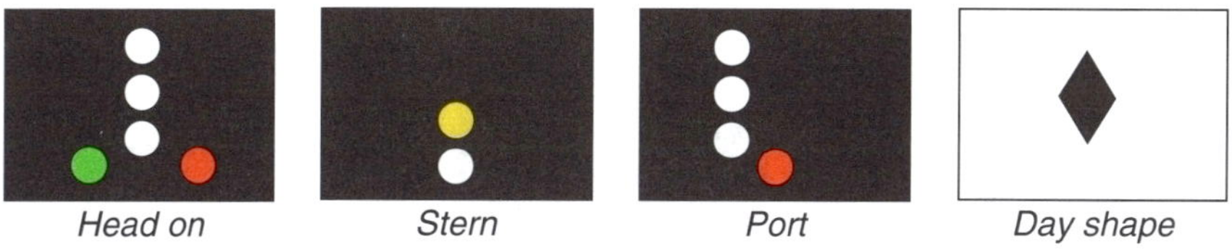

10. Vessel less than 50 meters long towing astern with tow over 200 meters in length (Rule 24(a))

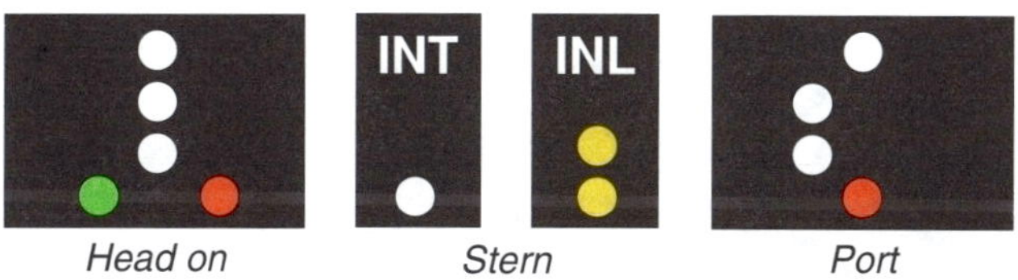

11. Vessel 50 meters or more in length pushing ahead or towing alongside (not part of composite unit) (Rules 24(c) and 23(a)(ii))

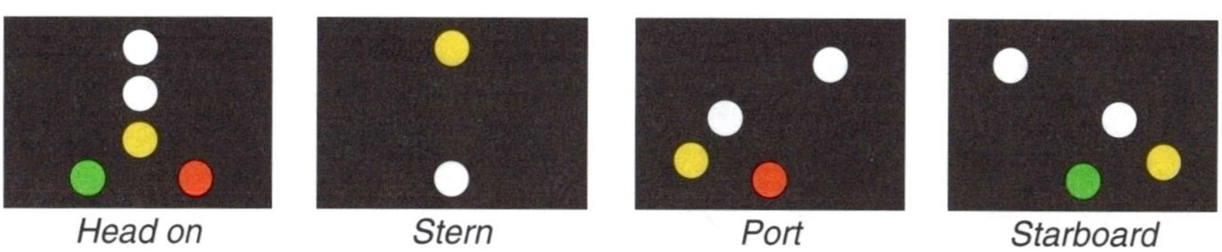

12. Air-cushion vessel in non-displacement mode—yellow light is flashing (Rule 23(b))

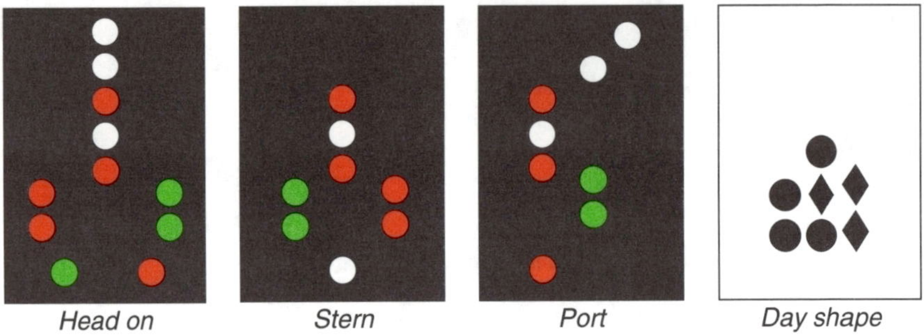

13. Vessel engaged in dredging or underwater operations (Rule 27(d))

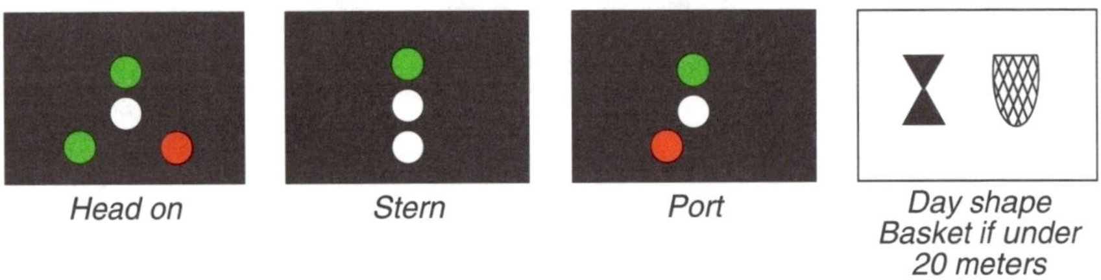

14. Vessel less than 50 meters long engaged in trawling (Rule 26(b))

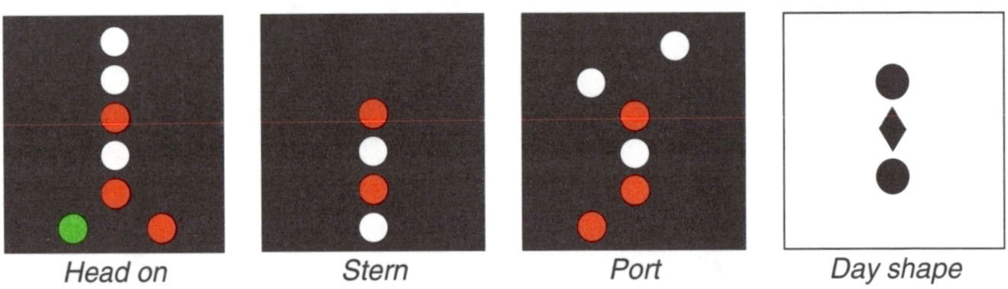

15. Vessel restricted in ability to maneuver, making way
(Rules 27(b) and 23(a)(ii))

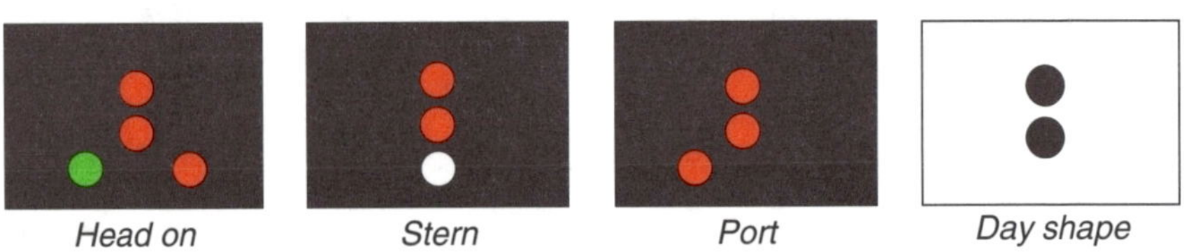

16. Vessel not under command, making way (Rule 27(d))

extraordinary operations often display both the required day shapes *and* lights at all times.

The burden of proof imposed by the U.S. Supreme Court under the *Pennsylvania* Rule[14] is not always impossible to carry, but as we have seen in chapter 2, it is ordinarily extremely difficult to prove that a statutory violation could not have caused or contributed to a collision. An exceptionally clear example of meeting the burden is found in the collision of the Motor Vessel *Dian* with the Tug *Seaspan Monarch,*[15] where a towed barge failed to display a starboard running light, but the *Dian* was approaching the tug and tow from the *port* side, so that she could not have seen the barge's green starboard light if it had been burning. And in *Moran Scow Corp. v. The Boston,*[16] it was held that the failure of a tug to extinguish two towing lights immediately after casting off the tow could not have confused the navigation of a colliding vessel. A simple inference of noncausality may also be drawn where the faults of a moving vessel involve grossly imprudent navigation, while the moored vessel was improperly lighted.

In another instance of exoneration from *Pennsylvania* Rule liability, the court found that a fog was so thick that the navigation lights on a towed barge could not have been seen if they had been burning.[17] An issue of the right to

---

14. *The Pennsylvania,* 86 U.S. 125 (1873). The rule is fully discussed in chapter 2, section A(1)(c).

15. *Hosei Kaiun Shoji Co. v. The Seaspan Monarch,* 1981 AMC 2162 (D Or. 1981).

16. 342 F. Supp. 216, 1972 AMC 2027 (SDNY 1972). Judge Levet found that the observing vessel had made a sharp left turn so that the tug's lights could not mislead or confuse, while lights on the barges were seen in sufficient time to avoid collision.

17. *Self Towing, Inc. v. Brown Marine Service, Inc.,* 651 F. Supp. 187, 1987 AMC 1068 (SD Ala. 1986), aff'd in part, rev'd in part, 837 F.2d 1501 (11th Cir. 1988). The moored vessel failed to display the all-round white light required by COLREGS Rule 30. See also *United States Fire Ins. Co. v. Allied Towing Corp.,* 966 F.2d 820, 1993 AMC 1276 (4th Cir. 1992).

In *In re Shaun Fisheries, Inc.,* 1984 AMC 2650 (D Or. 1983), a fishing vessel with no lookout failed to take action to avoid collision with a tug and barge similarly without a lookout, but being the give-way vessel in a crossing situation and not restricted in its ability to maneuver under COLREGS Rule 18, the absence of the towing day shape on the tug, although one was displayed on the barge, could be ignored. Both vessels were held equally at fault for the look-out failure; the court inferred that the absence of the day shape was irrelevant, since the fishing vessel never saw the tug and barge.

In *Hertz v. Consolidated Fisheries, Inc. The Diana Claire—The Crescent),* 213 F.2d 801, 1954 AMC 1164 (9th Cir. 1954), a fishing vessel's failure to hoist a fishing day shape was held noncontributory in a collision with a motorboat set on automatic pilot without anyone on deck and operating at 8 knots outside the entrance to San Francisco Bay.

In *Lind v. United States,* 156 F.2d 231, 1946 AMC 971 (2d Cir. 1946), a crossing collision at night in wartime, the gray-painted liberty ship *Abner Doubleday,* completely blacked out, with no navigational lights, spotted the trawler *Mary* twenty minutes before collision. Judge Learned Hand described the liberty ship as playing blindman's bluff at 9½ knots, while everyone on the trawler was cleaning fish, with the wheel lashed and the trawling gear out, "running blind" and lighted as brightly as a Christmas tree with every possible light except the lights required under old Rule 9(d) for trawling at night. The district court applied the *Pennsylvania* Rule to both vessels, found both to blame, and divided the damages equally (before *Reliable Transfer),* which would have wiped out the fishing vessel's owner. The Second Circuit, however, reversed and

exoneration from liability where the *Pennsylvania* Rule applies should not be decided on summary judgment, but after a factual hearing.[18]

4. *The "Positive-Negative" Rule in Relation to Lights*

This rule[19] is sometimes involved in cases relating to navigation lights, as it is when the sounding of a whistle signal is in dispute. The consequence of credible testimony that a vessel's lights were properly showing is that other vessels within the visibility range must have seen her, or will be required to explain why they did not.

The positive-negative rule is simply one of logic: the fact that a light was not seen, or that a whistle signal was not heard, does not necessarily mean that the light was not burning or that the signal was not sounded. While the rule does not create a "presumption" under the Federal Rules of Evidence, its place in judicial fact-finding is still significant.

In a fairly recent case, *Granholm v. The TFL Express,*[20] Judge Haight followed the traditional rule and accepted positive evidence that the required lights were lit over negative evidence that they were not, where the testimony concerning the lights was in balance i.e., similarly credible witnesses from each colliding vessel testified at cross purposes.[21] Of course, the court may believe the negative testimony of one witness and reject the positive testi-

---

imposed sole fault on the liberty ship. The court found that the liberty ship could not have been misled by the fishing vessel, as she had in fact plotted the contacts into collision, while the fishing vessel's look-out failure *could not* have contributed, since no lookout could have seen the blacked-out liberty. The analogy to a Christmas tree was also drawn in *Diamond State Telephone Co. v. Atlantic Refining Co.,* 205 F.2d 402, 406, 1953 AMC 1712 (3d Cir. 1953).

18. See *Cliffs-Neddrill Turnkey International v. The Rich Duke,* 947 F.2d 83, 1992 AMC 1 (3d Cir. 1991). Plaintiff's self-propelled oil drilling ship had been anchored 11 to 12 miles off Aruba and very near a heavily trafficked sea lane for thirty-five days. The Notice to Mariners warning of her presence, in the Dutch language, was not understood by the Korean officers of a tanker moving on a northerly course from Maracaibo to Delaware at 14 knots on autopilot. The anchored vessel's lights were not in accordance with COLREGS Rules 27(b)(i) and 30(a), but the lights were overwhelmed by 100 to 150 worklights of strengths of from 500 to 1,000 watts. Applying the presumption of fault against the moving vessel, the trial court granted plaintiff's motion for summary judgment, but the Third Circuit reversed for a factual hearing.

19. Griffin does not call it a "rule." See Griffin 627, where the author states: "The cases which accept affirmative in preference to negative evidence do not, of course, lay down a rule of law or even, in the strict sense, a rule of evidence. They merely emphasize the point that, when the affirmative evidence of a thing is of satisfactory quality, it is not ordinarily overcome by evidence that someone else did not observe the same thing."

20. 576 F. Supp. 435, 1984 AMC 943 (SDNY 1984). See also *Socony-Vacuum Oil Co. Inc. v. Charles C. Smith (The Sachem—The George A. Butler),* 179 F.2d 672, 1950 AMC 445 (5th Cir. 1950).

21. *Sun Oil Co. v. The Georgle,* 245 F. Supp. 537, 1966 AMC 662 (SDNY 1965), aff'd, 369 F.2d 406, 1967 AMC 1689 (2d Cir. 1966); *The Hampton Roads,* 1926 AMC 1510 (D Me. 1926).

mony of another; the rule properly applies only when the positive evidence and the negative evidence are equally credible.[22]

Section B. An Analysis of the Principal Light Rules

1. *Definitions and Visibility Requirements*

COLREGS Rule 21 and Inland Rule 21 (Definitions) are substantially identical, except that Inland Rule 21(b) adds a special provision concerning vessels of less than 12 feet in length, and also adds a paragraph (g), defining a "special flashing light."

The principal definitions contained in Rule 21 are of "masthead light" (a white 225-degree light showing from right ahead to 22.5 degrees abaft the beam on either side); "sidelights" (a green 112.5-degree light showing from right ahead to 22.5 degrees abaft the beam on the starboard side, and a red 112.5-degree light showing from right ahead to 22.5 degrees abaft the beam on the port side); and a "sternlight" (a white 135-degree light showing from right aft 67.5 degrees forward on each side). COLREGS Rule 22 and Inland Rule 22 are identical, except that Inland Rule 22 adds a requirement that a "special flashing light" have a minimum visibility of 2 miles.

Rule 22 provides that in vessels of 50 meters or more in length a masthead light must have a visibility of at least 6 miles, and that sidelights, sternlights, towing lights, and white, red, green, or yellow all-round lights must have a minimum visibility of 3 miles. The rule contains special provisions for vessels of less than 50 meters in length.

Detailed specifications concerning the required lights are contained in Annex I to COLREGS and in Annex I to the Inland Rules, so that a deck officer need commit to memory only the essential information as to the function, position, and predicted course of a vessel whose lights he sights. The visibility requirements for large vessels were increased by 1 mile from 1960 International Rule 2 (from 5 miles to 6 miles), and the number of compass points over which the light must show has been deleted in favor of degrees of arc. The term "masthead light" is used in the figurative sense—it does not mean that every vessel must have a mast; rather, it means that such a light must be raised above obstructions and all other lights. The definition of sternlight resembles that in Rule 10 of the 1960 International Rules, but flexibility in positioning the light is allowed by the addition of the words "as

---

22. *Capt'n Mark Co. v. The Sea Fever,* 692 F.2d 163, 1983 AMC 2651 (1st Cir. 1982).

nearly as practicable at the stern," in order to accommodate the increasing number of vessels with open configurations at the stern.

Annex I (8) to COLREGS replaced the visibility requirement of Rule 1(c)(x) of the 1960 Rules with a formula to determine luminous intensity of light in candelas, considering range of visibility and atmospheric transmissivity. Annex I (Section 84.13) to the Inland Rules is identical.

2. *Lights Required on Power-Driven Vessels Underway*

COLREGS and Inland Rule 23 conveniently brings together the *underway* provisions of 1960 International Rules 2, 7, and 10, but the basic provisions concerning lights on merchant vessels underway have not changed.

COLREGS and Inland Rule 23 prescribes the lights for power-driven vessels underway. Rule 23(a) requires a masthead light forward, a second masthead light abaft of and higher than the forward one (optional for vessels less than 50 meters long), sidelights, and a sternlight. Paragraph (a) of Inland Rule 23 is identical, except that it adds that a vessel less than 20 meters long need not exhibit the forward masthead light forward of amidships, but must exhibit it as far forward as is practicable.

COLREGS Rule 23 provides that an air-cushion vessel (e.g., hovercraft) when operating in the nondisplacement mode must exhibit the lights prescribed in paragraph (a) for power-driven vessels underway, plus an all-round flashing yellow light. Inland Rule 23(b) is identical, except that it adds, "where it can best be seen."

COLREGS Rule 23(c) and Inland Rule 23 (c) are identical: each permits a vessel less than 12 meters long to exhibit an all-round white light and sidelights, in lieu of the lights prescribed in paragraph (a) of the rule.

COLREGS Rule 23(c)(ii) provides that a power-driven vessel of less than 7 meters in length, with a speed not exceeding 7 knots, may, in lieu of the lights prescribed in paragraph (a) of the rule, exhibit an all-round white light, and if possible must also exhibit sidelights. There are no corresponding provisions in Inland Rule 23.

COLREGS Rule 23(c)(iii) provides that the masthead light or all-round white light on a power-driven vessel less than 12 meters long may be displaced from the fore and aft centerline if centerline fitting is not practicable, provided that the sidelights are combined in one lantern carried on the fore and aft centerline or as nearly as practicable on the same fore and aft line as the masthead light or the all-round white light. Again, there are no corresponding provisions in Inland Rule 23.

Inland Rule 23 adds a paragraph (d), which permits a power-driven vessel operating on the Great Lakes to carry an all-round white light in lieu of the second masthead light prescribed in paragraph (a). The light must be carried in the position of a second masthead light, and must have the same visibility.

3. *Towing Operations*[23]

COLREGS and Inland Rule 24(a) requires a power-driven vessel when towing astern to exhibit sidelights, a sternlight, a towing light in a vertical line above the sternlight and, instead of the light prescribed either in Rule 23(a)(i) or (a)(ii), two masthead lights in a vertical line. If the length of the tow exceeds 200 meters, the towing vessel must exhibit three such lights in a vertical line, and a diamond shape where it can best be seen. Under paragraph (b), when a pushing vessel and a vessel being pushed ahead are rigidly connected in a composite unit they are regarded as a power-driven vessel and must exhibit the lights prescribed for such a vessel in Rule 23.

COLREGS Rule 24(c) requires a power-driven vessel towing alongside or pushing (except in the case of a composite unit) to exhibit sidelights, a sternlight, and instead of the masthead lights prescribed in Rule 23(a)(i) or (a)(ii), two masthead lights in a vertical line. Inland Rule 24(a) requires two (yellow) towing lights in a vertical line, instead of the sternlight required by COLREGS Rule 24(c). Otherwise the provisions of paragraph (c) of both rules are the same.

COLREGS and Inland Rule 24(d) requires a power-driven vessel covered by Rule 24(a) or (c) to comply with Rule 23(a)(ii), i.e., to exhibit a second masthead light if she is 50 or more meters in length.

Under COLREGS Rule 24(g), inconspicuous, partly submerged vessels, or objects being towed must exhibit an all-round white light at each end, except that a dracone (described in *Oxford Encyclopedic Dictionary* [1991] as "a large flexible container for liquids, towed on the surface of the sea") is not required to exhibit a light at or near its forward end. If the vessel or object is 25 or more meters in length, two additional all-round white lights at the extremities of its breadth are required, and if it exceeds 100 meters in breadth, additional all-round white lights placed so that the distance between the lights does not exceed 100 meters. The towed vessel or object must also exhibit a diamond shape at or near its aftermost extremity, and if the tow's length exceeds 200 meters, an additional diamond shape forward. Inland Rule 24(g) is similar, but not identical to COLREGS Rule 24(g). A vessel or object being towed, other than one covered by Rule 24(g), is required by COLREGS and Inland Rule 24(d) to exhibit sidelights, a sternlight, and if the tow exceeds 200 meters in length, a diamond shape.

Rule 24(f)(i) of COLREGS and the Inland Rules requires a vessel being pushed ahead, not part of a composite unit, to exhibit sidelights at the forward end. The Inland Rule also requires a special flashing (yellow) light at the forward end.

Rule 24(f)(ii) requires a vessel being towed alongside to exhibit sidelights at the forward end and a sternlight.

---

23. For a discussion of the law of towage in relation to collision, see chapter 10.

COLREGS Rule 24(h) and Inland Rule 24(h) are substantially the same; both provide that where it is impracticable for a tow to exhibit the lights prescribed by Rule 24(e) or (g), all possible measures must be taken to light the tow at least to indicate its presence.

Inland Rule 24(i), applicable on the Mississippi (except below the Huey P. Long Bridge at New Orleans) and on waters specified by the Secretary of Transportation, requires a vessel ahead or alongside, except as Rule 24(b) applies, to exhibit sidelights and two (yellow) towing lights in a vertical line.

COLREGS Rule 24(i) and Inland Rule 24(j) are substantially identical. Under these paragraphs emergency tows undertaken by a vessel not normally engaged in towing are exempted from the towing lights requirements of COLREGS Rule 24(a) and (c) and in accordance with Rule 36 they must use all possible measures to indicate the relationship between the towing vessel and the vessel in need of assistance, as authorized by Rule 36. That rule authorizes a vessel to attract attention by light and sound signals that cannot be mistaken for any signal elsewhere authorized in the rules, or by directing the beam of her searchlight in the direction of the danger, in such a way as not to embarrass any vessel.[24] While COLREGS Rule 24 imposes distinct obligations for tugs and their tows, nevertheless, under the rule of *The Eugene F. Moran,*[25] fault liability may be imposed on both tug and tow when the required lights are not shown.

---

24. Cf. *Triangle Cement Co. v. Towboat Cincinnati,* 393 F.2d 936, 1968 AMC 892 (2d Cir. 1968). In a business decision rather than an emergency, a tug took an unmanned barge without the required lights under tow at night in the East River, New York Harbor, where collision with a downbound vessel soon occurred. A holding of liability of tug and barge (under the former rules) was affirmed, the barge for its absence of lights and the tug for attempting the tow with a barge unseaworthy as to lights. The Second Circuit held that the tug should have refused the tow.

25. 212 U.S. 466, 476 (1909). In the cited case the Tug *Matthews* was towing a railroad carfloat upriver, while a Moran tug was towing two mud scows (the *15D* and the *18D*) owned by the Henry Dubois Sons Co. ("Dubois") downriver. Neither mud scow was displaying the required lights. Both tugs and both mud scows were found at fault for a collision between the mud scow *15D* and the carfloat. The carfloat was not found at fault. The railroad proceeded *in rem* against both tugs and both mud scows in one case, while in a second case Dubois, as owner of the mud scow *15D,* proceeded *in rem* against both tugs. In the first case the railroad, as owner of the carfloat, was held entitled to recover damages equally from all four vessels. In the second case recovery for the damaged mud scow was assessed against both tugs *and* both mud scows, so that Dubois, as owner of both mud scows, had to bear half the total damages of the *15D* and of the carfloat. It was this result which was challenged in the Supreme Court, but the challenge was rejected.

Justice Holmes's opinion briefly mentioned the policy behind *in rem* proceedings (the convenient security furnished thereby), noting the similarity to *respondeat superior* in tort law. Justice Holmes then instructed us, "But after all a fiction is not a satisfactory ground for taking one man's property to satisfy another man's wrong, and it should not be extended." 212 U.S. 474. He then found a "difference in degree" between "mismanagement of the offending vessel" and "mismanagement of another vessel to which the immediate but innocent instrument of harm is

4. *Sailing Vessels and Oar-Propelled Vessels*

COLREGS Rule 25 has been drawn from Rules 5(a) and 7(c) of the 1960 International Rules. Inland Rule 25 is identical, except that Inland Rule 25(e), which requires a vessel proceeding under both sail and machinery to exhibit a conical shape, apex downward, makes the exhibition of such a shape optional for vessels under 12 meters in length.

COLREGS and Inland Rule 25(a) requires a sailing vessel underway to exhibit sidelights and a sternlight, but an amendment to COLREGS Rule 25(b) (followed in Inland Rule 25[b]) permits a combination lantern with sidelights and sternlight in one fixture, for vessels less than 20 meters long, to be carried at or near the top of the mast, "where it can best be seen." (It had previously been authorized only for vessels less than 12 meters long.) Sailing vessels of *less* than seven meters in length have the option of using an electric torch or lighted lantern with a white light, "which shall be exhibited in sufficient time to prevent collision." (Rule 25[d][i].) Such objects must be "ready at hand." The reason for such relaxation of the rules is the inability of such small craft to provide the power for sidelights and a sternlight, but such vessels ought not to be navigating at night under conditions other than dire emergency.[26] A similar provision for an electric torch or a lantern with a white light governs vessels under oars, but such vessels are scarcely likely to be moving with the speed of modern sailboats. (Rule 25[d][ii].)

5. *Fishing Vessels*

Under COLREGS and Inland Rule 3(d), a "vessel engaged in fishing" is any vessel fishing with nets, lines, trawls, or other fishing apparatus which restricts maneuverability, but does not include a vessel fishing with a trolling line or other fishing apparatus which does not restrict maneuverability. A trolling line moves casually through the water, usually with bait or a lure,

---

attached." Id. Thus, the common ownership of two of the offending mud scows did not affect the outcome.

Note the Supreme Court's recent choice of the pro rata share principle when one or more joint and several tort-feasors settle before a trial, which then proceeds against the nonsettling tort-feasors. See *McDermott, Inc. v. Amclyde,* 511 U.S. 202, 1994 AMC 1521 (1994).

26. *Linehan v. United States Lines,* 417 F. Supp. 678, 1979 AMC 1534 (D Del. 1976), involving a 1972 collision governed by former Rules 2 and 5, between an improperly lighted sailing vessel (the Yacht *Lotus*) and the S.S. *American Legend.* The yacht's engines were causing problems as the vessel proceeded down the Delaware River at night, and the yacht's master decided to switch from power to sail, thereby having to tack back and forth across the channel while the low battery charge and inoperable engines did not provide enough power to light the yacht's navigational lights to the required intensity. Thus, the intricate maneuvers of the yacht were invisible to the eye in the busy channel. The district court found the yacht 20 percent at fault and the merchant vessel 80 percent at fault. On appeal this was reversed and remanded, 559 F.2d 1208, 1979 AMC 1557 (3d Cir. 1977), and on remand the trial court changed the assessment to 30 percent against the yacht and 70 percent against the merchant vessel. 1979 AMC 1565 (D Del. 1977).

trailing behind a moving vessel. Trawls are large nets, bag-shaped, dragged along the ocean bottom, while driftnets or seines are traps used to snare swimming schools of fish. Lines with hooks and sinkers may be used with bait along the bottom or extending from any part of the ship, or from poles.

The fishing lights are required of all vessels actually engaged in fishing, regardless of size. (COLREGS and Inland Rule 26.) However, the day shape for a fishing vessel of less than 20 meters may be a basket, while all other fishing vessels must use a double cone, with the apex of each cone joined. Annex II to COLREGS and Annex II to the Inland Rules contain special provisions for additional lights when fishing vessels are operating in close proximity, as they often do when pursuing large schools of fish; the annexes distinguish between trawlers and purse seiners. Under COLREGS Rule 1(c), governments may make special rules for fishing fleet operations. Inland Rule 1(c) permits the Secretary of the (U.S.) Navy to do the same.

The expression "engaged in fishing" is not intended to be precisely limited to the period when fish are being caught. Rather, the shooting out and hauling in of nets and other apparatus are within the coverage of the rules. But as soon as the fishing vessel has terminated fishing operations, the lights required under COLREGS Rule 23 for ordinary vessels of similar size must be used.

While fishing, fishing vessels that are severely restricted in their ability to maneuver will be protected by Rule 18(a)(iii). Nevertheless, under Rule 18(c), fishing vessels must, so far as possible, keep out of the way of vessels not under command and vessels restricted in their ability to maneuver.[27]

The drafters of COLREGS Rule 26 drew upon 1960 International Rule 9 for most of its provisions. However, 1960 Rule 9(f) permitted fishing vessels to show a flare-up light and working lights to attract the attention of approaching vessels. While the flare-up light is no longer specifically provided for in COLREGS and Inland Rule 26, COLREGS and Inland Rule 36 permits a light that cannot be mistaken for any other authorized light. However, COLREGS Rule 36 ambiguously provides that "high intensity intermittent or revolving lights, such as strobe lights, shall be avoided." This 1981 amendment language, which is not contained in Inland Rule 36, seeks to have it both ways, using the mandatory *"shall,"* followed by the nonmandatory *"avoided"* instead of *"forbidden."* Nevertheless, COLREGS and Inland Rule 36 does permit the use of a searchlight beam in the direction of dangers such as trawls, nets, or lines. Further, in COLREGS and Inland Rule 30(c) working

---

27. In *Duque and Duarte, Inc. v. Geophysical Services, Inc.*, 401 F.2d 496, 1968 AMC 2284 (5th Cir. 1968), an oceanographic seismic research vessel, showing a proper day shape, was towing, underwater, a seismic cable some 7,800 feet long, when its tow was disrupted and damaged by a shrimp trawler seeking to be protected under former Rule 26 (COLREGS Rule 18), but the court refused to exonerate the fishing vessel because of the priority afforded to the research vessel by her signals and right of way.

lights may be used to illuminate the deck when a fishing vessel is anchored, and must be used if the vessel is 100 meters or more in length.

6. Vessels Not under Command; Vessels Restricted in Maneuverability

COLREGS Rule 27 contains provisions taken from 1960 International Rule 4, but it has changed the color of the shapes to black from red and white. There was no similar Inland Rule. COLREGS and Inland Rule 3(f) and 3(g) provide definitions of "vessel not under command"[28] and "vessel restricted in her ability to maneuver."[29] All vessels within the Rule 3(g) definition of vessels restricted in their ability to maneuver, except vessels engaged in mine-clearance operations, are included within the coverage of COLREGS and Inland Rule 27(b). A 1981 amendment added paragraph (f) to COLREGS Rule 27, specially dealing with mine clearance. Inland Rule 27 contains an identical paragraph. A government may, however, determine that a minesweeper is a vessel of special construction under COLREGS Rule 1(e), thereby authorizing those lights that the government determines to be in the closest possible compliance with COLREGS in respect of that vessel. Inland Rule 1(e) gives the (U.S.) Secretary of the Navy similar authority.

COLREGS Rule 27 and Inland Rule 27 are substantially identical. Rule 27(a) requires a vessel not under command to exhibit two all-round red lights in a vertical line and two balls or similar shapes in a vertical line, the lights and balls to be located where they can best be seen. When making way through the water the vessel must also exhibit sidelights and a sternlight.

Rule 27(b) provides that a vessel restricted in her ability to maneuver, except one engaged in mine-clearance operations, must exhibit (i) three all-round lights in a vertical line, the highest and lowest red and the middle one white; (ii) three shapes in a vertical line, the highest and lowest balls and the middle one a diamond; (iii) additionally, when making way through the water, a "masthead light or lights" ("masthead lights" in the Inland Rule), sidelights, and a sternlight. All such lights and shapes must be exhibited where they can best be seen.

Rule 27(b)(iv) provides that when at anchor a vessel restricted in her ability to maneuver, other than one engaged in mine-clearance, must, in addition to the lights and shapes prescribed in paragraphs (i) and (ii), supra, exhibit the lights and shapes prescribed in Rule 30, infra.

Rule 27(d) requires a vessel engaged in dredging or underwater operations, when restricted in her ability to maneuver, to exhibit, in addition to the lights required by Rule 27(b)(i), (ii), and (iii), two all-round red lights or two balls in a vertical line to indicate the side on which the obstruction exists,

---

28. "... [A] vessel which through some exceptional circumstance is unable to maneuver as required by these Rules and is therefore unable to keep out of the way of another vessel."

29. "... [A] vessel which from the nature of her work is restricted in her ability to maneuver as required by these Rules and is therefore unable to keep out of the way of another vessel."

and two similar green lights to indicate the side on which another vessel may pass. When at anchor she must exhibit the lights and shapes prescribed in Rule 27(d), instead of the lights and shapes prescribed in Rule 30.

Paragraphs (e) and (f) of Rule 27 contain special provisions for vessels engaged in diving and mine-clearance operations. Paragraph (g) exempts vessels of less than 12 meters in length from the requirements of the rule. Paragraph (h) warns that the signals are not signals of vessels in distress and requiring assistance; those signals are contained in Annex IV to COLREGS and in Annex IV to the Inland Rules.

7. *Vessels Constrained by Their Draft*

COLREGS Rule 28 provides that a vessel constrained by her draft *may*, in addition to the lights prescribed for power-driven vessels underway, exhibit where they can best be seen, three all-round red lights in a vertical line, or a cylinder. There is no Inland Rule 28, nor is there any Inland Rule providing for any special treatment of vessels constrained by their draft. COLREGS Rule 18(d), on the other hand, requires that if the circumstances admit, any vessel, other than one not under command or restricted in her ability to maneuver, must avoid impeding the safe passage of a vessel constrained by her draft and must exhibit the signals required by Rule 28. There is no comparable provision in the Inland Rules.

COLREGS Rule 3(h) defines the term"vessel constrained by her draft" as "a power-driven vessel which, because of her draft in relation to the available depth and width of navigable water is severely restricted in her ability to deviate from the course she is following." Since the Inland Rules give no special consideration to vessels constrained by their draft, there is no definition of the term in Inland Rule 3.

In discussing the lights and shape referred to in COLREGS Rule 28, Farwell states:

> The signal [i.e., the three red lights or a cylinder specified in the Rule] does not give right-of-way to the constrained vessel, but [COLREGS Rule] 18(d) directs other vessels to avoid impeding her. There have been complaints voiced that large ships are displaying these lights in areas where there are no constraints caused by depth of water or sea room, obviously hoping that other vessels will keep clear of them. In the event of a collision it is certain that the courts would look closely at the reasons why the three red lights were displayed.[30]

30. See *Farwell's Rules of the Nautical Road* 58 (7th ed.) by R. A. Smith.

8. Pilot Vessels

COLREGS and Inland Rule 29 are substantially identical. The rule requires vessels engaged on pilotage duty to exhibit, at or near the masthead, two all-round lights in a vertical line, the upper white and the lower red. When underway she must also display sidelights. When at anchor she must display the anchor lights and shapes prescribed in Rule 30, infra, in addition to the white and red lights. When not on pilotage duty a pilot vessel must exhibit the lights and shapes prescribed for a vessel of her length.

COLREGS Rule 29 maintains the content of 1960 Rule 8(b), but the obsolete provisions concerning sailing pilot vessels have been deleted, and the use of flare-up lights (at 10-minute intervals) to attract the attention of oncoming vessels is no longer specified. As we have seen, however, while COLREGS Rule 36 (Signals to Attract Attention) permits a light that cannot be mistaken for any other authorized light, it ambiguously states that, "high intensity intermittent or revolving lights, such as strobe lights, shall be avoided." It remains to be seen whether pilot vessels will cease to be the target of oncoming vessels as they have so often been in the past.

9. Anchored Vessels

COLREGS Rule 30 preserves the contents of 1960 International Rule 11, adding special provisions for small vessels. Thus, vessels less than 7 meters long, when anchored otherwise than in or near a narrow channel, fairway, anchorage, or where other vessels normally navigate, and grounded vessels less than 12 meters long, need not exhibit anchor lights.

COLREGS Rule 30 and Inland Rule 30 are identical, except that Inland Rule 30 contains a paragraph (g), providing that vessels less than 20 meters long, when anchored in a special anchorage area designated by the Secretary of Transportation, are not required to exhibit anchor lights.

Rule 30(b) permits a vessel less than 50 meters long to exhibit one all-round white light. Under Rule 30(a), a larger vessel must display an all-round white light or a ball in the fore part, and at a lower level, at or near the stern, a second all-round white light. Rule 30(c) requires a vessel of 100 or more meters in length also to use available working or equivalent lights to illuminate her decks. (Smaller vessels may, but are not required to, do the same.) This should improve the operational safety of those working the ship and highlights the vessel's status as anchored. The working lights must of course be extinguished as soon as the vessel is underway.

Rule 30(d) requires a grounded vessel to display the lights specified in Rule 30(a) or (b) and, if practicable, two all-round red lights in a vertical line and three balls in a vertical line.

The crucial distinction in collision law and in respect of a carrier's liability to shippers under the concept of due diligence "before and at the beginning of the voyage" is whether the vessel is underway or still anchored.[31] For generations seamen have used the expression "breaking ground" to indicate the moment that the anchor is no longer holding the ship to the bottom, or that lines are no longer holding her fast to a pier or other extension of the shore. It is considered that "breaking ground" is the moment when the ship is in fact underway and no longer anchored or moored, even though the entire process of weighing anchor can be lengthy, as the master may order engines and rudder to be used along with the anchor windlass in heaving in the anchor. American courts have been very severe in the assessment of fault against vessels anchored with improper lights.[32]

10. Seaplanes

COLREGS made no changes in the earlier rules governing seaplanes. Rule 31 simply provides that when it is impracticable for a seaplane to exhibit the lights required by Part C, she must exhibit lights and shapes as closely similar in characteristics as possible. Inland Rule 31 is identical.

31. In *Director General, India Supply Mission v. The Janet Quinn,* 335 F. Supp. 1329, 1972 AMC 1227 (SDNY 1971), an anchored vessel (the *Janet Quinn*) was held at fault for getting underway without lowering the day shape (an anchor ball) in the Bay of Suez. The vessel, being the give-way vessel, failed to give way to the hold-on vessel, resulting in a collision with the *Forest Lake.* The New York court dealt with subsidiary issues of general average and cargo damage, but the collision action between the vessels had been tried in London.

The distinction between being underway with way on and being underway with no way on continues to be crucial in determining the proper lights and shapes to be displayed. In *Savore v. Apache Towing Co.,* 282 F. Supp. 876, 1968 AMC 951 (ED La. 1968), a towed barge grounded on the bank of a narrow channel and its tug stood by in the channel with its engines running to keep the barge off the bank while displaying the lights for a vessel underway with tow under the 1960 Rules. The tug's lights were held to be correct.

32. See, e.g., *Davis v. Superior Oil Co.,* 510 F. Supp. 1162, 1981 AMC 2282 (ED La. 1981), where an insufficiently manned maneuvering crew boat with inoperable radar, proceeding at a 20-knot excessive speed, was held 30 percent at fault for a collision with an anchored trawler, but the trawler was held 70 percent at fault for displaying a green light atop the mast and white lights fore and aft. See, e.g., *Gaspar v. United States,* 460 F. Supp. 656, 1979 AMC 2232 (D Mass. 1978), where the United States was held in sole fault for a collision with a moving vessel, where the Coast Guard anchored its vessel in a navigable channel with improper anchor lights.

CHAPTER EIGHT

INTERNATIONAL AND INLAND RULES: PART D—SOUND AND LIGHT SIGNALS

Section A. Introduction

1. *Historical Background*

The worldwide phenomenon of fog is the most likely reason for the first use of vessel sound signals, despite the widely believed uncertainty of determining the direction from which a sound heard in fog has come.[1] Information concerning changes in a vessel's direction, conveyed by quick and efficient sound signals in the days before radar, very soon became a second reason for the use of such signals.

The sounding of fog signals by U.S. flag vessels has been required by statute at least since enactment of the Act of April 29, 1864,[2] the provisions of which were similar to the regulations adopted by the United Kingdom and France in 1863. Maneuvering signals were introduced in the International Rules of 1885, which applied to "all public and private vessels of the United States upon the high seas and in all coastal waters of the United States." The 1885 Rules[3] provided:

> In taking any course authorized or required by these regulations, a steamship underway may indicate that course to any other ship which she has in sight by the following signals on her steamwhistle, namely:

---

1. See R. Marsden, *Collisions at Sea,* 49–50 n. 64 (11th ed.) (hereinafter "Marsden"). The Supreme Court mentioned the problem of directional uncertainty in fog in *The Umbria,* 166 U.S. 404, 408 (1897). Judicial incredulity has been aroused when the excuse of "acoustic opacity" or uncertain direction of sound is accompanied by evidence of absent or defective look-out. See *The Leland,* 19 F.771 (ND Ill. 1884). See also *The City of New York,* 147 U.S. 72, 84–85 (1893), a sole-fault collision case where the Court said, "There is no such certainty of the exact position of a horn blown in a fog as will justify a steamer in speculating upon the probability of avoiding it by a change of the helm, without taking the additional precaution of stopping until its location is definitely ascertained." See also J. Griffin, *The American Law of Collision,* 320–32 (hereinafter "Griffin"), where the question of whether or not fog actually deadens and dissipates sound is discussed.

2. Ch. 69, art. 10, 13 Stat. 60: "Whenever there is a fog, whether by day or night, the fog signals described below shall be carried and used, and shall be sounded at least every five minutes, viz.: (a) Steamships underway shall use a steam whistle placed before the funnel, not less than eight feet from the deck. (b) Sailing ships underway shall use a fog-horn. (c) Steamships and sailing-ships when not underway shall use a bell."

3. Act of Mar. 3, 1885, ch. 354, art. 19, 23 Stat. 441.

> One short blast to mean "I am directing my course to starboard." Two short blasts to mean "I am directing my course to port." Three short blasts to mean "I am going full speed astern." The use of these signals is optional, but if they are used, the course of the ship must be in accordance with the signal made.

By the Act of August 19, 1890,[4] the permissive expression "may indicate" in the 1885 Rules was replaced by the mandatory "shall indicate." The introductory phrase was changed to read, "When vessels are in sight of one another, a steam vessel underway, in taking any course authorized or required by these rules, shall indicate that course by the following signals on her whistle or siren." The signals remained the same as in 1885. No change was made in 1948 or 1960. The only change made by COLREGS was the use of the term "altering my course" in place of "directing my course," the term used in the earlier rules.

2. *Definitions*

COLREGS defines "whistle" as any sound-signalling appliance capable of producing the prescribed blasts which complies with the specifications in Annex III to COLREGS. Inland Rule 32 is identical and refers to Annex III to those rules. The same rule defines "short blast" as one of about one second's duration, and "prolonged blast" as one of from four to six seconds' duration. The COLREGS and current U.S. Inland Rules definitions of "short blast" and "prolonged blast" are the same as in the 1960 International Rules and the earlier Inland Rules. However, the definition of "whistle" in Rule 32(a) of COLREGS and the current Inland Rules is new. The change was made in order to bring the definition into accord with the technical requirements of Annex III to COLREGS and Annex III to the Inland Rules.

3. *Equipment for Sound and Light Signals*

COLREGS and U.S. Inland Rule 33 provides that a vessel of 12 meters or more in length must have a whistle and a bell and one of 100 meters or more in length must, in addition, have a gong, the tone and sound of which cannot be confused with that of the bell. The bell or gong, or both, may be replaced by other equipment having the same respective sound characteristics, provided that manual sounding of the prescribed signals must always be possible. A vessel less than 12 meters long is not obliged to carry these sound-signalling appliances, but if she does not, she must have some other means of making an efficient sound signal.

COLREGS and the current Inland Rules put an end to the traditional "foghorn," except that Annex IV to COLREGS and Annex IV to the Inland

4. Ch. 802, art. 28.

Rules include among the signals to be used as distress signals "a continuous sounding with any fog signalling device." The rules for sound signals by vessels underway speak only of "whistles," and make no reference to any other sound sources, such as gongs, sirens, drums, guns, or cymbals. Note, however, that under COLREGS Rule 35(g) and Inland Rule 35(f), the bell and gong are retained for vessels anchored or grounded in fog. As with the navigational lights, the technical requirements have been removed from the rules and are now found in COLREGS Annex III and Inland Rules Annex III, which dictate fundamental frequency, range of audibility, intensity, directional properties, and positioning of the whistle.

As in the case of required lights, substitutes for the required sound apparatus are not permissible. Judicial hostility to substitutes can be found as early as the case that gave us the *Pennsylvania* Rule, where a sailing vessel under way in heavy fog was held in contributory fault for sounding a bell instead of the foghorn then required.[5]

Section B. Maneuvering Signals

1. *Under COLREGS : The Rudder Change Concept*

COLREGS Rule 34 provides that a power-driven vessel underway, when in sight of another, must indicate her maneuvers by sounding one short blast to mean "I am altering my course to starboard," two short blasts to mean "I am altering my course to port," and three short blasts to mean "I am operating astern propulsion." The whistle signals may be supplemented by light signals, repeated as appropriate, while the maneuver is being carried out. The light signals have the same meaning as the corresponding whistle signals, i.e., one flash means "I am altering my course to starboard," and two flashes means "I am altering my course to port." The duration of each flash must be about one second, the interval between flashes about one second, and the interval between successive signals at least ten seconds.

The light used for these signals, if fitted, must be an all-round white light, visible at a minimum range of 5 miles, and must comply with the provisions of Annex I to COLREGS and Annex I to the Inland Rules.

Under COLREGS Rule 34(c), when in sight of one another in a narrow channel or fairway, a vessel intending to overtake another must, in compliance with Rule 9(e)(i), indicate her intention by sounding on her whistle, two prolonged blasts followed by one short blast, meaning "I intend to overtake you on your starboard side," or two prolonged blasts followed by two short blasts, meaning "I intend to overtake you on your port side." If she

5. *The Pennsylvania,* 82 U.S. 125 (1873). For a discussion of the *Pennsylvania* Rule, see chapter 2. Concerning navigational lights, cf. chapter 7, notes 10–13.

agrees to the proposal, the vessel about to be overtaken, when acting in accordance with Rule 9(e)(i), must indicate her agreement by sounding on her whistle one prolonged, one short, one prolonged, and one short blast, in that order, whether the proposal was to pass on the starboard side or on the port side. If from any cause either vessel fails to understand the intentions or actions of the other, or is in doubt as to whether sufficient action is being taken by the other to avoid collision, the vessel in doubt must immediately indicate such doubt by giving at least five short and rapid blasts on the whistle. The signal may be supplemented by a light signal of at least five short and rapid flashes.

With reference to COLREGS Rule 34(a), the present progressive form of the verb—"I am altering"—can be reproduced in most modern languages. It means that as the whistle signal is given, the steering wheel and therefore the rudder are being turned, so that the vessel's heading is being changed to starboard or to port, as the case may be. Thus, under COLREGS, in meeting situations no whistle signal is sounded by either vessel unless she is obliged to make a change in heading. (See chapter 5, section D, supra.) Similarly, in crossing situations, where no change in heading by the hold-on vessel is ordinarily required, that vessel sounds no signal unless and until she is obliged to take avoiding action. (See chapter 5, section E, supra.) In overtaking situations, unless a change of heading by one or both of the vessels is required to permit a safe passing, neither vessel sounds a signal. (See chapter 5, section C, supra.)

2. *Under the U.S. Inland Rules: The Contractual Concept*

U.S. Inland Rule 34 provides that when power-driven vessels in sight of one another are meeting or crossing at a distance within half a mile of each other, each vessel underway, when maneuvering as authorized or required by the rules, must sound one short blast, meaning "I intend to leave you on my port side," or two short blasts, meaning "I intend to leave you on my starboard side," or three short blasts, meaning "I am operating astern propulsion."

A power-driven vessel hearing a one or two-blast signal from another must, if in agreement, sound the same whistle signal and take the steps necessary to effect a safe passing. But if, however, from any cause, the vessel hearing the first signal doubts the safety of the proposed maneuver, she must sound a danger signal and each vessel must take appropriate precautionary action until a safe passing agreement is reached. The whistle signals may be supplemented by light signals, one flash meaning "I intend to leave you on my port side," two flashes meaning "I intend to leave you on my starboard side," and three flashes meaning "I am operating astern propulsion." The light used must be an all-round white or yellow light, visible for at least 2 miles, synchronized with the whistle, and in compliance with the provisions of Annex I to each set of rules.

When in sight of one another, a power-driven vessel intending to overtake another power-driven vessel must indicate her intention by one short blast, meaning "I intend to overtake you on your starboard side," or two short blasts, meaning "I intend to overtake you on your port side." If she agrees, the power-driven vessel about to be overtaken must sound a similar sound signal. If in doubt she must sound a danger signal.

Rule 34(h) provides that if an agreement is reached between vessels in a meeting, crossing, or overtaking situation by using the radiotelephone prescribed by the Bridge-to-Bridge Radiotelephone Act,[6] the vessels are not obliged to sound the whistle signals prescribed by the rules, but may do so. If agreement is not reached, whistle signals must be exchanged in a timely manner.

It will be seen that under the Inland Rules concept, the signals of one and two short blasts are not "rudder" or "turning" signals, but signals of intention, i.e., of the manner in which vessels approaching on head-on, overtaking, or crossing courses intend to pass each other. Cross-signals must *never* be sounded, i.e., a signal of one short blast must never be answered with a two-blast signal, or a two-blast signal with a one-blast signal. But once a proposal is rejected by the sounding of a danger signal, either vessel may propose another method of passing.

For a century the "rudder" or "turning" concept has contrasted and conflicted with the contractual concept and created confusion in areas where inland and international waters meet. The difference between these two concepts is the most significant difference between COLREGS and the current Inland Rules. Some lessening of the conflict between the two concepts has occurred with the adoption of COLREGS Rule 34(c). As noted in chapter 4, section C, under COLREGS Rule 9(e)(i), in a narrow channel, when vessels are in sight of one another and an overtaking can take place only if the vessel to be overtaken has to take action to permit safe passing, the overtaking vessel must indicate her intention by sounding the signal prescribed in COLREGS Rule 34(c)(i). That signal is two prolonged blasts followed by one short blast if the proposal is to overtake on the starboard side of the vessel ahead, or two prolonged blasts followed by two short blasts if it is to overtake on the port side. If the vessel to be overtaken consents, she must reply with a signal of one prolonged, one short, one prolonged, and one short blast, in that order, whether the proposal was to pass on the port side or on the starboard side. If either vessel fails to understand the other's intentions or actions, or is in doubt as to whether the other is taking sufficient action to avoid collision, the vessel in doubt must indicate such doubt by sounding at least five short and rapid blasts on the whistle. This may be supplemented by a light signal of at least five short and rapid flashes.

6. 85 Stat. 165; 33 U.S.C. § 1207.

Another instance of the use of sound signals to indicate agreement under both sets of rules is to be found in COLREGS and Inland Rule 34(e), which requires a vessel nearing a bend or an area of a channel or fairway where other vessels may be obscured by an intervening obstruction to sound one prolonged blast. Any approaching vessel that may be within hearing around the bend or behind the obstruction must then answer with a prolonged blast.

In many instances, when two vessels agree on the manner in which they will pass each other in inland waters, one or both will in fact make a turn. Thus, if a port to port passing is agreed upon by two vessels approaching each other on reciprocal courses so as to involve risk of collision, each must turn to the right and pass port to port, after exchanging one-blast signals. But where risk of collision does not exist, and the vessels are shaped to meet or cross within a half mile of each other without any change of course by either, they must nevertheless exchange one-blast signals in accordance with Inland Rule 34(a).

Section C. Application of the Rules Relating to Maneuvering Signals

1. *Failure to Sound a Required Maneuvering Signal*

Failing to sound a required whistle signal is of course a statutory fault, and the violator therefore has the burden, under the *Pennsylvania* Rule, of proving that the failure could not have been causative. American Maritime Cases and the Federal Reporters are replete with decisions holding that the burden had not been met. Typical of these are *In re Bloomfield Steamship Co. (The Ronda—The Lucile Bloomfield);*[7] *In re Pacific Bulk Carriers, Inc. (The Atlantic Hope—The Sadoharu Maru);*[8] and *Oaksmith v. Garner (The Kiska—The Mayflower).*[9]

---

7. 298 F. Supp 1239, 1969 AMC 2205 (SDNY 1969), aff'd, 422 F.2d 728, 1970 AMC 521 (2d Cir. 1970). Among the faults charged to the *Bloomfield* was her failure to sound a one-blast signal on turning to starboard.

8. 639 F.2d 72, 1980 AMC 2530 (2d Cir. 1980). In addition to failure to sound the two blasts on turning to port, the *Atlantic Hope* had no lookout and failed to use available radar before colliding with the *American Aquarius* in international waters off Japan. The district court's 80 percent–20 percent allocation was modified to impose 100 percent fault on the *Atlantic Hope.*

9. 205 F.2d 262, 1953 AMC 1021 (9th Cir. 1953), decided under the former Inland Rules. The *Kiska* was held in sole fault for a number of violations, including not having and operating a whistle. Failure of the *Mayflower* to sound the danger signal was disregarded as noncontributory. The court found that the *Mayflower*'s use of a single 10-second whistle was not a proper substitute for the one short blast of about one second's duration required by the Inland Rules to be sounded by a vessel intending to overtake on the starboard side of the vessel ahead, despite the existence of a Great Lakes custom to exchange such signals. Nevertheless, this inordinately long whistle was found to be noncontributory because it could not have been confused with a two-blast signal. See also *In re S.S. Slobodna Plovidba,* 688 F. Supp. 1226, AMC 2307 (WD Mich. 1988).

In a fair number of cases, however, a failure to sound the required signal has been excused under the *in extremis* doctrine, or as noncausative because of remoteness. Operating at night in international waters 225 miles southeast of New York, the *Nashbulk* and the *Rutgers Victory* approached each other on crossing courses. The *Rutgers Victory*, the give-way vessel, had no lookout and her watch officer was not on the bridge. She failed to take action, while the *Nashbulk*, the hold-on vessel, maintained course and speed. Seeking to impose an equal division of damages, the *Rutgers Victory* argued that the *Nashbulk* was at fault under the then current 1897 Rules for failure to sound a one-blast signal on turning hard right at a distance of a half mile about one minute before collision, but the Second Circuit found the failure to signal to be noncontributory.[10] The case is notable for Judge Learned Hand's dissent. His view was that a danger signal would at least have served as a wake-up call.[11]

In *Mystic S.S. Corp. v. The Antonio Ferraz*,[12] the Second Circuit reached the same conclusion as did the court in *The Nashbulk*. In a meeting situation at the entrance to Chesapeake Bay, just outside inland waters, a barge in tow of the Tug *Betty Moran* collided with the *Antonio Ferraz*, which was entering the Bay. The tug's two-blast signal was not accompanied by a port turn, but in view of the *Antonio Ferraz*'s failure to maintain a look-out, the fault of the tug was found to be noncontributory.

Under the Inland Rules, the first duty of a vessel hearing one or two short blasts is to identify the proposer and then determine whether the proposed maneuver can be carried out in safety. This decision can only be made with

---

10. *National Bulk Carriers v. United States (The Nashbulk—The Rutgers Victory)*, 183 F.2d 405, 1950 AMC 1293 (2d Cir. 1950). The court of appeals disagreed with the district court as to the existence of an *in extremis* situation. In the view of the Second Circuit the right rudder order was not *in extremis*. Cf. *Maritrans v. The Faith I*, 800 F. Supp. 133, 1993 AMC 385 (D NJ 1992). See *The Steel Inventor*, 43 F.2d 958, 1930 AMC 1468 (2d Cir. 1930), where a course change without a whistle signal at a two- to three-mile distance and five minutes before collision was held to be noncontributory because too remote. In *International Bulktank Corp. v. The Shinto Maru*, 422 F. Supp. 982, 1977 AMC 37 (D Or. 1976), the omission of sound signals by both vessels in an overtaking situation in the Columbia River was held to be noncontributory, as both vessels were in constant touch by radiotelephone.

Other decisions involving the use or nonuse of bridge-to-bridge radiotelephone include *Gulfcoast Transit Co. v. The Anco Princess*, 1978 AMC 2471 (ED La. 1977) (tanker held 85 percent to blame for collision with tug whose one-blast proposal the tanker did not answer, and whose attempt to make radiotelephone contact she did not acknowledge); *Curtis Bay Towing Co. v. The Maryland Clipper*, 1979 AMC 2653 (D Md. 1977), reversed on other grounds, 599 F.2d 1313, 1979 AMC 2649 (4th Cir. 1979) (heavy voice traffic on the radiotelephone held no excuse for a failure to communicate with an unknown radar contact); *Penn Tanker Co. v. The Tug Exxon Massachusetts*, 1981 AMC 1903 (SDNY 1981) (overtaken vessel held at fault for failing to inform the overtaking vessel by radiotelephone of the danger of overtaking that would result when the overtaken vessel maneuvered to follow the bends in a narrow channel). See also *Southern Pacific Transp. Co. v. The Tug Captain Vick*, 443 F. Supp. 722, 1979 AMC 1404 (ED La. 1977).

11. 183 F. 2d at 410, 1950 AMC at 1300. "...[T]o arouse a vessel, which, as here for example, was giving every evidence of inattention, would seem to be even more desirable than to announce a change to an attentive vessel." Judge Hand's inability to find proportionate fault in this case led to his description of the former major-minor fault rule as "a sop to Cerberus."

12. 498 F.2d 538, 1974 AMC 545 (2d Cir. 1974).

full information as to the navigational situation. In the absence of full information, the responding vessel is required to sound the danger signal and be prepared to stop and reverse engines. These precautionary requirements are enforced by the courts, which hold that it is contributory fault to assent to an obviously dangerous proposal.[13]

2. *The Half-Mile Rule*

The current Inland Rules preserve the "half-mile rule" for vessels meeting or crossing in sight of one another. Such vessels are never to approach closer than a half mile without an exchange of whistle signals. Former Pilot Rule 312.2 required whistle signals to be given and answered, ". . . when passing or meeting at a distance within half a mile of each other, and whether passing to the starboard or port." There was a question as to whether the signal had to be sounded on sight if the vessels were then shaped to pass each other within a half mile, or whether it did not have to be sounded until the vessels had actually closed to a point within a half mile of each other. Griffin approved the latter reading of the former Pilot Rule.[14] Current Inland Rule 34(a), however, applies: "When power-driven vessels *are* in sight of one another *and* meeting or crossing" within a half a mile of each other. (Emphasis added.) It thus appears that two conditions must exist for the rule to apply: (a) the vessels must be in sight of one another, i.e., not obscured by fog or other condition of restricted visibility, or by an obstruction, and (2) they must in fact be meeting or crossing within a half mile of each other when the signals are sounded.

3. *The Danger Signal*

Judicial and legislative attitudes toward the danger signal have changed in recent years. Earlier versions of the International Rules had no provision for a signal to be given in cases of doubt, although some navigators adopted the practice of sounding the Morse code letter *U*—the signal for "You are standing

13. *Old Time Molasses Co. v. United States (The Barrance—The Colorado Springs—The San Pascual),* 31 F.2d 963, 1929 AMC 687 (5th Cir. 1929), reversing the district court's sole-fault holding; *The Seneca,* 35 F.2d, 707, 1929 AMC 1243 (2d Cir. 1929), modifying the district court's sole-fault holding; *Westfal-Larsen Co. v. Baltimore & Caroline Line (The Varanger—The Dora Weems),* 45 F.2d 608, 1931 AMC 1186 (4th Cir. 1931) (both vessels held at fault for collision during an overtaking in a narrow channel with a suction problem). Cf. *Warner Co. v. Independent Pier Co. (The Gulftrade),* 278 U.S. 1928 AMC 1815 (1928).

14. Griffin 202–05. The broader language of the current rule also eliminated the controversy over the application of the half-mile rule to crossing situations. Cf. *Cia. Carreto de Navigation, S.A. v. The Tug Sagamore (The Pilot—The Tug Sagamore),* 223 F. Supp. 598, 1964 AMC 585 (SDNY 1963) (holding the rule valid because not inconsistent with former Inland Rules, art. 18, Rule I, applicable to *meeting* situations; and *Mathieson Chemical Corp. v. The Tug Sadie (The Union Victory—The Tug Sadie and Tow),* 95 F. Supp. 221, 1951 AMC 270 (D Md. 1950) (holding the half-mile rule invalid because inconsistent with the statutory language).

into danger"—as a "wake-up" signal. The 1897 Inland Rules provided, in Art. 18, Rule III, for a signal of "several short and rapid blasts, not less than four," when either vessel failed to understand the course or intention of the other, from any cause. There was no change in Art. 18, Rule III until the current Inland Rules were enacted in 1980.

COLREGS Rule 34(d), as well as Inland Rule 34(d), now provide for a danger signal of five or more short and rapid blasts, which may be supplemented by a light signal of five or more short and rapid flashes, when vessels in sight of one another are approaching each other and from any cause either fails to understand the other's intentions or actions, or is in doubt as to whether the other is taking sufficient action to avoid collision.

There are many more reported decisions involving failure to sound a danger signal under the Inland Rules than under COLREGS because such a signal has been required in U.S. inland waters for so much longer than it has in international waters. It has been consistently held under both COLREGS and the Inland Rules that a failure to sound the danger signal as soon as there is an appearance of danger is a statutory fault, and that the *Pennsylvania* Rule is therefore applicable. Examples of decisions holding vessels at fault for failing to sound danger signals include *In re United States (The West Hartland);*[15] *The Fulton;*[16] *General Cable Corp. v. Pacific Atlantic Steamship Co. (The Commercial Mariner—The San Simeon);*[17] *In re Seiriki Kisen Kaisha (The Seiryu—The Stena Freighter);*[18] *Rich Ocean Car Carriers, S.A. v. The Sanko Diamond;*[19] *Union Oil Co. v. The Issaquena;*[20] *In re A.C. Dodge, Inc. (The Dodge—The Michael);*[21] *Henry Dubois*

15. 2 F.2d 834, 1925 AMC 47 (9th Cir. 1924) (risk of collision in a crossing situation).

16. 54 F.2d 467, 1932 AMC 232 (2d Cir. 1932) (meeting situation where there were crossed signals and no danger signal).

17. 63 F.2d 798, 1933 AMC 489 (2d. Cir. 1933) (*Pennsylvania* Rule applied to a failure to sound a danger signal in a meeting situation at night at a bend in the Delaware River Cherry Island Range. Judge Learned Hand's opinion enlarged the duty to sound the danger signal to situations where the proposed navigation is "plainly impracticable.")

18. 629 F. Supp. 1374, 1986 AMC 913 (SDNY 1986) (hold-on vessel in a crossing situation held 40 percent to blame for failing to maintain a proper look-out and failing to sound a danger signal when give-way vessel failed to keep out of the way.)

19. 1989 AMC 220 (MD Fla. 1988) (hold-on vessel in a crossing situation in international waters held 15 percent to blame for collision because of watch officer's unfamiliarity with vessel's maneuvering capabilities, failure to take timely avoiding action, and failure to sound a danger signal when give-way vessel failed to take prompt steps to keep out of the way).

20. 470 F.2d 875, 1973 AMC 493 (5th Cir. 1973) (Mississippi River collision at a narrow part of the river near Mile 865; Tug *Issaquena* was pushing twenty-five laden hopper barges [total tug and tow width 175 feet, length 1,145 feet], while Tug *L.W. Sweet* was pushing four empty barges [total tug and tow width 102.5 feet, length 648 feet]; the Fifth Circuit Court of Appeals affirmed the district court's holding that *Issaquena* should not have consented to *L.W. Sweet*'s proposal to overtake her, but should instead have rejected it by sounding a danger signal [under the then current Western Rivers Rules]).

21. 234 F.2d 374, 1956 AMC 1513 (2d Cir. 1956) (in head-on meeting in Delaware River, ascending tanker's one-blast port to port passing proposal was accepted by descending tanker, but a minute and a half later ascending tanker sounded a two-blast starboard to starboard passing signal, while holding speed. Descending tanker was held 50 percent to blame for failing to

Sons Co. v. A/S Ivarans Rederi;[22] *Alamo Chemical Co. v. The Overseas Valdes;*[23] *Afran Transport Co. v. The Transcolorado;*[24] *Ishikazi Kisen Co. v United States;*[25] *Hosei Kaiun Shoji Co. v. The Tug Seaspan Monarch;*[26] and *Wakefield v. The Veendam.*[27]

Under the former Inland Rules, U.S. courts sometimes found hold-on vessels in crossing situations at fault for failing to sound a danger signal when the give-way vessel failed to keep out of the way, but were reluctant to do so when the misunderstanding was not obvious or the danger was not readily apparent. However, where it is clear that the circumstances are such that a hold-on vessel should have sounded a danger signal, whether in inland or in international waters, the courts today do not hesitate to charge part of the blame for a collision to a hold-on vessel, as illustrated by *In re Seiriki Kisen Kaisha*[28] and *Rich Ocean Carriers v. The Sanko Diamond.*[29] Of course, when it is shown that the omission of a danger signal was not causative, no percentage of blame will attach to the omission. Thus, where the navigational situation is obvious to both vessels, no part of the blame will be ascribed to the vessel omitting the signal.[30]

A question on which the decisions are not in complete accord is whether, under the Inland Rules, if a maneuvering signal is not answered

---

sound a danger signal). This was before the proportionate fault rule was adopted in *United States v. Reliable Transfer Co.,* 421 U.S. 397, 1975 AMC 541 (1975).

22. 116 F.2d 492, 1941 AMC 214 (2d Cir. 1940). Judge Clark held that the failure to sound the danger signal could not have been noncontributory, where the uncertain movements of the other vessel had been observed for four minutes before the collision. See also *The Howard,* 256 F.987 (4th Cir. 1919).

23. 398 F. Supp. 1094, 1975 AMC 1762 (ED La. 1975) (descending tug with barge and ascending tanker approaching her dock each held 50 percent at fault for failing to sound danger signals).

24. 458 F.2d 164, 1972 AMC 1149 (5th Cir. 1972) (district court's holding of sole fault against give-way vessel modified by the Fifth Circuit Court of Appeals because stand-on vessel failed to sound danger signal and take avoiding action when give-way vessel failed to keep out of the way).

25. 510 F.2d 875, 1975 AMC 287 (9th Cir. 1975) (U.S. Army cargo vessel held 25 percent at fault for collision with a hydrofoil in the harbor of Kure, Japan).

26. 1981 AMC 2162 (D Or. 1981) (tug held 25 percent at fault for failing to sound danger signal before collision between a barge in tow of the tug and a cargo ship at the Columbia River bar).

27. 1980 AMC 2906 (WD Wash. 1980) (both-to-blame collision in Canadian waters governed by Canadian narrow channel rule. One vessel held 65 percent to blame for a number of faults, including failure to signal; the other held 35 percent at fault for failing to sound the danger signal. Judge Beeks said that the second vessel should have been in doubt as to the first vessel's intentions because of her failure to signal).

28. *In re Seiriki Kisen Kaisha,* supra note 18.

29. *Rich Ocean Carriers v. The Sanko Diamond,* supra note 19.

30. See, e.g., *United States v. Commonwealth and Dominion Line, Ltd. (The Port Philip—The Proteus),* 20 F.2d 729, 1927 AMC 1690 (2d Cir. 1927); *Bouchard Transportation Co., Inc. v. Connors Marine Co.,* 129 F.2d 110, 1942 AMC 972 (2d Cir. 1942); *Skibs A/S Orenor v. The Audrey,* 181 F. Supp. 697, 1960 AMC 723 (ED Va. 1960), aff'd, 287 F.2d 706, 1961 AMC 653 (4th Cir. 1961). (In the last cited case the district court stated that under the Inland Rules then in force the danger signal was "permissive but not mandatory," although its decision was not based on permissiveness. It is submitted that the statement was incorrect. The former Inland Rule, like the current Inland and COLREGS Rule, was worded mandatorily, not permissively.)

promptly it may be repeated, or whether a danger signal should be sounded instead. In *The Victory—The Plymothian*[31] the Supreme Court held that there was no fault in repeating a one-blast passing signal without hearing a reply. When the *Plymothian* repeated her one-blast signal, the *Victory* replied with two blasts. The *Victory* was held in sole fault. On the other hand, in *In re Oskar Tiedemann (The Elna II—The Mission San Francisco),*[32] involving a head-on meeting in the Delaware River, repeating a one-blast signal was held a fault. The court said that since there was doubt as to the navigational situation, the danger signal should have been sounded instead. In any case, a navigator who repeats a maneuvering signal should be prepared to take avoiding action and sound the danger signal immediately if the second signal is not answered.

Judge Learned Hand was a strong advocate of use of the danger signal. Thus, in *Cleary Bros. v. The Tug Dauntless,*[33] the majority held that a vessel was not at fault for repeating a one-blast signal just before a collision in the Kill Van Kull in New York Harbor. Judge Hand dissented, saying that in the absence of an agreement to the one-blast proposal a danger signal should have been sounded, because a reasonable master in the same position would have had doubts about the navigational situation. He noted, however, that in New York Harbor it was a common practice to repeat a signal to which no answer had been given.

In *McWilliams Blue Line, Inc. v. Card Towing Line, Inc. (The Thomas A. Feeney—The Edward Card)*[34] Judge Hand wrote for a unanimous court. Both vessels were held to blame for a head-on-meeting situation collision in the Hudson River, where one vessel repeated an unanswered one-blast signal a minute later. Judge Hand said that to repeat a proposal presupposes doubt, and that had the proposing vessel sounded a danger signal and turned hard right promptly after receiving no reply to the first signal, there would almost certainly have been no collision.

In *Merritt, Chapman & Scott Corp. v. Texas Co. (The Frank A. Furst—The Newark)*[35] Judge Hand wrote:

> The only debatable point is whether the *Furst*'s danger signal was a fault, and how far it excused the *Newark*. As we have already said, if the *Furst*, at rest, saw the *Newark*'s two running lights apparently bearing down upon her, it would be a harsh doctrine that she was not justified in uttering a cry of warning; but we do not wish to put our decision on that, because

31. 168 U.S. 410 (1897). See also *The Sicilian Prince,* 144 F. 951 (2d Cir. 1905).

32. 289 F.2d 237, 1961 AMC 1878 (2d Cir. 1961). See also *United States v. States Steamship Co. (The American Producer—The Dant),* 1971 AMC 642 (ND Cal. 1972), where a vessel was held at fault for twice repeating a passing signal instead of sounding a danger signal.

33. 178 F.2d 72, 1950 AMC 44 (2d Cir. 1949).

34. 168 F.2d 720, 1948 AMC 1137 (2d Cir. 1948). See also *Socony Vacuum Transportation Co. v. Gypsum Packet Co.,* 153 F.2d 773, 1946 AMC 309 (2d Cir. 1946).

35. 98 F.2d 719, 721, 1938 AMC 1060, 1066–67 (2d Cir. 1938).

> while we should not care to commit ourselves to the doctrine that it can never be a fault to blow a danger signal, we are at a loss to think of an occasion when it would be. The books do not contain a whisper that it ever is; and here at any rate it certainly was not. It is quite true that literally Rule III (33 Mason's U.S.C., sec. 203), does not call for a "danger signal" at all; it directs a master to blow only when he "fails to understand the course or intention of the other," and a purist might argue that it did not cover a case where he knew well enough that "course or intention," but wished to say that he thought it dangerous. But it has been universally interpreted as applying to cases where the master believes that safety requires a change of navigation, and by far the greater number of occasions of its use are just of that sort. We upheld this construction in *San Simeon,* 1933 A.M.C. 489, 63 F.(2d) 798, 801, and repeat that ruling now. Moreover, Rule I of the Pilot Rules calls it a "danger signal," and Rule 26 of the Great Lakes Rules (33 Mason's U.S.C., sec. 291), directs it as an answer to any signal which a master "deems . . . unsafe."

Under the Inland Rules a response to a passing signal is expected. But under COLREGS, when the maneuvering signals simply indicate the direction in which the vessel is turning, no response is required, and the repetition of a one- or two-blast signal may be confusing.[36]

Section D. "Fog" Signals

1. *Differences between COLREGS Rule 35 and Inland Rule 35*

Inland Rule 35 largely conforms to COLREGS Rule 35. This attempt at conformity required several substantial departures from the former Inland Rules. Thus, the former Inland Rule requirement that a power-driven vessel underway had to sound a prolonged blast at least once a minute has been replaced by a provision identical to that in COLREGS Rule 35(a), requiring a

---

36. Cf. *In re Cia. Nav. Lloyd Brasiliero (The Mandu—The Denderah),* 1939 AMC 1313 (EDNY 1939), modified on appeal as to allocation of fault, 114 F.2d 361, 1940 AMC 1150 (2d Cir. 1940). (*Mandu*'s repetition of a one-blast signal twice held not a fault under former International Rules.) It is submitted that the result would be otherwise under COLREGS, since the repetition of the one-blast signal indicated uncertainty, and therefore would require a danger signal. As to how long a master or watch officer should wait for a reply to a passing signal in waters where a reply is required, see *Partenreederei "Wallschiff" v. The Pioneer,* 164 F. Supp. 421, 1958 AMC 2511 (ED Mich. 1958), aff'd, 287 F.2d 886, 1961 AMC 660 (6th Cir. 1961), decided under the 1910 Brussels Collision Convention and under a Canadian rule identical to former U.S. Great Lakes Rule 26, which required a danger signal in case of doubt as to the intentions of another vessel. In charging one vessel (the *Pioneer*) with 5 percent of the fault, the court stated: "It cannot be said with mathematical nicety how many seconds a captain should wait for an answering signal. Thirty seconds, however, without action, followed by a danger signal, still without action and without full assurance of a safe passage, persuades this Court that he cannot completely exonerate Captain O'Leary [of the *Pioneer*] of fault."

prolonged blast at least every two minutes. And the former requirement that a manned vessel being towed must sound one prolonged blast followed by two short blasts at least once every minute has been replaced by a provision identical to the corresponding provision of COLREGS, which requires one prolonged blast followed by three short blasts at least every two minutes.

The only differences between COLREGS Rule 35 and Inland Rule 35 are (1) between paragraphs (c) and (d) of the COLREGS Rule and paragraph (c) of the Inland Rules, and (2) the inclusion of paragraph (j) of the Inland Rule, which has no counterpart in COLREGS. That paragraph provides that vessels of less than 20 meters in length, barges, canal boats, scows, or other nondescript craft are not required to sound the fog signals prescribed for anchored vessels when anchored in an area designated by the Secretary of Transportation. It will be noted that paragraph (c) of COLREGS Rule 35, requiring certain vessels to sound a prolonged blast, followed by two short blasts, applies to "a vessel constrained by her draft." Inland Rule 35(c) does not apply to such a vessel.

The remaining differences between paragraphs (c) and (d) of COLREGS Rule 35 and paragraph (c) of Inland Rule 35 are in draftsmanship. COLREGS Rule 35(d) provides that "a vessel engaged in fishing, when at anchor," and "a vessel restricted in her ability to maneuver when carrying out her work at anchor" must sound the signals prescribed in paragraph (c). That paragraph of the COLREGS Rule applies, *inter alia,* to "a vessel restricted in her ability to maneuver" and to "a vessel engaged in fishing." The drafters evidently intended that paragraph (c) should apply to such vessels when underway, while paragraph (d) specifically applies to such vessels when at anchor. The drafters of paragraph (c) of Inland Rule 35 presumably decided that there was no point in using a separate paragraph for the specified vessels when at anchor, as the signal required under the Inland Rule is the same for such vessels when at anchor as when underway. And so Inland Rule 35(c) specifically applies, *inter alia,* to a vessel restricted in her ability to maneuver and to a vessel engaged in fishing, "whether underway or at anchor."

Because there is no paragraph in Inland Rule 35 corresponding to paragraph (d) of COLREGS Rule 35, the result is that paragraphs lettered (e) to (j), inclusive, of COLREGS Rule 35 are lettered (d) to (i) in Inland Rule 35.

Inland Rule 35(f), which is identical to COLREGS Rule 35(g), provides that an anchored vessel must ring the bell rapidly for about five seconds at intervals of not more than a minute, and that a vessel 100 or more meters long must sound a gong rapidly for about five seconds, immediately after ringing the bell.

2. *When "Fog" Signals Must Be Commenced*

"Restricted visibility" is defined in COLREGS Rule 3 and in Inland Rule 3 as "any condition in which visibility is restricted by fog, mist, falling snow, heavy rainstorms, sandstorms or any other similar causes." The question of when conditions are such as to require a vessel to commence sounding "fog" signals is discussed in chapter 6.

3. Frequency of "Fog" Signals

It will be noted that under COLREGS and Inland Rule 35 fog signals to be sounded by the whistle must be sounded "at intervals of not more than 2 minutes," and that fog signals to be sounded by the bell or gong must be sounded at intervals of not more than 1 minute." It is not a violation of Rule 35 to sound fog signals at shorter intervals. In fact, there may be navigational situations where the presence of a number of small boats or obstructions of the kind that can cause "clutter" on radar screens may make it appropriate to sound fog signals at more frequent intervals than the minimums specified in Rule 35.

4. Failure to Sound "Fog" Signals When Required

Since failure to sound required fog signals is a statutory fault, the *Pennsylvania* Rule is of course applicable, and to escape liability if a collision occurs, the offending vessel must prove that her failure could not have been a contributing cause. There is authority, however, for excusing a failure to sound fog signals as noncontributory when the vessel guilty of the failure has already been located on the other vessel's radar screen. In *In re Hellenic Lines, Ltd.*[37] the Court of Appeals for the Fourth Circuit upheld the district court's conclusion that the *Hellenic Carrier* had met the *Pennsylvania* Rule burden of proving that her failure to sound fog signals was noncontributory, as fog signals would not have provided the other vessel (the *Lash Atlantico*), with any warning of the *Hellenic Carrier*'s presence and location which had not already been provided by the *Lash Atlantico*'s radar.

5. Sounding Improper "Fog" Signals

Just as failure to sound a required fog signal is a statutory fault creating a *Pennsylvania* Rule presumption, so too is the sounding of an improper signal. The most notorious case on this point is *Silver Line, Ltd. v. United States (The Chicago—The Silver Palm)*,[38] involving a 1933 both-to-blame collision in international waters off the California coast. At the time of the collision, the U.S. Navy's cruiser *Chicago* and the freighter *Silver Palm* were both proceeding at greatly excessive speeds in dense fog. The Court of Appeals for the Ninth Circuit held the *Chicago* at fault for sounding erroneous fog signals, as well as for

37. 730 F.2d 159, 162, 1984 AMC 2713, 2718 (4th Cir. 1984).
38. 94 F.2d 754, 1937 AMC 1427 (9th Cir. 1937).

excessive speed and failure to stop engines immediately upon hearing the fog signal of another vessel (the *Albion Star,* not the *Silver Palm*), apparently forward of her beam, as required by the International Rules then in force.

The first error with respect to fog signals lay in sounding a signal of two prolonged blasts on reducing speed when the *Chicago* heard the *Albion Star*'s fog signal. The second error lay in again sounding two prolonged blasts when the *Chicago* stopped engines just before she collided with the *Silver Palm.* The then current International Rules, like COLREGS, required a power-driven vessel making way through the water to sound one prolonged blast at least every two minutes, and a vessel underway with no way on to sound two prolonged blasts at the same interval. It appeared, however, that at the time of the collision, in the U.S. Navy a fog signal of two prolonged blasts meant that the engines were stopped, even though the vessel might have way on, as did the *Chicago.* In charging that vessel with fault in sounding the wrong signal the Ninth Circuit stated:

> The importance of this rule is shown by the fact that the violation of the rule imposes the severest burden of proof on the violator. He must prove not merely that probably the fault did not contribute to the collision, but that it could not have done so. *Ansaldo Savoia,* 176 Fed. 719, 722; *Old Colony,* 1931 A.M.C. 1459, 52 F.(2d) 992, 996; *Pennsylvania,* 86 U.S. 125, 136; *North Point,* 205 Fed. 958.[39] . . .
>
> That the Navy is not free to navigate without regard to the International Rules in the presence of opposing merchant ships has been repeatedly adjudicated in courts of admiralty. Judge Learned Hand's opinion in a libel in the Second Circuit, in which this Naval right was urged, condemns its assertion:
>
> "The International Rules . . . apply to 'all public and private vessels of the United States.'. . . If unfortunately it is impossible to equip submarines properly, they must take their chances until some provision has been made for them by law. We have no power to dispense with the statute, nor indeed has the Navy. *As they now sail they are unfortunately a menace to other shipping and to their own crews, as this unhappy collision so tragically illustrates.* We cannot say that they are not to be judged by the same standard as private persons. The safety of navigation depends upon uniformity; only so can reliance be placed upon what masters see at night." (Italics supplied [by the court]). *Ocean S.S. Co. v. U.S.,* 1930 A.M.C. 524, 38 F.(2d) 782, 786.
>
> See also as to other Naval vessels: *New England Maritime Co. v. U.S.,* 1932 A.M.C. 323, 55 F.(2d) 674, particularly at 677; *N.Y. & Cuba Mail S.S. Co. v. U.S.,* 1924 A.M.C. 1170, 300 Fed. 827, 1927 A.M.C. 230, 16 F.(2d)

39. 94 F.2d at 759, 1937 AMC at 1436.

945 (destroyer trial trip testing turbines); *Ozark,* 281 Fed. 281; *Watts v. U.S.,* 123 Fed. 105; *Thurlow v. U.S.,* 295 Fed. 905, 1924 A.M.C. 536.[40]

Because of the radically different implications of the two situations—underway with way on and underway with no way on, i.e., stopped—the courts have continued to require navigators to prove that signals of two prolonged blasts were not sounded while the vessel still had way on. But if a vessel with no way on has been properly sounding signals of two prolonged blasts, she must revert to signals of one prolonged blast once she gets underway. See, e.g., *A/B Svenska Amerika Linien v. Standard Oil Co. of New Jersey (The A.C. Bedford—The Kungsholm),*[41] in which Judge Learned Hand affirmed a district court decision holding the *A.C. Bedford* solely at fault for sounding fog signals of two prolonged blasts after stopping her engines, but while she still had way on. In the course of his opinion Judge Hand discussed the fog signals to be sounded by a vessel that has been stopped, but subsequently resumes her forward motion. He stated:

> When a vessel "under way" gives a series of two blasts in conformity with Article 15(b) she must be "stopped." The purpose is to advise all other vessels that in fact she is not moving, and that they may shape their navigation accordingly. The signal is an announcement to the other vessel quite the same as though she should say by her wireless: "I have stopped and you may pass. . . ."
>
> To meet this, the *Bedford* says that although a double blast does indeed mean that the vessel giving it is then lying to, it does not mean that she will remain so. Obviously she need not if the other vessel also blows that signal: in that case one of them must start up for the "danger of collision" ever to be "over." Hence, she says, it is always permissible for the "lying-to" vessel to start up, and she is bound not to repeat a double blast after she is under way.
>
> As we understand this argument, it would result that there might be an interval of substantially two minutes during which the "lying-to" vessel might be moving though her last signal indicated that she was still "stopped." We are not sure that, having once chosen to lie to, a vessel may later get under way at all except when the other vessel has indicated that she too is lying to; but we will not so hold. Assuming that she may start up, before doing so she must indicate her change of purpose; the one thing she may not do is to get underway, while leaving the other vessel under the impression that she is still "stopped." She must blow a

40. 94 F.2d at 761, 1937 AMC at 1439.

41. 105 F.2d 924, 1939 AMC 1104 (2d Cir. 1939). See also *The Ansaldo Savoia,* 276 F. 719 (ED Va. 1921), a both-to-blame decision holding one vessel at fault for sounding a fog signal for a vessel underway with no way on, although in fact she had considerable way on. The court found that she could not prove that the erroneous signal was not a cause of the collision.

signal of one blast at the very moment she turns in her order to the engine-room.[42]

Section E. Other Sound and Light Signals

1. *Bend Signals*

Rule 35(e) of COLREGS requires the sounding of one prolonged blast by a vessel nearing a bend or an area of a channel or fairway where other vessels may be obscured by an intervening obstruction. It further requires an answer of a prolonged blast by any vessel approaching within hearing around the bend or behind the obstruction. Inland Rule 35(e) is identical, except for the immaterial substitution of "This signal" as the opening words of the second sentence of paragraph (e) of Inland Rule 35 for "Such signal" in the corresponding paragraph of the COLREGS Rule. The bend signal should be considered in conjunction with Rule 9, the narrow channel rule, discussed in chapter 4, section G.

Interpretative problems arise from the use of the words "obscured" and "intervening obstruction." Thus, in *In re Schmidt Barge Lines, Inc.*,[43] involving a collision between a motorboat and a barge in tow of a tug on the Little Calumet River in Chicago, the motorboat owner contended that the tug was at fault for, among other things, failing to sound a bend signal in accordance with Rule 24(b) of the then current Western Rivers Rules. That rule provided that when the head of a tow was within 600 yards of a blind bend, a vessel pushing the tow was obliged to sound a bend signal of three distinct blasts of her whistle. Here, the motorboat was not around a bend in the river, but a view of the boat by those on the tug was obscured by the pilings and center pier of a bridge on the same side of the bend as the tug and tow. In affirming a decision exonerating the tug, the Seventh Circuit quoted from the district court's conclusions of law:

> There are many cases where the vessels failed to blow a bend signal at all and were found at fault for colliding with vessels rounding bends, but none of these cases is analogous, because this collision did not happen at a bend, and Moss [owner and operator of the motorboat] was never around the bend at any time when the *Mary R* was within 600 yards of the bend. *The law did not contemplate the sounding of a signal for the benefit of Moss, only for the benefit of vessels below the bend.* (Emphasis supplied by the court.)[44]

---

42. 105 F.2d at 924, 925, 1939 AMC at 1106–07.
43. 475 F.2d 428, 1973 AMC 1053 (7th Cir. 1973).
44. 475 F.2d at 431, 1973 AMC at 1057.

As in the case of other violations of the Sound and Light Rules, a failure to sound a bend whistle when one is required by Rule 34(e), being a statutory fault, imposes a *Pennsylvania* Rule burden on the violator to prove that the violation could not have caused or contributed to a collision.[45]

2. *Slip Whistles*

Inland Rule 34(g) provides that when a power-driven vessel is leaving a dock or berth she must sound a signal of one prolonged blast. There is no corresponding provision in COLREGS. This is immaterial in the United States, where, since all docks and berths are of course in inland waters they are subject to the Inland Rules. But the absence of such a provision in COLREGS may be material where the dock or berth is located in a country where COLREGS apply to domestic waters as well as the high seas, and there is no local rule requiring a slip whistle.

Again, a violation of Inland Rule 34(g) imposes on the violator the burden of proving that the violation could not have caused or contributed to a collision.[46] But at times one who violates the Rule succeeds in showing that the violation was not causative.[47] The whistle should be repeated at least until the vessel has a clear view of the fairway at the end of the slip.[48]

3. *Signals to Attract Attention*

COLREGS and Inland Rule 36 provides that if necessary to attract the attention of another vessel, a vessel may make light or sound signals that cannot be mistaken for any signal authorized elsewhere in the rules, or may direct the beam of her searchlight in the direction of the danger, in such a way as not to embarrass any vessel. The COLREGS Rule adds that any light to attract the attention of another vessel must be such that it cannot be mistaken for any aid to navigation, and that the use of high-intensity intermittent or revolving

45. *First National Bank of Chicago v. Material Services Corp.*, 597 F.2d 1110, 1980 AMC 817 (7th Cir. 1979).

46. *City of New York v. Morania No. 12, Inc.*, 357 F. Supp. 234, 1974 AMC 2155 (Sy.) (SDNY 1973). In this both-to-blame case, one of the vessels was held at fault for backing out of a slip without sounding either a slip whistle or a three-blast backing signal.

47. See *United States Lines Co. v. The Ocean Vagrant,* 85 F. Supp. 642, 1949 AMC 762 (SDNY 1949). In this both-to-blame case, the failure of a tug to sound a slip whistle on backing out from a slip into the river was held noncausative because the ship with which she collided had seen the tug at a distance of a half to three-fourths of a mile. However, the tug was held at fault for other reasons, including a failure to maintain a proper look-out.

48. *Reliable Fuel Supply Co. v. The Steamtug Dalzellea,* 109 F.2d 101, 1940 AMC 188 (2d Cir. 1940). Cf. *Rice v. United States,* 168 F.2d 219, 1948 AMC 1011 (2d Cir. 1948), where the captain of a tug leaving a slip stopped sounding a slip whistle before clearing some barges at the end of one of the piers forming the slip. The Second Circuit Court of Appeals said even if this was a fault it was noncausative, and then added that the then-existing major-minor fault rule should be applied in favor of the tug.

lights, such as strobe lights, must be avoided. There are no such provisions in the Inland Rule. Otherwise, Inland Rule 36 is identical to COLREGS Rule 36.

4. Distress Signals

COLREGS Rule 37 simply provides that a vessel in distress and requiring assistance must exhibit the signals described in Annex IV to "these Regulations." Inland Rule 37 is worded identically, except that the Inland Rule refers to "these Rules."

Paragraph 1 of Annex IV to COLREGS lists fifteen distress signals. Paragraph 87.1 of Annex IV to the Inland Rules lists the same fifteen signals and adds a sixteenth: "A high intensity white light flashing at regular intervals from 50 to 70 times per minute."

Paragraph 2 of Annex IV to COLREGS prohibits the use of any of the distress signals listed in paragraph 1, except to indicate distress and need of assistance. It also prohibits the use of other signals which may be confused with any of the listed signals. Paragraph 87.3 of Annex IV to the Inland Rules is worded identically.

Paragraph 3 of Annex IV to COLREGS draws attention to the relevant sections of the *International Code of Signals,* the *Merchant Ship Search and Rescue Manual,* and the following signals: (a) a piece of orange-colored canvas with either a black square and circle or other appropriate symbol (for identification from the air); and (b) a dye marker.

Paragraph 87.5 of Annex IV to the Inland Rules is identical, except that it draws attention to the International Telecommunication Union Regulations, as well as to the other regulations mentioned in the COLREGS Annex.

The distress signals provided for in both COLREGS and the Inland Rules that can be illustrated are shown in full color in the U.S. Coast Guard pamphlet on the Navigation Rules.[49]

---

49. See p. 124 of the pamphlet (1993 printing).

CHAPTER NINE

PILOTAGE IN COLLISION CASES

Section A. Definitions and Duties

1. *Types of Pilotage*

A pilot is an expert in the peculiar characteristics of internal waters who is licensed to direct or steer ships into or out of harbors or through dredged channels, canals, or straits.[1] There are, however, a number of different senses in which the term is used: (a) a "compulsory" pilot (a state-licensed individual who has a right to pilot a ship or collect a pilotage fee);[2] (b) a "noncompulsory" or "voluntary" pilot;[3] and (c) a "docking" pilot (usually an employee of a tugboat company who, with the use of a vessel's own power and steering equipment, together with the power and directional effort of one or more tugs, directs the vessel in intricate maneuvers to or from a wharf, pier, or other berth). Typically, the docking pilot, who is usually the master of one of the tugs servicing the ship, takes over from the compulsory pilot after the ship has entered a port, and directs the vessel to or from the place where cargo or passengers are taken on board or discharged from the vessel.[4]

Pilotage is an ancient institution.[5] Most nations have enacted legislative provisions mandating the use of locally licensed pilots for the arrival or departure of most types of merchant ships. The physical presence of a pilot on

1. Definition compiled from *Encyclopedia Britannica* (15th ed.) and *The Maren Lee,* 278 F. 918 (2d Cir. 1922); see also *Cooley v. Board of Wardens of the Port of Philadelphia,* 53 U.S. 299 (1851); *Atlee v. Northwest Union Packet Co.,* 88 U.S. 389, 396 (1874), holding that a river pilot must know the navigable channel, all permanent dangers and changes in currents, and the presence of sandbars or other dangers newly presented, which might cause injury to the vessel. This expertise, however, does not amount to strict liability for damage caused by sunken objects in unforeseeable locations. *Delta Transload Inc. v. The Navios Commander,* 818 F.2d 445, 1988 AMC 1155 (5th Cir. 1987). See generally, A. Parks & E. Cattell, Jr., *The Law of Tug, Tow, and Pilotage* (3d ed., 1994) (hereinafter "Parks & Cattell").

2. *Anderson v. Pacific Coast S.S. Co.,* 225 U.S. 187 (1912). See Parks & Cattell 991.

3. See *Homer Ramsdell Transportation Co. v. La Compagnie Générale Transatlantique,* 182 U.S. 406, 416 (1901), where the Court said that if no statute or regulation requires the presence of the pilot, and the master "is at liberty to take a pilot, or not, at his pleasure . . . the master acts voluntary [*sic*], although he is necessarily required to select from a particular class."

4. *Sun Oil Co. v. Dalzell Towing Co.* 287 U.S. 291, 1933 AMC 35 (1932); see also *National Distillers Products Corp. v. Boston Tow Boat Co.,* 134 F. Supp. 194, 1955 AMC 1925 (D Mass. 1955); *Federal Steam Navigation Co. v. The Tug Savannah,* 305 F. Supp. 1293 (SD Ga. 1969), and *Ross Towboat Co. v. The Bruarfoss,* 1982 AMC 1374 (D Mass. 1982).

5. See, e.g., Corpus Juris Civilis (533 A.D.) Digest 19.2.

such vessels may eventually become outmoded with the wider applicability of vessel traffic services, discussed in chapter 4.

2. *The Master's Duty of Supervision*

Maneuvers directed by pilots in congested waters frequently involve great risk of collision. They are usually governed by the special circumstances rule.[6] Because of this risk, a master has the duty to observe the pilot, question orders he considers inappropriate, or add warnings of appropriate degrees of intensity. Furthermore, in cases of immediate peril the master has the duty to relieve the pilot and resume the conn[7] because of his overriding obligation to provide for the safe navigation of the vessel.[8] The decision to intervene must be made when incompetence, inattention, or imprudence is obvious.

---

6. Rule 2, COLREGS and Inland Rules.

7. In *D/S Atalanta v. United States (The Sierra Leone),* 31 F.2d 961, 962, 1929 AMC 855, 856 (5th Cir. 1929), the court said: "The master is not entirely absolved of responsibility when a pilot is in charge, but before he is justified in replacing him, he should be sure that the pilot is for some reason incompetent." See also *Kingfisher v. Klarendon,* 651 F. Supp. 204, 1988 AMC 1270 (SD Tex. 1986), concerning the master's duty to intervene in the circumstances. Cases in which the vessel owner's negligence or the vessel's unseaworthiness joined with the pilot's negligence in allisions with bridges include *The Yorkmar,* 434 F. Supp. 715, 1977 AMC 805 (D Md. 1977), and *In re Gypsum Carrier Co.,* 465 F. Supp. 1050, 1979 AMC 1311 (SD Ga. 1979). "To have the conn" describes the position of a watch officer who is designated, by the authority of the master, to give orders to the helmsman on courses and speeds.

8. *The China,* 74 U.S. 53, 67–68 (1868): "It is the duty of the master to interfere in cases of the pilot's intoxication or manifest incapacity, in cases of danger which he does not foresee, and in all cases of great necessity. The Master has the same power to displace the pilot that he has to remove any subordinate officer of the vessel. He may exercise it or not, according to his discretion." See also *The Oregon,* 158 U.S. 186 (1895); D/S *Atalanta v. United States,* supra note 7; *The Brenta II,* 32 F.2d 209, 1929 AMC 897 (2d Cir. 1929); *Newfoundland Export & Shipping Co. v. United British S.S. Co. (The Framlington Court),* 69 F.2d 300, 1934 AMC 272 (5th Cir. 1934); *McGrath v. Nolan,* 83 F.2d 746, 1936 AMC 724 (9th Cir. 1936); *Union Shipping & Trading Co. v. United States,* 127 F.2d 771, 1942 AMC 709 (2d Cir. 1942) (American master and French pilot). But see *The Comanche,* 144 F.2d 101, 1944 AMC 1056 (2d Cir. 1944); *Bunge Corp. v. The Furness Bridge,* 558 F.2d 790, 1977 AMC 2109 (5th Cir. 1977); and *Burgess v. The Tamano,* 564 F.2d 964, 1977 AMC 1892 (1st Cir. 1977). Cf. *Owners of the Alexander Shukoff v. Owners of the Gothland,* [1921] 1 A.C. 216 (H.L. 1921).

In *Avondale Industries, Inc. v. International Maritime Carriers,* 15 F.3d 489, 1994 AMC 1555 (5th Cir. 1994), the master's duty to supervise the pilot was extended to tug assistance in an undocking and turning maneuver on the Mississippi River with two assisting tugs. The vessel had only her port engine available. The master knew that the pilot had released the bow tug, and had approved that decision, but did not know that the pilot had also released the stern tug. With only the one engine the vessel was unable to complete her turn, and struck a nearby drydock. The district court found no fault of the master, but the decision was reversed by the Fifth Circuit. Cf. *Kim Crest, S.A. v. The Sverdlovsk,* 753 F. Supp. 642, 1991 AMC 1364 (SD Tex. 1990), where it was held that the master of the Soviet ship properly intervened, but it was too late to avoid collision.

There is an analogy in the "turn-over" duties respecting the loading and unloading of vessels by stevedores, where damage or injury is suffered by a third party, and the question is whether the master has an obligation to intervene in the stevedoring operations. See *Howlett v. Birkdale Shipping Co.,* 512 U.S. 92, 1994 AMC 1817 (1994).

There is a direct connection between the rules governing pilotage operations and those concerning tugboats and their tows, but there is no special legal regime. General principles of maritime tort govern these relationships, under a negligence, rather than a strict liability standard.[9]

Section B. Compulsory Pilotage

The constitutional division of power between federal and state authorities is beyond the scope of this chapter.[10] The assumption here is that the pilot is operating lawfully as a compulsory pilot under federal or state law. The description of the compulsory pilot from the 1851 *Cooley* case is still accurate:

> Compulsory pilotage laws rest upon the propriety of securing lives and property exposed to the perils of a dangerous navigation, by taking on board a person peculiarly skilled to encounter or avoid them; upon the policy of discouraging the commanders of vessels from refusing to receive such persons on board at the proper times and places; and upon the expediency, and even intrinsic justice, of not suffering those who have incurred labor, and expense, and danger, to place themselves in a position to render important service generally necessary, to go unrewarded, because the master of a particular vessel either rashly refuses their proffered assistance, or, contrary to the general experience, does not need it.[11]

---

9. *The Manchioneal,* 243 F. 801 (2d Cir. 1917); *Andros Shipping Co. v. Panama Canal Co.,* 298 F.2d 720, 1962 AMC 870 (5th Cir. 1962). See also *United Fruit Co. v. Mobile Towing & Wrecking Co.,* 177 F. Supp. 297, 302, 1960 AMC 115 (SD Ala. 1959), where the court said, "The law requires due care and skill, but not infallibility."

10. Regulation and licensing of pilots involves concurrent federal and state powers. Watch officers on U.S. vessels are licensed by the United States Coast Guard, and their federal certificates may also include pilot licenses for specified waters. The three categories of pilots (compulsory, voluntary, and docking) discussed in this chapter are subject to state regulation and licensing. The leading case interpreting the federal commerce power during the age of Jacksonian democracy is *Cooley v. Board of Wardens of the Port of Philadelphia,* supra note 1. See also *Jackson v. Marine Exploration Co.,* 583 F.2d 1336, 1979 AMC 1331 (5th Cir. 1978). Under the *Cooley* doctrine, states are permitted to regulate the activities of pilots in state waters or state boundary waters until the Congress legislates to the contrary, i.e., preempts the field. A good example of federal preemption is *Ray v. Atlantic Richfield Co.,* 435 U.S. 151, 1978 AMC 527 (1978), where the antipollution legislation of the State of Washington imposed stricter requirements on oil tankers using Puget Sound than was required by federal legislation: All ocean-going oil tankers of a certain deadweight were required to carry a state-licensed pilot while navigating Puget Sound (an inlet of the Pacific Ocean surrounded by the State of Washington). Tankers not built with double bottoms and other protective devices had to operate in ballast or be assisted by tugs in Puget Sound. Very large (VLCC) and ultra-large (ULCC) tankers were excluded from the Sound. Wash. Rev. Code § 88.16. 170-88.16 190 (1988 Supp.). The Supreme Court rejected these state controls as preempted by federal statutes: the Coastal Licensing Act of 1793, 46 U.S.C. §§ 211–16; the Ports and Waterways Safety Act of 1972, 46 U.S.C. § 391(2); and an unspecified international agreement, undoubtedly the 1960 Safety of Life at Sea Convention.

11. Supra note 1; 53 U.S. at 312.

The Supreme Court has also provided a general description of the elements necessary for compulsory pilotage: "The requirement to take a licensed pilot or pay pilotage, together with the penalty imposed on a master who pilots his own foreign vessel, clearly impose compulsory pilotage."[12]

1. In Rem *Liability*

Under the general maritime law, the vessel herself is liable *in rem* in maritime tort for damages caused or contributed to by a vessel when under the conn of any type of pilot,[13] just as negligence of the ship's servants or agents is imputed to the ship. It is the service of the ship that produces the liability of the ship *in rem*. Accordingly, arrest of a colliding ship is an available remedy where the ship is under the conn of a compulsory pilot.[14]

In those States that have adopted the Brussels Collision Convention of 1910, compulsory pilotage is no defense to collision liability. In conformity with this principle a statutory limitation on the compulsory pilotage defense was enacted in the United Kingdom, overturning the older statute, which had given a defense to any action against the shipowner based on "the Neglect, Default, Incompetency or Incapacity" of a compulsory pilot.[15]

2. In Personam *Liability of Owners*

Under U.S. law, in compulsory pilotage cases there is no *in personam* liability of the vessel owner for damage caused by the pilot's fault, because the owner has no right to select the pilot.[16] Under this rationale there is no

---

12. *Homer Ramsdell Transp. Co. v. La Compagnie Générale Transatlantique,* supra note 3.

13. *The China,* supra note 8. In New York Harbor the outbound British Steamship *China* collided with the inbound American Sailing Vessel *Kentucky,* which sank. The *China* was under the conn of a compulsory pilot whose negligence was the sole cause of the collision. Defendant argued there could be no vessel liability *in rem* because there was no master-servant relationship between the owner and the pilot, the owner having had no choice as to which pilot would be hired. The Supreme Court rejected the argument on the ground that the pilot serves the vessel just as much as the master and crew hired by the owner. See also *Transorient Nav. Co. v. The Southwind,* 609 F. Supp. 634, 1985 AMC 2652 (ED La. 1985), modified in other respects, 788 F.2d 288 (5th Cir. 1986). A barge without navigating personnel, propulsion, or steering is liable for the faults of a compulsory pilot. *Amoco Oil v. The Montclair,* 766 F.2d 473, 1986 AMC 1420 (11th Cir. 1986).

See generally, Hunter, *Liability of Vessel for Negligent Act of Compulsory Pilot,* 8 J. Mar. L. & Com. 87 (1976), and Note, *In Rem Liability for a Vessel Under the Control of a Compulsory Pilot,* 10 Suffolk Transnational L. J. 159 (1986).

14. See *The Maren Lee,* 278 F. 918 (2d Cir. 1922); *Westfal-Larsen & Co. v. The Dora Weems,* 50 F.2d 724, 1931 AMC 1186 (4th Cir. 1931); and *Logue Stevedoring Co. v. The Tug Dalzellance,* 198 F.2d 369, 1952 AMC 1297 (2d Cir. 1952).

15. Brussels Collision Convention of 1910, art. 5. The Pilotage Act, 2 & 3 Geo. 5, ch. 31, § 15 (1913), repealing statutes going back to 1812 (The Pilotage Act, 52 Geo. 3, ch. 39, § 30, amended and reenacted in 1825, 1854, and 1894). See Bederman, *Compulsory Pilotage, Public Policy, and The Early Private International Law of Torts,* 64 Tulane L. Rev. 1033 (1990).

16. *Homer Ramsdell Transportation Co. v. La Compagnie Générale Transatlantique,* supra note 3; cf. *The China,* supra note 8. *Homer Ramsdell* was an action at common law for damage to a pier

master-servant relation with a compulsory pilot, and thus no imputed liability under the *respondeat superior* rule. Absence of *in personam* liability of the owner will, of course, leave claimants without any real remedy where the offending vessel has been sunk.

3. Nonliability of Pilot Associations

In cases of compulsory pilotage, where the offending vessel is lost, questions have arisen concerning the individual liability of the pilot and his pilot's association. Individual pilots are liable for their maritime torts, but they are usually not insured against liability, and they are usually asset-free.[17] In some states, however, pilots are bonded, and the injured party may seek to recover on the bond, although the amount of the recovery is likely to be very small.[18]

The leading case on the liability of voluntary unincorporated pilot associations is *Guy v. Donald,* decided in 1906.[19] Justice Holmes's opinion concerned a collision caused by the negligence of a compulsory pilot; the owners of the piloted vessel, having paid the other colliding vessel's claim for collision damages, sought to hold all members of the pilotage association liable for the amount paid. The Supreme Court rejected the claim of liability of the association and its members, since it could not select or discharge the members, who were licensed by the state, and could not control or direct them in the performance of their duties.[20] Plaintiffs had argued that the commingling of fees created a joint liability of the members of the association, but this argument was flatly rejected.[21]

The methods of operation of the association in *Guy v. Donald* have been closely followed by other pilots' associations, most of which are still uninsured. In *Guy,* the Commonwealth of Virginia had appointed a board of commissioners to license pilots, regulate them, and discipline their failings with the cooperation of the pilots' association, a voluntary, unincorporated body. Fees for pilotage were paid to the association on bills prepared by it, and the fees paid in to the association were deposited in a common fund from which

---

caused by the alleged fault of a compulsory pilot. Justice Gray said it could not have been brought in admiralty, 182 U.S. at 411, because the tort was inflicted on land. This was changed by the Act for the Extension of Admiralty Jurisdiction, 46 U.S.C. § 740. See *United States v. The President Van Buren,* 490 F.2d 504, 1974 AMC 1844 (9th Cir. 1973); *Texaco Trinidad, Inc. v. Afran Transport Co.,* 538 F. Supp. 1038, 1983 AMC 1582 (ED Pa. 1983), aff'd without opinion, 707 F.2d 1395, 1983 AMC 2408 (3d Cir. 1983); *Morania No. 4, Inc. v. The McAllister Sisters,* 778 F. Supp. 701, 1992 AMC 1272 (SDNY 1991), vacated, 869 F. Supp. 157 (SDNY 1992).

17. See *The China,* supra note 8, 74 U.S. at 68, where a recovery against the pilot is described as "mere delusion."

18. *The Fort Armstrong,* 51 F.2d 1063, 1931 AMC 1145 (D Ga. 1931); Cf. *McGrath v. Nolan,* supra note 8.

19. 203 U.S. 399 (1906).

20. 203 U.S. at 407–08.

21. 203 U.S. 408.

the business expenses of the association were paid before the profits were distributed among the members, according to the number of days each member had served on the active list.[22]

Section C. Voluntary or Noncompulsory Pilots

The difference between *in rem* liability and *in personam* freedom from liability in the compulsory pilot situation does not apply to voluntary pilotage. In this situation the vessel owner may have employed a licensed member of a pilotage association, although not required to do so. The decision to use a pilot when not required under penal or civil penalties is seen as a voluntary employment[23] in the service of the ship, so that the vessel and her owners (or charterers, if the vessel is operating under bareboat charter) become fully liable for all damages caused or contributed to by the actions of the pilot.[24]

1. Docking Pilots

A docking pilot—usually the master of one of the assisting tugs or a person employed by the tugboat company specially for the purpose of docking and undocking—can be the cause of collisions with other vessels or allisions with wharfs, piers, bridges, or aids to navigation.[25] The legal issues most often center on the interpretation of the "pilotage clause" discussed below. In these cases the docking pilot normally uses the power and steering capacity of the assisted ship as well as the power of the assisting tugs, and the basic principle of maritime tort law is that the docking pilot (and his employer, by reason of the doctrine of *respondeat superior*) is responsible and liable for the damages caused or contributed to by the pilot's fault.[26] The standard of liability is negligence, not a contractual warranty, and necessarily excludes liability for judgment calls where reasonable opinions may differ.[27] The care that the docking pilot must exercise is the same degree of prudence and skill

22. 203 U.S. at 404–05, 407. See also *D/S Atalanta v. United States,* supra note 8; *McGrath v. Nolan,* supra note 8; *Port of Seattle v. The Maria Rubicon,* 404 F. Supp. 302, 1976 AMC 109 (WD Wash. 1975); *General v. Delaware River Pilots' Association,* 254 F. Supp. 447, 1966 AMC 1734 (D Del. 1966); *United Fruit Co. v. Mobile Towing & Wrecking Co.,* 177 F. Supp. 297, 1960 AMC 115 (SD Ala. 1959); *O'Hare v. United States,* 1950 AMC 182 (WD Wash. 1949). Cf. *Spence v. S.E. Alaska Pilots' Assoc.,* 789 F. Supp. 1014, 1994 AMC 910 (D Alaska 1992).

23. *Homer Ramsdell Transportation Co. v. La Compagnie Générale Transatlantique,* supra note 3.

24. *United States v. The President Van Buren,* supra note 16; *The Helen,* 5 F.2d 54, 1925 AMC 267 (2d Cir. 1924); *California v. The Norfolk,* 1978 AMC 144 (ND Cal. 1977).

25. *Gray v. Johansson,* 287 F.2d 852, 1961 AMC 703 (5th Cir. 1961); *Logue Stevedoring Corp. v. The Dalzellance,* 198 F.2d 369, 1952 AMC 1297 (2d Cir. 1952); *International Terminal Operating Co. v. Cia. Naviera Aznar,* 198 F. Supp. 214, 1961 AMC 1758 (SDNY 1961); *Mathiasen Shipping Co. v. United States,* 87 F. Supp. 216, 1949 AMC 1831 (SDNY 1949); *O'Hare v. United States,* supra note 22; *The Niels R. Finsen,* 52 F.2d 795, 1931 AMC 1014 (SDNY 1931).

26. *In re Grace Line,* 517 F.2d 404, 1975 AMC 991 (2d Cir. 1975).

27. *D/S Atalanta v. United States,* supra note 8.

that a reasonable licensed pilot in similar circumstances must exercise—not the simple reasonably prudent person test, but the higher standard of the expert.[28]

2. *The Pilotage Clause*

Liability, as between a colliding vessel and a tugboat company as employer of a docking pilot whose negligence may have contributed to a collision, is customarily governed by contractual language that attempts to cut off the normal operation of *respondeat superior.*[29] The Supreme Court has tolerated pilotage clauses,[30] while holding similar clauses in towage contracts invalid.[31] Justice Black's expressed distinctions are not intellectually satisfying,[32] but it must be accepted that the pilotage clause will give protection to the actual employer of the docking pilot, while the towage clause has been held invalid.

Justification for judicial toleration of the pilotage clause is found today in risk-distribution analysis, the concept that ignores fault and seeks to reduce accident costs by channeling liability through an enterprise certain to be insured and certain to be able to pass along the costs of insurance to the users of the service.[33] Under this view, the economic gain is the avoidance of double insurance of the same risks by tugboat and towed vessel. The economic bargain results from the tugboat company offering a lower rate

---

28. See generally *Atlee v. Northwest Union Packet Co.,* supra note 1, 88 U.S. at 396. See also *Barbey Packing Co. v. The Stavros,* 169 F. Supp. 897, 1959 AMC 1542 (D Or. 1959).

29. *Sun Oil Co. v. Dalzell Towing Co.,* supra note 4.

30. Id.

31. *Bisso v. Inland Waterways Corp.,* 349 U.S. 85, 1955 AMC 899 (1955). See chapter 10, section C.

32. There are distinctions between a pilotage and a towage exemption clause which make it entirely reasonable to hold one valid and the other invalid. A pilotage clause exempts for the negligence of pilots only; a towage clause exempts from all negligence of all towage employees. Pilots hold a unique position in the maritime world and have been regulated extensively both by the states and federal government. Some state laws make them public officers, chiefly responsible to the state, not to any private employer. Under law and custom they have an independence wholly incompatible with the general obligations of obedience normally owed by an employee to his employer. Their fees are fixed by law and their charges must not be discriminatory. As a rule no employer, no person can tell them how to perform their pilotage duties. When the law does not prescribe their duties, pilots are usually free to act on their own best judgment while engaged in piloting a vessel. Because of these differences between pilots and towage employees generally, contracts stipulating against a pilot's negligence cannot be likened to contracts stipulating against towers' negligence.... [*Bisso v. Inland Waterways Corp.,* supra note 31, 349 U.S. at 93–94, 1955 AMC at 907.]

While *Sun Oil* concerned exculpation for the negligence of the tugboat company employee (the docking master), the Supreme Court in *Bisso* describes a compulsory pilot, member of a pilotage association, and not an employee of a corporate owner. Justice Douglas's concurrence notes, "I do not think we know enough about the economics and organization of this business to change the established rule. . ." 349 U.S. at 95, 1955 AMC at 932.

33. See Calabresi, *Some Thoughts on Risk Distribution and the Law of Torts,* 70 Yale L.J. 499 (1961). See also Note, *The Pilotage Clause: Albatross of Admiralty Law,* 64 B.U. L. Rev. 823 (1985).

to users of its employees' services in exchange for acceptance by shipowners of nonliability of the employer for the negligence of its employees.[34]

The form of the pilotage clause litigated in *Sun Oil Co. v. Dalzell Towing Co.*[35] read as follows:

> When the captain of any tug furnished to or engaged in the service of assisting a vessel which is making use of her own propelling power goes on board said vessel, it is understood and agreed that said tugboat captain or licensed pilot becomes the servant of the owners of the vessel assisted in respect to the giving of orders to any of the tugs furnished to or engaged in the assisting service and in respect to the handling of such vessel, and neither those furnishing the tugs and/or the pilot nor the tugs, their owners, agents or charterer shall be liable for any damage resulting therefrom.

The case was not one of collision but of the grounding of an oil tanker in New York Harbor in 1925, when the M/T *Sabine Sun,* assisted by three Dalzell tugs, was being maneuvered into a berth at Bergen Point, where the vessel grounded outside the dredged channel, resulting in substantial damage. The captain of the third tug to join the flotilla went on board the *Sabine Sun* and gave orders to the three assisting tugs, while simultaneously using the vessel's own power and steering.[36] Dalzell's defense to the Sun tanker's claim was the exculpatory language of the pilotage clause. There was, however, no single document containing the clause that had been signed by both parties for this docking. Instead the agreement was "reconstructed" from a telephone call from a Sun employee to a Dalzell employee, requesting tug service and docking, and prior dealings between the parties in which rate schedules, invoices, and receipts containing the printed pilotage clause had been used.[37]

The Supreme Court's brief opinion found that the pilotage clause did not resemble those earlier common carrier and public utility cases where exculpatory clauses were found to violate public policy.[38] Arm's length bargaining and absence of monopoly were key findings in favor of the clause and

---

34. See, e.g. *Twenty Grand Offshore, Inc. v. West India Carriers, Inc.,* 492 F.2d 679, 1974 AMC 2254 (5th Cir. 1974), a towage case dependent on the absence of monopolistic compulsion. Another towage clause case reproduced the almost ideal bargaining (favored by the economists of the University of Chicago school): *Crescent Towing & Salvage Co. v. Dixilyn Drilling Corp.,* 303 F.2d 237, 240–45, 1963 AMC 831 (5th Cir. 1962). The Supreme Court, however, could not discern any appreciable difference from *Bisso* and reversed *per curiam,* 372 U.S. 697, 1963 AMC 829 (1963).

35. *Sun Oil Co. v. Dalzell Towing Co., Inc.,* 55 F.2d 63, 64, 1932 AMC 149 (2d Cir. 1932), aff'd, 287 US. 291, 1933 AMC 35 (1932).

36. 287 U.S. at 293, 1933 AMC at 36.

37. Id.

38. As in *Liverpool & Great Western S.S. Co. v. Phenix Insurance Co.,* 129 U.S. 397 (1889) (liability for shippers' cargo damage claims held not exculpated by carrier's printed clause); *New York*

against the public policy arguments.[39] The Court had no problem with the fictitious employment aspect of the borrowed servant concept, finding it to be "well-established."[40] Accordingly, Sun Oil's claim was defeated by the pilotage clause.

The factual situation of the docking pilot going on board a vessel using her own power is the predicate for application of the clause. Other circumstances, such as tugboat negligence before docking or after undocking may come within the towage clause cases.[41] The situation is similar where the towed vessel is a dead ship without propulsion.[42]

The Second Circuit has strongly supported the validity of the pilotage clause against analogies to the towage clause and has given it a very broad reading, favoring tugboat companies in *Transpacific Carriers v. The Tug Ellen McAllister*[43] and *A/S Atlantica v. Moran Towing & Transp. Co.*[44] That court has refused to construe the language narrowly so as to deny coverage outside of the specified "orders to tugs" and "handling the vessel." The only relief for shipowners came in *Tankers and Tramps Corp. v. The Tugs Jane McAllister and Margaret M. McAllister,*[45] an unusual case where the tugboat company could not establish that the owner of a vessel not ordinarily calling at the port had been informed of the clause in writing. The First and Ninth Circuits[46] and district courts around the United States[47] have recently concurred in the validity of the 1933 pilotage clause. New York and other East Coast tugboat

---

Central Railroad Co. v. Lockwood, 84 U.S. 357 (1873) (railroad exculpation clause in a bill of lading held invalid).

In *Sun Oil Co.* plaintiff had argued the invalidity of the pilotage clause on the basis of *The Syracuse,* 79 U.S. 167 (1871), and *Cia. de Navegacion v. Fireman's Fund Ins. Co. (The Wash Gray),* 277 U.S. 66, 1928 AMC 924 (1928). Rejected in 1932, these cases reemerged to support the invalidity of the towage clause in *Bisso v. Inland Waterways Corp.,* supra note 31.

39. 287 U.S. 294. See generally, Zammit, *The Validity of the Pilotage Clause in Docking Assistance Contracts,* 3 J. Mar. L & Com. 71 (1971).

40. 287 U.S. 295. See generally, *Restatement (Second) of Agency* § 220 (1957).

41. *Boston Metals Corp. v. The Winding Gulf,* 349 U.S. 122, 1955 AMC 927 (1955), decided with *Bisso,* supra note 31.

42. *Gray v. Johansson,* 287 F.2d 852, 1961 AMC 703 (5th Cir. 1961).

43. 336 F.2d 371, 1964 AMC 2570 (2d Cir. 1964). See also *In re Marina Mercante Nicaraguense, S.A.,* 364 F.2d 118, 1966 AMC 2392 (2d Cir. 1966).

44. 498 F.2d 158, 1974 AMC 555 (2d Cir. 1974) (docking pilot's failure to order adequate tug power does not breach warranty of workmanlike service so as to impose liability on tugboat owner; pilotage clause upheld).

45. 358 F.2d 896, 1966 AMC 1205 (2d Cir. 1966). See also *In re Marina Mercante Nicaraguense, S.A.,* 248 F. Supp. 15, 1966 AMC 1777 (SDNY 1965), modified, 364 F.2d 118, 1966 AMC 2392 (2d Cir. 1966); *The West Eldera,* 104 F.2d 670, 1939 AMC 877 (2d Cir. 1939); *The Niels R. Finsen,* 52 F.2d 795, 1931 AMC 1014 (SDNY 1931).

46. *City of Boston v. The Texaco Texas,* 773 F.2d 1396, 1986 AMC 676 (lst Cir. 1985); *States Marine Corp. v. Victory Carriers, Inc.,* 272 F.2d 463, 1959 AMC 2164 (9th Cir. 1959); *Guangco v. Edward Shipping & Mercantile Co.,* 705 F.2d 360 (9th Cir. 1983); *Kane v. Hawaiian Independent Refinery Co.,* 690 F.2d 722, 1984 AMC 1323 (9th Cir. 1982).

47. *California v. The Jules Fribourg,* 140 F. Supp. 333, 1956 AMC 939 (ND Cal. 1956); *Pennsylvania R.R. Corp. v. The Beatrice,* 161 F. Supp. 136, 1958 AMC 1612 (SDNY 1958), aff'd, 275 F.2d 209, 1960 AMC 1408 (2d Cir. 1960); *National Distillers Products Corp. v. Boston Tow Boat Co.,* 134 F. Supp. 194, 1955 AMC 604 (D Mass. 1955); libel dismissed on rehearing, 1955 AMC 1925

companies have revised the clause.[48] Attempts to overturn the clause in certain harbors because of alleged monopoly conditions have not been successful.[49]

3. *Application of the Pilotage Clause to the Towed Vessel's Damage Claim*

This is the clearest case of the applicability of the pilotage clause and fits the facts of *Sun Oil Co. v. Dalzell.*[50] Even before the judicial popularity of risk distribution analysis,[51] appellate courts reined-in district court efforts to find exceptions to the clause.[52]

(D Mass. 1955); *Patterson Terminals, Inc. v. The Johannes Frans,* 209 F. Supp. 705, 1962 AMC 2623 (ED Pa. 1962).

48. The revised form of the pilotage clause used in New York and other East Coast ports reads:

> We do not furnish pilots or pilotage to vessels making use of or having available their own propelling power so that whenever any licensed pilot, or a captain of any tug which is furnished to or is engaged in the service of assisting a vessel making use of or having available her own propelling power, participates in directing the navigation of such vessel, or in directing the assisting tugs, from on board such vessel or from elsewhere, it is agreed that he becomes the borrowed servant of the vessel assisted and her owner or operator for all purposes and in every respect, his services while so engaged being the work of the vessel assisted, her owner and operator, and being subject to the exclusive supervision and control of the vessel's personnel. Any such service performed by any such person is beyond the scope of his employment for us and neither those furnishing the tugs or lending any such person, nor the tugs, their owners, agents, charterers, operators or managers shall be liable for any act or omission of any such person. The provisions of this paragraph may not be changed or modified in any manner whatsoever except by written instrument signed by an officer of this company.
>
> With respect to vessels that are not owned by the person or company ordering the tug service, it is understood and agreed that such person or company warrants that it has authority to bind the vessel owner to all the provisions of the preceding paragraphs, and agrees to indemnify and hold us harmless, and also those furnishing the tugs and the tugs, their owners, agents, charterers, operators and managers, from all damages and expenses that may be sustained or incurred in the event and in consequence of such person or company not having such authority.

See *Trinidad Corp. v. The Sister Katingo,* 280 F. Supp. 976, 1967 AMC 1561 (SDNY 1967); *Federal Steam Navigation Co. v. The Tug Savannah,* 305 F. Supp. 1293, 1970 AMC 115 (SD Ga. 1969); *Reederei Franz Hagen v. The Tug Resolute,* 400 F. Supp. 680, 1976 AMC 2133 (D Md. 1975); *Nippon Yusen Kaisha v. Zepher Shipping Corp.,* 1971 AMC 949 (D Mass. 1971); *Amerada Hess Corp. v. Ogden Saguenay Transport Co.,* 1980 AMC 900 (MD Fla. 1980); *Portland Pipe Line Corp. v. The Barcola,* 1982 AMC 2725 (D Me. 1982); *Ross Towboat Co. v. The Bruarfoss,* 1982 AMC 1374 (D Mass. 1982).

49. A suggestion of monopoly in San Juan, Puerto Rico, was alleged but not proved in *Aetna Ins. Co. v. The Tug John E. Berwind,* 129 F. Supp. 578, 1955 AMC 1296 (D P.R. 1955). Allegations of monopoly or collusion in New York Harbor were rejected in *Trinidad Corp. v. The Sister Katingo,* supra note 48. Allegations of virtual monopoly in Boston Harbor could not overcome precedent in *Nippon Yusen Kaisha v. Zepher Shipping Corp.,* supra note 48. In *Guangco v. Edward Shipping & Mercantile, S.A.,* supra note 46, the identical clause in the contracts of two competitors was upheld.

50. See supra notes 29–30, 35–45.

51. See supra note 33.

52. *Transpacific v. The Ellen F. McAllister,* 336 F.2d 371, 1964 AMC 2570 (2d Cir. 1964); *In re Marina Mercante Nicaraguense,* supra note 45 (2d Cir. decision); *A/S Atlantica v. Moran Towing & Transp. Co.,* 498 F.2d 158, 1974 AMC 555 (2d Cir. 1974); *Kane v. Hawaiian Independent Refinery, Co.,* 690 F.2d 722, 1984 AMC 1323 (9th Cir. 1984).

4. *Application of the Pilotage Clause to the Tugboat's Damage Claim*

Prior to 1955, by construing the fictitious employment language of the pilotage clause to make the docking pilot an employee of the vessel owner when maneuvers caused damage to one of the assisting tugs, the tugboat owners were able to recover these damages from the vessel owner.[53] That right to an affirmative recovery ceased as a result of the Supreme Court's decision in *United States v. Nielson.*[54] In short, the pilotage clause is a shield but not a sword to be used against the other contracting party.[55] Despite the Court's suggestion that the language might be clarified, parties to a pilotage clause have not been able to devise clear compromise language; thus the towed vessel is not liable for damage to the tug under the authority of *Nielson.*

5. *Application of the Pilotage Clause to Damage Claims of Third Parties: Indemnification of Tugboat Owners*

The contractual exculpation of the tugboat company, under the pilotage clause, of a contract between the company and the owner or operator of the towed vessel can have no effect on the rights of third parties sustaining damages in a collision. Third parties will be able to recover from those at fault, regardless of the contractual limitations in the contract between the pilot's actual employer and the vessel being piloted. Nevertheless, the tugboat owner can force the assisted vessel to indemnify it by application of the pilotage clause, even though under maritime tort principles both the tugboat

53. *Mathiasen Shipping Co. v. United States,* 87 F. Supp. 216, 1949 AMC 1831 (SDNY 1949); *Dalzell Co. v. The New York,* 77 F. Supp. 793, 1948 AMC 1230 (EDNY 1948).

54. 349 U.S. 129, 131–32, 1955 AMC 935 (1955), decided with *Bisso,* supra note 31:

> An agreement that one shall not be liable for negligence of a third person cannot easily be read as an agreement that one is entitled to collect damages for negligence of that third person. And there is no reason to stretch contractual language to force payment under circumstances like these. A person supplying his own employees for use by another in a common undertaking cannot usually collect damages because of negligent work by the employee supplied. Clear contractual language might justify imposition of such liability. But the contractual language here does not meet such a test and we do not construe it as authorizing respondent to recover damages from petitioner.

55. It may be helpful to note briefly the shifts in the Supreme Court's reasoning in the three cases decided on May 16, 1955, Justice Black having written all three majority opinions. In *Bisso,* supra note 31, decided 6–3 (towed vessel vs. tug owner), he held the towage clause invalid. Justice Frankfurter dissented on the basis of the clarity of the towage clause provisions, spotlighting the fictitious employment language as manifesting an intention that the tug should not be held liable for injury to the tow. In *Winding Gulf,* supra note 41, decided 6–2 (owner of towed dead ship v. third party colliding vessel), he held the towage clause invalid insofar as it purported to impose collision liability on the dead ship. Justice Frankfurter concurred, construing the indemnification provision to be unclear, while his *Bisso* colleagues in dissent (Justices Burton and Reed) continued their dissent on the basis of a broad view of the fictitious employment clause. Lastly, in *Nielson,* supra note 54, decided 6–2 (tugboat owner v. towed vessel), the pilotage clause was held unavailable to shift liability for plaintiff's employees' negligence to defendants. The Burton-Reed dissent emphasizes the fictitious employment language of the clause.

company as actual employer of the negligent docking pilot and the owner or operator of the assisted vessel, as fictitious employer *(in personam),* and the vessel herself as an instrumentality of the negligent conduct *(in rem)* would be jointly and severally liable to the third party.[56]

While the Supreme Court has not reviewed the indemnification aspect of the pilotage clause, unquestioned acceptance of the *Sun Oil* principle, even without the modern support of risk distribution analysis, will result in the continued absorption of the cost of third party damages by the assisted vessel's protection and indemnity insurer. Accordingly, collision damage to other vessels or allision damage to shore structures will be the responsibility and liability of the assisted vessel, although in fact caused by the negligence of the docking pilot.[57]

---

56. See *Societa per Azione de Navegazione Italia v. Los Angeles,* 31 Cal. 3d 446, 1982 AMC 2281 (S.C. Cal. 1982) (*in rem* process held unavailable in a state court).

57. *City of Boston v. The Texaco Texas,* 773 F.2d 1396, 1986 AMC 676 (1st Cir. 1985); *Consolidated Rail Corp. v. The Lagada Beach,* 1983 AMC 1242 (ED Pa. 1983). The Ninth Circuit has supplied the following rationale: "[T]here are substantial policy interests in permitting the parties to allocate risks among themselves, both in terms of acquisition and retention of appropriate insurance coverage and of effective management of sea-going vessels. Where access to insurance is considered, it is apparent that the pilotage clause assigned risk consistently with standard coverage, since the insurance commonly carried by sea-going vessels covers accidents under pilotage." *Kane v. Hawaiian Independent Refinery, Inc.,* supra note 52, at 690 F.2d 724, 1984 AMC at 1325. For the added complexity of foreign sovereign ownership (and possible immunity under the Foreign Sovereign Immunity Act, 28 U.S.C. §§ 1602–11), see Jarvis, *Confusion in the Harbor: Compulsory Pilots Collide with the Motorship FSU,* 6 N.W. J. of Int'l Bus. 1010 (1984).

CHAPTER TEN

COLLISIONS INVOLVING TUGS AND TOWS

Section A. Introduction

According to American Waterways Operators, Inc., the trade organization of the American tugboat industry, the industry consists of 600 towing and barge companies employing about 175,000 people, earning good wages, with about 7,000 tugs and 30,000 barges for use in harbors and internal waters. The industry carries 57 percent of all U.S grain, 30 percent of all petroleum for internal use, and an ever-increasing amount of hazardous chemicals. In 1990 the industry moved 775.3 million tons of cargo—15 percent of all domestic traffic.[1]

The tug and barge industry has survived severe competition with the rail and truck industries by offering the cheapest freight rates in the entire transportation field. In comparison with other modes of transportation, it is largely unregulated. Unfortunately, these cheap rates have been achieved through cost-cutting, sometimes at substantial expense to society because of human error casualties that result in heavy costs to insurers, shippers, other users of the waterways, maritime workers who are injured, and the families of those who are killed.

The majority of collisions and allisions in the tug and tow industry are the result of human error. The U.S. Coast Guard blamed human error for 7,664 of the 12,971 towage casualties over the twelve-year period from 1980 to 1991—about 60 percent of the total.[2] Very often the human error is the result of fatigue, since 16-hour days are not unknown in the industry, as the number of officers and other crew members has been drastically reduced to cut costs.[3]

---

1. Journal of Commerce (New York), Dec. 10, 1993, pp. 1A and 4A. See also A. Parks & E. Cattell, *The Law of Tug, Tow, and Pilotage,* 5–6, (3d. ed. 1994) (hereinafter "Parks & Cattell"). Any discussion of towage problems under U.S. law must first refer to this work, begun by the late Alex Parks, whose treatise is now in its third edition under Edward V. Cattell, Jr., with contributions from Tosh Hayashi of Halifax, Jonathan Lux and William Marsh of London, and Derrick R. Hentze of Sydney.

2. *Review of Marine Safety Issues Regarding Uninspected Towing Vessels,* U.S. Coast Guard, Office of Marine Safety, Security and Environmental Protection, and Office of Navigation Safety and Waterway Services, Report to the Commandant, Dec. 1, 1993, and Commandant's Action thereon.

3. *Shipboard Crew Fatigue, Safety and Reduced Manning,* Study by the Transportation Safety Center of the Department of Transportation (DOT-MARAD 84090014 of Nov. 1990.) (The maximum length of time that an officer may work in a 24-hour period is 12 hours. 46 U.S.C. § 8104[h]

Tugs function in a variety of ways, and thus it is not possible to generalize about types.[4] On the open ocean and in coastal transportation, the tug usually leads, with its stern hawser pulling the tow. In harbor maneuvers, such as the docking or undocking of a large vessel, there may be tugs assigned to push or pull at different positions on the vessel, as necessary. In river systems, the tug will probably be pushing barges made up into flotillas, some far greater in length and breadth than the largest single vessels afloat. The capacity of the tug to push or pull enormous loads has increased from the famous Second World War V4MA1 design of 2,320 horsepower, to the diesel tug with 15,000 horsepower or more. A new oceangoing tug may cost between $10 million and $20 million.[5]

Today the tug master has direct control of the engine from the bridge and instant communication with the tow and other vessels in the vicinity. No special navigational privileges arise merely because tugs and tows are awkward and difficult to maneuver; however, the unmaneuverability of a flotilla of tug and barges may be so extreme as to bring in the special circumstances rule.[6] The Inland Rules provide specially for the lights and shapes to be exhibited by tugs and tows, and for the fog signals they must sound when visibility is restricted,[7] but there is no special regime of law relating to collision avoidance where tugs and tows are involved.[8]

Section B. Liability Principles

1. *Negligence*

General principles of negligence are applied to collisions or allisions involving tugs and tows. The tort duties of care between tug and tow originate from

---

[1988] and 46 CFR 15.705. See also *An Assessment of Towing Vessel Manning Requirements,* U.S. Coast Guard, Office of Marine Safety, Security and Environmental Protection, July 1994.)

4. See Davey, *The Tug and Tow Relationship in the United States,* 70 Tul. L. Rev. 475 (1995).

5. Lloyd's List (London), Special Report on Towage and Salvage, Mar. 20, 1995, p. 4.

6. COLREGS Rule 2(b) "... [D]ue regard shall be had to all dangers of navigation and collision and to any special circumstances, including the limitations of the vessels involved. . . ." See *The Luzerne,* 204 F. 981 (2d Cir. 1913). Two tugs with flotillas were entering the East River in New York Harbor in a southerly direction, one from Hell Gate with a current of 4 mph, and the other from the Harlem River with a current of 1½ mph. Applying former Inland Rule 27 (the special circumstances rule) the Harlem River flotilla was held in sole fault for failing to hold back while the Hell Gate flotilla proceeded.

7. Cf. COLREGS Rules 24, 27(c), and 35(c) and (e).

8. *The Syracuse,* 79 U.S. 167 (1871); *The William H. Webb,* 81 U.S. 406 (1871); *The Margaret,* 94 U.S. 494 (1876); *The J.P. Donaldson,* 167 U.S. 599 (1897); *Stevens v. The White City,* 285 U.S. 195, 1932 AMC 468 (1932).

contract relationships,[9] but of course contractual provisions cannot be extended involuntarily to third parties to the relationship.[10]

Under negligence principles, the tug and its towed vessel are a unit, and the "dominant mind" of the unit is presumed to be the tug,[11] unless there is proof of independent fault of the towed vessel contributing to cause the collision.[12] The relationship of the tug to its tow is not that of bailor-bailee, insured-insurer, or shipper-carrier.[13] However, there may be circumstances when the shipper-carrier relationship exists, because the parties have intended to contract for affreightment of cargo rather than towage.[14]

2. *Navigational Duties of the Tug in Collision Cases*

The tug has the duty to exercise reasonable care in the circumstances and to perform in a workmanlike manner.[15] At the very least this duty of workmanlike

---

9. *The Syracuse,* supra note 8; *The Wash Gray,* 277 U.S. 66, 81, 1928 AMC 923, 925–27 (1928); *Bisso v. Inland Waterways Corp.,* 349 U.S. 85, 85–86, 1955 AMC 899–901 (1955).

10. See, e.g., *Boston Metals Co. v. The Winding Gulf,* 349 U.S. 122, 123, 1955 AMC 927, 928 (1955); *Pennsylvania R.R. Co. v. The Beatrice,* 275 F.2d 209, 211–14, 1960 AMC 1408, 1408–14 (1960).

11. *Sturgis v. Boyer,* 65 U.S. 110, 121–23 (1861); *The Civilta,* 103 U.S. 699, 701–02 (1880); *The Margaret,* supra note 8. See generally, Hooper & Van Hemmen, *Burdens of Proof Between Tugs and Tows,* 70 Tul. L. Rev. 531 (1995).

12. *Liverpool, Brazil & River Plate Steam Navigation Co. v. Brooklyn Eastern District Terminal,* 251 U.S. 48 (1919). The question was whether the value of the entire flotilla (all belonging to the owner of the tug) or the tug alone was to be surrendered in the limitation proceeding. Justice Holmes held that only the tug had to be surrendered, "... [F]or the purposes of liability the passive instrument of the harm does not become one with the actively responsible vessel by being attached to it." 251 U.S. at 52.

13. *Stevens v. The White City,* supra note 8, 285 U.S. at 200–02, 1932 AMC at 470–72. Negligence cannot be presumed from the damaged condition of the tow at the conclusion of the towage. (A new motorboat was towed across New York Harbor to Port Newark; the hull planking was found broken on arrival, but there was no evidence as to how the damage occurred.) See generally, Parrish, *Liabilities as between Tug and Tow,* 39 Fed. Ins. & Corp. Counsel Q. 275 (1989).

14. *Sacramento Navigation Co v. Salz,* 273 U.S. 326, 328, 1927 AMC 397, 398–99 (1927). The owner of a tug and a "dumb" barge had issued a bill of lading for carriage of a cargo of barley on the barge in the name of the barge only. The Supreme Court brought in the liability of the tug, describing the relation of both tug and barge to the barge's cargo as a single contract of affreightment and not two separate contracts. The Court said, "Towage service is the employment of one vessel to expedite the voyage of another. Here, while there was towage service, the contract actually made with respondent was not to tow a vessel but to transport goods, and plainly that contract was a contract of affreightment." 273 U.S. at 328, 1927 AMC at 398–99. See *In re D & H Corp. (The Tug Libra),* 1994 AMC 2285 (ED Va. 1993). Cf. *Mississippi Valley Barge Line v. T.L. James & Co.,* 244 F.2d 263, 267–68, 1957 AMC 1649, 1653–54 (5th Cir. 1957), holding that Harter Act defenses are unavailable for the towage of a barge from New Orleans to Tennessee and return; the tug was held liable when the barge careened, dumped the load of construction equipment, and sank. The late Judge John R. Brown suggested that incorporation of COGSA by reference into a towage contract would be invalid under the *Bisso* doctrine, supra note 9, discussed in section C, infra. See *Hercules v. Stevens Shipping Co.,* 698 F.2d 726, 737–39, 1983 AMC 1786, 1797 (5th Cir. 1983). See also *Pure Oil Co. v. The Caribbean,* 370 F.2d 121, 123, 1996 AMC 446, 447 (5th Cir. 1966).

15. *The Margaret,* supra note 8; *Stevens v. The White City,* supra note 8; *Winslow v. Thompson,* 134 F. 546, 549 (1st Cir. 1904); *National Transport Corp. v. Tug Abqaiq,* 294 F. Supp. 1080, 1086,

performance resembles the *res ipsa loquitur* presumption applied to falling objects in ordinary tort law; that is, a burden of explaining away the apparent negligence.[16] This is clearly a tort duty and not a warranty of workmanlike service arising out of contract.[17]

The particular grievous faults of tugs in collision cases are of three types: (a) the unseaworthiness of the tug, (b) the improper length of the towline, and (c) the unpreparedness or ignorance of the tug master respecting the conditions to be encountered.

(a) Tug Unseaworthiness. This may consist of general unseaworthiness due to age or improper maintenance,[18] or it may be particular to the job; e.g., insufficient power to accomplish the task[19] or improper composition of a

---

1970 AMC 203, 212 (SDNY 1968), aff'd, 418 F.2d 1241, 1970 AMC 213 (2d Cir. 1969), and *Offshore Co. v. G & H Offshore Towing Co.*, 262 F. Supp. 282, 286–87, 1966 AMC 2172, 2177–78 (SD Tex. 1966). See also *R.T.C. No. 20 Corp. v. The Tug Bronx*, 1981 AMC 2465, 2467 (SDNY 1981).

16. *The William H. Webb*, supra note 8, at 414 (the "duty of explanation arose because the tow had grounded on a shoal 10 miles off course); *Bisso v. Waterways Transportation Corp.*, supra note 9, (stranding gave rise to an obligation of satisfactory explanation); *Lehigh Valley Transportation Co v. Knickerbocker Steam Towage Co.*, 212 F. 708, 710 (2d Cir. 1914); *The Hardy*, 229 F. 985, 986 (9th Cir. 1916); *The Anaconda*, 164 F.2d 224, 228, 1947 AMC 1658, 1664 (4th Cir. 1947).

Res ipsa loquitur does not come from Roman law, but rather from a nineteenth-century English judge, Chief Baron Pollock, in *Byrne v. Boadle*, 159 Eng. Rep. 299 (Exchequer, 1863). In American law the facts do not speak softly of negligence; rather they *cry out* "Negligence." Thus, it might better be called *exclamat res ipsa* rather than *res ipsa loquitur*.

17. See *James McWilliams Blue Line, Inc. v. Esso Standard Oil Co.*, 245 F.2d 84, 86–87, 1957 AMC 1213, 1215–16 (2d Cir. 1957). Cf. *Fairmont Shipping Corp. v. Chevron National Oil Corp.*, 511 F.2d 1252, 1975 AMC 261 (2d Cir.). The warranty concept is disapproved in Parks & Cattell, 356–58. Cf. Alvey, *The Implied Warranty of Workmanlike Performance in Towage: A Viable Theory?* 7 [Tulane] Mar. Law. 1 (1982). Thus the contract of towage establishes the duty of care in the circumstances. In *Stevens v. The White City*, supra note 8, the Supreme Court said, "... In a suit against the tug for injury to the tow, the burden is upon the tow's owner to show that the injury was caused by a breach of that duty." 285 U.S. at 202, 1932 AMC at 472.

18. *The N.Y. Marine Co. No. 2—The Wessels*, 33 F.2d 272, 1929 AMC 978 (2d Cir. 1929); *The Admiral—The Cleveco*, 154 F.2d 605, 1946 AMC 933 (6th Cir. 1946); *The McAllister—The Cortlandt*, 18 F. Supp. 106, 107–8, 1937 AMC 293, 295 (EDNY 1937); *Dow Chemical v. Dixie Carriers*, 330 F. Supp. 1304, 1972 AMC 145 (SD Tex. 1972), aff'd, 463 F.2d 120, 1972 AMC 2137 (5th Cir. 1972); and *R.T.C. No. 20 Corp. v. The Tug Bronx*, supra note 15.

But see *Hendry v. Aircraft Rescue Vessels*, 113 F. Supp. 198, 1953 AMC 2115 (ED La. 1953) (tug without radio not thereby unseaworthy). Note, however, that in *The T.J. Hooper*, 60 F.2d 737, 1932 AMC 1169 (2d Cir.), Judge Learned Hand rejected the defense that absence of a radio for weather predictions was excusable because not then required by statute or trade custom.

19. *The Syracuse*, supra note 8, at 172–73; *W.E. Hedger Transportation Corp. v. The Tug Rob*, 122 F.2d 312, 1941 AMC 1201 (2d Cir. 1941); *Publicker Industries Inc. v. The Tugboat Neptune Co.*, 171 F.2d 48, 49–50, 1949 AMC 121, 123–24 (3d Cir. 1948); *The Severance*, 152 F.2d 916, 920–21, 1946 AMC 128, 135–36 (4th Cir. 1946); *Daniels v. Wienertor*, 1966 AMC 817 (MD Fla. 1966); *Universal Tramp Shipping Co. v. Irish Salt Mining Co.*, 1970 AMC 1783 (D Mass. 1970); *Nissho-Iwai American Corp. v. The Grand Day*, 1980 AMC 2882 (SDNY 1980); *Harbor Tug & Barge, Inc. v. Belcher Towing Co.*, 733 F.2d 823 (11th Cir. 1984).

Cf. *Farrell Lines Inc. v. The Birkenstein*, 207 F. Supp. 500, 1963 AMC 1846 (SDNY 1962). But see *The Frances*, 101 F.2d 30, 32–33, 1939 AMC 58, 62–63 (4th Cir. 1938); *United States v. The Westervelt*, 135 F. Supp. 596, 599–600, 1956 AMC 344, 348–49 (SDNY 1956); *The Tugs Jackson and Metropolitan No. 3*, 82 F. Supp. 595, 600–01, 1949 AMC 449, 458–60 (EDNY 1949).

flotilla of tug and barges.[20] Due care under the circumstances requires that the tug inspect its own towlines, and may even require that the tug inspect towlines belonging to the towed vessel, if the tow's towlines appear to be frayed or otherwise defective.[21]

(b) Improper Length of Towlines. COLREGS have no provisions governing the length of towlines. There are, however, such provisions in the Code of Federal Regulations implementing the Inland Rules.[22] The present rules on towing hawsers are set out below.[23] They are not as precise as earlier versions in the Pilot Rules for Inland Waters, Great Lakes, and Western Rivers. Note that the penalty for an unlawful towline is against the tug master's license.

---

20. See *Tidewater Marine Activities, Inc. v. American Towing Co.,* 437 F.2d 124, 1971 AMC 307 (5th Cir. 1970); *The Margaret Irving—The A.S. Sherman,* 47 F.2d 230, 1931 AMC 147 (2d Cir. 1931); *The Winona,* 1935 AMC 867 (SDNY 1935); *The Tug NL-5—Chesapeake Bay Bridge-Tunnel,* 1968 AMC 1427 (ED Va. 1968); *United States v. The Tug Parris Island (T-2 Tanker Midsection—The Chilula),* 215 F. Supp. 144, 148, 1963 AMC 643, 647–48 (ED N.C. 1963); *The U.P. No. 109,* 1931 AMC 1782 (EDNY 1931); *Barge No. 90 Corp. v. The Tug Helen L. Tracey,* 1964 AMC 145, 147 (SDNY 1964); and *Collier v. 3 A's Towing Co.,* 652 F. Supp. 576 (SD Ala. 1987).

21. *Slaten v. Hopemount Shipping Co. (In re Hoperange),* 345 F.2d 451, 1965 AMC 2203 (5th Cir. 1965) (petition to limit liability denied); *The H.S. Hayward,* 18 F.2d 75, 1927 AMC 489 (2d Cir. 1927). Cf. *Carlsen v. A. Paladini, Inc. (The Three Sisters),* 5 F.2d 387, 1925 AMC 828 (9th Cir. 1925), and *Pasco Marketing, Inc. v. Taylor Towing Service,* 554 F.2d 808 (8th Cir. 1977).

22. See 33 U.S.C. § 152, which requires the commandant of the U.S. Coast Guard to prepare regulations limiting the length of hawsers between towing vessels and seagoing barges in tow and the length of such tows within any of the inland waters of the United States designated and defined from time to time pursuant to 33 U.S.C. § 151. Such regulations have the force of law.

Section 151 authorizes the Secretary of the department in which the Coast Guard is operating (Transportation, in peacetime) to establish demarcation lines dividing the high seas from inland waters for the purpose of determining the applicability of "special navigational rules," (i.e., the Inland Rules, in lieu of COLREGS) and the applicability of each statute (such as § 152) that refers to § 151. The designated lines may not be located more than 12 miles from the base line from which the territorial sea is measured.

23. §163.01 *Application.*

> (a) The regulations in this part apply to vessels navigating the harbors, rivers, and inland waters of the United States except the Great Lakes and their connecting and tributary waters as far east as Montreal, the Red River of the North, the Mississippi River and its tributaries above Huey P. Long Bridge, and that part of the Atchafalaya River above its junction with the Plaquemine-Morgan City alternate waterway.
> (b) Seagoing barges and their towing vessels shall be subject to the requirements in this part under the provision of section 14 of the Act of May 28, 1908, as amended (sec. 14, 35 Stat. 428, as amended; 33 U.S.C. § 152). Under the provisions of section 15 of the Act of May 28, 1908, as amended (sec. 15, 35 Stat. 429; 33 U.S.C. § 153), the penalty for use of an unlawful towline shall be an action against the master of the towing vessel seeking the suspension or revocation of his license.

§163.05 *Tows of seagoing barges within inland waters.*

> (a) The tows of seagoing barges when navigating the inland waters of the United States shall be limited in length to five vessels, including the towing vessel or vessels.

§163.20 *Bunching of Tows.*

> (a) In all cases where tows can be bunched, it should be done.
> (b) Tows navigating in the North and East Rivers of New York must be bunched above a line drawn between Robbins Reef Light and Owls Head, Brooklyn, but the

The connection between vessels being towed astern and the tug is the towline or hawser, which is often visible. A very long towline can produce unmaneuverability, leading to collision and loss of the tug or tow. Prudent seamanship requires that the length of the hawser be determined in light of the volume, weight, and size of the tow as well as the condition of wind, wave, tide, and current. Tugs have been held at fault where the length of the towline is improper—usually too long, but occasionally too short. See, for example, *The H.M. Flagler—The Bern,*[24] where a 100-fathom towline was held excessively long, the court noting that towlines of over 75 fathoms in length require extraordinary care. In that case, a collision occurred in Kill Van Kull, New York Harbor, during a starboard to starboard passing (made necessary by low water and deep draft). The barge was caught in a tidal rip and drifted into the oncoming *Flagler.* The Second Circuit reasoned:

> We hold the *Bern* [the tug] liable, therefore, not because of the length of the hawser, but because, using a hawser the length she employed, she failed to control her tow and to keep it in line in tidewaters, and permitted it to swing across the *Flagler*'s bow. If the *Bern* had controlled her tow, this collision would never have happened.

Thus loss of control rather than length of hawser creates liability. The foreseeable peril is the power of the tug becoming insufficient to overcome the expectable forces of tide, wave, wind, and current.[25]

An example from a canal passage is *The John C. Enright—The William C. Fox.*[26] On the New York Barge Canal, at Lock No. 12 in the Mohawk River, the Tug *Fox* with a flotilla of four barges, eastbound with a hawser estimated at 300 feet long, contributed to a collision with vessels astern of its flotilla that then allided with the lock. The court found the *Fox* at fault, reasoning, "I think it is very clear that, if there had been a short hawser from the tug to the first two boats of the fleet, and the tug had continued into the lock keeping that hawser taut, the accident could not have occurred."[27]

---

quarantine anchorage and the north entrance to Ambrose Channel shall be avoided in the process of bunching tows.

(c) Tows must be bunched above the mouth of the Schuylkill River, Pa.

24. 1 F.2d 259, 263, 1924 AMC 1331 (2d Cir. 1924).

25. See *The Seneca Sun—The Tug Elizabeth S. Hooper and Tow,* 143 F. Supp. 258, 266, 1956 AMC 1519, 1530 (ED Pa. 1956), where the outbound tug's hawser was 1,100 feet longer than allowed under the then-applicable rule, contributing to the drifting of the barge into collision with the inbound tanker; *Newton Creek Towing Co. v. The Tug Christine Moran,* 115 F. Supp. 244, 247, 1953 AMC 2046, 2050 (SDNY 1953), involving two tugs with towed barges in New London Harbor, where the hawsers of both tugs exceeded the then-applicable rule (75-fathom limit), contributing to collision of the towed barges. Mutual fault of both tugs was found.

26. 36 F.2d 821, 1929 AMC 1694 (WDNY 1919), aff'd, 40 F.2d 588 (2d Cir. 1930). Rule 40 of The Barge Canal Rules provided, "In passing into and out of locks, no towing line in excess of fifty feet in length shall be used by towing floats." 36 F.2d at 822, 1929 AMC at 1694.

27. 36 F.2d at 822, 1929 AMC at 1694.

In *Tanker Hygrade No. 12 v. Moran Tug & Towing Co.*,[28] the district court placed sole fault on a tug whose barges in tow lost headway when the towline was slackened to an excessive length (from a total of 1,100 feet to a total of 2,800 feet) in Swash Channel, New York Harbor, so that the barges drifted across the channel and collided with the inbound tank barge, also under tow.

In *The Norsworthy—The Titan*,[29] the Tug *Titan* was held at fault for the stranding of its barge, *Norsworthy*, at Southwest Pass of the Mississippi River, after shortening the towline from between 1,400 and 1,500 feet to 150 feet, in preparation for entering the pass. The court found that the tow should have been lashed alongside or the hawser shortened further before risking the river currents. Thus, where the towline is inappropriately long, the tug is likely to be held liable for damages that result from a collision or allision.

Towlines can also be too short to accommodate the conditions of wind and wave. In *Val Line v. The Tug Harry R. Connors*,[30] the tug was towing a barge loaded with 200,000 gallons of oil on a short hawser, in the face of stiff winds and choppy seas. The bargee warned the tug master against the short hawser, but he ignored the warning. The towing hawser parted, and the tug damaged the barge, resulting in a finding of tug negligence.[31]

George W. Rogers Construction Corp. v. The Tug Ocean King[32] involved the capsizing of a pile driver being towed by a tug on Long Island Sound in calm weather; the court found that a combination of too short a hawser (about 150 feet) plus excessive speed of the tug caused the pile driver to flip over.[33]

Limitation of liability was denied in *The Michele*,[34] where one of the factors leading to the loss of life on a 900-horsepower tug was the short hawser. (The entire hawser length was estimated at between 600 feet and 1,000 feet and only 300 feet to 500 feet of it was out.) The tug (68.9 feet long) was towing a barge

---

28. 33 F. Supp. 149, 149–151, 1940 AMC 924, 924–28 (EDNY 1940), aff'd, 130 F.2d 256, 1942 AMC 1047 (2d Cir. 1942). See generally *White Stack Towing Corp. v. Bethlehem Steel Co. (The Bornholm—The Tug Fort Moultrie and Tow)*, 279 F.2d 419, 1960 AMC 2294 (4th Cir. 1960). The Tug *Fort Moultrie* and a laden barge with a 1,200-foot hawser, proceeding at 4.5 knots in heavy fog, collided in Chesapeake Bay off Point Lookout with the M/S *Bornholm*, proceeding in ballast and reducing speed from 10 knots to 4 knots. The tug's failure to shorten the hawser was found to be "glaring," while the ship's maneuvers were excused as *in extremis;* the court imposed sole fault on the tug. See also *Newton Creek Towing Co. v. The Tug Christine Moran*, supra note 25; and *American Hawaiian Steamship Co. v. The Tug Baldrock (The Ohioan)*, 1934 AMC 1282 (EDNY 1934). Near Scotland Lightship and Gedney Channel in New York Harbor in heavy fog the ocean Tug *Baldrock* with three barges on hawsers of 1,200 feet (4,400 feet total length of flotilla) collided with a 407-foot long steamship proceeding at 8 knots. The result was mutual fault; the tug was held at fault for failing to shorten the towing hawsers to the required maximum of 450 feet.

29. *Petroleum Navigation Co. v. Intracoastal Towing and Transportation Co. (The Norsworthy—The Titan)*, 1930 AMC 1506 (SD Tex. 1930), district court opinion corrected, and as corrected, aff'd, 1930 AMC 1709, 1709–12 (5th Cir. 1930).

30. 66 F. Supp. 125, 1946 AMC 429 (EDNY 1946).

31. Id.

32. 252 F. Supp. 657, 1965 AMC 2545 (SDNY 1965).

33. 252 F. Supp. at 655, 1965 AMC at 2556.

34. *Puamier v. The Barge BT 1793 (The Michele)*, 395 F. Supp. 1019, 1974 AMC 2637, 2651 (ED Va. 1974).

(203.5 feet long) on the open ocean from Miami to Richmond in November when it encountered heavy seas, listed to port, and then rolled over to port and sank as the barge dragged the tug underwater. The court explained:

> We cannot say whether the sinking occurred solely because the *Michele* was not powerful enough or big enough, or because the tow line was too short for a tow in rough seas. We conclude, rather, that all of these contributed to a substantial degree, and it is not necessary for the plaintiff to prove which cause contributed to the greatest degree or that one was the sole cause.[35]

The short hawser, furnished by the tug owner, had the decisive role in the denial of limitation.[36]

The boundary line between inland and international waters has been a major consideration in several of the towing hawser problem cases. Shifting from international waters (with no hawser length limit) to U.S. inland waters (with hawser length limits), or vice versa, presents problems in the applicability of the Inland Rules. Thus, in *Mystic Steamship Co. v. The Antonio Ferraz,*[37] where the maximum length under the Inland Rules was 450 feet (75 fathoms), but the towing hawser was 1,500 feet long, the court of appeals disregarded the length of tow violation when the collision occurred *after* the tug and tow had entered international waters, and the length of tow was not the proximate cause of the collision or the resulting damage.

In *Tiger Shipping Co. v. The Tug Carville,*[38] the towed vessel entered inland waters after coming from a foreign port. Heavy seas and adverse weather made the failure to shorten the towline from 1,200 feet to the required maximum of 450 feet an excusable error.

In *Brodospas v. United States,*[39] a submerged nuclear submarine, the *USS Von Steuben,* became entangled, due to her own fault, in a 3,400-foot towline from the Tug *Fairplay* to the dead ship *Sealady,* 40 miles outside of Cadiz Harbor, Spain. The tug was going ahead at a speed of 2 knots while shortening the ocean towline, when suddenly the tug began to go *in reverse.* The submarine then unexpectedly surfaced into the bottom of the tow. The United States' defense that the tug's towline was excessively long was rejected, and the government was held in sole fault.

The court rejected a defense based on the different standards between Inland and International Rules in *Sword Line v. The Tug Joseph H. Moran.*[40] The Moran tug, with two sludge barges carrying the solid product of New York City sewers, in tow with a 225-fathom hawser to the first barge and a

35. 395 F. Supp. at 1034, 1974 AMC at 2651.
36. Id.
37. 498 F.2d 538, 1974 AMC 545 (2d Cir. 1974).
38. 381 F. Supp. 1340, 1342–43, 1974 AMC 1957, 1960–61 (ED Va. 1974).
39. 1975 AMC 117 (SDNY 1974).
40. 57 F. Supp. 183, 184–85, 1944 AMC 1375, 1378–79 (EDNY 1944).

90-fathom hawser beyond to the second, and the incoming vessel, *Dixie Sword,* were operating in heavy fog at night in the vicinity of the Ambrose Light Ship (as it then was) at the entrance to New York Harbor. Both vessels were on northerly courses when they collided in international waters. The tug argued that having proceeded from the sludge dumping grounds in international waters, there was no obligation to shorten the towline until actual entry into inland waters. The court, however, rejected the tug's defense of absence of a rule on hawser length and applied the rule of "cautious" seamanship in the prevailing circumstances of adverse weather, stressing the fact that the tug was crossing a well-travelled ocean lane in a blanket of fog. The court held that the tug should have shortened the long hawsers, and accordingly found mutual fault.[41]

The important question regarding improper towlines is whether the *Pennsylvania* Rule burden of proof is applicable to the tug and tow situation. The Fifth Circuit applied the *Pennsylvania* Rule to the towage situation in *Candies Towing Co. Inc. v. The B & C Eserman.*[42] A Fourth Circuit case, *The Gezina—The G.W. Patterson,*[43] held that the tug's excessive towline was a condition and not a cause of the collision, so that the *Pennsylvania* Rule burden was not applicable.

(c) Tug Master Unpreparedness or Ignorance. Unfamiliarity with the waters or the special hazards of wind and tide is a frequent source of trouble (and collision) for tug masters who are expected to know everything on the charts as well as many things that are *not* on the charts, but which should be known to persons habitually navigating the specified waters.[44] This obliga-

---

41. 57 F. Supp. at 185, 1944 AMC at 1379. The court also considered it a fault that the barges did not give fog signals, even though not required to do so. Id. Further, the vessel's log appeared to have been altered and the bell books were not produced; thus it was impossible to prove that the vessel had stopped before collision.

42. 673 F.2d 91, 93–94, 1983 AMC 2033, 2036–37 (5th Cir. 1982). See also *Allied Chemical Corp. v. Hess Tankship Co.,* 661 F.2d 1044, 1052–53, 1982 AMC 1271, 1281–82 (5th Cir 1981); *Newton Creek Transportation Co. v. The Tug Christine Moran,* supra note 25; and *Wall v. William G. Fox,* 40 F.2d 588, 1930 AMC 907 (2d Cir. 1930).

43. 89 F.2d 300, 304–05, 1937 AMC 660, 665–67 (4th Cir. 1937), finding excessive hawser length (2,700 feet, instead of the required maximum of 1,400 feet for Inland Waters [Martha's Vineyard] still attached when preparing to anchor at Vineyard Haven could not have contributed to the collision). See also *Associated Dredging Co. v. Continental Marine Towing Co.,* 617 F. Supp. 961, 966 (ED La. 1985) (failure to lengthen the towing hawser excused as a cause of the capsizing of a towed dredge, in view of wave-wash damage from two large vessels); *Triboro Scow Corp. v. The Tug Lion,* 1942 AMC 745 (EDNY 1942).

44. The tug master must know water levels, depth of water and state of the tides, currents, ordinary obstructions, width and length of channels, and clearance of bridges. See *DiMillo v. Sheepscot Pilots, Inc.,* 870 F.2d 746, 1993 AMC 2699 (1st Cir. 1989); *Tug Ocean Prince, Inc. v. United States,* 584 F.2d 1151, 1978 AMC 1786 (2d Cir. 1978); *Mid-America Transportation Co. v. National Marine Service, Inc.,* 497 F.2d 776, 1974 AMC 1943 (8th Cir. 1974), on remand, 526 F.2d 629, 1976 AMC 389 (8th Cir. 1975); *Riverway Co. v. Spivey Marine & Harbor Services, Inc.,* 598 F. Supp. 909 (SD Ill. 1984); *Riverside Trawling Co. v. The Vulcan,* 60 F. Supp. 158, 1945 AMC 484 (ED La. 1945); *The Joseph Moran,* 1932 AMC 1000 (EDNY 1932). But see *The Mary J. Kennedy,* 1925 AMC 1250, 1252–53

tion of familiarity is in no way a strict liability of the tug; substantial "leeway" is afforded to tugs for "mere judgment errors."[45]

(d) Navigational Duties of the Towed Vessel in Collision Cases. Most importantly, the owner of the towed vessel is responsible for the seaworthiness of that vessel.[46] Potential faults of the tow include insufficient ballast of the tow,[47] overloading,[48] other failings of the tow making it unmaneuverable,[49] or interference by the tow in the normal operations of the tug.[50]

(EDNY 1925); *The Non-Pareil—The Eureka No. 33,* 15 F.2d 200, 1925 AMC 1160 (SDNY 1925), aff'd, 15 F.2d 202, 1926 AMC 1668 (2d Cir. 1926).

45. *The Margaret,* supra note 8; *Frank Jacobus Transportation Co. v. The Tug Alice Moran (The Imoan),* 67 F.2d 603, 1933 AMC 1626 (2d Cir. 1933); *Tug Ocean Prince, Inc. v. United States,* supra note 44; *American Tel. & Tel. Co. v. Steuart,* 1978 AMC 1680 (D Md. 1977); *Dick Towing Co. v. The Leo,* 202 F.2d 850, 856, 1953 AMC 498, 507–08 (5th Cir. 1953); *The Tug NL-5—Chesapeake Bay Bridge-Tunnel,* supra note 20; *Admiral Towing Co. v. Woolen (The Tug Companion),* 290 F.2d 641, 1961 AMC 2333 (9th Cir. 1961).

46. *Stevens v. East-West Towing Co.,* 649 F.2d 1104, 1982 AMC 2820 (5th Cir. 1981); *In re Berkley Curtis Bay Towing Co. Inc.,* 697 F.2d 288, 1984 AMC 1941 (2d Cir. 1982); *The Hercules,* 73 F. 255 (2d Cir. 1896); *The Eli B. Conine,* 233 F. 987 (2d Cir. 1916); *The Garden City,* 127 F. 298 (6th Cir. 1904); *The Radnor,* 21 F.2d 982, 1927 AMC 1875 (D Md. 1927); *In re Tug Beverly,* 1994 AMC 2437 (ED Pa. 1994).

47. *Curtis Bay Towing Co. v. Southern Lighterage Corp,* 200 F.2d 33, 1952 AMC 2034 (4th Cir. 1952); *Frederick Snare Corp. v. Moran Towing & Transp. Co.,* 195 F. Supp. 639, 1961 AMC 2605 (SDNY 1961); *The Director,* 1927 AMC 1295 (4th Cir. 1927); *South, Inc. v. Moran Towing & Transp. Co.,* 360 F.2d 1002, 1966 AMC 1987 (2d Cir 1966); *A.L. Mechling Barge Lines, Inc. v. Derby Co.,* 399 F.2d 304, 1968 AMC 1436 (5th Cir. 1968); *Nat G. Harrison Overseas Corp. v. The Tug Titan,* 516 F.2d 89, 1975 AMC 2257 (5th Cir. 1975), modified on other points, 520 F.2d 1104, 1975 AMC 2271 (5th Cir. 1975); *Moran Towing & Transp. Co. v. Bouchard Transp. Co.,* 373 F. Supp. 1, 1974 AMC 1513 (SDNY 1974).

Prior to adoption of the Federal Rules of Evidence, a presumption of unseaworthiness arose when a tow sank or foundered under normal weather and sea conditions. *South, Inc. v. Moran Towing & Transp. Co.,* supra; *The Radnor,* supra note 46; *Central R.R. of New Jersey v. The Tug Marie J. Turecamo,* 238 F. Supp. 145, 147, 1965 AMC 2570 (EDNY 1965); and *Frederick Snare Corp. v. Moran Towing & Transp. Co.,* supra. When the tug knows of the unseaworthy condition of the tow, the duty to use due care continues during the actual towage and until the towing service is ended. *The Heiderberg—The Mabel,* 94 F.2d 649, 651, 1938 AMC 240, 242–43 (2d Cir. 1938); *Henry DuBois Sons Co. v. Pennsylvania R.R. Co. (The Mercer),* 47 F.2d 172, 174, 1931 AMC 312, 314 (2d Cir. 1931). In *Hanover Ins. Co. v. Puerto Rico Lighterage Co.,* 553 F.2d 728, 730–31, 1977 AMC 850, 854–55 (1st Cir. 1977) the court sustained a finding that the collision was 95 percent the fault of the tug and only 5 percent the fault of the unseaworthy tow. By way of contrast, in *In re Tug Beverly, Inc.,* 1994 AMC 2437, 2440 (ED Pa. 1994), the sinking of a towed houseboat in unseaworthy condition was held 30 percent the fault of the tow, while the tug was charged with 70 percent of the fault for excessive speed and failure to inspect the condition of the tow.

48. See *Shamrock Towing Co. v. Schiavone - Bonomo Constr. Co.,* 275 F.2d 338, 1960 AMC 817 (2d Cir. 1960), affirming 173 F. Supp 39, 1960 AMC 628 (SDNY 1959).

49. *Bisso v. Inland Waterways Corp.,* supra note 9; *Dick Towing Co. v. The Leo,* supra note 45; *Lotz v. The Tug Elsie M,* 98 F. Supp. 246, 1951 AMC 1311 (SD Tex. 1950); *The Walter B. Pollock,* 1926 AMC 1019 (SDNY 1926). However, in *Shamrock Towing Co. v. Schiavone - Bonomo Constr. Corp.,* supra note 48, the tow owner was exonerated on proof of negligent loading by an independent stevedore.

50. See *In re Barrett (The Samcree),* 108 F. Supp. 710, 1953 AMC 159 (SDNY 1952), modified on other grounds, 209 F.2d 487 (2d Cir. 1954); *Neptune Transp. Co. v. Bartow,* 1957 AMC 2046 (SDNY 1957); *Allied Chemical and Dye Co. v. The Tug Christine Moran,* 303 F.2d 197, 1962 AMC

Section C. Negligence Clauses in Towage Contracts

Contracts between the tugboat owner and the owner of the towed vessel containing exculpatory clauses are very common. The essence of the towage contract is the agreement of the parties that the tug will skillfully and carefully move the towed object and deliver it in good condition to the agreed destination. The contract may explicitly state that the tug is not a common carrier, a bailee, or an insurer of the towed vessel. If such language is not explicit, it will be implied.[51]

Steam tugs began to be used in the United States about 1835 (even earlier in Scotland and England) and exculpatory clauses in towage contracts became common by 1860.[52] There are two types of exculpatory clauses—used singly or in combination. The *sole risk* clause states that "towage is at the sole risk of the towed vessel and the tugboat is not liable for any damages caused during the tow." The *fictitious employment* clause states that "the master and crew of the tug are employees of the towed vessel during the tow so that the towed vessel is liable for any negligent acts of these tugboat personnel." In 1955, however, total exculpation of the tug owner from liability for damage to the towed vessel caused by the tug's negligence was held to be against public policy; hence exculpatory clauses in towage contracts, either of the "sole risk of the towed vessel" type, or the fictitious employment of the master and crew of the tug by the towed vessel type, were invalid.[53]

In *Bisso* an oil barge collided with a bridge pier while the barge was being negligently towed by the Tug *Cairo* on the Mississippi River. The barge had no propulsion, steering, officers, or crew. The towage contract provided that the towage was at the sole risk of the towed vessel. It also provided that the tug's crew members were servants of the towed vessel, whether they were on the tug or not.[54] The district court dismissed the towed vessel's claim and the

---

1198 (2d Cir. 1962); the lower court had previously described barge crews as "feckless folk," 190 F. Supp. 703, 1961 AMC 2620 (SDNY 1961).

51. *Stevens v. The White City,* supra note 8.

52. *Orge v. New Steam-Tug Co.,* 31 L.T.R.O.S. 85 (1858). In the United Kingdom there have been for many years the "Standard Conditions for Towage and Other Services" that protect the tug owner "whilst towing." See generally, Bishop, *The Relationship between the Tug and Tow in the United Kingdom,* 70 Tul. L. Rev. 507 (1995). In the United States the Second Circuit had previously approved various towage exculpatory clauses and continues to approve *pilotage* clauses to the same effect. *A/S Atlantica v. Moran Towing & Transportation Co.,* 498 F.2d 158, 160–61, 1974 AMC 555, 559–60 (2d Cir. 1974). See also *The Oceanica,* 170 F. 893 (2d Cir. 1908), overruled in part by *Bisso,* supra note 9. The Ninth Circuit held towage exculpatory clauses invalid on the ground they violate public policy. *Mylroie v. British Columbia Mills Tug & Barge Co.,* 268 F. 449 (9th Cir. 1920), aff'd, 259 U.S. 1 (1922).

53. *Bisso v. Inland Waterways Corp.,* supra note 9. See Comment, *Exculpatory Provisions in Towage Contracts,* 49 Tul. L. Rev. 392 (1975). Cf. *Chile Steamship Co. v. McAllister Lighterage Line, Inc.,* 1956 AMC 1419 (SDNY 1955), where the special hazards of towage in ice were exculpated by a letter from the tugboat company.

54. 349 U.S. at 85-86, 1955 AMC at 901.

Fifth Circuit affirmed.[55] The Supreme Court reversed the Fifth Circuit by a vote of five to three, the rationale of the majority being the public policy to discourage negligence and to protect those requiring towage services from being overreached by those (possibly monopolies) who can drive hard and unfair bargains.[56] The Court's opinion attempted to distinguish the approved pilotage clause of *Sun Oil Co. v. Dalzell*[57] from the *Bisso* towage clause in a factually unconvincing manner, describing state compulsory pilots rather than docking pilots, who are at all times employees of the tug.[58]

Bisso was used on the same day as authority to strike down clauses making the towed vessel liable for all damage caused by the tug and tow through indemnification.[59] The obsolete U.S. Navy destroyer USS *Bancroft* (part of the pre-Second World War "destroyers for bases" lend-lease agreement with the United Kingdom) was being towed by the Tug *Peter Moran* to a ship-breaker for scrapping. The destroyer had no propulsion, steering, or crew when it collided with the *S.S. Winding Gulf* because the navigational lights of the destroyer were not functioning. Following a collision in heavy fog, the towed destroyer sank, and the *Winding Gulf* was badly damaged.[60] The district court found the tug negligent for failing to provide a crew to maintain the navigational lights and sound fog signals; the damages were divided equally.[61] The court of appeals affirmed the finding of tow liability, without the necessity for a finding of tug liability because of the exculpatory clause,[62] but the Supreme Court reversed by a vote of six to two on the basis of *Bisso*.[63]

Another case decided with *Bisso* and *The Winding Gulf—United States v. Nielson*[64]—again dealt with the fictitious employment clause, this time as a *sword* rather than a shield. Two Dauntless Towing Co. tugs were assisting the transfer of a vessel with her own power from Hoboken, New Jersey, to Brooklyn, New York, the captain of one tug having gone aboard the towed vessel as docking pilot. Negligence of the docking pilot caused one of the tugs to be crushed between the assisted vessel and a pier. The tug owner sued the towed vessel for the damage to its tug under the fictitious employment language, arguing that damage to its tug was caused while its employee was on board the assisted vessel as her temporary employee. The Supreme Court held that the release of the tug company from liability for damage by the tug did *not* authorize it "affirmatively to collect damages for injury to its own tug due to

55. 211 F.2d 401, 1954 AMC 648 (5th Cir. 1954), affirming 114 F. Supp. 713, 1953 AMC 1664 (ED La. 1953).

56. 349 U.S. at 89–91, 1955 AMC 903–04.

57. 287 U.S. 291, 1933 AMC 35 (1932).

58. 349 U.S. at 93–94, 1955 AMC at 907.

59. *Boston Metals Co. v. The Winding Gulf*, supra note 10.

60. 349 U.S. at 122, 1955 AMC at 927.

61. 72 F. Supp. 50, 1947 AMC 819 (D Md. 1947), aff'd, 209 F.2d 410, 1954 AMC 183 (4th Cir. 1954).

62. 209 F.2d 410, 1954 AMC 183 (4th Cir. 1954).

63. 349 U.S. at 122, 1955 AMC at 927.

64. 349 U.S. at 129, 1955 AMC at 935.

negligent pilotage by one of its own tug captains."[65] The Court's conclusion was not based on public policy, but rather on the ambiguity of the contractual language.[66]

Because of *Nielson*'s reliance on ambiguity, it was necessary, eight years later, to return to the question of validity of exculpatory towage contracts for damages to third parties. In *Dixilyn Drilling Corp. v. Crescent Towing & Salvage Co.,*[67] the contractual language specified that the towed vessel would indemnify the tug owner for "any damage claims urged by third parties." Furthermore, the tug was to be named as an assured in the towed vessel's P. & I. policy.[68] In this case the towed barge collided with a bridge pier. Both tug and tow paid the pier owner, and then in litigation between tug and tow, the district court upheld the indemnification agreement, holding the towed vessel solely liable.[69] The Fifth Circuit affirmed, distinguishing *Bisso,*[70] but the Supreme Court's terse *per curiam* opinion reversed: "We adhere to the rule laid down in *Bisso* and *Winding Gulf* and hold that the Court of Appeals was in error in failing to follow it."[71] It should be noted that the Supreme Court did not even comment on the trial court's finding that the tug owner was not in a monopoly position to drive a hard bargain.[72] Thus it is uncertain today what effect the *monopoly* component of the *Bisso* decision continues to have. Accordingly, contractual exculpations of tug owners from liability to the towed vessel because of the tug's own negligence still violate public policy and are invalid. Now, more than forty years after *Bisso* was decided, it is difficult to imagine that the Supreme Court would abandon precedent and overrule its decision directly; that, however, does not mean that it is impossible to circumvent it.

Section D. Insurance Coverage and Waiver of Subrogation

Since *Bisso,* bargaining on the cost of liability insurance has replaced the effort to draft exculpatory clauses to expose the towed vessel to the consequences of the tug's negligence. Justice Frankfurter suggested in his *Bisso* dissent that inequality of bargaining power could not be assumed in the tug and tow situation, and there was no reason why the tug owner could not shift

65. 349 U.S. at 131, 1955 AMC 937–38.

66. "A person supplying his own employees for use by another in a common undertaking cannot usually collect damages because of negligent work by the employee supplied. Clear contractual language might justify imposition of such liability. But the contractual language here does not meet such a test and we do not construe it as authorizing respondent to recover damages from petitioner." 349 U.S. at 131–32, 1955 AMC at 937.

67. 372 U.S. 697, 1963 AMC 829 (1963).

68. 372 U.S. at 698, 1963 AMC at 830.

69. 198 F. Supp. 788, 1961 AMC 943 (D Miss. 1961).

70. 303 F.2d 237, 1963 AMC 831 (5th Cir. 1962).

71. 372 U.S. at 698, 1963 AMC at 830.

72. 198 F. Supp. at 789–91, 1961 AMC at 944–45.

the financial consequences of the tug's faults to the tow's liability insurers, so that the user of towage services would have the choice of relying on the tug's insurers, with an additional cost for towage, or relying on its own P. & I. insurer, with a reduced cost for towage.[73] Accordingly, the owner of the towed vessel choosing the latter alternative will name the tug company as an additional assured, for which the vessel owner may (or may not) be required to pay an additional "premium." The towed vessel's owner will also now require a waiver of subrogation to claims against the tugboat company and the tugs employed in the tow.

The shift of insurance coverage from tug to towed vessel was attacked on the grounds of the public policy expressed in *Bisso*, in *Fluor Western Inc. v. G & H Offshore Towing Co.*,[74] where the towed vessel argued that the required waiver of subrogation in the insurance policy was the equivalent of an exculpation of the tug from the consequences of its own negligence, and hence void. The Fifth Circuit rejected the equivalency argument and enforced the waiver of subrogation.[75]

The Fifth Circuit's leading case, however, involved stronger facts and the court's approval of the shift of liability insurance with waiver of subrogation is now well established throughout the industry. *Twenty Grand Offshore, Inc. v. West India Carriers, Inc.*[76] involved clearly negligent action of the tug personnel whereby the towing hawser parted and the barge went aground. The owner of the towed barge had *not* named the tug as an additional insured and had not obtained the waiver of subrogation, all in breach of its obligation under the towage contract. The Fifth Circuit reversed the district

73. 349 U.S. at 117–19, 1955 AMC at 924–26.

74. 447 F.2d 35, 1972 AMC 406 (5th Cir. 1971). See also *Hartford Fire Ins. Co. v. Port Everglades Towing Co.*, 454 F.2d 276, 1972 AMC 316 (5th Cir. 1972) (waiver of subrogation contained in barge's hull insurance policy). See also *Willamette-Western Corp. v. Columbia Pacific Towing Corp.*, 466 F.2d 1390, 1972 AMC 2128 (9th Cir. 1972). See generally, Dixon & Canning, *The Continuing Erosion of Bisso—Waiver of Subrogation and Benefit of Insurance Clauses*, 44 Ins. Counsel J. 97 (1977).

75. 447 F.2d at 40, 1972 AMC at 413.

76. 492 F.2d 679, 685, 1972 AMC 2254, 2262 (5th Cir. 1974). See also *Dow Chemical Co. v. The Charles F. Detmar, Jr.*, 545 F.2d 1091 (7th Cir. 1976); *Dillingham v. The Collier Carbon*, 707 F.2d 1086, 1984 AMC 1990 (9th Cir. 1983). In *Twenty Grand Offshore*, supra, the towing agreement contained the following clauses:

> Owner [tugboat company] agrees to procure, pay for and maintain in full force and effect throughout the term of this agreement, hull and machinery insurances in an amount at least equal to the value of the vessel and full form protection and indemnity insurance with a limit in the amount of at least one million dollars ($1,000,000.00). Principal [the barge owner] shall be named as an additional assured in all of said policies and such policies shall contain a waiver of subrogation in favor of Principal.
>
> Principal agrees to procure, pay for and maintain in full force and effect through the term of this agreement, hull and machinery insurance in an amount at least equal to the value of the barge and full form protection and indemnity insurance with a limit of at least one million dollars ($1,000,000.00). Owner, the vessel, its master and crew shall be named as additional assureds in all of said policies and such policies shall contain a waiver of subrogation in favor of the owner, its master and crew. Proper evidence of such insurance shall be furnished Owner.

court's judgment in favor of the barge owner.[77] The question then became the amount of the towed vessel's damages covered by insurance. Accordingly, the tugboat company would remain liable for any damages *not* covered by insurance because of the tug's negligence, but the towed vessel would be responsible for the portion of its damages that should have been covered by its own insurance.[78] Subsequent cases have dealt with the effect of deductibles[79] and the inconsistencies created by a "maladroitly drafted instrument."[80]

Section E. Collisions between Tows and Other Vessels

When a vessel other than the tug or its tow (hereinafter the "third party") is damaged by the negligence of the tug or the tow, or both together, the question arises as to whether the faults of the tug are to be imputed to the tow or whether the faults of the tow should be imputed to the tug. Common law tort concepts of imputed liability (imputation of fault from agent to principal or from vehicle operator to vehicle owner) are *not* used in this situation.[81] Thus the negligence of the tug is not imputed to the tow, or vice versa.[82] Whether the tug or the tow is liable to the third party depends on which is the "dominant mind."[83]

---

77. 492 F.2d at 679, 1974 AMC at 2263. The Fifth Circuit reasoned that the insurance clauses were not the same type of clauses held invalid in *Bisso* and *Dixilyn,* and thus not exculpatory. Further, if the insurers had refused to pay, the tug owner would still have been liable to the towed vessel for the tug's negligence. 492 F.2d 683–85, 1974 AMC 2259–62.

78. Id.

79. *Seley Barges, Inc. v. The Tug El Leon Grande,* 396 F. Supp. 1020 (ED La. 1974), aff'd, 513 F.2d 628 (5th Cir. 1975).

80. *Dow Chemical Co. v. Ashland Oil, Inc.,* 579 F.2d 902, 903, 1979 AMC 1581, 1582 (5th Cir. 1978); *BASF Wyandotte Corp. v. The Tug Leander, Jr.,* 590 F.2d 96, 97, 1979 AMC 1721, 1722 (5th Cir. 1979). The rate bargaining and waiver of subrogation clause in *Dow Chemical,* supra, read as follows:

> Owner shall cause its hull, P & I and cargo underwriters either to waive subrogation as to Contractor or make Contractor an additional assured under Owner's policies covering the said tow; any expense in connection therewith to be for account of Owner. Neither the procuring of said insurance arrangements by Owner nor its failure in that regard shall affect the other provisions of this contract, the provisions of this paragraph being primarily for the protection of Owner with respect to its insurance.
>
> It is recognized and agreed by both parties hereto that the towage rate charged is based in part on the terms and conditions of this contract, without the benefits of which a higher towage rate would have been charged.

81. The tort law doctrine of imputed liability is reviewed in W. Keeton et al., *Prosser & Keeton on The Law of Torts,* §§ 69–74 at 499–533 (5th ed. 1984).

82. *Sturgis v. Boyer,* supra note 11, 65 U.S. at 121–23.

83. The only issue here is liability as between tug and tow. In the context of limitation of liability, the question is whether the tugboat must surrender (or post security for the value of) barges owned by the tug owner. In *Brown & Root Marine Operators, Inc. v. Zapata Off-shore Co.,* 377 F.2d 724, 727, 1967 AMC 2684, 2688 (5th Cir. 1967), the Fifth Circuit held that the value of the

1. *The Dominant Mind*

The vessel whose master and crew are in control of the towage operation is the dominant mind; accordingly, that vessel is alone liable for damage caused by the flotilla to third parties, unless there is independent negligence of one or more of the other flotilla vessels contributing to the damage.[84] When the tow strikes the third party vessel but the tow was not the dominant mind—having no crew, no propulsion, and no steering—the tow will not even be liable *in rem* for the damage.[85]

(a) The Tug as the Dominant Mind. The absence of propulsive power of the towed vessel is a prime consideration. Thus, in *The Fort George*,[86] where there was no propulsion capability in the tow and the tug provided the propulsion, it was held that the tug became the dominant mind and the tow had to follow the directions of the tug.[87] Contributory fault of the tow where the tug is the dominant mind can be found where the tow is unseaworthy,[88] has failed to follow the tug's directions,[89] or has breached a duty owing to the tug.[90]

---

entire flotilla of commonly owned and controlled tugs and barges had to be included in the limitation fund. See also *In re Drill Barge No. 2*, 454 F.2d 408, 411–12, 1972 AMC 1008, 1010–12 (5th Cir. 1972). Cf. *Liverpool, Brazil & River Plate Steam Navigation Co. v. Brooklyn Eastern District Terminal*, supra note 12. For purposes of applying the Steering and Sailing Rules, a flotilla comprised of tug and tow is considered a single unit. See *The Gladys*, 144 F. 653, 655 (2d Cir. 1906).

84. *Sturgis v. Boyer*, supra note 11; see also *The Margaret*, supra note 8. In *Naphtha Barge Co. v. Continental Navigation Co.*, 1978 AMC 501, 511 (ED La. 1977); and *Alter Co. v. The Miss Sue*, 536 F. Supp. 313, 316, 1983 AMC 302, 304 (ED La. 1982), "helper" tugs were exonerated and the dominant mind tug held fully liable.

85. *Sturgis v. Boyer*, supra note 11, 65 U.S. at 122–23. See also *Oil Transfer Corp. v. Westchester Ferry Corp.*, 173 F. Supp. 637, 1959 AMC 485 (SDNY 1958): ". . . [w]here responsibility for the joint navigation of two vessels has been taken over by one of them, the other is not liable *in rem* if her owner is not liable *in personam*, 173 F. Supp. at 640, 1959 AMC at 490."

But see *Amoco Oil v. The Montclair*, 766 F.2d 473, 475–76, 1986 AMC 1420, 1422–24 (11th Cir. 1985), where a barge without propulsive power, manned by a "riding crew," was held liable *in rem* for allision damage.

86. 183 F. 731, 732–33 (2d Cir. 1910). See also *The John D. Rockefeller*, 272 F. 67, 71 (4th Cir. 1921).

87. 183 F. at 732–33.

88. *In re Barrett (The Samcree)*, supra note 50. See also *P. Dougherty Co. v. United States*, 104 F. Supp. 711, 715–16, 1952 AMC 537, 542–43 (SDNY 1951), where the tug left a dead ship insecurely anchored with an incompetent crew on board, the members of which were held to remain employees of the tug owner; and *Ryan Walsh Stevedoring Co., Inc. v. James Marine Service, Inc.*, 557 F. Supp. 457, 460–61, 1983 AMC 2516, 2520–21 (ED La. 1983), aff'd, 729 F.2d 1457, 1984 AMC 3000 (5th Cir. 1984), where the tow was excused from contribution because the unseaworthiness of the tow was readily apparent. See also *S.C. Loveland, Inc. v. East West Towing Co.*, 415 F. Supp. 596, 605–06, 1978 AMC 2293, 2297–300 (SD Fla. 1976), aff'd, 608 F.2d 160, 1980 AMC 2947 (5th Cir 1979).

89. *Kinsman Marine Transport Co. v. Great Lakes Towing Co.*, 1975 AMC 837, 841 (ND Ohio 1975); *Montauk Oil Transportation Corp. v. The Tug Laurie Ann Reinauer*, 1974 AMC 2382, 2386 (SDNY 1974).

90. *Chevron U.S.A. Inc. v. Progress Marine, Inc.*, 1980 AMC 1637, 1639 (ED La. 1975) (failure to show proper lights); see also *The Sif*, 266 F. 166, 168 (2d Cir. 1920); and *The Gulfpenn—The Tug Dover—The Tug Susan A. Moran*, 1933 AMC 1086 (EDNY 1933) (summary of opinion).

The seaworthiness of a barge was brought into question in *Ryan Walsh Stevedoring Co. v. James Marine Service, Inc.,*[91] where the boom of a stern-mounted revolving crane (set in an elevated position) on the unmanned barge collided with the highest span of the Huey T. Long Bridge.[92] The tug argued that the positioning of the boom on the barge made it impossible for the barge to move safely from one site to another, and was thus not reasonably fit for its intended purpose, and unseaworthy.[93] However, the court rejected the tug's contention of nonliability, holding that it was solely responsible because the unseaworthiness was so obvious that the tug was negligent in proceeding on the job. The court said, "... [O]nce the master of the M/V *Hiawatha* took over the D/B *Frank L* without knowing the height of the boom or the vertical clearance of the bridge, all responsibility for the safe conduct of the voyage shifted to him."[94]

In *Kinsman Marine Transit Co. v. Great Lakes Towing Co.*[95] the dominant mind tug was held at fault in a collision where the tug imparted excessive sternway to the steamer it was towing. The court also found that the steamer had contributed to the collision because it had failed to respond promptly and properly to the tug's orders; accordingly, the damages were divided equally between tug and tow.[96] Similarly, in *Montauk Oil Transportation Co. v. The Tug L.A. Reinauer*[97] the tow was held at fault for failing to follow the tug captain's instructions to lower the booms on the barge that later collided with a bridge.

Again, in a dominant mind tug situation, the tow might be held solely liable for collision damage if the proximate cause of the collision was the negligence of the tow. In *In re Barrett,*[98] for example, the court held the tug free of fault in the towage of a vessel that had broken loose and drifted uncontrollably into collision. The court held that the tow was at fault for supplying a defective hawser to the tug, for a lack of authority and competence among the

---

91. Supra note 88.

92. Id., 557 F. Supp. at 459, 1983 AMC at 2517.

93. Id., 557 F. Supp. at 460–61, 1983 AMC at 2520.

94. Id., 557 F. Supp. at 462, 1983 AMC at 2522. Cf. *S.C. Loveland, Inc. v. East West Towing, Inc.*, supra note 88, 415 F. Supp. at 605, 1978 AMC at 2297, in which the court held that a barge that dragged anchor was not unseaworthy for failing to have a heavier anchor. The lower court held that the anchor was intended to be used only in emergencies for short periods of time, and that it was reasonably fit for this purpose. The crew of the tug should have known this and was thus negligent in leaving the barge unattended at anchor in an exposed area. See also *In re J.E. Brenneman Co.,* 782 F. Supp. 1021 (ED Pa. 1992); and *Frasier River Pile and Dredge Ltd. v. Empire Tug Boats, Ltd.,* 1995 AMC 1558 (Fed. Ct., Canada, 1995).

95. Supra note 89.

96. Id. at 841–42.

97. Supra note 89, 1974 AMC at 2386–87.

98. Supra note 50.

crew members aboard the tow, and in failing to maintain the anchors in a condition ready for immediate use.[99]

(b) The Towed Vessel as the Dominant Mind. Returning to the principle of *The Fort George,* that the tug providing the motive power will be the dominant mind, the parties may nevertheless alter this principle by agreement.[100] An agreement contradicting the dominant mind principle may be express or may be implied from the circumstances.[101] For example, the tow will be considered the dominant mind where the master and crew of the tow exclusively control both tug and tow from the tow, and the tug merely furnishes the motive power for the exercise.[102] In that situation, the tug is liable only for failing to follow the tow's orders, or for participation in an obviously dangerous maneuver.[103]

In *Dow Chemical Co. v. The Tug Thomas Allen,*[104] a tug and barge allided with an underwater gas pipeline while the tug and barge proceeded from one oil rig to another. The towed barge had chosen the route and directed the tug in accordance with the normal custom in the area.[105] The court held the tow at fault for directing the tug to proceed into shallow water, even though the tow's master knew that there were no charts of pipelines or guide boats available. However, the court held the tug was also at fault, for proceeding in the shallow area without chart or guide boat on a course the tug master understood to be dangerous.[106]

---

99. Id., 108 F. Supp. at 717, 1953 AMC at 169. See also *Chevron U.S.A. Inc. v. Progress Marine, Inc.,* supra note 90, where a tow was held solely at fault when the legs of an oil rig under tow struck underwater gas pipelines. The dominant mind tug had committed no negligence in navigation. The sole proximate cause of the collision was the failure of the tow to measure accurately the lengths of the legs of the rig. 1980 AMC at 1640–41.

100. Supra note 86, 183 F. at 732.

101. *Dow Chemical Co. v. The Tug Thomas Allen,* 349 F. Supp. 1354, 1363, 1974 AMC 781, 792 (ED La. 1972).

102. *Sturgis v. Boyer,* supra note 11, 65 U.S. at 122; *Old Time Molasses Co. v. United States,* 31 F.2d 963, 965, 1929 AMC 687, 690–91 (5th Cir. 1929); *The Beaverton,* 273 F. 535, 544 (SDNY 1919).

103. *Dow Chemical Co. v. The Tug Thomas Allen,* supra note 101. Actions were brought for personal injuries caused by fire on board the barge after an explosion resulting from the collision with the underwater gas pipeline.

104. Id.

105. Id., 349 F.Supp. at 1358–59, 1974 AMC at 783–87.

106. Id., 349 F.Supp. at 1363, 1974 AMC at 792.

CHAPTER ELEVEN

WATER POLLUTION FROM COLLISION

Section A. Introduction

Oil pollution has long been the subject of international treaties and state and federal legislation, as well as the general maritime law. Oil pollution regulation is divided between control of deliberate discharges[1] (which will not be considered here) and prevention and cleanup of accidental spills.[2] This chapter is concerned with removal costs and damages caused by cargoes of polluting substances or bunkers released from vessels as a result of collision. As of this writing (1997) there have been few collisions involving oil spills since adoption of the new pollution laws, and so most examples come from single-ship disasters in the carriage of crude oil. The discussion which follows

---

1. The first international regulatory scheme was the 1954 Convention for the Prevention of Pollution of the Seas by Oil, [1961] 12 U.S.T. 2989, T.I.A.S. 4900, 327 U.N.T.S. 3, in force in 1958, which prohibited discharges within specified zones of the high seas. The convention was amended by a 1962 Protocol extending the prohibited zones generally to 100 miles from land, [1966] 17 U.S.T. 1523, T.I.A.S. 6109, 600 U.N.T.S. 332, and was further amended by a protocol in 1969. [1976–77] 28 U.S.T. 1205, T.I.A.S. 8505, 600 U.N.T.S. 336, in force in 1978.

This convention was followed by the International Convention for the Prevention of Pollution From Ships (MARPOL), 12 Int'l Legal Mat. 1319 (1973), 6 *Benedict on Admiralty* Doc. 6–1 (rev. 7th ed., F. Wiswall editor-in-chief, *International Maritime Law Documents and Commentary*) (hereinafter "Benedict"), in force in 1983, which covers other polluting substances in addition to oil. Because the 1978 Protocol to the 1973 Convention came into force at the same time, the convention is usually referred to as MARPOL 73/78.

The 1982 United Nations Convention on the Law of the Sea (LOS), UN Doc A/CONF 62/122, 21 Int'l Legal Mat 1261 (1982), in force Nov. 16, 1994 greatly expands the provisions of public international law on the marine environment. This convention requires States to take all measures necessary to prevent pollution from any source, using the best practicable means. While the required 60 ratifications to bring the treaty into force did not come from developed, industrialized nations, the situation changed at the Special Session of the General Assembly in July 1994, and because of changes to seabed mining provisions, developed, industrialized nations signed the convention and began to deposit ratifications. As of this writing (1997) the United States has signed the convention but has not yet ratified it. See generally R. McGonicle & M. Zacher, *Pollution, Politics and International Law* (Berkeley, 1979); D. Abecassis & R. Jarashow, *Oil Pollution from Ships* (London, 1985); E. Gold, *Handbook on Marine Pollution* (Arendal, 1985); S. Pritchard, *Oil Pollution of the Sea: Environmental Aspects* (London, 1987).

2. International Convention on Civil Liability for Oil Pollution Damage, 973 U.N.T.S. 3, 6 Benedict, Doc. 6–3, 9, Int'l Legal Mat. 45 (1970) (hereinafter "CLC"). See generally, N. Healy, *The C.M.I. and IMCO Draft Conventions on Civil Liability for Oil Pollution*, 1 J. Mar. L. & Com. 93 (1969) and N. Healy, *The International Convention on Civil Liability for Oil Pollution Damage*, 1 J. Mar. L. & Com. 317 (1969). This convention, which entered into force in 1976, has not been ratified by the United States. A 1976 Protocol, 6 Benedict, Doc. 6–4, 16 Int'l Legal Mat. 617 (1977), came into force in 1981.

concerns (1) the liability of the vessel discharging the polluting substance for cleanup costs and damages, and (2) when the discharge results from collision, the liability of the other colliding vessel.

1. International Liability Schemes for Accidental Pollution

As of 1997 it was not possible for the United States to become a party to the international conventions on this subject because of the far greater liability of shipowners under the United States Oil Pollution Act of 1990 (OPA 90).[3] Nevertheless, a brief review of these conventions is provided for reference in those cases that are not subject to U.S. law and to which one or both of the conventions may be applicable.[4]

Under the conventions there are two levels of liability for an accidental oil spill. The first level is shipowner limited liability, provided in the 1969 Civil Liability Convention for Oil Pollution Damage (CLC).[5] The second level is the liability of a fund (also limited) provided by the users of cargo under the 1971 International Fund Convention on the Establishment of an International Fund for Compensation for Oil Pollution Damage[6] (Fund Convention).

The International Maritime Organization (I.M.O.) has produced an international convention dealing with hazardous and noxious substances (HNS) other than oil after twenty years of debate and the failure of one diplomatic conference on the subject. This convention covers all kinds of substances except oil, coal, and radioactive materials.[7] There are two tiers of liability in this single convention: shipowner liability rising progressively to

3. Pub. L. No. 101–380, 104 Stat. 486, codified in relevant part in 33 U.S.C. §§ 2701–61 (1992).

4. Neither the U.S. statute nor the 1969 CLC contain self-confining definitions or limitations to prevent overlapping exercises of jurisdiction by contracting States and the traditional Admiralty tort jurisdiction of U.S. courts. OPA 90 applies to the navigable waters and exclusive economic zones (EEZ) of the United States (33 U.S.C. § 2701 [21] and [8]).

OPA 90 also has a section on recovery by foreign claimants (33 U.S.C. § 2707), with a requirement for reciprocity (§2707[a][1][B]), limiting the applicability of OPA 90 to foreign discharges from an Outer Continental Shelf facility or deep water port, a vessel in U.S. navigable waters, a vessel carrying cargo between two U.S. ports, and a Trans-Alaska pipeline tanker. For U.S. admiralty jurisdiction over foreign-flag vessels polluting foreign territorial waters, see *In re Barracuda Tanker Corp. (The Torrey Canyon),* 281 F. Supp. 228, 1968 AMC 1711 (SDNY 1968), rev'd in part, 409 F.2d 1013, 1969 AMC 1442 (2d Cir. 1969); and *In re Oil Spill by Amoco Cadiz off the Coast of France on March 16, 1978,* 699 F.2d 909, 1983 AMC 1633 (7th Cir. 1983), and 954 F.2d 1279, 1992 AMC 913 (7th Cir. 1992). The general maritime law of oil pollution is discussed infra at notes 142–202.

5. See supra note 2.

6. International Convention on the Establishment of an International Fund for Oil Pollution Damage, 1110 U.N.T.S. 57, 6 Benedict Doc. 6–8, 11 Int'l Legal Mat. 284 (1972) (hereinafter "Fund Convention"). This treaty entered into force in 1978, but has not been ratified by the United States. In 1976 a protocol was added, 6 Benedict, Doc. 6–9, 16 Int'l Legal Mat. 621 (1977). A 1984 Protocol never entered into force and a new protocol to replace the 1984 Protocol was added in 1992. See infra note 36.

7. The Draft Convention on Liability and Compensation in Connection with Noxious and Hazardous Substances by Sea did not achieve the required two-thirds majority at the 1984 Diplomatic

SDRs (units of account) 100 million for a ship of 100,000 gross tons; and a second tier to be provided by a fund contributed to by cargo receivers after the shipowner limits have been exceeded.

2. *The 1969 Civil Liability Convention (CLC)*

This convention applies to all damages as well as cleanup expenses caused by oil pollution in the territory of contracting States.[8] In its original form, the CLC included the territorial sea[9] but not the contiguous zone.[10] A 1992 protocol, however, added the 200-mile exclusive economic zone (EEZ) of the coastal State.[11] Owner liability under the CLC is not dependent on residence, domicile, or allegiance to a contracting State, but rather on the presence of the vessel in territory subject to the convention.

Liability under the CLC is not absolute, since certain defenses are recognized: (a) acts of war, including civil war, insurrection, and hostilities, whether or not war has been declared; (b) acts of God, described in the convention as natural phenomena of an exceptional, inevitable, and irresistible character;[12] (c) intentional acts or omissions of third parties done with intent to cause damage;[13] (d) intentional or negligent acts or omissions of claimants;[14] and (e) negligent acts of governmental authorities in maintaining lights or other navigational aids.[15] The time bar on claims is three years from the date of the damage, and a statute of repose terminates actions six years from the date of the incident.[16] It will be seen that fault of the carrying vessel need not be shown to impose liability. Thus, seaworthiness is not a defense,

---

Conference. See Comment, *Liability for Shipments by Sea of Hazardous and Noxious Substances,* 17 Law & Pol. in Int'l Bus. 455 (1987), and De Bievre, *Liability and Compensation for Damage in Connection with the Carriage of Hazardous and Noxious Substances by Sea,* 17 J. Mar. L. & Com. 61 (1986). The new draft convention prepared by I.M.O. (Doc. LEG/64/4 of January 25, 1991) was adopted, with amendments, at the diplomatic conference on May 3, 1996.

8. CLC, art. II. This language will be replaced by art. 3 of the 1992 Protocol, extending the reach of the convention from the territorial sea to the EEZ. See also art. I(6).

9. CLC, art. II.

10. Under the 1958 Law of the Sea scheme, the contiguous zone is a water area less than 24 miles from the coastal State's baseline for determining the territorial sea. It is not territorial sea, and the coastal State's enforcement is limited to customs, fiscal, immigration, and sanitary laws. Convention on the Territorial Sea and Contiguous Zone, art. 24(1). Similar provisions are in the 1982 United Nations Convention on the Law of the Sea, art. 33(1).

11. The exclusive economic zone is an area extending 200 miles from the coastal State's baseline for determining the territorial sea. It is not territorial sea, but the coastal State has *"sovereign rights"* in the natural resources and the living resources, especially fisheries. 1982 Law of the Sea Convention, arts. 55–68 and art. 3 of the Protocol to the International Convention on Civil Liability for Oil Pollution Damage, (1992) 6 Benedict, Doc. 6–4B.

12. CLC art. III, 2(a).

13. CLC art. III, 2(b).

14. CLC art. III (3).

15. CLC art. III, 2(c).

16. CLC art. VIII.

even if there has been no failure to exercise due diligence to maintain the vessel in a seaworthy condition.

Limitation of the amount of the liability under the CLC was originally 2,000 Poincaré (gold) francs per ton of the ship's convention tonnage, subject to a maximum of 210 million francs.[17] In 1976 the unit of account was changed to the Special Drawing Right (SDR) of the International Monetary Fund. After 1976, the CLC provided for a limitation of SDRs 133 per gross ton, subject to a maximum of SDRs 14 million per incident.[18] If "actual fault or privity" of the owner is established, the liability may not be limited.[19]

A 1984 Protocol never entered into force and was replaced in 1992 by another protocol, increasing the maximum amount to SDRs 59.7 million. For ships of under 5,000 limitation tons, the limit was set at SDRs 3 million, and for ships of over 5,000 limitation tons, SDRs 420 per ton for every ton over 5,000, added to the base of SDRs 3 million.[20]

Under the 1992 Protocol, definitions of "ship," "oil," "pollution damage," and "incident" were reframed; the area of applicability was extended to the coastal State's EEZ, and changes in wording were made in eight of the twelve substantive articles of the 1969 Convention.[21] Claims must be brought in the courts of the contracting State or States where the injury occurred.[22] Judgments of such States are made enforceable in the courts of any State party to the CLC,[23] but the claimant's rights against other assets of the owner cease when the owner establishes a limitation fund under the convention. By the 1992 Protocol a list of six categories of parties against whom no claim may be made was added to the convention.[24]

3. *The 1971 Fund Convention*

Because the costs of the notorious 1967 oil spill from the VLCC tanker *Torrey Canyon* exceeded the 210 million Poincaré franc maximum that would have been recoverable under the CLC, dissatisfaction with the CLC amounts im-

17. CLC art. V.

18. Protocol to Amend the International Convention on Civil Liability for Oil Pollution Damage, Art. 6, 16 Int'l Legal Mat. 617 (1977). It entered into force in 1981.

19. CLC art. V(2).

20. Protocol to the International Convention on Civil Liability for Oil Pollution Damage, 1992, 6 Benedict, Doc. 6–4B. (The 1984 Protocol is printed at 15 J. Mar. L. & Com. 613 [1984].) See generally, Jacobsen & Yellen, *Oil Pollution: The 1984 London Protocols and The Amoco Cadiz,* 15 J. Mar. L. & Com. 467 (1984).

21. 1992 Protocol, supra note 20, arts. 2–11.

22. CLC art. IX (1). There is an obligation therein to give "reasonable notice of any such action" to defendants.

23. CLC art. X(1).

24. CLC, art. VI,1 (a); 1992 Protocol, infra note 36, art. 4 (2), listing: (a) servants or agents of owner or members of the crew; (b) pilot; (c) any charterer, manager, or operator; (d) any salvor with owner's consent; (e) any person taking preventative measures; and (f) all servants or agents of (c), (d), and (e).

periled chances of ratification. A supplementary system of liability compensation and indemnification was therefore added in 1971, based upon the creation of a fund to which consignees of oil cargoes must contribute in proportion to the tonnage actually received.[25] The compensation is payable out of the fund for pollution damage caused by any vessel[26] to any person suffering such damage who is "unable to obtain full and adequate compensation" under the CLC.[27] The shipowner who is held liable under the CLC will be partially indemnified.[28] Compensation may be payable from the fund even in circumstances where the CLC is not applicable.[29]

The fund's obligation to pay compensation is not absolute; there are certain defenses to liability: (a) war, hostilities, civil war or insurrection, or an incident caused by oil discharged from a warship or a government service vessel;[30] and (b) inability of the claimant to prove that the pollution damage resulted from an incident involving one or more ships.[31] Intentional or negligent acts or omissions of the claimant may result in loss of the right to recover.[32] The time bar on claims is three years from the date of damage, and a statute of repose terminates actions six years after the date of the incident.[33] The fund's obligation was originally limited to 450 million Poincaré francs per incident, which could be increased by the General Assembly of the Fund Organization to 900 million francs.[34] By a 1976 Protocol, the amounts were converted to SDRs 30 million and SDRs 60 million, respectively.[35] As in the case of the CLC, a 1984 Protocol never came into force and was replaced in 1992 by another protocol.[36] Under the 1992 Protocol the maximum amount of compensation is 135 million SDRs, including amounts payable under the

25. Of 150 oil spills analyzed from 1970 to 1980 by the U.S. Coast Guard, five involved cleanup costs in excess of $20 million. U.S. Coast Guard Executive Summary, *Benefit-Cost Analysis of Two International Conventions on Oil Pollution Liability and Compensation,* at 22 (1983). Costs of the *Torrey Canyon* spill (1967) were estimated at more than $16 million. See Patrick, *Liability, Compensation and Prevention of Oil Spills,* 1 Earth L. J. 301, 305 (1970). The Seventh Circuit affirmed an award of $205 million against the Amoco companies in favor of the French claimants in the *Amoco Cadiz* spill (1978). See *In re Oil Spill by Amoco Cadiz off the Coast of France on March 16, 1978,* 954 F.2d 1279, 1992 AMC 913 (7th Cir. 1992).

26. See Fund Convention, supra note 6, art. 10.

27. See Fund Convention, art. 4.

28. Cf. Fund Convention, art. 4 (2)(b).

29. Fund Convention, art. 4 (1). Three instances of inability to be fully compensated under CLC are given: (a) no CLC liability; (b) inability of the liable owner to pay; and (c) the damage exceeds the amount of the owner's limited liability.

30. Fund Convention, art. 4(1).

31. Fund Convention, art. 4(2)(a).

32. Fund Convention, art. 4(2)(b).

33. Fund Convention, art. 4(3).

34. Fund Convention, art. 6(1).

35. Protocol to Amend the International Convention on the Establishment of an International Fund for Oil Pollution Damage, 6 Benedict, Doc. 6–9, 16 Int'l Legal Mat. 621 (1977), in force in 1994. See art. III.

36. Protocol to the International Convention on the Establishment of an International Fund for Compensation for Oil Pollution Damage (1992), 6 Benedict, Doc. 6–9B. (The 1984 Protocol is printed at 15 J. Mar. L. & Com. 623 [1984].)

1992 CLC Protocol. That maximum amount may be increased to SDRs 200 million when there are three parties to the convention whose combined quantity of contributing oil exceeds 600 million tons.[37]

Section B. The U.S. Oil Pollution Act of 1990 (OPA 90)

1. Background of OPA 90

This complex and comprehensive legislation is the successor of earlier cleanup laws.[38] In addition, however, Congress relied on the 1980 Comprehensive Environmental Response, Compensation and Liability Act (CERCLA),[39] the "Superfund," in order that there be an antipollution regime for marine and nonmarine events that in almost every case would shift the full costs of cleanup and damages to the discharging vessel. Before 1990, legislation to stiffen penalties and increase liabilities had been stalled in Congress for fifteen years by attempts to balance protection of the environment with the needs of the tanker industry. The series of oil spills in 1989–90 in American waters, commencing with the disastrous *Exxon Valdez* spill of March 24, 1989,[40] firmed up public opinion for the need of more stringent legislation and produced overwhelming majorities in Congress that could not be dissuaded by boycott threats from the oil industry or suggestions of a presidential veto. The legislation was passed by the Senate on August 2, 1990, by a vote of 99–0[41] and by the House of Representatives on August 3, 1990, by a vote of 360–0.[42] It was signed into law, with regret, by President Bush on August 18, 1990. It became effective immediately, but it was not, however, made retroactive.[43]

37. 1992 Protocol, supra note 36, art. 6(3).

38. The Refuse Act of 1899, 33 U.S.C. § 407–16 (1985), made applicable to oil spills in *United States v. Standard Oil Co.,* 384 U.S. 224, 1966 AMC 1122 (1966); the 1972 Federal Water Pollution Control Act, as amended, 33 U.S.C. §§ 1251–1376 (1988); the 1974 Deepwater Port Act, 33 U.S.C. § 1501–24 and the 1973 Trans-Alaska Pipeline Authorization Act, 43 U.S.C. § 1653.

39. 42 U.S.C. §§ 9601–57 (1988). This statute does *not* under its provisions include oil as toxic waste cleanup.

40. 1990 U.S. Code Cong. & Admin. News 723–24, 750–51, and 776. Congress was alarmed that taxpayers had to pick up at least half the costs of cleanup from 1971 to 1982, the government having recovered only $49 million of the $124 million costs from responsible parties. See *Crude Legislation: Liability and Compensation under the Oil Pollution Act of 1990,* 23 Rutgers L. J. 597, 617 (1992).

41. Senate: 136 Cong. Record S11536-47 (Aug. 2, 1990).

42. House: 136 Cong. Record H 6933 (Aug. 3, 1990).

43. 33 U.S.C. § 2717 (e). See generally, Wagner, *The Oil Pollution Act of 1990: An Analysis,* 21 J. Mar. L. & Com. 569 (1990); Randle, *The Oil Pollution Act of 1990: Its Provisions, Interest & Effects,* 21 Envt'l. L. Rep. 10119 (1991); Rodriguez & Jaffe, *The Oil Pollution Control Act of 1990,* 15 Tulane Mar. Law J. 1 (1990); Edelman, *The Oil Pollution Act of 1990,* 8 Pace Env. L. Rev. 1 (1990); and Note, *The Oil Pollution Act of 1990: A Long Time Coming,* 2 Ford. Envt'l L. Rep. 59 (1990). Post-enactment threats to withdraw from the U.S. market and the reaction of the oil industry to the

OPA 90 does not replace the general maritime law of pollution damage applicable to incidents occurring outside U.S. territorial waters and EEZ. But within U.S. territorial limits and the EEZ, OPA 90 replaces statutes on cleanup and the general maritime law and tort law on damages. Congress and the president clearly understood that enactment of OPA 90 would make it impossible for the United States to ratify the CLC, the Fund Convention, and the 1976 and 1984 Protocols.[44] If there was any trade-off in the final package, it was that while liability limits for the existing fleet would be raised immediately, required changes in tanker construction would be postponed and phased in gradually over twenty-five years until 2015,[45] even though the useful life of an oil tanker is normally only twenty years.

2. *The OPA 90 Liability Regime*

The fault regime of the earliest laws relating to oil pollution was replaced in 1970 by the Water Quality Improvement Act which, with amendments, became the 1972 Federal Water Pollution Control Act (FWPCA). That act, like the CLC, recognized several defenses, but otherwise liability did not require proof of fault. But unlike the CLC it covered only federal government cleanup costs and the cost of preventive measures taken by the government to contain a spill or minimize its effects.

---

legislation can be studied in Petroleum Industry Research Foundation, *Transporting U.S. Oil Imports: The Impact of Oil Spill Legislation on the Tanker Market,* a report compiled for the U.S. Department of Energy, June 1992. See also Comment, *The Oil Pollution Act of 1990: Striking the Flags of Convenience,* 2 Colorado J. of Int'l Envt'l L. & P. 407 (1991), noting that 30 percent of the world's oil tankers fly the Liberian flag, as did the *Torrey Canyon,* the *Argo Merchant,* and the *Amoco Cadiz.*

44. 1990 U.S. Code Cong. & Admin. News 803–05 (House Report 125–27. In 33 U.S.C. § 3001, Congress expressed the pious hope that in the future the United States would be able to participate in an international regime at least as effective as federal and state laws in preventing pollution and compensating claimants.

45. 33 U.S.C. § 4115 (1992). The age of vessels is measured from the date of construction or the completion of a major conversion, whichever is later. (See 1990 U.S. Code Cong. & Admin. News 817–21) (1 House Report 139–42). All exemptions from the prohibition of existing single-hull tankers will expire by 2015. The scheme for gradual replacement of older design tankers is:

> *Tankers of over 30,000 gross tons* built before 1970 must be eliminated by 1995; those built after 1970 but before 1980 must be eliminated by 1997; and those built after 1980 must be eliminated by 2003.
>
> *Tankers of between 15,000 and 29,999 gross tons* built after 1955 but before 1965 must be eliminated by 1995; those built after 1965 but before 1970 must be eliminated by 1999; those built after 1970 but before 1980 must be eliminated by 2000; and those built after 1986 must be eliminated by 2005.
>
> *Tankers of between 5,000 and 14,999 gross tons* built after 1955 but before 1965 must be eliminated by 1995; those built after 1965 but before 1970 must be eliminated by 2000; and those built after 1970 must be eliminated by 2005.
>
> *Tankers of less than 5,000 gross tons* are exempt until 2015.

See also U.S. Code Cong. & Admin. News, 752, 763–65, 818–19 (House Report 139–41; Senate Report 4, 14–16).

OPA 90 went much further than FWPCA. The liability of a "responsible party" (the owner, operator, or demise charterer of the discharging vessel) was extended by OPA 90 to benefit private damage claimants. Governmental parties' rights to recover removal costs were further expanded. OPA 90 simply provides that each "responsible party"[46] is liable for removal costs and damages resulting from oil spills.[47] However, there are three complete defenses to liability: (a) act of God;[48] (b) act of war;[49] and (c) act or omission of a third party.[50] Each of these defenses is available only when it was the sole cause of the discharge. Furthermore, the defense can be lost where the responsible party or its agent or employee fails to report a spill,[51] fails to provide all reasonable cooperation and assistance in the removal,[52] or fails to comply with a lawful order.[53] Congressional intent to force vessel owners to take all measures necessary to mitigate the consequences of a spill can be read from

---

46. OPA 90, 33 U.S.C. § 2701 (32). The responsible party for a vessel is "... any person owning, operating or demise chartering the vessel." It is unclear whether the corporate veil between parents and subsidiaries may be pierced, as in the early case of *United States v. Ira S. Bushey & Sons, Inc.,* 363 F. Supp. 110, 1973 AMC 2639 (D Vt. 1973). Under CERCLA there are conflicting decisions on the corporate veil problem. See *United States v. Northeastern Pharmaceutical & Chemical Co.,* 810 F.2d 726 (8th Cir. 1986). Cf. *New York v. Shore Realty Corp.,* 759 F.2d 1032 (2d Cir. 1985); *Joslyn Manufacturing Co. v. T. L. James & Co.,* 893 F.2d 80 (5th Cir. 1990).

47. 33 U.S.C. § 2702. See 1990 U.S. Code Cong. & Admin. News 733 (Senate Report p. 11) and 780 (H.R. Rep. p. 102). Cf. the standard of strict, joint, and several liability of the 1972 FWPCA, 33 U.S.C. § 1251 (1988). The term "oil" refers to the definition in the 1972 FWPCA, 33 U.S.C. § 1251 (1988), amended so as to exclude oils that are hazardous substances as defined in the Comprehensive Environmental Response, Compensation and Liability Act of 1980 (CERCLA), 42 U.S.C. § 9601; See 33 U.S.C. § 2701 (23).

48. Id. 33 U.S.C. § 2703 (a)(1).

49. Id. 33 U.S.C. § 2703 (a)(2).

50. Id. 33 U.S.C. § 2703 (a)(3). A "third party" must be:

> ... other than an employee or agent of the responsible party or a third party whose act or omission occurs in connection with any contractual relationship with the responsible party (except where the sole contractual arrangement arises in connection with carriage by a common carrier by rail), if the responsible party establishes by a preponderance of the evidence, that the responsible party—
>
> > (A) exercised due care with respect to the oil concerned, taking into consideration the characteristics of the oil and in light of all relevant facts and circumstances; and
> > (B) took precautions against foreseeable acts or omissions of any sole third party and the foreseeable consequences of those acts or omissions; ...

Thus, where the third party is treated as the responsible party with respect to removal costs and damages, the original responsible party must settle claims in accordance with 33 U.S.C. § 2713, but is entitled to all rights of the claimant by subrogation to the extent of any claim already paid in recovery of damages from the fund or the third party. The absence of federal government negligence is a major change from the 1972 FWPCA defenses.

Section 2703(a)(4) excepts "any combination of paragraphs (1), (2) and (3)" [referring to the paragraphs cited notes 48, 49 and 50, supra, and this note].

51. 33 U.S.C. § 2703 (c)(1). Actual or constructive knowledge is required.

52. Id. 33 U.S.C. § 2703 (c)(2), provided it has been requested by a "responsible official," an expression not defined in the statute.

53. Id. 33 U.S.C. § 2703 (c)(3).

the way the defenses in the 1972 FWPCA have been rephrased:[54] Gross negligence or willful misconduct of a claimant will be a defense as to that particular claimant;[55] the time bar on damage claims is three years from the date of discovery of the injury;[56] and on cleanup claims it is six years from the completion of removal.[57]

3. Limitation of Liability under OPA 90

The global limitation of liability provided in the 1851 Limitation of Liability Act[58] is no longer applicable; only the provisions of OPA 90 can limit vessel owner liability for oil spills.[59] For tankers of over 3,000 gross tons, the liability of the shipowner per incident is limited to $1,200 per gross ton or $10 million, whichever is greater.[60] For tankers of less than 3,000 gross tons, the limit is $1,200 per gross ton or $2 million, whichever is greater.[61] For vessels other than tankers, the limit is $600 per gross ton or $500,000, whichever is greater.[62] For offshore facilities, removal costs are not limitable, but the limit of liability for damages is $75 million,[63] while deep-water ports and onshore facilities have a liability limit of $350 million.[64] These liability limits are to be adjusted by the President (i.e., by his designee), "to reflect significant increases in the Consumer Price Index . . . ," at three-year intervals.[65]

The right to limit liability, however, is lost if the oil spill results from gross negligence or willful misconduct,[66] violation of federal construction or operating safety regulations,[67] if there is a failure to report a spill, a failure to provide all reasonable cooperation and assistance in removal, or a failure to

54. 1990 U.S. Code Cong. & Admin. News 735–36 (Senate Report 13–15).

55. Id. 33 U.S.C. § 2703 (b).

56. Id. 33 U.S.C. § 2712 (h)(2). The provision reads: ". . . reasonably discoverable with the exercise of due care. . . ."

57. Id. 33 U.S.C. § 2712 (h)(1). The provision reads: ". . . within 6 years after the date of completion of all removal actions for that incident."

58. 46 U.S.C. §§ 183–89. See 1990 U.S. Code Cong. & Admin. News. 736 (Senate Report 14). In a case brought under the 1973 Trans-Alaska Pipeline Authorization Act, it was held that the 1973 act repealed the effect of the 1851 act on Trans-Alaska oil spills. *In re Glacier Bay,* 944 F.2d 577, 1992 AMC 448 (9th Cir. 1991).

59. 33 U.S.C. § 2702 (a). "Notwithstanding any other provision or rule of law. . ."

60. 33 U.S.C. § 2704 (a)(1).

61. 33 U.S.C. § 2704 (a)(1)(B)(ii).

62. 33 U.S.C. § 2704 (a)(2).

63. 33 U.S.C. § 2704 (a)(3).

64. 33 U.S.C. § 2704 (a)(4).

65. 33 U.S.C. § 2704 (d)(4).

66. 33 U.S.C. § 2704 (c)(1)(A). Congress has indicated that good faith compliance with regulations is a condition for limited liability. 1990 U.S. Code of Cong. & Admin. News 736 (Senate Report 14).

67. 33 U.S.C. § 2704 (c)(1)(B). The standards and regulations are federal and should not be trivial requirements unrelated to the discharge. 1990 U.S. Code Cong. & Admin. News 735 (Senate Report 14).

comply with a lawful order.[68] It will be noted that the provisions for loss of the right to limit (failure to report a spill,[69] failure to cooperate in removal,[70] and failure to comply with a lawful order[71]) are similar to the provisions for loss of defenses.

There are obvious uncertainties that will have to be resolved by decisions in the future: (a) given the fact that there are hundreds of construction and operating safety regulations, whether Congress intended that defenses or the right of limitation should be lost where there is a minimal causal relation between the failure to comply with a regulation and the oil spill; (b) what constitutes compliance with the "report of a spill" requirement, i.e., who is to make the report, what is to be reported, and to whom the report must be made; (c) what is the reasonable cooperation that can be required and by what type of federal officials; (d) when is there a failure to comply with a lawful order, i.e., who is to give the order, who is to receive the order, and what must its content be; and (e) when does the act or omission of an "agent," "employee," or independent contractor make a responsible party liable?

Because Congress has required "due diligence" and foresight to make available the defense of act of a third party[72] and has put statutory limitations on the exercise of all three complete defenses,[73] it is likely that the courts will give a very narrow reading to the defenses, as they did under the 1972 FWPCA.[74] Liability under OPA 90 is joint and several.[75] There is, however, no

---

68. 33 U.S.C. § 2704 (c)(2). Lack of financial ability as a reason for failure to clean up a spill may be considered if appropriate officials are *promptly* informed so as to permit alternative cleanup options. House Report (Committee on Public Works and Transportation) to accompany H.R. 1465, No. 101-242, p. 59.

69. Cf. 33 U.S.C. § 2703 (c)(1) and § 2704 (c)(2)(A).

70. Cf. 33 U.S.C. § 2703 (c)(3) and § 2704 (c)(2)(B).

71. Cf. 33 U.S.C. § 2703 (b) and § 2704 (c)(2)(C).

72. 33 U.S.C. § 2703 (a)(3)(A) and (B).

73. 33 U.S.C. § 2703 (c)(1), (2), and (3).

74. Under 33 U.S.C. § 1321 (f)(1), the vessel interests were not liable for a spill caused solely by an act of God, act of war, negligence of the United States, or the act or omission of a third party. *Liberian Poplar Transports v. United States,* 1992 AMC 2253 (Ct. Cl. 1992), (storm during discharge, causing lines to part, held not an act of God). See *St. Paul Fire & Marine Ins. Co. v. United States,* 4 Cl. Ct. 762, 768 (Ct. Cl. 1984) (act of God defense unavailable in settlement of soil beneath tanks); *United States v. Le Beouf Bros. Towing Co.,* 621 F.2d 787, 789, 1981 AMC 1947 (5th Cir. 1980) (crew member of tug towing tanker barge mistakenly opening valve, causing spill, held not a third party); *Tanker Hygrade No. 18, Inc. v. United States,* 526 F.2d 805, 1976 AMC 840 (Ct. Cl. 1975); *United States v. Hollywood Marine, Inc.,* 625 F.2d 524, 1981 AMC 2646 (5th Cir. 1980); *Frederick E. Bouchard, Inc. v. United States,* 583 F. Supp. 477, 1985 AMC 668 (D Mass. 1984); *In re Berkley Curtis Bay Co.,* 557 F. Supp. 335, 339, 1984 AMC 1934, 1940 (SDNY 1983), aff'd, 697 F.2d 288, 1984 AMC 1941 (2d Cir. 1983); cf. *Sabine Towing & Transp. Co. Inc. v. United States,* 1980 AMC 2600, 2609 (Ct. Cl. 1980); *Gasper v. United States,* 460 F. Supp. 656, 1979 AMC 2232 (D Mass. 1978); *Nunley v. The Dauntless Colocotronis,* 727 F.2d 455, 1984 AMC 2920 (5th Cir. *en banc* 1984); *United States v. The Big Sam,* 681 F.2d 432, 434, 1983 AMC 2730 (5th Cir. 1982); and *Burgess v. The Tamano,* 564 F.2d 964, 966, 1977 AMC 1892 (lst Cir. 1977). See also *In re Glacier Bay,* 746 F. Supp. 1379, 1991 AMC 739 (D Alaska 1990).

75. 33 U.S.C. § 2701 (17), referring to 33 U.S.C. § 1321. Third parties not involved in the transportation of oil cargoes may be deemed responsible parties where a "responsible party"

independent tort-type liability of federal officers or employees in a personal or individual capacity while acting within the scope of their employment.[76]

4. *Financial Responsibility under OPA 90*

The act places principal reliance for removal costs and damages on responsible parties and their insurers. Evidence of financial responsibility is required of all vessels, regardless of flag, using U.S. territorial waters.[77] In the same manner as the 1972 FWPCA, the responsible party for any vessel of more than 300 gross tons must furnish evidence of financial responsibility, in an amount equal to the maximum liability limit under § 2704.[78] Vessels unable to establish the required evidence can be denied entry to U.S. ports or can be detained or seized if already within U.S. waters.[79] Civil and administrative penalties of up to $25,000 per day can be imposed,[80] and direct actions against guarantors or insurers by claimants is permitted.[81]

5. *Absence of Preemption: State Laws*

While a new uniformity has been introduced into federal law by OPA 90, it specifically does *not* preempt state laws on oil pollution.[82] There are many unresolved questions concerning this absence of preemption: Does it apply only to the types and amounts of damages caused by the vessel from which the oil has been discharged? Does it apply to cargo owners whose liability was specifically excluded in OPA 90? Does it apply to earlier case law preempting

establishes that the discharge was caused solely by the act or omission of such third party. 33 U.S.C. § 2702 (d)(1)(A).

76. 33 U.S.C. § 2718 (d).

77. 33 U.S.C. § 2716 (a)(1–2).

78. 33 U.S.C. § 2716 (a) (1). This evidence can be liability insurance, a surety bond, a guarantee, a letter of credit, or qualification as a self-insurer, § 2716 (e). Financial responsibility requirements under the old law remained in effect under the authority of 33 U.S.C. § 1321 (p), until the new requirements were implemented. See Alcantara & Cox, *OPA 90 Certificates of Financial Responsibility*, 23 J. Mar. L. & Com. 369 (1992).

79. 33 U.S.C. § 2716 (b) (2) (B) for detention, and § 2716 (b) (3) for governmental seizure.

80. 33 U.S.C. § 2716 (a). See infra notes 110–15.

81. 33 U.S.C. § 2716 (f).

82. 33 U.S.C. § 2718; 1990 U.S. Code Cong. & Admin. News 272–78, 739–40, 770 (Senate Report 6, 17-18, 21) and 799 (House Report 121). See also Mitchell, *Preservation of State and Federal Authority under the Oil Pollution Act of 1990*, 21 Envt'l. L. J. 237 (1991). The theoretical support for the absence of preemption can be found in Justice Douglas's opinion in *Askew v. American Waterways Operators Inc.*, 411 U.S. 325, 1973 AMC 811 (1973), endorsing the State of Florida's police powers to impose strict and unlimited liability on vessel polluters. Nonliability aspects of federal preemption should not be affected. Cf. *Ray v. Atlantic Richfield Co.*, 435 U.S. 151, 1978 AMC 527 (1978), whereby Washington State was precluded from imposing more stringent standards for vessel construction than the federal government, excluding tankers larger than 125,000 DWT

regulation of vessel construction, manning, and operational standards? Thus, although under federal law there is strict liability of vessel owners, subject to the three complete defenses, and subject to the right to limitation—breakable by willful misconduct, gross negligence, or breach of statutory duties—the states retain the right to impose additional and unlimited liabilities. This absence of constitutional preemption applies to evidence of financial responsibility that may be required by states for vessels using state navigable waters, independent of the federal requirement.[83] Although some states have enacted new laws imposing stricter liabilities, the absence of preemption will also apply to state statutes enacted before OPA 90 and untested as to constitutionality. The wide divergences as to responsible parties, standards of liability, and limitation of that liability make exact analysis of risk exposure for insurance purposes impossible. Coastal state laws dealing with liability for pollution cleanup and damages are listed in the appendix.

6. *Governmental Removal and Procedure for Making Claims under OPA 90*

The goal of OPA 90 was prevention of spills and the effective and immediate removal of discharged oil. Accordingly, Congress expanded presidential powers[84] and mandated Coast Guard responsibilities to take over oil spill sites and respond to a disaster in the most effective manner. As a first step, "the President," i.e., his designee, designates the source or sources of any discharge or threatened discharge and notifies the relevant responsible party.[85]

A national contingency plan coordinates state and local governmental responses, together with private industry efforts. A national response team and ten regional response groups (one in each Coast Guard district) are mandated, although it is anticipated that private industry will supply most of the personnel and equipment for the removal.[86] After the source designation and the notification to the responsible party or guarantor, the responsible party has a five-day period within which to dispute the designation.[87] If the designation is not disputed, the responsible party or guarantor must, within fifteen days, begin a thirty-day period of advertising the procedure for presentation of claims for removal costs and damages, including natural resource damages.[88]

---

from navigating Puget Sound and requiring state pilots on coastwise or enrolled vessels. On federal preemption, see *International Paper Co. v. Ouillette,* 479 U.S. 481 (1987), and *State of Maryland Department of Natural Resources v. Kellum,* 51 F.3d 1220 (4th Cir. 1995).

83. 33 U.S.C. § 2719.
84. 33 U.S.C. § 4201.
85. 33 U.S.C. § 2714.
86. 33 U.S.C. § 4201. See 1990 U.S. Code Cong. & Admin. News 827 (House Report 148–51).
87. 33 U.S.C. § 2714 (a).
88. 33 U.S.C. § 2714 (b).

Claimants must first present all their claims to the responsible party or guarantor.[89] If the responsible party or guarantor denies the claim or it is not settled within ninety days of presentation, the claimant has the choice of commencing an action against the responsible party or guarantor or of making a claim against the Oil Spill Liability Trust Fund.[90] This fund is derived from a fee of five cents per barrel on imported oil levied on the oil industry, designed to produce a contingency fund of $1 billion per incident to remove discharges and compensate those damaged by spills who have not been otherwise compensated.[91] The purpose of the fund is to have compensation available when liability limits have been reached or the source of the spill remains unknown. (The new Oil Spill Liability Trust Fund consolidates funds available under the FWPCA,[92] the Deepwater Ports Act,[93] the Trans Alaska Pipeline Authorization Act,[94] and the Outer Continental Shelf Act.[95])

7. *Penalties under OPA 90*

While there was considerable debate over the effectiveness of criminal penalties to deter accidental spills, Congress was clear that failure to report a spill is antisocial conduct which should be subject to heavy criminal penalties[96] and result in the denial of civil defenses and the right of limitation of liability.[97] A civil penalty of $25,000 per day or up to $1,000 per barrel may be imposed on parties responsible for oil spills.[98] Civil penalties of up to $10,000 per violation may also be imposed for failure to comply with response plans.[99] For failure or refusal to comply with orders or regulations, a civil penalty of $25,000 per day or three times the government's removal costs may be imposed.[100]

---

89. 33 U.S.C. § 2713 (a). See also Kende, *Development and Presentation of the Pollution Victim's Claim,* 5 U.S.F. Mar. L. J. 203 (1993).

90. 26 U.S.C. § 9509. See 1990 U.S. Code Cong. & Admin. News 727, 730–32, and 754 (Senate Report 5-6, 9-10) and 790 (House Report 112). When the claimant presents a claim to this fund and is compensated, all rights, claims, and causes of action of the claimant are subrogated to the U.S. government. 33 U.S.C. § 2715 (a). Under 33 U.S.C. § 6001, the admiralty and maritime jurisdiction provision of the Constitution and the "saving to suitors" clause of 28 U.S.C. § 1333 are unaffected by the legislation.

91. 33 U.S.C. § 2712.

92. 33 U.S.C. § 1251 (FWPCA).

93. 33 U.S.C. § 1501.

94. 43 U.S.C. § 1651 ($100 million fund).

95. 43 U.S.C. § 1331.

96. 33 U.S.C. § 4301 (b), providing for imprisonment up to three years and fines up to $250,000 for an individual and $500,000 for an organization. 1990 U.S. Code Cong. & Admin. News 745–46 (Senate Rep. 23-24 and 831 (House Report 152).

97. See 33 U.S.C. § 2703(c)(1) and § 2704(c)(2)(D).

98. 33 U.S.C. § 4301 (b).

99. 33 U.S.C. § 4301 (b) and U.S. Code Cong. & Admin. News, p. 832 (House Report 153). For serious (or Class II) violations the penalty may be up to $10,000 per day, but not more than $125,000.

100. Id.

For willful failure or gross negligence in carrying out a presidential order, a minimum penalty of $100,000, or not more than $3,000 per barrel of discharged oil, may be imposed.[101] In imposing these penalties, the Administrator of the Environmental Protection Agency and the Secretary of Transportation are to consider the seriousness of the spill, the previous polluting record of the responsible parties, their culpability, and the attempts to mitigate the damage.[102]

8. Damages under OPA 90

In OPA 90 Congress has rewritten much of the law of damages, but not all of the old landmarks have been removed. Responding to the narrow reading of its earlier attempt to preserve the general maritime law and state law,[103] Congress has expanded the categories of damages once considered doubtful or unprovable.[104] For example, under the FWPCA the federal government could recover merely the expenses of preventing a threatened spill and the cleanup costs of a spill, but under OPA 90 the government may recover, as claimant or trustee, for damage to natural resources; physical or economic

101. 33 U.S.C. § 4301. Under FWPCA, personal fault is not required to establish grounds for a civil penalty under 33 U.S.C. § 1321 (b)(3). *Klatt v. United States,* 965 F.2d 743, 1992 AMC 2247 (9th Cir. 1992).

102. 33 U.S.C. § 4301 (b)(8).

103. See 33 U.S.C. § 1321 (*o*)(1): "Nothing . . . shall affect or modify in any way the obligations of any owner or operator of any vessel . . . to any person or agency under any provision of law for damages to any publicly owned or privately owned property resulting from a discharge of any oil. . . ." The first suggestion of the preemption of all other remedies of the federal government by the 1972 FWPCA is in *Steuart Transportation Co. v. Allied Towing Corp.,* 596 F.2d 609, 1979 AMC 1187 (4th Cir. 1979), based on the language in 33 U.S.C. § 1321 (f)(2): "notwithstanding any other provision of law."

In *Middlesex County Sewerage Authority v. National Sea Clammers Association,* 453 U.S. 1 (1981), a case dealing with pollution from sewage, the Supreme Court, using very broad language, noted that the scheme of federal controls in the 1972 FWPCA and the 1972 Marine Protection, Research and Sanctuaries Act, 33 U.S.C. § 1401, were broad enough to preempt federal common law nuisance. That opinion did not deal with whether the general maritime law had been preempted, but subsequent appellate cases reasoned as if it had been. See *United States v. Oswego Barge Corp.,* 664 F.2d 327, 1982 AMC 769 (2d Cir. 1981), holding that the federal government had no general maritime law cause of action for cleanup costs in excess of the statutory maximum in the FWPCA because of a presumed preemption of federal common law. Preemption was narrowly avoided in a subsequent case only because the defendant was not the discharging vessel, but the third party causing the collision and spill. *United States v. The Big Sam,* 681 F.2d 432, 1983 AMC 2730 (5th Cir. 1982). In *Conner v. Aerovox, Inc.,* 730 F.2d 835, 1984 AMC 2507 (1st Cir. 1984), private party claimants (commercial fishermen, lobstermen, and shellfishermen) were denied recovery in admiralty against the polluter of their fishing grounds because of preemption.

104. 33 U.S.C. § 2702. See 1990 U.S. Code Cong. & Admin. News, 780–82 (House Report 102–04; 726, 733–34 (Senate Report 5, 1112). See also Wagner, *Recoverable Damages under the Oil Pollution Act of 1990,* supra note 43.

losses to real or personal property; loss of subsistence use of natural resources; loss of revenues such as taxes, royalties, rents, fees, or net profit shares; loss of profits and earning capacity and costs of providing increased or additional public services during removal, and costs of assessing injury to natural resources, lost revenues, and economic losses for damage to federal lands. Claimants of "public services" damages also include state and local governments and American Indian tribes. Private claimants who own or lease property have expanded rights to recover economic losses.[105] However, a caveat is necessary: Congress has not included all foreseeable injuries or plaintiffs, and courts may in the future exclude claims and claimants under a narrow reading of OPA 90, or under a broad reading of the statute may include claims and claimants not now thought to be covered.

The damages rules are contained in the same section with the declaration of liability of responsible parties for removal costs and damages resulting from an oil pollution incident. Removal costs can be recovered by governmental parties.[106] Recovery of removal costs by "any person" is limited to those that are consistent with the national contingency plan.[107] The categories of damages, however, are divided between (a) those recoverable only by governmental claimants (specifically, loss of natural resources,[108] loss of revenues,[109] and costs of providing additional public services[110]), and (b) those recoverable by any claimant (specifically, destruction of real or personal property when the claimant is the owner,[111] loss of subsistence use from destroyed natural resources,[112] and loss of profits and earning capacity from the destruction of real property, personal property, or natural resources[113]).

(a) Recovery by Governmental Claimants. *Natural resources (33 U.S.C. Section 2702 [b][2][A]).* Congressional concern with public outrage at the needless deaths of seabirds and ocean mammals, and public concern over diminished

105. 33 U.S.C. § 2702 (b) (2) (B).
106. 33 U.S.C. § 2702 (b) (1) (A). Governmental parties are the United States, a state, or an Indian tribe.
107. 33 U.S.C. § 2702 (b) (1) (B).
108. 33 U.S.C. § 2702 (b) (2) (A).
109. 33 U.S.C. § 2702 (b) (2) (D) .
110. 33 U.S.C. § 2702 (b) (2) (F).
111. 33 U.S.C. § 2702 (b) (2) (B).
112. 33 U.S.C. § 2702 (b) (2) (C).
113. 33 U.S.C. § 2702 (b) (2) (E).

catches of fish and shellfish, are expressed in this provision for recovery by the trustee of the natural resources of the affected region. Under the *parens patriae* concept,[114] without specific statutory authority, courts had at times been confused as to the rights of the state and/or federal sovereign at common law. OPA 90 asserts the rights of the governmental trustee to recover for injury, destruction, loss of, or loss of use of natural resources, plus the reasonable costs of assessing the damage.[115] Natural resources are broadly defined as, "land, fish, wildlife, biota, air, water, ground water, drinking water supplies and other such resources."[116] Sovereign ownership rights are not required, as the natural resources definition also expanded the connection between the resource and the trustee as "belonging to, managed by, held in trust by, appertaining to, or otherwise controlled by the United States . . . any state or local government or Indian tribe or any foreign government."[117]

Although the trustee's nexus to the natural resource is ownership, management, trust, "appertaining to" (i.e., belonging properly as a function or part of the natural resources), or control, these can be seen as limitations on the right of recovery to proprietary relationships, similar to the § 2702 (b)(2)(B) restriction of the right to recover for physical damage or economic losses to the owner or lessor of real or personal property. Another provision of OPA 90 deals with the designation of trustees[118] and their functions,[119] and then specifies the measure of damages for loss of natural resources: "(A) the cost of restoring, rehabilitating, replacing or acquiring the equivalent of, the damaged natural resources; (B) the diminution in value of those natural resources pending restoration; plus (C) the reasonable cost of assessing those damages."[120] Double recovery for natural resource damages, including damage assessment, restoration, rehabilitation, replacement, or acquisition, is specifically forbidden.[121] Regulations for the assessment of

114. *Parens patriae* (literally "father of the fatherland") is the common law doctrine under which the crown in England and the state in the United States are the guardians of persons and property unable to protect themselves. See infra note 166.

115. 33 U.S.C. § 2702 (b) (2) (A).

116. 33 U.S.C. § 2701 (20).

117. Id.

118. 33 U.S.C. § 2706 (b).

119. 33 U.S.C. § 2706 (c).

120. 33 U.S.C. § 2706 (d) (1).

121. 33 U.S.C. § 2706 (d) (3).

natural resource damages[122] have the force and effect of a rebuttable presumption.[123]

Revenues (33 U.S.C. Section 2702 [b][2][D]). Another item of damages which governments may recover is the consequential net loss of " . . . taxes, royalties, rents, fees or net profit shares . . ." due to the injury, destruction or loss of real property, personal property, or natural resources.[124]

Public services (33 U.S.C. Section 2702 [b][2][F]). Net costs of increased or additional public services during or after removal activities may be recovered by governmental entities. Public services for protection against fire, safety, or health hazards are specifically listed,[125] but there is no language indicating whether these listed services are exclusive or merely examples.

(b) Recovery by All Claimants. *Real or personal property (33 U.S.C. Section 2702 [b][2][B]).* At first the inclusion of economic losses together with physical

---

122. 33 U.S.C. § 2706 (e)(1). Natural Resource Damage Assessment Rules (43 CFR Part 11), prepared by the Department of the Interior, was scorned in Congress as impermissibly narrow because of its efforts to impose market value and value of assessments. Congress intended that natural resources damage caused by an oil spill should be paid for by the responsible party, not the taxpayer. 1990 U.S. Code Cong. & Admin. News 737 (S. Rep. 15). The report states: ". . . [F]orests are more than board feet of lumber, and . . . seals and sea otters are more than just commodities traded on the market."

Natural Resource Damage Assessment Rules (43 CFR Part 11) had been prepared by the Department of the Interior under CERCLA. Under these rules there were Type A (Small) Spills , 43 CFR §§ 11.40—11.41; and Type B (Large) Spills, 43 CFR §§ 11.60–11.84. Type A rules provide easy valuations for small marine spills that can be made quickly. These rules were upheld in part in *Colorado v. Department of the Interior,* 880 F.2d 481 (DC Cir. 1989), using a computer model for coastal and marine environments. The court criticized the data base because the value of sea mammals such as whales and dolphins was not estimated. Type B rules stress that restoration of the natural resource is preferred to the equivalent value. See *Ohio v. Department of the Interior,* 880 F.2d 432 (DC Cir. 1989). The Type B rules were also criticized for failing to account fully for losses of natural resources. Under the amended rules, the trustee publishes a list of alternative restoration proposals, with strategies varying from replacement through intensive restoration to minimal human interference to allow for natural recovery. The trustee selects a proposal and explains its choice with the use of 10 factors relating costs to benefits.

The Natural Resource Damage Assessment Rules prepared by the U.S. National Oceanic and Atmospheric Administration (NOAA) became effective Feb. 4, 1996. These rules, required by OPA 90, were more than three years behind schedule. The rules, contained in a 308-page regulation, are designed for use by trustees designated under OPA 90, and become applicable when there has been an actual or substantial threat of an oil discharge not exempted by federal permit, and if natural resources or services are likely to be injured as a result of the spill. The next step is to determine whether restoration actions should be pursued, and this depends upon the likelihood of injuries or the actual existence of injuries. Response actions are not expected to address the injuries, and primary or compensatory restoration actions exist and are feasible to address the potential injuries. To evaluate the need for restoration, there follows a determination and quantification of the injury by reason of an analysis of the nature, degree, and extent of the injuries in space and time. Thereafter the trustees are to consider a reasonable range of alternative plans, select the plan, and publish a final plan for restoration. The rule approves the use of the method of damage assessment known as contingent valuation, whereby an estimate of the total value of a resource is obtained through the use of questionnaires.

123. 33 U.S.C. § 2706 (e)(2).

124. 33 U.S.C. § 2702 (b)(2)(D).

125. 33 U.S.C. § 2702 (b)(2)(F).

damages might indicate a general expansion of recoverable damages. However, Congress has attached these losses to "real or personal property which shall be recoverable by a claimant who owns or leases that property."[126] The question raised by the expressions "economic losses" and "claimant who . . . leases" is whether Congress intended thereby to overturn the specific holdings of *Robins Dry Dock*[127] and its progeny, *The Testbank*.[128] The legislative history is silent.[129] The difficulty lies in the statutory word "lease" instead of "charter party." Congress can be presumed to know the difference. Thus, textual analysis would indicate that *Robins* has not been affected by this provision.

Subsistence use of natural resources (33 U.S.C. Section 2702 [b][2][C]). Here, Congress deliberately permitted recovery, ". . . without regard to the ownership or management of the resources,"[130] but as far as the use of the resources is concerned, there has to be subsistence use. A restrictive interpretation of the provision was given in the *Cleveland Tankers* case.[131] Defendant's vessel, *The Jupiter,* exploded while unloading gasoline at a dock in the Saginaw River at Bay City, Michigan. The burning vessel broke free of her mooring and drifted into the navigation channel, where she sank, blocking all commercial navigation in the river for about a week.[132] Claimants in the shipowner's limitation of liability proceeding (a marina owner, a boat charterer, and a trucking company) sought recovery for economic losses due to the closing of the channel, citing § 2702 (b)(2)(C) (Subsistence Use) and § 2702 (b)(2)(E) (Profits and Earning Capacity) as the grounds for recovery. Respecting subsistence use only, the court required that the blocked river must have been used to obtain the minimum necessities of life.[133] Commercial fishermen might be permitted to recover under this test. While the *Cleveland Tankers* court's view of subsistence might be authorized by a dictionary definition, Congressional intent to preserve natural resources could have included recreational fishermen who eat their catches. The policy question would remain as to whether a dramatic increase in the number of individual claimants would violate Congressional purpose.

---

126. 33 U.S.C. § 2702 (b)(2)(B).

127. *Robins Dry Dock & Repair Co. v. Flint,* 275 U.S. 303, 1928 AMC 61 (1927). See infra, notes 169–86. See generally, Scowcroft, *Economic Loss in Admiralty: A Reexamination of Foundations,* 11 J. Mar. L. & Com. 267, 272 (1985); Owen, *Recovery for Economic Loss Under U.S. Maritime Law: Sixty Years Under Robins Dry Dock,* 18 J. Mar. L. & Com. 157 (1987); and Tetley, *Damages and Economic Loss in Marine Collision: Controlling the Floodgates,* 22 J. Mar. L. & Com. 539 (1991) .

128. *Louisiana ex rel. Guste v. The Testbank,* 752 F.2d 1019, 1985 AMC 1521 (5th Cir. *en banc* 1985).

129. 1990 U.S. Code Cong. & Admin. News. 736 (Senate Rep. 14-15).

130. 33 U.S.C. § 2702 (b)(2)(C).

131. *In re Cleveland Tankers,* 791 F. Supp. 669, 1992 AMC 1727 (ED Mich. 1992), aff'd, 67 F.3d 1200, 1996 AMC 151 (6th Cir. 1995).

132. Id., 791 F. Supp. at 671.

133. Id., 791 F. Supp. at 678. The owner of a marina that suffered smoke damage in addition to economic loss was allowed to recover. Id. at 679.

Profits and earning capacity (33 U.S.C. Section 2702 [b][2][E]). On the surface Section 2702 (b)(2)(B) (Real or Personal Property) and Section 2702 (b)(2)(E) (Profits and Earning Capacity) seem to be similar, in that both provisions include economic losses.[134] However, the nature of the claimants is different, as (B) limits recovery to a "claimant who owns or leases that property"[135] while (E) is available to *any* claimant.[136] Secondly, while (B)'s causation language is "resulting from destruction of real or personal property," a highly specific term of causation reminiscent of the *Palsgraf*[137] reasoning, the causation language of (E) "due to injury, destruction, or loss" of property or natural resources, is looser and more general. Thus fishermen need not own the natural resource to recover lost income due to damage to fisheries resources.

Cleveland Tankers[138] also involved a claim for loss of profits or impairment of earning capacity under section 2702 (b)(2)(E). The court denied recovery, since there was no proof that the claimant relied on the natural resource. It is submitted that this is an erroneous reading of the statute. Because Congress used "subsistence" in (C), a requirement of reliance on the property for the necessities of life made sense. However, there is no mandated reliance concept in this provision for loss of profits or impairment of earning capacity. It appears that the choice of words, "loss of profits," "due to the injury," and "any claimant" can support recovery of nonphysical losses without the case law barriers of *Robins Drydock* and *Testbank.*[139]

9. *Interest*

Claimants under OPA 90 may recover interest, including prejudgment interest, from vessel operators and owners.[140] No limitation is put on this liability.[141]

Section D. The General Maritime Law

Since Congress expressed no intent to curtail general maritime law recoveries for oil pollution damage occurring anywhere,[142] and since foreign parties

134. § 2702 (b)(2)(B) ("economic losses") and § 2702 (b)(2)(E) ("loss of profits").

135. 33 U.S.C. § 2702 (b)(2)(B).

136. 33 U.S.C. § 2702 (b)(2)(E).

137. *Palsgraf v. Long Island R.R. Co.,* 249 N.Y. 339, 162 N.E. 99 (1928), see infra, note 172.

138. Supra note 131.

139. Supra note 127 and infra note 145. Speculative costs and damages are clearly excluded under OPA 90. See 1990 U.S. Code Cong. & Admin. News 484 (Senate Rep.).

140. 33 U.S.C. § 2705. A responsible party's liability for interest begins 30 days after a claim is presented and continues until the claim is paid. The interest will be calculated at the average of the highest rate for commercial and finance company paper maturities, as published in the Federal Reserve Bulletin. § 2705 (b) (4).

141. 33 U.S.C. § 2705 (b)(5)(A).

142. See supra note 4.

can use OPA 90 only under limited circumstances,[143] the continued availability of the maritime tort remedy for oil spills outside of the territorial limits of OPA 90's applicability remains. Of course, Congress could forbid the use of U.S. courts to foreign claimants, as was done in the 1982 amendment to the Jones Act.[144] And the discretionary doctrine of *forum non conveniens* may be applied by the American forum to eliminate these cases.

1. Liability

The leading case on the pollution liability of a discharging vessel in collision is *The Testbank*.[145] On the Mississippi River, near the outlet to the Gulf of Mexico south of New Orleans, the inbound bulk carrier *Sea Daniel* was in collision with the outbound containership *Testbank*. As an immediate result of the impact of the two vessels, containers on the *Testbank* fell overboard into the river. One of the containers contained 12 tons of pentachlorophenol (PCP), which escaped into the river. As a consequence of this spill, the Mississippi River outlet and a 400-square-mile area of marshes and waterways were closed to navigation, as well as to commercial fishermen, shrimpers, crabbers, and oystermen, for a period of 19 days.[146]

Lawsuits were filed on behalf of the commercial fish and seafood businesses as well as shipping interests, recreational fishermen, seafood businesses, seafood restaurants, and marinas. The issue concerned the liability of the carrying vessel for the damages caused as a result of the discharge of the PCP.[147] On summary judgment motions the trial court dismissed all claims

---

143. 33 U.S.C. § 2707 (b). Claims may be made under OPA 90 for discharges of oil in or on the territorial sea, internal waters, or adjacent shoreline of a foreign country only if the discharge is from:

> 1. An Outer Continental Shelf facility or a deepwater port. "Outer Continental Shelf facility" is defined in 33 U.S.C. § 2701(25) without adding "of the United States," although such a limitation can be inferred. Section 2701(6) defines "deepwater port" under U.S. law (33 U.S.C. §§ 1501–24, the Deepwater Port Act of 1974).
> 2. A vessel in navigable waters, i.e., navigable waters of the United States (§ 2701[21]).
> 3. A vessel carrying oil as cargo between two places in the United States. (The cabotage laws against carriage of cargoes by foreign flag vessels between a loading port in the United States and a discharging port in the United States were still in effect as of 1997. See 46 U.S.C. § 883.)
> 4. A tanker that received the oil at the terminal of the pipeline constructed under the Trans-Alaska Pipeline Authorization Act (43 U.S.C. § 1651–55) for transportation to a place in the United States, if the discharge or threat occurs prior to delivery of the oil to that place.

144. 46 U.S.C. § 688 (b) (1988). See also, Baade, *Foreign Oil Disaster Litigation Prospects in the United States and the "Mid-Atlantic Settlement Formula,"* 7 J. Energy & Nat. Res. L. 125 (1989).

145. *State of Louisiana ex rel. Guste v. The Testbank,* 524 F. Supp. 1170, 1982 AMC 2246 (ED La. 1981), aff'd, 728 F.2d 748, 1984 AMC 2951 (5th Cir. 1984), aff'd *en banc* on rehearing, 752 F.2d 1019, 1985 AMC 1521 (5th Cir. 1985).

146. 752 F.2d at 1021, 1985 AMC at 1523.

147. Id.

by shipping interests, recreational fishermen, seafood businesses, seafood restaurants, and marinas, but retained the claims of commercial fishermen and commercial shrimpers, crabbers, and oystermen who made a commercial use of the embargoed waters.[148]

The general maritime law developed a nonstatutory cause of action for damage caused by oil pollution from a vessel resulting from fault.[149] Both right and remedy were based on maritime tort. These nonstatutory causes of action are available for all losses, i.e., cleanup expenses as well as damages to property.[150] Furthermore, there is no theoretical reason under the general maritime law not to include a nondischarging tort-feasor who contributed to the spill.

While the maritime tort of pollution is now clearly established, there was a period of time prior to the 1948 Admiralty Extension Act[151] when, because

148. 524 F. Supp. 1170, 1982 AMC 2246 (ED La. 1981), aff'd, 728 F.2d 748, 1984 AMC 2951 (5th Cir. 1984).

149. *State of California v. The Bournemouth,* 307 F. Supp. 922 (CD Cal. 1969). An oil spill damaged marine life in navigable waters. The court recognized a maritime lien created by the maritime tort of pollution in favor of the State of California to protect its marine environment; see also *Union Oil Co. v. Oppen,* 501 F.2d 558, 1975 AMC 416 (9th Cir. 1974); *State of Louisiana ex rel. Guste v. The Testbank,* supra note 145; and *National Sea Clammers Ass'n v. City of New York,* 616 F.2d 1222 (3d Cir. 1980), rev'd on other grounds sub nom., *Middlesex County Sewerage Auth. v. National Sea Clammers Ass'n,* supra note 103; *Burgess v. The Tamano,* 370 F. Supp. 247, 1973 AMC 1131 (D Me. 1973), aff'd mem. 559 F.2d 1200 (1st Cir. 1977); *Pruitt v. Allied Chemical Co.,* 523 F. Supp. 975 (ED Va. 1981); In *In re Oswego Barge Corp.,* supra note 103, the federal government's claim for cleanup costs in Canada was permitted under the general maritime law, although the claim for similar costs in U.S. waters was denied because of preemption under FWPCA.

150. Torts classified as "intentional," as opposed to "negligent" permit punitive damages as well as expanded consequential damages against tort-feasors. Negligent torts, however, are subject to restrictions based on the requirement that the resulting injury to the plaintiff must be within the foreseeable risk established by defendant's conduct or failure to act, as established in *Palsgraf v. Long Island R.R.,* 248 N.Y. 339, 162 N.E. 99 (1928). (See chapter 13.)

The *Palsgraf* consequential damages limitation was applied to narrow the nature of pollution damages by the Judicial Committee of the Privy Council in a case appealed from Australia, *Overseas Tankship (U.K.) Ltd. v. Morts Dock & Eng'r. Co. (Wagon Mound I),* [1961] A.C. 388, in which the vessel *Wagon Mound* discharged fuel in a careless manner, resulting in an oil spill which spread to a ship repair facility and a vessel moored at an adjacent pier. A workman at the repair facility was welding when the spilled oil was set on fire by hot metal and cotton waste from the welding. The oil fire spread to the moored ship, which was destroyed along with the pier. *Wagon Mound I* was the action of the owner of the pier destroyed by fire against the polluting vessel. Fire was not within the oil pollution risk, and so fire damage liability was denied. In *Wagon Mound II,* however, the owner of the moored ship brought a separate action (resulting in a separate finding of facts) and the Judicial Committee affirmed the liability of the polluting vessel for fire damage to the moored vessel because the polluter had not met the burden of adequate precautions (there being no rational explanation for the failure to prevent the oil pollution). *Overseas Tankship (U.K.) Ltd. v. The Miller S.S. Co.,(Wagon Mound II),* [1967] A.C. 617.

151. 46 U.S.C. § 740 (1982). Under the language of this statute, damage negligently caused by a vessel on navigable waters is actionable, even though consummated on land. The constitutionality of the statute was upheld in *United States v. Matson Nav. Co.,* 201 F.2d 610, 1953 AMC 272 (9th Cir. 1953), and was applied without question by the Supreme Court in *Gutierrez v. Waterman S.S. Corp.,* 373 U.S. 206, 1963 AMC 1649 (1963).

of the locality test previously applied by the Supreme Court,[152] a tort was not considered maritime if it originated on a vessel but was consummated on land, e.g., the entry of crude oil spilled from a vessel onto the property of a beachfront owner. It was the supposed inability of an admiralty court to fashion a remedy for land-owning plaintiffs that gave rise to the necessity of recognition of a common law tort for marine pollution.[153] Another factor was the purported inability of an admiralty court to enjoin future pollution nuisances.[154] There do not appear to be significant differences between the general maritime law tort and the common law tort.[155]

2. *Creation of Liability*

The proof required to establish a maritime tort against the vessel from which the polluting substance has come is proof of fault.[156] Policy arguments in favor of strict liability, instead of fault liability, have been rejected up to now,[157] but actions brought in admiralty under the general maritime law should

152. *The Plymouth,* 70 U.S. 20 (1866), where sparks and flames from a burning steamship spread to a wharf, whence it spread to a warehouse on the wharf. Libellant wharfinger's suit in admiralty against the vessel was dismissed for lack of jurisdiction, the Supreme Court holding that both the commission and consummation of the tortious act must take place on navigable waters.

153. *Taylor v. Boston, Cape Cod & N.Y. Canal Co.,* 224 Mass. 307, 112 N.E. 650 (1916); *Kerwin v. Mexican Petroleum Co.,* 267 F. 460 (D R.I. 1920); *Rose v. Socony-Vacuum Corp.,* 54 R.I. 411, 173 A. 627 (1934); *Magnolia Petroleum Co. v. Williams,* 222 Miss. 538, 76 So.2d 365 (1954); and *Brown v. Lundell,* 162 Tex. 84, 344 S.W.2d 863 (1961).

154. Traditional arguments about the unavailability of equitable remedies in admiralty were rejected by the Supreme Court in *Swift & Co. Packers v. Compania Colombiana del Caribe, S.A.,* 339 U.S. 684, 1950 AMC 1089 (1950). See also *Pino v. Protection Maritime Ins. Co.,* 599 F.2d 10, 1979 AMC 2459 (1st Cir. 1979).

155. The differences between federal common law and the general maritime law are examined in detail in the context of whether the 1972 FWPCA preempted general maritime law remedies in *National Sea Clammers,* supra note 103. See also Kalo, *Water Pollution and Commercial Fishermen: Applying General Maritime Law to Claims for Damages to Fisheries in Ocean and Coastal Waters,* 61 N.C. L. Rev. 313 (1983). With the adoption of comparative negligence by statute or decision in an overwhelming number of states since 1970, the difference between the comparative negligence defense in admiralty and the former rule whereby contributory negligence was a complete bar to recovery at common law is no longer very important.

156. *Salaky v. Atlas Tank Processing Corp.,* 120 F. Supp. 225, (SDNY 1953) rev'd, 208 F.2d 174, 1954 AMC 77 (2d Cir. 1954). Owners of small boats moored at a yacht basin alleged damages caused by oil pumped out of ships' bilges, but since they could not identify the particular polluter or the time and place of each spill, they could not establish the fault required for liability in tort. Cf. *In re New Jersey Barging Corp.,* 168 F. Supp. 925, 1955 AMC 2270 (SDNY 1958). See also later proceeding in the same case, 144 F. Supp. 340, 1956 AMC 1338, 168 F. Supp. 925, 1959 AMC 2532, where the pumpman of a barge of heating oil fell asleep and allowed an oil spill of 2,000 barrels which spread ¼ mile north and south of the New Haven discharge pier, affecting 155 beachfront properties; limitation of liability was granted.

157. *Esso Petroleum, Ltd. v. Southport Corp.,* [1956] A.C. 218 (H. L., 1956). After a tanker ran aground in the River Ribble near Liverpool, the master jettisoned 400 tons of fuel oil to lighten the vessel and the oil was carried by wind and tide onto plaintiff's beach, causing damage. While Lord Devlin suggested that an action based on the admiralty doctrine of unseaworthiness would have been possible if plaintiffs had pleaded and proved, e.g., that the source of the accident was

remain subject to the Limitation of Liability Act of 1851.[158] The difficulty, if not the impossibility, of proof of traditional fault by those suffering damage because of the enterprise of maritime transportation of petroleum and its products may in the future lead either to a standard of strict liability supported by the policy of legislative activity,[159] or to a reinterpretation of the common law standard of negligence, because the burden of proving adequate precautions has not been met.[160]

3. Assessment of Damages

In an earlier time, reimbursement of actual expenditures for cleanup was often all that was required to make whole the victims of maritime pollution. As stated, the 1972 FWPCA dealt only with the liability of a polluter to the federal government for cleanup.[161] Thus, at the outset, it is necessary to distinguish between cleanup or removal expenses and all other damages caused by a spill. In the category of "all other damages," most of the problems have come from (a) attempts to develop a formula to compensate for the lingering effects of pollution and the loss of use for aesthetic reasons; and (b) limitations on the consequential losses due to an oil spill because of legal remoteness; or (c) limitations on the nature of the damages themselves, such as "mere" economic loss, as opposed to actual physical damage.

(a) Compensation Formulas. In *In re New Jersey Barging Corp.*[162] a negligent oil discharge had spread ¼ mile north and south of the discharge pier in New Haven Harbor, affecting 155 beachfront property owners. The smells, hazards, and fouling of the beach and its installations lingered for at least four

---

a defective steering gear, the majority required evidence of negligence and found that the master had not been negligent in the circumstances; the lower court having rejected trespass and nuisance, the only issue for the court was common law negligence.

158. 46 U.S.C. §§ 183–89.

159. Modern doctrines of strict liability begin with the two appellate opinions in *Rylands v. Fletcher*, L.R., 1 Ex. 265 (1866), *aff'd*, L.R., 3 H.L. 330 (1868). See also *Read v. Lyons & Co.*, [1947] A.C. 156, confirming that enterprise liability attaches to the escape of inherently dangerous substances. See 1972 Ports and Waterways Safety Act, 33 U.S.C. §5 1221-36 (1982). See also *State of Maryland v. Amerada Hess Corp.*, 350 F. Supp. 1060, 1974 AMC 1003 (D Md. 1972).

The 1980 Comprehensive Environmental Response, Compensation and Liability Act, 42 U.S.C. §§ 9601-57, (CERCLA, the Superfund) has also created a strict liability for cleanup costs, 42 U.S.C. § 9607. See *United States v. Northeastern Pharmaceutical & Chemical Co.*, 810 F.2d 726, 733–34 (8th Cir. 1986); and *City of Philadelphia v. Stepan Chemical Co.*, 544 F. Supp. 1135, 1148. (ED Pa. 1983).

160. *Overseas Tankship (U.K.) Ltd. v. The Miller S.S. Co.*, [1967] A.C. 617 *(Wagon Mound II)* (supra note 150). In this action, foreseeability of the consequences of the careless oil spill was more easily established because of the failure to take adequate and cheap precautions to avoid the potential damage from the spill, where there would be no social utility under a rough cost-benefit analysis in not taking such precautions.

161. 33 U.S.C. § 1321.

162. 135 F. Supp. 97, 1955 AMC 2270; 144 F. Supp. 340, 1956 AMC 1338; 168 F. Supp. 925, 1959 AMC 2532, (SDNY, 1955, 1956, 1958).

years after the spill. Anticipating enormous damage suits, the barge owner petitioned to limit liability under the Limitation of Liability Act,[163] so that the issue of the formula for claims arose in the context of a limited fund. Beachfront property owners claimed $603,612, seeking to recover $8.00 per frontage foot for summer cottages and $12.00 per frontage foot for year-round homes, to compensate for loss of use. The commissioner to whom the issues of damages was referred rejected the formula, awarding only $54,423.93, basing the awards on evidence of actual out-of-pocket expenses, to which was added a small sum for inconvenience, annoyance, and discomfort by the decrease in use of the property for swimming, sunbathing, fishing, boating, and picnicking, and by loss of aesthetic value.[164]

In *Commonwealth of Puerto Rico v. The Zoe Colocotroni,*[165] the trial court sought to compensate the commonwealth, as *parens patriae,*[166] for the coastal ecosystem destroyed by an oil spill, by awarding the diminution in market value of the damaged area under a formula to replace trees, other flora, and even sediments.[167] The resulting amount ($5.5 million, based on a minimum of six cents per microorganism) was held to be "grossly disproportionate," and the court of appeals remanded for awards of damages based on ". . . the cost reasonably to be incurred by the sovereign . . . to restore or rehabilitate the environment in the affected area to its preexisting condition, or as close thereto as is feasible without grossly disproportionate expenditures," noting that the replacement purchase cost of the microorganisms could be appropriately considered.[168] These few cases seem to establish that compensation for oil spill damages must be tied very closely to actual costs to property owners, whether of cleanup or replacement, and that valuation formulas that bring in the processes of nature over time will not be approved, even though more accurate from a statistical point of view.

(b) Consequential Damages: Economic Loss. Consideration of this problem must always go back to the brief opinion of Justice Holmes in *Robins Dry Dock and Repair Co. v. Flint*[169] (decided before the *Palsgraf* case, but not inconsistent with it). *Robins* rejected a cause of action for negligent interference with contract simply because, "The law does not spread its protection so

---

163. 46 U.S.C. §§ 181–89. Protection of shipowners from all maritime claims was achieved in the original 1851 legislation and extension to nonmaritime claims was supposedly achieved by amendments to the statute in 1889, 23 Stat. 57, § 18, now 46 U.S.C. § 189 (1982). See *Richardson v. Harmon,* 222 U.S. 96 (1911).

164. 168 F. Supp. at 939, 1959 AMC at 2551.

165. 456 F. Supp. 1327, 1979 AMC 21 (D P.R. 1978), mod., 628 F. 2d 652, 1981 AMC 2185 (1st Cir. 1980).

166. Under *parens patriae* the sovereign becomes a trustee for the public. See *State of Maine v. The Tamano,* 357 F. Supp. 1097, 1973 AMC 1131 (D Me. 1973).

167. 628 F.2d at 671–72, 1981 AMC at 2196–97.

168. 628 F.2d at 675, 1981 AMC at 2221.

169. 275 U.S. 303, 1928 AMC 61 (1927).

far."[170] The case involved the claim of a time charterer (*not* the vessel owner, whose claim for loss of use was not involved) against the dry-dock company for two weeks' loss of use of a tramp steamer as a result of negligent damage to the vessel's propeller during dry-docking, required by the charter. The relevant charter contained an off-hire clause, so that the charterer did not have to pay hire during the repair period, but war conditions had made it possible for the charterer, as head charterer, to subcharter at fourteen times the rate in the prewar charter if the vessel had been operable.[171] The rejection of this loss of use claim by a nonowner of property became the foundation of a much broader doctrine against the recovery of mere economic losses or indirect consequential damages, unaccompanied by property damage. Justice Holmes's broad language, however, rejected tort-feasor liability to the charterer on a contract as well as a tort basis, and did not confine the resulting nonliability to admiralty law.

(c) The Theory of *Robins Dry Dock*. It is easier to describe the purpose and effect of *Robins* than it is to analyze the legal theory underlying the case, because in subsequent cases courts have understood it in different ways, and the Supreme Court has not returned to it. As used by courts of appeal, the *Robins Dry Dock* doctrine cuts off claims to limit the logic of the tort concepts of foreseeability. The "bright-line" rule of *The Testbank* attempts to fix meaningful limits to Justice Holmes's idea that the law does not spread its protection as far as a claim for negligent interference with contract. Thus, *Robins Dry Dock* is not merely a foreseeability case where there was no knowledge of the charter; nor is it simply a duty case where there was no privity of contract between charterer and repairer. No tort law principle can contain it; it is a pragmatic way to protect negligent tort-feasors from all the *possible* consequences of action.[172]

170. 275 U.S. at 309, 1928 AMC at 63. Justice Holmes was maddeningly vague when he wrote just before this line, ". . . No authority need be cited to show that, as a general rule, a tort to the person or property of one man does not make the tortfeasor liable to another merely because the injured person was under a contract with the other . . . ."

171. 275 U.S. at 307, 1928 AMC at 62. Note, however, that mandatory payments of hire even during breakdown periods under a "hell or high water" clause in a time charter will permit the charterer to recover from the negligent tort-feasor. *Venore Transp. Co. v. The Struma,* 583 F.2d 708, 1978 AMC 2146 (4th Cir. 1978).

The practical problem with *Robins* itself has always been the assumption that the existence of a charter in a merchant vessel situation is unknown to the tort-feasor. 275 U.S. at 309, 1928 AMC at 63. Of course, knowledge of the particular charter may not exist, but most tramp ships would probably be laid up unless on charter. Knowledge of the charter or business expectancy is apparently irrelevant under the "bright line" theory. See *East River Steamship Corp. v. Transamerica Delaval, Inc.,* 476 U.S. 858, 874–75, 1986 AMC 2027, 2041.

172. Just as Justice Holmes used admiralty tort theory to limit the consequences of tortious conduct in *Robins Dry Dock,* Chief Judge Cardozo (later Justice Cardozo of the U.S. Supreme Court) was doing the same thing for the common law of torts at the same time. In 1928 he wrote the opinion in *Palsgraf v. Long Island R.R. Co.,* 248 N.Y. 339, 162 N.E. 99 (1928), holding the railroad not liable to the intending passenger because the result (an explosion) was not within the foreseeable risk of defendant's conduct (careless handling of a passenger with a package). Non-

In *Burgess v. The Tamano,*[173] there was a spill of 100,000 gallons of crude petroleum at Portland, Maine, causing substantial damage to the rich marine environment. Commercial fishermen and commercial shellfish exploiters (clam diggers) were held entitled to recover for their actual losses and their economic losses because they made a direct and commercial use of the polluted coastal waters.[174] Denied claimants included restaurants, hotels, and motels, as well as owners and users of recreational facilities which had demanded compensation for the loss of tourist business when tourists ceased coming to the polluted area for rest and relaxation.[175] The theoretical justification of this result came from the common law tort of public nuisance, in that the commercial fishermen who lost catches of fish and shellfish suffered damages different in kind and degree from the damages of the entire community; their immediate livelihood had been lost, whereas the recreational facility owners who lost customers suffered nonimmediate losses similar to those of the entire community, and therefore not different in kind and degree from those of the community.[176]

---

liability was also the result in *H.R. Moch v. Rensselaer Water Co.,* 247 N.Y. 160, 159 N.E. 896 (1928), holding the water company not liable in tort for the loss of a warehouse by fire because there was not sufficient water to fight the fire, as required by a contract between the defendant and the city. Lastly, *Ultramares Corp. v. Touche, Niven & Co.,* 255 N.Y. 170, 174 N.E. 441 (1931), held that an accountant was not liable to a defrauded investor who relied on a negligently prepared balance sheet. That opinion cites *Robins* and outlines the policy to limit the consequences of negligence so as to prevent, "... liability in an indeterminate amount for an indeterminate time to an indeterminate class." 255 N.Y. at 179. Concerning economic loss, see *East River Steamship Corp. v. Transamerica Delaval, Inc.,* supra note 171. See also *Petition of Kinsman Transit Co. (Kinsman II),* 388 F.2d 821, 1968 AMC 293 (2d Cir. 1968), rejecting claims of riverfront property owners below the site of a ship-bridge allision for the increased costs in moving grain by rail and truck, where it was not possible to use the cheaper river transportation because of the blocked condition of the river. *Kinsman I* (338 F.2d 708, 1964 AMC 2503 (2d Cir. 1964), had permitted recovery by riverfront property owners above the site of the allision for flooding damage to property.

173. 370 F. Supp. 247, 1973 AMC 1939 (D Me. 1973), aff'd mem., 559 F. 2d 1200 (1st Cir. 1977).

174. Id., 370 F. Supp. at 250, 1973 AMC at 1942.

175. Id., 370 F. Supp. at 251. Note, however, that Maine is a common law state where the writ of trespass *quare clausum fregit* (q.c.f.) applies to any entry of the plaintiff's "close." Thus common law tort (trespass) might compensate beachfront hotel and restaurant owners whose property was actually invaded by the crude petroleum. Trespass q.c.f. normally permits expanded consequential and even punitive damages. See generally *Small v. United States,* 333 F.2d 702 (3d Cir. 1964).

176. Two nuisance cases are analogous: first, on the concept of damages different in kind and degree from the damages suffered by the community at large, see *Hampton v. North Carolina Pulp Co.,* 223 N.C. 535, 27 S.E.2d 538 (1943), a suit in public nuisance brought by commercial fishermen against the wood-pulp plant which had polluted the river. The court contrasted the rights of commercial fishermen whose livelihood was damaged with those of sport fishermen, recreational users, and other citizens whose aesthetic enjoyment of the river was diminished. See also *Maier v. Publicker Commercial Alcohol Co.,* 62 F. Supp. 161, 1946 AMC 968 (ED Pa. 1945), aff'd per curiam, 154 F.2d 1020 (3d Cir. 1946), a private nuisance suit in admiralty by the owner of barges which were moored, partially submerged, in a river near a sewer discharge from defendant's alcohol distillery, from which sour mash residue went directly into the barges, causing extra expenses to remove it and raise the vessels. There was a maritime tort of nuisance because of the continuing pollution from the distilling process. The case also involved the issue of violation of the pollution statutes as evidence of negligence.

In *Oppen v. Aetna Ins. Co. (Oppen I)*[177] there had been an escape of crude petroleum in 1969 from a well being drilled at a Union Oil Co. platform off Santa Barbara, California. The oil slick polluted the harbor and Santa Barbara Channel with its fishing grounds, preventing the use of these waters for fishing purposes. In *Oppen I* recreational fishermen and pleasure boat owners sued for physical damage to their vessels, plus damages for the loss of use of their vessels by interference with the right to navigate and fish the polluted waters. Recovery for the loss of use was denied, however, on the general principle that loss of use of a private leisure boat was not compensable. In *Union Oil Co. v. Oppen (Oppen II),*[178] however, commercial fishermen recovered their damages, including damages for loss of potential catch—a form of loss of use.[179]

Pruitt v. Allied Chemical Corp.[180] involved the deliberate discharge of the toxic chemical substance Kepone over a sixteen-month period by Life Science Products Co., which sold the product to Allied Chemical. The toxic waste was pumped into the sewer system of Hopewell, Virginia, eventually passing into the James River and thence into Chesapeake Bay, where migratory and local fish and shellfish were poisoned. (Kepone traces were subsequently found in fish caught in Upper Chesapeake Bay and off the New Jersey coast.) The claimants were commercial fishermen and shell fishermen, commercial oyster-bed lessors, recreational fishermen, tackle and bait shop owners, marina owners and, lastly, a group of businesses which

---

177. 485 F.2d 252 (9th Cir. 1973).

178. 501 F.2d 558 (9th Cir. 1974). Commercial fishermen were also permitted to recover economic losses (lost profits) in *Emerson G.M. Diesel, Inc. v. The Alaskan Enterprise,* 732 F.2d 1468, 1985 AMC 2069 (9th Cir. 1984). This holding, however, would not survive the Supreme Court's opinion in *East River Steamship Corp. v. Delaval Inc.,* supra note 171, rejecting economic loss claims in maritime product liability cases.

179. In *The Menominee,* 125 F. 530 (EDNY 1903), it was held that loss of prospective catches by fishermen was not compensable because too speculative. But in *Carbone v. Ursich,* 209 F.2d 178, 1954 AMC 169 (9th Cir. 1953), fishermen "on lays" recovered for loss of prospective catch.

180. 523 F. Supp. 975 (ED Va. 1981). Aspects of this doctrine denying recovery for economic loss are still controversial. Circuits aligned with *Robins* and *Testbank* are the First, Third, and Eleventh. See *Barber Lines A/S v. The Donau Maru,* 764 F.2d 50, 1985 AMC 2600 (1st Cir. 1985); *Getty Refining and Marketing Co. v. The Fadi B,* 766 F.2d 829, 1985 AMC 2579 (3d Cir. 1985); and *Hercules Carriers, Inc. v. Florida,* 720 F.2d 1201, 1984 AMC 2962 (11th Cir. 1983), aff'd *en banc,* 728 F.2d 1359, 1985 AMC 2396 (11th Cir. 1984). See Rizzo, *A Theory of Economic Loss and The Law of Torts,* 11 J. Legal Studies 281 (1981), and Note, *Negligent Interference With Contract: Knowledge as Standard for Recovery,* 63 Va. L. Rev. 813 (1977).

More recently, courts have held that economic losses *unrelated* to the oil spill may not be recovered, even though there has been physical contact with the oil. See *Naviera Maersk España, S.A. v. Cho-Me Towing, Inc.,* 782 F. Supp. 317, (ED La. 1992), and *In re Oriental Republic of Uruguay,* 821 F. Supp. 934 and 953, 1993 AMC 783 (D Del. 1993).

In other circuits economic loss alone is not determinative, as in *In re Kinsman Transit Co. (Kinsman II),* 388 F.2d 82, 1968 AMC 293 (2d Cir. 1968); *In re Bethlehem Steel Corp.,* 631 F.2d 441, 1980 AMC 2122 (6th Cir. 1980); *Venore Transportation Co. v. The Struma,* 583 F.2d 708, 1978 AMC 2146 (4th Cir. 1978); and *Union Oil Co. v. Oppen,* 501 F.2d 558, 1975 AMC 416 (9th Cir. 1974) *(Oppen II).* See supra notes 127–28; James, *Limitations on Liability for Economic Loss Caused by Negligence: A Pragmatic Appraisal,* 25 Vand. L. Rev. 43 (1972); Comment, *The Murky Waters of Robins Dry Dock: A Comparative Analysis of Economic Loss in Maritime Law,* 60 Tul. L. Rev. 995 (1986).

lost customers because of consumer fears of poisoned seafood, such as seafood restaurants, seafood retail stores, and seafood wholesalers. Recoveries by the commercial fishermen were approved, while they were denied to those businesses which suffered because of consumer fears.[181] Recoveries were approved under state law but not under maritime law for the businesses which serviced the recreational fishermen, as surrogate plaintiffs for the recreational fishermen themselves, whose provable damages were inconsequential.[182]

In *Louisiana ex rel. Guste v. The Testbank*[183] there was a full review of the *Robins Dry Dock* principles, which were strongly reaffirmed by the 10 to 5 en-banc decision of the Fifth Circuit.[184] The collision produced a chemical spill which required the closing of a Mississippi River ship channel and a river and marsh fishery for commercial fisheries and sportsmen. The economic loss claims of recreational fishermen, tackle and bait shop owners who lost customers, owners of boat rental businesses and marinas that also lost customers, together with wholesale and retail seafood businesses and seafood restaurants were all denied recovery because of the absence of physical damage to these plaintiffs.[185] The same general "bright line" rationale of *Robins* was used to deny the economic loss claims of shipping companies (whether owners or charterers) unable to use the closed channel and required to spend additional amounts to bypass it or suffer delay in moving cargoes.[186] (Claims of commercial fishermen were not involved in *The Testbank.*) In summary, the Fifth Circuit's "bright line" rejects recovery for economic loss unaccompanied by physical damage regardless of foreseeability and direct causation in tort and regardless of business expectancy or contractual relation.

---

181. Supra note 180, 523 F. Supp. at 976.

182. Id., 523 F. Supp. at 980.

183. Supra note 145.

184. 752 F.2d at 1020, 1032, 1985 AMC at 1522, 1542.

185. 752 F.2d at 1021, 1985 AMC at 1524. See also *BP North American Petroleum, Inc. v. The Robert E. Lee S.S.*, 993 F.2d 1193, 1993 AMC 2473 (5th Cir. 1993) and 999 F.2d 105, 1994 AMC 856 (5th Cir. 1994).

186. Id. See also *Akron Corp. v. The Cantigny,* 706 F.2d 151, 1984 AMC 2969 (5th Cir. 1983), and *In re Marine Navigation Sulphur Carriers, Inc.*, 638 F.2d 700 (4th Cir. 1981), (blocked channel and rerouting expense cases where recovery was also denied).

In *Stop and Shop v. Fisher,* 444 N.E.2d 368, 1986 AMC 2920, (Mass. 1986), no recovery was allowed for purely economic loss in the absence of physical damage to property, but under a public nuisance theory following a bridge and tow allision, there would be special pecuniary damage for loss of customer access to a store; however, the same court would not permit river-front businesses to recover economic losses by the simple expedient of characterizing federal admiralty claims as state law public nuisance. *Global Petroleum Corp. v. Northeast Petroleum Co.*, 539 N.E. 2d 1022 (Mass. 1989). Cf. *Petition of Kinsman Transit Co.,* 388 F.2d 821, 1968 AMC 293 (2d Cir. 1968) ("Kinsman II," opinion by Kaufman, J.); but see *Federal Commerce & Navigation Co., Ltd. v. The Marathonian,* 528 F.2d 907, 1975 AMC 2436 (2d Cir. 1975), where *Robins* was applied despite the reference to *Kinsman.*

In the litigation involving the 1978 *Amoco Cadiz*[187] oil spill off the coast of France, 220,000 tons (68 million gallons) of crude oil were let loose on the coasts of Brittany and Normandy from a VLCC supertanker 1,095 feet long and 167 feet wide, with a capacity of 230,000 deadweight tons. The ship's steering gear had completely failed and there were no alternative devices to control the steering; a salvage tug was unsuccessful in attempting to control the drift of the ship onto the rocks. The resulting oil slick, 80 miles long and 18 miles wide in places, polluted one fourth of the Brittany coast, ravaging the ecosystem and destroying commercial shellfish operations. Six months of effort by 4,400 men and 50 vessels were expended on the cleanup, at enormous cost. Joint and several liability of the owners and builders was based on improper design and construction of the steering gear and improper maintenance of the ship during its four-year life—especially in the deferred maintenance and the foreseeable signs of steering gear breakdown demonstrated by leakage and contamination of hydraulic fluid, ram scoring, and unwanted rudder movement.

The court of appeals made a number of changes in the district court's computation of damages, thereby increasing the damages owed by Amoco from $155 million to $205 million.[188] Amoco had objected to the admission of 1,236 documents as hearsay, and the court of appeals noted that the absence of agreement of the parties on the proof of damages condemned the trial judge to a morass of detail which, of necessity, included hearsay. The court of appeals could not find prejudice to Amoco's interests, especially in view of the way the court cut claims supported by clearly admissible evidence. In the view of the court of appeals, the alternative modes of proof in the *Manual for Complex and Multidistrict Litigation* should have been used. A multiplicity of claims by commercial fishermen and shell fishermen, aquaculture farmers, hotels, restaurants, ferries, communities, and regions were brought.[189] As a result of the court's evidentiary decisions, a relaxed standard of proof

187. *In re Oil Spill by the Amoco Cadiz off the Coast of France on March 16, 1978,* 491 F. Supp. 170 (ND Ill. 1979) aff'd, 699 F.2d 909 (7th Cir. 1983) and 954 F.2d 1279, 1992 AMC 913 (7th Cir. 1992). See also, Bartlett, *In re Oil Spill by the Amoco Cadiz—Choice of Law and a Pierced Corporate Veil Defeat the 1969 Civil Liability Convention,* 10 Mar. Law 1 (1985).

188. 954 F.2d 1320–37, 1992 AMC 962–89. Hearings on damages began in April 1986, resulting in a decision of the court (Chief Judge McGarr) on Jan. 11, 1988, and a report by Judge McGarr as special master on Feb. 21, 1989, following his retirement, which increased the amount of damages against the Amoco interests from the equivalent of $82.5 million to the equivalent of $115 million. (The award was made in French francs.) These awards were appealed by both claimants and defendant to the Seventh Circuit, which increased them to the equivalent of $205 million.

189. Testimony dealt with the destruction of oyster beds, destruction of an estimated 30,000 seabirds and the annual crop of commercial seaweed; and lost opportunities to take sole, crab, lobster, and other commercial fish; ecological damage to the coast and losses to the tourist industry, including losses of hotels, restaurants, ferries, municipalities, and touristic regions. Theoretical possibilities were rejected, along with estimates of future ecological improvement programs and delayed investment opportunities. The court relied heavily on estimates drawn up contemporaneously with the oil spill rather than those specially prepared for the trial, which

was applied with respect to many elements of damage sought by commercial users of the ocean, and there was recovery for precisely proven damages of the tourist industry.[190]

At an early stage of the litigation involving the *Exxon Valdez* oil spill, the U.S. District Court for the District of Alaska applied the general maritime law doctrine of *Robins Dry Dock* to claims in excess of the $100 million strict liability limit of the Trans-Alaska Pipeline Authorization Act (TAPAA).[191] Thus, under Alaska's law of strict liability without monetary limitation, or under federal law, claims for economic loss without proof of physical damage would be denied by application of *Robins Dry Dock* as part of the general maritime law. In contrast to that application of *Robins Dry Dock* are the claims falling directly under the TAPAA, where economic loss claimants—fish buyers, fish spotters, fish processors, and other shoreside businesses that suffered no physical damages to proprietary interests—would be permitted to recover for economic losses on the theory that TAPAA had preempted the application of the substantive general maritime law.[192] It should be noted that the TAPAA provision construed in *The Exxon Valdez* and *The Glacier Bay,* "[n]otwithstanding the provisions of any other law,"[193] is the same as the language of OPA 90.[194]

In *Ballard Shipping Co. v. Beach Shellfish Co.*[195] the First Circuit refused to apply *Robins Dry Dock* to claims of economic loss by shellfish dealers whose shellfishing activities were suspended for two weeks owing to the spill of

---

were hotly contested by the defendant. The principal beneficiary of the award was the French government, which had a large claim for cleanup costs. In the second report, oyster farmers were permitted additional costs for long-term damage.

190. 954 F. 2d 1304–12, 1992 AMC 941–50.

191. *In re Exxon Valdez,* 767 F. Supp. 1509, 1991 AMC 1482 (D Alaska 1991), in which the court stated that *Robins Dry Dock* would be the law of the case as to all parties, applicable to claims exceeding the $100 million TAPAA fund (Order No. 38). Subsequently, the court granted summary judgment against seafood wholesaler, processor, cannery employee, and tenderer plaintiffs (Order No. 174 [D Alaska 1994]).

Summary judgment was also granted against seven municipalities and against 95 area businesses that either (1) had no physical contact with the spilled oil; or (2) whose economic losses were *unrelated* to the oil spill, even though there may have been contact with the spilled oil (Order No. 189 [D Alaska 1994]).

Summary judgment was granted with respect to claims for price diminishment as to commercial fishermen whose fishing areas were not closed to fishing or contaminated as a result of the spill, but was denied with respect to commercial fishermen whose fishing areas were closed or partially closed as a result of the oil spill (Order No. 187 [D Alaska 1994]).

The Ninth Circuit put limits on claims under the TAPAA fund and denied recovery in a case where California drivers sought to recover from the fund for the increased costs of gasoline in California after the *Exxon Valdez* spill. *Benefiel v. Exxon Corp.,* 959 F.2d 805, 1992 AMC 1720 (9th Cir. 1992). See generally, Gallagher, *In the Wake of Exxon Valdez: Murky Legal Waters of Liability and Compensation,* 25 New Eng. L. Rev. 571 (1990).

192. *In re Glacier Bay,* 746 F. Supp. 1379, 1991 AMC 739 (D Alaska 1991). *Robins Dry Dock* was not applied in this case because the claims did not exceed the $100 million TAPAA fund.

193. 43 U.S.C. § 1653 (c) (1).

194. 33 U.S.C. § 2702 (a).

195. 32 F.3d 623, 1994 AMC 2705 (1st Cir. 1994).

300,000 gallons of heating oil into Narragansett Bay from the *World Prodigy* in June 1989 due to grounding on Brenton Reef. The shellfish dealers alleged negligence under the general maritime law and the Rhode Island Environmental Injury Compensation Act.[196] The district court dismissed, applying *Robins Dry Dock* to both claims, but the First Circuit reversed as to the state law claims where the statute specifically called for economic damages to be compensable. There would be no preemption of the state law for three reasons: (1) no act of Congress directly governed the case; (2) *Robins Dry Dock* was not a characteristic feature of the general maritime law but was an expression of a general rule of tort law that might be varied by state legislation; and (3) in balancing state and federal interests, the court came down in favor of the state interests in preventing pollution because of the provisions of OPA 90 (which was not enacted until more than a year after the Narragansett Bay spill), because Congress did not view liability for economic losses as an excessive burden on maritime commerce.

(d) Consequential Damages: Remoteness in Space and Time. In *Lloyd's Leasing Ltd. v. Conoco,*[197] a spill of 65,500 barrels of crude oil resulted from a grounding in Louisiana waters of the Gulf of Mexico. The crude washed up on Galveston Island, Texas, 70 miles from the site of the spill, where it was carried (or "tracked") onto the claimant's property—businesses and houses—by tourists and beachgoers, causing damage. This case also involved a limitation of liability proceeding, where an inadequate fund must be distributed pro rata. The appellate court rejected all the Galveston Island claims because of remoteness in space, although the dissenting judge would have awarded damages for physical loss, but not for loss of customers. The rationale of the majority was as follows: "While the appellee might reasonably anticipate that the oil would probably wash ashore somewhere, it had no reason to have anticipated that the oil would probably wash ashore in a heavily populated area and then be tracked into businesses and homes."[198] In reviewing the facts, the court noted that the coastline extends for 340 miles, only 60 of which are developed. Accordingly, the claims were rejected because the damages were not foreseeable.[199]

4. *Punitive Damages*

There is slender authority for the proposition that punitive damages can be awarded in cases of continued polluting operations classifiable as negligence but approaching intent,[200] as in those nuisance cases where the negligently

196. R.I. Gen. Laws, ch. 46-12.3.
197. 868 F.2d 1447, 1989 AMC 1552 (5th Cir. 1989).
198. 868 F.2d at 1449, 1989 AMC at 1555.
199. Id.
200. *Doralee Estates, Inc. v. Cities Service Oil Co.,* 569 F.2d 716 (2d Cir. 1977).

created nuisance has been brought to the attention of the defendant, who thereafter deliberately continues the nuisance.[201] Under normal tort law principles, punitive damages are not awarded in negligence cases.[202] While punitive damages are not likely to be awarded in the case of an accidental spill, the possibility remains that they might be allowed for deliberate spills and also in situations in which the contributing negligence is of a persistent nature, analogous to nuisance continued as a result of negligence.

Section E. Liability of the Nondischarging Vessel in Collision Cases

Interest now turns to the special considerations affecting the liability of a noncarrying vessel whose fault has caused or contributed to a collision resulting in pollution. Under the general maritime law, in a both-to-blame collision case the liability of the discharging vessel to governments for removal (or cleanup) would be like any other third-party liability which would be added to the damages of the discharging vessel for division of damages with the other colliding vessel or vessels.[203]

A complexity was introduced in the way courts construed the liabilities under the 1972 FWPCA, in that remedies other than the statutory remedy for government cleanup expenses of discharging vessels were preempted.[204] As FWPCA was amended the statutory remedy was, however, subject to a limitation of $600 per gross ton, with no cap.[205] Since the 1972 FWPCA did not deal with damage claims of pollution victims, these could be brought against the vessel or the owner of the carrying vessel by pollution victims,[206] and even by

201. *Morgan v. High Penn Oil Co.,* 238 N.C. 185, 77 S.E.2d 682 (1953).

202. C. McCormick, *Handbook of the Law of Damages* 280–82 (1935). Allowance of punitive damages under a Louisiana statute dealing with reckless handling or transportation of hazardous or toxic substances has been held not to conflict with or preempt federal law. *Zoila-Ortego v. B.J.-Titan Services,* 751 F. Supp. 633, 1991 AMC 1205 (ED La. 1990).

203. *Witte Marine Equipment Co. v. Texas City Refinery Co.,* 1961 AMC 157 (EDNY 1960). See generally *Moore-McCormack Lines v. The Esso Camden,* 244 F.2d 198, 1957 AMC 971 (2d Cir. 1957), and chapter 13.

204. The structure of the act was unclear. Section 1321 (f)(1) of 33 U.S.C. set up vessel liability, defenses, and limitation of liability, but dealt only with the discharging vessel. For the discharging vessel to be free of liability, someone or something other must have been the sole cause of the discharge. Subsection (g) of § 1321 applied the same regime as § 1321 (f)(1) to the sole cause third party, who had the same right to plead defenses and limitation of liability as the discharger. For the third-party vessel not to be liable, someone or something other must have been the sole cause of the discharge. (See, e.g., *United States v. LeBoeuf Bros. Towing Co.,* supra note 74.) Section 1321(h) of 33 U.S.C. is intended to deal with the party who has not discharged petroleum and who is not the sole cause of the spill. The other parties to the collision retain the right to force that party to contribute, under negligence law, to the cleanup costs under any appropriate remedy. The nondischarging, non-sole-fault party is also liable to the U.S. government under any appropriate remedy. (See, e.g., *United States v. Bear Marine Services,* 509 F. Supp. 710, 1982 AMC 2197 [ED La. 1980].)

205. 33 U.S.C. § 1321 (f)(1) as amended in 1977.

206. *United States v. City of Redwood City,* 640 F.2d 963, 1981 AMC 1519 (9th Cir. 1981).

the U.S. government,[207] either in admiralty as a maritime tort claim or under the "saving to suitors" clause under state law in trespass, negligence, or nuisance. All of these claims, however, were subject to global limitation of liability.[208] Thus, the rights against other vessels which in some way caused or contributed to the collision were not preempted by the 1972 FWPCA, even for cleanup costs and certainly not for damages of pollution victims. The complexity added by OPA 90 is that the damages of pollution victims are now added to the removal costs, which may be pursued by the federal or state governments.

As noted earlier, the discharging tanker owner's liability is subject to a limitation of liability of $1,200 per gross ton or $10 million, whichever is greater.[209] That liability is also imposed on a nondischarging vessel solely responsible for the discharge, since such a vessel becomes "the responsible party" under OPA 90.[210] However, the limit of that liability for nontanker vessels under OPA 90 is $600 per gross ton or $500,000, whichever is greater.

The nonpolluting nontanker vessel that has contributed to the collision without being its sole cause now appears to be governed by the liability regime of OPA 90. The language of 33 U.S.C. section 2702 (d)(2) indicates that a nontanker vessel that causes a spill is governed by the limitation of section 2704 (a)(2). This conclusion is strengthened by the language of section 2718 (a) specifically exempting state law imposing additional liability from the global limitation of liability (provided for in the Limitation of Liability Act, referred to as the Act of March 3, 1851) and section 2718 (c), exempting additional pollution liabilities under U.S. law from the global limitation of liability. This result is not entirely clear from the legislative history or the text of the statute. It may be that Congress intended to continue the use of the general maritime law of negligence to establish the nondischarging nontanker vessel's liability in contribution (subject to the global limitation of liability) because of the broad language of 33 U.S.C. section 2709 on contribution, whereby a civil action may be brought under OPA 90 or "another law." This is a very weak argument, however, and it may be that the courts will hold that the nontanker, nondischarging, non-solely responsible vessel cannot use the Limitation of Liability Act in defense of any claims brought under OPA 90 or under the general maritime law.

---

207. *United States v. Bear Marine Services,* supra note 202; *In re Berkley Curtis Bay Co.,* 557 F. Supp. 335, 1984 AMC 1934 (SDNY 1983), on remand from 1984 AMC 1941 (2d Cir. 1983).

208. See *In re Berkley Curtis Bay Co.,* 697 F.2d 288, 1982 AMC 2311 (2d Cir. 1982) (decision not to be cited).

209. 33 U.S.C. § 2704(a)(1) (1992).

210. 33 U.S.C. § 2701(32). Cf. *Steuart Transportation Co. v. Allied Towing Corp.,* supra note 103.

CHAPTER TWELVE

BOTH-TO-BLAME COLLISIONS: APPORTIONMENT OF LIABILITY

Section A. Historical Introduction

Historically, the consequences of a combination of faults of two or more vessels in collision have been difficult for courts to define. Various and conflicting rationales have been offered over the years: (1) neither vessel may recover because of the contributing faults of each; (2) the damages of the vessels involved must be divided equally; and (3) the damages of the vessels involved must be borne in proportion to their respective faults. These different solutions have been applied to resolve disputes between (or among) the colliding vessels themselves. Other problems arise when damages to third parties must be considered. The legal situation is presently stable in the United States, but to explain that stability it is first necessary to consider the alternatives rejected in the historical development.

1. The Former Rule of Equal Division of Damages

(a) English and Continental Origins. In 1975 the Supreme Court reformed a rule of its own making—the rule of equal division of damages in both-to-blame collisions—adopted in 1854 in *The Schooner Catharine v. Dickinson.*[1] That case has been harshly criticized as unjust and one that encouraged litigation. The equal division rule was originally settled because the Supreme Court considered that the law in the United States should be in accord with the rule in the United Kingdom and possibly other maritime States.

Despite early inconsistent decisions, the rule of equal division of damages in both-to-blame collisions was established in admiralty in *The Petersfield & The Judith Randolph*[2] in 1789, and restated in dicta in *The Woodrop-Sims*[3] in

1. *The Schooner Catharine v. Dickinson,* 58 U.S. 170 (1854).

2. *The Petersfield & The Judith Randolph,* 167 Eng. Rep. 596 (Adm. 1789).

3. *The Woodrop-Sims,* 165 Eng. Rep. 1422 (Adm. 1815). Despite the facts and the law on sole fault, the court (Sir William Scott, later Lord Stowell) described four possible solutions to collisions: (1) inevitable accident—no recovery by either vessel; (2) mutual fault—an equal division of damages between vessels; (3) sole fault of the single vessel damaged— no recovery for that vessel; (4) sole fault of the other vessel—recovery of damages.

Application of equal division of damages where the faults were unequal was approved by the House of Lords in an important Scottish case, *Hay v. Le Neve,* 2 Shaw's Rep. 395 (H. L. 1824).

1815. Arthur Browne in 1802 described the Roman law, the Laws of Oléron, and the Code of Visby, together with the text of Bynkershoek, as authority for the rule of equal division of damages in mutual fault collisions.[4]

(b) U.S. Origins of Equal Division. In the admiralty treatise by Flanders, published in 1852 before the decision in *The Schooner Catharine,* the author treats both-to-blame collisions:[5]

> If the collision was occasioned by the fault of both parties, the cost of damage is to be divided equally between them. It was said in the case of *Ralston v. States Rights* that this rule is applicable only where both parties are in fault at the time and in the acts which produced the collision, and where the faults are not egregiously unequal. This may be a just and proper qualification of the general rule, but it is certain that maritime law makes no distinction in apportioning the loss from difference in the value of the vessels, or the value of their cargoes, or the degree of their fault.

In that case the Court of Session, the highest court in the Scottish legal system, had divided the damages in proportion to the degree of fault chargeable to each of the parties (⅔ to ⅓). That decree was reversed by the House of Lords in favor of an equal division of the damages. In justifying this apparent inequity, Lord Gifford said:

> This principle of apportionment "grows out of an arbitrary provision in the law of nations, from views of general expediency, not as dictated by natural justice, nor possibly quite consistent with it." However, in a case of this kind, where both vessels are to blame, a court of admiralty will order the vessel most to blame to pay all the costs. . . . In such case it is the settled doctrine of the admiralty that the whole damage should be equally divided between the two vessels. . . . Those views of general expediency, upon which the rule we are now considering is founded, are thus satisfactorily stated by Valin: "No better means," he says, "of making the masters of small vessels, which are liable to be injured by the slightest shock, attentive to avoid collision than to keep the fear of paying for half the damages constantly before their eyes. And if it be said, that it would have been a shorter and more simple mode of adjustment to let each party bear the loss he had sustained, as arising from 'casus fortuitus,' an answer is, that then, the masters of large ships would have made light of collision with those of smaller burden. Upon the whole, therefore, no rule is so just as that of equal apportionment." 2 Shaw's Rep. at 397.

4. 2 A. Browne, *A Compendious View of the Civil Law and of the Law of the Admiralty,* 201–07 (London, 1802, a revision of the earlier Dublin edition of 1797). In describing the Roman Law, Browne states: "In case of accident, the loss was to be divided between both parties, in equal proportions; in case of wilful fault or negligence, the guilty person was to pay the whole . . ." In referring to Bynkershoek Browne states:

> If the injury has happened through fault, and that the fault of the sufferer, e.g. by not carrying lights at night, he plainly gets no reparation. If by the fault of the other, he pays the whole damage; but Bynkershoek imagines that the master of the ship only is liable, it being an act not authorized by the owners; and this may so far be true, that the owners shall not be liable beyond the value of the ships.

5. H. Flanders, *Treatise on Maritime Law,* 292–93 (Boston, 1852). Respecting joint and several liability to innocent cargo, see section D, infra.

The text subsequently cites *Hay v. Le Neve* and its conclusion, "Upon the whole, therefore, no rule is so just as that of equal apportionment."[6] This statement appears in modified form in *The Schooner Catharine* as the policy justification for the rule of equal division.[7] Before the equal division rule was recognized by the Supreme Court, it had been enthusiastically received by most of the lower federal courts.[8] In *The Schooner Catharine v. Dickinson*[9] the court settled the equal division rule in three short paragraphs of an opinion principally directed to a review of the facts of the collision itself; the lower court having found sole fault, the Supreme Court reversed. Mr. Justice Nelson wrote:[10]

> Upon this view of the case it becomes necessary to settle the rule of damages in a case where both vessels are in fault.
>
> The question, we believe, has never until now come distinctly before this court for decision. The rule that prevails in the district and circuit courts, we understand, has been to divide the loss. 9 Law Rep. 30.
>
> This seems now to be the well-settled rule in the English admiralty. . . [citing English cases].
>
> Under the circumstances usually attending these disasters, we think the rule dividing the loss the most just and equitable, and as best tending to induce care and vigilance on both sides, in the navigation.

Thus, the policy reason behind the equal division rule was a belief, incapable of proof, that it would deter the careless and produce greater maritime safety.

Section B. Proportional Fault

1. *The New Rule of* Reliable Transfer

After having heard argument on a review of the divided damages rule in *The Tug San Jacinto,*[11] the Supreme Court decided that case on another ground. Three years later, however, the Supreme Court reviewed the rule of divided

6. Supra note 3.

7. *The Schooner Catharine v. Dickinson,* supra note 1, 58 U.S. at 178.

8. *The Rival,* 20 F. Cas. 845 (No. 11, 867) (D Mass. 1846); *The Scioto,* 21 F. Cas. 774 (No. 12,508) (D Me. 1847); *The Bay State,* 2 F. Cas. 1091 (No. 1, 148) (SDNY 1848); *Ralston v. The States Rights,* 20 F. Cas. 201 (No. 11, 540) (ED Pa. 1836).

9. Supra note 1. The author of the opinion was Justice Samuel Nelson, a Jackson Democrat from New York, who wrote other famous admiralty decisions: *The Lexington,* 47 U.S. 344 (1848); *Hough v. Western Transportation Co. (The Plymouth),* 70 U.S. 20 (1866); and the dissent in *The Prize Cases,* 67 U.S. 635 (1864).

10. 58 U.S. at 177–78.

11. *Union Oil Co. v. The Tug San Jacinto,* 409 U.S. 140, 1972 AMC 2675 (1972). The opinion of Justice Rehnquist adds an additional gloss to the rule of moderate speed in fog (a speed sufficiently

damages in a single-vessel grounding rather than a collision case.[12] A coastal tanker, the *Mary A. Whelan,* ran aground at night at Rockaway Point outside New York Harbor, where the Coast Guard had failed to maintain its charted breakwater light.[13] The master of the tanker, however, had not employed available radar and charts and had set his course on the basis of intuition. There was Coast Guard negligence—breach of duty by personnel to maintain the light, which was a cause of the harm—and vessel owner negligence—again, breach of duty by employees in imprudent navigation, which was also a cause of the harm. Noting that a 75 percent–25 percent division would be more equitable, the trial court nevertheless said controlling precedent required an equal division of damages.[14] The decision was affirmed by the Second Circuit.[15]

After a review of the earlier cases[16] and a discussion of the proportional fault rule of the Brussels Collision Convention of 1910,[17] the Supreme Court concluded that the rule of an equal division of damages could no longer be justified; accordingly, the former rule, which had held on through "sheer inertia" and which was denigrated as "unnecessarily crude," "palpably unfair," and "inequitable," was abrogated.[18] The precise holding is important for its clues as to the way the new rule was to be interpreted. The Court held:

---

slow as to enable the vessel to stop within half the distance of the visibility). One vessel was held in sole fault. The case is discussed in chapter 4, section C, supra.

At the time of the discussions leading to the Brussels Collision Convention of 1910, it was assumed that the United States would quickly adopt the rule of proportional fault in collisions, since the Supreme Court had already approved the rule in personal injury actions. *The Max Morris,* 137 U.S. 1 (1890).

12. *United States v. Reliable Transfer Co.,* 421 U.S. 397, 1975 AMC 541 (1975), reversing 497 F.2d 1036, 1974 AMC 756 (2d Cir. 1974). On remand, the liability of the United States was fixed at 25 percent, the percentage originally suggested by the trial judge. See *Reliable Transfer Co. v. United States,* 522 F.2d 1381, 1975 AMC 1508 (2d Cir. 1975).

13. 421 U.S. 398–99. See also the district court decision, *Reliable Transfer Co. v. United States,* 1972 AMC 1757, 1763 (EDNY 1972).

14. 1972 AMC 1757 at 1764–66 (EDNY 1972).

15. 497 F.2d 1036, 1974 AMC 756 (2d Cir. 1974).

16. 421 U.S. at 402–03, 1975 AMC at 545–49. Earlier decisions critical of but following the precedent include *N.M. Patterson & Sons Ltd. v. City of Chicago,* 324 F.2d 254, 1963 AMC 2471 (7th Cir. 1963); *Tank Barge Hygrade, Inc. v. The Tug Gatco New Jersey,* 250 F.2d 485, 1958 AMC 1322 (3d Cir. 1957); *Ahlgren v. Red Star Towing & Transp. Co.,* 214 F.2d 618, 1954 AMC 1504 (2d Cir. 1954); and especially the dissent of Judge Learned Hand in *National Bulk Carriers, Inc. v. United States,* 183 F.2d 405, 410, 1950 AMC 1293, 1300 (2d Cir. 1950).

17. International Convention for the Unification of Certain Rules Relating to Collisions Between Vessels, Brussels 1910, UN Registration No. 134(a), 6 Benedict on Admiralty, Doc. 3-2 (7th ed. [rev.], F.L. Wiswall, Jr., editor-in-chief, volumes on treaties and related documents) (hereinafter "Benedict"). See 421 U.S. at 403–04, 1975 AMC at 546–47. The Court, at 421 U.S. 407, 1975 AMC at 549, also noted its own earlier precedent in maritime personal injury, *The Max Morris,* supra note 11.

18. 421 U.S. 405–07, 1975 AMC at 547–49. See generally Healy & Koster, *Reliable Transfer Co. v. United States: Proportional Fault Rule,* 7 J. Mar. L. & Com. 293 (1975); and Goschka, *Goodbye to All That!—The Unlamented Demise of the Divided Damages Rule,* 8 J. Mar. L. & Com.. 51 (1976); and Brown, *General Principles of Liability,* 51 Tul. L. Rev. 820 (1976).

> We hold that when two or more parties have contributed by their fault to cause property damage in a maritime collision or stranding, liability for such damage is to be allocated among the parties proportionately to the comparative degree of their fault, and that liability for such damages is to be allocated equally only when the parties are equally at fault or when it is not possible fairly to measure the comparative degree of their fault.[19]

Accordingly, all fault allocations prior to *Reliable Transfer* no longer have precedential value.

The Supreme Court's adherence to the formula of the Brussels Collision Convention of 1910, "degree of [their] fault[s]" should be noted carefully.[20] This choice of wording must be read along with the court's earlier formulation of the now-abandoned rule[21] and the many cases in which the Supreme Court had discussed *"fault"* in collision cases.[22] At this stage of development of the proportional division of damages in the United States, liability is based on the culpability of the vessel interests and not the degree of causation.[23]

Uncertainty about culpability alone may remain where the defendant is liable for personal injuries by operation of law through strict (i.e., non-fault) liability for defective products[24] and unseaworthiness.[25] Given the origin of these liabilities in public policies protecting consumers and seamen, however, it seems likely that the total measure of damages between collid-

19. 421 U.S. at 411, 1975 AMC at 552. The new rule was applied retroactively by the Fifth Circuit to reverse an equal division of damages in a 1966 collision. *Nutt v. Loomis Hydraulic Co.*, 552 F.2d 1126, 1977 AMC 2340 (5th Cir. 1977). Also note the remand in the case of a 1968 collision by the same court in *The Helena*, 529 F.2d 744, 1976 AMC 2022 (5th Cir. 1976). See also *Kinsman Marine Co. v. Great Lakes Towing Co.*, 532 F.2d 1073, 1976 AMC 493 (6th Cir. 1976).

20. 421 U.S. at 411, 1975 AMC at 552. Cf. 1910 Brussels Collision Convention, art. IV, ¶ 1: "If two or more vessels are in fault, the liability of each vessel is in proportion to the degree of the faults respectively committed. . . ." On the application of the convention by U.S. courts before *Reliable Transfer* in cases where the conflict of laws rule required application of the law of a convention country, see Paulsen, *Apportionment of Fault in Both-to-Blame Collision Cases*, Maritime Law Association Doc. No. 601 (1976).

21. *The Schooner Catharine v. Dickinson*, supra note 1.

22. *The Farragut*, 77 U.S. 334 (1870); *The Java*, 81 U.S. 189 (1872); *The Continental*, 81 U.S. 345 (1872); *The Great Republic*, 90 U.S. 20 (1874); *The Clara*, 102 U.S. 200 (1880); *The City of New York*, 147 U.S. 72 (1892); *The Oregon*, 158 U.S. 186 (1895).

23. See section C, infra; *Gele v. Wilson*, 616 F.2d 146, 148, 1981 AMC 462, 464 (5th Cir. 1980), apportioning liability on the basis of comparative degrees of fault, not according to the degrees of causation. The same circuit has applied the rule, however, in a situation normally regarded as one of passive (as opposed to active) negligence. *Loose v. Offshore Navigation, Inc.*, 670 F.2d 493, 1984 AMC 1216 (5th Cir. 1982). See also *Southern Natural Gas Co. v. Pontchartrain Materials, Inc.*, 711 F.2d 1251 (5th Cir. 1983), where the court applied *Reliable Transfer* to allocate damages among parties proportionately to their comparative faults, and not according to the degrees of causation. Cf. *The Helena*, 1976 AMC 2013, 2020–21 (ED La. 1976), where the court weighed both culpability and causation.

24. *Pan Alaska Fisheries, Inc. v. Marine Construction and Design Co.*, 565 F.2d 1129, 1978 AMC 2315 (9th Cir. 1977). See generally, *East River Steamship Corp. v. Transamerica Delaval, Inc.*, 476 U.S. 858, 1986 AMC 2027 (1986).

25. *Seas Shipping Co. v. Sieracki*, 328 U.S. 85, 1946 AMC 698 (1946); *Mitchell v. The Trawler Racer*, 362 U.S. 539, 1960 AMC 1503 (1960).

ing vessels will include third-party liabilities of vessel owners which do not involve traditional negligence-type fault in the sense of statutory violation, or breach of a duty of care imposed by trade custom or the "reasonably prudent person" standard.

2. *Inscrutable Fault and Impossible Allocation of Fault*

Although inscrutable fault cases are rare in practice, American courts have long recognized that in a collision case evidence of fault on either side may be absent, so that neither an inference of fault nor a factual finding of fault is possible; accordingly, losses remain where fate has left them and the courts will not interfere to shift them.[26] However, in its *Reliable Transfer* holding, the Supreme Court recognized that where fault of both vessels is provable, the court may be unable to measure the percentage differences in fault, in which case the damages must be divided equally. This limited continuation of life for the equal division of damages rule is not applied to traditional inscrutable fault causes, where there is no loss-shifting. The Supreme Court's dictum noted: ". . . [L]iability for such damages is to be allocated equally only when the parties are equally at fault *or when it is not possible fairly to measure the comparative degree of their fault.*"[27] (Emphasis added.)

3. *Abolition of Obsolete Doctrines after* Reliable Transfer

(a) The Major-Minor Fault Rule. Before *Reliable Transfer* the Supreme Court tried to reduce the unfairness of the equal division rule by an exception known as the major-minor fault rule, established in *The City of New York.*[28] In

26. *The Grace Girdler,* 74 U.S. 196 (1869); and *The Jumna,* 149 F. 171 (2d Cir. 1906). See *Wilson Marine Transit Co. v. Pennsylvania-Ontario Transp. Co.,* 191 F. Supp. 210 (ND Ohio 1960). Griffin, however, notes earlier inscrutable fault decisions where damages were divided equally, J. Griffin, *American Law of Collision* (1949) 620–21 (hereinafter "Griffin"). Although reversed on other grounds, the trial court divided damages equally, based on the "weight of authority of the ancient codes and of the continental writers. . ." in *The Comet,* 6 F. Cas. 195 (No. 3,050) (NDNY 1870), rev'd, 6 F. Cas. 200 No. 3051 (C.C. NDNY 1872). See also *Granholm v. The TFL Express,* 576 F. Supp. 435, 1984 AMC 943 (SDNY 1983) and 1984 AMC 972 (SDNY 1984); *Citadel Shipping Co. v. Consolidated Grain & Barge Co.,* 1983 AMC 1721 (ED La. 1983). See Chameides, *Inscrutable Fault in Collision Litigation,* 9 J. Mar. L. & Com. 363 (1978), and Owen, *The Origin and Development of Marine Collision Law,* 51 Tul. L. Rev. 759, 799 (1977).

27. 421 U.S. at 411. In favor of the proposition of equal division in cases of inability to measure faults is the clear mandate of the 1910 Brussels Collision Convention: ". . . [I]f, having regard to the circumstances, it is not possible to establish the degree of faults . . ., the liability shall be apportioned equally. . ."

28. 147 U.S. 72 (1893). Griffin dissects the concept in detail, Griffin 505–09. In essence, courts would close their eyes to slight faults on the part of one vessel which were overwhelmed by the gross faults of the other. The attempt to avoid extreme disparity of faults by equitable principles usually defeated logical analysis.

Reliable Transfer, however, the Court's dictum concluded that the rule had resulted in exchanging one unfairness for another.[29] Following the dictum, the Second Circuit abolished the major-minor fault rule in *Getty Oil Co. v. The Ponce de Leon.*[30]

(b) Last Clear Chance. This doctrine, derived from common-law tort, served a function similar to the admiralty major-minor fault rule. The Second Circuit first suggested that the doctrine might no longer be viable,[31] then explicitly held that last clear chance is no longer applicable in maritime collisions.[32]

(c) The *Pennsylvania* Rule. This outdated doctrine has survived *Reliable Transfer,* without serving any purpose.[33] We have urged (supra, chapter 2) that the rule should be abolished.

(d) Assumption of Risk. Assumption of risk has been held inapplicable to collision cases after *Reliable Transfer,*[34] but it was applied in an admiralty case in *De Sole v. United States,*[35] involving a yacht race during which two competing vessels were in collision. In the absence of congressional mandate, it is a grievous error for this outmoded concept to be resurrected in the face of *Reliable Transfer.*

---

29. 421 U.S. at 406, 1975 AMC at 548.

30. 555 F.2d 328, 1977 AMC 711 (2d Cir. 1977), affirming 409 F. Supp. 909, 1977 AMC 722 (SDNY 1976). On appeal from the 80 percent–20 percent division by the district court, the owner of an anchored vessel argued for sole fault or a 95 percent–5 percent division against a vessel proceeding at 12 knots in fog, but the court affirmed the 80 percent–20 percent allocation. Judge Mulligan said, 555 F.2d at 333, 1977 AMC at 717: "We read *Reliable* as a rejection not only of divided damages but as a repudiation of its illicit progeny, the major-minor approach."

Other cases holding that the major-minor fault rule is now obsolete include: *Trinidad Corp. v. The Keiyoh Maru,* 845 F.2d 818, 824, 1989 AMC 627, 635 (9th Cir. 1988); *Griffith v. Wheeling-Pittsburgh Steel Corp.,* 610 F.2d 116, 1980 AMC 833 (3d Cir. 1979); *Allied Chemical Corp. v. Hess Tankship Co.,* 661 F.2d 1044, 1982 AMC 1271 (5th Cir. 1981); *Neptune Marine Co. v. The Essi Camilla,* 714 F.2d 132, 1984 AMC 2983 (4th Cir. 1983); and *Western Pacific Fisheries, Inc. v. The President Grant,* 730 F.2d 1280 (9th Cir. 1984).

31. *Whitney Steamship Co. v. United States,* 747 F.2d 69, 1985 AMC 493 (2d Cir. 1984).

32. *Prudential Lines, Inc. v. McAllister Bros., Inc.,* 801 F.2d 616, 1987 AMC 231 (2d Cir. 1986).

33. See the discussion in chapter 2, supra.

34. *National Marine Services Inc. v. Petroleum Services Corp.,* 736 F.2d 272, 1987 AMC 840 (5th Cir. 1984). See also *Goldenrod Showboat, Inc. v. Waterways Winona, Inc.,* 1988 AMC 806 (ED Mo. 1986).

35. 1989 AMC 2739 (D Md. 1989). Despite the statutory language abolishing the defenses in N.Y.C.P.L.R. § 1411, "culpable conduct . . . including contributory negligence or assumption of risk," the New York Court of Appeals has restored the defense as a matter of public policy in both professional and nonprofessional sporting events; see *Akins v. Glens Falls City School District,* 53 N.Y. 2d 325 (1981) (spectator), and *Turcotte v. Fell,* 68 N.Y. 2d (1986) (professional jockey).

Section C. Causation and Culpability in Fault Doctrine

Unlike those portions of admiralty law where history or policy dictates liability without proof of fault, the Supreme Court[36] and the U.S. courts of appeals[37] have consistently and uniformly dealt with collision between vessels as a matter requiring proof of fault by violation of statutory rules[38] or by breach of a duty of care imposed either by trade custom[39] or by what is expected of the reasonably prudent person in similar circumstances.[40] Thus, being present at, or in the vicinity of, a collision of course is not enough to require contribution in damages; it is *culpability* on the part of each vessel participating in the collision (either before or after the impact) that must be proved. Less obvious, however, is the effect of degrees of causation in determining the percentage amounts chargeable to each vessel.

Because of the equal division of damages rule, which rewarded the party that demonstrated any fault of an opponent, the effect of causation on the percentage amount of fault assessed against a colliding vessel was not considered in the United States until the adoption of proportional fault in 1975 in *Reliable Transfer*[41] in language similar to the provisions of Article 4 of the 1910 Brussels Convention.[42]

According to Professor Berlingieri,[43] questions were raised at the Brussels Diplomatic Conference in 1910 concerning the exact meaning of the treaty language about fault, but, after discussion, no change was made. In that discussion the British delegation had suggested that *causation* should be considered in the apportionment of the loss. This view, supported by the Dutch and German delegations, introduced a bifurcated analysis: an objective

---

36. In *The Continental,* 81 U.S. 345 (1872), the Court said that a vessel is liable only ". . . on account of the negligence, unskillfulness or carelessness" of those in charge who have navigated her into collision. 81 U.S. at 354. See also *The Baltimore,* 75 U.S. 377 (1869); *The Farragut,* 77 U.S. 334 (1870); *The George Washington & The Gregory,* 76 U.S. 513 (1870); *Sears v. The Scotia,* 81 U.S. 170 (1872); *The Cayuga,* 81 U.S. 270 (1872); *The Java,* 81 U.S. 189 (1872); *The Great Republic,* 90 U.S. 20 (1874); *The Alabama and The Gamecock,* 92 U.S. 695 (1876); *The Atlas,* 93 U.S. 302 (1876); *The North Star,* 106 U.S. 17 (1882); *The Blue Jacket,* 144 U.S. 371 (1892); *The Oregon,* 158 U.S. 186 (1895); *The Chattahoochee,* 173 U.S. 540 (1899).

37. *The Lepanto,* 21 F. 651 (SDNY 1884), where the court said, "The basis of actions of this character is some fault in the vessel or person sued. Fault consists in the violation of some statutory rule of navigation, or in the failure to exercise due nautical skill or prudence." 21 F. at 655.

38. *The Pennsylvania,* 86 U.S. 125 (1874).

39. *The Newport News,* 105 F. 389 (4th Cir. 1900); *The Luzerne,* 204 F. 981 (2d Cir. 1913); *Union Oil Co. of California v. The Tug Mary Malloy,* 414 F.2d 669, 1969 AMC 2254 (5th Cir. 1969). Note, however, that custom can never overcome statutory rules. See *Lehigh Coal & Navigation Co. v. Compagnie Générale Transatlantique,* 12 F.2d 337, 1926 AMC 819 (2d Cir. 1926).

40. *Union Oil Co. v. The Tug San Jacinto,* supra note 11. See also *The H.F. Dimock,* 77 F. 226 (1st Cir. 1896), and the discussion of Former Rule 29, now Rule 2 of COLREGS and the Inland Rules, chapter 3, supra.

41. *United States v. Reliable Transfer Co.,* supra note 12.

42. Supra note 17.

43. Berlingieri, *Jurisdiction and Choice of Law in Collision Cases and an Overview of the Concept of Fault and Its Apportionment,* 51 Tul. L. Rev. 866, 874 (1977).

criterion (the causation element) and a subjective criterion (the seriousness of the fault).[44] While the treaty language remained unchanged, courts in Italy,[45] Germany,[46] France,[47] and the United Kingdom,[48] in accordance with their domestic legal theories, added a gloss to the treaty language on seriousness of causation in fixing the percentages of fault.

Sir Henry Brandon, later a Lord of Appeal, pointed out the development of the English rule at the Tulane Admiralty Law Institute Symposium on Collision.[49] Thus, only faults that have contributed to the vessels' damages are taken into account,[50] but thereafter, in making the proportional assessment, *causative potency*[51] as well as *culpability*[52] are considered. The nuances of causative potency and culpability are described in cases where the Court of Appeal has reversed the trial judge's apportionments,[53] and even more strongly where the House of Lords has subsequently reversed the Court of Appeal.[54]

At this formative stage of proportional fault in American law it will be important to have clearly reasoned decisions assigning the proportions of fault in order to determine the effect, if any, of both culpability and causative potency in striking the balance of liability. The Ninth Circuit did not speak clearly on the issue in *Pan Alaska Fisheries Association v. Marine Construction & Design Co.*,[55] where the court said that "whether we use the term comparative fault, contributory negligence, comparative causation, or even comparative blameworthiness, we are merely beating around the semantical bush seeking to achieve an equitable method of allocating the responsibility for an injury or loss."[56] Although the trial court had chosen a standard of "culpability"

---

44. Id.

45. Id. 875, *Rimorchiatori Napoletani c. Cantieri e Officine Meridionali,* 1933 Il Diritto Marittimo 37-38 (Judgment of Dec. 2, 1932).

46. Id. at 875–76.

47. Id. 876.

48. *The Miraflores & The Abadesa,* [1967] 1 A.C. 826 (H. L.).

49. Brandon, *Apportionment of Liability in British Courts under the Maritime Conventions Act of 1911,* 51 Tul. L. Rev. 1025 (1977).

50. 51 Tul. L. Rev. at 1028.

51. 51 Tul. L. Rev. at 1032, 1038–39.

52. 51 Tul. L. Rev. at 1032, 1038.

53. *The British Aviator,* [1965] 1 Lloyd's Rep. 271 (60 percent–40 percent apportionment modified to 50 percent–50 percent for failure of trial judge to consider seriousness of course change by the vessel held 40 percent to blame). See also *The Statue of Liberty,* [1971] 2 Lloyd's Rep. 277 (H. L.) (70 percent–30 percent apportionment division, modified to 85 percent–15 percent).

54. *The Almizar* [1971] 2 Lloyd's Rep. 290 (H. L.) (60 percent–40 percent trial court division modified to 40 percent–60 percent by the Court of Appeal, but modified by the House of Lords to 30 percent–70 percent because the vessel finally held 70 percent to blame was more blameworthy and her actions more causatively potent). See also *The Konigin Juliana,* [1974] 2 Lloyd's Rep. 353 (C.A.) ($\frac{2}{3}-\frac{1}{3}$ division modified to 50 percent–50 percent by the Court of Appeal, whose decision was in turn modified by the House of Lords to the original $\frac{2}{3}-\frac{1}{3}$, [1975] 2 Lloyd's Rep. 111 [H. L.]).

55. 565 F.2d 1129, 1978 AMC 2315 (9th Cir. 1977).

56. 565 F.2d at 1139, 1978 AMC at 2330.

alone,[57] the Ninth Circuit felt compelled to give equal support to "comparative causation."[58] The Fifth Circuit has also spoken on the issue of considering culpability alone in *Gele v. Wilson.*[59] Some lower-court decisions have attempted to combine culpability and causative potency.[60] We submit that in accordance with the plain language in *Reliable Transfer,* once causation is established, culpability alone should be the decisive factor in assessing the degree of fault chargeable to each vessel in a both-to-blame case.

Section D. Liability for Cargo Loss and Damage in Both-to-Blame Cases

1. Several Liability versus Joint and Several Liability of Tort-feasors for Cargo Loss and Damage

An issue that still separates the United States from a large part of the maritime world is the application of the proportional liability of colliding vessels to the innocent cargo interests; that is, whether liability to innocent cargo is to be borne by the colliding vessels, (a) *only* in proportion to the faults committed by each vessel, reserving also the carrier's immunity from liability to its own cargo for damage caused by nautical fault; or (b) both vessels being jointly and severally liable to cargo, subject to the carrier's nautical fault defense, and reserving the cargo's right to pursue the noncarrying vessel as a joint tort-feasor for 100 percent of the loss. The latter situation has been described as an indirect liability of a carrier to its own cargo when the third-party liabilities are added to the noncarrying vessel's collision damages for apportionment with those of the carrier. In addition to the nature of multiple tort-feasor liability is the issue of contribution between joint tort-feasors[61] and the nature of the immunity conferred upon carriers by the nautical fault

57. *Pan-Alaska Fisheries, Inc. v. Marine Construction & Design Co.,* 402 F. Supp. 1187 (WD Wash. 1975).

58. Supra note 55.

59. 616 F.2d 146, 1981 AMC 462 (5th Cir. 1980). A caveat here is the Fifth Circuit's citation of the district court opinion in *Pan Alaska Fisheries* (supra note 57), vacated by the Ninth Circuit, supra note 55.

60. *In re Seiriki Kisen Kaisha,* 629 F. Supp. 1374, 1986 AMC 913 (SDNY 1986); *Afran Transport Co. v. The Maria Venizelos,* 450 F. Supp. 621 (ED Pa. 1978).

61. While contribution among joint tort-feasors in collision cases was employed in *The North Star,* 106 U.S. 17 (1882), it was rejected in the context of maritime personal injury in *Pope & Talbot, Inc. v. Hawn,* 346 U.S. 406, 1954 AMC 1 (1953), but subsequently broadly recognized in *Cooper Stevedoring Co. v. Fritz Kopke, Inc.,* 417 U.S. 106, 1974 AMC 537 (1974). Many common-law courts rejected the possibility of enforced contribution among tort-feasors, with the result that this doctrine is usually based on statute. Cf. NYCPLR §§ 1401–04 and the Practice Commentary of the Hon. Joseph M. McLaughlin in Book 7B, *McKinney's Consolidated Laws of New York.*

defenses of the Harter Act,[62] the Hague-Visby Rules,[63] COGSA,[64] and many charter-party forms.

Alternative (a), supra, is now established in the several liability provision of the Brussels Collision Convention of 1910,[65] while alternative (b), supra, represents the traditional joint and several liability of U.S. law.[66] Both alternatives were debated in formulating early drafts of the Collision Convention.[67] It is obvious that alternative (a) would favor the interests of shipowners, whereas alternative (b) would favor the cargo interests (assuming that cargo insurance and subrogation were not involved). U.S. interests as a cargo-owning nation rather than a shipowning nation appeared to be affected adversely by the 1910 Convention, and this is the principal explanation of the failure of the United States to ratify it.

2. *The Rule of Several Liability*

Because of the peculiarities of admiralty jurisdiction in England before enactment of the 1873 Supreme Court of Judicature Act,[68] actions for cargo damage could be pursued at law *(in personam)* based on the contract having been made on land; or in admiralty *(in rem)* based on maritime tort. Under the common law, carriers were liable for damage as insurers,[69] but there were problems with the rule of no contribution between joint tort-feasors[70] and the fault of the carrying vessel being imputed to the cargo.[71] In admiralty, damages in both-to-blame collisions were customarily divided equally[72] so that in collision practice it was necessary for cargo to sue both colliding vessels. Subsequently, clauses in bills of lading, upheld in the English courts[73]

62. 46 U.S.C. § 192 (1982).

63. International Convention for the Unification of Certain Rules of Law Relating to Bills of Lading, Brussels, Aug. 25, 1924, as amended by Protocol to Amend the International Convention for the Unification of Certain Rules Relating to Bills of Lading, Brussels, Feb. 23, 1968, and the Further Protocol to Amend the International Convention for the Unification of Certain Rules Relating to Bills of Lading, Brussels, Dec. 21, 1979. See 6 Benedict, Docs. Nos. 1-1, 2, and 2-A.

64. 46 U.S.C. § 1303(2)(a).

65. Supra note 17.

66. See notes 78–82, infra.

67. Sweeney, *Proportional Fault in Both-to-Blame Collisions,* 1964 Il Diritto Marittimo (Special Edition, Studi in Onore di Giorgio Berlingieri) 549.

68. Supreme Court of Judicature Act of 1873, 36 & 37 Vict., ch. 66.

69. *Coggs v. Bernard,* 92 Eng. Rep. 107 (K.B. 1703).

70. At common law, suits by one tort-feasor against another were forbidden; see *Everet v. Williams,* Ex. 1725, where one highwayman sued another for an accounting. The case was dismissed, plaintiff and defendant were hanged, and the solicitors fined £50. Reported in L.Q. Rev. 197 (1893). See W. Prosser & W. Keeton, *The Law of Torts,* 336–47 (5th ed. 1984).

71. *Thorogood v. Bryan,* 137 Eng. Rep. 452 (H. L. 1849).

72. *The Woodrop-Sims,* supra note 3.

73. *Tattersall v. National Steamship Co.,* 12 Q.B. Div. 297 (1884), and *In re Missouri S.S. Co.,* 42 Ch. D. 321 (1889).

but rejected in the United States,[74] permitted the carrier to be exculpated from liability to its own cargo by a contractual clause. The English admiralty decision of *The Milan*[75] imposed the rule of several liability in admiralty cases and held that the statute of 1873[76] meant that cargo damaged in a both-to-blame collision would be compensated only to the extent of the proportional liability of the noncarrying vessel. The rule of *The Milan* became the rule of the Brussels Collision Convention of 1910.[77]

---

74. *Liverpool & Great Western Steamship Co. v. Phenix Ins. Co.*, 129 U.S. 397 (1888). For the background of the Harter Act, see Sweeney, *Happy Birthday, Harter: A Reappraisal of the Harter Act on its 100th Anniversary*, 24 J. Mar. L. & Com.. 1 (1993).

75. *The Milan*, 167 Eng. Rep. 167 (Adm. 1861). Mr. David Owen has given insight to *The Milan* in his symposium article, *The Origins and Development of Marine Collision Law*, 51 Tul. L. Rev. 759, 770–71 (1977). Dr. Lushington, who later became Admiralty Judge, had argued *Hay v. Le Neve*, 2 Shaw's Rep, 395 (H. L. 1824), supra note 3, as advocate for Hay, the shipowner whose vessel was ⅔ to blame in the collision with Le Neve's vessel. The issue argued was whether Hay had to pay ½ or ⅔ of the damages. The House of Lords decided in Hay's favor on the issue of half damages and awarded half damages to the cargo on Le Neve's vessel. Thirty-seven years later Dr. Lushington held that Cargo, represented by his son, could recover only half damages from the noncarrying vessel, contrary to the common-law rule of joint and several liability. Dr. Lushington the judge declared the rule of *Hay v. Le Neve* to be founded in equity and applied it. Mr. Owen concludes, "It is possible that the United States would be a party to the [1910 Collision] Convention today had Dr. Lushington been retained to represent Le Neve instead of Hay." (51 Tul. L. Rev. 771).

76. In the courts newly merged into the High Court of Justice, the former Admiralty Rules would govern admiralty cases where the admiralty and common-law rules were different. Supreme Court of Judicature Act of 1873, 36 & 37 Vict. ch. 66, § 25(9); ch. 85 § 25(9).

77. Supra note 17. (Translation of French original from Senate Doc. Executive K, 75th Cong. 1st Sess., April 29, 1937). See Art. 4 of the convention, which is reproduced in the appendix.

At the first meeting of the C.M.I. in Brussels in 1897 the goal was unification of differing legal approaches to collision law—principally differences between the laws of England and France. It was at this meeting that the proportional fault rule of the French legal system was combined with the British case law on several liability for cargo damage (*The Milan*, [1860] Lush. 388) to produce a compromise which would attract followers of both systems.

The 1899 C.M.I. meeting again specifically rejected joint and several liability to cargo. The delegates of the Maritime Law Association of the United States, which had been formed earlier in the year, were divided on the subject. The 1902 Hamburg C.M.I. meeting drafted treaty language rejecting joint and several liability for personal injury and death as well as cargo claims. American delegates strongly argued against this but were unsuccessful. At the C.M.I. meeting in Venice in 1907 an American delegate noted that the application of the proportional fault rule to cargo and personal injury claims was "not wise and is not just," stating that the United States, as a nation of cargo owners, was unlikely to support a convention containing such a provision.

Thereafter, a resolution of the U.S. MLA sought to achieve a compromise of the cargo liability issue by a reservation in the proposed convention of all rights afforded to cargo by the Harter Act. This maneuver was unsuccessful at the 1910 Diplomatic Conference in Brussels, and the best the American delegation could achieve was a reservation in an additional protocol whereby the United States declared that Article 4 of the convention should not affect the Harter Act. (This was, of course, before the Hague Rules Convention on risk allocation for cargo damage was adopted.)

The Collision Convention was *not* submitted to the Senate for advice and consent together with the Salvage Convention (ratified in 1912). In fact it was not submitted to the Senate until 1937. Shippers and cargo insurers remained opposed to the convention in 1937 because of its provision of several liability to cargo. Hearings were held in 1939, but no action was taken until 1947, when the convention was withdrawn as obsolete. (See C.M.I. Bulletins Nos. 1, 2, 4, 5, 6, and 10; MLA Doc. No. 161 [1930] and Executive K, 75th Cong. 1st Sess.).

3. *The Rule of Joint and Several Liability to Innocent Cargo*

In the United States, the Supreme Court has considered these questions as matters of public policy, having long ago weighed and rejected the arguments in favor of several liability. The leading cases on these problems in the context of actions for cargo damage brought by the cargo-owning interests against the shipowning interests will be developed chronologically, and the additional problem of cargo liability to carriers in general average will also be considered.

In *The Alabama and The Gamecock,*[78] both vessels in a both-to-blame collision were sued *in rem* by the cargo owner. The case is important for its treatment of cargo as "innocent" and the recognition of the right of cargo to full recovery. Accordingly, the decree provided that one-half of the cargo damages should be paid by each vessel, but, if either vessel were unable to pay its proportionate share, the cargo owner could recover the unpaid amount from the other vessel.[79]

In *The Atlas,*[80] the carrying vessel had sunk, and so the cargo insurer (by subrogation) proceeded against the surviving vessel for full damages. The district court found both vessels in fault, but awarded only one-half the

78. 92 U.S. 695 (1875). In an 1870 case, joint and several liability was imposed in a personal injury case arising out of a collision. *The George Washington & The Gregory,* 76 U.S. 513 (1870).

79. 92 U.S. at 696–97. At 92 U.S. 697 the court disapproved *The Milan,* supra note 75. See generally, Kasanin, *Cargo Rights and Responsibilities in Collision Cases,* 61 Tul. L. Rev. 880 (1977), and Waesche, *Cargo's Rights in Collision Cases,* 45 Tul. L. Rev. 781 (1971).

80. 93 U.S. 302 (1876). *The Atlas* involved a collision between a steamboat and a tug, which caused the loss of a canal boat in tow of the tug and cargo thereon. Justice Clifford wrote:

> Innocent parties in cases of the kind are entitled to full compensation, but the admiralty rule as between wrongdoers is that the combined amount of the damage shall be divided between the owners of the two offending vessels. . . . Strict justice would require, said Dr. Lushington, that the burden of making good the loss should fall upon the two delinquents in proportion to their delinquency, but in practice the proportion is impossible to be ascertained. Such a rule, if adopted, would be utterly impracticable, for the reason that the court cannot apportion the loss according to the quantum of neglect or culpability on the one side and the other; hence equal apportionment is the universal rule where there is mutual fault, even though fault on one side be much greater than the fault on the other. . . . Two admissions are made by the court in the case of *The Milan* which it is important to notice, as they are undoubtedly correct, and will afford much aid in disposing of the question involved in the present record: (1) That the owner of the cargo, in such a controversy, could recover for his whole loss in an action at law. (2) That the owner of the cargo, in such a case, is to be considered a perfectly innocent party . . . but the rule in admiralty is, that the loss in such a case must be apportioned between the offending vessels, as having been occasioned by the fault of both, but the rule of the common law and of the admiralty is the same where the suit is promoted by the innocent party, except that the moiety rule may be applied in the admiralty, if all the parties are before the court, and each of the wrongdoers is able to respond for his share of the damage. . . . Goods shipped as cargo, and their owners, as in the case before the court, are innocent of all wrong, and the owners of the cargo may sue the owners of one of the ships, or both, and they may sue at law or go into the admiralty, at their election, and having proved their case, they are as much entitled to full compensation in the admiralty as they would have been if they had elected to pursue their common law remedy. . . " 93 U.S. at 313–17.

damages sought.[81] This decree was reversed by the Supreme Court, which stated that the right of cargo to full compensation from joint tort-feasors was the same whether pursued in admiralty or at common law under the "saving to suitors" clause.[82]

The question then developed as to whether the 1893 Harter Act[83] had changed the situation because of its compromise provisions suppressing exculpatory clauses[84] but permitting carriers to enjoy a defense of nautical fault.[85] In *The Chattahoochee,*[86] the Supreme Court reaffirmed the joint and several liability rule of *The Atlas*[87] and the collision damages rule of *The North Star,*[88] so that the owners of innocent cargo could pursue the noncarrying vessel for 100 percent of its damages, and the noncarrying vessel would then be entitled to recover a portion of this third-party liability on a division of damages with the carrying vessel, a situation described as an indirect liability of the carrier to its own cargo, in the face of the congressional policy that provided carriers with the nautical fault defense. However, the Supreme Court did not read the language of the Harter Act immunity for nautical fault to go beyond the relation between the carrier and its own cargo,[89] and the so-called indirect liability of carriers was seen as the result of application of the joint tort-feasor status in a both-to-blame collision.[90] The case also noted that liabilities of the colliding vessels to third parties would be added to each vessel's collision damage claim.[91]

---

81. 93 U.S. at 309.

82. 93 U.S. at 317: "Goods shipped as cargo, and their owners, as in the case before the court, are innocent of all wrong; and the owners of the cargo may sue the owners of one of the ships, or both, and they may sue at law or go into the admiralty at their election. . . ." 93 U.S. at 317.

83. 46 U.S.C. §§ 190–96 (1996).

84. Under 46 U.S.C. § 190 clauses *relieving* the carrier of liability for negligence are invalid; Under 46 U.S.C. § 191 clauses *lessening* the carrier's obligation to use due diligence to furnish a seaworthy vessel are also invalid.

85. 46 U.S.C. § 192: "If the owner of any vessel . . . shall exercise due diligence to make the said vessel in all respects seaworthy and properly manned, equipped and supplied, neither the vessel, her owner or owners, agent, or charterers, shall become or be held responsible for damage or loss resulting from faults or errors in navigation or in the management of said vessel. . . ."

86. 173 U.S. 540 (1899). In an 1878 case the Supreme Court had approved a decree of 100 percent of the damages to innocent cargo where one of the colliding vessels was unable to pay her share. *The City of Hartford,* 97 U.S. 328 (1878).

87. 93 U.S. 302 (1876).

88. 106 U.S. 17 (1882).

89. 173 U.S. 540, 552–55 (1899). In the first case considered by the Court under the Harter Act, *The Delaware,* 161 U.S. 459 (1896), the Supreme Court quickly rejected the argument that the extremely broad language of the defenses—"If the owner of *any* vessel . . . neither the vessel, her owner or owners . . . shall . . . be held responsible for damage or loss resulting from faults or errors in navigation. . . ." meant that the colliding vessels were no longer liable to each other, holding that the context of the legislation was entirely the relation of carrier to its own cargo. (Emphasis supplied.)

90. 173 U.S. at 554–55.

91. 173 U.S. at 554. For application of this indirect liability of carrier rule in general average, see *Aktieselskabet Cuzco v. The Sucarseco (The Toluma),* 294 U.S. 394, 1935 AMC 412 (1935).

The question next considered was whether additional exculpatory language in the bill of lading could reverse the ruling of *The Chattahoochee*.[92] The North Atlantic Conferences prepared the Both-to-Blame Collision Clause[93] after the enactment of COGSA in 1936[94] and the rejection of the 1910 Brussels Collision Convention by a Senate Committee.[95] In *United States v. Atlantic Mutual Insurance Co. (The Esso Belgium—The Nathaniel Bacon)*,[96] the issue was described as the anomalous indirect liability of a carrier to its own cargo. This would be prevented by a bill of lading clause requiring the cargo interests to reimburse the carrier for any amounts for which it might be liable to the non-carrying vessel as a result of a both-to-blame collision.[97] The anomaly was said to result from the 100 percent nonliability if the carrier were solely at fault in the collision.[98] These arguments were rejected; the joint and several liability of *The Chattahoochee* and the earlier cases was reaffirmed.[99] The both-to-blame collision clause was held invalid as a matter of *public policy*,[100] finding no congressional intent in either the Harter Act or COGSA ". . . to alter the long-established rule that the full burden of the losses sustained by both ships in a both-to-blame collision is to be shared equally."[101]

4. *Effect of the Elimination of the Equal Division Rule*

Although in *United States v. Reliable Transfer Co.*[102] the equal division rule was repudiated and the proportional fault rule was adopted, since proportional fault and several liability to cargo are part of the Brussels Convention of

92. Supra note 89.

93. Several versions were in use over the years, but the clause litigated in *The Esso Belgium*, infra, is illustrative of the type:

> If the ship comes into collision with another ship as a result of the negligence of the other ship and any act, neglect or default of the Master, mariner, pilot or the servants of the Carrier in the navigation or in the management of the ship, the owners of the goods carried hereunder will indemnify the Carrier against any loss or liability to the other or non-carrying ship or her owners in so far as such loss or liability represents loss of, or damage to, or any claim whatsoever of the owners of said goods, paid or payable by the other or non-carrying ship or her owners to the owners of said goods and set off, recouped or recovered by the other or non-carrying ship or her owners as part of their claim against the carrying ship or Carrier. 343 U.S. at 238.

See also Paulsen, *Provable Damages in Collision Cases,* 51 Tul. L. Rev. 1047, 1059 (1977).

94. 46 U.S.C. §§ 1300–15 (1996).

95. See Hearings on Executive K, 75th Cong. 1st Sess. (1939). No vote of the full Senate was held.

96. 343 U.S. 236 (1952). Opinion by Justice Black; dissent of Justice Frankfurter, with concurrence of Justice Burton.

97. 343 U.S. at 241.

98. 343 U.S. at 241–42.

99. 343 U.S. at 240.

100. 343 U.S. at 242.

101. Id.

102. Supra note 12.

1910,[103] the argument was made that the policy decision to adopt proportional fault also mandated the rejection of joint and several liability.[104] This view has been rejected;[105] thus it would seem that congressional action will be necessary to overturn *The Chattahoochee,*[106] by treaty or legislation, or by both methods.[107]

In cases where the admiralty conflicts of law rules dictate application of the Brussels Collision Convention of 1910 (either because the collision was in foreign territorial waters or because both colliding vessels fly the flags of nations signatory to the convention), U.S. courts will observe the several liability rule and confine cargo's recovery to the percentage of fault of the noncarrying vessel[108] where the carrier's fault is "nautical," and the applicable statute, convention, or charter party contains a nautical fault exception.

Section E. Application of the Proportional Fault Rule in Collision Cases since 1975

". . . Liability for such damage is to be allocated among the parties proportionately to the comparative degree of their fault . . ."[109]

---

103. 421 U.S. at 411. In a noncollision case four years after *Reliable Transfer,* the Supreme Court, in dictum, noted that *Reliable Transfer* merely changed equal division to proportional fault and "did not upset the rule that the plaintiff may recover from one of the colliding vessels the damage concurrently caused by the negligence of both." *Edmonds v. Compagnie Générale Transatlantique,* 443 U.S. 256, 1979 AMC 1167 (1979).

104. It cannot be said that joint and several liability was overruled *sub silentio* in *Reliable Transfer,* since the opinion takes note of the rule without further comment. 421 U.S. 409 at n. 14. In *Alamo Chemical Transportation Co. v. The Overseas Valdes,* 469 F. Supp. 203, 1979 AMC 2033 (ED La. 1979), the court rejected joint and several liability to innocent cargo because of *Reliable Transfer,* but in *Allied Chemical Corporation v. Hess Tank Ship Co.,* 661 F.2d 1044, 1982 AMC 1271 (5th Cir. 1981), the Fifth Circuit overruled *Alamo* and held that joint and several liability to innocent cargo survived *Reliable Transfer.*

105. See *Vana Trading Co. v. The Mette Skou,* 556 F.2d 100, 1977 AMC 702 (2d Cir. 1977); *In re Flota Mercante Grancolombiana,* 573 F.2d 1290, 1978 AMC 1895 (2d Cir. 1977), affirming without opinion 440 F. Supp. 704 (SDNY 1977). See also *In re Oriental-Hero Castor,* 1976 AMC 1287 (SDNY 1976); *Linehan v. United States Lines,* 417 F. Supp. 678, 1979 AMC 1534 (D. Del. 1976), modified, 559 F.2d 1208, 1979 AMC 1557 (3d Cir. 1977), on remand 1979 AMC 1565 (D Del. 1979).

106. 173 U.S. 540 (1899).

107. Where they apply, the 1978 Hamburg Rules have eliminated the nautical fault (or negligent navigation and management) defenses, under a presumed fault rationale. Art. 5 and the Common Understanding annexed to the Rules, United Nations Conference on the Carriage of Goods by Sea, Hamburg, Mar. 31, 1978; Official Records, UN Doc. No. A/CONF. 89/14 (1981) at pp. 147–54, 17 I.L.M. 608 (1978), and 6 Benedict, Doc. No. 1-3. Elimination of the special carrier defense obviates the necessity for the cargo to seek a 100 percent recovery from the noncarrying vessel. Hence where the rules apply there is no longer a need for the joint and several liability rule as it affects cargo. It should be stressed that article 4 of the Brussels Collision Convention of 1910 provides for joint and several liability for personal injury and death claims. While article 5(7) of the Hamburg Rules provides that the carrier is not liable for more than that portion of the cargo loss attributable to its fault, overturning *The Chattahoochee* should be done by direct legislation rather than indirectly through a treaty provision.

108. See *In re Seiriki Kisen Kaisha,* 629 F. Supp. 1374, 1986 AMC 913 (SDNY 1986).

109. *United States v. Reliable Transfer Co.,* supra note 12, 421 U.S. at 411, 1975 AMC at 552.

1. The Standard for Review

As we have seen, the Supreme Court held in *Reliable Transfer* that equal division of damages between colliding vessels or other joint tort-feasors should be awarded "... only when the parties are equally at fault or when it is not possible fairly to measure the comparative degree of their fault."[110] Broad fractions ($\frac{2}{3} - \frac{1}{3}$; $\frac{1}{4} - \frac{3}{4}$; $\frac{2}{5} - \frac{3}{5}$) are quite acceptable[111] and trial courts may even risk reversal with overly precise allocations.[112]

Under the Supreme Court's decision in *McAllister v. Magnolia Petroleum Co.*,[113] the courts of appeals are not to reverse factual determinations of trial courts unless "clearly erroneous," thereby abolishing the admiralty appeal as a trial *de novo* and limiting severely the areas of inquiry on appeal. Nevertheless, use of improper legal standards as the basis on which factual findings and consequent allocations of fault are made will justify appellate courts going beyond the summary factual reviews permitted under the "clearly erroneous" standard.[114] Having said that, however, trial courts will always be more comfortable with analogies to decided cases in which the courts have reasoned their way through the evidence to produce a "rough sense of justice."[115] It should be emphasized, however, that this is always a reasoned process and not merely a mathematical calculation of the number of faults. A generalization after twenty-two years of the apportionment of fault is that violations of maneuvering rules are likely to result in greater percentages of fault than omissions from duties of due diligence or good seamanship.

---

110. Id. Professor Berlingieri's conclusion from a comparative study of the proportional fault rule is that: ". . . [C]ourts should depart from the rule of equal division of damages only when a different apportionment is clearly justified by the facts of the case, since Article 4 of the [1910 Collision] Convention, having established the proportionate fault rule, provides that if it is not possible to evaluate the degree of fault of each vessel, liability must be apportioned equally." Berlingieri, *Jurisdiction and Choice of Law in Collision Cases and an Overview of the Concept of Fault and Its Apportionment,* 51 Tul. L. Rev. 866, 878–79 (1977). The conclusion was drawn from the impossibility of attributing a greater or smaller degree of causation without the use of discretionary and nonuniform criteria. 51 Tul. L. Rev. 878.

111. As noted, since *The Max Morris,* 137 U.S. 1 (1890), the courts have used proportional degrees of fault in personal injury cases of all kinds. For a review of these allocations, see Owen and Moore, *Comparative Negligence in Maritime Personal Injury Cases,* 43 La. L. Rev. 941 (1983), and Owen, *The Origin and Development of Marine Collision Law,* 51 Tul. L. Rev. 759 (1977). See generally, V. Schwartz, *Comparative Negligence* (1974).

112. See *Flowers Transportation, Inc. v. The Peanut Hollinger,* 664 F.2d 112 (5th Cir. 1981). Nevertheless the "clearly erroneous" standard is applicable to the U.S. courts of appeals.

113. 357 U.S. 221 (1958). See also *United States v. United States Gypsum Co.,* 333 U.S. 364 (1948), and Rule 52(a) Fed. R. Civ. P.

114. *In re Interstate Co.,* 717 F.2d 752, 1983 AMC 2971 (2d Cir. 1983); *Inland Oil and Transport Co. v. Ark-White Towing Co.,* 696 F.2d 321 (5th Cir. 1983). See, e.g., *Hellenic Lines, Ltd. v. Prudential Lines, Inc.,* 813 F.2d 634, 1987 AMC 2470 (4th Cir. 1987).

115. *Palsgraf v. Long Island R.R. Co.,* 248 N.Y. 339 (1928). See dissent of Judge Andrews at 248 N.Y. 347: "What we do mean by the word 'proximate' is, that because of convenience, of public policy, of a rough sense of justice, the law arbitrarily declines to trace a series of events beyond a certain point." 248 N.Y. 352.

2. Examples of Apportionment

Set out below are examples of apportionments of fault made since *Reliable Transfer,* arranged according to percentages:

95 Percent–5 Percent Apportionment: *Hanover Ins. Co. v. Puerto Rico Lighterage Co.*[116] This case is unusual, not only because of the wide difference between the percentages of blame ascribed to each party, but because they were fixed by a jury, whose verdict was upheld on appeal. The case did not involve a collision, but damage to a "dead" U.S. Navy tug delivered to a drydock company for repairs to its propeller shaft. Following the repairs, the dry dock engaged another tug to tow the Navy tug to another pier within the harbor. During the towage, salt water entered the packing gland and caused extensive damage. The jury found the tugboat company 95 percent to blame for failing to inspect or inquire as to the seaworthiness of the tow, and the dry dock 5 percent to blame for failing to disclose to the tugboat company that coupling bolts located near the packing gland were loose. In upholding the jury's verdict the First Circuit stated: "In the interest of uniformity and justice, intrusion of appellate tribunals in this area should parallel the standards for review of damage awards. An appellate court is not a jury and appellant is not entitled to a trial *de novo* on the percentage findings."

90 Percent–10 Percent Apportionments: *Jones v. Texaco Panama, Inc. (The Texaco Ohio—The Little Chip).*[117] A 63-foot shrimp trawler overtaken by a 619-foot tanker was found 90 percent to blame for crossing ahead of the tanker, failing to hear or heed the tanker's warning signals, failing to keep a deck lookout, and failing to monitor its radio prior to collision. The court found that while both vessels violated statutory rules, the greater percentage of fault (90 percent) lay with the smaller, more maneuverable trawler, and only 10 percent with the much larger tanker, being less maneuverable.

Waterman Steamship Corp. v. Lauria Bros. and Co.[118] A steel-deck barge with defective "watertight" compartments sank in a navigable channel and created a hazard to navigation. A tug collided with the sunken barge seven minutes after the sinking. The court found that the sinking was foreseeable and held the barge owner 90 percent to blame. The tug was held 10 percent to blame for failing to heed a Coast Guard warning to stay out of the channel until the wreck's location had been verified.

Amoco Transport Co. v. The Mason Lykes.[119] An outbound tanker was held 10 percent to blame for a collision near the Galveston Channel Pilot Station

116. 553 F.2d 728, 1977 AMC 850 (1st Cir. 1977).

117. 428 F. Supp. 1333, 1977 AMC 1249 (ED La. 1977).

118. 1978 AMC 273 (SDNY 1978).

119. 550 F. Supp. 1264, 1983 AMC 1087 (SD Tex. 1982), rev'd (in other respects), 768 F.2d 659, 1986 AMC 563 (5th Cir. 1985).

because of her piecemeal course changes and failure to post a bow lookout, while an inbound cargo vessel was held 90 percent to blame because of her 14-knot speed in fog, failure to plot the approaching tanker on her radar, and changes of course to port while the tanker was forward of her beam.

85 Percent–15 Percent Apportionment: *Rich Ocean Car Carriers, S.A. v. The Sanko Diamond.*[120] The chemical tanker *Globe R. World,* the give-way vessel in a crossing situation, was held 85 percent to blame for a daylight collision with the bulk carrier *Sanko Diamond.* The *Globe R. World*'s faults were failing to give way, failing to maintain a proper look-out, and failing to take timely action to avoid collision. The *Sanko Diamond* was charged with 15 percent of the blame for failing to sound a danger signal and failing to take action when danger of collision became apparent.

80 Percent–20 Percent Apportionments: *Getty Oil Co. v. The Ponce de Leon.*[121] A finding of 80 percent blame against a moving vessel that collided with an improperly anchored vessel (20% to blame) was affirmed on appeal.

Tringali Bros. v. United States[122] *Whitney Steamship Co. v. United States.*[123] In each of these grounding cases, 80 percent of the blame was charged to a vessel and 20 percent to the government for fault of the U.S. Coast Guard.

Transorient Navigators Co. v. The Southwind.[124] The M/V *Southwind* and the M/V *Astros* were meeting port to port in the Mississippi. The *Southwind*'s pilot totally failed to anticipate the effect of a narrowing of the channel due to dredging operations, and the vessel sheered into the *Astros.* The *Southwind* was held 80 percent to blame and the government 20 percent to blame for the failure of the U.S. Army Corps of Engineers to publish changes in the conditions as a result of the dredging operations.

In re Gypsum Carrier, Inc.[125] A shoreside pulp mill was held 20 percent to blame for an allision of a freighter with a nearby railroad drawbridge, when emissions of smoke obscured the bridge lights and draw opening. The court held that the emissions created a public nuisance, and that the pulp mill was negligent in failing to correct a known hazard to navigation. The vessel was held 80 percent to blame for failing to maintain a proper look-out and have the vessel's radar properly manned, and for the pilot's failure to take into

---

120. 1989 AMC 220 (MD Fla. 1988).

121. 555 F.2d 328, 1977 AMC 711 (2d Cir. 1977), modifying 409 F. Supp. 903, 1977 AMC 722 (SDNY 1976). Cf. *In re Interstate Towing Co.,* 717 F.2d 752, 1983 AMC 2971 (2d Cir. 1983), modifying 1983 AMC 2980 (EDNY 1982), where the Second Circuit held it was an error to charge a vessel with only 20 percent of the blame for failing to maintain a proper look-out after the owner of a motorboat turned the operation of the boat over to an incompetent or inexperienced operator.

122. 630 F.2d 1089, 1982 AMC 271 (5th Cir. 1980).

123. 747 F.2d 69, 1985 AMC 493 (2d Cir. 1984).

124. 609 F. Supp. 634, 1985 AMC 2652 aff'd in part, rev'd in part, 788 F.2d 288 (5th Cir. 1986) (ED La. 1985); on remand from the Fifth Circuit, 714 F.2d 1358, 1985 AMC 1111 (5th Cir. 1983).

125. 1979 AMC 1311 (SD Ga. 1979).

account the existence of a known crosscurrent near the draw. The allision caused the drawbridge to collapse and fall into the river.

Gele v. Wilson.[126] A passenger on a boat was injured in a nighttime collision with an unmarked flare pipe protruding 10 feet above the water near a gas production platform. The flare pipe owner was held 80 percent to blame for violation of its statutory duty to mark the obstruction, and the boat was held 20 percent to blame for excessive speed.

Florida East Coast R.R. Co. v. Revilo.[127] The court applied the *Pennsylvania* Rule in charging a drawbridge owner with 80 percent of the blame for an allision of a tanker with the bridge, when the bridge owner was unable to prove that numerous violations of regulations by the bridge operator could not have contributed to the casualty. The tanker was charged with 20 percent of the blame for not maintaining an effective look-out and failing to sound a danger signal.

Alamo Chemical Co. v. The Overseas Valdez.[128] A descending tug with a barge in tow collided at night on the Mississippi with an ascending tanker approaching her dock. The tug was charged with 80 percent of the blame for failing to sound a danger signal and negligent navigation. The tanker was charged with 20 percent of the blame for failing to sound a danger signal and failing to maintain an effective look-out.

Newby v. The Kristen Gail.[129] A fishing vessel collided with a scow as she attempted to overtake the scow on Alaska's Egegik River. The overtaking vessel was held 80 percent to blame for failing to keep out of the way, while the scow was held 20 percent to blame for failing to maintain a proper look-out visually and by radar.

In re G.&G. Shipping Co.[130] In a head-on meeting situation off Puerto Rico, a 156-foot cargo ship of Anguillan flag sank after a sudden turn to port into the path of a 600-foot Dutch vessel. An unlicensed helmsman (who also served as cook, lookout, and longshoreman), unschooled in radar and incompetent in navigation, was at the helm of the Anguillan ship as the two vessels approached, both without lookouts; only the Dutch ship was aware of the other's presence. The Anguillan vessel was held 80 percent to blame for failing to maintain a proper look-out, failing to take action to avoid collision, and failing to give way. The Dutch vessel was held 20 percent to blame for failing to maintain a proper look-out, improper use of radar, failing to recognize and react to risk of collision, and failing to contact the Anguillan vessel on VHF radio. Limitation was denied to the Anguillan vessel.

---

126. 616 F.2d 146, 1981 AMC 462 (5th Cir. 1980).
127. 637 F.2d 1060, 1982 AMC 643 (5th Cir. 1981).
128. 398 F. Supp. 1094, 1975 AMC 1762 (ED La. 1975).
129. 937 F.2d 1439, 1992 AMC 149 (9th Cir. 1991).
130. 767 F. Supp. 398, 1994 AMC 170 (D P.R. 1991).

75 Percent–25 Percent Apportionments: *Moran Towing & Transp. Co. v. City of New York.*[131] The city was held 75 percent to blame for failing to raise a drawbridge fully, resulting in damage to a large crane mounted on a barge under tow. Although the bridge tender had sounded a signal for the tug and tow to proceed, the tug was held 25 percent to blame for the failure of the lookout to observe that the bridge had not been fully opened.

In re Potomac Transport, Inc.[132] While in most both-to-blame crossing cases the give-way vessel is charged with the greater degree of blame, here 75 percent of the blame was assessed against the stand-on vessel. The *Potomac,* recognizing her obligation to give way, made three course changes to starboard (30 degrees, 10 degrees, and 20 degrees), intending to come up under the stern of the *Baani,* the stand-on vessel. However, the changes were not large enough to be observed on the *Baani,* which wrongly assumed that the *Potomac* was maintaining course and speed. When collision was imminent, the *Baani* turned to port instead of to starboard, as recommended by Rule 17(c). The *Baani* was held at fault on this account, as well as for failing to use her radars and failing to contact the *Potomac* by VHF radio. The *Potomac* was held 25 percent to blame because her owner failed to prove that undermanning (the lack of a second mate) could not have contributed to the collision.

Elenson v. The Fortaleza.[133] This was a nighttime collision in dense fog in the "precautionary area" near Ambrose Light, where three vessel traffic schemes lead into New York Harbor, between a 700-foot containership and a 42-foot Bertram motor yacht. The yacht was held 75 percent to blame for proceeding on an imprudent course across shipping lanes, failing to have a lookout, failing to use her radar properly, and finally turning to port instead of to starboard. The containership was held 25 percent to blame for excessive speed (18 knots), failing to use her ARPA promptly and properly, and failing to take timely action to avoid collision.

Ishizaki Kisen Co. v. United States.[134] This case involved a collision in the harbor of Kure, Japan, between the *Kinsei-Go,* a Japanese passenger hydrofoil, and the *J-3793,* a U.S. Army cargo vessel. The hydrofoil, at 31½ knots, and the cargo vessel, at 13 knots, were on crossing courses. The *J-3793,* the hold-on vessel, was found 25 percent to blame for failing to sound a danger signal, while the hydrofoil was held 75 percent to blame for failing to keep out of the way.

Hosei Kaiun Shoji Co., Ltd. v. The Tug Seaspan Monarch.[135] The cargo ship *Dian* and the tug *Seaspan Monarch* collided at the Columbia River bar. The *Dian* was held 75 percent to blame for failing to maintain a proper look-out, and the *Seaspan Monarch* 25 percent to blame for failing to sound a danger

131. 620 F.2d 356, 1980 AMC 1414 (2d Cir. 1980).
132. 909 F.2d 42, 1991 AMC 190 (2d Cir. 1990).
133. 1992 AMC 1447 (SDNY 1991).
134. 510 F.2d 875, 1975 AMC 287 (9th Cir. 1975).
135. 1981 AMC 2162 (D Or. 1980).

signal, although for at least 20 minutes the tug was in doubt about the *Dian's* intentions.

Cottesbrooke Shipping Co. v. The Beishu Maru.[136] This collision occurred in a narrow channel of the Columbia River, in an upstream current. The upbound *Beishu Maru* was held 75 percent to blame for excessive speed in fog, making an excessively wide turn around a bend in the river, and improper look-out. The downbound *Conon Forest* was held 25 percent to blame for excessive speed in fog, failing to hold back, and improper look-out. Pilots of both vessels had been in frequent communication with each other before each observed the other on radar. The excessively wide turn made following an agreement to the contrary was the essential reason for the 75 percent allocation against the *Beishu Maru.*

Hood v. Knappton Corp.[137] Defendant's log raft broke away from its mooring and half of it drifted into a channel. Plaintiffs were engaged in a bass-fishing tournament, and were proceeding down the channel in "bass boats" at speeds of 40 to 55 MPH. The boats were damaged when they collided with the log raft, and one operator was injured. The court, citing *The Louisiana,*[138] applied the presumption that an unmoored vessel is presumed to be at fault if she drifts into collision and held the raft's owner 75 percent to blame. The "bass boats" were held 25 percent to blame for failing to maintain proper look-outs.

Royal Holland Lloyd Co. v. McAllister Brothers, Inc.[139] An inbound tug maneuvering with a scow on the wrong side of the narrow channel under the west side of the Verrazano Bridge in New York Harbor was held 75 percent to blame for failing to sound fog signals, failing to keep a proper aural or visual look-out, and failing to monitor the VHF radiotelephone. An outbound cargo ship with which the tug collided was held 25 percent to blame for excessive speed in fog.

In re Boston Fuel Transportation, Inc.[140] The tanker *Santos,* on entering Delaware Bay, observed towing lights ahead indicating a tug towing astern. She stopped to pick up a pilot, and then continued full ahead without ascertaining the position of the tow, which consisted of a large Navy houseboat. The tug stopped to shorten the towline, and a minute or so later the stern of the *Santos* collided with the tow's starboard side. The *Santos* was held 75 percent to blame for failing to ascertain the location of the tow after observing the tug's towing lights; failing to use her radar to ascertain whether the situation was overtaking, crossing, or meeting end-on; and failing to have a look-out at the bow. The tug was charged with 25 percent of the blame for failing

136. 1979 AMC 1205 (D Or. 1978).
137. 986 F.2d 329, 1993 AMC 928 (9th Cir. 1993).
138. 70 U.S. 164 (1866).
139. 1980 AMC 1839 (arb. at New York, 1980, R.H. Brown, Jr., sole arbitrator).
140. 433 F. Supp. 854, 1977 AMC 1168 (ED Pa. 1977).

to post a stern lookout and allowing the tug to drift while the hawser was being shortened.

Clayton Barge Line v. Bayou Liberty Corp.[141] An upbound and a downbound tug (with tows) each failed to maintain proper look-outs and to sound bend signals, but the court assessed 75 percent fault for a collision against the upbound tug, which had disregarded its previous passing agreement with the downbound tug.

G.&L. Towing Co. v. The Captain Wilfred.[142] A moving tug (with an empty barge in tow), entering Tiger Pass on the Mississippi under a strong current, collided with a stationary tug that was trying to hold another tug with a gash on its side on the river bank. The moving tug was held 75 percent to blame for failing to post a lookout and to sound a bend signal. The stationary tug was held 25 percent to blame for failure to have an operable bridge-to-bridge radiotelephone, obstructing the channel, and improper use of a searchlight by shining it onto the bridge of the approaching tug, in violation of 33 CFR 380.34.

70 Percent–30 Percent Apportionments: *Valley Towing Service, Inc. v. The American Wheat.*[143] A 70 percent–30 percent allocation was remanded because the district court had not taken the point-bend custom on the Mississippi into consideration and had held a downbound freighter only 30 percent to blame for failing to reduce speed and for improper use of radar, while the upbound tug, pushing three barges, had been held 70 percent to blame for excessive speed, failure to keep a proper look-out, failure to sound fog signals, and failure to confirm a passing agreement in accordance with the point-bend custom.

Stevens v. The Bonnie Doon.[144] Two fishing vessels collided on the high seas while one was "circling" and the other was crossing the circle. Neither vessel was maintaining a proper look-out. Under the industry custom of "fishing circles," when other vessels are aware that a fishing vessel is circling to pursue a school of fish, other vessels honor the circle and steer clear of the circling vessel. The district court assigned 70 percent of the blame against the vessel that had crossed the fishing circle and 30 percent against the other vessel. Finding that the custom did not contradict a statutory rule, the Ninth Circuit affirmed the apportionment.

Pelican Marine Carriers, Inc. v. City of Tampa.[145] The M/T *Louisiana Brimstone* was maneuvering to dock on the west side of 400-foot-wide Sparkman Channel, Florida, when she allided with the concrete cap on a sewer under

---

141. 1980 AMC 247 (ED La. 1978).
142. 1980 AMC 566 (ED La. 1979).
143. 618 F.2d 341, 1981 AMC 436 (5th Cir. 1980).
144. 655 F.2d 206, 1982 AMC 294 (9th Cir. 1981).
145. 791 F. Supp. 845, 1993 AMC 567 (MD Fla. 1992), aff'd w/o op., 4 F.3d 999, 1994 AMC 304 (11th Cir. 1993).

the channel that was not marked at the site or shown on the navigation charts. The sewer construction did not conform to the depth requirement of the construction permit and, accordingly, was an obstruction to navigation. The tanker was held 70 percent to blame for excessive speed and failing to make proper use of tugs and anchor in maneuvering, while the city was held 30 percent to blame for failure to mark the obstruction to navigation.

Davis v. Superior Oil Co.[146] A collision occurred on a moonless night between an anchored fishing trawler and a 78-foot crew boat engaged in carrying personnel to oil rigs in the vicinity. The trawler was held 70 percent to blame for having no proper anchor light, and the crew boat 30 percent to blame for excessive speed, inoperative radar, and having only one deckhand instead of the two required.

Mossbacher Production Co. v. Louisiana Materials Co.[147] This was actually a 70 percent–20 percent–10 percent apportionment. A self-propelled dredge was operating in Lake Pontchartrain with a dumb barge alongside. The barge grounded and was freed with the help of two tugs, whereupon it drifted into and damaged a gas well. The owner of the dredge and barge were held liable for 70 percent of the damages, because the captain of the dredge had no current license, navigated too close to the well, and abdicated his navigational responsibilities to the tugs. One tug was held 20 percent to blame for failing to ascertain whether the barge could have been moved out of a direct line with the well. The other was held 10 percent to blame because the captain made no attempt to ascertain what was required of him. The well was found free of any contributory fault.

65 Percent–35 Percent, 66 ⅔ Percent–33 ⅓ Percent, and 67 Percent–33 Percent Apportionments: These three allocations of percentages of blame are so close that they are being treated alike.

In re Hellenic Lines, Ltd.[148] The Fourth Circuit remanded a district court apportionment of 80 percent of the blame to one vessel for unseaworthiness (inoperable radars) and 18-knot speed in heavy fog, and 20 percent to the other vessel for 14-knot speed. On remand the district court held each vessel 50 percent to blame. On a second appeal, the Fourth Circuit revised the apportionment to 65 percent–35 percent because the district court had included failure to plot as an element of negligence on the part of the vessel eventually held 35 percent to blame, although that element had already been found noncontributory.

Canal Barge Co. v. China Ocean Shipping Co.[149] The M/V *Huatonghai* was proceeding up the middle of the Mississippi below Algiers Point (opposite

146. 510 F. Supp. 1162, 1981 AMC 2282 (ED La. 1981).

147. 1981 AMC 1458 (ED La. 1980).

148. 730 F.2d 159, 1984 AMC 2713 (4th Cir. 1984), 813 F.2d 634, 1987 AMC 2470 (4th Cir. 1987).

149. 770 F.2d 1357, 1986 AMC 2042 (5th Cir. 1985).

New Orleans) when she reached a starboard-to-starboard passing agreement with the Tug *Elaine Jones,* downbound with eight loaded barges in tow. About a half mile ahead of the *Elaine Jones* was the Tug *Delta Tenn,* which had arranged a starboard-to-starboard passing with the *Huatonghai,* which was accomplished with great difficulty. To pass the *Huatonghai* the *Elaine Jones* turned left. The *Huatonghai* passed safely at full speed, but the tug was taken up by the current and was swept into collision with a wharf and two vessels moored at the wharf. The court of appeals affirmed a decision charging the *Huatonghai* ⅔ to blame for excessive speed, forcing a starboard-to-starboard passing knowing that the *Elaine Jones* would have to hug the point, and failing to stop or slow down to permit the tug to clear the point before passing. The tug was held ⅓ to blame for failing to insist on a port-to-port passing and failing to make it clear that she wanted to hug the point.

Cement Division, National Gypsum Co. v. City of Milwaukee.[150] The S.S. *E.M. Ford,* loaded with bulk cement, was awaiting arrival of her sister ship so that both could enjoy winter layup berths in the Milwaukee inner harbor. A temporary berth in the outer harbor was arranged after assurances by the city's superintendent that it was safe, despite knowledge of dangerous wave surges and unsafe conditions in winter storms. On Christmas Eve 1979, with a skeleton crew on the ship and the city employees on holiday, a violent storm struck Milwaukee, with waves of 15 feet in the outer harbor. The ship was torn loose from her moorings, pounded against the dock, and eventually sank after the crew and assisting tugboats had abandoned her. Plaintiff sued the city for the loss of the ship ($6,500,000), while the city sought $250,000 for damage to the dock caused by the pounding. The district court found the shipowner 96 percent to blame for failing to employ a standby master, failing to maintain ship-to-shore radiotelephone communication, and failing to monitor the weather. The city was found 4 percent to blame for failing to warn of wind and wave conditions, failing to order that the ship remain manned or moved to another berth, and allowing the temporary layup. The unusual numerical fault allocation caught the attention of the court of appeals, which concluded that the district court had apportioned liability in accordance with the damages each party had suffered. Since the shipowner's damages were twenty-six times greater than defendant's, this resulted in the 96 percent to 4 percent allocation. The court of appeals modified the allocation, charging the ship with two-thirds of the blame, and the city with one-third.

Creole Shipping Ltd. v. Diamandis Pateras, Ltd.[151] The M/V *Pyramid Veteran,* moored at a pier in Mobile Harbor, at which the depth of water was 40 feet, was damaged by "suction," causing her to strike the pier, when the M/V *Panagos D. Pateras,* drawing 36 feet, passed by. The *Pateras* alleged that she was

150. 915 F.2d 1154, 1991 AMC 1002 (7th Cir. 1990), aff'd on other grounds, 115 S.Ct. 2091, 1995 AMC 1882 (1995).

151. 410 F. Supp. 313, 1977 AMC 189 (SD Ala. 1976), aff'd, 554 F.2d 1348, 1977 AMC 1648 (5th Cir. 1977).

proceeding at bare steerageway, while the *Veteran* alleged that the speed was excessive. In holding the *Pateras* ⅔ to blame, the court said that she should have proceeded at a speed below steerageway, relying on the tugs to provide steering. The *Veteran* was found ⅓ to blame for slack mooring lines.

In re Texaco, Inc.[152] In an unusually fine-tuned allocation, a tanker was held 67 percent to blame for a collision with an unlighted, partially completed oil and gas platform in the Gulf of Mexico. The tanker's faults included "running the rigs" rather than following the fairway, failing to correct a blind spot on the vessel's radar, and failing to ensure that the master had up-to-date navigational information. Of the balance of 33 percent, 5 percent was assessed against the platform's owner, 12 percent against the general construction company, and 16 percent against a subcontractor, all for failure to repair warning lights that had been destroyed in a hurricane before the collision.

In re Sincere Navigation Corp. (The Helena).[153] The trial court's allocation of equal division of damages was remanded in the case of a head-on collision between the cargo ship *Helena* and the U.S.C.G. Cutter *White Alder* on the Mississippi, which caused the deaths of seventeen Coast Guard crewmen. On remand,[154] Judge Rubin (then District Judge) held the *Helena* 35 percent to blame for excessive speed, absence of lookouts, and inability to see small vessels ahead of her. The *White Alder* was held 65 percent to blame for being undermanned, unexpectedly crossing the *Helena*'s bow, failing to respond to a passing signal, violating the points and bends custom, failure to answer radio calls, and absence of a lookout. Summarizing, Judge Rubin said:

> It is profitless to attempt to weigh fault against fault as if each shortcoming could be measured in some sort of scale. Both vessels were at fault and actively so. The errors of neither were minor. Each vessel committed acts that contributed to the collision. No single act of either can be completely disentangled. But the *White Alder*'s unexplained sheer into the course of the *Helena* was the fateful and final act of negligence.
>
> However, the fault does not appear to have been equal. I conclude that the *White Alder*'s faults were more than half again as responsible as the *Helena*'s, but not as great as twice as much.[155]

Flowers Transportation, Inc. v. The Peanut Hollinger.[156] A grain barge sank while being unloaded. The owner was held 65 percent to blame for failing to take adequate steps to determine its condition. The owner of the fleet in which the barge had been placed was held 35 percent to blame. In making up

152. 570 F. Supp. 1272, 1985 AMC 1650 (ED La. 1983).
153. 529 F.2d 744, 1976 AMC 2022 (5th Cir. 1976).
154. 1976 AMC 2013 (ED La. 1976).
155. 1976 AMC at 2021–23.
156. 664 F.2d 112, 1983 AMC 302 (mem.) (5th Cir. 1981), affirming 526 F. Supp. 611 (ED La. 1980).

a tow including the barge, which had to be taken from the fleet to the grain elevator, the fleet's employee, although he knew the barge had been damaged, negligently failed to place it in the best position in the tow for a damaged barge. As a result the barge sustained further damage while under tow. In affirming the 65 percent–35 percent allocation of fault the Fifth Circuit said: "Comparative fault cannot be apportioned with formulaic precision. Because the decision made appears to us to be at least roughly correct, Rule 52(a) bars our intervention to attempt to make a more fastidious, which would not necessarily be a more correct, adjustment."[157]

Guidry v. LeBeouf Bros. Towing Co.[158] In an overtaking situation in the Intracoastal Waterway involving two tugs, each with tows, both vessels were held at fault and damages were allocated 65 percent against the overtaking vessel for excessive speed and failure to keep clear, and 35 percent against the overtaken vessel for failure to have an operable horn to sound a danger signal.

Alaska Packers Ass'n, Inc. v. The East Point.[159] Both colliding crab-fishing vessels failed to maintain a proper look-out and to sound appropriate whistle signals, but 65 percent blame was assessed against the one that attempted a port-to-port passing and was at the time of the collision in charge of unlicensed crewmen whose visibility was obstructed by an unauthorized enclosure erected on the forward deck.

Humble Transportation Co. v. United States.[160] A tanker was held 65 percent to blame for a grounding at the entrance channel to New Haven Harbor. The pilot was found negligent for attempting the passage, in view of the vessel's size, the prevailing weather conditions, and his knowledge that channel buoys were off-station. The U.S. Coast Guard was held 35 percent to blame for failing to use heavier sinkers to prevent ice from causing the buoys to drift.

Wakefield v. The Veendam.[161] A fishing vessel was held 65 percent to blame and a passenger liner 35 percent to blame for a collision in Canadian waters. The incompetently manned fishing vessel was a "casualty in being," since she could not comply with the lookout, radar, sound signal, and other rules of COLREGS, and her starboard propeller and rudder were inoperable. The liner, informed by radio of the fishing vessel's midchannel course, was guilty of the cardinal faults of unsafe speed (18 knots) and failure to detect and plot by radar the fishing vessel's approach.

Alamo Barge Lines, Inc. v. Rim Maritime Co.[162] An underpowered and negligently navigated tug with three barges in tow collided with a chemical tanker anchored outside the designated anchorage area of the Mississippi at Baton

157. 664 F.2d at 114.
158. 398 F. Supp. 952, 1975 AMC 1780 (ED La. 1975).
159. 421 F. Supp. 48, 1976 AMC 2228 (WD Wash. 1976).
160. 1980 AMC 594 (SDNY 1976).
161. 1980 AMC 2906 (WD Wash. 1980).
162. 596 F. Supp. 1026, 1985 AMC 2540 (ED La. 1984).

Rouge; the blame was apportioned 65 percent against the tug and 35 percent against the ship, whose statutory anchorage violation precluded reliance on the presumption of fault on the part of a moving vessel.

In re Ocean Foods Boat Co.[163] The fishing vessel *McKinley* collided with the cargo ship *Tosca.* A temporary deckhand was at the wheel of the fishing vessel, watching the radar screen, but the constant bearing and decreasing distance of the *Tosca* did not alarm him. The chief mate on watch on the *Tosca* heard the report of a radar contact, which proved to be the *McKinley.* He engaged the ARPA, but could not get a radar contact. Seven minutes later the *McKinley* was dead ahead; last-minute evasive actions on both vessels were unsuccessful, and the *Tosca* struck and sank the *McKinley.* The *McKinley* argued that it was an end-on meeting situation, while the *Tosca* urged it was a crossing. The court found the difference between their two courses varied between 17 degrees and 23 degrees, and that accordingly it was a crossing situation, that the *McKinley* was the give-way vessel, and that the *Tosca* was the hold-on vessel. Allocating blame on the basis of culpability, the court found the *McKinley* 65 percent to blame, based on the helmsman's incompetent navigation and improper look-out (failure to recognize risk of collision), failure to give way in a crossing situation, and failure to take action to avoid collision. The *Tosca* was held 35 percent to blame for failure to make effective use of her ARPA, for improper look-out, and for failure to slow and take prompt action to avoid collision.

Alkmeon Naviera, S.A. v. The Marina L.[164] Two cargo vessels collided in heavy fog (visibility 200 meters) off Baja California. The *Theokeetor* was proceeding at full speed on a course of 340 degrees (T), with one operable radar set at the 12-mile range, while the *Marina L* was also proceeding at full speed on a course of 161 degrees (T). Ten minutes before collision the *Theokeetor,* observing the *Marina L* on radar on a collision course, 3.5 miles distant, ordered hard right rudder and sounded one blast. Four minutes before collision the *Theokeetor* continued her right turn and again sounded one blast. Two minutes before collision the *Theokeetor* stopped her engines. The *Theokeetor* did not appear on the *Marina L*'s radar until five minutes before collision, at a distance of 2.3 miles. The *Marina L* turned 8 degrees to port (in violation of COLREGS Rule 19[d]), sounding a two-blast signal, again turned to port, sounding another two blasts, and then stopped her engines. One minute before collision the *Marina L* heard the *Theokeetor*'s one-blast signal and went hard right, then full astern. The *Marina L* struck the *Theokeetor* broadside. The district court found that each vessel was equally at fault for immoderate speed and improper use of radar, but made a 60 percent–40 percent allocation against the *Marina L* because of her maneuvering faults. On appeal, the *Theokeetor* urged an 80 percent–20 percent division

163. 692 F. Supp. 1253, 1989 AMC 579 (D Or. 1988).
164. 633 F.2d 789, 1982 AMC 153 (9th Cir. 1980).

against the *Marina L,* while the *Marina L* urged a 50 percent–50 percent allocation. The *Marina L* also urged the applicability of COLREGS Rule 16(b) (hearing another's fog signal) but the court applied Rule 16(c) (detecting another vessel's presence). Judge Kennedy (later Justice Kennedy of the U.S. Supreme Court) held that the trial court's apportionment of fault must stand, rejecting the *Marina L*'s citation of *The Verena,*[165] because U.S. courts must affirm apportionments unless, after a review of all the evidence, the appellate court has a definite and firm conviction that a mistake has been committed.

Fathom Expeditions, Inc. v. The Gavrion.[166] The tanker *Gavrion,* the give-way vessel in a crossing situation, and the treasure-hunting vessel *Fathom II,* the hold-on vessel, collided off the Florida coast. The *Fathom II* was cut in two and sank. The *Gavrion* was held 60 percent to blame for failing to keep out of the way, her rudder having failed to respond properly to the pilot's hard left order, and her whistle having failed to work. The *Fathom II* was held 40 percent to blame for failing to maintain a proper look-out.

Paul Lin, Inc. v. The Rondys.[167] The fishing vessel *Paul Lin,* on a course of 60 degrees (T) collided with another fishing vessel, the *Rondys,* on a generally clear day with patches of fog. Both vessels were held at fault for excessive speed and failing to recognize that there was risk of collision. However, the court allocated 60 percent of the blame to the *Rondys* for her failure to observe that it was obviously a crossing and not an end-on meeting situation.

Nissho-Iwai American Corp. v. The Grand Day.[168] A dead ship in tow of a tug that was to take her to Taiwan grounded in Hong Kong Harbor. The tug and tow were both found unseaworthy in failing to prepare a proper plan for the towage. The court also found the tug at fault for undertaking the towage although she was insufficiently powered, and was using an excessively long towing wire for towage through treacherous currents close to shallow water. Sixty percent of the damages were assessed against the tug and 40 percent against the tow, which had only one anchor; the anchor winch was not working properly, and it was decided to cut the anchor chain in order to free the vessel so that the towage could commence on a favorable tide.

Mechling v. Tri-State Marine, Inc.[169] During expectable high water on the Illinois River barges broke away and drifted into a dam and docks, causing damage. The owner of the tugs, who was operator of a barge shuttle service and responsible for securing the barges, was held 60 percent to blame for improper mooring, and the operator of the barge fleeting area 40 percent to blame for failing to inspect the barges and strengthen the mooring lines.

165. [1961] 2 Lloyd's Rep. 127 (C.A.).
166. 402 F. Supp. 390, 1975 AMC 1391 (MD Fla. 1975).
167. 494 F. Supp. 242, 1981 AMC 2300 (WD Wash. 1980).
168. 1980 AMC 2882 (SDNY 1980).
169. 1981 AMC 2601 (ND Ill. 1981).

Consolidated Rail Corp. v. The Legada Beach.[170] A docking pilot, knowing of an obstruction at a coal-loading pier in Philadelphia created by the coal-loader's operating cab extending out over navigable waters, was held 60 percent to blame for an allision of the piloted vessel with the pier. The pier operator was held 40 percent to blame for failure to abate the obstruction.

Cumberland County Utilities Authority v. The Delbar.[171] A county utilities authority was held 60 percent to blame for failure to light a warning sign at a sewer outfall line in a navigable river that was struck by a tug at night. The tug was held 40 percent to blame for disregarding the relevant Loran charts and the local Notice to Mariners.

In re Seiriki Kisen Kaisha (The Seiryu—The Stena Freighter).[172] The collision occurred on a clear night, 8.5 miles off the western end of Cuba. Both vessels were proceeding at full speed, on automatic pilot, the *Seiryu* en route from Panama to Houston, and the *Stena Freighter* from Miami to Panama. *The Stena Freighter's* watch officer correctly concluded his vessel was the hold-on vessel on a course crossing that of the *Seiryu,* while the *Seiryu*'s watch officer erroneously believed the vessels were on reciprocal courses. He did nothing until two or three minutes before the collision, when he turned left across the *Stena Freighter*'s bow, without sounding a whistle signal. Meanwhile, the *Stena Freighter*'s watch officer, believing the *Seiryu* would pass clear, busied himself with taking and plotting a fix, and let the helmsman, the only other person on deck, go below to call the next watch. The *Stena Freighter*'s bow collided with the *Seiryu*'s starboard side amidships and almost cut her in two. Fortunately, the *Seiryu*'s crew were able to climb aboard the *Stena Freighter* without injury before the *Stena Freighter* pulled away from the *Seiryu,* which then sank like a rock.

The court charged the *Seiryu,* which confessed fault, with 60 percent of the blame, for failing to keep out of the way of the *Stena Freighter,* the hold-on vessel, and finally turning left instead of right, without signalling. *The Stena Freighter* was held 40 percent to blame for failing to maintain a proper lookout, and failing to sound a danger signal when it should have been apparent that the *Seiryu* was not fulfilling her duty, as the give-way vessel, to keep out of the *Stena Freighter's* way.

50 Percent–50 Percent Apportionments: *Healy v. The Tug Falcon.*[173] A yacht, the *Bounty,* accompanied by another yacht, the *Three Bells,* was proceeding southerly in heavy fog from Cape May, New Jersey, to Cape Henry, Virginia, while the tug *Falcon,* with a barge on a 1200-foot hawser, was proceeding northerly from Norfolk, Virginia, to Kearney, New Jersey, when the *Bounty*

170. 1983 AMC 1242 (ED Pa. 1982).

171. 604 F. Supp. 383, 1984 AMC 1856 (D N.J. 1984).

172. 629 F. Supp. 1374, 1986 AMC 913 (SDNY 1986). Other aspects of this case are discussed in chapter 1, section C, and chapter 5, section D.

173. 541 F.2d 277, 1977 AMC 361 (4th Cir. 1976).

collided with the *Falcon*'s towline and tow off the eastern shore of Virginia. The district court analyzed the faults as equal, specifying the *Bounty*'s excessive speed (6–8 to 11 knots), her failure to maintain a look-out, failing to notify the *Three Bells* of radar failure, and failing to observe the *Falcon*'s fog signals. The tug's faults were failure to observe the fog signals of the *Three Bells* and the *Bounty*, especially after the *Bounty* encountered the towline, and failure to monitor the radio emergency frequency. On appeal, the court of appeals said that the trial court erred in finding the *Falcon* at fault for failing to monitor the emergency frequency, since monitoring was not required of vessels the size of the tug. The district judge, however, had advised the court of appeals that deletion of the monitoring fault, ". . . would not alter findings or the result of the case."[174]

Portacci v. Moran Towing & Transp. Co.[175] Personal injuries resulted from a collision of a fishing vessel with a tug. The district court apportioned the fault equally. The fishing vessel had no working radio and failed to maintain a proper look-out, while the tug did not have proper running lights and failed to sound a danger signal. The district court held that the vessels were "mutually at fault." On appeal, the Fifth Circuit remanded for a new apportionment, since mutual fault does not imply equal fault; the expression could mean 90 percent–10 percent as well as 50 percent–50 percent.

LoVuolo v. Gunning.[176] Plaintiff, proceeding at night out of Boston inner harbor at 10 knots in his 23-foot open speedboat, collided with defendant's 32-foot cabin cruiser, which was proceeding into the harbor, also at 10 knots. The situation was a crossing one, with the speedboat the hold-on vessel. Defendant cut the engines of the cabin cruiser but failed to take any other action. Plaintiff turned hard right in an unsuccessful attempt to avoid collision. The district court held the vessels equally to blame, but the court of appeals remanded. The principal issue on the appeal was whether Rule 8 (Action to Avoid Collision) overrode (or "trumped") the other rules. In holding that it did not, the court of appeals agreed with the district court that neither vessel maintained a proper look-out, but noted that the district court had failed to consider plaintiff's status as the hold-on vessel under the crossing rules. In remanding, the court of appeals stated: "In making this reapportionment the district court should keep in mind that a finding of equal fault is now the exception rather than the rule."[177]

Granholm v. The TFL Express.[178] This case is a model of a factual analysis on which a fault allocation can be based. It concerned a high-seas collision between the sailing yacht *Olympus Camera,* proceeding from Newport, Rhode Island, to Lisbon, and the containership *TFL Express,* proceeding from

174. 541 F.2d at 278, 1977 AMC at 362.
175. 615 F.2d 293, 1981 AMC 895 (5th Cir. 1980).
176. 925 F.2d 22, 1991 AMC 1651 (1st Cir. 1991).
177. 925 F.2d at 28, 1991 AMC at 1660.
178. 576 F. Supp. 435, 1984 AMC 943 (SDNY 1983).

Wilmington, North Carolina, to Rotterdam. The *Olympus Camera*'s owner was sailing his vessel alone, on a qualifying heat for a single-handed sailing race scheduled to be held later in the year. At about 2230 hours, while the owner was sleeping below, with the yacht on automatic pilot, the mainsail out to port and the No. 1 Genoa out to starboard, the yacht was struck by the *TFL Express*. That vessel was proceeding at 18 knots and was apparently unaware that a collision had occurred until she heard and responded to the yacht's Mayday. The *TFL Express* was then 4 miles beyond the stricken yacht. The *TFL Express*'s wheelhouse radar was not operating, but was on standby. The court held that there was no obligation to keep the radar activated under the circumstances. The lookout had reported no traffic in the vicinity prior to going below for tea. The *TFL Express* was held 50 percent to blame for failure to maintain a proper and attentive look-out. The yacht was also held 50 percent to blame for failure to maintain a proper look-out—the single-handed sailor having gone below to rest at night, near a recognized transatlantic route for large vessels, instead of during the day, when the yacht could have been seen more easily. Concluding a detailed review of the facts, Judge Haight noted that there was no basis for distinguishing between the faults of the *TFL Express* and the *Olympus Camera*.[179]

Alter Co. v. Carol D. Eymard, Inc.[180] Off Algiers Point, opposite New Orleans, the Tug *Bayou Andre,* proceeding northbound, pushing two loaded barges, proposed overtaking the Tug *Margaret A. Eymard,* pushing three barges, which was also northbound. The *Eymard* agreed to an overtaking on her starboard side, and as the *Bayou Andre* was attempting to overtake, her lead barge struck the middle barge of the *Eymard*'s flotilla. The tugs were held equally to blame, the *Bayou Andre* for proposing to overtake at Algiers Point, where eddies and currents made such a maneuver dangerous, and the *Eymard* for agreeing to the proposal. The *Eymard* was also charged with failure to have a proper lookout. The captain, who acted as lookout, had no sight in one eye. The *Bayou Andre* was also held at fault for failing to sound a danger signal when danger of collision became apparent. Each vessel was charged with 50 percent of the blame.

Capital Marine Supply, Inc. v. The City of Port Allen.[181] The Tug *City of Port Allen* was heading down the Mississippi in dense fog with six barges in tow. The Tug *Ashley* and tow were proceeding upriver with no operable radar. Instead of following the point-bend custom she proposed a port-to-port passing, to which the *Port Allen* agreed. The tugs were held equally to blame for the collision that followed, the *Ashley* for proposing an imprudent passing and for her inability to determine her own position and that of the *Port Allen* because of lack of an operable radar. The *Port Allen* was faulted for failing to maneuver

179. 576 F. Supp. at 447, 1984 AMC at 958.
180. 1982 AMC 1008 (ED La. 1981).
181. 1981 AMC 1576 (ED La. 1980).

properly after having agreed to an imprudent passing proposal, and for taking no evasive action although she knew that the *Ashley* had no operable radar, and observed, with her own radar, that there was danger of collision.

Penn Tanker Co. v. The Tug Massachusetts.[182] A tug pushing one barge in Arthur Kill, a narrow waterway in New York Harbor, asked permission to overtake a large tanker assisted by two tugs at her bow. The tanker agreed that the tug could pass on either side, and the tug proceeded to pass on the port side. When the tug was at the tanker's port quarter, the tanker turned right to follow a slight bend in the channel, making several changes in engine speed. The turn caused the tanker's stern to pivot toward the barge the tug was pushing. The tanker urged the tug to back down, but the tanker's port quarter collided with the starboard side of the barge while the tug was attempting to "back and fill." The tanker and the tug were held equally at fault, the tanker for failing to inform the tug of the danger of overtaking at the bend in the channel, and for failing to sound a danger signal. The tug was held at fault for attempting to overtake at a place where a turn should have been anticipated, and for failing to sound an overtaking signal.

Verdin v. Sea-Land Services, Inc.[183] A small fishing vessel and a large motor ship collided in clear weather in the Mississippi Gulf Outlet. The motor ship sounded several overtaking signals without receiving a reply. When she was 500 feet from the fishing vessel, she sounded a danger signal and cut her 10-knot speed. The fishing vessel began moving to starboard, while the motor ship moved to port and struck the fishing vessel's stern. The fishing vessel was held 50 percent to blame for failing to maintain a proper look-out and for impeding the passage of a larger vessel in a narrow channel, in violation of Inland Rule 9. The motor ship was also held 50 percent to blame for excessive speed in a narrow channel and for failing to keep out of the way of a vessel being overtaken.

Pennzoil Producing Co. v. Offshore Express, Inc.[184] An offshore supply boat was held 50 percent to blame for striking and damaging a pipeline crossing under the Houma Navigation Canal under fog conditions. The court found that the vessel's owners were aware of the presence of the pipeline and of the fact that on the night of the casualty the canal was in a low-water stage. The court further found that the captain of the supply boat, who was at the wheel, was negligent in failing to follow the configuration of the deep-water channel and veering into the pipeline area. The owner of the pipeline was also held 50 percent to blame because the pipeline had been neither covered nor marked.

182. 1981 AMC 1903 (SDNY 1981).

183. 1992 AMC 2579 (ED La. 1992).

184. 735 F. Supp. 195, 1990 AMC 1895 (ED La. 1990), aff'd, 943 F.2d 1465, 1994 AMC 1034 (5th Cir. 1991).

Sweeney v. Car/Puter International Corp.[185] Two large motor yachts, one 45 feet long and the other 72 feet long, were proceeding together at high speeds on the Atlantic Intracoastal Waterway, creating huge wakes, which caused a passenger in a small pleasure boat to be tossed about the boat in such a way that she sustained severe injuries. Each of the motor yachts was found at fault for failing to maintain a proper look-out and proceeding at excessive speed under the circumstances, and each was held liable for half the passenger's damages.

In re Shaun Fisheries, Ltd.[186] A fishing vessel and a tug with a tow were on crossing courses off the Oregon coast. The tug, the port-hand vessel, failed to give way, while the fishing vessel took no avoiding action until collision was inevitable. The collision caused the loss of the fishing vessel and her crew. The court divided the damages equally.

48 Percent–26 Percent–26 Percent Apportionment: *Maute v. United States.*[187] Two powerboats collided in the Florida Intercoastal Waterway, where the U.S. Coast Guard had placed confusing navigational markers, causing the two operators to be misled. In an unusual allocation, the court charged one operator with 48 percent of the blame and the other operator and the Coast Guard each with 26 percent.

185. 521 F. Supp. 276, 1982 AMC 622 (D S.C. 1981).
186. 1984 AMC 2650 (D Or. 1983).
187. 1987 AMC 2502 (SD Fla. 1987).

CHAPTER THIRTEEN

SHIPOWNERS' DAMAGES IN COLLISION CASES

Section A. Introduction

1. Conventions and Rules

The Brussels Collision Convention of 1910[1] was prepared by the Comité Maritime International (C.M.I.) over the years from 1897 to 1910, to regulate the liability principles to be applied in collision cases.[2] While the convention has not been adopted by the United States, American courts are frequently called upon to apply it, as in the case of high-seas collisions between ships of countries that have subscribed to it. Furthermore, the U.S. Supreme Court, in *Reliable Transfer Co. v. United States,*[3] has adopted its principal feature—the proportionate fault rule—which is now part of the U.S. general maritime law. The United States has failed to adopt two other C.M.I. conventions directly concerned with collision—the 1952 Convention on Civil Jurisdiction in Collision Cases[4] and the 1952 Convention on Penal Jurisdiction in Collision Cases.[5]

Conventions that are concerned primarily with other subjects but at times are involved in collision cases include those on arrest of ships, bills of lading, salvage, water pollution, and limitation of liability, all briefly discussed in chapter 1. The Limitation Convention is discussed in further detail

---

1. International Convention for the Unification of Certain Rules Relating to Collisions between Vessels, Sept. 23, 1910, 212 Consol. Treaty Series 178, 6A Benedict on Admiralty, Doc. No. 3-2 (7th ed. [rev.], 1996, F. Wiswall, editor-in-chief, *International Maritime Law Documents and Commentary* (hereinafter "Benedict"), I *Transport Laws of the World,* I/E/I (1977) (D. Hill & M. Evans, eds.). The official text is in French, 212 Consol. Treaty Series, 178. The United States is not a party. See Note, *The Difficult Quest for a Uniform Maritime Law: Failure of the Brussels Convention to Achieve International Agreement on Collision Liability, Liens and Mortgages,* 64 Yale L.J. 878 (1955). See also Senate Executive K, 75th Cong. 1st Sess. (1937).

2. J. Sweeney, *Proportional Fault in Both to Blame Collisions: Studi in Onore di Giorgio Berlingieri,* Sp. Ed. Il Diritto Marittimo 549 (1964), tracing the historical development of the 1910 Collision Convention by the Comité Maritime International (C.M.I.).

3. 421 U.S. 397, 1975 AMC 541 (1975).

4. International Convention for the Unification of Certain Rules Relating to Civil Jurisdiction in Matters of Collision, Brussels, May 10, 1952; entered into force Sept. 14, 1955, 439 U.N.T.S. 217, 6 Benedict Doc. 3-1.

5. International Convention for the Unification of Certain Rules Relating to Penal Jurisdiction in Matters of Collision, Brussels, May 10, 1952; entered into force Nov. 30, 1955, 439 U.N.T.S. 233, 6 Benedict Doc. 3-3.

in chapter 14, the 1989 Salvage Convention in chapter 15, and the Convention on Civil Liability for Oil Pollution in chapter 11.

More recently a C.M.I. subcommittee, under the chairmanship of the late Jean Warot, prepared Rules on Compensation for Damages in Collision Cases, which have become known as "The Lisbon Rules," the initial draft having been prepared at the C.M.I. Lisbon Conference in 1985.[6] The rules consist of definitions, lettered rules dealing with immediacy and directness, *"restitutio in integrum,"* avoidable consequences, and burden of proof, followed by numbered rules on total loss, repairable damage to vessels, damage to property on board vessels, currency exchange, and interest. The Lisbon Rules were not intended as a draft of an international convention or a model statute, but rather as a set of rules recommended for voluntary adoption, as are the York-Antwerp Rules of 1994, relating to general average.

At its Rio de Janeiro Conference in 1977, the C.M.I. approved a draft Convention on Jurisdiction, Choice of Law and Recognition and Enforcement of Judgments in Collision Cases. As of 1997 the International Maritime Organization (I.M.O.) Legal Committee intended to consider the draft after it had dealt with matters considered more pressing. This draft convention is discussed in chapter 1.

2. *Appellate Review of Decisions on Collision Damages*

In analyzing older cases on collision damages, a date that must be taken into consideration is 1954, when the Supreme Court, in *McAllister v. United States,*[7] finally abolished the old rule that an admiralty appeal was a trial *de novo*. Since then, the U.S. courts of appeals have been reviewing findings of fact made by a district court only under the "clearly erroneous" standard, and have no longer been making independent findings of fact based on their own evidentiary conclusions. Rule 52a of the Federal Rules of Civil Procedure has been applicable to admiralty cases since 1966. Under that rule the trial court's determination of damages is treated as a finding of fact, and is therefore not reviewable on appeal unless "clearly erroneous."[8] This standard makes review of awards of collision damages difficult, because the challenger must prove that the trial court clearly made a mistake.[9]

---

6. 18 J. Mar. L. & Com. 577 (1987). See Warot, *A Comment on the Lisbon Rules on Compensation for Damages in Collision Cases,* 18 J. Mar. L. & Com. 583 (1987).

7. 348 U.S. 19, 1954 AMC 1999 (1954).

8. See *United States v. United States Gypsum Co.*, 333 U.S. 364 (1948); *Darling v. Scheimer,* 444 F.2d 514, 1971 AMC 1868 (9th Cir. 1971); *Daniels Towing Service, Inc. v. Nat Harrison Assoc.*, 432 F.2d 103, 1970 AMC 2250 (5th Cir. 1970); *Alkmeon Naviera, S.A. v. The Marina L,* 633 F.2d 789, 1982 AMC 153 (9th Cir. 1980).

9. See *Inland Oil and Transport Co. v. Ark-White Towing Co.*, 696 F.2d 321 (5th Cir. 1983); *Stevens v. The Bonnie Doon,* 731 F.2d 1433, 1985 AMC 363 (9th Cir. 1984); *Marcona v. The Shifty III,* 615 F.2d 206, 1981 AMC 468 (5th Cir. 1980).

3. Bifurcated Trials

The admiralty custom, made possible by the absence of a jury, is that in trials of collision cases, issues of liability can be separated from issues of damages, and those issues can be heard either by the court or by a commissioner appointed by the court. This custom is now preserved in the Federal Rules of Civil Procedure.[10] Most issues of damages in collision litigation are ultimately settled, but where they are not, the custom avoids the expense of trying those issues with respect to the damages sustained by a vessel held solely at fault.

4. Punitive Damages

It is assumed in this chapter that the damages suffered by the parties in a collision case resulted from negligence, rather than from an intentional tort, i.e., harmful or offensive conduct done with the purpose of causing the collision, or with knowledge that a collision is substantially certain to follow defendant's conduct. This is not to say, however, that "intentional" collisions are unknown.[11]

A noncollision case, *Protectus Alpha Navigation Co. v. North Pacific Grain Growers, Inc.*,[12] is an illustration of an intentional maritime tort resulting in an award of punitive damages. In that case representatives of a dock owner ordered lines to a vessel on fire to be cut while fire fighters were still on board fighting the fire. The court held that the callous and deliberate disregard of the safety of human life justified an award of punitive damages.

An illustration of a situation where punitive damages were initially awarded in a collision case but disallowed on appeal is the *The Cedarville—The Topdalsfjord*,[13] in which the district court found the following faults of the master justified an award of punitive damages against the owner: maintaining full speed in fog, failure to follow courses designated by the Coast Guard, failure to sound a danger signal when approaching another vessel, failure to reduce speed to bare steerageway and to reverse when the approaching vessel failed to answer a one-blast signal. The trial court held these actions to

10. Rule 42(b), Fed. R. Civ. P.:

> (b) Separate Trials. The court, in furtherance of convenience or to avoid prejudice, or when separate trials will be conducive to expedition and economy, may order a separate trial of any claim, cross-claim, counterclaim, or third-party claim, or of any separate issue or of any number of claims, cross-claims, counterclaims, third-party claims, or issues, always preserving inviolate the right to jury trial.

Appeals are allowed from interlocutory judgments in admiralty when only damage issues remain open. See 28 U.S. Code § 1292(a)(3).

11. See Marsden, *The Law of Collisions at Sea* 44 (11th ed., K. McGuffie, editor; vol. 4 of British Shipping Laws) (hereinafter "Marsden"), citing Dr. Lushington's judgment in *The James Seldon,* (1886) 1 A.&E. 62, 64, and *The Ida,* (1860) Lush. 6. See also Rest. Torts 2d, § 29(13).

12. 767 F.2d 1379, 1986 AMC 56 (9th Cir. 1985). See also *Ralston v. The States Rights,* 20 F. Cas. 201 (No. 11540) (ED Pa. 1836).

13. 276 F. Supp. 163, 1967 AMC 1965 (ND Ill. 1967).

"constitute wilful and wanton misconduct directly related to the collision and the subsequent loss of life and personal injury." The trial record further supported the conclusion that the vessel owner vested sole and exclusive discretion in the masters of its vessels, "and that the above departures from the Rules were routine practices ratified by the highest echelon" of the vessel's corporate owner. Punitive damages were decreed against the owner because of what the court found was callous disregard of the safety of the vessel's crew and the ratification of the practice of proceeding at full speed in fog in the Straits of Mackinac.

On appeal, the Sixth Circuit reversed,[14] holding that punitive damages were *not* recoverable against the owner of a vessel for the act of the master (in attempting to beach rather than abandon the ship) unless it could be shown that the owner authorized or ratified the acts of the master either before or after the accident. Punitive damages would be recoverable if the acts complained of were those of an unfit master and the owner was reckless in employing him.[15]

5. *Remedies of Claimants*

Collisions caused by fault are maritime torts, and accordingly give rise to maritime liens for the damages sustained, enforceable by the arrest of the offending vessel by *in rem* process under Fed. R. Civ. P. Suppl. Rule C.[16] Claims for such damages may also be enforced against the owner or bareboat charterer of the offending vessel *in personam,* except in the unusual case of a collision caused by the sole fault of a compulsory pilot. If the defendant cannot be "found" within the federal district where the action is brought, its tangible property within the district may be attached and its bank accounts or other credits may be garnished to obtain jurisdiction, in accordance with Suppl. Rule B. It may also be possible to attach property of the defendant under an attachment statute of the state wherein the district court is located. Maritime torts enjoy a high priority in the ranking of liens, coming only after *custodia legis* expenses, wage liens of seamen and longshore workers employed directly by the ship, and salvage liens.

14. *United States Steel Corp. v. Fuhrman,* 407 F.2d 1143, 1969 AMC 252 (6th Cir. 1969). See also *W.G. Bush & Co. v. Sioux City & N.O. Barge Lines, Inc.,* 1977 AMC 2491 (MD Tenn. 1977).

15. 407 F.2d at 1148, 1969 AMC at 259.

16. *The John G. Stevens,* 170 U.S. 113 (1898); see also *The China,* 74 U.S. 53 (1869); *The Barnstable,* 181 U.S. 464 (1901); Biele, *Maritime Liens Arising out of Collision,* 51 Tul. L. Rev. 1134 (1977); Friedell & Healy, *An Introduction to In Rem Jurisdiction and Procedure in the United States,* 20 J. Mar. L. & Com. 55 (1989). *The John G. Stevens* involved a dispute between collision damage claimants and materialmen. The decision favored the collision claimants. In a dispute with seamen on wages, however, the seamen were preferred, *The C.J. Saxe,* 145 F. 749 (SDNY 1906).

6. *American and English Approaches to Negligence*

The British Admiralty Court—as part of the old Probate, Divorce and Admiralty Division of the High Court, and as part of the Queen's Bench Division since 1970—has had great experience in collision cases and has developed a substantial jurisprudence on subtle issues of collision damages. This learning was once available in Roscoe's treatise on Collision Damages;[17] that treatise is now incorporated in Marsden, which, in turn, is part of the British Shipping Laws Series.[18] Nevertheless, a caveat is in order here, because the negligence principles on which cases prior to publication of the latest edition of Marsden were decided are not the same as those which have long governed American cases. The difference in approach arises from the 1921 decision of the Court of Appeal in the *Polemis*[19] case, which contains an opinion by Lord Justice Scrutton, a very experienced maritime judge.[20] *Polemis* permitted recovery where there was a direct causal link between the negligent act and the damage suffered, although the nature of the damage could not have been anticipated.[21] *Polemis* is reminiscent of ancient common-law thinking on the writ of trespass, which required direct causation, whereas the writ of trespass on the case, the forerunner of modern negligence law, permitted recovery of damages where the causation was indirect.[22] Accordingly, English negligence law permitted recovery of damages, "so long as the damage [was] in fact *directly traceable* to the negligent act. . . ."[23]

Modern American negligence principles have developed from the famous opinion of Chief Judge Cardozo of the New York Court of Appeals (later Justice Cardozo of the U.S. Supreme Court) in *Palsgraf v. Long Island*

---

17. E. Roscoe, *Measure of Damages in Marine Collisions* (3d ed. 1929).
18. Supra note 11.
19. *In Re Arbitration between Polemis and Furness, Withy & Co.,* [1921] 3 K.B. 560 (C.A.).
20. Lord Justice Scrutton wrote:

> To determine whether an act is negligent, it is relevant to determine whether any reasonable person would foresee that the act would cause damage; if he could not, the act is not negligent. But if the act would or might probably cause damage, the fact that the damage it in fact causes is not the exact kind of damage one would expect is immaterial, so long as the damage is in fact directly traceable to the negligent act, except that they could not avoid its results. Once the act is negligent, the fact that its exact operation was not foreseen is immaterial. . . .

21. The case arose as an arbitration between owners and time charterers for the total loss of a chartered vessel due to the negligence of stevedores for whose actions charterers were responsible. The arbitrators found that "the ship was lost by fire; that the fire arose from a spark igniting the petrol vapor in the hold; that the spark was caused by the falling board [dropped by the stevedores] coming into contact with some substance in the hold; and that the causing of the spark could not reasonably have been anticipated from the falling of the board, though some damage to the ship might reasonably have been anticipated. . . ." Charterers alleged that the total-loss damages were too remote, but the direct causation theory expounded in the Court of Appeal justified the full award, which was affirmed.
22. *Leame v. Bray,* 3 East 593, 102 Eng. Rep. 724 (K.B. 1802). See also *Brown v. Kendall,* 60 Mass. 292 (1850).
23. See *In re Arbitration between Polemis and Furness, Withy & Co.,* supra note 19.

R.R. Co.,[24] "codified" in the first Restatement of Torts.[25] The *Palsgraf* principle was adopted in the admiralty context by Chief Judge Friendly of the U.S. Court of Appeals for the Second Circuit in *Petition of Kinsman Transit Co.* in 1964.[26]

In *Palsgraf,* recovery of damages was determined by the specific risk which the defendant had created, since the orbit of danger as disclosed to the eye of reasonable vigilance is the orbit of the legal duty,[27] and "The risk reasonably to be perceived defines the duty to be obeyed and risk imports relation; it is risk to another or to others within the range of apprehension. . . ."[28] In other words, the result (plaintiff's injury) must be within the specific risk set up by defendant's conduct. Accordingly, direct causation is not determinative in American law, but rather the test is whether the plaintiff's damage is a result *within the risk reasonably to be foreseen* by the defendant. While *Kinsman* accepts the *Palsgraf* principle, it adds the gloss that the *exact* kind of injury need not be foreseeable, as long as injury of some kind *is* foreseeable.[29]

British and American theories were brought closer together in 1961 in the first *Wagon Mound* decision of the Judicial Committee of the Privy Council.[30] Accordingly, since 1961 it has been possible to say that the negligence principles underlying both English and American cases on damages are the same.

Underlying the collision damages rules, whether for total loss or for repairable damage, is the standard or maxim, *restitutio in integrum*—restoring the wholeness. It has been lifted from Roman civil law applicable to obliga-

---

24. 248 N.Y. 339, 162 N.E. 99 (1928).

25. Restatement of Torts § 281. See also § 443, comment e.

26. 338 F.2d 708, 1964 AMC 2503 (2d Cir. 1964). See also *In re Alva S.S. Co.,* 262 F. Supp. 328, 1967 AMC 2363 (SDNY 1966), aff'd after issue became moot, 616 F.2d 605, 1980 AMC 857 (2d Cir. 1980).

27. *Palsgraf,* supra note 24, 248 N.Y. at 342.

28. Id. at 344.

29. *Kinsman,* supra note 26, 338 F.2d at 726, 1964 AMC at 2529: "We go only so far as to hold that where, as here, the damages resulted from the same physical forces whose existence required the exercise of greater care than was displayed and were of the same general sort that was expectable, unforeseeability of the exact developments and of the extent of the loss will not limit liability. . . ."

30. *Overseas Tankship (U.K.) Ltd. v. Mort's Dock & Engineering Co. (Wagon Mound No. 1),* [1961] 1 Lloyd's Rep. 1 (P.C.). This case arose out of an oil spill in the harbor of Sydney, Australia. The oil spread out 600 feet from the tanker source to plaintiff's wharf, causing minor pollution damage. It was then ignited by cotton waste on the surface, which had been ignited by molten metal from acetylene torch operations, causing a major fire which damaged the wharf and ships alongside. On the theory that fire damage was not within a foreseeable pollution risk, the plaintiff wharf owner's negligence action was dismissed. See Fleming, *The Passing of Polemis,* 39 Can. Bar Rev. 489 (1961). A later action relating to the same incident by another plaintiff, but with a new fact finding, resulted in recovery of damages by the owners of the ships burnt by the fire, *Overseas Tankship (U.K.) Ltd. v. Miller Steamship Co. (Wagon Mound No. 2),* [1967] 1 A.C. 617 (P.C.1966). See also Goodhart, *The Brief Life Story of the Direct Consequences Law in English Tort Law,* 53 Va. L. Rev. 857 (1961).

tions generally and has even been applied in public international law to duties between nations.[31] It has a lengthy history in English and American admiralty law and has often been cited by the U.S. Supreme Court.[32] This does not, however, mean that it is free of criticism because of age; Judge Learned Hand has warned us about it, in dissent, as "...one of those scraps of Latin which serve only to bemuse the user and usually the hearer."[33] *Restitutio in integrum* simply refers to the court's function of ensuring that the tortfeasor pays compensation to the victim in an amount that restores the victim's property rights in damaged objects as nearly as possible to their position just before the collision; it is a rule of reasonableness, not perfection.

Section B. Damages in Total Loss Cases

1. General Principles

Where a vessel has sunk as a result of collision and cannot be raised and restored to useful service in an economical manner, i.e., where she has become

---

31. Paulsen, *Provable Damages in Collision Cases,* 51 Tul. L. Rev. 1047 (1977) (hereinafter "Paulsen"), wherein the maxim is described as a "useless shibboleth."

The phrase can sometimes act as a dangerous substitute for clear thinking, especially where it can be used to represent both the objective test of "market" value and the more subjective test of "fair" value. Roscoe traced the history of this expression and concluded:

> There is no connection between the use of this phrase in Roman law and in modern maritime law. It appears to have been taken from Roman law and transferred to English law merely because it conveyed in a convenient and terse form the idea of the Court of Admiralty that damages should, if possible, place the innocent party in the same pecuniary position as if no injury had been done to him. It denotes a spirit of generosity towards the innocent party rather than a desire to limit his remedies by a stringent application of the doctrine that damages must not be too remote. The phrase further implies accuracy of estimation, because a man cannot be fully compensated for a loss payable in money unless the pecuniary loss which he has suffered is accurately and carefully measured. E. Roscoe, *The Measure of Damages in Actions of Maritime Collisions* 6 (3d ed. 1929).

From Dr. Lushington's earlier discussion we derive the admiralty idea of market value. *The Clyde,* 1 Swabey 23, 24 (1856):

> In order to ascertain this [value], there are various species of evidence that may be resorted to—for instance, the value of the vessel when built. But that is only one species of evidence, because the value may furnish a very inferior criterion whereby to ascertain the value at the moment of destruction. The length of time during which the vessel has been used, and the degree of deterioration suffered, will affect the original price at which the vessel was built. But there is another matter infinitely more important than this—known to even the most unlearned—the constant change which takes place in the market. It is the market price which the Court looks to, and nothing else, as the value of the property.

32. *The Baltimore,* 75 U.S. 377, 385 (1869); *The Potomac,* 105 U.S. 630, 631 (1881); *The Umbria,* 166 U.S. 404, 421 (1897); *Standard Oil Co. v. Southern Pacific Railroad Co. (The Proteus—The Cushing),* 268 U.S. 146, 158, 1925 AMC 779 (1925).

33. *The Zeller No. 12 v. Nessa Corp.,* 166 F.2d 32, 35, 1948 AMC 418, 423 (2d Cir. 1948) (dissent).

an actual or constructive total loss, the courts will measure the owner's damages by the market value of the vessel just before her destruction, assuming that there is a market for similar vessels. Market value can best be established by evidence of actual contemporaneous sales. Where there is no market, the courts will seek a substitute for market value, e.g., in the reproduction cost depreciated by age, or by any other method that fairly reflects the true value of the vessel. These basic propositions are established by the leading Supreme Court case on the subject, *Standard Oil Co. v. Southern Pacific Railroad Co. (The Proteus—The Cushing).*[34]

Collect freight lost because the cargo cannot be delivered is also included in the measure of damages for total loss. Salvage value of a wreck, if any, is deducted from the market value in computing the value of the vessel in total loss cases.[35]

Rule I of the Lisbon Rules provides that in the case of a total loss the claimant is entitled to damages equal to the cost of purchasing a similar vessel in the market on the date of the collision and that where no similar vessel is available, the claimant is entitled to recover the value of the vessel on that date, "calculated by reference to the type, age, condition, nature of operation of the vessel and any other relevant factors." The rule further provides that damages recoverable in total loss cases also include salvage, general average, and other charges and expenses reasonably incurred; sums for which the claimant has become legally liable and has paid to third parties by reason of contractual, statutory, or other legal obligations; the net collect freight; and the value of bunkers and ship's gear lost as a result of the collision and not included in the value of the vessel as ascertained in accordance with the rule. Finally, the rule provides that, subject to reimbursement for any claim for loss of freight, the claimant is entitled to compensation for the loss of use of the vessel for the period reasonably necessary to find a replacement, whether the vessel is actually replaced or not.

2. *Market Value*

In *The Proteus—The Cushing,* Justice Butler crystallized the *restitutio in integrum* concept, writing:[36]

> It is fundamental in the law of damages that the injured party is entitled to compensation for the loss suffered. Where property is destroyed by wrongful act, the owner is entitled to its money equivalent, and thereby to be put in as good position pecuniarily as if his property had not been

34. Supra note 32.

35. *The Umbria,* supra note 32; *The Scotland,* 105 U.S. 24 (1886); *B & M Towing Co. v. Wittliff,* 258 F.2d 473, 1959 AMC 145 (5th Cir. 1958).

36. *The Proteus—The Cushing,* supra note 32, 268 U.S. at 155–56, 1925 AMC at 782.

> destroyed. In case of total loss of a vessel, the measure of damages is its market value, if it has a market value, at the time of destruction. . . .

The courts have frequently encountered considerable difficulty in ascertaining market value of a vessel because, in the international shipping world, depressed economic conditions and a corresponding glut of ships have alternated with wartime scarcity. Further, government ownership of vessels, government subsidies, and flags of convenience all combine to distort the classical idea of a free market.

3. Establishing Value When There Is No Market

In *The Proteus—The Cushing*, supra, after considering the rule governing in cases where there is a market, the Supreme Court continued:

> Where there is no market value such as is established by contemporaneous sales of like property in the way of ordinary business, as in the case of merchandise bought and sold in the market, other evidence is resorted to.
>
> The value of the vessel lost properly may be taken to be the sum which, considering all the circumstances, probably could have been obtained for her on the date of the collision; that is, the sum that in all probability would result from fair negotiations between an owner willing to sell and a purchaser desiring to buy.[37]

---

37. Id. Other cases concerning market value problems include the following: *Oliver J. Olson & Co. v. The Marine Leopard,* 356 F.2d 728, 1966 AMC 1064 (9th Cir. 1966), holding that if there is ample evidence of market value through contemporaneous sales of similar vessels, it is error for a commissioner to exclude such evidence and to rely on reproduction cost less depreciation. Certain of the contemporaneous sales were of vessels of foreign registry and without coastwise privileges. Furthermore, the motives of their owners for selling them were challenged, but the court held that the admissibility of evidence of contemporaneous sales was not affected by these factors.

Barton v. Borit (The Miami Mae I), 316 F.2d 550, 1969 AMC 216 (3d Cir. 1969), involving loss in the Virgin Islands of a 40-foot catamaran built the year before in Portugal for $12,000. The Third Circuit held that the trial court erred in failing to explore evidence of a market for such catamarans and instead based its award of $23,000 upon a finding that the reproduction cost in the Virgin Islands would have been $23,000, plus $2,500 for sails and miscellaneous equipment. The court said that only if it appears that there is no market for similar boats may a court resort to replacement cost, as depreciated.

In Re Bankers Trust Co. (The Edgar M. Queeny—The Corinthos), 658 F.2d 103, 1982 AMC 1098 (3d Cir. 1981). The Third Circuit said that in fixing a tanker's market value, the district court had correctly considered a sufficient number of appropriate factors, including the contemporaneous sale price of a similar vessel (adjusted for differentiating factors of age, speed, and tonnage) as well as opinions of appraisers and the vessel's value under charter.

The Second Circuit, however, has not stated the substitutes for market value in terms of a definite rule. In *Ozanic v. United States (The Petar),* 165 F.2d 738, 1948 AMC 340 (2d Cir. 1948), the commissioner valued two old wooden but still useful barges in good condition at $10,000. They had no market or replacement value, as no comparable barges existed or would ever again be built. The commissioner based his findings on real value reasonably considering "all

Where there is no market and it is necessary to look to other evidence of value, there may be a problem of admissibility because of the *res inter alios acta* rule, the common-law concept that a thing done between others may not be relevant to the case in litigation. Illustrative of limitations on the type of evidence that may be considered is *Bloomfield Steamship Co. v. Brownsville Shrimp Exchange (The Genevieve Peterkin—The Linda Lee)*,[38] where the court refused to admit authenticated copies of U.S. Customs House records of the sale of fishing vessels somewhat similar to the shrimp trawler which had been lost, because merely nominal considerations were usually stated in the documents.

A listing of the types of evidence which may be used as a substitute for evidence of market value is found in *Carl Sawyer, Inc. v. Poor (The Fire Island)*[39] where the Fifth Circuit wrote:

> But in cases where no market value has been established by recent and comparable sales, other evidence is admissible touching value such as the opinion of marine surveyors, engineers, the cost of reproduction less depreciation, the condition of repair which the vessel was in, the uses to which it can be put, the amount of insurance that the underwriters have issued, and the like.

With respect to insurance, it would seem more realistic to use appraisals for insurance purposes rather than the amount for which a vessel is insured under a valued policy on hull and machinery, which may be considerably higher or, occasionally, lower than the market value. However, the insured value has been considered in some cases.[40]

The following are examples of the types of problems that can be encountered in total loss cases where there is no market: In *Almirante Steamship Corp. v. United States (The Almirante—The Hisko)*[41] a refrigerator ship owned by an American company, registered in the United States but built in the United Kingdom, sank as a result of a collision. There was no market, as the vessel had been requisitioned, and the district court looked to reproduction cost in the United States less depreciation, whereas the respondent (the United

---

the relevant facts." Against claims of no value, because no market, the valuation was affirmed, since the determination of value cannot be reduced to inexorable rules.

The composite nature of evidence admitted to establish a substitute for market value is shown in *Sun Oil Co. v. The Fernview,* 1968 AMC 1996 (SDNY 1968), where the vessel's operational history, future operations, useful service expectancy, and insured values were considered.

In addition to the decisions noted above, *see O'Brien Bros. v. The Tug Helen B. Moran,* 160 F.2d 502, 1947 AMC 493 (2d Cir. 1947); *United States v. Eastern S.S. Lines, Inc. (The George Washington),* 171 F.2d 589, 1949 AMC 243 (1st Cir. 1948); *Carl Sawyer, Inc. v. Poor (The Fire Island),* 180 F.2d 962, 1950 AMC 873 (5th Cir. 1950); and *United States v. The Tug Holland,* 164 F. Supp. 741, 1958 AMC 1904 (D Md. 1958).

38. 243 F.2d 869, 1957 AMC 1247 (5th Cir. 1957).

39. Supra note 37.

40. Id. See also *Brodospas v. United States.* 1976 AMC 1849 (SDNY 1976); *Sun Oil Co. v. The Fernview.* 1968 AMC 1996 (SDNY 1968); *United States v. The Tug Holland,* supra note 37.

41. 54 F.2d 540, 1932 AMC 7 (2d Cir. 1931).

States) had urged that the figure should be determined by the use of reproduction costs in the United Kingdom. The Second Circuit said:

> . . . Reconstruction cost less depreciation for age is not an absolute measure of a vessel's value, but only one of the relevant facts. . . . The libellant is entitled to be restored to the position it would have been in had no tort been committed, that is, to get the value on September 6, 1918, of a British built *Almirante* flying an American flag and going under requisition when she reached port. If she was less valuable because British built, then reconstruction costs should be estimated on British rather than American prices.[42]

In *Boston Iron & Metal Co. v. The Winding Gulf*[43] the district court was presented with the unusual problem of an obsolete Canadian destroyer, one of five purchased at bargain rates, lost in collision while being towed to ship breakers for scrapping. The plaintiff scrap company's claim was based on the net value of the metal which would have been salvaged ($46,449), whereas respondent estimated the value of the obsolete destroyer at the purchase price ($6,591), plus the cost of towage to the point of collision ($3,048). Since the terms of the contract of sale provided that the vessel could be used only for scrap, there was no question here as to the market value of a destroyer as a destroyer. However, there was a market for this class of destroyer for scrap. The court awarded $15,000, rejecting the respondent's contention that any sum in excess of $10,000 would necessarily involve compensation for lost profits, which are not generally recoverable in total loss cases.[44]

---

42. Id., 54 F.2d at 541, 1932 AMC at 9.

43. 85 F. Supp. 806, 1949 AMC 1149 (D Md. 1949), aff'd, 209 F.2d 410, 1954 AMC 183 (4th Cir. 1954) rev'd on other grounds, 349 U.S. 122, 1955 AMC 927 (1955), see chapter 9 supra. The obsolete destroyer I-24, purchased for scrap value, was sunk and became a total loss as a result of a collision. The purchase price had been $6,591 at Sydney, Nova Scotia. The expense to the purchaser of towing her to the point of loss was $3,048.91. The cost of five similar destroyers purchased by the same ship-breaker at approximately the same time was $7,000 each for two and $6,591 each for the remaining three. The purchaser maintained a stockpile of old destroyers and other vessels for scrapping. The value claimed by the ship-breaker was $46,449.32, based upon an estimate of the net value of the metal which would have been salvaged, but this was disregarded in favor of the fair and reasonable value at the time of the collision, found by the court to be $15,000.

44. The court said, at 85 F. Supp. 812, 1945 AMC 1158–59:

> This contention results from too slavish an application of the rule of damages applicable to lost merchandise and fails to recognize the important distinction between value and profits. Value reflects an object's worth as of a certain past or present date, without regard for what it would or might be worth at a future date in a changed economic situation. This latter element is the profit element (which, when applicable, is only one element in the measure of damages) and has no application when the correct and only element and measure of damages is value at the present or a past date. The fact that the value of an article is more than its initial cost does not amount to an award of profits and the difference cannot be so denominated. This increase results from the owner's skill and perspicacity and from changes in the economic situation. . . .

Inevitably, the parties will resort to experts, whose testimony frequently cannot be reconciled; thus, the result is likely to be a compromise between extremes, as seen in *Carl Sawyer, Inc. v. Poor (The Fire Island)*:[45] ". . . Suffice it to say that upon controverted testimony the Commissioner fixed the value well between the limits of the highest and lowest values in evidence, and that there is substantial evidence to support even a higher value. . . ."

In *United States v. The Bessemer (The Manhattan—The Bessemer)*[46] the problem was the loss of a government dredge that had been sunk in the Delaware River; there was no market for a government dredge, and so the court had to find some substitute and took the cost of reproduction as the preferred method of valuation in the circumstances.

In *Ozanic v. United States (The Petar)*[47] the Second Circuit succinctly stated the problem: "The questions which must be resolved are whether all relevant factors which the law requires to be given effect were duly considered and, if so, whether the evidence adequately supports the finding."[48]

Here, a Yugoslav flag vessel, requisitioned by the flag State for the British service in World War II, had originally cost $171,000 and was 32 years old when sunk by a U.S. tanker in 1942. At the hearing before the commissioner, The *Petar*'s experts valued the vessel at $210,000 (based on a 1942 reproduction cost of $500,000, depreciated at the rate of 2½ percent), whereas the government's experts valued the vessel at $110,000 (based on roughly the same reproduction cost, depreciated at the rate of 5 percent). The commissioner split the difference, allowing $170,000, and his award was confirmed by the district court.[49] The commissioner's reasoned report accepted the *Petar*'s valuation up to a point, but increased the amount of depreciation because the vessel had been requisitioned; its rate of hire was fixed, and the amount of war risk insurance coverage available was lower because of the great submarine danger.

In *American Mail Line v. Skagit River Navigation & Trading Co. (The President Madison)*,[50] the Ninth Circuit listed substitutes for market value thus:

> Failing market value, a court of admiralty may estimate the worth of a lost ship by all relevant evidence, including original cost less depreciation, cost of construction less depreciation, the earnings of the vessel, her condition at the time of loss, her probable life expectancy before she was

45. Supra note 37, 180 F.2d at 963, 1950 AMC at 874.

46. 1935 AMC 227 (ED Pa. 1934 and 1935), aff'd, sub nom. *The Manhattan*, 85 F.2d 427, 1936 AMC 1168 (3d Cir. 1936).

47. Supra note 37.

48. Id., 165 F.2d at 740, 1948 AMC at 342.

49. 68 F. Supp. 296 (SDNY 1946), aff'd, 165 F.2d 738, 1948 AMC 340 (2d Cir. 1948). See also *United States v. Eastern S.S. Lines, Inc. (The George Washington)*, supra note 37, where there was no market because of war and the simple formula applied was reproduction cost less annual depreciation at 5 percent.

50. 91 F.2d 835, 1937 AMC 1375 (9th Cir. 1937).

lost, and prior statements of the owner as to her value, for tax or other purposes.

In this case, the court used as a test of value the term "going concern value." Under this concept, a court may consider evidence of loss of earning power which the owner might suffer, as shown by the unusual capacity of the sunken vessel to earn a net profit and the probability of a long life. The vessel was found to be in first-class condition, with a probable future life of fifteen years or more. The vessel earned about $8,680 annually in an increasing river trade, and the court of appeals found the "going concern" value to be fully justified.

In *Pan American Petroleum and Transport Co. v. Kenneally (The I.C. White—The Blanche C. Pendleton),*[51] the loss of the Schooner *Blanche C. Pendleton* took place during a collapse of the market in the 1922 recession. The vessel had been built two years before at the peak of shipbuilding costs for $155,000. Respondent's experts testified that her market value was $30,000 to $35,000. The owner contended that the vessel was of such peculiar construction that there was no market for her, other than for scrap, and therefore claimed reproduction costs. The court of appeals stated that in the absence of a market, evidence of replacement cost less depreciation might be acceptable, but immediately qualified its statement with this language: ". . . if the evidence showed that it was earning for him a fair return on such value, or, if the fact were otherwise, to an amount which would make good to him the diminution of his earnings. . . ."[52]

In this case the commissioner had allowed the reproduction cost less depreciation ($103,000). The circuit court of appeals rejected that theory and reduced the award to $70,477 (twice the alleged market value), asserting that the district court had erred in using reproduction cost less depreciation alone, placing an unfair burden on the tort-feasor (probably because reproduction costs are likely to be higher than other valuations). Cost of replacement was a factor to be used in evaluating other evidence, but it should not have been given the principal weight, much less should it have been treated as controlling.[53]

In the case of unique vessels built for special purposes, such as cable laying, hydrographic studies, or dredging,[54] it would appear that the "going concern" rule would not be applicable if there was a very narrow, virtually single-use purpose which had ceased to exist. Logically, this could also be argued for naval vessels, although there might be some doubt with respect to service ships such as naval oilers, which could be used in commerce.

---

51. 295 F.593, 1924 AMC 382 (4th Cir. 1924).
52. Id., 295 F. at 595, 1924 AMC at 384.
53. Id., 295 F. at 597, 1924 AMC at 387.
54. See *The City of Alexandria,* 40 F. 697 (SDNY 1889), which concerned an unique dredge to which substantial alterations had been made at great expense over a period of time.

Therefore, reproduction cost less an arbitrary depreciation progressively graduated would be the proper measure for at least most naval vessels.

4. *Constructive Total Loss*

This is essentially a marine insurance concept, but it may be applied even when no marine insurance question is involved. Apart from insurance, a vessel is a constructive total loss when the cost of salvage and repairs would exceed the vessel's market value at the time and place of the collision or other casualty, or when repairs would not be physically practicable or economically feasible.[55] A large ship still afloat might not be considered a constructive total loss if she could be salvaged and repaired so as to be useful, at a cost less than her market value when repaired, although then fit for a different service than the one in which she had been engaged before the casualty. Customary usage is an important factor in constructive total loss analysis. Under the maxim *restitutio in integrum,* an owner of a vessel damaged in collision has a right to have her restored so as to make her fit for her customary use, and not an inferior use. In the English courts the rule is stated in terms of the reasonable owner. Thus, when a vessel is so badly damaged by a collision that a prudent uninsured owner would not repair her, the vessel will be considered a constructive total loss.[56]

In *The Reno,*[57] a thirty-year-old ferryboat had been sunk in the Hudson River at Albany in 12 feet of water. The owners did not arrange a joint survey of the amount of repairs necessary, ordering repairs without obtaining any preliminary bids. The total cost of repairs and raising the wreck was $1,800, whereas the market value for the ferryboat was $600. The Second Circuit stated:

> If she was not a total loss, then the measure of damages is the reasonable expense of raising and repairing her to an extent sufficient to put her in as good condition as she was before the collision. The burden is upon the owner to prove the amount of his loss, either by showing the vessel to have been a total loss, actually or constructively, or by showing the extent and cost of necessary repairs and the incidental expenses.[58]

The Second Circuit modified the decree and reduced the award to $600 plus interest from the time of collision.

In *United States v. The Holland (The Nyland—The E. Kirby Smith—The Holland),*[59] the problem was finding the value, for constructive total loss pur-

---

55. See *O'Brien Bros., Inc. v. The Tug Helen B. Moran,* supra note 37. See also *Hewlett v. The Barge Bertie,* 418 F.2d 654, 1969 AMC 2238 (4th Cir. 1969).
56. See E. Roscoe, *Measure of Damages in Marine Collisions,* supra note 17.
57. 134 F. 555 (2d Cir. 1905).
58. Id., 134 F. at 556.
59. Supra note 37.

poses, of a liberty ship which was no longer used for carriage of cargo, but to store surplus wheat for the Agriculture Department. At the time of the collision this floating silo was being towed down the James River to Norfolk, Virginia, from an anchorage on the James where she had been laid up for 10 years. The government decided not to make repairs, which would have cost approximately $275,000, and sold the vessel for scrap, at a price of $147,000. The other interests contended that the ship was not worth more than the $147,000 scrap value. The government sought the reasonable cost of repairs, arguing that the owner of a vessel declared a constructive total loss should receive the estimated cost of repairs unless that cost would exceed the value of the ship before the collision, without deducting the amount received as scrap value after the collision. The district court rejected this argument and allowed $203,722 damages, based on the diminution in the market value of the vessel on account of the collision, i.e., the value before the collision less the scrap value.[60]

Respecting incidental costs in constructive total loss cases, in *Edwards v. Wilmington Transportation Co. (The Catalina—The Arbutus),*[61] a pleasure yacht had been so extensively damaged that she was declared a constructive total loss. The district court's award was made up of the market value of the yacht ($22,000), plus the cost of salvage ($2,215), the cost of a watchman ($34), the master's salary ($150), storage ($400), and survey fees ($375), less the amount received from the sale of the wreck ($2,100), or a total of $23,074.

5. *Loss of Profitable Use in Total Loss Cases*

Under U.S. law there is no right of recovery for loss of profitable use in total loss cases, in contrast to Rule I(d) of the Lisbon Rules. In an 1897 case, *The Umbria,*[62] the owners of the French *Iberia,* sunk in collision with the British *Umbria* off Long Island, included in their statement of damages a claim for the profits which they would probably have received from a charter party fixed two weeks before the collision. The lower courts rejected the claim, as did the Supreme Court. Justice Brown wrote:

> There is nothing in the peculiar facts of the case to take it out of the general rule that in cases of total loss by collision damages are limited to the value of the vessel, with interest thereon, and the net freight pending at the time of the collision. The probable net profits of a charter may be considered in cases of delay, occasioned by a partial loss [i.e., repairable damage] where the question is as to the value of the use of the vessel pending her repairs. In such cases the net profits of a charter, which she would have performed except for the delay, may be treated as a basis for

60. Id., 164 F. Supp. at 743, 1958 AMC at 1908.
61. 18 F. Supp. 461, 1937 AMC 401 (SD Cal. 1937).
62. Supra note 32.

> estimating the value of her use. . . . But in cases of total loss the probable profits of a charter not yet entered upon, are always rejected.[63]

In this case, there was a market, and so the market value of the lost vessel could be ascertained, but the claimants were seeking lost profits as additional consequential damages. The principle of *The Umbria* has been interpreted and extended by the U.S. Court of Claims[64] to the effect that where there has been a total loss, the plaintiff is not entitled to recover charter hire of a vessel of like capacity for the time required to construct a new vessel, citing *The Umbria.* Furthermore, no detention claim will be allowed where the vessel is a total loss.[65] The English rule is the same.[66] No reported American decision has been found that has distinguished or reinterpreted *The Umbria* by expressly granting consequential damages for lost profits in cases of total loss. However, by applying the "going concern" value test discussed above, a court may in effect be allowing a recovery for lost profits.

6. *Incidental Expenses in Total Loss Cases*

(a) Repatriation of the Crew. The expenses of repatriating the crew after a total loss should be recoverable. However, the present limitation in the case law is that to recover these expenses as damages it must be shown that the law of the ship's flag gives seamen a right to repatriation if their ship is lost.

In *Ozanic v. United States (The Petar),*[67] the claimant repatriated the crew in wartime and introduced evidence of the contract between the owners and the seamen's union, which required repatriation, but there was no evidence of the applicable law of the flag State (Yugoslavia). The Second Circuit would not assume that Yugoslav law required repatriation, and accordingly denied the claim for repatriation expenses.[68]

The 1926 Convention on Repatriation of Seamen,[69] sponsored by the International Labour Organization (ILO), imposes a duty of repatriation on shipowners. It is submitted that the cases decided since 1926 requiring evi-

63. Id., 166 U.S. at 422.

64. *Hubbard v. United States,* 1941 AMC 1483 (Ct. Claims 1941). See also *A&S Transportation Co. v. The Fajardo,* 688 F.2d 1, 1983 AMC 10 (1st Cir. 1982).

65. *The Umbria,* supra note 32. See also *O'Brien Bros. v. The Tug Helen B. Moran,* supra note 37; *The Urbubamba—The Tug Coot,* 171 F. Supp. 735, 1959 AMC 2505 (SDNY 1959); *Etheridge v. The Hellenic Laurel,* 1977 AMC 2453 (SDNY 1977). See Note, *Loss of Use as an Item of Damages in Admiralty Collision Cases,* 12 U. San Francisco L. Rev. 311 (1978).

66. Marsden, supra note 11 at 516. See *The Empress Eugenie,* Lush. 138 (Adm. 1860).

67. Supra note 37.

68. 165 F.2d at 744, 1948 AMC at 347–48.

69. The Convention on the Repatriation of Seamen (ILO Convention No. 23 of June 23, 1926) entered into force on April 16, 1928. It has been ratified by Belgium, Bulgaria, China, Colombia, Cuba, Estonia, France, Germany, Iraq, Ireland, Italy, Liberia, Luxembourg, Mexico, the Netherlands, Nicaragua, Poland, Spain, Uruguay, and Yugoslavia. It was amended in 1946 as to the final articles of the convention by ILO Convention No. 80 and the 1926 text as amended has

dence that the law of the flag mandated repatriation were wrongly decided. A general maritime law duty to repatriate seamen should now be inferred from the adoption of this convention.

In *The Lynn—The Ventura,*[70] a claim of expenses incurred by the owner of a fishing vessel for the recovery of twenty-three bodies of the crew was not contested, and the expenses were allowed as consequential damages. The district court commented that it "would unquestionably have been considered something less than inhuman [*sic*] had [the owners] not made this reasonable expenditure. . . ."[71]

(b) Loss of Personal Effects. In total loss cases, damages for loss of the personal effects of the crew are recoverable from the party or parties at fault.[72]

(c) Wreck Marking and Removal. The marking and removal of wrecks sunk in the navigable waters of the United States are statutory duties.[73] Under the broad policy of the Rivers and Harbors Act,[74] as interpreted by the Supreme Court in *Wyandotte Transport Co. v. United States,*[75] a party negligently causing a sinking may not shift the obligation of wreck removal or payment of damages resulting from collision with the wreck, either to a nonnegligent wreck owner or to the United States. That case noted the possibility of obtaining damages and even injunctive relief against the negligent tort-feasor, in addition to the latter's liability for criminal penalties and civil fines for failure to cause the prompt removal of the wreck,[76] after having marked it immediately after the sinking[77] and keeping it marked until removal. Congress amended the Wreck Act in 1986 to require the owner, without proof of its negligence,

---

been published in 38 U.N.T.S. 315 and as Doc. 9-32 in 6A Benedict. It was revised in 1987 by ILO Convention No. 166 of October 9, 1987, denominated "Revised Convention Concerning the Repatriation of Seafarers," which entered into force on July 3, 1991. An ILO Recommendation on Maritime Personnel not covered by the 1926 Convention was Recommendation No. 27 of June 23, 1926, concerning the Repatriation of Masters and Apprentices.

70. 1957 AMC 716 (D Mass. 1956), aff'd, 242 F.2d 526, 1957 AMC 605 (1st Cir. 1957).

71. Id., 1957 AMC at 717.

72. *New England Maritime Co. v. United States (The Childs—The Mills),* 1934 AMC 1493 (D Mass. 1933), aff'd, 1934 AMC 1511 (1st Cir. 1934).

73. See 33 U.S.C. §§ 409–12, 414–15.

74. 33 U.S.C. §§ 401–65.

75. 389 U.S. 191, 1967 AMC 2553 (1967).

76. 33 U.S.C. § 409 (1995). See *City of New York v. Morania No. 12, Inc.,* 357 F. Supp. 234, 1974 AMC 2155 (SDNY 1973). See also *Nunley v. The Dauntless Colocotronis,* 727 F.2d 455, 1984 AMC 2920 (5th Cir. 1984) (*en banc*), on remand 661 F. Supp. 1096, 1988 AMC 1445 (ED La. 1987), aff'd in part, reversed in part, 863 F.2d 1190, 1993 AMC 1676 (5th Cir. 1989).

77. 33 U.S.C. § 409. See also 33 CFR § 64.01 - 10a and 33 CFR § 245.60. Marking is a nondelegable duty of the owner that the Coast Guard *may* perform (without relieving the owner of responsibility). See 14 U.S.C. § 86 and *Inland Tugs Co. v. Ohio River Company,* 709 F.2d 1065, 1984 AMC 1943 (6th Cir. 1983). Cf. *Lane v. United States,* 529 F.2d 175, 1976 AMC 66 (4th Cir. 1975), holding that the Coast Guard's failure to mark a sunken vessel is an abuse of authority. What constitutes negligence in marking depends on the circumstances of each case. See *Somerset Seafood Co. v. United States,* 193 F.2d 631, 637 1951 AMC 230 (4th Cir. 1951).

to remove the wreck or to reimburse the United States for the cost of wreck removal.[78] Since the statute is concerned with the danger of collision with the wreck, it is not necessary to remove a wreck sunk in water sufficiently deep as to preclude collision.[79]

In *University of Texas v. United States,*[80] the owner of an oceanographic vessel, which negligently collided with a tanker and caused her to collide with and sink a government-owned dredge, was held liable *in personam* for the government's costs of removing the wreck of the dredge from the navigable channel. Tort-feasors are liable for the cost of removing wrecks from privately owned slips and piers,[81] as well as from the navigable waters of the United States.

(d) Salvage. The cost of raising a sunken vessel by salvors—operating either under contract or otherwise—may be part of collision damages. In *Oliver J. Olson & Co. v. The Marine Leopard,*[82] a both-to-blame collision occurred off the coast of California between the coastwise lumber carrier *Howard Olson,* then in ballast, and a steamship, causing the *Olson* to sink in a shallow-water shipping lane. Removal of the wreck as an obstacle to navigation was essential, either by blowing it up or by raising and removing it. The cost of a survey of the wreck to determine the feasibility of salvage and the costs of salvage were held properly included in the collision damages.

(e) Pollution Cleanup Costs and Damages. Under the Oil Pollution Act of 1990 (OPA 90),[83] the owner of a vessel that is the source of an oil spill is a "responsible party" and is strictly liable for cleanup costs and damages of property owners. The statute provides that the strict liability is joint and several. Thus, all vessels involved in a collision are potentially liable,[84] with very limited defenses, i.e., act of God, act of war, and act or omission of a third party. Even these defenses are qualified by requirements of reporting the spill and cooperation with the cleanup authorities.[85] In a collision case, if an oil spill is caused solely by the fault of another vessel, the vessel spilling the oil would

78. Pub. Law No. 99 - 662, Title IX, § 939(a), 100 Stat. 4199, amending 33 U.S.C. § 409.

79. See *Bunge Corp. v. Agri-Transp. Corp.,* 721 F.2d 1005, 1983 AMC 1931 (5th Cir. 1983).

80. 557 F.2d 438, 1977 AMC 2607 (5th Cir. 1977). This is a joint and several obligation with the other colliding vessel. *The Esso Seattle v. The Guam Bear,* 314 F. Supp. 1339, 1970 AMC 1592 (ND Cal. 1970). See also *Nunley v. The Dauntless Colocotronis,* supra note 76.

81. See *O'Brien Bros. Inc. v. The Tug Helen B. Moran,* supra note 37. In *The Barrenfork,* 13 F.2d 72, 1926 AMC 1040 (4th Cir. 1926), an action was brought by the United States against the Virginia Railway for the loss of a government tug that sank at the pier because of the railway employees' careless loading of coal. The Fourth Circuit said that the sunken tug had become an obstacle to navigation. The railway itself had insisted that the tug be removed, and the court therefore approved an award of the expense as "part of the damage proximately caused by its wrong doing."

82. Supra note 37.

83. 33 U.S.C. §§ 2701–61.

84. See chapter 11, supra.

85. 33 U.S.C. § 2703(c).

have a good defense to a claim under OPA 90, in accordance with the "act or omission of a third party" exception to liability. In a both-to-blame case, the colliding vessels would be jointly liable, but one paying more than an amount corresponding to her percentage of blame should be entitled to recover a contribution from the other for her percentage.

Polluting substances other than oil are governed by the 1980 Comprehensive Environmental Response, Compensation and Liability Act (CERCLA or Super Fund Act).[86] That statute also makes responsible parties strictly liable for removal of the spill, physical damage to property, and economic losses. The liability is joint.[87]

Section C. Damages in Partial Loss Cases

1. *Basic Principles*

In legal theory, the measure of damages in partial loss cases is the difference between the value of the damaged vessel immediately before the collision and her value immediately after it.[88] On rare occasions there is no difference, as when a vessel being towed to the breakers for scrapping sustains minor collision damage, which does not affect her seaworthiness for the towage operation and does not result in any appreciable delay. A still rarer example would be superficial cosmetic damage to an old collier, which has no effect on her seaworthiness or her suitability for the carriage of coal, and again does not delay her appreciably. But in the vast majority of cases, there is a diminution in value, great or small, and the diminution is measured by the cost of salvage or towage (if necessary), repairs, expenses incidental to repairs, and detention damages for the time lost to the vessel on account of the collision, particularly for repairs.

Rule II of the Lisbon Rules provides that in partial loss cases the claimant is entitled to recover as damages the cost of temporary repairs reasonably effected, and the reasonable cost of permanent repairs, including any necessary dry-docking, gas-freeing, or tank cleaning, port charges, supervision and classification surveys, and dry-dock dues and/or wharfage for the time occupied in carrying out the repairs. The rule further provides that when collision repairs are carried out in conjunction with owner's work essential to seaworthiness, or with essential repair work arising out of another incident, or are deferred and made during a routine dry-docking, the damages include dry-dock dues, wharfage, and other time-based charges only to the

86. 42 U.S.C. §§ 9601-75.

87. 42 U.S.C. § 9607(a).

88. *Pan American Petroleum & Transport Co. v. United States,* 27 F.2d 684, 1928 AMC 1347 (2d Cir. 1928). See also *New Jersey Shipbuilding & Dredging Co. v. The Salutation,* 37 F.2d 337, 1930 AMC 202 (2d Cir. 1930); *The William E. Ferguson,* 108 F. 984 (2d Cir. 1901).

extent that the period to which those charges relate has been extended on account of the collision repairs.

2. *Unseaworthiness as a Condition Precedent to Recovery for the Cost of Immediate Dry-docking and Repairs*

Because of the high cost of dry-docking a vessel for repairs and the practice of regular dry-docking for classification and safety, the question frequently arises as to whether there is an immediate need for collision repairs because seaworthiness has been affected, or whether collision repairs can be postponed until a regularly scheduled dry-docking. Where seaworthiness is not affected by the collision, repairs of collision damage should be postponed until the vessel's next regularly scheduled dry-docking.[89] The necessity for repairing collision damage immediately will, *ipso facto,* establish the owner's right to recover detention damages sustained during the repair period. When collision damage renders the vessel unseaworthy, the owner may recover dry-docking costs from the tort-feasor, even though owner's repairs are made simultaneously. It has been held that this is so despite the fact that dry-docking for owner's other purposes may have been scheduled for a time in the near future.[90]

If repairs of damage not connected with the collision are necessary in order to put the vessel in a seaworthy condition, a careful apportionment between owner's repairs and collision repairs should be made in the repair bills rendered by the shipyard; apportionment may also be required to determine the detention damages. However, if owner's repairs not connected with the collision are not required to make the vessel seaworthy and do not extend

---

89. See *Eagle Transport Co. v. United States (The San Tirso—The Pocahontas),* 109 F.2d 929, 1940 AMC 351 (2d Cir. 1940), where the collision damage did not render the vessel unseaworthy, and she proceeded to London from the harbor where the vessels collided. En route she encountered severe weather that rendered her unseaworthy and for which dry-docking and permanent repairs were performed at London. The Second Circuit rejected dry-docking claims against the tort-feasor for expenses and detention damages.

See also *Skibs A/S Dalfonn v. The Alabama,* 373 F.2d 101, 1967 AMC 267 (2d Cir. 1967), where the action of the Coast Guard was unclear as to whether immediate dry-docking was necessary. After the January 1958 collision in the Delaware River, a temporary cement patch was installed in the bow and the vessel proceeded to Providence and then to Galveston, where collision repair and owner's work was performed in February 1958, owner's work having been previously scheduled for June 1958. In denying recovery of the dry-docking for collision repairs, the court discussed the problem of unseaworthiness as a condition precedent for immediate dry-docking.

In *Valdesa Cia. Naviera v. Frota Nacional de Petroleiros (The Cape Araxos),* 348 F.2d 33, 1965 AMC 1796 (3d Cir. 1965), a grounding case, the court reduced the repairable damage claim by the amount saved by the postponement of the next regular dry-docking (due in five months). Furthermore, since the dry-docking was not required because of unseaworthiness, the actual cost of dry-docking was reduced by the amount of an average annual dry-docking to reflect the savings to the owner.

90. *Atlantic Refining Co. v. Matson Navigation Co.,* 253 F.2d 777, 1958 AMC 1316 (3d Cir. 1958). Cf. *Moore-McCormack Lines, Inc. v. The Esso Camden,* 244 F.2d 198, 1957 AMC 971 (2d Cir. 1957).

the time required for collision repairs, there need be no apportionment of the total repair period for detention purposes.[91]

3. Surveys

The costs of classification society survey fees and owner's survey fees are clearly recoverable as damages.[92] Underwriters' survey fees, on the other hand, are usually not recoverable,[93] unless there has been no owner's survey and the underwriters' survey is for the purpose of protecting the owner as well as the underwriters, in which case the survey costs will be allowed.[94]

In many cases a principal area of dispute is the apportionment of the costs of collision repairs and owner's repairs. Apportionment is also relevant to some incidental expenses and detention. The solution, as a practical matter, will normally be found in arranging for a joint survey of the collision damage to be conducted by experts appointed by the owners or operators of the colliding vessels. Such a survey should of course be held as soon as possible after the collision. The survey report will itemize the damage found and set forth the surveyors' recommendations concerning repairs.

In *United States v. The Evansville (The Evansville—The Marblehead),*[95] the commissioner, whose report was confirmed by the district court, said that a vessel owner who fails to invite the opposing party to attend a prompt survey of collision damage assumes the heavy burden of justifying all the items claimed.[96] The U.S.S. *Marblehead,* a cruiser, was damaged in collision, and the court said that failure to allow a survey by the tort-feasor had long been condemned as the cause of expense, delay, and trouble, and that there was no reason the rule should not apply to naval vessels as well as to commercial ships.[97] Surveys are usually prepared "without prejudice" to either party. Thus, in *Waldie v. Hudson River Day Line (The Hendrik Hudson—The Scully),*[98] one of the parties treated the amounts estimated in the survey reports as if they were contractual limits on recoveries, but the court held that the survey could not be regarded as an agreement fixing the damages at the amounts specified.

The virtual impossibility of proving at a later time that the cause of a particular item of damage was the collision, rather than some prior or later incident, is readily apparent when the repairs are not made immediately. On the

---

91. *Rederei A/B Soya v. Evergreen Marine Corp.,* 1972 AMC 1555 (ED Va. 1971). See also *Pan American Petroleum & Transport Co. v. United States,* supra Note 88.

92. See Rule II of the Lisbon Rules; *American Steamship Co. v. The Tugs Delaware and Maryland,* 1941 AMC 1417 (WDNY 1941).

93. *The Priscilla,* 55 F.2d 32, 37, 1932 AMC 334, 335 (1st Cir. 1932).

94. *Reliable Transfer Co. v. United States,* 1973 AMC 930 (EDNY 1973), aff'd, 497 F.2d 1036 (2d Cir. 1974), rev'd on other grounds, 421 U.S. 397, 1975 AMC 541 (1975).

95. Id., 1941 AMC 62 (EDNY 1940).

96. Id., at 64–65.

97. Id.

98. 52 F.2d 239, 1931 AMC 1396 (SDNY 1931).

other hand, when the experts for both sides have concurred in finding what physical damage was caused by the collision, and have signed a joint survey report, it will be very difficult for an owner to establish a claim for any item of damage not listed in the report.[99]

4. *Repair Bills*

(a) Repairs Reasonably Required. Because of the common practice of holding joint surveys, the question of the reasonableness of individual items of repair bills will not often be at issue. Owners are expected to be reasonable, so that where repairing a vessel to "brand-new" condition is unreasonable, the owner will be able to recover only the cost of repairs reasonably required to restore the vessel to a serviceable and seaworthy condition, plus compensation for any remaining reduction in the value of the vessel,[100] rather than the cost of repairs made to restore the vessel to a "like-new" condition.[101]

(b) Overtime. In *United States v. The Holland* (a three-way collision),[102] because of overtime work, collision repairs which had originally been estimated to require eighteen working days were completed in eleven working days, thus saving ten days of detention (including Saturdays and Sundays). The court allowed the amount of the repair bill, including overtime, to the extent that the damages were minimized thereby. Since the owners had not obtained the approval of the owners of the other vessels involved to incur the overtime, they could not recover any more than the saving.

In *Cia. Punta Alta v. Dalzell (The Marjory v. Dalzell)*,[103] the commissioner dealt with the question of the good faith and good business practice involved in a claim for double time on Sunday. Since the repairs could have been be-

99. *Pinto v. The Fernwood,* 507 F.2d 1327, 1976 AMC 744 (1st Cir. 1974), where defendants' surveyor did not see damage to the interior of the hull until permanent repairs were made two years after the collision. A denial of the cost of repairs was affirmed.

100. See *Pennsylvania R.R. Co. v. Downer,* 11 F.2d 466, 1926 AMC 772 (2d Cir. 1926); *Atkins v. Alabama Drydock Co.,* 195 F. Supp. 944, 1961 AMC 909 (SD Ala. 1960); *Bleakley Transportation Co. v. Colonial Sand & Stone Co.,* 1956 AMC 1115 (report of Elliott B. Nixon, commissioner, rejecting hypothetical claims), aff'd, 245 F.2d 576, 1957 AMC 1746 (2d Cir. 1957); *United States v. The Tug Holland,* supra note 37. Repairable loss charges are reviewed in *Diesel Tanker Ira S. Bushey, Inc. v. The Tug Bruce A. McAllister (The Ira S. Bushey—The Tug Bruce A. McAllister,* 1995 AMC 806 (SDNY 1994).

Obviously, if repairs increase the value of the vessel beyond her precollision value, the tort-feasor cannot be charged for such costs. Thus, in *Starved Rock Scenic Boat Co. v. La Salle,* 1961 AMC 662 (ND Ill. 1961), recovery of the cost of structural repairs lengthening a vessel by one foot and increasing the carrying capacity by five passengers was denied.

101. *Bleakley Transportation Co. v. Colonial Sand & Stone Co.,* supra note 100; *Zeller Marine Corp. v. Nessa Corp.,* 68 F. Supp. 795, 799, 1947 AMC 43, 47 (SDNY 1946), aff'd, 166 F.2d 32, 1948 AMC 418 (2d Cir. 1948).

102. Supra note 37.

103. 1958 AMC 2016 (SDNY 1957).

gun on a Friday, he disallowed the double time but allowed ordinary overtime.

In *Emile v. The Texas (The Maryland—The Texas),*[104] it was noted that while a shipowner may make its own repairs, it cannot hold the tort-feasor liable for more time than would reasonably have been consumed by more expert workmen at the nearest "reasonably available and efficient shipyard."

5. *Incidental Expenses in Partial Loss Cases*

Where vessel unseaworthiness on account of a collision results in the need for immediate temporary or permanent repairs, recovery will be allowed for underwater inspection,[105] salvage expenses,[106] towage and pilotage to places of repair,[107] owner's and classification surveys,[108] unloading and reloading of cargo,[109] gas-freeing (of tankers),[110] wharfage,[111] watchmen,[112] general average expenses,[113] and contributions in general average.[114]

When immediate repairs are unnecessary, a number of the incidentals will still be recoverable, including underwater inspection, salvage, surveys, and general average contributions. Out-of-pocket expenses for crew wages

104. 1924 AMC 1573 (SD Fla. 1924). See also *Bleakley Transportation Co. v. Colonial Sand & Stone Co.,* supra note 100; *United Overseas Express Lines, Inc. v. Medluck Cia. Naviera,* 785 F.2d 1320 (5th Cir. 1986).

105. See *Rodi v. Dean (The Lady Lu—The Harolmi III),* 138 F.2d 309, 1944 AMC 650 (7th Cir. 1943) (collision of two yachts; damages were confined to repair costs); *Thomson v. United States,* 266 F.2d 852, 1959 AMC 1345 (4th Cir. 1959) (collision of a yacht with the wreck of the U.S.S. *Texas*; damages were confined to salvage, repair costs, and crew wages because of certainty of amounts).

106. *Haden Co. v. Southern Steamship Co. (The City of Houston—The Lola),* 46 F.2d 791, 1931 AMC 601 (5th Cir. 1931); *United States v. Reliable Transfer Co.,* supra note 94.

107. *Crain Bros. v. Dusquesne Slag Co.,* 273 F.2d 948, 1960 AMC 2415 (3d Cir. 1959); *The Oneida,* 84 F. 716 (D W.Va.1898); *Burns Bros. v. Erie R.R. Co.,* 79 F. Supp. 948, 1948 AMC 1161 (EDNY 1948); *The Integrity—The Raritan,* 54 F.2d 978 1932 AMC 108 (2d Cir. 1932), aff'd, 287 U.S. 170, 1932 AMC 1487 (1932); *United States v. Standard Oil Co.(The Clarke's Wharf),* 1960 AMC 2106 (SDNY 1960); *M.L. Gosney v. The Green Island,* 1969 AMC 2121 (ED La. 1969), aff'd, 426 F.2d 260, 1970 AMC 1117 (5th Cir. 1970); *Jones v. Bender Welding Co.,* 581 F.2d 1331, 1979 AMC 1300 (9th Cir. 1979).

108. *New Jersey Shipbuilding & Dredging Co. v. The James McWilliams (The Dredge No. 9),* 40 F.2d 130, 1930 AMC 1055 (2d Cir. 1930).

109. *Cargill, Inc. v. The Tug Frank A. Lowery,* 1955 AMC 572, 1956 AMC 297 (NDNY 1955), aff'd on opinion below, 251 F.2d 845, 1958 AMC 842 (2d Cir. 1958). Cf. *McDonough Marine Service, Inc. v. The Royal Street,* 465 F. Supp. 928, 1982 AMC 2701 (ED La. 1979), where recovery of the cost of removing solidified crude oil from a barge at a cost five times the barge's value was denied.

110. See *Bouchard Transportation Co., Inc. v. The Tug Ocean Prince,* 691 F.2d 609, 1982 AMC 2944 (2d Cir. 1982), reversing the trial court's denial of gas-freeing costs.

111. *The Conqueror,* 166 U.S. 110, 134–35 (1897).

112. Id. See Justice Cardozo's criticism in *Brooklyn Eastern District Terminal v. United States,* 287 U.S. 170, 175, 1932 AMC 1487, 1490 (1932).

113. *Oliver J. Olson & Co. v. The Marine Leopard,* supra note 37; *Cia. Punta Alta v. Danzell,* 162 F. Supp. 926, 1958 AMC 2007 (SDNY 1958).

114. See *Alamo Chemical Transportation Co. v. The Overseas Valdez,* 1979 AMC 2033, 2055.

and consumables during repairs are also recoverable, but may be subject to "skeleton crew" treatment.

6. *Estimated Cost of Repairs of Unrepaired Damage*

There is no requirement that the repair work must actually have been completed before a recovery of damages can be made.[115] As we have seen, in partial-loss cases, the obligation of the tort-feasor is to compensate the owner for the difference between the value of the vessel immediately before the collision and her value immediately after it.[116] Respecting unrepaired damage, there are two different situations. The first is when the repairs will never be made because the vessel is to be sold or not returned to her former service.[117] The second is when the repairs may or may not be made at some future date, at the convenience of the owner.[118] In addition to the estimated repair costs, the plaintiff may seek to recover the estimated dry-docking costs[119] and the estimated detention damages,[120] but the fact that repairs were not immediately necessary and were not in fact made will defeat claims of this type.

Expert testimony backed up by a joint survey report is the most reliable and accurate method of proof of the cost of repairable damage, even though surveys are not conclusive. No special method of determining relevance, competency, and credibility is necessary. However, when the survey findings cannot be backed up by observations of repairs actually made, two factors stand out: the thoroughness with which the joint survey was conducted, and the timing of the survey, which, as we have noted, should be made as soon after a collision as possible. The reputation of the surveyors and the amount of time spent on the survey may be evidence of its thoroughness, while claims of damage unrelated to the collision and the effects of market fluctuations and price changes will be avoided when the survey takes place promptly.

Another consideration where repairs have not been effected is the place where repairs could have been made. The cost of repairs varies significantly because of differences in the cost of labor and materials. In *Horton & Horton v. Bordagain Shipping Co. (The Tug June S—The Bordapian),*[121] plaintiffs offered evidence of the estimated cost of repairs at an American shipyard. Defendant argued that the repair costs should be based on Japanese or Spanish shipyard costs, which were then roughly ⅔ of the American costs. Defendant argued that plaintiffs' recovery must be based on the lowest cost of repairs to avoid

115. *United Overseas Express Lines, Inc. v. Medluck Cia. Naviera,* supra note 104.

116. *Pan American Petroleum & Transport Co. v. United States (The Norman Bridge—The Rapidan),* supra note 88.

117. See id. See also *United Overseas Express Lines, Inc. v. Medluck Cia. Naviera,* supra note 104.

118. *Horton & Horton, Inc. v. Bordagain Shipping Co. (The June S.—The Bordapian),* 418 F.2d 306, 1969 AMC 2113 (5th Cir. 1969).

119. See Marsden 376.

120. See Marsden 377.

121. Supra note 118.

an inequitable windfall. The Fifth Circuit rejected defendant's argument and approved an award based on the estimated cost of repairs at an American yard. The court distinguished cases where the owner had chosen the most expensive of several available yards and also distinguished cases where the repairs were actually effected at a lower cost and the plaintiff sought to recover the higher cost shown in the initial appraisal. Important factors in the determination were that the ship's home port was in the United States and not in Spain or Japan, and that there was no evidence of the vessel frequently voyaging to either Spain or Japan. In dictum, the court said that even if the repairs would be made in the future at a lower cost, the plaintiff was entitled to the repair costs it had been awarded, based on the rationale that permits recovery of the estimated cost of repairs even if no repairs are made.[122]

A formidable problem for an owner may be the tort-feasor's contention that the reason no repairs were made was that they were impracticable and the vessel should be considered a total loss, thereby limiting recovery to the market value of the vessel before collision. In resolving this argument, the court should consider only the circumstances existing at the time of the collision, because the owner's recovery is determined by the estimated cost of repairs immediately following the collision. Events subsequent to the collision that might influence the decision not to repair should not affect the practicability or impracticability of repairing the vessel.[123]

Special problems arise when the owner sells the vessel in unrepaired condition. The question then is whether there was a diminution in price because of the unrepaired collision damage. The answer will depend upon when the sale price was fixed. In *Detroit & Cleveland Navigation Co. v. The Elbert H. Gary*,[124] plaintiff's dock was damaged in an allision and was later purchased, unrepaired, by the City of Detroit. Prior to the allision the city had sought to take the dock by eminent domain; the price set by the city was challenged and an appeal was pending at the time of the allision. The original condemnation price was subsequently affirmed. Plaintiff's collision damage action against the tort-feasor was dismissed because plaintiff had suffered no loss; it was therefore not entitled to the estimated cost of repairs, since the condemnation price accurately reflected the market value of the dock prior to collision.

By contrast, however, in a Ninth Circuit case,[125] plaintiff (the United States) was awarded estimated repair costs, although the vessel was later sold unrepaired at a price fixed by a statute enacted after the collision, which did

122. Id., 418 F.2d at 307, 1969 AMC at 2114. See also *China Union Lines, Ltd. v. States Steamship Co. (The Illinois—The Union Star)*, 378 F.2d 356, 1967 AMC 1725 (9th Cir. 1967), involving a subsidized vessel.

123. Id.

124. 161 F. Supp. 570, 1958 AMC 2112 (ED Mich. 1958). See also *The L-1—The Philadelphia*, 10 F. Supp. 43, 1935 AMC 250 (ED Pa. 1935) (vessel scrapped).

125. *Shipowners & Merchants Tugboat Co. v. United States*, 205 F.2d 352, 1953 AMC 1978 (9th Cir. 1953), affirming 103 F. Supp. 152, 1952 AMC 483 (ND Cal. 1952). In *M. & J. Tracy, Inc. v. The*

not take the collision damage into account. Defendant argued that the United States had suffered no harm since the full statutory price was paid. The district court found that the statutory price was irrelevant, and that plaintiff was entitled to the decrease in value immediately following the collision. In affirming, the Ninth Circuit pointed out that the government could just as easily have sued before enactment of the statutory sales law, in which case it would have been entitled to recover the estimated repair costs.[126]

Section D. Detention Damages in Repairable Damage Cases

1. *General Observations*

Damages for loss of use are usually called "detention" and sometimes loosely referred to as "demurrage," although that term is actually contractual and not delictual. In clear distinction from a total loss situation, where damages for loss of use are not allowed,[127] detention damages are recoverable in partial loss cases, but the amount of recovery will be affected by a number of factors that reflect the owner's business operations.

A dictum in *The Umbria* contrasted the repairable loss situation: "The probable net profits of a charter may be considered in cases of delay occasioned by a partial loss where the question is as to the *value of the use* of the vessel pending her repairs."[128] (Emphasis added.) In dictum in *The Conqueror,*[129] a case involving a yacht seized by the customs authorities, the court discussed the rules for computing loss of use damages in collision cases as an analogy to the loss of use problem in the case of a wrongful seizure of a vessel. Justice Brown wrote:

> That the loss of profits or of the use of a vessel pending repairs, or other detention, arising from a collision or other maritime tort, and commonly spoken of as "demurrage" is a proper element of damage, is too well settled both in England and America to be open to question. It is equally well settled, however, that demurrage will only be allowed when *profits* have actually been, or may be reasonably supposed to have been lost, and the *amount of such profits* is proven with reasonable certainty. . . . The best evidence of damage suffered by detention is the sum for which

B.F. Guinan, 40 F.2d 277, 1930 AMC 219 (EDNY 1930), the coal boat *Cape Franklin* was damaged by the barge *B.F. Guinan* in April 1924 and temporary repairs were then made. Permanent repairs had not been made by the time of the trial on damages in 1930, although the vessel had continued to trade. The 1924 survey amount ($1,214) was accepted as proper, rather than the tort-feasor's 1930 estimate of $880, which had been approved by the commissioner.

126. Id., 105 F.2d at 352.

127. *The Umbria,* supra note 32.

128. Id., 166 U.S. at 421.

129. Supra note 111, 166 U.S. at 110.

vessels of the same size and class can be chartered in the market. Obviously, however, this criterion cannot be often applied, as it is only in the larger ports that there can be said to be a market price for the use of vessels. . . . In the absence of such market value, the value of her use to her owner in the business in which she was engaged at the time of the collision is a proper basis for estimating damages for detention, and the books of the owner, showing her earnings about the time of her collision, are competent evidence of her probable earnings during the time of her detention. . . . The mere opinions of witnesses, unfortified by any data, as to what the earnings would probably have been, are usually regarded as too uncertain and conjectural to form a proper basis for estimation, though in a few cases they seem to have been received. . . .[130] (Emphasis added.)

A question arises about the terms "profits," as used in *The Conqueror,* and "value of use," as used in *The Umbria:* whether "profits" is an intentional limitation on the right to recover damages, or whether it is merely illustrative of an easy example of the value of use. In any event, there has been much dispute in cases of vessels of peculiar usage, public vessels, and pleasure vessels that are not clearly engaged in the carriage of passengers and cargo for profit. In view of the truly unique circumstances of *The Conqueror,* and in view of the Lisbon Rules, it is suggested that the commercial profit criterion of that decision is outmoded.

Generally, shipowners can clearly recover damages for loss of use when there has been a loss of profits, proven with substantial certainty.[131] This does not always mean that the shipowner must show that it has lost charter hire under a breakdown clause or its equivalent. As in other branches of tort law, the courts are hesitant to accept proof of loss of profits because of the highly speculative nature of the testimony offered and suspicions of the partiality and veracity of witnesses; accordingly, the reasonable certainty of the proof is always a necessary element of a detention claim.

When dealing with vessels operated for a commercial purpose, it is first necessary to consider whether the collision damage has rendered the vessel unseaworthy so that immediate repairs are necessary, with the attendant loss of profitable employment, or whether the repairs can be made at a time when the vessel is regularly scheduled to undergo dry-docking, overhaul, and owner's repairs, if any.[132] If repairs are not immediately necessary to restore

130. Id., 166 U.S. at 125–27. See also *The Ames & Carroll No. 20,* 66 F.2d 413, 1933 AMC 1320 (2d Cir. 1933).

131. *Moore McCormack Lines v. The Esso Camden,* 244 F.2d 198, 1957 AMC 971 (2d Cir. 1957); *Skibs A/S Gylfe v. The Trujllo,* 209 F.2d 386, 387–88, 1954 AMC 233 (2d Cir. 1954). Circumstantial proof is not thereby excluded. *The North Star,* 151 F. 168, 175 (2d Cir. 1907). Cf. *Bolivar County Gravel Co. v. Thomas Marine Co.,* 585 F.2d 1306, 1979 AMC 1806 (5th Cir. 1978).

132. *Skibs A/S Dalfonn v. The Alabama,* supra note 89. See also *Hellenic Lines, Ltd. v. Sinclair Refining Co.,* 206 F. Supp. 383, 1966 AMC 326 (ED Va. 1962).

seaworthiness, and the collision repairs can be deferred to the next regularly scheduled overhaul, there can be no detention damages because the vessel will be out of service in the ordinary course of business. If, however, the collision repairs during the regular overhaul extend the repair period beyond the time needed for owner's work, then the owner may recover detention damages for the time lost on account of the extension.[133]

In *The Potomac,*[134] involving a collision between two steamboats on the Mississippi River, the libellant's vessel, the *Robert E. Lee,* was a passenger and cargo carrying vessel making weekly trips between New Orleans and Vicksburg, Mississippi. During the repair period the *Robert E. Lee* missed three trips. Libellant claimed that the proper way to measure the loss was to compute the average profits for six and a half months before the collision and allocate an amount based on that average to the three missed trips, which was the method followed by the commissioner. The court approved, but stated the following as the general principle:

> In order to make full compensation and indemnity for what has been lost by the collision, *restitutio in integrum,* the owners of the injured vessel are entitled to recover for the loss of her use, while laid up for repairs. When there is a market price for such use, that price is the test of the sum to be recovered. When there is no market price, evidence of the profits that she would have earned if not disabled is competent.[135]

2. *Vessels under Time Charter*

The clearest case of detention or loss of use occurs when a vessel under time charter goes "off hire" because of collision damage repairs, pursuant to an "off hire" or "breakdown" clause in the charter, such as clause 17 of the 1993 New York Produce Exchange Form[136] and clause 11 of the Baltic and International Maritime Conference ("Baltime") Form.[137]

---

133. Cia. *Pelineon de Navegacion, S.A. v. Texas Petroleum Co.,* 540 F.2d 53, 56, 1976 AMC 1245 (2d Cir. 1976); *Demetrius Maritime Co., Ltd. v. The Connecticut,* 463 F. Supp. 1108 (SDNY 1979); *Pan American Petroleum & Transport Co. v. United States (The Norman Bridge—The Rapidan),* supra note 88; *Bouchard Transportation Co., Inc. v. The Tug Ocean Prince,* supra note 110.

134. 105 U.S. 630 (1881).

135. Id.

136. Text of clause 17:

> "Off Hire." In the event of loss of time from deficiency and/or default and/or strike of officers or crew, or deficiency of stores, fire, breakdown of, or damages to hull, machinery or equipment, grounding, detention by arrest of the Vessel, (unless such arrest is caused by events for which the charterers, their servants, agents or subcontractors are responsible), or detention by average accidents to the Vessel or cargo unless resulting from inherent vice, quality or defect of the cargo, drydocking for the purpose of examination or painting bottom, or by any other similar cause preventing the full working of the Vessel, the payment of hire and overtime, if any, shall cease for the time thereby lost. . . .

137. Text of clause 11:

Courts have readily concluded that the fact that the time charter was being performed at the time of the collision establishes the regular employment of the vessel and the amount that would have been earned but for the collision.[138] The exact amount of hire lost must be computed by deducting any savings effected during the off-hire period.[139]

3. *Vessels Operating for Owner's Account*

The clear cases do not produce litigation, but a number of questions have arisen based on the size and character of the vessel owner's fleet and any parent-subsidiary relationship between owner and charterer. In order to escape the consequences of a profitable high-rate charter, tort-feasors may argue that an available (and cheaper) "spare boat" could have been used, or that a substitute vessel might have been chartered for the detention period at the same or a lower rate than that being paid for the use of the damaged vessel. These arguments may be advanced under the doctrine of avoidable consequences or the duty of the victim to mitigate (or minimize) the damages.[140] There are few maritime cases involving these concepts, but it may be that in the future courts will impose these principles of tort law.

Common carriers operating a liner service may have problems in proving detention claims, especially in volatile markets where freight rates may accelerate or decelerate rapidly. Because of conference agreements and the need to file tariffs with the Federal Maritime Commission to ensure immunity from antitrust action (as of 1997), it is not possible for these owners to respond to market developments quickly. However, vessel owners who make their ships available for the tramp trade under voyage charters are more directly at the mercy of market forces, and market volatility may even require that the vessel be laid up temporarily rather than be chartered at a loss or a minimal profit. These owners are permitted to prove expectable losses with

---

Suspension of Hire etc.

> (a) In the event of drydocking or other necessary measures to maintain the efficiency of the Vessel, deficiency of men or Owners' stores, breakdown of machinery, damage to hull or other accident, either hindering or preventing the working of the Vessel and continuing for more than twenty-four consecutive hours, no hire to be paid in respect of any time lost thereby during the period in which the Vessel is unable to perform the service immediately required. Any hire paid in advance to be adjusted accordingly.

138. *Moore McCormack Lines, Inc. v. The Esso Camden,* supra note 131. See also *Cia. Pelineon de Navegacion, S.A. v. Texas Petroleum Co.,* supra note 133, where an option to extend the charter was exercised; *Skou v. United States,* 478 F.2d 343 (5th Cir. 1973) (a detention award was reversed where the vessel interests received full hire during a repair period).

139. E.g., crew wages saved will be deducted from charter hire lost. *The Brand,* 224 F. 321 (3d Cir. 1915).

140. See *Ellerman Lines, Ltd. v. The President Harding,* 288 F.2d 288, 1961 AMC 2137 (2d Cir. 1961), where reasonableness of unloading cargo was challenged; *Southport Transit Co. v. Avondale Marine Ways,* 234 F.2d 947, 1956 AMC 1498 (5th Cir. 1956).

reasonable certainty by circumstantial evidence.[141] There is no requirement that the owner prove that specific cargoes were not carried or that available voyage charters were not fixed because of the collision damage.[142]

(a) Substitute Vessels. In the case of a liner service, where the vessel owner is committed to operating on a fixed weekly or monthly schedule, the cost of hiring a substitute vessel for the period of repairs is regularly allowed.[143] It should be noted that it is the cost of hiring a vessel that may be introduced in evidence; there is no requirement that a substitute vessel be actually chartered and put in service during the detention period.[144] However, purely hypothetical evidence of the probable cost of hiring a substitute vessel is unacceptable.[145]

(b) "Spare Boats." A special situation occurs where the shipowner also carries its own products in its own fleet of vessels, maintaining one or more vessels at all times for use in emergencies. This gives rise to the "spare boat" problem, where another vessel (or spare boat) of the owner's fleet is used instead of chartering a replacement. Tort-feasors argue there has been no loss, but in these cases what it would have cost to hire a substitute vessel may be proved, although a spare boat was in fact used, and the spare boat would not have been otherwise employed during the detention period.[146]

---

141. See generally *Williamson v. Barrett,* 54 U.S. 100 (1851); *Standard Oil Co. v. Glendola S.S. Corp., (The Glendola),* 47 F.2d 206, 1931 AMC 302 (2d Cir. 1931), where the vessel owner was a large oil company with a constant demand for oil shipments. During the actual detention period the company rearranged the schedules of its other vessels to move the cargoes that the damaged vessel would have moved. Despite the rearranged schedules, not all of the cargoes could be carried. A backlog accumulated and it was necessary to hire a substitute vessel. The fact that the chartered vessel entered the service of the owner of the damaged vessel after completion of the detention period did not affect its status as a substitute vessel. See also *Sinclair Refining Co. v. The American Sun,* 188 F.2d 64, 67, 1951 AMC 845 (2d Cir. 1951), where the cost of a substitute vessel was permitted even though other reasonable means of moving the oil cargoes—such as a pipeline and railroad tank cars—were in fact used to handle the backlog.

142. *Slater v. Texaco, Inc.,* 506 F. Supp. 1099, 1113 (D Del. 1981); *Midland S.S. Line, Inc. v. City of Chicago,* 1964 AMC 1393 (ND Ill. 1963).

143. *Standard Oil Co. v. Glendola S.S. Corp. (The Glendola),* supra note 141; *Sinclair Refining Co. v. The American Sun,* supra note 141; *Pocahontas S.S. Co. v. The Detroiter,* 1948 AMC 349 (SDNY 1947).

144. See *Moore—McCormack Lines Inc. v. The Esso Camden,* supra note 131; *Skibs A/S Gylfe v. The Trujillo,* supra note 131; *Slater v. Texaco,* supra note 142; and *The Carolinian—The San Clemente,* 1943 AMC 758, 770 (ND Cal. 1943).

145. In *The North Star,* supra note 131, where the owner of several Great Lakes ships declined cargoes for a ship damaged in a collision, detention damages were denied despite these cargo proffers, because with the approach of winter, the Great Lakes sailing season was drawing to a close and the owner had already laid up his other ships. See also *Inland Oil & Transport Co. v. Ark-White Towing Co.,* 696 F.2d 321 (5th Cir. 1983).

146. The "spare boat" argument was advanced in two cases involving New York Harbor ferries: *The Cayuga,* 81 U.S. 278 (1871); and *The Favorita,* 85 U.S. 598 (1873). In both cases the fact that the ferry operator used a spare boat did not diminish the detention damages. In *The Emma Kate Ross,* 50 F. 845 (3d Cir. 1892), an excursion steamer required 21 days of repair. She had

The multinational oil companies' problems were described in *Sinclair Refining Co. v. The American Sun.*[147] In the forty-six years since that case was decided, there have been changes in the companies' business methods such that the production, transportation, and distribution functions are now usually distributed among subsidiary corporations, often of several different countries.[148] These changes are discussed in the lengthy opinions in *The Amoco Cadiz.*[149]

(c) The Three-Voyage Rule. In the absence of clear proof of profits earned by identical vessels on the same routes at the same time, it will be necessary to utilize a number of alternative methods to calculate damages for loss of use sustained by owners who operate vessels on their own account. The three-voyage rule considers the profits earned on the voyage immediately before the collision and the voyage immediately after it, and the profits that would have been earned on the collision voyage if the collision had not occurred. Revenue that would have been produced on the three voyages is then adjusted by deducting ordinary operating expenses and adding "out of pocket" expenses made necessary by the period of dry-docking and repairs, producing the "average daily earnings" by which the number of detention days will be multiplied.

Regular employment is a preliminary requirement for the three-voyage rule, a circumstance that may make recovery of detention damages difficult for vessels going back into service after a period of layup. Even proof of available cargoes and charters will not be enough if the owner cannot prove a willingness to have seized the opportunities had the collision not occurred.

Moore McCormack Lines, Inc. v. The Esso Camden[150] illustrates the three-voyage rule in fixing detention damages. The case involved a mutual fault collision in Chesapeake Bay between an Esso tanker and a Moore McCormack Line vessel, the *Halsted,* which was just beginning a regularly scheduled voyage to Baltic Sea ports. The *Halsted* underwent immediate collision repairs for seventeen days and then resumed her interrupted Baltic voyage. On

---

been chartered for 20 of the 21 days. The owner hired a substitute for eight of the 21 days and used a spare boat for the other 13. The owner sought detention damages based on the charter hire of the substitute. The Third Circuit affirmed, but on the theory that owner's detention damages for eight days consisted of the charter hire of the substitute ($110 per day), and then compensated him for the use of his spare boat at the same rate.

In *Brooklyn Eastern District Terminal v. United States,* 287 U.S. 170, 1932 AMC 1487 (1932), the spare boat was maintained for emergencies and was in fact used to deal with the cargoes that would have been carried during the detention of the damaged vessel. The owner was permitted to recover the market rate of hiring a similar vessel or the cost of maintaining the spare boat during the repairs. See also *United States v. The John R. Williams,* 144 F.2d 451, 1944 AMC 1061 (2d Cir. 1944).

147. Supra note 141.

148. Id.

149. *In re Oil Spill by Amoco Cadiz, off the Coast of France on March 16, 1978,* 491 F. Supp. 170, 1980 AMC 143 (ND Ill. 1979), aff'd, 699 F.2d 909, 1983 AMC 1633 (7th Cir. 1983).

150. Supra note 90.

returning from it, however, it was too late in the season for another Baltic voyage, and so the vessel was diverted to the South American service. The district court approved the commissioner's report, which showed that the libellant had proved a precollision Baltic voyage of 59 days, the collision Baltic voyage of 78 days, and the postcollision South American voyage of 104 days. The court of appeals affirmed the use of the three-voyage, 241-day period to arrive at the average daily earnings, despite libellant's argument that it was unfair to include the postcollision South American voyage, on which the profit was less than half ($42,978) that of the collision voyage ($95,710).

The three-voyage rule is not applied mechanically; rather, courts consider the proof which most accurately reflects the lost earnings.[151] In *Skibs A/S Gylfe—The Trujillo,*[152] the three-voyage rule was not applied because the postcollision charter market was declining rapidly. At the time of the collision, the owner was negotiating a charter that was never fixed because of the collision, but the court accepted an estimate of what the average daily net profit would have been under the proposed charter, since that figure was very close to the average daily net profit on the collision voyage and the postcollision voyage.

In contrast, in *Cie. Maritime Normande v. United States, (The Quevilly—The Sampson),*[153] the precollision voyage was excluded from consideration because the charter rate for that voyage was greatly below that for the collision voyage and the postcollision voyage rates, which were subject to the rapid inflation resulting from commencement of the First World War.

In *United States v. Standard Oil Co. (The Clarke's Wharf),*[154] involving a collision on a ballast voyage, the court used ten voyages, as stipulated by the parties—five before the collision and five after the collision—to arrive at the average daily profit. The problem for the court was the method of arriving at the average net earnings. Libellant's method was to compute the net earnings for each voyage, total them, and divide the total by ten to arrive at an average daily profit. Under libellant's method the detention damages would have been $20,329. Respondent, however, contended that the gross earnings for the ten voyages should be added together before deducting the total expenses for those voyages to produce the net earnings for the total number of days taken to perform the voyages, from which the number of days taken for the collision repairs should be deducted, to arrive at the average daily net earnings. Under respondent's method the detention damages would have been $16,503. The commissioner followed respondent's method, by analogy to the language of Judge Lumbard in *Moore McCormack Lines, Inc. v. The Esso*

151. See *Pocahontas S.S. Co. v. The Detroiter,* supra note 143, where the War Shipping Administration had authorized higher maximum freight rates just before the collision. The postcollision voyage, at a rate close to the authorized maximum, was found to be more nearly representative of the value of the use of the vessel during the detention period.

152. Supra note 131.

153. 1938 AMC 347 (SDNY 1938).

154. 1960 AMC 2106 (SDNY 1960).

Camden, taking "the average daily earnings over the entire period of the three voyages in evidence."[155]

(d) Naval and Coast Guard Vessels: Skeleton Crews. In these situations, we confront the problem as to whether detention compensates for lost profits or provable losses. Very often the owner has no commercial, profit-making intention, yet some courts have imposed the standards of commercial operations as a limitation on recoveries. Thus, in *The Chicago—The Silverpalm,* the commissioner said: "Palpably, a government vessel, such as the U.S.S. *Chicago* [a cruiser], is engaged in activity that is, commercially speaking, purely of an infructuous nature. There are no lost profits involved."[156]

Recent American cases have not ruled authoritatively on the question, but the U.S. Navy usually does not make ordinary detention claims. Instead, it claims out-of-pocket expenses during the repair period in place of detention damages. English jurisprudence, however, provides a useful guide for claims of this kind. In *The Astrakhan,*[157] a British merchant vessel collided with a Danish warship. The defendant opposed the detention claim on the ground that as there was no war during the repair period, there had been no loss of use. The vessel had been scheduled to be laid up during part of the repair period. The court rejected defendant's argument and apportioned the claim, noting that the King of Denmark was entitled to use his vessel for any purpose: aggressive, defensive, or merely ceremonial.

In *Admiralty Commissioners v. The Chekiang,*[158] the light cruiser HMS *Cairo* collided with a merchant vessel just prior to the time for the warship's annual overhaul, when both collision repairs and annual refitting were carried out simultaneously. An apportioned detention claim was approved. A usable lifetime of twenty years was assumed and 5 percent per annum interest on the capital value of the vessel was allowed. The thirty-six days in the repair yard were apportioned—twenty days for collision repairs and sixteen days for annual overhaul. An award for the pay and allowances of the officers and crew was also approved.

The House of Lords dealt with another naval case, *The Susquehanna,*[159] at the same time. In that case the admiralty claimed detention for the collision damage repair period of a naval tanker, the *Prestol,* based on the going rate for the charter of a similar vessel. The Lords rejected this proof, as the admiralty would not have put the tanker out on the charter market. They held that the proof must closely reflect the use which the admiralty would have made of

155. 244 F.2d 198 at 201, 1957 AMC 971 at 974 (2d Cir. 1957).

156. 1937 AMC 498 (ND Cal. 1937), aff'd, 94 F.2d 754, 1937 AMC 1427 (9th Cir. 1937). In *The A.A. Raven,* 231 F. 380 (3d Cir. 1916), the U.S. Navy had not even claimed detention damages before the commissioner. The Navy raised the question on appeal, but the Third Circuit refused to consider the issue, as it was not raised below.

157. [1910] A.C. 172 (H.L.).

158. [1926] A.C. 637 (H.L.).

159. [1926] A.C. 655 (H.L.).

the tanker if there had been no collision: the admiralty might prove the loss of use of the capital value of the vessel during repairs, even though other admiralty tankers were rescheduled to take the place of the *Prestol.*

As noted above, the U.S. Navy claims for its actual costs in lieu of ordinary detention damages during a period of shipyard collision repairs. These include consumable supplies and the wages and subsistence of the officers and crew. Expenditures for fuel and stores have not been a problem, but crew wages and subsistence have been a contested issue. The argument is made that it is unfair to require the tort-feasor to pay for the wages and subsistence of a full crew during repairs.

In *The A.A. Raven,*[160] repairs to a government dredge occupied forty days, although the government agreed to a reduction to twenty-one days as the reasonable time for repairs. The ship's entire complement of fifty-eight remained on board during the repairs, but the commissioner awarded only the cost of a skeleton crew of ten for the twenty-one day period. On appeal, the court allowed the wages of the entire crew for the twenty-one day period because it was a prudent business decision to keep a highly skilled crew together rather than risk the loss of their expertise if they were dispersed. Following the prudent business decision rationale of *The A.A. Raven,* the court in *The Nantasket*[161] refused to allow the cost of crew wages where repairs were never in fact made and the crew was not specially selected and trained.

In *The Commonwealth,*[162] a collision involving the U.S.S. *New Hampshire,* a battleship, required three days of temporary repairs and ninety days of permanent repairs. The vessel's full complement consisted of 11 officers and 232 enlisted men. The commissioner allowed the cost of the entire complement during temporary repairs but cut the allowance for wages to 8 officers and 62 enlisted men for permanent repairs, the repair period having been described as an excellent opportunity for training. Dry-docking expenses were denied because no other government dry dock was occupied during the period.

In *The Chicago—The Silverpalm,*[163] the full complement of the cruiser *Chicago* was 45 officers and 495 enlisted men. The commissioner allowed the wages of a skeleton crew of 17 officers and 261 enlisted men during the five-month repair period. The explanation was that there must be a skeleton crew large enough to maintain the ship in as good condition, exclusive of the collision damage, as she was in on arrival at the shipyard. The commissioner rejected the defendant's contention that the Navy should have removed all of the regular crew or retained merely a minimum number as watchmen, but he also rejected the Navy's contention that it was entitled to recover the cost of maintaining the ship at all times as a fighting unit with a full complement.

160. Supra note 156.
161. 290 F. 813 (1st Cir. 1923).
162. 297 F. 651 (1st Cir. 1923).
163. Supra note 156.

In fact, the complement of naval vessels is not ordinarily reduced during shipyard repairs, although the period may be used for crew leaves and school periods.

In *The Evansville—The Marblehead*[164] the full complement of the cruiser *Marblehead* was 33 officers and 435 enlisted men. The commissioner allowed the wages of a skeleton crew of 5 officers and 90 enlisted men during the fifty-day repair period, while in *The Delmarva—The U.S.S. LST 389,*[165] the naval vessel was not assigned to the fleet for operations, but was used only for training. Since the repair period was only eight days, the commissioner allowed the wages of the usual permanent group of 7 officers and 54 enlisted men. Lastly, in *The Hawaiian—The Larchgrove,*[166] a requisitioned merchant vessel required eleven and a half days for temporary repairs and four months for permanent repairs. The commissioner allowed the full navy crew during temporary repairs but only a skeleton crew during permanent repairs.

(e) Fishing Vessels. In former times, fishing vessels with small crews operated on "lays," or shares of the profits of the voyage,[167] while modern fishing vessels and fishing "factories" usually hire crews on wages. The share system raised the issue of lost catches, and speculative evidence was usually involved in these cases. Despite early misgivings, English courts have accepted evidence of the actual catches of other vessels fishing in the same area at the same time as the damaged vessel.[168]

Mistrust of the proferred evidence led American courts to confine the inquiry to the collision voyage itself[169] or to the precollision and collision voyages, excluding evidence of postcollision earnings.[170] Even evidence of earnings of other vessels at the time of the collision voyage has been rejected[171] or subjected to intense and searching criticism.[172] More recently, some courts

164. 1941 AMC 62 (EDNY (1941).

165. 1945 AMC 1332 (ED Va. 1945).

166. 1935 AMC 809 (SDNY 1933).

167. See *Carbone v. Ursich,* 209 F.2d 178, 1954 AMC 169 (9th Cir. 1953). Cf. *The Clipper—The Eunice Lillian,* 194 F. Supp. 827, 1961 AMC 1530 (D Mass. 1961); *The California—The Curlew,* 105 F. Supp. 428, 1952 AMC 508 (D Mass. 1952).

168. See Marsden 362–63, 390.

169. The ideal proof was provided in *The Fannie F. Hickey,* 1931 AMC 794 (D Mass. 1931), where the collision occurred at the fishing grounds. The vessel had already been fishing there for one and a half days and had had a good catch. Cf. *The Aurora—The Karankawa,* 64 F. Supp. 502, 1945 AMC 235 (ED La. 1945), aff'd, 153 F.2d 224, 1946 AMC 506 (5th Cir. 1946), where loss of use was allowed but evidence of loss of earnings on the collision voyage was denied because of a lengthy period of squally weather.

170. In *Atchison, Topeka & Santa Fe R.R. v. California Sea Products Co. (The Lansing),* 51 F.2d 466, 1931 AMC 1470 (9th Cir. 1931), the whaler was delayed in reaching the whaling ground by the collision. Evidence of kills by other whaling vessels after the collision was rejected, largely because it was a new and untried whaling ground and the only evidence was the number of whales subsequently caught.

171. *The Menominee,* 125 F. 530 (EDNY 1903).

172. *The Aurora—The Karankawa,* supra note 169.

have accepted evidence that all participants had had a successful season during the time of the collision voyage.[173]

In *Nicodemisen v. The Dartmouth,*[174] Judge Aldrich said he would accept either proof of net profits plus all expenses not saved, or gross profits less expenses saved, having reasoned that either method should reach the same result.

(f) Pleasure Craft. Owners of vessels maintained entirely for purposes of personal pleasure are usually denied detention damages on the authority of *The Conqueror.*[175] In the view of Justice Brown, "...there must be a loss of profits in a commercial sense."[176] In this noncollision case, the Collector of Customs at New York seized Frederick Vanderbilt's English-built motor yacht for nonpayment of duty. The vessel had been purchased in England for $75,000 in 1891 and entered in the Royal Mersey Yacht Club of Liverpool in order to fly the British flag, while at the same time her owner claimed the benefits of U.S. citizen ownership. Mr. Vanderbilt eventually won his argument with the collector in the lower court, and the yacht was released from seizure. He then sought to collect detention damages for the period of 161 days the yacht was under the control of the collector. The collector's control, however, was limited to the presence of one watchman, while Mr. Vanderbilt's crew remained on board during the thirty-three-day period the vessel was anchored in the stream off Stapleton Anchorage until moved to a berth in Erie Basin, at which time the crew was reduced to five. The district court awarded $15,000 detention damages and $6,742 expenses, sums that shocked the conscience of the Supreme Court, which reversed and remanded.[177]

Justice Brown was very skeptical of plaintiff's friendly witnesses—three yacht brokers who testified that the hire for such a vessel during the detention period would have been $15,000, over and above expenses. Noting that the testimony was given "without practical illustrations," he rejected not only the evidence but the claim for detention, since there was not an iota of testimony that the owner would ever have chartered to others the vessel that he had bought for his personal pleasure. Thus, the *Conqueror* would never be engaged in commercial pursuits.[178] Further, the Court took judicial notice that the yachting season in northern waters was almost over at the time of the seizure. There was no evidence of a potential tropical cruise, and merely the suggestion that the owner might have desired to use the vessel on a winter cruise, a contingency too remote to justify any detention damages. The

173. *Eastes v. Superior Oil Co.,* 65 F. Supp. 998, 1946 AMC 1398 (WD La. 1946), aff'd, 160 F. 2d 189, 1947 AMC 1742 (5th Cir. 1947).

174. 158 F. Supp. 417, 1958 AMC 2134 (D Mass. 1958).

175. Supra note 111.

176. Id., 166 U.S. at 125.

177. Id., 166 U.S. at 133.

178. Id., 166 U.S. at 134.

Court did allow out-of-pocket expenses of the owner for wages and consumables of the entire crew at the exposed anchorage (for 33 days) and the wages and consumables of a skeleton crew in berth (for 128 days).[179]

Considering all the circumstances surrounding this unusual case, it is submitted that it does not stand for a general rule that detention damages should be denied whenever a vessel does not earn commercial profits, even though that has been its precedential result.[180] Today it is unlikely that large pleasure craft would not be used at least some of the time for business conferences and business entertainment, and so there is no longer a need to preserve the *Conqueror*'s dislike of conspicuous consumption by denial of detention damages.

4. *Detention Claims of Time or Voyage Charterers*

The leading case on this subject is still *Robins Dry Dock & Repair Co. v. Flint,*[181] not a collision case, which holds that a time charterer cannot recover from the tort-feasor for loss of use caused by the tort-feasor's negligence during dry-docking and repair of the time-chartered vessel. The time charter of the S.S. *Bjornefjord* contained clauses requiring dry-docking every six months and providing for cessation of hire during the dry-docking periods. According to schedule, the ship entered defendant's dry dock on August 1, 1917, but the ship's propeller was so badly damaged during the maneuver that a new propeller had to be fitted and the period in dry-docking was extended to August 15, resulting in the charterer being unable to employ the vessel at the high wartime rates for two weeks. The dry dock owner contended it had no knowledge of the existence of the charter until August 10. Owners settled their claim with the dry dock. The charterer claimed loss of use damages during the off-hire period, even though the tort-feasor was liable to the owner for the repairable damage and for the time charter hire lost as a result of the breakdown.

The district court awarded detention damages to the charterer on a third-party beneficiary theory. The court of appeals rejected this theory and also rejected the district court's alternative theory, i.e., that the time charterer had a property interest in the vessel. Nevertheless, the court of appeals affirmed the result, on a bailment-type theory that the charterer somehow shared in the whole loss, for which the owner would be trustee for the charterer if the owner recovered an award for the charterer's loss of use. This theory was firmly rejected by the Supreme Court, which held that "The respondents [the charterers] have no claim either in contract or in tort. . . ."[182] Justice Holmes framed the question for the Court thus: ". . .whether

179. Id.

180. Id.

181. 275 U.S. 303, 1928 AMC 61 (1927).

182. Id., 275 U.S. at 309, 1928 AMC at 64.

the respondents have an interest protected by the law against unintended injuries inflicted upon the vessel by third persons who know nothing of the charter." His answer was a resounding negative, to which he applied the pithy phrase, "The law does not spread its protection so far."[183] The weakest part of his opinion, however, was the rationale: ". . .[N]o authority need be cited to show that as a general rule, at least, a tort to the person or property of one man does not make the tortfeasor liable to another merely because the injured person was under a contract with that other unknown to the doer of the wrong."[184] Accordingly, there could be no recovery for the economic losses sustained by the time charterer. Despite criticisms, the exact holding remains valid.[185] Bareboat (demise) charterers, on the other hand, do have a sufficient "property" interest in the vessel to recover for loss of use.[186]

An exception to *Robins Dry Dock* is found in *Venore Transport Co. v. The Struma,*[187] where the charter required the charterer to continue to pay charter hire during the repair period, "come hell or high water," i.e., there was no off-hire clause providing for cessation of hire during breakdown periods. Viewing *Robins* as based on a remoteness rationale, the appellate court in *Venore* permitted the charterer to recover the charter hire actually paid out to the owner during the repair period. In this exception to *Robins,* the "hell or high water" requirement of payment of hire to the owner during the breakdown period had shifted the risk of loss of use from the owner to the time charterer.[188]

5. *The "New-for-Old" Doctrine in Repairable Damage Cases*

Avoidance of unjust enrichment of the victim at the expense of the careless tort-feasor is the basis of the "new-for-old" doctrine in insurance law, whereby the value of the increased life expectancy of the property because of its repair is deducted from the recoverable repair costs. At the present time, no deduction "new for old" is made from the recoverable cost of ship repairs.[189] The new-for-old doctrine, however, is clearly applied to repair costs of shoreside

183. Id., 275 U.S. at 309, 1928 AMC at 63.

184. Id.

185. *Federal Commerce & Navigation Co. v. The Marathonian,* 392 F. Supp. 908, 913–16, 1975 AMC 738 (SDNY), aff'd, 528 F.2d 907, 1975 AMC 2436 (2d Cir. 1975); *Cia. de Navegacion Porto Ronco v. The American Oriole,* 1976 AMC 433 (ED La. 1975). See also *State of Louisiana ex rel. Guste v. The Testbank,* 752 F.2d 1019, 1985 AMC 1521 (5th Cir. 1985); *Pennzoil Producing Co. v. Offshore Express, Inc.,* 943 F.2d 1465, 1473 (5th Cir. 1991).

186. See *Leary v. United States,* 81 U.S. 607 (1872). See generally, James, *Limitations on Liability for Economic Loss Caused by Negligence: A Pragmatic Appraisal,* 25 Vand. L. Rev. 43 (1972).

187. 583 F.2d 708, 1978 AMC 2146 (4th Cir. 1978). See also *Amoco Transportation Co. v. The Mason Lykes,* 768 F.2d 659, 1986 AMC 563 (5th Cir. 1985).

188. See *Pruitt v. Allied Chemical Corp.,* 523 F. Supp. 975, 981 (ED Va. 1981), in which *Venore* is described as eminently just.

189. See generally *Shepard S.S. Co. v. United States,* 111 F.2d 110, 1940 AMC 373 (2d Cir. 1940); *Oregon v. The Tug Go-Getter,* 468 F.2d 1270, 1973 AMC 243 (9th Cir. 1972).

structures.[190] As with other elements of damages, proof of depreciation is necessary before the court will reduce the allowance for repairs on a new-for-old basis.[191] New for old will not be applied even in shoreside cases where there is no proof of enhanced value or extended useful life.[192]

Since the 1855 decision in *The Schooner Catharine v. Dickinson,*[193] it has been assumed that damage to the hull must be repaired to keep the vessel in seaworthy condition, and that these repairs may affect undamaged parts of the hull. Yet these necessary repairs never raised the issue of a windfall or unjust enrichment for the owner. No deductions for previous wear and tear are made for repairs to hulls damaged in collision.[194] This rule of nondeduction is also applied where repairs are not made.[195] Where there has been a replacement of worn-out equipment, the "new-for-old" deduction may even be applied to ship repairs.[196]

---

190. *General American Transportation Co. v. The Patricia Chotin,* 120 F. Supp. 246, 1954 AMC 923 (ED La. 1954) (dock and dock pilings—reduction of one quarter); *Jemison v. The Duplex,* 163 F. Supp. 947, 1958 AMC 707 (SD Ala. 1958) (wharf-reduction of 20 percent); *Patterson Terminals Inc. v. The Johannes Frans,* 209 F. Supp. 705, 1962 AMC 2623 (ED Pa. 1962) (deduction for betterment of a dolphin [20 percent] and for its age and previous collisions [50 percent]); *Seaboard Air Line Rail Co. v. Marine Industries, Inc.,* 237 F. Supp. 10, 1966 AMC 1552 (EDSC 1964) (bridge—50 percent reduction); *Oakdene Compress & Warehouse Co. v. The Cities Service Norfolk,* 242 F. Supp. 148 (EDSC 1965) (wharf—40 percent reduction); *Elgin, Joliet & Eastern Railway Co. v. American Commercial Line,* 317 F. Supp. 175, 1970 AMC 1707 (ND Ill. 1970) (bridge—20 percent reduction); *Portland Pipeline Corp. v. The Barcola,* 1982 AMC 2725 (D Me. 1982) (34 percent reduction of protective panel of a pile); *Weyerhaeuser Co. v. The Atropos Island,* 777 F. 2d 1344, 1986 AMC 1016 (9th Cir. 1985) (fender pilings, railings, and docks surfaces—remand for depreciation). See Pritchett, *Ship to Shore Allison Damages: The Problem of Remedial Disuniformity in the Federal Courts,* 11 J. Mar. L. & Com. 333 (1980).

191. *City of New Orleans v. American Commercial Barge Lines, Inc.,* 662 F.2d 1121, 1982 AMC 1296 (5th Cir. 1981). See the opinion of the same circuit concerning the useful life of a bridge. No deduction was made. In *In re Canal Barge Co.,* 480 F.2d 11, 1973 AMC 843 (5th Cir. 1973), a pier—deduction; *Freeport Sulphur Co. v. The Hermosa,* 526 F.2d 300, 1977 AMC 508 (5th Cir. 1976), where the court noted two situations: (1) the straight line depreciation where the expected useful life after repairs is the same as at the time of the acquisition of the property; (2) where the repairs extend the useful life of the property to a different degree than the expected useful life at time of acquisition. These formulas were suggested only for repairs extending useful life and not for repairs enhancing the value of the property.

192. *Oregon v. The Tug Go-Getter,* supra note 190 (pier of a bridge); *Hinfin Realty Corp. v. The Poling Bros. No. 7,* 348 F. Supp. 1391, 1972 AMC 2465 (EDNY 1972) (a forty-year-old dock); *In re The Elaine Jones,* 480 F.2d 17, 1975 AMC 2098 (5th Cir. 1973) (a bridge).

193. 58 U.S. 170 (1855).

194. *The Baltimore,* 75 U.S. 377 (1869).

195. *Appeal of Waterman S.S. Corp.,* 1974 AMC 2061, 2068 (Armed Services Board of Contract Appeals, 1974).

196. A dictum in *Pillsbury Co. v. Midland Enterprises, Inc.,* 715 F. Supp. 738, 765, 1989 AMC 2113 (ED La. 1989), suggests that the new-for-old rule is applicable to both repair and replacement.

But see *Sheppard S.S. Co. v. United States,* 111 F.2d 110, 113, 1940 AMC 573, 578 (2d Cir. 1940), where the court suggested that the rule might be different if the part replaced was not in good condition at the time of the collision.

In *The Silver Moon—The Tug Cleveland,* 1959 AMC 1172, 1173 (EDNY 1959), a case of a collision between two barges, the estimated cost of repairs to one of the barges was reduced by one quarter because of its previously deteriorated state. A new-for-old deduction was made from the value of an old wooden vessel in a vessel-drilling rig collision in *Atkins v. Alabama Drydock and Shipbuilding Co.,* 195 F. Supp. 944, 1961 AMC 909 (SD Ala. 1960).

Section E. Interest on Damages

Rule IV of the Lisbon Rules provides that in total loss cases interest is recoverable from the date of the collision to the date of payment, and that for all other claims it runs from the date the loss was sustained or the expense was incurred to the date of payment. Under American law, on the other hand, an award of prejudgment interest in collision cases is within the discretion of the trial judge, as stated in the recent Supreme Court decision in *City of Milwaukee v. Cement Division, National Gypsum Co.*[197] The award itself or the failure to make an award of interest may be challenged as an abuse of the court's discretion. Generally, prejudgment interest will be awarded where the tortfeasor is held in sole fault.[198] Similarly, where the vessel is a total loss or a constructive total loss, prejudgment interest is usually awarded.[199] Contests can be expected where there has been a repairable damage collision claim resulting from mutual fault.

The Supreme Court's 1995 opinion on prejudgment interest in a mutual-fault collision did not hold that interest should be granted in all cases, but indicated that a very narrow exception existed for peculiar or exceptional circumstances.[200] However, the case decided that difference of opinion of the parties as to liability is not an exceptional circumstance, nor is disparity in the faults of the respective vessels.[201]

The Supreme Court's opinion was the climax of a sixteen-year controversy between the owner of the *E.M. Ford* and the City of Milwaukee over damage to the steamship in a violent winter storm on Christmas Eve, 1979, while the ship was berthed at a city pier. The shipowner sought collision repair damages of $4.5 million, alleging negligence in the assignment of the ship to a berth known to the city to be unsafe in heavy winds, in breach of the city's duty as wharfinger. The ship broke loose and crashed into the headwall of the slip, causing $250,000 damage to the pier, for which the city counterclaimed in the shipowner's suit, denying any fault and alleging sole fault of the owner for leaving the ship virtually unmanned over the Christmas holiday, with no means to monitor weather conditions or summon help. In 1986 the trial judge found the ship 96 percent to blame and the city 4 percent to

---

197. 515 U.S.189, 1995 AMC 1882 (1995). See generally, Annotation, *Award of Prejudgment Interest in Admiralty Suits,* 34 A.L.R. Fed. 126-270 (1977), updated annually. Statements of the general rule before *City of Milwaukee* may be found in *In re Banker's Trust Co. (The Edgar M. Queeny—The Corinthos),* supra note 37, and *In re The Vulcan,* 553 F.2d 489 (5th Cir. 1977) (cost of borrowing by the victim).

198. *Fireman's Fund Insurance Co. v. Standard Oil Co.,* 339 F.2d 148, 1965 AMC 1252 (9th Cir. 1964); *Darling v. Scheinmer,* 444 F.2d 514, 1971 AMC 1868 (9th Cir. 1971).

199. See *In re Bankers Trust Co.,* supra note 37; *Mecom v. Levingston Shipbuilding Co.,* 622 F.2d 1209, 1217 (5th Cir. 1980) (unjustifiable delay); *American Zinc Co. v. Foster,* 441 F.2d 1100, 1972 AMC 536 (5th Cir. 1971).

200. *City of Milwaukee v. Cement Division, National Gypsum Co.,* supra note 197, 515 U.S. at 196, 1995 AMC at 1889.

201. Id., 515 U.S. at 198, 1995 AMC at 1887–89.

blame. This allocation was reversed by the Seventh Circuit, which found the ship ⅔ to blame and the city ⅓ to blame.[202] While the parties agreed that ⅓ of the ship's physical damage amounted to $1,677,541, the shipowner claimed prejudgment interest of $5,317,857, which the city contested. The district judge denied prejudgment interest as inequitable for two reasons: (1) the city was only ⅓ at fault, and (2) the status of the municipality, the source of the payment of interest being the taxpayers. The Seventh Circuit again reversed the trial judge,[203] holding that *Reliable Transfer* had abolished mutuality of fault as a reason for denying interest.[204]

Because of a difference between the rule of the Ninth Circuit[205] and that of the Fifth Circuit[206] the Supreme Court granted certiorari and affirmed, 8–0. (Justice Breyer did not participate in the decision.) Justice Stevens reviewed the question of interest in admiralty decrees from 1796 on and found that denial of interest in mutual fault cases required peculiar or exceptional circumstances. The city's justification of denial because of a legitimate difference of opinion as to liability was rejected as unexceptional, and the city's justification because of disparity in fault was also rejected, since the disparity had already been taken into consideration in the proportional assessment of damages, so that denial of prejudgment interest would unfairly penalize a party twice for the same fault.[207] The Court did not address the issue of the status of the municipality.

Since *City of Milwaukee,* the reasons for denying interest would seem to be severely limited. Bad faith in asserting an excessive or insupportable claim and unwarranted delay in making the claim seem to be the only reasons which fit the Supreme Court's conditions of peculiar and exceptional circumstances for the denial of prejudgment interest. Under the Suits in Admiralty Act,[208] interest (at 4 percent) may be awarded against the government "as ordered by the court," but under the Public Vessels Act, it may run only from the date of judgment.[209] The date from which prejudgment interest may be awarded against private parties is within the discretion of the trial judge. This seems to be affected by the intensity of the financial impact upon the payor. Thus, there are partial loss cases in which prejudgment interest was allowed from the date of the collision.[210]

---

202. 915 F.2d 1154, 1991 AMC 1002 (7th Cir. 1990).

203. 31 F.3d 581, 1995 AMC 1453 (7th Cir. 1994).

204. Supra note 3.

205. *Alkmeon Naviera S.A. v. The Marina L.,* supra note 8.

206. *Inland Oil and Transport Co. v. Ark-White Towing Co.,* supra note 9.

207. *City of Milwaukee v. Cement Division, National Gypsum Co.,* supra note 197, 515 U.S. at 199, 1995 AMC at 1889. Since equal division of damages in both-to-blame cases where the faults are not equal was terminated in *Reliable Transfer,* supra note 3, allowance of prejudgment interest as a method of ameliorating the harsh rule of equal division is no longer necessary. Cf. *Afran Transport Co. v. The Bergechief,* 285 F.2d 119, 120, 1961 AMC 213, 214 (2d Cir. 1960).

208. 46 App. U.S.C. §§ 741–52.

209. 46 App. U.S.C. §§ 781–90.

210. See, e.g., *Union Oil Co. v. The Issaquena,* 339 F. Supp. 1011, 1972 AMC 2175 (ND Miss. 1971), aff'd, 470 F.2d 875, 1973 AMC 493 (5th Cir. 1973). However, in the case cited, only the

Other cases concerning the commencement of interest in collision cases are cited in the notes.[211]

The rate of interest is usually the same as the rate the damaged party would have to pay on a short-term loan obligation. In *City of Milwaukee,* the Supreme Court did not review the rate of interest, but the Seventh Circuit suggested that the city should pay an average of the prime rate for the years in question, influenced by the city's status as a credit-worthy municipality, which should result in a rate of interest resembling that charged to the city for short-term unsecured loans.[212]

In the United States, postjudgment interest is governed in federal cases by statute. Under 28 U.S.C. § 1961 (a), interest on a final judgment is payable at a rate determined by the public auction of fifty-two-week U.S. Treasury Bills immediately prior to the date of the judgment.

Section F. Rates of Exchange

Rule 5 of the Lisbon Rules provides *inter alia* that unless otherwise agreed, losses and expenses are to be converted from the currency in which they are incurred into SDRs at the exchange rate prevailing on the date they were incurred. Under American law, location of the collision is the essential factor in deciding how the rate of exchange is to be fixed. Unfortunately, at the present time, rates of inflation and currency devaluations have not been determinative factors. Thus, conflict of law rules originating at a time of currency stability are applied even in periods of volatility.

For collisions in U.S. territorial waters or on the high seas, U.S. courts will apply the rate of exchange prevalent when the amount became definite or liquidated.[213] For example, in a total loss or constructive total loss case, the rate of exchange on the day of collision governs. But in repairable-damage

---

plaintiff had suffered damages. The date of the collision is usually selected in cases of total loss. *Independent Bulk Transportation Inc. v. The Morania Albaco,* 676 F.2d 23, 25, 1982 AMC 1535 (2d Cir. 1982). See *Afran Transport v. The Bergechief,* supra note 208; *In re Bankers Trust Co.,* supra note 37; *The Hygrade No. 24, Inc. v. The Dynamic,* 233 F.2d 444, 447, 1956 AMC 1032 (2d Cir. 1956).

211. *Sinclair Refining Co. v. The Green Island,* supra note 107; *Afran Transport Co. v. The Bergechief,* supra note 207; *In re Bankers Trust Co. (The Edgar M. Queeny—The Corinthos),* supra note 37; *The Hygrade No. 24, Inc. v. The Dynamic,* 233 F.2d 444, 447, 1956 AMC 1032 (2d Cir. 1956); *In re Canal Barge Co.,* 323 F. Supp. 805, 823 (ND Miss. 1971); *American Oil Co. v. The Lacon,* 398 F. Supp. 1181, 1973 AMC 1900, aff'd, 496 F.2d 1405, 1974 AMC 2679 (5th Cir. 1974). In a constructive total loss case the district judge overruled the commissioner to begin interest at the time of payment for repairs. *The Manhattan,* 10 F. Supp. 45, 1935 AMC 242 (ED Pa. 1935), aff'd, 85 F.2d 427, 1936 AMC 1168 (3d Cir. 1936).

212. See *Cement Division, National Gypsum Co. v. City of Milwaukee,* 31 F.3d 581, at 587, 1995 AMC 1453, at 1462 (7th Cir. 1994).

213. See *Skibs A/S Gylfe v. The Trujillo,* supra note 131, 209 F.2d at 387–88, 1954 AMC at 237–38, where the Norwegian ship *Gylfe* collided with the *Trujillo* on departure from Aruba. The *Gylfe* returned to Aruba for temporary repairs, then completed her voyage and returned to Scandinavia, where different portions of the permanent repairs were effected in Norway, Sweden,

cases the rate of exchange prevalent on the day of payment of the expenditure for repairs or other items attributable to the collision will be applied. In cases of collisions occurring in the territorial waters of other nations, but tried in the United States, the courts will apply the rate of exchange in effect on the judgment date.[214] In salvage cases, at least, the court may, in its discretion, award additional amounts to compensate for exchange-rate fluctuations.[215] No case has been found as of this writing (1997) making a similar adjustment of collision damages.

The date of the termination of the adventure is the essential factor for the conversion of general-average expenses into U.S. currency.[216] Similarly, claims for general-average contributions accrue at the port of destination and delivery of the cargo,[217] and if that port is outside the United States, in the absence of an agreement to the contrary, it would follow that conversion into U.S. currency should also be made as of that date.

---

and Denmark. Owners of both vessels agreed the *Gylfe* would recover 90 percent of her damages, but the *Trujillo*'s owners argued for the judgment-day rate before the commissioner, who rejected the argument. The district court confirmed the commissioner's report, and its decision on this point was affirmed by the Second Circuit. The court reasoned that the general maritime law of the high-seas collision would fix the loss when the tort was committed, but since the loss was not immediately ascertainable, it would be fixed as of the date of expenditure. See also *Jamaica Nutrition Holdings Ltd. v. United Shipping Co.*, 643 F.2d 376, 1981 AMC 2883 (5th Cir. 1981); *Eagle Oil & Shipping Co. v. The Jim Brown*, 104 F. Supp. 271, 1952 AMC 1395 (SD Tex. 1952).

See generally, Note, *Conversion Date of Foreign Money Obligations*, 65 Col. L. Rev. 490 (1965), and Note, *Conversion of Judgments Measured in Foreign Currencies*, 39 Wash. & Lee L. Rev. 165 (1982).

214. *Shaw, Savill, Albion & Co. v. The Fredericksburg*, 189 F.2d 952, 1951 AMC 1273 (2d Cir. 1951) (applying the judgment-day rate for a 1946 collision in British territorial waters. Nonmaritime authority cited was *Deutsche Bank Filiale Nurnberg v. Humphrey*, 272 U.S. 517 (1926), involving the alien property custodian, applying German law.

215. B. V. Bureau Wijsmuller v. United States *(The Furer)*, 1979 AMC 2331 (SDNY 1979), decided by Judge Haight, aff'd, 633 F.2d 202, 1980 AMC 2993 (2d Cir. 1980). See also *B.V. Bureau Wijsmuller v. United States (The Pioneer Commander)*, 702 F.2d 333, 1983 AMC 1471 (2d Cir. 1983), in which the court awarded a 27 percent "equitable uplift" where the applicable statutory rate of interest was 4 percent under 46 U.S.C. § 746.

Note that in the United Kingdom, the court may award judgment in the currency in which the expenses were incurred, or in the plaintiff's currency, or in English currency. See *The Despina R.* [1979] 1 Lloyd's Rep. 1 (H. L. 1978). See Note, *The Need to Retreat from Inflexible Conversion Rules—An Equitable Approach to Judgment in Foreign Currency*, 22 Santa Clara L. Rev. 871 (1982).

216. *Det Forenede Dampskibs Selskab v. Insurance Co. of North America (The Arkansas)*, 31 F.2d 658, 1929 AMC 581 (2d Cir. 1929). General-average expenses were incurred in Norway and England and the voyage terminated in New York, where the general average was stated after a considerable delay. The issue was whether the rate of exchange on the date of the statement or the rate on the date of termination of the adventure should govern. The lower court chose the date of termination of the venture, even though the amount of contribution was then indefinite, and the court of appeals affirmed.

217. *United States v. Atlantic Mutual Insurance Co. (The Arkansas)*, 298 U.S. 483, 1936 AMC 993 (1936). See also *Chandris v. Argo Insurance Co., Ltd.*, [1963] 2 Lloyd's Rep. 65, where the court stressed that issuance of the statement itself is unnecessary, and that a claim for general-average contributions can properly be made on the basis of the necessary facts then available.

Since the cause of action arises on the termination of the adventure rather than on the issuance of the statement, an action against the United States for a general-average contribution must be commenced within two years of the termination of the voyage. See 46 App. U.S.C. § 745 (Suits in Admiralty Act) and 46 App. U.S.C. § 782 (Public Vessels Act).

CHAPTER FOURTEEN

SHIPOWNERS' LIMITATION OF LIABILITY IN COLLISION CASES

Section A. Introduction

Despite the controversy surrounding the policy of limitation of liability[1] and its potential for abuse, the subject cannot be ignored in any treatment of the law of collision. In the United States, shipowners may initiate limitation proceedings without waiting to be held liable, but there is a very short time bar (six months)[2] on this right. While limitation of liability in the United States is essentially defensive in the substantive sense that it permits the shipowner and its insurers to reduce the amount of its potential exposure to liability, it is also offensive in the procedural sense,[3] in that the shipowner may initiate proceedings which, through the issuance of the court's injunction, can forestall litigation in other courts in the United States, state or federal and, under limited circumstances, even prevent litigation abroad.[4] The materials in this

1. See Black, J., dissenting, in *Maryland Casualty Co. v. Cushing,* 347 U.S. 409, 437, 1954 AMC 837, 859 (1954): "Many of the conditions in the shipping industry which induced the 1851 Congress to pass the [Limitation of Liability] Act no longer prevail. And later Congresses, when they wished to aid shipping, provided subsidies paid out of the public treasury rather than subsidies paid by injured persons." See also *University of Texas Medical Branch v. United States,* 557 F.2d 438, 441, 1977 AMC 2607, 2608 (5th Cir. 1977), where the Limitation Act is described as "hopelessly anachronistic."

2. 46 App. U.S.C. § 185.

3. *Hartford Accident & Indemnity Co. v. Southern Pacific Co.,* 273 U.S. 207, 1927 AMC 402 (1927). For a more extensive history of the subject, see Donovan, *The Origins and Development of Limitation of Shipowners' Liability,* 53 Tul. L. Rev. 999 (1979).

4. Fed. R. Civ. P., Supp. Rule F(3). In *British Transport Commission v. United States (The Duke of York—The Haiti Victory),* 354 U.S. 129, 1957 AMC 1151 (1957), a British ferry collided with a U.S. government transport in the English Channel, causing great loss of life and damage to the ferry. The government could not obtain jurisdiction of the British owner in the United States. However, when the government petitioned to limit its liability in a U.S. court, the British ferry owner filed a claim for $1.5 million in the limitation proceeding. The U.S. court found the British ferry solely to blame, denied the ferry's claim, and gave the government judgment on its counterclaim. The ferry owner argued that it could not be held liable on the counterclaim, as it could not be forced to defend in the United States, but the Supreme Court rejected the argument and held that having filed a claim in the government's limitation proceeding, the British claimant had thereby subjected itself to the jurisdiction of the U.S. court with respect to all matters arising out of the collision.

In *The Salvore,* 36 F.2d 712, 1930 AMC 23 (2d Cir. 1929), cargo claimants attached the shipowner's vessels in New York in an action for the losses caused by a fire aboard the *Salvore* while in dry dock. The shipowner petitioned to limit liability in New York, and then sued the cargo claimants in Italy for wrongful attachment. The cargo claimants moved for an order requiring

chapter are by no means intended as a complete treatment of the law of limitation of liability.[5] Rather, the chapter is essentially concerned with the principal problems of limitation law which should be considered by a collision lawyer in determining whether or not to initiate a limitation proceeding, and if so, where.

1. *International Perspective*

(a) U.S. Forum. When a complaint (formerly called a petition), for limitation of liability is filed in a U.S. district court, the court will apply U.S. limitation of liability law to the case, regardless of the flag of the vessel whose owners seek limitation.[6] However, if the casualty occurred in the territorial waters of a foreign State under whose laws limitation is considered substantive, it will apply the law of that State to such questions as the composition of the limitation fund.[7] Since most foreign limitation of liability statutes and conventions appear to be procedural, they will not be enforced in the United States. Thus, the principal concern of shipowners against whom large claims can be enforced in the United States must be with the statute enacted in

---

the shipowner to dismiss the Italian suits, but the motion was denied by the district court. On appeal, the decision was reversed. The Second Circuit held that the limitation petitioners could be forced to abandon the foreign litigation, stating, at 36 F. 2d 714, 1930 AMC at 26:

> The court below having obtained prior jurisdiction of the parties, and the appellee having sought that same jurisdiction in its limitation proceedings, unquestionably gave the court the power to deal with the appellee before it as equity and justice required. It could have refused the injunction in the limitation proceedings, or it could have granted the injunction only upon condition that the appellee willingly litigated all the controversies arising, including the subject-matter of the claims filed in the Italian actions. The court could not restrain the trial in the Italian courts, but it could restrain or stay the limitation proceedings within its jurisdiction.
>
> The court first securing jurisdiction has the authority and power of enjoining the parties to the litigation from proceeding in another jurisdiction. And the court has an undoubted authority to control all persons and things within its own territorial limits.

5. See *Tulane Admiralty Law Institute Symposium on Limitation of Liability,* 53 Tul. L. Rev. 999–1420 (1979), for a more extensive treatment.

6. 46 App. U.S.C. § 183(a); *The Scotland,* 105 U.S. 24 (1881); *The Titanic,* 233 U.S. 718 (1914).

7. *Black Diamond S.S. Corp. v. Robert Stewart & Sons Ltd. (The Norwalk Victory),* 336 U.S. 386, 1949 AMC 393 (1949), which mandates a determination as to whether limitation of liability in a State in whose territorial waters a casualty occurs is substantive or merely procedural. If procedural, it will not be enforced in the United States under the precedent of *The Titanic,* supra note 6. But the foreign law will be applied if it is found to be substantive. Decisions concerning determination of the question as to whether the foreign law is substantive or procedural in nature include *In re Chadade S.S. Co.,* 266 F. Supp. 517, 1967 AMC 1843 (SD Fla. 1967) (Panamanian law); *In re Ta Chi Navigation (Panama) Corp.,* 416 F. Supp. 371, 1976 AMC 1895 (SDNY 1976) (Panamanian law); *In re Geophysical Service, Inc.,* 590 F. Supp. 1346, 1984 AMC 2413 (SD Tex. 1984) (Canadian law); *In re Bethlehem Steel Corp. v. Marriott Corp.,* 631 F.2d 441, 1980 AMC 2122 (6th Cir. 1980) (Canadian law); *In re Compania Gijonesa de Navegacion, S.A. (The Cimadevilla),* 590 F. Supp. 241, 1985 AMC 1469 (SDNY) (Spanish law); *Cliffs-Neddrill Turnkey International-Oranjestad v. The Rich Duke,* 734 F. Supp 142, 1990 AMC 1583 (D Del. 1990) (law of The Netherlands Antilles); and *In re K.S. Line Corp.,* 596 F. Supp. 1268, 1985 AMC 722 (D Alaska 1984) (Korean law).

1851,[8] enabling the American merchant marine to compete with the merchant fleet of the United Kingdom, where limitation of shipowners' liability had been provided by statute since 1734. The policy of the U.S. statute has not been completely reconsidered by Congress since its enactment in 1851, although it was amended in 1871, 1884, 1935, 1936, and 1984.

(b) Foreign Limitation of Liability. Unification of this aspect of maritime law has been a principal concern of the Comité Maritime International (C.M.I.), which has produced three conventions on the subject—those adopted in 1924,[9] 1957,[10] and 1976.[11] There were indications in the early maritime codes that shipowners' liabilities after a disaster could be limited to the value of the vessel or wreck, if it was abandoned to the claimants. This concept of abandonment is still found in codes which follow the French Code de Commerce of 1804.[12] (It is also found in the U.S. Limitation of Liability Act, which gives the shipowner the option of surrendering his interest to a trustee for the benefit of claimants.[13] This option, however, has very seldom been exercised.) Despite the lingering effect of the 1924 and 1957 Conventions, which have been denounced by most of the States that had adopted them and replaced by the 1976 Convention, attention will be directed to the special features of that Convention, which entered into force on December 1, 1986, but has not been adopted by the United States.

The American statute restricts the right of limitation to owners (including charterers who man, victual, and supply the vessel at their own expense,[14] i.e., bareboat charterers). The 1976 Convention, on the other hand, permits limitation of liability by anyone involved in the management, operation, or

---

8. 46 App. U.S.C. §§ 181–89 (1995). The original statute, 9 Stat. 635, was enacted in response to the liabilities imposed on the carrier in *The Lexington,* 47 U.S. 344 (1848). The statute was initially interpreted by the Supreme Court in *Norwich & New York Transportation Co. v. Wright,* 80 U.S. 104 (1872). Section 181 of 46 App. U.S.C. (§ 2 of the Act, as amended), concerns the carriage of bullion and other precious cargo, and § 182 (§ 1 of the Act), usually referred to as the "fire statute," relates to loss of or damage to cargo by fire. Section 183a., not to be confused with § 183(a), has been repealed and replaced by § 183(e). Section 183b. relates to stipulations limiting time for filing claims and commencing suit, and § 183c. invalidates contractual provisions purporting to avoid or lessen liability for wrongful death or personal injury. The discussion in this chapter is limited to the remaining sections.

9. International Convention Relating to the Limitation of Liability of Owners of Seagoing Ships, Brussels, 1924, 6 Benedict on Admiralty, Doc. No. 5-1 (7th ed. [Rev.], F. L. Wiswall, Jr., Editor-in-Chief, *International Maritime Law Documents and Commentary*) (hereinafter "Benedict").

10. International Convention for the Unification of Certain Rules Relating to the Limitation of Liability of Owners of Seagoing Ships, Brussels, 1957, 6 Benedict, Doc. No. 5-2.

11. International Convention on Limitation of Liability for Maritime Claims, 6 Benedict, Doc. No. 5-4. (Entered into force Dec. 1, 1986; hereinafter "1976 Convention").

12. Code de Commerce, Art. 216. See A. Rein, *International Variations on Concepts of Limitation of Liability,* 53 Tul. L. Rev. 1259 (1979). A survey of limitation in 29 legal systems is provided in K. Pineus and G. Rohreke, *Limited Liability in Collision Cases,* a Comité Maritime International (C.M.I.) publication (1981).

13. Section 4 of the Act, 46 App. U.S.C. § 185.

14. Section 5 of the Act, 46 App. U.S.C. § 186.

liability insurance of vessels. The claims which can be limited include claims for (a) loss of life, personal injury, or loss of or damage to property occurring on board or in direct connection with the operation of the ship, or with salvage operations; (b) delay in the carriage by sea of cargo, or of passengers and their luggage; (c) other losses resulting from infringement of rights, except contractual rights, occurring in direct connection with the operation of the ship or with salvage operations; (d) wreck removal; and (e) removing or destroying cargo or rendering it harmless. Also subject to limitation under the 1976 Convention are "claims of a person other than the person liable in respect of measures taken in order to avert or minimize loss for which the person liable may limit his liability in accordance with this Convention, and further loss caused by such measures."[15]

As will be seen, the amount of the potential limitation fund is known before any disaster occurs since, under the 1976 Convention, the amount is based on tonnage rather than on the value of the vessel after the casualty. This is a decided advantage to hull underwriters, who are interested because of the running-down clause in the usual hull policy, P & I clubs, and other P & I insurers. The intention of the drafters of the 1976 Convention was to make the limitation amount virtually unbreakable by eliminating the concept of "actual fault and privity" of the shipowner, the American counterpart of which ("privity or knowledge") has caused limitation to be denied in many proceedings brought in the United States. This was accomplished by setting up a single exception to limitation: "the personal act or omission" of the party claiming the right to limit liability, "committed with the intent to cause such loss, or recklessly and with knowledge that such loss would probably result."[16]

The 1976 Convention, like the U.S. Limitation Act, effectuates a marshaling of claims by barring parties who have filed claims against the fund

---

15. 1976 Convention, supra note 11, art. 2.

16. 1976 Convention, supra note 11, art. 4. The unit of account is the Special Drawing Right (SDR) of the International Monetary Fund (art. 8). The system can be described as one based on adjusted gross tonnage, with limitation amounts decreasing as the tonnage increases. Except in respect of passengers, the limits under art. 6 are as follows:

> (a) for personal injury and death: vessels of not over 500 tons: 333,000 SDRs; vessels in excess of 500 tons: 333,000 SDRs, plus 500 SDRs for each ton from 501 to 3,000 tons; 333 SDRs for each ton from 3,001 to 30,000 tons; 250 SDRs for each ton from 30,001 to 70,000 tons; and 167 SDRs for each ton over 70,000 tons.
>
> (b) for any other claims: vessels of not over 500 tons: 167,000 SDRs; vessels in excess of 500 tons: 167,000 SDRs, plus 167 SDRs for each ton from 501 to 30,000; 167,000 SDRs, plus 125 SDRs for each ton from 30,001 to 70,000; 167,000 SDRs, plus 83 SDRs for each ton over 70,000.

In respect of claims for injury to or death of passengers, the limit is 46,666 SDRs multiplied by the number of passengers the ship is authorized to carry, but not exceeding 25 million SDRs. See 1976 Convention, supra note 11, art. 7. An American case, *In re Tecomar, S.A.*, 765 F. Supp. 1150, 1991 AMC 2432 (SDNY 1991), interpreting the 1976 Convention as the law of the port of loading (Germany), denied both limitation of liability per unit and global limitation because of reckless maintenance of the vessel involved.

from proceeding against any other property of the party by or on behalf of whom the fund has been created.[17] Under English law, as under U.S. law, in both-to-blame collision cases, a claim against the other colliding vessel is postponed until the claims of innocent parties, such as cargo owners, have been fully satisfied or the fund has been exhausted.[18]

Because of the wide divergence between ownership interests and the flags flown by many vessels at the present time, and the great volume of third-world-country carriage (by fleets belonging neither to the exporting nor the importing State), disputes about jurisdiction of the courts over the several parties involved in a high-seas collision will occur with frequency as each party seeks out the most favorable forum for its claims. (The pejorative description is "forum shopping.")[19]

In section 5 of the U.S. Limitation of Liability Act, 46 App. U.S.C. section 185, after outlining the steps to be taken by a shipowner seeking limitation, Congress provided that "Upon compliance with the requirements of this section all claims and proceedings against the owner with respect to the matter in question shall cease." This language is repeated in Rule F(3), Suppl. Rules, Fed. R. Civ. P., with the further provision: "On application of the plaintiff the court shall enjoin the further prosecution of any action or proceeding against the plaintiff or his property with respect to any claim subject to limitation in the action."[20]

Since Congress did not prescribe the international effect to be given to a limitation injunction, a presumption will run against any suggestion of international recognition.[21] This flat statement, however, is subject to the caveat

---

17. 1976 Convention, supra note 11, art. 13.

18. See Thomas, *British Concepts of Limitation of Liability,* 53 Tul. L. Rev. 1205, 1245–48 (1979).

19. See *In re Bloomfield Steamship Co.,* 422 F.2d 728, 1970 AMC 521 (2d Cir. 1970), in which District Judge Palmieri (sitting by designation on the Second Circuit Court of Appeals) answered the charge of forum shopping in limitation of liability proceedings:

> That interested parties here have engaged in extensive far-flung litigation is not surprising. The owners of ships moving in international trade and colliding in international waters may well expect to be involved in legal proceedings in more than one country. Forum shopping in this context is not a term of opprobrium but a way of life and each party seeks what appears to be the best legal haven (422 F.2d at 736, 1970 AMC at 533).

It should be noted that the uncertainties of the multiple fora, described infra, might be alleviated as to signatory States by the provisions of the 1976 Convention, supra note 11, art. 13.

20. Fed. R. Civ. P., Suppl. Rule F (3). It is customary for the plaintiff shipowner's counsel to prepare the draft order and include it with the other papers accompanying the complaint for the ex parte preliminary proceeding.

21. See *American Banana Co. v. United Fruit Co.,* 213 U.S. 347 (1909); *McCulloch v. Sociedad Nacional de Marineros de Honduras,* 372 U.S. 10, 1963 AMC 283 (1963); and *Equal Employment Opportunity Commission v. Arabian American Oil Co.,* 499 U.S. 244 (1991). The obvious consequence of this is that claimants who do not pursue their rights in the United States may bring actions against the plaintiff shipowner in foreign courts. Cf. *British Transport Commission v. United States*

that equitable procedures govern limitation proceedings, so that parties subject to U.S. jurisdiction under Rule 4, Fed. R. Civ. P., and even those in an adversarial relationship in litigation in the United States, can be forced to discontinue actions abroad against the plaintiff shipowner.[22] Consequently, the injunction prohibiting claims outside the limitation proceeding will be effective in the United States, and may be effective abroad in the sense that parties in an adversarial relationship in the United States, as for example, opponents in collision litigation or claimants in a limitation proceeding, can be ordered to discontinue foreign litigation. The corollary is that litigation outside the United States between parties not in an adversarial relationship in the United States will not be enjoined.[23]

Section B. Précis of U.S. Limitation of Liability

1. Venue

The offensive aspect is demonstrated by the procedure for choosing the venue of limitation of liability proceedings. The governing rule[24] provides that a limitation proceeding must be brought by the shipowner in the district where the vessel has been arrested, and if not arrested, where the shipowner has been sued. If neither an arrest nor a suit is pending, it must be brought where the vessel lies. If none of the previous alternatives is applicable, it may be brought in any district court. Liberal transfer "to any district" is provided, but the court may dismiss where "venue is wrongly laid." In view of the short time bar, the selection of the correct venue is essential.[25]

(The Duke of York—The Haiti Victory), supra note 4. In *The Titanic,* supra note 6, two British subjects who had filed claims in the American limitation proceeding were permitted to withdraw their claims so that they might pursue them in England.

22. *The Salvore,* supra note 4. See also *A.C. Dodge, Inc. v. J.M. Carras, Inc.,* 218 F.2d 911, 1955 AMC 706 (2d Cir. 1955). Chief Justice Taft, a great admirer of equity, described limitation as "... the administration of equity in an admiralty court," *Hartford Accident & Indemnity Co. v. Southern Pacific Co.,* 273 U.S. 207, 215, 1927 AMC 402 (1927).

23. *The Titanic,* supra note 6, and 225 F. 747 (2d Cir.1915); *British Transport Commission v. United States (The Duke of York—The Haiti Victory),* supra note 4; *Bloomfield Steamship Co. v. Haight,* 363 F.2d 872, 1967 AMC 660 (5th Cir. 1966); *In re Bloomfield Steamship Co.,* supra note 19. See also *In res Ta Chi Navigation (Panama) Corp. v. (The Eurypylus),* supra note 7; *In re Compania Gijonesa de Navegacion, S.A. (The Cimadevilla),* supra note 7; *In re Bethlehem Steel Corp.,* supra note 7.

24. Suppl. Rule F (9), Fed. R. Civ. P.

25. *In re Bloomfield Shipping Co.,* 227 F. Supp. 615, 1964 AMC 1563 (ED La. 1964), aff'd, 363 F.2d 872, 1967 AMC 660 (5th Cir.1966); *In re Far Eastern Shipping Co.,* 460 F. Supp. 107, 1979 AMC 322 (SDNY 1978); *In re St. George Packing Co., Inc.,* 1990 AMC 2848 (ED La. 1990); see also *In re Bankers Trust Company (The Puerto Rican),* 640 F. Supp. 11, 1986 AMC 67 (ED Pa. 1985). For a contrary result, see *In re Connecticut National Bank (The Omi Yukon),* 687 F. Supp. 111, 1989 AMC 791 (SDNY 1988).

2. *Time Bar*

The time bar of the rule,[26] deriving from the 1936 amendment to 46 U.S.C. section 185, involves some uncertainty, but one provision is crystal clear: where there are multiple claims, in order to obtain a concursus or marshaling of the claims, and to be sure of obtaining a pro rata reduction in the amount of liability upon a showing of the absence of privity, the shipowner must file a complaint for limitation within six months of receipt of the first written notice of claim. Because of the possibility of a letter, telefax message, or other communication respecting the collision or other casualty being subsequently construed as a claim in writing, prudent practice dictates that the date of the casualty be considered as the date from which the six months allowed for filing a complaint for limitation begins to run.[27]

The circuits are presently divided on the question as to whether the six-month time bar applies to limitation pleaded in an answer to a complaint filed by a claimant, as well as to the filing of a complaint for limitation filed by the shipowner. The Sixth Circuit[28] regards the 1936 amendment of the Limitation Act as a congressional response to previous abuse of the limitation privilege, and as requiring a strict construction of any language permitting limitation of a claimant's right to a full recovery. Thus it applies the six-month time bar to pleading limitation in an answer.

The Second,[29] Third[30] and Fifth[31] Circuits, on the other hand, hold the opposite view. Thus, the Second Circuit has noted that the right to seek limitation by way of an answer to a complaint in an action brought by a claimant was not a target of the 1936 amendment, as the timing of such an action (absent laches) is in the hands of the claimant, and not the shipowner. Even in circuits where invoking the right to limit in an answer filed after six months

---

26. Fed. R. Civ. P. Suppl. Rule F (1).

27. See *In re N.Y.T.R. Transportation Corp.,* 1985 AMC 2827 (EDNY 1985). See also *In re Okeanos Research Foundation,* 704 F. Supp. 412, 1989 AMC 1677 (SDNY 1989), where the court distinguished letters held to be "notices of claim" from the letter before the court, which was held not to constitute a notice. In *Sook v. Great Pacific Shipping Co.,* 632 F.2d 100, 1981 AMC 1232 (9th Cir. 1980), representatives of members of the crew of a vessel that sank at sea sued the shipowner in Korea. That suit was voluntarily dismissed and plaintiffs sued under the Jones Act, 46 App. U.S.C. § 688, in the District Court for the Northern District of California. The owner then filed a complaint for limitation, which the representatives moved to dismiss on the ground that the Korean suit was a notice of claim, and the limitation proceeding was not filed within six months of the suit. The Ninth Circuit affirmed a district court decision holding that the Korean suit was not a "notice of claim," since under Korean law claims for wrongful death or personal injury of crew members are not subject to limitation, and the claims referred to in the Limitation Act are claims that are subject to limitation.

28. *Cincinnati Gas & Elec. Co. v. Abel (The Reddy Kilowatt),* 533 F.2d 1001, 1976 AMC 567 (6th Cir. 1976).

29. *Deep Sea Tankers v. The Long Branch,* 258 F.2d 757, 1959 AMC 28 (2d Cir. 1958). See also *Murray v. New York Central Railroad Co.,* 287 F.2d 152, 1961 AMC 1118 (2d Cir. 1961).

30. *The Chickie,* 141 F.2d 80, 1944 AMC 635 (3d Cir. 1944).

31. *Signal Oil and Gas Co. v. The Barge W-107,* 654 F.2d 1164, 1982 AMC 2603 (5th Cir. 1981) (quoting from *The Chickie,* supra note 30), and see *In re Vatican Shrimp Co. (The Vatican),* 820 F.2d 674, 1987 AMC 2426 (5th Cir. 1987).

has been held permissible, it is extremely risky, unless it is absolutely certain that there can only be one claim. An obvious example is a case where there are a number of claims, all for cargo damage, and each claimant files a complaint in a different district, after expiration of six months. This could result in the shipowner being held liable up to the limitation amount in each of several courts. The lesson is that for a shipowner to obtain the maximum advantage from the Limitation of Liability Act, a complaint for limitation, accompanied by security in approved form and amount, should be filed within six months of the date of the collision or other casualty.

3. The Limitation Fund

(a) General Rules Governing Constitution of the Fund. As noted, section 5 of the Limitation Act[32] gives a shipowner the option of either (a) depositing in court the amount of its interest in the vessel and "pending freight," or security therefor, or (b) transferring its interest to a court-appointed trustee for the benefit of the claimants. Since a transfer is scarcely ever made, this discussion will be limited to the constitution of the fund represented by the security accompanying the complaint for limitation.

Substantial "up-front" money may be required to establish the fund, e.g., because the surety company may want a large amount of collateral before issuing a bond. And preliminary proceedings may be instituted by claimants seeking to have the amount of the security tendered by the shipowner increased. If the shipowner were to fail to comply with a court order requiring such an increase, it could result in dismissal of the complaint for limitation.[33]

Until relatively recent times, commercial vessels were usually owned by single individuals, or "on shares" by groups of individuals. In the latter case, any individual share owner who was not chargeable with "privity or knowledge" was entitled to limitation of liability to the value of his or her interest in the vessel and the "pending freight." Now that commercial vessels are almost invariably owned by corporations, there is ordinarily only a single interest to be considered—the interest of the corporate owner. That interest is the value of the vessel, free and clear of liens,[34] and the "pending freight."

The Limitation Act does not prescribe when the value of the vessel is to be taken, i.e., whether before or after the casualty with respect to which limitation of liability is sought. However, in the first limitation case to come before it, *The City of Norwich (I) (Norwich & N.Y. Transp. Co. v. Wright)*,[35] the

32. 46 App. U.S.C. § 185.

33. See *In re Kingston Shipping Co., Inc.*, 1982 AMC 134 (MD Fla. 1981); *In re Dammers & Vanderheide*, 836 F.2d 750, 1988 AMC 1674 (2d Cir. 1988); *In re Slobodna Plovidba*, 1987 AMC 2209 (WD Mich. 1987).

34. Gilmore & Black, *The Law of Admiralty* 951–52 (2d ed.) (hereinafter "Gilmore & Black"), citing 3 Benedict 458 (6th ed. 1940).

35. 80 U.S. 104 (1871).

Supreme Court held that the value to be taken is the value at the end of the casualty voyage, and this interpretation of the Limitation Act has been followed ever since. This of course means that if the vessel has sunk in deep water or has otherwise become a total loss on the casualty voyage, the value of the owner's interest in the vessel is zero, unless the owner has valid outstanding claims against third parties that are representative of the vessel, such as a claim for unrepaired collision damage arising on a prior voyage.[36] If the vessel survives, the owner's interest in the vessel is her value at the end of the casualty voyage, plus the value of any outstanding claims against third parties that are representative of the vessel.

In 1886 the Supreme Court decided, by a 5-to-4 vote, that the proceeds of insurance on the vessel are not part of the limitation fund.[37] The majority reasoned that insurance proceeds are not representative of the vessel; that insurance is something the owner is not obliged to obtain, and that if the owner chooses to obtain insurance for its own benefit, it should be entitled to keep the proceeds.

The term "pending freight," as used in the Limitation Act, has been given a very broad interpretation. It means not only collect freight, which in modern times is usually either minimal or nonexistent, but freight already collected or earned, charter hire, and passenger monies, whether collected or to be collected.[38]

(b) Personal Injury and Death Claims. Section 3(b) of the Limitation Act[39] provides that in the case of "any seagoing vessel," if the portion of the fund applicable to death and injury claims is less than $420 multiplied by the vessel's limitation tonnage, that portion must be increased to an amount equal

36. See *O'Brien v. Miller*, 168 U.S. 287 (1897); *Phillips v. Clyde Steamship Co.*, 17 F.2d 250, 1927 AMC 341 (4th Cir. 1927); *The Bleakley No. 76*, 55 F.2d 725, 1932 AMC 307 (SDNY 1932); *Oliver J. Olson & Co. v. The Marine Leopard*, 356 F.2d 728, 1966 AMC 1064 (9th Cir. 1966). Note, however, that the Fifth Circuit has held that the shipowner's claims against third-party tort-feasors for indemnity or contribution for personal injury or death need not be included in the fund. *Guillot v. Cenac Towing Co.*, 366 F.2d 898, 1966 AMC 2685 (5th Cir. 1966).

37. *Place v. Norwich & N.Y. Transp. Co. (The City of Norwich [II])*, 118 U.S. 468 (1886). The policy involved was a fire policy, and the shipowner had to sue the insurer to recover the insured amount. *Norwich & N.Y. Transp. Co. v. Western Mass. Ins. Co.*, 34 Conn. 561, 18 F. Cas. 447 (No. 10,363) (CC D. Conn. 1886). See also *The Great Western*, 118 U.S. 520 (1886), and *The Scotland*, supra note 6.

38. See *The Main v. Williams*, 152 U.S. 122 (1894), where the Supreme Court gave broad readings to both "pending" and "freight," interpreting the statutory language as requiring the inclusion in the limitation fund of all of the gross earnings of the casualty voyage, from the carriage of either merchandise or passengers.

39. 46 App. U.S.C. § 183(b). While the 1936 amendments to the act provided for an increase in the death and injury claimants' share of the fund to a maximum of $60 per ton, this was increased in 1984 to $420 per ton. Under Section 3(c) of the act, 46 App. U.S.C. § 183(c), the limitation tonnage is computed by deducting the crew spaces from the gross tonnage, whereas under art. III (7) of the 1976 Convention the limitation tonnage is computed by adding the engine room spaces to the net tonnage. The result is about the same under both regimes. If the limitation tonnage is in dispute, a naval architect will be needed to establish its precise amount.

to $420 per ton, to be available only for the payment of death and injury claims. Paragraph (d) of the same section provides that the owner of any such seagoing vessel shall be liable in respect of loss of life or bodily injury "arising on distinct occasions" to the same extent as if no other loss of life or bodily injury had occurred.

(c) Property Damage Claims. With respect to property damage, all limitable claims arising on the voyage are subject to the same limitation. Thus, assume that a collision occurs, and a colliding vessel whose owners are seeking limitation remains sufficiently seaworthy to proceed on her scheduled voyage. If another liability-creating incident occurs during the voyage, liabilities for property damage occurring on both occasions are treated together for limitation purposes. But personal injury and death claims arising on each occasion are treated separately, in the case of seagoing vessels. Thus, if limitation is allowed, the owner can be held liable to death and injury claimants for a maximum of $840 per ton of the vessel's limitation tonnage, i.e., to a maximum of $420 in respect of each incident.

In *In re Alva Steamship Co. (The Alva Cape),*[40] there was a collision, explosion, and fire, with great loss of life and personal injury. Twelve days later, during an effort to inert the vessel's cargo tanks, there was another explosion on the burned-out hulk, causing the vessel to sink, with further loss of life and personal injury. The issue before the court was the narrow one of whether the owner should be required to post security for two personal injury and wrongful death funds of $60 per ton each (the then-current limit, which was later increased to $420). The court held that security should be posted for two funds, one for the claims arising out of the initial collision, explosion, and fire, and one for the subsequent explosion and sinking.

The 1936 Amendments made no change affecting property claimants. Where limitation is granted they remain entitled to a pro rata share of the basic fund. Thus, if the fund is $500,000, the limitation tonnage is 5,000 tons, the provable property claims total $100,000, and the provable death and injury claims total $900,000, the property claimants will receive their pro rata share of the fund ($50,000). Since the death and injury claimants' pro rata share of the fund ($450,000) is less than $420 multiplied by the limitation tonnage ($2,100,000), they will receive the full amount of their provable damages ($900,000).

4. *"Privity or Knowledge"*

The most difficult problem for the shipowner seeking limitation is usually in meeting the heavy burden of proving that the acts or omissions leading to the

40. 262 F. Supp. 328, 1967 AMC 2363 (SDNY 1966).

casualty were not within its "privity or knowledge."[41] This is essentially a burden of proving a negative.[42] Thus today, the most common reason for a denial of limitation is the owner's failure to prove the absence of privity or knowledge in any negligence or unseaworthiness causing or contributing to the loss.[43] The elements of the shipowner's proof are:

1. Seaworthiness of the vessel's hull and equipment;[44]
2. Competence of the crew, including proper licensing, training, and shipboard experience;[45]
3. A cause of the loss not involving privity, e.g., negligent navigation by a qualified watch officer, or elimination of all possible causes which would involve privity where the cause cannot be shown precisely;[46]

---

41. 46 App. U.S.C. § 183(a); *Coryell v. Phipps,* 317 U.S. 406, 410 (1943): "The burden of establishing a lack of privity or knowledge under 46 U.S.C. § 183(a) [now 46 App. U.S.C. § 183(a)] is on those who seek its benefit."

42. See *In re Hercules Carriers, Inc.,* 506 F. Supp. 962, 1983 AMC 2409 (MD Fla. 1983).

43. See *The Argent,* 1940 AMC 508, 509 (SDNY 1915): "If lack of actual knowledge were enough, imbecility, real or assumed, on the part of owners would be at a premium." Id. (constructive knowledge of an improper navigational light in place for a year and a half.); *In re Ta Chi (Panama) Navigation Corp.,* supra note 7 (improper manning).

See generally *Spencer Kellogg & Sons v. Hicks (The Linseed King),* 285 U.S. 502, 1932 AMC 503 (1932). A hostile judicial attitude toward limitation may be observed in this case, where the owner had a company launch to carry workers from New York City to its factory on the west side of the Hudson River. The launch was not of sufficient strength to operate in icy conditions on the river, and the master had received written instructions not to operate the launch under those conditions. Nevertheless, the launch was operated on an icy day, when it ran into an ice floe and sank, causing more than 80 deaths by drowning. The court denied limitation, reasoning that the written directive was insufficient to establish absence of privity or knowledge in the negligence of the master; further steps were required to prevent the launch from operating in icy conditions. Professors Gilmore and Black interpret the case as establishing that the duty to control employees increases with the possibility of control. Gilmore & Black 877. See also *Continental Oil Co. v. Bonanza Corp.,* 677 F.2d 455, 1983 AMC 387 (5th Cir. 1982); *Avera v. Florida Towing Co.,* 322 F.2d 155, 165, 1963 AMC 2110 (5th Cir. 1963), quoting the first edition of Gilmore & Black 704.

See *In re Marine Sulphur Queen,* 460 F.2d 89, 1972 AMC 1972 (2d Cir. 1972), where the owners could not disprove privity or knowledge in the sinking of a converted sulphur carrier because of the owner's knowledge of the conversion plans. The conversion was found to have made the vessel unseaworthy. Note that under 46 App. U.S.C. § 183(d) in respect of loss of life or bodily injury, the privity or knowledge of the master of a seagoing vessel at or before commencement of each voyage is imputed to the owner. This provision is inapplicable to property damage claims. See *Moore-McCormack Lines, Inc. v. Armco Steel Co. (The Mormackite),* 272 F.2d 873, 1960 AMC 185 (2d Cir. 1959); Gilmore & Black 923–25.

44. *In re Farrell Lines, Inc.,* 530 F.2d 7, 1976 AMC 1639 (5th Cir. 1976).

45. *The Tug Ocean Prince v. United States,* 584 F.2d 1151, 1978 AMC 1786 (2d Cir. 1978); *In re Ta Chi Navigation (Panama) Corp.,* supra note 7; *In re Hercules Carriers, Inc.,* supra note 42; *Brister v. A.W.I., Inc.* 946 F.2d 350, 1993 AMC 1990 (5th Cir. 1991); *In re Oil Spill by the Amoco Cadiz,* 954 F.2d 1279, 1992 AMC 913 (7th Cir. 1992).

46. *In re Flota Mercante Grancolombiana,* 440 F. Supp. 704, 1979 AMC 156 (SDNY 1977), aff'd w/o op., 573 F.2d 1290 (2d Cir 1977).

4. Absence of actual control of the activity causing the loss by corporate officers, directors, managing agents, or managerial employees of the owner.[47]

In contrast to English law, American decisions have imputed to the owner the privity or knowledge of supervisory employees, such as marine superintendents, superintendent engineers, and even port captains, regardless of formal title.[48] To defeat limitation, English law requires the privity or knowledge of an *alter ego* of a corporate owner, i.e., someone higher up on the corporate structure, such as a director.[49]

Generalizations respecting privity or knowledge are likely to be misleading. Accordingly, summarized below are some fairly recent cases in which the owner has successfully proved absence of privity or knowledge, and some in which limitation has been denied because of the owner's inability to prove its absence.

Decisions granting limitation: In *Gibney v. Wright*[50] an improperly secured fuel tank on a 30-foot racing sloop was held not a defect the owner should have discovered through reasonable inspection, as it would have been impossible to inspect the tank without cutting away some portion of the cockpit sole or cabin bulkhead. In *In re Farrell Lines, Inc.*[51] the district court's denial of limitation, based on an alleged inadequacy of procedures, personnel, and equipment to prevent human error was reversed; the vessel's allision with a bridge was held caused by the helmsman's erroneous execution of a pilot's rudder order. In *In re Valley Line Co.*[52] a tug master's miscalculation, resulting in a collision with a barge, was held not within the attributable knowledge or means of knowledge of which the owner or his superintendent was

47. *In re Hercules Carriers Inc.*, supra note 42; *Waterman Steamship Corp. v. Gay Cottons,* 414 F.2d 724, 1969 AMC 1682 (9th Cir. 1969) (owner's failure to have an operable radio direction finder; the one on board had not been accurately calibrated over a five-year period).

48. *Coleman v. Jahncke Service, Inc.*, 341 F.2d 956, 1965 AMC 535, (5th Cir. 1965); *China Union Lines, Ltd. v. A.O. Andersen & Co.*, 364 F.2d 769, 1966 AMC 1653 (5th Cir. 1966). See *In re P. Sanford Ross, Inc.*, 204 F. 248, 251 (2d Cir. 1913): "[T]he . . . test is not as to their being [corporate] officers in a strict sense but as to the largeness of their authority." See also *Great Atlantic & Pacific Tea Co. v. Lloyd Brasileiro,* 159 F.2d 601, 1947 AMC 306 (2d Cir. 1947), decided under 46 App. U.S.C. §182 (the "fire statute") (traffic manager authorized to maintain the vessel, hire the crew, settle claims, and make contracts); *Pennzoil Producing Co. v. Offshore Express, Inc.*, 943 F.2d 1465 (5th Cir. 1991) (allision of offshore utility vessel with a natural-gas pipeline; limitation denied on the basis of knowledge of the general manager that masters of these utility vessels operated the vessels in fog, with resulting accidents. See also *Greater New Orleans Expressway Commission v. The Tug Claribel,* 222 F. Supp. 521, 1964 AMC 967 (ED La. 1964) (superintendent of tug company).

49. *The Garden City,* [1982] 2 Lloyd's Rep. 382 (Q.B.Adm.Ct.). Cf. *The Marion,* [1983], 2 Lloyd's Rep. 15, aff'd [1984] A.C 563 (H.L.); *F.T. Everard & Sons, Ltd. v. London and Thames Haven Oil Wharves Ltd. (The Anonity),* [1961] 2 Lloyd's Rep. 118 (C.A.); *The Lady Gwendolen,* [1964] 2 Lloyd's Rep. 99 (Adm.); see also *Lennard's Carrying Co. v. Asiatic Petroleum Co.,* [1915] A.C. 705.

50. 517 F.2d 1054, 1975 AMC 2071 (5th Cir. 1975).

51. 530 F.2d 7, 1976 AMC 1639 (5th Cir. 1976).

52. 564 F. Supp. 612 (ED Mo. 1983).

bound to avail himself. In *Hellenic Lines, Ltd. v. Prudential Lines, Inc.*[53] the second mate's inability to plot radar contacts, while known to the owner, was held overcome by the owner's instruction that the master was to be summoned to the bridge in low visibility. Thus, the second mate's failure to call the master and his navigational errors were held not within the owner's privity or knowledge. In *In re Seiriki Kisen Kaisha*[54] the practice of permitting the helmsman-lookout on a fully automated ship to go below to call the next watch was held not improper under ordinary conditions, but it was a fault to follow the practice when another vessel was close by. While the shoreside management was aware of the practice under ordinary conditions, they were not privy to the watch officer's permitting the helmsman-lookout to go below with another vessel close by, and limitation was therefore granted. The other vessel was also held to blame, and was denied limitation because her watch officer, whose negligent navigation was a primary cause of the collision, did not have a proper license.

Decisions denying limitation: In *The Ocean Eagle*[55] a tanker overloaded by seven inches broke in two at a harbor entrance, causing a massive oil spill. The overloading had produced sagging stresses in the hull. The owner knew of overloadings on at least nine previous voyages and had failed to make up a loading manual, as required by safety regulations. The owner's destruction of loading records from previous voyages was held to justify an inference that the vessel was overloaded with its privity and knowledge, and limitation was therefore denied. In *In re Flota Mercante Grancolombiana*[56] a localized power failure on the bridge incapacitated the gyrocompass and the manual and push-button steering controls and contributed to a both-to-blame collision. The fact that there had been two previous unexplained power failures persuaded the court that negligent inspection and servicing of the electrical system was within the owner's privity. *Empress Lineas Maritimas, S.A. v. United States*[57] involved a collision between a freighter and a U.S. Coast Guard cutter that was found caused by navigational errors of the cutter's commanding officer, affected by his medical condition. While his condition was known to his superior officers, they failed to conduct a more probing inquiry to determine whether it might affect his ability to perform his duties as commanding officer. In *Verdin v. C&B Boat, Inc.*[58] limitation was denied in a wrongful death case because of the owner's constructive knowledge of a failure to maintain safety equipment. In *In re Hercules Carriers, Inc.*[59] a vessel allided with a bridge as a result of unseaworthiness and negligence, causing the collapse of the

53. 813 F.2d 634, 1987 AMC 2470 (4th Cir. 1987), on remand from *In re Hellenic Lines, Ltd.*, 730 F.2d 159, 1984 AMC 2713 (4th Cir. 1984).

54. 629 F. Supp. 1374, 1986 AMC 913 (SDNY 1986).

55. 1974 AMC 1629 (D P.R. 1974).

56. 440 F. Supp. 704, 1979 AMC 156 (SDNY 1977), aff'd w/o op., 573 F.2d 1290 (2d Cir. 1977).

57. 730 F.2d 153, 1984 AMC 1698 (4th Cir. 1984)

58. 860 F.2d 150 (5th Cir. 1988).

59. 506 F. Supp. 962, 1983 AMC 2409 (MD Fla. 1983)

bridge, with heavy loss of life. The owner's unwritten policy was to place the pilot rather than the master in ultimate command in pilotage waters, so that the master's failure to countermand negligent orders of the pilot caused the allision. Limitation was denied for this reason and others, including the lack of a shipboard training program and the owner's failure to check the licenses of the chief and second mates (which were in fact fraudulent), although the management knew of a problem of fraudulent licenses in the fleet. In *In re Chevron Transport Co.*[60] a tanker collided with a dredge flotilla, the management personnel of the tanker owner having failed to distribute to the masters of vessels in the fleet a notice to mariners concerning the presence of the dredge. Limitation was therefore denied. In *In re Thebes Shipping Co. (The Argo Merchant)*[61] a tanker went aground, broke in two, and sank, causing a massive oil spill; limitation was denied because of general gross mismanagement and neglect of the owners, who were thus in privity with the improper, slipshod navigational practices of the master. Furthermore, persistent failures of the gyrocompass and radio direction finder rendered the ship unseaworthy. There was ample notice to the management, because the deck logs contained irregular true-course entries having no rational relationship to the magnetic compass entries. In *In re Cameron Boat Rentals, Inc.*[62] an oil rig crew boat struck and sank an anchored wooden pleasure fishing boat, causing death and personal injuries. Limitation was denied because pilots ignorant of radar fundamentals were hired and their maintenance of excessive speed and failure to keep a proper look-out caused the disaster.

Section C. Limitation of Liability in Both-to-Blame Collision Cases

1. *The Single Liability Rule*

At the outset it should be noted that much judicial thinking has centered around the almost ideal situation where the colliding vessel interests and all possible claimants are proceeding in the same court, where, additionally, the contending shipowners have filed complaints for exoneration from, or limitation of, liability. Since claimants remain free to select a favorable forum outside the United States, however, it is not always possible to force a single forum, regardless of efficiency.[63]

The judicial goal is a single judgment, essentially a shortcut, where the one judgment determines all issues, including not only the liability issues but the right of each owner to limit and the constitution and distribution of the

60. 613 F. Supp. 1428 (MD Fla. 1985), modified, 832 F.2d 1540, 1988 AMC 2278 (11th Cir. 1987).
61. 486 F. Supp. 436, 1980 AMC 1686 (SDNY 1980).
62. 683 F. Supp. 577 (WD La. 1988), on remand from 819 F.2d 1140 (5th Cir. 1987).
63. See *The Salvore,* supra note 4.

fund of the shipowner on the "paying end." Because of the difficulty sometimes encountered in achieving this goal today, a court must devise solutions for those situations in which only a part of the collision-limitation puzzle has been referred to it. The place to begin is the 1882 Supreme Court decision in *The North Star—The Ella Warley,*[64] involving a collision between two steamships in an end-on meeting situation, one entering and the other leaving New York Harbor. The inbound *Ella Warley* sank and was a total loss; the outbound *North Star* was badly damaged, but survived to be arrested *in rem* in an action brought by the *Ella Warley*'s owners. The *North Star*'s owners filed a cross-libel (counterclaim) against the *Ella Warley*'s owners, and the libel and cross-libel were tried together. The result was both-to-blame, and the circuit court divided the damages equally under the American rule then in force,[65] rendering a decree in favor of the *Ella Warley*'s owners for the amount by which their damages exceeded one-half the total damages of both parties.

Neither owner petitioned for limitation, but the Supreme Court described the *Ella Warley*'s total-loss situation as the equivalent of one where her owners had filed a limitation petition.[66] (At the time *The North Star* was decided, an owner was permitted to delay seeking limitation until after being held liable.) The Court noted that the *North Star* would probably not be entitled to limit because the faulty positioning of her sidelights was attributable to her owners and was a contributing cause of the collision. The *Ella Warley*'s owners contended that, as their vessel was a total loss, the Limitation Act protected them against any liability to the *North Star*'s owners, they were entitled to recover half their damages from the *North Star*'s owners, and that the latter were not entitled to any deduction in respect of the *North Star*'s damages, i.e., that limitation should be applied *before* a balance was struck between the damages of the two vessels. This contention was flatly rejected by the Supreme Court, which affirmed the decree of the circuit court as written. The Court thus established the rule that in both-to-blame collision cases, limitation is applied only after a balance has been struck, and then, in the absence of privity or knowledge, it is applied to the balance which would otherwise be owing by one owner to the other. The rule was stated by the Court as follows: "When this resulting liability of one party to the other has been ascertained, then, and not before, would seem to be the proper time to apply the rule of limited responsibility, if the party decreed to pay is entitled to it. It will enable him to avoid payment pro tanto of the balance found against him."[67] While the rule was adopted at a time when damages were divided equally in both-

64. 106 U.S. 17 (1882).

65. *The Schooner Catharine v. Dickinson,* 58 U.S. 170 (1855).

66. 106 U.S. at 29: "The *Ella Warley* by her loss discharged her portion of the common burden, and so much more as the amount that would thus be decreed in her favor. Her delivery to the waves was tantamount to her surrender into court in case she had survived."

67. 106 U.S. at 20. See *The Manitoba,* 122 U.S. 97 (1897), interpreting *The North Star,* and applying it to a situation where the damages were very unequal ($85,818 and $7,470, respectively) although the vessels' faults were equal.

to-blame collision cases, regardless of the respective degrees of blame, it remains valid under the proportional fault rule in force in the United States since *Reliable Transfer.*[68]

The following is an example of its application in a case where Vessel A is 75 percent and Vessel B 25 percent to blame for a collision causing A $100,000 and B $200,000 in damages:

A's 75 percent share of total damages:	$225,000
A's own damages:	–100,000
Single liability of A to B before limitation:	$125,000
B's own damages:	$200,000
B's 25 percent share of total damages:	–75,000
Single liability of A to B before limitation:	$125,000

If A is held entitled to limitation, A's fund is $80,000, and there are no other claims against the fund, then B will receive A's entire fund ($80,000) and will have to bear the remaining $45,000 of the $125,000 B would have received from A if limitation had been denied.

Assuming there is no reversal on appeal, as there is only a single liability, i.e., the liability of A to B, and no cross-liability of B to A, then whether or not B has filed a complaint for limitation will be of no consequence. Nor, if B *has* filed a complaint, will it be of any consequence whether or not B has been able to prove absence of privity or knowledge.

In the example given, it is presupposed that any third-party claims for which each vessel is liable have been paid or secured and included in the collision damages of the party or parties paying or securing the claims.[69] It is also presupposed that any claims representative of Vessel A, such as outstanding claims for unrepaired collision damage arising on a prior voyage, have been included in A's limitation fund.[70] Other illustrations of adjustments in both-to-blame collision cases involving limitation will be found in the appendix.

2. *Innocent Claimants' Right to Priority*

This section describes the application of equitable principles[71] in the distribution of an inadequate limitation fund. In the marshaling of claims and the distribution of the fund, a district court, as a court of admiralty, will apply the equitable principle of subordination or postponement of claims of parties without "clean hands" (such as the other colliding vessel in a both-to-blame case) until all claimants innocent of fault have been paid in full or the fund

68. 421 U.S. 397, 1975 AMC 541 (1975).
69. *The Albert Dumois,* 177 U.S. 240 (1900).
70. *O'Brien v. Miller,* supra note 36.
71. *Hartford Accident and Indemnity Co. v. Southern Pacific Co. (The Bolikow),* supra note 22, 1927 AMC 402 (1927).

has been exhausted.[72] Thus, valid cargo, personal injury, and wrongful death claims have priority over the claim of the other colliding vessel if she is also to blame. Application of the priority rule can sometimes lead to strange results, as will be seen from the following example:

Assume Vessel B, in ballast, and Vessel C, with cargo, are both to blame for navigational errors causing a high-seas collision resulting in $100,000 in damage to B, $1,000,000 in damage to C, and $1,000,000 in damage to C's cargo; that each vessel seeks limitation in the same court, and that each is granted the right to limit. Assume, further, that each vessel is of a 1910 Brussels Collision Convention State, and that the carriage of C's cargo was subject to the Brussels Bill of Lading Convention (the Hague Rules). If the court were to assess 60 percent of the blame against C and 40 percent against B, C would pay nothing to cargo because of the Hague Rules errors in navigation defense. Before limitation, B would be liable to cargo for $400,000 (40 percent of $1,000,000), without any right to indemnification. Before limitation, B would be liable to C for $340,000, computed as follows:

C's damages:	$1,000,000
B's damages:	+100,000
Total:	$1,100,000
	×.40
B's share:	$ 440,000
B's own damages:	–100,000
B's liability to C before limitation:	$ 340,000

If B's fund was $500,000, C's Cargo would receive $400,000 (40 percent of $1,000,000), and C would receive the remaining $100,000 of B's fund. But if the court were to assess 50 percent of the blame against each vessel, the result would be that C's Cargo would receive $500,000 (50 percent of $1,000,000), thereby exhausting the fund, so that C would receive nothing. Thus, while C's Cargo would fare better with a 50 percent-50 percent division than with a 60 percent-40 percent division in B's favor, C would actually fare better with a 60 percent-40 percent division in B's favor than with a 50 percent-50 percent division.

3. Conclusion

As we have seen, the single liability rule of *The North Star* in both-to-blame collision cases remains valid today. But results under the rule may vary greatly,

72. *The Mauch Chunk,* 154 F.2d 182 (2d Cir. 1907). See also *The Catskill,* 95 F. 700 (SDNY 1899); *In re A. C. Dodge, Inc.,* 282 F.2d 86, 1961 AMC 233 (2d Cir. 1960); *In re Marina Mercante Nicaraguense, S.A.,* 248 F. Supp. 15, 1966 AMC 1777 (SDNY 1965), modified, 364 F.2d 118, 1966 AMC 2392 (2d Cir. 1966); *Oliver J. Olson & Co. v. The Marine Leopard,* 356 F.2d 728, 1966 AMC 1064 (9th Cir. 1966). Cf. *Moore-McCormack Lines v. Richardson,* 295 F.2d 583, 1962 AMC 804 (2d Cir. 1961); *The Virginia,* 266 F. 437 (D Md. 1920).

depending upon a number of factors. These include the governing law, i.e., whether it is American (or Liberian[73]) or that of a 1910 Collision Convention State; the percentage of blame chargeable to each vessel; if there is cargo damage, the nature of the fault chargeable to the carrying vessel, i.e., whether it was solely an error in navigation, or whether unseaworthiness or improper manning was a cause; whether the package limitation is applicable; whether the governing contract of carriage is a bill of lading subject to COGSA or the Harter Act, in which case a "both-to-blame" collision clause would be invalid, or whether it is a charter party that did not incorporate the terms of either statute by reference, in which case the clause would be valid.

73. The Liberian Maritime Law incorporates by reference the general maritime law of the United States.

CHAPTER FIFTEEN

SALVAGE AND GENERAL AVERAGE IN COLLISION CASES

Section A. Review of the Elements of Salvage

A collision may produce a sinking or stranding, or cause a vessel to drift without power. Accordingly, salvors and their tugs will be involved in many collision situations.[1]

Salvage, whether contractual or noncontractual (usually called "pure salvage"), is an independent doctrine in Anglo-American law. It is descended from the ancient codes of the general maritime law, and has been the subject of two international conventions: the 1910 Salvage Convention[2] and the 1989 Salvage Convention.[3] The 1989 Convention entered into force in 1996. It was intended to replace the 1910 Convention and has done so in the States that have ratified it, which include the United States, Canada, and the United Kingdom. There are also federal statutes[4] and a considerable body of case law and literature[5] on the subject.

1. See e.g., *In re Yamashita-Shinnihon Kisen,* 305 F. Supp. 796, 1969 AMC 2102 (D Or. 1969), involving a collision between the Japanese *Suwaharu Maru* and the Liberian *Mandoil II* 300 miles west of the mouth of the Columbia River. The *Mandoil* was eventually towed to Nootka Sound, B.C., by the tug *Sudbury* under a Lloyd's Open Form Salvage Agreement, and the *Suwaharu Maru* was eventually towed to Victoria, B.C., by the tug *Arthur Foss* for a contract towage fee of $30,050. Judge Beeks's decision in a consolidated proceeding of the limitation petitions of both vessels contains an interesting discussion of problems of pure salvage, contract salvage, and life salvage that can arise following a collision. It is often forgotten that the master and crew of a salving vessel as well as her owner have salvage rights. See *Squires v. Ionian Leader,* 100 F. Supp. 829, 1952 AMC 161 (D N.J. 1951); *Sobonis v. The National Defender,* 298 F. Supp. 631, 1969 AMC 1219 (SDNY 1969).

2. Convention for the Unification of Certain Rules With Respect to Assistance and Salvage At Sea, Brussels, Sept. 23, 1910, T.S. No. 576, 37 Stat. 1670 (hereinafter "1910 Convention"). The official text, in French, appears at 37 Stat. 1658. The 1910 Convention entered into force March 1, 1913, but was suspended during the First and Second World Wars. See I. Wildeboer, *The Brussels Salvage Convention* (1965). For the intent of Congress to conform U.S. law to the 1910 Convention, see *The Impoco,* 287 F. 400 (SDNY 1922).

3. International Convention on Salvage, London, April 20, 1989, I.M.O. Doc. LEG 60/12. The text is reprinted at 20 J. Mar. L. & Com. 589-602 (1989).

4. 46 App. U.S.C. §§ 729 (life salvage). See also 10 U.S.C. §§ 7361–65 (salvage by U.S. naval vessels); 19 U.S.C. § 1310 (duty-free status of salvaged merchandise); 43 U.S.C. §§ 2101–6 (the Abandoned Shipwrecks Act); 46 App. U.S.C. §§ 721–25 (strandings on U.S. and foreign coasts); 46 App. U.S.C. §§ 741–52 and §§ 781–90 (actions against the United States for salvage services rendered to government vessels and cargoes); 46 U.S.C. §§ 2303–4 (the Stand-By Act, as amended—duty to provide assistance at sea); 33 U.S.C. §§ 409, 411–16, 418, 502 (the Wreck Act); 18 U.S.C. § 1658 (crime of plundering a distressed vessel).

5. The leading American text, by Martin J. Norris, has now been incorporated in 3A *Benedict on Admiralty* (7th ed. rev. 1993) (hereinafter "Benedict"). See also E. Brady, *Marine Salvage*

The public policy behind salvage is the encouragement of daring individuals to rescue maritime property in peril at sea or in other navigable waters, and to discourage theft. Thus, the reward which successful salvors are entitled to receive distinguishes salvage from the reimbursement of out-of-pocket expenses which persons saving lives and nonmaritime property may obtain under the common law.[6]

Today, most collision salvage will be performed under a contract, usually on the Lloyd's Open Form Salvage Agreement (LOF).[7] In order to avoid problems of unconscionability or compulsion[8] in the negotiation of salvage contracts for stipulated amounts, the amount of the award is left open in

---

Operations (1960); G. Brice, *The Maritime Law of Salvage* (2d. ed. 1993); and W. Kennedy, *The Law of Civil Salvage* (5th ed. 1987, K. McGuffie, ed.) for the English law. See also G. Darling & C. Smith, *LOF 90 and the New Salvage Convention* (1991); and E. Vincenzini, *International Salvage Law* (1992). Additional textual treatment can be found in G. Gilmore & C. Black, *The Law of Admiralty* (2d ed. 1975) (hereinafter "Gilmore & Black"); T. Schoenbaum, *Admiralty and Maritime Law* (2d ed. 1994); W. Tetley, *Maritime Liens and Claims* (1985); and G. Robinson, *The Law of Admiralty* (1939).

See also Parks, *The 1910 Brussels Convention, the United States Salvage Act of 1912 and the Arbitration of Salvage Cases in the United States,* 57 Tul. L. Rev. 1457 (1983); Bessemer Clark, *The Role of Lloyd's Open Form,* [1980] 3 LMCLQ 297; Gold, *Marine Salvage: Towards a New Regime,* 20 J. Mar. L. & Com. 407 (1989); and Kerr, *The 1989 Salvage Convention: Expediency or Equity?* 20 J. Mar. L. & Com. 506 (1989).

6. *The Blackwall,* 77 U.S. 1, 14 (1870): "Public policy encourages the hardy and adventurous mariner to engage in these laborious and sometimes dangerous enterprises, and with a view to withdraw from him every temptation to embezzlement and dishonesty, the law allows him, in case he is successful, a liberal compensation . . . ." See *Mason v. The Blaireau,* 6 U.S. 240 (1804), for a comparison of land law and the maritime law of salvage. See also *Rest. Restitution* § 2 (officious conferring of benefit) (1936). Under the common law, "rescuers" were officious intermeddlers. In equity they were left unrewarded, as volunteers. Cf. French *Code Civil,* art. 1372, the *"gestion d'affaires"* concept, encouraging rescue of property, a descendant of the Roman law *"negotiorum gestio."*

7. Lloyd's Open Form 1995, replacing earlier LOF forms (NO CURE-NO PAY), made available from the Corporation of Lloyd's since 1892. An American decision concerning the master's authority to bind cargo to the LOF form (and, under the circumstances of the case, rejecting such authority) is *American Metal Co., Ltd. v. The Belleville,* 284 F. Supp. 1002, 1970 AMC 633 (SDNY 1968).

LOF 1995 (clause 14) provides that the master of the vessel signs as agent for the vessel, cargo, freight, bunkers, stores, and other property, and the respective owners thereof. English law requires a "true agency of necessity" in order to bind the cargo owner. See *Industrie Chimiche Italia Centrale v. Alexander G. Tsavliris & Sons Maritime Co. Ltd.,* [1990] 1 Lloyd's Rep. 516 (C.A. 1990), where a salvage award against cargo under the LOF form was reversed, on the ground that the master did not have the authority to bind the cargo interests to the contract without their consent, since the facts were not such as to create an agency of necessity.

8. *The Jessomene,* 47 F. 903 (D Cal. 1891); *Magnolia Petroleum Co. v. National Oil Transport,* 281 F. 336 (5th Cir. 1923); *Scott v. Four Hundred and Forty-five Tons of Coal,* 39 F. 285 (D Conn. 1889); *Higgins v. The Tri-State,* 99 F. Supp. 694, 1951 AMC 862 (SD Fla. 1951), for examples of salvage contracts not enforced.

Cf. *The Elfrida,* 172 U.S. 186 (1898) (contract enforced as not unconscionable despite appearance of unreasonable compensation). Contract salvage will be awarded where the efforts are successful within a limited time, the contract having been made without a mistake of fact, or fraud, or compulsion. There is a presumption in favor of the contract even though the price agreed turns out to be greater than the services were actually worth. See *Osal Marine Services, Inc. v. The Panasea,* 1993 AMC 1930 (WD Wash. 1992); and *Flagship Marine Services, Inc. v. Belcher Towing Co.,* 966 F.2d 602, 1992 AMC 2901 (11th Cir. 1992).

LOF agreements. If the parties cannot agree on the amount after a successful salvage operation, the issue is submitted to arbitration by an arbitrator appointed by the Committee of Lloyd's,[9] and English law will apply. LOF further provides for a right of appeal to an appeal arbitrator, who is also appointed by the Committee of Lloyd's.[10]

A successful salvor has a maritime lien for salvage,[11] but not title to the salved property, unless the owner has abandoned title. The maritime lien for salvage has the second highest position in the ladder of priorities of maritime liens, ranking only after maritime liens for wages of the master and crew.[12] In fact, at a time when wages depended on the safe prosecution of the voyage, salvage liens were sometimes ranked ahead of wage liens, on the theory that but for the efforts of the salvors, no wages would have been earned. This chapter will be concerned with maritime property that has an identifiable owner, and not with marine archaeology or treasure salvage. Under the law of finds, usually involved in marine archaeology, it is possible to obtain an award of title when the property has been definitely abandoned by the owner.

---

9. See LOF 1995, clause 1 (c) and (g). In addition to the law of England (including English salvage law), LOF 1995 incorporates Articles 1, 8, 13, and 14 of the 1989 Salvage Convention (supra note 3). The arbitrator is appointed by the Committee of Lloyd's (clause 6a). There are no formal rules of evidence (clause 9a[i]). An earlier edition of the LOF received a positive endorsement from the House of Lords in *Admiralty Commissioners v. The Valverda,* [1938] A. C. 173.

The LOF 1995 differs radically from the earlier forms (except the 1994 form), in that it provides a "safety net" to compensate a salvor who is unsuccessful in salving property, but whose efforts prevent or minimize damage to the marine environment. This is a departure from the general maritime law principle of "no cure, no pay."

In *In re Oil Spill by Amoco Cadiz off Coast of France,* 639 F.2d 789, 1981 AMC 2407 (7th Cir. 1981), the LOF London Arbitration Clause was held applicable to disputes under the agreement in addition to disputes concerning the amount of an award. The dispute in question concerned the claim of Amoco, an American company, against Bugsier, a German salvage company, for alleged negligence in the attempt of one of its tugs to salvage the *Amoco Cadiz.*

In *Jones v. Sea Tow Services,* 30 F.3d 360, 1994 AMC 2661 (2d Cir. 1994), where all the parties were American, the court refused to apply the London arbitration provision of LOF to a claim for salvage of a pleasure craft. Refusal to require arbitration in London of a purely local American dispute may have been the impetus, in part, for the new one-page "U.S. Open Form Salvage Agreement," code name "MARSALV," offered by the Society of Maritime Arbitrators, Inc., since 1995.

10. See LOF 1995, clause 11(d).

11. *The Sabine,* 101 U.S. 384 (1879). In addition to the claim of the owner of the salving vessel, there is an independent claim by her crew. *Squires v. The Ionian Leader,* supra note 1; *Nicholas E. Vernicos Shipping Co. v. United States,* 349 F.2d 465, 1965 AMC 1673 (2d Cir. 1965); *Goldade v. The Seattle Star,* 1992 AMC 808 (Arbitration at Seattle, 1991), except when the crew is employed by a professional salvage company. *W.E. Rippon & Son v. United States (The Ocklawaha),* 1964 AMC 2695 (SDNY 1963), modified on other grounds (reduction of the amount of the award), 348 F.2d 627, 1967 AMC 153 (2d Cir. 1965); Norris (3A Benedict) § 81.

12. *In re Ta Chi Navigation (Panama) Corp., S.A.,* 583 F. Supp. 1322, 1985 AMC 1367 (SDNY 1984); *The William Leishar,* 21 F.2d 862 (D Md. 1927). Of course, "expenses of justice," e.g., for wharfage furnished to a vessel in the custody of a court, outrank all maritime liens. *New York Dock Co. v. The Poznan,* 274 U.S. 117, 1927 AMC 723 (1927).

The Abandoned Shipwrecks Act of 1988[13] is applicable when an abandoned wreck is embedded in the land at the bottom of the coastal sea. Under the Act the states, rather than the federal government, are responsible for protecting the natural resources and shipwreck sites so that efforts will be made for their recovery, consistent with historical value, scientific archaeological principles, and environmental integrity.[14] The act, however, removes the law of salvage and the law of finds from the area to which the statute applies[15]—a congressional alteration of the traditional maritime law, which was nationalized under Article III, clause 1 of the U.S. Constitution.

Underlying both contractual and pure salvage are basic requirements, which will be briefly summarized:[16]

1. Maritime property: a vessel,[17] cargo, or freight monies[18] must be involved.[19]

---

13. Pub. L. 100-298, 43 U.S.C. §§ 2101–06 (1996). By § 2105(c) the title of the United States is transferred to the state in or on whose submerged lands the shipwreck is located. See *Zych v. Unidentified Wrecked and Abandoned Vessel,* 941 F.2d 525, 1992 AMC 532 (7th Cir. 1991).

14. 43 U.S.C. § 2101 (1996).

15. 43 U.S.C. § 2106(a).

16. See *The Blackwall,* 77 U.S. 1 (1870). A British vessel loaded with sacks of grain caught fire while at anchor in San Francisco Harbor. Eventual success in extinguishing the fire was due to the work of fire department personnel. Plaintiff's tug was used to carry pumping engines and firemen to the fire, to put a line on the ship during the fire, and then to tow the ship to safety after the fire was extinguished. Plaintiff's activities, in combination with others, took an hour. In approving an award in plaintiff's favor, against defendant's objections that the fire had been extinguished by the fire department in pursuance of a public duty, so that no salvage situation existed, the Supreme Court succinctly defined salvage: "Salvage is the compensation allowed to persons by whose assistance a ship or her cargo has been saved, in whole or in part, from impending peril on the sea, or in recovering such property from actual loss, as in cases of shipwreck, derelict, or recapture. Success is essential to the claim . . . ." See also *The Clarita and The Clara,* 90 U.S. 1 (1874); and *Allseas Maritime S.A. v. The Mimosa,* 812 F.2d 243, 1987 AMC 2515 (5th Cir. 1987). Professors Gilmore and Black note that the formal requisites of an act of salvage bear a close family resemblance to those of a general average act. See Gilmore & Black 534.

17. In *Cope v. Vallete Dry Dock Co.,* 119 U.S. 625 (1887), a floating dry dock permanently moored (for twenty years) to the shore was held not the subject of a salvage claim by those rescuing the dry dock after a collision.

18. When freight is collect it is subject to salvage, because it is saved when the ship is saved from a marine peril by salvors.

19. In *The Steamship Jefferson,* 215 U.S. 130 (1909), the vessel was undergoing repairs in a dry dock when fire broke out. The court below held that there was no marine peril and that the law of salvage was therefore inapplicable to successful efforts to extinguish the fire. The Supreme Court reversed, holding that salvage was applicable to vessels whether at sea, at a pier, or in dry dock. See also *Taylor v. 42 Foot Egg Harbor Hull,* 1995 AMC 582 (D N.J. 1994).

It is likely that the legal tests applied in maritime tort cases may be applied to the question of what is maritime property in salvage cases, i.e., that the property must be involved in a traditional maritime activity. See *Executive Jet Aviation, Inc. v. City of Cleveland,* 409 U.S. 249, 1973 AMC 1 (1972); *Foremost Insurance Co. v. Richardson,* 457 U.S. 668, 1982 AMC 2253 (1982); *Sisson v. Ruby,* 497 U.S. 358, 1990 AMC 1801 (1990); *Jerome B. Grubart, Inc. v. Great Lakes Dredge & Dock Co.,* 513 U.S. 527, 1995 AMC 913 (1995).

2. Marine peril: there must be some kind of danger[20] to the vessel,[21] or her cargo,[22] or both, from the natural or artificial actions of the seas, winds, waves, or nearness of the shore.
3. Voluntariness: the salvor or salvors must owe no legal duty[23] to perform the service.

---

20. See *Treasure Salvors, Inc. v. The Unidentified Wrecked and Abandoned Sailing Vessel (La Nuestra Señora de Atocha),* 569 F.2d 330, 1978 AMC 1404 (5th Cir. 1978), in which the government contested plaintiff's salvage claim on the ground that no marine peril then existed respecting the wreck of a Spanish treasure ship sunk in a hurricane off the Marquesas Keys of Florida in 1622. The court rejected this argument, holding that the wreck was still in peril of being lost through the actions of the elements, noting, "Marine peril includes more than the threat of storm, fire or piracy to a vessel in navigation." Cf. *Klein v. Unidentified Vessel,* 758 F.2d 1511, 1985 AMC 2970 (11th Cir. 1985). See also *Platoro Limited, Inc. v. Unidentified Remains of a Vessel,* 695 F.2d 893, 1984 AMC 2288 (5th Cir. 1983), involving another Spanish treasure ship sunk in a hurricane off the Texas coast in 1555; *Markakis v. The Volendam,* 486 F. Supp. 1103, 1980 AMC 915 (SDNY 1980), where the master and crew of the *Monarch Sun* were allowed salvage claims against the *Monarch Star,* of the same ownership, when the latter vessel lost power and drifted; *Fort Myers Shell and Dredging Co. v. The Barge NBC 512,* 404 F.2d 137, 1969 AMC 186 (5th Cir. 1968), where the court took into consideration the possibility of stranding after a towing hawser had parted. In *The Benison,* 36 F. 793 (SDNY 1888), following a collision, the bow and stem of the *Benison* were carried away to the collision bulkhead, which was in danger of giving way; thus, although the sea was calm, the towage by the salving steamship was perilous.

21. *Wiggins v. 1,100 Tons, More or Less, of Italian Marble,* 186 F. Supp. 452, 1960 AMC 1774 (ED Va. 1960); *St. Paul Marine Transport Co. v. Cerro Sales Corp.,* 312 F. Supp. 338 (D Hawaii 1970).

22. *The Gerbeviller,* 34 F.2d 825 (D Mass. 1929); *B.V. Bureau Wijsmuller v. United States,* 702 F.2d 333 (2d Cir. 1983); *Flagship Marine Services, Inc. v. Belcher Towing Co.,* 761 F. Supp. 793, 1992 AMC 181 (SD Fla. 1991), rev'd on other grounds, 966 F.2d 602, 1992 AMC 2901 (11th Cir. 1992); *Taylor v. 42 Foot Egg Harbor Hull,* supra note 19.

23. *The Clarita and The Clara,* supra note 16. See generally, *The Fisher's Hill,* 218 F.2d 631, 1955 AMC 697 (2d Cir. 1955); *Clifford v. The Islander,* 751 F.2d 1, 1985 AMC 1855 (1st Cir. 1984); *Nunley v. The Dauntless Colocotronis,* 863 F.2d 1190, 1993 AMC 1676 (5th Cir. 1989), on defendant's burden of proof.

Nonvoluntariness is clearest where municipal firemen of the jurisdiction where the ship is located perform the services. See, e.g., *Firemen's Charitable Association v. Ross,* 60 F. 456 (5th Cir. 1893). But when volunteer firemen put out a fire originating outside their jurisdiction, salvage may be awarded. *Bowers v. The European,* 44 F. 484 (SD Fla. 1890).

The voluntariness issue respecting crew members of the salved vessel turns on the permanent duty relationship owed to the vessel. Theoretically, when the order "abandon ship" is given, the relationship terminates. See *The Georgiana,* 245 F. 321 (1st Cir. 1917); *Baretich v. United States,* 97 F. Supp. 600, 1951 AMC 1812 (SDNY 1951). However, case law does not fully support such a facile distinction. In *Bertel v. Panama Transport Co.,* 202 F.2d 247, 1953 AMC 471 (2d Cir. 1953), during a fire on board an oil tanker, the master ordered "abandon ship" but plaintiffs, who were in the engine room, did not hear the order, remained at their posts, and then extinguished the fire. Their salvage claims were denied, as their duty to the ship had not ended with the master's order, which was construed as one for a mere temporary abandonment to save lives, rather than a permanent abandonment which would terminate the relationship. See also *The Matt W. Ransom,* 58 F. Supp. 1008, 1945 AMC 254 (D Md. 1945); and *Lavall v. United States,* 92 F. Supp. 532, 1950 AMC 1016 (SDNY 1950).

No similar duty to the ship rests on passengers, but the duty of self-preservation will result in the denial of salvage claims where the acts do not amount to extraordinary services to save the ship. *The Connemara,* 108 U.S. 352 (1883). For an example of extraordinary services, see *Towle v. The Great Eastern,* 24 F. Cas. 25 (No. 14, 110) (SDNY 1864).

There is a policy against recovery of salvage by U.S. Coast Guard personnel, even though search and rescue are not mandatory. No such policy inhibits recovery by U.S. Navy or U.S. Air Force personnel. See *United States v. Amoco Co. (The Amoco Virginia),* 417 F.2d 164, 1969 AMC

4. Success: the salvor's efforts—whether singly or jointly with others[24]—must save all or part of the venture, i.e., the vessel, cargo, and freight (if at risk.)[25]

Section B. Property Rights of the Salved Vessel Owner; Consequences of Abandonment

Salvage law enforces the property rights of owners of salved vessels, while at the same time ensuring a fair reward to the successful salvor. Thus, one purpose of the tradition that the master should be the last person to abandon a foundering vessel is to protect the owners' right to refuse salvage offers in order to seek more favorable towage or contract salvage terms.[26] But the owner's right to risk the vessel by refusing salvage must give way before the rights of other participants in the common venture, including the cargo interests,[27]

1761 (5th Cir. 1969). See also *In re Sun Oil Co.*, 342 F. Supp. 976, 1972 AMC 2258 (SDNY 1972), aff'd, 474 F.2d 1048, 1973 AMC 572 (2d Cir. 1973). As a result of collision, the bow of the *Maumee Sun* became embedded in the hull of the *American Pilot,* whose master ordered the two ships to be lashed together until removal of the oil cargo of the *Maumee Sun.* The *American Pilot*'s officers and crew filed salvage claims against the *Maumee Sun,* which were rejected, as the services were found not voluntary, in partial reliance on the Stand-By Act, 33 U.S.C. former §§ 367–68, (now repealed and replaced), but also relying on the idea that the alleged salvors were guaranteeing their own safety as well as the safety of the *Maumee Sun* by the lashings ordered by their master.

24. *The Blackwall,* supra note 16; *The Sabine,* supra note 11; *B.V. Bureau Wijsmuller v. United States,* supra note 22; *Reynolds v. The Tug Patrice McAllister,* 572 F. Supp. 1131, 1984 AMC 1303 (SDNY 1983); *Flagship Marine Services, Inc. v. Belcher Towing Co.,* supra note 22. Unsuccessful efforts are not penalized unless damage is caused by gross negligence or willful misconduct. See generally, *In re Amoco Cadiz,* 1984 AMC 2123 (ND Ill. 1984); and *Allseas Maritime S.A. v. The Mimosa,* supra note 16.

25. *In re Sincere Navigation Corp.*, 327 F. Supp. 1024, 1971 AMC 2270 (ED La. 1971); *In re Ta Chi Navigation (Panama) Corp. S.A.,* supra note 12; *Faneuil Advisors, Inc. v. The Sea Hawk,* 50 F.3d 88, 1995 AMC 1504 (1st Cir. 1995), where salvage lien priority over a preferred ship mortgage was denied on an abandoned vessel in state custody, secured to a pier but not in danger of sinking.

26. See *The J.C. Pfluger,* 109 F. 93 (ND Cal. 1901); *Squires v. The Ionian Leader,* supra note 1. In *In re Ta Chi Navigation (Panama) Corp., S.A.,* supra note 12, a Greek flag steamship began to tow a burning Liberian vessel which had been abandoned by her crew, against the wishes of the owner, who had already retained a professional salvor's services. The owner obtained a court order for the surrender of the vessel to the professional salvor, and the steamship owner's salvage claim was denied. See also *Grauwiller v. King,* 131 F. Supp. 630, 1955 AMC 1236 (EDNY 1955), aff'd, 229 F.2d 153, 1956 AMC 319 (2d Cir. 1956).

27. *The Odenwald,* 71 F. Supp. 314, 1947 AMC 666 (D P.R. 1947), aff'd, 168 F.2d 47, 1948 AMC 888 (1st Cir. 1948). A U.S. Navy crew was awarded salvage for salving a German commerce raider scuttled by her crew, despite the general policy of the U.S. Navy not to press salvage claims. While the German government might have approved the deliberate action of the crew during the "neutrality patrol" period before the United States entered the Second World War, the court could not ignore the rights of cargo owners and the Swiss mortgagee in the vessel, which carried commercial cargo. (Since the United States was not yet in the war, the U.S. Navy could not take the vessel as a prize. However, the salvage libel had the effect of immobilizing the ship for the duration of the war).

crew,[28] and passengers.[29] As long as the shipowner is in actual or constructive possession of the vessel through the master, officers, and crew, he can control any salvage problems that may arise.[30] Thus, there can be no forced salvage of the vessel until the moment the peril begins to destroy her and threaten human lives. The law has never required acceptance of salvage service by the shipowner under all circumstances. But when the vessel is abandoned in fact, any salvor may attempt to rescue her from peril.[31] This effective abandonment is considered as occurring at the time when no reasonably prudent person would refuse salvage.[32]

Abandonment, however, is of two types: (1) a temporary abandonment ordered by the master or other person in charge of the vessel for the safety of life, as in a fire at sea which appears to be out of control[33]; and (2) a permanent abandonment, as when the shipowner expressly or implicitly relinquishes title to the vessel.[34] After a physical abandonment of the vessel by master, officers, and crew, the owner may seek contract salvage (or towage). If the cost of salvage and repairs would exceed the vessel's value when repaired, under the usual hull policy forms the owner may tender abandonment of title to the vessel to the hull underwriters as a constructive total loss.[35] It should be noted, however, that the permanent abandonment of a vessel in the navigable waters of the United States will not terminate the owner's obligations under the Wreck Act,[36] which are to mark the wreck with a buoy or

---

28. See *Peninsular & Oriental Steam Navigation Co. v. Overseas Oil Carriers, Inc.,* 553 F.2d 830, 1977 AMC 283 (2d Cir. 1977). A remedy in *quantum meruit* for actual expenses was provided where there was no basis for a claim for life salvage, since there was no property saved from a marine peril. A passenger ship with medical personnel changed course to come to the aid of a crew member who had suffered a heart attack on a merchant vessel without medical personnel.

29. *The Veendam,* 46 F. 489 (SDNY 1891).

30. *Bonifay v. The Paraporte,* 145 F. Supp. 879, 1956 AMC 1898 (ED Va. 1956). See also the 1910 Convention, supra note 2, art. 3: "Persons who have taken part in salvage operations, notwithstanding the express and reasonable prohibition on the part of the vessel . . . have no right to any remuneration." But see *The Snow Maiden,* 159 F. Supp. 30, 1958 AMC 272 (D Mass. 1958). The first "salvor" or finder on the scene was granted equitable restraining orders on competing American salvors in *Columbus-America Deep Search, Inc. v. The Unidentified Wrecked and Abandoned Sailing Vessel,* 1988 AMC 2957 (ED Va. 1988), reversed on other grounds, 974 F.2d 450, 1992 AMC 2705 (4th Cir. 1992). See also *R.M.S. Titanic, Inc. v. Wrecked and Abandoned Vessel,* 924 F. Supp. 714, 1996 AMC 2481 (ED Va. 1996).

31. *The Gerbeviller,* supra note 22. In *Brady v. The African Queen,* 179 F. Supp. 321, 1960 AMC 69 (ED Va. 1960), the vessel went aground with little expectation of being refloated. Owners abandoned the vessel to hull underwriters, who engaged contract salvors. They failed to refloat the vessel, and the underwriters announced that the vessel was permanently abandoned. Several months later plaintiff refloated and separated the stern section. In an *in rem* proceeding, plaintiff was awarded the entire proceeds of a sale.

32. See *Bunge Corp. v. Agri-Trans Corp.,* 542 F. Supp. 961, 1983 AMC 1931 (ND Miss. 1982), aff'd in part, vacated in part, 721 F.2d 1005 (5th Cir. 1983).

33. *Bertel v. Panama Transport Co.,* supra note 23; *Drevas v. United States,* 58 F. Supp. 1008, 1945 AMC 254 (D Md. 1945).

34. *Martha's Vineyard Scuba Headquarters, Inc. v. Unidentified Wrecked and Abandoned Steam Vessel,* 833 F.2d 1059, 1988 AMC 1109 (1st Cir. 1987).

35. See American Hull Syndicate form of hull policy in appendix 9.

36. 33 U.S.C. §§ 409, 411–16, 418, 502.

beacon during the day and a lantern at night[37] until removal by the owner[38] or by the U.S. government at the expense of the owner.[39]

Abandonment of title by the shipowner, or by the hull underwriters if title has been properly abandoned to them, will have the consequence that one who locates and takes possession of the vessel will be awarded title in accordance with the law of finds.[40] Under American law, the first finder of abandoned property on the high seas to reduce it to effective possession acquires title to the property.[41] More than discovery is necessary for title, although the reduction to possession may be by mechanical means.[42] Under English law, cargo abandoned to the sea was Crown property outside the law of salvage.[43]

Section C. Special Defenses to Salvage Claims

Admiralty courts have traditionally refused to reward salvors' faults by applying equitable principles, such as the "clean hands" doctrine, to reduce or deny an award or disqualify a particular salvor[44] guilty of fraud, deceit, or other willful, unlawful conduct relating to the matter in dispute.[45] Conduct

---

37. See *Inland Tugs Co. v. Ohio River Co.*, 709 F.2d 1065, 1984 AMC 1943 (6th Cir. 1983). Cf. *Allied Chemical Corp. v. Hess Tankship Co. of Delaware*, 661 F.2d 1044, 1982 AMC 1271 (5th Cir. 1981) (good faith but unsuccessful search for a wreck).

38. *Wyandotte Transportation Co. v. United States*, 389 U.S. 191, 1967 AMC 2553 (1967). Wreck removal costs are not subject to limitation of liability. See *In re Chinese Maritime Trust, Ltd.*, 478 F.2d 1357, 1973 AMC 1110 (2d Cir. 1973); *In re Sincere Navigation Corp.*, supra note 25; *In re Plimsoll Marine, Inc.*, 1992 AMC 765 (ED La. 1991). Cf. *In re Compania Nacional de Navegacion*, 463 F. Supp. 330, 1979 AMC 730 (D C.Z. 1978).

39. *Wyandotte Transportation Co. v. United States*, supra note 38.

40. See *Martha's Vineyard Scuba Headquarters, Inc. v. Unidentified, Wrecked and Abandoned Steam Vessel*, supra note 34; *Hener v. United States*, 527 F. Supp. 350, 1982 AMC 847 (SDNY 1981).

41. *Treasure Salvors, Inc. v. The Unidentified Wrecked and Abandoned Sailing Vessel (La Nuestra Señora de Atocha)*, supra note 20.

42. *Columbus-America Discovery Group, Inc. v. The Unidentified, Wrecked and Abandoned Vessel (The Central America)*, 1989 AMC 1955 (ED Va. 1989), reversed on other grounds, 974 F.2d 450, 1992 AMC 2705 (4th Cir. 1992). See also *Brady v. The African Queen*, supra note 31.

43. Under English law, flotsam, jetsam, and lagan were "Droits of the Admiralty." 2 A. Browne, *A Compendious View of the Civil Law and of the Law of The Admiralty*, 46–54 (London, 1802).

44. See *The Boston*, 3 F. Cas. 932, (No. 1673) (C.C. D Mass. 1833), in which Justice Story applied the equitable maxims of clean hands and utmost good faith. See also *Aetna Insurance Co. v. Hattersley*, 1984 AMC 2837 (D Or. 1983).

45. *The Clarita and The Clara*, supra note 16. Later recognition of the equity "clean hands" doctrine may be found in *Johnson v. Yellow Cab Transit Co.*, 321 U.S. 383 (1944), where defendants, Oklahoma state officers, had seized plaintiff carrier's shipment of liquor to the officers' club at a federal reservation, Fort Sill. Defendant argued lack of clean hands, but the Supreme Court answered:

> We may assume that because of the clean hands doctrine a federal court should not, in an ordinary case, lend its judicial power to a plaintiff who seeks to invoke that power for the purpose of consummating a transaction in clear violation of law. But this does not mean that courts must always permit a defendant wrongdoer to retain the profits of his wrongdoing merely because the plaintiff himself is possibly guilty of transgressing the law in the

which might be described as unjust, unfair, or founded on an impure motive may be enough to deny or diminish an award.[46] Specific situations in which salvage claims have been denied or reduced are of the following types:

1. Misbehavior, such as looting the salvaged property;[47]
2. Reckless or grossly negligent salvage operations, or a "distinguishable injury";[48]
3. Fault of the salvaging vessel in causing a collision necessitating the salvage services;[49]
4. Barratry and fraud.[50]

> transactions involved. The maxim that he who comes into equity must come with clean hands is not applied by way of punishment for an unclean litigant, but upon considerations that make for the advancement of right and justice. . . . 321 U.S. at 387.

46. See generally, *Carmen v. Fox Film Corp.*, 269 F. 928 (2d Cir. 1920); *Aetna Ins. Co. v. Hattersley*, 1984 AMC 2387 (D Ore. 1989) and Chafee, *Coming Into Equity with Clean Hands*, 47 Mich. L. Rev. 1065 (1949).

47. *The Bello Corrunes*, 19 U.S. 152 (1821); *Danner v. United States*, 99 F. Supp. 880, 1951 AMC 1495 (SDNY 1951); *The Norseman*, 1967 AMC 1531 (D P.R. 1967); *Empacadora Del Norte, S.A. v. The Finnco Victoria*, 1983 AMC 1235 (SD Tex. 1982). See also *The Island City*, 66 U.S. 121 (1861); and *Merritt & Chapman Derrick & Wrecking Co. v. About Four Hundred Barrels of Wine*, 159 F. 406 (3d Cir. 1908); *The Cape Race*, 18 F.2d 79, 1927 AMC 628 (2d Cir. 1927). See also the U.S. Criminal Code, 18 U.S.C. § 1658 (1996) (Crime of Plundering Vessels Wrecked, Lost, Stranded or Cast Away).

48. *The Noah's Ark*, 292 F.2d 437, 1961 AMC 1641 (5th Cir. 1961) and *The Noah's Ark*, 322 F.2d 3, 1964 AMC 59 (5th Cir. 1963). See also *P. Dougherty Co. v. United States*, 207 F.2d 626, 1953 AMC 1541 (3d Cir. 1953), where the court noted the overwhelming weight of opinion that salvors are not liable for damage to the salved vessel during salvage operations, "absent gross negligence or wilful misconduct." But see *Serriss v. Ferguson*, 84 F. 202 (2d Cir. 1897), and *The Cape Race*, 18 F.2d 79, 1927 AMC 628 (2d Cir. 1927), where the negligent manner in which the salving tug approached a barge adrift in Hell Gate caused the tug to lose its salvage claim and be held liable for collision damage to the barge. See also *Martinez v. Puerto Rico Marine Management, Inc.*, 755 F. Supp. 1001, 1990 AMC 2655 (SD Ala. 1990).

For the English rule concerning salvor liability for negligent salvage, see *B.V. Bureau Wijsmuller v. The Tojo Maru*, [1971] 1 Lloyd's Rep. 341, [1972] A.C. 242 (H.L.). See *In re Alva Steamship Co.*, 616 F.2d 605, 1980 AMC 857 (2d Cir. 1979), concerning the joint liability of a negligent salvor and the owner of a salvaged vessel for a second explosion after a collision and a first explosion.

49. *The Clarita and the Clara*, supra note 16.

50. *The North Carolina*, 40 U.S. 15 (1841); *Church v. Seventeen Hundred and Twelve Dollars*, 5 F. Cas. 669 (No. 2713) (D Fla. 1853); *Higgins v. The Tri-State*, supra note 8; *Jackson Marine Corp. v. The Blue Fox*, 845 F.2d 1307, 1988 AMC 2740 (5th Cir. 1988) (fraudulent salvage contract); *Black Gold Marine, Inc. v. Jackson Marine Co.*, 759 F.2d 466, 1986 AMC 137 (5th Cir. 1985).

Cf. *Unnamed Master and Crew v. Certain Unnamed Vessel*, 592 F. Supp. 1191 (SD Fla. 1984). Salvage rather than title to an abandoned derelict was awarded to salvors who rescued a 38-foot motorboat carrying marijuana that had been abandoned by its operators, believing the salvors to be police.

On the effect of misconduct, see generally, 1 J. Story, *Equity Jurisprudence*, § 99:

> Misconduct which will bar relief in a court of equity need not necessarily be of such a nature to be punishable as a crime or to constitute the basis of a legal action. Under this maxim, any willful act in regard to the matter in litigation which would be condemned and pronounced wrongful by honest and fair minded men will be sufficient to make the hands of the applicant unclean.

Section D. Salvage of One Colliding Vessel by the Other

1. When the Salvor Is in Fault for a Collision

The leading decision is *The Clarita and The Clara.*[51] Negligent efforts of the Tug *Clarita* to salvage a ferryboat on fire at a pier in Hoboken, New Jersey, led to a collision between the ferry, under tow of the *Clarita,* with the anchored *Clara.* The *Clarita* used hemp hawsers to tow the ferry onto a flat area of relative safety, but the hawsers burned and the ferry drifted onto the *Clara,* which also caught fire. The *Clara* fire was extinguished by the *Clarita* after the ferry sank. The *Clara* sued for the collision damage and the *Clarita* cross-libeled for salvage. The Supreme Court recognized that a salvor must have "clean hands" in claiming salvage, and said:

> . . . [I]t is very clear that if the vessel in fault renders assistance to the one not in fault, the former cannot make any claim for salvage either from the other vessel or the cargo on board as it is her duty to render every assistance in her power . . . and it is expressly decided that salvors are not entitled to reward for saving property which they had by their own wrongful acts contributed to place in jeopardy. . . .[52]

While *The Clarita* and *The Clara* dealt with a sole-fault collision, the rationale of that decision has been applied in a both-to-blame case to deny a recovery.[53] Note that this denial of recovery, based on application of equitable principles, occurred in 1892, under the influence of the then-current rule of equal division of damages in both-to-blame collision cases and before the principle of proportional fault in collision cases was introduced in the United States in 1975.[54] Note also that part of the rationale for the original rule was the statutory duty to stand by, since under the stand-by statute then in force the failure to comply resulted in a presumption of fault.[55] That statute has since been repealed and replaced by one requiring colliding vessels to stand by each other, but creating no presumption when there is a failure to do so.[56]

---

51. Supra note 16.

52. *The Clarita and The Clara,* supra note 16, 90 U.S. at 18. See also *Vessel Engineering & Development Corp. v. The Barge ZPC 404,* 1989 AMC 2782 (D Or. 1989), where the tug whose towed barge separated due to tug negligence was denied an award for a later rescue of the abandoned tow. See *The Pine Forest,* 129 F. 700 (1st Cir. 1904); *The Mishawaka,* 10 F. Supp. 722, 1935 AMC 701 (D Me. 1935). See also *Champion International Corp. v. The Lash Pacifico,* 569 F. Supp. 1557, 1984 AMC 444 (SDNY 1983), and *S.C. Loveland Co. v. The Barge Arlington,* 1982 AMC 704 (ED La. 1980).

53. *The Minnie C. Taylor,* 52 F. 323 (SDNY 1892). See also *Lynch v. Chew,* 159 F. 182 (ED Pa. 1908) (not a collision case).

54. *United States v. Reliable Transfer Co.,* 421 U.S. 397, 1975 AMC 541 (1975), discussed in chapter 12.

55. 33 U.S.C. former § 367. Cf. 46 U.S.C. §§ 2303 and 2304.

56. See chapter 2, section A(8).

2. *Proportional Faults of Salvors and Salvaged Vessel*

The effect of adoption of the proportional fault principle should cause the courts to permit a salvage claim where the faults of the claimant colliding vessel are minor or technical only. As of 1997 it was not possible to say definitively at what point the salvor's faults will be held so serious as to bring in the rationale of *The Minnie C. Taylor*.[57]

3. *When the Salving Vessel Is Free of Fault*

When the salvaging vessel is entirely free of fault for a collision, she will be entitled to a salvage award for salvaging the other colliding vessel.[58]

Section E. Review of the Fundamentals of General Average

General average is the earliest known doctrine of maritime law; the Justinian Digest ascribes it to the ancient Rhodians.[59] Under traditional definitions, the doctrine requires pro rata contributions from those benefited, to help make up the losses suffered by one or more interests in a maritime venture singled out for deliberate sacrifice or for the making of extraordinary expenditures, for the purpose and with the effect of saving the other interests from an imminent peril impending over the whole.[60] Thus, in the usual case, three elements must be established: (1) a common peril; (2) a transfer of the peril affecting the whole to a part of the venture; and (3) success. However, under the 1994 York-Antwerp Rules,[61] which are now incorporated by reference in

57. Supra note 53.

58. See *Star Towing Co. v. The Barge ORG 6504*, 301 F. Supp. 819 (ED La. 1969), where an unseaworthy lash barge foundered while being properly towed, causing water damage to a cargo of plywood. The barge was held solely liable to cargo.

59. "It is provided by the Rhodian Law that if merchandise is thrown overboard to lighten the ship, the loss occasioned for the benefit of all must be made good by the contribution of all." 2 Digest of Justinian 385 (ca. 533 A.D.) (Moore translation, 1909), Digest 14.2.1.

"Average" in the context of general average has nothing to do with mathematics. The word was derived from the French "avarie" and the Spanish and Italian "avaria," which came from an Arabic word meaning damage to a ship or goods. Thus, the term "general average" describes a loss to be shared by all participants in a marine venture, whereas "particular average" describes a loss assessed against an individual participant.

60. See *The Star of Hope*, 76 U.S. 207 (1870). Cf. *Navigazione Generale Italiana v. Spencer Kellogg & Sons, Inc. (The Mincio)*, 92 F.2d 41, 1937 AMC 1506, (2d Cir. 1937) where the court said, "[W]e think the 'imminency' of the peril is not the critical test. If the danger be real and substantial, a sacrifice or expenditure made in good faith for the common interest is justified, even though the advent of any catastrophe may be distant or indeed unlikely. . . ."

61. The 1994 York-Antwerp Rules (Y.A.R.) are reproduced in full at 6 Benedict 64-28 (Doc. No. 4-6). For a discussion of the rules see section F, infra. Earlier editions are discussed in Buglass, *Marine Insurance and General Average* (3d ed. 1991) (hereinafter "Buglass"); and in Felde, *General Average and the York-Antwerp Rules*, 27 Tul. L.R. 406 (1953).

Y.A.R., Rule A, defines a general average act as follows: "There is a general average act when, and only when, any extraordinary sacrifice is intentionally and reasonably made or inmost contracts of affreightment, if damage occurring on the first stage of a voyage is discovered at a port of call, expenses incurred to enable the vessel to continue to destination are recoverable in general average, even though the vessel is not then in any danger.

An example of a deliberate sacrifice is the jettisoning of part of the cargo on the master's orders, for the purpose of lightening and refloating a grounded vessel.[62] Another is the master's decision to work the ship's engines in a successful effort to refloat a vessel grounded by the stern, knowing that it will probably result in the sanding of the engines.[63] Perhaps the most common examples of extraordinary expenditures allowed in general average are expenses incurred in putting into a port of refuge for repairs following a collision or other casualty. Port of refuge expenses allowed in general average include those for crew wages earned and for provisions, fuel, and stores consumed during the prolongation of the voyage; port charges; handling of cargo, fuel, or stores on board; and discharging and reloading of cargo, when necessary for the common safety, or to enable repairs to be made.[64] The cost of temporary repairs made at a port of loading, call, or refuge for the common safety, or of damage caused by a general-average sacrifice, is also allowed in general average.[65] The cost of permanent repairs of damage caused by a collision or other casualty is of course a particular average expense and not recoverable in general average, as such damage is accidentally, and not voluntarily caused.

Section F. The York-Antwerp Rules

While there is frequently a sense of urgency surrounding salvage law, general average is the preserve of average adjusters—specialists who perform the sometimes very complicated and time-consuming task of ascertaining the losses and expenses chargeable in general average and the values of the interests benefited by the sacrifice or extraordinary expenditures. There may be scores of these interests, as in the case of a general ship carrying cargo for a multitude of shippers. In such a case it may take several years before the "general average statement" is completed. In England, average adjusters are mostly members of firms that limit their services to adjusting general and particular average. In the United States, on the other hand, most adjusters

---

curred for the common safety for the purpose of preserving from peril the property involved in a common maritime adventure." See also *Ralli v. Troop,* 157 U.S. 386 (1895), and Section 66 of the British Marine Insurance Act, 1906, 6 Edw. 7, c. 41, which contains a more detailed definition.

62. Y.A.R., Rules I and II.

63. Y.A.R., Rule VII.

64. Y.A.R., Rules X, XI, and XII.

65. Y.A.R., Rule XIV.

are members of insurance brokerage firms specializing in marine insurance, or at least having important marine insurance departments.

The charter party, bill of lading, or other contract of carriage customarily stipulates where a general average is to be stated, but the selection of the adjusters is usually made by the shipowners, although they represent all of the interests involved. Average adjusters are organized in a number of national and international associations, some of which have their own rules of practice, which are generally similar, but not identical. However, the fundamental rules governing general average *are* quite uniform. They are not based upon legislation or treaty; rather they depend on the agreement of the parties to a bill of lading, voyage charter, or other contract of affreightment. The rules almost universally agreed upon are the York-Antwerp Rules (Y.A.R.), the edition of which current in 1997 was adopted at the Conference of the C.M.I., held at Sydney, Australia, in 1994. As stated, the rules are incorporated by reference in the overwhelming majority of bills of lading, charter parties, and other contractual arrangements between the parties to the venture: the ship and her owner, the freight interests, and the cargo and its owners. The centrality of these rules in modern shipping comes from the fact that marine insurers—whether hull, cargo, P & I, or third party liability—all presuppose that in almost every case the parties involved in a collision or other marine casualty involving cargo will have agreed to the application of the 1994 York-Antwerp Rules.[66]

The original Y.A.R. were drafted by the International Law Association (I.L.A.) in 1877. The I.L.A. was founded in Brussels in 1873 as a consequence of the American Civil War (1861–65) and the Franco-Prussian War (1870–71). Before the Comité Maritime International (C.M.I.) was founded in 1897, problems of international maritime law and related matters were dealt with by the I.L.A.

One of the most immediate problems facing the international insurance industry in the 1870s was the difference between the English and the French substantive and procedural rules governing general average. It was mainly to reconcile these differences that the I.L.A. formulated the Y.A.R. in 1877. The

66. There have been at least two attempts to adopt rules other than the Y.A.R. On Jan. 1, 1975, the China Council for the Promotion of International Trade promulgated a set of "Provisional Rules for General Average Adjustment," which are reproduced in 6 Benedict at 4-74 (Doc. No. 4-10). As of 1997, these were still incorporated in bills of lading issued by Chinese steamship companies.

In 1990, a number of shipping companies trading on the Danube, including companies of (West) Germany, Bulgaria, Austria, Hungary, Romania, Yugoslavia, the former U.S.S.R., and the former Czechoslovakia, adopted the "Danube Rules on General Average" as an integral part of the Agreement on General Terms of Carriage of Goods in International Communication on the Danube. The rules were to "come into force for all carriage of goods with the exception of cases when another agreement is made by participants in General Average."

The Rules of Practice of the following national general average associations are reproduced in 6 Benedict: American (Doc. No. 4-8); Canadian (Doc. No. 4-11); United Kingdom (Doc. No. 4-9); Japanese (Doc. No. 4-12).

rules were thereafter revised in 1890, 1924, 1950, 1974, and 1994, and one amendment was made in 1990. The most recent revisions were made at conferences of the C.M.I., with the cooperation of the various associations of average adjusters and other maritime organizations.[67]

The 1994 Y.A.R. consist of a "Rule of Interpretation," a "Rule Paramount," seven lettered rules setting forth general principles, and twenty-two numbered rules (Roman numerals) dealing with specific general average situations and problems. The "Rule of Interpretation" in the 1994 Rules reads: "Except as provided by the Rule Paramount and the numbered Rules, general average shall be adjusted according to the lettered Rules." Thus, in the event of a conflict between a lettered rule and a numbered rule, the numbered rule governs. The Rule Paramount was introduced in the 1994 Rules. It simply provides that "In no case shall there be any allowance for sacrifice or expenditure unless reasonably made or incurred."

A good illustration of a conflict between a lettered rule and a numbered rule is found in *Eagle Terminal Tankers, Inc. v. Insurance Co. of the U.S.S.R. (The Eagle Courier)*.[68] The U.S. flag *Eagle Courier,* under charter to carry grain to the former U.S.S.R., sailed from Port Arthur, Texas, on a voyage to Leningrad (now St. Petersburg), with a planned refueling stop at Rotterdam. After arrival at that port, it was found that the vessel's propeller had been badly damaged from striking some unknown underwater object during the first stage of the voyage. Part of the cargo was discharged, the vessel was dry-docked, her propeller was repaired, and after reloading she continued on to Leningrad, where she arrived safely.

The cargo owners and their insurers refused to contribute in general average, and the shipowners sued. The cargo interests pointed to Rule A of the 1974 York-Antwerp Rules then in force, which provided: "There is a general average act when, and only when, any extraordinary sacrifice or expenditure is intentionally and reasonably made or incurred for the common safety for the purpose of preserving from peril the property involved in a common maritime adventure." The district court agreed, and held that since the expenses incurred at Rotterdam were not made for the purpose of preserving the vessel and cargo from peril, they were not recoverable in general average.[69] On appeal, the Second Circuit reversed, citing Rule X of the 1974 York-Antwerp Rules, under which expenses of a general average nature were recoverable in general average when made at a port of call, if made for the safe prosecution of the voyage, as well as when made for the common safety. The court then cited the Rule of Interpretation of the 1974 Rules, which was identical to the corresponding rule of the 1994 Rules quoted above, except

---

67. A detailed history of the Y.A.R. is included in R. Lowndes & G. Rudolph, *The Law of General Average* (10th ed. 1975 by J. Donaldson [now Lord Donaldson], C. Staughton [later Lord Justice Staughton], and D. Wilson).

68. 637 F.2d 890, 1981 AMC 137 (2d Cir 1981).

69. 489 F. Supp. 920, 1980 AMC 2023 (SDNY 1980).

that of course it made no reference to the Rule Paramount, which was not introduced until 1994. It will be seen that Rule A of the 1974 (and 1994) Rules is in line with the traditional definitions of general average, whereas the portion of Rule X involved in *The Eagle Courier* is a departure from them.

Section G. Disputed Claims for General Average Contributions

Unless the parties otherwise agree, e.g., by a bill of lading or charter party provision, a statement of general average is not legally binding.[70] However, such statements are seldom challenged on grounds of inaccuracy. There is therefore relatively little litigation concerning general average, except for cases where cargo interests challenge the shipowners' claim for a contribution on the ground that the sacrifice or extraordinary expenditure was made necessary by the shipowners' failure to exercise due diligence to make the vessel seaworthy and properly manned, equipped, and supplied. Such claims are frequently asserted as counterclaims in actions for cargo damage involving the same issues.

The Harter Act of 1893[71] generally codified the general maritime law nullifying clauses purporting to relieve the carrier of liability for unseaworthiness or negligence,[72] but it made two principal exceptions: first, the carrier was permitted to exempt itself from liability for losses caused by unseaworthiness not resulting from a lack of due diligence to make the vessel seaworthy and properly manned, equipped, and supplied;[73] second, if the carrier had used due diligence to make the vessel seaworthy in all respects, it was not liable for losses caused by errors in the navigation or management of the vessel.[74]

In *The Irrawady*,[75] a carrier seeking general average contributions argued that since under the Harter Act carriers who had used due diligence to make the vessel in all respects seaworthy and properly manned, equipped, and supplied were not liable for loss or damage caused by errors in navigation and management, the carrier should be entitled to recover general average contributions, even though the general average expenditures were necessitated by such errors. The Supreme Court disagreed; it held that the act was a

70. See *Empire Stevedoring Co. v. Oceanic Adjusters, Ltd.*, 315 F. Supp. 921, 1971 AMC 795 (SDNY 1970).

71. 46 App. U.S.C. §§ 190–96.

72. Sections 1 and 2 (46 App. U.S.C. §§ 190 and 191).

73. By prohibiting clauses lessening, weakening, or avoiding the carrier's obligation to use due diligence with respect to seaworthiness, section 2 of the Harter Act, 46 App. U.S.C. § 191, implicitly permitted the inclusion of clauses exonerating the carrier from liability for loss or damage caused by unseaworthiness where it was not the result of a failure to exercise due diligence. See *The Carib Prince*, 170 U.S. 655 (1898).

74. 46 App. U.S.C. § 192.

75. 171 U.S. 187 (1896).

shield, but not a sword; it created defenses, but did not create an affirmative right to recover general-average contributions where no such right had existed before its enactment. The carriers' response to *The Irrawady* was to include in their bills of lading a clause designed to parallel the scheme of the Harter Act exceptions to liability. The clause gave the carrier the right to recover general average contributions under circumstances where the Act would provide defenses to claims for cargo loss or damage.

In 1912 the Supreme Court sustained the validity of the clause in *The Jason,*[76] despite the argument of cargo interests that the clause violated the public policy against exculpatory clauses whereby a carrier purported to exempt itself from liability for its own negligence. The clause has ever since been known as the *Jason* clause.

Shortly before COGSA[77] was enacted in 1936, the Supreme Court decided *The Isis,*[78] which gave a very literal reading to Section 3 of the Harter Act.[79] It held that where the cause of cargo loss or damage is an error in navigation or management, the owner is not entitled to exoneration under Section 3 unless it can prove that it had exercised due diligence to make the vessel seaworthy *in all respects*—even in respects wholly unrelated to the negligence in navigation or management that caused the loss or damage.

While the Harter Act has not been repealed, it has been superseded by COGSA in the foreign trade, except for the periods prior to loading and subsequent to discharge,[80] and by contract it may be entirely superseded by COGSA in domestic trades.[81] Under COGSA, a carrier is not liable for cargo loss or damage resulting from a collision or stranding, even if caused in whole or in part by the carrier's fault, unless a contributing cause was the carrier's failure to exercise due diligence to make the vessel seaworthy, and properly manned, equipped, and supplied.[82] Following enactment of COGSA the *Jason* clause was tailored to fit that statute, as well as the Harter Act and charter party clauses similar to the provisions of COGSA. The clause in general use as of 1996 reads as follows:

> In the event of accident, danger, damage, or disaster, before or after commencement of the voyage resulting from any cause whatsoever, whether due to negligence or not, for which, or for the consequences of which, the Carrier is not responsible by statute, contract or otherwise, the goods, shippers, consignees, or owners of the goods shall contribute with the Carrier in general average to the payment of any sacrifices, losses, or expenses of a general average nature that may be made or incurred,

76. 225 U.S. 32 (1912).
77. 46 App. U.S.C. §§ 1300–1312.
78. 290 U.S. 333, 1933 AMC 1565 (1933).
79. 46 App. U.S.C. § 192.
80. 46 App. U.S.C. §§ 1311 and 1312.
81. 46 App. U.S.C. § 1312.
82. 46 App. U.S.C. §§ 1304(1) and 1304(2)(p).

and shall pay salvage and special charges incurred in respect of the goods.[83]

The most significant aspect of a both-to-blame collision as it affects general average is the effect of the American rule of joint and several liability to notionally innocent cargo. In *Aktieselskabet Cuzco v. The Sucarseco,*[84] the Supreme Court held that contributions which the cargo interests were required to make to the carrying vessel toward general average expenses incurred following a both-to-blame collision can be recaptured by means of an action against the noncarrying vessel for 100 percent of the cargo damages, including cargo's general average contributions. The noncarrying vessel may then include all of these third-party liabilities as part of her collision damages for apportionment with the carrying vessel. The result is that in a both-to-blame case, because of the operation of the rule of joint and several liability,[85] the carrying vessel is indirectly liable to her own cargo for a return of a percentage of the general average contributions made by the cargo interests corresponding to the carrying vessel's degree of blame.

83. 2 Benedict 186.
84. 294 U.S. 394, 1935 AMC 412 (1935).
85. See *The Chattahoochee,* 173 U.S. 540 (1899).

CHAPTER SIXTEEN

MARINE INSURANCE IN COLLISION CASES

Section A. Introduction

1. Collision Losses and Liabilities Covered by Marine Insurance

Marine insurance so pervades collision cases that no collision text would be even reasonably comprehensive without at least a brief treatment of the subject, to the extent that it impacts on the law of collision.[1]

Collision is a marine peril, and loss of or damage to maritime property—vessels, cargoes, collect freights, and other insurable interests—as a result of a collision is covered under the standard perils clause of a marine insurance policy. Hull and machinery policies customarily include "running down" or "collision" clauses, insuring against either 75 percent or 100 percent of the liability of the insured shipowner for loss of or damage to another ship or vessel and her cargo as a result of a collision. A collision may necessitate general average, salvage, and "sue and labor" expenses in respect of the insured property, all of which are covered under standard forms of marine insurance policies.

If a vessel is entered in a shipowners' protection and indemnity ("P & I") association or "club," or the owners are otherwise insured against P & I risks, they are entitled to indemnity from the club or other P & I insurer in respect of any amounts which they have become liable to pay and have paid for cargo loss or damage on the insured vessel resulting from a collision, and for injury to and wrongful death of persons, whether on that vessel or the other colliding vessel.

---

1. Among the leading texts and articles on marine insurance and related subjects are A. Parks, *The Law and Practice of Marine Insurance and Average* (1987) (hereinafter "Parks"); J. Arnould, *The Law of Marine Insurance* (16th ed. 1981 by Sir Michael Mustill [later Lord Mustill] and J. Gilman, hereinafter "Arnould"); E. Hardy - Ivamy, *Marine Insurance* (3d ed. 1981); W. Birch Reynardson, *The History and Development of P. & I. Insurance: The British Scene,* 43 Tul. Law Rev. 457 (1969) (hereinafter "Birch Reynardson"); *Templeman on Marine Insurance* (5th ed. 1981); S. Braekhus & A. Rein, *Handbook of P. & I. Insurance* (2d ed. 1979); L. Buglass, *Marine Insurance and General Average in the United States* (3d ed. 1991); A. Parks and E. Cattell, *The Law of Tug, Tow, & Pilotage* (3d ed. 1994); Tulane Admiralty Law Institute, *Symposium on the Hull Policy,* 41 Tul. L. Rev., 232-435 (1967); Tulane Admiralty Law Institute, *Symposium on the P. & I. Policy,* 43 Tul. Law Rev., 457-696 (1969); Tulane Admiralty Law Institute, *Symposium on Marine Insurance,* 66 Tul. Law Rev. 257-509 (1991); American Maritime Cases, *Five-Year Digests,* 1923–1997.

When the "running down" or "collision" clause in the hull and machinery policy is a "three-fourths" clause, the P & I insurance covers the remaining one-fourth of any liability for collision damage caused to another ship or vessel. P & I insurance also covers liabilities paid for collision damage to fixed objects, such as piers, wharves, bridges, buoys, and lights; for removal or disposal of obstructions, wrecks, or cargoes; and may also cover liability for pollution damage and cleanup costs.

2. *The Applicable Law: The General Maritime Law and* Wilburn Boat

American courts continue to be guided to a considerable extent by English decisions, even though English law is mainly in statutory form and American law is not. Thus British and Commonwealth decisions will be cited together with American decisions on the same points. The U.S. Supreme Court has often stated that there are special reasons for the United States to keep in harmony with the marine insurance law of England, and in general to "accord respect to established doctrines of English maritime law."[2] The lower courts almost universally applied this concept prior to the Supreme Court's unsettling decision in *Wilburn Boat Co. v. Fireman's Fund Ins. Co.;*[3] and there appears to have been little tendency to depart from the concept even since *Wilburn.*[4] Until *Wilburn,* marine insurance was clearly governed by the general maritime law.[5] As of 1997 a U.S. Maritime Law Association committee was considering means of reinstating the general maritime law to the extent it had been supplanted by *Wilburn.*[6] One means under consideration was the introduction of draft legislation tracking the 1906 British Marine Insurance Act. Another was preparation of a restatement of the law of marine insurance.

The Wilburn brothers were the owners of a small houseboat operating on Lake Texoma, an inland lake between Oklahoma and Texas. They sold the boat to a corporation in which they were the sole stockholders, the boat

2. *Standard Oil v. United States,* 340 U.S. 54, 1951 AMC 1 (1950); *Queen Ins. Co. v. Globe & Rutgers Fire Ins. Co.,* 263 U.S. 487, 1924 AMC 107 (1924); *Calmar S.S. Corp. v. Scott,* 345 U.S. 427, 1953 AMC 952 (1953).

3. 348 U.S. 310, 1955 AMC 467 (1955).

4. See, for example, *The Honeybrook,* 6 F.2d 736, 1925 AMC 717 (2d Cir. 1925); *The Eastern Prince—The Roustabout,* 173 F.2d 955, 1950 AMC 377 (9th Cir. 1950); *Landry v. Steamship Mut. Underwriting Ass'n,* 177 F. Supp. 143, 1960 AMC 54 (D Mass. 1960), aff'd, 281 F.2d 484, 1960 AMC 1650 (1st Cir. 1960) ("The court is not aware of any pertinent difference between British and American law"); *Northwestern Mutual L.I. Co. v. Linard,* 498 F.2d 556, 1974 AMC 877 (2d Cir. 1974) ("Great weight is to be given to English decisions in the field of marine insurance"); and *Lenfest v. Coldwell,* 525 F.2d 717, 1975 AMC 2489 (2d Cir. 1975) ("American courts look to British law for meaning and definition in the field of marine insurance"). The British courts have likewise recognized the desirability of compatibility of English with American law in the field of marine insurance. See *Cory v. Burr,* 9 Q.B.D. 463, 469 (C.A. 1882), aff'd, 8 App. Cas. 393 (H.L. 1883).

5. See *Insurance Co. v. Dunham,* 78 U.S. 1 (1870); *De Lovio v. Boit,* 7 F. Cas. 418 (No. 3776) (C.C.D Mass. 1815); *Queen Ins. Co. v. Globe & Rutgers Fire Ins. Co.,* 263 U.S. 487, 1924 AMC 107 (1924).

6. See MLA Report, Sept. 30, 1995.

was mortgaged, and instead of being used for private pleasure purposes it was chartered and used to carry passengers for hire. The policy issued by the defendant insurance company contained warranties prohibiting all three actions of the owners. The boat was destroyed by fire while moored on the lake. The underwriters denied liability on grounds of breach of warranty, and the corporate owner sued on the policy in a Texas state court. The action was removed to the federal court on grounds of diversity of citizenship.

The assured contended that under Texas law the breaches of warranty were immaterial, as they did not contribute to the loss. The underwriters argued that a causal connection between the breach and the loss was unnecessary under the general maritime law. The district court denied recovery on the policy; the Fifth Circuit affirmed on the narrow issue of whether state law or general maritime law governed. The Supreme Court divided three ways. The majority reversed and remanded with instructions to apply appropriate state law, finding that there was no established rule of the general maritime law about the effect of breach of a warranty. Justice Frankfurter concurred with the result but disagreed with the reasoning, although his language is often used to explain the case as one of "essentially localized incidence." Justices Reed and Burton dissented.

Although the court recognized its historic rule-making function in admiralty cases, it refused to formulate a warranties rule, stating that making a choice of rules involved policy considerations which Congress was peculiarly suited to make. Justice Reed, in dissenting, correctly noted that all prior decisions supported the necessity of uniform rules in marine insurance cases above all else, and urged that sound judicial policy dictated that American marine insurance law be kept in harmony with that of England, under which a breach of warranty is a defense to an action on a marine policy, even if the breach did not contribute to the loss. The trend after *Wilburn* appears to be that the decision will be restricted to cases involving policy warranties.[7] And notwithstanding *Wilburn,* the courts are continuing to apply general maritime law principles to marine insurance cases.[8]

---

7. *Indemnity Ins. Co. of North America v. California Stevedore and Ballast Co.,* 307 F.2d 513, 1962 AMC 2507 (9th Cir. 1962); *U.S. Fire Ins. Co. v. Gulf States Marine & Mining Co.,* 262 F.2d 565, 1959 AMC 397 (5th Cir. 1959).

8. See *Strachan Shipping Co. v. Koninklyke Nederlandsche, etc.,* 301 F.2d 741, 1964 AMC 1925 (5th Cir. 1962); *McCross v. Ratnaker Shipping Co.,* 265 F. Supp. 827, 1967 AMC 291 (D Md. 1967); *Crosson v. N.V. Stoomvaart Mij "Nederland,"* 409 F.2d 865, 1969 AMC 1363 (2d Cir. 1969); *Stanley Scott v. Makah Development,* 496 F.2d 525, 1974 AMC 934 (9th Cir. 1974); *Wells Fargo v. London S.S. Owners Mut. Ins. Ass'n,* 408 F. Supp. 626, 1976 AMC 592 (SDNY 1976).

A *Wilburn Boat* analysis requires courts to determine three issues when state law is urged as determinative in a dispute on marine insurance: (1) Is there an applicable admiralty precedent? (2) Are there state policies or local interests that outweigh available admiralty precedent? and (3) Will the application of state law have a harmful effect on the uniformity of the general maritime law? A succinct example of this analysis can be found in *Steelmet, Inc. v. Caribe Towing Co.,* 779 F.2d 1485, 1488, 1986 AMC 1641, 1645 (11th Cir. 1986). See also MacChesney, *Marine*

Section B. The Running Down (Collision) Clause

1. *Coverage under the Running Down Clause*

(a) The Origin of the Clause. The decision in *De Vaux v. Salvador*[9] led to the inclusion in hull policies of a "running down" or "collision" clause, whereby the hull and machinery underwriters insure the risk of liability of the owner of the insured vessel for damage done by that vessel in collision with another vessel.[10] As first adopted (and as now still current in the Institute Time Hulls form of the Institute of London Underwriters), the clause only covered three-fourths of the owner's collision liability to the other vessel. It was thought that by limiting the coverage to three-fourths, thereby compelling the owners (or their P & I club) to bear one-fourth of the liability, greater care would be exercised by the owners in the selection of the master and crew. American forms (of which the 1977 American Institute Hulls (AIH) form is the most common example) invariably cover four-fourths of the owner's collision liability. The running down clause is set forth in the AIH form.[11]

(b) "Collision" under the Running Down Clause. The opening phrase of the AIH form running down clause, "And it is further agreed that," provides coverage supplementary to the basic hull coverage. Thus, the underwriters may incur liability under the running down clause in addition to liability to the insured for total or partial loss arising out of the collision. For example, a vessel may be sunk and totally lost in a collision, and at the same time the insured owners may be found liable to the other vessel for the damage done to her. In that instance, the hull underwriters will be liable to the insured owners for the agreed value of their vessel and, in addition, under the running down clause they will be liable for the damages paid to the other vessel, up to the agreed value.[12]

Insurance and the Substantive Maritime Law: A Comment on Wilburn Boat, 57 Mich. L. Rev. 555 (1959).

The *Wilburn Boat* concept was extended to corporate excess of loss policies in a dispute in the aftermath of the oil spill into Prince William Sound, Alaska, by the tanker *Exxon Valdez* in March 1989. See *Youell v. Exxon Corporation,* 48 F.3d 105, 1995 AMC 1147 (2d Cir. 1995), case remanded, 116 S. Ct. 43, 1996 AMC 2997 (1995). On remand the Second Circuit adhered to its view that an important federal admiralty question was involved that required federal adjudication; accordingly, the declaratory judgment action was reinstated. *Youell v. Exxon Corporation,* 74 F.3d 373, 1996 AMC 752 (2d Cir. 1996), cert. denied, 135 L.Ed. 2d 203 (June 10, 1996). The New York declaratory judgment action and the Texas state court action both proceeded until settled in 1996.

9. (1836) 5 L.J.K.B. 134, 111 E.R. 845.

10. *De Vaux v. Salvador* was followed in *General Mutual Ins. Co. v. Sherwood,* 55 U.S. 351 (1847).

11. See lines 158–84 of the AIH form in appendix 9.

12. See *New York Trap Rock Corp.,* 1956 AMC 469 (Arbitration at New York, Gregory S. Rivkins, Sole Arbitrator, 1955); *Adelaide Steamship Co. v. The Crown (The Warilda)* (1926) A.C. 172.

(c) "Ship or Vessel" under the Running Down Clause. The question of what is a ship or vessel within the meaning of the clause has caused some difficulty. For example, in *Chandler v. Blogg,*[13] the insured vessel collided with a barge which had just been sunk in a collision with another vessel. The barge was raised the next day, taken to her home port, and repaired. The court, apparently impressed by the fact that the barge was so promptly raised, applied a "navigability" test and held that it was still a "vessel," and that underwriters were therefore liable under the running down clause.

By contrast, in *Pelton S.S. Co. Ltd. v. North of England Protecting and Indemnity Association (The Zelo),*[14] the insured vessel collided with the wreck of another vessel upon which salvage efforts were then being conducted rather unsuccessfully. The collision with the insured vessel caused additional damage which made any salvage operations hopeless. The owners of the insured vessel claimed against hull underwriters under the running down clause, and the latter refused to pay on the ground that the wreck was no longer a "vessel." The insured then brought suit against the P & I insurers, who paid one-quarter of the loss but refused to pay the remaining three-quarters, on the ground that the wreck was a "vessel" at the time of collision. The court, in concluding that the wreck was a "vessel," applied a test as to whether or not any reasonably minded owner would have continued salvage operations just prior to the collision in the hope of completing recovery and repairing her. In doing so, the "navigability" test applied in *Chandler v. Blogg* was disapproved.[15]

Where an insured tug collided with the anchor of another vessel, it was held that a collision had occurred with a "vessel."[16] However, in *Trinidad Corp. v. American S.S. Owners Mut. P. & I. Ass'n.,*[17] it was held that a pipeline and pontoon attached to a dredge were not parts of a "vessel." The insured vessel ran into the dredge's pipeline and pontoon, forcing the pontoon into contact with another vessel and causing damage to the pipeline, the pontoon, and the other vessel. After an exhaustive analysis of the English cases, the court held that the collision did not occur with the dredge itself, that there was no collision with a "vessel," and that consequently the loss fell within the ambit of the P & I policy which, in that instance, covered liability

13. [1898] 1 Q.B. 32, 8 Asp. Mar. Law Cas. 349.

14. 22 Ll. L. Rep. 510 (K.B. 1925).

15. See note 16, infra. In this connection, see *Burnham v. China Mut. Ins. Co.,* 189 Mass. 100, 75 N.E. 74, 109 Am.St.Rep. 627 (1905), where the insured vessel struck a wrecked vessel which had sunk several hours before and had not been raised. Although it was possible to raise her, the cost would have exceeded her value when raised. The court held that the insured vessel had not come into collision with another "vessel" within the meaning of the running down clause.

16. *Re Margetts and Ocean Accident and Guarantee Corporation,* [1901] 2 K.B. 792, 9 Asp. Mar. Law Cas. 217.

17. 130 F. Supp. 46, 1955 AMC 1280 (SDNY 1955), aff'd, 229 F.2d 57, 1956 AMC 1464 (2d Cir. 1956).

for damage to "any fixed or moveable object or property whatsoever, except another vessel or craft."

In *Polpen Shipping Co. v. Commercial Union Assurance Co.*[18] a flying boat was held not to be a ship or vessel within the intendment of the running down clause.

In *Merchants' Marine Ins. Co. v. North of England Protecting and Indemnity Association,*[19] a pontoon barge with a crane permanently mounted on it, with no motive power of its own, not capable of being steered, and with no rudder, having been moved only five or six times in twelve years, was held not to be a vessel. On the other hand, in *The Coelleda—The Swallow*[20] it was held that the hull of a former naval sloop, stripped of her fittings and for many years used for the storage of gunpowder, permanently anchored in a river and not attached to or moored to the shore, was a "ship or vessel" within the meaning of the running down clause.

In *Lehigh & Wilkes-Barre Coal Co. v. Globe & Rutgers Fire Ins. Co. (The Honeybrook),*[21] barges struck rock abutments and the bank of a canal while under tow. The court held that this was not a "collision" as comprehended by the clause. In that instance, the clause covered "collision with any other vessel, craft or structure, floating or otherwise."

Thus, the courts seem to have proceeded on an *ad hoc* basis, on the theory that a "ship or vessel" may be hard to define, but that one knows a ship or vessel when one sees one.[22]

Notwithstanding the apparent breadth of the running down clause, certain categories of risks are wholly excluded, e.g., removal or disposal of obstructions and wrecks, and injury to real and personal property of every

---

18. [1943] K.B. 161, 74 Ll. L. Rep. 157, 1943 AMC 438.

19. 26 Ll. L. Rep. 201 (C.A. 1926).

20. 1932 AMC 1044 (Arbitration at New York, John W. Griffin, Sole Arbitrator [1932]).

21. 6 F.2d 736, 1925 AMC 717 (2d Cir. 1925). See also *Bennett S.S. Co. v. Hull Mutual S.S. Protection Society,* [1914] 3 K.B. 57, 12 Asp. Mar. Law Cas. 522. A number of the cases involving this point have arisen with respect to tug and tow. The most controversial is *McCowan v. Baine & Johnston (The Niobe).* [1891] A.C. 401, 7 Asp. Mar. Law Cas. 89 (H.L.). There, the *Niobe* was in tow of the Tug *Flying Serpent,* which collided with and sank the *Valetta.* The *Valetta*'s owners brought suit against the tug and the *Niobe* and recovered damages against both. After the *Niobe*'s owners had paid the *Valetta,* they sued their underwriters on the running down clause. Recovery was allowed even though the *Niobe* never came into contact with the *Valetta.* The judgment clearly followed the doctrine that a tug and tow are legally regarded as one vessel and, in this case, the command and control of the flotilla rested with the crew of the tow.

The *Niobe* antedated *Devonshire (Owners) v. Owners of the Barge Leslie,* [1912] A.C. 634, 12 Asp. Mar. Law Cas. 210 (H.L.), where Lord Atkinson said that "the question of the identity of the tow with the tug that tows her is one of fact, not law, to be determined upon the particular facts and circumstances of each case." This brought the English rule into conformity with the rule in the United States. See *Sturgis v. Boyer,* 65 U.S. 110 (1861). The *Niobe* was severely criticized in *Western Transit Co. v. Brown,* 161 F. 869 (2d Cir. 1908), and *The Richmond,* 161 F. 871 (2d Cir. 1908).

22. *Merchants Marine Ins. Co. v. North of England P. & I. Assoc.,* 26 Ll. L. Rep. 201 (C.A. 1926) (per Scrutton, L.J.)

description, other than vessels and property thereon.[23] The present forms of P & I certificates of entry and the rules they incorporate pick up the risks currently excluded under the running down clause and, in fact, have been described as a "complement" to collision liability insurance in hull and machinery policies.

It has been said that the uninsured one-quarter of collision liability under the standard English clause led shipowners to attempt to protect themselves by placing the remaining one-quarter liability with "Protection" Associations. The first "club" was formed to cover "extra risks not covered by ordinary marine policies on ships with a collision or running down clause therein," that is, excess collision liability and liability for loss of life and personal injury.[24] Today, the P & I clubs are usually incorporated companies. The club itself is therefore the insurer, and any right of action the member may have lies against the club and not the other members, the consideration being the assured's obligation to contribute to the losses of the other members and the expenses of the club.[25]

2. *Hybrid Clauses*

Running down clauses are not necessarily limited in their scope to collisions with "vessels," but depend upon the wording of the clause in the particular hull policy. In *Mancomunidad del Vapor "Frumiz" v. Royal Exchange Assurance,*[26] the clause read "collision with any object (ice included) other than water," and was held to cover a stranding and bumping on rocks, and in *Vestey Bros. v.*

23. *Trinidad Corp. v. American S.S. Owners Mutual P. & I. Ass'n,* 130 F. Supp. 46, 1955 AMC 1280 (SDNY 1955), aff'd, 229 F.2d 57, 1956 AMC 1464 (2d Cir. 1956).

24. Birch Reynardson, supra note 1. Also, prior to *De Vaux v. Salvador,* supra note 9, mutual associations, called "hull clubs," competed with underwriters at Lloyd's, although the coverage supplied by them does not appear to have been extensive. Some of the hull clubs did insure their members against third-party liabilities to crew members, passengers, and cargo. There was a logical and natural transition from hull clubs to protection and indemnity clubs. The first protection and indemnity club, the Shipowners Mutual Protection Society (now the Britannia Steam Ship Insurance Association) was formed in 1854.

25. *North-Eastern 100A S.S. Insurance Association v. Red S. Steamship Co.,* 22 T.L.R. 692, 12 Com. Cas. 26, (C.A. 1906). Most P & I insurance is provided by the sixteen mutual associations forming the International Group of Shipowners Protection and Indemnity Associations, commonly referred to as the "clubs," which insure more than 90 percent of the world's oceangoing tonnage. When a steamship company "enters" a vessel with one of the clubs, it receives a "certificate of entry" which incorporates by reference the rules of the particular club. Among other things, the rules set forth the liabilities covered. The clubs in the International Group pool their larger losses and the group reinsures its catastrophic losses with Lloyd's and scores of other underwriters around the world.

While the evidence of the P & I insurance provided by the clubs is a "certificate of entry" and the rules it incorporates, evidence of P & I insurance provided by other insurers is called a "policy," and that term is sometimes used herein, although in a particular case cited the contract of insurance may have been called a "certificate of entry." P & I insurance is discussed further in § F, infra.

26. [1927] 1 K.B. 567, 17 Asp. Mar. Law Cas. 205, 26 Ll. L. Rep. 191.

Motor Union Ins. Co.,[27] a clause reading "collision with ice or any other substance other than water" was held to cover a collision of the vessel with the chain of a gate while navigating through a lock.

In *Harding v. Amer. Univ. Ins. Co.,*[28] a vessel's propeller shaft struck an unidentified submerged object while the vessel was proceeding through shoal waters. The court held that striking a submerged object is a "peril of the sea," and the fact that such a striking is not a collision and therefore not covered by the running down clause did not mean that the loss was not covered by the perils clause; the two clauses provided distinct rights of recovery unrelated to one another.

In *The Munroe,*[29] the clause covered collision with "any . . . sunken . . . wreck." The vessel ran aground and on the tide falling she was found to be resting amidships on the wreck of a vessel sunk more than a year before. The vessel subsequently shifted her position off the wreck and onto a bank of iron ore which, two or three years earlier, had formed part of the cargo of another vessel. It was held that the policy covered the insured's loss.

In *Union Marine Ins. Co. v. Borwick,*[30] the policy covered collision with "piers, or stages, or similar structures." Two vessels covered by the policy went adrift in a storm and onto the toe of a breakwater, whereupon they went to pieces. It was held to be a collision and not a mere stranding.

3. *Specially Constructed Endorsements*

It is not uncommon to find specially constructed endorsements tacked on to other existing forms used as P & I policies and certificates of entry with P & I clubs, or as general liability policies. Thus, the towage exclusion in a P & I certificate of entry may be deleted and a new endorsement added which essentially provides the same coverage as Forms A, B, C, or D of the American Hull Institute clauses, or the same coverage as will be found in special tug hull policies. In the case of a general liability policy, the "watercraft exclusion" may be deleted and a towers' liability endorsement added.

For example, in *Bee Line Transportation Co. v. Connecticut Fire Insurance Company of Hartford (The Wyoming),*[31] the language used was quite similar to that of one of the insuring clauses in the Form "C" endorsement. Compare,

---

27. 10 Ll. L. Rep. 194, 270 (1910). See also *Newton Creek Towing Co. v. Aetna Ins. Co.,* 163 N.Y. 114, 57 N.E. 302 (1900), where a boat lashed to the starboard side of a tug and projecting 45 to 50 feet beyond it was damaged by being forced through a heavy ice floe in the night, when the tug's master could not see whether the ice was so heavy or dangerous that he should stop. The contract of towers' liability insurance covered the tow for any damage caused by "collision"; the court held that the term "collision" covered damage sustained by striking the heavy ice floe.

28. 130 So.(2d) 86, 1962 AMC 2423 (State of Fla., Dist. Ct. of App., 1st Dist.). Compare, however, *Cline v. Western Assur. Co.,* 101 Va. 496, 44 S.E. 700 (1903).

29. [1893] P. 248, 7 Asp. Mar. Law Cas. 407.

30. [1895] 2 Q.B. 279, 8 Asp. Mar. Law Cas. 71.

31. 76 F.2d 759, 1935 AMC 670 (2d Cir. 1935).

for example, the language in *Bee Line,* supra, reading: ". . . And it is further agreed that this policy shall also extend to and cover the said vessel's legal liability for any collision and/or grounding and/or stranding and/or loss or damage which may occur to any vessel or vessels or craft while in tow of said vessel, subject to all the terms and conditions of this clause," with the latter portion of the insuring clause in the Form "C" endorsement, reading: ". . . And it is further agreed that this policy shall also extend to and cover the legal liability of the Vessel hereby insured arising from any collision, grounding, stranding or sinking which may occur to any Vessel(s) or Craft(s) while in tow of said vessel." In *Bee Line,* the phrasing "said vessel's legal liability for any collision and/or grounding and/or stranding and/or loss or damage" was held to be sufficiently broad to cover the tug's legal liability to the owner of the cargo on the tow. The court cited *Marine Transit Corp. v. Northwestern Fire & Marine Ins. Co.*[32]

In *Bluewaters, Inc. v. Boag,*[33] a standard printed form of hull policy was issued, at lower than normal rates, which had attached to it an Institute form labeled "American Institute Time (Hulls)," at the top of which was typed "In so far as applicable." The typed portion of the policy provided for coverage against total and/or constructive total loss only. The printed institute clause, however, included running down coverage. The insured vessel collided with another vessel. A suit ensued in which the insured vessel owner prevailed but incurred attorneys' fees in defending the suit. Suit was then brought by the insured owner against his underwriters, seeking recoupment of a portion of the attorneys' fees. The trial court held that the policy was an integrated document and since it was clearly limited to total and constructive total loss, the institute "rider" was not applicable, and consequently the running down clause in the institute form did not provide collision liability coverage.

4. Tug and Tow Problems under the Running Down Clause

When a multitude of interests are involved, such as when a tow commonly owned with its tug, or separately owned by a third party, collides with another vessel, apportionment of the ultimate liability among underwriters, regardless of whether liability exists at all, can become unbelievably complex. The running down clause in standard forms has been amended to remove a problem resulting from the single ownership of two or more vessels. The addition of the language, "in consequence of the insured vessel being at fault," seems to have had the intended effect.[34] A lawyer confronted with the problem of

32. 67 F.2d 544, 1933 AMC 1631 (2d Cir. 1933).

33. 320 F.2d 833, 1964 AMC 71 (lst Cir. 1963).

34. *Harbor Towing Co. v. Atlantic Mutual Ins. Co.,* 189 F.2d 409, 1951 AMC 1070 (4th Cir. 1951), involved a negligent tug which caused its innocent barge to collide with another vessel. The tug and barge were owned by the same person. The Fourth Circuit held that the running

analyzing liability under applicable insurance policies in a collision case involving a tug and its tow must consider the following questions:

1. Does the hull policy on the tug, either directly (as in the McLelland Tug Hull Form, No. 1706) or by endorsement (as in Form "C") provide running down coverage with respect to its tow and cargo on the tow?
2. Does the P & I policy or the applicable club rule provide coverage and, if so, to what extent?
3. Is either the tug or the tow entitled to limit liability and, if so, what is the impact upon the extent of recoverable damages?
4. What impact, if any, does the cross-liabilities provision in the running down clause have upon ultimate coverage and the consequent recovery of damages?
5. What impact does the sister-ship provision in the running down clause have with respect to ultimate coverage and the consequent recovery of damages?

Section C. Cross-insurance Endorsements

Cross-insurance endorsements may be arranged by the owners of the tug and the owners of the tow, a practice which is now very common in the towing industry. Such endorsements are a relatively new development and have only recently received judicial approbation.[35]

There is, of course, a distinct difference between an outright exculpatory clause purporting to relieve the tug of all consequences of its own negligence, and a clause in the contract between the owner of the tug and the owner of the tow that each will procure appropriate insurance on its vessel and name the other as an additional assured, with a waiver of subrogation. The leading case is *Twenty Grand Offshore v. West India Carriers,*[36] where the tug

down clause covered only the insured vessel's liability and could not be stretched to protect the owner of a vessel not at fault, even though the same person owned both vessels.

The same result was reached in *The Norman Kelly,* 1923 AMC 959 (Ohio Sup. Ct. 1923). The facts were the same in *The Fanny D (Eggers v. Southern S.S. Co.),* 112 F.2d 347, 1940 AMC 1101 (5th Cir. 1940), but there the Fifth Circuit held that the fact that the barge was not liable *in rem* as the offending thing did not prevent a recovery, as coverage under the policy was not restricted to cases in which the insured vessel was at fault, and was broad enough to cover the *in personam* liability of its owner.

Compare *Driftwood Land and Timber, Ltd. v. U.S. Fire Ins. Co.,* [1954] O.R. 733, aff'd, [1954] O.W.N. 935; [1955] 1 D.L.R. 176, 1955 AMC 844 (Court of Appeal, Canada), where the insurance was "in respect of" a barge. The insured also owned a tug. While the tug was towing the barge, the tug crew negligently allowed the barge to strike and damage a dock. It was held that the damage was not covered, as the intent of the policy was to cover the insured only in its capacity as owner of the barge, and not in respect of the operation of the tug.

35. See chapter 10, supra notes 73–80.

36. 492 F.2d 679, 1974 AMC 2254 (5th Cir. 1974).

lost the barge under tow when the towing hawser parted and the barge went aground. In a subsequent limitation proceeding, the court held the tug owner liable and denied limitation, finding negligence and privity, and awarded the barge owner its damages. The finding of negligent towage was not contested on appeal. The towage agreement provided that the owner of the tug would procure and pay for hull and machinery and P & I insurance, naming the owner of the tow as an additional assured and waiving subrogation. The agreement contained essentially identical provisions requiring the owner of the tow to procure like insurance, naming the tug owner, the tug, and its crew as additional assureds, and waiving subrogation. The tug owner did procure the requisite insurance; the barge owner failed to have the tug owner and its tug named as additional assureds and failed to procure waivers of subrogation.

The district court, concluding that *Bisso*[37] forbade tug owners to do indirectly what could not be done directly, held the insurance clauses invalid. The Fifth Circuit, citing *Fluor Western v. G. & H. Offshore Towing Co.*,[38] held such clauses valid and not exculpatory *per se* in the context of *Bisso,* stating:

> We can discern no basic difference between *Fluor Western* and this case. The fact that it *[Fluor Western]* involved cargo insurance and cargo damage rather than barge insurance and barge damage is a distinction without a difference. *Fluor Western,* as does the instant case, involved a towing agreement, and simply because cargo laden aboard the tow was damaged, rather than the tow itself, can conceptually make no difference....
>
> We conclude that the provision in the towing agreement requiring each party to fully insure its vessel, to effect a waiver of subrogation, and to name the other party as an additional assured, is not an exculpatory clause of the type invalidated in *Bisso* and *Dixilyn.*[39]

The logic of the decision is self-evident and seemingly has set at rest the question of cross-insurance clauses.[40]

37. *Bisso v. Inland Waterways Corp.*, 349 U.S. 85, 1955 AMC 899 (1955).

38. 447 F.2d 35, 1972 AMC 406 (5th Cir. 1972).

39. *Dixilyn Drilling Corp. v. Crescent Towage & Salvage Co.*, 372 U.S. 697, 1963 AMC 829 (1963).

40. See also *Tenneco Oil Co. v. The Tug Tony and Coastal Towing Corp.*, 324 F. Supp. 834, 1971 AMC 2336 (SD Tex. 1971); *Slade v. Samson Towing Co.*, 327 F. Supp. 555, 1971 AMC 2342 (ED Tex. 1971); *Hartford Fire Ins. Co. v. Port Everglades Towing Co.*, 454 F.2d 276, 1972 AMC 316 (5th Cir. 1972); *BASF Wyandotte v. The Tug Leander Jr.*, 590 F.2d 96, 1979 AMC 1721 (5th Cir. 1979). Cf. *Dow Chemical Co. v. Ashland Oil, Inc.*, 579 F.2d 902, 1979 AMC 1581 (5th Cir. 1978); *Dow Chemical Co. v. The Charles F. Detmar, Jr.*, 545 F.2d 1091 (7th Cir. 1976); *PPG Industries, Inc. v. Ashland Oil, Inc.*, 592 F.2d 138, 1979 AMC 2056 (3d Cir. 1979).

Section D. The Basis of Liability under the Running Down Clause

1. *Tort and Contract*

The first paragraph of the standard running down clause originally provided that it only came into play when the insured vessel was at fault and the assured actually paid damages. In short, the liabilities contemplated by the clause referred to those arising from "tort," rather than from contractual obligations. This was first established in *Furness, Withy & Co., Ltd. v. Duder,*[41] where the insured vessel was under tow and collided with the tug due to the tug's negligence. Under the U.K. Towing Conditions then in effect, she was contractually obligated to pay for the damage to the tug. The court held that this was a liability created by contract and not by tort, and that the running down clause therefore did not apply.

A comparable situation arose in *Hall Bros. Steamship Co. v. Young,*[42] where the assured was obliged under French law to pay for damage sustained by a French pilot boat which collided with the assured's vessel through no fault of the latter. The court held, in essence, that payment was made because of the provisions of French law and not by reason of collision liability *per se.* Under an amended version of the running down clause the problem of the requirement of liability in tort has been resolved: the language now provides for coverage, "in consequence of the vessel being at fault."[43]

---

41. [1936] 2 K.B. 461, 2 All E.R. 119, 55 Ll. L. Rep. 52.

42. [1939] 1 All E.R. 809, 63 Ll. L. Rep. 143 (C.A.). See also *Taylor v. Dewar,* [1864] 33 L.J.Q.B. 141, 122 E.R. 754, where the owners of the *Roven,* which had run down another vessel, were required to pay wrongful death damages to the representatives of the crew of the vessel run down, and the running down clause was held not to apply.

43. The question seems to have first arisen in the United States in *The Norman Kelly,* supra note 34, where the barge *Norman Kelly* was insured under a hull policy which contained a running down clause reading:

> And it is further agreed that if the ship hereby insured shall come into collision with any other ship or vessel, and the Assured shall in consequence thereof become liable to pay, and shall pay by way of damages to any other person or persons any sum or sums not exceeding . . . we, the Assurers, will pay the Assured such proportion of such sum or sums so paid.

The barge, while in tow of a commonly owned tug, collided with a steamer, causing damage to both the steamer and the barge. In a suit by the steamer, the court found the collision was caused by the sole negligence of the tug. The tug and barge owner then sought to recover from the underwriters on the barge hull policy the amount it had paid to the steamer interests. The court said:

> . . . The liability as a result of such collision must be such a liability as would permit the third person or persons to recover in a suit at law for the damage done. . . . Unless the collision occurred by the fault of the barge, and such fault was either a proximate or contributing cause of the collision, there could be no liability on the part of [the owner] in its capacity as *owner of the barge* to pay any third person for any damage resulting from said collision. (Emphasis added.)

Cf. *The Fanny D (Eggers v. Southern S.S. Co.),* supra note 34; *Harbor Towing Co. v. Atlantic Mutual Ins. Co.,* supra note 34 (the barge was not "at fault," and so there was no coverage). See also *The London*

2. *Indemnity and Liability*

The standard form of running down clause provides, in part, that the underwriters will pay the assured when "in consequence of the Vessel being at fault" the assured "shall become liable to pay *and shall pay* by way of damages . . . any sum or sums in respect of such collision." In nearly all jurisdictions, this renders the policy one of indemnity and not of liability.[44]

In *The Narco—The Lolita,*[45] the *Narco* collided with the *Lolita,* whose owners then filed an action against the *Narco,* her owners, and Nardelli, her charterer. Nardelli, in turn, impleaded the hull underwriters, seeking recovery under the hull policy in the event the *Narco* should be held liable. After decisions in the lower court and on appeal, it was held on rehearing that the running down clause covered Nardelli up to the full amount of the policy. The case was remanded. No further evidence was taken, and the charterer was awarded the full amount of the policy, plus his attorney's fees expended in establishing liability under it. The case was again appealed. The Fifth Circuit, in a difficult opinion, held that since Nardelli had paid nothing on the judgment in favor of the *Lolita,* the requirement of "payment" precluded him from recovery, i.e., the policy was one of indemnity and not liability and there could be no recovery in the absence of proof that payment had actually been made. Nardelli did, however, recover his attorneys' fees, as these were actually incurred and paid.

State law, however, may have a dramatic effect upon the classification of a policy as being one of indemnity rather than liability. Thus, in *Liman,*[46] the court held that under New York law, an insurer under an indemnity policy is not relieved of its obligation to indemnify the assured by showing that the funds enabling the assured to pay claims were advanced by a third party or financed in some other fashion.[47]

S.S. Owners' Ass'n v. The Grampian S.S. Co., [1890] 24 Q.B.D. 663 (C.A.); *Field S.S. Co. v. Burr* [1899] 1 Q.B. 579 (C.A.); *Stuyvesant Ins. Co. v. Nardelli (The Narco—The Lolita),* 258 F.2d 718, 1958 AMC 2404 (5th Cir. 1958), modified, 286 F.2d 600, 1961 AMC 1999 (5th Cir. 1961); *The Augusta—The Detroit,* 290 F. 685, 688, 1923 AMC 754, 757 (4th Cir. 1923); *The Ariosa and The D-22,* 144 F.2d 262, 1944 AMC 1035 (2d Cir. 1944).

44. *The Narco—The Lolita,* supra note 43; *Cucurillo v. American S.S. Owners Mut. Protection & Indemnity. Ass'n. Inc.,* 1969 AMC 2334 (N.Y. Sup. Ct., N.Y. County, 1969); *Liman, Trustee v. American S.S. Owners Mut. Protection & Indemnity Ass'n. Inc.,* 299 F. Supp. 106, 1969 AMC 1669 (SDNY 1969), aff'd, 417 F.2d 627, 1971 AMC 814 (2d Cir. 1971); *Ahmed v. American S.S. Owners Mut. Prot. & Indemn. Ass'n. Inc.,* 640 F.2d 993, 1981 AMC 897 (9th Cir. 1981), on remand 1982 AMC 1228 (ND Cal. 1982).

45. Supra note 44.

46. Id.

47. Cf. *Orion Ins. Co. v. Firemens Fund Ins. Co. (The Barcelona),* 46 Cal. App. 3d 374, 1975 AMC 1183 (Cal. Dist. Ct. of Appeal, 2d Dist. 1975); *Saunders v. Austin W. Fishing Corp.,* 352 Mass. 169, 224 N.E. 2d 215, 1967 AMC 986 (Sup. Jud. Ct., Mass. 1967).

3. *Exceptions under the Running Down Clause*

Under the exceptions proviso, the running down clause in the 1977 AIH form does not extend to any sum which the assured may become liable to pay or shall pay with respect to:

> (a) removal or disposal of obstructions, wrecks or their cargoes under statutory powers or otherwise pursuant to law;
> (b) injury to real or personal property of every description;
> (c) the discharge, spillage, emission or leakage of oil, petroleum products, chemicals or other substances of any kind or description whatsoever;
> (d) cargo or other property on or the engagements of the Vessel;
> (e) loss of life, personal injury or illness.
>
> Provided, further, that exclusions (b) and (c) above shall not apply to injury to other vessels or property thereon except to the extent that such injury arises out of any action taken to avoid, minimize or remove any discharge, spillage, emission or leakage described in (c) above.

The liabilities enumerated in the proviso are, however, recoverable by the shipowner from its P & I insurers under the usual club rules.[48]

4. *Legal Costs of Attack or Defense*

The running down clause in the AIH form provides in subsection (b): "... In cases where, with the consent in writing of a majority (in amount) of Hull Underwriters, the liability of the Vessel has been contested, or proceedings have been taken to limit liability, the Underwriters will also pay a like proportion of the costs which the Assured shall thereby incur or be compelled to pay." The covenant to pay costs is supplementary to the earlier provision of the clause and, therefore, costs are payable in addition to the maximum liability with respect to damages, which, in the case of the running down clause in the AIH form, is the agreed value stated in the policy.[49]

The coverage with respect to costs was inserted in the running down clause as a consequence of *Xenos v. Fox,*[50] in which it was held (under the clause as it then read) that the costs of defending a claim for collision damages, even though successful, could not be recovered under the clause, nor

---

48. See, e.g., Rule 2, § 10, of The Rules of the United Kingdom Mutual Steam Ship Assurance Association (Bermuda) Limited (commonly known as the U.K. P & I Club), 7A Benedict § 1.01.

49. The last several lines of paragraph (a) of the clause (relating to liability for damages) contain a proviso that underwriters' liability with respect to any one collision shall not exceed their proportionate part of the agreed value of the vessel; no such proviso appears with respect to paragraph (b), relating to liability for costs.

50. [1869] L.R. 4 C.P. 665 (Ex. Ch.). See also *Cunard S.S. Co. v. Marten,* [1902] 2 K.B. 624, 9 Asp. Mar. Law Cas. 342, aff'd, [1903], 2 K.B. 511, 9 Asp. Mar. Law Cas. 452 (C.A.).

as sue and labor expenses, inasmuch as such costs were not incurred to prevent loss of or damage to the insured vessel herself.

The underwriters' willingness to bear costs is not altogether altruistic, as the paramount objective is to minimize liabilities to third parties, as far as possible. As costs of defense, they are borne by the hull underwriters under the clause.[51] Obviously, damage to the insured vessel is of no concern to the P & I insurers (except to the extent that it may affect the value of the vessel for limitation of liability purposes), nor are they interested in the costs applicable to obtaining a recovery from the other colliding vessel. One would assume that if the insured vessel were found solely at fault, all costs incurred, including those expended to limit liability, should be considered as costs of defense. However, this does not necessarily follow as a practical matter, because at the time legal proceedings are in progress, lawyers for the insured vessel are almost invariably defending her and, at the same time, pressing claims against the other colliding vessel. The actual outcome will of course not be known until the trial has been concluded and the court has rendered its decision. As a matter of practice, the allocation of legal expenses and costs among the parties in interest is a function of the average adjusters and, in practice, such costs are commonly treated as general costs, with the underwriters or other interests involved each paying their share.[52]

Costs fall rather neatly into three classes: general, attack, and defense:

(a) General Costs. These are incurred in endeavoring to establish liability up to the time liability is definitely established, including investigation of the facts, interviewing witnesses, attending hearings of regulatory agencies such as the U.S. Coast Guard, and attending depositions on the issue of liability. These usually embrace efforts to prove that the other vessel was to blame and that the insured vessel was not, or at least that the other vessel was more to blame than her owners concede. Also included are any other costs which cannot be specifically attributed to attack or defense, i.e., that are common to both attack and defense and that must be apportioned rateably over the amounts involved.

(b) Attack Costs. These are costs which relate to prosecuting the claim against the other colliding vessel. Examples are preparation of and filing the

---

51. This is true, of course, under American practice, where the collision clause covers four-fourths of the shipowners' liability; under English practice, where the clause covers only three-fourths of the shipowners' liability, the P & I insurers customarily cover the remaining one-fourth, and are therefore interested to that extent in the payment of costs.

52. In a typical collision involving two vessels, each carrying cargo, the average adjuster must apportion costs among the three parties involved with respect to the insured vessel: the owner, as to deductibles and uninsured losses such as detention; the hull underwriters, as to hull damage and liabilities and costs under the running down clause; and the P & I insurers (in most instances), as to death and personal injury claims, claims of cargo on the insured vessel, and other claims of a P & I nature.

complaint or counterclaim against the other vessel; arranging for service of process; arranging for the arrest of the other vessel or obtaining security in lieu of an arrest; examining evidence in support of claims for physical and detention damages of the insured vessel; and obtaining evidence as necessary, including payment of the expenses of witnesses called solely for the purpose of proving the damages of the insured vessel, as distinguished from those called in connection with establishing liability of the other vessel. Costs incurred in attempting to defeat the other vessel's right to limit liability or relating to the size of her limitation fund also fall within this category.

The average adjuster apportions the attack costs over the various items of any recovery made, or, if recovery has been denied, over the various interests which would have benefited from a successful outcome. For example, costs referable to efforts to recover for physical damage are charged to the hull underwriters; costs relating to the vessel's detention claim are charged to the owner, if, as is usual, it is not insured against loss of use.

(c) Defense Costs. These are costs which specifically relate to defending the other vessel's claim. Included are preparation of the answer to the other vessel's complaint; arranging for posting security to release the insured vessel from arrest, or to avoid arrest; and investigating and contesting the other vessel's damages. Also included are costs incurred in filing and prosecuting limitation proceedings on behalf of the insured vessel.

The average adjuster here apportions the defense costs among the interests benefited or intended to be benefited, i.e., the hull underwriters with respect to those claims falling within the running down clause and P & I insurers with respect to any claims falling within the scope of the policy or club rules, such as personal injury and death claims, claims of cargo on the insured vessel, and other claims of a P & I nature.

Under English law, "costs" are discretionary, but in sole-fault cases are usually awarded to the successful party alone. In both-to-blame cases they are usually divided, but not necessarily in proportion to the respective degrees of blame.[53] The rule in the United States is similar.[54]

It should be observed that the AIH clause with respect to costs provides that they must be incurred with the "consent in writing of a majority (in amount) of Hull Underwriters." This does not mean, however, that vessel owners should not take the necessary steps to preserve and protect their own interests, as well as those of their underwriters, even before it is possible to

---

53. *The Osprey,* [1967] 1 Lloyd's Rep. 76. For a detailed discussion of the English practice concerning costs in collision cases, see Marsden 317–33.

54. See Fed. R. Civ. P. 54(d); *Ore Carriers of Liberia, Inc. v. Navigen Co.,* 305 F. Supp. 895, 1971 AMC 508 (SDNY 1969), aff'd per curiam, 435 F.2d 549, 1971 AMC 513 (2d Cir. 1970). Unlike the practice in England, under American law "costs" do not include an allowance on account of the fees of the successful party's lawyers, but only such items as premiums on a surety bond posted to release a vessel from arrest, or to avoid an arrest, court filing fees, witness fees, etc.

obtain such consent. For example, such obviously necessary steps as arranging a survey of the other vessel and interviewing witnesses should be undertaken without delay and will invariably be treated by underwriters as costs of defense. It should be remembered that, in the United States, statements reduced to writing may be discoverable by the opposing party.[55]

As noted above, the allocation of legal expenses and costs among the various parties in interest is generally a matter for average adjusters. In this connection, in the United States these are generally apportioned in accordance with Rule XX of the Association of Average Adjusters of the United States, reading as follows:[56]

> In cases involving collisions, the legal costs and/or other expenses incurred to determine liability either by court action, arbitration or determination by consent of the parties shall be apportioned rateably over the full provable damages, excluding interest and costs, of the claim and counter-claim which have been or would have been allowed.
>
> Nothing contained in this rule shall affect those legal costs and/or other expenses incurred specifically for the purpose of defense or recovery which shall be charged accordingly.[57]

Section E. Sister-Ship Clauses

When two vessels in common ownership are involved in a collision, it is impossible to resolve the question of blame by legal proceedings, because a shipowner cannot be legally liable to itself and therefore cannot sue itself.[58] It was to avoid this inequity arising simply out of an accident of ownership that the sister-ship clause was devised.

There are two sister-ship clauses in the AIH form. The clause relating to collision will be found as part of the running down clause and reads:

> The principles involved in this clause shall apply to the case where both vessels are the property, in part or in whole, of the same owners or charterers, all questions of responsibility and amount of liability as between the two vessels being left to the decision of a single Arbitrator, if the parties can agree upon a single Arbitrator, or failing such agreement, to the decision of Arbitrators, one to be appointed by the Assured and one to be appointed by the majority (in amount) of Hull Underwriters interested; the two Arbitrators chosen to choose a third Arbitrator before

55. See *Leviathan, Inc. v. The Alaska Maru,* 86 F.R.D. 8, 1981 AMC 301 (D Wash. 1980).

56. The rules are reprinted in 2 Parks 1204 ff.

57. For the corresponding rule of the Canadian Average Adjusters' Associations see 2 Parks 710.

58. *Simpson v. Thomsen,* [1877] 3 App. Cas. 279 (H.L.). See also *The Augusta—The Detroit,* 1924 AMC 872 (D Md. 1924), aff'd, 5 F.2d 773, 1925 AMC 756 (4th Cir. 1925).

> entering upon the reference, and the decision of such single Arbitrator, or of any two of such three Arbitrators, appointed as above, to be final and binding.

The other clause is part of the general average and salvage clause of the AIH form and reads:

> In the event of salvage, towage or other assistance being rendered to the Vessel by any vessel belonging in part or in whole to the same Owners or Charterers, the value of such services (without regard to the common ownership or control of the vessels) shall be ascertained by arbitration in the manner provided for under the Collision Liability clause in this Policy, and the amount so awarded so far as applicable to the interest hereby insured shall constitute a charge under this Policy.

In English policies, the sister-ship clause follows the running down clause in the London Institute Clauses and is worded as follows:

> Should the Vessel hereby insured come into collision with or receive salvage services from another vessel belonging wholly or in part to the same Owners or under the same management, the Assured shall have the same rights under this Policy as they would have were the other vessel entirely the property of Owners not interested in the Vessel hereby insured; but in such cases the liability for the collision or the amount payable for the services rendered shall be referred to a sole arbitrator to be agreed upon between the Underwriters and the Assured.

It will be seen that under the sister-ship clause, the assured shipowner can recover its detention damages if its vessel is not to blame, or a proportion of its detention damages on a cross-liabilities basis when both vessels are to blame. If the principle of cross-liabilities were not applied, underwriters would simply pay for the damage suffered by each vessel and the shipowner would not recover any part of its detention damages. The same principle applies when salvage services and, under the AIH form, when towage services are rendered by one vessel to another vessel owned by the same entity.

It is customary in sister-ship collisions, when one vessel is clearly responsible for the collision and the other is wholly innocent, to request underwriters' approval to present the claim for damage to the innocent vessel on the policy covering that particular vessel, thus obviating the necessity for an arbitration. Moreover, if no detention claims are involved, the claims are often stated as particular average claims under the respective policies on the vessels and the liability question becomes moot. However, if there is any doubt about liability for the collision damage and detention claims involved, it is necessary to follow the arbitration provisions.[59]

59. Other decisions explaining the principles governing sister-ship provisions under the running down clause include *The Industry—The Commerce,* 1939 AMC 717 (Arbitration at New

Section F. Protection and Indemnity Insurance

1. Losses Covered

(a) General Coverage. As noted in section B, supra, the first "protection" club was formed to cover extra risks, such as excess collision liabilities, not covered by the running down clause of an ordinary marine policy on a ship.[60] Shortly thereafter, the *Westenhope* was lost off South Africa, after having deviated from the port of original destination. The owners were obliged to pay for the loss of cargo on board, and the club refused to reimburse the owners. In due course, the club rules were amended to provide coverage against most types of cargo claims, and "indemnity" was added to the description of the risks covered.

There are now many different types of coverage offered by P & I clubs in addition to the original coverage of the excess collision liability not covered by the hull policy.[61] In general, such contracts are construed in the same way as any other insurance contracts, i.e., in the light of the purpose of the insurance.

In *Seaboard Shipping Corp. v. Jocharanne Tugboat Corp.*,[62] the court noted that P & I policies are intended to apply chiefly to situations not covered by other insurance, and thereupon upheld a "no contribution" clause where the assured had expended sums for sue and labor expenses and its hull underwriters sought to recoup a portion of them from the P & I insurers. The court reached this conclusion, even though the efforts and sums expended

York, Roger D. Englar, Sole Arbitrator); *Aetna Ins. Co. v. Henry DuBois Sons Co. (The Ariosa—The D-22)*, 144 F.2d 262, 1944 AMC 1035 (2d Cir. 1944); *Bushey & Sons v. Tugboat Underwriting Syndicate,* 1975 AMC 392 (SDNY 1975).

60. See Birch Reynardson, supra note 1. See also *Report of Advanced Study Group No. 109 of the Insurance Institute of London,* presented at a special meeting of members, Jan. 8, 1957.

61. As a result of legislation over the years and the imposition of new liabilities on shipowners, P & I insurers have continually added new risks to the coverages originally provided. For example, there are freight, demurrage, and defense associations associated with the P & I clubs, associations covering shipbuilders' and ship repairers' liabilities, and "strike" clubs. Moreover, there are employers' liability-type policies which carry special endorsements, such as the Marina Operators' Liability policy construed in *Pillgrem v. Cliff Richardson Boats, Ltd.*, [1977] 1 Lloyd's Rep. 297 (Supreme Ct. of Ontario 1976), and comprehensive personal liability policies (with special endorsements), such as the one construed in *Security National Ins. Co. v. Sequoyah Marina, Inc.*, 246 F.2d 830, 1958 AMC 143 (10th Cir. 1958).

62. 461 F.2d 500, 1972 AMC 2151 (2d Cir. 1972). See also *Cunard S.S. Co. v. Marten,* [1903] 2 K.B. 511 (C.A.); *Caballery v. Sea-Land Services,* 1973 AMC 479 (D R.I. 1973); *Lanasse v. Travelers Ins. Co.*, 450 F.2d 580, 1972 AMC 818 (5th Cir. 1972); *Bee Line Transp. Co. v. Connecticut Fire Ins. Co. of Hartford,* 76 F.2d 759, 1935 AMC 670 (2d Cir. 1935); *American Ins. Co. v. Keane,* 233 F.2d 354, 1956 AMC 488 (D.C. Cir. 1956) (combination hull and P & I policy covering a racing yacht); *Hinkle & Finlayson v. Globe & Rutgers Fire Ins. Co.*, 1936 AMC 1289 (mem.) (N.Y. State Court of Appeals); *Security National Ins. Co. v. Sequoyah Marina Inc.*, 246 F.2d 830, 1958 AMC 143 (10th Cir. 1958).

may well have avoided possible explosion, abandonment, and other liabilities which otherwise would have fallen upon the P & I insurers.[63]

For the purposes of the discussion which follows, references are to the American Steamship Owners Mutual Protection and Indemnity Association (ASM) form, revised February 20, 1972. Modern P & I policies cover such diverse risks as liability for loss of life, personal injury, and illness of any person except employees covered by any workmen's compensation act; repatriation expenses; excess collision liabilities (e.g., the one-fourth liability for damage to ships and vessels not covered by a three-fourths running down clause in a hull policy); liability for damage to docks, buoys, and other fixed objects; wreck removal expenses; liability for cargo loss and damage; fines and penalties; mutiny and misconduct; quarantine expenses; expenses incurred with respect to landing injured or sick seamen and passengers; inability to recover cargo's proportion of general-average liabilities;[64] expenses of investigation and defense; and expenses in the club's interest incurred with the authorization of the club.

(b) Collision Coverage. The ASM form provides coverage for:

> Liability for loss or damage arising from collision of the insured vessel with another ship or vessel where the liability is of a type, character, or kind which would not be covered in any respect by the following portions of the Four-Fifths Collision Clause in the American Institute Hull Clauses (January 18, 1970) form including the June 4, 1970 Collision Clause Amendment A.[65]

Thus, in general terms, liability under the ASM P & I form for collision liability (except with respect to fixed objects) is limited to those risks excluded by the "exclusions" clause in the hull policy running down clause.

---

63. A very similar form, in common use in the United States, particularly on the inland waterways, is the SP-23 (Rev. 1/56). A comparison of the two forms will be found in "Marine P & I Policy Annotations, 1982," prepared by the Admiralty & Maritime Law Committee, Section of Tort and Insurance Practice, American Bar Association, in cooperation with the Committee on Marine Insurance, General Average, and Salvage of the Maritime Law Association of the United States.

64. This refers only to contributions claimed from cargo which cannot be collected because of owner's breach of the contract of affreightment, e.g., a failure to exercise due diligence to make the vessel seaworthy.

65. As we have seen, English running down clauses, as a general rule, still cover only three-fourths of the collision liability, whereas in the American market four-fourths clauses are customary. It should be noted, however, that not all vessels are entered in P & I clubs, and some that are entered for most P & I risks are not entered for excess collision liability. For example, the Netherlands Hull Form includes a four-fourths collision clause which is very broad in scope. Builders' risks and institute port risks in the London market also include full collision clauses, and, moreover, include certain P & I risks. Yachts (which are ineligible for entry in the clubs) are customarily protected by special clauses, including full collision coverage with P & I supplements.

Exclusion (d) of the AIH running down clause concerns the joint and several liability problem under American law, where if both vessels are at fault in any degree, the cargo may recover in full from the noncarrying vessel, and the carrying vessel is then obligated to pay to or credit the noncarrying vessel with an amount representing the carrying vessel's share of the blame. This indirect liability is excluded under the AIH running down clause, but is covered by the ASM P & I form, and under the rules of the other clubs constituting the International Group.

With reference to exclusion (e), hull underwriters have never, under any standard form of hull policy, covered claims for loss of life, personal injury, or illness which, like the other exclusions in the proviso of the collision clause, come within the ambit of the P & I policy. The ASM form, moreover, contains a proviso which explicitly provides that the P & I coverage does not extend to any liability, direct or indirect, in respect of the engagements of or the detention of or loss of time of the insured vessel. The ASM form also includes cross-liabilities and sister-ship provisions essentially similar to those found in a hull running down clause.

Thus it is the function of P & I insurance to respond (subject to its own exclusions) to liabilities otherwise excluded by the running down clause of the hull policy.[66] It is, indeed, a "supplement" to the hull policy, as was pointed out in *Trinidad Corp. v. American S.S. Owners Mut. P & I Ass'n.*[67]

It should be emphasized that the ASM form recognizes that the vessel covered might be a tug, in which case, the reference in the P & I policy to the appropriate running down clause in the hull policy must be amended to reflect the correct scope of coverage under the P & I policy. Therefore, the ASM form provides that with respect to tugs, the collision clause in the American Institute Tug Form, January, 1954 (Revised November 30, 1959) is deemed incorporated in lieu of the usual collision clause.[68]

---

66. Buglass gives, as examples, expenses incurred in removing oil from the sea or shore, or deliberately destroying a vessel to prevent pollution. See Buglass at 364.

67. 130 F. Supp. 46, 1955 AMC 1280 (SDNY 1955), aff'd, 229 F.2d 57, 1956 AMC 1464 (2d Cir. 1956).

68. See the clause in the ASM form under "Risks Excluded," reading:

> In every case where this policy insures tugs, Clause (b) of Paragraph (6) and Clause (c) of Paragraph (29) shall be deemed to refer to the American Institute Tug Form, January, 1954 (Revised November 30, 1959) instead of the American Institute Hull Clauses (January 18, 1970) Form including the June 4, 1970 Collision Clause Amendment A and Paragraph (3) shall be deemed to incorporate the Collision Clause contained in said policy (American Institute Tug Form, January, 1954 (Revised November 30, 1959) instead of the Collision Clause quoted in said Paragraph (3) and the following clause shall be substituted for and supersedes Clause (d) of Paragraph (29) namely:
>
> "Loss of or damage to any vessel or vessels in tow and/or their cargoes, whether such loss or damage occurs before, during or after actual towage; provided, that this exception shall not apply to claims under Paragraph (1) of this policy [i.e., claims for loss of life or personal injury]."

Since there is coverage under a P & I policy or club rules for full collision damage liability only if the insured vessel collides with some object other than a ship or vessel, many of the decisions involving the interplay of the running down clause in the hull policy with the P & I policy have devolved around the question of whether the object with which the insured vessel collided was, or was not, a "ship or vessel."[69]

(c) Excess Collision Liability. In certain circumstances, where a vessel owner carries insufficient hull insurance to pay collision losses in full, an "excess" collision liability can result. This was the situation in *Landry v. Steamship Mut. Underwriting Association.*[70] There, the owner had insured the vessel for $20,000 and obtained P & I insurance for $50,000. The insured vessel collided with another, whose damages amounted to more than $24,000. The vessel owner paid the $24,000, received $20,000 from his hull underwriters, and thereafter brought suit against the P & I insurers for the $4,000 difference. Much to the latters' surprise, the court held that the vessel owner could recover for the excess liability from the P & I insurers. As a consequence, P & I insurers in the United States amended their policies to exclude this excess liability. The amended ASM form, for example, provides (in paragraph 29[c]) that there shall be no liability by reason of:

> Any loss, damage, sacrifice or expense of a type, character or kind which would be payable under the terms of a policy written on the American Institute Hull Clauses (January 18, 1970) Form including the June 4, 1970 Collision Clause Amendment A, and a policy written on the American Institute Increased Value and Excess Liabilities Clauses (January 18, 1970) Form *whether or not the insured vessel is fully covered under those policies by insurance and excess insurance sufficient in amount to pay in full and without limit all such loss, damage, sacrifice or expense.* [The italicized portion is the new amendment].[71]

A similar question was raised in *Stuyvesant Ins. Co. v. R. Leloup Shrimp Co.,*[72] where the P and I portion of the policy contained language essentially similar to that involved in *Landry,* supra. However, there was a second exclu-

69. See § B(c) supra.

70. 177 F. Supp. 142, 1960 AMC 54 (D Mass. 1960), aff'd, 281 F.2d 482, 1960 AMC 1650 (1st Cir. 1960).

71. The English clubs apparently regard the excess collision liability as an important part of their cover, as, incidentally, do the Scandinavian clubs, notwithstanding that they, like the ASM, leave four-fourths of the collision liability with the hull underwriters. Keeping in mind that the London Institute Hulls policy covers only three-fourths of the collision liability, the clubs not only cover the remaining one-fourth, whether or not it exceeds the insured value of the entered vessel but, in addition, once hull underwriters have paid out the maximum under their policy, (i.e., three-fourths of the insured value), then *if the vessel is fully insured,* the clubs will cover the entirety of the collision liability above that amount. If the vessel is underinsured, the owner may be faced with an uninsured liability in part.

72. 333 F. Supp. 233, 1972 AMC 1286 (SD Tex. 1972).

sionary clause which provided, in essence, that liability was excluded for any loss "in connection with *any accident covered under* the Four-fourths Running Down Clause. . . ." The court, noting that there was a difference between *loss covered by* and *an accident covered by* the policy, held that it was clear that the *accident* there involved (the collision) was, in fact, covered under the running down clause and, consequently, the excess collision liability confronting the owner was not covered.

It should be emphasized that coverage under P & I insurance applies to liabilities that do not fall within the scope of a specified type of hull policy running down clause. Whether the owner's hull policy actually contains a collision clause of the type specified is immaterial. In fact, it is immaterial whether or not the owner's hull policy includes any form of running down clause. The P & I insurer's liability is measured by what coverages the specified form of running down clause would have provided rather than whether such insurance was actually maintained by the assured.[73] The collision liabilities for which the P & I insurers undertake to indemnify, i.e., those excluded by the proviso of the running down clause, are in fact duplicated in other portions of the policy. For example, removal of wrecks (excluded by paragraph [a] of the proviso) is specifically covered under paragraph (6) of the ASM form. Loss of life, injury, and illness (excluded by paragraph [e] of the proviso) are specifically covered under paragraph (1) of the ASM form; injury to real or personal property of every description (excluded by paragraph [b] of the proviso) is specifically covered by paragraph (5) of the ASM form; oil pollution, etc. (excluded by paragraph [c] of the proviso) is specifically covered by paragraph (13) of the ASM form; and loss of or damage to cargo on the insured vessel (excluded by paragraph [d] of the proviso) is specifically covered by paragraph (7) of the ASM form. In addition, the ASM form also specifically covers, in paragraph (4), liability for loss of or damage to any other vessel or craft, or property on board, caused otherwise than by collision of the insured vessel with another vessel or craft; i.e., what might be classified as "quasi-collision" claims, such as for swell damage, for forcing another vessel aground, or for causing her to collide with a third vessel or other object.

A fortiori, it matters little, then, in construing the coverages provided by P & I insurance, whether the loss or damage was occasioned by a collision or by some other event, so long as the event is otherwise covered by some relevant insuring clause in the policy. The legal construction of the P & I insurance provision is the same, whether that event was a collision or some other insured casualty.

73. *DeBardeleben Coal Corp. v. P & I Underwriting Syndicate,* 34 So.2d 62 (La. App. 1948).

2. *Direct Actions Against P & I Insurers*

In most cases, when there is no question of solvency, a P & I club, as a convenience to its member, will advance the funds needed to satisfy a judgment or consummate a settlement in respect of a cargo, personal injury, or other claim covered under the club rules, without insisting that the member first pay the judgment or settlement. But where a member becomes insolvent, the club will invoke the "pay to be paid" provisions of the rules. This may lead to the institution of an action by the injured party directly against the club under a "direct action" statute. The New York Insurance Law permits direct actions against insurers in certain instances if the insured becomes insolvent, but the law specifically excludes P & I and other marine insurance from its coverage.[74]

For many years it was assumed by the Fifth Circuit and other federal courts that the Louisiana "direct action" statute[75] was applicable to P & I insurance.[76] However, in *Backhus v. Transit Casualty Co.*,[77] the Supreme Court of Louisiana held that P & I insurance was "marine insurance" within the meaning of section 22-611A of the Louisiana Insurance Law, which expressly excludes marine insurance from its coverage. *Backhus* was followed by the Fifth Circuit in *Grubbs v. Gulf International Marine, Inc.*[78]

The United Kingdom Direct Action Statute[79] provides, in section 1(1):

> Where under any contract of insurance . . . [the assured] is insured against liabilities to third parties which he may incur, then . . . (b) in the case of the insured being a company, in the event of a winding-up order[80] being made, . . . if, either before or after that event, any such liability . . . is incurred by the insured, his rights against the insurer under the contract in respect of the liability shall . . . be transferred to and vested in the third party to whom the liability was so incurred.

Section 1(4) provides: "Upon a transfer under subsection (1) . . . , the insurer shall . . . be under the same liability to the third party as he would have been under to the insured . . . ."

---

74. New York Insurance Law, §§ 3420 (i), 2117(b). See *Cucurillo v. American S.S. Owners Mutual Protection & Indemnity Association*, 1969 AMC 2334 (Sup. Ct., N.Y. County 1969), which cites former section numbers of the law.

75. La. Rev. Stat. §§ 22-655.

76. See, e.g., *Cushing v. Maryland Casualty Co.*, 198, F.2d 536, 1952 AMC 1803 (5th Cir. 1952), modified, 347 U.S. 409, 1954 AMC 837 (1954); *Crown Zellerbach Corp. v. Ingram Industries, Inc.*, 783 F.2d 1296, 1986 AMC 1471 (5th Cir. 1986 *en banc*) (overruling *Olympic Towing Corp. v. Nebel Towing Co.*), 419 F.2d 230, 1969 AMC 1571 (5th Cir. 1969 [*en banc*]).

77. 549 So. 2d 283, 1990 AMC 417 (La. 1989).

78. 975 F.2d 186, 1993 AMC 164 (5th Cir. 1992).

79. The Third Parties (Rights Against Insurers) Act, 1930, 20 & 21 Geo. 5, ch. 25.

80. In the United Kingdom, the term "bankruptcy" applies to an insolvent individual; "winding up" is used in the case of an insolvent company.

The applicability of the British statute to P & I insurance despite a "pay to be paid" provision was debated for many years. Finally, two cases, *The Fanti*[81] and *The Padre Island,*[82] came before the courts. Both involved unsatisfied cargo damage awards against insolvent shipowners. In each case, the shipowning company was wound up, and the cargo interests sued under the statute to recover from the owner's P & I club. In *The Fanti,* Justice Staughton (later Lord Justice Staughton of the Court of Appeal), held for the cargo interests, while Justice Saville, in *The Padre Island,* decided in favor of the P & I club. The Court of Appeal heard the two cases together. It affirmed *The Fanti* and reversed *The Padre Island.*[83] The court reasoned that the pay-to-be-paid provisions of the rules of the respective clubs were impossible to perform once the statutory transfers of the members' rights to the third parties had occurred, and that the third parties were therefore entitled to recover, even though the clubs' members had not paid the claims. The House of Lords reversed, holding that the right transferred by the statute was a right conditional upon the happening of a certain event, i.e., the payment of the claim, and that the right remained conditional after the statutory transfer to the third party; since the condition of payment had not been met by either shipowner, the clubs concerned had no liability to the cargo interests.[84] The holding will presumably be applied to running down clauses and other insurance containing "pay-to-be-paid" provisions, as well as to P & I coverage.

81. [1987] 2 Lloyd's Rep. 299 (Q.B., Comm'l Ct.).
82. [1987] 2 Lloyd's Rep. 529 (Q.B., Comm'l Ct.).
83. [1989] 1 Lloyd's Rep. 239 (C.A.).
84. *Firma C-Trade S.A. v. Newcastle Protection & Indemnity Ass'n (The Fanti),* and *Socony Mobil Oil Co. v. West of England Mut. Ins. Ass'n (London) Ltd. (The Padre Island),* [1990] 2 Lloyd's Rep. 191 (H.L.). Compare *Charter Reinsurance Co. Ltd. v. Fagan,* [1996] 2 Lloyd's Rep. 113 (H.L.), where the House of Lords held that reinsurance syndicates must pay claims against an insolvent reinsurer, even though the underlying insurance claims have not been paid in full.

CHAPTER SEVENTEEN

OFFICIAL INVESTIGATIONS OF COLLISIONS

Section A. Introduction

Assistance in litigation between private parties is *not* the purpose of official investigations by the U.S. Coast Guard, the U.S. Navy, or the National Transportation Safety Board, although the facts developed in these investigations may be determinative in subsequent civil litigation. The purpose of these investigations is safety at sea. Thus, substantial freedom from strict rules of procedure and evidence is customarily permitted to accommodate this purpose. Furthermore, there is almost never adequate time to prepare for one of these investigations, and lawyers for private parties who will eventually litigate collision issues in a civil case will be unable to control the development of the investigation.

1. U.S. Coast Guard Investigations

The U.S. Coast Guard investigates "marine casualties or accidents" which involve (a) any non-public vessel, regardless of flag, if they take place upon the navigable waters of the United States, or (b) any U.S. flag nonpublic vessel, regardless of where the incident occurs.[1] A "public vessel" may be a commissioned vessel of the U.S. Navy or Coast Guard. The term also includes vessels used for other public purposes, if they are not engaged in trade, and are owned outright by the U.S. government.[2] The term "marine casualty or accident" includes a collision, among other things.[3]

An owner, agent, master, or other person in charge of a vessel involved in a marine casualty must notify the Coast Guard of the casualty as soon as possible if it results in: (a) the creation of a hazard to navigation or the environment; (b) the loss of certain of the vessel's systems; (c) adverse effects on the vessel's seaworthiness; or (d) loss of life, personal injury, or damage to prop-

1. 46 U.S.C. § 6101–6308; 46 CFR §§ 4.03-1(a) and 4.07-1(a). By amendment to 46 U.S.C. § 6101, the U.S. Coast Guard may investigate casualties involving foreign flag ships carrying U.S. passengers. The statute was held to apply to a collision between two foreign flag vessels in *Veldhoen v. United States,* 35 F. 3d 222, 1995 AMC 317 (5th Cir. 1994).

2. 46 CFR § 4.03-40.

3. 46 CFR § 4.03-1(b).

erty in excess of $25,000.[4] In addition to the notice, a written report must be submitted to the Coast Guard within five days.[5]

2. *Failure to Report an Incident*

A person who fails to make the required report is liable to the United States for a civil penalty of $1,000.[6] The failure to report a marine casualty in a timely manner can have other consequences as well. In *Taylor v. Bouchard Transportation Co.*,[7] the defendants sought to exclude a Coast Guard report of an accident from civil litigation. They contended the report was untrustworthy because the Coast Guard investigation was not conducted in a timely manner.[8] The court was undecided as to whether a delay of six months between an incident and the start of an investigation would necessarily render a report untimely. However, since the defendants had not reported the accident until four months after it occurred, the court ruled against them, any delay having been partly the result of their failure to comply with the reporting requirement of the law.[9]

3. *Initiation of an Investigation*

Once the Coast Guard receives information of a marine casualty or accident, it will customarily initiate some type of investigation at once.[10] The investigation has several purposes. First, it is meant to determine the cause of the accident and whether any failure of material was involved.[11] It is also intended to determine whether there were any acts of misconduct, inattention to duty, negligence, or willful violation of the law which would require disciplinary proceedings.[12] Finally, it is used to determine whether the incident should be further investigated by a more formal marine board of investigation.[13] The Commandant of the Coast Guard or the appropriate district commander designates an investigating officer to conduct the investigation.[14] The investigating officer has the power to administer oaths, subpoena witnesses, require

---

4. 46 CFR § 4.05-1.
5. 46 CFR § 4.05-10.
6. 46 U.S.C. § 6103(a).
7. 1991 AMC 2423 (SDNY 1991).
8. See infra, subsection 7, concerning factors, including timeliness, which make a report trustworthy.
9. 1991 AMC at 2425.
10. 46 CFR § 4.07-1.
11. 46 CFR § 4.07-1(c)(1) and (2). These findings can be used to make recommendations to prevent the recurrence of similar casualties.
12. 46 CFR § 4.07-1(c)(3). See also section B, infra, for a discussion of suspension and revocation proceedings.
13. 46 CFR § 4.07-1(c)(5).
14. 46 CFR § 4.03-30.

persons to answer questionnaires, and require the production of documents and records.[15]

4. Conduct of an Informal Investigation

The investigating officer is required to open the investigation by announcing the statutory authority for the proceeding and to advise all parties in interest that they have the right to be represented by counsel, that they may examine and cross-examine witnesses, and that they may call witnesses on their own behalf.[16] "Parties in interest" include any person who has a direct interest in the investigation, such as an owner or charterer of the vessel involved, or persons whose conduct is under investigation, including any persons on either of the colliding vessels, or on other vessels involved, and even shoreside personnel.[17]

5. Formal Investigations

At any time during an investigation, the commandant may designate a more formal marine board of investigation ("board") to conduct an investigation, if it appears that it would promote safety of life and property at sea or would be in the public interest.[18] At that point the preliminary investigation ceases and all materials and information which the investigating officer has gathered is turned over to the board.[19]

The board has the same powers to subpoena witnesses and to require the production of information and documents as an investigating officer.[20] Similarly, the chairman of a marine board of investigation is required to open the investigation with the same statement regarding statutory authority and the rights of the parties as an informal investigating officer is required to make.[21] Board sessions are open to the public[22] and a complete record of the proceedings is kept.[23]

6. Deliberation and Report

Upon completion of an investigation, the investigating officer or the board, as the case may be, must make a report of the facts, together with opinions

15. 46 CFR § 4.07-5.
16. 46 CFR § 4.07-7.
17. 46 CFR § 4.03-10.
18. 46 CFR § 4.09-1.
19. 46 CFR § 4.07-55.
20. 46 CFR § 4.09-5.
21. 46 CFR § 4.07-7.
22. 46 CFR § 4.09-17.
23. 46 CFR § 4.09-20.

and recommendations.[24] The report of a preliminary investigation is forwarded through the Coast Guard chain of command to the commandant, with endorsements indicating approval, or disapproval and remand, and any action which has been taken.[25] The report of a marine board of investigation is finally submitted to the commandant for his consideration.[26] These Coast Guard investigative records and reports are made available to the public.[27] The right to representation and the right to transcripts of the proceedings are important to ensure administrative regularity and to satisfy due process.

In *United States v. Lober,*[28] the defendants challenged the authority of a Coast Guard investigation, particularly its power to issue subpoenas, contending that the hearings failed to satisfy due process. The court held that the proceedings had satisfied due process because there was no showing of substantial prejudice.[29] Significant in the court's reasoning was the fact that the investigating officer began each hearing with the required opening statement apprising the parties of their rights. Also significant was the fact that parties in interest who were added during the course of the proceedings were given transcripts of the prior hearings.

7. *Admissibility of Reports*

Chapter 2, section D, deals with the evidentiary process and the admissibility of investigative reports. In 1996, Congress enacted a statute[30] providing that Coast Guard reports of marine casualties shall neither be admissible in civil litigation nor be subject to discovery. There is an exception for administrative proceedings initiated by the United States. Nevertheless, Coast Guard members and Department of Transportation employees may testify as to "factual matters" with the express permission of the Secretary of Transportation, who is not to withhold consent if the information is not available elsewhere or is not obtainable by other means. The prohibition, however, does not prevent the government from calling Coast Guard members as expert witnesses.[31]

A controversy had existed over whether Coast Guard investigative reports and records should be admitted, in whole or in part, as evidence in judicial proceedings. The Federal Rules of Evidence provide a public records exception to the hearsay rule. Rule 803(8) allows courts to admit into evidence: "records, reports, statements or data compilations, in any form, of

---

24. 46 CFR §§ 4.07-10 and 4.09-20.
25. 46 CFR § 4.07-10.
26. 46 CFR § 4.07-20.
27. 46 CFR § 4.13-1.
28. 630 F.2d 335 (5th Cir. 1980).
29. "In an administrative proceeding, proof of denial of due process requires a showing of substantial prejudice." Id. at 337, 338.
30. 46 U.S.C. § 6308(a).
31. 46 U.S.C. § 6308(b).

public offices or agencies, setting forth . . . (c) in civil actions and proceedings . . . factual findings resulting from an investigation made pursuant to authority granted by law, unless the sources of the information or other circumstances indicate lack of trustworthiness." From the enactment of the Federal Rules of Evidence in 1975 until 1988 there was disagreement among the circuits regarding the meaning of the term "factual findings."[32] A majority of the circuits favored a broad interpretation of the term, which would include evaluative conclusions and opinions.[33] The minority felt that the term "factual findings" was used to distinguish between the facts and the opinions in a report, and therefore refused to admit into evidence portions of public records which contained opinions.[34]

With respect to Coast Guard investigative reports, the minority had further support for its view in the language of the Coast Guard regulations. The regulations provide that the purpose of investigations is to "tak[e] appropriate measures for promoting safety of life and property at sea, *and [is] not intended to fix civil or criminal responsibility*."[35] The courts in both *In re American Export Lines. Inc.*[36] and *Smith v. Ithaca Corp.*[37] cited this language as an important factor which weighed against the evidentiary use of evaluative conclusions or opinions contained in such reports.[38]

The conflict between the circuits was finally addressed by the Supreme Court in 1988 in *Beech Aircraft Corp. v. Rainey*.[39] This case concerned the admission of a report of the U.S. Navy's Judge Advocate General ("JAG") into evidence. Like a Coast Guard investigative report, a JAG report is divided into fact, opinion, and recommendation sections.[40] The Court of Appeals for the Eleventh Circuit had held that it was bound by the Fifth Circuit precedent of *Smith v. Ithaca Corp.*,[41] and therefore concluded that the opinions contained in the JAG report should not have been admitted in evidence.[42] The Supreme Court reversed and held that portions of investigative reports otherwise admissible under Rule 803(8)(c) of the Federal Rules of Evidence

---

32. See *Beech Aircraft Corp. v. Rainey*, 488 U.S. 153, 158, 1989 AMC 441, 446 (1988), discussed in Paulsen and Lambert, *Admissibility of Government Agency Reports in Maritime Cases*, 21 J. Mar. L. & Com. 111 (1990).

33. Id.

34. See *In re American Export Lines, Inc.*, 73 F.R.D. 454, 458 (SDNY 1977); *Smith v. Ithaca Corp.*, 612 F.2d 215, 222, 1981 AMC 1029 (5th Cir. 1980).

35. 46 CFR § 4.07-1(b). (Emphasis added.)

36. 73 F.R.D. 454, 1977 AMC 2632 (SDNY 1977).

37. 612 F.2d 215, 1981 AMC 1029 (5th Cir. 1980).

38. 73 F.R.D. at 458, 1977 AMC at 2636; 612 F.2d at 222, 1981 AMC at 1039.

39. Supra note 32.

40. 488 U.S. at 157, 1989 AMC at 442–43.

41. *Rainey v. Beech Aircraft Corp.*, 827 F.2d 1498, 1500 (11th Cir. 1987). In *Bonner v. City of Prichard*, 661 F.2d 1206, 1207 (11th Cir. 1981) (*en banc*), following the division of the old Fifth Circuit into two circuits (the Fifth and the Eleventh), the Eleventh Circuit adopted as precedents decisions of the former Fifth Circuit rendered prior to October 1, 1981.

42. 827 F.2d at 1500–1501.

are not inadmissible merely because they state an opinion or conclusion.[43] After a review of prior decisions, statutory language, and legislative history, the Court concluded that Rule 803(8)(c) assumes admissibility of the entire report in the first instance, and then provides a safeguard against the admission of unreliable evidence in the final clause by requiring a trustworthiness inquiry.[44] This clause gives the trial judge the discretion to exclude all or any portion of a report which is untrustworthy.[45]

The Advisory Committee on the Federal Rules of Evidence proposed a nonexclusive list of factors to assist in the trustworthiness determination. These are: (1) the timeliness of the investigation; (2) the investigator's skill or experience; (3) whether a hearing was held; and (4) possible bias when reports are prepared with a view toward possible litigation.[46]

Section B. Proceedings for the Suspension and Revocation of Licenses, Certificates, and Documents

In order to maintain standards of competence, which are of course essential to the promotion of safety at sea,[47] the Coast Guard has the authority to take administrative action against holders of Coast Guard licenses, certificates, and documents.[48] The Coast Guard may initiate an investigation any time it appears that a person is incompetent, or has been guilty of misconduct, negligence, or an act in violation of law or regulation while acting under the authority of a license, certificate, or document issued by the Coast Guard.[49] In the case of a marine casualty or accident, the investigation into the incident will automatically include an inquiry into whether a holder of a Coast Guard license, certificate, or document contributed to the casualty through misconduct, inattention to duty, negligence, or willful violation of law.[50]

1. *Preferral of Charges*

After an investigation, the investigating officer may prefer charges against the holder of a Coast Guard license, certificate, or document (the "respondent"), seeking suspension or revocation in an administrative proceeding.[51]

43. 488 U.S. at 170, 1989 AMC at 453.
44. 488 U.S at 167, 1989 AMC at 451.
45. Id.
46. Advisory Committee Notes on Fed. R. Evid. 803(8), 28 U.S.C. App., p. 725 (cited in *Beech Aircraft* at 488 U.S. 167, 1989 AMC at 451, n. 11.) See *Taylor v. Bouchard Transportation Co., Inc.,* 1991 AMC 2423 (SDNY 1991), and *In re Munyan,* 143 F.R.D. 560 (D N.J. 1992), for a treatment of trustworthiness factors in Coast Guard investigative report cases.
47. 46 CFR § 5.5.
48. 46 CFR § 5.1.
49. 46 CFR § 5.101(a)(1) and (2).
50. 46 CFR § 4.07-1(3).
51. 46 CFR § 5.105(a).

The investigating officer prepares charges[52] and specifications,[53] together with a notice of the time, date, and place of the hearing, and serves them upon the respondent.[54] At the time of service, the respondent is also advised of the nature of the suspension and revocation proceedings, the right to representation at the hearing, and the right to have witnesses, records, and other evidence subpoenaed.[55]

2. *Administrative Hearings*

The hearing in a suspension and revocation proceeding is presided over and exclusively controlled by an administrative law judge in accordance with the Administrative Procedure Act.[56] The general procedures to be followed at a hearing are outlined in the suspension and revocation proceedings regulations.[57] However, slight deviations from these procedures are not necessarily reversible errors if the respondent is not prejudiced by the deviations.[58]

3. *Conduct of the Proceeding*

After opening the hearing, the administrative law judge will advise the respondent of his or her right to be represented by counsel, to have witnesses and evidence subpoenaed, to examine or cross-examine witnesses, to introduce evidence into the record, and to testify or remain silent.[59] This is followed by a reading of the charges, with the respondent's answers. To each charge the respondent must answer with a denial of the charge, a response of "no contest," or an admission.[60] Assuming a denial, both the investigating

---

52. A charge is the designation of an act or offense, in general terms. It must be supported by one or more specifications. 46 CFR § 5.23.

53. A specification sets forth the facts which form the basis of a charge. It enables the respondent to identify the act or offense so that a defense can be prepared. It must set forth the basis of jurisdiction, the date and place of the act or offense charged, and the facts which constitute it. 46 CFR § 5.25.

In *Woods v. United States Dep't of Transportation,* 681 F.2d 988 (5th Cir. 1982), the appellant challenged the Coast Guard's admonishment for negligence because, he contended, the specifications against him were defective. The court held that the specifications were sufficient to apprise the appellant of the offense and the underlying facts, and therefore affirmed the Coast Guard action. Id. at 990.

54. 46 CFR § 5.107(a) and (b).

55. 46 CFR § 5.107(d).

56. 46 CFR § 5.501(a). An administrative law judge is any person designated by the Commandant pursuant to the Administrative Procedure Act (5 U.S.C. § 551–59) to conduct a hearing. 46 CFR § 5.19.

57. 46 CFR § 5.501(d).

58. See *Wardell v. DOT, National Transportation Safety Board (NTSB),* 884 F.2d 510 (9th Cir. 1989). The petitioner objected to the testimony of a witness who was present during the hearing in violation of the general rule that witnesses will be excluded from the hearing room. 46 CFR § 5.517. The court held that the petitioner was not prejudiced by this error. Id. at 514.

59. 46 CFR § 5.519.

60. 46 CFR § 5.527.

officer and the respondent, or his or her representative, are given the opportunity to make an opening statement,[61] to submit evidence,[62] to make arguments,[63] and to submit proposed findings and conclusions.[64]

4. *Deliberation and Decision*

The administrative law judge makes findings and a separate conclusion for each charge and specification.[65] The judge then enters an order which recites the disposition of the case. For each charge that is found "not proved," the order will state that the charge is dismissed. For each charge that is found "proved," the administrative law judge may order an admonishment, suspension, with or without probation, or a revocation.[66] The respondent is served with a complete written decision[67] and is advised of his or her right to appeal to the commandant if a finding of "proved" has been rendered against him or her.[68]

5. *Appeal from an Adverse Finding*

On appeal, the only matters which may be considered by the commandant are rulings on motions or objections which were not waived, clear errors on the record, and jurisdictional questions.[69] The respondent must file a written notice of appeal within thirty days after service of the complete written decision.[70] The completed appeal must be submitted to the commandant within sixty days of service of the decision.[71] The commandant may affirm, reverse, alter, or modify the decision, or may remand the case for further proceedings.[72] Except in the case of a remand, the commandant's decision is the final agency action.[73]

---

61. 46 CFR §§ 5.529 and 5.531.
62. 46 CFR §§ 5.537–5.557.
63. 46 CFR § 5.559.
64. 46 CFR § 5.561.
65. 46 CFR § 5.563.
66. 46 CFR § 5.567. Revocation is mandatory when a charge of misconduct for wrongful possession, use, sale, or association with dangerous drugs is found proved. It is also mandatory if the respondent has been "a user of, or addicted to the use of, a dangerous drug, or has been convicted for a violation of the dangerous drug laws . . . and such charge is found proved." 46 CFR § 5.59.
67. 46 CFR § 5.571.
68. 46 CFR §§ 5.573 and 5.701(a).
69. 46 CFR § 5.701(b).
70. 46 CFR § 5.703(a).
71. 46 CFR § 5.703(c).
72. 46 CFR § 5.705.
73. Id.

6. *Collateral Estoppel*

An issue which has arisen in connection with Coast Guard suspension and revocation proceedings is whether a prior administrative determination may be used as the basis for collateral estoppel in subsequent civil proceedings. This issue was addressed by a state court in *Shannon v. Moffett.*[74] In that case, the defendant's license was suspended after a Coast Guard administrative proceeding had determined that he had operated his boat negligently. In a subsequent civil action, the defendant argued that the finding of negligence should not be afforded collateral estoppel treatment because he had not had a full and fair opportunity to contest the issue. The Oregon Court of Appeals rejected this argument, ruling that the Coast Guard proceeding had been conducted in accordance with the Administrative Procedure Act, and any proceeding conducted in that manner would seem to offer a full and fair opportunity to contest an issue.[75]

The court did, however, find other factors which compelled it to deny collateral estoppel. One factor was the language in the Coast Guard regulation providing that investigations "are not intended to fix civil or criminal responsibility."[76] Another factor was that Coast Guard proceedings are not required to adhere strictly to the rules of evidence observed by the courts.[77] The court was concerned that the finding of negligence might have been based on evidence which would not be admissible in an Oregon court.[78] A third factor was that the hearing was conducted by a single administrative law judge, and that if his finding of negligence were given collateral estoppel effect, the defendant would be denied his right to a jury trial.[79] Although the court considered none of these individual factors controlling, it held that the combination of these and other factors were enough for denial of collateral estoppel.[80]

A federal case addressing the collateral estoppel issue is *Wentworth v. Cole.*[81] In that case the U.S. District Court for the District of Hawaii gave collateral estoppel effect to a finding of negligence in a Coast Guard revocation proceeding. The court first determined that the Coast Guard proceeding had satisfied the Ninth Circuit's requirements for fairness.[82] Significantly,

---

74. 604 P.2d 407 (Or. App. 1979).

75. Id. at 409.

76. Id. at 410 (citing 46 CFR § 4.07-1[b]). The court did recognize that the cited language appeared in Part 4 of 46 CFR, which governs the investigation of marine casualties and accidents, and not in Part 5, which governs suspension and revocation proceedings such as were conducted in this case. Therefore, the court found that the language was not controlling on the issue of collateral estoppel, but it was some indication that collateral estoppel should not be used.

77. 46 CFR § 5.537.

78. 604 P.2d at 411.

79. Id.

80. Id.

81. 1990 AMC 253 (D Hawaii 1989).

82. Id. at 255–56.

the defendant had been given an adequate opportunity to litigate the issue of negligence. The court next held that the plaintiffs were entitled to the use of offensive collateral estoppel because, among other reasons, the defendant had every incentive to litigate the earlier proceeding fully and vigorously, and there were no procedural opportunities available to him in the second proceeding that had not been available in the first.[83]

The *Cole* court specifically rejected the reasoning used in *Shannon*. First, it pointed out that the language in the Coast Guard regulations cited by the *Shannon* court was contained in Part 4 of 46 CFR and applied to investigations, while the license revocation proceeding was conducted pursuant to Part 5 of 46 CFR and was an adjudication. The court stressed that "[a]djudications are very different from investigations."[84] The *Cole* court next noted that courts have given collateral estoppel effect to administrative agency determinations despite the fact that the agency had different rules of evidence. Therefore, the court held that even if the administrative law judge had considered evidence that would be inadmissible in court, that would not support the denial of collateral estoppel unless there was a showing of unfairness.[85] Finally, the court cited a Supreme Court decision finding that the presence or absence of a jury was not significant with respect to the use of collateral estoppel.[86]

Section C. U.S. Naval Investigations

1. Fact-finding Bodies

A U.S. Naval fact-finding body consists of an officer, or group of officers, appointed for the primary purpose of finding and reporting "facts," and in some instances for the additional purpose of expressing "opinions" and making "recommendations." It is purely "advisory" in nature. Thus, its opinions do not constitute final determinations or legal judgments, and its recommendations are not binding on reviewing authorities.[87]

There are three types of fact-finding bodies. The first is a court of inquiry, which is the most formal of all, consisting of three or more commissioned

83. Id. at 256–57.

84. Id. at 259–60. The court cited the comparable provision in Part 56, which reads: "The administrative actions against a license, certification or document are remedial and not penal in nature. These actions are intended to help maintain standards for competence and conduct essential to the promotion of safety at sea. 46 CFR § 5.5." The court felt that the section's silence with respect to collateral estoppel effect indicated that it should be given to adjudications under Part 5 because the agency certainly knew how to suggest expressly that collateral estoppel effect should not be given.

85. Id. at 260–61.

86. Id. at 261 (citing *Parklane Hosiery Co. v. Shore,* 439 U.S. 322 [1979]).

87. Manual of the Judge Advocate General of the Navy (hereinafter "JAGMAN") § 0201(c).

officers as members and a commissioned officer as counsel to the court. It has the power to subpoena witnesses and it always takes testimony under oath.[88] Persons subject to the Uniform Code of Military Justice (UCMJ) whose conduct is subject to inquiry must be designated as parties. Persons subject to the code or employed by the Department of Defense who have a direct interest in the subject of the inquiry must be designated parties upon a request made to the court.

The second type is a formal investigation, consisting of one or more commissioned officers. If more than one, it is called a "board of investigation." The appointing order may direct that the body take all testimony under oath and record all proceedings verbatim. A formal investigation is convened by a written appointing order. It may, if the circumstances warrant, be convened by oral or message orders, which are later confirmed in writing. The order may be modified at any time so as to change the membership of the investigative body, or limit or increase its scope, or provide additional instructions.

The third type is an informal fact-finding body, consisting of one or more officers, senior enlisted persons, or civilian employees of the Department of the Navy. It may be convened orally or in writing and ordinarily does not take testimony under oath or record it verbatim, and it utilizes informal procedures in collecting evidence. Most important, it may not designate any persons as parties to the investigation. Neither a formal fact-finding body nor an informal one has the power to subpoena civilian witnesses; only a court of inquiry has that power. When a formal fact-finding body is convened under Article 139 of the UCMJ and chapter 10 of the JAG Manual, it has power to subpoena naval witnesses by virtue of Article 139.[89]

2. *Procedures of Courts of Inquiry and Formal Investigations*

(a) Convening the Investigation. Any commanding officer, officer in charge, or a higher authority may convene a court of inquiry or a formal investigation. A board first meets at the time and place designated in the appointing order to determine the manner in which the investigation will proceed. The appointing order is read by the counsel for the investigation, or, if none exists, by the junior member, to learn the instructions prescribed by the convening authority for conducting the investigation. Those instructions are binding on the investigation and the method of proceeding is limited or extended thereby.[90]

88. JAGMAN § 0204.

89. Art. 139 (10 U.S.C. § 939) deals with investigations conducted as a result of complaints to the military that military personnel have willfully damaged or taken private property.

90. JAGMAN § 0409.

(b) Counsel for the Investigation. The primary duties of counsel for the investigation are to bring out all of the relevant facts, in an impartial manner, without regard to the effect on the persons concerned;[91] to arrange for the hearing room and necessary equipment and assistance; and to call all witnesses. Since there is no power to subpoena civilian witnesses, they may only be requested to appear, or the board may go to them. The counsel also administers the oath to all witnesses, reporters, and interpreters; supervises the recording of proceedings and the preparation of the record; remains in closed sessions (even if not a member of the board); and if the board so requests, assists the board in drafting its findings, opinions, and recommendations.

(c) Parties to the Investigation. The JAG Manual defines a party as an individual who has properly been designated as such in connection with a court of inquiry or a formal fact-finding body.[92] It should be noted that no person is designated a party before an informal board of investigation. Both the convening authority and, under certain circumstances, the investigative body have the power to designate persons as "parties." The convening authority may designate persons as "parties" in the appointing order if they are known at that time or become known at any other time during the investigation. The investigative body (court of inquiry or formal fact-finding body) has the power to designate parties only if such power is specifically delegated in the appointing order; such designation is made a matter of record.[93] Where it appears that a party is no longer involved to a material degree in the matter being investigated, the designation as a party will be withdrawn by the investigative body. This may be done either at the request of the party or on the motion of the investigative body itself.[94]

Designation as a party means that the person is "subject to inquiry" or has a "direct interest." A person's conduct or performance of duty is "subject to inquiry" when disciplinary action may follow; the individual's rights or privileges may be affected, or his or her personal reputation or professional standing may be jeopardized. A person has a "direct interest" in the subject of inquiry when the findings, opinions, or recommendations may reflect questionable or unsatisfactory performance of duty, or may relate to a matter over which he or she has a duty or right to exercise official control. Nonmilitary personnel may not be designated as parties without the express authorization of the Secretary of the Navy. The sole purpose and effect of designating an individual as a party is to afford a hearing respecting possibly adverse information concerning conduct or performance of duty, or relating to a matter over which there is a duty or right to exercise official control. It is not

91. JAGMAN § 0505.
92. See generally, JAGMAN §§ 0301–06.
93. JAGMAN § 0302.
94. JAGMAN § 0304.

desirable to designate parties to investigations unless the subject matter of the inquiry is so extremely complex, or involves such disputed issues of fact, that a grave risk of substantial injustice to the individual would exist if the rights of a party during the investigation were not afforded to the individual. Any party to the investigation has the right to be given due notice of the designation; to be present during the proceedings (but not when the investigation is cleared for deliberations); to be represented by counsel; to examine and to object to the introduction for consideration by the fact-finding body, physical and documentary evidence, and statements or testimony of witnesses; to cross-examine witnesses not called by the party; to introduce evidence; and to testify as a witness. In a proceeding conducted by a formal fact-finding body, a party may be called by counsel for the investigation or by any other party to testify, whether or not "formally charged" with an offense at the time called. In a court of inquiry, a party who has been charged with an offense may not be called as a witness unless he or she requests it. Once the party takes the stand, he or she has only those rights that any other witness has, i.e., rights under Article 31 UCMJ.[95] If a person is on the stand at the time he or she is designated a party, all of the person's testimony previously given remains in the record. Lastly, a party has a right to make an unsworn statement to be included in the record of proceedings. Such a statement may be oral or written and may be made by the party or by his or her counsel.

(d) Evidence. A formal investigation is not bound by the strict rules of evidence prescribed for courts-martial. However, general observance of the spirit of such rules should be followed where practicable, in order to promote an orderly procedure and increase the probability of a full, fair, and impartial investigation. Constitutional and statutory provisions must be observed. The board should protect every witness from improper questions, harsh or insulting treatment, and unnecessary inquiry into private affairs. Depositions may be used under the same rules as those prescribing their use in a court-martial. Affidavits may also be used under certain circumstances.[96] After all the evidence is in, each party may make an unsworn statement. After all statements have been made, the counsel for the investigation and each party may present arguments to the board.

3. The Report

(a) Findings of Fact. The investigation should set forth in its "findings of fact" only those facts which it finds supported by believable evidence in the

95. To be informed of the suspected offense, the right to remain silent, and the right to have counsel appointed for a party unable to pay therefor. Art. 31 UCMJ.

96. JAGMAN §§ 0506 and 0421.

record.[97] Each fact should be set forth clearly, concisely, chronologically, and separately.

(b) Opinions. Opinions are given only if the appointing order so directs or if called for by a controlling regulation. Any opinion given must be supported by the facts found.[98] Opinions may properly include inferences drawn from the facts, opinions as to performance of duty by persons concerned, opinions as to performance of equipment involved, and opinions required by regulations.

(c) Recommendations. Recommendations are made only if the appointing order so directs. Any recommendation given must be based upon the opinions set forth and should be specific as to its nature.[99]

4. Action by Reviewing Authorities

The convening authority of the investigation reviews the record and takes action thereon, setting forth comments and an approval or disapproval, in whole or in part, of the proceedings, findings, opinions, and recommendations. The convening authority may also return the record to the investigative body for further investigation, by an endorsement indicating what further action is desired. After the record has been acted upon, it is forwarded to the Judge Advocate General, via appropriate reviewing authorities in the chain of command.[100]

5. Admiralty Claims Involving Naval Vessels

(a) U.S. Government Liability for Damage Caused by Public Vessels. Liability for suit and settlement authorization are not coextensive; each has definite limitations. Suits involving admiralty matters primarily may be brought against the United States under one of two acts—the Suits in Admiralty Act[101] and the Public Vessels Act.[102] The Suits in Admiralty Act prescribes the procedure for maintaining suit against the United States in connection with the operation of merchant vessels by the government. The Public Vessels Act extended the government's waiver of sovereign immunity to "damage caused by public vessels of the United States," i.e., naval, Coast Guard, and other vessels engaged in public service, as distinguished from

97. JAGMAN § 0430.
98. JAGMAN § 0431.
99. JAGMAN § 0432.
100. JAGMAN § 0210.
101. Act of Mar. 9, 1920, 41 Stat. 525, 46 U.S.C. App. §§ 741–52.
102. Act of Mar. 3, 1925, 43 Stat. 1112, 46 U.S.C. App. §§ 781–90.

government-owned merchant vessels. Basically, although not exclusively, this liability is a tort liability.

"Swell" damage is within the coverage of the Public Vessels Act,[103] as is damage to fish nets and floating or fixed lobster pots. Also within its coverage are cargo damage and personal injury or death experienced by longshore workers and other personnel who are not attached to the public vessel.

Broadening of the interpretation of the Public Vessels Act occurred in *Canadian Aviator Ltd. v. United States (The Cavelier).*[104] In that case, a privately owned vessel sailing in convoy during World War II was directed by the commanding officer of the U. S. Navy escort vessel *YP249* to follow her into Delaware Bay. Through the alleged negligence of the officer, the *Cavelier* was led over a submerged wreck, with resulting damage. In a suit under the Public Vessels Act, the government excepted to the libel (complaint) on the ground that it failed to state a cause of action.

The government argued, and the district court agreed, that "damage caused by a public vessel," within the meaning of the Public Vessels Act, was damage inflicted by the vessel as the "physical instrument" causing the harm, as in a collision case, and that here the damage was caused, not by the escort as a "physical instrument," but rather by the personal negligence of her commanding officer.[105] The court of appeals affirmed, although for somewhat different reasons,[106] but the Supreme Court reversed, stating: "The libel avers that she [the *Cavalier*] was under orders by the naval authorities to proceed directly astern of the *YP249;* for all practical purposes she was as firmly fastened to the stern of the *YP249* as if she had been in tow."[107] While U.S. Navy vessels may not be arrested under *in rem* process, government liability under the Public Vessels Act permits application of the principles of *in rem* liability, as well as *in personam* liability.[108]

The 1948 legislation extending admiralty jurisdiction[109] has two further aspects of concern to the Navy Department: the first is the provision that the Public Vessels Act, or the Suits in Admiralty Act, as the case may be, shall be the exclusive remedy for any damage falling within the coverage of the applicable statute. The second provision precludes suit until six months after claim has been filed with the government department or agency operating the injuring vessel. The "cooling-off" period of six months affords the government an opportunity to effect settlement of claims. In 1961 the Federal

---

103. *Ladd v. United States,* 97 F. Supp. 80, 1951 AMC 1186 (ED Va. 1951), aff'd, 193 F.2d 929, 1952 AMC 277 (4th Cir. 1952).

104. 324 U.S. 215, 1945 AMC 265 (1945).

105. 52 F. Supp. 211, 1943 AMC 744 (D N.J. 1943).

106. 142 F.2d 709, 1944 AMC 752 (3d Cir. 1944).

107. 324 U.S. at 229, 1945 AMC at 276.

108. 324 U.S. at 226–28, 1945 AMC at 273–75.

109. 46 U.S.C. App. § 740.

Tort Claims Act was amended to exclude any claims that might be brought under the Public Vessels Act or the Suits in Admiralty Act.[110]

Surveys, both of the naval vessel and of the privately owned vessel, are absolutely essential in the Navy Department's admiralty claims settlement procedure. The requirement applies not only to collisions but to all damage covered by the Public Vessels Act.

(b) Navy Department Admiralty Claims Settlement. Prior to 1944, the Navy Department's settlement authorization was very much restricted. Settlements, when approved by the Secretary, were transmitted to Congress for action. Payment was effected by the General Accounting Office after a congressional appropriation. Congress has since provided greatly increased settlement authorization for "damage caused by a vessel in the naval service" and for "compensation for towage and salvage service."[111] The limit on the Secretary's settlement authorization is $1 million. The Act of July 3, 1944, was amended to permit the Secretary to delegate his settlement authorization in matters where the required payment is not in excess of $10,000. The settlement authorization specifically allows the Secretary to "compromise or settle claims." The settlement, when made by the Secretary, is final and conclusive for all purposes, any law to the contrary notwithstanding. The settlement does not become binding on the claimant until the claimant actually accepts the amount involved. Payments of admiralty claims are made out of the claims appropriation for the Department of Defense. Settlements in litigated admiralty matters are paid by the Department of Justice out of its appropriations, where the amount paid does not exceed $100,000. Payments over that amount must be obtained by congressional appropriation in each case. The availability of U.S. Navy funds for immediate payment, after settlement is reached, constitutes a material advantage in inducing settlement. The Judge Advocate General of the Navy or the Deputy Judge Advocate General, may approve settlements where the amount paid or received does not exceed $10,000.

(c) Affirmative Navy Department Admiralty Claims. The Navy Department possesses the same monetary settlement authorization with respect to its affirmative admiralty claims as it does in connection with claims for damages caused by naval vessels. The authority is the reciprocal of the vessel damage settlement statute.[112]

110. 28 U.S.C. § 2679, 2680(d).

111. Act of July 3, 1944, Section 7, 58 Stat. 726, as amended by 60 Stat. 803, 70A Stat. 472, and 79 Stat. 212, codified at 10 U.S.C. § 7622.

112. 10 U.S.C. § 7623.

Section D. National Transportation Safety Board Investigations

With the establishment of the Department of Transportation in 1967, Congress created the National Transportation Safety Board (NTSB) within that department.[113] In 1975, Congress separated the board from the department, making it an independent federal agency to promote safety in transportation. Its function is to investigate accidents, report the facts, conditions, and circumstances and the cause or probable cause or causes of accidents, and to recommend ways to prevent similar accidents.[114] While the board may investigate accidents in maritime transportation and in all modes of transportation subject to federal regulations,[115] it must be remembered that the methodology and procedures of the board were developed in its investigation of aviation accidents.[116] It is entirely possible that there may be both a Coast Guard investigation and an NTSB investigation of the same incident.[117]

113. Pub. L. No. 89-670 of Oct. 15, 1966, 80 Stat. 931, codified in relevant part at former section 49 U.S.C. § 1441.

114. Independent Safety Board Act of 1974. Pub. L. No. 93-633 of Jan. 3, 1975, 88 Stat. 2166, former 49 U.S.C. § 1901. See also 49 CFR § 845.11.

115. 49 U.S.C. § 1131 (a) 1 (E). See also 49 CFR § 800.3. That statement of NTSB functions specifies: ". . . major marine casualties and marine accidents involving a public and non-public vessel or involving Coast Guard functions." See further, 49 CFR § 850.15:

> (a) The Board may conduct an investigation under the Act of any major marine casualty or any casualty involving public and nonpublic vessels. . . .
> (b) The Board shall conduct an investigation under the Act when:
>
> > (1) The casualty involves a Coast Guard and a nonpublic vessel and at least one fatality or $75,000 in property damage; or
> > (2) The Commandant and the Board agree that the Board shall conduct the investigation, and the casualty involves a public and a nonpublic vessel and at least one fatality or $75,000 in property damage; or
> > (3) The Commandant and the Board agree that the Board shall conduct the investigation, and the casualty is a major marine casualty which involves significant safety issues relating to Coast Guard safety functions.

116. The Air Commerce Act of 1926 authorized the Aeronautics Branch of the Commerce Department to investigate the causes of aviation accidents; however, that function was assumed by the Air Safety Board of the Commerce Department in 1933. In 1940, under the Civil Aeronautics Act of 1938, the Bureau of Safety of the Civil Aeronautics Board assumed the investigatory function continuing until the creation of the Department of Transportation, in which the old Bureau of Air Safety became the National Transportation Safety Board in 1967. Inclusion of the NTSB within DOT terminated with the Independent Safety Board Act of 1974. See note 114 supra. Nevertheless, the procedures for aircraft accident investigation (49 CFR § 830) are separate from the rules for other modes of transportation (49 CFR § 845).

117. See 49 CFR § 850.3. Where there are separate proceedings, however, duplication is to be avoided, "as much as possible." See 49 CFR § 850.3 (b). Deferral of NTSB investigation to the Coast Guard is not permitted where there is an allegation of federal government misfeasance or nonfeasance. See 49 CFR § 850.25 (a).

1. *Investigations*

NTSB hearings are described by the regulations as "fact finding proceedings with no formal issues and no adverse parties," and are relieved from compliance with the Administrative Procedures Act.[118] Unless national security classified matter is involved, the hearings are open to the public.[119] The proceedings are recorded verbatim.

Respecting marine casualties, the Bureau of Accident Investigation, one of nine staff components of the NTSB, has the crucial task of conducting investigations, recommending public hearings, preparing probable cause recommendations for the board, or actually making the probable cause determination when delegated to do so by the board.[120]

The decision to hold a public hearing is made by the NTSB on notice in the Federal Register.[121] The selection of the member of the board[122] to be chair of the particular board of inquiry is made by the NTSB; thereafter, the selection of NTSB employees to make up the board of inquiry is made by the chair.[123]

Unless the board of inquiry is designated for expedited treatment, the regulations require a prehearing conference[124] with the parties[125] to advise them of the witnesses and exhibits. Parties are to proffer additional documentary evidence, exhibits, or the names of additional witnesses at that time.[126]

The chair of the board of inquiry has substantial powers to move the investigation along: to admit or refuse evidence, to dispose of procedural requests, and to take "any other action necessary or incident to the orderly conduct of the hearing.[127] The board has power to subpoena witnesses or evidence from any place in the United States.[128]

---

118. 49 CFR § 845.2. See 5 U.S.C. § 554.

119. 49 CFR § 845.3.

120. 49 CFR § 800.2 (e) and 49 CFR § 800.25 for delegated authority.

121. 49 CFR § 845.10. The chairman may make the determination regarding catastrophic accidents when a quorum of the board is not available. Three of the five members constitute a quorum (49 U.S.C. § 1111 [f]).

122. The National Transportation Safety Board consists of five members appointed by the President and confirmed by the Senate for five-year terms. The President designates the chairman and vice chairman for two-year terms. As with other agencies, no more than three members are to be appointed from the same political party. Members continue to serve even after the expiration of their terms until their successors are appointed and qualified. See 49 U.S.C. § 1111, Pub. L. No. 103-272 of July 5, 1994; 108 Stat. 746. See generally, 1994 U.S. Code Cong. & Admin. News. 818.

123. 49 CFR § 845.11. Respecting the authority of the board, see 49 U.S.C. § 1113.

124. 49 CFR § 845.23.

125. See infra note 129–32.

126. In the absence of such a proffer, the party may be precluded from introducing such evidence, although the chairman may admit it "for good cause shown." See 49 CFR § 845.23 (c).

127. 49 CFR § 845.20. See also 49 CFR § 845.25 respecting determinations of materiality, relevancy, and competency of evidence by the chairman, and 49 CFR § 845.26 respecting exclusion of nonpertinent or cumulative evidence.

128. 49 U.S.C. § 1113 (a) (2)–(4). See *N.T.S.B. v. Carnival Cruise Lines, Inc.*, 723 F. Supp. 1488, 1989 AMC 2730 (SD Fla. 1989), for failure to enforce an NTSB subpoena on foreign flag

2. *Parties to the Investigation*

The chair must designate as parties to the hearing, "...those persons, agencies, companies, and associations whose participation in the hearing is deemed necessary in the public interest and whose special knowledge will contribute to the development of pertinent evidence."[129] While parties have the right to be "accompanied, represented, or advised by counsel,"[130] the regulations specifically exclude as counsel for parties those lawyers who represent claimants or insurers.[131] Parties may "examine" witnesses after the board or its technical panel has concluded its examination, but this is clearly not a right to cross-examine. Lastly, parties may submit proposed findings, including findings of probable cause and proposed safety recommendations.[132] The usual parties so designated are: the relevant divisions of the Department of Transportation, the common carriers involved, and the manufacturer of the transportation vehicles or the component parts involved. The board, however, will generally exclude as parties the victims of the accident and those experts retained for and provided by victims. Although not designated as parties, potential defendants in future litigation arising out of the accident have also been permitted to "participate" in the examination of witnesses. The board stresses that in the interest of a full factual report, Congress has put no restrictions on its activities; accordingly the board will insist on its right to be selective in its choice of witnesses and experts, but this wide discretion can be abused.[133]

3. *Report and Reconsideration*

The board will report the probable cause or causes and the facts, conditions, and circumstances of all accidents in a standard format, but where the board determines that the accident warrants it, there will be a detailed narrative.

---

vessels in collision in international waters. See supra note 1 concerning an amendment to the statute.

129. 49 CFR § 845.13. The board does not permit "corporate" type entities to appear as parties through their "legal" employees.

130. 49 CFR § 845.24.

131. 49 CFR § 845.13 (b): "No party shall be represented by any person who also represents claimants or insurers. Failure to comply with this provision shall result in loss of status as a party." See Clemen and Long, *Representing Potential Litigants as Parties to N.T.S.B. Public Hearings: Some Problems in Search of Solution*, 56 J. Air L. & Com. 969 (1991).

132. 49 CFR § 845.27.

133. The board's discretion can clearly be abused. See *Miller v. Rich*, 845 F.2d 190 (9th Cir. 1988), where the owner of an aircraft that had crashed sought to compel the presence of his experts at the disassembly of the aircraft engine by the NTSB. The district court denied the order. On a second appeal, the Ninth Circuit held that while the NTSB regulations did not compel the presence of the aircraft owner's representatives, it was an abuse of discretion to refuse to allow the owner's expert to observe the disassembly of the engine, especially since the board gave no rational explanation for the exclusion of the expert.

Appropriate recommendations to the operational agencies of the government that have regulatory authority may also be made.[134]

Parties have the right to request a reconsideration or modification of board findings only where the request is based on new evidence or a detailed showing that the board's findings are erroneous.[135] The request for reconsideration is served on all other parties, who then have ninety days to comment on the request.[136] In unusual cases the board may permit oral argument.[137]

4. Admissibility of NTSB Reports in Litigation

Congressional policy clearly forbids the use of NTSB accident reports in any litigation growing out of casualties or accidents investigated by the NTSB.[138] The regulations explain the desire to preserve the impartiality of the board, to avoid embroiling the board in controversial issues not related to its duties, to avoid spending public funds for non-board purposes, and to ensure that board employees' time is used only for official purposes.[139]

Nevertheless, NTSB employees are permitted to testify as to "the factual information they obtained during the course of the investigation; including factual evaluations embodied in their factual accident reports."[140] As a testimonial aid the report may be used to refresh recollection.[141] Such testimony by NTSB employees is tightly controlled by the NTSB general counsel and is usually available only by written interrogatory or by deposition at the NTSB employees' assigned station, most often the NTSB office in Washington, D.C.[142]

---

134. 49 CFR § 845.40 and 49 CFR § 850.20. See 49 U.S.C. § 1135 for reports to the Secretary of Transportation.

135. 49 CFR § 845.41 (a). The right is also extended to "other persons having a direct interest in the accident investigation." However, reconsideration will not be accorded to parties who failed to submit proposed findings, nor will the board reconsider claims which are repetitious of previously submitted proposed findings. Final orders of the NTSB may be appealed to the appropriate court of appeals. 49 U.S.C. § 1153 (a).

136. 49 CFR § 845.41 (b).

137. 49 CFR § 845.41 (c).

138. 49 U.S.C. § 1154 (b), incorporating former 49 U.S.C. § 1441 (e) of the 1958 Federal Aviation Act and 49 U.S.C. § 1903 (c) of the 1974 Independent Safety Board Act. See generally Legislative History of Pub. L. No. 103-272, in 1994 U.S. Code Cong. & Admin. News, 818. See also Welch and Faulk, *The Use of Aviation Accident Reports by Civil Litigants: The Historical Development of 49 U.S.C. § 1441 (e)*, 9 Pepperdine Law Rev. 583 (1982). See also 49 CFR § 835.2: ". . . no part of these reports may be admitted as evidence or used in any suit or action for damages growing out of any matter mentioned in such reports."

See S. Rep. No. 93-1192, 93d Cong., 2d Sess., 44 (1974). In *Protectus Alpha Navigation Co. v. North Pacific Grain Growers, Inc.*, 767 F.2d 1379, 1986 AMC 56 (9th Cir. 1986), the NTSB report was excluded to the extent that it expressed conclusions as to the probable cause of the accident. Cf. *Petition of Cleveland Tankers, Inc.*, 821 F. Supp 463, 1993 AMC 865 (ED Mich. 1992).

139. 49 CFR § 835.1. See also 49 CFR § 835.3 concerning the board's experts' opinions.

140. 49 CFR § 835.3 (b).

141. 49 CFR § 835.4.

142. 49 CFR §§ 835.5–835.8.

Section F. Penal Proceedings in Collision Cases

Jurisdiction in penal cases involving collisions is discussed briefly in chapter 1, section (B) 3. As there stated, while penal proceedings may be brought against persons charged with misconduct in connection with collisions involving American vessels, very few such cases have thus far been reported. Instead, the master or a member of the crew of a vessel accused of misconduct or negligence resulting in a collision, a stranding, or other casualty is more likely to be subjected to disciplinary proceedings. As we have seen in earlier sections of this chapter, these are conducted by the U.S. Coast Guard in the case of merchant vessels and by a naval court of inquiry or other naval investigatory body in the case of U.S. naval vessels.

One of the few reported penal proceedings involving a collision is *United States v. Diehl,*[143] where the master of the coast-wise passenger ship *City of Rome* was prosecuted for negligence, and under 33 U.S.C. former sections 367[144] and 368,[145] for failure to stand by[146] following a collision with a U.S. Navy submarine, the U.S.S. *S51,* which was operating on the surface. Captain Diehl, the *City of Rome's* master, observed a white light ahead, and as no sidelights came into view, he assumed he was coming up on a vessel displaying her sternlight. In fact, the *S51* was crossing his vessel's bow from starboard to port, but the unrefuted evidence was that the submarine's sidelights were improperly located, so that the glow of the white light made it impossible to see the red light until it was too late to avoid the collision. The submarine sank in two minutes and only three of her crew survived. The jury found Captain Diehl not guilty of the charge of negligence and of the charge of failure to stand by. The court approved the verdict.

One of the by-products of the increased interest in improvement of the marine environment in recent years has been the attempt to criminalize negligent discharges of oil and other polluting substances from vessels. As of 1996 the most widely known case of this kind was *Alaska v. Hazelwood,*[147] the prosecution of the master of the *Exxon Valdez* for the stranding of that vessel in Prince William Sound and the consequent oil pollution of coastal areas on

143. 1927 AMC 1844 (D Mass. 1927). The AMC report is of the charge to the jury, during the course of which the court summarized the evidence and the applicable law in considerable detail.

144. With modifications, now 46 U.S.C. § 2303.

145. With modifications, now 46 U.S.C. § 2304.

146. The Stand-By Act formerly created a presumption of fault on the part of a vessel whose master failed to stand by following a collision. The presumption has been abolished, but the act, as modified, still subjects the master or other person in charge of the vessel to a fine of not more than $1,000, or imprisonment for not more than two years for failing to stand by. The vessel is liable *in rem* to the government for the fine. For a further discussion of the Stand-By Act, see chapter 2, section A(8).

147. 3AN-S89-7217 CR, 3AN-S89-7218(CR), unreported, but cited in Russo, *Criminal Liability in Marine Accidents,* 7 University of San Francisco L.J. 151 (1994) (hereinafter *Criminal Liability*).

a massive scale. Also indicted were the Exxon Corporation and its marine subsidiary, Exxon Shipping Company, owner of the vessel. Captain Hazelwood was charged under environmental statutes for the negligent discharge of oil, and under general penal statutes for criminal mischief, reckless endangerment, and operating a vessel while intoxicated.[148] Captain Hazelwood's case ended in his acquittal of all felony charges, but resulted in a conviction for a Class B misdemeanor: negligent discharge of oil. Exxon was separately charged with several felonies and misdemeanors and pleaded guilty to two Class A misdemeanors based on a negligent violation of the Clean Water Act[149] and a strict liability violation of the Migratory Bird Treaty Act.[150] The fact that these charges were instituted illustrates the serious problem that can now result from a marine oil spill—the possibility of the criminal prosecution of the ship's master or other personnel, the officers and directors of a corporate owner, and the owner itself. Although the *Exxon Valdez* incident was not a collision, the same principles would of course apply if it had been, except that in a collision case there might be the additional complication of an attempt to impose sole or contributory fault on the other colliding vessel.

The prosecutions following the *Exxon Valdez* stranding are discussed in Russo, *Criminal Liability in Marine Accidents,*[151] in which the author points out that environmental statutes are now treated as public welfare statutes, which were initially concerned with pure food and drug laws.[152] With respect to public welfare statutes, the traditional doctrine of *mens rea*—the necessity of showing a criminal intent to convict a person of a crime—has been abandoned, with the result that criminal liability may be imposed for simple negligence or may even be based upon strict liability, without a showing of traditional criminal *mens rea.*[153]

That a requirement of *mens rea* may be dispensed with in marine accident cases even when water pollution is not involved is indicated by *State of Florida v. Gruen.*[154] Defendant was charged with operating a vessel without a lookout and operating her improperly in restricted visibility, resulting in a boating accident. A county court granted defendant's motion to dismiss the

148. Id., at 152, n. 3.

149. See 33 U.S.C. § 1319(c).

150. 16 U.S.C. §§ 703, 707(a).

151. Supra note 147.

152. *Criminal Liability,* supra note 147, at 153–54, citing *United States v. Dotterwich,* 320 U.S. 277, 253 (1922).

153. *Criminal Liability,* supra note 147, at 153.

154. 1992 AMC 276 (Fla. Dist. Ct. App., 3d Dist. 1991). The report does not indicate the nature of the "boating accident" resulting in the charges against the defendant, but as the charges involved failure to maintain a look-out and improper navigation in restricted visibility, the "accident" was probably a collision or allision. There is likewise no indication why the prosecution was conducted by the state, under a state statute which presumably echoed the Inland Rules, rather than by the federal government, under the Inland Rules as such.

information on the ground that the state statute[155] under which defendant was charged was unconstitutional because it was vague and lacked a *mens rea* requirement. The state appealed, and the Florida District Court of Appeals (Third District) reversed. In its *per curiam* decision the court stated:

> The legislature has the power to declare conduct criminal and attach criminal sanctions to such conduct . . .
>
> The legislature's power is first limited by the nature of the proscribed conduct. In *State v. Oxx,* 417 So.2d 287, 289 (Fla. 5th DCA 1982), the court explained the distinction between statutes codifying crimes recognized at common law and statutes that proscribe conduct not prohibited at common law. In the common-law crimes or crimes *"mala in se,"* the intent for the offense is deemed inherent in the offense, even if the statute fails to specify intent as an element. Id. at 289. But crimes proscribing conduct not prohibited at common law or crimes *"mala prohibita,"* which usually result from neglect, do not require any criminal intent. Id.
>
> In the instant case, the defendant is charged with violating the duties of care imposed by the legislature in enacting §327.33. The statute proscribes a crime resulting from reckless or careless operation of a vessel; it describes a crime *"malum prohibitum."* Accordingly, the legislature properly disposed of criminal intent.
>
> The legislature's power may be further restricted by the due process clause of the Constitution. This "constitutional restriction may come into play where the statute imposes an affirmative duty to act and then penalizes the failure to comply. In such an instance, if the failure to act otherwise amounts to essentially innocent conduct, the failure of the penal statute to require some specific intent may violate due process." Id. at 290.[156]

---

155. § 327.33(3)(a), Florida Statutes (1989).
156. 1992 AMC at 277–78.

APPENDIX 1

THE INTERNATIONAL REGULATIONS FOR PREVENTING COLLISIONS AT SEA (COLREGS) (AS AMENDED TO JANUARY 6, 1997)

A. AUTHORS' INTRODUCTORY NOTE

COLREGS were adopted as the Convention on the International Regulations for Preventing Collisions at Sea, signed by twenty-five States on October 20, 1972, at a diplomatic conference held in London. As of 1997 it had been adhered to by eighty-seven other States. The United Kingdom ratified it on June 28, 1974, Canada on March 7, 1975, and the United States on November 23, 1976. It entered into force on July 15, 1977. As of 1997 the Convention had been amended three times, and the amendments are incorporated in the text of the Convention that follows.

The U.S. Congress adopted the Regulations as national legislation by a statute enacted July 27, 1977.[1]

Following 6A Benedict Doc. 3-4 there is a complete list of the States that have ratified or acceded to the Convention, with dates of ratification or accession, and the dates when it entered into force in the various States. The list is followed by the texts of reservations and declarations of a number of States. These are mostly irrelevant to the Regulations as navigational rules. They relate to such matters as the dispute between Argentina and the United Kingdom with respect to sovereignty of the Falkland Islands (Malvinas).

The thirty-eight Rules constituting COLREGS, and the four Annexes to the Rules, are set forth following 33 U.S.C. § 1602.

B. STATUTORY PROVISIONS PRECEDING COLREGS

33 U.S.C. § 1601. Definitions

For the purposes of this chapter—

(1) "vessel" means every description of watercraft, including nondisplacement craft and seaplanes, used or capable of being used as a means of transportation on water; and

---

1. Pub. L. No. 95-75, § 3, 91 Stat. 30, 33 U.S.C. § 1602.

The full text of the Convention in its original form appears at 28 UST 3459, TIAS 8587, and 1050 UNTS 16. As amended, it appears at TIAS 10672, 1143 UNTS 346, and 6A Benedict on Admiralty, Doc. 3-4 (7th ed.[rev.], F. L. Wiswall, Jr., Editor-in-Chief, *International Maritime Law Documents and Commentary,* hereinafter "Benedict").

There are minor differences in punctuation, spelling, and capitalization between the Convention and the U.S. implementing legislation; with a few immaterial exceptions what follows is the text of the Convention as it appears in Benedict.

(2) "high seas" means all parts of the sea that are not included in the territorial sea or in the internal waters of any nation.

33 U.S.C. § 1602. International Regulations

(a) Proclamation by President; effective date
The President is authorized to proclaim the International Regulations for Preventing Collisions at Sea, 1972 (hereinafter referred to as the "International Regulations"). The effective date of the International Regulations for the United States shall be specified in the proclamation and shall be the date as near as possible to, but no earlier than, the date on which the Convention on the International Regulations for Preventing Collisions at Sea, 1972 (hereinafter referred to as the "Convention"), signed at London, England, under date of October 20, 1972, enters into force for the United States. The International Regulations proclaimed shall consist of the rules and other annexes attached to the Convention.

(b) Publication of proclamation in Federal Register
The proclamation shall include the International Regulations and shall be published in the Federal Register. On the date specified in the proclamation, the International Regulations shall enter into force for the United States and shall have effect as if enacted by statute.

(c) Amendment of International Regulations
Subject to the provisions of subsection (d) of this section, the President is also authorized to proclaim any amendment to the International Regulations hereafter adopted in accordance with the provisions of article VI of the Convention, and to which the United States does not object. The effective date of the amendment shall be specified in the proclamation and shall be in accordance with the provisions of the said article VI. The proclamation shall include the adopted amendment and shall be published in the Federal Register. On the date specified in the proclamation, the amendment shall enter into force for the United States as a constituent part of the International Regulations, as amended, and shall have effect as if enacted by statute.

(d) Notification to Congress of proposed amendments; Congressional resolution of disapproval

(1) Upon receiving a proposed amendment to the International Regulations, communicated to the United States pursuant to clause 3 of article VI of the Convention, the President shall promptly notify the Congress of the proposed amendment. If, within sixty days after receipt of such notification by the Congress, or ten days prior to the date under clause 4 of article VI for registering an objection, whichever comes first, the Congress adopts a resolution of disapproval, such resolution shall be transmitted to the President and shall constitute an objection by the United States to the proposed amendment. If, upon receiving notification of the resolution of disapproval, the President has not already notified the Inter-Governmental Maritime Consulta-

tive Organization[2] of an objection to[3] the United States to the proposed amendment, he shall promptly do so.

(2) For the purposes of this subsection, "resolution of disapproval" means a concurrent resolution initiated by either House of the Congress, the matter after the resolving clause of which is to read as follows: "That the ___________ (the ___________ concurring) does not favor the proposed amendment to the International Regulations for Preventing Collisions at Sea, 1972, relating to ___________ , and forwarded to the Congress by the President on ___________ .", the first blank space therein to be filled with the name of the resolving House, the second blank space therein to be filled with the name of the concurring House, the third blank space therein to be filled with the subject matter of the proposed amendment, and the fourth blank space therein to be filled with the day, month, and year.

(3) Any proposed amendment transmitted to the Congress by the President and any resolution of disapproval pertaining thereto shall be referred, in the House of Representatives, to the Committee on Merchant Marine and Fisheries, and shall be referred, in the Senate, to the Committee on Commerce, Science, and Transportation.[4]

C. INTERNATIONAL REGULATIONS

PART A - GENERAL

RULE 1

Application

(a) These Rules shall apply to all vessels upon the high seas and in all waters connected therewith navigable by seagoing vessels.

(b) Nothing in these Rules shall interfere with the operation of special rules made by an appropriate authority for roadsteads, harbours, rivers, lakes or inland waterways connected with the high seas and navigable by seagoing vessels. Such special rules shall conform as closely as possible to these Rules.

(c) Nothing in these Rules shall interfere with the operation of any special rules made by the Government of any State with respect to additional station or signal lights, shapes or whistle signals for ships of war and vessels proceeding under convoy, or with respect to additional station or signal lights or shapes for fishing vessels engaged in fishing as a fleet.

2. Now the International Maritime Organization (I.M.O.).
3. So in original. Probably should be "by."
4. Pub. L. 95-75, § 3, July 27, 1977, 91 Stat. 308. The Presidential Proclamations concerning the amendments appear in the notes following 33 U.S.C.A. § 1602. The House Merchant Marine and Fisheries Committee was abolished in 1995. Some of its functions were assumed by the National Security, Transportation & Infrastructure, Public Lands, Resources, and Agricultural Committees.

These additional station or signal lights, shapes or whistle signals shall, so far as possible, be such that they cannot be mistaken for any light, shape or signal authorized elsewhere under these Rules.

(d) Traffic separation schemes may be adopted by the Organization for the purpose of these Rules.

(e) Whenever the Government concerned shall have determined that a vessel of special construction or purpose cannot comply fully with the provisions of any of these Rules with respect to the number, position, range or arc of visibility of lights or shapes, as well as to the disposition and characteristics of sound-signalling appliances, such vessel shall comply with such other provisions in regard to the number, position, range or arc of visibility of lights or shapes, as well as to the disposition and characteristics of sound-signalling appliances, as her Government shall have determined to be the closest possible compliance with these Rules in respect of that vessel.

RULE 2

Responsibility

(a) Nothing in these Rules shall exonerate any vessel, or the owner, master or crew thereof, from the consequences of any neglect to comply with these Rules or of the neglect of any precaution which may be required by the ordinary practice of seamen, or by the special circumstances of the case.

(b) In construing and complying with these Rules due regard shall be had to all dangers of navigation and collision and to any special circumstances, including the limitations of the vessels involved, which may make a departure from these Rules necessary to avoid immediate danger.

RULE 3

General definitions

For the purpose of these Rules, except where the context otherwise requires:

(a) The word "vessel" includes every description of water craft, including non-displacement craft and seaplanes, used or capable of being used as a means of transportation on water.

(b) The term "power-driven vessel" means any vessel propelled by machinery.

(c) The term "sailing vessel" means any vessel under sail provided that propelling machinery, if fitted, is not being used.

(d) The term "vessel engaged in fishing" means any vessel fishing with nets, lines, trawls or other fishing apparatus which restrict manoeuverability, but does not include a vessel fishing with trolling lines or other fishing apparatus which do not restrict manoeuverability.

(e) The word "seaplane" includes any aircraft designed to manoeuvre on the water.

(f) The term "vessel not under command" means a vessel which through some exceptional circumstances is unable to manoeuvre as required by these Rules and is therefore unable to keep out of the way of another vessel.

(g) The term "vessel restricted in her ability to manoeuvre" means a vessel which from the nature of her work is restricted in her ability to manoeuvre as required by these Rules and is therefore unable to keep out of the way of another vessel. The term "vessels restricted in their ability to maneuver" shall include but not be limited to:

(i) a vessel engaged in laying, servicing or picking up a navigation mark, submarine cable or pipeline;
(ii) a vessel engaged in dredging, surveying or underwater operations;
(iii) a vessel engaged in replenishment or transferring persons, provisions or cargo while underway;
(iv) a vessel engaged in the launching or recovery of aircraft;
(v) a vessel engaged in mineclearance operations;
(vi) a vessel engaged in a towing operation such as severely restricts the towing vessel and her tow in their ability to deviate from their course.

(h) The term "vessel constrained by her draught" means a power-driven vessel which, because of her draught in relation to the available depth and width of navigable water, is severely restricted in her ability to deviate from the course she is following.

(i) The word "underway" means that a vessel is not at anchor, or made fast to the shore, or aground.

(j) The words "length" and "breadth" of a vessel mean her length overall and greatest breadth.

(k) Vessels shall be deemed to be in sight of one another only when one can be observed visually from the other.

(l) The term "restricted visibility" means any condition in which visibility is restricted by fog, mist, falling snow, heavy rainstorms, sandstorms or any other similar causes.

PART B - STEERING AND SAILING RULES

Section I - Conduct Of Vessels In Any Condition Of Visibility

RULE 4

Application

Rules in this Section apply in any condition of visibility.

RULE 5

Look-out

Every vessel shall at all times maintain a proper look-out by sight and hearing as well as by all available means appropriate in the prevailing circumstances and conditions so as to make a full appraisal of the situation and of the risk of collision.

RULE 6

Safe speed

Every vessel shall at all times proceed at a safe speed so that she can take proper and effective action to avoid collision and be stopped within a distance appropriate to the prevailing circumstances and conditions.

In determining a safe speed the following factors shall be among those taken into account:

(a) By all vessels:
   (i) the state of visibility;
   (ii) the traffic density including concentrations of fishing vessels or any other vessels;
   (iii) the manoeuverability of the vessel with special reference to stopping distance and turning ability in the prevailing conditions;
   (iv) at night the presence of background light such as from shore lights or from back scatter of her own lights;
   (v) the state of wind, sea and current, and the proximity of navigational hazards;
   (vi) the draught in relation to the available depth of water.

(b) Additionally, by vessels with operational radar:
   (i) the characteristics, efficiency and limitations of the radar equipment;
   (ii) any constraints imposed by the radar range scale in use;
   (iii) the effect on radar detection of the sea state, weather and other sources of interference;
   (iv) the possibility that small vessels, ice and other floating objects may not be detected by radar at an adequate range;
   (v) the number, location and movement of vessels detected by radar;
   (vi) the more exact assessment of the visibility that may be possible when radar is used to determine the range of vessels or other objects in the vicinity.

RULE 7

Risk of collision

(a) Every vessel shall use all available means appropriate to the prevailing circumstances and conditions to determine if risk of collision exists. If there is any doubt such risk shall be deemed to exist.

(b) Proper use shall be made of radar equipment if fitted and operational, including long-range scanning to obtain early warning of risk of collision and radar plotting or equivalent systematic observation of detected objects.

(c) Assumptions shall not be made on the basis of scanty information, especially scanty radar information.

(d) In determining if risk of collision exists the following considerations shall be among those taken into account:
   (i) such risk shall be deemed to exist if the compass bearing of an approaching vessel does not appreciably change;
   (ii) such risk may sometimes exist even when an appreciable bearing change is evident, particularly when approaching a very large vessel or a tow or when approaching a vessel at close range.

RULE 8

Action to avoid collision

(a) Any action taken to avoid collision shall, if the circumstances of the case admit, be positive, made in ample time and with due regard to the observance of good seamanship.

(b) Any alteration of course and/or speed to avoid collision shall, if the circumstances of the case admit, be large enough to be readily apparent to another vessel observing visually or by radar; a succession of small alterations of course and/or speed should be avoided.

(c) If there is sufficient sea room, alteration of course alone may be the most effective action to avoid a close-quarters situation provided that it is made in good time, is substantial and does not result in another close-quarters situation.

(d) Action taken to avoid collision with another vessel shall be such as to result in passing at a safe distance. The effectiveness of the action shall be carefully checked until the other vessel is finally past and clear.

(e) If necessary to avoid collision or allow more time to assess the situation, a vessel shall slacken her speed or take all way off by stopping or reversing her means of propulsion.

(f) (i) A vessel which, by any of these Rules, is required not to impede the passage or safe passage of another vessel shall, when required by the circumstances of the case, take early action to allow sufficient sea room for the safe passage of the other vessel.

(ii) A vessel required not to impede the passage or safe passage of another vessel is not relieved of this obligation if approaching the other vessel so as to involve risk of collision and shall, when taking action, have full regard to the action which may be required by the Rules of this part.

(iii) A vessel the passage of which is not to be impeded remains fully obliged to comply with the Rules of this part when the two vessels are approaching one another so as to involve risk of collision.

RULE 9

Narrow channels

(a) A vessel proceeding along the course of a narrow channel or fairway shall keep as near to the outer limit of the channel or fairway which lies on her starboard side as is safe and practicable.

(b) A vessel of less than 20 metres in length or a sailing vessel shall not impede the passage of a vessel which can safely navigate only within a narrow channel or fairway.

(c) A vessel engaged in fishing shall not impede the passage of any other vessel navigating within a narrow channel or fairway.

(d) A vessel shall not cross a narrow channel or fairway if such crossing impedes the passage of a vessel which can safely navigate only within such channel or fairway. The latter vessel may use the sound signal prescribed in Rule 34(d) if in doubt as to the intention of the crossing vessel.

(e) (i) In a narrow channel or fairway when overtaking can take place only if the vessel to be overtaken has to take action to permit safe passing, the vessel intending to overtake shall indicate her intention by sounding the appropriate signal prescribed in Rule 34(c)(i). The vessel to be overtaken shall, if in agreement, sound the appropriate signal prescribed in Rule 34(c)(ii) and take steps to permit safe passing. If in doubt she may sound the signals prescribed in Rule 34(d).

(ii) This Rule does not relieve the overtaking vessel of her obligation under Rule 13.

(f) A vessel nearing a bend or an area of a narrow channel or fairway where other vessels may be obscured by an intervening obstruction shall navigate with particular alertness and caution and shall sound the appropriate signal prescribed in Rule 34(e).

(g) Any vessel shall, if the circumstances of the case admit, avoid anchoring in a narrow channel.

RULE 10

Traffic separation schemes

(a) This Rule applies to traffic separation schemes adopted by the Organization and does not relieve any vessel of her obligation under any other Rule.

(b) A vessel using a traffic separation scheme shall:

(i) proceed in the appropriate traffic lane in the general direction of traffic flow for that lane;

(ii) so far as practicable keep clear of a traffic separation line or separation zone;

(iii) normally join or leave a traffic lane at the termination of the lane, but when joining or leaving from either side shall do so at as small an angle to the general direction of traffic flow as practicable.

(c) A vessel shall, so far as practicable, avoid crossing traffic lanes but if obliged to do so shall cross on a heading as nearly as practicable at right angles to the general direction of traffic flow.

(d) (i) A vessel shall not use an inshore traffic zone when she can safely use the appropriate traffic lane within the adjacent traffic separation scheme. However, vessels of less than 20 metres in length, sailing vessels and vessels engaged in fishing may use the inshore traffic zone.

(ii) Notwithstanding subparagraph (d)(i), a vessel may use an inshore traffic zone when en route to or from a port, offshore installation or structure, pilot station or any other place situated within the inshore traffic zone, or to avoid immediate danger.

(e) A vessel other than a crossing vessel or a vessel joining or leaving a lane shall not normally enter a separation zone or cross a separation line except:

(i) in cases of emergency to avoid immediate danger;

(ii) to engage in fishing within a separation zone.

(f) A vessel navigating in areas near the terminations of traffic separation schemes shall do so with particular caution.

(g) A vessel shall so far as practicable avoid anchoring in a traffic separation scheme or in areas near its terminations.

(h) A vessel not using a traffic separation scheme shall avoid it by as wide a margin as is practicable.
(i) A vessel engaged in fishing shall not impede the passage of any vessel following a traffic lane.
(j) A vessel of less than 20 metres in length or a sailing vessel shall not impede the safe passage of a power-driven vessel following a traffic lane.
(k) A vessel restricted in her ability to manoeuvre when engaged in an operation for the maintenance of safety of navigation in a traffic separation scheme is exempted from complying with this Rule to the extent necessary to carry out the operation.
(l) A vessel restricted in her ability to manoeuvre when engaged in an operation for the laying, servicing or picking up of a submarine cable, within a traffic separation scheme, is exempted from complying with this Rule to the extent necessary to carry out the operation.

Section II - Conduct Of Vessels In Sight Of One Another

RULE 11

Application

Rules in this Section apply to vessels in sight of one another.

RULE 12

Sailing vessels

(a) When two sailing vessels are approaching one another, so as to involve risk of collision, one of them shall keep out of the way of the other as follows:
  (i) when each has the wind on a different side, the vessel which has the wind on the port side shall keep out of the way of the other;
  (ii) when both have the wind on the same side, the vessel which is to windward shall keep out of the way of the vessel which is to leeward;
  (iii) if a vessel with the wind on the port side sees a vessel to windward and cannot determine with certainty whether the other vessel has the wind on the port or on the starboard side, she shall keep out of the way of the other.
(b) For the purposes of this Rule the windward side shall be deemed to be the side opposite to that on which the mainsail is carried or, in the case of a square-rigged vessel, the side opposite to that on which the largest fore-and-aft sail is carried.

RULE 13

Overtaking

(a) Notwithstanding anything contained in the Rules of Part B, Sections I and II, any vessel overtaking any other shall keep out of the way of the vessel being overtaken.
(b) A vessel shall be deemed to be overtaking when coming up with another vessel from a direction more than 22.5 degrees abaft her beam, that is, in

such a position with reference to the vessel she is overtaking, that at night she would be able to see only the sternlight of that vessel but neither of her sidelights.

(c) When a vessel is in any doubt as to whether she is overtaking another, she shall assume that this is the case and act accordingly.

(d) Any subsequent alteration of the bearing between the two vessels shall not make the overtaking vessel a crossing vessel within the meaning of these Rules or relieve her of the duty of keeping clear of the overtaken vessel until she is finally past and clear.

RULE 14

Head-on situation

(a) When two power-driven vessels are meeting on reciprocal or nearly reciprocal courses so as to involve risk of collision each shall alter her course to starboard so that each shall pass on the port side of the other.

(b) Such a situation shall be deemed to exist when a vessel sees the other ahead or nearly ahead and by night she could see the masthead lights of the other in a line or nearly in a line and/or both sidelights and by day she observes the corresponding aspect of the other vessel.

(c) When a vessel is in any doubt as to whether such a situation exists she shall assume that it does exist and act accordingly.

RULE 15

Crossing situation

When two power-driven vessels are crossing so as to involve risk of collision, the vessel which has the other on her own starboard side shall keep out of the way and shall, if the circumstances of the case admit, avoid crossing ahead of the other vessel.

RULE 16

Action by give-way vessel

Every vessel which is directed by these Rules to keep out of the way of another vessel shall, so far as possible, take early and substantial action to keep well clear.

RULE 17

Action by stand-on vessel

(a) (i) Where by any of these Rules one of two vessels is to keep out of the way the other shall keep her course and speed.

(ii) The latter vessel may however take action to avoid collision by her manoeuvre alone, as soon as it becomes apparent to her that the vessel required to keep out of the way is not taking appropriate action in compliance with these Rules.

(b) When, from any cause, the vessel required to keep her course and speed finds herself so close that collision cannot be avoided by the action of the give-way vessel alone, she shall take such action as will best aid to avoid collision.

(c) A power-driven vessel which takes action in a crossing situation in accordance with sub-paragraph (a)(ii) of this Rule to avoid collision with another power-driven vessel shall, if the circumstances of the case admit, not alter course to port for a vessel on her own port side.

(d) This Rule does not relieve the give-way vessel of her obligation to keep out of the way.

RULE 18

Responsibilities between vessels

Except where Rules 9, 10 and 13 otherwise require:

(a) A power-driven vessel underway shall keep out of the way of:
- (i) a vessel not under command;
- (ii) a vessel restricted in her ability to manoeuvre;
- (iii) a vessel engaged in fishing;
- (iv) a sailing vessel.

(b) A sailing vessel underway shall keep out of the way of:
- (i) a vessel not under command;
- (ii) a vessel restricted in her ability to manoeuvre;
- (iii) a vessel engaged in fishing.

(c) A vessel engaged in fishing when underway shall, so far as possible, keep out of the way of:
- (i) a vessel not under command;
- (ii) a vessel restricted in her ability to manoeuvre.

(d)
- (i) Any vessel other than a vessel not under command or a vessel restricted in her ability to manoeuvre shall, if the circumstances of the case admit, avoid impeding the safe passage of a vessel constrained by her draught, exhibiting the signals in Rule 28.
- (ii) A vessel constrained by her draught shall navigate with particular caution having full regard to her special condition.

(e) A seaplane on the water shall, in general, keep well clear of all vessels and avoid impeding their navigation. In circumstances, however, where risk of collision exists, she shall comply with the Rules of this Part.

Section III - Conduct Of Vessels In Restricted Visibility

RULE 19

Conduct of vessels in restricted visibility

(a) This Rule applies to vessels not in sight of one another when navigating in or near an area of restricted visibility.

(b) Every vessel shall proceed at a safe speed adapted to the prevailing circumstances and conditions of restricted visibility. A power-driven vessel shall have her engines ready for immediate manoeuvre.

(c) Every vessel shall have due regard to the prevailing circumstances and conditions of restricted visibility when complying with the Rules of Section I of this Part.

(d) A vessel which detects by radar alone the presence of another vessel shall determine if a close-quarters situation is developing and/or risk of collision exists. If so, she shall take avoiding action in ample time, provided that when such action consists of an alteration of course, so far as possible the following shall be avoided:
   (i) an alteration of course to port for a vessel forward of the beam, other than for a vessel being overtaken;
   (ii) an alteration of course towards a vessel abeam or abaft the beam.

(e) Except where it has been determined that a risk of collision does not exist, every vessel which hears apparently forward of her beam the fog signal of another vessel, or which cannot avoid a close-quarters situation with another vessel forward of her beam, shall reduce her speed to the minimum at which she can be kept on her course. She shall if necessary take all her way off and in any event navigate with extreme caution until danger of collision is over.

PART C - LIGHTS AND SHAPES

RULE 20

Application

(a) Rules in this Part shall be complied with in all weathers.

(b) The Rules concerning lights shall be complied with from sunset to sunrise, and during such times no other lights shall be exhibited, except such lights as cannot be mistaken for the lights specified in these Rules or do not impair their visibility or distinctive character, or interfere with the keeping of a proper look-out.

(c) The lights prescribed by these Rules shall, if carried, also be exhibited from sunrise to sunset in restricted visibility and may be exhibited in all other circumstances when it is deemed necessary.

(d) The Rules concerning shapes shall be complied with by day.

(e) The lights and shapes specified in these Rules shall comply with the provisions of Annex I to these Regulations.

RULE 21

Definitions

(a) "Masthead light" means a white light placed over the fore and aft centreline of the vessel showing an unbroken light over an arc of the horizon of 225 degrees and so fixed as to show the light from right ahead to 22.5 degrees abaft the beam on either side of the vessel.

(b) "Sidelights" means a green light on the starboard side and a red light on the port side each showing an unbroken light over an arc of the horizon of 112.5 degrees and so fixed so as to show the light from right ahead to 22.5 degrees abaft the beam on its respective side. In a vessel of less than 20 metres in length the sidelights may be combined in one lantern carried on the fore and aft centreline of the vessel.

(c) "Sternlight" means a white light placed as nearly as practicable at the stern showing an unbroken light over an arc of the horizon of 135 degrees and so fixed as to show the light 67.5 degrees from right aft on each side of the vessel.

(d) "Towing light" means a yellow light having the same characteristics as the "sternlight" defined in paragraph (c) of this Rule.

(e) "All-round light" means a light showing an unbroken light over an arc of the horizon of 360 degrees.

(f) "Flashing light" means a light flashing at regular intervals at a frequency of 120 flashes or more per minute.

RULE 22

Visibility of Lights

The lights prescribed in these Rules shall have an intensity as specified in Section 8 of Annex I to these Regulations so as to be visible at the following minimum ranges:

(a) In vessels of 50 metres or more in length:
—a masthead light, 6 miles;
—a sidelight, 3 miles;
—a sternlight, 3 miles;
—a towing light, 3 miles;
—a white, red, green or yellow all-round light, 3 miles.

(b) In vessels of 12 metres or more in length but less than 50 metres in length:
—a masthead light, 5 miles; except that where the length of the vessel is less than 20 metres, 3 miles;
—a sidelight, 2 miles;
—a sternlight, 2 miles;
—a towing light, 2 miles;
—a white, red, green or yellow all-round light, 2 miles.

(c) In vessels of less than 12 metres in length:
—a masthead light, 2 miles;
—a sidelight, 1 mile;
—a sternlight, 2 miles;
—a towing light, 2 miles;
—a white, red, green or yellow all-round light, 2 miles.

(d) In inconspicuous, partly submerged vessels or objects being towed:
—a white all-round light, 3 miles.

RULE 23

Power-driven vessels underway

(a) A power-driven vessel underway shall exhibit:
(i) a masthead light forward;
(ii) a second masthead light abaft of and higher than the forward one; except that a vessel of less than 50 metres in length shall not be obliged to exhibit such light but may do so;
(iii) sidelights;
(iv) a sternlight.

(b) An air-cushion vessel when operating in the non-displacement mode shall, in addition to the lights prescribed in paragraph (a) of this Rule, exhibit an all-round flashing yellow light.

(c) (i) A power-driven vessel of less than 12 metres in length may in lieu of the lights prescribed in paragraph (a) of this Rule exhibit an all-round white light and sidelights;

(ii) A power-driven vessel of less than 7 metres in length whose maximum speed does not exceed 7 knots may in lieu of the lights prescribed in paragraph (a) of this Rule exhibit an all-round white light and shall, if practicable, also exhibit sidelights;

(iii) the masthead light or all-round white light on a power-driven vessel of less than 12 metres in length may be displaced from the fore and aft centreline of the vessel if centreline fitting is not practicable, provided that the sidelights are combined in one lantern which shall be carried on the fore and aft centreline of the vessel or located as nearly as practicable in the same fore and aft line as the masthead light or the all-round white light.

RULE 24

Towing and pushing

(a) A power-driven vessel when towing shall exhibit:

(i) instead of the light prescribed in Rule 23(a)(i) or (a)(ii), two masthead lights in a vertical line. When the length of the tow, measuring from the stern of the towing vessel to the after end of the tow exceeds 200 metres, three such lights in a vertical line;

(ii) sidelights;

(iii) a sternlight;

(iv) a towing light in a vertical line above the sternlight;

(v) when the length of the tow exceeds 200 metres, a diamond shape where it can best be seen.

(b) When a pushing vessel and a vessel being pushed ahead are rigidly connected in a composite unit they shall be regarded as a power-driven vessel and exhibit the lights prescribed in Rule 23.

(c) A power-driven vessel when pushing ahead or towing alongside, except in the case of a composite unit, shall exhibit:

(i) instead of the light prescribed in Rule 23(a)(i), two masthead lights forward in a vertical line;

(ii) sidelights;

(iii) a sternlight.

(d) A power-driven vessel to which paragraphs (a) or (c) of this Rule apply shall also comply with Rule 23(a)(ii).

(e) A vessel or object being towed, other than those mentioned in paragraph (g) of this Rule, shall exhibit:

(i) sidelights;

(ii) a sternlight;

(iii) when the length of the tow exceeds 200 metres, a diamond shape where it can best be seen.

(f) Provided that any number of vessels being towed or pushed in a group shall be lighted as one vessel,
   (i) a vessel being pushed ahead, not being part of a composite unit, shall exhibit at the forward end, sidelights;
   (ii) a vessel being towed alongside shall exhibit a sternlight and at the forward end, sidelights.

(g) An inconspicuous, partly submerged vessel or object, or combination of such vessels or objects being towed, shall exhibit:
   (i) if it is less than 25 metres in breadth, one all-round white light at or near the forward end and one at or near the after end except that dracones need not exhibit a light at or near the forward end;
   (ii) if it is 25 metres or more in breadth, two additional all-round white lights at or near the extremities of its breadth;
   (iii) if it exceeds 100 metres in length, additional all-round white lights between the lights prescribed in sub-paragraphs (i) and (ii) so that the distance between the lights shall not exceed 100 metres;
   (iv) a diamond shape at or near the aftermost extremity of the last vessel or object being towed and if the length of the tow exceeds 200 metres an additional diamond shape where it can best be seen and located as far forward as is practicable.

(h) Where from any sufficient cause it is impracticable for a vessel or object being towed to exhibit the lights or shapes prescribed in paragraph (e) or (g) of this Rule, all possible measures shall be taken to light the vessel or object towed or at least to indicate the presence of such vessel or object.

(i) Where from any sufficient cause it is impracticable for a vessel not normally engaged in towing operations to display the lights prescribed in paragraph (a) or (c) of this Rule, such vessel shall not be required to exhibit those lights when engaged in towing another vessel in distress or otherwise in need of assistance. All possible measures shall be taken to indicate the nature of the relationship between the towing vessel and the vessel being towed as authorized by Rule 36, in particular by illuminating the towline.

RULE 25

Sailing vessels underway and vessels under oars

(a) A sailing vessel underway shall exhibit:
   (i) sidelights;
   (ii) a sternlight.

(b) In a sailing vessel of less than 20 metres in length the lights prescribed in paragraph (a) of this Rule may be combined in one lantern carried at or near the top of the mast where it can best be seen.

(c) A sailing vessel underway may, in addition to the lights prescribed in paragraph (a) of this Rule, exhibit at or near the top of the mast, where they can best be seen, two all-round lights in a vertical line, the upper being red and the lower green, but these lights shall not be exhibited in conjunction with the combined lantern permitted by paragraph (b) of this Rule.

(d) (i) A sailing vessel of less then 7 metres in length shall, if practicable, exhibit the lights prescribed in paragraph (a) or (b) of this Rule, but if she does not, she shall have ready at hand an electric torch or lighted lantern showing a white light which shall be exhibited in sufficient time to prevent collision.

(ii) A vessel under oars may exhibit the lights prescribed in this Rule for sailing vessels, but if she does not, she shall have ready at hand an electric torch or lighted lantern showing a white light which shall be exhibited in sufficient time to prevent collision.

(e) A vessel proceeding under sail when also being propelled by machinery shall exhibit forward where it can best be seen a conical shape, apex downwards.

RULE 26

Fishing vessels

(a) A vessel engaged in fishing, whether underway or at anchor, shall exhibit only the lights and shapes prescribed in this Rule.

(b) A vessel when engaged in trawling, by which is meant the dragging through the water of a dredge net or other apparatus used as a fishing appliance, shall exhibit:

(i) two all-round lights in a vertical line, the upper being green and the lower white, or a shape consisting of two cones with their apexes together in a vertical line one above the other; a vessel of less then 20 metres in length may instead of this shape exhibit a basket;

(ii) a masthead light abaft of and higher than the all-round green light; a vessel of less than 50 metres in length shall not be obliged to exhibit such a light but may do so;

(iii) when making way through the water, in addition to the lights prescribed in this paragraph, sidelights and a sternlight.

(c) A vessel engaged in fishing, other than trawling, shall exhibit:

(i) two all-round lights in a vertical line, the upper being red and the lower white, or a shape consisting of two cones with apexes together in a vertical line one above the other; a vessel of less than 20 metres in length may instead of this shape exhibit a basket;

(ii) when there is outlying gear extending more than 150 metres horizontally from the vessel, an all-round white light or a cone apex upwards in the direction of the gear;

(iii) when making way through the water, in addition to the lights prescribed in this paragraph, sidelights and a sternlight.

(d) A vessel engaged in fishing in close proximity to other vessels may exhibit the additional signals described in Annex II to these Regulations.

(e) A vessel when not engaged in fishing shall not exhibit the lights or shapes prescribed in this Rule, but only those prescribed for a vessel of her length.

RULE 27

Vessels not under command or restricted in their ability to manoeuvre

(a) A vessel not under command shall exhibit:

(i) two all-round red lights in a vertical line where they can best be seen;

   (ii) two balls or similar shapes in a vertical line where they can best be seen;
   (iii) when making way through the water, in addition to the lights prescribed in this paragraph, sidelights and a sternlight.

(b) A vessel restricted in her ability to manoeuvre, except a vessel engaged in mineclearance operations, shall exhibit:
   (i) three all-round lights in a vertical line where they can best be seen. The highest and lowest of these lights shall be red and the middle light shall be white;
   (ii) three shapes in a vertical line where they can best be seen. The highest and lowest of these shapes shall be balls and the middle one a diamond;
   (iii) when making way through the water, a masthead light or lights, sidelights and a sternlight, in addition to the lights prescribed in subparagraph (i);
   (iv) when at anchor, in addition to the lights or shapes prescribed in subparagraphs (i) and (ii), the light, lights or shape prescribed in Rule 30.

(c) A power-driven vessel engaged in a towing operation such as severely restricts the towing vessel and her tow in their ability to deviate from their course shall, in addition to the lights or shapes prescribed in Rule 24(a), exhibit the lights or shapes prescribed in sub-paragraphs (b)(i) and (ii) of this Rule.

(d) A vessel engaged in dredging or underwater operations, when restricted in her ability to manoeuvre, shall exhibit the lights and shapes prescribed in sub-paragraphs (b)(i), (ii) and (iii) of this Rule and shall in addition, when an obstruction exists, exhibit:
   (i) two all-round red lights or two balls in a vertical line to indicate the side on which the obstruction exists;
   (ii) two all-round green lights or two diamonds in a vertical line to indicate the side on which another vessel may pass;
   (iii) when at anchor, the lights or shapes prescribed in this paragraph instead of the lights or shape prescribed in Rule 30.

(e) Whenever the size of a vessel engaged in diving operations makes it impracticable to exhibit all lights and shapes prescribed in paragraph (d) of this Rule, the following shall be exhibited:
   (i) three all-round lights in a vertical line where they can best be seen. The highest and lowest of these lights shall be red and the middle light shall be white;
   (ii) a rigid replica of the International Code flag "A" not less than 1 metre in height. Measures shall be taken to ensure its all-round visibility.

(f) A vessel engaged in mine clearance operations shall in addition to the lights prescribed for a power-driven vessel in Rule 23 or to the lights or shape prescribed for a vessel at anchor in Rule 30 as appropriate, exhibit three all-round green lights or three balls. One of these lights or shapes shall be exhibited near the foremast head and one at each end of the fore yard. These lights or shapes indicate that it is dangerous for another vessel to approach within 1000 metres of the mine clearance vessel.

(g) Vessels of less than 12 metres in length, except those engaged in diving operations, shall not be required to exhibit the lights and shapes prescribed in this Rule.

(h) The signals prescribed in this Rule are not signals of vessels in distress and requiring assistance. Such signals are contained in Annex IV to these Regulations.

RULE 28

Vessels constrained by their draught

A vessel constrained by her draught may, in addition to the lights prescribed for power-driven vessels in Rule 23, exhibit where they can best be seen three all-round red lights in a vertical line, or a cylinder.

RULE 29

Pilot vessels

(a) A vessel engaged in pilotage duty shall exhibit:
  (i) at or near the masthead, two all-round lights in a vertical line, the upper being white and the lower red;
  (ii) when underway, in addition, sidelights and a sternlight;
  (iii) when at anchor, in addition to the lights prescribed in sub-paragraph (i), the light, lights or shape prescribed in Rule 30 for vessels at anchor.

(b) A pilot vessel when not engaged on pilotage duty shall exhibit the lights or shapes prescribed for a similar vessel of her length.

RULE 30

Anchored vessels and vessels aground

(a) A vessel at anchor shall exhibit where it can best be seen:
  (i) in the fore part, an all-round white light or one ball;
  (ii) at or near the stern and at a lower level than the light prescribed in sub-paragraph (i), an all-round white light.

(b) A vessel of less than 50 metres in length may exhibit an all-round white light where it can best be seen instead of the lights prescribed in paragraph (a) of this Rule.

(c) A vessel at anchor may, and a vessel of 100 metres and more in length shall, also use the available working or equivalent lights to illuminate her decks.

(d) A vessel aground shall exhibit the lights prescribed in paragraph (a) or (b) of this Rule and in addition, where they can best be seen:
  (i) two all-round red lights in a vertical line;
  (ii) three balls in a vertical line.

(e) a vessel of less than 7 metres in length, when at anchor, not in or near a narrow channel, fairway or anchorage, or where other vessels normally navigate, shall not be required to exhibit the lights or shape prescribed in paragraphs (a) and (b) of this Rule.

(f) A vessel of less than 12 metres in length, when aground, shall not be required to exhibit the lights or shapes prescribed in sub-paragraphs (d)(i) and (ii) of this Rule.

RULE 31

Seaplanes

Where it is impracticable for a seaplane to exhibit lights and shapes of the characteristics or in the positions prescribed in the Rules of this Part she shall exhibit lights and shapes as closely similar in characteristics and position as is possible.

PART D - SOUND AND LIGHT SIGNALS

RULE 32

Definitions

(a) The word "whistle" means any sound signalling appliance capable of producing the prescribed blasts and which complies with the specifications in Annex III to these Regulations.
(b) The term "short blast" means a blast of about one second's duration.
(c) The term "prolonged blast" means a blast of from four to six seconds' duration.

RULE 33

Equipment for sound signals

(a) A vessel of 12 metres or more in length shall be provided with a whistle and a bell and a vessel of 100 metres or more in length shall, in addition, be provided with a gong, the tone and sound of which cannot be confused with that of the bell. The whistle, bell and gong shall comply with the specifications in Annex III to these Regulations. The bell or gong or both may be replaced by other equipment having the same respective sound characteristics, provided that manual sounding of the prescribed signals shall always be possible.
(b) A vessel of less than 12 metres in length shall not be obliged to carry the sound signalling appliances prescribed in paragraph (a) of this Rule but if she does not, she shall be provided with some other means of making an efficient sound signal.

RULE 34

Manoeuvering and warning signals

(a) When vessels are in sight of one another, a power-driven vessel underway, when manoeuvering as authorized or required by these Rules, shall indicate that manoeuvre by the following signals on her whistle:
one short blast to mean "I am altering my course to starboard";
two short blasts to mean "I am altering my course to port";
three short blasts to mean "I am operating astern propulsion".

(b) Any vessel may supplement the whistle signals prescribed in paragraph (a) of this Rule by light signals, repeated as appropriate, whilst the manoeuvre is being carried out:

(i) these light signals shall have the following significance:
one flash to mean "I am altering my course to starboard";
two flashes to mean "I am altering my course to port";
three flashes to mean "I am operating astern propulsion";

(ii) the duration of each flash shall be about one second, the interval between flashes shall be about one second, and the interval between successive signals shall be not less than ten seconds;

(iii) the light used for this signal shall, if fitted, be an all-round white light, visible at a minimum range of 5 miles, and shall comply with the provisions of Annex I to these Regulations.

(c) When in sight of one another in a narrow channel or fairway:

(i) a vessel intending to overtake another shall in compliance with Rule 9(e)(i) indicate her intention by the following signals on her whistle:
two prolonged blasts followed by one short blast to mean "I intend to overtake you on your starboard side";
two prolonged blasts followed by two short blasts to mean "I intend to overtake you on your port side".

(ii) the vessel about to be[5] overtaken when acting in accordance with Rule 9(e)(i) shall indicate her agreement by the following signal on her whistle:
one prolonged, one short, one prolonged and one short blast, in that order.

(d) When vessels in sight of one another are approaching each other and from any cause either vessel fails to understand the intentions or actions of the other, or is in doubt whether sufficient action is being taken by the other to avoid collision, the vessels in doubt shall immediately indicate such doubt by giving at least five short and rapid blasts on the whistle. Such signal may be supplemented by a light signal of at least five short and rapid flashes.

(e) A vessel nearing a bend or an area of a channel or fairway where other vessels may be obscured by an intervening obstruction shall sound one prolonged blast. Such signal shall be answered with a prolonged blast by any approaching vessel that may be within hearing around the bend or behind the intervening obstruction.

(f) If whistles are fitted on a vessel at a distance apart of more than 100 metres, one whistle only shall be used for giving manoeuvering and warning signals.

RULE 35

Sound signals in restricted visibility

In or near an area of restricted visibility, whether by day or night, the signals prescribed in this Rule shall be used as follows:

(a) A power-driven vessel making way through the water shall sound at intervals of not more than 2 minutes one prolonged blast.

---

5. The word "the" in the original, an obvious typographical error, has been changed to "be."

(b) A power-driven vessel underway but stopped and making no way through the water shall sound at intervals of not more than 2 minutes two prolonged blasts in succession with an interval of about 2 seconds between them.

(c) A vessel not under command, a vessel restricted in her ability to manoeuvre, a vessel constrained by her draught, a sailing vessel, a vessel engaged in fishing and a vessel engaged in towing or pushing another vessel shall, instead of the signals prescribed in paragraphs (a) or (b) of this Rule, sound at intervals of not more than 2 minutes three blasts in succession, namely one prolonged followed by two short blasts.

(d) A vessel engaged in fishing, when at anchor, and a vessel restricted in her ability to manoeuvre when carrying out her work at anchor, shall instead of the signals prescribed in paragraph (g) of this Rule sound the signal prescribed in paragraph (c) of this Rule.

(e) A vessel towed or if more than one vessel is towed the last vessel of the tow, if manned, shall at intervals of not more than 2 minutes sound four blasts in succession, namely one prolonged followed by three short blasts. When practicable, this signal shall be made immediately after the signal made by the towing vessel.

(f) When a pushing vessel and a vessel being pushed ahead are rigidly connected in a composite unit they shall be regarded as a power-driven vessel and shall give the signals prescribed in paragraphs (a) or (b) of this Rule.

(g) A vessel at anchor shall at intervals of not more than one minute ring the bell rapidly for about 5 seconds. In a vessel of 100 metres or more in length the bell shall be sounded in the forepart of the vessel and immediately after the ringing of the bell the gong shall be sounded rapidly, for about 5 seconds in the after part of the vessel. A vessel at anchor may in addition sound three blasts in succession, namely one short, one prolonged and one short blast, to give warning of her position and of the possibility of collision to an approaching vessel.

(h) A vessel aground shall give the bell signal and if required the gong signal prescribed in paragraph (g) of this Rule and shall, in addition, give three separate and distinct strokes on the bell immediately before and after the rapid ringing of the bell. A vessel aground may in addition sound an appropriate whistle signal.

(i) A vessel of less than 12 metres in length shall not be obliged to give the above-mentioned signals but, if she does not, shall make some other efficient sound signal at intervals of not more than 2 minutes.

(j) A pilot vessel when engaged on pilotage duty may in addition to the signals prescribed in paragraphs (a), (b) or (f) of this Rule sound an identity signal consisting of four short blasts.

RULE 36

Signals to attract attention

If necessary to attract the attention of another vessel any vessel may make light or sound signals that cannot be mistaken for any signal authorized elsewhere in these Rules, or may direct the beam of her searchlight in the direction of the danger, in such a way as not to embarrass any vessel. Any light to attract the attention of another vessel shall be such that it cannot be mistaken for any aid to navigation. For the purpose of this Rule the use of high intensity intermittent or revolving lights, such as strobe lights, shall be avoided.

RULE 37

Distress signals

When a vessel is in distress and requires assistance she shall use or exhibit the signals described in Annex IV to these Regulations.

PART E - EXEMPTIONS

RULE 38

Exemptions

Any vessel (or class of vessels) provided that she complies with the requirements of the International Regulations for Preventing Collisions at Sea, 1960, the keel of which is laid or which is at a corresponding stage of construction before the entry into force of these Regulations may be exempted from compliance therewith as follows:

(a) The installation of lights with ranges prescribed in Rule 22, until four years after the date of entry into force of these Regulations.

(b) The installation of lights with colour specifications as prescribed in Section 7 of Annex I to these Regulations, until four years after the date of entry into force of these Regulations.

(c) The repositioning of lights as a result of conversion from Imperial to metric units and rounding off measurement figures, permanent exemption.

(d) (i) The repositioning of masthead lights on vessels of less than 150 metres in length, resulting from the prescriptions of Section 3(a) of Annex I to these Regulations, permanent exemption.

(ii) The repositioning of masthead lights on vessels of 150 metres or more in length, resulting from the prescriptions of Section 3(a) of Annex I to these Regulations, until nine years after the date of entry into force of these Regulations.

(e) The repositioning of masthead lights resulting from the prescriptions of Section 2(b) of Annex I to these Regulations, until nine years after the date of entry into force of these Regulations.

(f) The repositioning of sidelights resulting from the prescriptions of Section 3(b) of Annex I to these Regulations, until nine years after the date of entry into force of these Regulations.

(g) The requirements for sound signal appliances prescribed in Annex III to these Regulations, until nine years after the date of entry into force of these Regulations.

(h) The repositioning of all-round lights resulting from the prescription of Section 9(b) of Annex I to these Regulations, permanent exemption.

D. ANNEXES TO THE INTERNATIONAL REGULATIONS

ANNEX I: POSITIONING AND TECHNICAL DETAILS OF LIGHTS AND SHAPES

1. DEFINITION

The term "height above the hull" means height above the upper-most continuous deck. This height shall be measured from the position vertically beneath the location of the light.

2. VERTICAL POSITIONING AND SPACING OF LIGHTS

(a) On a power-driven vessel of 20 metres or more in length the masthead lights shall be placed as follows:
 (i) the forward masthead light, or if only one masthead light is carried, then that light, at a height above the hull of not less than 6 metres, and, if the breadth of the vessel exceeds 6 metres, then at a height above the hull not less than such breadth, so however that the light need not be placed at a greater height above the hull than 12 metres;
 (ii) when two masthead lights are carried the after one shall be at least 4.5 metres vertically higher than the forward one.

(b) The vertical separation of masthead lights of power-driven vessels shall be such that in all normal conditions of trim the after light will be seen over and separate from the forward light at a distance of 1000 metres from the stem when viewed from sea level.

(c) The masthead light of a power-driven vessel of 12 metres but less than 20 metres in length shall be placed at a height above the gunwale of not less than 2.5 metres.

(d) A power-driven vessel of less than 12 metres in length may carry the uppermost light at a height of less than 2.5 metres above the gunwale. When, however, a masthead light is carried in addition to sidelights and a sternlight, or the all-round light prescribed in Rule 23(c)(i) is carried in addition to sidelights, then such masthead light or all-round light shall be carried at least 1 metre higher than the sidelights.

(e) One of the two or three masthead lights prescribed for a power-driven vessel when engaged in towing or pushing another vessel shall be placed in the same position as either the forward masthead light or the after masthead light; provided that, if carried on the aftermast, the lowest after masthead light shall be at least 4.5 metres vertically higher than the forward masthead light.

(f) (i) The masthead light or lights prescribed in Rule 23(a) shall be so placed as to be above and clear of all other lights and obstructions except as described in sub-paragraph (ii).
 (ii) When it is impracticable to carry the all-round lights prescribed by Rule 27(b)(i) or Rule 28 below the masthead lights, they may be carried above the after masthead light(s) or vertically in between the forward masthead light(s) and after masthead light(s), provided that in

the latter case the requirement of Section 3(c) of this Annex shall be complied with.

(g) The sidelights of a power-driven vessel shall be placed at a height above the hull not greater than three quarters of that of the forward masthead light. They shall not be so low as to be interfered with by deck lights.

(h) The sidelights, if in a combined lantern and carried on a power-driven vessel of less than 20 metres in length, shall be placed not less than 1 metre below the masthead light.

(i) When the Rules prescribe two or three lights to be carried in a vertical line, they shall be spaced as follows:

   (i) on a vessel of 20 metres in length or more such lights shall be spaced not less than 2 metres apart, and the lowest of these lights shall, except where a towing light is required, be placed at a height of not less than 4 metres above the hull;

   (ii) on a vessel of less than 20 metres in length such lights shall be spaced not less than 1 metre apart and the lowest of these lights shall, except where a towing light is required, be placed at a height of not less than 2 metres above the hull gunwale;

   (iii) when three lights are carried they shall be equally spaced.

(j) The lower of the two all-round lights prescribed for a vessel when engaged in fishing shall be at a height above the sidelights not less than twice the distance between the two vertical lights.

(k) The forward anchor light prescribed in Rule 30(a)(i), when two are carried, shall not be less than 4.5 metres above the after one. On a vessel of 50 metres or more in length this forward anchor light shall be placed at a height of not less than 6 metres above the hull.

3. HORIZONTAL POSITIONING AND SPACING OF LIGHTS

(a) When two masthead lights are prescribed for a power-driven vessel, the horizontal distance between them shall not be less than one half of the length of the vessel but need not be more than 100 metres. The forward light shall be placed not more than one quarter of the length of the vessel from the stem.

(b) On a power-driven vessel of 20 metres or more in length the sidelights shall not be placed in front of the forward masthead lights. They shall be placed at or near the side of the vessel.

(c) When the lights prescribed in Rule 27(b)(i) or Rule 28 are placed vertically between the forward masthead light(s) and the after masthead light(s) these all-round lights shall be placed at a horizontal distance of not less than 2 metres from the fore and aft centreline of the vessel in the athwartship direction.

4. DETAILS OF LOCATION OF DIRECTION-INDICATING LIGHTS FOR FISHING VESSELS, DREDGES AND VESSELS ENGAGED IN UNDERWATER OPERATIONS

(a) The light indicating the direction of the outlying gear from a vessel engaged in fishing as prescribed in Rule 26(c)(ii) shall be placed at a horizontal distance of not less than 2 metres and not more than 6 metres away from the two all-round red and white lights. This light shall be placed not higher than the all-round white light prescribed in Rule 26(c)(i) and not lower than the sidelights.

(b) The lights and shapes on a vessel engaged in dredging or underwater operations to indicate the obstructed side and/or the side on which it is safe to pass, as prescribed in Rule 27(d)(i) and (ii), shall be placed at the maximum practical horizontal distance, but in no case less than 2 metres, from the lights or shapes prescribed in Rule 27(b)(i) and (ii). In no case shall the upper of these lights or shapes be at a greater height than the lower of the three lights or shapes prescribed in Rule 27(b)(i) and (ii).

5. SCREENS OF SIDELIGHTS

The sidelights of vessels of 20 metres or more in length shall be fitted with inboard screens painted matt black, and meeting the requirements of Section 9 of this Annex. On vessels of less than 20 metres in length the sidelights, if necessary to meet the requirements of Section 9 of this Annex, shall be fitted with inboard matt black screens. With a combined lantern, using a single vertical filament and a very narrow division between the green and red sections, external screens need not be fitted.

6. SHAPES

(a) Shapes shall be black and of the following sizes:
   (i) a ball shall have a diameter of not less than 0.6 metre;
   (ii) a cone shall have a base diameter of not less than 0.6 metre and a height equal to its diameter;
   (iii) a cylinder shall have a diameter of at least 0.6 metre and a height of twice its diameter;
   (iv) a diamond shape shall consist of two cones as defined in (ii) above having a common base.

(b) The vertical distance between shapes shall be at least 1.5 metre.

(c) In a vessel of less than 20 metres in length shapes of lesser dimensions but commensurate with the size of the vessel may be used and the distance apart may be correspondingly reduced.

7. COLOUR SPECIFICATION OF LIGHTS

The chromaticity of all navigation lights shall conform to the following standards, which lie within the boundaries of the area of the diagram specified for each colour by the International Commission on Illumination (CIE).

The boundaries of the area for each colour are given by indicating the corner co-ordinates, which are as follows:

(i) White

x	0.525	0.525	0.452	0.310	0.310	0.443
y	0.382	0.440	0.440	0.348	0.283	0.382

(ii) Green

x	0.028	0.009	0.300	0.203
y	0.385	0.723	0.511	0.356

(iii) Red

x	0.680	0.660	0.735	0.721
y	0.320	0.320	0.265	0.259

(iv) Yellow

x	0.612	0.618	0.575	0.575
y	0.382	0.382	0.425	0.406

8. INTENSITY OF LIGHTS

(a) The minimum luminous intensity of lights shall be calculated by using the formula:

$I = 3.43 \times 10^6 \times T \times D^2 \times K^{-D}$

where I is luminous intensity in candelas under service conditions,

T is threshold factor 2×10^{-7} *lux,* D is range of visibility (luminous range) of the light in nautical miles, K is atmospheric transmissivity.

For prescribed lights the value of K shall be 0.8, corresponding to a meteorological visibility of approximately 13 nautical miles.

(b) A selection of figures derived from the formula is given in the following table:

Range of visibility; (luminous range) of light in nautical miles, D:	Luminous intensity of light in candelas for K = 0.8
1	0.9
2	4.3
3	12
4	27
5	52
6	94

NOTE: The maximum luminous intensity of navigation lights should be limited to avoid undue glare. This shall not be achieved by a variable control of the luminous intensity.

9. HORIZONTAL SECTORS

(a) (i) In the forward direction, sidelights as fitted on the vessel shall show the minimum required intensities. The intensities must decrease to reach practical cut-off between 1 degree and 3 degrees outside the prescribed sectors.

(ii) For sternlights and masthead lights and at 22.5 degrees abaft the beam for sidelights, the minimum required intensities shall be maintained over the arc of the horizon up to 5 degrees within the limits of the sectors prescribed in Rule 21. From 5 degrees within the prescribed sectors the intensity may decrease by 50 percent up to the prescribed limits; it shall decrease steadily to reach practical cut-off at not more than 5 degrees outside the prescribed sectors.

(b) All-round lights shall be so located as not to be obscured by masts, topmasts or structures within angular sectors of more than 6 degrees, except anchor lights prescribed in Rule 30, which need not be placed at an impracticable height above the hull.

10. VERTICAL SECTORS

(a) The vertical sectors of electric lights as fitted, with the exception of lights on sailing vessels underway shall ensure that:
   (i) at least the required minimum intensity is maintained at all angles from 5 degrees above to 5 degrees below the horizontal;
   (ii) at least 60 per cent of the required minimum intensity is maintained from 7.5 degrees above to 7.5 degrees below the horizontal.

(b) In the case of sailing vessels underway the vertical sectors of electric lights as fitted shall ensure that:
   (i) at least the required minimum intensity is maintained at all angles from 5 degrees above to 5 degrees below the horizontal;
   (ii) at least 50 percent of the required minimum intensity is maintained from 25 degrees above to 25 degrees below the horizontal.

(c) In the case of lights other than electric these specifications shall be met as closely as possible.

11. INTENSITY OF NON-ELECTRIC LIGHTS

Non-electric lights shall so far as practicable comply with the minimum intensities, as specified in the Table given in Section 8 of this Annex.

12. MANOEUVERING LIGHT

Notwithstanding the provisions of paragraph 2(f) of this Annex the manoeuvering light described in Rule 34(b) shall be placed in the same fore and after vertical plane as the masthead light or lights and, where practicable, at a minimum height of 2 metres vertically above the forward masthead light, provided that it shall be carried not less than 2 metres vertically above or below the after masthead light. On a vessel where only one masthead light is carried the manoeuvering light, if fitted, shall be carried where it can best be seen, not less than 2 metres vertically apart from the masthead light.

13. APPROVAL

The construction of lights and shapes and the installation of lights on board the vessel shall be to the satisfaction of the appropriate authority of the State whose flag the vessel is entitled to fly.

ANNEX II: ADDITIONAL SIGNALS FOR FISHING VESSELS FISHING IN CLOSE PROXIMITY

1. GENERAL

The lights mentioned herein shall, if exhibited in pursuance of Rule 26(d), be placed where they can best be seen. They shall be at least 0.9 metre apart but at a lower level than lights prescribed in Rule 26(b)(i) and (c)(i). The lights shall be visible all around the horizon at a distance of at least 1 mile but at a lesser distance than the lights prescribed by these Rules for fishing vessels.

2. SIGNALS FOR TRAWLERS

(a) Vessels when engaged in trawling, whether using demersal or pelagic gear, may exhibit:
  (i) when shooting their nets: two white lights in a vertical line;
  (ii) when hauling their nets: one white light over one red light in a vertical line;
  (iii) when the net has come fast upon an obstruction: two red lights in a vertical line.

(b) Each vessel engaged in pair trawling may exhibit:
  (i) by night, a searchlight directed forward and in the direction of the other vessel of the pair;
  (ii) when shooting or hauling their nets or when their nets have come fast upon an obstruction, the lights prescribed in 2(a) above.

3. SIGNALS FOR PURSE SEINERS

Vessels engaged in fishing with purse seine gear may exhibit two yellow lights in a vertical line. These lights shall flash alternately every second and with equal light and occultation duration. These lights may be exhibited only when the vessel is hampered by its fishing gear.

ANNEX III: TECHNICAL DETAILS OF SOUND SIGNAL APPLIANCES

1. WHISTLES

(a) Frequencies and range of audibility. The fundamental frequency of the signal shall lie within the range 70-700 Hz.
The range of audibility of the signal from a whistle shall be determined by those frequencies, which may include the fundamental and/or one or more higher frequencies, which lie within the range 180-700 Hz (± 1 per cent) and which provide the sound pressure levels specified in paragraph 1(c) below.

(b) Limits of fundamental frequencies. To ensure a wide variety of whistle characteristics, the fundamental frequency of a whistle shall be between the following limits:
  (i) 70-200 Hz, for a vessel 200 metres or more in length;
  (ii) 130-350 Hz, for a vessel 75 metres but less than 200 metres in length;
  (iii) 250-700 Hz, for a vessel less than 75 metres in length.

(c) Sound signal intensity and range of audibility. A whistle fitted in a vessel shall provide, in the direction of maximum intensity of the whistle and at a distance of 1 metre from it, a sound pressure level in at least one 1/3rd-octave band within the range of frequencies 180-700 Hz (± 1 percent) of not less than the appropriate figure given in the table below.

Length of vessel in metres	*1/3-octave band level at 1 metre in dB referred to 2×10^{-5} N/m²*	*Audibility range in nautical miles*
200 or more	143	2.0
75 but less than 200	138	1.5
20 but less than 75	130	1.0
Less than 20	120	0.5

The range of audibility in the table above is for information and is approximately the range at which a whistle may be heard on its forward axis with 90 per cent probability in conditions of still air on board a vessel having average background noise level at the listening posts (taken to be 68 dB in the octave band centered on 250 Hz and 63 dB in the octave band centered on 500 Hz).

In practice the range at which a whistle may be heard is extremely variable and depends critically on weather conditions; the values given can be regarded as typical but under conditions of strong wind or high ambient noise level at the listening post the range may be much reduced.

(d) Directional properties. The sound pressure level of a directional whistle shall be not more than 4 dB below the prescribed sound pressure level on the axis at any direction in the horizontal plane within ±45 degrees of the axis. The sound pressure level at any other direction in the horizontal plane shall be not more than 10 dB below the prescribed sound pressure level on the axis, so that the range in any direction will be at least half the range on the forward axis. The sound pressure level shall be measured in that 1/3rd-octave band which determines the audibility range.

(e) Positioning of whistles. When a directional whistle is to be used as the only whistle on a vessel, it shall be installed with its maximum intensity directed straight ahead.

A whistle shall be placed as high as practicable on a vessel, in order to reduce interception of the emitted sound by obstructions and also to minimize hearing damage risk to personnel. The sound pressure level of the vessel's own signal at listening posts shall not exceed 110dB (A) and so far as practicable should not exceed 100 dB (A).

(f) Fitting of more than one whistle. If whistles are fitted at a distance apart of more than 100 metres, it shall be so arranged that they are not sounded simultaneously.

(g) Combined whistle systems. If due to the presence of obstructions the sound field of a single whistle or of one of the whistles referred to in paragraph 1(f) above is likely to have a zone of greatly reduced signal level, it is recommended that a combined whistle system be fitted so as to overcome this reduction. For the purposes of the rules a combined whistle system is to be regarded as a single whistle. The whistles of a combined system shall be located at a distance apart of not more than 100 metres and arranged to be sounded simultaneously. The frequency of any one whistle shall differ from those of the others by at least 10 Hz.

2. BELL OR GONG

(a) Intensity of signal. A bell or gong, or other device having similar sound characteristics shall produce a sound pressure level of not less than 110 dB at a distance of 1 metre from it.

(b) Construction. Bells and gongs shall be made of corrosion-resistant material and designed to give a clear tone. The diameter of the mouth of the bell shall be not less than 300 mm for vessels of 20 metres or more in length, and shall be not less than 200 mm for vessels of 12 metres or more but of less than 20 metres in length. Where practicable, a power-driven bell striker is recommended to ensure constant force but manual operation shall be possible. The mass of the striker shall be not less than 3 per cent of the mass of the bell.

3. APPROVAL

The construction of sound signal appliances, their performance and their installation on board the vessel shall be to the satisfaction of the appropriate authority of the State whose flag the vessel is entitled to fly.

ANNEX IV: DISTRESS SIGNALS

1. The following signals, used or exhibited either together or separately, indicate distress and need of assistance:
   (a) a gun or other explosive signal fired at intervals of about a minute;
   (b) a continuous sounding with any fog-signalling apparatus;
   (c) rockets or shells, throwing red stars fired one at a time at short intervals;
   (d) a signal made by radiotelegraphy or by any other signalling method consisting of the group • • • — — — • • • (SOS) in the Morse Code;
   (e) a signal sent by radiotelephony consisting of the spoken word "Mayday";
   (f) the International Code Signal of distress indicated by N.C.;
   (g) a signal consisting of a square flag having above or below it a ball or anything resembling a ball.
   (h) flames on the vessel (as from a burning tar barrel, oil barrel, etc.)
   (i) a rocket parachute flare or a hand flare showing a red light;
   (j) a smoke signal giving off orange-colored smoke;
   (k) slowly and repeatedly raising and lowering arms outstretched to each side;
   (l) the radiotelegraph alarm signal;
   (m) the radiotelephone alarm signal;
   (n) signals transmitted by emergency position-indicating radio beacons;
   (o) approved signals transmitted by radio communication systems.
2. The use or exhibition of any of the foregoing signals except for the purpose of indicating distress and need of assistance and the use of other signals which may be confused with any of the above signals is prohibited.

3. Attention is drawn to the relevant sections of the International Code of Signals, the Merchant Ship Search and Rescue Manual and the following signals:
   (a) a piece of orange-colored canvas with either a black square and circle or other appropriate symbol (for identification from the air);
   (b) a dye marker.

E. STATUTORY PROVISIONS FOLLOWING COLREGS AND THE ANNEXES THERETO

33 U.S.C. § 1603. Vessels subject to International Regulations

Except as provided in section 1604 of this title and subject to the provisions of section 1605 of this title, the International Regulations, as proclaimed under section 1602 of this title, shall be applicable to, and shall be complied with by

(1) all vessels, public and private, subject to the jurisdiction of the United States, while upon the high seas or in waters connected therewith navigable by seagoing vessels, and

(2) all other vessels when on waters subject to the jurisdiction of the United States.

33 U.S.C. § 1604. Vessels not subject to International Regulations

(a) The International Regulations do not apply to vessels while in the waters of the United States shoreward of the navigational demarcation lines dividing the high seas from harbors, rivers, and other inland waters of the United States.[6]

(b) Whenever a vessel subject to the jurisdiction of the United States is in the territorial waters of a foreign state the International Regulations shall be applicable to, and shall be complied with by, that vessel to the extent that the laws and regulations of the foreign state are not in conflict therewith.[7]

33 U.S.C. § 1605. Navy and Coast Guard vessels of special construction or purposes

(a) Certification for alterative compliance
Any requirement of the International Regulations with respect to the number, position, range, or arc of visibility of lights, with respect to shapes, or with respect to the disposition and characteristics of sound-signaling appliances, shall not be applicable to a vessel of special construction or purpose, whenever the Secretary of the Navy, for any vessel of the Navy, or the Secretary of the department in which the Coast Guard is operating, for any other vessel of the United States, shall certify that the vessel cannot comply fully with that requirement without interfering with the special function of the vessel.

(b) Closest possible compliance by vessels covered by certification for alternative compliance

6. Pub.L. No. 95-75, § 4, July 27, 1977, 91 Stat. 309.

7. Pub.L. No. 95-75, § 5, July 27, 1977, 91 Stat. 309; Pub.L. No. 96-591, § 6(1), Dec. 24, 1980, 94 Stat. 3434.

Whenever a certification is issued under the authority of subsection (a) of this section, the vessel involved shall comply with the requirement as to which the certification is made to the extent that the Secretary issuing the certification shall certify as the closest possible compliance by that vessel.

(c) Publication of certifications in Federal Register
Notice of the certifications issued pursuant to subsections (a) and (b) of this section shall be published in the Federal Register.

(d) Issuance of certification for a class of vessels
A certification authorized by this section may be issued for a class of vessels.[8]

33 U.S.C. § 1606. Special rules for ships of war, vessels proceeding under convoy, and fishing vessels engaged in fishing as a fleet

(a) The Secretary of the Navy is authorized to promulgate special rules with respect to additional station or signal lights or whistle signals for ships of war or vessels proceeding under convoy, and the Secretary of the department in which the Coast Guard is operating is authorized to promulgate special rules with respect to additional station or signal lights for fishing vessels engaged in fishing as a fleet.

(b) The additional station or signal lights or whistle signals contained in the special rules authorized under subsection (a) of this section shall be, as far as possible, such that they cannot be mistaken for any light or signal authorized by the International Regulations. Notice of such special rules shall be published in the Federal Register and, after the effective date specified in such notice, they shall have effect as if they were a part of the International Regulations.[9]

33 U.S.C. § 1607. Implementation by rules and regulations; authority to promulgate

The Secretary of the department in which the Coast Guard is operating is authorized to promulgate such reasonable rules and regulations as are necessary to implement the provisions of this chapter and the International Regulations proclaimed hereunder.[10]

33 U.S.C. § 1608. Civil Penalties

(a) Liability of vessel operator for violations
Whoever operates a vessel, subject to the provisions of this chapter, in violation of this chapter or of any regulation promulgated pursuant to section 1607 of this title, shall be liable to a civil penalty of not more than $5,000 for each such violation.

(b) Liability of vessel for violations; seizure of vessel
Every vessel subject to the provisions of this chapter, other than a public vessel being used for noncommercial purposes, which is operated in violation of this chapter or of any regulation promulgated pursuant to section 1607

8. Pub.L. No. 95-75, § 6, July 27, 1977, 91 Stat. 309; Pub.L. No. 96-591, § 6(2), Dec. 24, 1980, 94 Stat. 3434.

9. Pub.L. No. 95-75, § 7, July 27, 1977, 91 Stat. 310.

10. Pub.L. No. 95-75, § 8, July 27, 1977, 91 Stat. 310.

of this title, shall be liable to a civil penalty of not more than $5,000 for each such violation, for which penalty the vessel may be seized and proceeded against in the district court of the United States of any district within which such vessel may be found.

(c) Assessment of penalties; notice; opportunity for hearing; remission, mitigation, and compromise of penalty; action for collection
The Secretary of the department in which the Coast Guard is operating may assess any civil penalty authorized by this section. No such penalty may be assessed until the person charged, or the owner of the vessel charged, as appropriate, shall have been given notice of the violation involved and an opportunity for a hearing. For good cause shown, the Secretary may remit, mitigate, or compromise any penalty assessed. Upon the failure of the person charged, or the owner of the vessel charged, to pay an assessed penalty, as it may have been mitigated or compromised, the Secretary may request the Attorney General to commence an action in the appropriate district court of the United States for collection of the penalty as assessed, without regard to the amount involved, together with such other relief as may be appropriate.[11]

11. Pub.L. No. 95-75, § 9, July 27, 1977, 91 Stat. 310; Pub.L. No. 96-591, § 6(3), (4), Dec. 24, 1980, 94 Stat. 3435.

THE INLAND NAVIGATION RULES (AS AMENDED TO JANUARY 6, 1997)

A. AUTHORS' INTRODUCTORY NOTE

The Inland Navigation Rules were enacted December 24, 1980, as Pub.L. No. 96-591; 94 Stat. 3415: 33 U.S. Code 2001-38. The Rules and portions of Rules set out below are those that differ materially from the corresponding Rules of COLREGS. Where there is no difference, or where the difference is immaterial, the Inland Rule or portion of a Rule is not set out, but there is a cross reference to the corresponding provision of COLREGS. Differences considered immaterial are those in punctuation, spelling (American vice English) and, in a few instances, choice of words (e.g., "anchored" vice "at anchor," "these Rules" vice "these Regulations" and "that" vice "such"). The same practice has been followed with respect to the Annexes to the Inland Rules (Appendix 2B).

B. INLAND NAVIGATION RULES

PART A - GENERAL

RULE 1

Application

(a) These Rules apply to all vessels upon the inland waters of the United States, and to vessels of the United States on the Canadian waters of the Great Lakes to the extent that there is no conflict with Canadian law.

(b) (i) These Rules constitute special rules made by an appropriate authority, within the meaning of Rule 1(b) of the International Regulations.

(ii) All vessels complying with the construction and equipment requirements of the International Regulations are considered to be in compliance with these Rules.

(c) Nothing in these Rules shall interfere with the operation of any special rules made by the Secretary of the Navy with respect to additional station or signal lights and shapes or whistle signals for ships of war and vessels proceeding under convoy, or by the Secretary with respect to additional station or signal lights and shapes for fishing vessels engaged in fishing as a fleet. These additional station or signal lights and shapes or whistle signals shall, so far as possible, be such that they cannot be mistaken for any light, shape, or signal authorized elsewhere under these Rules. Notice of such special rules shall be published in the Federal Register and, after the effective date specified in such notice, they shall have effect as if they were a part of these Rules.

(d) Traffic separation schemes may be established for the purpose of these Rules. Vessel traffic service regulations may be in effect in certain areas.

(e) Whenever the Secretary determines that a vessel or class of vessels of special construction or purpose cannot comply fully with the provisions of any of these Rules with respect to the number, position, range, or arc of visibility of lights or shapes, as well as to the disposition and characteristics of sound-signalling appliances, the vessel shall comply with such other provisions in regard to the number, position, range, or arc of visibility of lights or shapes, as well as to the disposition and characteristics of sound-signalling appliances, as the Secretary shall have determined to be the closest possible compliance with these Rules. The Secretary may issue a certificate of alternative compliance for a vessel or class of vessels specifying the closest compliance with these Rules. The Secretary of the Navy shall make these determinations and issue certificates of alternative compliance for vessels of the Navy.

(f) The Secretary may accept a certificate of alternative compliance issued by a contracting party to the International Regulations if he determines that the alternative compliance standards of the contracting party are substantially the same as those of the United States.

RULE 2

Responsibility

[Rule 2 is the same as COLREGS Rule 2.]

RULE 3

General Definitions

For the purpose of these Rules and this Act, except where the context otherwise requires:

[Paragraphs (a) to (g) are the same as COLREGS Rule 3(a) to (g).]

(h) The word “underway” means that a vessel is not at anchor, or made fast to the shore, or aground;

(i) The words “length” and “breadth” of a vessel means her length overall and greatest breadth;

(j) Vessels shall be deemed to be in sight of one another only when one can be observed visually from the other;

(k) The term “restricted visibility” means any condition in which visibility is restricted by fog, mist, falling snow, heavy rainstorms, sandstorms, or any other similar causes;

(l) “Western Rivers” means the Mississippi River, its tributaries, South Pass, and Southwest Pass, to the navigational demarcation lines dividing the high seas from harbors, rivers, and other inland waters of the United States, and the Port Allen-Morgan City Alternate Route, and that part of the Atchafalaya River above its junction with the Port Allen-Morgan City Alternate Route including the Old River and the Red River;

(m) “Great Lakes” means the Great Lakes and their connecting and tributary waters including the Calumet River as far as the Thomas J. O’Brien Lock and Controlling Works (between mile 326 and 327), the Chicago River as far as the east side of the Ashland Avenue Bridge (between mile 321 and 322), and the Saint Lawrence River as far east as the lower exit of Saint Lambert Lock;

(n) "Secretary" means the Secretary of the department in which the Coast Guard is operating;

(o) "Inland Waters" means the navigable waters of the United States shoreward of the navigational demarcation lines dividing the high seas from harbors, rivers, and other inland waters of the United States and the waters of the Great Lakes on the United States side of the International Boundary;

(p) "Inland Rules" or "Rules" mean the Inland Navigational Rules and the annexes thereto, which govern the conduct of vessels and specify the lights, shapes, and sound signals that apply on inland waters; and

(q) "International Regulations" means the International Regulations for Preventing Collisions at Sea, 1972, including annexes currently in force for the United States.

PART B - STEERING AND SAILING RULES

Subpart I - Conduct of Vessels in Any Condition of Visibility

RULE 4

Application

Rules in this subpart apply in any condition of visibility.

RULE 5

Look-out

[Rule 5 is the same as COLREGS Rule 5.]

RULE 6

Safe Speed

[Rule 6 is the same as COLREGS Rule 6.]

RULE 7

Risk of Collision

[Rule 7 is the same as COLREGS Rule 7.]

RULE 8

Action to Avoid Collision

[Paragraphs (a) to (e) are the same as COLREGS Rule 8(a) to (e).]

(f) Early action to allow room for safe passage

(i) A vessel which, by any of these Rules, is required not to impede the passage or safe passage of another vessel shall, when required by the circumstances of the case, take early action to allow sufficient sea room for the safe passage of the other vessel.

(ii) A vessel required not to impede the passage or safe passage of another vessel is not relieved of this obligation if approaching the other vessel so as to involve risk of collision and shall, when taking action, have full regard to the action which may be required by the Rules of this part.

(iii) A vessel the passage of which is not to be impeded remains fully obliged to comply with the Rules of this part when the two vessels are approaching one another so as to involve risk of collision.

RULE 9

Narrow Channels

[Paragraph 9(a)(i) is the same as COLREGS Rule 9(a).]

(ii) Notwithstanding paragraph (a)(i) and Rule 14(a), a power-driven vessel operating in narrow channels or fairways on the Great Lakes, Western Rivers, or waters specified by the Secretary, and proceeding downbound with a following current shall have the right-of-way over an upbound vessel, shall propose the manner and place of passage, and shall initiate the maneuvering signals prescribed by Rule 34(a)(i), as appropriate. The vessel proceeding upbound against the current shall hold as necessary to permit safe passing.

[Paragraphs 9(b) and (c) of Rule 9 are the same as COLREGS Rule 9(b) and (c).]

(d) A vessel shall not cross a narrow channel or fairway if such crossing impedes the passage of a vessel which can safely navigate only within that channel or fairway. The latter vessel shall use the danger signal prescribed in Rule 34(d) if in doubt as to the intention of the crossing vessel.

(e) (i) In a narrow channel or fairway when overtaking, the power-driven vessel intending to overtake another power-driven vessel shall indicate her intention by sounding the appropriate signal prescribed in Rule 34(c) and take steps to permit safe passing. The power-driven vessel being overtaken, if in agreement, shall sound the same signal and may, if specifically agreed to take steps to permit safe passing. If in doubt she shall sound the danger signal prescribed in Rule 34(d).

[Paragraphs e(ii), (f) and (g) are the same as COLREGS Rule 9(e)(ii), (f) and (g).]

RULE 10

Traffic separation schemes

[Rule 10 is now the same as COLREGS Rule 10.]

Subpart II - Conduct of Vessels in Sight of One Another

RULE 11

Application

Rules in this subpart apply to vessels in sight of one another.

RULE 12

Sailing Vessels

[Rule 12 is the same as COLREGS Rule 12.]

RULE 13

Overtaking

[Rule 13 is the same as COLREGS Rule 13.]

RULE 14

Head-on Situation

(a) Unless otherwise agreed, when two power~driven vessels are meeting on reciprocal or nearly reciprocal courses so as to involve risk of collision each shall alter her course to starboard so that each shall pass on the port side of the other.

[Paragraphs (b) and (c) are the same as COLREGS Rule 14(b) and (c).]

(d) Notwithstanding paragraph (a) of this Rule, a power-driven vessel operating on the Great Lakes, Western Rivers, or waters specified by the Secretary, and proceeding downbound with a following current shall have the right-of-way over an upbound vessel, shall propose the manner of passage, and shall initiate the maneuvering signals prescribed by Rule 34(a)(1), as appropriate.

RULE 15

Crossing Situation

(a) When two power-driven vessels are crossing so as to involve risk of collision, the vessel which has the other on her starboard side shall keep out of the way and shall, if the circumstances of the case admit, avoid crossing ahead of the other vessel.

(b) Notwithstanding paragraph (a), on the Great Lakes, Western Rivers, or waters specified by the Secretary, a power-driven vessel crossing a river shall keep out of the way of a power-driven vessel ascending or descending the river.

RULE 16

Action by Give-way Vessel

[Rule 16 is the same as COLREGS Rule 16.]

RULE 17

Action by Stand-on Vessel

[Rule 17 is the same as COLREGS Rule 17.]

RULE 18

Responsibilities Between Vessels

[Paragraphs (a), (b), (c) and (d) are the same as COLREGS Rule 18(a), (b), (c) and e), respectively. There is no paragraph of Inland Rule 18 corresponding to Paragraph (d) of COLREGS Rule 18.]

Subpart III - Conduct of Vessels in Restricted Visibility

RULE 19

Conduct of Vessels in Restricted Visibility

[Rule 19 is the same as COLREGS Rule 19.]

PART C - LIGHTS AND SHAPES

RULE 20

Application

[Rule 20 is the same as COLREGS Rule 20.]

RULE 21

Definitions

(a) "Masthead light" means a white light placed over the fore and aft centerline of the vessel showing an unbroken light over an arc of the horizon of 225 degrees and so fixed as to show the light from right ahead to 22.5 degrees abaft the beam on either side of the vessel, except that on a vessel of less than 12 meters in length the masthead light shall be placed as nearly as practicable to the fore and aft centerline of the vessel.

(b) "Sidelights" mean a green light on the starboard side and a red light on the port side each showing an unbroken light over an arc of the horizon of 112.5 degrees and so fixed as to show the light from right ahead to 22.5 degrees abaft the beam on its respective side. On a vessel of less than 20 meters in length the sidelights may be combined in one lantern carried on the fore and aft centerline of the vessel, except that on a vessel of less than 12 meters in length the sidelights when combined in one lantern shall be placed as nearly as practicable to the fore and aft centerline of the vessel.

[Paragraphs (c), (d), (e) and (f) are the same as COLREGS Rule 21(c), (d), (e) and (f).]

(g) "Special flashing light" means a yellow light flashing at regular intervals at a frequency of 50 to 70 flashes per minute, placed as far forward and as nearly as practicable on the fore and aft centerline of the tow and showing an unbroken light over an arc of the horizon of not less than 180 degrees nor more than 225 degrees and so fixed as to show the light from right ahead to abeam and no more than 22.5 degrees abaft the beam on either side of the vessel.

RULE 22

Visibility of Lights

The lights prescribed in these Rules shall have an intensity as specified in Annex I to these Rules, so as to be visible at the following minimum ranges:

(a) In a vessel of 50 meters or more in length:
—a masthead light, 6 miles;
—a sidelight, 3 miles;
—a sternlight, 3 miles;
—a towing light, 3 miles;
—a white, red, green or yellow all-round light, 3 miles; and
—a special flashing light, 2 miles.

(b) In a vessel of 12 meters or more in length but less than 50 meters in length:
—a masthead light, 5 miles; except that where the length of the vessel is less than 20 meters, 3 miles;
—a sidelight, 2 miles;
—a sternlight, 2 miles;
—a towing light, 2 miles;
—a white, red, green or yellow all-round light, 2 miles; and
—a special flashing light, 2 miles.

(c) In a vessel of less than 12 meters in length:
—a masthead light, 2 miles;
—a sidelight, 1 mile;
—a sternlight, 2 miles;
—a towing light, 2 miles;
—a white, red, green or yellow all-round light, 2 miles; and
—a special flashing light, 2 miles.

(d) In an inconspicuous, partly submerged vessel or object being towed:
—a white all-round light, 3 miles.

RULE 23

Power-driven Vessels Underway

[Paragraphs (a), (b) and (c) are the same as COLREGS Rule 23(a), (b) and (c), except that Inland Rule 23(b) adds, at the end, "where it can best be seen."]

(d) A power-driven vessel when operating on the Great Lakes may carry an all-round white light in lieu of the second masthead light and sternlight prescribed in paragraph (a) of this Rule. The light shall be carried in the position of the second masthead light and be visible at the same minimum range.

RULE 24

Towing and Pushing

[Paragraphs (a) and (b) are the same as COLREGS Rule 24 (a) and (b).]

(c) A power-driven vessel when pushing ahead or towing alongside, except as required by paragraphs (b) and (i) of this Rule, shall exhibit:

(i) instead of the light prescribed either in Rule 23(a)(i) or 23(a)(ii), two masthead lights in a vertical line;
(ii) sidelights; and
(iii) two towing lights in a vertical line.

(d) A power-driven vessel to which paragraphs (a) or (c) of this Rule apply shall also comply with Rule 23(a)(i) and 23(a)(ii).

[Paragraph (e) is substantially the same as Paragraph (e) of COLREGS Rule 24(e).]

(f) Provided that any number of vessels being towed alongside or pushed in a group shall be lighted as one vessel, except as provided in paragraph (iii)—
(i) a vessel being pushed ahead, not being part of a composite unit, shall exhibit at the forward end, sidelights and a special flashing light;
(ii) a vessel being towed alongside shall exhibit a sternlight and at the forward end, sidelights and a special flashing light; and
(iii) when vessels are towed alongside on both sides of the towing vessels a stern light shall be exhibited on the stern of the outboard vessel on each side of the towing vessel, and a single set of sidelights as far forward and as far outboard as is practicable, and a single special flashing light.

(g) An inconspicuous, partly submerged vessel or object being towed shall exhibit:
(i) if it is less than 25 meters in breadth, one all-round white light at or near each end;
(ii) if it is 25 meters or more in breadth, four all-round white lights to mark its length and breadth;
(iii) if it exceeds 100 meters in length, additional all-round white lights between the lights prescribed in subparagraphs (i) and (ii) so that the distance between the lights shall not exceed 100 meters: *Provided*, That any vessels or objects being towed alongside each other shall be lighted as one vessel or object;
(iv) a diamond shape at or near the aftermost extremity of the last vessel or object being towed; and
(v) the towing vessel may direct a searchlight in the direction of the tow to indicate its presence to an approaching vessel.

[Paragraph (h) is the same as COLREGS Rule 24(h).]

(i) Notwithstanding paragraph (c), on the Western Rivers (except below the Huey P. Long Bridge on the Mississippi River) and on waters specified by the Secretary, a power-driven vessel when pushing ahead or towing alongside, except as paragraph (b) applies, shall exhibit:
(i) sidelights; and
(ii) two towing lights in a vertical line.

(j) Where from any sufficient cause it is impracticable for a vessel not normally engaged in towing operations to display the lights prescribed by paragraph (a), (c) or (i) of this Rule, such vessel shall not be required to exhibit those lights when engaged in towing another vessel in distress or otherwise in need of assistance. All possible measures shall be taken to indicate the nature of the relationship between the towing vessel and the vessel being assisted. The searchlight authorized by Rule 36 may be used to illuminate the tow.

RULE 25

Sailing Vessels Underway and Vessels Under Oars

[Paragraphs (a)-(d) are the same as COLREGS Rule 25(a)-(d).]

(e) A vessel proceeding under sail when also being propelled by machinery shall exhibit forward where it can best be seen a conical shape, apex downward. A vessel of less than 12 meters in length is not required to exhibit this shape, but may do so.

RULE 26

Fishing Vessels

[Rule 26 is substantially the same as COLREGS Rule 26.]

RULE 27

Vessels Not Under Command or Restricted in Their Ability to Maneuver

[Paragraphs (a) and (b) are the same as COLREGS Rule 27(a) and (b), except that "masthead light or lights" in COLREGS Rule 27(b)(iii) reads "masthead lights" in Inland Rule 27(b)(iii).]

(c) A vessel engaged in a towing operation which severely restricts the towing vessel and her tow in their ability to deviate from their course shall, in addition to the lights or shapes prescribed in subparagraphs (b)(i) and (ii) of this Rule, exhibit the lights or shape prescribed in Rule 24.

[Paragraphs (d), (e), (f), (g) and (h) are the same as COLREGS Rule 27(d), (e), (f), (g) and (h), except that "for anchored vessels" is added at the end of Inland Rule 27(d)(iii) and "instead" is added after "the following shall" in Inland Rule 27(e).]

RULE 28

[Reserved]

[As of 1997 there was no Inland Rule 28.]

RULE 29

Pilot Vessels

[Rule 29 is substantially the same as COLREGS Rule 29.]

RULE 30

Anchored Vessels and Vessels Aground

[Paragraphs (a)-(f) are the same as COLREGS Rule 30(a)-(f).]

(g) A vessel of less than 20 meters in length, when at anchor in a special anchorage area designated by the Secretary, shall not be required to exhibit the anchor lights and shapes required by this Rule.

RULE 31

Seaplanes

[Rule 31 is the same as COLREGS Rule 31.]

PART D - SOUND AND LIGHT SIGNALS

RULE 32

Definitions

[Rule 32 is the same as COLREGS Rule 32.]

RULE 33

Equipment for Sound Signals

[Rule 33 is the same as COLREGS Rule 33.]

RULE 34

Maneuvering and Warning Signals

(a) When power-driven vessels are in sight of one another and meeting or crossing at a distance within half a mile of each other, each vessel underway, when maneuvering as authorized or required by these Rules:

(i) shall indicate that maneuver by the following signals on her whistle: one short blast to mean "I intend to leave you on my port side"; two short blasts to mean "I intend to leave you on my starboard side"; and three short blasts to mean "I am operating astern propulsion".

(ii) upon hearing the one or two blast signal of the other shall, if in agreement, sound the same whistle signal and take the steps necessary to effect a safe passing. If, however, from any cause, the vessel doubts the safety of the proposed maneuver, she shall sound the danger signal specified in paragraph (d) of this Rule and each vessel shall take appropriate precautionary action until a safe passing agreement is made.

(b) A vessel may supplement the whistle signals prescribed in paragraph (a) of this Rule by light signals:

(i) These signals shall have the following significance: one flash to mean "I intend to leave you on my port side"; two flashes to mean "I intend to leave you on my starboard side"; three flashes to mean "I am operating astern propulsion";

(ii) The duration of each flash shall be about 1 second; and

(iii) The light used for this signal shall, if fitted, be one all-round white or yellow light, visible at a minimum range of 2 miles, synchronized with the whistle, and shall comply with the provisions of Annex I to these Rules.

(c) When in sight of one another:

(i) a power-driven vessel intending to overtake another power-driven vessel shall indicate her intention by the following signals on her whistle: one short blast to mean "I intend to overtake you on your starboard side"; two short blasts to mean "I intend to overtake you on your port side"; and

(ii) the power-driven vessel about to be overtaken shall, if in agreement, sound a similar sound signal. If in doubt she shall sound the danger signal prescribed in paragraph (d).

[Paragraphs (d), (e) and (f) are the same as COLREGS Rule 34(d), (e) and (f).]

(g) When a power-driven vessel is leaving a dock or berth, she shall sound one prolonged blast.

(h) A vessel that reaches agreement with another vessel in a meeting, crossing, or overtaking situation by using the radiotelephone as prescribed by the Bridge-to-Bridge Radiotelephone Act (85 Stat. 165; 33 U.S.C. 1207), is not obliged to sound the whistle signals prescribed by this Rule, but may do so. If agreement is not reached, then whistle signals shall be exchanged in a timely manner and shall prevail.

RULE 35

Sound Signals in Restricted Visibility

In or near an area of restricted visibility, whether by day or night, the signals prescribed in this Rule shall be used as follows:

[Paragraphs (a) and (b) are the same as COLREGS Rule 35(a) and (b).]

(c) A vessel not under command; a vessel restricted in her ability to maneuver, whether underway or at anchor; a sailing vessel; a vessel engaged in fishing, whether underway or at anchor; and a vessel engaged in towing or pushing another vessel shall, instead of the signals prescribed in paragraphs (a) or (b) of this Rule, sound at intervals of not more than 2 minutes, three blasts in succession; namely, one prolonged followed by two short blasts.

[Paragraphs (d), (e), (f), (g) and (h) are the same as Paragraphs (e) (f), (g), (h) and (i), respectively, of COLREGS Rule 35, except that in Inland Rule 35(g) the reference is to Paragraph (f) of the Rule, and in Inland Rule 35(i) the reference is to Paragraphs (a), (b) and (f) of the Rule.]

(j) The following vessels shall not be required to sound signals as prescribed in paragraph (f) of this Rule when anchored in a special anchorage area designated by the Secretary:

(i) a vessel of less than 20 meters in length; and

(ii) a barge, canal boat, scow, or other nondescript craft.

RULE 36

Signals to Attract Attention

If necessary to attract the attention of another vessel, any vessel may make light or sound signals that cannot be mistaken for any signal authorized elsewhere in these Rules, or may direct the beam of her searchlight in the direction of the danger, in such a way as not to embarrass any vessel.

RULE 37

Distress Signals

When a vessel is in distress and requires assistance she shall use or exhibit the signals described in Annex IV to these Rules.

PART E - EXEMPTIONS

RULE 38

Exemptions

Any vessel or class of vessels, the keel of which is laid or which is at a corresponding stage of construction before December 24, 1980, provided that she complies with the requirements of—

- (a) The Act of June 7, 1897 (30 Stat. 96), as amended (33 U.S.C. 154-232) for vessels navigating the waters subject to that statute;
- (b) Section 4233 of the Revised Statutes (33 U.S.C. 301-356) for vessels navigating the waters subject to that statute;
- (c) The Act of February 8, 1895 (28 Stat. 645), as amended (33 U.S.C. 241-295) for vessels navigating the waters subject to that statute; or
- (d) Sections 3, 4, and 5 of the Act of April 25,1940 (54 Stat.163), as amended (46 U.S.C. 526 b, c, and d) for motorboats navigating the waters subject to that statute; shall be exempted from compliance with the technical Annexes to these Rules as follows:
  - (i) the installation of lights with ranges prescribed in Rule 22, until 4 years after the effective date of these Rules, except that vessels of less than 20 meters in length are permanently exempt;
  - (ii) the installation of lights with color specifications as prescribed in Annex I to these Rules, until 4 years after the effective date of these Rules, except that vessels of less than 20 meters in length are permanently exempt;
  - (iii) the repositioning of lights as a result of conversion to metric units and rounding off measurement figures, are permanently exempt; and
  - (iv) the horizontal repositioning of masthead lights prescribed by Annex I to these Rules:
    - (1) on vessels of less than 150 meters in length, permanent exemption.
    - (2) on vessels of 150 meters or more in length, until 9 years after the effective date of these Rules.
  - (v) the restructuring or repositioning of all lights to meet the prescriptions of Annex I to these Rules, until 9 years after the effective date of these Rules;
  - (vi) power-driven vessels of 12 meters or more but less than 20 meters in length are permanently exempt from the provisions of Rule 23(a)(i) and 23 (a)(iv) provided that, in place of these lights, the vessel exhibits a white light aft visible all round the horizon; and
  - (vii) the requirements for sound signal appliances prescribed in Annex III to these Rules, until 9 years after the effective date of these Rules.

C. ANNEXES TO THE INLAND NAVIGATION RULES

Author's Note: The Annexes to the Inland Navigation Rules were promulgated by the Secretary of Transportation pursuant to Section 3 of the Act embodying the Rules, Pub.L. No. 96-591, § 3, Dec. 24, 1980, 94 Stat. 3433, 33 U.S.C. § 2071, which provides:

> The Secretary may issue regulations necessary to implement and interpret this act. The Secretary shall establish the following technical annexes to these Rules: Annex I, Positioning and Technical Details of Lights and Shapes; Annex II, Additional Signals for Fishing Vessels Fishing in Close Proximity; Annex III, Technical Details of Sound Appliances; and Annex IV, Distress Signals. These annexes shall be as consistent as possible with the respective annexes to the International Regulations. The Secretary may establish other technical annexes, including local pilot rules.

ANNEX I: POSITIONING AND TECHNICAL DETAILS OF LIGHTS AND SHAPES

§ 84.01 Definitions.[1]

[Paragraph (a) is the same as COLREGS Annex I, § 1.]

(b) The term "practical cut-off" means, for vessels 20 meters or more in length, 12.5 percent of the minimum luminous intensity (Table 84.15(b)) corresponding to the greatest range of visibility for which the requirements of Annex I are met.

(c) The term "Rule" or "Rules" means the Inland Navigation Rules contained in Sec. 2 of the Inland Navigational Rules Act of 1980 (Pub. L. 96-591, 94 Stat. 3415, 33 U.S.C. 2001, December 24, 1980) as amended.

§ 84.03 Vertical positioning and spacing of lights.

(a) On a power-driven vessel of 20 meters or more in length the masthead lights shall be placed as follows:

- (1) The forward masthead light, or if only one masthead light is carried, then that light, at a height above the hull of not less than 5 meters, and, if the breadth of the vessel exceeds 5 meters, then at a height above the hull not less than such breadth, so however that the light need not be placed at a greater height above the hull than 8 meters;
- (2) When two masthead lights are carried the after one shall be at least 2 meters vertically higher than the forward one.

[Paragraph (b) is the same as COLREGS Annex I, § 2(b).]

[Paragraph (c) is the same as COLREGS Annex I, § 2(c).]

(d) The masthead light, or the all-round light described in Rule 23(c), of a power-driven vessel of less than 12 meters in length shall be carried at least one meter higher than the sidelights.

(e) One of the two or three masthead lights prescribed for a power-driven vessel when engaged in towing or pushing another vessel shall be placed in the same position as either the forward masthead light or the after masthead

1. Author's Note: References are to sections of Title 33, Ch. 1, Subchapter E, Code of Federal Regulations (CFR), as amended to January 6, 1997.

light, provided that the lowest after masthead light shall be at least 2 meters vertically higher than the highest forward masthead light.

[Paragraph (f)(1) is the same as COLREGS Annex I, § 2(f)(i).]

(2) When it is impracticable to carry the all-round lights prescribed in Rule 27(b)(i) below the masthead lights, they may be carried above the after masthead light(s) or vertically in between the forward masthead light(s) and after masthead light(s), provided that in the latter case the requirement of § 84.05(d) shall be complied with.

(g) The sidelights of a power-driven vessel shall be placed at least one meter lower than the forward masthead light. They shall not be so low as to be interfered with by deck lights.

(h) [Reserved]

[As of 1997 there was no Paragraph (h) of Inland Rules Annex I, § 84.03.]

(i) When the Rules prescribe two or three lights to be carried in a vertical line, they shall be spaced as follows:

(1) On a vessel of 20 meters in length or more such lights shall be spaced not less than 1 meter apart, and the lowest of these lights shall, except where a towing light is required, be placed at a height of not less than 4 meters above the hull;

[Subparagraphs (2) and (3) are the same as COLREGS Annex I, § 2(i)(ii) and (iii).]

[Paragraphs (j) and (k) are the same as COLREGS Annex I, §§ 2(j) and (k).]

§ 84.05 Horizontal positioning and spacing of lights

(a) Except as specified in paragraph (b) of this section, when two masthead lights are prescribed for a power-driven vessel, the horizontal distance between them shall not be less than one quarter of the length of the vessel but need not be more than 50 meters. The forward light shall be placed not more than one half of the length of the vessel from the stem.

(b) On power-driven vessels 50 meters but less than 60 meters in length operated on the Western Rivers, and those waters specified in § 89.25, the horizontal distance between masthead lights shall not be less than 10 meters.

[Paragraph (c) is the same as COLREGS Annex I, § 3(b).]

(d) When the lights prescribed in Rule 27(b)(i) are placed vertically between the forward masthead light(s) and the after masthead light(s) these all-round lights shall be placed at a horizontal distance of not less than 2 meters from the fore and aft centerline of the vessel in the athwartship direction.

§ 84.07 Details of location of direction-indicating lights for fishing vessels, dredgers and vessels engaged in underwater operations

[Section 84.07 is the same as COLREGS Annex I, § 4.]

§ 84.09 Screens

(a) The sidelights of vessels of 20 meters or more in length shall be fitted with mat black inboard screens and meet the requirements of § 84.17. On vessels of less than 20 meters in length, the sidelights, if necessary to meet the requirements of § 84.17, shall be fitted with mat black inboard screens. With a combined lantern, using a single vertical filament and a very narrow division between the green and red sections, external screens need not be fitted.

(b) On power-driven vessels less than 12 meters in length constructed after July 31, 1983, the masthead light, or the all-round light described in Rule 23(c) shall be screened to prevent direct illumination of the vessel forward of the operator's position.

§ 84.11 Shapes

[Section 84.11 is the same as COLREGS Annex I, § 6, except that it omits the specifications of a cylinder.]

§ 84.13 Color specification of lights

(a) The chromaticity of all navigation lights shall conform to the following standards, which lie within the boundaries of the area of the diagram specified for each color by the International Commission on Illumination (CIE), in the "Colors of Light Signals", which is incorporated by reference. It is Publication CIE No. 2.2. (TC-1.6), 1975, and is available from the Illumination Engineering Society, 345 East 47th Street, New York, NY 10017. It is also available for inspection at the Office of the Federal Register, Room 8401, 1100 L Street N.W., Washington, D.C. 20408. This incorporation by reference was approved by the Director of the Federal Register.
[Paragraph (b) is the same as COLREGS Annex I, § 7, second paragraph.]

§ 84.15 Intensity of lights

[Section 84.15 is the same as COLREGS Annex I, § 8, except that it does not include the Note at the end of COLREGS § 8.]

§ 84.17 Horizontal sectors

[Paragraph (a) is the same as COLREGS Annex I, § 9(a).]

(b) All-round lights shall be so located as not to be obscured by masts, topmasts or structures within angular sectors of more than 6 degrees, except anchor lights prescribed in Rule 30, which need not be placed at an impracticable height above the hull, and the all-round white light described in Rule 23(d), which may not be obscured at all.

§ 84.19 Vertical sectors

(a) The vertical sectors of electric lights as fitted, with the exception of lights on sailing vessels underway and on unmanned barges, shall ensure that:
   (1) At least the required minimum intensity is maintained at all angles from 5 degrees above to 5 degrees below the horizontal;
   (2) At least 60 percent of the required minimum intensity is maintained from 7.5 degrees above to 7.5 degrees below the horizontal.

[Paragraph (b) is the same as COLREGS Annex I, § 10(b).]

(c) In the case of unmanned barges the minimum required intensity of electric lights as fitted shall be maintained on the horizontal.

[Paragraph (d) is the same as COLREGS § 10(c).]

§ 84.21 Intensity of non-electric lights

[Section 84.21 is the same as COLREGS Annex I, § 11.]

§ 84.23 Maneuvering light

Notwithstanding the provisions of § 84.03(f), the maneuvering light described in Rule 34(b) shall be placed approximately in the same fore and aft vertical plane as the masthead light or lights and, where practicable, at a minimum height of one-half meter vertically above the forward masthead light, provided that it shall be carried not less than one-half meter vertically above or below the after masthead light. On a vessel where only one masthead light is carried the maneuvering light, if fitted, shall be carried where it can best be seen, not less than one-half meter vertically apart from the masthead light.

§ 84.25 Approval. [Reserved]

[As of 1997 there was no § 84.25 in Annex I to the Inland Rules.]

ANNEX II: ADDITIONAL SIGNALS FOR FISHING VESSELS FISHING IN CLOSE PROXIMITY

§ 85.1. General

The lights mentioned herein shall, if exhibited in pursuance of Rule 26(d), be placed where they can best be seen. They shall be at least 0.9 meter apart but at a lower level than lights prescribed in Rule 26(b)(i) and (c)(i) contained in the Inland Navigational Rules Act of 1980. The lights shall be visible all around the horizon at a distance of at least 1 mile but at a lesser distance than the lights prescribed by these Rules for fishing vessels.

§ 85.3 Signals for trawlers

[Section 85.3 is the same as COLREGS Annex II, § 2.]

§ 85.5 Signals for purse seiners

[Section 85.5 is the same as COLREGS Annex II, § 3.]

ANNEX III: TECHNICAL DETAILS OF SOUND SIGNAL APPLIANCES

Subpart A - Whistles

§ 86.01 Frequencies and range of audibility.

The fundamental frequency of the signal shall lie within the range 70-525 Hz. The range of audibility of the signal from a whistle shall be determined by those frequencies, which may include the fundamental and/or one or more higher frequencies, which lie within the frequency ranges and provide the sound pressure levels specified in § 86.05.

§ 86.03 Limits of fundamental frequencies.

To ensure a wide variety of whistle characteristics, the fundamental frequency of a whistle shall be between the following limits:

(a) 70-200 Hz, for a vessel 200 meters or more in length;

(b) 130-350 Hz, for a vessel 75 meters but less than 200 meters in length;
(c) 250-525 Hz, for a vessel less than 75 meters in length.

§ 86.05 Sound signal intensity and range of audibility.

A whistle on a vessel shall provide, in the direction of the forward axis of the whistle and at a distance of 1 meter from it, a sound pressure level in at least one 1/3-octave band of not less than the appropriate figure given in Table 86.05 within the following frequency ranges (± 1 percent):

(a) 130-1200 Hz, for a vessel 75 meters or more in length;
(b) 250-1600 Hz, for a vessel 20 meters but less than 75 meters in length;
(c) 250-2100 Hz, for a vessel 12 meters but less than 20 meters in length.

Table 86.05

Length of vessel in meters	*Fundamental frequency range (Hz)*	*For measured frequencies (Hz)*	*1/3-octave band level at 1 meter in dB referred to 2×10^{-5} N/m^2*	*Audibility range in nautical miles*
		130-180	145	
200 or more	70-200	180-250	143	2
		250-1200	140	
		130-180	140	
75 but less than 200	130-350	180-250	138	1.5
		250-1200	134	
		250-450	130	
20 but less than 75	250-525	450-800	125	1.0
		800-1600	121	
		250-450	120	
12 but less than 20	250-525	450-800	115	0.5
		800-2100	111	

NOTE: [The Note is the same as the Note following COLREGS Annex III, § 1(c).]

§ 86.07 Directional properties.

The sound pressure level of a directional whistle shall be not more than 4 dB below the sound pressure level specified in § 86.05 in any direction in the horizontal plane within ±45 degrees of the forward axis. The sound pressure level of the whistle at any other direction in the horizontal plane shall not be more than 10 dB less than the sound pressure level specified for the forward axis, so that the range of audibility in any direction will be at least half the range required on the forward axis. The sound pressure level shall be measured in that one-third octave band which determines the audibility range.

§ 86.09 Positioning of whistles.

(a) When a directional whistle is to be used as the only whistle on the vessel and is permanently installed, it shall be installed with its forward axis directed forward.

[Paragraph (b) is the same as the second paragraph of COLREGS Annex III, § 1(e).]

§ 86.11 Fitting of more than one whistle.

If whistles are fitted at a distance apart of more than 100 meters, they shall not be sounded simultaneously.

§ 86.13 Combined whistle systems.

(a) A combined whistle system is a number of whistles (sound emitting sources) operated together. For the purposes of the Rules a combined whistle system is to be regarded as a single whistle.

(b) The whistles of a combined system shall:

(1) Be located at a distance apart of not more than 100 meters,

(2) Be sounded simultaneously,

(3) Each have a fundamental frequency different from those of the others by at least 10 Hz, and

(4) Have a tonal characteristic appropriate for the length of vessel which shall be evidenced by at least two-thirds of the whistles in the combined system having fundamental frequencies falling within the limits prescribed in § 86.03, or if there are only two whistles in the combined system, by the higher fundamental frequency falling within the limits prescribed in § 86.03.

NOTE: If due to the presence of obstructions the sound field of a single whistle or of one of the whistles referred to in § 86.11 is likely to have a zone of greatly reduced signal level, a combined whistle system should be fitted so as to overcome this reduction.

§ 86.15 Towing vessel whistles.

A power-driven vessel normally engaged in pushing ahead or towing alongside may, at all times, use a whistle whose characteristic falls within the limits prescribed by § 86.03 for the longest customary composite length of the vessel and its tow.

Subpart B - Bell or gong

§ 86.21 Intensity of signal.

[Section 86.21 is the same as COLREGS Annex III, § 2(a).]

§ 86.23 Construction.

Bells and gongs shall be made of corrosion-resistant material and designed to give a clear tone. The diameter of the mouth of the bell shall be not less than 300 mm for vessels of more than 20 meters in length, and shall be not less than 200 mm for vessels of 12 to 20 meters in length. The mass of the striker shall be not less than 3 percent of the mass of the bell. The striker shall be capable of manual operation.

NOTE: When practicable, a power-driven bell striker is recommended to ensure constant force.

Subpart C - Approval

§ 86.31 Approval. [Reserved]

[As of 1997 there was no § 86.31 in Annex III to the Inland Rules.]

ANNEX IV: DISTRESS SIGNALS

§ 87.1 Need of assistance.

The following signals, used or exhibited either together or separately, indicate distress and need of assistance:

[Paragraphs (a) to (n) are the same as COLREGS Annex IV, §§ (a) to (n).]

(o) Signals transmitted by radiocommunication systems.

(p) A high intensity white light flashing at regular intervals from 50 to 70 times per minute.

§ 87.3 Exclusive use.

[Section 87.3 is the same as COLREGS Annex IV, § 2.]

§ 87.5 Supplemental signals.

Attention is drawn to the relevant sections of the International Code of Signals, the Merchant Ship Search and Rescue Manual, the International Telecommunication Union Regulations and the following signals:

(a) A piece of orange-colored canvas with either a black square and circle or other appropriate symbol (for identification from the air);

(b) A dye marker.

ANNEX V: PILOT RULES

§ 88.01 Purpose and applicability

This Part applies to all vessels operating on United States inland waters and to United States vessels operating on the Canadian waters of the Great Lakes to the extent there is no conflict with Canadian law.

§ 88.03 Definitions.

The terms used in this part have the same meaning as defined in the Inland Navigational Rules Act of 1980.

§ 88.05 Copy of Rules.

After January 1, 1983, the operator of each self propelled vessel 12 meters or more in length shall carry on board and maintain for ready reference a copy of the Inland Navigation Rules.

§ 88.09 Temporary exemption from light and shape requirements when operating under bridges.

A vessel's navigation lights and shapes may be lowered if necessary to pass under a bridge.

§ 88.11 Law enforcement vessels.

(a) Law enforcement vessels may display a flashing blue light when engaged in direct law enforcement or public service activities. This light must be located so that it does not interfere with the visibility of the vessel's navigation lights.

(b) The blue light described in this section may be displayed by law enforcement vessels of the United States and the States and their political subdivisions.

§ 88.12 Public safety activities.

(a) Vessels engaged in government sanctioned public safety activities, and commercial vessels performing similar functions, may display an alternately flashing red and yellow light signal. This identification light signal must be located so that it does not interfere with the visibility of the vessel's navigation lights. The identification light signal may be used only as an identification signal and conveys no special privilege. Vessels using the identification light signal during public safety activities must abide by the Inland Navigation Rules, and must not presume that the light or the exigency gives them precedence or right of way.

(b) Public safety activities include but are not limited to patrolling marine parades, regattas, or special water celebrations; traffic control; salvage; firefighting; medical assistance; assisting disabled vessels; and search and rescue.

§ 88.13 Lights on barges at bank or dock.

(a) The following barges shall display at night and, if practicable, in periods of restricted visibility the lights described in paragraph (b) of this section:
   (1) Every barge projecting into a buoyed or restricted channel.
   (2) Every barge so moored that it reduces the available navigable width of any channel to less than 80 meters.
   (3) Barges moored in groups more than two barges wide or to a maximum width of over 25 meters.
   (4) Every barge not moored parallel to the bank or dock.

(b) Barges described in paragraph (a) of this section shall carry two unobstructed white lights of an intensity to be visible for at least one mile on a clear dark night, and arranged as follows:
   (1) On a single moored barge, lights shall be placed on the two corners farthest from the bank or dock.
   (2) On barges moored in group formation, a light shall be placed on each of the upstream and downstream ends of the group, on the corners farthest from the bank or dock.
   (3) Any barge in a group, projecting from the main body of the group toward the channel, shall be lighted as a single barge.

(c) Barges moored in any slip or slough which is used primarily for mooring purposes are exempt from the lighting requirements of this section.

(d) Barges moored in well-illuminated areas are exempt from the lighting requirements of this section. These areas are as follows:

Chicago Sanitary Ship Canal

(1) Mile 293.2 to 293.9
(3) Mile 295.2 to 296.1
(5) Mile 297.5 to 297.8
(7) Mile 298 to 298.2
(9) Mile 298.6 to 298.8
(11) Mile 299.3 to 299.4
(13) Mile 299.8 to 300.5
(15) Mile 303 to 303.2
(17) Mile 303.7 to 303.9
(19) Mile 305.7 to 305.8
(21) Mile 310.7 to 310.9
(23) Mile 311 to 311.2
(25) Mile 312.5 to 312.6
(27) Mile 313.8 to 314.2
(29) Mile 314.6
(31) Mile 314.8 to 315.3
(33) Mile 315.7 to 316
(35) Mile 316.8
(37) Mile 316.85 to 317.05
(39) Mile 317.5
(41) Mile 318.4 to 318.9
(43) Mile 318.7 to 318.8
(45) Mile 320 to 320.3
(47) Mile 320.6
(49) Mile 322.3 to 322.4
(51) Mile 322.8
(53) Mile 322.9 to 327.2

Calumet Sag Channel

(61) Mile 316.5

Little Calumet River

(71) Mile 321.2
(73) Mile 322.3

Calumet River

(81) Mile 328.5 to 328.7
(83) Mile 329.2 to 329.4
(85) Mile 330, west bank to 330.2
(87) Mile 331.4 to 331.6
(89) Mile 332.2 to 332.4
(91) Mile 332.6 to 332.8

Cumberland River

(101) Mile 126.8
(103) Mile 191

§ 88.15 Lights on dredge pipelines.

Dredge pipelines that are floating or supported on trestles shall display the following lights at night and in periods of restricted visibility.

(a) One row of yellow lights. The lights must be:
   (1) Flashing 50 to 70 times per minute,
   (2) Visible all around the horizon,
   (3) Visible for at least 2 miles on a clear dark night,
   (4) Not less than 1 and not more than 3.5 meters above the water,
   (5) Approximately equally spaced, and
   (6) Not more than 10 meters apart where the pipeline crosses a navigable channel. Where the pipeline does not cross a navigable channel the lights must be sufficient in number to clearly show the pipeline's length and course.

(b) Two red lights at each end of the pipeline, including the ends in a channel where the pipeline is separated to allow vessels to pass (whether open or closed). The lights must be:

(1) Visible all around the horizon, and
(2) Visible for at least 2 miles on a clear dark night, and
(3) One meter apart in a vertical line with the lower light at the same height above the water as the flashing yellow light.

D. INLAND NAVIGATION RULES: IMPLEMENTING RULES

Subpart A - Certificate of Alternative Compliance

§ 89.1 Definitions

As used in this subpart:

"Inland Rules" refers to the Inland Navigation Rules contained in the Inland Navigational Rules Act of 1980 (Pub.L. 96-591) [33 U.S.C. §§ 2001-2038] and the technical annexes established under that act.

"A vessel of special construction or purpose" means a vessel designed or modified to perform a special function and whose arrangement is thereby made relatively inflexible.

"Interference with the special function of the vessel" occurs when installation or use of light, shapes or sound-signalling apliances under the Inland Rules prevents or significantly hinders the operation in which the vessel is usually engaged.

§ 89.3 General

Vessels of special construction or purpose which cannot fully comply with the light, shape, and sound signal provisions of the Inland Rules without interfering with their special function may instead meet alternative requirements. The Chief of the Marine Safety Division in each Coast Guard District Office makes this determination and requires that alternative compliance be as close as possible with the Inland Rules. These regulations set out the procedure by which a vessel may be certified for alternative compliance. The information collection and recordkeeping requirements in §§ 89.5 and 89.18 have been approved by the Office of Management and Budget under OMB control number 2115-0074.

§ 89.5 Application for a certificate of alternative compliance

(a) The owner, builder, operator, or agent of a vessel of special construction or purpose who believes the vessel cannot fully comply with the Inland Rules light, shape, or sound signal provisions without interference with its special function may apply for a determination that alternative compliance is justified. The application must be in writing, submitted to the Chief of the Marine Safety Division of the Coast Guard District in which the vessel is being built or operated, and include the following information:
  (1) The name, address, and telephone number of the applicant.
  (2) The identification of the vessel by its:
    (i) Official number;
    (ii) Shipyard hull number;
    (iii) Hull identification number; or
    (iv) State number, if the vessel does not have an official number or hull identification number.
  (3) Vessel name and home port, if known.

(4) A description of the vessel's area of operation.
(5) A description of the provision for which the Certificate of Alternative Compliance is sought, including:
(i) The Inland Rules Rule or Annex section number for which the Certificate of Alternative Compliance is sought;
(ii) A description of the special function of the vessel that would be interfered with by full compliance with the provision of that Rule or Annex section; and
(iii) A statement of how full compliance would interfere with the special function of the vessel.
(6) A description of the alternative installation that is in closest possible compliance with the applicable Inland Navigation Rules Rule or Annex section.
(7) A copy of the vessel's plans or an accurate scale drawing that clearly shows
(i) The required installation of the equipment under the Inland Rules.
(ii) The proposed installation of the equipment for which certification is being sought, and
(iii) Any obstructions that may interfere with the equipment installed in:
(A) The required location; and
(B) The proposed location.
(b) The Coast Guard may request from the applicant additional information concerning the application.

§ 89.9 Certificate of alternative compliance: contents

The Chief of the Marine Safety Division issues the Certificate of Alternative Compliance to the vessel based on a determination that it cannot comply fully with Inland Rules light, shape, and sound signal provisions without interference with its special function. This Certificate includes:
(a) Identification of the vessel as supplied in the application under § 89.5(a)(2).
(b) The provision of the Inland Rules for which the Certificate authorizes alternative compliance;
(c) A certification that the vessel is unable to comply fully with the Inland Rules light, shape, and sound signal requirements without interference with its special function;
(d) A statement of why full compliance would interfere with the special function of the vessel;
(e) The required alternative installation;
(f) A statement that the required alternative installation is in the closest possible compliance with the Inland Rules without interfering with the special function of the vessel;
(g) The date of issuance;

(h) A statement that the Certificate of Alternative Compliance terminates when the vessel ceases to be usually engaged in the operation for which the certificate is issued.

§ 89.17 Certificate of alternative compliance: termination

The Certificate of Alternative Compliance terminates if the information supplied under § 89.5(a) or the Certificate issued under § 89.9 is no longer applicable to the vessel.

§ 89.18 Record of certification of vessels of special construction or purpose

(a) Copies of Certificates of Alternative Compliance and documentation concerning Coast Guard vessels are available for inspection at the Chief, Marine Safety and Environmental Protection, U.S. Coast Guard Headquarters, 2100 Second Street S.W., Washington, DC 20593-0001.
(b) The owner or operator of a vessel issued a Certificate shall ensure that the vessel does not operate unless the Certificate of Alternative Compliance or a certified copy of that Certificate is on board the vessel and available for inspection by Coast Guard personnel.

Subpart B - Waters Upon Which Certain Inland Navigation Rules Apply

§ 89.21 Purpose

Inland Navigation Rules 9(a)(ii), 14(d), and 15(b) apply to the Great Lakes, and along with 24(i), apply on the "Western Rivers" as defined in Rule 3(1), and to additional specifically designated waters. The purpose of this Subpart is to specify those additional waters upon which Inland Navigation Rules 9(a)(ii), 14(d), 15(b), and 24(i) apply.

§ 89.23 Definitions

As used in this subpart:

"Inland Rules" refers to the Inland Navigation Rules contained in the Inland Navigational Rules Act of 1980 (Pub.L. 96-591) [33 U.S.C. §§ 2001-2038] and the technical annexes established under that act.

§ 89.25 Waters upon which Inland Rules 9(a)(ii), 14(d), and 15(b) apply

Inland Rules 9(a)(ii), 14(d), and 15(b) apply on the Great Lakes, the Western Rivers, and the following specified waters:

(a) Tennessee-Tombigbee Waterway.
(b) Tombigbee River.
(c) Black Warrior River.
(d) Alabama River.
(e) Coosa River.
(f) Mobile River above the Cochrane Bridge at St. Louis Point.
(g) Flint River.
(h) Chattachoochee River.
(i) The Apalachicola River above its confluence with the Jackson River.

§ 89.27 Waters upon which Inland Rule 24(i) applies

(a) Inland Rule 24(i) applies on the Western Rivers and the specified waters listed in § 89.25(a) through (i).

(b) Inland Rule 24(i) applies on the Gulf Intracoastal Waterway from St. Marks, Florida, to the Rio Grande, Texas, including the Morgan City-Port Allen Alternate Route and the Galveston-Freeport Cutoff, except that a power-driven vessel pushing ahead or towing alongside shall exhibit the light required by Inland Rule 24(c), while transiting within the following areas:

(1) St. Andrews Bay from the Hathaway Fixed Bridge at Mile 284.6 East of Harvey Locks (EHL) to the DuPont Fixed Bridge at Mile 295.4 EHL.

(2) Pensacola Bay, Santa Rosa Sound and Big Lagoon from the Light "10" off of Trout Point at Mile 176.9 EHL to the Pensacola Fixed Bridge at Mile 189.1 EHL.

(3) Mobile Bay and Bon Secour Bay from the Dauphin Island Causeway Fixed Bridge at Mile 127.7 EHL to Little Point Clear at Mile 140 EHL.

(4) Mississippi Sound from Grand Island Waterway Light "1" at Mile 53.8 EHL to Light "40" off the West Point of Dauphin Island at Mile 118.7 EHL.

(5) The Mississippi River at New Orleans, Mississippi River-Gulf Outlet Canal and the Inner Harbor Navigation Canal from the junction of the Harvey Canal and the Algiers Alternate Route at Mile 6.5 West of Harvey Locks (WHL) to the Michoud Canal at Mile 18 EHL.

(6) The Calcasieu River from the Calcasieu Lock at Mile 238.6 WHL to the Ellender Lift Bridge at Mile 243.6 WHL.

(7) The Sabine Neches Canal from Mile 262.5 WHL to Mile 291.5 WHL.

(8) Bolivar Roads from the Bolivar Assembling Basin at Mile 346 WHL to the Galveston Causeway Bridge at Mile 357.3 WHL.

(9) Freeport Harbor from Surfside Beach Fixed Bridge at Mile 393.8 WHL to the Bryan Beach Pontoon Bridge at Mile 397.6 WHL.

(10) Matagorda Ship Channel area of Matagorda Bay from Range "K" Front Light at Mile 368.7 WHL to the Port O'Connor Jetty at Mile 472.2 WHL.

(11) Corpus Christi Bay from Redfish Bay Day Beacon "55" at Mile 537.4 WHL when in the Gulf Intracoastal Waterway main route or from the north end of Lydia Ann Island Mile 531.1A when in the Gulf Intracoastal Waterway Alternate Route to Corpus Christi Bay LT 76 at Mile 543.7 WHL.

(12) Port Isabel and Brownsville Ship Channel south of the Padre Island Causeway Fixed Bridge at Mile 665.1 WHL.

E. INLAND NAVIGATION RULES: INTERPRETATIVE RULES

§ 90.1 Purpose.

(a) This part contains the interpretative rules for the Inland Rules. These interpretative rules are intended as a guide to assist the public and promote compliance with the Inland Rules.

§ 90.3 Pushing vessel and vessel being pushed: Composite unit.

Rule 24(b) of the Inland Rules states that when a pushing vessel and a vessel being pushed ahead are rigidly connected in a composite unit, they are regarded as a power-driven vessel and must exhibit the lights prescribed in Rule 23. A "composite unit" is interpreted to be the combination of a pushing vessel and a vessel being pushed ahead that are rigidly connected by mechanical means so they react to sea and swell as one vessel. Mechanical means does not include lines, wires, hawsers, or chains.

F. VIOLATIONS OF THE INLAND NAVIGATION RULES

Title 33 U.S.C. § 2072 provides:

(a) Liability of operator for civil penalty
Whoever operates a vessel in violation of this chapter, or of any regulation issued thereunder, or in violation of a certificate of alternative compliance issued under Rule 1 is liable to a civil penalty of not more than $5,000 for each violation.

(b) Liability of vessel for civil penalty; seizure of vessel
Every vessel subject to this chapter, other than a public vessel being used for noncommercial purposes, that is operated in violation of this chapter, or of any regulation issued thereunder, or in violation of a certificate of alternative compliance issued under Rule 1 is liable to a civil penalty of not more than $5,000 for each violation, for which penalty the vessel may be seized and proceeded against in the district court of the United States of any district within which the vessel may be found.

(c) Assessment of civil penalty by Secretary; collection
The Secretary may assess any civil penalty authorized by this section. No such penalty may be assessed until the person charged, or the owner of the vessel charged, as appropriate, shall have been given notice of the violation involved and an opportunity for a hearing. For good cause shown, the Secretary may remit, mitigate, or compromise any penalty assessed. Upon the failure of the person charged, or the owner of the vessel charged, to pay an assessed penalty, as it may have been mitigated or compromised, the Secretary may request the Attorney General to commence an action in the appropriate district court of the United States for collection of the penalty as assessed, without regard to the amount involved, together with such other relief as may be appropriate.

(d) Withholding of clearance

(1) If any owner, operator, or individual in charge of a vessel is liable for a penalty under this section, or if reasonable cause exists to believe that the owner, operator, or individual in charge may be subject to a penalty under this section, the Secretary of the Treasury, upon the request of the Secretary, shall with respect to such vessel refuse or revoke any clearance required by section 4197 of the Revised Statutes of the United States (46 App.U.S.C. 91).

(2) Clearance or a permit refused or revoked under this subsection may be granted upon filing of a bond or other surety satisfactory to the Secretary.

APPENDIX 3

STATUTES[1]

A. EXTRACT FROM THE LIMITATION OF LIABILITY ACT (46 U.S.C. Appendix §§ 181-189)

§ 183. Amount of liability

(a) Privity or knowledge of owner; limitation
The liability of the owner of any vessel, whether American or foreign, for any embezzlement, loss, or destruction by any person of any property, goods, or merchandise shipped or put on board of such vessel, or for any loss, damage, or injury by collision, or for any act, matter, or thing, loss, damage, or forfeiture, done, occasioned, or incurred, without the privity or knowledge of such owner or owners, shall not, except in the cases provided for in subsection (b) of this section, exceed the amount or value of the interest of such owner in such vessel, and her freight then pending.

(b) Seagoing vessels; losses not covered in full
In the case of any seagoing vessel, if the amount of the owner's liability as limited under subsection (a) of this section is insufficient to pay all losses in full, and the portion of such amount applicable to the payment of losses in respect of loss of life or bodily injury is less than $420 per ton of such vessel's tonnage, such portion shall be increased to an amount equal to $420 per ton, to be available only for the payment of losses in respect of loss of life or bodily injury. If such portion so increased is insufficient to pay such losses in full they shall be paid therefrom in proportion to their respective amounts.

(c) Tonnage of seagoing vessels
For the purposes of this section the tonnage of a seagoing steam or motor vessel shall be her gross tonnage without deduction on account of engine room, and the tonnage of a seagoing sailing vessel shall be her registered tonnage: Provided, That there shall not be included in such tonnage any space occupied by seamen or apprentices and appropriated to their use.

(d) Loss of life or bodily injury arising on distinct occasions
The owner of any such seagoing vessel shall be liable in respect of loss of life or bodily injury arising on distinct occasions to the same extent as if no other loss of life or bodily injury had arisen.

(e) Privity imputed to owner
In respect of loss of life or bodily injury the privity or knowledge of the master of a seagoing vessel or of the superintendent or managing agent of the

1. As of the end of 1997 Title 46, U.S. Code, was in the process of a revision that may change the numbering of the statutes without changing the content.

owner thereof, at or prior to the commencement of each voyage, shall be deemed conclusively the privity or knowledge of the owner of such vessel.

(f) "Seagoing vessel" defined

As used in subsections (b), (c), (d), and (e) of this section and in section 183b of this title, the term "seagoing vessel" shall not include pleasure yachts, tugs, towboats, towing vessels, tank vessels, fishing vessels or their tenders, self-propelled lighters, nondescript self-propelled vessels, canal boats, scows, car floats, barges, lighters, or nondescript non-self-propelled vessels, even though the same may be seagoing vessels within the meaning of such term as used in section 188 of this title, as amended.

§ 183b. Stipulations limiting time for filing claims and commencing suit

(a) Time periods

It shall be unlawful for the manager, agent, master, or owner of any seagoing vessel (other than tugs, barges, fishing vessels and their tenders) transporting passengers or merchandise or property from or between ports of the United States and foreign ports to provide by rule, contract, regulation, or otherwise a shorter period for giving notice of, or filing claims for loss of life or bodily injury, than six months, and for the institution of suits on such claims, than one year, such period for institution of suits to be computed from the day when the death or injury occurred.

(b) Claims not barred for failure to give notice

Failure to give such notice, where lawfully prescribed in such contract, shall not bar any such claim—

(1) If the owner or master of the vessel or his agent had knowledge of the injury, damage, or loss and the court determines that the owner has not been prejudiced by the failure to give such notice; nor

(2) If the court excuses such failure on the ground that for some satisfactory reason such notice could not be given; nor

(3) Unless objection to such failure is raised by the owner.

(c) Mental incompetents; minors, wrongful death actions

If a person who is entitled to recover on any such claim is mentally incompetent or a minor, or if the action is one for wrongful death, any lawful limitation of time prescribed in such contract shall not be applicable so long as no legal representative has been appointed for such incompetent, minor, or decedent's estate, but shall be applicable from the date of the appointment of such legal representative: *Provided, however,* That such appointment be made within three years after the date of such death or injury. . . .

§ 184. Apportionment of compensation

Whenever any such embezzlement, loss, or destruction is suffered by several freighters or owners of goods, wares, merchandise, or any property whatever, on the same voyage, and the whole value of the vessel, and her freight for the voyage, is not sufficient to make compensation to each of them, they shall receive compensation from the owner of the vessel in proportion to their respective losses; and for that purpose the freighters and owners of the property, and the owner of the vessel, or any of them, may take the appropriate proceedings in any court, for the purpose of apportioning the sum for which the owner of the vessel may be liable among the parties entitled thereto.

§ 185. Petition for limitation of liability; deposit of value of interest in court; transfer of interest to trustee

The vessel owner, within six months after a claimant shall have given to or filed with such owner written notice of claim, may petition a district court of the United States of competent jurisdiction for limitation of liability within the provisions of this chapter and the owner (a) shall deposit with the court, for the benefit of claimants, a sum equal to the amount or value of the interest of such owner in the vessel and freight, or approved security therefor, and in addition such sums, or approved security therefor, as the court may from time to time fix as necessary to carry out the provisions of section 183 of this title, or (b) at his option shall transfer, for the benefit of claimants, to a trustee to be appointed by the court his interest in the vessel and freight, together with such sums or approved security therefor, as the court may from time to time fix as necessary to carry out the provisions of section 183 of this title. Upon compliance with the requirements of this section all claims and proceedings against the owner with respect to the matter in question shall cease.

§ 186. Charterer may be deemed owner

The charterer of any vessel, in case he shall man, victual, and navigate such vessel at his own expense, or by his own procurement, shall be deemed the owner of such vessel within the meaning of the provisions of title 48 of the Revised Statutes relating to the limitation of the liability of the owners of vessels; and such vessel, when so chartered, shall be liable in the same manner as if navigated by the owner thereof.

§ 187. Remedies reserved

Nothing in sections 182, 183, 184, 185, and 186 of this title shall be construed to take away or affect the remedy to which any party may be entitled, against the master, officers, or seamen, for or on account of any embezzlement, injury, loss, or destruction of merchandise, or property, put on board any vessel, or on account of any negligence, fraud, or other malversation of such master, officers, or seamen, respectively, nor to lessen or take away any responsibility to which any master or seaman of any vessel may by law be liable, notwithstanding such master or seaman may be an owner or part owner of the vessel.

§ 188. Limitation of liability of owners applied to all vessels

Except as otherwise specifically provided therein, the provisions of sections 182, 183, 183b–187, and 189 of this title shall apply to all seagoing vessels, and also to all vessels used on lakes or rivers or in inland navigation, including canal boats, barges, and lighters.

B. VESSEL BRIDGE-TO-BRIDGE RADIOTELEPHONE ACT (33 U.S.C. §§ 1201-1208)

§ 1201. Statement of purpose

It is the purpose of this chapter to provide a positive means whereby the operators of approaching vessels can communicate their intentions to one another through voice radio, located convenient to the operator's navigation station. To effectively accomplish this, there is need for a specific frequency or frequencies dedicated to the exchange of navigational information, on navigable waters of the United States.

§ 1202. Definitions

For the purpose of this chapter—

(1) "Secretary" means the Secretary of the Department in which the Coast Guard is operating;
(2) "power-driven vessel" means any vessel propelled by machinery; and
(3) "towing vessel" means any commercial vessel engaged in towing another vessel astern, alongside, or by pushing ahead.

§ 1203. Radiotelephone requirement

(a) Vessel coverage; exchange of navigational information
Except as provided in section 1206 of this title—
  (1) every power-driven vessel of twenty meters or over in length while navigating;
  (2) every vessel of one hundred gross tons as measured under section 14502 of Title 46, United States Code, or an alternative tonnage measured under section 14302 of that title as prescribed by the Secretary under section 14104 of that title, and upward carrying one or more passengers for hire while navigating;
  (3) every towing vessel of twenty-six feet or over in length while navigating; and
  (4) every dredge and floating plant engaged in or near a channel or fairway in operations likely to restrict or affect navigation of other vessels—

shall have a radiotelephone capable of operation from its navigational bridge or, in the case of a dredge, from its main control station and capable of transmitting and receiving on the frequency or frequencies within the 156-162 Mega-Hertz band using the classes of emissions designated by the Federal Communications Commission, after consultation with other cognizant agencies, for the exchange of navigational information.

(b) Vessels upon navigable waters of United States inside high seas lines
The radiotelephone required by subsection (a) of this section shall be carried on board the described vessels, dredges, and floating plants upon the navigable waters of the United States inside the lines established pursuant to section 151 of this title.

§ 1204. Radiotelephone for exclusive use of master, person in charge, or pilot; frequency listening watch; portable radiotelephone equipment

The radiotelephone required by this chapter is for the exclusive use of the master or person in charge of the vessel, or the person designated by the master or person in charge to pilot or direct the movement of the vessel, who shall maintain a listening watch on the designated frequency. Nothing contained herein shall be interpreted as precluding the use of portable radiotelephone equipment to satisfy the requirements of this chapter.

§ 1205. Radiotelephone capability; maintenance; restoration; consequences of loss: navigation of vessel

Whenever radiotelephone capability is required by this chapter, a vessel's radiotelephone equipment shall be maintained in effective operating condition. If the radiotelephone equipment carried aboard a vessel ceases to operate, the master shall exercise due diligence to restore it or cause it to be restored to effective operating condition at the earliest practicable time. The failure of a vessel's radiotelephone equipment shall not, in itself, constitute a violation of this chapter, nor shall it obligate the master of any vessel to moor or anchor his vessel; however, the loss of radiotelephone capability shall be given consideration in the navigation of the vessel.

§ 1206. Exemptions; terms and condition

The Secretary may, if he considers that marine navigational safety will not be adversely affected or where a local communication system fully complies with the intent of this concept but does not conform in detail, issue exemptions from any provisions of this chapter on such terms and conditions as he considers appropriate.

§ 1207. Regulations

(a) Operating and technical conditions and characteristics; frequencies, emission, and power of radiotelephone equipment
The Federal Communications Commission shall, after consultation with other cognizant agencies, prescribe regulations necessary to specify operating and technical conditions and characteristics including frequencies, emission, and power of radiotelephone equipment required under this chapter.

(b) Enforcement
The Secretary shall, subject to the concurrence of the Federal Communications Commission, prescribe regulations for the enforcement of this chapter.

§ 1208. Penalties

(a) Master, person in charge, or pilot subject to penalty
Whoever, being the master or person in charge of a vessel subject to this chapter, fails to enforce or comply with this chapter or the regulations, hereunder; or
Whoever, being designated by the master or person in charge of a vessel subject to this chapter to pilot or direct the movement of the vessel, fails to enforce or comply with this chapter or the regulations hereunder—
Is liable to a civil penalty of not more than $500 to be assessed by the Secretary.

(b) Vessels subject to penalty; jurisdiction
Every vessel navigating in violation of this chapter or the regulations hereunder is liable to a civil penalty of not more than $500 to be assessed by the Secretary for which the vessel may be proceeded against in any district court of the United States having Jurisdiction.

(c) Remission or mitigation

Any penalty assessed under this section may be remitted or mitigated by the Secretary upon such terms as he may deem proper.

C. EXTENSION OF ADMIRALTY JURISDICTION ACT (46 U.S.C. Appendix § 740)

The admiralty and maritime jurisdiction of the United States shall extend to and include all cases of damage or injury, to person or property, caused by a vessel on navigable water, notwithstanding that such damage or injury be done or consummated on land.

In any such case suit may be brought in rem or in personam according to the principles of law and the rules of practice obtaining in cases where the injury or damage has been done and consummated on navigable water: *Provided,* That as to any suit against the United States for damage or injury done or consummated on land by a vessel on navigable waters, the Public Vessels Act [46 App. U.S.C. §§ 781-790] or Suits in Admiralty Act [46 App. U.S.C. §§ 741-752], as appropriate, shall constitute the exclusive remedy for all causes of action arising after June 19, 1948, and for all causes of action where suit has not been hitherto filed under the Federal Tort Claims Act: *Provided further,* That no suit shall be filed against the United States until there shall have expired a period of six months after the claim has been presented in writing to the Federal agency owning or operating the vessel causing the injury or damage.

D. SUITS IN ADMIRALTY ACT (46 U.S.C. Appendix §§ 741-751)

§ 741. Exemption of United States vessels and cargoes from arrest or seizure

No vessel owned by the United States or by any corporation in which the United States or its representatives shall own the entire outstanding capital stock or in the possession of the United States or of such corporation or operated by or for the United States or such corporation, and no cargo owned or possessed by the United States or by such corporation, shall, in view of the provision herein made for a libel in personam, be subject to arrest or seizure by judicial process in the United States or its possessions: *Provided,* That this chapter shall not apply to the Panama Canal Commission.

§ 742. Libel in personam

In cases where if such vessel were privately owned or operated, or if such cargo were privately owned or possessed, or if a private person or property were involved, a proceeding in admiralty could be maintained, any appropriate nonjury proceeding in personam may be brought against the United States or against any corporation mentioned in section 741 of this title. Such suits shall be brought in the district court of the United States for the district in which the parties so suing or any of them, reside or have their principal place of business in the United States, or in which the vessel or cargo charged with liability is found. In case the United States or such corporation shall file a libel in rem or in personam in any district, a cross libel in personam may be filed or a set-off claimed against the United States or such corporation with the same force and effect as if the libel had been filed by a private party. Upon application of either party the cause may, in the discretion of the court, be transferred to any other district court of the United States.

§ 743. Procedure in cases of libel in personam

Such suits shall proceed and shall be heard and determined according to the principles of law and to the rules of practice obtaining in like cases between private parties. A decree against the United States or any corporation mentioned in section 741 of this title may include costs of suit, and when the decree is for a money judgment, interest at the rate of 4 per centum per annum until satisfied, or at any higher rate which shall be stipulated in any contract upon which such decree shall be based. Interest shall run as ordered by the court. Decrees shall be subject to appeal and revision as provided in other cases of admiralty and maritime jurisdiction. If the libelant so elects in his libel, the suit may proceed in accordance with the principles of libels in rem wherever it shall appear that had the vessel or cargo been privately owned and possessed a libel in rem might have been maintained. Election so to proceed shall not preclude the libelant in any proper case from seeking relief in personam in the same suit. Neither the United States nor such corporation shall be required to give any bond or admiralty stipulation on any proceeding brought hereunder.

§ 744. Release of privately owned vessel after seizure

If a privately owned vessel not in the possession of the United States or of a corporation described in section 741 of this title is arrested or attached upon any cause of action arising or alleged to have arisen from previous possession, ownership, or operation of such vessel by the United States or by such corporation, such vessel shall be released without bond or stipulation therefor upon the suggestion by the United States, through its Attorney General or other duly authorized law officer, that it is interested in such cause, desires such release, and assumes the liability for the satisfaction of any decree obtained by the libelant in such cause, and thereafter such cause shall proceed against the United States in accordance with the provisions of this chapter.

§ 745. Causes of action for which suits may be brought; limitations; exceptions; actions which may not be revived; interest on claims

Suits as authorized by this chapter may be brought only within two years after the cause of action arises: *Provided,* That where a remedy is provided by this chapter it shall hereafter be exclusive of any other action by reason of the same subject matter against the agent or employee of the United States or of any incorporated or unincorporated agency thereof whose act or omission gave rise to the claim: *Provided further,* That the limitations contained in this section for the commencement of suits shall not bar any suit against the United States brought hereunder within one year after December 13, 1950, if such suit is based upon a cause of action whereon a prior suit in admiralty or an action at law was timely commenced and was or may hereafter be dismissed solely because improperly brought against any person, partnership, association, or corporation engaged by the United States to manage and conduct the business of a vessel owned or bareboat chartered by the United States or against the master of any such vessel: *And provided further,* That after June 30, 1932, no interest shall be allowed on any claim prior to the time when suit on such claim is brought as authorized by section 742 of this title unless upon a contract expressly stipulating for the payment of interest.

§ 746. Exemptions and limitations of liability

The United States or a corporation described in section 741 of this title shall be entitled to the benefits of all exemptions and of all limitations of liability accorded by law to the owners, charterers, operators, or agents of vessels.

§ 747. Seizures in foreign jurisdictions

If any vessel or cargo within the purview of sections 741 and 744 of this title is arrested, attached, or otherwise seized by process of any court in any country other than the United States, or if any suit is brought therein against the master of any such vessel for any cause of action arising from, or in connection with, the possession, operation, or ownership of any such vessel, or the possession, carriage, or ownership of any such cargo, the Secretary of State of the United States in his discretion, upon the request of the Attorney General of the United States, or any other officer duly authorized by him, may direct the United States consul residing at or nearest the place at which such action may have been commenced to claim such vessel or cargo as immune from such arrest, attachment, or other seizure, and to execute an agreement, undertaking, bond, or stipulation for and on behalf of the United States, or the Maritime Administration, or a corporation described in section 741 as by said court required, for the release of such vessel or cargo, and for the prosecution of any appeal; or may, in the event of such suits against the master of any such vessel, direct said United States consul to enter the appearance of the United States, or of the Maritime Administration, or of such corporation, and to pledge the credit thereof to the payment of any judgment and cost that may be entered in such suit. The Attorney General is vested with power and authority to arrange with any bank, surety company, person, firm, or corporation in the United States, its Territories and possessions, or in any foreign country, to execute any such aforesaid bond or stipulation as surety or stipulator thereon, and to pledge the credit of the United States to the indemnification of such surety or stipulator as may be required to secure the execution of such bond or stipulation. The presentation of a copy of the judgment roll in any such suit, certified by the clerk of the court and authenticated by the certificate and seal of the United States consul claiming such vessel or cargo, or his successor, and by the certificate of the Secretary of State as to the official capacity of such consul, shall be sufficient evidence to the proper accounting officers of the United States, or of the Maritime Administration, or of such corporation, for the allowance and payment of such judgments: *Provided, however,* That nothing in this section shall be held to prejudice or preclude a claim of the immunity of such vessel or cargo from foreign jurisdiction in a proper case.

§ 748. Payment of judgment, award, or settlement

Any final judgment rendered in any suit herein authorized, and any final judgment within the purview of sections 744 and 747 of this title, and any arbitration award or settlement had and agreed to under the provisions of section 749 of this title, shall, upon the presentation of a duly authenticated copy thereof, be paid by the proper accounting officers of the United States out of any appropriation or insurance fund or other fund especially available therefor; otherwise there is appropriated, out of any money in the Treasury of the United States not otherwise appropriated, a sum sufficient to pay any such judgment or award or settlement.

§ 749. Arbitration, compromise, or settlement of claims

The Secretary of any department of the Government of the United States, or the board of trustees of a corporation mentioned in section 741 of this title, are, and each is, authorized to arbitrate, compromise, or settle any claim in which suit will lie under the provisions of sections 742, 744, and 750 of this title.

§ 750. Recovery for salvage services by vessel or crew [Omitted]

§ 751. Disposition of moneys recovered by United States [Omitted]

§ 752. Reports as to awards and settlements [Omitted]

E. PUBLIC VESSELS ACT (46 U.S.C. Appendix §§ 781-790)

§ 781. Libel in admiralty against or impleader of United States

A libel in personam in admiralty may be brought against the United States, or a petition impleading the United States, for damages caused by a public vessel of the United States, and for compensation for towage and salvage services, including contract salvage, rendered to a public vessel of the United States: *Provided,* That the cause of action arose after the 6th day of April, 1920.

§ 782. Venue of suit; application of provisions of chapter 20

Such suit shall be brought in the district court of the United States for the district in which the vessel or cargo charged with creating the liability is found within the United States, or if such vessel or cargo be outside the territorial waters of the United States, then in the district court of the United States for the district in which the parties so suing, or any of them, reside or have an office for the transaction of business in the United States; or in case none of such parties reside or have an office for the transaction of business in the United States, and such vessel or cargo be outside the territorial waters of the United States, then in any district court of the United States. Such suits shall be subject to and proceed in accordance with the provisions of chapter 20 of this title or any amendment thereof, insofar as the same are not inconsistent herewith, except that no interest shall be allowed on any claim up to the time of the rendition of judgment unless upon a contract expressly stipulating for the payment of interest.

§ 783. Cross libel, set-off, or counterclaim

In the event of the United States filing a libel in rem or in personam in admiralty for damages caused by a privately owned vessel, the owner of such vessel, or his successors in interest, may file a cross libel in personam or claim a set-off or counterclaim against the United States in such suit for and on account of any damages arising out of the same subject matter or cause of action: *Provided,* That whenever a cross libel is filed for any cause of action for which the original libel is filed by authority of this chapter, the respondent in the cross libel shall give security in the usual amount and form to respond to the claim set forth in said cross libel unless the court, for cause shown, shall otherwise direct; and all proceedings on the original libel shall be stayed until such security shall be given.

§ 784. Subpoenas to officers or members of crews

No officer or member of the crew of any public vessel of the United States may be subpoenaed in connection with any suit authorized under this chapter without the consent of the Secretary of the department or the head of any independent establishment of the Government having control of the vessel at the time the cause of action arose, or of the master or commanding officer of such vessel at the time of the issuance of such subpoena.

§ 785. Suits by nationals of foreign government

No suit may be brought under this chapter by a national of any foreign government unless it shall appear to the satisfaction of the court in which suit is brought that said government, under similar circumstances, allows nationals of the United States to sue in its courts.

§ 786. Arbitration, compromise, or settlement

The Attorney General of the United States is authorized to arbitrate, compromise, or settle any claim on which a libel or cross libel would lie under the provisions of this chapter, and for which a libel or cross libel has actually been filed.

§ 787. Payment of judgments or settlements

Any final judgment rendered on any libel or cross libel herein authorized, and any settlement had and agreed to under the provisions of section 786 of this title, shall, upon presentation of a duly authenticated copy thereof, be paid by the proper accounting officer of the United States out of any moneys in the Treasury of the United States appropriated therefor by Congress.

§ 788. Lien not created against public vessels

Nothing contained in this chapter shall be construed to recognize the existence of or as creating a lien against any public vessel of the United States.

§ 789. Exemptions and limitations of liability

The United States shall be entitled to the benefits of all exemptions and of all limitations of liability accorded by law to the owners, charterers, operators or agents of vessels.

§ 790. Reports by Attorney General [Omitted]

F. EXTRACT FROM THE RIVERS AND HARBORS APPROPRIATION ACT OF 1899, AS AMENDED (33 U.S.C. §§ 401-418)

§ 409. Obstruction of navigable waters by vessels; floating timber; marking and removal of sunken vessels

It shall not be lawful to tie up or anchor vessels or other craft in navigable channels in such a manner as to prevent or obstruct the passage of other vessels or craft; or to sink, or permit or cause to be sunk, vessels or other craft in navigable channels; or to float loose timber and logs, or to float what is known as sack rafts of timber and logs in streams or channels actually navigated by steamboats in such manner as to obstruct, impede, or endanger navigation. And whenever a vessel, raft, or other craft is wrecked and sunk in a navigable channel, it shall be the duty of the owner, lessee, or operator of such sunken craft to immediately mark it with a buoy or beacon during the day and a lighted lantern at night, and to maintain such marks until the sunken craft is removed or abandoned, and the neglect or failure of the said owner, lessee or operator so to do shall be unlawful; and it shall be the duty of the owner, lessee or operator of such sunken craft to commence the immediate removal of the same, and prosecute such removal diligently, and failure to do so shall be considered as an abandonment of such craft, and subject the same to removal by the United States as provided for in sections 411 to 416, 418, and 502 of this title.

G. EXTRACT FROM THE OIL POLLUTION ACT OF 1990 ("OPA 90") (33 U.S.C. §§ 2701-2805)

§ 2701. Definitions

For the purposes of this Act, the term—

. . .

(32) "responsible party" means the following:

(A) VESSELS. In the case of a vessel, any person owning, operating, or demise chartering the vessel.

. . .

§ 2702. Elements of Liability

(a) IN GENERAL.—Notwithstanding any other provision or rule of law, and subject to the provisions of this chapter, each responsible party for a vessel or a facility from which oil is discharged, or which poses the substantial threat of a discharge of oil, into or upon the navigable waters or adjoining shorelines or the exclusive economic zone is liable for the removal costs and damages specified in subsection (b) that result from such incident.

(b) COVERED REMOVAL COSTS AND DAMAGES.—

(1) REMOVAL COSTS.— The removal costs referred to in subsection (a) are—

(A) all removal costs incurred by the United States, a State, or an Indian tribe under subsection (c), (d), (e), or (*l*) of section 1321 of this title, as amended by this Act, under the Intervention on the High Seas Act (33 U.S.C. 1471 et seq.), or under State law; and

(B) any removal costs incurred by any person for acts taken by the person which are consistent with the National Contingency Plan.

(2) DAMAGES.— The damages referred to in subsection (a) are the following:

(A) NATURAL RESOURCES.— Damages for injury to, destruction of, loss of, or loss of use of, natural resources, including the reasonable costs of assessing the damage, which shall be recoverable by a United States trustee, a State trustee, an Indian tribe trustee, or a foreign trustee.

(B) REAL OR PERSONAL PROPERTY.— Damages for injury to, or economic losses resulting from destruction of, real or personal property, which shall be recoverable by a claimant who owns or leases that property.

(C) SUBSISTENCE USE.— Damages for loss of subsistence use of natural resources, which shall be recoverable by any claimant who so uses natural resources which have been injured, destroyed, or lost, without regard to the ownership or management of the resources.

(D) REVENUES.— Damages equal to the net loss of taxes, royalties, rents, fees, or net profit shares due to the injury, destruction, or loss of real property, personal property, or natural resources, which shall be recoverable by the Government of the United States, a State, or a political subdivision thereof.

(E) PROFITS AND EARNING CAPACITY.— Damages equal to the loss of profits or impairment of earning capacity due to the injury, destruction, or loss of real property, personal property, or natural resources, which shall be recoverable by any claimant.

(F) PUBLIC SERVICES.— Damages for net costs of providing increased or additional public services during or after removal activities, including protection from fire, safety, or health hazards, caused by a discharge of oil, which shall be recoverable by a State, or a political subdivision of a State.

(c) EXCLUDED DISCHARGES.— This title does not apply to any discharge—

(1) permitted by a permit issued under Federal, State, or local law;

(2) from a public vessel; or

(3) from an onshore facility which is subject to the Trans-Alaska Pipeline Authorization Act (43 U.S.C. 1651 et seq.).

(d) LIABILITY OF THIRD PARTIES.—

(1) IN GENERAL.—

(A) THIRD PARTY TREATED AS RESPONSIBLE PARTY.— Except as provided in subparagraph (B), in any case in which a responsible party establishes that a discharge or threat of a discharge and the resulting removal costs and damages were caused solely by an act or omission of one or more third parties described in section 2703(2)(3) of this title (or solely by such an act or omission in combination with an act of God or an act of war), the third party or parties shall be treated as the responsible party or parties for purposes of determining liability under this subchapter.

(B) SUBROGATION OF RESPONSIBLE PARTY.— If the responsible party alleges that the discharge or threat of a discharge was caused solely by an act or omission of a third party, the responsible party—

(i) in accordance with section 2713 of this title, shall pay removal costs and damages to any claimant; and

(ii) shall be entitled by subrogation to all rights of the United States Government and the claimant to recover removal costs or damages from the third party or the Fund paid under this subsection.

(2) LIMITATION APPLIED.—

(A) OWNER OR OPERATOR OF VESSEL OR FACILITY.—If the act or omission of a third party that causes an incident occurs in connection with a vessel or facility owned or operated by the third party, the liability of the third party shall be subject to the limits provided in section 2704 of this title as applied with respect to the vessel or facility.

(B) OTHER CASES.— In any other case, the liability of a third party or parties shall not exceed the limitation which would have been applicable to the responsible party of the vessel or facility from which the discharge actually occurred if the responsible party were liable.

§ 2703. Defenses to Liability

(a) COMPLETE DEFENSES.— A responsible party is not liable for removal costs or damages under section 2702 of this title if the responsible party establishes, by a preponderance of the evidence, that the discharge or substantial threat of a discharge of oil and the resulting damages or removal costs were caused solely by—

(1) an act of God;

(2) an act of war;

(3) an act or omission of a third party, other than an employee or agent of the responsible party or a third party whose act or omission occurs in connection with any contractual relationship with the responsible party (except where the sole contractual arrangement arises in connection with carriage by a common carrier by rail), if the responsible party establishes, by a preponderance of the evidence, that the responsible party—

(A) exercised due care with respect to the oil concerned, taking into consideration the characteristics of the oil and in light of all relevant facts and circumstances; and

(B) took precautions against foreseeable acts or omissions of any such third party and the foreseeable consequences of those acts or omissions; or

(4) any combination of paragraphs (1), (2), and (3).

(b) DEFENSES AS TO PARTICULAR CLAIMANTS.—A responsible party is not liable under section 2702 of this title to a claimant, to the extent that the incident is caused by the gross negligence or willful misconduct of the claimant.

(c) LIMITATION ON COMPLETE DEFENSE.—Subsection (a) does not apply with respect to a responsible party who fails or refuses—

(1) to report the incident as required by law if the responsible party knows or has reason to know of the incident;

(2) to provide all reasonable cooperation and assistance requested by a responsible official in connection with removal activities; or

(3) without sufficient cause, to comply with an order issued under subsection (c) or (e) of section 1321 of this title, as amended by this Act, or the Intervention on the High Seas Act (33 U.S.C. 1471 et seq.).

§ 2704. Limits on Liability

(a) GENERAL RULE.—Except as otherwise provided in this section, the total of the liability of a responsible party under section 2702 of this title and any removal costs incurred by, or on behalf of, the responsible party, with respect to each incident shall not exceed—
  (1) for a tank vessel (except a tank vessel on which the only oil carried as cargo is an animal fat or vegetable oil as those terms are used in section 2720 of this title), the greater of—
    (A) $1,200 per gross ton; or
    (B) (i) in the case of a vessel greater than 3,000 gross tons, $10,000,000; or
      (ii) in the case of a vessel of 3,000 gross tons or less, $2,000,000;
  (2) for any other vessel, $600 per gross ton or $500,000, whichever is greater;
  (3) for an offshore facility except a deepwater port, the total of all removal costs plus $75,000,000; and
  (4) for any onshore facility and a deepwater port, $350,000,000.

(b) DIVISION OF LIABILITY FOR MOBILE OFFSHORE DRILLING UNITS.—
  (1) TREATED FIRST AS TANK VESSEL.— For purposes of determining the responsible party and applying this chapter and except as provided in paragraph (2), a mobile offshore drilling unit which is being used as an offshore facility is deemed to be a tank vessel with respect to the discharge, or the substantial threat of a discharge, of oil on or above the surface of the water.
  (2) TREATED AS FACILITY FOR EXCESS LIABILITY.— To the extent that removal costs and damages from any incident described in paragraph (1) exceed the amount for which a responsible party is liable (as that amount may be limited under subsection [a][1] of this section), the mobile offshore drilling unit is deemed to be an offshore facility. For purposes of applying subsection (a)(3) of this section, the amount specified in that subsection shall be reduced by the amount for which the responsible party is liable under paragraph (1).

(c) EXCEPTIONS.—
  (1) ACTS OF RESPONSIBLE PARTY.— Subsection (a) of this section does not apply if the incident was proximately caused by—
    (A) gross negligence or willful misconduct of, or
    (B) the violation of an applicable Federal safety, construction, or operating regulation by,

  the responsible party, an agent or employee of the responsible party, or a person acting pursuant to a contractual relationship with the responsible party (except where the sole contractual arrangement arises in connection with carriage by a common carrier by rail).
  (2) FAILURE OR REFUSAL OF RESPONSIBLE PARTY.— Subsection (a) of this section does not apply if the responsible party fails or refuses—
    (A) to report the incident as required by law and the responsible party knows or has reason to know of the incident;

(B) to provide all reasonable cooperation and assistance requested by a responsible official in connection with removal activities; or

(C) without sufficient cause, to comply with an order issued under subsection (c) or (e) of section 1321 of this title, as amended by this Act, or the Intervention on the High Seas Act (33 U.S.C. 1471 et seq.).

(3) OCS FACILITY OR VESSEL.— Notwithstanding the limitations established under subsection (a) of this section and the defenses of section 2703 of this title, all removal costs incurred by the United States Government or any State or local official or agency in connection with a discharge or substantial threat of a discharge of oil from any Outer Continental Shelf facility or a vessel carrying oil as cargo from such a facility shall be borne by the owner or operator of such facility or vessel.

. . .

H. OVERVIEW OF COASTAL STATE LAWS ON OIL POLLUTION DAMAGES AND CLEANUP

Alabama: Act Regarding Liability for Persons Responding to Oil Spills, Alabama Code, § 22.22-1 et seq., copying some language of OPA '90 and providing for non-liability for removal costs or damages resulting from actions in the course of rendering care, assistance or advice consistent with the National Contingency Plan or otherwise directed by the Federal On-Scene Coordinator or similar state official, but this non-liability does not apply to responsible parties.

Alaska: Alaska Statutes §§ 46.03.710-850, criminalizes oil pollution, whether reckless or negligent (§ 46.03.759). Civil penalties for discharges of oil (limited to $500,000,000) are provided in a statutory civil action without requiring proof of fault for pollution damages, unlimited in amount (§ 46.03.760). Liability is imposed on the owner; operator; demise charterer; the owner of the oil cargo at the time of loading (where loading occurred within state jurisdiction) and the person causing or permitting the discharge.

California: Cal. Water Code § 13350 and Water, Harbor & Navigation Code § 293 et seq. imposes absolute liability for damages and a comprehensive scheme for regulation of the transport of petroleum, together with the establishment of a compensation fund. Damages include economic loss and damages to natural resources. Under § 294 (g) (l) a-e, the following elements of damage may be proven: a. Injury or harm to real or personal property; b. Business loss, including loss of income; c. Costs of cleanup, removal or treatment of natural gas, oil or drilling waste; d. Cost of wildlife rehabilitation; e(i), Injury to natural resources or wildlife, and loss of use and enjoyment of public beaches, and e(ii), Monitoring cleanup costs.

Liability can be imposed on the owner, operator, lessee or demise charterer of any vessel or marine facility or the person accepting responsibility for the vessel or facility; the owner or transporter of the discharged oil is also liable for the damage. Evidence of financial responsibility up to $1,000,000,000 must be provided by the year 2000. In addition to defenses for war, intentional or criminal acts of third parties, negligence or intentional acts of the claimant, there are defenses for "unanticipated exceptional grave natural disasters (which could not have been avoided with due diligence)," natural seepage not caused by a responsible party, and discharge or leaking of oil from a private pleasure boat.

Connecticut: Conn. Gen. Stat. Ann. Title 22a-Ch. 466K requires the development and implementation of oil spill contingency plans and requires tank ships and tank barges to carry floating boom retention devices. There is strict liability of "any person, firm or corporation which directly or indirectly. . . causes. . . discharge, spillage, uncontrolled loss or seepage of oil" for all containment and removal costs and civil penalties. (Title 22 a §§ 451, 454c, 457 a and b.) The criminal penalty can be up to a $500,000 fine and one year imprisonment; the civil penalty can be up to $500,000 per violation or $30 per gallon spilled.

Delaware: Del. Code Ann. Title 7, § 6201 et seq. provides for joint and several strict liability for all cleanup costs and damages, but the liability is limited to $300 per gross ton up to a maximum of $30 million or $250,000, whichever is greater. Liability is placed on the owner, demise charterer and any person responsible for operating, manning, victualing and supplying the polluting vessel.

Florida: The Pollutant Discharge Prevention and Control Act, Fla. Stat. Ann. § 376.011 et seq. establishes a strict liability for damages, while cleanup costs can be recovered up to $1,200 per gross ton or $10 million, whichever is greater. Civil and criminal penalties may be imposed. The responsible party for an oil spill is any vessel, its agents or servants. Defenses are act of war; act of a state, federal or municipal government, unforeseeable act of God; act or omission of a third party; and a federal or state permit.

Georgia: Ga. Code Ann. § 12-5-20 et seq. Liability is based on negligence or intent in causing or permitting oil to be spilled, discharged or deposited, but the amount of the liability is unlimited for both cleanup and damages.

Hawaii: Rev. Stat. § 342 D-1 et seq. The statute provides that a liable party (any individual, partnership or firm which discharges a pollutant or allows it) is strictly liable for all costs of removal and damages for injury to, destruction of, or loss of natural resources.

Louisiana: Rev. Stat. § 30: 2025, § 30: 2071. The strict liability of any person who discharged or allowed the discharge of oil, together with limitation of liability amounts, have been copied from OPA '90. The Coastal Environment Protection Trust Fund has been established, and the law also provides for civil and criminal penalties.

Maine: Maine Revised Statutes Annotated (M.R.S.A.), Title 38, §§ 541 et seq. The statute provides for removal of prohibited discharges and establishes the Maine Coastal and Inland Surface Oil Clean-up Fund. Those liable include any person, vessel, licensee, agent or servant who permits or suffers an illegal discharge from a vessel. Licensees of marine terminals are liable for all acts and omissions of servants and agents from the time the vessel enters state waters until the vessel leaves state waters, without proof of negligence.

Maryland: Ann. Code, §§ 4-401-411. The person responsible for oil spillage is strictly liable (without limitation of amount) to any other person for any damage to his real or personal property directly caused by the spillage (§ 4-409). The statute provides for the collection of a "compensatory fee" (§ 4-408) from the person responsible for any oil spillage, and establishes the Maryland Oil Disaster Containment, Clean-Up and Contingency Fund (§ 4-411). Liable parties are the vessel owner or operator and the owner of the discharged oil. There are exceptions to criminal responsibility for emergency imperiling life or property, unavoidable accident, collision or stranding, or authorization by permit.

Massachusetts: The Oil and Hazardous Material Release Prevention and Response Act, Mass. G.L.A. Chapter 21 (§ 27) and Chapter 21 E, was influenced by the provisions of CERCLA. The vessel owner, operator, demise charterer, and any person who caused or is legally responsible for the release of oil is liable, without regard to fault, for all costs of assessment, containment and removal, and for injury to and destruction or loss of natural resources, without limitation as to amount, and is liable to any person for damage to his real or personal property. The defenses are act of God, act of war or act of a third party not in contractual relations.

Mississippi: Air and Water Pollution Control Law, Miss. Code Ann. § 49-17-1 et seq. imposes strict liability for cleanup costs and restoration of natural resources on any person who causes pollution of any state waters.

New Hampshire: N.H.R.S.A. Ch. 146A § 1 et seq. Requires restoration of natural resources and imposes strict liability of the operator or other person who directly or indirectly causes a discharge of oil in state waters. The liability is unlimited as to amount, for cleanup and removal costs. Damages to pollution victims may be doubled.

New Jersey: The Spill Compensation and Control Act (N.J. Stat. Ann. Title § 58: Ch. 10-23.11 et seq.) provides for an Environmental Fund to pay for all cleanup and removal costs; the Fund's recovery of damages from responsible parties is without regard to fault, but limited in amount to $150 per gross ton for each vessel. However, any person who has discharged oil (including the owner, operator or demise charterer of the vessel) is strictly liable, jointly and severally, for all cleanup and removal costs.

New York: McKinney's Consol. Laws (Ch. 37) N.Y. Nav. Law § 170 et seq. Strict liability, without regard to fault, is imposed on any person who has discharged petroleum (including a vessel owner, operator or demise charterer) for all cleanup and removal costs and all direct and indirect damages, but is limited to $1,200 per gross ton, unless there is gross negligence or willful misconduct, in which case the owner or operator will be liable for the full amount of cleanup, removal costs and damages. The New York Environmental Protection and Spill Compensation Fund has also been established in this legislation.

North Carolina: N.C. Gen. Stat. § 143-215.75 et seq. The statute establishes strict liability of any person having control over oil, including any person using, transferring, storing or transporting oil immediately prior to discharge (including carriers and bailees). The liability is unlimited in amount and covers all cleanup costs and damages plus civil and criminal penalties.

Oregon: Or. Rev. Stat., Title 36, Chapter 46b et seq. The statute prohibits the entry of oil into state waters, regardless of the cause of the entry or the fault of the person having control over the oil, or regardless whether the entry is the result of intentional or negligent conduct, accident or other cause. The defenses are act of God, act of war or sabotage, negligence of the United States Government or the State of Oregon, an act or omission of a third party, and the express authorization of the Dept. of Environmental Quality or a federal on-scene coordinator to cause the entry. Liability is imposed on any person owning or having any control over any oil or hazardous material spilled or released or threatening to spill or release. It is strict liability for cleanup and damages. An Oil Spill Prevention Fund and an Oil Spillage Control Fund were also established.

Rhode Island: The Environmental Injury Compensation Act (R.I. Gen. Laws § 46-12-1 et seq.) imposes a strict, unlimited liability for cleanup because of violations of rules, and provides for an action for damages caused by negligence, against any person who places a pollutant in a location where it is likely to enter state waters. It exempts those (other than persons responsible for the discharge) who render care, assistance or advice with respect to amelioration of environmental damage.

South Carolina: S.C. Code Ann. § 48-43-10 et seq. The statute imposes strict liability for cleanup costs on any person who directly or indirectly causes a discharge, with defenses similar to those in the 1972 F.W.P.C.A.: acts of God, war or sabotage, negligence of the United States or the state, act or omission of a third party and permitted discharge. Civil and criminal penalties are also imposed.

Texas: The Oil Spill Prevention and Response Act (Vernon Texas Codes Annotated, Water Code § 26.261 et seq.) establishes a Coastal Protection Fund of $50 million for response costs and damages related to unauthorized discharges of oil. The fund is liable for all proven, reasonable response costs, natural resource damages and all other proven damages. The purpose of the legislation is to support and complement OPA '90, and it creates liability of the owner, operator, and demise charterer of a vessel from which a spill emanates, or any other person who causes, suffers, allows, or permits a spill or discharge. The legislation imposes civil penalties of up to $25,000 per day and criminal penalties of $10,000 for each offense, $25,000 for a willful or negligent violation and $50,000 for a repeated willful or negligent violation. The civil penalties may not be assessed if the discharge was promptly reported and there were reasonable cleanup efforts.

Virginia: Va. Code Ann. (State Waters, Ports and Harbors) § 621-44.2 et seq. Strict liability for all cleanup costs, loss of natural resources and damages of pollution victims is imposed, but limited to $500 per gross ton or $10 million, with defenses of acts of God, acts of war or acts or omissions of third parties. Civil and criminal penalties are also imposed.

Washington State: The Oil and Hazardous Substance Spill Prevention and Response Act, Wash. Rev. Code Ann. Ch. 90.48 et seq. requires contingency plans, and imposes strict liability, unlimited in amount, on any person owning oil or having control over oil that enters state waters. Civil and criminal penalties are provided. There are also special regulations for the navigation of Puget Sound and the Strait of Juan de Fuca.

INTERNATIONAL CONVENTIONS

A. EXTRACT FROM ANNEX TO THE SAFETY OF LIFE AT SEA CONVENTION, 1974 (SOLAS 1974)[1]

CHAPTER V - Safety of Navigation

REGULATION 12

Shipborne Navigational Equipment

(a) For the purpose of this Regulation "constructed" in respect of a ship means a stage of construction where:
   (i) the keel is laid; or
   (ii) construction identifiable with a specific ship begins; or
   (iii) assembly of that ship has commenced comprising at least 50 tonnes or 1 per cent of the estimated mass of all structural material, whichever is less.

(b) (i) Ships of 150 tons gross tonnage and upwards shall be fitted with:
      (1) a standard magnetic compass, except as provided in sub-paragraph (iv);
      (2) a steering magnetic compass, unless heading information provided by the standard compass required under (1) is made available and is clearly readable by the helmsman at the main steering position;
      (3) adequate means of communication between the standard compass position and the normal navigation control position to the satisfaction of the Administration; and
      (4) means for taking bearings as nearly as practicable over an arc of the horizon of 360°.
   (ii) Each magnetic compass referred to in sub-paragraph (i) shall be properly adjusted and its table or curve of residual deviations shall be available at all times.
   (iii) A spare magnetic compass, interchangeable with the standard compass, shall be carried, unless the steering compass mentioned in sub-paragraph (i) (2) or a gyro compass is fitted.
   (iv) The Administration, if it considers it unreasonable or unnecessary to require a standard magnetic compass, may exempt individual ships or

1. With amendments to and including Amendment of December 9, 1994, which entered into force July 1, 1996.
The convention is reprinted in full in 6A Benedict, Doc 14-1.

classes of ships from these requirements if the nature of the voyage, the ship's proximity to land or the type of ship does not warrant a standard compass, provided that a suitable steering compass is in all cases carried.

(c) Ships of less than 150 tons gross tonnage shall, as far as the Administration considers it reasonable and practicable, be fitted with a steering compass and have means for taking bearings.

(d) Ships of 500 tons gross tonnage and upwards constructed on or after 1 September 1984 shall be fitted with a gyro compass complying with the following requirements:

(i) the master gyro compass or a gyro repeater shall be clearly readable by the helmsman at the main steering position;

(ii) on ships of 1,600 tons gross tonnage and upwards a gyro repeater or gyro repeaters shall be provided and shall be suitably placed for taking bearings as nearly as practicable over an arc of the horizon of 360°.

(e) Ships of 1,600 tons gross tonnage and upwards, constructed before 1 September 1984 when engaged on international voyages, shall be fitted with a gyro compass complying with the requirements of paragraph (d).

(f) Ships with emergency steering positions shall at least be provided with a telephone or other means of communication for relaying heading information to such positions. In addition, ships of 500 tons gross tonnage and upwards constructed on or after 1 February 1992, shall be provided with arrangements for supplying visual compass readings to the emergency steering position.

(g) Ships of 500 tons gross tonnage and upwards constructed on or after 1 September 1984 and ships of 1,600 tons gross tonnage and upwards constructed before 1 September 1984 shall be fitted with a radar installation. From 1 February 1995, the radar installation shall be capable of operating in the 9 GHz frequency band. In addition, after 1 February 1995, passenger ships irrespective of size and cargo ships of 300 tons gross tonnage and upwards when engaged on international voyages, shall be fitted with a radar installation capable of operating in the 9 GHz frequency band. Passenger ships of less than 500 tons gross tonnage and cargo ships of 300 tons gross tonnage and upwards but less than 500 tons gross tonnage may be exempted from compliance with the requirements of paragraph (r) at the discretion of the Administration, provided that the equipment is fully compatible with the radar transponder for search and rescue.

(h) Ships of 10,000 tons gross tonnage and upwards shall be fitted with two radar installations, each capable of being operated independently of the other. From 1 February 1995, at least one of the radar installations shall be capable of operating in the 9 GHz frequency band.

(i) Facilities for plotting radar readings shall be provided on the navigating bridge of ships required by paragraph (g) or (h) to be fitted with a radar installation. In ships of 1,600 tons gross tonnage and upwards constructed on or after 1 September 1984 the plotting facilities shall be at least as effective as a reflection plotter.

(j) (i) An automatic radar plotting aid shall be fitted on:

(1) ships of 10,000 tons gross tonnage and upwards, constructed on or after 1 September 1984;

(2) tankers constructed before 1 September 1984 as follows:

(aa) if of 40,000 tons gross tonnage and upwards by 1 January 1985;

(bb) if of 10,000 tons gross tonnage and upwards but less than 40,000 tons gross tonnage, by 1 January 1986;

(3) ships constructed before 1 September 1984, that are not tankers, as follows:

(aa) if of 40,000 tons gross tonnage and upwards by 1 September 1986;

(bb) if of 20,000 tons gross tonnage and upwards, but less than 40,000 tons gross tonnage, by 1 September 1987;

(cc) if of 15,000 tons gross tonnage and upwards, but less than 20,000 tons gross tonnage, by 1 September 1988.

(ii) Automatic radar plotting aids fitted prior to 1 September 1984 which do not fully conform to the performance standards adopted by the Organization may, at the discretion of the Administration, be retained until 1 January 1991.

(iii) The Administration may exempt ships from the requirements of this paragraph, in cases where it considers it unreasonable or unnecessary for such equipment to be carried, or when the ships will be taken permanently out of service within two years of the appropriate implementation date.

(k) When engaged on international voyages ships of 1,600 tons gross tonnage and upwards constructed before 25 May 1980 and ships of 500 tons gross tonnage and upwards constructed on or after 25 May 1980 shall be fitted with an echo-sounding device.

(l) When engaged on international voyages ships of 500 tons gross tonnage and upwards constructed on or after 1 September 1984 shall be fitted with a device to indicate speed and distance. Ships required by paragraph (j) to be fitted with an automatic radar plotting aid shall be fitted with a device to indicate speed and distance through the water.

(m) Ships of 1,600 tons gross tonnage and upwards constructed before 1 September 1984 and all ships of 500 tons gross tonnage and upwards constructed on or after 1 September 1984 shall be fitted with indicators showing the rudder angle, the rate of revolution of each propeller and in addition, if fitted with variable pitch propellers or lateral thrust propellers, the pitch and operational mode of such propellers. All these indicators shall be readable from the conning position.

(n) Ships of 100,000 tons gross tonnage and upwards constructed on or after 1 September 1984 shall be fitted with a rate-of-turn indicator.

(o) Except as provided in Regulations I/7(b)(ii), I/8 and I/9, while all reasonable steps shall be taken to maintain the apparatus referred to in paragraphs (d) to (n) in efficient working order, malfunctions of the equipment shall not be considered as making a ship unseaworthy or as a reason for delaying the ship in ports where repair facilities are not readily available.

(p) When engaged on international voyages, ships of 1,600 tons gross tonnage and upward shall be fitted with a radio direction-finding apparatus. The Administration may exempt a ship from this requirement if it considers it unreasonable or unnecessary for such apparatus to be carried or if the ship is provided with other radionavigation equipment suitable for use throughout its intended voyages.

(q) Until 1 February 1999, ships of 1,600 tons gross tonnage and upwards constructed on or after 25 May 1980 and before 1 February 1995, when engaged on international voyages, shall be fitted with radio equipment for homing on the radiotelephone distress frequency.

(r) All equipment fitted in compliance with this Regulation shall be of a type approved by the Administration. Equipment installed on board ships on or after 1 September 1984 shall conform to appropriate performance standards not inferior to those adopted by the Organization. Equipment fitted prior to the adoption of related performance standards may be exempted from full compliance with those standards at the discretion of the Administration, having due regard to the recommended criteria which the Organization might adopt in connection with the standards concerned.

(s) A rigidly connected composite unit of a pushing vessel and associated pushed vessel, when designed as a dedicated and integrated tug and barge combination shall be regarded as a single ship for the purpose of this Regulation.

(t) If the application of the requirements of this Regulation necessitates structural alterations to a ship constructed before 1 September 1984, the Administration may allow extension of the time limit for fitting the required equipment not later than 1 September 1989, taking into account the first scheduled dry-docking of such a ship required by the present Regulations.

(u) Except as provided elsewhere in this Regulation, the Administration may grant to individual ships exemptions of a partial or conditional nature, when any such ship is engaged on a voyage where the maximum distance of the ship from the shore, the length and nature of the voyage, the absence of general navigation hazards, and other conditions affecting safety are such as to render the full application of this Regulation unreasonable or unnecessary. When deciding whether or not to grant exemptions to an individual ship, the Administration shall have regard to the effect that an exemption may have upon the safety of all other ships.

B. INTERNATIONAL CONVENTION FOR THE UNIFICATION OF CERTAIN RULES OF LAW WITH RESPECT TO COLLISIONS BETWEEN VESSELS

(Signed at Brussels, September 23, 1910. Entered into force March 1, 1913. Not in force in the United States as of 1997.)

ARTICLE 1

Where a collision occurs between sea-going vessels or between sea-going vessels and vessels of inland navigation, the compensation due for damages caused to the vessels, or to any things or persons on board thereof, shall be settled in accordance with the following provisions, in whatever waters the collision takes place.

ARTICLE 2

If the collision is accidental, if it is caused by force majeure, or if the cause of the collision is left in doubt, the damages are borne by those who have suffered them.

This provision is applicable notwithstanding the fact that the vessels, or any one of them, may be at anchor (or otherwise made fast) at the time of the casualty.

ARTICLE 3

If the collision is caused by the fault of one of the vessels, liability to make good the damages attaches to the one which has committed the fault.

ARTICLE 4

If two or more vessels are in fault the liability of each vessel is in proportion to the degree of the faults respectively committed. Provided that if, having regard to the circumstances, it is not possible to establish the degree of the respective faults, or if it appears that the faults are equal, the liability is apportioned equally.

The damages caused, either to the vessels or to their cargoes or to the effects or other property of the crews, passengers, or other persons on board, are borne by the vessels in fault in the above proportions, and even to third parties a vessel is not liable for more than such proportion of such damages.

In respect of damages caused by death or personal injuries, the vessels in fault are jointly as well as severally liable to third parties, without prejudice however to the right of the vessel which has paid a larger part than that which, in accordance with the provisions of the first paragraph of this Article, she ought ultimately to bear, to obtain a contribution from the other vessel or vessels in fault.

It is left to the law of each country to determine, as regards such right to obtain contribution, the meaning and effect of any contract or provision of law which limits the liability of the owners of a vessel towards persons on board.

ARTICLE 5

The liability imposed by the preceding Articles attaches in cases where the collision is caused by the fault of a pilot, even when the pilot is carried by compulsion of law.

ARTICLE 6

The right of action for the recovery of damages resulting from a collision is not conditional upon the entering of a protest or the fulfilment of any other special formality.

All legal presumptions of fault in regard to liability for collision are abolished.

ARTICLE 7

Actions for the recovery of damages are barred after an interval of two years from the date of the casualty.

The period within which an action must be instituted for enforcing the right to obtain contribution permitted by paragraph 3 of Article 4, is one year from the date of payment.

The grounds upon which the said periods of limitation may be suspended or interrupted are determined by the law of the court where the case is tried.

The High Contracting Parties reserve to themselves the right to provide, by legislation in their respective countries, that the said periods shall be extended in cases where it has not been possible to arrest the defendant vessel in the territorial waters of the State in which the plaintiff has his domicile or principal place of business.

ARTICLE 8

After a collision, the master of each of the vessels in collision is bound, so far as he can do so without serious danger to his vessel, her crew and her passengers, to render assistance to the other vessel, her crew and her passengers.

He is likewise bound so far as possible to make known to the other vessel the name of his vessel and the port to which she belongs, and also the names of the ports from which she comes and to which she is bound.

A breach of the above provisions does not of itself impose any liability on the owner of a vessel.

ARTICLE 9

The High Contracting Parties whose legislation does not forbid infringements of the preceding Article bind themselves to take or to propose to their respective Legislatures the measures necessary for the prevention of such infringements.

The High Contracting Parties will communicate to one another as soon as possible the laws or regulations which have already been or may be hereafter promulgated in their States for giving effect to the above undertaking.

ARTICLE 10

Without prejudice to any Conventions which may hereafter be made, the provisions of this Convention do not affect in any way the law in force in each country with regard to the limitation of shipowners' liability, nor do they alter the legal obligations arising from contracts of carriage or from any other contracts.

ARTICLE 11

This Convention does not apply to ships of war or to Government ships appropriated exclusively to a public service.

ARTICLE 12

The provisions of this Convention shall be applied as regards all persons interested when all the vessels concerned in any action belong to States of the High Contracting Parties, and in any other cases for which the national laws provide.

Provided always that—

1. As regards persons interested who belong to a non-contracting State, the application of the above provisions may be made by each of the contracting States conditional upon reciprocity.

2. Where all the persons interested belong to the same State as the court trying the case, the provisions of the national law and not of the Convention are applicable.

ARTICLE 13

This Convention extends to the making good of damages which a vessel has caused to another vessel, or to goods or persons on board either vessel, either by the execution or non-execution of a manoeuvre or by the non-observance of the regulations, even if no collision has actually taken place.

[Articles 14-17, and an "Additional Article" are omitted. They concern (1) the right of a Contracting Party to call for a fresh conference, within three years after the Convention enters into force, to consider amendments; (2) accessions; (3) entry into force; (4) denunciations, and (5) the right of a Contracting Party to delay giving effect to Article 5 until the Contracting Parties reach agreement on limitation of liability.]

C. INTERNATIONAL CONVENTION ON CERTAIN RULES CONCERNING CIVIL JURISDICTION IN MATTERS OF COLLISION

(Signed at Brussels, May 10, 1952. Entered into force September 14, 1959. Not in force in the United States as of 1997.)

ARTICLE 1

(1) An action for collision occurring between seagoing vessels, or between seagoing vessels and inland navigation craft, can only be introduced:
  (a) either before the Court where the defendant has his habitual residence or a place of business;
  (b) or before the Court of the place where arrest has been effected of the defendant ship or of any other ship belonging to the defendant which can be lawfully arrested, or where arrest could have been effected and bail or other security has been furnished;
  (c) or before the Court of the place of collision when the collision has occurred within the limits of a port or in inland waters.
(2) It shall be for the plaintiff to decide in which of the Courts referred to in § 1 of this article the action shall be instituted.
(3) A claimant shall not be allowed to bring a further action against the same defendant on the same facts in another jurisdiction, without discontinuing an action already instituted.

ARTICLE 2

The provisions of Article 1 shall not in any way prejudice the right of the parties to bring an action in respect of a collision before a Court they have chosen by agreement or to refer it to arbitration.

ARTICLE 3

(1) Counterclaims arising out of the same collision can be brought before the Court having jurisdiction over the principal action in accordance with the provisions of Article 1.
(2) In the event of there being several claimants, any claimant may bring his action before the Court previously seized of an action against the same party arising out of the same collision.
(3) In the case of a collision or collisions in which two or more vessels are involved nothing in this Convention shall prevent any Court seized of an action by reason of the provisions of this Convention, from exercising jurisdiction under its national laws in further actions arising out of the same incident.

ARTICLE 4

This Convention shall also apply to an action for damage caused by one ship to another or to the property or persons on board such ships through the carrying out of or the omission to carry out a manoeuvre or through non-compliance with regulations even when there has been no actual collision.

ARTICLE 5

Nothing contained in this Convention shall modify the rules of law now or hereafter in force in the various contracting States in regard to collisions involving warships or vessels owned by or in the service of a State.

ARTICLE 6

This Convention does not affect claims arising from contracts of carriage or from any other contracts.

ARTICLE 7

This Convention shall not apply in cases covered by the provisions of the revised Rhine Navigation Convention of October 17, 1868.

ARTICLE 8

The provisions of this Convention shall be applied as regards all persons interested when all the vessels concerned in any action belong to States of the High Contracting Parties.

Provided always that:

(1) As regards persons interested who belong to a non-contracting State, the application of the above provisions may be made by each of the contracting States conditional upon reciprocity,
(2) Where all the persons interested belong to the same State as the court trying the case, the provisions of the national law and not of the Convention are applicable.

ARTICLE 9

The High Contracting Parties undertake to submit to arbitration any disputes between States arising out of the interpretation or application of this Convention, but this shall be without prejudice to the obligations of those High Contracting Parties who have agreed to submit their disputes to the International Court of Justice.

[Articles 10-16, relating to signature, ratification, entry into force, amendments, denunciations, etc., are omitted.]

D. INTERNATIONAL CONVENTION FOR THE UNIFICATION OF CERTAIN RULES RELATING TO PENAL JURISDICTION IN MATTERS OF COLLISION OR OTHER INCIDENTS OF NAVIGATION

(Signed at Brussels, May 10, 1952. Entered into force Nov. 20, 1955. Not in force in the United States as of 1997.)

ARTICLE 1

In the event of a collision or any other incident of navigation concerning a sea-going ship and invoking the penal or disciplinary responsibility of the master or of any other person in the service of the ship, criminal or disciplinary proceedings may be instituted only before the judicial or administrative authorities of the State of which the ship was flying the flag at the time of the collision or other incident of navigation.

ARTICLE 2

In the case provided for in the preceding Article, no arrest or detention of the vessel shall be ordered, even as a measure of investigation, by any authorities other than those whose flag the ship was flying.

ARTICLE 3

Nothing contained in this Convention shall prevent any State from permitting its own authorities, in cases of collision or other incidents of navigation, to take any action in respect of certificates of competence or licences issued by that State or to prosecute its own nationals for offences committed while on board a ship flying the flag of another State.

ARTICLE 4

This Convention does not apply to collisions or other incidents of navigation occurring within the limits of a port or in inland waters.

Furthermore the High Contracting Parties shall be at liberty, at the time of signature, ratification or accession to the Convention, to reserve to themselves the right to take proceedings in respect of offences committed within their own territorial waters.

ARTICLE 5

The High Contracting Parties undertake to submit to arbitration any disputes between States arising out of the interpretation or application of this Convention, but this shall be without prejudice to the obligations of those High Contracting Parties who have agreed to submit their disputes to the International Court of Justice.

[Articles 6-10, relating to ratification, accession, entry into force, etc., are omitted.]

E. INTERNATIONAL CONVENTION ON LIMITATION OF LIABILITY FOR MARITIME CLAIMS

(IMCO No. 77.04.E. Signed at London, November 19, 1976. Entered into force December 1, 1986. Not in force in the United States as of 1997.)

CHAPTER I. THE RIGHT OF LIMITATION

ARTICLE 1

Persons entitled to limit liability

1. Shipowners and salvors, as hereinafter defined, may limit their liability in accordance with the rules of this Convention for claims set out in Article 2.
2. The term "shipowner" shall mean the owner, charterer, manager and operator of a seagoing ship.
3. Salvor shall mean any person rendering services in direct connexion with salvage operations. Salvage operations shall also include operations referred to in Article 2, paragraph 1(d), (e) and (f).
4. If any claims set out in Article 2 are made against any person for whose act, neglect or default the shipowner or salvor is responsible, such person shall be entitled to avail himself of the limitation of liability provided for in this Convention.
5. In this Convention the liability of a shipowner shall include liability in an action brought against the vessel herself.
6. An insurer of liability for claims subject to limitation in accordance with the rules of this Convention shall be entitled to the benefits of this Convention to the same extent as the assured himself.
7. The act of invoking limitation of liability shall not constitute an admission of liability.

ARTICLE 2

Claims subject to limitation

1. Subject to Articles 3 and 4 the following claims, whatever the basis of liability may be, shall be subject to limitation of liability:
   (a) claims in respect of loss of life or personal injury or loss of or damage to property (including damage to harbour works, basins and waterways and aids to navigation), occurring on board or in direct connexion with the operation of the ship or with salvage operations, and consequential loss resulting therefrom;
   (b) claims in respect of loss resulting from delay in the carriage by sea of cargo, passengers or their luggage;

(c) claims in respect of other loss resulting from infringement of rights other than contractual rights, occurring in direct connexion with the operation of the ship or salvage operations;
(d) claims in respect of the raising, removal, destruction or the rendering harmless of a ship which is sunk, wrecked or abandoned, including anything that is or has been on board such ship;
(e) claims in respect of the removal, destruction or the rendering harmless of the cargo of the ship;
(f) claims of a person other than liable in respect of measures taken in order to avert or minimize loss for which the person liable may limit his liability in accordance with this Convention, and further loss caused by such measures.

2. Claims set out in paragraph 1 shall be subject to limitation of liability even if brought by way of recourse or for indemnity under a contract or otherwise. However, claims set out under paragraph 1(d), (e) and (f) shall not be subject to limitation of liability to the extent that they relate to remuneration under a contract with the person liable.

ARTICLE 3

Claims excepted from limitation

The rules of this Convention shall not apply to:
(a) claims for salvage or contribution in general average;
(b) claims for oil pollution damage within the meaning of the International Convention on Civil Liability for Oil Pollution Damage, dated 29 November 1969 or of any amendment or Protocol thereto which is in force;
(c) claims subject to any international convention or national legislation governing or prohibiting limitation of liability for nuclear damage;
(d) claims against the shipowner of a nuclear ship for nuclear damage;
(e) claims by servants of the shipowner or salvor whose duties are connected with the ship or the salvage operations, including claims of their heirs, dependents or other persons entitled to make such claims, if under the law governing the contract of service between the shipowner or salvor and such servants the shipowner or salvor is not entitled to limit his liability in respect of such claims, or if he is by such law only permitted to limit his liability to an amount greater than that provided for in Article 6.

ARTICLE 4

Conduct barring limitation

A person shall not be entitled to limit his liability if it is proved that the loss resulted from his personal act or omission, committed with the intent to cause such loss, or recklessly and with knowledge that such loss would probably result.

ARTICLE 5

Counterclaims

Where a person entitled to limitation of liability under the rules of this Convention has a claim against the claimant arising out of the same occurrence, their respective claims shall be set off against each other and the provisions of this Convention shall only apply to the balance, if any.

CHAPTER II. LIMITS OF LIABILITY

ARTICLE 6

The general limits

1. The limits of liability for claims other than those mentioned in Article 7, arising on any distinct occasion, shall be calculated as follows:
   (a) in respect of claims for loss of life or personal injury,
      (i) 333,000 Units of Account for a ship with a tonnage not exceeding 500 tons,
      (ii) for a ship with a tonnage in excess thereof, the following amount in addition to that mentioned in (i):
      for each ton from 501 to 3,000 tons, 500 Units of Account;
      for each ton from 3,001 to 30,000 tons, 333 Units of Account;
      for each ton from 30,001 to 70,000 tons, 250 Units of Account; and
      for each ton in excess of 70,000 tons, 167 Units of Account.
   (b) in respect of any other claims,
      (i) 167,000 Units of Account for a ship with a tonnage not exceeding 500 tons,
      (ii) for a ship with a tonnage in excess thereof the following amount in addition to that mentioned in (i):
      for each ton from 501 to 30,000 tons, 167 Units of Account;
      for each ton from 30,001 to 70,000 tons, 125 Units of Account;
      and for each ton in excess of 70,000 tons, 83 Units of Account.
2. Where the amount calculated in accordance with paragraph 1(a) is insufficient to pay the claims mentioned therein in full, the amount calculated in accordance with paragraph 1(b) shall be available for payment of the unpaid balance of claims under paragraph 1(a) and such unpaid balance shall rank rateably with claims mentioned under paragraph 1(b).
3. However, without prejudice to the right of claims for loss of life or personal injury according to paragraph 2, a State Party may provide in its national law that claims in respect of damage to harbour works, basins and waterways and aids to navigation shall have such priority over other claims under paragraph 1(b) as is provided by that law.
4. The limits of liability for any salvor not operating from any ship or for any salvor operating solely on the ship to, or in respect of which he is rendering salvage services, shall be calculated according to a tonnage of 1,500 tons.
5. For the purpose of this Convention the ship's tonnage shall be the gross tonnage calculated in accordance with the tonnage measurement rules

contained in Annex 1 of the International Convention on Tonnage Measurement of Ships, 1969.

ARTICLE 7

The limit for passenger claims

1. In respect of claims arising on any distinct occasion for loss of life or personal injury to passengers of a ship, the limit of liability of the shipowner thereof shall be an amount of 46,666 Units of Account multiplied by the number of passengers which the ship is authorized to carry according to the ship's certificate, but not exceeding 25 million Units of Account.
2. For the purpose of this Article "claims for loss of life or personal injury to passengers of a ship" shall mean any such claims brought by or on behalf of any person carried in that ship:
   (a) under a contract of passenger carriage, or
   (b) who, with the consent of the carrier, is accompanying a vehicle or live animals which are covered by a contract for the carriage of goods.

ARTICLE 8

Unit of Account

1. The Unit of Account referred to in Articles 6 and 7 is the Special Drawing Right as defined by the International Monetary Fund. The amounts mentioned in Articles 6 and 7 shall be converted into the national currency of the State in which limitation is sought, according to the value of that currency at the date the limitation fund shall have been constituted, payment is made, or security is given which under the law of that State is equivalent to such payment. The value of a national currency in terms of the Special Drawing Right, of a State Party which is a member of the International Monetary Fund, shall be calculated in accordance with the method of valuation applied by the International Monetary Fund in effect at the date in question for its operations and transactions. The value of a national currency in terms of the Special Drawing Right, of a State Party which is not a member of the International Monetary Fund, shall be calculated in a manner determined by that State Party.
2. Nevertheless, those States which are not members of the International Monetary Fund and whose law does not permit the application of the provisions of paragraph 1 may, at the time of signature without reservation as to ratification, acceptance or approval or at the time of ratification, acceptance, approval or accession or at any time thereafter, declare that the limits of liability provided for in this Convention to be applied in their territories shall be fixed as follows:
   (a) in respect of Article 6, paragraph 1(a) at an amount of:
      (i) 5 million monetary units for a ship with a tonnage not exceeding 500 tons;
      (ii) for a ship with a tonnage in excess thereof, the following amount in addition to that mentioned in (i):
      for each ton from 501 to 3,000 tons, 7,500 monetary units;

for each ton from 3,001 to 30,000 tons, 5,000 monetary units;
for each ton from 30,001 to 70,000 tons, 3,750 monetary units; and
for each ton in excess of 70,000 tons, 2,500 monetary units; and

(b) in respect of Article 6, paragraph 1(b), at an amount of:
   (i) 2.5 million monetary units for a ship with a tonnage not exceeding 500 tons;
   (ii) for a ship with a tonnage in excess thereof, the following amount in addition to that mentioned in (i):
   for each ton from 501 to 30,000 tons, 2,500 monetary units;
   for each ton from 30,001 to 70,000 tons, 1,850 monetary units; and
   for each ton in excess of 70,000 tons, 1,250 monetary units; and

(c) in respect of Article 7, paragraph 1, at an amount of 700,000 monetary units multiplied by the number of passengers which the ship is authorized to carry according to its certificate, but not exceeding 375 million monetary units.

Paragraphs 2 and 3 of Article 6 apply correspondingly to sub-paragraphs (a) and (b) of this paragraph.

3. The monetary unit referred to in paragraph 2 corresponds to sixty-five and a half milligrammes of gold of millesimal fineness nine hundred. The conversion of the amounts referred to in paragraph 2 into the national currency shall be made according to the law of the State concerned.
4. The calculation mentioned in the last sentence of paragraph 1 and the conversion mentioned in paragraph 3 shall be made in such a manner as to express in the national currency of the State Party as far as possible the same real value for the amounts in Article 6 and 7 as is expressed there in units of account. States Parties shall communicate to the depositary the manner of calculation pursuant to paragraph 1, or the result of the conversion in paragraph 3, as the case may be, at the time of the signature without reservation as to ratification, acceptance or approval, or when depositing an instrument referred to in Article 16 and whenever there is a change in either.

ARTICLE 9

Aggregation of claims

1. The limits of liability determined in accordance with Article 6 shall apply to the aggregate of all claims which arise on any distinct occasion:
   (a) against the person or persons mentioned in paragraph 2 of Article 1 and any person for whose act, neglect or default he or they are responsible; or
   (b) against the shipowner of a ship rendering salvage services from that ship and the salvor or salvors operating from such ship and any person for whose act, neglect or default he or they are responsible; or
   (c) against the salvor or salvors who are not operating from a ship or who are operating solely on the ship to, or in respect of which, the salvage

services are rendered and any person for whose act, neglect or default he or they are responsible.

2. The limits of liability determined in accordance with Article 7 shall apply to the aggregate of all claims subject thereto which may arise on any distinct occasion against the person or persons mentioned in paragraph 2 of Article 1 in respect of the ship referred to in Article 7 and any person for whose act, neglect or default he or they are responsible.

ARTICLE 10

Limitation of liability without constitution of a limitation fund

1. Limitation of liability may be invoked notwithstanding that a limitation fund as mentioned in Article 11 has not been constituted. However, a State Party may provide in its national law that, where an action is brought in its Courts to enforce a claim subject to limitation, a person liable may only invoke the right to limit if a limitation fund has been constituted in accordance with the provisions of this Convention or is constituted when the right to limit liability is invoked.
2. If limitation of liability is invoked without the constitution of a limitation fund, the provisions of Article 12 shall apply correspondingly.
3. Questions of procedure arising under the rules of this Article shall be decided in accordance with the national law of the State Party in which action is brought.

CHAPTER III. THE LIMITATION FUND

ARTICLE 11

Constitution of the fund

1. Any person alleged to be liable may constitute a fund with the Court or other competent authority in any State Party in which legal proceedings are instituted in respect of claims subject to limitation. The fund shall be constituted in the sum of such of the amounts set out in Articles 6 and 7 as are applicable to claims for which that person may be liable, together with interest thereon from the date of the occurrence giving rise to the liability until the date of the constitution of the fund. Any fund thus constituted shall be available only for the payment of claims in respect of which limitation of liability can be invoked.
2. A fund may be constituted, either by depositing the sum, or by producing a guarantee acceptable under the legislation of the State Party where the fund is constituted and considered to be adequate by the Court or other competent authority.
3. A fund constituted by one of the persons mentioned in paragraph 1 (a), (b) or (c) or paragraph 2 of Article 9 or his insurer shall be deemed constituted by all persons mentioned in paragraph 1(a), (b) or (c) or paragraph 2, respectively.

ARTICLE 12

Distribution of the fund

1. Subject to the provisions of paragraphs 1, 2 and 3 of Article 6 and of Article 7, the fund shall be distributed among the claimants in proportion to their established claims against the fund.
2. If, before the fund is distributed, the person liable, or his insurer, has settled a claim against the fund such person shall, up to the amount he has paid, acquire by subrogation the rights which the person so compensated would have enjoyed under this Convention.
3. The right of subrogation provided for in paragraph 2 may also be exercised by persons other than those therein mentioned in respect of any amount of compensation which they may have paid, but only to the extent that such subrogation is permitted under the applicable national law.
4. Where the person liable or any other person establishes that he may be compelled to pay, at a later date, in whole or in part any such amount of compensation with regard to which such person would have enjoyed a right of subrogation pursuant to paragraphs 2 and 3 had the compensation been paid before the fund was distributed, the Court or other competent authority of the State where the fund has been constituted may order that a sufficient sum shall be provisionally set aside to enable such person at such later date to enforce his claim against the fund.

ARTICLE 13

Bar to other actions

1. Where a limitation fund has been constituted in accordance with Article 11, any person having made a claim against the fund shall be barred from exercising any right in respect of such claim against any other assets of a person by or on behalf of whom the fund has been constituted.
2. After a limitation fund has been constituted in accordance with Article 11, any ship or other property, belonging to a person on behalf of whom the fund has been constituted, which has been arrested or attached within the jurisdiction of a State Party for a claim which may be raised against the fund, or any security given, may be released by order of the Court or other competent authority of such State. However, such release shall always be ordered if the limitation fund has been constituted:
   (a) at the port where the occurrence took place, or, if it took place out of port, at the first port of call thereafter; or
   (b) at the port of disembarkation in respect of claims for loss of life or personal injury; or
   (c) at the port of discharge in respect of damage to cargo; or
   (d) in the State where the arrest is made.
3. The rules of paragraphs 1 and 2 shall apply only if the claimant may bring a claim against the limitation fund before the Court administering that fund and the fund is actually available and freely transferable in respect of that claim.

ARTICLE 14

Governing Law

Subject to the provisions of this Chapter the rules relating to the constitution and distribution of a limitation fund, and all rules of procedure in connexion therewith, shall be governed by the law of the State Party in which the fund is constituted.

CHAPTER IV. SCOPE OF APPLICATION

ARTICLE 15

1. This Convention shall apply whenever any person referred to in Article 1 seeks to limit his liability before the Court of a State Party or seeks to procure the release of a ship or other property or the discharge of any security given within the jurisdiction of any such State. Nevertheless, each State Party may exclude wholly or partially from the application of this Convention any person referred to in Article 1 who at the time when the rules of this Convention are invoked before the Courts of that State does not have his habitual residence in a State Party or does not have his principal place of business in a State Party or any ship in relation to which the right of limitation is invoked or whose release is sought and which does not at the time specified above fly the flag of a State Party.
2. A State Party may regulate by specific provisions of national law the system of limitation of liability to be applied to vessels which are:
   (a) according to the law of that State, ships intended for navigation on inland waterways;
   (b) ships of less than 300 tons.

   A State Party which makes use of the option provided for in this paragraph shall inform the depositary of the limits of liability adopted in its national legislation or of the fact that there are none.
3. A State Party may regulate by specific provisions of national law the system of limitation of liability to be applied to claims arising in cases in which interests of persons who are nationals of other States Parties are in no way involved.
4. The Courts of a State Party shall not apply this Convention to ships constructed for, or adapted to, and engaged in, drilling:
   (a) when that State has established under its national legislation a higher limit of liability than that otherwise provided for in Article 6; or
   (b) when that State has become party to an international convention regulating the system of liability in respect of such ships.

   In a case to which sub-paragraph (a) applies that State Party shall inform the depositary accordingly.
5. This Convention shall not apply to:
   (a) air-cushion vehicles;
   (b) floating platforms constructed for the purpose of exploring or exploiting the natural resources of the sea-bed or the subsoil thereof.

CHAPTER V. FINAL CLAUSES

[ARTICLE 16 Omitted]

ARTICLE 17

Entry into force

[PARAGRAPHS 1, 2 AND 3 Omitted]

4. In respect of the relations between States which ratify, accept, or approve this Convention or accede to it, this Convention shall replace and abrogate the International Convention relating to the Limitation of the Liability of Owners of Sea-going Ships, done at Brussels on 10 October 1957, and the International Convention for the Unification of Certain Rules relating to the Limitation of Liability of the Owners of Sea-going Vessels, signed at Brussels on 25 August 1924.

[ARTICLES 18–23 Omitted]

Signatories: Denmark, Finland, France, Federal Republic of Germany, Norway, Spain, Sweden and the United Kingdom.

For a list of States ratifying or adhering to the Convention, together with the texts of the declarations and reservations of Argentina, Belgium, France, Japan, the former German Democratic Republic, the former Federal Republic of Germany, The Netherlands, Norway, Poland, Sweden, Switzerland and the United Kingdom, see 6 Benedict 5-44.

F. PROTOCOL OF 1996 TO AMEND THE CONVENTION ON LIMITATION OF LIABILITY FOR MARITIME CLAIMS, 1976

(Signed at London, May 2, 1996. Not yet in force as of late 1997.)

THE PARTIES TO THE PRESENT PROTOCOL,

CONSIDERING that it is desirable to amend the Convention on Limitation of Liability for Maritime Claims, done at London on 19 November 1976, to provide for enhanced compensation and to establish a simplified procedure for updating the limitation amounts,

HAVE AGREED as follows:

ARTICLE 1

For the purposes of this Protocol:

1. "Convention" means the Convention on Limitation of Liability for Maritime Claims, 1976.
2. "Organization" means the International Maritime Organization.
3. "Secretary-General" means the Secretary-General of the Organization.

ARTICLE 2

Article 3, subparagraph (a) of the Convention is replaced by the following text:

(a) claims for salvage, including, if applicable, any claim for special compensation under Article 14 of the International Convention on Salvage 1989, as amended, or contribution in general average;

ARTICLE 3

Article 6, paragraph 1 of the Convention is replaced by the following text:

1. The limits of liability for claims other than those mentioned in Article 7, arising on any distinct occasion, shall be calculated as follows:
   (a) in respect of claims for loss of life or personal injury,
      (i) 2 million Units of Account for a ship with a tonnage not exceeding 2,000 tons,
      (ii) for a ship with a tonnage in excess thereof the following amount in addition to that mentioned in (i):
      for each ton from 2,001 to 30,000 tons, 800 Units of Account;
      for each ton from 30,001 to 70,000 tons, 600 Units of Account; and
      for each ton in excess of 70,000 tons, 400 Units of Account,
   (b) in respect of any other claims,
      (i) 1 million Units of Account for a ship with a tonnage not exceeding 2,000 tons,
      (ii) for a ship with a tonnage in excess thereof the following amount in addition to that mentioned in (i):
      for each ton from 2,001 to 30,000 tons, 400 Units of Account;
      for each ton from 30,001 to 70,000 tons, 300 Units of Account; and
      for each ton in excess of 70,000 tons, 200 Units of Account.

ARTICLE 4

Article 7, paragraph 1 of the Convention is replaced by the following text:

1. In respect of claims arising on any distinct occasion for loss of life or personal injury to passengers of a ship, the limit of liability of the shipowner thereof shall be an amount of 175,000 Units of Account multiplied by the number of passengers which the ship is authorized to carry according to the ship's certificate.

ARTICLE 5

Article 8, paragraph 2 of the Convention is replaced by the following text:

2. Nevertheless, those States which are not members of the International Monetary Fund and whose law does not permit the application of the provisions of paragraph 1 may, at the time of signature without reservation as to ratification, acceptance or approval or at the time of ratification, acceptance, approval or accession or at any time thereafter, declare that the limits of liability provided for in this Convention to be applied in their territories shall be fixed as follows:
   (a) in respect of Article 6, paragraph 1(a), at an amount of:

(i) 30 million monetary units for a ship with a tonnage not exceeding 2,000 tons;

(ii) for a ship with a tonnage in excess thereof the following amount in addition to that mentioned in (i):
for each ton from 2,001 to 30,000 tons, 12,000 monetary units;
for each ton from 30,001 to 70,000 tons, 9,000 monetary units; and
for each ton in excess of 70,000 tons, 6,000 monetary units; and

(b) in respect of Article 6, paragraph 1(b), at an amount of:

(i) 15 million monetary units for a ship with a tonnage not exceeding 2,000 tons;

(ii) for a ship with a tonnage in excess thereof the following amount in addition to that mentioned in (i):
for each ton from 2,001 to 30,000 tons, 6,000 monetary units;
for each ton from 30,001 to 70,000 tons, 4,500 monetary units; and
for each ton in excess of 70,000 tons, 3,000 monetary units; and

(c) in respect of Article 7, paragraph 1, at an amount of 2,625,000 monetary units multiplied by the number of passengers which the ship is authorized to carry according to its certificate.

Paragraphs 2 and 3 of Article 6 apply correspondingly to subparagraphs (a) and (b) of this paragraph.

ARTICLE 6

The following text is added as paragraph 3bis in Article 15 of the Convention:

3bis. Notwithstanding the limit of liability prescribed in paragraph 1 of Article 7, a State Party may regulate by specific provisions of national law the system of liability to be applied to claims for loss of life or personal injury to passengers of a ship, provided that the limit of liability is not lower than that prescribed in paragraph 1 of Article 7. A State Party which makes use of the option provided for in this paragraph shall inform the Secretary-General of the limits of liability adopted or of the fact that there are none.

ARTICLE 7

Article 18, paragraph 1 of the Convention is replaced by the following text:

1. Any State may, at the time of signature, ratification, acceptance, approval or accession, or at any time thereafter, reserve the right:
   (a) to exclude the application of Article 2, paragraphs 1(d) and (e);
   (b) to exclude claims for damage within the meaning of the International Convention on Liability and Compensation for Damage in Connection with the Carriage of Hazardous and Noxious Substances by Sea, 1996 or of any amendment or protocol thereto.

   No other reservations shall be admissible to the substantive provisions of this Convention.

ARTICLE 8

Amendment of limits

1. Upon the request of at least one half but in no case less than six, of the States Parties to this Protocol, any proposal to amend the limits specified in Article 6, paragraph 1, Article 7, paragraph 1 and Article 8, paragraph 2 of the Convention as amended by this Protocol shall be circulated by the Secretary-General to all Members of the Organization and to all Contracting States.
2. Any amendment proposed and circulated as above shall be submitted to the Legal Committee of the Organization (the Legal Committee) for consideration at a date at least six months after the date of its circulation.
3. All Contracting States to the Convention as amended by this Protocol, whether or not Members of the Organization, shall be entitled to participate in the proceedings of the Legal Committee for the consideration and adoption of amendments.
4. Amendments shall be adopted by a two-thirds majority of the Contracting States to the Convention as amended by this Protocol present and voting in the Legal Committee expanded as provided for in paragraph 3 on condition that at least one half of the Contracting States to the Convention as amended by this Protocol shall be present at the time of voting.
5. When acting on a proposal to amend the limits, the Legal Committee shall take into account the experience of incidents and, in particular, the amount of damage resulting therefrom, changes in the monetary values and the effect of the proposed amendment on the cost of insurance.
6. (a) No amendment of the limits under this Article may be considered less than five years from the date on which this Protocol was opened for signature nor less than five years from the date of entry into force of a previous amendment under this Article.
   (b) No limit may be increased so as to exceed an amount which corresponds to the limit laid down in the Convention as amended by this Protocol increased by six per cent per year calculated on a compound basis from the date on which this Protocol was opened for signature.
   (c) No limit may be increased so as to exceed an amount which corresponds to the limit laid down in the Convention as amended by this Protocol multiplied by three.
7. Any amendment adopted in accordance with paragraph 4 shall be notified by the Organization to all Contracting States. The amendment shall be deemed to have been accepted at the end of a period of eighteen months after the date of notification, unless within that period not less than one-fourth of the States that were Contracting States at the time of the adoption of the amendment have communicated to the Secretary-General that they do not accept the amendment, in which case the amendment is rejected and shall have no effect.
8. An amendment deemed to have been accepted in accordance with paragraph 7 shall enter into force eighteen months after its acceptance.
9. All Contracting States shall be bound by the amendment, unless they denounce this Protocol in accordance with paragraphs 1 and 2 of Article 12 at

least six months before the amendment enters into force. Such denunciation shall take effect when the amendment enters into force.

10. When an amendment has been adopted but the eighteen-month period for its acceptance has not yet expired, a State which becomes a Contracting State during that period shall be bound by the amendment if it enters into force. A State which becomes a Contracting State after that period shall be bound by an amendment which has been accepted in accordance with paragraph 7. In the cases referred to in this paragraph, a State becomes bound by an amendment when that amendment enters into force, or when this Protocol enters into force for that State, if later.

ARTICLE 9

The Convention and this Protocol shall, as between the Parties to this Protocol, be read and interpreted together as one single instrument.

2. A State which is Party to this Protocol but not a Party to the Convention shall be bound by the provisions of the Convention as amended by this Protocol in relation to other States Parties hereto, but shall not be bound by the provisions of the Convention in relation to States Parties only to the Convention.
3. The Convention as amended by this Protocol shall apply only to claims arising out of occurrences which take place after the entry into force for each State of this Protocol.
4. Nothing in this Protocol shall affect the obligations of a State which is a Party both to the Convention and to this Protocol with respect to a State which is a Party to the Convention but not a Party to this Protocol.

FINAL CLAUSES

[ARTICLE 10 Omitted]

ARTICLE 11

Entry into force

1. This Protocol shall enter into force ninety days following the date on which ten States have expressed their consent to be bound by it.
2. For any State which expresses its consent to be bound by this Protocol after the conditions in paragraph 1 for entry into force have been met, this Protocol shall enter into force ninety days following the date of expression of such consent.

[ARTICLES 12–15 Omitted]

G. EXTRACT FROM THE INTERNATIONAL CONVENTION RELATING TO THE ARREST OF SEA-GOING SHIPS, 1952

([439 UNTS 193] Signed at Brussels, May 10, 1952. Entered into force Feb. 24, 1956. Not in force in the United States as of 1997.)

ARTICLE 1

In this Convention the following words shall have the meanings hereby assigned to them:

(1) "Maritime Claim" means a claim arising out of one or more of the following:
- (a) damage caused by any ship either in collision or otherwise;
- (b) loss of life or personal injury caused by any ship or occurring in connexion with the operation of any ship;
- (c) salvage;
- (d) agreement relating to the use or hire of any ship whether by charterparty or otherwise;
- (e) agreement relating to the carriage of goods in any ship whether by charterparty or otherwise;
- (f) loss of or damage to goods including baggage carried in any ship;
- (g) general average;
- (h) bottomry;
- (i) towage;
- (j) pilotage;
- (k) goods or materials wherever supplied to a ship for her operation or maintenance;
- (l) construction, repair or equipment of any ship or dock charges and dues;
- (m) wages of Masters, Officers, or crew;
- (n) Master's disbursements, including disbursements made by shippers, charterers or agent on behalf of a ship or her owner;
- (o) disputes as to the title to or ownership of any ship;
- (p) disputes between co-owners of any ship as to the ownership, possession, employment, or earnings of that ship;
- (q) the mortgage or hypothecation of any ship.

(2) "Arrest" means the detention of a ship by judicial process to secure a maritime claim, but does not include the seizure of a ship in execution or satisfaction of a judgment.

(3) "Person" includes individuals, partnerships and bodies corporate, Governments, their Departments, and Public Authorities.

(4) "Claimant" means a person who alleges that a maritime claim exists in his favour.

ARTICLE 2

A ship flying the flag of one of the Contracting States may be arrested in the jurisdiction of any of the Contracting States in respect of any maritime claim, but in respect of no other claim; but nothing in this Convention shall be deemed to extend or restrict any right or powers vested in any governments or their departments, public authorities, or dock or harbour authorities under their existing domestic laws or regulations to arrest, detain or otherwise prevent the sailing of vessels within their jurisdiction.

ARTICLE 3

(1) Subject to the provisions of para. (4) of this article and of article 10, a claimant may arrest either the particular ship in respect of which the maritime claim arose, or any other ship which is owned by the person who was, at the time when the maritime claim arose, the owner of the particular ship, even though the ship arrested be ready to sail; but no ship, other than the particular ship in respect of which the claim arose, may be arrested in respect of any of the maritime claims enumerated in article 1, (o), (p) or (q).

(2) Ships shall be deemed to be in the same ownership when all the shares therein are owned by the same person or persons.

(3) A ship shall not be arrested, nor shall bail or other security be given more than once in any one or more of the jurisdictions of any of the Contracting States in respect of the same maritime claim by the same claimant: and, if a ship has been arrested in any of such jurisdictions, or bail or other security has been given in such jurisdiction either to release the ship or to avoid a threatened arrest, any subsequent arrest of the ship or of any ship in the same ownership by the same claimant for the maritime claim shall be set aside, and the ship released by the Court or other appropriate judicial authority of that State, unless the claimant can satisfy the Court or other appropriate judicial authority that the bail or other security had been finally released before the subsequent arrest or that there is other good cause for maintaining that arrest.

(4) When in the case of a charter by demise of a ship the charterer and not the registered owner is liable in respect of a maritime claim relating to that ship, the claimant may arrest such ship or any other ship in the ownership of the charterer by demise, subject to the provisions of this Convention, but no other ship in the ownership of the registered owner shall be liable to arrest in respect of such maritime claim. The provisions of this paragraph shall apply to any case in which a person other than the registered owner of a ship is liable in respect of a maritime claim relating to that ship.

ARTICLE 4

A ship may only be arrested under the authority of a Court or of the appropriate judicial authority of the contracting State in which the arrest is made.

ARTICLE 5

The Court or other appropriate judicial authority within whose jurisdiction the ship has been arrested shall permit the release of the ship upon sufficient bail or other security being furnished, save in cases in which a ship has been arrested in respect of any of the maritime claims enumerated in article 1, (o) and (p). In such cases the Court or other appropriate judicial authority may permit the person in possession of the ship to continue trading the ship, upon such person furnishing sufficient bail or other security, or may otherwise deal with the operation of the ship during the period of the arrest.

In default of agreement between the parties as to the sufficiency of the bail or other security, the Court or other appropriate judicial authority shall determine the nature and amount thereof.

The request to release the ship against such security shall not be construed as an acknowledgment of liability or as a waiver of the benefit of the legal limitations of liability of the owner of the ship.

ARTICLE 6

All questions whether in any case the claimant is liable in damages for the arrest of a ship or for the costs of the bail or other security furnished to release or prevent the arrest of a ship, shall be determined by the law of the Contracting State in whose jurisdiction the arrest was made or applied for.

The rules of procedure relating to the arrest of a ship, to the application for obtaining the authority referred to in Article 4, and to all matters of procedure which the arrest may entail, shall be governed by the law of the Contracting State in which the arrest was made or applied for.

ARTICLE 7

(1) The Courts of the country in which the arrest was made shall have jurisdiction to determine the case upon its merits if the domestic law of the country in which the arrest is made gives jurisdiction to such Courts, or in any of the following cases namely:
   (a) if the claimant has his habitual residence or principal place of business in the country in which the arrest was made;
   (b) if the claim arose in the country in which the arrest was made;
   (c) if the claim concerns the voyage of the ship during which the arrest was made;
   (d) if the claim arose out of a collision or in circumstances covered by article 13 of the International Convention for the unification of certain rules of law with respect to collisions between vessels, signed at Brussels on 23rd September 1910;
   (e) if the claim is for salvage;
   (f) if the claim is upon a mortgage or hypothecation of the ship arrested.

(2) If the Court within whose jurisdiction the ship was arrested has not jurisdiction to decide upon the merits, the bail or other security given in accordance with article 5 to procure the release of the ship shall specifically provide that it is given as security for the satisfaction of any judgment which may eventually be pronounced by a Court having jurisdiction so to decide; and the Court or other appropriate judicial authority of the country in which the claimant shall bring an action before a Court having such jurisdiction.

(3) If the parties have agreed to submit the dispute to the jurisdiction of a particular Court other than that within whose jurisdiction the arrest was made or to arbitration, the Court or other appropriate judicial authority within whose jurisdiction the arrest was made may fix the time within which the claimant shall bring proceedings.

(4) If, in any of the cases mentioned in the two preceding paragraphs, the action or proceeding is not brought within the time so fixed, the defendant may apply for the release of the ship or of the bail or other security.

(5) This article shall not apply in cases covered by the provisions of the revised Rhine Navigation Convention of 17 October 1868.

ARTICLE 8

(1) The provisions of this Convention shall apply to any vessel flying the flag of a Contracting State in the jurisdiction of any Contracting State.

(2) A ship flying the flag of a non-Contracting State may be arrested in the jurisdiction of any Contracting State in respect of any of the maritime claims enumerated in article 1 or of any other claim for which the law of the Contracting State permits arrest.

(3) Nevertheless any Contracting State shall be entitled wholly or partly to exclude from the benefits of this convention any government of a non-Contracting State or any person who has not, at the time of the arrest, his habitual residence or principal place of business in one of the Contracting States.

(4) Nothing in this Convention shall modify or affect the rules of law in force in the respective Contracting States relating to the arrest of any ship within the jurisdiction of the State of her flag by a person who has his habitual residence or principal place of business in that State.

(5) When a maritime claim is asserted by a third party other than the original claimant, whether by subrogation, assignment or otherwise, such third party shall, for the purpose of this Convention, be deemed to have the same habitual residence or principal place of business as the original claimant.

ARTICLE 9

Nothing in this Convention shall be construed as creating a right of action, which, apart from the provisions of this Convention, would not arise under the law applied by the Court which was seized of the case, nor as creating any maritime liens which do not exist under such law or under the Convention on maritime mortgages and liens, if the latter is applicable.

ARTICLE 10

The High Contracting Parties may at the time of signature, deposit or ratification or accession, reserve:

(a) the right not to apply this Convention to the arrest of a ship for any of the claims enumerated in paragraphs (o) and (p) of article 1, but to apply their domestic laws to such claims;

(b) the right not to apply the first paragraph of article 3 to the arrest of a ship within their jurisdiction for claims set out in article 1 paragraph (q).

[ARTICLES 11 and 12 Omitted]

H: EXTRACTS FROM THE CONVENTION ON STANDARDS OF TRAINING, CERTIFICATION AND WATCHKEEPING FOR SEAFARERS (STCW)

Authors' Note: The International Convention on Standards of Training, Certification and Watchkeeping for Seafarers (STCW) was prepared by IMCO (predecessor of I.M.O.) at a diplomatic conference in 1978. The United States and 104 other nations have ratified or adhered to the Convention. Operational requirements are set forth in six sets of Regulations in the Annex to the Convention. These Regulations provide international standards for training and certificating masters, chief mates, engineering officers, radio officers and officers in charge of a watch. In addition, there are Regulations on Deck Department watchkeeping, Engineering Department watchkeeping, and Radio Department watchkeeping, as well as special requirements for tankers and emergency, safety, medical care and survival functions.

Article XII of the Convention provides a swift and easy process for amending the Convention and Annex through tacit consent, whereby amendments adopted by a two-thirds majority in the I.M.O. Maritime Safety Committee or a two-thirds majority of the delegates to a diplomatic conference may prepare amendments that will be deemed accepted two years after the date on which they are communicated to the State Parties, unless more than one third of the Parties (whose combined gross tonnage is not less than fifty percent of world tonnage of ships of more than 100 gross registered tons) object to the amendments. In the absence of objection, the amendments enter into force six months after the date of the deemed acceptance.

The Maritime Safety Committee considered a proposed revision of the Convention in 1994, which was adopted at a diplomatic conference in June - July 1995. A review of the proposed changes before their adoption was authored by Christopher Young, *Comprehensive Review of the STCW Convention : An Overview.*[2]

The provisions concerning Deck Department watchkeeping and look-outs had been contained in Chapter II, Regulation II/1 of the 1978 Convention. They have been preserved but rearranged and are now to be found in a new Chapter VIII of the Annex, "Watchkeeping Regulations," and Chapter VIII of the STCW Code, "Standards regarding Watchkeeping." These are reproduced below from I.M.O. Publication 938 E.

---

2. 26 J. Mar. L. & Com. 1-55 (1995).

STCW ANNEX

CHAPTER VIII

Watchkeeping

Regulation VIII/1

Fitness for duty

Each Administration shall, for the purpose of preventing fatigue:

.1 establish and enforce rest periods for watchkeeping personnel; and

.2 require that watch systems are so arranged that the efficiency of all watchkeeping personnel is not impaired by fatigue and that duties are so organized that the first watch at the commencement of a voyage and subsequent relieving watches are sufficiently rested and otherwise fit for duty.

Regulation VIII/2

Watchkeeping arrangements and principles to be observed

1 Administrations shall direct the attention of companies, masters, chief engineer officers and all watchkeeping personnel to the requirements, principles and guidance set out in the STCW Code which shall be observed to ensure that a safe continuous watch or watches appropriate to the prevailing circumstances and conditions are maintained in all seagoing ships at all times.

2 Administrations shall require the master of every ship to ensure that watchkeeping arrangements are adequate for maintaining a safe watch or watches, taking into account the prevailing circumstances and conditions and that, under the master's general direction:

.1 officers in charge of the navigational watch are responsible for navigating the ship safely during their periods of duty, when they shall be physically present on the navigating bridge or in a directly associated location such as the chartroom or bridge control room at all times;

.2 radio operators are responsible for maintaining a continuous radio watch on appropriate frequencies during their periods of duty;

.3 officers in charge of an engineering watch, as defined in the STCW Code and under the direction of the chief engineer officer, shall be immediately available and on call to attend the machinery spaces and, when required, shall be physically present in the machinery space during their periods of responsibility; and

.4 an appropriate and effective watch or watches are maintained for the purpose of safety at all times, while the ship is at anchor or moored and, if the ship is carrying hazardous cargo, the organization of such watch or watches takes full account of the nature, quantity, packing and stowage of the hazardous cargo and of any special conditions prevailing on board, afloat or ashore.

STCW CODE

CHAPTER VIII

Standards regarding watchkeeping

Section A-VIII/1

Fitness for duty

1 All persons who are assigned duty as officer in charge of a watch or as a rating forming part of a watch shall be provided a minimum of 10 hours of rest in any 24-hour period.

2 The hours of rest may be divided into no more than two periods, one of which shall be at least 6 hours in length.

3 The requirements for rest periods laid down in paragraphs 1 and 2 need not be maintained in the case of an emergency or drill or in other overriding operational conditions.

4 Notwithstanding the provisions of paragraphs 1 and 2, the minimum period of ten hours may be reduced to not less than 6 consecutive hours provided that any such reduction shall not extend beyond two days and not less than 70 hours of rest are provided each seven-day period.

5 Administrations shall require that watch schedules be posted where they are easily accessible.

Section A-VIII/2

Watchkeeping arrangements and principles to be observed

PART 1—CERTIFICATION

1 The officer in charge of the navigational or deck watch shall be duly qualified in accordance with the provisions of chapter II, or chapter VII appropriate to the duties related to navigational or deck watchkeeping.

2 The officer in charge of the engineering watch shall be duly qualified in accordance with the provisions of chapter III, or chapter VII appropriate to the duties related to engineering watchkeeping.

PART 2—VOYAGE PLANNING

General requirements

3 The intended voyage shall be planned in advance, taking into consideration all pertinent information, and any course laid down shall be checked before the voyage commences.

4 The chief engineer officer shall, in consultation with the master, determine in advance the needs of the intended voyage, taking into consideration the requirements for fuel, water, lubricants, chemicals, expendable and other spare parts, tools, supplies and any other requirements.

Planning prior to each voyage

5 Prior to each voyage the master of every ship shall ensure that the intended route from the port of departure to the first port of call is planned, using adequate and appropriate charts and other nautical publications necessary for the intended voyage, containing accurate, complete and up-to-date in-

formation regarding those navigational limitations and hazards which are of a permanent or predictable nature and which are relevant to the safe navigation of the ship.

Verification and display of planned route

6 When the route planning is verified taking into consideration all pertinent information, the planned route shall be clearly displayed on appropriate charts and shall be continuously available to the officer in charge of the watch, who shall verify each course to be followed prior to using it during the voyage.

Deviation from planned route

7 If a decision is made, during a voyage, to change the next port of call of the planned route, or if it is necessary for the ship to deviate substantially from the planned route for other reasons, then an amended route shall be planned prior to deviating substantially from the route originally planned.

PART 3—WATCHKEEPING AT SEA

Principles applying to watchkeeping generally

8 Parties shall direct the attention of companies, masters, chief engineer officers and watchkeeping personnel to the following principles, which shall be observed to ensure that safe watches are maintained at all times.

9 The master of every ship is bound to ensure that watchkeeping arrangements are adequate for maintaining a safe navigational watch. Under the master's general direction, the officers of the navigational watch are responsible for navigating the ship safely during their periods of duty, when they will be particularly concerned with avoiding collision and stranding.

10 The chief engineer officer of every ship is bound, in consultation with the master, to ensure that watchkeeping arrangements are adequate to maintain a safe engineering watch.

Protection of marine environment

11 The master, officers and ratings shall be aware of the serious effects of operational or accidental pollution of the marine environment and shall take all possible precautions to prevent such pollution, particularly within the framework of relevant international and port regulations.

PART 3-1—PRINCIPLES TO BE OBSERVED IN KEEPING A NAVIGATIONAL WATCH

12 The officer in charge of the navigational watch is the master's representative and is primarily responsible at all times for the safe navigation of the ship and for complying with the International Regulations for Preventing Collisions at Sea, 1972.

Look-out

13 A proper look-out shall be maintained at all times in compliance with rule 5 of the International Regulations for Preventing Collisions at Sea, 1972 and shall serve the purpose of:

.1 maintaining a continuous state of vigilance by sight and hearing as well as by all other available means, with regard to any significant change in the operating environment;

.2 fully appraising the situation and the risk of collision, stranding and other dangers to navigation; and

.3 detecting ships or aircraft in distress, shipwrecked persons, wrecks, debris and other hazards to safe navigation.

14 The look-out must be able to give full attention to the keeping of a proper look-out and no other duties shall be undertaken or assigned which could interfere with that task.

15 The duties of the look-out and helmsperson are separate and the helmsperson shall not be considered to be the look-out while steering, except in small ships where an unobstructed all-round view is provided at the steering position and there is no impairment of night vision or other impediment to the keeping of a proper look-out. The officer in charge of the navigational watch may be the sole look-out in daylight provided that on each such occasion:

.1 the situation has been carefully assessed and it has been established without doubt that it is safe to do so;

.2 full account has been taken of all relevant factors, including, but not limited to:
—state of weather,
—visibility,
—traffic density,
—proximity of dangers to navigation, and
—the attention necessary when navigating in or near traffic separation schemes; and

.3 assistance is immediately available to be summoned to the bridge when any change in the situation so requires.

16 In determining that the composition of the navigational watch is adequate to ensure that a proper look-out can continuously be maintained, the master shall take into account all relevant factors, including those described in this section of the Code, as well as the following factors:

.1 visibility, state of weather and sea;

.2 traffic density, and other activities occurring in the area in which the vessel is navigating;

.3 the attention necessary when navigating in or near traffic separation schemes or other routeing measures;

.4 the additional workload caused by the nature of the ship's functions, immediate operating requirements and anticipated manoeuvres;

.5 the fitness for duty of any crew members on call who are assigned as members of the watch;

.6 knowledge of and confidence in the professional competence of the ship's officers and crew;

.7 the experience of each officer of the navigational watch, and the familiarity of that officer with the ship's equipment, procedures, and manoeuvring capability;

.8 activities taking place on board the ship at any particular time, including radiocommunication activities, and the availability of assistance to be summoned immediately to the bridge when necessary;

.9 the operational status of bridge instrumentation and controls, including alarm systems;

.10 rudder and propeller control and ship manoeuvring characteristics;

.11 the size of the ship and the field of vision available from the conning position;

.12 the configuration of the bridge, to the extent such configuration might inhibit a member of the watch from detecting by sight or hearing any external development; and

.13 any other relevant standard, procedure or guidance relating to watchkeeping arrangements and fitness for duty which has been adopted by the Organization.

Watch arrangements

17 When deciding the composition of the watch on the bridge, which may include appropriately qualified ratings, the following factors, *inter alia*, shall be taken into account:

.1 at no time shall the bridge be left unattended;

.2 weather conditions, visibility and whether there is daylight or darkness;

.3 proximity of navigational hazards which may make it necessary for the officer in charge of the watch to carry out additional navigational duties;

.4 use and operational condition of navigational aids such as radar or electronic position-indicating devices and any other equipment affecting the safe navigation of the ship;

.5 whether the ship is fitted with automatic steering;

.6 whether there are radio duties to be performed;

.7 unmanned machinery space (UMS) controls, alarms and indicators provided on the bridge, procedures for their use and limitations; and

.8 any unusual demands on the navigational watch that may arise as a result of special operational circumstances.

Taking over the watch

18 The officer in charge of the navigational watch shall not hand over the watch to the relieving officer if there is reason to believe that the latter is not capable of carrying out the watchkeeping duties effectively, in which case the master shall be notified.

APPENDIX 5

THE C.M.I. LISBON RULES ON COMPENSATION FOR DAMAGES IN COLLISION CASES, 1987
(6 Benedict Doc. No. 3-4 A)

DEFINITIONS

In these Rules, the following words are used with the meaning set out below:

"Vessel" means any ship, craft, machine, rig or platform whether capable of navigation or not, which is involved in a collision.

"Collision" means any accident involving two or more vessels which causes loss or damage even if no actual contact has taken place.

"Claimant" means any person, corporate body or legal entity to whom damages are due in respect of loss or damage (excluding death and personal injury) as a result of a collision.

"Damages" means the financial compensation payable to the Claimant.

"Total Loss" means an actual total loss of the vessel or such damage to the vessel that the cost of saving and repairing her would exceed her market value at the time of the collision.

"Property" means cargo, goods and other things on board a vessel.

"Freight" means the remuneration payable for the carriage by the vessel of property or passengers or for the use of the vessel.

"Detention" means the period of time during which the Claimant is deprived of the use of the vessel.

RULE A

These Rules are available for adoption in cases where damages are claimed following a collision. Their adoption does not imply an admission of liability.

RULE B

When a vessel is involved in a collision, these Rules shall apply to the assessment of the damages. These Rules shall not extend to the determination of liability or affect rights of limitation of liability.

RULE C

Subject to the application of the numbered rules the Claimant shall be entitled to recover only such damages as may reasonably be considered to be the direct and immediate consequence of the collision.

RULE D

Subject to the application of Rule C and of the numbered Rules, damages shall place the Claimant in the same financial position as he would have occupied had the collision not occurred.

RULE E

The burden of proving the loss or damage sustained in accordance with these Rules shall be upon the Claimant. Damages shall not be recoverable to the extent that the person against whom the claim is made is able to show that the Claimant could have avoided or mitigated the loss or damage by the exercise of reasonable diligence.

RULE I

Total Loss

1. In the event of a vessel being a total loss, the Claimant shall be entitled to damages equal to the cost of purchasing a similar vessel in the market at the date of the collision. Where no similar vessel is available, the Claimant shall be entitled to recover as damages the value of the vessel at the date of the collision calculated by reference to the type, age, condition, nature of operation of the vessel and any other relevant factors, less the residual or net salvage value of the vessel after the collision.
2. Damages recoverable in the event of a total loss shall also include:
    (a) Reimbursement of salvage, general average and other charges and expenses reasonably incurred as a result of the collision.
    (b) Reimbursement of sums for which the Claimant has become legally liable and has paid to third parties in respect of such liability, arising out of the collision by reason of contractual, statutory or other legal obligations.
    (c) Reimbursement for the net freight lost and the value of bunkers and ship's gear lost as a result of the collision and not included in the value of the vessel ascertained in accordance with Rule I.1. above.
    (d) Subject to reimbursement for any claim for loss of freight under paragraph (c) above, compensation for the loss of use of the vessel for the period reasonably necessary to find a replacement whether the vessel is actually replaced or not. Such compensation to be calculated in accordance with Rule II, less any interest which the Claimant may be entitled to receive under Rule IV in respect of the said period.

RULE II

Damage to Vessel

1. In the event of a vessel being damaged but not being a total loss as defined in these Rules, the Claimant shall be entitled to recover as damages:
    (a) The cost of temporary repairs reasonably effected, and the reasonable cost of permanent repairs.

        The cost of those repairs shall include but not be limited to the cost of any necessary drydocking, gasfreeing or tank cleaning, port charges, supervision and classification surveys, together with drydock dues and/or wharfage, for the time occupied in carrying out such repairs.

However, when the collision damage repairs are carried out in conjunction with Owners' work which is essential to the seaworthiness of the vessel or with essential repair work arising out of another incident or are deferred to and carried out at a routine docking, the damages shall include but not be limited to drydock dues, wharfage and/or other time-based charges only to the extent that the period to which such charges relate has been extended by reason of the collision damage repairs.

(b) Reimbursement of salvage, general average and other charges and expenses reasonably incurred as a result of the collision.

(c) Reimbursement of sums, for which the Claimant has become legally liable and has paid to third parties in respect of such liability, arising out of the collision by reason of contractual, statutory or other legal obligations.

(d) Reimbursement for the net freight lost and the cost of replacing bunkers and vessel's gear lost as a result of the collision and not included in the cost of repairs under Rule II 1.(a).

2. Damages recoverable shall also include:

(a) Subject to reimbursement for any claim for loss of freight under Rule II.1(d), compensation for the net loss of earnings arising from the collision. This compensation shall be assessed by establishing the gross earnings of the vessel lost during detention, calculated by reference to the vessel's earnings or by reference to the earnings of comparable vessels in the same trade and then deducting from the gross earnings the operating costs which would normally have been incurred in order to achieve the gross earnings, such as hire payable, crew and bunker costs, port disbursements and insurance.

(b) Operating costs and expenses actually incurred during detention, other than those included under Rule II.1.

3. In the interpretation of Rule II.2, the following particular provisions will also apply:

(a) When detention occurs during the performance of a voyage charterparty and such detention does not entail cancellation of the charterparty, compensation shall be calculated by applying the average net earnings on the two voyages prior to and the two voyages subsequent to the detention.

When no reference to two prior and two subsequent voyages is possible, the net earnings on other relevant voyages or if there are no other relevant voyages on the voyage during which the collision took place shall form the basis of compensation.

If in consequence of such detention the charterparty is cancelled, and freight remains unearned compensation shall include the net freight lost.

(b) When detention occurs while the vessel is being operated on a liner service, compensation for detention shall be assessed as follows:

i. when detention occurs during the voyage which the vessel is performing at the time of the collision, by applying to the detention the net daily earnings for that voyage, computed for the time the voyage would have taken had the collision not occurred,

ii. when detention occurs other than during the voyage which the vessel is performing at the time of the collision, by applying to the detention the average net earnings on the two voyages prior to and the two voyages subsequent to the detention. When reference to two prior and two subsequent voyages is not possible, the basis of the computation will be the net earnings on other relevant voyages. If there are no other relevant voyages the compensation will be assessed by reference to the net earnings of a similar vessel operating in a similar trade.

(c) When detention occurs while the vessel is performing under a time charter, compensation shall include the net loss of hire during the detention. If in consequence of such detention the charterparty is cancelled, compensation shall include the net hire which would have been paid during the unperformed portion of the charter, allowance being made for any actual net earnings during that portion.

4. When collision damage repairs are carried out in conjunction with Owners' work which is essential to the seaworthiness of the vessel or with essential repair work arising out of another incident or are deferred to and carried out at a routine docking, damages shall include compensation for detention only to the extent that the period under repair is extended by reason of the collision damage repairs.

RULE III

Property on Board

1. The Claimant shall be entitled to recover damages when property has been lost or damaged in consequence of the collision.
2. In the case of property having a commercial value such damages shall be calculated as follows:

   (a) If such property is lost, the Claimant shall be entitled to reimbursement of the market value at the port of destination at the time when it should have arrived, less any expenses saved.

   When such market value cannot be determined, the value of the property shall be the shipped value plus freight and the cost of insurance if incurred by the Claimant, plus a margin for profit assessed at no more than 10% of the value of the property calculated as above.

   (b) If such property is damaged, the Claimant shall be entitled to damages equal to the difference between the value of the property in sound condition at destination and its value in damaged condition.

   Where physical damage to such property arises from the prolongation of the voyage following the collision, the compensation shall be fixed on the same basis. However, where the loss arises from a fall in the market during such prolongation there shall be no right to damages.

3. In the case of any other property the Claimant shall be entitled to recover:

(a) Where the property has been lost or is irreparable: its value or the reasonable cost of its replacement;

(b) Where the property is damaged and can be repaired: the reasonable cost of repairs, but not exceeding its value or the reasonable cost of its replacement.

RULE IV

Interest

1. Interest on damages is recoverable in addition to the principal sum.
2. For claims under Rule I.1, interest shall run from the date of the collision to the date of payment.

   For all other claims, interest shall run from the date the loss was sustained or the expense was incurred to the date of payment.
3. Where under Rule V the damages are to be calculated in Special Drawing Rights (SDR), the rate of interest shall be the average London rate for three months SDR linked deposits in the period that interest runs; otherwise the rate of interest shall be ten per cent per annum.

RULE V

Currency

Unless the parties have agreed to apply a specific currency in the calculation of their damages the following procedure shall be adopted:

—losses or expenses shall be converted from the currency in which they are incurred into Special Drawing Rights (SDR) at the rate of exchange prevailing on the day the losses or expenses were incurred.

—the final amounts due shall be calculated in SDR and the balance due shall be paid to the Claimant in the currency of his choice at the rate of exchange prevailing on the date of payment.

—where no official SDR exchange rate is quoted for the currency, conversions to and from SDR shall be made by reference to U.S. dollars.

AGREEMENT

RE: ....(o)

The parties hereto agree that their respective claims arising out of the above incident shall be assessed in accordance with the Lisbon Rules 1987.

The damages shall be calculated in

....(x)

(o) Insert names of ships involved and date/place of collision.

(x) If a currency is not specified, Rule V provides that the damages will be calculated in Special Drawing Rights (SDR).

APPENDIX 6

C.M.I. DRAFT CONVENTION FOR THE UNIFICATION OF CERTAIN RULES CONCERNING CIVIL JURISDICTION, CHOICE OF LAW, AND RECOGNITION AND ENFORCEMENT OF JUDGMENTS IN MATTERS OF COLLISION

(Approved at the Plenary Session of the 31st C.M.I. Conference, Rio de Janeiro, September 30, 1977.)

PRELIMINARY

Article 1

(1) This Convention shall govern jurisdiction, choice of law, and recognition and enforcement of judgments in collision actions, including recourse actions, for damages resulting from:
  a) loss of or damage to a vessel;
  b) loss of or damage to property on board a vessel.

For the purposes of this Convention "collision" means contact between two or more vessels, one of which at least is seagoing, and any other accident involving such vessels, arising from a manoeuvre, or a failure to manoeuvre, or from a failure to comply with any applicable rules of navigation, statutory or otherwise, even if no actual contact has occurred.

(2) This Convention shall not apply to:
  a) ships of war or government vessels appropriated exclusively to a public non-commercial service, other than ferries;
  b) claims which are capable of being founded in contract.

TITLE I - JURISDICTION

Article 2

(1) Unless the parties otherwise agree, the plaintiff may prosecute such an action only in a Court of a State Party to this Convention:
  a) where the defendant has his habitual residence or domicile, or principal place of business; or
  b) in the internal waters or territorial sea of which the collision has occurred; or
  c) where a vessel involved in the collision (other than the plaintiff's own vessel) or a vessel under the same ownership lawfully subject to arrest, has been arrested or security has been provided to avoid arrest on account of the collision; or

d) where the defendant has property subject to attachment under the law of that State and such property has been attached or security has been provided to avoid attachment on account of the collision; or

e) where a limitation fund has been properly constituted by the defendant in accordance with the law of that State on account of the collision.

(2) If an action is pending in one State Party, any further action brought in another State Party by the same plaintiff against the same defendant to recover for the same damage shall be stayed unless and until the previous action has been discontinued, or, if the Court so permits, stayed.

If judgment has been rendered on the merits in an action in one State Party, a party to such action shall not be permitted to bring a further action against the other party or parties to such action on the same facts in another State Party, unless, in the case of a successful party, the judgment cannot be fully satisfied in the State where it was rendered, in accordance with the law of that State.

Article 3

In the event of there being more than one claim to which this Convention applies arising out of the same collision, action on any such claim, whether by counterclaim or otherwise, may be brought against any party or parties to the proceedings before the Court seized of the original action.

TITLE II - CHOICE OF LAW

Article 4

Unless the parties otherwise agree, when a collision occurs in the internal waters or territorial sea of a State the law of that State shall apply, and when a collision occurs in waters beyond the territorial sea, the law of the Court seized of the case shall apply, except that when all of the vessels involved are registered or otherwise documented or, if not registered or otherwise documented, owned in the same State, the law of that State shall apply, wherever the collision occurs.

Provided, however, that in cases involving vessels registered or otherwise documented in, or, if not registered or otherwise documented, owned in different States, the Court seized of the case shall apply any Convention to which all of such States have given effect.

Provided, further, that to the extent that it is established that the law of all of such States is in accordance with the principles of a convention, the Court seized of the case shall, to that extent, apply such law.

Notwithstanding anything contained in this article, any relevant local navigational rules or regulations, statutory or otherwise, shall apply.

Article 5

The law applicable as provided in Article 4 shall be the law governing:

(1) the basis of liability;

(2) the grounds for exemption from liability and any division of liability;

(3) the kinds of damage for which compensation may be due;

(4) the quantum of damages;

(5) the persons who may claim damages in their own right;
(6) the liability of a principal for the acts or omissions of his agent, or of an employer for the acts or omissions of his employee, or of a vessel or her owner or operator for the acts or omissions of a pilot;
(7) the question whether a right to damages may be assigned or inherited;
(8) the burden of proof and presumptions;
(9) the rules concerning prescription.

The application of a law declared applicable under this title may be refused only when such application would be incompatible with public policy.

Article 6

Wherever reference is made in this title to the law of a State, the law referred to is the internal law of that State.

TITLE III - RECOGNITION AND ENFORCEMENT OF JUDGMENTS

Article 7

(1) This title applies to the recognition and enforcement of judgments, including judgments in limitation actions, rendered by a Court of a State Party in cases governed by this Convention, provided that the successful party is entitled to execution thereon under the law of the State where rendered.
(2) Such judgments shall be recognized and enforced in a State Party under the conditions laid down in the following article, provided that such State and the State wherein the judgment was rendered have concluded a Supplementary Agreement to this effect.
(3) This Title shall not apply to judgments rendered before the entry into force of the Supplementary Agreement provided for in the preceding paragraph, unless that Agreement otherwise provides.
(4) The Supplementary Agreement shall continue to be applicable to judgments in respect of which recognition or enforcement proceedings have been instituted before any denunciation of that Agreement takes effect.

Article 8

(1) A party seeking recognition or enforcement of a judgment shall furnish:
  a) a complete authenticated copy of the judgment;
  b) authenticated copies of all documents necessary to establish that the judgment fulfills the conditions of Article 7;
  c) such translations of the documents referred to in sub-paragraphs (a) and (b) of this paragraph as may be required by the Court of the State wherein recognition or enforcement is sought.
(2) Recognition or enforcement of a judgment may be refused only if the Court is satisfied that:
  a) the Court which rendered the judgment did not have jurisdiction under this Convention; or
  b) the judgment was obtained by fraud; or

c) recognition or enforcement of the judgment would be incompatible with the public policy of the State wherein recognition or enforcement is sought; or
d) the judgment debtor was not given reasonable notice of the proceedings and a fair opportunity to present his case.

(3) Enforcement of a judgment shall be refused to the extent that the judgment has been satisfied.

TITLE IV - GENERAL PROVISIONS

Article 9

This Convention shall be without prejudice to the provisions of any other conventions or treaties to which any of the States Parties are or shall become parties.

This Convention shall not apply to limitation of liability except as provided in Title III in respect of judgments in limitation actions.

Questions of procedure and any questions not otherwise regulated by this Convention shall be governed by the law of the Court seized of the case.

In respect of relations between States which ratify or accede to it, this Convention shall replace and abrogate the International Convention on Certain Rules Concerning Civil Jurisdiction in Matters of Collision, signed at Brussels on 10th May 1952, to the extent that the provisions of the two conventions are incompatible.

(Author's Note: This draft convention was submitted by the Comité Maritime International to the International Maritime Organization (I.M.O.) following the C.M.I. Rio de Janeiro Conference. The I.M.O. Legal Committee intended to consider it at its May 1978 meeting, but set it aside for consideration of oil pollution problems following the *Amoco Cadiz* disaster of March 1978, and later for consideration of the C.M.I. Draft Convention on Salvage. The draft has not been rejected, but as of 1997 there was no indication of when it would be considered by the Legal Committee.)

APPENDIX 7

LOF 1995

LLOYD'S

STANDARD FORM OF

SALVAGE AGREEMENT

> NOTES
>
> *1. Insert name of person signing on behalf of Owners of property to be salved. The Master should sign wherever possible.*
>
> *2. The Contractor's name should always be inserted in line 4 and whenever the Agreement is signed by the Master of the Salving vessel or other person on behalf of the Contractor the name of the Master or other person must also be inserted in line 4 before the words "for and on behalf of." The words "for and on behalf of" should be deleted where a Contractor signs personally.*
>
> *3. Insert place if agreed in clause 1(a)(i) and currency if agreed in clause 1(e).*

(APPROVED AND PUBLISHED BY THE COUNCIL OF LLOYD'S)

NO CURE – NO PAY

On board the____________________

Dated___________

IT IS HEREBY AGREED between Captain[1]__________________________________ for and on behalf of the Owners of the "__________________________________" her cargo freight bunkers stores and any other property thereon (hereinafter collectively called "the Owners") and________________________for and on behalf of ______________ (hereinafter called "the Contractor"[2]) that:–

1. (a) The Contractor shall use his best endeavors:–

(i) to salve the " __________________________________ " and/or her cargo freight bunkers stores and any other property thereon and take them to[3] __________ __________________________or to such other place as may hereafter be agreed either place to be deemed a place of safety or if no such place is named or agreed to a place of safety and

(ii) while performing the salvage services to prevent or minimize damage to the environment.

(b) Subject to the statutory provisions relating to special compensation the services shall be rendered and accepted as salvage services upon the principle of "no cure–no pay."

(c) The Contractor's remuneration shall be fixed by Arbitration in London in the manner hereinafter prescribed and any other difference arising out of this Agreement or the operations thereunder shall be referred to Arbitration in the same way.

(d) In the event of the services referred to in this Agreement or any part of such services having been already rendered at the date of this Agreement by the Contractor to the said vessel and/or her cargo freight bunkers stores and any other property thereon the provisions of this Agreement shall apply to such services.

(e) The security to be provided to the Council of Lloyd's (hereinafter called "the Council") the Salved Value(s) the Award and/or any Interim Award(s) and/or any Award on Appeal shall be in[3] ________________________________ currency.

(f) If clause 1(e) is not completed then the security to be provided and the Salved Values(s) the Award and/or Interim Award(s) and/or Award on Appeal shall be in Pounds Sterling.

(g) This Agreement and Arbitration thereunder shall except as otherwise expressly provided be governed by the law of England, including the English law of salvage.

PROVISIONS AS TO THE SERVICES

2. *Definitions:* in this Agreement any reference to "Convention" is a reference to the International Convention on Salvage, 1989, as incorporated in the Merchant Shipping (Salvage and Pollution) Act 1994 (and any amendment thereto). The terms "Contractor" and "services"/ "salvage services" in this Agreement shall have the same meanings as the terms "salvor(s)" and "salvage operation(s)" in the Convention.

3. *Owners Cooperation*: The Owners their Servants and Agents shall co-operate fully with the Contractor in and about the salvage including obtaining entry to the place named or the place of safety as defined in clause (1). The Contractor may make reasonable use of the vessel's machinery gear equipment anchors chains stores and other appurtenances during and for the purpose of the salvage services free of expense but shall not unnecessarily damage abandon or sacrifice the same or any property the subject of this Agreement.

4. *Vessel Owners Right to Terminate*: When there is no loner any reasonable prospect of a useful result leading to a salvage reward in accordance with Convention Article 13 the owners of the vessel shall be entitled to terminate the services of the Contractor by giving reasonable notice to the Contractor in writing.

PROVISIONS AS TO SECURITY

5. (a) The Contractor shall immediately after the termination of the services or sooner notify the Council and where practicable the Owners of the amount for which he demands salvage security (inclusive of the costs expenses and interest) from each of the respective Owners.

(b) Where a claim is made or may be made for special compensation, the owners of a vessel shall on the demand of the Contractor whenever made provide security for the Contractor's claim for special compensation provided always that such demand is made within two years of the date of termination of the services.

(c) The amount of any such security shall be reasonable in the light of the knowledge available to the Contractor at the time when the demand is made. Unless otherwise agreed such security shall be provided (i) to the Council (ii) in a form approved by the Council and (iii) by persons firms or corporations either acceptable to the Contractor or resident in the United Kingdom and acceptable to the Council. The Council shall not be responsible for the sufficiency (whether in amount or otl.erwise) of any security which shall be provided nor for the default or insolvency of any person firm or corporation providing the same.

(d) The owners of the vessel their Servants and Agents shall use their best endeavors to ensure that the cargo owners provide their proportion of salvage security before the cargo is released.

6. (a) Until security has been provided as aforesaid the Contractor shall have a maritime lien on the property salved for his remuneration.

(b) The property salved shall not without the consent in writing of the Contractor (which shall not be unreasonably withheld) be removed from the place to which it has been taken by the contractor under clause 1(a). Where such consent is given by the Contractor on condition that the Contractor is provided with temporary security pending completion of the voyage the Contractor's maritime lien on the property salved shall remain in force to the extent necessary to enable the Contractor to compel the provision of security in accordance with clause 5(c).

(c) The Contractor shall not arrest or detain the property salved unless:-

(i) security is not provided within 14 days (exclusive of Saturdays or Sundays or other days observed as general holidays at Lloyd's) after the date of the termination of the services or
(ii) he has reason to believe that the removal of the property salved is contemplated contrary to clause 6(b) or
(iii) any attempt is made to remove the property salved contrary to clause 6(b).

(d) The Arbitrator appointed under clause 7 or the Appeal Arbitrator(s) appointed under clause 13(d) shall have power in their absolute discretion to include in the amount awarded to the Contractor the whole or part of any expenses reasonably incurred by the Contractor in:-

(i) ascertaining demanding and obtaining the amount of security reasonably required in accordance with clause 5.
(ii) enforcing and/or protecting by insurance or otherwise or taking reasonable steps to enforce and/or protect his lien.

PROVISIONS AS TO ARBITRATION

7. (a) Whether security has been provided or not the Council shall appoint an Arbitrator upon receipt of a written request made by letter telex facsimile or in any other permanent form provided that any party requesting such appointment shall if required by the Council undertake to pay the reasonable fees and expenses of the Council and/or any Arbitrator or Appeal Arbitrator(s).

(b) Where an Arbitrator has been appointed and the parties do not proceed to arbitration the Council may recover any fees costs and/or expenses which are outstanding.

8. The Contractor's remuneration and/or special compensation shall be fixed by the Arbitrator appointed under clause 7. Such remuneration shall not be diminished by reason of the exception to the principle of "no cure–no pay" in the form of special compensation.

REPRESENTATION

9. Any party to this Agreement who wishes to be heard or to adduce evidence shall nominate a person in the United Kingdom to represent him failing which the Arbitrator or Appeal Arbitrator(s) may proceed as if such party had renounced his right to be heard or adduce evidence.

CONDUCT OF THE ARBITRATION

10. (a) The Arbitrator shall have power to:-

(i) admit such oral or documentary evidence or information as he may think fit
(ii) conduct the Arbitration in such manner in all respects as he may think fit subject to such procedural rules as the Council may approve
(iii) order the Contractor in his absolute discretion to pay the whole or part of the expense of providing excessive security or security which has been unreasonably demanded under clause 5(b) and to deduct such sum from the remuneration and/or special compensation
(iv) make Interim Award(s) including payment(s) on account on such terms as may be fair and just
(v) make such orders as to costs fees and expenses including those of the Council charged under clauses 10(b) and 14(b) as may be fair and just.

(b) The Arbitrator and the Council may charge reasonable fees and expenses for their services whether the Arbitration proceeds to a hearing or not and all such fees and expenses shall be treated as part of the costs of the Arbitration.

(c) Any Award shall (subject to Appeal as provided in this Agreement) be final and binding on all the parties concerned whether they were represented at the Arbitration or not.

INTEREST & RATES OF EXCHANGE

11. *Interest*: Interest at rates per annum to be fixed by the Arbitrator shall (subject to Appeal as provided in this Agreement) be payable on any sum awarded taking into account any sums already paid:-

(i) from the date of termination of the services unless the Arbitrator shall in his absolute discretion otherwise decide until the date of publication by the Council of the Award and/or Interim Award(s) and
(ii) from the expiration of 21 days (exclusive of Saturdays and Sundays or other days observed as general holidays at Lloyd's) after the date of publication by the Council of the Award and/or Interim Award(s) until the date payment is received by the Contractor or the Council, both dates inclusive.

For the purpose of sub-clause (ii) the expression "sum awarded" shall include the fees and expenses referred to in clause 10(b).

12. *Currency Correction*: In considering what sums of money have been expended by the Contractor in rendering the services and/or in fixing the amount of the Award and/or Interim Award(s) and/or Award on Appeal the Arbitrator or Appeal Arbitrator(s) shall to such an extent and in so far as it may be fair and just in all the circumstances give effect to the consequences of any change or changes in the relevant rates of exchange which may have occurred between the date of termination of the services and the date on which the Award and/or Interim Award(s) and/or Award on Appeal is made.

PROVISIONS AS TO APPEAL

13. (a) Notice of Appeal if any shall be given to the Council within 14 days (exclusive of Saturdays and Sundays or other days observed as general holidays at Lloyd's) after the date of the publication by the Council of the Award and/or Interim Award(s).

(b) Notice of Cross-Appeal if any shall be given to the Council within 14 days (exclusive of Saturdays and Sundays or other days observed as general holidays at Lloyd's) after notification by the Council to the parties of any Notice of Appeal. Such notification if sent by post shall be deemed received on the working day following the day of posting.

(c) Notice of Appeal or Cross-Appeal shall be given to the Council by letter telex facsimile or in any other permanent form.

(d) Upon receipt of Notice of Appeal the Council shall refer the Appeal to the hearing and determination of the Appeal Arbitrator(s) selected by it.

(e) If any Notice of Appeal or Cross-Appeal is withdrawn the Appeal hearing shall nevertheless proceed in respect of such Notice of Appeal or Cross-Appeal as may remain.

(f) Any Award on Appeal shall be final and binding on all the parties to that Appeal Arbitration whether they were represented either at the Arbitration or at the Appeal Arbitration or not.

CONDUCT OF THE APPEAL

14. (a) The Appeal Arbitrator(s) in addition to the powers of the Arbitrator under clauses 10(a) and 11 shall have power to:-

(i) admit the evidence which was before the Arbitrator together with the Arbitrator's notes and reasons for his Award and/or Interim Award(s) and any transcript of evidence and such additional evidence as he or they may think fit.

(ii) confirm increase or reduce the sum awarded by the Arbitrator and to make such order as to the payment of interest on such sum as he or they may think fit.

(iii) confirm revoke or vary any order and/or Declaratory Award made by the Arbitrator.

(iv) award interest on any fees and expenses charged under paragraph (b) of this clause from the expiration of 21 days (exclusive of Saturdays and Sundays or other days observed as general holidays at Lloyd's) after the date of publication by the Council of the Award on Appeal and/or Interim Award(s) on Appeal until the date payment is received by the Council both dates inclusive.

(b) The Appeal Arbitrator(s) and the Council may charge reasonable fees and expenses for their services in connection with the Appeal Arbitration whether it proceeds to a hearing or not and all such fees and expenses shall be treated as part of the costs of the Appeal Arbitration.

PROVISIONS AS TO PAYMENT

15. (a) In case of Arbitration if no Notice of Appeal be received by the Council in accordance with clause 13(a) the Council shall call upon the party or parties concerned to pay the amount awarded and in the event of non-payment shall subject to the Contractor first providing to the Council a satisfactory Undertaking to pay all the costs thereof realize or enforce the security and pay therefrom to the Contractor (whose receipt shall be a good discharge to it) the amount awarded to him together with interest if any. The Contractor shall reimburse the parties concerned to such extent as the Award is less than any sums paid on account or in respect of Interim Award(s).

(b) If Notice of Appeal be received by the Council in accordance with clause 13 it shall as soon as the Award on Appeal has been published by it call upon the party or parties concerned to pay the amount awarded and in the event of non-payment shall subject to the Contractor first providing to the Council a satisfactory Undertaking to pay all the costs thereof realize or enforce the security and pay therefrom to the Contractor (whose receipt shall be a good discharge to it) the amount awarded to him together with interest if any. The Contractor shall reimburse the parties concerned to such an extent as the Award on Appeal is less than any sums paid on account or in respect of the Award or Interim Award(s).

(c) If any sum shall become payable to the Contractor as remuneration for his services and/or interest and/or costs as the result of an agreement made between the Contractor and the Owners or any of them the Council in the event of non-payment shall subject to the Contractor first providing to the Council a satisfactory Undertaking to pay all the costs thereof realize or enforce the security and pay therefrom to the Contractor (whose receipt shall be a good discharge to it) the said sum.

(d) If the Award and/or Interim Award(s) and/or Award on Appeal provides or provide that the costs of the Arbitration and/or of the Appeal Arbitration or any part of such costs shall be borne by the Contractor such costs may be deducted from the amount awarded or agreed before payment is made to the Contractor unless satisfactory security is provided by the Contractor for the payment of such costs.

(e) Without prejudice to the provisions of clause 5(c) the liability of the Council shall be limited in any event to the amount of security provided to it.

GENERAL PROVISIONS

16. *Scope of Authority*: The Master or other person signing this Agreement on behalf of the property to be salved enters into this Agreement as agent for the vessel her cargo freight bunkers stores and any other property thereon and the respective Owners thereof and binds each (but not the one for the other or himself personally) to the due performance thereof.

17. *Notices*: Any Award notice authority order or other document signed by the Chairman of Lloyd's or any person authorized by the Council for the purpose shall be deemed to have been duly made or given by the Council and shall have the same force and effect in all respects as if it had been signed by every member of the Council.

18. *Sub-Contractor(s)*: The Contractor may claim salvage and enforce any Award or agreement made between the Contractor and the Owners against security provided under clause 5 if any on behalf of any Sub-Contractors his or their Servants or Agents including Masters and members of the crews of vessels employed by him or by any Sub-Contractors in the services provided that he first provides a reasonably satisfactory indemnity to the Owners against all claims by or liabilities to the said persons.

19. *Inducements prohibited*: No person signing this Agreement or any party on whose behalf it is signed shall at any time or in any manner whatsoever offer provide make give or promise to provide demand or take any form of inducement for entering into this Agreement.

For and on behalf of the Contractor	**For and on behalf of the Owners of property to be salved.**
(To be signed either by the Contractor personally or by the master of the salving vessel or other person whose name is inserted in line 4 of this Agreement.)	(To be signed by the Master or other person whose name is inserted in line 1 of this Agreement.)

INTERNATIONAL CONVENTION ON SALVAGE, 1989

The following provisions of the Convention are set out for information only.

Article 1

Definitions

(a) *Salvage Operation* means any act or activity undertaken to assist a vessel or any other property in danger in navigable waters or in any other waters whatsoever

(b) *Vessel* means any ship or craft, or any structure capable of navigation

(c) *Property* means any property not permanently and intentionally attached to the shoreline and includes freight at risk

(d) *Damage to the environment* means substantial physical damage to human health or to marine life or resources in coastal or inland waters or areas adjacent thereto, caused by pollution, contamination, fire, explosion or similar major incidents

(e) *Payment* means any reward, remuneration or compensation due under this Convention

Article 6

Salvage Contracts

1. This Convention shall apply to any salvage operations save to the extent that a contract otherwise provides expressly or by implication.

2. The master shall have the authority to conclude contracts for salvage operations on behalf of the owner of the vessel. The master or owner of the vessel shall have the authority to conclude such contracts on behalf of the owner of the property on board the vessel.

Article 8

Duties of the Salvor and of the Owner and Master

1. The salvor shall owe a duty to the owner of the vessel or other property in danger:

(a) to carry out the salvage operations with due care;

(b) in performing the duty specified in subparagraph (a), to exercise due care to prevent or minimize damage to the environment;

(c) whenever circumstances reasonably require, to seek assistance from other salvors; and

(d) to accept the intervention of other salvors when reasonably requested to do so by the owner or master of the vessel or other property in danger; provided however that the amount of his reward shall not be prejudiced should it be found that such a request was unreasonable.

2. The owner and master of the vessel or the owner of other property in danger shall owe a duty to the salvor:

(a) to co-operate fully with him during the course of the salvage operations;

(b) in so doing, to exercise due care to prevent or minimize damage to the environment; and

(c) when the vessel or other property has been brought to a place of safety, to accept redelivery when reasonably requested by the salvor to do so.

Article 13

Criteria for Fixing the Reward

1. The reward shall be fixed with a view to encouraging salvage operations, taking into account the following criteria without regard to the order in which they are presented below:

(a) the salved value of the vessel and other property;

(b) the skill and efforts of the salvors in preventing or minimizing damage to the environment;

(c) the measure of success obtained by the salvor;
(d) the nature and degree of the danger;
(e) the skill and efforts of the salvors in salving the vessel, other property and life;
(f) the time used and expenses and losses incurred by the salvors;
(g) the risk of liability and other risks run by the salvors or their equipment;
(h) the promptness and use of vessels or other equipment intended for salvage operations;
(i) the availability and use of vessels or other equipment intended for salvage operations;
(j) the state of readiness and efficiency of the salvor's equipment and the value thereof.

2. Payment of a reward fixed according to paragraph 1 shall be made by all of the vessel and other property interests in proportion to their respective salved values.

3. The rewards, exclusive of any interest and recoverable legal costs that may be payable thereon, shall not exceed the salved value of the vessel and other property.

Article 14

Special Compensation

1. If the salvor has carried out salvage operations in respect of a vessel which by itself or its cargo threatened damage to the environment and has failed to earn a reward under Article 13 at least equivalent to the special compensation assessable in accordance with this Article, he shall be entitled to special compensation from the owner of that vessel equivalent to his expenses as herein defined.

2. If, in the circumstances set out in paragraph 1, the salvor by his salvage operations has prevented or minimized damage to the environment, the special compensation payable by the owner to the salvor under paragraph 1 may be increased up to a maximum of 30% of the expenses incurred by the salvor. However, the Tribunal, if it deems it fair and just to do so and bearing in mind the relevant criteria set out in Article 13, paragraph 1, may increase such special compensation further, but in no event shall the total increase be more than 100% of the expenses incurred by the salvor.

3. Salvor's expenses for the purpose of paragraphs 1 and 2 means the out-of-pocket expenses reasonably incurred by the salvor in the salvage operation and a fair rate for equipment and personnel actually and reasonably used in the salvage operation, taking into consideration the criteria set out in Article 13, paragraph 1(h), (i) and (j).

4. The total special compensation under this article shall be paid only if and to the extent that such compensation is greater than any reward recoverable by the salvor under article 13.

5. If the salvor has been negligent and has thereby failed to prevent or minimize damage to the environment, he may be deprived of the whole or part of any compensation due under this article.

6. Nothing in this article shall affect any right of recourse on the part of the owner of the vessel.

APPENDIX 8

ILLUSTRATIONS OF ADJUSTMENTS IN BOTH-TO-BLAME COLLISION CASES

In the illustrations set out below the following facts are assumed, unless it is otherwise indicated:

1. Vessel A's damages total $560,000.
2. Vessel B's damages total $40,000.
3. Vessel A is found 60% at fault for errors in navigation, except that in Case No. 4 A's fault is in improper manning, with A's "privity or knowledge."
4. Vessel B is found 40% at fault for errors in navigation.
5. Cargo, if any, is carried on Vessel A under the U.S. Carriage of Goods by Sea Act (COGSA).
6. The package limitation of COGSA is not involved.
7. Owners of A and B institute limitation proceedings in the same court and the two proceedings are consolidated.
8. Each vessel's limitation fund is $100,000.
9. B is not guilty of "privity or knowledge."
10. In Cases Nos. 1, 2 and 3, A's fault is not within the "privity or knowledge" of A's owner.

Case No. 1

(Under either U.S. collision law or the 1910 Collision Convention.)

A's damages:		$560,000
B's damages:	(+)	40,000
Total collision damages:		$600,000
A's 60% share:	(–)	360,000
B's 40% share:		$240,000
Damages already sustained by B:	(–)	40,000
B's liability to A before limitation:		$200,000

A recovers B's entire limitation fund ($100,000) and absorbs the remainder of its damages. B suffers its damages of $40,000 plus the loss of its limitation fund ($100,000).

Recapitulation

A's net loss:	$460,000	(damages of $560,000, less $100,000 recovered from B's limitation fund)
B's net loss:	(+) 140,000	(damages of $40,000, plus its limitation fund of $100,000)
Total cost of collision:	$600,000	

Case No. 2

(Under U.S. collision law)

(The facts are the same as in Case No. 1, except that Vessel A is carrying cargo, which sustains collision damages of $100,000.)

A's damages:		$560,000
B's hull and detention damages:	$40,000	
B's payment or commitment to pay 100% of damages of A's Cargo:	(+) 100,000	
B's total damages:		(+) 140,000
Total collision damages:		$700,000
A's 60% share:		(–) 420,000
B's 40% share:		$ 280,000
Total damages already sustained by B:		(–) 140,000
Balance owing by B to A before limitation:		$140,000

Cargo, being "innocent," takes precedence over A, a joint tort-feasor, in the distribution of B's limitation fund, even though A is shielded from affirmative liability to its Cargo by the "nautical fault" exception of COGSA. Cargo is therefore made whole by the recovery of B's entire limitation fund of $100,000. A must bear its own damages ($560,000).

Recapitulation

A's net loss:	$560,000	(its damages)
B's net loss:	140,000	(its damages of $40,000, plus its limitation fund of $100,000)
Cargo's net loss:	(+) 0	(its damages of $100,000, less B's limitation fund of $100,000)
Total cost of collision:	$700,000	

Case No. 3

(Under the 1910 Collision Convention)

The facts are the same as in Case No. 2.

A's damages:		$560,000
B's vessel damages:	(+)	40,000
Total vessel damages:		$600,000
A's 60% share:	(–)	360,000
B's 40% share:		$240,000
Vessel damages already sustained by B:	(–)	40,000
Balance owing by B to A before limitation:		$200,000
B's 40% share of A's Cargo's damages:	(+)	40,000
B's total liability before limitation:		$240,000

A's "innocent" Cargo takes precedence over A, a joint tort-feasor, as a claimant against B's limitation fund, although A is shielded by the "nautical fault" exception of COGSA against affirmative liability to its Cargo. A's Cargo therefore recovers the full amount of B's 40% liability to it ($40,000) from B's fund, and A recovers the remaining $60,000 of the fund. A's Cargo bears the $60,000 of its damages remaining after its recovery of $40,000 from B's fund.

Recapitulation

A's net loss:		$500,000	($560,000 damages, less $60,000 recovered from B's limitation fund)
B's net loss:		140,000	($40,000 damages, plus its limitation fund of $100,000)
A's Cargo's net loss:	(+)	60,000	($100,000 damages, less $40,000 recovered from B's fund)
Total cost of collision:		$700,000	

Case No. 4

(Under either U.S. collision law or the 1910 Collision Convention)

The facts are the same as in Cases Nos. 2 and 3, except that the collision was caused by errors in navigation by B and the improper manning of A, with the "privity or knowledge" of A's owner.

A's own damages:		$560,000
B's own damages:	(+)	40,000
Total vessel damages:		$600,000
A's 60% share:	(–)	360,000
B's 40% share:		$240,000
Damages already sustained by B:	(–)	40,000
Balance owing by B to A before limitation:		$200,000
Amount of liability of B to A's Cargo before limitation:	(–)	40,000
Total liability of B before limitation:		$240,000

As A's liability to its Cargo is based on improper manning with A's "privity or knowledge," A is not shielded from liability by the "nautical fault" exception of COGSA, and could not have limited its liability if its limitation fund had been less than $60,000. A's Cargo therefore recovers 60% ($60,000) of its damages from A.

A's Cargo recovers the remaining 40% ($40,000) of its damages from B's fund.

A recovers the balance of B's fund ($60,000).

Recapitulation

A's net loss:		$560,000	(damages of $560,000, plus $60,000 payment or commitment to A's Cargo, less $60,000 recovered from B's fund)
B's net loss:		140,000	(damages of $40,000, plus its limitation fund of $100,000)
A's Cargo's net loss:	(+)	0	(damages of $100,000, less $60,000 recovered from A and $40,000 recovered from B's fund)
Total cost of collision:		$700,000	

AMERICAN INSTITUTE HULL CLAUSES (JUNE 2, 1977)

To be attached to and form a part of Policy No. .... of the ....
....

The terms and conditions of the following clauses are to be regarded as substituted for those of the policy form to which they are attached, the latter being hereby waived, except provisions required by law to be inserted in the Policy. All captions are inserted only for purposes of reference and shall not be used to interpret the clauses to which they apply.

ASSURED

This Policy insures ....
....
.... hereinafter referred to as the Assured.

If claim is made under this Policy by anyone other than the Owner of the Vessel, such person shall not be entitled to recover to a greater extent than would the Owner, had claim been made by the Owner as an Assured named in this Policy.

Underwriters waive any right of subrogation against affiliated, subsidiary or interrelated companies of the Assured, provided that such waiver shall not apply in the event of a collision between the Vessel and any vessel owned, demise chartered or otherwise controlled by any of the aforesaid companies, or with respect to any loss, damage or expense against which such companies are insured.

LOSS PAYEE

Loss, if any, payable to..
....
.... or order.

Provided, however, Underwriters shall pay claims to others as set forth in the Collision Liability clause and may make direct payment to persons providing security for the release of the Vessel in Salvage cases.

VESSEL

The Subject Matter of this insurance is the Vessel called the ....
or by whatsoever name or names the said Vessel is or shall be called, which for purposes of this insurance shall consist of and be limited to her hull, launches, lifeboats, rafts, furniture, bunkers, stores, supplies, tackle, fittings, equipment, apparatus, machinery, boilers, refrigerating machinery, insulation, motor generators and other electrical machinery.

In the event any equipment or apparatus not owned by the Assured is installed for use on board the Vessel and the Assured has assumed responsibility therefor, it shall also be considered part of the Subject Matter and the aggregate value thereof shall be included in the Agreed Value.

Notwithstanding the foregoing, cargo containers, barges and lighters shall not be considered a part of the Subject Matter of this insurance.

DURATION OF RISK

From the .... day of .... 19...... , ... time
to the .... day of .... 19...... , ... time

Should the Vessel at the expiration of this Policy be at sea, or in distress, or at a port of refuge or of call, she shall, provided previous notice be given to the Underwriters, be held covered at a pro rata monthly premium to her port of destination.

In the event of payment by the Underwriters for Total Loss of the Vessel this Policy shall thereupon automatically terminate.

AGREED VALUE

The Vessel, for so much as concerns the Assured, by agreement between the Assured and the Underwriters in this Policy, is and shall be valued at................................ ....Dollars.

AMOUNT INSURED HEREUNDER

....Dollars.

DEDUCTIBLE

Notwithstanding anything in this Policy to the contrary, there shall be deducted from the aggregate of all claims (including claims under the Sue and Labor clause and claims under the Collision Liability clause) arising out of each separate accident, the sum of $ ...., unless the accident results in a Total Loss of the Vessel in which case this clause shall not apply. A recovery from other interests, however, shall not operate to exclude claims under this Policy provided the aggregate of such claims arising out of one separate accident if unreduced by such recovery exceeds that sum. For the purpose of this clause each accident shall be treated separately, but it is agreed that (a) a sequence of damages arising from the same accident shall be treated as due to that accident and (b) all heavy weather damage, or damage caused by contact with floating ice, which occurs during a single sea passage between two successive ports shall be treated as though due to one accident.

PREMIUM

The Underwriters to be paid in consideration of this insurance .... Dollars being at the annual rate of .... per cent., which premium shall be due on attachment. If the Vessel is insured under this Policy for a period of less than one year at pro rata of the annual rate, full annual premium shall be considered earned and immediately due and payable in the event of Total Loss of the Vessel.

RETURNS OF PREMIUM

Premium returnable as follows:

Pro rata daily net in the event of termination under the Change of Ownership clause;

Pro rata monthly net for each uncommenced month if it be mutually agreed to cancel this Policy;

For each period of 30 consecutive days the Vessel may be laid up in port for account of the Assured,

cents per cent. net not under repair, or

cents per cent. net under repair;

provided always that

(a) a Total Loss of the Vessel has not occurred during the currency of this Policy;

(b) in no case shall a return for lay-up be allowed when the Vessel is lying in exposed or unprotected waters or in any location not approved by the Underwriters;

(c) in the event of any amendment of the annual rate, the above rates of return shall be adjusted accordingly;

(d) in no case shall a return be allowed when the Vessel is used as a storage ship or for lightering purposes.

If the Vessel is laid up for a period of 30 consecutive days, a part only of which attaches under this Policy, the Underwriters shall pay such proportion of the return due in respect of a full period of 30 days as the number of days attaching hereto bears to 30. Should the lay-up period exceed 30 consecutive days, the Assured shall have the option to elect the period of 30 consecutive days for which a return is recoverable.

NON-PAYMENT OF PREMIUM

In event of non-payment of premium 30 days after attachment, or of any additional premium when due, this Policy may be cancelled by the Underwriters upon 10 days written or telegraphic notice sent to the Assured at his last known address or in care of the broker who negotiated this Policy. Such proportion of the premium, however, as shall have been earned up to the time of cancellation shall be payable. In the event of Total Loss of the Vessel occurring prior to any cancellation or termination of this Policy full annual premium shall be considered earned.

ADVENTURE

Beginning the adventure upon the Vessel, as above, and so shall continue and endure during the period aforesaid, as employment may offer, in port or at sea, in docks and graving docks, and on ways, gridirons and pontoons, at all times, in all places, and on all occasions, services and trades; with leave to sail or navigate with or without pilots, to go on trial trips and to assist and tow vessels or craft in distress, but the Vessel may not be towed, except as is customary or when in need of assistance, nor shall the Vessel render assistance or undertake towage or salvage services under contract previously arranged by the Assured, the Owners, the Managers or the Charterers of the Vessel, nor shall the Vessel, in the course of trading operations, engage in loading or discharging cargo at sea, from or into another vessel other than a barge, lighter or similar craft used principally in harbors or inland waters. The phrase "engage in loading or discharging cargo at sea" shall include while approaching, leaving or alongside, or while another vessel is approaching, leaving or alongside the Vessel.

The Vessel is held covered in case of any breach of conditions as to cargo, trade, locality, towage or salvage activities, or date of sailing, or loading or discharging cargo at sea, provided (a) notice is given to the Underwriters immediately following receipt of knowledge thereof by the Assured, and (b) any amended terms of cover and any additional premium required by the Underwriters are agreed to by the Assured.

PERILS

Touching the Adventures and Perils which the Underwriters are contented to bear and take upon themselves, they are of the Seas, Men-of-War, Fire, Lightning, Earthquake, Enemies, Pirates, Rovers, Assailing Thieves, Jettisons, Letters of Mart and Counter-Mart, Surprisals, Takings at Sea, Arrests, Restraints and Detainments of all Kings, Princes and Peoples, of what nation, condition or quality soever, Barratry of the Master and Mariners and of all other like Perils, Losses and Misfortunes that have or shall come to the Hurt, Detriment or Damage of the Vessel, or any part thereof, excepting, however, such of the foregoing perils as may be excluded by provisions elsewhere in the Policy or by endorsement thereon.

ADDITIONAL PERILS (INCHMAREE)

Subject to the conditions of this Policy, this insurance also covers loss of or damage to the Vessel directly caused by the following:

Accidents in loading, discharging or handling cargo, or in bunkering;

Accidents in going on or off, or while on drydocks, graving docks, ways, gridirons or pontoons;

Explosions on shipboard or elsewhere;

Breakdown of motor generators or other electrical machinery and electrical connections thereto, bursting of boilers, breakage of shafts, or any latent defect in the machinery or hull, (excluding the cost and expense of replacing or repairing the defective part);

Breakdown of or accidents to nuclear installations or reactors not on board the insured Vessel;

Contact with aircraft, rockets or similar missiles, or with any land conveyance;

Negligence of Charterers and/or Repairers, provided such Charterers and/or Repairers are not an Assured hereunder;

Negligence of Masters, Officers, Crew or Pilots;

provided such loss or damage has not resulted from want of due diligence by the Assured, the Owners or Managers of the Vessel, or any of them. Masters, Officers, Crew or Pilots are not to be considered Owners within the meaning of this clause should they hold shares in the Vessel.

DELIBERATE DAMAGE (POLLUTION HAZARD)

Subject to the conditions of this Policy, this insurance also covers loss of or damage to the Vessel directly caused by governmental authorities acting for the public welfare to prevent or mitigate a pollution hazard, or threat thereof, resulting directly from damage to the Vessel for which the Underwriters are liable under this Policy, provided such act of governmental authorities has not resulted from want of due diligence by the Assured, the Owners, or Managers of the Vessel or any of them to prevent or mitigate such hazard or threat. Masters, Officers, Crew or Pilots are not to be considered Owners within the meaning of this clause should they hold shares in the Vessel.

CLAIMS (GENERAL PROVISIONS)

In the event of any accident or occurrence which could give rise to a claim under this Policy, prompt notice thereof shall be given to the Underwriters, and

(a) where practicable, the Underwriters shall be advised prior to survey, so that they may appoint their own surveyor, if they so desire;

(b) the Underwriters shall be entitled to decide where the Vessel shall proceed for docking and/or repair (allowance to be made to the Assured for the actual additional expense of the voyage arising from compliance with the Underwriters' requirement);

(c) the Underwriters shall have the right of veto in connection with any repair firm proposed;

(d) the Underwriters may take tenders, or may require in writing that tenders be taken for the repair of the Vessel, in which event, upon acceptance of a tender with the approval of the Underwriters, an allowance shall be made at the rate of 30 per cent. per annum on the amount insured, for each day or pro rata for part of a day, for time lost between the issuance of invitations to tender and the acceptance of a tender, to the extent that such time is lost solely as the result of tenders having been taken and provided the tender is accepted without delay after receipt of the Underwriters' approval.

Due credit shall be given against the allowances in (b) and (d) above for any amount recovered:

(1) in respect of fuel, stores, and wages and maintenance of the Master, Officers or Crew, allowed in General or Particular Average;

(2) from third parties in respect of damages for detention and/or loss of profit and/or running expenses;

for the period covered by the allowances or any part thereof.

No claim shall be allowed in Particular Average for wages and maintenance of the Master, Officers or Crew, except when incurred solely for the necessary removal of the Vessel from one port to another for average repairs or for trial trips to test average repairs, in which cases wages and maintenance will be allowed only while the Vessel is under way. This exclusion shall not apply to overtime or similar extraordinary payments to the Master, Officers or Crew incurred in shifting the Vessel for tank cleaning or repairs or while specifically engaged in these activities, either in port or at sea.

General and Particular Average shall be payable without deduction, new for old.

The expense of sighting the bottom after stranding shall be paid, if reasonably incurred especially for that purpose, even if no damage be found.

No claim shall in any case be allowed in respect of scraping or painting the Vessel's bottom.

In the event of loss or damage to equipment or apparatus not owned by the Assured but installed for use on board the Vessel and for which the Assured has assumed responsibility, claim shall not exceed (1) the amount the Underwriters would pay if the Assured were owner of such equipment or apparatus, or (2) the contractual responsibility assumed by the Assured to the owners or lessors thereof, whichever shall be less.

No claim for unrepaired damages shall be allowed, except to the extent that the aggregate damage caused by perils insured against during the period of the Policy and left unrepaired at the expiration of the Policy shall be demonstrated by the Assured to have diminished the actual market value of the Vessel on that date if undamaged by such perils.

GENERAL AVERAGE AND SALVAGE

General Average and Salvage shall be payable as provided in the contract of affreightment, or failing such provision or there be no contract of affreightment, payable at the Assured's election either in accordance with York-Antwerp Rules 1950 or 1974 or with the Laws and Usages of the Port of New York. Provided always that when an adjustment according to the laws and usages of the port of destination is properly demanded by the owners of the cargo, General Average shall be paid accordingly.

In the event of salvage, towage or other assistance being rendered to the Vessel by any vessel belonging in part or in whole to the same Owners or Charterers, the value of such services (without regard to the common ownership or control of the vessels) shall be ascertained by arbitration in the manner provided for under the Collision Liability clause in this Policy, and the amount so awarded so far as applicable to the interest hereby insured shall constitute a charge under this Policy.

When the contributory value of the Vessel is greater than the Agreed Value herein, the liability of the Underwriters for General Average contribution (except in respect to amounts made good to the Vessel), or Salvage, shall not exceed that proportion of the total contribution due from the Vessel which the amount insured hereunder bears to the contributory value, and if, because of damage for which the Underwriters are liable as Particular Average, the value of the Vessel has been reduced for the purpose of contribution, the amount of such Particular Average damage recoverable under this Policy shall first be deducted from the amount insured hereunder, and the Underwriters shall then be liable only for the proportion which such net amount bears to the contributory value.

TOTAL LOSS

In ascertaining whether the Vessel is a constructive Total Loss the Agreed Value shall be taken as the repaired value and nothing in respect of the damaged or break-up value of the Vessel or wreck shall be taken into account.

There shall be no recovery for a constructive Total Loss hereunder unless the expense of recovering and repairing the Vessel would exceed the Agreed Value. In making this determination, only expenses incurred or to be incurred by reason of a single accident or a sequence of damages arising from the same accident shall be taken into account, but expenses incurred prior to tender of abandonment shall not be considered if such are to be claimed separately under the Sue and Labor clause.

In the event of Total Loss (actual or constructive), no claim to be made by the Underwriters for freight, whether notice of abandonment has been given or not.

In no case shall the Underwriters be liable for unrepaired damage in addition to a subsequent Total Loss sustained during the period covered by this Policy.

SUE AND LABOR

And in case of any Loss or Misfortune, it shall be lawful and necessary for the Assured, their Factors, Servants and Assigns, to sue, labor and travel for, in, and about the defense, safeguard and recovery of the Vessel, or any part thereof, without prejudice to this insurance, to the charges whereof the Underwriters will contribute their proportion as provided below. And it is expressly declared and agreed that no acts of the Underwriters or Assured in recovering, saving or preserving the Vessel shall be considered as a waiver or acceptance of abandonment.

In the event of expenditure under the Sue and Labor clause, the Underwriters shall pay the proportion of such expenses that the amount insured hereunder bears to the Agreed Value, or that the amount insured hereunder (less loss and/or damage payable under this Policy) bears to the actual value of the salved property, whichever proportion shall be less; provided always that their liability for such expenses shall not exceed their proportionate part of the Agreed Value.

If claim for Total Loss is admitted under this Policy and sue and labor expenses have been reasonably incurred in excess of any proceeds realized or value recovered, the amount payable under this Policy will be the proportion of such excess that the amount insured hereunder (without deduction for loss or damage) bears to the Agreed Value or to the sound value of the Vessel at the time of the accident, whichever value was greater; provided always that Underwriters' liability for such expenses shall not exceed their proportionate part of the Agreed Value. The foregoing shall also apply to expenses reasonably incurred in salving or attempting to salve the Vessel and other property to the extent that such expenses shall be regarded as having been incurred in respect of the Vessel.

COLLISION LIABILITY

And it is further agreed that:

(a) if the Vessel shall come into collision with any other ship or vessel, and the Assured or the Surety in consequence of the Vessel being at fault shall become liable to pay and shall pay by way of damages to any other person or persons any sum or sums in respect of such collision, the Underwriters will pay the Assured or the Surety, whichever shall have paid, such proportion of such sum or sums so paid as their respective subscriptions hereto bear to the Agreed Value, provided always that their liability in respect to any one such collision shall not exceed their proportionate part of the Agreed Value.

(b) in cases where, with the consent in writing of a majority (in amount) of Hull Underwriters, the liability of the Vessel has been contested, or proceedings have been taken to limit liability, the Underwriters will also pay a like proportion of the costs which the Assured shall thereby incur or be compelled to pay.

When both vessels are to blame, then, unless the liability of the owners or charterers of one or both such vessels becomes limited by law, claims under the Collision Liability clause shall be settled on the principle of Cross-Liabilities as if the owners or charterers of each vessel had been compelled to pay to the owners or charterers of the other of such vessels such one-half or other proportion of the latter's damages as may have been properly allowed in ascertaining the balance or sum payable by or to the Assured in consequence of such collision.

The principles involved in this clause shall apply to the case where both vessels are the property, in part or in whole, of the same owners or charterers, all questions of responsibility and amount of liability as between the two vessels being left to the decision of a single Arbitrator, if the parties can agree upon a single Arbitrator, or failing such agreement, to the decision of Arbitrators, one to be appointed by the Assured and one to be appointed by the majority (in amount) of Hull Underwriters interested; the two Arbitrators chosen to choose a third Arbitrator before entering upon the reference, and the decision of such single Arbitrator, or of any two of such three Arbitrators, appointed as above, to be final and binding.

Provided always that this clause shall in no case extend to any sum which the Assured or the Surety may become liable to pay or shall pay in consequence of, or with respect to:

(a) removal or disposal of obstructions, wrecks or their cargoes under statutory powers or otherwise pursuant to law;
(b) injury to real or personal property of every description;
(c) the discharge, spillage, emission or leakage of oil, petroleum products, chemicals or other substances of any kind or description whatsoever;
(d) cargo or other property on or the engagements of the Vessel;
(e) loss of life, personal injury or illness.

Provided further that exclusions (b) and (c) above shall not apply to injury to other vessels or property thereon except to the extent that such injury arises out of any action taken to avoid, minimize or remove any discharge, spillage, emission or leakage described in (c) above.

PILOTAGE AND TOWAGE

This insurance shall not be prejudiced by reason of any contract limiting in whole or in part the liability of pilots, tugs, towboats, or their owners when the Assured or the agent of the Assured accepts such contract in accordance with established local practice.

Where in accordance with such practice, pilotage or towage services are provided under contracts requiring the Assured or the agent of the Assured:

(a) to assume liability for damage resulting from collision of the Vessel insured with any other ship or vessel, including the towing vessel, or
(b) to indemnify those providing the pilotage or towage services against loss or liability for any such damages,

it is agreed that amounts paid by the Assured or Surety pursuant to such assumed obligations shall be deemed payments "by way of damages to any other person or persons" and to have been paid "in consequence of the Vessel being at fault" within the meaning of the Collision Liability clause in this Policy to the extent that such payments would have been covered if the Vessel had been legally responsible in the absence of any agreement. Provided always that in no event shall the aggregate amount of liability of the Underwriters under the Collision Liability clause, including this clause, be greater than the amount of any statutory limitation of liability to which owners are entitled or would be entitled if liability under any contractual obligation referred to in this clause were included among the liabilities subject to such statutory limitations.

CHANGE OF OWNERSHIP

In the event of any change, voluntary or otherwise, in the ownership or flag of the Vessel, or if the Vessel be placed under new management, or be chartered on a bareboat basis or requisitioned on that basis, or if the Classification Society of the Vessel or her class therein be changed, cancelled or withdrawn, then, unless the Underwriters agree thereto in writing, this Policy shall automatically terminate at the time of such change of ownership, flag, management, charter, requisition or classification; provided, however, that:

(a) if the Vessel has cargo on board and has already sailed from her loading port, or is at sea in ballast, such automatic termination shall, if required, be deferred until arrival at final port of discharge if with cargo, or at port of destination if in ballast;

(b) in the event of an involuntary temporary transfer by requisition or otherwise, without the prior execution of a written agreement by the Assured, such automatic termination shall occur fifteen days after such transfer.

This insurance shall not inure to the benefit of any transferee or charterer of the Vessel and, if a loss payable hereunder should occur between the time of change or transfer and any deferred automatic termination, the Underwriters shall be subrogated to all of the rights of the Assured against the transferee or charterer in respect of all or part of such loss as is recoverable from the transferee or charterer, and in the proportion which the amount insured hereunder bears to the Agreed Value.

The term "new management" as used above refers only to the transfer of the management of the Vessel from one firm or corporation to another, and it shall not apply to any internal changes within the offices of the Assured.

ADDITIONAL INSURANCES

It is a condition of this Policy that no additional insurance against the risk of Total Loss of the Vessel shall be effected to operate during the currency of this Policy by or for account of the Assured, Owners, Managers, Operators or Mortgagees except on the interests and up to the amounts enumerated in the following Sections (a) to (g), inclusive, and no such insurance shall be subject to P.P.I., F.I.A. or other like term on any interests whatever excepting those enumerated in Section (a); provided always and notwithstanding the limitation on recovery in the Assured clause a breach of this condition shall not afford the Underwriters any defense to a claim by a Mortgagee who has accepted this Policy without knowledge of such breach:

(a) DISBURSEMENTS, MANAGERS' COMMISSIONS, PROFITS OR EXCESS OR INCREASED VALUE OF HULL AND MACHINERY, AND/OR SIMILAR INTERESTS HOWEVER DESCRIBED, AND FREIGHT (INCLUDING CHARTERED FREIGHT OR ANTICIPATED FREIGHT) INSURED FOR TIME. An amount not exceeding in the aggregate 25% of the Agreed Value.

(b) FREIGHT OR HIRE, UNDER CONTRACTS FOR VOYAGE. An amount not exceeding the gross freight or hire for the current cargo passage and next succeeding cargo passage (such insurance to include, if required, a preliminary and an intermediate ballast passage) plus the charges of insurance. In the case of a voyage charter where payment is made on a time basis, the amount shall be calculated on the estimated duration of the voyage, subject to the limitation of two cargo passages as laid down herein. Any amount permitted under this Section shall be reduced, as the freight or hire is earned, by the gross amount so earned. Any freight or hire to be earned under the form of Charters described in (d) below shall not be permitted under this Section (b) if any part thereof is insured as permitted under said Section (d).

(c) ANTICIPATED FREIGHT IF THE VESSEL SAILS IN BALLAST AND NOT UNDER CHARTER. An amount not exceeding the anticipated gross freight on next cargo passage, such amount to be reasonably estimated on the basis of the current rate of freight at time of insurance, plus the charges of insurance. Provided, however, that no insurance shall be permitted by this Section if any insurance is effected as permitted under Section (b).

(d) TIME CHARTER HIRE OR CHARTER HIRE FOR SERIES OF VOYAGES. An amount not exceeding 50% of the gross hire which is to be earned under the charter in a period not exceeding 18 months. Any amount permitted under this Section shall be reduced as the hire is earned under the charter by 50% of the gross amount so earned but, where the charter is for a period exceeding 18 months, the amount insured need not be reduced while it does not exceed 50% of the gross hire still to be earned under the charter. An insurance permitted by this Section may begin on the signing of the charter.

(e) PREMIUMS. An amount not exceeding the actual premiums of all interest insured for a period not exceeding 12 months (excluding premiums insured as permitted under the foregoing Sections but including, if required, the premium or estimated calls on any Protection and Indemnity or War Risks and Strikes insurance) reducing pro rata monthly.

(f) RETURNS OF PREMIUM. An amount not exceeding the actual returns which are recoverable subject to "and arrival" or equivalent provision under any policy of insurance.

(g) INSURANCE IRRESPECTIVE OF AMOUNT AGAINST:—Risks excluded by War, Strikes and Related Exclusions clause; risks enumerated in the American Institute War Risks and Strikes Clauses; and General Average and Salvage Disbursements.

WAR STRIKES AND RELATED EXCLUSIONS

The following conditions shall be paramount and shall supersede and nullify any contrary provisions of the Policy.

This Policy does not cover any loss, damage or expense caused by, resulting from, or incurred as a consequence of:

(a) Capture, seizure, arrest, restraint or detainment, or any attempt thereat; or

(b) Any taking of the Vessel, by requisition or otherwise, whether in time of peace or war and whether lawful or otherwise; or

(c) Any mine, bomb or torpedo not carried as cargo on board the Vessel; or

(d) Any weapon of war employing atomic or nuclear fission and/or fusion or other like reaction or radioactive force or matter; or

(e) Civil war, revolution, rebellion, insurrection, or civil strife arising therefrom, or piracy; or

(f) Strikes, lockouts, political or labor disturbances, civil commotions, riots, martial law, military or usurped power; or

(g) Malicious acts or vandalism, unless committed by the Master or Mariners and not excluded elsewhere under this War Strikes and Related Exclusions clause; or

(h) Hostilities or warlike operations (whether there be a declaration of war or not) but this subparagraph (h) not to exclude collision or contact with aircraft, rockets or similar missiles, or with any fixed or floating object, or stranding, heavy weather, fire or explosion unless caused directly by a hostile act by or against a belligerent power which act is independent of the nature of the voyage or service which the Vessel concerned or, in the case of a collision, any other vessel involved therein, is performing. As used herein, "power" includes any authority maintaining naval, military or air forces in association with a power.

If war risks or other risks excluded by this clause are hereafter insured by endorsement on this Policy, such endorsement shall supersede the above conditions only to the extent that the terms of such endorsement are inconsistent therewith and only while such endorsement remains in force.

PRELIMINARY ACTS

EXTRACT FROM THE RULES OF THE SUPREME COURT OF ENGLAND AND WALES (PRELIMINARY ACTS)[1]

18.- (1) In an action to enforce a claim for damage, loss of life or personal injury arising out of a collision between ships, the following provisions of this rule shall apply unless the Court otherwise orders.

(2) The plaintiff must within 2 months after service of the writ on any defendant and the defendant must within 2 months of acknowledging issue or service of the writ file in the appropriate registry a document in two parts (in these rules referred to as a preliminary act) containing a statement of the following:

Part One

(i) the names of the ships which came into collision and their ports of registry;

(ii) the length, breadth, gross tonnage, horsepower and draught at the material time of the ship and the nature and tonnage of any cargo carried by the ship;

(iii) the date and time (including the time zone) of the collision;

(iv) the place of the collision;

(v) the direction and force of the wind;

(vi) the state of the weather;

(vii) the state, direction and force of the tidal or other current;

(viii) the position, the course steered and speed through the water of the ship when the other ship was first seen or immediately before any measures were taken with reference to her presence, whichever was the earlier;

(ix) the lights or shapes (if any) carried by the ship;

(x) (a) the distance and bearing of the other ship if and when her echo was first observed by radar;

(b) the distance, bearing and approximate heading of the other ship when first seen;

(xi) what light or shape or combination of lights or shapes (if any) of the other ship was first seen:

(xii) what other lights or shapes or combinations of lights or shapes (if any) of the other ship were subsequently seen before the collision, and when;

1. Order 75, r. 18, with amendment effective Oct. 1, 1990.

(xiii) what alterations (if any) were made to the course and speed of the ship after the earlier of the two times referred to in article (viii) up to the time of the collision, and when, and what measures (if any) other than alterations of course or speed, were taken to avoid the collision, and when;
(xiv) the heading of the ship, the parts of each ship which first came into contact and the approximate angle between the two ships at the moment of contact;
(xv) what sound signals (if any) were given, and when;
(xvi) what sound signals (if any) were heard from the other ship, and when.

Part Two

(i) a statement that the particulars in Part One are incorporated in Part Two;
(ii) any other facts and matters upon which the party filing the preliminary act relies;
(iii) all allegations of negligence or other fault which the party filing the preliminary act makes;
(iv) the remedy or relief which the party filing the preliminary act claims;

(3) Part Two of the preliminary act shall be deemed to be the pleading of the person filing the preliminary act (in the case of the plaintiff his statement of claim and in the case of the defendant his defence and, where appropriate, his counterclaim) and the provisions of these rules relating to pleadings shall apply to it save insofar as this rule and rule 20 provide otherwise.

(4) The Court may order that Part Two of the preliminary act need not be filed by the plaintiff or defendant and give directions for the further conduct of the action.

(5) Every preliminary act shall before filing be sealed by the proper officer and be filed in a sealed envelope which shall not be opened except as provided in paragraph (7) or by order of the court.

(6) A plaintiff must serve notice of filing his preliminary act on every defendant who acknowledges issue or service of the writ within 3 days of receiving notice of that acknowledgement or upon filing his preliminary act, whichever is the later. A defendant must, upon filing his preliminary act, serve notice that he has done so on the plaintiff and on every other defendant who has acknowledged issue or service of the writ.

(7) Any party may inspect and bespeak a copy of the preliminary act of any other party upon filing in the appropriate registry a consent signed by that other party or his solicitor.

(8) Order 18, rule 20 (close of pleadings) shall not apply; and for the purposes of Order 18, rule 14 (denial by joinder of issue), Order 20, rule 3 (amendment of pleadings without leave) and Order 24, rules 1 and 2 (discovery of documents) the pleadings shall be deemed to be closed —

(a) at the expiration of 7 days after service of the reply or, if there is no reply but only a defence to counterclaim, after service of the defence to counterclaim pursuant to leave given under rule 20, or

(b) if neither a reply nor a defence to counterclaim is served, at the expiration of 7 days after the last preliminary act in the action was served pursuant to paragraph (9) below.

(9) Within 14 days after the last preliminary act in the action is filed each party must serve on every other party a copy of his preliminary act.

(10) At any time after all preliminary acts have been filed any party may apply to the Court for an order that —

(a) one or more parties file in the registry particulars of the damages claimed by them and serve a copy thereof on every other party, and

(b) that the damages be assessed prior to or at the trial on liability. The application must be made by summons to the appropriate registrar even if it is made after the issue of a summons for directions.

(11) When an order is made under paragraph (10) the claim or claims concerned shall be treated as referred to the appropriate registrar for assessment and rules 41 and 42 shall apply unless the registrar otherwise directs.

(12) In this rule "the appropriate registry" means the Admiralty and Commercial Registry or, if the action is proceeding in a district registry, that registry; and references to "the appropriate registrar" shall be construed accordingly.

APPENDIX 11

EXTRACT FROM *THE MASTER'S ROLE ON COLLECTING EVIDENCE*

(CHAPTER 9 - COLLISIONS)

Introduction

This chapter examines the type of evidence required where the ship has been involved in a collision. It is likely that in the aftermath of a collision, lawyers and surveyors acting for owners and their insurers will come aboard the vessel and play an active role in gathering evidence necessary to bring or defend claims for damage. However, they will rely heavily on the Master and the crew to provide much of the evidence.

This chapter deals with the following:—

- Evidence required prior to a collision—
  - Working charts,
  - Movement books;
- Evidence required after a collision—
  - General,
  - Vessel under pilotage or in congested waters,
  - Vessel moored or anchored;
- Involvement of lawyers.

In the appendix to this chapter checklists and a case history are provided. The reader should also refer to chapters 7 and 8 in the event that salvage services are required or a general average incident occurs as a result of the collision.

Evidence Prior to a Collision

Evidence recording the daily routine of the vessel will be crucial in determining how and why a collision occurred. This type of evidence will include copies of the vessel's rough log books. It is imperative, therefore, that all sections of the log book are completed fully and accurately at all times. . . . Sounding records are also likely to be important.

Working charts and movement books are two items of evidence which have particular relevance in collision investigations.

Working Charts

The Master should ensure that chart positions are left precisely as plotted and that positions which do not match others are not erased.

---

1. Compiled by a special Working Group of the Northeast Branch of the [British] Nautical Institute and reprinted by the Steamship Mutual Underwriting Association (Bermuda) Ltd., with whose kind permission the extract is reprinted here.

Attorneys litigating collision actions in the U.S. courts usually prepare memoranda of interviews with prospective witnesses, rather than signed statements, which are discoverable by opposing counsel. See *Hickman v. Taylor,* 329 U.S. 495, 1947 AMC 1 (1947).

As a large number of collisions occur under pilotage or in congested waters, the Master also should ensure that the general practice of marking charts while on passage is continued while the vessel is under pilotage. Particular care should be taken to plot the vessel's location on the chart, for example, by indicating the distances abeam off buoys.

Movement Books

The Master should ensure that movement books are kept in ink and that any alterations are made in ink, signed, and dated by the person making the alterations. The material deleted should be scored out with a single line leaving the writing underneath legible. The use of correction fluid should not be permitted.

The Master should also ensure that times are recorded as accurately as possible. Finally, he should ensure that printer outputs from telegraph recorders and the engine room are retained as part of the movement book.

Evidence after a Collision

General

If possible, the Master and the crew should collect, record, and preserve as much detail of the collision as they can immediately after an incident. The type of evidence discussed below is of particular importance. The Master should ensure that a note of the following is made:

1. The vessel's position at the time of the incident —
   Every effort should be made to fix and confirm the position from more than one source;
2. The exact time of the collision—
   The accuracy of the clocks on the bridge and in the engine room as well as the accuracy of automatic recorders such as course recorders, telegraph loggers, and data loggers should be verified. The personal watches of the members of the crew who witnessed the incident should be checked. If a reflective plotter was in use prior to a collision, the crew member operating the plotter should ensure that he has made a note (not on the screen) of any marks accompanied by a time on the screen;
3. The heading of the vessel at the time of the collision—
   It is important that the course recorder is marked in ink to indicate the time when the vessel collided, although care should be taken not to spoil the trace. If a course recorder is not available, the heading of the vessel should be determined by some other method which also should be recorded;
4. An estimate of the angle of blow by or to the other vessel;
5. An estimate of the speed of each of the vessels at the time of the collision—
   The estimates can be verified at a later date by other data such as photographs and logs;
6. Any alterations of course and speed prior to a collision—
   If possible, this note should be verified by a second person or equipment recording.

In addition, the Master should ensure that all crew members on the bridge as well as other members of the crew who witnessed the incident, record their account of events which occurred prior to and after the incident. The Master also should ensure that any independent witnesses to the incident are identified. He should record the names of all the vessels in the vicinity and attempt to obtain the names and addresses of the operators and duty officers of these vessels by VHF.

Finally, the Master should ensure that any scraps of paper which have been disposed of in the waste paper basket on the bridge are retained as these may contain the key as to why and how a collision occurred.

Vessel under Pilotage or in Congested Waters

As stated above, many collisions take place when a vessel is under pilotage or in congested waters. In such cases, the actions of the person controlling the vessel immediately before the vessel was involved in a collision, are particularly relevant in determining the cause of the collision. The Master, in addition to gathering the evidence discussed in the preceding sections, should ensure that the watch keeper, helmsman, the look-out, and any other persons on the bridge at the time of the collision make a complete record of events. The pilot also should be requested to make a written account of the events before he leaves the vessel. A note should be made of the pilot's name, address, and telephone number.

The Master should record speed log readings and make a note of the state of the tide at the time of the collision. An estimate of tidal current is unlikely to be accurate, however, a note of the time of observed slack water will be useful when calculations are being made from the tide tables. The Master should note that S.A.L. logs may be inaccurate in freshwater.

Vessel Moored

It is generally the view that unless there is evidence that the moored or anchored vessel contributed in some way to the collision, the vessel underway is liable for the damage.

Regardless of whether the Master is on the colliding vessel, he should ensure the following information is obtained:

1. Whether or not the moored vessel or an adjacent vessel was testing her main engines in such a way as to contribute to the incident;
2. Whether or not the moorings on the moored vessel were defective, slack, or ineffective in any way;
3. An estimate of the tidal direction and strength;
4. The identity of witnesses on shore; and
5. Photographs of damage to own vessel, and if possible, of the damage to the other vessel.

As many of the incidents which take place when the vessel is moored are minor incidents, the insurers of both vessels may not require a joint survey, but will rely heavily on the Master's evidence. It is important, therefore, that the Master's report of the incident gives a detailed record of the damage.

Involvement of Lawyers

As stated above, lawyers are likely to play a significant role in gathering evidence in the aftermath of a collision. While the investigating lawyers are likely to be appointed by the vessel's insurers and will not be directly representing the interests of the Master and crew, these interests do to a certain degree coincide with those of the insurers. Therefore, the lawyers may advise the Master and the crew of their legal position and if the circumstances merit it, recommend that the crew or their union appoint their own lawyers.

Finally, there is an understanding between lawyers that if they represent owners of another vessel, they will not question crew members of the opponent's vessel. Therefore, the Master should ensure that crew members identify any persons to whom they make statements.

Checklist

1. Courses steered during four hours before collision (time, position, altered course to);
2. Weather conditions at time of collision:
   a. Direction and force of wind,
   b. Direction and height of sea,
   c. Direction and height of swell,
   d. Visibility,
   e. Last weather forecast;
3. State of tide and currents;
4. Personnel on bridge at or immediately before collision;
5. Position fixing system(s) in use;
6. First observation of other vessel:
   a. By what means,
   b. Distance and bearing,
   c. Lights and shapes observed,
   d. Aspect,
   e. Apparent course,
   f. Time;
7. Course of own ship at time of first observation;
8. Speed of own ship at time of first observation;
9. Action taken by own vessel at time of first observation;
10. Subsequent observations:
    a. Times,
    b. Distance and bearing;
11. First vessel sighting:
    a. Time,
    b. Distance and bearing,
    c. Lights observed,
    d. Aspect,
    e. Apparent course;
12. Steps taken to plot other vessel (e.g. reflection plot, formal plot);
13. Record of actions of both vessels including times up to the time of collision (including engine movement);
14. Sound signals made and when made;
15. Sound signals heard and when heard;
16. Details of any communications between vessels before collision;
17. Time of collision;
18. Position of collision (state how obtained);
19. Angle of contact between vessels (if possible take photographs or make a drawing);
20. Heading of own vessel at time of collision;
21. Heading of other vessel at time of collision;

22. Speed of other vessel at time of collision;
23. Description of movements of both vessels after collision;
24. Details of communications after collision;
25. Names of other vessels in vicinity when collision occurred;
26. Communications with other vessels in vicinity;
27. If vessel under pilotage, name, address, and telephone number of pilot—see also the evidence listed in the section 'Vessel under Pilotage or in Congested Waters;'
28. If the vessel is moored at the time of collision, see the evidence listed in the section 'Vessel Moored;'

In addition to the above information, the Master should ensure that:

1. All witnesses of the incident write an account of the collision and the events leading up to the collision;
2. The practice of marking charts is continued while the vessel is under pilotage, and chart positions are left precisely as plotted;
3. Recording telegraph printer output and other printer output from the engine room are retained as part of the movement book;
4. Accuracy of clocks on bridge and in engine room, as well as automatic recorders are verified;
5. Course recorder marked in ink to indicate collision;
6. Operator of reflective plotter makes note marks;
7. A full photographic record of events is made;
8. Scraps of paper on which course calculations may have been made are retained.

Finally, the Master should ensure that the following general information is noted:

1. Details of vessel:
    a. Name,
    b. Nationality,
    c. Port of registry,
    d. Vessel's general description,
    e. Radio equipment on board,
    f. Vessel's complement (details of rank and qualifications),
    g. Watchkeeping arrangements,
    h. Navigational equipment on board;
2. Name and port of registry of other ship;
3. Date of collision;
4. Approximate area of collision;
5. Details of voyage:
    a. From where to where was the vessel going,
    b. Time of sailing,
    c. Draughts on sailing (forward, mid, and aft),
    d. Intended course to next port.

APPENDIX 12

BIBLIOGRAPHY

Berlingieri, F., ed. *The Travaux Préparatoires of the 1910 Collision Convention and of the 1952 Arrest of Ships Convention.* Antwerp: CMI Headquarters, 1997.

Blank, J. S. *Modern Towing.* Centreville, Md.: Cornell Maritime Press, 1989.

Buzek, F. J., and F. M. C. Holdert, *Collision Cases—Judgments and Diagrams,* 2d ed. London: Lloyd's of London Press, 1990.

Cahill, R. A. *Collisions and Their Causes,* 2d ed. Houston, Tex.: Nautical Books, 1997.

Cockcroft, A. N., and J. N. F. Lameijer. *A Guide to the Collision Avoidance Rules: International Regulations for Preventing Collisions at Sea,* 4th ed. London: Stanford Maritime, Ltd. 1990.

Farnsworth, B. A., and L. C. Young. *Nautical Rules of the Road.* Centreville, Md.: Cornell Maritime Press, 1990.

Griffin, J. W. *The American Law of Collision.* Baltimore: American Maritime Cases, Inc., 1949.

Marsden, R. G. *The Law of Collisions at Sea,* 11th ed. Edited by K.C. McGuffie. London: Stevens & Sons, 1961.

Meadows, J. F., and D. F. Sears. *Ship Collisions: Technical and Legal Aspects.* 63 Am Jur Trials 346, 1997.

Parks, A., and E. V. Cattell, Jr. *The Law of Tug, Tow, and Pilotage,* 3d ed. Centreville, Md.: Cornell Maritime Press, 1994.

Smith, R. A., ed. *Farwell's Rules of the Nautical Road,* 7th ed. Annapolis, Md.: Naval Institute Press, 1994.

Sturt, R. H. S. *The Collision Regulations.* London: Lloyd's of London Press, 1991.

Tate, W. H. *A Mariner's Guide to the Rules of the Road.* Annapolis, Md.: Naval Institute Press, 1978.

U.S. Coast Guard. *Navigation Rules—International—Inland.* Washington, D.C.: United States Government Printing Office, 1995.

The following eleven articles all appear in the Tulane Admiralty Law Institute Symposium on the American Law of Collision, 51 Tulane L. Rev. 759 (1977), and are listed here alphabetically by author: Berlingieri, F., *Jurisdiction and Choice of Law in Collision Cases and an Overview of the Concept of Fault and Its Apportionment;* Biele, E. C., *Maritime Liens Arising Out of Collision;* Brandon, H.V., *Apportionment of Liability in British Courts Under the Maritime Conventions Act of 1911;* Brown, R. H., Jr., *General Principles of Liability;* Buglass, L. J., *General Average Contributions as Provable Damages in Collision Cases;* Jacobsen, D. A., *Technology and Liability;* Lugenbuhl, C. E., and A. A. Maki, Jr., *River Navigation;* McCoy, H. E., *The American Law of Collision Practice, Procedure and Evidentiary Matters;* Owen, D. R., *The Origins and Development of Marine Collision Law;* Paulsen,

G. W., *Provable Damages in Collision Cases;* Young, J. F., *Evidence Rules and Burden of Proof in Collision Cases.*

Note: For a more extensive bibliography of books published before 1977, see D. R. Owen, *Collision Law: A Bibliography* (an appendix to his article, *The Origins and Development of Marine Collision Law*).[1] See also M. Newman, *Maritime Law: An Annotated Bibliography of Essential Publications.*[2]

Articles on collision law contained in the first twenty-five volumes of the *Journal of Maritime Law and Commerce* are indexed at 27 J. Mar. L. & Com. 1, 143–44 (1996).

1. 51 Tulane L. Rev. 759 (1977).
2. 15 J. Mar. L. & Com. 585 (1984).

INDEX

ISBN 0-87033-505-7